A DICTIONARY OF THE HAWAIIAN LANGUAGE

A DICTIONARY
OF THE
HAWAIIAN LANGUAGE

TO WHICH IS APPENDED AN
ENGLISH-HAWAIIAN VOCABULARY
AND A
CHRONOLOGICAL TABLE OF REMARKABLE EVENTS

BY LORRIN ANDREWS

WITH AN INTRODUCTION TO THE NEW EDITION BY
NOENOE K. SILVA
ALBERT J. SCHÜTZ

A DICTIONARY OF THE HAWAIIAN LANGUAGE
Written by Lorrin Andrews
Illustration Consultant Kimo Armitage
Illustrated by Ronald Lee
Book Design by Holly S. Yokomichi
Keystroke by Holly S. Yokomichi and Lynda Emery
Proofed by Noenoe K. Silva, Albert J. Schütz,
Kimo Armitage and M. Nohea Stibbard

Published and distributed by
ISLAND HERITAGE
PUBLISHING

94-411 KŌ‘AKI STREET, WAIPAHU, HAWAI‘I 96797-2806
Orders: (800) 468-2800 • Information: (808) 564-8800
Fax: (808) 564-8877
www.islandheritage.com

ISBN 0-89610-393-5
First Edition, Third Printing - 2010

CONTENTS

Lorrin Andrews's Dictionary:
A Bridge to Nineteenth-Century Hawaiian Thought

Reading the literature in Hawaiian that was produced in the hundred years or so between the advent of writing and the tragic loss of Hawaiian as a national and community language yields many treasures. For scholars and lovers of Hawaiian literature, the many newspapers and books are replete with history, literary masterpieces, poetry, and representations of daily life. They offer us views of Hawaiian history and culture rarely, if ever, seen in the English language depictions of Hawai'i and Hawai'i's indigenous people. I have argued elsewhere for the importance of reading Hawaiian language sources for understanding the past, particularly in the fields of history and anthropology. A more complete understanding of traditional Hawaiian cultures and historical events is also needed to understand the politics of the present day. Translations of important Hawaiian works suffer from various problems: Samuel Kamakau's original "Ka Moolelo o Kamehameha I," for example, was not translated in its entirety nor in its original order for the English version *Ruling Chiefs of Hawai'i*. Even worse, Hawaiian culture has been viewed as extinct (even though more of us are alive now than in 1900), so most of the attention paid by translators of the twentieth century was to ethnological texts. Texts that speak to the historical agency of our people, or that document our proud history of struggle against colonialism, are largely missing from translated works. Reading the nineteenth and twentieth century archive in the original can do much to restore the gaps and erasures in our histories.

For most of us living today, however, our grandparents or great-grandparents were the last to speak Hawaiian as their first and main language. English was imposed as part of the cultural and later political takeover by the United States, and two, three, or more generations of Kanaka 'Ōiwi were thus deprived of learning the language of their parents and grandparents. Now, through the tremendous efforts of many dedicated people, many of us are able to read what our ancestors of the nineteenth and twentieth century wrote in their own language to their peers, and just as consciously to us, their mo'opuna (descendants). Although we are educated enough to read, we do not share the living culture and language as they were when these documents were written. Kawena Pukui wrote in 1949:

> As we move farther off into modern times from ancient times it is increasingly difficult to understand the kaona ["inner meaning"]. We have left the old atmosphere and associations, and it is no longer possible to re-create them (in Schütz 1994, 210).

How then do we begin to understand the language and lives depicted in these writings? Most of us use a collection of reference books while we read. These include, first and foremost, Mary Kawena Pukui and Samuel Elbert's *Hawaiian Dictionary*, both 1971 and 1986 editions; Pukui's *ʻŌlelo Noeau: Hawaiian Proverbs and Poetical Sayings*; Pukui, Elbert, and Mookini's *Place Names of Hawaiʻi*; and Lorrin Andrews's A *Dictionary of the Hawaiian Language*.

Lorrin Andrews's study of the Hawaiian language led him to a deep appreciation of its poetry. Poetry in Hawaiian is difficult to understand, requiring years of study. In Andrews's own words, "It is rather remarkable that many foreign residents commence and prosecute the study of the Hawaiian language with considerable success, so as to speak, write and transact ordinary business in it; who, on attempting to read and translate a Hawaiian *mele*, are brought to a dead stand in the first or second line!" His respect for the skill of the composer of Hawaiian poetry is evident, as well: "... the poet or haku mele is considered as possessing a degree of skill and ingenuity beyond the mass of common minds. Among Hawaiians the *oihana haku mele*, the skill of the poet, has been honored from time immemorial." To understand the poetry, the reader or listener must be versed in a whole system of symbolic language, which is based in common cultural knowledge, including historical events and persons, plant and animal life, place names, wind and rain names, and so forth. Andrews actually did immerse himself in the language and culture necessary to begin an understanding of Hawaiian poetry. As Schütz notes, he produced (partial) translations of the famous epic poems "Haui ka lani" and "Kualii." I myself do not possess sufficient knowledge to evaluate these translations, but do believe that for Andrews even to have attempted a translation is indicative of substantial knowledge. That body of knowledge is partially available to us today in his dictionary.

The Andrews dictionary was produced when the language was used by nearly everyone in Hawaiʻi; thus, its purpose was to assist speakers using a living language. By contrast, the Pukui-Elbert dictionary was created during a time when Hawaiian was assumed to be lost as a living language, and so the dictionary was meant to help translators. This results in different information in the two books. For example, Andrews explains certain cultural concepts in addition to giving the English translation, while Pukui and Elbert tend to just give the translation. Here is Andrews's entry for *ka-pu*:

> A general name of the system of religion that existed formerly on the Hawaiian Islands, and which was grounded upon numerous restrictions or prohibitions, keeping the common people in obedience to the chiefs and priests; but many of the *kapus* extended to the chiefs themselves.

This is followed by the regular entries of translations. And here is the Pukui-Elbert entry for *kapu*:

> Taboo, prohibition; special privilege or exemption from ordinary taboo; sacredness; prohibited, forbidden ...

Furthermore, while Pukui-Elbert is based on Andrews's dictionary, it does not include every word and meaning Andrews recorded. At times, when scholars are unable to find words in Pukui-Elbert, they find them in Andrews. One example is the word *ka-ka-o-ko*, which Andrews says is an adjective meaning 'dull; slow; crooked.' Sometimes a word is in Pukui-Elbert, but the meaning implied by the context does not seem to be there. Again, the scholar would go to Andrews and would often find different meanings there. One example is *hoʻomakakī*, which Pukui-Elbert defines as 'to look at with hatred; to plan revenge or evil.' Andrews gives this meaning, but also offers an additional meaning, "to beg; to ask." Another is *hohō*, for which Andrews gives the additional meaning of 'snow.'

Some differences in meaning apparently reflect the different value systems of the nineteenth-century Protestant missionaries and the twentieth-century Hawaiian, as in the entries for the term *kahiau*. Pukui and Elbert give a positive value to the word: "to give generously or lavishly with the heart and not with expectation of return." But Andrews gives the word distinctly negative meanings: 'to give away lavishly and inconsiderately; lavish of gifts; wasting of property by indiscriminate giving.' Andrews's entry reflects the culture of the missionaries (and capitalism), which valued accumulation, while Pukui's definition reflects the Hawaiian culture that values generous giving. When readers use both dictionaries together, they are able to make better sense of the variety of nineteenth-century texts: many texts, including newspaper articles concerning nearly every aspect of Hawaiian life, were written by missionaries or other foreigners. Furthermore, not all texts in Hawaiian reflect a singular Hawaiian culture or value system, which, in any case, never did exist. Access to an alternative set of meanings helps us to be more careful and precise in our reading and analysis.

I would not recommend that anyone use Andrews without Pukui-Elbert. Pukui-Elbert provides the modern reader the pronunciation that is entirely missing in Andrews. As Schütz explains, Andrews evidently could not always distinguish or recognize the glottal stop as a productive sound, nor did he pay attention to the long vowels that we now mark with the kahakō (macron). He lists *na-o* as one word, for example, where Pukui-Elbert lists *nao* as one entry, and *naʻo* as another. Pukui-Elbert also gives us the twentieth-century understanding of words.

One of the most interesting aspects of the Andrews dictionary is that some entries appear entirely in Hawaiian with no English translation. The last meaning Andrews gives for *na-o* is 'he waiulaula, he waiahulu.' Pukui-Elbert tells us that *nao* can mean 'dark red dye; red,' which is most likely the meaning of Andrews's *waiulaula*. The word or phrase *waiahulu* does not appear at all in Pukui-Elbert. We gain extra knowledge here, then, by attending to Andrews's giving *waiahulu* as an additional meaning for *nao*. The Pukui-Elbert entry for *wai* includes the meanings 'color' and 'dye,' but the entry for *ʻahulu* does not refer to color, except for the meaning 'discolored.' Andrews's entry for *a-hu-lu* says, "… ua *ahulu* ke kai, i. e., dirty or green, not blue or clear." Using the two dictionaries together, we are now able to construct an additional meaning for *nao* not available in Pukui-Elbert: 'dirty or discolored water.'

It is also interesting and pleasurable for the reader fluent in Hawaiian to read the entries written entirely in Hawaiian, with no English explanation at all. Here is an example: *Pu-a, s. A pae pu mai a hiki laua (mau mea heenalu) mauka, e lana ana kekahi mouo, ua kapaia kela mea he pua.* (They floated toward shore together until they (two surfers) reached land, a buoy or fishnet float was floating [there], that thing is called a *pua.*) Here Andrews does not give a regular dictionary entry; rather he provides an example of the use of the word. However, it is beneficial to us today to observe which words were considered synonyms at that time, and how meanings of words were explained without resorting to English. It is hoped that it will not be too long before a dictionary solely in Hawaiian is created. Andrews's entries serve as inspiration for such a project.

I encourage all readers, and particularly scholars, to keep the Andrews dictionary beside their other standard reference works; it will no doubt add to their understanding and appreciation of Hawaiian texts.

Noenoe K. Silva
July 2002

LORRIN ANDREWS AND HIS DICTIONARY

Of all the members of the Hawaiian mission in the nineteenth century, the Reverend Lorrin Andrews was the one most closely connected with the study of the Hawaiian language. Although he published a grammar in 1854, he is best remembered for his contributions to lexicography. Based on a short "vocabulary" (1836), his *Dictionary of the Hawaiian Language* (1865), was the only full-scale Hawaiian dictionary available for nearly a century. A second edition was published in 1893, and a revised edition in 1922. Although the *Hawaiian-English Dictionary* by Mary Kawena Pukui and Samuel H. Elbert (1986) was so greatly expanded that it could not be called merely a revision, it was based on Andrews's work.

* * * * *

Andrews was born on April 29, 1795, in East Windsor, Connecticut. He was educated at Jefferson College, Pennsylvania, and Princeton Theological Seminary in New Jersey. He married Mary Ann Wilson on August 16, 1827, and a little less than a month later was ordained. He and his wife were members of the "Third Company"—sixteen missionaries appointed by the American Board of Commissioners for Foreign Missions, along with three Hawaiians (a teacher, a shoemaker, and an aide to one of the missionaries) and a Tahitian (an aide to another missionary). This group sailed from Boston on the *Parthian* on November 3, 1827, and after having "suffered an unusual share of discomforts, from the discourtesy of the captain, and others,"[1] they arrived at Honolulu nearly five months later. Shortly afterward, Andrews was assigned to the Lahaina station on Maui.

The fact that Andrews arrived in Hawai'i in the ninth year of the mission is significant. By that time, the major obstacle to teaching, translating, and printing had been overcome: after six years of experimentation and controversy, his colleagues had decided on what would serve as the foundation for all further work with the Hawaiian language—an efficient alphabet.

The Alphabet

Although Hawaiian had been written since the time of Captain Cook's visit, its sounds had never been studied systematically. For this reason, explorers and other visitors varied widely in the way they wrote Hawaiian words, since they usually used the spelling conventions of their native language.

But Hawaiian needed its own alphabet, not one based on that of another language. At first, the main problem seemed to be how to write the vowels. For a short time, the missionaries wrote some of the vowel letters with numbers, but they discarded that system when they saw how confusing it was. In late 1821, influenced by the decisions already made in Tahiti, the missionaries decided to write the vowels in the so-called foreign or continental (e.g., Italian), not the English, way. The result was a perfect match between the sounds and the letters—at least for the short vowels.

The consonants, however, presented a different problem. As visitors to Hawai'i in the first two decades of the nineteenth century gradually discovered, certain consonants varied, not only from place to place, but even from speaker to speaker in the same area. These were the troublesome groups:

$$t - k \qquad b—p \qquad l—r—d \qquad v—w$$

In other words, whether a speaker said, for example, *hale* or *hare*, the word still meant house. Native speakers were consulted again and again, and the results were the same: it simply didn't matter which of the sounds in the group was used.

In the spoken language, this variation presented no difficulties. But for compiling a dictionary, the problem is obvious: how does someone look up a word if there are several ways to spell it?

In 1826, the missionaries put the question to a vote, deciding on *k*, *p*, *l*, and *w* and discarding the other letters, except to write foreign borrowings. With two exceptions—the glottal stop and vowel length (which those who knew the language could usually infer through context)—this efficient alphabet made it very easy for Hawaiians to read and write their own language. Thus, when Andrews arrived two years later, literacy was well underway, and the path was clear for serious study of the language—not only for works *in* Hawaiian, but also for works *about* Hawaiian.

Andrews's first years in Hawai'i were a time of triumph for the missionary teachers. In 1829, there were more than 46,000 students in the schools,[2] and more than 100,000 copies of various books and pamphlets, mostly in Hawaiian, were printed at the Mission press.[3]

But the large number of students also meant that the American missionaries and teachers could not handle all the work alone. Early on, it was necessary to use local teachers in the flourishing schools, but sometimes the teachers themselves could not read and write beyond the level of the first primers. To raise the quality of the teachers, and to begin training them for the ministry as well, a missionary seminary was established in 1831 at Lahainaluna, with Andrews as its head. It opened with twenty-five pupils; enrollment was increased to sixty-seven by the end of the year. Its program was ambitious, beginning with courses in arithmetic, geometry, trigonometry, sacred geography, Hawaiian grammar, and languages in the first year, and adding courses in algebra, navigation, surveying, history, natural philosophy, church history, astronomy, and chemistry in the next three years.[4] Andrews served as principal and teacher in this environment for over ten years, and his work in higher education could not help but fuel his interest in the Hawaiian language. His translated works include not only the book of Proverbs, but a number of textbooks on subjects as diverse as geography, animals, geometry, surveying, and navigation. In the middle of his stay at Lahainaluna, he published his first collection of Hawaiian words.

A Vocabulary of Words in the Hawaiian Language (1836)

Even before the missionaries arrived in Hawaii, word collecting was a serious endeavor—they believed some kind of formalization, or "fixing," of the vocabulary was a prerequisite for language learning and translation. The first vocabulary referred to in the mission records is that of 'Ōpūkaha'ia, prepared at Cornwall, Connecticut, but it has disappeared. As far as we know, none of the First Company of missionaries even referred to the manuscript in their journals. But 'Ōpūkaha'ia was certainly the inspiration for those who followed him, particularly Elisha Loomis, the first printer.

In the preface to his *Vocabulary*, Andrews explained that in 1834 the Mission had selected him to prepare this work. He did not have to start with a completely clean slate, because several of his colleagues, including Loomis, had been compiling vocabulary lists from the very beginning.

The *Vocabulary* contains about 5,700 entries. Headwords are divided into syllables, which might be an aid to pronunciation had Andrews's concept of a syllable been more accurate. The source of most of the errors is his omission of the glottal stop, which none of the missionary-linguists recognized as a consonant. Instead, they seemed to interpret it as a way to separate two identical vowels, or to keep two different vowels from forming a diphthong. For example, a hyphen between identical vowels is a fairly reliable sign that there is a glottal stop in that position, as in *a-a-hu* ('a'ahu), 'clothing.' However, hyphens between unlike vowels could mean one of two things: either that a glottal stop separated them, or that Andrews did not consider that this particular vowel sequence was a diphthong. Thus, judging from his use of hyphens, it appears that for Andrews, *ai* and *au* were diphthongs, but *ae* and *ao* were not. Moreover, in practice he was not entirely consistent, as he missed the separation (that is, the glottal stop) in some very common words, such as *'a'ole* (negative), which he spelled *ao-le*.

Andrews's only recognition of the glottal stop in writing followed a convention begun as early as 1823. Since words such as *kou* 'your' and *ko'u* 'my' could not be distinguished through context, it was necessary to separate them by writing an apostrophe in the second. He did not call the sound a consonant, but instead "a slight break in the pronunciation."

Even though the label "vocabulary" suggests a word list, certain features of this work approach those of a full-scale dictionary or grammar. Note the following comment on the pronunciation of /a / :

> A, the first letter of the Hawaiian alphabet. Its sound is generally that of the English *a* in father, ask, &c. but it has sometimes, when standing before the consonants *k, l, m, n*, and *p*, a short sound somewhat resembling the short *u* in *mutter*; as in *paka, malimali, lama, mana, napenape*,[5] &c. pronounced nearly as we should pronounce pukka, mullymully, lumma, munna, nuppy-nuppy.

Oddly, this prominent phonetic feature was ignored in the sections on pronunciation in the most recent Hawaiian grammar and dictionary.

Andrews himself had no illusions about the scope or accuracy of the *Vocabulary*. In the introduction, he listed a number of its faults, treating it, we assume, as a work in progress. But the fuller dictionary did not appear until nearly thirty years later.

Dictionary of the Hawaiian Language (1865)

According to Andrews, this dictionary grew out of his interest in Hawaiian poetry. As preparation for its study, "he was induced to collect specimens of the language of common life." But this collection was for his own use. In 1860, when he had completed about four-fifths of the work with no plans for publication, he discovered that, without his knowledge, the Legislature had appropriated funds for printing his work.

Does Andrews's dictionary indeed reflect "the language of common life"? Perhaps a partial answer to this question lies in its preface (reprinted in this work), with its detailed list of sources. From a lexicographic point of view, it reveals several aspects of Andrews's linguistic philosophy. First (and most important), he insisted that native speakers should be the authorities for defining words. Next, his comments show two important attitudes about usage. He had his own ideas about a "standard" Hawaiian, preferring material "written by Chiefs to other Chiefs, and such as were written by one intelligent Hawaiian to another." He added that he "sought after the best and purest Hawaiian he could obtain." Finally (and consistent with a common nineteenth-century missionary stance), his policy of selection was more prescriptive than descriptive, for he excluded "low, filthy, vulgar language of ignorant and sensual depravity." (Even so, the Reverend Lorenzo Lyons wrote in 1878 that this work still contained "some bad words that ought not to appear in a dictionary.")

A contemporary mission publication, *The Friend*, kept its readers apprised of the birth of the dictionary as a printed book. In March 1864, it announced that the printing had begun, and several months later it whetted the reading public's appetite by printing a sample page. When the dictionary was finally ready for sale (June 1865), it turned out to be the most expensive work printed in Hawai'i, other than the Bible. (The book sold for $5.00, and Andrews received $1.00 per copy.) The editor suggested that the government give Andrews a grant for further work, but he was not optimistic that his advice would be taken.

The period between the *Vocabulary* and the *Dictionary* was one of rapid growth in the educated public's knowledge of Polynesian and other Austronesian languages. However, Andrews lagged behind even some of his colleagues in his refusal to recognize the glottal stop as a full-fledged consonant. Thus, in this area, the faults of the *Vocabulary* were not corrected.

This seemingly simple omission, along with the unfortunate failure to mark long vowels, had a far-reaching effect on the form of the entry words. As it is, users must sort through, for example, fifteen entries spelled simply *a*, and twenty-four spelled *a-a*. Moreover, because Andrews treated such pairs as *oli* 'chant' and *'oli* 'joy' as the same word, his confusion is reflected in his definition: 'to sing with a joyful heart'.

According to Andrews's own estimate, this work contains about 15,500 entries. However, although this count may be technically accurate, it is somewhat inflated because many words were entered twice: once as a noun, and once as a verb. For example, *nui* 'size', and *nui* 'to be great'. Some words are entered three times: *mai-kai* [*maika'i*] 'good' appears as an adjective, a noun, and a verb.

The order of the entries is the same as that in the *Vocabulary*—that is, according to the Hawaiian alphabet. The vowels are first, followed by the consonants, and finally by foreign consonants. The words in this last section are, of course, borrow-ings—mostly from English, but also Hebrew, Chaldean, Syrian, Latin, and Greek. The number was increased from the forty-one in his *Vocabulary* to one hundred sev-enty-five. However, the latter figure does not accurately reflect the number of loan-words adapted into the language, since it includes only those words beginning with the extraneous consonants. Other borrowings are scattered throughout the diction-ary—for example, *laiki* 'rice', *pena* 'paint', *ki* [*kī*] 'key', and *waina* 'wine'.

Andrews added an English-Hawaiian glossary of about 4,225 words, with entries based on those in George Pratt's Samoan dictionary (1862).

Since Andrews had already published his grammar, he could refer to this work in his dictionary. Examples of this cross-referencing can be found by looking up almost any grammatical marker, or words that behave in a special way, such as *hiki* 'be able to:'

Hiki is often used with other verbs as a kind of helping verb. *Gram.* § 171.

or *loa'a* 'gotten:'

Loaa is mostly confined in its meaning to a passive or neuter sense … *Gram.* § 232.

As Andrews did with his *Vocabulary*, he "pre-reviewed" his *Dictionary* by listing what he saw as its faults. Nor were his colleagues entirely uncritical. In 1878, the Reverend Lorenzo Lyons, "acknowledged the best Hawaiian scholar living," dis-cussed some of these faults.[6] From the time of publication, he had added new entries and corrected old ones. After noting that much of the dictionary was "good, and correct, and helpful and enlightening," he raised some important issues: incor-rect definitions, the problems caused by not writing the glottal stop, a need to spec-ify whether a word should be preceded by *ka* or *ke*, and no indication of pronunci-ation. As mentioned above, even prudery entered the argument: Lyons objected to some of the words included.

Lyons planned to revise the work, but the large number of copies still in stock made a revision financially impractical. He added that the supply of dictionaries might outlast the Hawaiian race, a statement that gives us a revealing look at one of the concerns of the Mission at that time.

But the supply of dictionaries outlasted Lyons himself, who died in 1886. Ironically, only a few years later (1893), the earlier prediction was proven wrong, and it became necessary to print another edition—without the revisions Lyons had felt so strongly about and had worked so long for.

* * * * *

Strictly speaking, the *Dictionary* was not a Mission production, since Andrews had distanced himself from the organization on a matter of principle:[7]

> About 1840 [1842], his mind was so strongly impressed with the iniquity of the system of American slavery that he resigned his position as a missionary of the American Board, because funds for its support were received from the slave States.

After leaving the Mission, he headed a printing office and bindery at Lahainaluna, and taught music and penmanship. He opened a school for his own and other children; he also served as Seamen's Chaplain in Lahaina from 1844–45. He was appointed judge of the Court of O'ahu in Honolulu in 1845. He served in other posts as well: he was a member of the Superior Court of Law, secretary of the Privy Council, first associate justice of the Supreme Court, and judge of probate and divorce cases. He resigned as judge in 1855, but the Hawaiian government helped support him with an annuity.[8]

Late in life, Andrews continued his work on translation, but this time from Hawaiian to English:

> In his later years, Judge Andrews translated the ancient *mele*, *Haui ka lani* and *Kualii* [Kūali'i]. Their sonorous rhythms, faithfully rendered in English, recall earlier poetical work on the Hawaiian Bible[,] which is one of the greatest monuments left by missionaries to Hawaii.[9]

About a year before his death, Andrews became nearly blind, but still continued his literary work with the help of a secretary.[10] He died on September 29, 1868, leaving a widow, five children, and several grandchildren. The funeral was held in his home in Nu'uanu Valley, and he was buried in O'ahu Cemetery.

Lorrin Andrews's Published Works on Language[11]

n.d. Vocabulary ["of words in the Hawaiian language, not dated, but, judging from the penmanship, written a few years after the lexicon." From Gay Slavsky's (expert on Hawaiian books) annotation.] The lexicon referred to is the first part of the bound ms.: A Pocket Hebrew Lexicon, Translated and Enlarged from the Manual Lexicon of J. Simonis. Punahou: Cooke Library.

1829. *He Hope no ka Pi-A-Pa.* O'ahu: Mission Press.

[183-]. A Vocabulary of Hawaiian Words with English Definitions Illustrated by

Short Sentences in the English Language. Ms. (unidentified hand); [Oʻahu? 183-]. Houghton Library, Harvard University; Hamilton Library, University of Hawaiʻi at Mānoa, microfilm S10110.

1832 [1834]. Essay on the Best Practicable Method of Conducting Native Schools at the Sandwich Islands. Read at the General Meeting of the Mission, June 13, 1832, by Lorrin Andrews, Principal of the High School at Lahaina. Appendix 3 of the *Annual Report of the ABCFM read at the 25th Annual Meeting* (1834), pp. 156–68.

1836a. *A Vocabulary of Words in the Hawaiian Language*. Lahainaluna: Press of the High School. Judd, Bell, and Murdoch #142.

1836b. Remarks on the Hawaiian Dialect of the Polynesian Language. *Chinese Repository* 5 (May 1836 to April 1837), Article II: 12–21.

[1837a]. *He Piliolelo no ka Olelo Beritania* {A grammar of the English language}. Lahainaluna: Press of the High School. 40 pp. Judd, Bell, and Murdoch #161. [Andrews was the translator.]

1837b. *Ke Kumu Kahiki: Oia ka Mea e Ao ai i na Hua a me ka Hookui, a me ka Heluhelu ana i ka Olelo Beretania* {The foreign teacher: A way to teach the letters and spelling, and reading in the English language}. 1837. Lahainaluna: Press of the High School. Judd, Bell, and Murdoch #147.

1838. Peculiarities of the Hawaiian Language. *The Hawaiian Spectator* 1(4):392–420.

1841. *He mau Haawina no ka Olelo Beretania* {A few lessons in English}. Lahainaluna: Press of the High School. Judd, Bell, and Murdoch #222. 2d ed. 1844. *He mau Haawina no ka Olelo Beritania. Ka Lua o ka Pai ana.* Honolulu: Mea Pai Palapala a na Misionari. Judd, Bell, and Murdoch #273.

1843. *O ke Kokua no ko Hawaii Poe Kamalii e Ao ana i ka Olelo Beritania* {The assistant for Hawaiian youths in learning the English language}. Lahainaluna: Press of the High School. Judd, Bell, and Murdoch #263.

1854. *Grammar of the Hawaiian Language*. Honolulu: Mission Press. Judd, Bell, and Murdoch #324. 2d ed. 1885. Honolulu: Thrum. Judd, Bell, and Murdoch #324.

1860. Degrees of Relationship in the Language of the Hawaiian Nation. Typescript copy of ms. Dated Honolulu, August 1860. Bernice Pauahi Bishop Museum Library.

1864. Value of the Hawaiian and English Languages in the Instruction of Hawaiians. In *Hawaiian Evangelical Association's Proceedings ... 3 June to 1 July 1863*, pp. 94–107. Boston: Marvin.

1865. *A Dictionary of the Hawaiian Language, to which is Appended an English-Hawaiian Vocabulary and a Chronological Table of Remarkable Events*. Honolulu: Whitney. Judd, Bell, and Murdoch #213. Reprinted 1893. Revised by Henry H. Parker, 1922 (Honolulu: Board of Commissioners of Public Archives of the Territory of Hawaii). Facsimile ed., with introduction by Terence Barrow, 1974 (Rutland, VT: Tuttle).

1870. Notes on the Hawaiian Degrees of Relationship. In *Systems of Consanguinity and Affinity of the Human Family*, ed. by Lewis Morgan, 451–57. Washington, D.C.: Smithsonian.

1875. Remarks on Hawaiian Poetry. *The Islander* 1:26, 27, 30, 31, 35.

1922. *A Dictionary of the Hawaiian Language*. Revised by Henry H. Parker. Bernice P. Bishop Mus. Spec. Publ. no. 8. Honolulu: Board of Commissioners of Public Archives of the Territory of Hawaii.

Lorrin Andrews's Translations[9]

English to Hawaiian

Catechism on Genesis
Lama Hawaii (Newspaper)
Maps of Universal Geography
Linear Drawing
Maps of Sacred Geography
Atlas of Colored Maps
English and Hawaiian Lessons
Reading Books for Schools
Skeleton Maps
Animals of the Earth with Chart
Geographical Questions
Bible Class Book (Abbot and Fisk)
First Book for Teaching English
First Lessons in Geography
Geometry, Surveying and Navigation
Sabbath Whaling, a tract

Hawaiian to English

The *mele* "Haui ka Lani" (*The Islander* 1:31, 36, 42, 47, 55, 64, 72, 79, 80, 89, 97, 104) and "Kualii"

More on Hawaiian Dictionaries

For discussions of Hawaiian dictionaries in greater detail, see Schütz 1994 and Ashford 1987.

References

Ashford, Marguerite K.   1987. The Evolution of the Hawaiian Dictionary and Notes on the Early Compilers, with Particular Attention to Manuscript Resources of the Bishop Museum Library. *Bishop Museum Occasional Papers* 27.1–24.

Bingham, Hiram.   1847. *A Residence of Twenty-one Years in the Sandwich Islands; or the Civil, Religious, and Political History of Those Islands; comprising a particular view of the missionary operations connected with the introduction and progress of*

Christianity and civilization among the Hawaiian people. Hartford, CT: Huntington; New York: Converse.

The Friend. [A missionary periodical, originally titled *The Temperance Advocate, and Seamen's Friend*.]

Judd, Bernice; Janet E. Bell; and Clare G. Murdoch. 1978. *Hawaiian Language Imprints 1822–1899. A Bibliography*. Honolulu: Hawaiian Mission Children's Society and University of Hawaii Press.

Missionary Album. Portraits and Biographical Sketches of the American Protestant Missionaries to the Hawaiian Islands. 1969. Enlarged from the edition of 1937. Sesquicentennial Edition. Honolulu: Hawaiian Mission Children's Society.

Missionary Herald. [A publication of the American Board of Commissioners for Foreign Missions (ABCFM).]

Morse, Peter. 1970. *Lorrin Andrews: Pioneer of Many Talents*. [Honolulu: Honolulu Academy of Arts.]

Pratt, George. 1862. *A Samoan Dictionary: English and Samoan, and Samoan and English, with a Short Grammar of the Samoan Dialect*. [Malua]: London Missionary Society Press.

Pukui, Mary Kawena, and Samuel H. Elbert. 1986. *Hawaiian-English Dictionary*. Honolulu: University of Hawaii Press.

Schütz, Albert J. 1994. *The Voices of Eden: A History of Hawaiian Language Studies*. Honolulu: University of Hawaii Press.

Albert J. Schütz
July 2002

NOTES

Except for corrections to obvious English misspellings, the content of the original dictionary has not been changed.

[1] Bingham 1847:326.

[2] Bingham 1847:335, 370.

[3] Judd, Bell, and Murdoch 1978:17–19.

[4] Bingham 1847:423–24.

[5] All these words except the last show a noticeable raising of the /a/. Those followed by /i/ in the next syllable are examples of assimilation (to the high vowel); the raising of sequences of /as is not so easily explained on phonetic grounds, but also occurs in modern Hawaiian, as well as in Micronesian languages and languages of Vanuatu.

[6] *The Friend*, 2 September 1878, p. 73.

[7] *The Missionary Herald* 65:42.

[8] *The Missionary Herald* 65:42.

[9] *Missionary Album*, p. 27.

[10] *The Missionary Herald* 65:43.

[11] Schütz 1994:389–92.

[12] *Missionary Album*, p. 25

AUTHOR'S PREFACE.

IT was the intention of the Author of this volume to make some extended remarks concerning the character, peculiarities and extent of the Hawaiian Language, by way of Preface or Introduction; but the want of physical strength, and especially of mental energy, has induced him to forgo such an attempt and be contented with a mere History of the manner in which this Dictionary has come into existence. The History of Hawaiian Lexicography is short. For the first effort the Author will quote from the preface of "A Vocabulary of Words in the Hawaiian Language" as follows:

"At a General Meeting of the Mission in June, 1834, it was voted, `That Mr. Andrews prepare a *Vocabulary of the Hawaiian Language.*' At the same time a wish was earnestly expressed and often repeated, that the work should not be delayed, but should be printed as soon as possible; and it was fully understood and expected that the work would necessarily be an imperfect one.

"On receiving the above appointment from the Mission, the Compiler set about a review of his materials for the compilation of a Vocabulary. The materials at hand and from which the following work has been compiled were the following:

"1. A vocabulary of words collected mostly, it is believed, by Mr. Loomis, formerly a member of this Mission. This was transcribed by the Compiler on his voyage from the United States, and put to use in 1828. In using it, his object was to insert every new word which he saw in print or understood in conversation or could obtain in any other way, besides correcting such mistakes as had been made in transcribing from the copy of Mr. Loomis. It was also a point with him to insert, if possible, the authority. Owing, however, to his ignorance of the Language at the time, many mistakes were made both in the orthography of the words and in the definitions.

"2. A vocabulary of words arranged, it is believed, in part by Mr. Ely, at the request of the Mission, and finished by Mr. Bishop. A copy of this was received and transcribed by the Compiler in the summer of 1829. Every other page was left blank for the insertion of new words, and for any such other corrections or additions as should be important. In using this manuscript, the same method was taken as with the Vocabulary of Mr. Loomis. New words and new definitions of words before collected, increased the size of the book to a considerable extent.

"On the slightest review of these irregular masses of materials, it was manifest that the labor of a thorough examination of every word, either by consulting intelligent Natives or by examining the *usus loquendi* from such manuscripts as could be obtained, or from the books that had been printed, must necessarily be a very protracted labor—the labor of some years at least. In consideration, therefore, of the urgent desire that something should be commenced in the form of a Vocabulary, and that a work having any pretensions to perfection must be slow in its progress, and protracted in its completion—and as the Compiler was burdened with labors of another kind—he judged it best to reduce the materials he had on hand to order in the best manner his time would permit. He has done so, without looking for any new words or extending the definitions of such as were collected, or consulting any native with regard to the propriety or impropriety of any definition. He feels it his duty, therefore, to forewarn those who may consult the following Vocabulary that they will often be disappointed. *It is by no means a perfect Vocabulary of the Hawaiian Language.*"

Such is the History of the Vocabulary. The printing was commenced at Honolulu in 1835, but finished at the press of the then High School at Lahainaluna and published early in 1836. It consisted of 132 pages octavo, and contained a little over 6,000 words, and has been the principal Vocabulary in use until the present time.

OF THE PRESENT DICTIONARY.

As soon as the aforementioned Vocabulary was published, the Author had several copies bound with blank leaves for making corrections and inserting new words, and continued his reading of Hawaiian documents both printed and written—giving the preference in all cases to such as were written by Chiefs to other Chiefs, and such as were written by one intelligent Hawaiian to another. As many of these written documents were never printed and were ephemeral in their nature, no reference could be made to them except by quoting a short sentence containing the word in question. No works of Foreign Authors—i. e., Foreigners writing Hawaiian—have been referred to except a very few school books, such as the *Anahonua* (Surveying), the *Anatomia*, a short treatise on Anatomy by Dr. Judd; *Hoikehonua* (Geography), and a few others. The translation of the Bible, however, from the great care exercised in translating—the frequent and thorough reviews by parties distinct from the original translators—and in all cases with Hawaiians sitting by and assisting, who were distinguished for intelligence and skill in their own language—is the principal exception. That has been considered and treated as a *classic*, and numerous references have been made to it accordingly. It may be remarked, however, that as the Hawaiian Bible has been under a revision for two or three years past, and is now being printed in the United States, *some* of the references in the Dictionary may not apply to this new edition of the Bible. With these exceptions, the authorities for the definition of words, so far as the Author is concerned have been drawn from Manuscripts written by Hawaiians or from printed pages originally written by such. The Author has ever sought after the best and purest Hawaiian he could obtain. As he has had no use for the low, filthy, vulgar language of ignorant and sensual depravity that must ever exist where there is no purifying principle to counteract it, his book may appear deficient in low terms, too common even now. A good many, it is to be feared, have crept in unawares along with better company, but they have never been sought after.

Besides two interleaved volumes filled up by the Author himself, he has been permitted to draw from the following sources:

1st. From a Manuscript of Dr. Baldwin, of Lahaina. This manuscript was especially useful, not so much for definitions fully written out, as for its suggestions of what might be and what should be further investigated. In noting down the ideas that appeared to belong to the word under review, he appears to have had a shrewd Hawaiian at his elbow. Some of his definitions have been copied in entire, but the most are mixed up with those of the Author, making the article more full. Hence this general acknowledgment is all that can appear in the work.

2nd. Mr. Richards' book. This was a printed volume of the Vocabulary bound up like the Author's with blank leaves. In his Missionary work, and especially after he became a Teacher for the Chiefs, Mr. Richards obtained quite a stock of new words; but it is to be regretted that his engagements did not allow him time to define them well. He frequently obtained a new word, but instead of giving a radical definition, merely mentioned that the *Princess* or *Hoapili* or some other Chief used the word, *apparently* meaning so and so, leaving the Author to find out as best he could the *real* meaning of the word. It was, however, of considerable help to the Author.

3d. The volume of Rev. A. Bishop has also rendered assistance to the Author. Having a blank interleaved book, he corrected or improved many definitions of the printed Vocabulary, and also added upwards of two hundred new words.

4th. The Author is also indebted to Dr. Judd in the same way: i. e., by allowing the Author the use of his interleaved Vocabulary. Besides his work on *Anatomy* into which he introduced the Hawaiian names of the bones, muscles and ligaments of the human system, he has collected in his Vocabulary a good number of words belonging to the colloquial department.

5th. The Vocabulary of S. M. Kamakau. This was designed to be a vocabulary of Hawaiian words with Hawaiian definitions. This work was commenced and carried on by Mr. Kamakau through the instigation, if not the expense of the Rev. J. S. Emerson while Professor at the Seminary of Lahainaluna. Its value as a vocabulary is diminished, not for want of information in the writer, but for want of skill in making definitions. Instead of giving a definition in other words, he merely added the *synonyms* of the word in question. The work, however, was of value to the Author, for these synonyms increased the number of words which finally found their way into the Dictionary. For all these helps, the Author desires to make due acknowledgment.

Still there has been ample room for the exercise of the Author's own judgment. The different departments in which he has been called to act, as that of a Missionary, a Teacher in the Seminary at Lahainaluna, a Magistrate in the different Courts of the Kingdom and Secretary of the Privy Council, in all which the Hawaiian Language was used, have brought before him a great variety of forms of speech, and perhaps also, a greater variety of the senses in which many words are used than could have been obtained had he been confined to any one department. But after all, as he reviews his Dictionary, he feels that he has nothing to boast of. The deficiencies are still great. Much will remain for the Author's successors to do before the genius, extent and peculiarities of the Hawaiian Language will be fully developed.

There are several departments of the language the words of which are but feebly represented in this Dictionary. That which relates to the imaginative in the Kaaos or Legends of different classes,—that which relates to what may be termed their philosophical views, i.e., their mode of accounting for natural phenomena, as the creation of their own islands,—the Origin of their Religious rites,—and especially the power of imagination displayed in their Meles and the consequent richness of their language for expressing the nicest shades of love, of hatred, of jealousy and revenge, and the language employed by the priests when drawing on their gods for assistance, are but partially presented in the definitions of this Dictionary. The Kaao of Laieikawai is almost the only specimen of that species of language which has been laid before the public. Many fine specimens have been printed in the Hawaiian periodicals, but are neither seen nor regarded by the foreign community. Volumes more of the same quality as Laieikawai might be collected and printed and whose moral influence would be no worse on Hawaiian minds than the famous Scott's Novels are on English readers. The study of these Kaaos would demonstrate that the Hawaiians possessed a language not only adapted to their former necessities, but capable of being used in introducing the arts of civilized society, and especially of pure morals, of law and the religion of the Bible.

The number of words in this Dictionary is about 15,500. The Author would here state that four-fifths of the work were completed before he had any intimation that it would ever be printed. It was written solely for his own amusement and information, and preparatory to a more full investigation of those departments of the language above mentioned. He has been desirous for many years of going more fully into the study of Hawaiian poetry, and as a preparation to it he was induced to collect specimens of the language of common life; hence the origin of this Dictionary. An appropriation of money for a Dictionary passed by the Legislature of 1860 without his knowledge, was the first intimation the Author had that such a work was desired by the Foreign community on the Islands.

Much praise is due to the Managers of the Office of the *Advertiser* for the correctness of the printing. Seldom is a book of this size printed with so few typographical errors. The public will also feel indebted to Professor Alexander for assiduous attention not only in one reading of each proof sheet, but in suggesting improvements in the language of definitions. The work is now submitted to a candid public. The Author hopes and prays that as God has spared his life to bring it to a close, he will in some way make it useful to the increase of intelligence in this Hawaiian Kingdom.

LORRIN ANDREWS.

HONOLULU, April, 1865.

NOTICES TO THE READER.

The Reader will notice that the *Order* of words in the Dictionary does not follow the order of letters in the English Alphabet, but they follow the order in which they stand in the Hawaiian *first books* for children, viz.: 1st, the vowels; 2d, the Hawaiian consonants; and 3d, such foreign consonants as have been introduced in connection with foreign words. (See the Alphabet below.)

In arranging the definitions, where there are several attached to a word, the Author has endeavored first to ascertain, if possible, the radical idea of the word in its simplest form, and from that he has used his best judgment in arranging in the order of their sequence the various derived significations. How far he has succeeded must be left to the judgment of the Reader.

The Reader of Hawaiian will notice that many words begin with the letters *hoo*. In looking in the Dictionary for such words, he may not find them; thus, *hoonaauao* will not be found under the letter *H*. Throw off then the *hoo* and look for *naauao, v.*, and there it will appear, and so of many others.

The sounds of the vowels will appear in the Alphabet below, and in the same order as they stand in the Dictionary.

Hawaiian Vowels.

- A as heard in *arch, ask,* &c.
- E as in *hate, late,* &c.
- I as in *ee* in English, or as *i* in *pique*.
- O as long in *note*.
- U as *oo* in *coo*.

Hawaiian Consonants

- H
- K
- L
- M
- N
- P
- W

as in English.

Foreign Consonants pronounced as in English.

- B.
- D.
- F.
- G.
- R.
- S.
- T.
- V.
- Z.

L.A.

ABBREVIATIONS.

Books of the Bible are abbreviated and italicized, followed by chapter and verse number. A list of these abbreviations appears at the beginning of the Hawaiian Bible. JBM refers to an entry in *Hawaiian Language Imprints, 1822–1899*, by Bernice Judd, Janet E. Bell, and Clare G. Murdoch.

adj.	adjective
adj. pron.	adjectival pronoun
adv.	adverb
Ana. Hon.	*Ke Anahonua 'The Geometry'* JBM 97–101
Anah.	*Ke Anahonua 'The Geometry'* JBM 97–101
Anahon.	*Ke Anahonua 'The Geometry'* JBM 97–101
Anat.	*Anatomia 'Anatomy'* JBM 166
art.	article
Chald.	Chaldean
comp.	compound
conj.	conjunction, conjugation
dem.	demonstrative
dist., distrib.	distributive
Eng.	English
fig.	figurative
freq., frequent.	frequentative
Gr.	Greek
Heb.	Hebrew
imperat.	imperative
int., interrog.	interrogative
interj.	interjection
Kam., Kamak	S.M. Kamakau's vocabulary
Kan. Haw.	*Kānāwai* ... (Hawaiian Laws 1841–42)?
Laieik.	*Laieikawai: Ka Hiwahiwa o Paliuli* JBM 395, 546
Lat.	Latin
met.	metaphorical
num.	number, numerical
part.	participle, particle
pass.	passive
perf.	perfect
pers.	person, personal
prep.	preposition
pron.	pronoun, pronominal
s.	substantive (noun)
sim.	simple
simp.	simple
sing.	singular
subj.	subjunctive
syn.	synonymous
Syr.	Syrian
v.	verb

A.J.S.

HAWAIIAN-ENGLISH

A DICTIONARY
OF THE
HAWAIIAN LANGUAGE.

A

A, in Hawaiian, as in most other languages, is the first letter of the alphabet; "because, if pronounced open as *a* in *father*, it is the simplest and easiest of all sounds." *Encyc. Amer.* Its sound, in Hawaiian, is generally that of *a* in *father, ask, pant,* &c.; but it has, sometimes, when standing before the consonants *k, l, m, n,* and *p,* a short sound, somewhat resembling the short *u,* as in *mutter,* but not so short. Thus *paka, malimali, lama, mana, napenape,* are pronounced somewhat as we should pronounce *pukka, mullymully, lumma, munna, nuppynuppy,* &c.; reference being had only to the first vowel of each word. It has also in a few words, a sound nearly resembling (but not so strong) that of *au* or *aw* in English; as *iwaho, mawaho,* pronounced somewhat as *iwauho, mawauho.* To foreigners who merely *read* the language, the common pronunciation of *a* as in *father* is near enough for all practical purposes; but to those who wish to speak it, the mouth of a Hawaiian is the best directory.

A is used for various parts of speech, and, of course, has various significations.

A, *adv.* When; then; there; until. With verbs in a narrative tense, it signifies when, and when, &c.; as, *a hiki mai ia,* when he arrived. With *nei* it signifies a designation of place, as mai *a nei* aku, from here (this place) onward. Until, as noho oia malaila *a make,* he lived there *until* he died. NOTE.— A *nei* is often written as one word, and then it signifies *here,* present place. A when pronounced with a protracted sound, signifies a protracted period of time, or distance, or a long continued action; as, holo ae la ia *a—a* hiki i ka aina kahiki, he sailed a long time (or a long distance) *until* he reached a foreign country.

A, *conj.* And; and then; and when.

When it connects verbs, it usually stands by itself; as, holo ka waa, *a* komo iho, the canoe sailed *and* sank. When it connects nouns, it is usually joined with *me;* as, haawi mai oia i ka ai *a me* ke kapa, he furnished food *and* clothing. A with *me* signifies and, and also, besides, together with, &c. When emphatic, it is merely a disjunctive. *Lunk.* 6:39. NOTE.— In narration, it frequently stands at the beginning of sentences or paragraphs, and merely refers to what has been said, without any very close connection with it. In many cases, it is apparently euphonic, or seems to answer no purpose, except as a preparatory sound to something that may follow; as, akahi no oukou *a* hele i keia ala, never before have you passed this road. *Gram.* § 166.

A, *prep.* Of; to; in connection with motion, e hoi oe *a* ka hale, return *to* the house, (*hiki i*) understood. *Laieik.* 12. Unto; at; belonging. It designates the properties of relation, possession and place; and is often synonymous with *o,* but more generally distinct, giving another shade of meaning and implying a more close connection. *Gram.* § 69, 3.

A, *int.* Lo; behold. It is expressive of surprise, disappointment, astonishment or admiration. It is similar in meaning to *aia hoi, eia hoi, aia ka.*

A, *v.* To burn, as a fire; ua *a* mai ke ahi, the fire *burns;* ua *a* mai ke ahi ma ka waha, the fire *burned* in their mouths.

    2. To burn, as a lamp: to blaze, as a flame.

    3. FIG. To burn, as jealousy. *Hal.* 79:5. As anger. *Nah.* 11:1.

    4. *Hoo* or *ho.* To cause to burn, i. e., to kindle; to light, as a lamp; to kindle, as a fire. Also with *ho* doubled, as *hohoa,* to dry; na hua i *hohoa ia,* dried fruits. *Oihk.* 2:14. See the reduplicate form AA and HOO. *Gram.* § 212.

A, *adj.* Fiery; burning; he lua *a*, a fiery pit.

A, *s.* The jawbone; the cheek bone. *Hal.* 3:7. A luna, upper jaw; a lalo, lower jaw.

A, *s.* The name of an instrument made of smooth bone, and used formerly for piercing or killing an unborn child. It was called the *a* oo, the piercing *a*; also *a* koholua. See KOHOLUA.

A, *s.* Name of broken lava from the volcano; probably so called from being burnt. See A, *v.* Ke *a* o Kaniku a me Napuuapele.

A, *s.* Name of the white spots that appear in poi when pounding.

A, *s.* Name of a large sea bird often caught by natives; also called aaianuhea-kane, feathers white.

A, *s.* Name of a small fish that bites at a hook; called also aakimakau.

A, *s.* Name of the Hawaiian alphabet; also the first sheet on which it was printed.

A-A, *v.* A doubled. See A, verb, before. To burn fiercely or furiously, as a fire; to burn constantly. *Oihk.* 6:9.

2. FIG. To kindle; to burn furiously, as anger. *Nah.* 11:33.

3. *Hoo.* To cause to kindle; to burn, as a fire; to light, as a lamp.

4. FIG. To burn, as anger. *Kin.* 30:2.

5. To rage; to be angry.

A-A, *adj.* Burning; raging, as a fire, he ahi *aa* loa; also as anger.

A-A, *s.* A burning; a lighted fire, &c. *Laieik.* 78.

A-A, *v.* To be bold; to dare. *Nah.* 14:44.

2. To tempt; to challenge. *Puk.* 17:2. To defy. 1 *Sam.* 17:10.

3. To venture, ua *aa* anei oe e hele i ke kaua? Ua *aa* anei oe e hele i ke alii?

4. To accept a challenge; to act presumptuously. *Kanl.* 1:43. He *aa* ka manao; he wiwo ole.

A-A, *s.* A daring; tempting. *Nah.* 14:22.

A-A, *adj.* Spiteful; quick angry; also roguish; mischievous.

A-A, *v.* To gird; tie around, as a loose garment.

A-A, *s.* A belt; a girdle.

A-A, *v.* To make a noise, as in trying to speak, as a dumb person; hence,

2. To be dumb, ua *aa* ka leo.

A-A, *adj.* Silent; still; lonely, as a house uninhabited; he *aa* ko ka hale, the people of the house are *silent*.

A-A, *s.* Dumbness; inability to speak intelligibly; also a dumb person. *Puk.* 4:11. I loheia e na *aa* lololohe; i mau *aa* lolo kuli.

A-A, *s.* The small roots of trees or plants. *Iob.* 8:17. Also called weli.

2. The veins or arteries for blood, from their resemblance to the fine roots of trees, aole lakou i ike ke koko maloko o na *aa*. *Anat.* 1.

3. FIG. The lower part of the neck.

4. Offspring.

A-A, *s.* A pocket; a bag. *Iob.* 14:17. SYN with *eke*. Aa moni, a purse; a scrip; a bag to carry provisions in for a journey; aole kanaka *aa* ole, no man without his scrip; a bag for weights (of money.) *Kanl.* 25:13. The name of the envelop for a fœtus. *Laieik.* 190. Kuu kaikaina i ka *aa* hookahi.

A-A, *s.* A dwarf; a small person. *Oihk.* 21:20. Kanaka poupou *aa*; ua ike au i kahi keiki i komoiii, *aa* no hoi ke kino.

A-A, *s.* See A above. Broken lava, i. e., sand, earth, stones and melted lava, cooled and broken up; hence

A-A, *adj.* Stony; abounding with lava; rough with broken lava, as ground to walk over, or to work in. See A, broken lava, above.

A-A, *s.* A covering for the eyes.

A-A, *s.* See A above. Name of a bird that hunts fish during the day, but flies back to the mountains in the evening.

A-A, *s.* The caul of animals; *aa* maluna o ke eke, the *caul* above the liver. *Puk.* 29:13. The midriff. *Oihk.* 3:4.

A-A, *s.* Name of a sea breeze at Lahaina and some other places on the islands.

A-A, *s.* Name of the cloth-like covering, near the roots of cocoanut leaves, *aa* niu. Hence,

2. The name of a coarse kind of cloth, he *aa* haole.

3. The outer husk of the cocoanut; the skin of the banana, same as *paaa*.

A-A, *s.* Chaff; hulls; the outside of seeds or fruit. *Ier.* 23:28.

A-A, *s.* Name of a reddish fish. See A above.

A-A, *v.* To send love in compliment; as, e *aa* mai ana o mea ma ia oe; the answer would be, Anoai wale laua, or welina wale laua, or aloha wale laua.

A-A-A, *adj.* Hospitable; friendly; kind to strangers, he makamaka aloha; SYN. with *haaa.*

A-A-A, *adj.* Uninhabited, as a house or village; lonely.

A-A-A, *s.* A house without inhabitants; also a low or humble dwelling, he hale *aaa,* aole kiekie.

A-A-A-KI, *v.* To bite often. See AKI, to bite.

A-A-E, *s.* See AA, fine roots. A kalo patch where the kalo is pulled.

2. The young shoots of kalo remaining in the ground after the old is pulled. SYN. with *oha,* as, pau ke kalo i ka hukiia, o ka *oha* wale no koe, oia ka *aae.*

A-AE, *s.* A certain form of commencing worship anciently.

    Aae, e kaulei, e lelei, e ku i kiona
    Ia oe e Kahamuili.

A-AE-A, *s.* A word used by children in addressing parents before they can speak plainly.

A-AI, *v.* See AI, to eat. To eat to satiety; to consume much.

2. To increase or grow, as an ulcer.

3. To ulcerate; to eat or make progress, as a sore.

4. FIG. To give pain; irritate. 2 *Tim.* 2:17. Aole hoi e *aai* ka hewa iloko o ka poe e ku paa ana, sin will not *increase* in those who stand fast.

A-AI, *adj.* Eating; increasing; continuing, as a sore; he mai *aai,* an increasing sore, he lepera *aai* ia. *Oihk.* 13:51.

A-AI, *s.* The progress or continuance of a sore.

A-AI, *s.* The action of the surf at high tide, when dashing ashore and then receding, thus wearing away the gravel; spelled also *aei.*

A-AI, *s.* Name of the net used to catch the fish opelu and maomao; as, *aai* opelu, the opelu net; *aai* maomao, the maomao net; also written *aei.*

A-A-IA-NU-HEA-KA-NE, *s.* Name of a bird. See A above.

A-A-I-O-LE, *adj.* Aai, to grow, and *ole,* not. Falling before ripe, as bread-fruit; applied to men who die before their time, i. e., before maturity.

A-A-I-O-LE, *s.* The bread-fruit which is ripe and fallen down of itself.

A-A-I-NA, *adv.* Loudly; strongly, as a sound, kani *aaina;* also continually. See

AAI, to increase.

A-AO, *adj.* Greedy, as dogs; always ready to eat, or seize food.

AA-O, *adj.* A species of tall, wild banana, he maia *aao.*

A-A-O-KO-KO, *adj.* Aa, vein or artery, and *koko,* blood. Epithet of any substance red hot, as fire, iron, stone, &c.; probably from the raging or rapid flow of blood.

A-AU, *s.* See AU. To swim dispersedly; a flock, as of birds when frightened; a school, as of fish as they come together and frightened; suddenly separate.

2. A slight ripple on the surface of calm water by a light breeze.

A-AU, *v.* To ripple mildly, as a calm sea, by a slight wind.

2. To separate, as a flock of birds when frightened, or a school of fish.

    Ka lele *aau* o ka manu o Kiwaa,
    The frightened flight of the birds of Kiwaa.
    Ka *aau* mai Kukona ke koae,
    The flock from Kukona, the koae.
    Ke koae nui hulu meamea,
    The great feathered koae.

A-AU-A, *s.* Epithet of a woman as she begins to advance in age, has wrinkles about the eyes, &c.

A-AU-A, *adj.* Strong scented, as the skin of a hog in dressing.

A-A-HA, *s.* Name of some kind of outside covering for a dish. He ipu i hanaia i ka *aaha* a paa, the cup was held with the *aaha,* and tightly.

A-A-HI, *s.* A, bag, and *ahi,* fire. A bag in which fire and fire materials were carried; he kieke *ahi.*

A-A-HI, *s.* Name of the iliahi or sandal-wood when young.

A-A-HI, *v.* See definition of AAMOO. Perhaps *a* and *ahi,* to burn, as with lust.

A-A-HO, *v.* To put up pia in small packages, that it may keep sweet.

A-A-HO, *s.* A container in which pia is put up.

A-A-HU, *s.* See AA, kind of cloth, and AHU, a fine mat. An outside garment. *Kin.* 27:15. A cloak, a garment thrown loosely over the shoulders.

2. A robe. *Iob.* 29:14. A covering for ornament; *aahu* kapa maikai, the dress of a dandy, i. e., dandyism. NOTE.—The *aahu* was formerly some kind of kapa; mamua, *aahu* kapa, mahope, *aahu* lole.

3. The bark of the mulberry soaked in water for making kapa.

4. *Aahu* kaua, armor. 1 *Sam.* 17:38.

A-A-HU, *v.* To cover with kapa; to

cover, as with a cloak.

2. To put on or wear clothes; to put on one's garment.

3. FIG. *Iob.* 29:14. *Aahu* iho au i ka pono, I have clothed myself with righteousness.

4. *Hoo.* To clothe one; to provide clothes for one. *Kin.* 3:21; *Oihk.* 8:7. SYN. with hookomo kapa.

A-A-HU-A, *v.* Pass of the foregoing for *aahuia. Gram.* § 211. Clothed; dressed; covered.

A-A-HU-A, *v.* To speak reproachfully; to use words of strong contempt for one.

A-A-HU-A-LII, *adj. Aa,* dwarf, and *hua-lii,* diminutive. Small; low in stature; defective in bodily structure; noinoi.

A-A-HU-A-LII, *s.* The name of a god.

A-A-HU-A-POO, *s. Aahu,* covering, and *poo,* head. A covering or clothing for the head; a defense in time of peril; a shield in war. 2 *Oihl.* 14:8. A buckler. 2 *Oihl.* 23:9. Connected with mahiole and palekaua.

A-A-HU-I, *s. Aa,* vein, and *hui,* pain, ache.

1. LIT. An aching vein.

2. A desire for pleasure, attended with some sense of pain. Pau ke *aahui,* ke aa-koni oloko, the painful desire within has ceased.

A-A-HU-U-LA, *s. Aahu* and *ula,* red. A cloak or royal dress adorned with red feathers, considered very valuable; o ka *aahuula,* he waiwai makamae nui ia.

A-A-HU-KA-PU, *s. Aahu,* garment, and *kapu,* forbidden. A consecrated or holy garment. *Puk.* 28:2.

A-A-HU-MA-KA-LOA, *v. Aahu,* garment, *malo* and *loa,* long malo. To clothe one, or put on the long malo; ua aahuia ka maloloa, nolaila, he *aahumakaloa.*

A-A-HU-MA-MO, *s. Aahu* and *mamo,* a yellow bird. A large yellow robe worn by the king or high chief; no ka hanohano nui o ka *aahumamo.*

A-A-HU-PA-WE-HE, *s. Aahu,* garment, and *pawehe,* which see. A garment made of a kind of mat called pawehe; nolaila i ole-loia'i i *aahupawehe* hiwa na ka makani.

A-A-KA, *v.* To complain, as a person of a perverse or sour temper; to grumble; chide; find fault; to strive. *Nah.* 20:13. Iole makou e *aaka* a koea iho, that we may not think hard and refuse.

2. To be very dry; to be exceedingly thirsty.

3. To burst or crack open, as a ripe melon or banana.

4. To be hard, severe, as labor or toil; aole i *aakaia* ka hana a na haku, the work for the lords was not hard.

A-A-KA, *s.* Harsh speaking against one; a grumbling; a fault-finding.

A-A-KA, *s.* Name of a species of sandalwood. When young it is called *naio;* when old and when mature, it is odoriferous. It is very durable when used for house posts.

A-A-KA, *adj.* Coarse; illiberal; fault-finding; hard; severe. *Sol.* 8:13.

2. Peeled; skinned, as a banana.

3. Dry, as the coral of the reef at low tide.

A-A-KA, *v.* 5th conj. of *aka.* See *Gram.* § 209. To laugh at; to ridicule.

A-A-KA-KA, *s. A,* to burn, and *akaka,* clearly. The clear burning or splendor of the heavenly bodies in a clear night.

A-A-KI, *v.* 5th conj. of *aki.* To bite frequently; to bite in two; to bite, as the bark from a stick, or the rind from sugar cane.

2. To grate the teeth; ua *aaki* ke kui, ua make loa, he *grates* his teeth, he is dying.

3. To feel the severe pangs of child-birth.

A-A-KI, *v.* To surround or come upon one, as darkness; ua pouli loa, ke *aaki* mai nei ka poeleele.

2. To experience palpable darkness. *Puk.* 10:21.

3. To be caught or held by a thing; ua holo ia kanaka i ka moana, ua *aaki* i ke koa a paa, that man sailed out upon the ocean, he is *caught* in the coral, and is fast.

4. To come upon, as a fit of love; ua *aaki* paa ia ke aloha wela iluna ona. *Laieik.* 197.

A-A-KI, *adj.* Thick; obscure, as darkness. *Iob.* 38:9.

A-A-KI, *s.* A biting; ka naho manini nui, he *aaki* nei i ka limu.

A-A-KI-MA-KAU, *s.* A hook-biting fish; the name of a small fish noted for its readiness to bite at a hook. See A.

A-A-KO, *v.* 5th conj. of *ako.* To cut or clip off, as the spray of the sea when the surf strikes against a bluff of perpendicular rocks and is met by a wind from the land, and cuts or clips off the spray.

A-A-KO, *v.* Used in the imperative; be quick; go to work, &c.

A-A-KO, *s. Ako,* the name of a disease.

1. The furor uteriensis of females; insatiable desire of coition; *aako* kahi mai i ka hana hewa.

2. The itch; he maneo; he lalawe. This

last form of the word expresses the name of the last stage of the disease, followed by death. A primary stage is expressed by *ako*, to itch.

A-A-KO-KO, *s.* *Aa*, vein, and *koko*, blood. A vein; a blood vein. *Anat.* 45.

A-A-KO-NI, *s.* *Aa*, vein, and *koni*, to throb. Hence, an artery, perhaps; pau ke aahui, ke aalihui, ke *aakoni* oloko.

A-A-LA, *v.* 5th conj. of *ala*, to perfume. To emit a perfume; to be fragrant. *Isa.* 3:24.

2. To smell of perfumery. *Hal.* 45:8. *Aala* i ka ihuana ka uka o Kawela.

A-A-LA, *adj.* *Ala*, odoriferous; *aala* ka hala, sweet the hala; *aala* ka rose, sweet the rose; o na kaikuwahine *aala* o Aiwohikupua. *Laieik.* 62.

A-A-LA, *s.* *Ala.* An odor.

2. A kind of scrofulous sore, so called from the smell.

3. Fig. He *aala* no o Kaahumanu, a sweet perfume is Kaahumanu.

A-A-LA-I-O-A, *s.* Name of a wild ferocious man who lived in the forest; hence,

2. Wildness; ferocity; a savage appearance; kuku ka *aalaioa*.

A-A-LA-I-HI, *s.* A species of fish, small and yellow.

A-A-LA-KAI, *adj.* See **ALAKAI.** Large; plump; full fleshed.

A-A-LE-LE, *s.* *Aa*, vein, and *lele*, to jump. An artery, from its motion. *Anat.* 8.

A-A-LI, *s.* A small or low place between two larger ones; he puali.

A-A-LII, *s.* Name of a hard timber; more generally *alii*.

A-A-LI-NA-NUI, *adj.* Large, fat and weak, as a fat man.

A-A-LO, *v.* 5th conj. of *alo.* To dodge often; to dodge, as one does a stone.

A-A-LO-LE, *s.* *Aa*, cloth of cocoanut leaves. The name first given to cloth by the people of Kauai.

A-A-LO-LO, *s.* *Aa* and *lolo*, the brain. A nerve; *aalolo* hoao. *Anat.* 7. *Aalolo* lohe, the auditory nerve.

A-A-LU, *s.* Dim. of *alu.* A ravine; a small brook, valley or ravine.

A-A-MA, *v.* To stretch out the hands for the purpose of catching something.

2. To steal small articles; to pilfer.

A-A-MA, *s.* That motion of the hands when a person would try to seize hold of something while it rolls down a pali.

2. The act of stealing or pilfering.

3. A black crab living on a rocky shore.

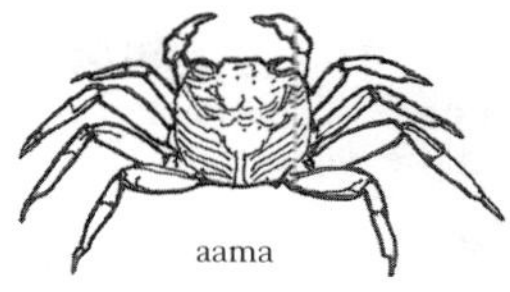

aama

4. Name of a four-footed animal in the sea.

A-A-MA, *s.* A person who speaks rapidly, concealing from one and communicating to another.

2. One who is expert in gaining knowledge.

A-A-MO, *adj.* Insatiable in lust; never satisfied; applied to females; he wahine *aamo*, ana ole.

A-A-MOO, *s.* See **AA.** The cloth-substance around cocoanut leaves; a veil; thin white cloth; o ka mea keokeo e lalahi ana i ka *moo*, he mea lahilahi a puaweawe; whatever is light, thin, as thin cloth.

A-A-MOO, *adj.* Light; thin, as cloth; o ka inoa o ka lole lahilahi loa.

A-A-NA, *v.* To speak angrily; to fret; olelo *aana* mai oia.

A-A-NA-PUU, *v.* To crook in different directions; to be small and large, i. e., to be uneven in size, as a rope.

A-A-NEI, *adv.* An interrogative adverb, and marks a question like *anei*; sometimes it is used of place, as pehea *aanei* la oe? where are you in the matter?

A-A-NE-MA, *v.* To be jealous of a man's friend, or to discover jealousy.

A-A-NO, *v.* The 7th conj. of *ano.* Hoo. To change one's form; to become another in appearance; ua *hooano* no oukou he poe akamai; to feign; to pretend to be something one is not.

A-A-NI-U, *s.* See **AA** and **NIU,** cocoanut. The covering like a coarse cloth around cocoanut leaves; a hookahekahe ma ka *aaniu*.

A-A-PA, *adj.* Presumptuous, as when a drunken man lies down on a precipice.

A-A-PI, *v.* 5th conj. of *api.* To bend, as the gills of a fish; to spring or warp, as a board.

A-A-PO, *v.* 5th conj. of *apo*, to catch. To snatch, as several persons at once; to catch at, as several hands at the same thing.

2. To receive readily in the mind; to grasp mentally, as a truth; ke *aapo* nei makou a malama.

A-A-PO, *adj.* Ready, quick to receive knowledge; quick at apprehension; he *aapo* ka naau o na kamalii.

A-A-PO, *s.* One who snatches.

2. One who learns quickly; a ready scholar.

A-A-POO, *s.* The skin, flesh and sinews on the back of the neck; he *aapoo* ka mea ma ka ai he *aapoo* bipi. *Kam.*

A-A-PU, *s.* See APU, a cup. A thin piece of wood, such as will bend up.

2. A concave vessel.

3. A valve of a vein. *Anat.* 45.

A-A-PU, *v.* To warp or bend, as a board in the sun.

2. To wrinkle or ruffle, as cloth; mimino. See AAPI.

3. *Hoo.* To turn the hollow of the hand upward; e *hooaapu* ae i kou poho lima.

A-A-PU-A, *s.* *Aa*, bag, and *pua*, an arrow. An arrow case; a quiver. *Iob.* 39:23; *Kin.* 27:3.

A-A-PUU-PUU, *s.* A capsular ligament. *Dr. J.*

A-A-WA, *s.* See AWA. Name of a species of fish, reddish and striped; he ia kokoke like ke ano me ko ka ea.

2. Also the name of a tree.

3. Name of an insect that destroys sweet potatoes; ua make ka mala uala i ka hoopalu, i ke pai, i ka peelua a me ka *aawa*.

A-A-WE, *v.* 5th conj. of *awe.* Used imperatively with *mai*, bring here; with *aku*, take away.

A-E, *v.* To pass, physically or mentally, from one state, condition, or place, to another.

1. *Specifically*, to break a kapu, ua *ae* lakou iluna o kahi laa; to violate a law or agreement, i. e., to transgress, as a law, to break a covenant. *Ios.* 7.11; *Hal.* 89:34.

2. To pass over, as the mind, i. e., to yield assent to the thought or opinion of another; to assent to the request of another; to say yes to a request or to an affirmation.

3. To permit, grant permission for a thing to be done; he mea *ae ia*, a thing permitted or allowed.

4. To pass physically from one place to another, from one situation to another, as from land on board a ship; ua *ae* aku lakou iluna o ka moku, iluna o ka lio, to *embark*, to *mount* a horse. *Hoo.*, conj. 3. To cause to pass from one place to another, from one person to another; to transfer.

5. To raise or lift up, as the head, with joy, e *ae* ko oukou poo no ka olioli.

6. To mount, as a horse or a mule. 2 *Sam.* 13:29.

7. To be sea-sick; to throw up from the mouth; to vomit; he mea luai ka moku, o ka *ae* wale aku no.

A-E, *s.* Assent, expressed by one person to the thought or opinion of another; approval of the conduct or opinion of another; consent; agreement.

A-E, *adj.* Consenting; agreeing; he olelo *ae like*, an agreement.

A-E, *s.* Name of an east wind.

2. A species of sea moss.

A-E, *s.* The water or liquid as wrung from the leaves of vegetables, as kalo, &c.; he *ae* kalo, he *ae* wauki, he ohi.

A-E, *s.* An irregular movement of the ocean; he wahi ano ia ma ka moana, a ma ka *ae* kai, a ma ka aina.

2. The coming in and receding of the sea upon the shore; the flux and reflux of the tide. See AEKAI.

A-E, *verbal directive. Gram.* § 234, 4. Implies an oblique motion of the verb, either up, down, or sideways. It often follows after nouns, also adjectives, as aohe kanaka e *ae*, there is no *other* man.

A-E, *adv.* See verb 2. Yes; the expression of affirmation, approbation or consent; opposed to *aole*, or *aohe.* With *paha*, as *ae paha*, a polite way of assenting when full belief is withheld; *ae ka paha*, even so, be it so.

A-E-A, *v.* To wander away from a place; mai ko'u alo aku, aole oe e *aea*, from my presence, do not wander away; to wander from place to place. *Nah.* 14:33.

2. To wander; go astray morally. *Hal.* 58:3.

3. To remove; to be removed; to go to another place. *Ier.* 4:1.

4. To live unsteadily; as, i kona wa i ona ai, nui kona *aea* ana, in his seasons of drunkenness, he lived principally here and there.

5. To toss or throw back the head, as a person with pride, as a horse on putting on a bridle; e *aea* ae ke poo o ka lio i ke kaulawaha.

A-E-A, *s.* A vagabond; an outcast. *Isa.* 11:12. He *poe aea*, fugitives. *Lunk.* 12:4.

2. The name of the rope connecting two fish nets. See KUKAI.

A-E-A, *adj.* Wandering; unstable; shifting a place; he one *aea* ke one o Hoohila; unsettled, as kanaka *aea*; a vagabond; wandering about. *Kin.* 4:12.

A-E-A, *adj.* Wanderingly, in a loose unstable manner.

AE-AE, *v.* Conj. 13 of *ae*, 4. To be a frequent transgressor, he *aeae* oe maluna o kahi kapu.

2. To step over a thing often.

3. To work over and over, as in pounding poi, until very fine.

4. To be or become very small or fine, as dust. 2 *Nal.* 23:6.

5. To interrupt one in his speech.

AE-AE, *adj.* Comminuted; small or fine, as dust; fine, as poi well pounded; he poi *aeae,* he poi uouo, he wali.

2. Dark, obscure, as a vision, indistinctly seen; po *aeae,* a night of indistinct vision, not totally dark, i. e., light and darkness mixed.

AE-AE-KAI, *v.* See AE, before. The ebbing and flowing of the sea.

A-EI, *s.* Name of the net used in catching the opelu and the maomao.

2. A kind of rope of the medium size.

A-EI, *s.* See AAI, before. Oia ka malama e kalai ai i ka kuku *aei* o Pelu.

A-EI-O-LE, *s.* See AAIOLE. Bread-fruit, ripe and fallen down, he ulu haule wale.

AE-O-KA-HA-LO-A, *s.* A kind of kapa made of wauke, and colored with charcoal, kuina *aeokahaloa.*

AE-KAI, *s.* The name of the place in the sea where the surf breaks; o kahi o ke kai i poi iho ai, he *aekai* ka inoa.

A-E-LO, *adj.* Rotten; applied to eggs. FIG. Ua like makou me na hua *aelo.*

AE-LO-A, *s.* The north-east trade wind on the ocean; same as *moae.*

AE-NEI, *v.* To be here; to be present; to be in existence. *Mat.* 2:18. NOTE.— This word seems to be compounded of *ae,* No. 4, expressive of a passing or transfer, and *nei,* which refers to present time or present place; something not fixed or exactly defined, but near by, either in time or place, as *at this present.*

AE-NEI, *adv.* Now, i. e., about this time, just now, within a short time past or future.

2. Here; hereabouts; near by; not far off; ua holo *aenei,* he has just now sailed; ua olelo *aenei,* he has lately spoken; ua make *aenei* no ke alii, the king died a short time ago; ua hele *aenei* no kahi i noho ai, he is gone a little ways to his place of residence.

A-E-NEI, *s.* Breadfruit. See AAINEI.

AE-SE-LO-NA, *s.* *Heb.* Name of an unclean bird, so translated in *Kanl.* 14:13.

A-E-TO, *s.* *Gr.* An eagle. *Puk.* 19:4; *Hoik.* 12:14.

AI, *v.* To eat; to consume food, as persons or animals.

2. To devour, as animals.

3. To destroy, consume, as fire. *Nah.* 16:35.

4. To consume; spoken of the sword, 2 *Sam.* 2:26.

5. To eat, consume, as a sore; aole *ai* ka mai, the disease has made no advance. *Oihk.* 13:5.

6. To taste, eat, enjoy the benefits of, have the profits of, as land; e *ai* i ka aina. *Nah.* 32; 19th conj., 3d hoo.

7. To cause to eat, i. e., compel or induce to eat; huhu loa ia (Kekuokalani) i ka *hoai* noa ana a lakou i ke alii (Liholiho), he was very angry at them for causing the king to eat freely, i. e., contrary to kapu.

8. To have sexual intercourse; applied to both sexes; also to animals. *Kin.* 30:41.

AI, *s.* Food; vegetable food, in distinction from *ia,* meat. Ai oo, ripe food; *ai* maloo, dried food; *ai* maka, green food, vegetables. NOTE.—*Ai,* food, is the representative of property generally.

AI, *adj.* Consuming; destroying; spoken of fire.

AI, *adv.,* for *aia.* There; near by, but not in contact; *ai* no iloko o ka hale, *there* in the house.

2. There, at another place, however distant; there; when; as, Auhea o Kekuaokalani? Ai ae no mauka mai. Where is Kekuaokalani? *There he is* coming by land.

AI, *verbal directive.* Gram. § 242. It has reference, generally, to a preceding noun, verb or adverb, expressive of time, place, cause, manner or instrument; often contracted, thus, hana'i, for hana ai.

AI, *s.* The neck; he *a-i* ko ke kanaka, oia kahi e hui ai ke poo me ke kino, man has a *neck,* it is that which unites the head with the body. A-i oolea, a stiff neck.

2. *Figuratively,* perverseness; disobedience. *Puk.* 33:3.

A-I-A, *v.* To be or show one's self contrary to the gods.

2. To disregard the will of the gods; to be ungodly in practice.

3. To have the character of an ungodly person. *Ier.* 23:11. See HAIHAIA.

A-I-A, *s.* An unprincipled or ungodly person. *Hal.* 14:1.

2. The practice of ungodliness itself; he hoomaloka; he hoole akua.

A-I-A, *adj.* Ungodly; irreligious.

2. Bad, sore, watery, as the eye; onohi-*aia,* a sore or watery eye.

A-I-A, *adv.* There, referring to place; *aia* malaila ka hana ana, *there* the work is doing.

2. Then, referring to time, generally in

connection with some other event. *Nah.* 10:3.

A-I-A, *interj.* Expressive of admiration or surprise, of triumph or contempt. *Aia hoi,* behold! see there; *aia ka,* there now! *Ios.* 9:12. *Aia* la, there you have it! an expression of triumph with contempt. *Hal.* 35:21.

AI-AI, *v.* To reduce to very small particles; to make small. *Kanl.* 9:21. To reduce to powder.

AI-AI, *v.* Found only in 15th conj. *Hoo.* To make white; splendid; to beautify; e *hooaiai* ana i ke kula o Lele, beautifying the upland of Lele.

AI-AI, *s.* Brightness; clearness; ua like ke keokeo me ka *aiai. Puk.* 24:10.

AI-AI, *adj.* Bright, as moonlight; fair; white. *Iob.* 25:5. He malamalama *aiai.* 2 *Sam.* 23:4. Pure, as milk. 1 *Pet.* 2:2. Clear, as glass. *Hoik.* 21:18. Pure, as gold. *Hoik.* 21:21. White, clean, as linen. *Hoik.* 19:8.

A-I-AI, *adv.* Nearly.

AI-AI-A-KU-U-LA, *s.* Name of god, the son of Hinahele, his mother, and Kuula, his father. He was a god of fishermen; he akua lawaia.

AI-AI-NA, *v.* Ai, to eat, and *aina,* land. LIT. To eat the land, i. e., to enjoy, to possess land; to own land; aole ia i *aiaina,* he did not possess land.

AI-AU, *v.* To pray or poison to death, as was formerly practiced.

   2. To show covetousness in asking; as, ua *aiau* aku i ka hai, he coveted what was another's. Similar to *aluna* and *makee.*

AI-A-HU-A, *v.* To break secretly the kapus of the gods, but to observe them openly; to act hypocritically.

   2. To conspire secretly against one.

   3. To defraud one's landlord by withholding the tax and using it himself.

   4. To pray to death. Similar to *anaana.*

AI-A-HU-A, *s.* A term applied to those who disregard the kapu while others observe it. When the kapu is generally disregarded it is called *ainoa;* hence,

   2. A hypocrite; an irreligious person.

AI-A-HU-A, *adj.* Irreligious; unmindful of the kapu; nani ke kanaka aiahua. See AIAHULU.

AI-A-HU-LU, *v.* To pray or poison to death.

   2. To procure the death of another by any fraudulent means, or for any political or selfish purpose. NOTE.—The agent of the intrigue is called kalaiino, niania, pao-

paonohonia. See these words in their places.

AI-A-HU-LU, *s.* Food baked a long time in the oven till it is brown.

AI-A-HU-PU-AA, *adj.* See AI and AHU-PUAA. A division of country; he alii *aiahupuaa,* enjoying the office and perquisites of an overseer of land. *Laieik.* 34.

AI-A-KA-KAI, *s.* Ai, food, and *akakai,* a rush. New, fresh, sweet food, like poi newly pounded; he ai hou, he ai manalo. Such food is also called *pololei.*

AI-A-LA-A-LA, *s.* Ai, to eat, and *ala,* or *alaala,* odoriferous. The scrofula.

AI-A-LII, *v.* Ai and *alii,* chief. E hoohanohano, to enjoy the ease, honor and dignity of a chief; to act the chief. See NALI-NALI.

AI-A-LO, *s.* Ai, to eat, and *alo,* in front. To eat before.

   1. The people about the chief; his attendants, in distinction from the poe makaainana; kanaka *aialo* no ke alii.

   2. A prince or princess; those about a king. *Sol.* 31:4. Pau loa na makaainana a me na *aialo* i ka pii iuka, all the common people and those about the chief went up the mountain.

   3. A small division of land less than an ahupuaa; na kanaka o na aina, a me na ahupuaa, a me na *aialo.*

   4. One who is a hanger on and lives lazily with a chief and eats his food.

AI-A-NA, *s. Eng.* The Hawaiian pronunciation of *iron;* a flat iron.

AI-A-NA, *adj.* Walking wearily up and down precipices; he hele aikena, he maloeloe.

AI-A-NEI, *adv.* There; just by; not far off.

AI-E, *v.* Ai, to eat, and *e,* before hand, i. e., to eat or enjoy a thing before it is paid for; from the custom of paying for work before it was done, and the pay consumed.

   1. To owe; to be indebted; aole oia (o Kamehameha) i *aie,* he (Kamehameha) never went into debt.

   2. To enjoy something yet to be paid for; e lawe e i ka waiwai a mahope hookaa.

AI-E, *s.* Indebtedness; the state of being in debt; he poe *aie* kakou, we are debtors.

   2. A debt; that which is due for any cause; e lawe *aie,* to go in debt for a thing. *Neh.* 5:2. E haawi *aie,* to give (lend) on usury. *Kanl.* 23:20.

AI-E, *adj.* In debt; owing; under obligation to render some equivalent for something received.

AI-E, *adv.* E haawi *aie,* to give to be paid again.

AI-EA, *s.* Fatigue; weariness.

AI-EA, *s.* Name of a species of tree found on Lanai and other islands used for finishing off canoes.

AI-I-LI-LO-KO, *v.* Ai, to enjoy, *ili,* the skin, surface (of land,) *loko,* that which is contained in something else. To have or possess a division of land less than an ahupuaa.

AI-O, *v.* The exclamation of one who commands others to pull, or lift altogether; e holo, e ale, e miha, *aio!*

A-I-OE-OE, *s.* A-i, the neck, and *oeoe,* long. A long neck; applied,

1. To animals, as to *nene,* a goose, a terrapin, the camelopard.

2. To persons. NOTE.—This was the distinctive appellation which the Hawaiians first gave to the missionaries' wives, on account of the fashion of their bonnets (in 1820,) which gave them the appearance of long necks. No ka loloa o ka *a-i* a me ka *oeoe* o ka papale, kapa aku na kanaka ia lakou, Aioeoe. *Mooolelo Hawaii,* p. 39.

AI-O-HA-HA, *s.* Ai, food, and *ohaha,* plump. Vegetables, kalo or potatoes, full sized and good.

AI-O-HA-LAU, *s.* Ai, food, and *oha,* the lower part of kalo tops, and *lau,* leaf. Food, of the kalo tops, often fed to swine.

A-I-U-HA-U-HA, *s.* A-i, the neck, and *uha-uha.* A stiff or cramped neck.

AI-U-HA-U-HA, *s.* Ai, to eat, and *uha-uha,* riotous. Epithet of a lower class of chiefs; eating riotously, or riotous eaters.

AI-HA-HA, *s.* Ai, food, and *haha,* skin of kalo tops. The food of poor people; e *aihaha* ana na luwahine.

AI-HA-LA-LE, *v.* Ai, eat, and *halale,* to sup up, as a liquid. To be lazy; to do nothing; to be the reproach of others; to eat the food of others without work. See LOMALOMAAIHALALE.

AI-HA-MU, *s.* Ai, food, and *hamu,* remnants of food.

1. The food left after a meal, especially when little is left.

2. Crumbs and scrapings, that which is burned on to the stones of the oven.

AI-HA-MU, *v.* Ai, to eat, and *hamu,* refuse food.

1. To eat refuse food.

2. To eat up clean; ua *aihamuia* kau mala uala.

3. Applied as an epithet of reproach to

the poe kahuna anaana, the priests who practiced sorcery.

AI-HE-A, *int. adv.* Ai, there, and *hea,* where. At, or towards what place? the answer, *ailaila,* there. NOTE.—The *a* may be *a* No. 2. NOTE.—And *ihea* the auialo of *hea.* See *Gram.* § 165, p. 93.

AI-HU-A-WAA, *v.* To pass from one place to another and find a dwelling place.

AI-HU-A-WAA, *adj.* He poe *aihuawaa,* wanderers that have not settled down in any place.

AI-HU-E, *v.* Ai, food and *hue,* to steal. LIT. To steal food. But ai represents property of all kinds. See AI, *s.* NOTE.—Hence, to steal generally; to take another's property secretly and without leave; to steal a person. *Kanl.* 24:7.

AI-HU-E, *s.* A thief; one who steals.

AI-HU-E-A,

AI-HU-E-IA, } *v.* These are all passive forms of the verb *aihue;*

AI-HU-E-HI-A, } to be stolen. For these forms, see *Gram.* § 211:

AI-HU-E-LI-A, } 1st, 2d.

AI-HU-E, *adj.* Found in all the above forms. Stolen; taken secretly.

AI-KA-HA-U-LA, *s.* See MOEKAHAULA. A dreaming of committing adultery or fornication; a lascivious dream.

AI-KA-NE, *v.* Ai, No. 8, and *kane,* male.

1. To cohabit, as male with male, or female with female.

2. To commit sodomy; hence

AI-KA-NE, *s.* An intimate friend of the same sex; a friend or companion of the same sex.

2. Those who mutually give and receive presents, being of the same sex.

3. Sodomy; dissoluteness of habit.

AI-KA-PA, *v.* Ai, to enjoy, and *kapa,* side, edge, border. To own one-half of a thing; applied to anything of which one-half belongs to one person and one-half to another.

AI-KA-PU, *v.* Ai, to eat, and *kapu,* fobidden.

1. To eat according to the restrictions of the kapu.

2. To obey the rules of the tabu (kapu) system, i. e., to observe the ceremonies of the kapu. NOTE.—It is the opposite of *ainoa.*

AI-KA-PU, *s.* The observance of the rules of the kapu; yielding obedience to them; hooikaika lakou ia ia e hoopaakiki me ka *aikapu,* they encouraged him to be firm by the kapu.

AI-KE-NA, *v.* To compel to work when one is already fatigued; to cause a groaning or complaint for hard usage.

AI-KE-PA, *v.* Ai and *kepa,* to scrape off, as dirt from a stone.

1. To level off; to rabbet, as the edge of a board.

2. To lap over; to cut a thing off obliquely so as to make uneven parts.

AI-KE-PA, *adj.* Being cut obliquely off, so as to make uneven parts; o ko'u ia, ua oki *aikepa* ia aku nei a uuku loa, my fish, it is cut off *obliquely,* and is very small; he lole i oki *aikepa* ia a pono ole, the cloth is cut off *obliquely,* and not straight.

AI-KE-PA-KE-PA, *v.* To quarrel, as a man and his wife when another intercedes; he wahine nuku *aikepakepa* lua.

AI-KI, *v.* Abbreviation of the word *hoa-iki.* To peep privately, or to look slyly; i lele i ke kapu a pa i ka *aiki.*

AI-KO-LA, *v.* See AKOLA. Used only in conj. 13. *Hoo.* To despise; to spurn from; to triumph over; to treat contemptuously. *Hal.* 22:24.

2. FIG. Applied to trees; to rejoice over, in view of victory. *Isa.* 14:8. See also HOONAIKOLA, another form of the same word.

AI-KO-LA, *s. Hoo.* The subject of scorn or derision; he mea *hoaikola* a akaaka hoi, a subject of scorn and derision. *Hal.* 79:4. See HOAIKOLA.

AI-KO-LA, *int.* An expression of triumph mixed with contempt, as *aha! Ezek.* 25:3.

AI-KU, *v.* Ai, to eat, and *ku,* to stand. LIT. To eat standing.

1. To eat in an improper manner.

2. FIG. To do a thing contrary to rule or ceremony.

3. To break a kapu similar to *aia.* Aiku was an offense against the gods.

A-I-KU, *s.* A-i, the neck, and *ku,* to stand. A standing collar for a jacket.

AI-KU, *s.* Name of a disease; the croup, from the disposition to hold the head erect.

AI-KU-KU-KU, *v.* To be sick with swelling in the mouth and legs; ua *aikukuku* ma ka waha, he has a swelling in the mouth; ua *aikukuku* ma ka wawae, aole ola, he has swelled legs, he will not live.

AI-KU-KU-KU, *s.* The swelling and soreness of the mouth and legs, like the large itch.

AI-KU-PUU, *s.* Ai, food, and *kupuu.* Dry food, as baked kalo or other vegetables.

AI-LA, *s. Eng.* Oil; *aila* kukui, lamp oil; *aila* mura, ointment. *Sol.* 27:9. NOTE.— The Hawaiian words are *momona, konahua,* &c.

AI-LA, *s.* The name of the tree; called also *koli.*

AI-LAI-LA, *adv.* Ai (see AI, *adv.*) and *laila,* there. In answer to the interrogative *aihea;* there; by the side of; in that place; there; there it is.

AI-LA-LO, *adv.* Ai, *adv.,* and *lalo,* down. Down; down under; down there; *ailalo* kahi i make ai, *down there* is the place where he died.

AI-LE-A, *v.* Ai, *v.* 8, and *lea,* pleasure. To copulate, as male and female; spoken of men and animals.

AI-LE-PE, *v.* Ai and *lepe,* the comb of a cock.

1. To turn up and back.

2. To ruck, as the skin when broken, or as kapa when ruffed.

AI-LE-PE, *adj.* Turned up; rucked; as the skin when broken; as kapa when ruffed.

AI-LE-PO, *s.* Ai, to eat, and *lepo,* dirt. An expression applied to a multitude of fish. The application is not clear.

A-I-LI, *v.* To pant; to gasp for breath.

2. To pull up, as a bush; e uhuki.

3. To pull up, as a hook with a fish on it; o ka *aili* ae no ia i ke aho lou ka ia i ka makau, he pulled up his hook line, the hook was the fish. See KAILI.

AI-LI-A, *v.* Pass. of *aili* for *ailiia.*

AI-LII, *v.* Ai and *lii* for *alii.* To enjoy the dignity of the chief; to be noble.

AI-LI-HI, *v.* Ai, to eat, enjoy, and *lihi,* a border, edge.

1. To possess or enjoy a piece of land only in part, as some corner, end or out side, while the main part is denied. See AIKAPA.

2. To pay only a part of a debt and withhold the remainder; ua hookaa mai i kekahi a ua *alihi* aku no i kekahi, he paid some and withheld some (of the debt.)

3. To disregard the kapu in respect to trading.

AI-LI-HI, *s.* A creditor; he mea i *aili-hiia,* a person paid only in part; he inoa no kekahi mea.

AI-LO-LO, *s.* The name of a religious performance when a hog was offered in sacrifice; a part of it was eaten at the time of offering.

AI-LO-LO, *v.* To teach the art of *lua* and the practice of *anaana;* sorcery and the practice of soldiery, so as to be a proficient. Ua ao i ka lua, a ua make ke kanaka, ua *ailolo*. Ua ao i ka anaana, ua make ke kanaka, ua *ailolo*. Ua ao i ke koa, ua ku i ka moku, a ua *ailolo*.

AI-LO-LO, *adj*. Disobedient, as a child, and thus destroys himself; one that destroys himself through his own evil courses; it belongs to persons of all classes; he keiki hoolohe ole, a ua lele i ka pali no ke kolohe, a ua make *ailolo* ka hookuli, he was a disobedient child, he leaped a precipice through mischief, he died through disobedience, &c.; ua make no ke kanaka hewa no ka hookuli *ailolo* no ia lakou.

AI-LO-LO, *s*. He inoa no kekahi mea.

AI-LU-NA, *adv*. There above; up; upwards.

AI-MA-HA-HA, *s*. A kind of hard kalo, difficult to make into good poi.

AI-MA-LU, *v*. Ai, to eat, and *malu*, secretly.
1. To transgress or break a law secretly.
2. To eat with one contrary to kapu; he *aimalu* ka poe ai puupuu o na 'lii, the stewards of the chiefs transgressed.

AI-MO-KU, *s*. Ai, to eat, enjoy, and *moku*, a district. A person who holds the rank of a chief over some district or island; one who enjoys the honors and profits of such a post without really owning the land; e pau kona *aimoku* ana, his authority is ended. *Laieik*. 34.

AI-MO-KU, *adj*. Having the authority of a chief; he kane *aimoku*, epithet of a person acting for a chief, a lieutenant, one who enjoys the fruits of the land but pays a part to the owner; na 'lii *aimoku*, governors. *Ezr*. 8:36; *Eset*. 3:12.

AI-NA, *s*. Ai, to eat, enjoy, and *na*, contraction of *ana* (the participial termination of words equivalent to *Eng*. ing. See *Gram*. § 204, 2.) An eating; the means of eating, i. e., the fruits of the land; hence,
1. Land generally; a farm; a field; a country; an island. In this sense it is SYN. with moku, or mokupuni; elua inoa i kapaia ma ka mokupuni, he *moku* kekahi, a he *aina* kekahi, an island has two names, *moku* is one, and *aina* is the other. *D. Malo*. 7:1.
2. Any taxable privilege, as the right of fishing, the right to sell things in market, &c.
3. Any means of obtaining a living; e kii au e hao i kela waiwai, no ka mea, o ko'u *aina* no o ka hao wale aku, I will go and rob that property, because it is my means of living to rob. *Haw. Hist*.

AI-NA, *s*. A contraction of *ai ana*. See above. An eating; a meal.

AI-NA, *adj*. Eating; dining; papa *aina*, an eating table; hale *aina*, one of the six houses of an establishment; he hale *aina* oia kekahi, the eating house is one.

AI-NA, *s*. The snap of a gun; the jar of a door; the report of lightning. See PAPAINA.

AI-NA, *v*. LIT. Being eaten. Used passively; to be destroyed; to be devoured; eaten up. Aina o Hawaii e ka pele, Hawaii is eaten by the volcano; aina ke kanaka e ka mano, the man was devoured by a shark; aina ka ai e ka puaa, the food was eaten by a hog.

AI-NA, *s*. Pain; grief; weariness; disappointed affection; he kena, luhi, he lea.

AI-NA-O-LE, *v*. To eat silently, gently, without noise; e ai mahie, e mukamuka, e ainaole.

AI-NA-HOO-I-LI-NA, *s*. Aina, land, and *hooilina*, to inherit. An inheritance, i. e., land inherited. 2 *Oihl*. 20:11. An inherited portion. *Iob*. 24:8.

AI-NA-KE-A, *s*. Aina, eating, and *kea*, species of cane. See KOKEA. The eating of sugar-cane till dry and white.

AI-NE-A, *v*. To labor in vain; to be weary with hard toil. See INEA.

AI-NE-MA-NE-MA, *v*. Ai, and *nema*. To reproach; to vilify.

AI-NO-A, *v*. Ai, to eat, and *noa*, free from restraint. To eat freely, without regarding the kapu; to break kapu by eating; to disregard the kapus in one's manner of living.

AI-NO-A, *s*. Ai and *noa*. Implying a release from kapu; the opposite of *aikapu*; freedom from the restraints of kapu; o ka *ainoa*, oia ka hoomaka ana e pau ai ia mau kapu, the eating freely, i. e., (the disregarding the kapu,) that was the beginning of the destruction of the kapu system. *Ainoa* was the general term, and universally applied when the nation threw off idolatry. *Haw. Hist*.

AI-NO-A, *s*. Name of those persons who first ate together, men and women, contrary to the kapu.

AI-PA (e-pa), *s*. *Heb*. Name of a dry measure; an epha. *Nah*. 5:15.

AI-PAA, *s*. Ai, food, and *paa*, hard. Hard food; food, that is, kalo prepared for keeping.

AI-PA-LAI, *s*. A name for scrofula. The word is said to have originated with Kamehameha I., meaning the same as *aialaala*.

AI-PO-O-LA, *s.* He *aipoola*, he like me ka puupoola i ka moni.

AI-PO-O-LA, *s.* He hana mahiai, a mahope kalua ka mea ai no ka luhi o ka hana ana; he kaumaha paha o ka mea i hanaia, he *aipoola.*

AI-PO-O-LA, *adj.* Ua paa i ka hana, he hana *hoaipoola.*

A-I-PUU, *s.* A-*i*, neck, and *puu*, a bunch.

   1. A bunch on the shoulder from carrying heavy burdens.

   2. Name of the person who has such a bunch.

   3. The name of a disease; also called *leholeho.* Ka pilikia no ke kau ana mai o ka mai *aipuu* a e anai mai, the difficulty from the attack of the disease *aipuu* causing waste, &c.; he kokua leholeho.

AI-PUU-PUU, *v.* Ai, food, and *puupuu*, to divide out. See PUU.

   1. *Hoo.* To serve out provisions to others; to supply with provisions.

   2. To serve or wait on at table.

   3. To act as a servant in any manner.

AI-PUU-PUU, *s.* A servant who prepares food; a steward; a cook; a servant generally; originally, applied to stewards of chiefs.

AI-PU-HI-U, *s.* The release from the restrictions of kapu; it has the same meaning as *ainoa*, but is seldom used.

AI-PU-KA, *s.* See IPUKA, a gate. *Ipuka* is the correct orthography.

AI-PU-NI, *v.* To go around; to circumambulate, as a tract of country; like *kaapuni.*

A-I-WA (e-i-wa), *num. adj.* The simple form is *iwa.* Nine; the number nine.

A-I-WA-I-WA, *v.* To be very good, beneficent and kind, or the contrary. *Aiwaiwa* refers to the excess of character, very good or very bad. *Aiwaiwa* ke kanaka akamai i ka naauao; *aiwaiwa* no hoi ke alii lokomaikai; *aiwaiwa* no hoi ke keiki kolohe. *Aiwaiwa* refers to a person accomplished with learning; it applies to a very kindhearted chief; it also applies to a mischievous child.

AI-WA-I-WA, *s.* A remarkable person or animal; applied to the fabulous dog Kalahumoku, of Tahiti; a ike aku la ia Kalahumoku i ke *aiwaiwa* o Tahiti. *Laieik.* 108.

AI-WA-I-WA, *v.* To look long and steadily at a person or thing; *aiwaiwa* nui i ka nana loihi a ike, he persevered in looking for a long time.

AI-WAI-U, *adj.* Ai, to eat, and *waiu*, milk. Milk-eating; epithet of a sucking child; an infant. *Isa.* 49:15. LIT. A milk-

eater.

AO, *v.* To be or become light or day, as in the morning; ua *ao* ka po, the night has become light. *Oih.* 12:18.

   2. To awake, as from a vision or dream.

   3. To come to one's right mind or self-possession.

   4. To teach; instruct. *Luk.* 11:1.

   5. To enlighten; instruct in one's duty or conduct. *Oihk.* 10:11.

   6. To reprove; take heed; beware; to warn. *Kin.* 31:24.

   7. To regard with reverence; to obey.

   8. To charge strictly.

   9. To learn to do a thing; to learn, to study, as a language; e na kumu e, e *ao* oukou i ka olelo Hawaii, O teachers, study the Hawaiian language.

   10. To copy the example of others. *Kanl.* 18:9. In the imperative, e *ao*, look out; watch; be on your guard; take heed. *Ios.* 22:5.

AO, *v.* Found only in hoo., conj. 3. To tempt; to try; to prove. *Dan.* 12:10.

   2. To try one's conduct or fitness for a duty. *Lunk.* 7:4.

   3. To try; assay. *Kanl.* 4:34.

   4. To try to do a thing, to ascertain whether it can be done; e *hoao* e ae oe mamua a maopopo, a ina maopopo, alaila hana, try first whether the thing is feasible, if feasible, then do it.

   5. To try; taste of, i. e., suffer, as pain or death. *Mat.* 16:18. To tempt, as the Holy Spirit. *Oih.* 5:9.

   6. To try, i. e., to cohabit before marriage.

   7. To exhibit or practice the shameless conduct of the sexes as in former times.

AO, *s.* Light; day, in distinction from *po*, night. *Kin.* 1:5. For the different periods of time through the night, see *Laieik.* 30.

   2. The world. *Hal.* 89:11. O ke *ao* nei, o keia *ao*, this world; o kela *ao*, the future world; na wahi *ao*, heavenly places. *Epes.* 1:3.

   3. Light; applied to the light-green of fresh leaves of plants or trees; the green fresh buds; a kupu, a lau, a loa, a *ao*, a muo, a liko; the middle or new leaf of plants; as, *ao* ko, *ao* kalo.

   4. Knowledge; instruction; ke *ao* ana, doctrine.

A-O, *s.* A cloud. *Puk.* 14:19. Ao pouli, a dark cloud. *Puk.* 14:20. Na mea nana i ke *ao*, observers of clouds. *Kanl.* 18:14.

AO, *adj.* Enlightened; informed; instructed; mostly connected with *naau*, as naau*ao*, and written as one word.

Ao, *s.* Dried kalo or potatoes (i. e., kalo or potatoes baked and dried,) used for food.

2. Sea-bread or any hard bread was called *ao* by Hawaiians when they first saw it.

Ao, *s.* Art., ka. Name of a species of bird. *Laieik.* 29.

A-O-A, *v.* To howl, as a dog or wolf.

2. To howl or wail for grief for the loss of friends; to howl for a calamity that has come upon one. *Isa.* 13:6.

3. To cry, as one in distress and anguish. *Iak.* 5:1. To howl, as in despair. *Ioel.* 1:5.

A-O-A, *s.* A howling, as of a dog or ravenous beast; a wailing for the dead.

A-O-A, *adj.* Howling, as of a ravenous beast. *Isa.* 13:21. Holoholona *aoaoa*, howling beasts. Hence, cross; angry; rough in language.

A-O-A, *s.* A snail; he pupu.

2. Also the name of a species of small fish.

A-O-A, *s.* Name of a tree, not found on these islands, but in some foreign country; often spoken of in the ancient meles.

Ao-AO, *s.* The side of a thing, as land, country; the coast of a country. Ma ka *aoao* o Puna a me Kau ka holo ana, along the shore of the Puna and Kau was the sailing. Pehea na *aoao* o Ferani? What are the boundaries of France?

2. *Trop.* A way, habit, manner, peculiar to any one. *Oih.* 17:2. A course of life. *Hal.* 1:1 and 6.

Ao-AO, *v.* To accustom; to practice; e hoomaamaa. See MAA. To repeat frequently.

2. To teach; to give instruction to one how to act on occasion. *Laieik.* 12.

A-O-AO, *v.* To make one's escape from justice; to depart secretly from fear of being taken; e *aoao* malu ana, i mahuka, to escape secretly, to run away.

2. To show or point out a way for one to go; *aoao* aku la o mea, eia ko alanui.

Ao-AO, *s.* What one has been taught to say or do; kahea iho la e like me ke *aoao* ana, he called out as he had been instructed. *Laieik.* 170.

A-OA-OA, *s.* Name of a pleasant sea-breeze at Honolulu; he paa o *aoaoa* lani.

Ao-AO-NU-I, *s.* The name of a species of broad fish; he ia kino palahalaha.

Ao-A-KU-A, *s.* Ao, for *wao*, a desert place, and *akua*, God. A lonely place; generally a barren place; a desert. More properly written *waoakua*, the region of the gods, ghosts, hobgoblins, &c. See WAO-

AKUA. NOTE.—The proper orthography is *auakua*.

Ao-AO-WE-LA, *s.* A species of fish of a green color.

A-O-E, *adv.* One of the forms of the adverb of negation; *aohe, aole, aoe,* no, not, nor, a universal negative.

A-OE, *v.* See OE. To move along with a rustling, rippling noise, as a wave of the sea; to make a noise like a rippling wave; *aoe* ka ale o ka moana, the slight wave of the ocean ripples, &c. he hele wale no e like me ka *aoe*.

A-OO, *s.* See A oo under A. Name of an instrument for destroying unborn children, &c. See KOHOLUA.

A-O-O, *adj.* See Oo, to be mature. Epithet of a full grown man when all his faculties of body and mind have come to maturity; he *aoo* ia, he is full grown.

A-O-O-NO-HI, *s.* He *aoonohi* ulaula; an expression signifying that a storm is near.

Ao-O-PU-A, *s.* Ao, cloud, and *pua*, an arrow. Sharp-pointed clouds as they appear in the sky; me he mau *aoopua* la e kau ana, pela ke kau ana o ka make maluna o na kanaka, as sharp-pointed clouds hang in the sky, so death hangs over men.

Ao-U-LI, *s.* Ao, a cloud, and *uli*, blue.

1. A blue cloud, i. e., the sky, the firmament.

2. The visible arch of heaven; aia iluna lilo ke *aouli* la, there above is the sky.

3. The stars collectively; the host of heaven. 2 *Oihl.* 33:5.

4. Heaven itself. *Hal.* 89:6. NOTE.— In *grammar*, it is used for mood; as, *aouli* hai, indicative *mood*; *aouli* kauoha, imperative *mood*; *aouli* kuihe, subjunctive *mood*; *aouli* kuwale, infinitive *mood*.

A-O-HE, *adv.* No; not; not at all; by no means. See AOLE and AOE.

Ao-HAA,
Ao-HE-IO,
Ao-HE-IO-HOI,
Ao-HE-HOI,
Ao-HE-O-KA-NA-MAI, } *adv.* Used as adverbs and interjections. What! How great! Truly so; a confirmation of the declaration of another; also, surprising; admirable; never so many, &c.

Ao-HE-LE, *v.* Ao, to teach, and *hele*, to go.

1. To teach as one travels; to preach traveling about; ua *aohele* o Kaahumanu me ka hoohuli i na kanaka a pau ma ka pono, Kaahumanu went about teaching the people and turning them to do what was right.

2. To declare; publish, as a law; as a chief when he went from place to place; *aohele na 'lii i na kanawai.*

Ao-ho-ku, *v.* Ao, to teach, and *hoku*, a star. To teach astronomy.

Ao-ho-ku, *s.* Astronomy as a science; also an astronomer; *pepehiia ae la ke alii moku a me ka mea aohoku,* the captain of the ship was slain and the astronomer.

Ao-ka, *v.* To be crushed or chewed finely for swallowing.

A-o-ka-o-ka, *v.* See OKA. To pulverize; make fine; to bruise or pound fine; *aweluawelu.* See OKAOKA.

A-o-ka-a-o-ka, *s.* Any fine particles of matter, as saw-dust, lees of wine, dregs of any liquid; hence,

2. An offensive smell, as connected with such matter.

Ao-ka-ha-ea, *s.* Ao, cloud, and *kahaea.* A kind of cloud as it appears in the heavens; *he aokahaea i kinohinohiia.*

Ao-ku, *s.* The name of a rain; he ua *aoku.*

A-o-le (ole)**,** *adv.* An adverb of denying, refusing; no; not; a universal negative; for euphony's sake, it takes different forms; as, *aohe, aole, ohe, ole,* and *aoe.* The form *ole* is privative in its meaning, and may be added to almost any adjective, noun (proper names excepted,) or verb in the language. It is equivalent to the English inseparable negative particles, *less, in, un,* &c. See OLE.

A-o-le, *v.* To not; not to do; *aole* oia i hana, he did it not.

2. To deny; refuse to do a thing; *aole* ae la ia i hoopono ia ia, ia manawa, he refused (he did not) reform himself at that time.

3. Not to be; no existence. *Hal.* 37:36. *Aole* e ole, a phrase signifying the strongest affirmation, as, it cannot but be, it cannot be otherwise, it will not fail of being so, there is no *not* in the case, &c. NOTE.— the sense 2, to deny, is more generally found under the form *ole, v.,* 3d conj. hoo., which see.

A-o-le-e-o-le, *adv.* See AOLE above. It cannot but be. LIT. It cannot be not.

A-o-le-io-hoi, *adv.* See under AOHAA. How very! *Mat.* 6:23. *Aole loa,* God forbid. *Luk.* 20:16.

A-o-le-pa-ha, *adv.* A strong affirmation; how true; true indeed; so it is.

A-o-le-hoi-na, *adv.* A very affectionate salutation; now used only among the old people; the modern term is *aloha.*

Ao-loa, *s.* Ao, cloud, and *loa,* long. A comparison of clouds, as high and low; applied also to men, as more or less honorable; o Ku ke *aoloa,* o Ku ke *aopoko,* Ku is the long cloud, Ku is the short cloud. See AOPOKO.

Ao-mi-lo, *v.* To procure abortion; oo no lakou i na keiki, *aomilo* a hahai, ua nui na kamalii i make. NOTE.—The methods of procuring abortion were numerous and various.

A-o-ne, *s.* Dirt; he lepo, he lau one. See ONE, sand.

A-o-no, *adj. num.* See ONO, the simple form. Six; with other forms, *eono,* ke *ono,* he *ono.*

A-o-no-ka, *adv.* A contracted poetical phrase for aole no ka e kala, not lately done, long ago.

Ao-nu-i-hoo-la-ho-la-ho, *s.* The name of a broad mass of clouds extending over a great space.

2. A mass of pillar clouds as seen at night.

Ao-po-ko, *s.* See AOLOA. LIT. A short cloud. FIG. Men of little weight of character.

Au, *pers. pron.,* 1st per. sing. I; when prefixed or preceded by the emphatic o, as o *au,* the compound sound resembles that of *w*; hence it has the forms *au,* o *au, wau,* and o *wau;* the o is no part of the word, and should be written separately.

A'u, *pron.* So written for *aau,* one *a* dropped and the apostrophe supplied. It is the *auipili,* one of the oblique cases of *au,* I. See *Gram.* § 124. Of me; mine. There is a sensible break in the pronunciation, to distinguish it from *au,* the 1st person, and from *au,* of the 2d person next below.

Au, *pron.* With a more protracted, smooth pronunciation than the foregoing, one of the auipili cases of the 2d per. sing. of *oe. Gram.* § 132. Thine; of thee.

Au, *s.* The handle or helve of an axe. *Kanl.* 19:5. The staff of a spear. 1 *Sam.* 17:7. The handle of a sword. *Lunk.* 3:22. The handle of an auger, &c.; *au* koi, *au* pahi.

Au, *s.* The current in the ocean; *au* maloko o ka moana; o kahi o ke kai e wili ana, he *au* ia; he *wili au* kahi inoa.

2. The grain in wood.

3. The motion of the hand in mixing poi.

4. An action of the mind; as, ke *au* wale nei no ko'u manao e ake e pulelo iki ae, my mind is exercising, &c. See AU, *v.,* below.

Au, *s.* The gall of animals. *Oihk.* 3:4; *Iob.* 16:13; *Met. Oih.* 8:23.

Au, *s.* Time; a period of time, more or

less definitely designated, as the reign of a king. *Ier.* 28:1.

2. The time of one's life; i ke *au* ia Kalaniopuu; i ke *au* o Liholiho, in the time of Kalaniopuu, &c.

3. A season. *Oih.* 11:28. A portion of time.

Au, *s.* A territory; district of country; generally compounded with other qualifying words; as, *auakua,* a desert, a place of gods, ghosts, &c. See AUAKUA. *Aukanaka,* an inhabited country; *aupuni,* a large region, &c. NOTE.—*Au* is the term representing all places where food grows; as *kaha* represents such places as are on or near the shore where food does not grow. This applies mostly to the leeward side of the islands.

Au, *v.* To swim; ua *au* na kanaka i ka moana, a pakele i ka make, the people swam the ocean and escaped death.

2. To float on the surface of water; to turn, as the eyes to look at something; i na ua ike oe e *au* ana kona maka. *Laieik.* 145. SYN. with nana ia.

3. *Hoo.,* 3d conj. To cause to swim, to float; *hooau* hele aku la i na pahu o lakou, they floated along their (water) casks.

4. To convey, as on a raft. 2 *Oihl.* 2:16.

5. To swim through the water by the exertions of the arms and other limbs; poho ka uhane o ka poe make i ka moana, aole paha e hiki ke *au* iuka, the souls of those who sink in the ocean are lost, they are not able to swim ashore. Used imperatively, to quicken, to hasten; more generally doubled, as *auau,* which see.

Au, *s.* Name of a fish with a sharp nose.

2. Name of a soft porous stone.

Au, *v.* To long after, or be wholly bent on; to be fully engaged in a course of conduct; alaila, *au* loa wau i na ino o ke ao nei, then I was wholly engrossed in the vileness of the world; makemake, puni, lilo loa. See AU, current, above.

Au-a, *v.* To dislike to part with property; to be stingy in giving.

2. To keep back what should be given to another; to withhold. *Sol.* 11:24.

3. Not to give a thing asked for; to be stingy.

4. To think so much of a thing as not to part with it. *Kin.* 45:20. Ua hewa no kahi *aua* ana o na Lunaauhau, some of the stinginess of the Lunaauhaus is wrong.

5. To look with regret upon a thing.

6. To forbid; withhold. *Kin.* 30:2.

7. To refuse assent to a proposal; not to be pleased with it. *Laieik.* 140.

Au-a, *s.* The name of a fish.

Au-a, *s.* Stinginess; closeness.

Au-a, *s.* The voice of the bird alala.

Au-a, *adj.* Close; hard parsimonious; stingy; he pi, he paa.

Au-ae, *s.* See AUWAE, the chin. A lana ka *auae* kahi uuku.

Au-ae, *adj.* Expert; cunning; provident.

Au-ae, *v.* To be lazy; to spend time idly; e kalauea, e kaialili.

Au-ae, *s.* Laziness, indolence; one who spends time idly.

Au-ae-puu, *v.* For *auwaepuu.* Hoo. To be lazy, indolent.

Au-au, *v.* Conj. 6 of *au,* to swim. To bathe in water, as a person. *Puk.* 2:5.

2. To wash; cleanse with water. *Oihk.* 15:5.

3. To take out wrinkles from a piece of cloth. *Hoo.,* conj. 3. To wash; cleanse, &c.

4. Used imperatively, to excite; hasten; e *auau* aku kakou, e wikiwiki; e *auau* mai oe, come quickly, e wikiwiki mai oe; used also with *ho.* See HOAUAU.

Au-au, *s.* A bathing; washing; ua hele i ka *auau,* he is gone to bathe.

Au-au, *adj.* Of, or belonging to bathing; as, he wai *auau;* wahi *auau.*

Au-au, *s.* Name of a certain aho (a small stick) to be thatched first in the process of building a heiau.

Au-au, *s.* Name of a long slim fish; the guard-fish that swims near the surface of the water.

Au-au, *s.* A snare for catching and killing birds; he pahele e make ai ka manu; he *auau* manu.

Au-au, *s.* The stalk of loulu made into a spear; he ihe.

Au-au-nei. Probably for *auanei,* which see.

Au-au-pa-pa-o-he, *v.* Also *aupapaohe.* Name of a fish, a variety of the species *auau.*

Au-au-wa-ha, *s.* Au, a place, *au* doubled and *waha,* a mouth. To dig a furrow or ditch; to dig up into furrows, as for planting. *Hoo.* To make a furrow by digging. *Hal.* 14:7. See AUWAHA.

Au-a-ku-a, *s.* Also written *wauakua* and *waoakua.* Au, a place, and *akua,* a god.

1. A region remote from inhabitants, and supposed to be the haunts of spirits, ghosts, hobgoblins, &c.

2. A desolate place; uninhabited. *Isa.* 13:9. He anoano kanaka ole.

Au-a-lii, *adj.* Name of a kapu sacred

to Kama, an ancient chief of Maui; o ka noekole *aualii* kapu o Kama.

Au-a-lo, *s. Au,* place, and *alo,* in front. A shed or veranda adjoining a house for storing canoes, calabashes, and other property.

Au-a-mo, *s. Au,* a handle, and *amo* to carry. A stick or pole with which burdens are carried across the shoulder. 1 *Oihl.* 15:15. A staff or pole for carrying a burden. *Puk.* 25:13. Hale *auamo,* a palanquin. *Mel. Sol.* 3:9. A yoke. *Kanl.* 21:3. Fig. A burden; service. *Mat.* 11:30.

Au-a-mo, *v.* To carry on the shoulders or back; e halihali, e mamaka; to carry on a stick across the shoulder. See above.

Au-a-mo-e, *v. Auamo,* to bear, and *e,* extra. To bear a very heavy load, so as to sprain or bruise the neck; e *auamoe* me ka nanaha o ka a-i, to carry a load with the straining of the neck.

Au-a-na, *v.* Also written *auwana. Au,* to swim, and *ana,* the participial termination *ing.* A swimming off. The word has its origin in the overturning of a canoe, when men and all the cargo of the canoe float off in different directions.

1. To be scattered; dispersed, as things disperse in the upsetting of a canoe.

2. To go astray, as the mind; *auwana* hewa ka naau; to be wandering, as the thoughts.

3. To scatter from each other, as people.

4. To go here and there in search of something. *Puk.* 5:12.

5. *Hoo.* To scatter; disperse abroad; to cause to wander; to go from place to place. *Kin.* 20:13. Ua *hooauwanaia* ka poe hewa i ka make, the wicked are scattered in death. See Auwana.

Au-a-na, *adj.* Scattered; wandering; dispersed.

Au-a-nei, *adv. Au,* time, and *anei,* now, here, &c. It refers to an indefinite future time, but not far off; hereafter; by and by; soon; used only after verbs. E ua *auanei,* ke opiopi mai nei ke ao, it will rain soon, the clouds are folding up; e ino *aua-nei,* ke okupukupu mai la ka hao ino. Note.—After a word ending with *a,* it is often written *uanei.*

Au-e, *int.* Also *auwe.* O; oh! woe to; alas; O dear; expressive of regret, of grief, of pain, of disappointment; *aue* ka make! *aue* ke ano e! See Auwe.

Au-e, *v.* See also Auwe. To cry; to weep; to lament for any loss, suffering or calamity.

Au-i, *v.* To decline, as the sun in the afternoon. 1 *Nal.* 18:29.

2. To be turned aside in a course; a i ka moana, *auiia* ka waa e ka ale, when on the ocean, the canoe was turned aside by a wave.

3. To vary from a direct line; to turn aside, as the head; ua *aui* ae nei ka la; ua *aui* ae nei ka ia.

4. To swell, as the sea, in great rollers.

5. To pass by a certain time.

6. To shun a blow by inclining the head.

7. To roll up roughly, as high waves of the sea; ke *aui* mai la ka nalu; *aui* mai la ka ale o ke kai. Conj. 9. *Au-i-au-i,* to roll up, as the sea, &c.

Au-i-au-i, *v.* See Aui, *v.,* above. To roll up, as a high sea.

Au-i, *s.* A wave of the sea; a billow. *Isa.* 48:18. He *aui* no ka nalu.

2. The name for case in grammar. *Gram.* § 99.

Au-i-a-le, *s. Aui* and *ale.* A swell of the sea, not a small wave; so called from the motion, passing by.

Au-i-na, *s. Aui,* to decline, and *ana,* the participial termination. The declining or turning aside; i ka *auina* la, at sun declining, that is, in the afternoon. *Laieik.* 49. See Auwina.

Au-o-lo, *s. Au* and *olo,* to vibrate. A tabernacle; a temporary house. *Iob.* 27:18. An out-house for sheltering canoes; he *au-olo* waa; also written *auwolo.*

Au-o-lo, *adj.* Belonging to a temporary building; ahaaina *auolo,* feast of tabernacles. *Kanl.* 16:13.

Au-ha, *s.* A shed or house for putting canoes to screen them from the sun; he auolo no ka waapa. See Auolo.

Au-hai, *v.* To tear; to rend, as clothes. See Uhai.

Au-hau, *v.* To put a people under tribute. *Lunk.* 1:28. To tax; assess a tax.

2. To exercise lordship; to exact of one. *Neh.* 5:10. Note.—In ancient times every article of value was taxed, to be paid in kind; at present, the *auhau* dala is the great thing.

Au-hau, *s.* A tax; a revenue for the benefit of chiefs; kahi *auhau,* a place for collecting taxes; similar to *hookupu.*

Au-hau, *s.* Name of a species of wood for making spears; he hau ka ihe e kaua ai, he *auhau* kekahi ihe, the spears for war are made of hau, some spears are made of *auhau.*

Au-hau-hu-i, *s.* A religious ceremony

in the *hoopiopio*; perhaps, to strike regularly.

Au-hau-ma-u-le, *s.* I na *auhaumaule* ka pa, ua huna ia malalo o ka weuweu.

Au-hau-pu-ka, *v.* To beg; to ask for a thing. Syn. with *noi*, but more modest. See Noi, Makilo, Apiki, &c.

Au-hau-pu-ka, *s.* A beggar; one who solicits favors of chiefs; he *auhaupuka* na kanaka noi wale.

2. Beggary; a system of living by beggary; ma ka *auhaupuka* e loaa ai ka ai a me ke kapa, by begging they obtain food and clothing.

Au-ha-ka, *s.* Epithet of a man with long, spindling legs, like the legs of a horse; he kanaka wawae loloa *auhaka* loihi, e like me ka lio wiwi *auhaka*.

Au-ha-ka, *adj.* A man tall, poor and thin, especially his legs; spindle-legged; me he wawae *auhaka* la ka eaea.

Au-he-a, *adv. int.* Au, place, and *hea*, what.

1. Where? what place?

2. A call of attention to what one has to say; *auhea* oe? *auhea* oukou? where art thou? where are you?

Au-hee, *v.* Au, to swim, and *hee*, to melt, causing an intensive.

1. To melt; to flow, as a liquid.

2. To flee from one; to slip off from danger; *auhee* mai la ka auwaa, the fleet of canoes hurried off (from fear;) to flee, as from temptation.

3. To flee or be put to flight in battle. 1. *Oihl.* 10:1. To be scattered; disappear.

4. Used imperatively, go away; let me alone; forbear. 2 *Oihl.* 35:21.

5. *Hoo.* To put to flight, to rout, as an enemy. *Oihk.* 26:8.

6. To drive away; to dispel, as darkness. See Hee.

Au-hee, *v.* To be destitute; to be bereaved; to be deprived of all comforts; to make desolate.

> Ua lilo kuu aina, ua *auhee* au,
> My land is gone, I am poor.
> Ua make kuu wahine, ua *auhee* au,
> My wife is dead, I am bereaved.
> Ua wela kuu hale, ua *auhee* au,
> My house is burned, I am destitute.
> Ua make kuu alii, ua *auhee* makou,
> My chief is dead, we are friendless.

Au-he-le, *v.* Au and *hele*, to move.

1. To cut out clothes, i. e., to move round, as with shears or scissors in cutting out clothes. This is a modern word, or at least a modern use of the word; equivalent to *helehele*.

2. To sail from one place to another; *auhele* au ma ka moana, a pae mauka, I sailed about on the ocean, and then went ashore; *auhele* makou a pae i o.

Au-ho-la, *s.* See Hola. The name of the plant with which fish are intoxicated and caught. See Auhuhu.

Au-ho-la, *v.* From the foregoing. To catch fish by means of the *auhola* or *hola*.

Au-ho-nu-a, *s.* Au, time, and *honua*, earth. The time of the earth, i. e., as long as the world has stood, of old time, from the beginning.

Au-hu-hu, *s.* A shrub; the name of a plant used in poisoning or intoxicating fish, that they may be caught. See Auhola.

Au-hu-la-a-na, *adj.* The act of swimming round a pali where there is no road; he poe *auhulaana* no ka pali; those swimming round the pali; ke hele la ka poe *auhulaana* o Milolii ma Kauai.

Au-hu-li, *v.* Au and *huli*, kalo tops for planting.

1. To thrust downwards, as in planting kalo; to plant kalo.

2. To send downwards; to drive away.

3. To overturn, as a kingdom.

Au-hu-li-hi-a, *v.* Pass. of *auhuli*, with *h* inserted. *Gram.* § 48. To be overturned; to be dispossessed of land and tenements; to be turned off or driven from house and home; to be driven to ruin. *Hal.* 9:17. *Auhulihia* ke aupuni a lilo aku i ka mea e, the kingdom is overturned and gone to another.

Au-hu-li-hi-a, *s.* A change of governments or rulers; an overturn of government; a revolution.

Au-hu-lu, *v.* To stick together, as little things, by wetting them in the mouth.

Au-ka, *v.* To be wearied, fatigued with doing a thing. *Ier.* 6:11.

Au-ka, *adj.* Tired; weary, as of sitting still.

Au-ka, *s.* A bar, as of soap.

2. A bar of unwrought silver, iron or gold. *Ios.* 7:21.

3. In *architecture*, a fillet. *Puk.* 27:10.

4. A bar of a city gate. 1 *Nal.* 4:13.

A-u-ka, *v.* A, prep.; of and *uka*, inland. To belong inland, or up country; *auka* aku nei ma kona hoi mai nei.

Au-ka-hi, *adj.* Au and *kahi*, to cut smooth.

1. Smooth, without knots or protuberances, as a canoe; he waa *aukahi*, aole lala, aole opuupuu, a canoe, smooth, no knots, no protuberances.

2. Level and straight, as a floor; smooth and straight throughout; hookahi ano o ka *au* o ka laau.

3. Straight and smooth, as a looking-glass.

4. Applied also to a well composed speech; correct; eloquent.

Au-ka-ka, *s.* *Au*, wave, and *kaka*, hook. A place far out at sea where fish are caught; o ka pililua o lawaia o ke *aukaka*.

Au-ka-ku, *s.* Name of a fish with a sword snout.

Au-ka-na-ka, *s.* *Au*, place, and *kanaka*, men. A place or region where men are found, in distinction from *auakua*, region of the gods.

1. *Emphatically*, a thickly peopled place; he wahi kanaka, he wahi paapu, a lehulehu.

2. The habited world. *Mat.* 24:14.

Au-ke-la, *v.* *Au*, to swim, and *kela*, to excel. To swim ahead of others.

Au-ki, *s.* For *lauki*. The *ki* leaf; also,

2. A species of fish.

Au-koi, *s.* A disease in the groin, resulting from pollution; he ewai, he *auwakoi*.

Au-ku, *v.* *Au*, to swim, and *ku*, to stand.

1. To swim or sail uprightly, as a vessel rising and pitching in a heavy sea; *auku* ka ihu i ka makani; to stand up, as the bow of a vessel by the wind, from the resemblance to a man's position in swimming uprightly in a rough sea.

2. To toss up the nose, as an expression of pride, anger or contempt for a thing; *auku* ka ihu o ka wahine huhu wale, the angry woman turns up her nose; *auku* iluna ka ihu o ke kanaka haaheo, the nose of the proud man is turned up.

3. To climb, as a man, up a precipice.

4. To rise up, as the end of the nose at a bad smell, or the end of a canoe in a surf.

Au-ku, *s.* *Au* and *ku*. A stream, so shallow that a person can wade through with his clothes on; a shallow stream, not deep.

2. Name of a road or path leading up hill.

Au-ku and **Au-kuu,** *s.* Name of a bird which makes a loud, yelling noise at night; a sea-bird.

Au-kuu, *s.* The action of a person vomiting.

2. A kind of fish-hook.

Au-kuu, *s.* The name of a bird; me he *aukuu* la ke kau i ke ahua, as an *aukuu*, lights on a bank; ua hoolikeia ke kanaka hana hewa me ka *aukuu*, a bad man is likened to an *aukuu*; no ka mea, he ahua kahi e kau ai ka *aukuu*, because the *aukuu*

sits on a bank; nolaila i olelo mai ka poe kahiko; hence the ancients say:

> Me he *aukuu* la ke kau i ke ahua,
> As the *aukuu* sits upon a sand bank,
> Alaalawa na maka me he pueo la,
> Its eyes looking about like an owl.

Au-ku-ku, *s.* A swelling up of the water of the sea; the rise and rapid flow of water in a river; moana ke kai kele a ka *aukuku* ke kae ka hohonu.

Au-la, *adj.* Stinted, as vegetables; barren, as ground; he palakai, he *aula*, he ponalo.

Au-lau, *s.* A bundle of cane or other leaves bound together, used in taking fish. See AUMAIEWA.

Au-la-ma, *v.* To give or cause light around. See LAMA. He kolikukui, i *aulamaia*.

Au-le-le, *v.* To fly off in flocks, as many kinds of birds.

Au-le-pe, *s.* Name of a long slim fish.

Au-lii, *adj.* Neat; nice; excellent.

Au-li-ke, *v.* *Au*, to swim, and *like*, alike. To swim evenly; to swim abreast, as two or more persons.

Au-li-ke, *adj.* Even and smooth from end to end, as a piece of timber; he laau *aulike*, a straight, smooth piece of timber; he aukahi.

Au-li-ko-lo-ma-nu, *s.* A beautiful, well-formed person.

2. Any article beautifully made.

3. An expression of commendation or praise, connected with boasting or pride of one's circumstances or privileges, as being skillful, expert or reflecting.

Au-li-ma, *s.* *Au*, a handle, and *lima*, the hand. The name of the stick held in the hand when rubbing to produce fire. The name of the stick rubbed is *aunaki*. NOTE.—The action of rubbing is *hia*.

Au-ma, *s.* See PAIAUMA. A person in distress or pain, so as not to be still.

Au-mai-e-wa, *s.* Many persons engaged in taking fish and using the lau halaakia.

Au-ma-ka, *s.* *Au*, a handle, and *maka*. A pole to carry baggage on. See MAMAKA.

Au-ma-ku-a, *s.* Name of a class of ancient gods who were considered able and trustworthy; na akua i ka po, o na *aumakua* i ke ao, gods of the night, gods of the day; o Kiha i ka po, o Liloa i ka po, o Umi i ka po, o Mea i ke ao.

Au-ma-ku-a, *adj.* He akua *aumakua*, able, that may be trusted as a child trusts to a parent; ua ola ke akua *aumakua*. Kukuluia ka hale no ko Kamehameha mau iwi, i mea e hoolilo ai ia ia i akua *aumakua*, a house was built for Kamehameha's bones that he might become a *substantial* god.

Au-ma-ku-a, *s.* A person so called who provided for a chief or for chiefs; a trusty, steadfast servant; one who is not easily provoked to leave his place.

A-u-me-u-me, *v.* A and *ume,* to pull, draw out. To contend, to strive for a thing in order to obtain it from another; to pull from one to another; *aumeume* na kanaka i ka ia, the people contended for the fish; *aumeume* na kanaka i ka lole, the people contended for the cloth.

A-u-me-u-me, *s.* A pulling from one person to another in contention; an acting with opposition and force; he huki aku, huki mai, a puepue, there was pulling this way and that with force; he ola nae, he ola *aumeume,* there was life, however, but life with *contention.*

Au-mi-ha, *s.* Au and *miha.* To float off in the air, as miasma; contagion; evil influence supposed to attend the graves of the dead.

Au-mi-hi, *v.* Au and *mihi.* To sorrow; to repent; to grieve for the loss of a thing. See Mihi.

Au-mi-ki, *s.* Water kept in a calabash, and the chief drinks awa, (which is very bitter,) then drinks this water, which he thinks is sweet.

Au-mo-a-na, *s.* Swimming the ocean; name of a class of Kamehameha's laws.

Au-moe, *s.* Au, time, and *moe,* to sleep. The season when the world is asleep; night. *Specifically,* midnight. *Puk.* 11:4.

Au-mu, *s.* A place for baking; an oven; he wahi e kalua ai i ka ai; a place for cooking food. See Umu and Imu.

Au-mu, *v.* To bake; to cook by baking or burying under ground.

Au-mu, *adj.* Epithet of the stones of an oven, that is, oven stones; pohaku *aumu.*

Au-na, *s.* A collection or flock of birds; as, *auna* kolea, a flock of koleas; *auna* kolea e wili ana me he *auna* manu la, a *flock* of koleas mingling together like a *flock* of birds.

Au-na-ki, *s.* The name of the stick rubbed upon in obtaining fire by friction. See Aulima.

Au-nei, syn. with *auanei.* A particle referring to future time, but not distant. 1 *Sam.* 31:4. Soon; pretty soon; by and by.

Au-pa-pa, *v.* To be poor; to lose one's property. Fig. Ohina *aupapa,* the swimming board is lost. Same as pau ka waiwai.

Au-pa-pa, *adj.* A man who, in swimming on a board through the surf, loses his board; hence,

2. A person who has lost his property, i. e., his board was his dependence.

Au-pa-pa-o-he, *s.* Name of a fish similar to auaupapaohe, a species of the auau.

Au-pu-la, *v.* To catch fish with a net when the pulale is used; he mea e loaa i ka ia e like me ka lau, a thing for obtaining fish like the lau.

Au-pu-ni, *s.* Au, a place, and *puni,* around.

1. A region of country governed by a chief or king. Note.—Originally the word did not imply a large country, as there were formerly several *aupunis* on one island. At present, the word is used to signify,

2. A kingdom; the dominion and jurisdiction of a king.

Au-pu-ni, *v.* To be in an undisturbed state; to be in a state of peace and quietness, as a kingdom.

2. To exist or be known as a kingdom; ua *aupuni* keia pae aina, these islands are at peace.

3. To become a kingdom. *Ezek.* 16:13

Au-pu-ni, *adj.* Relating to the kingdom or government; he hana *aupuni,* government work; he mau lio *aupuni,* horses, the property of the government.

Au-wa, *v.* A different orthography for *aua.* See Aua. To forbid; refuse a favor when asked. *Luk.* 6:29.

Au-waa, *s.* Au, a place, and *waa,* a canoe. A cluster or fleet of canoes; o ka nui o ka *auwaa,* ua pau i ka lukuia, the greater part of the fleet of canoes was destroyed; any number of canoes in company; e hoomakaukau i ko lakou *auwaa* iho, to get ready their own canoes.

Au-waa-lau-ki, *s.* *Auwaa* and *lau ki,* ki leaves. Ki leaves folded up so as to sail for children's sport.

Au-wa-a-la-lua, *s.* The name of a species of fish; he wahi mea holo maloko o ke kai, e like me ka waa, an animal that sails in the sea like a canoe.

Au-wae, *s.* The chin of a person; *auwae,* kahi malalo o ka waha, the *auwae* is the place below the mouth.

2. The jog cut in the top of the post of a Hawaiian house. See Auae.

Au-wae-ai-na, *s.* A present out of respect to the hakuaina of a hog or other fruits of the land. Note.—When a land was transferred to a new owner, and he reinstated the people upon it, they usually bring a present from the land; this present of hogs, food, kapa, fish, nets, &c., was called *auwaeaina.*

AU-WAE-PUU, *s.* Laziness; indifference. See AUAEPUU.

AU-WAI, *s.* *Au*, furrow, and *wai*, water. A brook; a small water course. *Sol.* 21:1. The outlet of a pool. *Isa.* 7:3. The general name for streams used in artificial irrigation.

AU-WAI-HI-KI or **AUWAIAHIKI,** *s.* A running disease in the groin from impure habits; he wai ma ke kumu uha, he aukoi, he ewai, he auwakoi; a swelling in the groin and under the arms.

AU-WA-HA, *s.* *Au* and *waha*, mouth. An opening of the ground, as a furrow; plowed ground. 1 *Sam.* 14:14. A ditch. *Sol.* 23:27. A channel; a place dug like a pit. *Hal.* 7:15. He lua loihi i eli ia a puni ke kihapai, a long pit dug around the garden. See AUAUWAHA.

AU-WA-HA, *v.* To make a groove in wood; to cut forked, like the foot of a rafter on a Hawaiian house.

2. *Hoo.* To make a ditch or furrow, i. e., to plow. *Iob.* 1:14; *Mik.* 3:12.

AU-WA-KO-I, *s.* He auwaiahiki; a swelling in the groin, a bubo.

AU-WAA-LA-KI, *s.* Name of the little ships which children make of cane leaves; *auwaalaki* hooholoholo. See AUWAALAUKI.

AU-WA-NA, *v.* See AUANA. In this, like many other cases, the *w* is a mere expletive, as the words may be written both ways and the pronunciation continue the same.

1. To wander; to go from place to place. *Ios.* 5:6; *Iob.* 1:7.

2. To scatter; disperse, as an army. 2 *Oihl.* 18:16.

3. *Hoo.* To cause to wander, &c. *Kin.* 20:13.

4. To go astray morally; to deviate from the path of rectitude. *Kanl.* 13:6.

AU-WE, *v.* Also *aue.* To express an affection of the mind, as love, grief, disappointment, &c.

2. To mourn for one beloved. *Kanl.* 34:8.

3. To cry to one for help. 2 *Nal.* 4:1. To cry in great distress. *Hal.* 18:6.

4. To groan; to sigh; to groan inwardly. *Ioh.* 11:33. See AUE.

AU-WE, *s.* The cry of persons lamenting for the sick or dying; lamentation for any great loss or calamity.

2. Affection; love.

AU-WE, *int.* See AUE. An exclamation of wonder, or surprise, of fear, of pity or affection, as oh! woe! alas! 2 *Nal.* 6:5. *Auwe* kakou, alas for us! 1 *Sam.* 4:7, 8. *Auwe* ka lehulehu o ka poe i poho, alas for the multitude of those who were lost!

2. Also an expression of execration or cursing. *Mal.* 1:14.

AU-WI, *v.* See AUI. To decline; to incline from a perpendicular.

2. To move off; to pass along, as the sun is supposed to do; to decline, as the day. *Rom.* 13:12.

AU-WI-LI, *s.* *Au*, tide, and *wili*, to turn. A returning tide; he nalu mauka aku, an outward current.

AU-WI-NA, *s.* A declining, &c. See AUINA.

AU-WI-NI-WI-NI, *s.* *Au* and *wini*, sharp pointed. The sharp end of a potato leaf drooping with the rain; he *auwiniwini* ke au'o ka uala luea i ka ua.

AU-WO-LO. See AUOLO.

A-HA, *num. adj.* See HA. Four; the number four; also *eha.*

A-HA, *s.* A company or assembly of people for any purpose. *Puk.* 35:1. Often compounded with some qualifying word; as, *ahaaina, ahaolelo, ahakanaka, ahahookolokolo, ahamokomoko,* &c. See these compounds, which are sometimes written in one word, and sometimes divided. *Ahaakohipa,* a company for shearing sheep. 2 *Sam.* 13:23.

A-HA, *s.* Name of a certain prayer connected with a kapu; ina walaau ke kanaka i ka *aha*, make no ia, if a man should make a noise during the *prayer*, he would die, i. e., he would be guilty of an offense for which he would forfeit his life. The name originated in the fact that cocoanut fiber (see AHA, below) is very strong when braided into strings; so this prayer, with its rigid kapus, was supposed to be very efficacious in holding the kingdom together in times of danger.

2. The success or answer of a prayer, or such a proper performance of prayer as to insure success; loaa ka kakou *aha*, we have received our *prayer*, i. e., *the answer*; ua lilo ka *aha*, alaila, e pule hou, the *prayer* is lost (of no avail,) then pray again.

A-HA, *s.* A cord braided from the husk of the cocoanut.

2. A cord braided from human hair.

3. Strings made from the intestines of animals; ka naau i mea *aha* moa, the intestines for strings to tie fowls with; he *aha* pulu niu; he *aha* waa a me ka *aha* hoa waa, a cord for tying and strengthening a

canoe in a storm; he *aha* palaoa, he lau-oho i hili uilo ia.

A-HA, *s.* Name of a small piece of wood, around which was wound a piece of kapa, and held in the hand of the priest while offering sacrifices.

2. Name of a kind of kapa made on Molokai.

A-HA, *s.* The earwig.

2. The name of a species of long fish swimming near the surface of the water.

A-HA, *inter. pron.* Declinable with the definite article; indeclinable with the indefinite. *Gram.* § 159. *Heaha*, what? often united with the article; why? for what reason? *Hal.* 68:16. No *keaha?* i *keaha?* It is also used as an interrogative adverb, why?

A-HA, *v.* To what; to do, &c.; e *aha* ana oia? what shall he do? Of course it is used only in the interrogative. *Ioh.* 20:21.

A-HA. An interjection of surprise, wonder, &c. Ua heluhelu lakou, *aha*; ua loaa lakou e moe ana, *aha*.

A-HA, *v.* To stretch the cord by which the first posts of a house were put down or set straight; e kii i ke kaula e *aha* ai, fetch the rope to make straight with.

2. FIG. *Aha*, oia ka ana a me ka *aha* pololei no ke aupuni, *aha*, that is, to measure and *direct straightly* the government.

A-HA, *s.* Used in the expressions, ua like na *aha*, the sides are equal; *aha* like, meaning side—*measure* perhaps.

A-HA-AI-NA, *s.* *Aha*, a company, and *aina*, eating.

1. A company for eating.

2. A feast for pleasure or enjoyment; *ahaaina* olioli, a joyful feast.

3. A feast as a celebration of a past event. *Puk.* 12:14. *Ahaaina* is often qualified by the following word; as, *ahaaina* hebedoma, a feast of weeks. *Puk.* 34:22. *Ahaaina* kauhale lewa, feast of tabernacles. *Oihk.* 23:34. *Ahaaina* laa, a solemn feast. *Nah.* 15:3. *Ahaaina* moliaola, feast of the passover. 2 *Oihl.* 35:18.

4. The food for the company in such cases. *Ahaaina* awakea, a dinner; *ahaaina* ahiahi, a supper.

A-HA-AI-NA, *v.* *Aha*, company, and *aina*, to eat.

1. To collect together for eating.

2. To eat together; to feast; to partake of a banquet; to hold a feast. *Puk.* 5:1.

A-HA-A-HA, *v.* To go or walk in a mincing or irregular manner. *Hooahaaha*, hele *hooahaaha*, hele *hoohaha*.

A-HA-A-HA, *adv.* Sitting squarely; uprightly, &c.

A-HAI, *v.* To take away; to carry off; to bear away. *Laieik.* 13. Hence,

2. To flee; to be routed, as men in battle.

3. To flee from fear; to forsake the care of; ua *ahai* na makua i na keiki, aole hoihoi hou mai i ke kula, the parents took no care of the children, and did not send them back to school.

4. To arrive, as a set day or proper time for doing a thing; *ahai* ia ka la e hakaka ai.

A-HAI, *s.* The name of a pillar, wood or stone, which a chief sets up in memory of some great exploit. The exploit itself is a *pao* (arch.) Alaila, kau ka *ahai* maluna iho o na pao.

A-HAI, *adj.* Breaking off and carrying away; ka manu *ahai* kanu awa e, the bird *clipping* the twig of a tree and planting it elsewhere, poetical.

A-HAI-HAI, *adj.* See above. Ka manu *ahaihai* kanu awa e, the bird breaking off the awa plants.

A-HA-I-KI, *s.* *Aha*, assembly, and *iki*, small. A small party for private conversation; a small council or collection of people; a secret council respecting war or an emergency.

A-HAI-LO-NO, *s.* See AHAI. The person who alone survives or escapes after a battle, or a canoe out of a fleet, all others being taken or lost; pepehiia a pau, aohe *ahailono*. *Laieik.* 104. See next page of *Laieik.* 105.

A-HA-I-NU, *v.* *Aha*, a company, and *inu*, to drink. To partake at a drinking feast. *Eset.* 7:1.

A-HA-I-NU, *adj.* Relating to banqueting or to a drinking feast; a wine-drinking feast. *Ier.* 51:39. Hale *ahainu*. *Mel. Sol.* 2:4.

A-HA-I-NU-A-WA, *s.* *Aha* and *inu*, to drink, and *awa*. An assembly for drinking awa; he *ahainuawa* no na kanaka kahu akua hoomanamana ia Nahienaena, an assembly for drinking awa by the protectors of the god worshipped by Nahienaena.

A-HA-I-NU-WAI-NA, *s.* *Aha*, *inu* and *waina*. A wine feast; a feast for drinking wine. *Eset.* 7:7.

A-HA-I-NU-RA-MA, *s.* An assembly for drinking rum or any alcoholic drinks, formerly practiced by chiefs and people.

A-HA-O-LE-LO, *s.* *Aha*, a company, and *olelo*, to speak.

1. A council; a body of chiefs assembled to regulate public affairs.

2. A consultation.

3. In modern times, a legislature; a body to consult and enact laws for the good of the kingdom.

A-HA-O-LE-LO, *v.* *Aha,* assembly, and *olelo,* to speak. To take council; to consult together to get the united wisdom of all present; *ahaolelo* iho la na 'lii, the chiefs held a consultation. 2 *Oihl.* 10:6. In modern times, to meet and consult, as the legislative bodies of Nobles and Representatives, to make and adopt laws for the nation.

A-HA-HA, *v.* See HA, to breathe. To pant; to breathe hard on account of heat, as a hog or a dog from a chase; ua *ahaha* ka ilio i ka wela, a i ka maloeloe i ka loa, the dog panted hard from heat and from long weariness.

A-HA-KA-NA-KA, *s.* *Aha,* assembly, and *kanaka,* men. A great company; a multitude; an assembly. *Lunk.* 20:2. Na kanaka lehulehu, paapu.

A-HA-KEA, *s.* Name of a species of yellowish wood used for rims of canoes. It is also used for making poi boards, canoe paddles, &c.

A-HA-LI-KE, *adj.* *Aha,* four, and *like,* alike. Four sides alike or equal; a quadrangular; aoao *ahalike.* *Puk.* 28:16. Like na aoao, like ka loa me ka laula; four square. *Ezek.* 40:47.

A-HA-LI-KE, *s.* Name of the square bone in the wrist joint; he iwi *ahalike* maloko o ka pulima.

A-HA-LU-A-LI-KE, *adj.* Four sided, with two sides parallel. *Anah.* 43.

A-HA-LU-NA-KA-NA-WAI, *s.* A court room; a judgment hall. *Luk.* 22:66. Court; sanhedrim.

A-HA-MA-HA, *s.* The part of the face in front of the ears; ma ka aoao elua, ma kela maha ma keia maha.

A-HA-MA-HA, *s.* A feint; a show, a sham fight.

A-HA-MA-KA, *s.* A kapa fastened at each end between two posts and swinging between; na kapa e kau ana ma ka manuea mai hope a mua, he moe lewa.

2. A brave man skilled in a knowledge of the lua and of war.

A-HA-MA-KA, *s.* An assembly for prayers.

A-HA-MO-A, *s.* Name of the assembly collected at a cock-fight; he *ahamoa* o ka naau o ke kanaka; ua kau ia i *ahamoa.*

A-HA-MO-KO-MO-KO, *s.* *Aha,* meeting, and *mokomoko,* boxing. An assembly for boxing; a boxing match. *Laieik.* 21.

A-HA-WA, *v.* To collect together, as water, to overflow a low place; ua ahua, ua *ahawa.*

A-HE, *adv.* Used for *ae,* yes. Ae, oia no; *ahe,* he oiaio paha; yes, so it is; yes, it is perhaps true; *ahe,* kuhi au ua hala lakou, aole ka! *ahe,* pela kou manao ea?

A-HE, *s.* A slight or hacking cough; he *aheahe,* he mai kunu.

A-HE, *s.* Anything light, gentle or soft, as a light breeze, ke *ahe* makani puulena. *Laieik.* 34. Ahe koolauwahine, he makani *aheahe* ka makani.

A-HE, *s.* A wind; a slight breeze.

A-HE-A, *int. adv.* When; used only with reference to the future. *Hal.* 101:2.

A-HE-A, *adv.* Used only with the future; when? at what time? Ahea ka ina o ke keiki e ku imua; *ahea* ka inoa o ke alii; *ahea* no la nalo ka moe ke aahi la i ka pili o ka houpo.

A-HE-A-HE, *s.* See AHE. A light gentle breeze.

2. A faint diminishing sound; he kamumu o ke *aheahe* malie, a sound of a still, small voice. 1 *Nal.* 19:12. Aheahe ka makani ma Pu; *aheahe* mai ke kaiaulu o Waianae.

A-HE-A-HE, *adj.* A cough; a hacking cough; i ka manawa *aheahe,* ke kau *aheahe* make o Kahalaia ma laua o Humehume, in the time of coughing, there lighted a deadly cough upon Kahalaia and Humehume.

A-HE-A-HE-A, *adj.* Warm, as water by standing in the sun.

A-HE-A-HE, *v.* To be hungry; he pololi; *aheahe* kahi opu i ka pololi.

A-HE-A-KA, *s.* A shade; shadow. See AKA.

A-HE-KO-LO, *s.* *Ahe* and *kolo,* to creep. A slight breeze; *ahekolo* ka makani, aheahe malie, a creeping, gentle wind.

A-HE-KO-LO, *v.* To creep; to crawl along; ke i ae la e *ahekolo* kana hele, he says he walks creeping along.

A-HE-LE, *s.* A snare; used in a former translation for *pahele.* *Ier.* 18:22. A snare; same as *pahele,* but is more used.

A-HE-WA, *v.* A and *hewa,* wrong, sin.

1. To turn off the eyes, as one cross-eyed.

2. To plead against one.

3. To condemn for a crime or fault.

4. To cause to be under a curse. *Lunk.* 21:18. To condemn one. 2 *Sam.* 1:16. Hoo. Ua *hooahewaia* oia e make, he is condemned to die.

A-HE-WA, *s.* Evil; condemnation. *Ier.* 29:11.

A-HE-WA. A hanai aku *ahewa* ae ka waha loaa ka hale.

A-HE-WA-IA, *s.* Punishment; condemnation. 1 *Sam.* 28:1.

2. The state of being accused or under a curse. *Kin.* 3:14. E ka poe i *ahewaia*, ye cursed. *Mat.* 25:41.

A-HE-WA-HE-WA, *s.* Name of a tree on the mountains.

A-HI, *s.* A fire; he *ahi* e a ana, a burning fire.

A-HI, *s.* Name of the fish called albicore.

A-HI-A, *adj.* See AHIAHIA.

A-HI-A (ehia), *int. adv.* How many? *Ahia* ka nui o ka waiwai? how many articles of property? See EHIA. NOTE.—There is a nice distinction in the use of *ahia* and *ehia*, difficult to understand; in many cases they are synonymous.

A-HI-AI-HO-NU-A, *s. Ahi*, fire, *ai*, to eat, and *honua*, earth. Epithet of a volcano; earth-eater or consumer.

A-HI-AI-HO-NU-A, *adj.* Earth-consuming, as a volcano; constantly burning; unquenchable.

A-HI-A-HI, *s.* The after part of the day; ua aui ai ka la; the afternoon; towards night; ua napoo ka la; evening. *Sol.* 7:9. NOTE.—When it is dark it is *po*.

A-HI-A-HI, *v.* To be or become evening; a *ahiahi* iho la, hoi mai ia, when it was evening he returned.

A-HI-A-HI, *v.* To spread slanderous reports; e olelo ino.

2. To complain falsely of another; e niania.

3. To defame; to tell tales; e holoholo-olelo, to reveal secrets.

A-HI-A-HI, *s.* A false report concerning one; a defamation; a slander.

A-HI-A-HI-A, *adj.* Obscure; faded; dim, as colors in kapa or calico; kohu maikai ole; as cloth having lost color; *ahiahia* ke koko, the blood is colorless; applied to the uncolored parts of dyed cloth or kapa; he *ahiahia* ka palapala, the writing is dim, not plain; ulaula *ahiahia*, faded red, that is, purple. 2 *Oihl.* 3:14.

A-HI-U, *s.* The name of a wind.

A-HI-U, *adj.* Wild; untamed, as a horse; he aa; aole laka mai. See HIHIU.

A-HI-HI, *v.* To be united with another or with others in mischief or error.

2. To conspire with; to be involved with another or others, as in ignorance; ua *ahihi* pu aku la laua ilaila, they were both involved in that matter; *ahihi* i ka naaupo. See HIHI and HIHIA.

A-HI-HI, *s.* Name of a tree or shrub in Nuuanu; he lei no ka huakaihele o Kona.

A-HI-KO-LI, *v.* To cut off even, as in trimming a lamp.

A-HI-KU (ehiku), *num. adj.* Seven; with the article, the seventh. *Gram.* § 110, 1st. The root is *hiku*.

A-HI-NA, *s.* A gray color.

A-HI-NA, *adj.* A and *hina*, gray hairs. Applied to Molokai; Molokai *ahina*, gray Molokai, from the fog around the top.

A-HI-NA, *adj.* Gray, as the head of an old man; he poo *ahina*; applied to a dry tree; he laau *ahina*. See HINA and POO-HINA.

A-HI-NA-HI-NA, *s.* Name of a species of grass.

2. Name of a plant living in cold, dry places; so named from its color, a light silver gray; known as the "silver sword."

3. The life-everlasting plant.

A-HI-NA-HI-NA, *adj.* Very light blue; gray; slate color. *Oihk.* 13:37.

A-HO, *v.* To be patient, submissive, humble; to be merciful, kind; to be ready to do a kind act. See the compounds AHONUI and AHOLOA.

A-HO, *v.* (Impersonal.) It is easier; it is better; it is less severe; e *aho* nau e kokua mai ia makou, it is better for you to help us; it implies a comparison. 2 *Sam.* 18:3. E *aho* nae ko lakou hope i ko kakou, their end, however, will be more tolerable than ours; it is better that, &c. *Nah.* 14:2. It had been better if, &c. *Ios.* 7:7. It is better, preferable; e *aho* iki no ke hoi kakou, it will be a little better for us to return; e *aho* no ka hele mamuli o ka noho ana me ka pilikia, it is better to go than to stay in perplexity.

A-HO, *s. Art.,* ke. The natural breathing of a person; the breath; hence,

2. Patience; i nui ke *aho*, let the breath be long, i. e., be patient.

3. MET. Spirit; courage. *Ios.* 2:11. Resolution; also kindness.

A-HO, *s. Art.,* ke. A line; a cord, as a fish line; ke *aho* lawaia; a kite string; ke kakaiapola a me ke *aho*; alaila, hoolele aku i ka lupe i ka lewa, a paa aku ma ke *aho*, (prepare) the kite tail and the string, then send off the kite into the air, but hold fast by the string.

A-HO, *s. Art.,* ka. The name of the small sticks used in thatching.

A-HO-AI-O-LE, *s.* An aho or string too short; not long enough for the purpose.

A-HO-LE, *s.* Name of a species of white

fish.

A-HO-LE-HO-LE, *s.* Name of a species of fish. See AHOLE above.

A-HO-LOA, *adj.* Aho, patient, and *loa*, long. Patient; long suffering. See AHONUI.

A-HO-LOA, *s.* Aho, a cord, and *loa*, long. A long string for fishing or sounding in deep water; he *aholoa* loa i ka mio; he *aholoa* i ka luu ilalo o ka moana.

A-HO-NA, *v.* Ahona a kui maoli aku kela, lele liilii. *Laieik.* 42.

A-HO-NU-I, *v.* Aho, patient, and *nui*, much. To be patient, gentle, kind, &c. 1 *Tes.* 2:7. See AHOLOA.

A-HO-NU-I, *s.* Aho, patient, and *nui*, much. Forbearance; long suffering; patience.

A-HO-NU-I, *adj.* Patient; enduring; long suffering. *Puk.* 34:6.

A-HU, *v.* To gather or collect together. *Kin.* 43:11. Ahu iho la i kahakai, hu ae la ka lolo, they gathered them together (dead bodies) on the sea shore, the brains flowed; to collect one's food where there is little.

> Ahu iho ka hoka i ka pakai,
> Ku i ka pakai ka mea haku ole,
> Lele ae no ka manu i Houa,
> Hapapa wale iho no ka hokahoka.

To collect but gain little; *ahu* wale iho no, aole wahi kapa; *ahu* wale iho, aole ai; *ahu* wale iho no i ka oneanea.

2. To lay up, as in a store-house; to lay up for future use, as goods. *Mat.* 6:19. To store in the memory.

3. To lie strewed over the ground. *Puk.* 16:3.

4. To cover one with a cloak; to be merely covered. *Iob.* 26:6. To clothe.

5. *Hoo.* To collect what is scattered.

6. To fall together, as men slain in battle.

7. To keep; treasure up, as anger; *hooahu* iho la i ka huhu maluna o kela poe, he kept in reserve his anger for that company.

8. To pile up, as stones. *Ios.* 8:29. To gather up; glean, as a field. *Rut.* 2:7.

9. To bring condemnation upon.

10. To reply to; to object to something said. *Rom.* 9:20.

A-HU, *s.* See AHA. An assemblage or collection of things; *ahu* ai, a place for storing food; a collection of provisions. 2 *Oihl.* 11:11. Wahi *ahu*, a place for something. *Iob.* 28:1. Ahu pohaku, a pavement; a heap, as of stones. *Kin.* 31:46.

2. A heap of stones as a way mark. *Ier.* 31:21.

3. As a memorial. *Ios.* 7:26.

A-HU, *adj.* Storing; collecting; hale *ahu*, a store-house. *Iob.* 38:22.

A-HU, *s.* A fine mat; a coarse one is *moena*; a mat for covering a canoe; o ka uhi ana i ka *ahu*, ea, oia ka mea e pale aku i kekahi ale, the spreading over a mat, that is what will keep off some of the waves; *ahuao, ahu* mokoloa.

A-HU-A, *s.* See AHU, collection. Any place elevated in the manner of a high path.

2. A bank in the sea; a bank formed by the sand at a mouth of a river; hence,

3. A ford; a place for passing a stream or river. *Ios.* 2:7; *Lunk.* 3:28. He puu; a hillock; he kiekie ma kekahi aoao.

A-HU-A, *v.* To be raised up on a platform; ua *ahua*, ua ahawa.

A-HU-AO, *s.* The young and tender leaves of the hala for making mats; ahu moena, ahu pawehe, *ahuao.*

A-HU-A-HU, *s.* Young sprouts or shoots from layers, as from sugar-cane.

2. A boy or girl that grows up quickly.

A-HU-A-HU, *adj.* Angry; fretful; unwilling, as when one receives orders to work, and from fatigue or indolence he is unwilling, he is then *ahuahu.*

A-HU-A-HU, *v.* To be sullen; unwilling to do a thing ordered.

A-HU-A-HU, *adv.* Unwillingly; fretfully.

A-HU-A-LA-LA, *v.* To lie slain, as many bodies slain in battle; aia hoi, e *ahualala* kukui ana ka heana, behold, they were dead bodies fallen to the earth. 2 *Oihl.* 20:24.

A-HU-A-WA, *s.* A species of strong rush of which cords are made; the leaves are made into hats.

2. The name of the cord itself; mai hoka au i ke *ahuawa.*

A-HU-E, *v.* See HUE, to lie. To steal; to take without liberty. See AIHUE.

2. To double up; to turn up, as a piece of kapa or paper.

A-HU-I, *s.* A bunch or cluster of fruit, as bananas, grapes, or hala.

A-HU-I-LI, *v.* To lie sick; to be weak; e *ahuili* auanei ka poe hooko i ka eha.

A-HU-I-WAI-NA, *s.* Ahui, a cluster, and *waina*, grapes. A bunch or cluster of grapes. *Hoik.* 14:18.

A-HU-MO-E-NA, *s.* A figured, fine mat, or a fine mat of small figures of different colors. *Laieik.* 112.

A-HU-U-A, *s.* A heap; a pile; a collection of things; he *ahuua* waiwai, he *ahuua* kiekie, a pile of goods, a high heap.

A-HU-U-A, *v.* To heap up; to put in heaps; ke *ahuua* mai la. See AHU.

A-HU-U-LA, *s.* *Ahu*, a garment, and *ula*, red.

1. A red feathered cloak; a cloak made of the feathers of the oo and the red feathers of the iiwi, worn by kings and high chiefs; a gorgeous dress. *Laieik.* 112.

2. A kind of fish net; ka upena puni, a haku a maikai.

A-HU-HI-NA-LO, *s.* A garment or cloth made of the hala leaf.

A-HU-KU, *v.* To stone; to bury with stones or other missiles; e hailuku, e hoo nou, e hooulua.

A-HU-LAU, *s.* A pestilence among men. *Hab.* 3:5. A murrain among cattle. *Puk.* 9:3. A sickness like a pestilence. NOTE.— The most destructive raged while Kamehameha lived the first time at Oahu; Kamehameha himself was attacked, but recovered. Thousands were swept off by it at that time; probably in 1804.

A-HU-LAU, *adj.* Epidemic; pestilential; mai *ahulau*, a pestilence. *Oihk.* 26:25.

A-HU-LAU, *v.* To have the pestilence; to die with it; ua *ahulau* ae la na kanaka i ka make.

A-HU-LI-U, *adj.* Heated hot, as stones in the oven; heated to whiteness; *ahuliu* ka imu, the oven is exceedingly hot.

A-HU-LU, *v.* To be overdone, as food cooked too much; ua *ahulu* loa ka umu ai, ua ulaula ka ai, to be too hot.

A-HU-LU, *adj.* Overdone, as food; baked too much; cooked hard.

2. Spoiled, as eggs, or medicines by long lying.

3. Unnatural in appearance; dirty; defective; ua *ahulu* ke kai, i. e., dirty or green, not blue and clear.

A-HU-LU-HU-LU, *s.* A species of small, red fish; some kind of mechanical tool; koi *ahuluhulu*.

A-HU-NA-LII, *s.* A small chief.

A-HU-NA-LII, *adj.* A colored kapa; he mamaki *ahunalii*, he mamaki i hooluuia, a colored mamaki kapa.

A-HU-PA-WE-HE, *s.* *Ahu*, mat, and *pawehe*. Name of a kind of striped mat made on Niihau; he *ahupawehe* no Niihau.

A-HU-PU-AA, *s.* *Ahu*, collection, and *puaa*, hog.

1. Name of one of the smaller divisions of a country, made up of several ili, and under the care of a head man; a hog paid the tax of that district to the king. He *ahupuaa* o Wailuku; o na aina maloko o Wailuku, he ili, he moo.

2. A city; a village; a settlement, as the capital of said *ahupuaa*.

A-HU-WAI-WAI, *adj.* *Ahu*, collection, and *waiwai*, property. The property of a treasury; belonging to a place for storing property. *Oihl.* 9:26. Hale *ahuwaiwai*, a store-house.

A-HU-WA-LE, *v.* To be in plain sight, as a hill, or a house on a hill.

A-KA, A particle set before verbs to express carefulness, regularity of proceeding, &c.; as, *aka* hele, go carefully; *aka* holo, sail or run slowly; *aka* hana, work carefully; *aka* noho, sit quietly.

A-KA, *conj.* But; if not; on the other hand. The word is generally used to express strong opposition of idea.

A-KA, *s.* The shadow of a person; the figure or outline of a thing; a similitude or likeness. *Nah.* 12:8. NOTE.—The shade of a tree or house is *malu*.

2. The dawn or light of the moon before rising.

3. The knuckle joints; the protuberances of the ankle joints; the joints of the back bone.

4. FIG. A shadow; frailty; impotence. *Isa.* 30:2.

A-KA, *v.* To light up, as the moon before rising; ua aha ka mahina? kokoke puka, ua *aka* mai la, how is the moon? it is near rising, it lights up.

2. To go up and down, as on a hilly road. (See No. 2 above, joints of the back-bone.)

3. To be split or peeled up, as the bark of a tree.

4. To be torn off, as the kaupaku of a house; ua *aka* ke kaupaku o ka hale.

A-KA, *v.* To laugh; to deride; i ko'u noonoo ana i keia kumu manao, ua *aka* iki mai no ka pono, in thinking of this composition, I smiled at its correctness. (The 13th conj., *akaaka*, is more generally used.)

A-KAA, *v.* To break open, as a seal. *Hoik.* 5:2. To tear or take up, as a mat.

A-KAA, *adj.* Anything broken up; not cohering; he *akaa* wale, he pipili ole.

A-KA-A-KA, *v.* See AKA, to laugh. To laugh; to laugh at. *Sol.* 4:9. *Hoo.* To cause to laugh, to have joy. *Kin.* 21:6.

A-KA-A-KA, *s.* Laughter; exhilaration of spirits. *Hal.* 126:2.

A-KAA-KAA, *v.* See AKAA, to break up. To fall off, as the old thatching of a house.

2. To break up, as the roof or sides of a house; ua *akaakaaia* e ka mea kolohe, it was pulled off by some mischievous one.

A-KAA-KAA, *s.* The falling off of the

scarf-skin after a course of drinking awa.

>Ua mahuna i ka awa,
>Ua *akaakaa* ka ili,
>He puahilohilo ke kua i ka lepo,
>Ua *akaakaa*.

A-KAA-KAA, *adj.* Poor; destitute.

A-KAA-KAI, *s.* Bulrushes out of which mats and bags are made.

2. Onions have taken the same name from the similarity of the tops. *Nah.* 11:5.

A-KA-I-KI, *v.* *Aka*, to laugh, and *iki*, a little.

1. To be pleased; to smile; to be gratified on receiving a favor; *akaiki* lakou me ka olioli no ka loaa o ko lakou waiwai, they smiled with pleasure on obtaining their property.

2. To laugh in one's sleeve; to laugh secretly; na hoa nohoi i kani ai ka *akaiki* i ua wahi la, the companions also *chuckled* at us in that place.

3. To sneer at. See AKAAKA.

A-KA-I-KI, *s.* A rejoicing in consequence of hope; desire in proportion to the prospect of receiving a thing.

A-KA-OO, *s.* *Aka*, shadow, and *oo*, ripe. A full grown shadow; applied to a person who is close, hard or stingy.

A-KA-O-LE-LO, *v.* *Aka* and *olelo*. To speak cautiously; to speak deliberately, advisedly.

A-KAU, *adj.* The right; on the right; lima *akau*, the right hand; ma ka aoao *akau*, on the right side. In *geography*, the person is supposed to stand with his face to the west; hence the right hand is towards the north, and his left to the south. Aoao *akau*, *north* side; aoao *hema*, *south* side; welau *akau*, *north* pole, &c.

A-KA-HA, *s.* Name of a tree. One species has long leaves and grows inland; one species by the sea. It is a hard tree, like the uwea; also called *ekaha*.

A-KA-HAI, *v.* *Aka*, with care, and *hai*, to speak. To be tender of heart; meek. *2 Nal.* 22:19.

A-KA-HAI, *s.* *Aka*, with care, and *hai*, to speak. Meekness; modesty; gentleness. *Nah.* 12:3. Poe *akahai*, the meek. *Zep.* 2:3.

A-KA-HAI, *adj.* Modest; gentle, &c. *Sol.* 15:1. Soft in speech.

A-KA-HE-LE, *v.* See AKA and HELE, to go. To go slowly or moderately in doing a thing; to go carefully; the opposite of *hikiwawe*. E hikiwawe mai i ka lohe, e *akahele* hoi i ka olelo, be quick to hear; but slow to speak. Used also imperatively; beware; be cautious; e *akahele* ka pepehi mai o oukou i ke akua, beware of your striking the god; e *akahele* ka huhu, mai hikiwawe, be slow to anger, not quick.

A-KA-HE-NE-HE-NE, *v.* *Aka*, to laugh and *henehene*, to ridicule. To laugh to scorn; to laugh in derision or mockery. *Neh.* 2:19.

A-KA-HI, *s.* The number one; root, *kahi*.

A-KA-HI, *adv.* One; once; just now; expressive of greatness or superiority. *Emphatically*, *akahi* no au i lohe i ka hekili, *once* have I heard it thunder, i. e., thunder loudly; *akahi* no au i ike i ka ino, *once* have I witnessed a storm, i. e., never so great a one before.

A-KA-HI-A-KA-HI, *adv.* LIT. Once by once; of little experience; a novice. *1 Tim.* 3:6. Aole ka mea *akahiakahi* e holo i ka ino o make auanei i ka moana a pae kupapau aku i Lanai, let not the inexperienced sail out in a storm lest he die in the ocean and his dead body float ashore on Lanai.

A-KA-KA, *v.* To be plain; to be clear, as a thought or the expression of an idea; to be distinct, intelligible, as language.

2. To be clear, transparent, as glass. *Hoik.* 22:1; *Anat.* 2. Clear, as a liquid.

3. *Hoo.* To make plain; to expound, demonstrate; to bring to light.

4. To set up boundary lines.

A-KA-KA, *adj.* Clear, as water.

2. Lucid; bright, as the moon.

3. Certain; distinct; transparent; he *akaka*, kokoke like me ke aniani kona *akaka* ana, clear, almost like glass.

A-KA-KA, *adv.* *Akaka* loa, very plainly; very clearly. *Ioan.* 10:24.

A-KA-KA, *adj.* Rent; torn; dead. See NAKAKA.

A-KA-KA-LA-NI, *s.* Poetical for *akalani*. A heaven of light; a great light; the heavens much lighted; he *akakalani* no ka Uhane Hemolele. *Mel. Creat.*

A-KA-KA-NE, *s.* Name of a small bird found in the mountains.

A-KA-KE, *adj.* Spry; light, as one walking or running; not loaded; he *akake* no kau, you are spry, quick at walking.

A-KA-KI-WI, *v.* To set up on the edge.

A-KA-KU, *v.* To cease; to abate; to grow calm, as wind, rain, surf, anger; ua *akaku* mai ka makani, the wind has abated; ua *akaku* mai ka ua; *akaku* mai ka ino o ke kaikoo; to be gentle; quiet.

A-KA-KU, *s.* A subsiding of a storm, wind, &c.

2. A delirium; a trance. *Oih.* 10:10.

An ecstasy; vision. 2 *Oihl.* 26:5. He moe uhane. *Hoo.* A vision. *Oih.* 26:19.

A-KA-KU, *adj.* Gentle, &c. *Tit.* 3:2.

A-KA-KUU, *v.* To be settled; calmed; quieted; appeased; ua *akakuu* mai ka huhu o ke alii i na kanaka, the anger of the chief towards the people is appeased; ua *akakuu* mai ke alii, aole inu rama hou, the mind of the chief is settled, he will drink no more rum.

A-KA-KUU, *adj.* Gentle; quiet; kind; calm. *Tit.* 3:2.

A-KA-LA, *s.* A berry, something like a strawberry; a raspberry.

A-KA-LA, *s.* A kind of cloth, e like me ka lole alaihi.

A-KA-LA, *s.* The end of a house. See KALA.

A-KA-LAU. See KINOAKALAU and WAI-LUA. A ghost that appears to some people, but not to others.

A-KA-LEI, *s.* See LEI. A lei worn on the neck.

A-KA-LA-NI, *s.* See AKAKALANI above. A heavenly shadow; a splendid light.

A-KA-MAI, *v.* To be wise; makemake au e *akamai* oukou a pau, I wish that you may all become wise; mostly used in the causative. *Hoo.* To be or become wise; to make wise; skillful. *Sol.* 3:7. To think one's self wise.

A-KA-MAI, *s.* Wisdom; skill; ingenuity. *Hoo.* Exhibiting wisdom. 1 *Kor.* 2:1.

A-KA-MAI, *adj.* Wise; skillful; ingenious; expert; sagacious; learned; *akamai* ma ka naau. *Puk.* 28:3.

A-KE, *v.* To desire. *Nah.* 23:10. To wish for a thing; *ake* nui no lakou e haule ka ua, they greatly desired that rain should fall; to pant after; *ake* nui kahi poe i ka waiwai, certain people greatly desire property; to wish to do a thing; *ake* no na kamalii e paani; to be willing; *ake* no na kanaka i ka hewa.

A-KE, *v.* To blab; to tattle; to prate; to slander; tell lies; e wahahee; e imi hala; to go about talking nonsense.

A-KE, *s.* A lie; a falsehood; a slanderous report of one; noho o Lahainaluna i ke *ake*, the people of Lahainaluna live under slanderous reports.

A-KE, *s.* The liver of an animal. *Puk.* 29:13. Akepaa, same.

A-KE is a general name for several internal organs, qualified by different terms; see below.

A-KE-A, *adj.* Broad; spacious; open; not crowded; public; ua kaawale ka hale, ua *akea* oloko.

A-KE-A, *adv.* Openly; publicly; ua hana *akea* ia, it was done publicly.

A-KE-A, *v.* To be broad or wide, as a land.

2. To be separate, as different things, a space being between them; ua *akea* ka aina, aole pilikia. Mostly used in the causative sense.

3. *Hoo.* To enlarge; widen out. *Isa.* 54:2.

4. To make room for one, i. e., to set free from difficulty, and supply one's wants. *Kanl.* 12:20.

5. To enlarge one's heart. *Isa.* 60:8. To become generous.

A-KE-A, *s.* A broad open space; a place not concealed.

A-KE-A-KA-MAI, *s. Ake,* desire, and *aka-mai,* skill. A lover of wisdom; epithet of a philosopher. *Oih.* 17:18.

A-KE-A-KE, *s.* Name of a bird.

A-KE-A-KE, *adj.* See AKE, to desire. Quick; ready; smart, especially to do a kindness; cheerful in entertaining strangers.

A-KE-A-KE-A, *v.* To fade, as kapa or cloth colored; to lose the color; to fade out; he *akeakea* ka ulaula, he ula *akeakea* ka palapala, the red is faded out, a faded red is the printing.

A-KEU-KEU, *adj.* Active; ready; skillful; receiving kindly one's friends. SYN. with he mikimiki, he oleole. See AKEAKE.

AKE-KE, *s.* A singular little animal of the sea.

2. A small quantity of dust; aole nui o ka lepo.

A-KE-KE,   } *s.* A species of bird. See
A-KE-KE-KE, } KEKE.

A-KE-KEE, *s.* Name of a little brown bird resembling the wren found on the mountain of Waialeale on Kauai; it was formerly worshipped by the natives as the god of the mountain.

A-KE-LE-KE-LE, *s.* An escape from great danger, as a person in a canoe in a storm; he *akelekele* wale no ka pakele, mai make.

A-KE-LOA,   } *s. Ake,* liver, and *loa,*
A-KE-NI-AU, } long. The spleen.

A-KE-MA-KA-NI, *s.* The lungs. See AKE-MAMA.

A-KE-MA-MA,   } *s. Ake,* liver, and
A-KE-PA-HOO-LA, } *mama,* light. The lungs; the lights; oia ke ake e hanu ai, that is the lungs by which we breathe.

A-KE-NA, *v.* To be proud; boasting; to be high minded; proud of some favor received; ua *akena* mai o Poki i na mea pono o ke Akua ana i ike ai, Poki was boasting of the favors which God had permitted him to see; *akena* ia ia iho, to boast of one's self; to behave boastingly, as in war, joined with singing.

A-KE-NA, *adv.* Proudly; loftily; boastingly.

A-KE-NA, *s.* Pride; haughtiness; feeling of superiority over others.

A-KE-NA-KE-NA. An intensive of the foregoing in all its meanings.

A-KE-NI-AU, *s.* See AKELOA above. The spleen.

A-KE-PA, *s.* The name of a bird.
 2. A sprightly, active man.

A-KE-PA, *adj.* Sprightly; active; turning this way and that.

A-KE-PA-KE-PA, *v.* To stand up every way, as uncombed hair; *akepakepa* mai la na ia ma ke opi a pau, the fish were cut cross ways and every way.

A-KE-PAA, *s.* The liver. *Oihk.* 3:4.

A-KE-PAA-HO-O-LA, *s.* The lights, &c. See AKEMAMA.

A-KE-RI-DA, *s. Heb.* Uhini *akerida*, a grasshopper. *Oihk.* 11:22.

A-KI, *v.* To bite; to bite in two, as a thread; to bite, as in peeling sugar-cane or cocoanut; e *aki* i ke ko, e *aki* i ka niu.
 2. To backbite; to speak reproachfully of one behind him; to taunt. *Ezek.* 5:15.
 3. To spread false reports; *aki* wahahee, e ake e hewa ka mea hewa ole; to slander. *Hal.* 50:20. NOTE.—Some of the meanings of *aki* are similar to *ake*. This verb has various forms; as, *aki, aaki, aaaki, aki-aki,* which see in their places.

A-KI, *v.* To begin to heal or scar over, as a wound.
 2. To lop or double down, as the top of a sail when there is much wind; *aki* ko oukou pea; from *aki*, locks of hair, &c.; see below.

A-KI, *s.* Locks of hair left behind the head, while all above is shorn off; he lauoho *aki* loloa mahope; ka *aki* lauoho pupuni waiwai.
 2. Backbiting; speaking ill of another.

A-KI, *s.* The stools on which canoes are placed when standing on shore.

A-KI, *adj.* Backbiting; reviling. *Rom.* 1:30.

A-KI, *s.* A disease; the headache.

A-KI-A, *s.* Name of an intoxicating shrub; its qualities are like the auhuhu; it is also called *haakea*. The

akia

bark is used to poison fish in fresh water as auhuhu is in salt.

A-KI-A-HA-LA, *s.* Name of a tree; also called *puahanui*.

A-KI-A-KI, *v.* See AKI. To bite in two repeatedly.
 2. To take away by little and little.
 3. To nibble, as a fish at a hook.
 4. To pilfer; he aihue liilii.

A-KI-A-KI, *s.* A backbiter; a reviler; a slanderer. 1 *Kor.* 6:10.

A-KI-A-KI, *s.* A disease; the dog colic.

A-KI-A-KI, *s.* Name of a species of seaweed adhering to the rocks; it is eaten for food.

A-KI-O-HA-LA, *s.* Name of a plant; the marshmallows; the same perhaps as akia hala above.

A-KI-U, *adv.* Used in a prayer as follows: Akele *akiu* kelekele *akiu*, kau aku *akiu* iluna ke kau lua he wai akane, &c.

A-KI-U-KI-U, *v.* See KIU. To act the part of a spy; to search into; to penetrate.

A-KI-U-KI-U, *adj.* Searching; penetrating; a me ka makani *akiukiu* kipe pua hala o Puakei, the searching wind pelting the hala blossoms of Puakei.

A-KI-HI-A-LO-A, *s.* Name of a small yellow bird; o ka *akihialoa*, he manu hulu lenalena.

A-KI-HI-PO-LE-NA, *s.* Name of a small bird with red feathers.

A-KI-HOO-LA-NA, *s. Aki*, stools for canoes, and *hoolana*, to float. A dry dock; ka hana ana i ka *akihoolana* i ke awa o Honolulu, building a *dry dock* in the harbor of Honolulu.

A-KI-KI, *s.* A dwarf; a person of full age, but a child in size; he keiki kahiko, aole nui.

A-KII-KII, *s.* Name of a round fish net to catch the pahuhu in; he upena *akiikii*.

A-KI-LOU, *s. Aki*, to bite, and *lou*, a hook. A hook biter, that is, a thief. NOTE.—Thieves formerly supplied themselves with hooked rods to assist in obtaining articles of property; hence *akilou*, to apply the hook, was to steal.

A-KI-LOU, *v. Aki* and *lou*, to bend over. To eat secretly the food of another.

A-KI-LO-LO, *s.* The name of a fish; a species of small fish.

A-KO, *v.* To cut, as with scissors; to cut, clip off; to crop off. *Ezek.* 17:4.
 2. To pluck, as flowers or fruit. *Hal.*

80:12. To shear, as sheep. *Kin.* 31:19. To cut off, as hair. *Ier.* 7:29. Ua *ako* ia ka lauoho; ua *ako* ia i ka hulu o ka hipa; ua *akoia* ka lau o ka nalu i ka makani.

3. To clip off, as the wind the top of the surf.

A-KO, *v.* To thatch; to cover a house with thatch; ua akoia ka hale.

A-KO, *s.* The art of thatching; ua pau ka hale i ke *ako*; mea *ako* hale, a house thatcher; mea *ako* hipa, a sheep shearer.

A-KO, *s.* Name of a disease of females of bad character; he *ako* na wahine hana hewa; he *ako* ka mai o na wahine hana hewa.

A-KO-A, *s.* Kapa of a snuff color; so named from the dye made of the *akoa* tree; he kapa i kuku ia ma ka *akoa*; he paupau *akoa*.

A-KO-A-KO, *v.* See AKO. To move, as the lips in speaking to one's self. 1 *Sam.* 1:13.

2. To itch in the throat before coughing; akahi no ka *akoako* o kuu puu no ka maneo, uncommon is the tickling of my throat on account of itching.

3. To have a hacking cough in the throat.

A-KO-A-KO, *v.* *Akoako* ka ale, to swell up, as a wave just before breaking; kuku ka lili o ka nalu.

A-KO-A-KO-A, *v.* To assemble, as people for business.

2. To collect together what is separated; ua *akoakoa* na kanaka ma ka hale pule, the people are assembled at the meeting house. *Hoo.* To gather together, as men. *Kin.* 34:30.

3. To collect together, as waters. *Puk.* 15:8. To come together again, as a dispersed people. *Kanl.* 30:3. E hoouluulu ae ma kahi hookahi.

A-KO-A-KO-A, *adj.* Assembled; collected.

A-KO-A-KO-A, *adv.* Collectively, in heaps; e waiho *akoakoa*, to lay down in heaps. 2 *Oihl.* 31:6.

A-KO-A-KO-A, *s.* The horned coral.

2. Coral generally. *Ezek.* 27:16.

3. A precious stone. *Iob.* 28:18.

A-KO-HE-KO-HE, *s.* Name of a small bird making its nest on the ground.

A-KO-LA, *v.* To triumph over the ills or misfortunes of another. *Hal.* 94:3. To triumph, as over an enemy; *hooakola* mai oia ia lakou me ka olelo ana, *akola!* he triumphed over them, exclaiming hurrah! *akola!* pakele mai nei no au, well done! I have just escaped. See AIKOLA. *Honaikola* is another form.

A-KO-LA, *int.* An exclamation of triumph of any kind; a word of contempt

for not getting a thing, or for losing.

A-KO-LA, *s.* Name of a fruit found on Hawaii.

A-KO-LE, *v.* See KCLE. To make or render one's self poor. SYN. with e hooilihune, e hoowaiwai ole.

A-KO-LE, *adj.* Poor, in consequence of squandering one's property.

A-KO-LE-A, *s.* Name of a species of shrub, grass, or fern.

A-KO-LO, *adv.* A cant word, expressive of contempt.

A-KO-LO, *v.* A for *aa,* and *kolo* to run. To run into small roots, as potatoes, and bear no fruit.

A-KO-LO, *adj.* Running and branching, as roots of plants; good above and small below. SYN. with aakolo, he kolo pu.

A-KO-LOA, *s.* A species of fern.

A-KO-LU, *adj. num.* See KOLU. Three; the number three; also written *ekolu.*

A-KU, *v.* To follow.

A-KU, A verbal directive. See *Gram.* § 233, 2, and § 236. In Hawaiian, the motion or action of verbs is supposed to be towards one (*mai,*) or from one (*aku,*) or upwards (*ae,*) or downwards (*iho,*) or side ways, which is also ae. Aku is mostly connected with verbs, sometimes with nouns and adverbs; it implies motion or tendency *from* one, *onward,* &c.; as, e hele *aku,* to go *off,* go *from* one; the opposite of e hele *mai,* to come *towards* one. In narrative tenses the verbal directives are generally followed by the syllable *la;* as, hele *aku la* oia, he went *off;* noho *iho la* ia, he sat *down,* or he dwelt.

A-KU, *s.* Name of a species of fish, smooth, round; the bonito; the name of one of the two fish that accompanied Pili in his voyage to these islands; *aku* helped paddle (haluku) the canoe, and *opelu* calmed the winds when too strong. D. *Malo* 4:13. See OPELU.

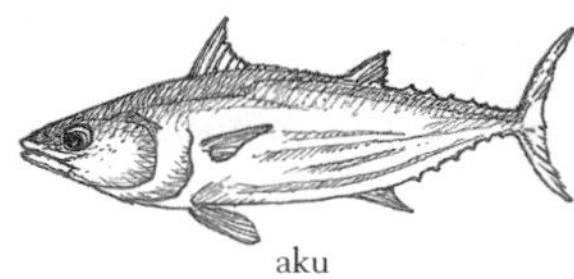
aku

A-KU, *adj.* Clear; unclouded; spoken of the moon when fully up; he *aku* ka mahina, the moon is clear.

A-KU-A, *s.* Among Hawaiians, formerly, the name of any supernatural being, the object of fear or worship; a god. The term, on the visit of foreigners, was applied to artificial objects, the nature or properties of which Hawaiians did not understand, as the movement of a watch, a compass, the self-striking of a clock, &c. At present, the word *Akua* is used for the true God, the Deity, the object of love and obedience as well as fear.

2. The name of the night when the moon was perfectly full; a akaka loa o ia poepoe ana, o *Akua* ia po; hence it would seem that the ancient idea of an *Akua* embraced something incomprehensible, powerful, and yet complete, full orbed. The names of the four principal gods of the Hawaiians were Ku, Lono, Kane, and Kanaloa.

A-KU-A-AU-MA-KU-A, *s.* *Akua*, *au*, time, and *makua*, parent. The ancestors of those who died long ago, and who have become gods; the spirits of former heroes.

A-KU-A-U-LU, *s.* *Akua*, god, and *ulu*, to inspire. The god which came upon one and inspired him to speak; the god of inspiration.

A-KU-A-HAI-A-MIO, *s.* *Akua*, god, *hai*, to speak, and *amio*, to be silent. A god speaking silently.

A-KU-A-HA-NAI, *s.* *Akua*, god, and *hanai*, to feed.

1. The god that fed poison to people; the god of poison; hence,

2. Poison itself; he *akuahanai* ka rama, rum is a poisonous god, a he moonihoawa ka aie, and a poison toothed lizard (serpent) is going into debt.

A-KU-A-HOO-U-NA-U-NA, *s.* *Akua*, god, and *hoouna*, to send. A class of gods who were sent on errands like Mercury of the Greeks; the names of some of them were Keawenuikauohilo, Kapo, Kapua, Kamakukou, and many others.

A-KU-A-KII, *s.* *Akua*, god, and *kii*, an image.

1. The god represented by an image; hence,

2. An idol; a god made. *Oihk.* 26:1; *Isa.* 31:7.

A-KU-A-KU, *adv.* Up and down, as an uneven road; having the form of stairs; he ala *akuaku*.

A-KU-A-KU, *adv.* Sailing, as over a rough sea, or traveling over a rough road; hele *akuaku* ma ke ala; holo *akuaku* ka moku; with one end up, then down.

A-KU-A-KU, *s.* A species of rush.

A-KU-A-KU, *adj.* Done in a hurry; therefore, badly done; he *akuaku* iho kou, you were in a great hurry; he *akuaku* kana

hana, his work is badly done.

A-KU-A-LA-PU, *s.* *Akua*, god, and *lapu*, a ghost. A ghost; a spectre; an apparition; an evil spirit. NOTE.—According to the old people, the poe *akualapu* were the spirits of deceased persons seen in the night about burying and other places for the purpose of frightening people.

A-KU-A-LE-LE, *s.* *Akua*, god, and *lele*, to fly. A meteor; an *ignis fatuus*. NOTE.—When the Hawaiians were first shown the representation or imaginary picture of an angel, they at once called it an *akualele*, a flying god.

A-KU-A-NO-HO, *s.* Name of a class of gods supposed to be the spirits of men deceased; they were supposed to dwell with, or be over men as guardians.

A-KU-E, *s.* A short, low woman; he wahine poupou.

A-KU-I-KU-I, *v.* See KUI, to strike. To strike often, as with a stick in order to drive fish into a net.

A-KU-I-KU-I, *s.* Name of a particular fish net. See AKUIKUI above. Also, the name of the stick used to drive fish into the *kuikui*.

A-KU-HE, *v.* To be black, blue or dark colored. See KUKUHE.

A-KU-KA-PI-HE, *s.* The juice of the tree called koko, used among Hawaiians as a cathartic.

A-KU-KU, *s.* The standing up of water when wind and current are opposite; me he *akuku* nalu la i poi iloko o ka malama o Kaulua. *Laieik.* 167.

A-KU-LE, *s.* Name of a species of fish.

A-KU-LE, *s.* An epithet of an aged person; an old man or woman. See ELEMAKULE.

A-KU-LI, *v.* To collect in a stream of water, as leaves, blossoms, &c.

2. To dam up the water by such collection; ua *akuli* ka wai, a ua halana; a ua *akuli* ka lau o ka laau iloko o ka wai.

> Akuli ka pua o ka laau i ka wai,
> Lulana ahu i ka ae waililua,
> He wai hoopaa ia nolaila
> No ua 'kua la, o Maua, o Limaloa.

A-KU-LI-KU-LI, *s.* A kind of water herb, perhaps purslain; he mea ulu ma ka aina, ma na aliali, a he *papapa* kekahi inoa.

A-KU-LU, *s.* A species of color or colors; he *akulu* moe wai, a eleele uliuli.

A-KU-LU, *s.* Name of a species of fish.

A-KU-MU, *adj.* Broken or cut off till very short; applied to anything cut or broken off piece by piece, as a pin in mending, or a pencil in sharpening.

A-LA, *v.* To wake from sleep; to watch, i. e., to keep from sleep.

2. To rise up, as from a sleeping posture; e hikilele oia ma ka hiamoe ana. *Puk.* 10:23. *Ala* ku e, to rise up against one. *Puk.* 15:7.

3. To rise up, as a new generation of people; to come forward. *Lunk.* 2:10.

4. *Hoo.* To cause one to rise; to lift up; to rise from the dead.

5. To raise up; excite to action; to stir up, as the mind. *2 Pet.* 3:1.

6. To stir up; excite to evil. *Puk.* 23:1.

7. To raise up, as a deliverer or benefactor. *Lunk.* 3:9.

8. To repair, as a broken down wall. *Neh.* 3:4.

A-LA, *v.* To anoint; to dress a sore or a limb. *2 Sam.* 19:24.

A-LA, *s.* A round, smooth stone; a pebble, such as has been worn by the water; he pohaku maloko o ka muliwai. *1 Sam.* 17:40 and 49. *Ala* o ka maa, a sling stone. *Zek.* 9:15.

A-LA, *s.* A path; way; road; often *alanui*, great road; it is used in some places as synonymous with *kuamoo*; he kahi e hele ai; kuu aku ana keia i ke *ala*; po oloko i ke *ala*. *Laieik.* 62.

A-LA, *adj.* Round or oval, as a smooth stone or bullet; hence, heavy; kaumaha, e like me ka *ala* o kahawai, heavy, as a smooth stone in a water course. See ALA, a round smooth stone.

A-LA, *adj.* Spicy; perfumed; aromatic.

A-LA, *adj.* Fair eyed, but blind; *ala* ka maka, e like me ko ka elemakule, dim sighted, as an old person.

A-LA, *s.* A variety of kalo, tough and stringy.

A-LA-A, *v.* To work with the oo in cultivating or digging off green sward.

A-LA-A, *s.* A kind of tree.

A-LA-A-LA, *s.* *Ala*, round, &c. A scrofulous sore; an ulcer, particularly on the neck; the ringworm; poha ka *alaala* me kukae uli.

A-LA-A-LA, *s.* A soft substance in the squid used for bait in fishing; he *alaalahee*.

2. Soft, flabby flesh; soft and tough, as some kinds of food.

3. The name of potatoes that grow on the leaf of the potato.

A-LA-A-LA, *adj.* Scrofulous.

A-LA-A-LAE, *adj.* Hard, or half cooked, as kalo; aohe maneo, moa puehuehu, he

maneo ia.

> Ku i Hawaii ke one,
> *Alaalae* ke one,
> He pehu ka mai, he liki ka lau.

A-LA-A-LAI, *s.* Name of a bird.

A-LA-A-LAI, *s.* The name of a kalo patch formed by bending down the rushes and covering them with dirt and irrigating it; hence

A-LA-A-LAI, *s.* Argillaceous earth.

A-LA-A-LA-HEE, *s.* The spawn or black substance found in the squid. See ALA-ALA. He *alaalahee* me kahi kukui inamona, the spawn of the squid with kukui nuts as a relish.

A-LA-A-LA-PU-LOA, *s.* A plant with small yellow blossoms; called also *uhola*, a species of useless shrub; auhea o mea? aia i kula i ka *alaalapuloa*, i. e., gone on a wild goose chase, or on a fool's errand.

A-LA-A-LA-PU-LOA, *s.* The name of a species of fish of the squid kind; he *alaala puloa* me ka wekaweka no.

A-LA-A-LA-WA, *v.* The compound, frequentative, poetical form of *alawa*; to look frequently one way and the other, as in fear of being seen; *alaalawa* ka maka o ka aihue, *alaalawa* na maka me he pueo la, the eyes of the thief look this way and that, they look here and there like an owl.

A-LA-A-LA-WAI-NUI, *s.* Name of a large tree whose fruit is used in dying.

A-LA-A-LA-WAI-NUI, *s.* Name of a small plant growing in stony places; he a ahi ulu liilii ma ke ahu pohaku.

A-LA-A-MAO-MAO, *s.* Name of a god of the winds; the Eolus of the Hawaiian Islands.

> Huai mai ka ipu makani,
> *Alaamaomao* ke akua makani.

A-LA-A-PA-PA, *s.* The name of a kind of dance; he *alaapapa* kahi hula.

A-LA-A-PA-PA, *v.* To disclose to another what one has said of his character.

A-LAE, *s.* Name of a bird with a red skin on the upper part of its bill; oia ka mea (o Mauiakalani) nana i imi i ke ahi, a loaa i ka *alae*, he it was (Mauiakalani) who being in search of fire, found the *alae*; *alae*, he moa eleele loa, a very black fowl. The *alae* was formerly worshipped as a god, especially the *alae* keokeo, the white *alae*.

A-LA-EA, *s.* Red dirt; a kind of Spanish brown dug from the earth.

2. Any red coloring matter; red ochre. *Isa.* 44:13.

A-LA-EA, *adj.* Relating to the practice of the priest offering the yearly sacrifice;

hele mai ke kahuna *alaea* me ke kanaka, nana e lawe ka ipu *alaea*.

A-LA-EA, *adj.* Red, as the flesh of the fish aku and ahi. See foregoing. Huki koke ka io *alaea* a me na io a pau; name of a muscle. *Anat.* 50.

A-LA-EA, *s.* The fore part of the thigh.

A-LA-EA, *s.* A family, tribe or clan.

2. The descendants of servants; the descendants of Keopuolani are the *alaea* of Nahienaena.

A-LA-E-LA, *adv.* Poetic for *aia la*, there it is.

A-LAI, *v.* To obstruct; to hinder one in any way; ua *alai* ia e ka hilahila a hiki ole ke pane aku, he or she was hindered by shame and could not answer. *Laieik.* 127. To block up a door or passage by sitting down in it.

2. To form a circle round one for his defense in danger.

3. To defend; oppose one.

4. To be so thronged as not to see out. NOTE.—The double form, *alalai*, is more generally used. Ua *alai* ia, ua paapu loa, aole ike aku kahi mea, he was thronged thickly, he could not see out.

A-LAI-A, *s.* A small, thin surf board.

A-LA-I-HI, *s.* A species of small red fish.

2. Name of a red cloth.

A-LA-I-KI, *s.* The practice of quartering in one's house or seizing one's property when a chief traveled with his people.

A-LAI-LA, *adv.* Refers both to time and place; *there*, when place is referred to; *then*, when reference is made to time. Like many other adverbs, it is declinable with the simple prepositions. *Gram.* § 68 and § 165, 2d.

A-LA-O, *s.* Name of a class of heiaus.

A-LA-O, *s.* The eating of the oopu or other fish raw, and even before dead; ka *alao* mai no i na wahi oopu, a me na wahi opae.

A-LA-OU. Ua like me *alao*. See the foregoing.

A-LA-O-LO-LI, *s.* *Ala*, path, and *ololi*, narrow. A narrow path; a lane, as of a city.

A-LA-O-MA, *v.* To receive into the mouth; to swallow greedily, as a fish the bait; *alaoma* ka waha o ka oopu a me ke aholehole i ke koe; the mouths of the oopu and the aholehole greedily swallow the worm; alaume momoni.

A-LA-U, *v.* To knock with the knuckle on anything hard, as a board; olou.

A-LAU, *s.* Place where a wind is parted, as the east wind at Hana, Maui.

A-LAU-A, *v.* To look upon one's self with admiration; e *alaua* ana ia ia iho me ka manao ua nani oia.

A-LAU-KA, *s.* Badness; worthlessness; vileness; the offscouring or dregs of society; he hana inoino pupuka *alauka*.

A-LA-U-KA, *adj.* Vile; bad; worthless; slovenly; negligent; pupuka.

A-LA-U-LA, *s.* *Ala*, road, and *ula*, red.

1. A streak of light, such as is seen after the setting and before the rising sun. *Kin.* 32:24. Hence,

2. The first dawn of the morning. *Hal.* 46:5. The early dawn or first gleam of morning light. *2 Pet.* 1:19.

A-LA-U-LA, *s.* Red dust in a road; the red dust of a pali; red dust generally.

2. A kind of red chalk in which nothing will grow.

3. A kind of sea-weed, blackish; a species of limu.

A-LA-U-ME, *v.* See ALAOMA.

A-LAU-WA-HIO, *s.* A species of bird, small and yellow. See LAUWI.

A-LA-HA-KA, *s.* *Ala*, a path, and *haka*, open.

1. A ladder. *Kin.* 28:12.

2. A rough road, with many ravines or chasms. *Laieik.* 71.

A-LA-HEE, *s.* Name of a tree; a species of tree, very hard, of which instruments were made to till the soil with; o na oo mahiai i ka wa kahiko, o ka ulei a o ke *alahee*, the diggers for farming in ancient times were made of ulei and *alahee*.

A-LA-HII, *s.* A species of wood; bastard sandal-wood.

2. A row or hem, as on a mat.

A-LA-HOU-AN-A, *s.* *Ala*, to rise, and *hou*, again, and the participial termination *ana*. A rising again; a rising from the dead. *Oih.* 24:15. A resurrection.

A-LA-HO-NU-A, *s.* The south-west direction from Hilo; ke ala ana i ka manawa i makemake ole ai; o ke *alahonua* ana mamua, aole i hiki i ka manawa.

A-LA-HU-LA, *v.* To break a certain kapu; ua *alahula* kahi kapu, ua noa ke kanawai.

2. *Alahula* Puuloa, he hele na Kaapahau.

3. To make a road through one's house or farm by constantly passing through it; ua lilo i alanui hele mau ma ia wahi.

A-LA-HU-LA, *s.* A thoroughfare; a path or place much frequented; ua maa i ka ikeia, ua hele pinepine ia.

2. A road made on a pali on which a stranger cannot go, only traveled by resi-

dents.

2. A place where it is necessary to swim past a cliff that intercepts the passage along the beach, as Elelu on Hawaii.

A-LA-KAI, *v.* *Ala*, road, and *kai*, to lead.

1. To lead along the path; to guide or conduct one on a road. *Puk.* 13:17.

2. To lead, as captives. *2 Oihl.* 6:36.

3. To take, as a person, from one place to another. *2 Oihl.* 8:11.

4. To lead, as an animal; *alakai* ke keiki i ka puaa, the child leads the hog; ua *alakaiia* ka lio i ka pa. *Hoo.* To cause to lead. *Ezek.* 39:28.

A-LA-KAI, *s.* *Ala*, path, and *kai*, the sea. He *alakai* ke alanui hulaana o na pali, a path where one must swim around a projecting cliff or bluff.

A-LA-KAI, *s.* *Ala*, road, and *kai*, to lead. A leader; conductor; guide. *Heb.* 13:7.

A-LA-KAI, *adj.* Large; pot-bellied; plump.

A-LA-KAI-MAU-NA, *s.* *Alakai*, guide, and *mauna*, mountain. A guide on the mountains and inland; what a pilot is on board ship.

A-LA-KO, *v.* *Ala*, path, and *ko*, to drag along.

1. To drag along the ground.

2. To lead, as a criminal; kindred with *alakai*. *Hal.* 28:3. E kauo, e huki.

3. To trail, as a gown in the dust; he *aloko* mai i ka lepo, to drag in the dirt.

4. To draw or influence one. *Hos.* 11:4.

A-LA-LA, *s.* Name of a bird; a species of raven on Hawaii; so named from its cry, resembling that of a child. *Laieik.* 29.

A-LA-LA, *v.* To cry, as the young of animals. *Mik.* 1:8.

A-LA-LA, *s.* The cry of young animals; a crying; weeping; a bleating, crying, &c., of flocks. *1 Sam.* 15:14. The squealing of hogs. *Laieik.* 17.

A-LA-LA, *s.* A specie of potato with fruit on the leaves. See ALAALA.

A-LA-LAI, *v.* *Ala*, road, and *lai*.

1. To hinder one from doing a thing.

2. To obstruct one's road. *Iob.* 19:8.

3. To be in the way of another; ua *alalai* mai oia i ko'u hele ana, he hindered me in my passage; he keakea.

A-LA-LAI, *v.* To consecrate; to render sacred by coming in contact with some sacred object.

A-LA-LAU-WA, *s.* A species of small fish; called so when small or young; when larger or older they are called *aweoweo*.

A-LA-LA-LA, *v.* To spread out tobacco leaves over or before a fire to dry for use.

A-LA-LE-HE, *adj.* Sick; weak; hungry, as a child; he ukuhi ohemo na keiki, omino, *alalehe*, ka *alalehe*, ka uwe wale.

A-LA-LO, *s.* A, jaw, and *lalo*, under. The lower jaw of men and animals; the lower mandible of a bird.

A-LA-LO-A, *s.* *Ala*, path, and *loa*, long. a highway, path, &c. SYN. with alanui. *Nah.* 20:17.

A-LA-MA-A-WE-I-KI, *s.* *Ala*, path, *maawe*, any small substance, and *iki*, little. A small, narrow, indistinct path; it is applied to the departure of the soul when one dies; he is said to have gone along the *alamaaweiki*, i. e., the untrodden path; he alaololi.

A-LA-MA-KA-HI-NU, *s.* Name of a stone at Maiao, flat and shining; applied to a disobedient child; he *alamakahinu* i ke alii.

A-LA-ME-A, *v.* To be too ripe; rotten, as anything lying out in the rain; ua kapule *alamea* i ka ua.

A-LA-ME-A, *s.* The name of a species of hard stone from volcanoes, out of which stone axes were made.

A-LA-MO-LE, *s.* A species of stone.

A-LA-NA, *s.* A present made by a chief to a priest to procure his prayers.

2. A present made to a god; he makana e haawi aku ai i ke akua.

3. An oblation or free will offering for any purpose. *Puk.* 18:12.

4. A sacrifice. *Puk.* 29:28. *Alana* hoano, a holy oblation. *Ezek.* 48:10. He *alana* ka mea e haawiia aku ai e kalaia mai ai ka hala o ka mea lawehala.

5. A fee prepaid to a physician to attend upon a sick person.

A-LA-NA, *v.* To give or bring a present as an offering. *Oihk.* 12:14. To offer a sacrifice. *Hal.* 66:15.

A-LA-NA, *adj.* A and *lana*, to float. Light, not heavy; easily floating on the water; he hookomo ole; not sinking.

A-LA-NA, *s.* *Alala*, to cry, and *ana*. A crying; the voice of suffering or of complaint; ke oho *alana* makuakahi, the voice of complaint from an only parent.

A-LA-NA-A-LO-HA, *s.* *Alana*, offering, and *aloha*, love. A peace offering; an offering for making peace with another to procure one's favor; he alana e aloha mai o hai ia ia.

A-LA-NA-KU-NI, *s.* *Alana* and *kuni*, to burn. An offering to procure the death of a sorcerer; e make ai ka mea nana i ana-ana; a burnt offering.

A-LA-NA-MO-LI-A, *s.* An offering made to the gods to procure a curse; he alana e molia i kipi aina, to curse the rebels; ke alana e molia i ka mamala ku i ka pa; he alana e molia i ka olulo pae i kapa.

A-LA-NE-O, *adj.* *Ala*, path, and *neo*, silent.

1. Clear; serene; unclouded, as the atmosphere on the mountains; *alaneo* ka uka, aole ao, clear was the upland, no clouds.

2. Desolate; without people, as a country; *alaneo* kauhale, aole kanaka. *Ier.* 50:3. See NEONEO.

A-LA-NE-O, *s.* The name of a disease where the patient is swelled greatly in every part except the face; he olelo a na kahuna lapaau; ina olelo aku i ka mai, pela he *alaneo* kou mai, o ke ano o ia olelo, he mai kanaka ole, aole lehulehu o kanaka nana e kii i ka laau.

2. A class of gods, males only.

3. The name of a cloak or royal robe made of the feathers of the mamo only; o ka aahuula i hanaia i ka hulu mamo wale no ua kapaia he *alaneo*.

4. Clear weather; no clouds.

A-LA-NI, *s.* The name of the mountain on Lanai and some other places.

A-LA-NI, *s.* Name of a timber tree used in fitting up canoes.

A-LA-NI, *s.* *Eng.* The Hawaiian pronunciation of the word *orange*; an orange, a foreign fruit; also, the name of the tree.

A-LA-NI, *s.* Name of a land breeze at Lanai, from the name of the mountain.

A-LA-NI, *s.* Name of a species of limu, bitter, and very similar to the limu lipoa.

A-LA-NI-A, *adj.* Smooth, as the ocean, without wave or ripple; aole apuupuu, he *kalania*.

A-LA-NI-HO, *s.* *Ala*, path, and *niho*, tooth. Name of the long strips of tattoo made on the skin by means of a shark's tooth.

A-LA-NU-I, *s.* *Ala*, path, and *nui*, large. A highway; a road; a frequented path. See ALALOA. In some places *kuamoo* is used.

A-LA-PA, *adj.* Ugly; poor; thin in flesh, as a hog.

A-LA-PA-HI, *v.* To spread false reports; to slander. 2 *Sam.* 19:27.

2. To deceive; to lead others astray.

3. To deceive, as a demagogue.

A-LA-PA-HI, *s.* Slander; detraction; falsehood; he *alapahi* moe ipo ka nana; a lie; false speaking.

A-LA-PA-HI, *adj.* Olelo *alapahi*, a slanderous or false report. *Neh.* 14:36.

A-LA-PA-KUI, *adj.* Exceedingly fragrant, too much so, or too strong to be pleasant.

A-LA-PA-PII-MOO-KU, *s.* A mean man of no character who goes before the king; ka mea ino pii i kahi o ke alii.

A-LA-PII, *v.* *Ala*, path, and *pii*, to ascend. A ladder; stairs. 2 *Nal.* 9:13. An ascent. 1 *Nal.* 10:5. He alahaka, he ala-ulii; he *alapii* pali ino o Wahinekapu.

A-LA-PU-KA, *adj.* Having scrofulous sores, as on the neck, legs, &c.

2. Applied to kalo which has spots of dry-rot; he kalo *alapuka*.

A-LA-WA, *v.* To look on one side, then on the other, as one who is afraid of being seen; e hoi oukou me ko oukou maka *alawa* ole io a io.

2. To look up, as one downcast.

3. To lift up the eyes in pride. *Isa.* 37:23.

4. To lift up the eyes to see a thing. *Ioan.* 4:35. To take a survey. *Isa.* 60:4.

5. To turn the eyes in an oblique direction. *Kin.* 33:5.

6. To turn one's head to look about.

7. To be lifted or turned up, as the eyes; *alawa* ae la kona mau maka.

A-LA-WA, *s.* A turning of the eyes to look behind; he *alawa* na maka i hope e ike i ka poe e hele mai ana.

A-LA-BA-TA,   } *adj.* *Gr.* Alabaster; he
A-LA-BA-TE-RO, } ipu *alabata*. *Luk.* 7:37.

A-LE, *v.* To swallow, in various senses; e moni aku.

1. When anything disagreeable is to be taken.

2. To drink in, as water.

3. To drink in, as the earth drinks water.

4. To swallow up, as the earth. *Nah.* 16:32. To absorb; to swallow, as a flood; to destroy.

5. To overpower, as an army. 2 *Sam.* 17:16. *Ale* wale, to swallow without choking.

6. Ke *ale* mai, to come up into, as tears into the eyes; as poets say, the tears *welled* up in her eyes.

A-LE, *s.* A wave; a billow put in motion by the wind; a wave of the sea. *Iob.* 9:8. Aloia mai ai na *ale* ino o Lae Hao, having escaped the raging *billows* of Cape Horn; make iho nei ia iloko o ka *ale* o Pailolo, he was lately drowned in the *waves* of Pailolo; loi ale no i ke alia o kolo. FIG. *Ale* o ka make. 2 *Sam.* 22:5. Holo pipi ka *ale* o ka moana, the crest of a wave; ka *ale*, water put in motion; ka *ale* wai hau a ke 'kua, *water* of snow of the god. NOTE.—It was supposed that the gods made the snow.

A-LE-A, *s.* See LEA. Having a pleasant voice for singing; agreeable, as the voice.

A-LE-A-LE, *v.* 13th conj. of *ale.* To make into waves; to stir up, as water; to trouble; to toss about, as restless waters. *Epes.* 4:14. *Aleale* ka wai, ua piha a *aleale* ke keakea. *Hoo.* To stir up, as water. *Ioan.* 5:4.

A-LE-A-LE, *s.* A moving, swelling, stirring, as the waves of the sea; as water any where.

A-LE-A-LE-A, *s.* A sharp, white, small shell fish found near the shore; he pupu *alealea.*

A-LE-O, *adj.* High; applied to a house or a room; a look-out on a house top.

A-LEU-LEU, *s.* Old kapa or mats; also applied to all kinds of bad kapa.

A-LE-KU-MA, } *s. Heb.* A later ortho-
A-LE-GU-MA, } graphy for *aleguma*; name of a timber tree, as below; name of a tree found in the deserts of Arabia; the algum tree. 2 *Oihl.* 2:8. Also, by a change of letters, *alemuga.* See below. Supposed by Kitts to be the sandal-wood.

A-LE-LE, *v.* To go or act as a messenger.
   2. To go or act as a spy.
   3. To look or examine the condition of another. See LELE.

A-LE-LE, *s.* See LELE and ELELE. A messenger; one sent on business; he *alele* wau i hoounaia mai nei, I am a messenger sent hither. *Laieik.* 79. See LUNA.

A-LE-LE, *s.* A messenger of a chief; an ambassador. See ELELE.

     He kiu ka pua kukui;
     He *alele* hooholo na ke Koolau.—*Mele.*

A-LE-HE, *s.* A snare; a noose; he ahele; he pahele.

A-LE-LO, *s.* The tongue, of man or animals. *Puk.* 11:7; 2 *Sam.* 23:2. See ELELO.

A-LE-LO, *s.* The tongue; he *alelo* wana ka ono, he ono ke *alelo* wana, he okulikuli.

A-LE-MA-NA-KA, *s. Eng.* An almanac; the first was published in Hawaiian in 183—.

A-LE-MO-NE, *adj. Eng.* of an almond.

A-LE-MO-NE, *s.* A hazel. *Kin.* 30:37. The almond tree. *Kekah.* 12:15.

A-LE-MU-GA, } *s.* See ALEKUMA above.
A-LE-KU-MA, }

A-LE-PA, *s. Gr. Alepa,* alpha; name of the first letter of the Greek alphabet; hence,

the first, ka mua. *Hoik.* 21:6.

A-LE-WA-LE-WA, *s.* A cloud or smoke floating in the atmosphere; hookaa ka punohu ka *alewalewa.*

A-LE-GU-MA, *s.* See ALEKUMA above.

A-LI, *s.* A scar on the face. *Isa.* 1:6.

A-LI, *v.* To have a scar on the cheek; ua *ali* ka papalina i ka mai; to have a scar anywhere.
   2. *Hoo.* To shake; to wave; to move to and fro, &c. *Nah.* 5:25. See HOALI.

A-LI-A, *v.* To wait; to stop one when doing a thing; to restrain. 2 *Sam.* 24:16.
   2. Used *imperatively,* stop; wait; applied to a person in the way; take care; stand aside. 1 *Sam.* 15:16.

A-LI-A, *s.* A large flat surface where it is white with salt; he *alia* hoohaahaa paakai; loi ale no i ke *alia* okolo salt bed.

A-LI-A, *s.* The name of two sticks carried by a person before the god of the year.

A-LI-A, *adv.* By and by; after a little.

A-LI-A-LI, *adj.* White, as snow or paper; he wai *aliali,* he keokeo; he huali.

A-LI-A-LI, *v.* Ua *aliali,* to have scars; to be rough with scars; to be scarred; ua kalikali, kokoke e piha; ukali ae no hoi; hulihuli.

A-LI-A-LI-A, *s.* He *alialia* paakai, a bed where salt is dried; he *alialia* manu; na *alialia* o na wai puna huihui. See ALIA above.
   2. Ground which is smooth, dry and barren, as that which is baked in the sun, or covered with salt.

A-LI-A-NE, *adv.* A word of similar import with *nane* and i *nane,* let us see, show it to me, &c.; as *aliane,* referring to something spoken of, let us see; let me see.

A-LII, *s.* Name of a hard timber tree, used for posts of houses and other purposes; also called *aalii.*

A-LII, *s.* A chief; one who rules or has authority over other men; a king, qualified by various epithets.
   1. Ke *alii moi,* the supreme executive.
   2. Ke *alii aimoku,* a chief over a division, i. e., a governor under the *alii* moi.
   3. *Alii koa,* a chief over soldiers, i. e., a general, leader of an army. 2 *Sam.* 2:8.
   4. *Alii okana,* chief of a district. *Luk.* 9:7.

A-LII, *v.* To act the chief; to be chief or principal. *Kin.* 1:16. To rule over men. *Oihk.* 26:17. To govern. *Kin.* 37:8.
   2. *Hoo.* To crown one a king; to make one a king; to make one's self a king; to rule; to have power or influence with.

A-LII, *adj.* Mea noho *alii,* a ruler. *Puk.*

22:28. *Alii weliweli*, king of terrors. *Iob.* 18:14.

A-LII-KOA, *s.* A general of an army. 2 *Sam.* 2:18.

A-LII-PA-PA, *s.* Name of a child where the mother was a chief and the father not.

A-LII-WA-HI-NE, *s. Alii* and *wahine,* woman. A Queen. *Mat.* 11:44.

A-LI-U-LI-U, *adv.* A long time.

A-LI-HI, *s. H* inserted; a captain of a company. *Ios.* 10:24. *Alihi kaua,* a general.

A-LI-HI, *s.* The lines of a fish net; o ke kaula ma ka pikoni.

2. The cords holding the sinkers of a net.

3. The upper part of a calabash strap; he *alihi* no ke koko o ka umeke; o ka *alihi* maluna o ka waa e kalai hou a haahaa ka niao o ka *alihi* maluna o ka umeke; ma ka *alihi* moana, e pili aku ana i kumu lani, at the *edge* of the ocean, i. e., where the ocean and sky meet. *D. Malo* 5:13.

A-LI-HI, *v.* To be ready to work for the sake of gain, but at other times absent.

A-LI-HI, *adv.* Unwillingly.

A-LI-HI-KAU-A, *s. Alihi* (alii) and *kaua,* war. A general; commander; one who directs in battle. 1 *Nal.* 16:16.

A-LI-HI-LA-NI, *s.* The horizon.

A-LI-HI-LE-LE, *s.* Name of a drag-net; the net for taking the anae.

A-LI-KA-LI-KA, *adj.* Clammy; sticky; tough, as kalo baked; as mud.

2. Stingy; not liberal.

A-LI-KE-A-LI-KE, *s.* See LIKE. One-half; an equal division of a thing.

A-LI-KI-LI-KI, *v.* See LIKI; see OPUOHAO. To be swelled tight as the skin can hold, as in the dropsy.

2. To be girded tightly.

A-LI-MA (e-li-ma), *adj.* Five; the number five. See LIMA.

A-LI-MA, *s.* See AULIMA, the stick held in the hand in rubbing to obtain fire.

A-LI-MA.

> *Alima* hea ko alakai,
> Ke ani peahi la ia Limaloa
> I hoapili no manu a kepa ka ua—he.

A-LI-NA, *v.* To be defiled or contaminated, as by marrying one of low birth; mai moe oukou i ka poe keiki a ka poe kauwa, o *alina* auanei ka oukou mau keiki; applied to a chief who married a low woman and had children of low order; *alina* oe i kou mare ana i kau kauwa.

2. To be scarred, as one burned badly; to be scarred by scrofula; ua *alina* oe i ke ahi.

3. To have spots or blemishes on one's person.

4. *Morally,* to be disgraced or implicated in sin.

5. To be filthy, as food; ua *alina* loa o Mea; ua *alina* ka kakou, ua makole.

A-LI-NA, *s.* A low servant; a slave.

A-LI-NA, *adj.* Low; degraded.

A-LI-NA-LI-NA, *s.* A shell fish of the sea; the young or small of the opihi.

2. A mark; a sign; nearly SYN. with hoailona.

A-LO, *v.* To elude or dodge the stroke of a weapon. 1 *Sam.* 18:11.

2. To pass over from one place to another; ua *alo* aku nei na kaulua i na kumu i Molokai.

3. To skip or pass over something; e *alo* i kekahi la, e hana i kekahi la.

4. To pass through the water by swimming; to extend the hands in swimming.

5. To set one's self against; to be opposed to; e *alo* ia ia, to face him; to turn and front him.

6. To meet some difficulty or resisting force or opposition; ua nui ka makou hana i ke *alo* ana me na haku i ka maka o ke kaua, we have much work to do in resisting with our masters the front of the war.

7. To resist boldly, as a difficulty; face, as an enemy in danger. *Ios.* 8:20. E *alo* i na ino a pau e hiki mai ana e like me kaua i *alo* hoomanawanui ai i ka la o ka makalii.

8. To double, as a cape; e *aloia* mai ai na ale o Lae Hao.

9. To face; to be against. *Lunk.* 20:48. To resist. *Puk.* 23:29.

10. To consume; devour.

11. *Hoo.* To pass away; forget. *Isa.* 40:27.

12. To shun; eschew. 1 *Pet.* 3:11.

A-LO, *s.* The front; the face; the presence of one. *Kin.* 3:8. Ma ke *alo*, before; in front.

2. The breast or belly. *Kin.* 3:14. Ua hiki mai i ko'u *alo* nei, it has come to my *front,* i. e., to me; ma kona *alo* iho, directly in front of him. *Ios.* 6:20. Ma ke *alo* alii, persons living with and in the favor of the chief.

A-LO, *s.* The name of a four-footed animal in the sea.

A-LO-A-LO, *v.* Double form of *alo.* To turn this way and that; to look one way and another, as if in fear, or about to do mischief. *Puk.* 2:12. *Aloalo* na maka o ka aihue.

A-LO-A-LO, *v.* See ALO. To dodge; to flee from, as a shower, i. e., to run from one tree to another; *aloalo* ua, *aloalo* makani, kipakipa, pukauhale, to dodge the rain, &c.

A-LO-A-LO, *v.* To go after, as a servant; to bring things; to wait on; he ai puupuu, he poi puupuu.

A-LO-E, *s.* Eng. Aloes. *Mel. Sol.* 4:14.

A-LOI-LOI, *s.* A species of small fish.

A-LO-HA, *v.* To love; to regard with affection; to desire.

2. To have pity or compassion upon.

3. To show mercy; to be merciful as a habit. *Mat.* 5:7. To spare. *Ezek.* 7:9.

aloiloi

4. To salute at meeting or parting. 1 *Sam.* 10:4.

5. To salute contemptuously; *aloha* ino kaua, alas for us two. NOTE.—*Aloha*, as a word of salutation, is modern; the ancient forms were anoai, welina, &c.

6. *Hoo.* To give thanks as an act of worship. 1 *Oihl.* 25:3.

A-LO-HA, *s.* A word expressing different feelings; as, love; affection; gratitude; kindness; pity; compassion; grief; the modern common salutation at meeting and parting.

A-LO-HA, *adj.* Loving; beloved; favored.

A-LO-HA-IA. A verbal from the verb *aloha* above used as a noun. Favor; kindness; loaa ia ia ke *alohaia* mai, he obtained favor; favor; good will. *Kin.* 33:10.

A-LO-HA-I-NO, *int.* *Aloha* and *ino.* An intentive; it expresses great love, pity or compassion for a person in a suffering condition. It is also used by way of contempt, as poor fellow! good enough for you!

A-LO-HA-LO-HA, *v.* To love much.

2. *Hoo.* To give thanks; to express affection for; to bless in worship. 2 *Sam.* 22:50.

3. To salute. 2 *Sam.* 8:10.

4. To speak kindly to; to entreat gently. *Luk.* 15:28.

A-LO-HI, *v.* To shine; to become shining or bright; to reflect brightness. *Isa.* 9:1. *Alohi* e like me ka la i ke awakea. FIG. To shine, as christian character. *Pil.* 2:15.

A-LO-HI, *s.* A bright shining; brightness; splendor.

A-LO-HI-LO-HI, *s.* Splendor; brightness. *Hoik.* 21:11. Light. *Isa.* 59:9. Sparkling, as the eye; ka inoa he akua i ke *alohilohi* o na maka, I thought they were gods by the *brightness* of their eyes.

A-LO-HI-LO-HI, *adj.* Malamalama *alohi-*

lohi, bright light. *Iob.* 37:21.

A-LO-HI-LO-HI, *v.* To shine brightly. *Luk.* 17:24. To shine, as light. *Dan.* 12:3.

A-LO-LO, *adv.* Exclamation of triumph at the ills of another, as the fall of an enemy. See LOLO.

A-LO-LU-A, *adj.* Two-sided; double-faced; applied to men and things; moena *alolua,* a double mat, having two faced sides.

A-LO-PE-KE, *s.* Gr. A fox. *Lunk.* 15:4.

A-LO-PI-HE, *s.* *Alo* and *pihe,* the sound of mourning as it floats in the air.

A-LU, *v.* To combine, as several persons in aiding another either in a good or bad cause.

2. To give aid or assistance. *Oih.* 21:28. To help, as in quarrels where one is likely to be killed and several aid in effecting his escape.

3. To unite together, as several persons for a particular object.

4. To be connected, as the joints of the human body.

5. To adhere to; to act with; e *alu* aku mahope; make o Manono no ka nui o kona *aluia,* Manono died for the strength of her *adherence* to him.

A-LU, *v.* To relax; hang down; be weak. *Puk.* 17:11.

2. To bend the knees; to courtesy.

3. To stoop down, as in entering a low door; to stoop down, as in hiding behind a low object; *alu* ae la maua e pee ana. *Laieik.* 207.

4. To ruff up, as a mat; ua alu na moena i ka nakuia.

5. *Hoo.* To loosen, as the tongue. *Mar.* 7:31.

A-LU, *s.* The lines of the hand.

2. A gutter; a ravine; kahawai awawa; a road descending a hill.

3. A courtesy.

4. The muscles of the eye. *Hal.* 76:4.

5. The skin and soft parts of men, fish, and all animals, when the bones are taken out. See ALUALU.

6. A name given to women who have borne children. See ALUALU.

A-LU, *adj.* Combined; acting together; he mau ilio *alu* i ka hakaka.

A-LU-A (e-lu-a), *num. adj.* The number two; two. See LUA.

A-LU-A, *adj.* A word signifying admiration; it applies to what is good, great, admired, &c.; the *a* is often dropped; as, aohe ona *lua,* there is none like him. See LUA. Ka inoa o ka ona no kona waiwai (iho), o ka mahuna *alua,* surely drunken ness (by awa) has its own reward, the wonderful scaling of the skin. *Laieik.* 35.

A-LU-A-LU, *v.* *Alu*, doubled; 13th conj. of *alu*. To come upon one.

2. To follow; pursue; overpower. *Kanl.* 32:30.

3. To pursue, as an enemy. *Kin.* 14:15; 1 *Sam.* 17:52.

4. To chase. *Ios.* 23:10.

5. To persecute. 1 *Tes.* 2:15.

6. To be wrinkled, as the cheeks and forehead of old persons.

A-LU-A-LU, *s.* The flexible skin or hide of an animal; he *alualu* bipi.

2. The soft parts of flesh when the bones are taken out; the appearance is flabby, loose and wrinkled, &c.

3. The fetus of animals or men; kanuia ka, *alualu* i ka lepo, the *fetus* was buried in the dust.

4. The skins, rinds and refuse of melons after the substance is eaten; ua aiia na ipu, a o ka *alualu* wale no koe.

A-LU-A-LU, *adj.* Loose; flabby; premature; shapeless, as an untimely birth. *Laieik.* 12. Slack, as a rope or string.

2. Uneven; rough; full of lines.

3. He ili *alualu*, a loose skin; applied to an untimely birth; he keiki *alualu*, ua like me ka iewe ke ano, an imperfect child like a placenta.

A-LU-A-LU-A, *s.* A crack, as in the wall of a house. *Oihk.* 14:3.

2. A rough road, full of ravines and difficult passes; he *alualu* inoino ke alanui e hele ai i Kahakuloa.

3. A second-hand garment, full of wrinkles.

4. The name given to the numeration table, beginning thus: *elua lua aha*, two twos are four; ma ke *alualua* ko lakou ao ana i ka helu, through the multiplication table they learn arithmetic.

A-LU-HEE, *adj.* Loose, as a bundle not well bound; hanging flabbily.

A-LU-KA, *v.* To jumble together, as parts of two stories.

2. To mix together, as contributions for different purposes or different taxes.

3. To mix together, so as not to distinguish.

4. *Hoo.* To cause a mixture, as above; e ao o *hoaluka* i ka waiwai hookupu; similar to *huikai*.

A-LU-KA, *s.* The uniting or mixing together of things of different or opposite qualities; ke *aluka* o ka hewa o ka pono.

A-LU-LI, *v.* To turn the head on one side; he *aluli* ke poo, he kekee.

A-LU-LU, *adj.* Quick; in a hurry; he hopuhopu *alulu* kona hele ana no ka lohe ana he make.

A-LU-LU, *adv.* Quickly; hastily; holo hopuhopu *alulu* aku la makou a ee maluna o ka waa.

A-LU-NA, *s.* A, the jaw, and *luna*, upper, over. The upper part of the mouth of a person; of the bill of birds; of the mouth of animals. *Laieik.* 104. The roof of the mouth. *Hal.* 137:5. The upper jaw.

A-LU-NU, *v.* See LUNU. To defraud. 1 *Sam.* 12:3, 4. To be overbearing in a bargain. *Oihk.* 19:13. To oppress; to be hard upon one. *Kanl.* 24:14.

2. To accuse falsely. *Luk.* 3:14.

3. To be desirous of possessing property.

A-LU-NU, *s.* Oppression. *Isa.* 30:12. Usury. *Neh.* 5:16. Extortion; covetousness. *Isa.* 57:17. He *alunu*, an extortioner.

A-LU-NU, *adj.* Covetous; greedy of gain; waiwai *alunu*, property unlawfully taken. *Puk.* 18:21. Waiwai *alunu* is also lucre. 1 *Sam.* 8:3. *Alunu* is opposed to *lokomaikai*. *Isa.* 32:5.

A-LU-NU-WA-LE, *s.* A strong desire to take what is another's; extortion; robbery.

A-MA, *s.* The longitudinal stick of the outrigger of a canoe.

A-MA, *adj.* Satisfied; satiated, as with food.

2. Talkative; revealing secrets; tattling; he ahiahi: he waha *ama* ia hai, a mouth revealing to others. See AMAAMA.

A-MA, *v.* To offer to the gods ohias and melons; mostly found in the conj. haa and hoo; as, *hoama*, *haama*, &c; *haama* ka ohia; *haama* i ka ipuhaole; akahi no a *haama* ae i ka ipu aimaka. See AMAMA, to offer, &c.

A-MA-A-MA, *v.* See AMA 2. To reveal secrets; to tell another's faults; to slander; *amaama* ka waha i ka hai i ka hewa o ka mea e.

A-MA-A-MA, *adj.* Slanderous, as the mouth of one ever ready to speak evil; he waha *amaama*, ka leieoi, ka waha hiki wawe i ke kamailio ma na olelo i manaoia e huna.

A-MA-A-MA, *s.* A species of fish; young mullet perhaps.

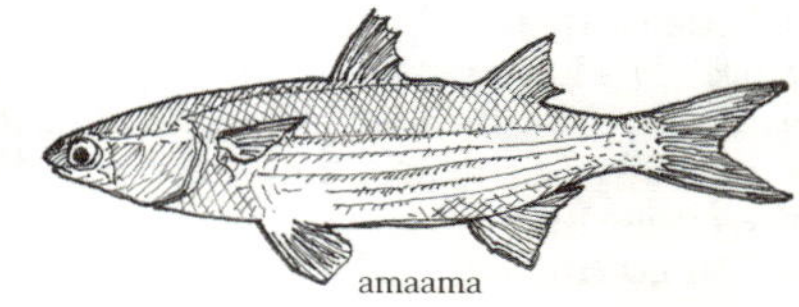

amaama

A-MA-A-MAU, *v. Ama,* satisfied with food, and *amau,* still.

1. To eat much; to be satisfied with food; e ai nui i ka ai me ka *amaamau.*

2. To eat quickly or fast, as one who is hungry and has a keen appetite.

A-MAU, *v.* To hush up; to keep one from speaking or complaining; ua *amau* aku au e noho malie, aole pono e pane mai. See HAMAU.

A-MA-UI, *s.* A species of small bird.

A-MAU-MAU, *adj.* A god growing among the ferns on the mountains; i na 'kua *amaumau* o ke kula.

A-MAU-MAU, *s.* The fern; the brake.

A-MA-KA-MI-KA, *v.*
See AMIKA, to desire food. To desire food, as we say, his mouth waters for it.

amaumau

2. To have a desire for that which cannot be obtained.

A-MA-KI-HI, *s.* Name of a small yellow bird; he manu hulu lenalena ia.

A-MA-KI-KA, *s.* A species of small bird.

A-MA-MA, *v.* Conj. 9th of *ama,* to offer, &c. To give over to the gods in sacrifice.

2. To offer sacrifice as an act of worship. *Hoik.* 8:3. O ke kino uhane ole e waiho ana, *amama* ae la ke alii, the body lying without life the king offered in sacrifice; ua *amamaia,* aku la i kona akua ia Kaili, he was sacrificed to his god Kaili; to offer prayers; *amama,* ua noa, like our term Amen to a prayer. *Laieik.* 104.

A-MA-MA, *s.* The offering of a sacrifice; ka *amama* ana i ke kanaka i ke akua.

A-MA-NA, *s.* Two sticks crossing each other at oblique angles.

2. The branches of a tree in the form of the letter Y.

A-MA-NA, *adj.* Crossing; put together in the form of a cross or gallows; na laau *amana* i kauia'i o Kuhama; he aleo kahi hale, he *amana* kekahi hale.

A-MA-NA, *v. Amana* mau ke kani ana o ka pu; *amama* mau ke kani o ka pu a ka anela.

A-MA-RA, *s. Eng.* The Hawaiian orthography for the word *armorer;* a blacksmith. 1 *Sam.* 13:19. NOTE.—The first ships that visited the islands were ships of war or of discovery, and their blacksmiths were called *armorers;* hence the word.

A-ME-NE, *adj. Eng.;* from the *Heb.* Amen; so be it; truly; pela no.

A-ME-NE, *s. Heb.* Ka *amene,* an epithet of Jesus Christ as a true and faithful Savior. *Hoik.* 3:14.

A-ME-TU-SE-TE, *s. Gr.* An amethyst; a precious stone. *Hoik.* 21:20; also, *Puk.* 28:19.

A-MI, *v.* To turn, as upon hinges; as a door; as the lid of a chest, &c.; to move back and forwards; to make any motion back and forth; to swing back and forth, as a gate; to move up and down, as the chin in eating.

A-MI, *s.* A hinge; a butt for a door. *Sol.* 26:14.

2. A joint of a war harness. 1 *Nal.* 22:34. Joint of an animal. *Epes.* 4:16. Joint of a limb. *Dan.* 5:6.

3. A small worm which, in crawling, doubles itself up; he peelua kuapuu.

4. A swinging, pendulous motion.

5. The name of a long slim fish; he ia kino oeoe.

A-MI-A-MI, *adj.* Elastic; pendulous.

2. A term used to reproach one just married; ka *amiami* ana o ka puaa.

A-MI-O, *v.* To walk or move still and slyly, so as not to be heard; maanei no i *amio* iho nei a nalowale, he came here silently just now and is gone; mai kukulu aku oe i ke kukui ma ka puka; to flare, as the blaze of a lamp in the wind; he *amio* ka makani, e pio auanei; to move silently this way and that.

A-MI-O, *s.* That which enters silently, as death; as a fish floats unseen and comes not to the top; a gentle moving to and fro.

A-MI-KA, *v.* To desire food or drink.

A-MI-KA, *s.* A desire or relish for food.

A-MI-KA-MI-KA, *v.* See AMIKA. To eat, but not enough; the desire is for more; aole i onoono iho kahi puu i ka mea ai, aole i *amikamika* iho; aole ona o ka awa, aole *amikamika* iho.

A-MI-KA-MI-KA, *s.* A remainder wished for.

A-MO, *v.* To wink, as the eye. 1 *Kor.* 15:52.

2. To twinkle, as a star; ke *amo* mai la ka hoku; often doubled, as *amoamo;* applied to the winking of any animal. See IMO.

A-MO, *v.* To bear or carry a burden on the shoulder. *Puk.* 27:7. To bear or bring along a weight; to carry.

2. FIG. To perform difficult offices of any kind. *Puk.* 18:22. SYN. with lawe. *Oihl.* 15:2.

3. *Hoo.* To put upon the shoulders of one. NOTE.—To carry on the back is *haawe;*

to carry under the arm is *hii.*

A-MO, *s.* A burden carried on the shoulders.

A-MO-A, *v.* Pass. for *amoia;* also *amoaia;* a double passive ua laweia.

A-MO-A-MO, *v.* To be high; to be raised up, as a high precipice; to rise high, as the crest of a wave; *amoano* iluna o ka pali o Kihiopua; *amoamo* iluna ka lau o ka nalu.

A-MO-A-MO, *v.* See AMO, to wink. To wink repeatedly.

A-MO-A-MO, *s.* A winking; a twinkling, as of the eye or a star; a sudden change of the wind.

A-MO-E, *s.* For *aumoe;* midnight; e holo, ua nui ke kai o ke *amoe.*

A-MOO-MOO, *s.* Work for women; he kuku *amoomoo,* he palaholo ke kapa.

A-MOO-MOO, *s.* A kind of fish; a small fish, also the *ulua.*

A-MO-HU-LU, *s.* E papani ka *amohulu* o ia nei; a lascivious word.

A-MO-MO, *s.* The general name of odoriferous herbs mentioned in *Hoik.* 18:13. Latin, *amomus.*

A-MO-PU-U, *adj.* Lean; thin in flesh; hakake, olala; a word used in caviling.

A-MU, *v.* To shear or shave the hair from the head. *Oih.* 18:18. To trim the hair; ua kolikoliia no a *amu.*

A-MU, *adj.* Relating to shearing or shaving; he pahi *amu,* a razor. 1 *Sam.* 1:11: He lauoho *amo* no kona, he has his hair *cut.*

A-MU,   ⎫   *v.* To use profane lan-
A-MU-A-MU, ⎭   guage; to revile; *amuama* i ke Akua. to blaspheme; *amuamu* i ka huahaule, to curse the friendless.

A-MU-A-MU, *s.* A cursing; a reviling; reproaching; ka *amuamu* ana i ke alii me ka hoohiki ino, a cursing of the king with profanity; he *kuamuamu,* a reviling of sacred things. *Hal.* 10:7.

> Ke *amuamuia* la i ka ue wale,
> O ka ue wale iho no ia.
> O ka ke kamalii hana'na no ia.

A-MU-E-MU-E, *v.* To feel the chilling breeze of a cold morning when the skin contracts with cold; to suffer the same from being long in the water.

A-MU-KU, *v.* See MUKU, to cut short. To cut off; to cut in pieces. See OMUKU.

A-MU-MU, *adj.* Blunt on the edge; dull, as a tool. See KUMUMU.

A-MU-MU, *s.* Bluntless; dullness, as a tool.

A-MU-PU, *s.* A word of reproaching or reviling; he kanaka *amupu,* small, insignificant.

A-NA, *v.* To suffer; to undergo, as an experiment of healing in sickness.

2. To be grieved; troubled. *Oih.* 16:18.

3. To be affected at contempt or vile treatment. *Hal.* 123:3, 4.

A-NA, *v.* To measure. *Hoik.* 21:16.

2. To measure in any way; e hiki ia'u ke *ana* i ka loa, a me ka laula, a me ka hohonu, a me ke kiekie o keia mea; *met.*

3. *Ana* wau i kou pono a me kou hewa. I measured your good and your evil; no ke *ana* ana, in measuring. *Oihk.* 19:35. Mea *ana* hora, a dial. *Isa.* 38:8. *Hoo.* To set apart; to set aside. *Puk.* 16:33. To restrain; keep back. *Oih.* 5.2

A-NA, *v.* To be satiated; satisfied, as the eye with seeing. *Kekah* 1:8.

2. To have a sufficiency of property. *Kekah.* 5:10.

3. FIG. To drink sufficiently, as the sword drinks blood, i. e., to be revenged. *Isa.* 34:6.

4. *Hoo.* To satiate, as with food. *Ier.* 31:25. As with drink. *Hal.* 104:11. Ua *ana,* it is enough. *Sol.* 30:15.

A-NA, *adj.* Satisfied, as with food, having eaten sufficiently; maona.

A-NA, *v.* To praise much and covet another's wealth.

A-NA, *s.* Grief; sadness; sorrow; trouble from the conduct of others.

2. The feelings of a parent towards a child that refuses his instructions; a mixed feeling of weariness, anger and love. *Oih.* 16:18.

3. Fatigue from hard labor or toil.

A-NA, *s.* A measure, as for cloth. *Puk.* 26:2. A measure of any kind. *Kanl.* 25:14. *Ana* ohe, a measuring rod. *Ezek.* 40:3.

A-NA, *s.* A kind of light stone found in the sea, used by nurses to cure the ea, or the white fur on the tongue; also used in rubbing and polishing off canoes and wooden calabashes.

A-NA, *s.* A cave; a den formed by rocks. *Kin.* 19:30; *Ios.* 10:16.

2. Name of a hollow place in the mouth by which the voice is modified. *Anat.* 11.

3. A cave for the retreat of the vanquished; a place where the conquered are found.

A-NA, *pron.* The oblique case of the pronoun, third person sing.; of him; of her; of it; his; hers. *Gram.* § 139. *Auipili.*

A-NA, The participial termination of verbs answering to the Eng. *ing;* as, lawe *ana,* carry*ing;* hana *ana,* work*ing;* but it has some peculiarities.

1. The *ana* is not united with the verb as *ing* is in Eng.

2. The *ana* may be separated from the verb, and any qualifying word or words, and also the verbal directives may come between. *Gram.* § 233. As, e kukulu hale *ana* ia, he is build house *ing*; e hopu bipi *ana*, he is catch cattle *ing*, &c. In many cases the participial termination *ana* becomes united with a noun and becomes a participial noun; in which case the first *a* of the *ana* is dropped, or coalesces with the last letter of the preceding word, and they both become one word; as *hopena* for *hope ana*; *haawina* for *haawi ana*, &c.

A-NA-A-NA, *v.* To practice divination or sorcery by prayer; e *anaana* ana ia kakou, they were practicing sorcery upon us.

A-NA-A-NA, *s.* A kind of sorcery or prayer used to procure the death or a curse upon one. *Nah.* 22:7.

2. Witchcraft. 1 *Sam.* 15:23. Divination. *Ier.* 14:14.

A-NA-A-NA, *adj.* Diving; consulting divinations; kahuna *anaana*, a diviner. *Kanl.* 18:10. Pule *anaana*, a praying one to death.

A-NA-A-NA, *adj.* In small balls, as the dung of sheep or goats; he *anaana* ka lepo o ke kao a me ka hipa; *anaana* ka lepo i ka ai liilii.

A-NA-A-NA, *v.* To be in a tremor, as the muscles after great fatigue; *anaana* pu na wawae i ka maloeloe i ka hele ana.

A-NA-A-NA-PU, *v.* To undulate, as the air under a hot sun.

2. To flash, as lightning; ka *anaanapu* ana o ka uila ma ka po; to send forth light.

3. To crook often; to have many crooks. See ANAANAPUU; also ANAPA.

A-NA-A-NA-PUU, *adj.* Bent; crooked; out of a straight line; he kaula *anaanapuu* o ka hilo ana; he lopi *anaanapuu* ana; he anuu hanuu loa o *anaanapuu*.

A-NA-A-NE-A, *adj.* Stupid; palaka.

A-NA-A-NAI, *v.* Frequentative of *anai*.

A-NA-AI-NA, ⎫ *s.* An eating circle.
A-NAI-NA, ⎭ 2. A congregation of people for any purpose, provided a space be left in the center; a congregation. *Puk.* 29:4.

A-NA-AI-NA, *v.* Ana, to measure, and *aina*, land. To survey or measure land.

A-NA-AI-NA, *s.* Land surveying. See above. Anahonua.

A-NAE, *s.* Name of a species of fish; o Kaulua, oia ka malama e pae mai ai ka pua *anae*.

A-NA-E, *v.* See ANA E. *Hoo.* To set aside; to set apart. *Puk.* 16:23, 33.

A-NAE, *s.* A species of fish; the mullet.

A-NAI-NA, *v.* To assemble around a person or place; to meet around a thing. *Hoik.* 5:11.

A-NAI-NA, *s.* An assembly; a multitude. *Ezek.* 23:42.

A-NAI, ⎫ *v.* To rub; to rub out grain
A-NA-A-NAI, ⎭ with the hand. *Luk.* 6:1.

2. To grind; to scour; to brush down thatching; to polish; kalai a maikai, *anai* a pakika. *Oihl.* 6:28. To smooth. *Isa.* 41:7. Hence,

3. To blot out; cut off; destroy. *Puk.* 17:14. To lay waste. *Isa.* 5:6. To blot out. *Oih.* 13:19.

4. FIG. To nullify one's character or pretensions. 1 *Kor.* 1:28.

A-NA-A-NAI, *v.* To be angry; perhaps to nestle.

A-NA-A-NAI, *adj.* Angry.

A-NAI-NA-KA-NA-KA, *s.* See ANAINA. A congregation of people. *Hal.* 7:7. An assembly of men. *Kanl.* 31:30.

A-NAI-NAI, *v.* To rub often; to polish, &c. See ANAI, conj. 9th.

A-NAU, *v.* To pace, as a horse.

2. To go about irregularly from house to house.

3. To traipse up and down.

A-NA-HA, *s.* The reflection of glancing of light; the flashing of light.

A-NA-HA-NA-HA, ⎫ *s.* Repeated reflec-
A-NA-HA-NA-PA, ⎭ tion or gleaming of light.

A-NA-HO-NU-A, *v.* Ana, to measure, and *honua*, flat land. To survey land.

A-NA-HO-NU-A, *s.* Land measuring; geometry; me ka ike aku i ke *anahonua*.

2. The title of a school book, *geometry*.

A-NA-HU-A, *s.* A tall man bending over; stoop-shouldered; ke *kanahua*, he oohu.

A-NA-HU-A, *s.* The second son of Luahoomoe; he kahuna makapo, akamai, he akua no ka poe mahiai; the god of husbandmen.

A-NA-HU-LU, *v.* To arrive at, or amount to the number ten; applied to days; a *anahulu* ae, alaila hiki mai, when ten days had passed he arrived.

A-NA-HU-LU, *s.* A period of ten days; a decade. 1 *Sam.* 25:38. A malaila i noho loihi ai ekolu *anahulu*. *Laieik.* 61.

A-NA-KA, *s.* *Heb.* A ferret. *Oihk.* 11:30.

A-NA-KI-MA, *s.* *Heb.* Name of a people

mentioned in the books of Deuteronomy and Joshua remarkable for their size. *Ios.* 11:21. They lived mostly in the south and south-west parts of Canaan.

A-NA-KO-I, *s.* A swelling in the groin. See HAHAI.

A-NA-LI-O, *s.* General name of the stars near the horizon at any point of the compass. See ANALIPO.

A-NA-LI-PO, *s.* Name of the place supposed to be beyond the stars, i.e, out of sight, but really below the horizon.

A-NA-MI-U, *v.* To break off the root which unites the potato to the main root; e emiemi iho la lakou i ka uala nui a hahai ae la ie ke *anamiu* o ka uala.

A-NA-NA, *v.* Conj. 9th of *ana*, to measure.

A-NA-NA, *s.* A common, but indefinite measure formerly used; the length of the arms and body when both arms were extended, to the ends of the longest fingers.

2. A fathom.

A-NA-NI-O, *s.* The root which holds the potato to the main root; e mohai ke *ananio.*

A-NA-NU, *s.* See LAULELE. Name of a plant used for food, boiled.

A-NA-PA, *v.* To shine with reflected light, as the moon reflected from the water; like the sun reflected from a mirror.

2. To flash like lightning, or like the burning of gunpowder.

3. To light suddenly.

A-NA-POA-NA, *s.* A machine to measure weight; a balance. *Sol.* 16:11.

A-NA-PAU, *v.* To turn; to bend; to warp; to turn, as on hinges; to crook round.

A-NA-PAU, *s.* A crook in a thing; a bending; a turning; a hinge.

A-NA-PA-NA-PA, *s.* The dazzling of the sun on any luminous body, such as strikes the eyes with pain.

A-NA-PA-NA-PA, *s.* A species of tree, the bark of which is used for soap.

A-NA-PA-NA-PA, *s.* A species of limu.

A-NA-PU, *s.* A flash of light. *Mat.* 24:27. See ANAPA. *Hoo.* To send forth lightning. *Hal.* 144:6. See ANAANAPU.

2. To burn; scorch, as the direct rays of the sun; e wela ana ka wawae i ka la.

3. To quiver, as the rays of the sun on black lava.

A-NA-PU, *s.* A glimmering, as of light.

A-NA-PUU, *v.* To crook, as a rafter, or as a rope large in some places and small in others.

A-NA-PUU, *s.* A corner formed by two lines meeting.

A-NA-PUU, *adj.* Contorted; blunt.

A-NA-PU-NA-PU, *s.* Heat or light reflected, or both; the light and heat of reflection.

A-NA-PU-NI, *v. Ana,* to measure, and *puni,* around. To encompass, as a boundary line. See ANAHONUA 10.

A-NA-PU-NI, *s.* A circle.

A-NA-WAE-NA, *s. Ana,* measure, and *waena,* middle. A diameter of a circle. *Anah.* 23.

A-NA-WAE-NA-LOA, *s.* As above. LIT. A long diameter, that is, the diameter of an ellipse the long way. *Anah.* 24.

A-NA-WAE-NA-PO-KO, *s.* The short or conjugate diameter of an ellipsis. *Anah.* 24.

A-NA-TO-MI-A, *s. Gr.* The science of dissecting animal bodies; applied mostly to human bodies.

2. Name of the book teaching that science.

A-NE, *v.* To eat, as small insects eat wood.

2. To be near doing a thing; to like to do it, but not quite; as *ane* aku au e hoonou i ka pohaku, I was near throwing a stone. See ANEANE. *Ane* like iki, it is almost like.

A-NE, *s.* Name of a small insect that eats wood, but is not itself visible.

2. The worm dust of wood; powder-post.

3. The cutaneous disease called ring-worm.

4. A soft stone used in polishing wood; also written *ana.*

A-NE, *adj.* Light, as worm-eaten timber; not heavy; mama.

A-NE, *adv.* With difficulty; scarcely; nearly; generally followed by *ole; ane* haalele ole ia ia, it hardly leaves him; *ane* hiki ole ke hali, which can scarcely be carried.

A-NE-A, *v.* For *aneia;* pass. of *ane;* to be worm-eaten; to be light, as worm-eaten wood; to be dry, as timber.

A-NE-A, *s.* The dry-rot of wood, occasioned by heat, or the action of insects; applied to timber very old; also to other things. See ANOA.

A-NE-A, *s.* The heat of the sun; more properly the apparent vibration of the air caused by the heat of the sun.

A-NE-A, *adj.* Insipid; tasteless, as the inside of worm-eaten food, or of poor food; applied to persons having no appetite for food, on account of oppressive heat; exhausted, as men, by hunger, by long abstinence, by long sleep, or by diving in deep water. See KANEA and ANEANE.

A-NE-A-NE, *v.* To be exhausted, as a man with hunger or by long abstinence; by long sleep, or by diving in deep water.

2. To blow softly, as a light breeze or zephyr.

3. To be almost something; to be almost at a place. *Laieik.* 71. *Aneane* oia e hoohiki ino aku i kona akua, he almost cursed his god. *Laieik.* 158. Almost to do something. *Oih.* 19:27. See ANE.

A-NE-A-NE, *s.* A jest; a kind of jocose denial to a request.

2. A vacancy of the stomach for want of food or from sickness; he *aneane* no la; he *aneane* pupuka no la; he *aneane* pono la; he *aneane* hiki no la.

A-NE-A-NE, *adj.* See ANE above. Faint; feeble; low; weak, as a sick person.

A-NE-A-NE, *adv.* See ANE. Nearly; almost; in danger of; liable to; applied to number; he *aneane* pono ole ko'u noho ana maanei; *aneane* make, unto death, almost dead. *Lunk.* 16:16.

A-NEE, *v.* To hitch or move along, like a cripple; to walk on one's knees.

2. To go about from house to house begging; aia no oia ma ka huahuelo kahi i *anee* ai.

A-NEE, *s.* One who goes from house to house telling fortunes, begging, or for any such purpose; a beggar.

A-NEE, *adj.* Moving about from place to place; going about begging; kanaka *anee*, a beggar; a fortune teller.

A-NEE-NEE, *s.* Mats old and worn; he wahi moena *aneenee* uuku, a small mat about a fathom long.

A-NEI, *v.* See NEI. To sweep off; to cause to disappear.

A-NEI, *adv.* The sign of a question, used after verbs or nouns; as, mai *anei* oia? is he sick? ua holo *anei* ia? has he sailed? he mai *anei*?

A-NEI, *adv.* Here; in this place; like maanei; mai *anei* aku. *Kin.* 50:25. I ko kakou hoi ana *anei* a hiki i Kauai, on our returning along this way till we reach Kauai. *Laieik.* 87.

A-NE-HE, *v.* To be on the alert; ready for a start, as a cat for a mouse; as a bird to fly.

2. To be ready to seize upon a person or thing when circumstances require.

A-NE-HE-NE-HE, *v.* The double root of the above; to be prepared; all ready to do a thing; to be on the look out to do it. *Oih.* 21:35.

A-NE-HE-NE-HE, *s.* Violence; disorder, &c., as of a mob.

A-NE-HO, *s.* He hala.

A-NE-LA, *s. Eng.* An angel; a messenger from heaven. *Puk.* 14:19.

A-NE-NE. See ANEENEE.

A-NE-WA, *adj.* Indolent; sleepy.

A-NE-WA, *v.* To be inactive, as asleep.

A-NE-WA-NE-WA, *v.* To be as dead.

2. To be in a fainting fit; unconscious, as men; as fish poisoned with hola.

3. In *morals*, to be unmindful of evils around us. See KUNEWANEWA. Ke *anewanewa* kakou hoolono io ana ke kihi, huna pala iki ke akamai.

A-NE-TE-LO-PE,
A-NE-TE-LO-PA, } *s. Eng.* An antelope. *Mel. Sol.* 2:7; 1 *Nal.* 4:23.

A-NE-TO, *s. Eng.* An herb; anise. *Mat.* 23:23

A-NI, *v.* To pass over a surface, as the hand over a table.

2. To draw a net over the surface of the water.

3. To beckon one with the hand; to make signs secretly to one.

> *Ani* malu ka ike ilaila
> I ka mauli hoaalona wale,
> Aloha opa, opa he ake.

4. To blow softly, as a gentle breeze; ke *ani* nei ka makani, ke *ani* peahi la ia Limaloa, the wind blows softly, it fans Limaloa with a fan.

A-NI, *adj.* Drawing; dragging, as a net for fish; he upena *ani*.

A-NI-A, *v.* To be hard and smooth on the surface.

A-NI-A, *adj.* Smooth and even. See NIANIA, ANIANIA and MANIANIA.

A-NI-A-NI, *s.* A glass; a mirror; a looking-glass. *Puk.* 38:8. He *aniani* nana helehelena; he *kilo* kekahi inoa; called by Hawaiians *kilo*.

A-NI-A-NI, *v.* See ANI 4. To cool; to refresh one heated; *aniani* mai la ka makani. *Oih.* 27:13. To blow gently, as a wind; *aniani* puka alohi na ka haole paha la; *aniani* poaeae na make o Kuawili.

A-NI-A-NI, *adj.* Agreeable; cool; refreshing.

A-NI-A-NI-A, *adj.* See ANIA. Smooth and even, as the surface of a planed board; smooth, as the sea in a calm; applied also to the skin when burnt hard; he paapaa ili mawaho no ka lapalapa o ke ahi.

A-NI-HA, *v.* To be provoked at the mischief of one; to be angry at a person on account of lying and deception.

2. To be hardened in crime; capable of committing any offense.

A-NI-HA-NI-HA, *v.* To be near obtaining an object and fail; *anihaniha* makou e pae, a loaa ka makani.

A-NI-HA-NI-HA, *adj.* Easily provoked; captious; caviling.

A-NI-HI-NI-HI, *s.* Kalo tops; he kalo, he *anihinihi*, he oha. See ONINIHI.

A-NI-HI-NI-HI, *v.* See NIHI. Near to falling off a pali; to stand in a dangerous place.

A-NI-NI, *adj.* Small; dwarfish; stinted, as men or animals.

A-NO, *s.* Likeness; resemblance; image of a thing.

2. The meaning of a word or phrase.

3. The moral quality of an action, as good or evil, or the moral state of the heart.

4. The character of a person, as to his life and manners; the explanation of a thing obscure. *Kin.* 41:8.

A-NO, *v.* To have a form or appearance.

2. With *hou*, to change the form or appearance of a person or thing; e *ano* ae, to become new. *Oihk.* 13:16. To change the state of things.

3. With *hoo*, to boast; to glory; to hallow; to consecrate. *Kin.* 2:3.

4. To transform; to change the external appearance.

5. With *e*, to set apart to another purpose; to consecrate. *Hal.* 4:3.

6. With *hou*, to change; to transform. 2 *Kor.* 11:13.

7. With *e*, to change, as the countenance, from mirth to sadness and fear. *Dan.* 5:10.

A-NO, *s.* Fear; dread; ua kau mai ke *ano* ia'u la, fear fell upon me; ke kau mai la ke *ano* hewa ia oe.

A-NO, *v.* To be in fear; *ano* wale mai la no au. See ANO or ANOANO. To be silent; solitary, as a deserted village; ua pau i ke kaua, hauaia na kanaka a pau i ka hana.

A-NO, *adv.* Now; at the present time; *ano* nei, *ano* la. 1 *Sam.* 2:16. Soon.

2. Often used more as an expression of earnestness or certainty of something doing, or to be done, than of anything literally doing *now*. *Puk.* 6:1.

3. It is used after some other event has been spoken of as a consequence. *Ios.* 1:2. Ina no *ano*, even now. 1 *Nal.* 14:14.

A-NO-A, *adv.* Same as *ano* above. Now; at this time; immediately; *anoa* no hele; ahea hele? *anoa* no.

A-NO-AI, *adv.* But; except; lest; perhaps; malia paha.

A-NO-AI, *adv.* A warm salutation; as, aloha, welina; a salutation; a bow; a courtesy.

A-NO-A-NO, *s.* Seeds; the seeds of fruit, as apple, onion, melon, &c. *Nah.* 20:5.

2. The semen of males. *Oihk.* 15:16.

3. Descendants; children of men. *Ezek.* 44:22. NOTE.—The fruit itself is *hua*; also, the seeds incased in pods or husks are called *hua*; *anaono* oili, seeds destitute of meat.

A-NO-A-NO, *s.* A solemn stillness.

2. A sacred, hallowed place. See ANO, *s.*, fear; dread.

A-NO-A-NO, *adj.* Solitary; still; retired. *Hal.* 17:12. He wahi *anoano*, mehameha loa no ka makau i ka make; aohe lua o ka noho ana i ua kula *anoano* kanaka ole nei.

A-NO-E, *v.* To be different from something else; to take a different form or character. See ANO and E.

A-NO-I, *v.* To desire very strongly; to covet; e *anoi* ana na alii wahine.

A-NO-I, *s.* A thirst; a strong desire for a thing; eia ka pono, o ka noonoo, o ka *anoi*, o ke ake e loaa.

A-NO-HO, *s.* A custom; a practice, as strict as a law; ina e ku ke kanaka i ka *anoho* ana o ko ke alii ipuwai auau, a me ka *anoho* ana o kona kapa, make no ia.

A-NO-LA-NI, *adj.* Ano, character, and *lani*, heaven. A modern coined word perhaps; of heavenly character; good; pure; he manao *anolani*, he naau *anolani*, he kino *anolani*. 1 *Kor.* 15:40.

A-NO-NA-NO-NA, *s.* An ant. *Sol.* 6:6. See NONANONA. Name of a periodical formerly printed at the islands; aloha oe e *Anonanona*.

A-NO-NI, *v.* To mix together several ingredients, as different kinds of food; to make a garment of different textures of cloth; to mix together falsehood and truth; to corrupt. 2 *Kor.* 2:17.

2. To ponder with anxiety, as an act of the mind; to revolve in one's mind.

3. To be agitated with anxiety; to be troubled in mind, so as not to sleep. *Dan.* 2:1.

4. To be in doubt or suspense what judgment to form respecting one's meaning. See ANONONI.

A-NO-NI-NO-NI, *v.* See ANONI. To doubt; to be in suspense as to the result of a thing; ua *anoninoni* ka pakele ana i ka make.

A-NO-NI-NO-NI, *adj.* Doubtful; uncertain; he pono *anoninoni* na paani nawaliwali.

2. Angry.

A-NO-NO-NI, *v.* See ANONI. To doubt; to hesitate; to be in suspense, as one in an inquiring state of mind.

A-NU, *adj.* Cold; hui, huihui.

A-NU, *s.* Cold; the absence of warmth; ua make au i ke *anu*, I am dead with the cold; huihui ko'u mau wawae i ke *anu.*

A-NU, *v.* To be cold; to feel cold; ua *anu* au i kahi kapa ole, I am cold, having no clothes; *anu* aku la o Maunakea i ka hoilo, Maunakea feels cold in the winter.

A-NU-A, *s.* A pile, as of mats piled one upon another.

A-NU-A-NU, *adj.* Cold; huihui. See ANU.

A-NU-A-NU, *s.* Cold; chilliness. *Hal.* 147:17.

A-NU-A-NU-A, } *s.* A rainbow. *Kin.* 9:13;
A-NU-E-NU-E, } *Ezek.* 1:28.

A-NUU, *v.* To sprain, as a muscle; hina iho la au maluna o ka papaa lepo a *anuu* kuu kua, eha loa iho la, I fell upon the hard ground and sprained my back, with great pain.

A-NUU, *s.* A sprain by a false step.

A-NUU, *s.* A building in a sacred inclosure formed by long poles overhung near the top, which also were tied and covered with white pieces of kapa.

2. A high place in the heiau before which the idols stood, and where the victims were laid. *Laieik.* 164.

A-NUU, *s.* A rest or jog in a wall. 1 *Nal.* 6:6.

2. Stairs or steps for ascending a height. *Ezek.* 40:6. *Anuu* wili, winding stairs. 1 *Nal.* 6:8.

3. A ledge of rocks. 1 *Nal.* 7:28.

4. Jogs or steps in ascending a steep place.

5. In *music,* a tone.

A-NUU, *s.* Name of a ship formerly at the islands; no ka naaupo, ua kapaia aku e makou ka moku he anuu. *Lam. Haw.* 11:4, 3.

A-NUU-HA-PA, *s.* In *music, anuu,* a tone, and *hapa,* a part. A semitone.

A-NUU-NUU, *v.* To strike; to beat; to pound, as kapa.

2. *Hoo.* E *hooanuunuu* ai ke poo, to raise, to elevate the head.

A-NUU-NUU, *s.* See ANUU. Stairs; steps for ascending or descending. *Neh.* 3:15.

2. A plaid in a plaided garment.

A-NUU-NUU, *adj.* Having steps like stairs; provided with or made with steps; e ku kakou, a pii aku i ke alanui *anuunuu,* let us arise and go up the road made with steps; formed in the manner of stairs; he papale *anuunuu;* rough, as a bad road.

A-NU-HE (e-nu-he), *s.* A large worm that destroys the leaves of vegetables; he peelua, he poko.

A-NU-HE-NU-HE, *adj.* Rarely done, as food not sufficiently cooked.

2. Rough with cold, *anuhenuhe* ka ili i ke anu, the skin is pimpled with cold.

A-NU-HE-NU-HE, *s.* The eating of bad food, fish, or meat, that is spoiled.

A-NU-HE-NU-HE, *s.* Name of a species of fish, also of limu.

A-NU-LU, *v.* To be covetous; to be greedy, &c. See ALUNU, by change of syllables.

A-NU-NE-NU-NE, *v.* To mix up, as hash; awiliwili.

A-NU-NU, *s.* Change of *n* for *l.* See ALUNU. An oppressor; one greedy of gain.

A-NU-NU, *adj.* See ALUNU. Oppressive; hard; extortionate; he makee, he paa.

A-PA, *s.* A roll; a bundle, as a piece of cloth, or a ream of paper.

A-PA, *adj.* Meddling; officious; busy; mischievous, as a child; careless; blundering; slow; tardy; nahili, he lohi.

A-PAA, *s.* Name of a wind; i kuipeia e ka makani *apaa,* he was knocked down flat by the wind *apaa.*

2. Name of a region of country below the *ma'u* or *waokanaka* on the side of the mountains.

A-PA-A-PA, *v.* To be evilly disposed; to be treacherous; to deceive; to be mischievous.

A-PA-A-PA, *s.* Guile; deceit; evil generally. 1 *Pet.* 2:22. That which is untrue; false in opposition to truth and stability. *Rom.* 1:25. Haalele i ka oiaio no ka mea *apaapa,* forsook the truth for a false thing.

2. One who frequently changes his situation.

A-PA-A-PA, *adj.* Unsettled; unstable; irresolute.

2. Without truth; deceitful; lalau wale iho no ka olelo.

3. Careless; without thought; kapulu. See APA.

A-PAA-PAA, *s.* Name of a wind at Kohala.

A-PAA-PAA, *adj.* Firm; hard; compact, as a well made road; he alanui *apaapaa,* aole pueho o ka lepo.

A-PAA-PAA, *s.* The name of a species of fish; he ula *apaapaa.*

A-PAA-PA-NI, *v.* To oppose one with words; to reply quickly; to overwhelm with words.

2. To make one forget the subject of dispute.

A-PAA-PA-NI, *s.* A speech in opposition;

a rapid reply. See APANI.

A-PAI, s. A deep, long fish net for catching the opae.

A-PA-HU, v. To cut up; to cut square off, as a piece of timber.

2. To cut in pieces; to chop off; to cut in two, as pieces of wood or sugar-cane.

3. To stuff food into one's mouth.

A-PA-HU, s. Pieces cut off or cut in two, as wood, sugar-cane, &c.

2. A kind of pau.

A-PA-HU, adj. Marked; distinguished by some mark or dress or cut of the hair; nani na kanaka *apahu.*

A-PA-HU, s. The sound of a trumpet; the bursting forth of a sound suddenly; the sound from a sudden falling of a substance.

A-PA-KAU, v. To seize upon; to lay hold of; to hold on to, as on falling.

2. To lay hold of things and displace them, as a child.

3. To give thoughtlessly, as a man gives away his food until it is all gone.

A-PA-LI, v. To go into the presence of a chief, and on account of shame, return without making a request.

A-PA-LI-PA-LI, v. To hurry; to hasten.

A-PA-NA, s. A fragment; a patch; a piece; a slice; a piece, as of bread; a portion; *apana* poohiwi, a shoulder piece for a garment. *Puk.* 39:4. A piece of any substance; of a human body. *Lunk.* 19:29. A division of people. 1 *Nal.* 16:21. *Apana* V., a sector of a circle. *Anahon. Apana* uuku, a little piece. *Ioan.* 6:7.

A-PA-NA-PO-AI, s. *Apana* and *poai,* to surround. A segment of a circle. *Anah.* 23.

A-PA-NE, s. A species of bird much valued on account of its red feathers.

2. A species of the lehua, the ohia, with red blossoms, which are food for birds.

A-PA-NE, adj. Red on the flesh when burned; hence, applied to anger.

2. Red; flushed with anger.

A-PA-NI, v. To go from house to house tattling and doing nothing valuable; he mea hele kauhale e *apani* ana ia hale aku ia hale aku me ka holoholo kauhale.

A-PA-NI-PA-NI. See APANI above and APAAPANI.

A-PA-PA, v. To deceive. See APAAPA.

A-PA-PA, s. Name of a strong wind blowing over Kohala Point.

A-PA-PA-NE, s. The name of a bird on Hawaii; a i kani aku ka leo o ka *apapane. Laieik.* 29. It has red feathers. Hulu *apapane,* the red feathers of the *apapane.*

A-PE, s. A plant with broad leaves, acrid to the taste, like kalo, but more so; it is eaten for food in times of scarcity.

A-PE-A-PE, adj. Full of knots, as a string; full of small round stones, as a road.

A-PE-A-PE, s. The motion of the gills of a fish in water; the breathing of a fish. See API.

2. The name of a remarkable plant found near the top of Waialeale on Kauai; length of stalk, twenty feet or over; leaves, six feet in diameter, somewhat resembling, in shape, the ape; the leaf is round and attached to the stem in the center.

A-PE-A-PE-A, s. A species of squid not eaten; he *apeapea* noloko o ke kai.

A-PEE-PEE, s. A species of limu; he limu *apeepee.*

A-PE-U, s. A species of poor mats; ua lawe aku au i *apeu* moena; large mats, but very poor ones.

A-PEU-PEU, adj. See the foregoing. *Apeupeu* applies to kapa as well as mats.

A-PE-RI-LA, s. *Eng.* Name of the month April.

A-PI, v. To gather together, as people to one spot; to bring into a small compass, as baggage; e *api* mai a uuku.

A-PI, v. To flap, as the gills of a fish when breathing out of water.

2. To shake, as a cocoanut leaf in the breeze.

3. To tremble, as the liver of a hog when killed.

4. To throb; to beat; as the pulse.

5. To be greedy; to covet this and that thing.

A-PI, s. The gills of a fish; same as *mahamaha.*

2. The fins with which a fish swims.

3. The beating of the pulse.

4. Greediness; covetousness; ke *api* o ka ia nui pimoe.

5. A small net.

6. The name of a very flat fish.

A-PI-A-PI, s. The drinking (breathing) of a fish in the water.

2. The flowing of water or of blood in the veins.

A-PII, s. A species of large kalo.

A-PII-PII, s. Name of a species of shrub or bush.

A-PII-PII, adj. Curling, as the hair; he lauoho *apiipii.*

A-PI-KA-PI-KA, adj. Spotted. See OPI-KOPIKO.

A-PI-KI, v. To sport at the expense of

another; to be roguish; to act mischievously.

2. To beg; to live at the expense of others.

A-PI-KI, *s.* Sleight; cunning; craft. *Eps.* 4:14.

A-PI-KI, *adj.* Roguish; mischievous; lawless; addicted to roguish tricks.

2. Deceitful; he hoopunipuni; he lei *apiki*, he lei ilima.

A-PI-KI, *adj.* Of or belonging to the *ilima*, yellow flowers, &c.

A-PI-KI-PI-KI, *v.* To fold up, as a piece of kapa.

2. To spread out one upon another for the purpose of folding, as sheets of paper, kapa, cloth, &c.

3. To multiply thoughts.

A-PI-KI-PI-KI, *s.* A kind of agitation of the mind; anxiety; doubt.

2. A particular kind of kapa.

A-PI-PI (ho-a-pi-pi), *adj.* United; joined together, as the two canoes of a double canoe; he mau waa elua i *hoapipiia.*

A-PO, *v.* To catch at, as with the hand; to hook in.

2. To span or reach round. 1 *Nal.* 7:15. To put one's arm around another. *Laieik.* 117.

3. To receive; to embrace, as a long-absent friend. *Kin.* 29:13.

4. To fall upon one, as an expression of affection. *Kin.* 33:4.

5. To contain, hold or encircle. 1 *Nal.* 8:27.

6. To receive, as into the mind; to apprehend intellectually. *Oih.* 8:27.

7. To receive and embrace, as a truth. *Ioan.* 17:18.

8. To receive; to take out of sight, as a cloud. *Oih.* 1:9.

A-PO, *s.* A hoop; a band; *apo* hao, an iron hoop; in *grammar,* kaha *apo,* the sign of a parenthesis, thus: ( ); a ring or clasp for the fingers or arm; *apo* gula, a golden ring. *Puk.* 25:12. He *apo* gula pepeiao, a golden ear-ring. *Puk.* 32:2. In *geometry,* a circle. FIG. *Apo* o ka make, bands of death. *Oih.* 2:24. A certain kind of belt worn by women.

> *Apo* na poe a ka ua kuahine,
> Noho hoomakue i ka uka o Kahui
> Ka hookohukohu puahi ole a ka ua.

A-PO, *s.* The union of the cheek bone with the iwi maha. *Anat.* 11.

A-PO, *s.* A particular variety of sweet potatoes.

A-PO-A-PO, *v.* See APO. To catch at frequently; to snatch or scramble for; to seize upon a person or thing; to seize or

come upon one, as fear; *apoapo* ka naau i ka makau; to be troubled with doubt, anxiety; *apoapo* ka oili; to be troubled with jealousy. *Mat.* 2:3. *Apoapo,* lelele ka oili, to palpitate, as the heart.

A-PO-A-PO, *s.* A catching; a seizing; a forcing.

A-PO-A-PO, *s.* A bunch, as of kalo; a hill of potatoes; he apuepue.

A-POO, *v.* To go from house to house, doing no work; ua *apoo* hele i kauhale i ka ua.

A-POO, *s.* An idle, lazy person who goes from house to house; aia i ka *apoo* kauhale.

A-POO-POO, *s.* A deep or hollow place, as the hollow of the hand or foot; the frog or hollow place of a horse's foot.

A-PO-HAO, *s. Apo,* hoop, and *hao,* iron.

1. An iron hoop. See APO.

2. A name formerly of the king's guard.

A-PO-KAU, *v.* To take hold of and displace. See APAKAU.

A-PO-KE, *v.* To cut up into short pieces.

A-PO-KE, *s.* A short piece cut off.

A-PO-LI-MA, *s.* See APO and LIMA, hand. A signet; a finger ring. *Kin.* 38:18.

A-PO-NO, *v.* To approve; to treat as innocent. 2 *Oihl.* 6:23. The opposite of *ahewa.*

2. To justify; to be accepted. *Puk.* 28:38.

3. *Hoo.* To exculpate from blame. *Kin.* 44:16.

4. To clear, as one charged with a crime. *Puk.* 34:7. The opposite of *ho'ohewa. Kanl.* 25:1.

A-PO-NO-IA, *s. Hoo.* Justification; treatment of one as just. *Rom.* 9:30.

A-PO-PE-PEI-AO, *s. Apo,* a ring; and *pepeiao,* ear. A ring for the ear; an ear-ring.

A-PO-PO, *adv.* LIT. When the night nights, i. e., to-morrow. *Lunk.* 19:9. *Apopo* kela la aku, day after to-morrow.

A-PO-GU-LA, *s. Apo,* ring, and *gula,* gold. A gold ring, but often applied to an ear-ring of any material.

A-PU, *v.* To run after; to chase with a design of overtaking another.

2. To devour food greedily.

A-PU, *s.* A cup made of cocoanut shell for drinking awa; he *apu* ka iwi o ka niu.

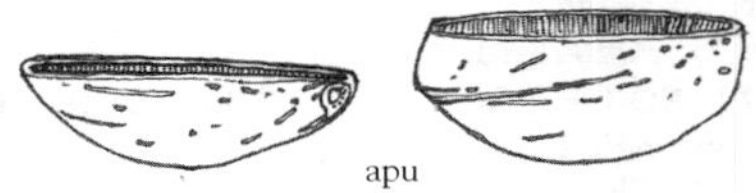
apu

2. A dish; a cup of any material.

3. MET. Affliction; suffering; he kiaha; also,

4. Water in which kalo has been soaked, a kind of medicine; *apu* kalo, *apu* laau; the cup gives name to the drink.

A-PU-A, *v.* To be disloyal; to disregard or disobey the orders of his chief.

A-PU-A, *s.* A man who disobeys or disregards the commands of his chief.

A-PU-A, *s.* A shell or cup for scooping up the oopu; he *apua* oopu.

A-PU-AI, *s.* A variety of kalo.

A-PU, } *s.* A file; a rasp. 1 *Sam.*
A-PU-A-PU, } 13:20.

2. The beard of a fish-hook.

A-PU-AU-HU-HU, *s.* *Apu,* cup, and *auhuhu,* the poison plant. A cup for containing the auhuhu.

A-PU-A-PA-LE-LEO, *v.* *Apua,* to disobey, *pale,* to reject, and *leo,* voice. To disobey; not to comply with a command.

A-PU-A-PA-LE-LEO, *s.* Epithet of a chief who obeyed not the word of the priest.

A-PU-A-WA, *s.* *Apu,* cup, and *awa,* a plant. The awa cup; a cup out of which awa was drank.

A-PU-E-PU-E, *v.* See Pue, to force. To solicit one of the other sex.

2. To strive; to contend, as two persons endeavoring to get the same thing; *apuepue* na kanaka i ka ai i ka manawa wi.

A-PU-E-PU-E, *s.* Strife between two persons to get the same thing; attempting to get what another wants.

2. A difficulty; a contention; hiki *apuepue,* to obtain with difficulty.

3. A bunch of kalo; a hill of potatoes. See Apoapo.

A-PU-E-PU-E, *adv.* With strife; with difficulty. *Mat.* 19:23.

A-PUU-PUU, *adj.* See Puu. Rough; uneven, as land; as a road. *Isa.* 45:2. Full of hillocks.

A-PUU-PUU, *s.* Hillocks; rough places; e hoomania i na *apuupuu* a palahalaha ae, smooth down the rough places till they are smooth.

A-PU-KA, *v.* To hide; to secrete; to steal.

A-PU-KA, *s.* Deceit; treachery.

2. A thief; e manaoia oia no he *apuka,* he shall be considered as having stolen. *Kan. Haw.*

3. *Apuka,* in law, is forgery.

A-PU-KO-HE-O-HE-O, *s.* *Apu,* cup, and *koheoheo,* causing death.

1. The cup in which deadly ingredients were mixed, and out of which they were drank, such as auhuhu and awa.

2. Fig. O ka hewa, oia ka *apukoheoheo* e

make ai na kanaka a pau i ke ao nei, sin is the cup of death causing all people to die.

A-PU-LU, *v.* To wax old; ready to be laid aside. *Isa.* 31:6.

A-PU-LU, *adj.* Old; worn out; he waa *apulu,* an old canoe; he upena *apulu,* a worn out mat; *apulu* is applied to *things* as *elemakule* is to *men.*

A-PU-LU, *s.* A shred, or anything old and rotten or decayed, as a garment, a house, a canoe, &c.; he wahi *apulu* hale, the ruins of a house; he wahi *apulu* kapa, a remnant of a garment, &c.

A-PU-NI, *s.* The name of a day supposed to be inauspicious to one's enemies; e hee ai kou hoapaio ia oe, no ka mea o *apuni* keia la, he la hee.

A-PU-NI, *v.* To come together, as two persons, and scold and threaten and curse one another, but separate without fighting.

A-WA, *v.* To converse earnestly.

A-WA, *s.* Name of a plant, of a bitter acrid taste, from which an intoxicating drink is made.

2. The name of the liquor itself expressed from the root of the plant; the drinking of *awa* causes the skin to crack and flake off for a time; i ka manawa e inu ai kekahi i ka *awa,* he maikai kona ili ke nana aku; a mahope, mahuna ka ili, nakaka, puehoeho, inoino loa ke nana aku.

3. Bitterness, from the name of the plant.

A-WA, *s.* Fine rain; mist; he ua *awa,* ma ka manuna ia ua.

2. A species of fish.

A-WA, *s.* A harbor; a landing place; an entrance between two reefs; he *awa* o Kou ma Oahu, he *awa* ku moku; he nui na *awa* hookomo waa, there is the harbor of Kou on Oahu where ships anchor.

A-WA-A, *v.* To dig, as a ditch or a pit; kohi, eli, kulepe, ekuia a awaawaa.

A-WAA, *s.* A ditch, trench or pit dug deep; a hole; a cave.

2. A famine, or the consequences of a famine.

A-WAA-WAA, *v.* To make a groove; *awaawaa* waena, to make a hole in the center.

A-WAA-WAA, *v.* To dig; to throw up dirt; to root, as a hog; kohi, eli, awaa, kulepe, ekuia a *awaawaa.*

A-WA-A-WA, *adj.* Sour; bitter; sharp; pungent, as rum, pepper, orange skin, &c.; unpleasant to the taste; salt, as sea-water; brackish; no ka *awaawa* o ka wai, hookoni.

2. Met. Hard to deal with.

3. Harsh in manners, as a person. *Luk.*

19:21, 22.

A-WA-A-WA, *s.* Bitterness; sourness; pungency to the taste.

A-WA-A-WA, *v.* To be bitter, &c. *Hoik.* 10:10. See AWA.

A-WA-A-WA, *s.* A mist; a spray. See AWA above.

A-WAI, *s.* Name of a disease; a swelling in the groin; he *awai* ma ke kumu o ka uha.

 2. A bunch; a cluster; he *awai* kalo, a bunch of kalo; he *awai* huihui waina, a bunch of grapes.

A-WAI, *v.* To bind or tie up.

A-WAI, *s.* A place to stand on when addressing a multitude. *Neh.* 8:4.

 2. A raised platform; a scaffold; a pulpit. *2 Oihl.* 6:3.

A-WAI, *s.* A bundle or something tied up; lewa ka *awai* o ka paipu.

A-WAI-A-HI-KI, *s.* A swelling in the groin; a bubo. See AWAI.

A-WA-HE-WA, *v.* To miss; to overlook; to make a mistake.

A-WA-HE-WA, *s.* A mistake; an error, when the physician thought that a god had the direction of the disease or sent it.

A-WA-HI-A, *v.* The passive of *awa* for *awaia,* h inserted. *Gram.* § 48. To be bitter to the taste.

 2. FIG. *Hoo.* To make bitter; severe; to be hard in treatment of men. *Kol.* 3:19. MET. To cause to be laborious, painful, toilsome. *Puk.* 1:14.

A-WA-HIA, *s.* Bitterness; sourness; ka awaawa; ka mulea.

A-WA-HI-A, *adj.* Bitter, like gall; like the apuawa; he mulemule.

A-WA-HI-A, *s.* A mist or spray. See AWAAWA and AWA.

A-WA-HU-A, *adj.* Surly; regardless of everybody; obstinate; perverse.

 2. Unwilling to attend to one's duty; regardless of the will of the gods and the duties of religion; he aia, lokoino.

A-WA-KE-A, *s.* The time of day when the sun is the highest; noon; midday.

 2. The name of the god who opened the gate of the sun; o *Awakea* ka mea nana i wehe ke pani o ka la, kahi i noho ai o Ka-onohiokala.

A-WA-KE-AU, *s.* Living together a great distance off and a long time ago; loihi loa o ka hele ana a me ka noho ana ma kahi hookahi; kahiko, liuliu.

A-WA-LA, *v.* To pull steadily and carefully, as a fisherman afraid of losing his fish. *Lam. Haw.* 45:43. *Awala* i ke aho.

 2. To work steadily and with energy; *awala* ae la ia me ka huki ae i kana hee iluna o ka waa, he pulled steadily and drew his squid into the canoe.

A-WA-LE, *adj.* A, burning, and *wale.* Burnt very much; burnt of itself.

A-WA-LII, *s.* Name of a hard stone out of which kois were made.

A-WA-LOA, *s.* A place where the bones of chiefs were hid; he iwi kau i ka *awaloa.*

A-WA-LU, *adj. num.* Eight; the number eight; also *ewalu.* See WALU.

A-WA-PU-HI, *s.* The ginger root; the bastard ginger, the smell odoriferous, used for dyeing.

A-WA-WA, *s.* The opposite of *mauna.* *Ios.* 9:1. A valley; he kahawai; a low, level place with high ground on each side. *Nah.* 24:6.

 2. The space between two prominences.

 3. The space between the fingers of the hand and the toes of the feet.

 4. The space between the branches of a river; he wahi poopoo loihi, a long deep place. See WA.

A-WE, *v.* To carry; to bring, as it is followed with *mai* or *aku;* e *awe* aku, to carry off; e *awe* mai, to bring here; generally written *lawe.* PASS. To be borne, carried. *Isa.* 46:3. Hookahi mea ana i *awe* aku la mai ko kakou alo aku; alaila, puolo ae la a paa, *awe* mai la aloko nei, then tie up the bundle fast, bring it in here.

A-WE, *s.* A burden; that which is carried.

A-WE, *s.* The tails of the squid; na *awe* o ka hee.

A-WE-A-WE, *v. Hoo.* To make small; to diminish; to render of small account; e maawe.

A-WE-A-WE, *s.* The curling of the water in the wake of a ship.

 2. The track or wake of a ship.

 3. The tails or arms of a squid; he waiu no ka hee malalo o ke *aweawe.*

A-WE-A-WE, *adj.* Beautiful; handsome; applied to men and women.

A-WE-A-WE, *adj.* White; slimy, as the fæces in some diseases. See WALEWALE, *adj.*

A-WE-A-WE, *s.* Tied up in a bundle; bound tight; he laulau *aweawe* no ka haawe.

A-WE-A-WE, *adj.* Well mixed; applied to poi.

A-WE-A-WE-A, *v.* To see in a slight degree; to catch a glimpse of an object.

 2. To act the part of a weawea or procurer; to act the pimp. See WEAWEA.

A-WE-A-WE-A, *s.* A glimpse; a half

sight of an object.

A-WE-A-WE-A, *adj.* Spotted; variegated with spots of different colors; he *aweawea* ulaula; obscure; not plain; *aweawea* ka lohe.

A-WE-A-WE-A, *s.* The seeds of green fruit, as squashes, melons, &c.

A-WE-A-WE-A, *adv.* Dimly to the sight; not plainly seen; faintly; ike *aweawea* aku la oia he wahi onohi ma Koolau, o Hawaii. *Laieik.* 26.

A-WE-O-WE-O, *s.* A shrub or small tree resembling pig-weed, sometimes eaten by Hawaiians.

A-WE-O-WE-O, *s.* Name of a species of reddish fish. See ALALAUWA.

A-WE-O-WE-O, *adj.* Applied to some fish; a iho aku la i ka paeaea aweoweo. *Laieik.* 206.

A-WEU-WEU, *s.* A species of wild or mountain kalo; called also the *mamauea.*

A-WE-KA, } *adj.* Deceitful; dis-
A-WE-KA-WE-KA, } honest; parsimonious.

A-WE-KA, } *s.* Deceit; dishon-
A-WE-KA-WE-KA, } esty; one who refuses to pay a forfeit.

A-WE-LA, } *s.* A species of fish;
A-WE-LA-WE-LA, } he puhi *awela*; a variety probably of the kala.

A-WE-LA-WE-LA, *adj.* Escaping, as a fish from a net; ke kukai *awelawela*; he poniu, he kaihi.

A-WE-LE, *s.* The running of a man sent on an errand; aka, i lilo ka *awele* ka pahu i kekahi nana ke eo.

A-WE-LU, *adj.* See WELU. Torn; ragged; worn to holes, as a kapa, he wahi kapa *awelu* kona i haawiia'ku.

A-WE-LU-WE-LU, *v.* To be torn; to be ragged, as a kapa; nahaehae, weluwelu.

A-WI-A-WI, *s.* A plant, used to stop bleeding.

A-WI-HA, } *v.* To have a glimpse
A-WI-HA-WI-HA, } of a thing. See AWE-AWEA.

A-WI-HA, } *s.* A glimpse; an im-
A-WI-HA-WI-HA, } perfect sight.

A-WI-HI, *v.* To wink; to ogle; to look obliquely; to eye; to look at one with jealousy. 1 *Sam.* 18:9.

A-WI-HI, *s.* Ka poe *awihi* hoowalewale, enchanters. *Ier.* 27.9.

A-WI-KI, *v.* IMP. Be quick; hasten.

A-WI-KI-WI-KI, *s.* A vine bearing black berries about the size and shape of American blackberries; they are used as a medicine, operating both as an emetic and cathartic; ke okole o makiki.

A-WI-LI, *v.* To mix together different ingredients.

2. To make a garment of different textures of cloth.

3. To wind; to twist about a thing; to entwine. *Iob.* 8:17.

4. To be agitated with conflicting emotions. See WILI.

A-WI-LI-WI-LI, *v.* The intensive of *awili* above.

A-WI-WI, *v.* To quicken; to hasten; to expedite; to accelerate. SYN. with wikiwiki.

A-BA, *s. Heb.* Father; he makuakane.

A-BI-BA, *s. Heb.* Name of a month. *Puk.* 13:4.

A-CI-DA, *s. Eng.* An acid; he mea omo i ka puna. *Anat.* 2.

A-DA-MA, *s. Eng.* Adamant. *Zek.* 7:12.

A-DO-BI-E, *s. Sp.* A species of brick made of earth and water mixed with grass or straw and dried in the sun.

A-GA-TA, *s. Eng.* An agate; a precious stone. *Ezek.* 27:16.

A-GA-TI, *s. Eng.* Name of a precious stone; an agate. *Puk.* 28:19. See above.

A-GO-ZA, *s. Heb.* A nut. *Mel. Sol.* 6:11.

A-RE-DE-A, *s. Heb.* Name of an unclean bird. *Kanl.* 14:18.

A-RE-ZA, *s. Heb.* Name of a tree; the cedar or fir. *Lunk.* 9:15.

A-SA-RI-O, *s. Gr.* A farthing. *Mat.* 10:29.

E.

E, the second letter of the Hawaiian alphabet. It represents the sound of the long slender *a* in English, or its sound is like that of *e* in *obey*. It is sometimes commuted for *a*, as in the numericals from *elua*, alua, to *eiwa*, aiwa; also in *alelo*, the tongue, *elelo*; *mahana*, warm, *mehana*. In an unaccented syllable at the end of a word, it sound is similar to that of the English *y*, as *ope*, opy; *mahope*, mahopy, &c.

E, *adv.* Synonymous with and a contraction for *ae*; yes. *E*, yes, is more familiar, and not so dignified and respectful as *ae*. See AE.

E, *adv.* Other; another; strange; new; mea *e*, a stranger, a strange thing; kanaka *e*, a stranger; often SYN. with malihini. *Nah.* 15:15.

E, *adv.* From; away; e holo *e* lakou, they will flee *from*; e puhi *e*, blow *away*; i kai lilo e, at sea afar *off*.

E, *prep.* By. As a preposition, it is mostly used after passive verbs to express the agent; as, ua *ahewaia* oia e ke alii, he *was condemned by* the chief. Many verbs have no sign of a passive voice, the construction of the sentence alone determines it, and the *e* thus situated helps determine the point as much as anything; nui loa hoi ka poe daimonio i mahiki aku e ia. *Gram.* § 105,11.

E standing before nouns marks the aui-hea or *vocative* case; it also often follows the same case; as, *e* ka lani *e*, O *chief. Gram.* § 105,8.

E is used also to call or invite attention to what one is about to say; a contraction, perhaps of *ea.* NOTE.—*E* is mostly used at the beginning of an address, and *ea* in the middle, or if a single sentence, only at the end.

E following either active, passive or neuter verbs signifies *before* hand, and serves to mark a kind of second future tense of the verb; as, lohe *e* au, I heard *before*; hiki *e* mai oia, he had arrived *first. Gram.* § 190, 2d.

E is the sign of the imperative mood, and generally of the infinitive also, though after *hiki* and *pono* the *e* of the infinitive is changed into *ke. Gram.* § 191 and 193. E is also the sign of the future tense. *Gram.* § 190, 1.

'E. After a word ending in *a*, *'e* is a contraction for *ae.*

E, *v.* To enter, as into a country or city.

2. To dash upon, as waves upon the deck of a ship; aohe o kana mai o ka nui o na ale i e maluna o ka moku. See EE.

E-A, *v.* To raise up, as a person bowed down.

2. To lift or throw up.

3. To raise up, as from the grave. *Iob.* 7:9.

4. To mount or go up upon, as an ancient bed. *Hal.* 132:3.

5. To rise up, as water. *Puk.* 15:8.

6. *Hoo.* To be thrown or raised up, as land out of the ocean; ua *hoea* mai na aina mai loko mai o ka moana, the land was thrown up out of the ocean.

7. To rise in sight, as a cloud. 1 *Nal.*

18:44. To heave in sight, as a ship; a *hoea* mai makai aku o Hilo, she *hove in sight* off Hilo.

8. To rise up, as out of the water. *Kin.* 41:2, 3.

9. To stir up, excite, as the affections; ia manawa ka *hoea* ana mai o ka hai, at that time was the exciting of other's love.

E-A, *s.* A species of turtle much valued on account of the shell.

2. The shell itself; he *ea* kuu wakawaka. *Eset.* 1:6. Put for ivory. NOTE.—The *ea* was forbidden to women to eat, under the kapu system.

E-A, *s.* A species of fish somewhat similar to the hilu, aawa and poou.

E-A, *s.* Takes *ke* for its article. Spirit; vital breath; the breath of life.

2. Life itself; oiai ke *ea*, while life lasts.

3. The natural breath of life. 1 *Tes.* 2:8. E kaili aku ke *ea*, to die. *Kin.* 25:8.

4. The breath of man or beast. *Kekah.* 3:21. Nani ka lokomaikai o ke Akua i kona haawi ana mai i ke *ea* o ke kanaka. *Hal.* 78:39. SYN. with hanu. *Isa.* 42:5.

5. He makani ku malie, oia ka makani e hanu ai kakou, the breathable air.

E-A, *s.* The thrush or aphthæ, a disease of children; *art.,* ka.

E-A, *s.* Dirt, dust raised by the wind.

> Ea me he opua hiki kakahiaka la,
> Me he mea la o Hoku o Mahealani
> Ka hukiku o ka waa la i ka lae.

E-A, *adj.* Dirty; dusty, as when the air is full of dust.

E-A, *int.* The expression of a call to one's attention, as aloha oukou, *ea*, to which a reply is expected; generally *ae*, aloha.

E-A is used in answer to a call, more familiar and disrespectful than *eo. Ea* is also used by a speaker to call the attention of his hearers to some particular point which he is about to state; its frequency of use is according to the taste of the speaker; it is brought out generally, in the middle of a sentence. *Lunk.* 7:3. Sometimes it commences a speech. 1 *Sam.* 9:5.

E-A, *s.* In *music*, the highest part; the *air.*

E-A, *adj.* Windy; noisy; without effect; he *ea* ka waha i ke ao ana i ke keiki hookuli, wahapaa; noisy; clamorous; assenting to the commands of a parent, but not obeying; disobedient.

E-A, *s.* Ku ka *ea* o Lahainaluna i ka lepo; dust raised by the wind, but not a whirlwind.

E-A, *adj.* Strong smelling, as meat or

food kept too long. See EAEA.

E-A-E-A, *adj.* Dignified; honorable; high. SYN. with hanohano, hiehie, eaea kai. Me he wawae, kuhaka la ka *eaea.*

E-A-E-A, *s.* See EA, *adj.* above. The strong, offensive smell of meat; *eaea,* paoa, hauna, hohono; *eaea* ka iloli o ka mano o Koolau; *eaea* ke hohono o ka palani (ba-rani.)

E-A-E-A, *v.* To cover the eyebrows, as a fisherman, to shade the eyes while look-ing into deep water for fish; ka lawaia nui i *eaea* na kuemaka i ehuehu na lihilihi.

E-A-E-A, *v.* To be covered with dust, as one out in the wind where the dust is flying; *eaea* na kamalii o Lahainaluna i ka lepo.

EA-EA-KAI, *s.* That which is covered with sea drops or the spray of the sea.

E-A-HA, *adv. int.* See E. E, sign of the future tense, and *aha,* what. How? what? used with the future, as *heaha* is with the present and past; *eaha* ia oe? how will it be with you? what will become of you? *Eaha* ana oukou? what will you be about?

E-E, *v.* See E, to dash upon. To mount; to get upon anything higher, as a horse; to leap upon; to get on board a ship; *ee aku la maluna o ka moku;* to get into a carriage. 1 *Nal.* 12:18. To go aboard a vessel.

2. *Hoo.* To receive on board a ship; to put upon, as a saddle upon a horse. *Kin.* 22:3. To set or put one up, as upon a horse. *Kin.* 31:17.

3. To pass from one carriage to another. 2 *Oihl.* 35:24. *Ee maluna o ka waa; ee maluna o ka lio.* See AE, 4.

E-E, *adj.* Out of sight; at a great dis-tance. See E, *adv.*

E-E, *adv.* Opposite to; adversely; against. 1 *Tim.* 6:20.

E-E, *adj.* He hulu *ee* no ka manu oo, that is, the yellow feathers under the wing (or the *ee*) of the oo, oia ka lei hulu manu.

E-E, *adj. Hoo.* A rising; a sweeping; as, kai *hoee. Dan.* 9:26.

E-E, *s.* The armpit. See POEE and POAEAE. Same under the wing of fowls.

E-E, *adj.* Maloo, kaee; dry; not wet.

E-E, *adj.* Caressing; inviting; kind; he makamaka *ee,* he iike, he lokomaikai, he koe ole, aole wawau.

E-E-E, *v.* To rise up. See EE, to mount. To rise up from one's seat to steal some-thing. Hence,

2. To be mischievous.

E-E-A, *v.* To rise up frequently. See EA.

E-E-A, *adj.* See the foregoing. Quick; ready; expert.

E-E-E-LU, *s.* The top of a tree when cut off.

E-EI, }
E-EI-E-HI-E-HI, } Some of the words of a filthy song sung at a
E-KI-KI-LAU, } great day of the Princess.

E-E-I-NA, *v.* To creak; to grate, as one thing against another; to crepitate. See UUINA.

E-EU, *adj.* Alert; ready to obey orders.

E-E-HI, *v.* To tramp up; to kick up, as dust. See EHI and HEHI.

E-E-HI-A, *v.* Passive, *h* inserted, for *eeia.* See E, another; strange. To fear great-ly; to be afraid; to be dreadful. *Kin.* 28:17.

2. To lop the ears, as an animal, through fear or shame.

3. Applied to men whose countenances droop with fear; kindred with *makau,* but stronger; also written *ehia.*

E-E-HI-A, *s. Art.,* ke. Fear; dread; reverence; awe. 2 *Oihl.* 17:10.

2. A vision.

E-E-HI-A, *adj.* Fearful; dreadful; awful. *Kin.* 28:17.

2. Trembling with fright, occasioned by a dream or vision.

E-E-KE, *v.* To start away, as a person from danger; to shrink back.

2. The motion of one's hand when he has burnt his finger.

3. To twinge or writhe, as with great pain.

4. To start, as with fear; e puiwa; *eeke mai la ia i ka wela i ke ahi.*

E-E-KE, *adj.* Excellent, &c. See EKE.

E-E-KE, *s.* A starting from fear; a shrinking from the contact with fire or any fearful object.

2. The shrinking or contracting of a rope in length.

E-E-KE, *s.* A species of crab in the sea.

E-E-KE, *adj.* Excellent; nice; applied to a canoe, &c. See EKE, *adj.*

E-E-KE-LOI (ka-e-ke-loi), *s.* To drum with the fingers on the pahu and sing at the same time.

E-E-LO-KO-A, *s.* A storm at Waimea from the north-east.

E-E-NA, *adj.* O ka pua *eena* ole ia o ka moku? Wild; untamed, as children in a school.

2. Skillful; applied to birds and fish that discover the snare or net.

E-E-NE, *v.* To tremble for, as for one in danger; *eene* aku i ka mea aneane haule.

2. To be astonished at, or ashamed of

one for lying or committing other evil.

3. To tremble for one violating the kapu of the chiefs, as a child ignorantly climbing on the person of a chief, which was death.

E-E-PA, *s.* See EPA. Forgery; deceit; treachery.

E-E-WA, *v.* Ewa, ewaewa; to mock; to make mouths at; to vex.

E-I, *adv.* A particle of place; here; similar to *eia*; *ei ae*, here; close by; *ei ae, ke hele mai nei, here,* he is coming now.

E-IA, *adv.* Here; in this place; used in answer to the question auhea oe? *Ans. Eia* wau la, here am I. NOTE.—*Eia,* here, is in contrast with *aia,* there.

EI-A, *adj. pron.* This. SYN. with keia.

EI-NEI, *comp. pron.* This one, present; this person; this thing.

E-I-WA, *num. adj.* See IWA. Nine; the number nine; also written *aiwa.*

E-O, *v.* See O. To answer to a call; to say *here* to one calling. *Iob.* 13:22. No ka mea, ua *eo* kakou i ke Akua; penei ko kakou *eo* ana ia ia.

E-O, *s.* The answer to a call.

E-O, *v.* To gain or win in a bet or wager; ua *eo* wau ia oe, I have gained you, i. e., the bet. *Laieik.* 97. E ko.

2. To give as an equivalent in a bargain; to have made an honest, *bona fide* bargain; no ka mea, *eo* ko kaua kuai ana me ka ae like.

E-O, *adj.* See EO, *v.,* to gain. Finished; made an end of; complete; puni *eo,* a full accomplishment.

E-O, *s.* A calabash or other vessel brimful of food; he aloha i ka ipu ka *eo.*

E-O-E-KA-LA, (*adv.* phrase) for eole e kala; long ago; not lately.

E-O-LA-NI, *adj.* Stretching or reaching up to heaven, i. e., very high; *eolani* na kia o ka moku kiekie.

E-O-NO, *num. adj.* Six. See AONO. Simple form, *ono.*

EU, *v.* To rise up, as one who has been sitting.

2. To ascend from an humble to an exalted situation.

3. To excite or stir up one to do a thing. 1 *Nal.* 21:15. O aku la o Poki ia Kalaiwahi, *eu,* hoi, kaua ma Oahu, Poki said to Kalaiwahi, come on (up,) let us two return to Oahu.

4. *Hoo.* To collect; to call out, as a company of soldiers on an emergency; to excite to tears; ia manawa, e *hoeu* ana ke aloha, e hoolale ana i na wai maka. The

root, *eu,* is often doubled, giving intensity; as, *hooeueu,* to excite, stir up, rouse to action. See EUEU.

EU, *s.* A rising up to do something; aole ana *eu* ae, he did not get up, i. e., did not exert himself.

2. In the abstract, mischief; theft; murder, and the like. *Laieik.* 104. NOTE.—Ka *eu* also means a peculiar sensation of the skin, a creeping numbness, like *maeele* or *malanai;* holo ka *eu* ma ka lae.

EU, *adj.* Disobedient; mischievous; he wahapaa.

E-U, *v.* To live; to crawl here and there, as worms in a putrid, dead body; *eu* ka ilo, apuupuu ka ili, *eu* ka nalo, *eu* ka naio, *eu* mai ka opae; e nee, e kolo paha.

2. To steal; not quite so strong as *aihue.*

3. To trouble by asking favors.

E-U-A-NE-LIO, *s.* Gr. The gospel; the life and labors of Jesus Christ as described by one of the Evangelists.

2. The system of salvation as revealed in the New Testament. *Mat.* 11:5; *Gal.* 1:6. Ke kauoha hou, ka olelo maikai.

EU-EU, *v.* 13th conj. of *eu;* see above. *Hoo.,* conj. 15th. To stir up; to influence one to action. 2 *Pet.* 1:13. Often SYN. with hoala.

2. To stir up one to perform his duty. 2 *Oihl.* 24:6. *Eueu* ka lehelehe o ka wahine nuku wale, the lips of a scolding woman make trouble.

EU-EU, *s.* A stirring up; an excitement. 2 *Pet.* 1:12, 13.

E-U-LU, *v.* To cut or crop off a branch with some smaller branches; e oki aku i ka *eulu* me na lala liilii; "no ka lau ka *eulu* pipili ka lani, oki ka honua." See ULU, to grow.

E-U-LU, *s.* See ULU, to grow. A branch cut off to be planted again; a layer.

2. The top and branches of a tree which are cut off and left as good for nothing.

E-U-NU-HA, *s.* Gr. A eunuch; one castrated. *Mat.* 19:12.

E-U-NU-HA, *v.* Gr. *Hoo.* To make one a eunuch. *Mat.* 19:12.

E-U-WE-KE, *v.* To open; to take off, as a man takes off irons from one confined.

2. To burst open.

3. To dash upon, as a wave does a double canoe by rising between them.

E-HA, *v.* To be hurt; to be sore; to be painful; to suffer; *eha* ka naau, the heart is pained. *Hoo.* To suffer in any way, as in sickness or pain, or by punishment according to law, justly or unjustly. 1 *Pet.*

4:15, 16. FIG. To cause hurt; to grieve one. *Epes.* 4:30.

E-HA, *s.* Pain; soreness of any kind; sorrow; suffering of punishment; a hurt; affliction. 1 *Sam.* 1:11.

E-HA, *adj.* Sore; painful; hurtful.

E-HA, *num. adj.* Four; the number four. See AHA and HA.

E-HA-E-HA, *v.* Conj. 13 of *eha. Hoo.* To give pain; to afflict. *Nah.* 29:7. To chastise; to punish; *Kanl.* 8:5. To grieve, i. e., to cause grief to one. *Hal.* 95:10. To vex. *Kin.* 21:12.

E-HA-E-HA, *s.* Suffering; torment; pain; grief.

E-HA-E-HA, *adj.* Intensely painful. 1 *Nal.* 12:4.

E-HA-E-HA, *adv.* Painfully; grievously.

E-HA-HA, *v.* To loll; to pant, as a dog or hog after violent exercise, or with heat. See AHAHA.

E-HE, *adj.* Huluiia mai kuu lani kuu alii *ehe*.

E-HE-A, *v.* To call; to call aloud; perhaps the imperative mood of *hea*, to call. See KAHEA.

E-HE-E-HE, *v.* To cough; to cough slightly; to hack.

E-HE-E-HE, *adj.* Pertaining, or belonging to a cough; mai *eheehe*.

E-HE-U, *s.* The wing of a fowl; na mea *eheu*, winged animals. *Kin.* 1:21. FIG. Care; protection; eia no au iloko o na *eheu* o ko kaua makuahine; the wing, as of an eagle. *Puk.* 19:4. Oukou, e na hoa (scholars of the Sem.) o na *eheu* o ke kaka-hiaka nui. *Eheu* takes both forms of the article *ka* and *ke*. See EHEHEU.

E-HE-U, *adv.* As wings; as if with wings. *Isa.* 40:31.

E-HE-HEU, *s.* A wing. See EHEU.

E-HE-NA, *v.* See HEHENA.

E-HI, *v.* To tread upon; to trample down; to kick. See HEHI and HAHI.

E-HI-A, *int. adv.* How many?

E-HI-A, *v.* See EEHIA.

E-HI-E-HI, *v.* To slander; to spread evil reports of one. See AHIAHI.

E-HI-KU, *num. adj.* Seven; also *ahiku* and *hiku*.

E-HI-NA, *adj.* Reddish; sandy; applied to the hair.

E-HI-PA, *v.* To crook; to bend.

E-HI-PA, *s.* A crook.

E-HI-PA, *adj.* Crooked.

E-HO, *s.* A stone idol; he akua o Lono-kaeha.

2. A collection of stone gods.

3. A monument; a stone pillar set up as a memorial. *Kin.* 28:18; also *Kin.* 35:14. Name of a pile of stones set up to attract the attention of fishermen.

4. A swelling of bunch internal, a kind of disease.

5. Name of a stone put inside of an animal in cooking.

E-HO-E-HO, *v.* See EHO, 3.

E-HU, *s.* The spray of the surf.

2. The steam of boiling water. See MAHU and KEHU.

3. One of the servants of the king.

E-HU, *v. Hoo.* To drive away; to scare away, as hogs or hens.

E-HU, *adj.* Red or sandy haired; ruddy in countenance; florid. 1 *Sam.* 16:12.

E-HU-A-HI-A-HI, *s.* LIT. The red of the evening.

2. An epithet of old age.

E-HU-A-WA, *s.* A species of strong grass or rush from which cords are made; also written *ahuawa*.

E-HU-E-HU, *s.* A strong wind blowing severely; aka huhumanu *ehuehu* ka makani, inoino lepolepo ka moana; hakukai ka ale o ka moana i ka *ehuehu* o ka makani.

2. Darkness arising from dust, fog or vapor.

E-HU-E-HU, *adv.* Angrily; furiously; in a raging manner, as the wind. See EHU. Ku *ehuehu*, huhu, inaina.

E-HU-KA-KA-HI-A-KA, *s.* LIT. The red of the morning; an epithet of youth. See EHUAHIAHI.

E-KA, *s.* Costiveness; filth.

2. Name of a sea breeze at Kona.

E-KA, *s.* The upper part of a bunch of bananas; he lila wale no mai ka *eka* luna a hiki i ka pola.

E-KA, *s. Eng.* An acre (of land); a measured quantity. *Isa.* 5:10.

E-KA, *adj.* Dirty; unclean; foul. *Isa.* 57:20.

2. Costive; filthy.

3. Curly, as a Negro's hair.

E-KA-E-KA, *adj.* See EKA. Dirty; covered with filth; very dirty.

E-KA-HA, *s.* Name of a parasitical plant.

2. Name of a hard kind of bush which grows in the sea.

3. Also the name of a fern-like plant.

E-KA-HA-KA-HA, *s.* Name of a species of sea-weed.

2. Name of a plant, large, long leaf.

E-KA-KU, *s.* The rolling of a stone down

a pali; kaa ka pohaku, ula ka pali, he ahaia? he *ekaku.*

E-KA-LE-SI-A, *s.* Gr. A church; a body of professing Christians. *Oih.* 8:1.

2. He *ekalesia,* a church member.

E-KE, *s.* A pocket; a bag; a small sack. *Luk.* 9:3. *Eke* kala, a money bag; a purse. *Ioan.* 12:6. SYN. with hipuu.

2. Name of a kind of net; properly, the bottom or bag part of the net.

E-KE, *adj.* Excellent; nice; applied to canoes; perhaps to other things.

E-KE-E-KE, *v.* To be in pain; to be pained, as the bowels on pressure.

2. To be pained, as the mind stung by an offense.

E-KE-E-KE, *s.* A piercing, stinging pain.

2. Displeasure, arising from an offense.

3. The feeling one has when that which he prizes is spoken against or injured.

E-KE-E-KE, *adj.* Hurt; pained, as the striking at something hard.

E-KE-E-KE, *v.* To brush off, as a fly or insect.

E-KE-E-KE, *adj.* Excellent; nice, &c. See EKE, *adj.*

E-KE-E-KEI, *v.* To be too short. *Hoo.* To shorten; to make short. See EKEKEI.

E-KE-U, *s.* A wing of a bird. *Hal.* 17:8. SYN. with ehue. See EKEKE and EKEKEU.

E-KE-U, *adj.* Proud; haughty; applied to a person neatly dressed, who despises others. SYN. with HAAHEO.

E-KE-KE,   ⎫ *s.* A wing; the wing of a
E-KE-KE-U, ⎭ bird. See EHEU and EKEU.

E-KE-KEI, *adj.* Short; too short; shorter than something else; applied to clothes, strings, &c.

E-KE-KEU, *s.* A wing, &c. See EKEKE above.

E-KE-KE-MU, *v.* To open or move the lips, as in speaking, but without sound.

E-KE-MU, *v.* To open, as the mouth.

2. To utter by the organs of speech. 2 *Kor.* 12:4.

3. To speak audibly or intelligibly. *Kin.* 24:21.

4. To speak out; to reply to a question. *Kin.* 45:3.

5. To answer in reply. *Ios.* 22:21.

6. To come forth in any way.

7. To operate as a cathartic.

E-KI, *adj.* See ELAUEKI. Pertaining to the top of a ki leaf.

E-KI-KI-LAU, See EEI. A word used in a dirty mele.

E-KO,   ⎫ *s.* Dirt; filth, &c. Spoken
E-KO-E-KO, ⎭ of a person unwashed.

E-KO,   ⎫ *adj.* Dirty; filthy, as in
E-KO-E-KO, ⎭ former times, when it was kapu to bathe. See EKA.

E-KO-LU, *adj. num.* Three; the number three; also *akolu.* See KOLU.

E-KU, *v.* To root, as a pig; (*motio foeti in utero*); to dig in the ground, as a plow. *Laieik.* 107.

E-KU-LE, *s.* A species of fish.

E-LAA,   ⎫ *adv.* Together with; along
E-LAA-HOI, ⎭ with; likewise; thus; in like manner; as also; the same; alike; the same as; penei, *elaa* ka mea ole ana. See LAA.

E-LAU, *s.* The straight top of a tree, or of a sugar-cane.

2. The end of one's finger; the point of a bayonet; the bearded part of a spear.

3. The commencement of a breeze of wind.

4. The pointed end of a substance. See WELAU and WELELAU.

E-LAU-E-KI, *s.* A bayonet.

E-LAU-I-KI, E-LA-WAI-KI, or **E-LAU-WAI-KI,** *s.* The top of the ki leaves.

E-LE, *v.* To be dark; black; to be dark colored; not clear.

E-LE. An intensive added to many words; very; much; greatly, &c.

E-LE-AO, *s.* Name of a worm that destroys food; he ilo, he mea e make ai ka ulu o ka ai.

E-LE-E-LE, *adj.* See ELE. Dark colored; black; blue; dark red; brown. See ULIULI; also LIPOLIPO.

E-LE-E-LE, *s.* Darkness; ua like ka *eleele* me ka uliuli.

E-LE-E-LE, *adv.* Darkly, without much light; ke hele *eleele* nei au, I walk in darkness. *Iob.* 30:28.

E-LE-E-LE-KU, *v.* To fly to pieces; to break easily. See ELEKU below.

E-LE-E-LE-KU, *adj.* Easily broken; similar to *helelei;* pohaku *eleku.*

2. Unhandsome; unsightly; applied to a homely, lean, or insignificant person; a good for nothing man.

E-LE-E-LE-PI, *adj.* Dashing different ways, as waves affected by different winds.

2. Applied to men of different minds; as, *eleelepi* ka waha o kanaka.

E-LEI-O, *v.* To go after anything privately, as a mouse after poi.

E-LE-U, *adj.* Alert.

E-LE-U-LI, *s.* A kind of kapa; kapa

eleuli no Puna.

E-LE-HEI, *adj.* Too short for the purpose designed; one leg too short; as an oopa, wawae pokoli. See EKEKEI.

E-LE-HEI, *s.* Shortness; want of length; i ka *elehei*, i ka mumuku.

E-LE-HEU, *s.* Anger; rage.

E-LE-HEU, *adj.* Angry; very angry; in a raging manner.

E-LE-KA, *s. Eng.* The elk; an animal. *Lam. Haw.* 6:1.

E-LE-KU, *v.* To fly to pieces. See ELE-ELEKU.

E-LE-KU, *adj.* Easily broken; similar to *helelei*; pohaku *eleku*.
2. A good for nothing man; a coward; applied to a homely, lean or mean insignificant person. See ELEELEKU.

E-LE-KU, *s.* A species of stone; he pohaku *eleku*, a brittle stone.

E-LE-LE, *s.* A messenger; one sent by authority. *Nah.* 21:21. An ambassador; ka mea i hoounaia'ku; a representative to transact the business of another; one sent to carry news. 1 *Sam.* 4:17. Often SYN. with luna.

E-LE-LO, *s. Art.,* ke. The tongue of man or beast; the organ of speech; the instrument of communicating good or evil. *Iob.* 20:16. See ALELO and LELO.

E-LE-LO-LU-A, *adj.* Tongue-tied.

E-LE-LO-LU-A, *s.* A tongue-tied person.

E-LE-LU, } *s.* A cockroach, *elelu* lii-
E-LE-LE-LU, } lii, the small cockroach; *elelu* papa, the flat, broad cockroach.

E-LE-MA-KU-LE, *v.* To be or become old; to have the evidence of decay; mostly applied to men; sometimes, FIG., to other things. *Heb.* 8:13.

E-LE-MA-KU-LE, *s.* An old man; an aged man; olelo ino aku la ia i kekahi mau *elemakule*, he spoke reproachfully to certain old men; ukiuki iho la ua mau *elemakule* la. Mostly applied to persons; sometimes to things—the works of creation. *Hal.* 102:26.

E-LE-MA-KU-LE, *adj.* Old; aged; decaying, as men advanced in life, but often indefinite. When one has not seen a child for some time, and the child has grown considerably, he exclaims, ka, ua *elemakule* no, why, he has become an old man. NOTE.—The same idea applied to an old woman would be *luahine*.

E-LE-MI-O, *v.* To taper off to a point.

E-LE-MI-O, *adj.* Tapering to a point.

E-LE-MI-HI, *s.* Name of a four-footed animal in the sea.

E-LE-PAI-O, *s.* A species of bird, *Laieik.* 29. Also,
2. A species of kalo with spotted leaves.

Elepaio, Oahu variety

E-LE-PA-NE, *s.* The sea elephant; a seal; a walrus.

E-LE-PA-NE or **E-LE-PA-NI,** *s. Eng.* The elephant.

E-LE-PA-NE, *adj.* Niho *elepane*, ivory. 1 *Nal.* 10:22.

E-LE-PI, *s.* Name of a four-footed animal found in the sea.

E-LI, *v.* To loosen or break up earth; to dig in the ground, as a pit, hole or ditch; e kohi; e *eli* oukou i ka lua a poopoo, dig the pit until it is deep; alaila, e kanu aku i ka laau, then plant the tree; ua *eli* lakou i ka auwaha a hohonu, they dug a ditch very deep.

E-LI-E-LI, *v.* To dig repeatedly. See above.

E-LI-E-LI, *Elieli* kapu, *elieli* noa.

E-LI-MA, *num. adj.* Five; the number five; also *alima*. See LIMA.

E-LO, *adj.* Wet; to soak, as kapa with rain; pulu kahi kapa i ka ua, *elo* wale, a kapa was wet with rain, and *all soft*.

E-LO-E-LO, *adj.* Very wet. See ELO. Ua pulu *eloelo* wale ko lakou aahu i ka waimaka, their robes were *soaked soft* with their tears.

E-LO-E-LO, *v.* To moisten; to make wet; o Kaelo keia malama, ke *eloelo* nei na huihui i ke kai, o Kaelo ia ke *eloelo* nei i ka ua.

E-LO-WA-LE, *v.* To be wet; dirty; defiled.

E-LU, *v.* To crumble to pieces.

E-LU-A, *num. adj.* Two; the number two. See ALUA and LUA.

E-MA-NU-E-LA, *s. Heb.* God with us; Emmanuel; a name of Jesus Christ. *Mat.* 1:23.

E-ME-RA-LA, *s. Eng.* Name of a precious stone. *Puk.* 28:18. An emerald.

E-MI, *v.* To fall behind, as one of several persons walking together.
2. To decrease in number.
3. To retire back; ebb; subside, as the tide; to diminish in quantity. *Kin.* 8:1.
4. To take an humble place after occupying one higher.
5. To think one's self of little consequence.
6. To despond; to flag, as the mind or

spirits; to fail, as the courage.

7. *Hoo.* To diminish. *Puk.* 21:10. To shorten; to make few; to sink back with fear; ke *hoemi* nei lakou i kau hana.

E-MI, *s.* In *music,* a flat; the character b.

E-MI-E-MI, *v.* See above. To fall behind, &c.; e *emiemi* iho la lakou i ka uala nui a hahai ae la i ke anamiu o ka uala.

E-MI-E-MI, *adv.* Backwardly; lazily; falling behind; mai hele *emiemi* i hope, mai hopohopo, mai makau, e hele aku i mua, do not fall behind, tremble not, fear not, go ahead.

E-MI-KU-A, *v.* To go backward.

E-MO, *v.* To be long; to delay; to put off; not much used, except with the negative *ole*; as, *emoole,* which see below.

E-MO, *s.* A waiting; a delay.

E-MO-O-LE, *s.* Quickness; dispatch; he hikiwawe. *Kin.* 27:22. Suddenness. *Gal.* 1:6.

E-MO-O-LE, *adj.* Emo and ole. Quickly; soon; active; punctual; aole emo! O how quickly!

E-MO-O-LE, *adv.* Suddenly. *Oih.* 2:2.

E-MU, *v.* To cast away; to throw away. *Hoo.* The same; e hookuke, e kipaku.

E-NA, *v.* To be in a rage, as in anger.

2. To burn, as fire; ua *ena* loa ka ula o ka mai, the sick person is red with heat; ke *ena* loa ae nei, wena.

E-NA, *adj.* Red hot; raging, as fire; epithet of an oven when red hot; applied also to anger.

2. Angry; wild; untamed, as an animal; full of fury.

3. Jealous, as a bird of a snare, or fearful, as a villain of good men; threatening, as some kinds of clouds that threaten a storm.

E-NA-E-NA, *v.* To burn, as a raging fire; to be hot. *Kanl.* 32:22. Spoken of anger.

2. To be strongly offensive to the smell, as the stench of a dead carcass; *enaena* ka pilau o ka lio make; ua *enaena* Kilauea i ka pele.

3. *Hoo.* To heat, as an oven. *Hos.* 7:4.

E-NA-E-NA, *s.* A raging, furious heat. *Dan.* 3:19.

E-NE, *v.* To creep, as a child first attempting; ua *ene* ke keiki, the child has begun to creep.

2. To creep along; to get near an object; *ene* aku la au e pehi i ka pohaku. *Hoo.* Hooene aku la na kahuna i ka laau halalo.

E-NE, *s.* The commencement of a child's creeping.

E-NEI, *adv.* For *nei*; here; this place; this neighborhood. *Kol.* 4:9. Mahea ko *enei* kamalii? where are the children of this place? See ANEI, here.

E-NE-HE, *v.* See ANEHE. To be ready to do a thing; prepared for it; *enehe* aku no ka lima e lalau, the hand was ready to catch hold; *enehe* aku la laua e holo aku.

E-NE-MI, *s.* *Eng.* An enemy. *Puk.* 23:22. He mea e ku e ai. *Nal.* 21:20.

E-NE-NE, *v.* 9th conj. of *ene.* To move itself, as a thing of life.

2. To bore a small hole in order to make a larger.

3. To file or rasp gently.

4. *Hoo.* To move itself, as a chicken in the shell. *Lam. Haw.* 12:2, 1.

E-NO, *v.* To be wild, easily made afraid, as an animal partially tamed. See HOO.

E-NO-E-NO. See MAENCENO.

E-NU-HE, *s.* A species of worm, large and striped. See ANUHE. On Maui it is called *peelua.* He puko, he peelua. NOTE.— The word is used for worm, generally in a moral sense, that is.

2. A poor, helpless, despicable creature. *Hal.* 22:6. Worms. *Kanl.* 28:39. FIG. Applied to men. *Isa.* 41:14.

3. A caterpillar. *Ier.* 51:14.

E-PA, *v.* To be deceived, to be led into error.

2. To be deceitful.

3. To steal.

4. To backbite, e wahahee, e hoopunipuni, e alapahi.

5. *Hoo.* To act basely or treacherously; also, *epaepa* with hoo; auhea oukou e ka poe i kapa ae nei, he pono ka *hooepaepa*? *Epa* wahahee, to get up a lie or false report. *Hal.* 119:69.

E-PA, *s.* One who is false to his trust.

2. An act of villainy; fraud, or artifice.

3. Falsehood; forgery, by getting property in the name of another; haku *epa,* one who speaks falsely to the hurt of another.

E-PA, *adj.* False; deceitful.

E-PA, *s.* *Heb.* Name of a Hebrew measure; an ephah. *Lunk.* 6:19; *Puk.* 16:36.

E-PA-E-PA, *v.* See EPA above.

E-PO-DA, *s.* *Heb.* An ephod; a part of the official dress of a Jewish high priest. 1 *Sam.* 2:18.

E-WA, *v.* To crook; to twist; to bend out of shape.

2. To act improperly; to pervert.

3. To mock; to vex; to trouble. *Hoo.* Hooewa ae mahope kuai ka hale; e *hoewa* ae ma ke kua; e *hoewa* aku ma ke kala; *hoewa* nuku mua; he *sneered* at the house and afterwards bought it; it was *crooked*

on the back side, it was *crooked* at the end, it was *crooked* in front. *Anat.* Generally in the reduplicated form.

E-WA-E-WA, *v.* To mock; to vex; to render one uncomfortable.

2. To act unjustly or unrighteously; to pervert justice. *Ezek.* 18:25.

3. *Hoo.* To cause mockery; vexation, &c. See MAEWA and MAEWAEWA.

E-WA-E-WA, *s.* Injustice; a turning aside from right. *Hal.* 9:8.

E-WA-EWA, *adj.* Unequal; unjust; irregular in structure, as an irregular bone. *Anat.* 4.

2. Grinning or expressing anger; applied to the mouth and eyes; as, he maka *ewaewa*, he waha *ewaewa*.

E-WA-E-WA, *adv.* Unjustly, respecting persons in judgment. *Kol.* 3:15. With partiality. 1 *Tim.* 5:21.

E-WA-E-WA-I-KI, *s.* A lohe oe i ka leo o ka *ewaewaiki* e hoonene ana. *Laieik.* 149. The imaginary voice of a female spirit who had died, and her unborn infant with her.

2. Name of a bird on Hawaii.

E-WAI, *s.* A swelling under the armpit or groin; also *awai*; he auwakoi.

E-WA-LU, *num. adj.* Eight; the number eight; also *awalu* and *walu*.

E-WE, *v.* To grow again after being cut off, as a stalk of sugar-cane; ke *ewe* ka aa; alaila kukulu na 'lii a pau i *ewe* ai, he heiau hoouluulu ua ia.

E-WE, *s.* The navel string.

2. Ke *ewe* o ka huamoa, the *white* of an egg. *Iob.* 6:6.

3. The abdominal aorta; he *ewe*, ke *ewe*.

4. The place of one's birth and where his ancestors before him were born; kona *ewe* hanau. See IEWE, placenta.

E-WE-WE, *s.* The love, affection and remembrance one has for the place of his birth and where he has spent his first years; o ke aloha mai ia oukou me ke *ewewe* o ka noho pu ana, malaila mai no ke aloha ana ia oukou.

E-BO-NI, *s. Eng.* Ebony, a species of black wood. *Ezek.* 27:15.

E-DE-NA, *s. Heb.* Name of the garden planted for our first parents. *Kin.* 2:8.

E-VA-NE-LI-O, *s. Gr.* The gospel; the history of Jesus Christ; the news of salvation. See EUANELIO. *Mar.* 1:1.

I.

I, the third letter of the Hawaiian alphabet. Its sound is that of *ee* in English, or that of the French *i*.

I is the medium of communication between an active transitive verb or a verb of motion and its object. See *Gram.* § 105, p. 49, *d* and *e*; also, *Gram.* Syntax, Rule 19. Before proper names of persons and pronouns, the *i* becomes *ia*. See note *Gram.* p. 49.

I has a variety of significations, and is used for a variety of purposes.

I, *prep.* To; towards; in; at; unto; by; for; in respect of; above; more than; on account of, &c.

I, *adj.* Stingy.

I, *adv.* When; while; if.

I, *conj.* If; that; a contraction perhaps of *ina*.

I. A sign. 1st. Of the imperfect tense of verbs.

2. A sign of the subjunctive mood; a contraction of *ina*.

3. As a sign of a tense, it often has the meaning of a potential; that; as, ua hai aku au i lohe oukou, I have spoken, *that* you might hear. See *Gram.* § 209, subj. mood, 4th form.

4. The sign of the imperative mood, passive in certain cases; as *i* kukui, *i* wai, *i* noho, bring a lamp, water, &c.

'I with an apostrophe before it, is a contraction after *a* of the preceding word, for *ai*; as, malaila kahi i waihoia'i ka waiwai, for waihoia *ai*.

I, *v.* To speak; to say, in connection with the thing spoken or said. *Kin.* 1:3 and 20.

2. To address one; to make a speech to one; often SYN. with olelo. *Kin.* 3:1. *I* mai la ia *i* ka wahine, he *said* to the woman (after this follows what was said.)

3. To say within one's self. *Kanl.* 18:21.

4. To pronounce a single word, as a signal. *Lunk.* 12:6.

5. To give an appellation, and SYN. with kapa. *Isa.* 32:5. To designate the name of a person. *Oih.* 9:36.

I, *v.* To beget, as a father.

I, *s.* Name of the papaia fruit and tree.

See II.

IA, *v. Hoo.* To enter; to be received, as into the mouth.

IA, *v.* To beat or pound, as in making kapa.

IA, *s.* The name of the mallet used in beating kapa.

IA, *prep.* Used before proper names of persons, and before pronouns, as *i* is before common nouns. See I, *prep.* It signifies, to; of; for; by; with; on account of; in respect of, &c. See *Gram.* § 126, 6.

IA, *adv.* In the beginning of a sentence, and before a pronoun, it refers to time; when; at that time, &c.; as *ia* lakou i noho ai ilaila, *while* they lived there; *ia* manawa, make iho la ke alii, at *that* time the chief died.

IA, *pers. pron.,* third pers. sing. He; she; it; more rarely in the sense of *it*, for which Hawaiians use a periphrasis; thus: *ia* kanaka, *ia* wahine, *ia* mea, kela, keia, &c. *Gram.* § 137, 140, 3d.

IA, *pron. adj.* This; that; according as the thing referred to is present or absent.

IA annexed to verbs, forms the passive voice of all the conjugations; as, ua *alohaia* mai kakou, we *are beloved.* This sign of the passive voice may be annexed to the verb and form one word, or it may be separated, one or more words intervening; as, ua *lawe* malu *ia* ke dala, the money *was taken* secretly. *Gram.* § 211. NOTE.—Sometimes letters are inserted before the *ia*; as *awahia,* it is bitter, for *awaia.*

I-A, *s.* A fish; the general name of all sea animals, also those in fresh water; ua kapaia na mea a pau ma ke kai he *ia*, o na mea holo a me na mea holo ole; aia no kekahi mau *ia* maloko o ka wai mauka o ka aina.

    2. Meat of any kind, in distinction from *ai*, vegetable food; o ka *ia* wale no i koe ia ia, the *fish* only remained to him (i. e., Dagon). 1 *Sam.* 5:4. NOTE.—The names of the fish formerly kapu for women to eat were: kumu, moano, ulua, honu perhaps, and the ea.

IA, *s.* Pronounced *yah. Eng.* A yard in length.

I'A, *s.* The galaxy or milky way.

IA-O, *s.* Name given to a small fish used for bait.

    2. Name of a bird somewhat like the moho.

IA'-U, *pron. pers.,* 1st pers. A contraction of *ia au*; the auialo (accusative or objective case) of *au*; me; to me; for me; by me, &c. *Gram.* § 126, 6th auialo.

IA-U, *s.* Name of a species of small fish.

I-A-HA, *adv. int.* See AHA. For what? to what? *iaha* la ka makemake? for what is the desire?

I-A-HO-NA, *v.* To be near to death, but desirous of living; to wish to live or recover from sickness; *iahona* paha a ike aku, o kuu make paha ia. *Laieik.* 180.

I-A-KO, *s.* The number forty; a round or whole number, as we say, a dozen; it is applied mostly, if not exclusively, to counting kapas; perhaps to a few other things; a me ka *iako* kapa he nui loa, and the very many *forties* of kapas.

I-A-KO, *s.* Name of the arched sticks which connect a canoe with its outrigger; o ka *iako* waa, o ka hau ka *iako* paa.

I-A-KO, *s.* The name of a class of persons skilled in clearing, emptying and refitting a canoe upset in a storm at sea; ka poe i aoia i ka holo moana a me ka luu kai i na *iako*, oia ka poe i aoia e kamai ka huli pu.

I-A-LO-A, *v.* To embalm. *Kin.* 50:2. To bury dead bodies with perfumes; to preserve dead bodies by salting them.

I-A-LO-A, *s.* A dead body embalmed and preserved; a lawe ae la oia i kona mau *ialoa* a pau. *Laieik.* 123.

IA-LO-KO, *s. Ia,* prep., and *loko*, internal. That which is inside; what belongs inside. See LOKO.

IA-NA, *s. Heb.* A word translated *owl* in *Isa.* 13:21. The ostrich perhaps.

IA-NEI, *adv. Ia,* prep., and *nei*, here. Here; at this place. *Isa.* 45:14.

IA-NU-A-RI, *s. Eng.* The name of the first month in the year, adopted by Hawaiians from the Romans through the English. The name of the Hawaiian month nearly corresponding is Kaelo. See *D. Malo* 12:6.

IA-WI, *s.* Name of a small red bird.

IA-GU-A, *s. Eng.* Name of the animal jaguar.

IA-SE-PI, *s. Gr.* A jasper; a precious stone. *Puk.* 28:20; *Hoik.* 21:11.

IE, *v.* To insult; to provoke; to pick a quarrel.

IE, *s.* Canvas; *ie* nani, fine linen; white cotton cloth, lole *ie.*

    2. A vine used in making baskets, also in decorating their persons; he *ie* o ka nahele-hele.

    3. A material braided into hats by the women; he ulana *ie* papale ka na wahine hana.

4. Name of a stick used in beating kapa; he *ie* kuku.

IE, *adj.* Flexible; limber, like cloth or a vine; he lole *ie*, he kanaka *ie* ke ona i ka rama, a man is limber (like cloth) when he is drunk; he lapa; he noho *ie*, he papale *ie*, he ipu *ie*.

I-E-I-E, *s.* The leaves of the ie formerly used in decorating the gods of Hawaii, generally made into wreaths; he *ieie* huewai, he *ieie* hula.

I-E-I-E, *adj.* He poo *ieie* no Hilo; a kind of lei for the head used by Hilo people.

ieie

I-E-I-E, *v.* To be decorated with leaves; to be dressed in wreaths.

2. *Hoo.* To be ennobled; to be dignified.

I-E-I-E, *adj. Hoo.* Proud; pompous; light minded.

I-E-I-E-WA-HO, *s.* Name of the sea or channel between Oahu and Kauai, hoi mai no ma ka moana o ka *Ieiewaho*, he returned by the ocean of the *Ieiewaho*.

I-E-I-E-WE, *s.* The envelop of a fetus; placenta; secundines feminarum parturientium.

2. The uterus; the womb; ka aa, ka alualu.

IE-HO-VA, *s. Heb.* The name of the one eternal, living and true God, in opposition to all other gods. *Isa.* 45:5, 6. His name and attributes have been accepted by Hawaiians.

I-E-WE, *s.* The navel string connecting the new-born infant with the mother.

2. The infant itself; a young one just born. *Kanl.* 28:57.

3. The after-birth.

I-E-LE, *s.* A chief; a king; he alii, ke alii.

I-E-SE-RU-NA, *s. Heb.* A poetical name for the Israelitish people, signifying upright, beloved. *Kanl.* 32:15—33:5.

I-I, *adj.* Sour; mouldy; musty, as food injured by long standing. SYN. with punahelu.

2. Covetous; close; niggardly.

I-I, *v.* To be mouldy, &c., as food; ua *ii* loa ka ai.

2. To be lost; forgotten, as something formerly known; ua *ii* na olelo kahiko, ua nalowale.

I-I, *s.* Mould; rust; anything indicating age or decay.

I-I, *v.* To collect; to gather up, as small things; to bring together. See NOII. Ua ko waa, ke *ii* nei ka aha.

I-I, *s.* A gathering together; a collecting, as of small things; ka noii, ua hele i ka *ii* hana; he pii no i ka *ii* poaaha, they go up to collect mulberry bark.

I-I, *s.* A rejoicing with an audible voice, like a chant; o ka mea lea i ke olioli, aia a loaa ka *ii* iloko o ka puu; a singing in the throat, like the gurgling of water running from a calabash; e olaola ana me he huewai la; oia ka *ii*.

I-I, *s.* A heavy weight, difficult to lift; he kaumaha, he koikoi ka pupu.

I-I, *s.* A person hard hearted, cruel and selfish; ka *hooii* puahi ole a ka ua iuka wale no e haakeke ai.

I-I, *s.* Name of a bird, partly red, bill hooked. See APANE. He manu liilii ulaula; he apapane kekahi inoa.

2. Name of a species of fish around Molokai; ka pua *ii*.

3. A kind of fern.

4. Name of the papaia; also written *i*.

I-I, } *adj.* Stinted; unthrifty; choked
I-I-I, } with weeds; applied to vegetables or animals.

2. Mortified or humbled, as a person by the overbearing conduct of another; restrained.

3. Tight, as a rope in a hole.

4. Close; parsimonious. See II 2.

I-I-A-AO, *s.* Hard mouldy poi.

I-I-I, *s.* A child of slow growth, many years, little stature; aole nae ka *iii* loa, a nonoi no hoi; aia he uuku nui ae. Ua ike au i kahi keiki i komo *iii*, aa no hoi ke kino ke nana aku.

I-I-I, *adj.* Little; small; dwarfish; he puaa *iii*, a small hog; he laau *iii*, a small tree; also, ka pulu *iii*, little cotton; ka ipulu *iii*.

I-I-I, *s.* Smallness; littleness; inferiority, ka *iii*, ka aa, ke noinoi, ke kupalii.

2. Name of a plant eaten in time of scarcity.

I-I-I, *v.* To choke; to restrain; to hedge up.

I-I-I-KA, *s.* A scar; a contraction of the skin from a wound.

I-I-I-NA, *v.* To desire strongly. See IINI.

I-I-KA, *adj.* Small; little in size; he wahi manini *iika*, a small manini, i. e., a kind of fish; ke kalo *iika*, the little kalo; he wiwi, he olala.

I-I-KE, *adj.* See IKE, to know. Quick

to learn; ready; smart; having gained knowledge.

I-I-MO, *v.* See IMO. To wink repeatedly; to wink often.

2. To convey some idea by winking. *Sol.* 6:13.

I-I-NI, *v.* To desire; to wish for; to long after. *Kin.* 31:30.

2. To fear or expect the loss of a thing which we very much love.

3. To desire strongly to have or do a thing. 2 *Sam.* 13:39. Ke *iini* nei ka naau i ka pono, the heart desires that which is good.

I-I-NI, *s.* A strong desire; ka *iini* nui, the greatly loved one. *Laieik.* 114. Ka makemake nui me ka ikaika.

I-I-WI, *s.* A small red bird; also *iawi.*

I-I-WI-PO-LE-NA, *s.* The name of a bird mentioned in *Laieikawai* 29, 80 and 149.

I-O, *s.* A species of bird; a hawk.

I-O, *s.* Name of a game.

I-O, *s.* Lean flesh; the animal muscle. *Anat.* 3. A muscle; he *io* ku e, an antagonistic muscle. *Anat.* 26.

2. Flesh in general. *Puk.* 29:14.

3. Flesh, i. e., person. *Oihk.* 16:4.

4. One's flesh, i. e., kindred; relation. *Kin.* 29:14. Io maha, the muscle on the side of the head.

I-O, *s.* Part; portion; reality; truth; verity. *Ezek.* 12:23.

I-O, *s.* A forerunner; one who announces the approach of a chief.

I-O, *adj.* True; real; not imaginary; ua paa ka manao o kanaka he akua *io* no o Lono, the minds of the people were firm that Lono (Captain Cook) was a *real* god.

I-O, *adv.* Truly; really; verily; certainly; *oiaio*, truth. *Io* is a strong intensive. Pela *io* no ka hana ana a lakou; aohe *io* o ka hewa, the wickedness is great.

I-O, *adv.* I, prep., and *o*, there. Yonder; aia no ia *io*, there he is yonder. See O. *Io* ia nei, adverbial phrase, hither and thither.

I-O, *prep.* Nearly SYN. with *ia*; used before proper names and pronouns. To; towards. *Iob.* 5:1. But implying motion.

I-O, *v.* To flee; to hasten away with fear.

I-O, *v.* To be loaded with bundles; ua alaulau.

I-O-E-NA, *adj.* Wild; savage; untamed, as a wild, ferocious animal; he piena, hihiu.

I-O-I-O, *v.* To peep, as a chicken; also *piopio.* *Isa.* 10:14. Misprinted *oioi*; to chatter. *Isa.* 38:14. To whisper, as ghosts were supposed to do. See HANEHANE.

I-O-I-O, *adj.* Peeping, as a chicken; he manu *ioio*, a swallow. *Ier.* 8:7.

I-O-I-O, *v.* To look this way and that, as a thief about to steal; *ioio* na maka o ka hohe wale.

I-O-I-O, *v.* To appear above water, as a shark's fin when swimming about; *ioio* kuala o ka mano i ka ili kai.

I-O-I-O, *v.* To project upwards, as a point of a mountain; *ioio* ae ana o Puuonioni e oni ae ana e like me Maunakea.

I-O-I-O-LE-A, *adj.* Brisk; lively; light in traveling; mama ma ka hele ana; also,

2. Angry; quick tempered.

I-O-I-O-LE-PO, *s.* A bearer of tidings; a messenger to carry news.

I-O-KU-PU, *s.* *Io*, flesh, and *kupu*, to grow up. A polypus, name of a disease in the nose; a gum-boil; lampers in a horse.

I-O-LA-NA, *v.* See LANA. To float in the air, as a bird.

I-O-LE, *s.* A mouse. *Oihk.* 11:29. *Iole* nui, a rat or rabbit; a mole. *Isa.* 2:20.

I-O-LEA, *adj.* Wild; untamed, as an animal; he puaa *iolea*, hihiu.

I-O-LE-NU-I, *s.* A rat, especially the large wharf-rat.

I-O-LE-RA-BA-TI, *s.* Hawaiian name for the rabbit, a foreign animal.

I-O-LIU, *s.* The lean flesh inside the backbone of beef, &c., adjoining the ribs. NOTE.—The flesh outside is called *uhau.*

IO-MA-HA, *s.* See IO, muscle, and MAHA, side of the head, temple. The muscle on the temple or *temple muscle. Anat.* 6.

I-O-MO, *v.* To throw a stone into the air which falls into the water.

2. To leap, as a person into the water, provided he does not spatter the water. *Hoo.* the same.

I-O-PO-NO, *s.* Name of a class of persons formerly who were entrusted with the care of the king, and whose business it was to guard his person and effects, lest some one should obtain his spittle and garments, and thus have power to pray him to death. The poe *iopono* were generally high chiefs.

2. A friend; a relation of one whose faithfulness might be trusted; he hoahanau *iopono* no kela nou, ua make no oe he *iopono.*

I-U, *s.* Name of a particular kapu relating to females.

I-U, *adj.* Prohibited; sacred; tabooed; applied to everything within the reach of the kapu; *iu* kahi o ke alii, ano, makau, *sacred* is the place of the chief, it is consecrated, it is to be feared.

I-U, *s.* A consecrated place; he kapu ke alii, noho i ka *iu* la, the king is kapu, he sits in the *sacred place.*

I-U, *v.* Hoo. To lay a kapu for a particular time; e *hooiu* aku i kekahi manawa.

I-U-I-U, *v.* To be afar off; high up; to live in some sacred, kapu place. NOTE.— The ideas of *far off* or *high up* seem to be connected with sacredness, or separation from everything common. See HEMOLELE.

I-U-I-U, *s.* A place supposed to be afar off or high up above the earth or beneath the ocean, sacred to the dwelling place of God; ke Akua noho i ka *iuiu*, the God dwells afar off; i ka welau o ka makani, at the further end of the wind; he onohi ku i ka moana, an eye-ball standing in the ocean, i. e., the center of the ocean.

I-U-I-U, *adj.* What is high up or afar off; he poiuiu, he poliuliu.

I-U-KA, *adv.* I, prep., towards, and *uka*, inland. A direction opposite from the sea; inland; up the mountain.

IU-LAI, *s. Eng.* Name of the modern seventh month, July, answering to Kaaona of the ancient Hawaiian division.

IU-NI-PE-RA, *s. Eng.* Name of a tree not found on these islands; juniper; laau *iunipera.* 1 *Nal.* 19:4.

IU-PI-TA, *s. Eng.* The planet Jupiter; the Hawaiian name is *Kaawela.*

IU-BI-LE, *s. Heb.* A year of release from service. *Oihk.* 25:9, 11.

IU-BI-LE, *adj.* Of or pertaining to jubilee or the year of release; makahiki *iubile. Oihk.* 25:28.

IU-DAI-O, *s.* A Jew; a descendant of Abraham.

I-HA, *v.* To be intent upon; persevering at; to desire greedily; ua *iha* wale no, he gives his whole attention.

I-HA-I-HA, *adj.* Firmly drawn, as a rope; ua *ihaiha* ke kaula, ua maloeloe, strained.

I-HA-I-HA, *adj.* Ua *ihaiha* ka puukole i ka mimi, ua iheihe; ua hele a *ihaiha* wale ka poe hana hewa, e hana mau ma ka hewa; to draw in, restrain, as one desiring to fulfill a call of nature, and is restrained by the presence of some one; so also having a desire to lasciviousness.

I-HE, *s.* A spear, *Ios.* 8:18. *Ihe* hulali, a glittering spear; a javelin. *Nah.* 25:7. He *ihe* pakelo; *ihe* pahee a me na *ihe* o, the hand staves and the spears.

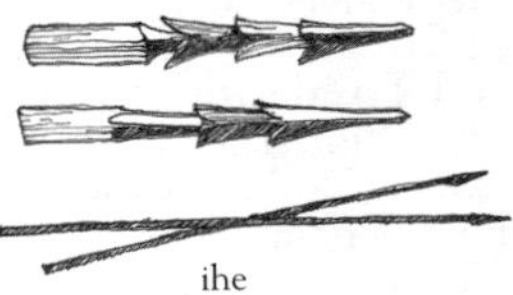

ihe

I-HE-A, *adv. int.* I and *hea*, where? To what place? whither? *ihea* oukou? where are you going?

I-HEE, *adj.* Still, quiet, as the weather; he *ihee* no ka la malie.

I-HEE, *v.* To run from; to escape, e *ihee* ana i ka ia (kawelo) i ka mua o na waa.

I-HEE-HEE, *v.* To pour into; to slip easily, as oil into a bottle; e *iheehee* ana i ka aila iloko o ka huewai.

I-HE-I-HE, *s.* A species of fish of the sword kind, but small; kaawili *iheihe.*

I-HI, *v.* To peel off the bark from a stick. *Kin.* 30:37.

2. To peel; to flay the skin from an animal; e *ihi* i ka ai, to take the skin from food (kalo or potatoes); e *ihi* i ka ili o ka manini, to peel the skin from the manini (a species of kalo); e hoopohole, e maihi; ua *ihi* ka la, ua wela ka pahoehoe, the sun is peeled off, i. e., the clouds, the smooth rocks are hot; ua *ihi* ke kapu o ke alii, the kapu is taken off. LIT. Peeled off.

I-HI, *s.* The name of a plant growing on the mountains, the root, used in native medicines, slightly cathartic; also,

2. A plant like the pig-sorrel, which is called *ihi* makole.

I-HI, *adj.* Sacred; hallowed. *Hal.* 72:19. Generally applied to high chiefs.

I-HI-I-HI, *adj.* Sacred; holy; *Ios.* 24:19. No mixture of evil. *Isa.* 6:3.

2. Majestic; dignified. See IHI, *adj.*

I-HI-I-HI, *s.* See IHI above. Name of a plant; he *ihiihi* makole, he *ihiihi* ai.

I-HI-I-HI, *interj.* An expression of surprise at seeing anything uncommon or out of the ordinary course of things; he huaolelo kahaha, a word expressive of astonishment.

I-HI-I-HI, *v.* Hoo. To put on dignity or importance.

I-HI-HI, *adj.* Angry; cross; offended; unsociable; he kanaka *ihihi*, displeased with; disaffected to; parsimonious; he kanaka *ihihi*, e aua no, stingy.

I-HI-HI, *v.* To neigh, as a horse.

I-HI-MA-NU, *s.* Name of a large creature of the ocean, one and a half or two feet in diameter; perhaps *hihimanu* is a better orthography. *Hueu.*

I-HO, *v.* To go down; to descend, as from a higher to a lower place. *Nah.* 12:5. To go down from an eminence. *Puk.* 19:24. E *iho* ana i ka pali, descending a precipice.

2. *Hoo.* To cause to descend; to bring down, as a punishment. 1 *Nal.* 2:9.

3. To cause to fall. *Ezek.* 26:20.

I-HO, *s.* The pith of a vegetable; he *iho* laau ka mea mawaena o ka laau, the *pith* of a tree is what is in the center of the tree.

2. In *geography*, the pole of the earth; he *iho* ko ka honua a puka ma na aoao elua, the earth has a pith (pole) coming out at both sides; ka *iho* kukui. See IHOIHO.

I-HO, *s.* Name of the inferior kapas in a set, the best being the kilohana.

I-HO. A verbal directive, which implies,

1. Motion or tendency downward.

2. It implies succession, and is used much in narrative tenses; generally followed by *la. Gram.* § 233, § 234, 3d, § 237, § 239.

I-HO is also used after adverbs of time, and expresses succession of time; as, mahope *iho*, after that. *Lunk.* 1:1. *Iho* nei, just now.

I-HO, following nouns or pronouns, is equivalent to *self* or *selves*; as, e malama ia oukou *iho*, take care of your *selves*; eia ko'u manao no'u *iho*, here is my opinion of *myself*. It is equivalent to *own* after a possessive; as, kona *iho*, his *own*.

I-HO-I-HO, *s.* The solid, heavy part of timber; the heart; something solid inside of something soft; hele mai ia me ka pu a me ka pololu a me ka *ihoiho* kukui.

I-HO-I-HO-KU-KUI, *s.* A string of kukui nuts, used for torches.

I-HO-LE-NA, *s.* A species of banana which were permitted to be eaten under the kapu system; eia na maia a Papa e ai ai, o ka popolu, o ka *iholena.*

I-HO-NA, *s. Iho* and *ana.* A descending; going down; a path descending a hill.

I-HO-PE, *adv. I*, prep., and *hope*, end. Back; backward. *Heb.* 10:38, 39.

I-HU, *s.* The nose of a person. *Isa.* 65:5. The snout of an animal. *Sol.* 11:22. The bill of a bird; the bowsprit of a ship; the fore part of a canoe, &c.; e homai ka *ihu*, give me a kiss. *Laieik.* 72. NOTE.—Hawaiians kissed by touching noses. *Laieik.* 119.

Oia ka manawa e loaa'i kou *ihu* i ke keiki Kauai; a proverbial expression, or it may be a misprint for *ike. Laieik.* 126.

I-HU-A-NU, *s. Ihu*, nose, and *anu*, cold.

1. Name of a wind upland of Kawela; o ka *ihuanu*, he makani ia no Kawela, mauka mai.

2. Name of an odoriferous tree or shrub of that place.

I-HU-O-LA-O-LA, *s. Ihu*, nose, and *olaola*, to snore.

1. A breathing hard; a snoring.

2. A snoring nose.

I-HU-HA-NU-NU, *adj. Ihu*, nose, and *hanunu*, to breathe hard. A hard breathing nose; hard breathing; snoring.

I-HU-I-HU, *adj.* A word used in contemning another.

I-HU-KU, *v. Ihu*, nose, and *ku*, to stand. To turn up the nose in anger or contempt. See IHUPII.

I-HU-KU, *s.* Anger; contempt.

I-HU-KU-KA-NI, *adj. Ihu, ku* and *kani*, to sound. Hard breathing.

I-HU-MAA, *adj.* Disobedient; mischievous; manomano ke keiki *ihumaa* oe, you are a child of frequent disobedience.

I-HU-NA, *adj.* Mischievous, applied to persons; kolohe.

I-HU-NA-NA, *adj.* Snoring; a snoring person. See IHUNONO below.

I-HU-NO-NO, *v. Ihu*, nose, and *nono*, to snore. To snore in one's sleep. See NONOO and NONE.

I-HU-PA-PA, } *adj. Ihu*, nose, and *papa*,
I-HU-PE-PE, } flat, or *pepe*, mashed. Depressed; flat or depressed nosed.

I-HU-PE-PE, *s.* A flat nosed person. *Oihk.* 21:18. Puka *ihu*, a nostril. *Nah.* 11:20.

I-HU-PII, *v. Ihu*, nose, and *pii*, to go up. To turn up the nose in contempt.

I-HU-PII, *s.* A word of contempt. LIT. A turned up nose.

I-KA, *v.* To float ashore, as a drowned person; a ao ia po, *ika* ia aku la ia kanaka iuka o Ukumehame; to be driven on shore by the surf.

2. To be turned aside, as a vessel by the wind aud current. *Oih.* 27:41.

3. To fall off, as a vessel before the wind.

4. To run before the wind. *Hoo.* To be thrown up on the bank of a kalo patch.

I-KA, *s.* Name of the sides of a kalo patch, or of a mala where the grass is thrown; oia ka mea e malu ai na *ika*, i lilo ole ka mea kanu a kekahi i kekahi.

I-KA, *adj.* Drifting; inclined to fall off before the wind; making leeway.

I-KAI, *adv.* *I*, prep., towards, and *kai*, sea. Towards the sea; the opposite of *iuka*, towards inland.

I-KAI-KA, *v.* See IKA 3 and 4. To exercise muscular strength; to be strong; ua *ikaika* kona lima, his arm was strong.

2. To be strong mentally or morally; to be courageous; persevering; energetic. *Kanl.* 31:6.

3. *Hoo.* To make strong, as one weak in body.

4. To be courageous in mind.

5. To be persevering in business.

6. To exhort one to be strong, energetic, persevering, &c.

I-KAI-KA, *s.* Strength; power; valor; zeal; perseverance.

I-KAI-KA, *adj.* Strong; hardy; persevering.

I-KAI-KA, *adv.* Strongly; perseveringly. 1 *Oihl.* 10:2.

I-KE, *v.* To see, perceive by the eye.

2. To see, perceive mentally, i. e., to know; understand.

3. A form of sending love to an absent one; as, e *ike* aku oe ia mea, do you salute such a one.

4. To receive, as a visitor or a messenger.

5. To know; to have carnal knowledge of. *Kin.* 4:1 and 19:5.

6. *Hoo.* To exhibit; to show; to point out; to cause to know; to give testimony in a court concerning one.

I-KE, *s.* Knowledge; instruction; ka *ike*, the person having knowledge. *Puk.* 4:11. Understanding. *Kanl.* 4:6. A parting salutation; as, e *ike*.

I-KE-A, *v.* Used for *ikeia*, the passive of *ike*. *Gram.* § 211. It has also the regular passive *ikeia*. To be seen; to be known; to appear. *Puk.* 16:10.

2. *Hoo.* To be exhibited; manifested.

I-KE-A-KA, *v.* *Ike*, to know, and *aka*, clear. To know clearly; to perceive distinctly. SYN. with ikepaka, ikelea.

I-KE-I-KE, *v.* See IKE. To see; to know, &c. *Hoo.* To explain; to exhibit; to show; to bear witness. *Sol.* 10:32.

I-KE-I-KE, *s.* *Hoo.* A testimonial; a superscription.

I-KE-I-KE, *adj.* Showing; witnessing.

I-KE-MA-KA, *s.* *Ike*, to see, and *maka*, the eye. An eye witness; one that sees with his own eyes, or knows a thing of his own knowledge; a witness. *Ier.* 32:10.

I-KE-MA-KA, *v.* *Ike*, to see, and *maka*, the eye. To know positively; to see with the eyes.

I-KI, *adj.* Small, diminutive; little; often used in compounds; as, *kamaiki, keiki*, the little one, &c.; he wahi mea uuku, he liilii.

I-KI, *adv.* Not at all; nearly; ke hookoe *iki* nei no ka aie o ke aupuni, there remains very little of the government debt.

I-KI, *v.* *Hoo.* To spare; to hold back; to make small. *Isa.* 54:2.

I-KI-I-KI, *v.* To be pressed; to be compelled to do a thing; to be compelled to act or not to act against one's will.

2. To be weary of refraining from. *Ier.* 20:9.

3. To pant for breath, as one dying.

I-KI-I-KI, *s.* A confinedness; want of room.

2. A close, tight room.

3. Severe pain; panting for breath; strangulation; the pangs of death.

4. A siege of a city. *Ier.* 19:9

I-KI-I-KI, *adj.* Close and hot, as the confined air of a crowded room.

2. Tight, as a bandage or clothes made too small.

I-KI-I-KI, *s.* Name of the fifth month of the Hawaiian year.

I-KI-KI, *s.* Disquietness; suffering. *Hal.* 38:2. Stifling for want of air; hot.

I-KI-KI, *s.* See IKIIKI above and OIKIKI. Name of a month, May.

I-KI-MA-KU-A, *s.* Name of a kind of stone out of which the maika stones were made.

I-KO, *v.* To imitate. SYN. with hoko.

I-KO-I, *s.* A buoy; a float. See LALEA.

I-KU, *int.* A word of encouragement to persons about to exert themselves in any exercise, thus: *iku*, ikuku, oinana, oimokuo, oia, o ka holo no ia.

I-KU-A, *s.* Ancient name of one of the months; also written *ikuwa*; October.

I-KU-I-KU, *s.* An offensive smell. SYN. with okaoka.

I-KU-WA, *s.* Name of one of the Hawaiian months. See the above.

I-KU-WA, *adj.* A lohe oe i ka leo *ikuwa* (bird singing) a na manu. *Laieik.* 149.

I-KU-WA, *v.* Ka leo o na kahuli e *ikuwa* ana; singing like birds. *Laieik.* 149.

I-LA, } *s.* A dark spot on the skin; he
I-LAA, } wahi eleele iki ma ke kino.

I-LAI-LA, *adv.* The auialo of *laila*; there; in that place; to that place. *Gram.* § 165:2.

I-LAI-LAU. See LAULELE.

I-LA-LO, *adv.* The auialo of *lalo*, down; down; downwards; below. *Gram.* § 161.

I-LA-MU-KU, *s.* An officer whose business it was to enforce the orders of a chief, or of a judge.

2. An executioner; a destroyer. *Kanl.* 16:18.

3. An executive officer. 1 *Oihl.* 23:4.

4. In modern times, a marshal; a sheriff.

I-LI, *v.* To strike, rub or scrape on the ground, as a canoe, boat or ship. *Kin.* 8:4,

2. To strike or run aground, as a ship; to strike a rock.

3. To be cast away; ua *ili* ka moku a nahaha, the ship stranded and was broken up.

4. To rest on land, as a boat when the water subsides; to stick fast.

5. To lay upon one, as good or bad, i. e., to make responsible. *Nah.* 18:1.

6. To come upon one, as a good or a blessing. *Kanl.* 28:2. Also,

7. As a curse or evil. *Kanl.* 28:15.

8. To fall or come to one, as an inheritance, or to become one's by inheritance. *Ios.* 24:32.

9. To inherit, as land. *Kin.* 15:8.

10. To pass over, as the moon over the surface of the ocean; ua *ili* ka mahina maluna o ka *ili* o ke kai.

11. *Hoo.* To cause one to inherit, as an estate, i. e., to give one an inheritance.

12. To bring upon one, as evil, i. e., to come upon one, as a judgment; to fasten the charge of evil upon one.

13. To count or consider a thing as belonging to one; to impute, or attribute something to one, &c. *Kin.* 15:6.

14. To attribute to another a plan which was partly his own; *hooili* aku la na ke kahuna wale no ka olelo, a huna i kana iho, he attributed the plan to the priest, and concealed his own part.

15. To cause a transfer of property or a kingdom to another; i *hooili* pono aku ai o Kaahumanu i ke aupuni no Liholiho, that Kaahumanu might *transfer* the kingdom to Liholiho as his.

16. To lade, as a beast of burden; to take in, as a passenger on board a ship; ke *hooili* nei i ka ukana o ka moku.

17. To be stopped, as a stone rolling down a hill, i. e., to strike.

18. Applied also to a person pursued in battle until he is angry with the pursuer, and turns upon his adversary with such fury that he also runs in turn.

I-LI, *s.* The stranding of a ship on a shore or rock.

2. The descent of property from parents to children.

3. To dashing of one thing against another.

I-LI, *s.* The skin of a person or animal. *Iob.* 16:15. Eia mai na *ili* o kanaka, he keokeo kekahi, he ulaula kahi, he eleele kekahi.

2. The bark of a tree; the outer rind of any vegetable; the husk or shuck of fruit.

3. The surface of the ground or sea; na ka la e hoomalamalama i ka *ili* o ka honua, the sun enlightens the surface of the earth; maluna o ka *ili* kai kona hele, his going was upon the surface of the sea.

4. Mea *ili*, whatever is made of skin. *Nah.* 31:21.

5. The surface of any substance; elua no ano o na *ili*, o ka *ili* laumania, a o ka *ili* hualala. *Anahon.*

I-LI, *s.* The name of a small district of land, next smaller than an ahupuaa. There are thirty-three *ilis* in the ahupuaa of Honolulu.

I-LI, *s.* A small smooth stone worn by the water; a pebble.

I-LI, *s.* In *geometry*, a side; a surface; *ili* o ke kai, surface of the sea; *ili* o ka aina, surface of the land.

I-LI-AU, *s.* A species of bush in the for est; nana aku he ka moloua ka *iliau.*

I-LI-A-HI, *s.* Sandal-wood; a deeply scented, hard wood, formerly a wood of traffic.

I-LI-E, *s.* A kind of vine; with its roots scars are made in the skin in mourning for the dead or *kumakena.* The operation is called *kuni.*

I-LI-I-LI, *s.* See ILI above. Small, smooth stones worn by the water; pebbles. *Sol.* 26:8. Gravel. *Isa.* 48:19.

2. Small stones used in playing at konane. *Laieik.* 38.

I-LI-I-LI, *v. Hoo.* To collect; to gather in, as the fruits of harvest. *Isa.* 17:5.

2. To gather up; to pick up, as fuel. *Nah.* 15:32.

3. To gather, as grapes of a vintage. *Kanl.* 24:20, 21.

4. To collect together, as small pieces of anything.

5. To obtain, as property. *Kin.* 12:5. Wa *hooiliili* ai, harvest time. Note.—Hooiliili is the opposite of *hoolei. Ioan.* 6:12.

I-LI-I-LI, *s. Hoo.* A gathering in; a col lection; a harvest.

I-LI-O, *s.* A dog; *ilio* hihiu, a wolf; *ilio* hahai, a greyhound. *Sol.* 30:31.

2. The cross beam of a house.

3. Fig. A catamite. *Hoik.* 22:15.

4. A stingy, close man.

I-LI-O, *adv.* I hele aku, ea, mai, maka-maka *ilio* i ka huelo ka ike, a proverbial expression: the end of a friendship that once existed, false friendship remains.

I-LI-O-E-HA, *s.* A species of fish.

I-LI-O-HA, *s.* A species of limu having broad leaves; he limu lau palahalaha.

2. Also a plant with small leaves.

I-LI-O-HAE, } *s.* Epithet of a wolf;
I-LI-O-HI-HIU-HAE, } a fierce, cross dog. *Lam. Haw.* 23:1, 1.

I-LI-O-LE-LO, *v.* Ili and *olelo*, to talk. To go about tattling; retailing scandal; e imi olelo, hooholoholo olelo.

I-LI-O-MA-KA, *s.* Ili, skin, and *omaka*, prepuce. The foreskin. See OMAKA.

I-LI-HAU, *s.* The bark of the hau tree, of which ropes are made; he kaula *ilihau*.

I-LI-HEE, *s.* A shrub, the bark of whose root is very acrid; also *hiliee*.

I-LI-HE-LO, *s.* Name of the class of farmers who worked but little; o ka poe mahiai liilii, ua kapaia lakou he mahiai *ilihelo*.

I-LI-HIA, *v.* To be astonished at an event. *Oihk.* 26:32.

2. To be offended, as with a servant who has done mischief.

3. To be in great fear; ua *ilihia* makou i ka makau maoli.

4. *Hoo.* To cause fear or trepidation; me he mea la e *hooilihia* ka olelo a na kahuna.

I-LI-HI-A, *adj.* Quick tempered.

I-LI-HI-A, *s.* Great fear; trepidation; he makau, he weliweli.

I-LI-HI-LAU-NA, *v.* To reach or arrive at; to associate with.

I-LI-HO-LO, *s.* Name of those who worked at mahiai only part of the day. See ILIPILO.

I-LI-HU-NE, *adj.* Ili, skin, and *hune*, poor, i. e., poor to the skin. Poor; destitute of property; without clothing.

I-LI-HU-NE, *v.* To be poor; without prop-erty. 2 *Sam.* 12:1. The opposite of *waiwai*. *Hoo.* To make or cause one to become poor. 1 *Sam.* 2:7.

I-LI-KAI, *s.* Ili, surface, and *kai*, sea. LIT. The surface (skin) of the sea; the sur-face of any substance.

I-LI-KAI, *adj.* Horizontal; kaha *ilikai*, a horizontal line. *Ana. Hon.* 4.

I-LI-KA-LA, } *s.* Ili, skin, and *kala*, rough;
I-LI-KA-NI, } epithet of the shark skin. The skin stretched over and fastened to a cocoa-

nut shell, which formed a kind of drum; penei e hana'i, o ka puniu, o ka *ilikala* (shark skin paha,) ka pili me ka pilali o ke kukui, a paa, kakoo me ke kaula a maloo, waiho a maloo, alaila, hookani iho me ka uhane.

I-LI-KI, *v.* To dash; to strike against,

1. As a weapon of war.

2. As rain in a storm.

3. As water in a torrent; i ka manawa e kaua ai, *iliki* iho la ka pohaku me ka laau, nahoahoa ke poo; i ko laua hele ana i ka makaikai a Koolau, *iliki* iho ana ka ua; aole o kanamai o ka *iliki* ana mai a ka wai o na kahawai.

I-LI-KI, *s.* A dashing; a striking against, &c.

I-LI-KI, *s.* A varnish made of the kukui bark, laui, opuumaia, &c.

I-LI-KO-NA, *s.* A wart; a small, hard protuberance on the skin; he puupuu ino paakiki, wanawana liilii.

I-LI-KO-LE, } *adj.* Ili, skin and *kole*,
I-LI-KO-NE, } raw. Very poor; destitute, so much that life is undesirable; e aho ka make ia Milu, loaa ke akua o ka po, it is better to die by Milu and be received by the god of night.

I-LI-KO-LE, *adj.* Not thoroughly ripe, as the cocoanut; not oolea loa; he niu *ilikole*.

I-LI-LI-HIA, *adj.* See ILIHIA. Excited; filled with fear.

2. Dignified; full of dread.

I-LI-LU-A, *s.* Ili, skin, and *lua*, second.

1. The second or new skin; applied to old age.

2. The seventh stage of life—wrinkled skin.

3. An aged person; he pakaka ka ili.

I-LI-LU-NA, *s.* Ili, skin, and *luna*, upper; above. LIT. The upper skin, i. e., the sur-face of a thing; the top.

I-LI-MA, *s.* A shrub with green and yel-low flowers; the shrub is used for fuel. See APIKI. He apiki, he lei apiki.

2. The name of a region next below the apaa on the side of the mountains.

I-LI-MA-NO, *s.* Ili, skin, and *mano*, shark. LIT. The shark skin; used for making drum heads; oia ka ili i hanaia i ka pahu haekeeke.

I-LI-NA, *s.* A burying place where many are buried (where only one is buried, it is called *hunakele*); a grave. *Oihl.* 34:4. With *kupapau*, a burying place. *Kin.* 49:30. A sepulchre. *Neh.* 2:5. A tomb; same as *hale kupapau*.

2. *Hoo.* An inheritance. *Kanl.* 18:2. A possession. *Kin.* 48:4.

3. An heir; one to whom an estate or inheritance has fallen or is to fall; he mea e hooili ai ka waiwai a ka mea i make.

I-LI-NA-WAI, *s.* *Ilina* and *wai,* water. A place where a brook loses itself in the ground. LIT. The grave of the water.

I-LI-PA-LA-PA-LA, *s.* *Ili,* skin, and *palapala,* to write. A skin written upon; a parchment. *2 Tim.* 4:13.

I-LI-PI-LO, *s.* Name of the farmers who worked all day till dark; o ka poe mahiai nui a po ka la, ua kapaia lakou he mahiai *ilipilo;* those who worked little were called *ilihelo.*

I-LI-WAI, *adj.* *Ili,* surface, and *wai,* water. Horizontal; level. *Ana. Hon.* 4. He kaha *iliwai,* a horizontal line. See ILIKAI.

I-LI-WA-HI-WA-HI, *s.* *Ili,* skin, and *wahi,* covering. A sword scabbard.

I-LO, *s.* A maggot; a body worm. *Iob.* 7:5.
2. A worm consuming vegetables. *Puk.* 16:20.
3. Worms of various kinds; na *ilo* ilima, na *ilo* baka, na *ilo* liilii e ulu ae ana ma ka nahelehele.

I-LO-I-LO, *v.* To be wormy; full of worms, as meat, or as worms on vegetables; ua *iloilo* ka ia, ua kau ia nae e ka *iloilo* liilii. *Hoo.* Ua *hooiloilo* ke kahuna e make.

I-LO-I-LO, *adj.* Wormy; full of worms or maggots.

I-LO-KO, *prep.* I and *loko,* internal. In; inside of; within. *Gram.* § 161.

I-LO-LI, *s.* A strong smell; scent; applied to the shark; ka *iloli* o ka mano.
2. The unpleasant sensations of pregnancy.

I-LU-NA, *prep.* I and *luna,* above. Up; upward; upon; above. *Gram.* § 161.

I-LU-NA, *adv.* Up; upward.

I-MI, *v.* To search for a thing as lost; to look after with a view to find.
2. To seek, as for knowledge, for riches, for pleasure.
3. E *imi* hala, to seek some evil against one; to devise devices. *Ier.* 18:18. To seek occasion against. *Dan.* 6:4, 5.

I-MI-I-MI, *v.* Freq. of the foregoing. To seek earnestly or diligently for a thing; ua *imiimi* wahi dala no ke kino; ua *imiimi* wahi noho hou aku.

I-MI-HA-LA, *v.* To seek occasion against. See IMI above.

I-MI-HA-LE, *s.* Epithet of one who is a seeker of property, in distinction from one who is to possess it, who is the *noho hale;* o Kamehameha ka *imihale,* o Liholiho ka noho hale.

I-MI-HA-LE, *v.* To seek an inheritance for one's children, as Kamehameha did and left it for his children.

I-MI-HIA, *v.* Pass. of *imi* for *imiia.* To be sought; looked for. *Ezek.* 5:17; also 6:1.

I-MI-O-LE-LO, *v.* *Imi* and *olelo,* word, speech.
1. To lie; to obtain a thing by false statements.
2. To prattle; to tell tales; to slander.

I-MO, *v.* To wink. *Hal.* 35:19. See AMO. Conj. 5th, *iimo,* to wink; to triumph, as one in mischief. *Sol.* 6:13.
2. To snap, as the eyes on drinking something very acid.
3. To twinkle, as a star; *imo* ou iho na maka o ke koa, kuku ka lihilihi, okalakala ka hulu o ke koa, pai o kukae me ka naau.

I-MO, *s.* E lele i ka *imo* o ka lani; a look; a looking.

I-MO-I-MO, *v.* See above. To wink repeatedly; to wink fast. *Iob.* 15:12. Ua *imoimo* na maka i ka ue.

I-MO-I-MO, *adv.* Very high; very far off; at a great distance; poiuiu loa; ua kauia na hua o ka niu iluna loa, a *imoimo* ke nana aku, the fruit of the cocoanut hangs very high, it is *very high* (there is winking) to look at it.

I-MU, *s.* A place for baking made by heating stones underground; an oven for baking vegetables or meat. *Puk.* 7:28. See also UMU.

I-MU-A, *prep.* I and *mua,* first. Before; in front of; in presence of; *imua* no o Kekuokalani a make; aole i hoi ihope, *imua* no ka poe koa a make.

I-MU-LI, *prep.* I and *muli,* remainder. Behind; coming after; in the rear.

I-MU-LOA, *s.* *Imu* and *loa,* long. A long oven; an oven for baking men.

I-MU-LOA, *v.* To perform the process of baking men, sometimes as offerings to the gods and sometimes for medicinal purposes.

I-NA, *v.* To judge; to set in order; to settle a difficulty.
2. To pry up; to raise by means of a lever.
3. To sound, as from a distance; e *ina* mai ka leo o mea e hea mai.
4. To modulate or ease off, as the syllables at the end of a mele line; *ina* leo; *hooina* leo, same.

I-NA, Used in an imperative inviting sense, come on; go to; let us do (something); mostly in the plural; *ina* kakou, &c. *Kin.* 11:4; also 37:20. *Adverbially,* be quick;

used in exhortation, to make speed; *ina* hoi. *Luk.* 20:14. Come on, let us do this or that; *ina* no, though; albeit. *Ezek.* 2:6.

I-NA, *s.* A species of sea egg; poke *ina*; he ia poepoe kalakala.

I-NA, *adv.* With *no*, for indeed.

I-NA, *conj.* If; it implies condition, and is usually followed by a corresponding *ina*, answering to *then*, in the last member of the sentence; as *ina* i makemake mai oe ia mea, *ina* ua kii mai oe, *if* you had desired that thing, *then* (if) you would have come for it.

I-NA, *interj.* O that. *Iob.* 29:2. I wish that. *Neh.* 22:29. Would to God. *Puk.* 16:3. *Ina* no wau i make nou, O that I had died for thee. 2 *Sam.* 18:33. *Ina* aole makou e hiki mai, O that we had not come. *Laieik.* 67.

I-NAI, *s.* The little delicacies which give relish to food; condiments.

I-NAI-NA, *v.* To hate. *Kin.* 37:4. To be angry with; to grieve.

   2. To have the feelings hurt by another's conduct; to abhor; to dislike. *Oihk.* 26:15.

   3. *Hoo.* To excite one's anger or rage. *Ier.* 32:31.

I-NAI-NA, *v.* To shake; to move; to stir; paonioni.

I-NAI-NA, *s.* Anger; hatred. *Kin.* 3:15. Malice; wrath.

   2. The reddish evacuation which precedes labor; ua hemo ka *inaina* o ke keiki, kokoke paha ka manawa e hanau ai.

I-NAI-NA,   } *adj.* Angry; abominable;
I-NAI-NA-IA, }   hateful; causing one to be angry. *Oihk.* 18:29, 30.

I-NA-HE-A, *adv. int.* When? at what time? referring only to past time; *inahea* oe i hele mai ai? when did you come? inehinei, yesterday.

I-NA-LE-O, *s.* Any word which stands before nouns to limit and direct the sense; in *grammar*, a preposition.

I-NA-LU-A, *s.* A basket used in catching fish; he huehue, he laau hihi, he mea hopu ia.

I-NA-MO-NA, *s.* The meat of the kukui nut roasted and pounded up with salt as a relish for food.

I-NA-NA, *v.* To walk about idly, without any definite object; to loaf about.

I-NA-NA,   } *v.* IMP. Let me see; let me
I-NA-NE, }   hear; show it to me; exhibit it, &c. according to the subject. NOTE.— The last form, *inane*, is better language than the other.

I-NE, *conj.* If; used less frequently than *ina*. See INA, *conj.*

I-NEA, *s.* Fruitless labor; hard toil with little reward; na hoa o keia *inea*, o ka poe nana a waele.

I-NE-A, *adj.* Hard to be obtained, costing much time and labor with liability to loss; o kuu hoapili, hoa *inea*, my companion, a friend *hard to be obtained*; o keia wahi *inea*, this *hard living* place. *Hoo.* E o'u hoa *hooinea*, O my *long tried* friend.

   2. Deceitful; vain; useless. *Sol.* 11:18. He hana *inea* ka hewa, sin is labor without reward; he hana *inea* ka inu rama, rum drinking does not pay.

I-NEI, *adv.* Here. See IANEI.

I-NE-HI-NEI,   } *adv.* Yesterday. *2 Nal.*
I-NEI-HI-NEI, }   9:26. *Inehinei* kela la aku, day before yesterday. *Fig. Iob.* 8:9. See NEHI.

I-NE-KA,   } *s. Eng.* Ink; Hawaiian word
I-NI-KA, }   waieleele. 3 *Ioan.* 13.

I-NI-HA, *s.* An inch.

I-NI-I-NI-KI, *v.* To pinch a little; to pinch often or frequently. See next word.

I-NI-KI, *v.* To pinch with thumb and finger; to snatch away; to carry off; kaili, lawe lilo; to pinch off, as the bud of a plant.

I-NI-KI-NI, *s. Eng.* Indians; applied to the aborigines of America; he nui na lahui *Inikini* e noho ana ma Amerika, many are the tribes of *Indians* in America.

I-NO, *v.* To hurt; to injure; to render uncomfortable; oia ka mea e *ino* ai ke kino, that is what *injures* the body.

   2. To be or become worthless. *Ier.* 18:4.

   3. *Hoo.* To disfigure. *Oihk.* 19:27. To trouble with evil. *Puk.* 7:27.

   4. To punish; to afflict; to suffer evil.

   5. To reproach; to vex; to tease; to harass.

   6. To curse.

I-NO, *s.* Iniquity. *Puk.* 37:7. Depravity; anything which is contrary to the general good.

   2. The poor quality of a thing; eia kekahi, o ke *ino* o ka pepa a me ka inika, the *poor quality* of the paper and ink.

   3. The substance in the intestines; honowa.

   4. *Hoo.* Violence; iniquity; cursing.

   5. A gale; a storm of wind and rain; he *ino* huhu, a horrible tempest.

I-NO, *adj.* Bad; wicked; vile; sinful; mea *ino*, an abomination; an evil thing. *Mat.* 24:15.

I-NO, *adv.* Badly; wickedly.

I-NO, A strong intensive, used in both a good and bad sense; it expresses very great feeling of affection or hatred; aloha *ino, very great* love, or with a peculiar tone of voice, very great contempt; he mea minamina *ino* ka waa, a thing of *very great* loss is the canoe.

I-NO-I-NO, *v.* See INO above. To make sad; to be grieved; no ke aha la i *inoino* ai kou maka? why is your countenance *sad?* *Neh.* 2:2.

2. To be very tempestuous, as the sea. *Iona.* 1:13.

3. *Hoo.* To defile; to deface; to pollute.

I-NO-I-NO, *s.* Badness; worthlessness; indecency; ua like ka *inoino* me ka pupuka, a me ka pelapela, a me ke alauka.

2. A bad disposition; a mind for doing harm. *Laieik.* 101.

I-NO-I-NO, *adj.* Very poor; lean; miserable; despicable.

I-NO-A, *s.* A name; name of a person, place or thing.

I-NO-A, *Kainoa,* an adverbial expression; just as if; I thought; *kainoa* ua pau loa na kanaka Hawaii i ka ike au, I *thought* all the people of Hawaii knew how to swim; it is connected with some degree of surprise, or contrariety of opinion.

I-NU, *v.* To drink, as water or any liquid.

2. *Hoo.* To cause to drink. *Nah.* 20:8.

3. To give drink to; to water, as a flock. NOTE.—This verb sometimes takes the syllable *ha* between the causative *hoo* and the verb; as *hoohainu. Kin.* 24:14.

I-NU, *s.* Drink; any liquid for drinking; he *inu* awa, awa drinking.

> Inu aku i ka awa o Koukou
> Ka awa lau hinalo aala
> Awa o Mamalahoa he hoa—e.

I-NU-WAI, *s. Inu,* to drink, and *wai,* water. Name of a sea breeze at Lehua on Kauai.

I-NU-WAI, *s.* Epithet of such Hawaiians as have signed the total abstinence pledge; ka poe puali *inuwai,* the army of *water drinkers.*

I-PO, *v.* To cohabit before marriage or without marriage; to practice lasciviousness; to commit fornication.

I-PO, *s.* A sweetheart; a paramour. *Ier.* 4:30.

I-PO-I-PO, *adj. Hoo.* Making lascivious gestures while eating. 1 *Pet.* 4:3. Ahaaina *hooipoipo,* a lascivious feast.

I-PU, *s.* A general name for all kinds of gourds, calabashes, melons, pumpkins, &c.

2. A general name for small containers, as dish, cup, mug, tumbler, &c. *Kanl.*

23:25. Each kind is designated by some additional word expressive of its quality or use, which see under their own names.

I-PU-AI, *s.* A vessel (calabash) for containing food; a me kana mau *ipuai.*

I-PU-AI-MA-KA, *s. Ipu, ai* and *maka,* green; fresh. A melon; a fruit to be eaten raw. *Nah.* 11:5.

I-PU-A-HI, *s. Ipu,* cup, and *ahi,* fire. A censer. *Nah.* 4:14.

I-PU-A-LA, *s. Ipu,* cup and *ala,* odoriferous. A box for containing odors; also a musk-melon.

I-PU-AU-AU, *s. Ipu* and *auau,* to wash. A wash-basin; a laver. *Puk.* 30:18.

I-PU-A-WA, *s. Ipu* and *awa,* bitter. The bitter calabash.

I-PU-A-WA-A-WA, *s.* See above. The bitter or poison calabash.

I-PU-IA, *s. Ipu* and *ia,* meat; fish. A meat dish; a flesh pot. *Puk.* 16:3.

I-PU-I-NI-KA, *s. Ipu* and *inika,* ink. An inkstand.

I-PU-HAO, *s. Ipu* and *hao,* iron. An iron pot. 2 *Nal.* 4:38.

I-PU-HA-O-LE, *s. Ipu* and *haole,* foreigner. A foreign *ipu,* i. e., a water-melon.

I-PU-HO-LOI, *s. Ipu* and *holoi,* to wash. A laver; a wash-basin. 1 *Nal.* 7:38.

I-PU-HO-LO-HO-LO-NA, *s. Ipu* and *holoholona,* crawling things. A calabash for fishing worms. *Lam. Haw.* 25:4, 3.

I-PU-KA, *s.* See PUKA. A door; a gate; a place for entering a house or an inclosure. *Puk.* 32:27. A window; the gate of a city.

I-PU-KA-IA, *s.* A calabash for containing fish (*ka* inserted); o ke aloha ka mea i oi aku ka maikai mamua o ka umeki poi a me ka *ipukaia,* love is that which excels in excellency the poi dish and the *fish bowl.*

I-PU-KA-LUA, *s.* The name of a vegetable.

I-PU-KA-PU-A-HI, *s. Ipu* and *kapuahi,* a fire place. A censer. *Oih.* 16:12.

I-PU-KU-KUI, *s. Ipu* and *kukui,* fruit of the kukui. A candlestick; a lamp. *Puk.* 25:31.

I-PU-KU-NI-A-LA, *s. Ipu* and *kuni,* to burn, and ala, incense. A censer. *Nah.* 16:6.

I-PU-LA-AU, *s. Ipu* and *laau,* wood. A wooden vessel. *Oihk.* 15:12.

I-PU-LEI, *s.* Applies to a person with a large body and small legs; a word of reproach to the people of Kohala; *ipulei* Kohala na ka moaeku.

I-PU-LE-PO, *s. Ipu* and *lepo,* earth; clay. An earthern vessel. *Oihk.* 15:12. A cup; a potter's vessel. *Hal.* 2:9.

I-PU-LU, *s. Pulu* iii, *ipulu* iii. See PULU. The *i* does not belong to the word. Fine pulu, in distinction from *pulu haapu.*

I-PU-NUI, *s. Ipu* and *nui,* large. The sea of Solomon's temple. 2 *Nal.* 25:16.

I-PU-PU, *s. Ipu* and *pu,* fruit of the squash kind. A pumpkin; a squash.

I-PU-WAI-AU-AU, *s.* A wash-bowl; ina lawe ia mai kona *ipuwaiauau;* this epithet used to be applied to those who kept the genealogies of the chiefs, because they managed to wash the characters of the chiefs so far as their pedigree was concerned; ua kapaia ka poe kuauhau he *ipuwaiauau* no na alii e hoomaemae ai.

I-PU-BA-KA, *s. Ipu* and *baka* (*Eng.*), tobacco. A tobacco pipe.

I-PU-TI, *s. Ipu* and *ti* (*Eng.*), tea. A teapot.

I-WA, *num. adj.* Nine; the number nine; also *aiwa* and *eiwa.*

I-WA, *s.* A thief; the word comes from *Oiwa,* a notorious thief who lived long ago and obtained the surname of *Oiwahue,* i. e., Oiwathief.

I-WA, *s.* The name of a large bird with black feathers.

I-WAE-NA, *prep.* In the midst; between; among.

iwa

I-WAE-NA-KO-NU, *s.* The center of a circle; the middle; in the midst of. *Lunk.* 20:42.

I-WA-I-WA, *adj.* Learned; intelligent; skillful. See AIWAIWA.

2. Also the name of a plant; he mea ulu e like me ka palaa, ua ulana pa ia me ka papale mauu.

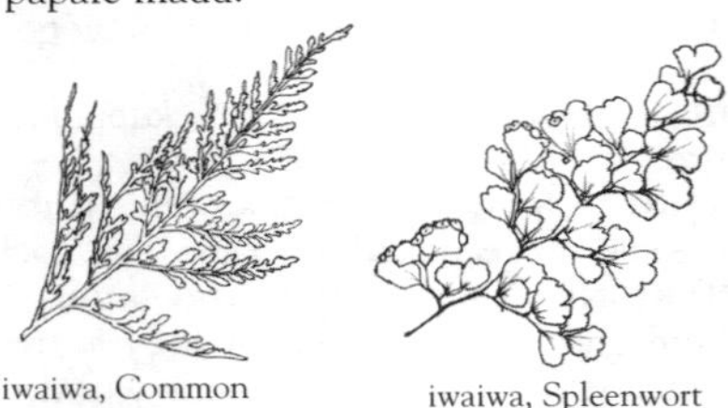

iwaiwa, Common Maidenhair variety

iwaiwa, Spleenwort variety

I-WA-HO, *prep. I* and *waho,* out of. Out; out of; without.

I-WA-KA-LU-A, *num. adj.* Twenty; the number twenty; with the article it becomes a noun.

I-WI, *s.* A bone.

2. The midrib of a vegetable leaf.

3. The side of an upland field of kalo.

4. A cocoanut shell; the rind of sugarcane.

5. The stones stuck up along the boundaries of ilis, or rather lands; sometimes a low stone wall; e kuhikuhi i ka iwi o ko ka poe kahiko wahi i mahiai, to point out the boundary stones of the places where the ancients cultivated.

6. Any hard broken material; the remnants of other things, as corn cobs, the remains of lime pits; paiwi.

7. Used FIG. for near kindred. *Kin.* 29:14. Alaila pomaikai kaua, ola na *iwi* iloko o ko kaua mau la elemakule. *Laieik.* 9. Then we two shall be happy, our *descendants* shall live in the days of our old age. See the names of some of the bones of the human frame below. He *iwi* halua oe; he *iwi* kau i ka awaloa, reproachful epithets.

I-WI, *s.* The name of a small bird with red feathers; o ka *iwi,* he ulaula ka hulu.

I-WI, *v.* To turn aside; to be crooked, as the eyes of cross-eyed persons.

I-WI, } *adj.* Crooked; pointed;
I-WI-I-WI, } curved, as most bones are; ina i ehuehu me ke kikala, he hulu *iwi* ia puaa.

I-WI-A, *s. Iwi* and *a,* the jaw. A jawbone. *Lunk.* 15:15.

I-WI-AO-AO, *s. Iwi* and *aoao,* side. A side bone; the rib. 2 *Sam.* 2:23.

I-WI-I-WI, *adj.* Poor in flesh; thin. LIT. Bony.

I-WI-A-LA-LO, *s. Iwi* and *a,* jaw, and *lalo,* under. The under jawbone.

I-WI-A-LU-NA, *s. Iwi* and *a,* jaw, and *luna,* upper. The upper jawbone.

I-WI-E-LE-LO, *s. Iwi* and *elelo,* the tongue. The tongue bone. *Anat.* 14.

I-WI-O-LE, *s.* Name of certain kinds of koi or adz; o ka *iwiole* kekahi koi.

I-WI-O-PE-A-PE-A, *s.* Name of a bone in a person's head. *Anat.* 8. The bat-bone.

I-WI-U-LU-NA, *s. Iwi* and *uluna,* pillow. The bone of the upper arm. LIT. The pillow bone.

I-WI-U-MAU-MA, *s. Iwi* and *umauma,* breast. The breast bone.

I-WI-HI-LO, *s. Iwi* and *hilo,* thigh. The thigh bone. *Anat.* 21.

I-WI-HOE-HOE, *s. Iwi* and *hoehoe,* paddle. The shoulder bone; the shoulder blade.

I-WI-HO-PE, *s.* The skull bone of the back part of the head. *Anat.* 7.

I-WI-HU-A, *s. Anat.* 6.

I-WI-KA, *s. Iwi* and *ka.* A bone near the

seat.

I-WI-KA-E-LE (i-wi-ka-la), *s.* The hull of a ship; the body of a canoe; kalai ia ka *iwikaele.*

I-WI-KA-LA-KU-A, *s.* The bones of a fish which run up from the backbone.

I-WI-KA-LA-LO, *s.* The bones of a fish which run down from the backbone.

I-WI-KA-NA-KA, *s. Iwi* and *kanaka,* human being. A human bone. *Nah.* 19:16.

I-WI-KA-NA-NA, *s.* Name of a bone in the front part of the head. *Anat.* 8.

I-WI-KA-NO, *s. Iwi* and *kano,* handle. The bone of the fore arm which joins the wrist.

I-WI-KE-E-LE, ⎱ *s.* The keel of a ship or
I-WI-KE-LE, ⎰ boat. See IWIKAELE.

I-WI-KU, *s. Iwi* and *ku,* to stand. One of the bones of the lower leg. *Anat.* 21.

I-WI-KU-A-MOO, *s. Iwi* and *kuamoo,* lizard. The bones of the back; the backbone.

I-WI-KU-A-MOO, *s.* One who attended the person of a high chief, executed his or-ders, &c.; ko ke alii mau *iwikaumoo* ponoi. *Laieik.* 35. See ILAMUKU and POELAMUKU.

I-WI-LAE, *s.* The bone of the forehead. *Anat.* 6.

I-WI-LEI, *s.* The shoulder bone; the collar bone; also,

2. The measure of a yard, i. e., from the breast bone to the end of the longest finger.

I-WI-MA-HA, *s.* The cheek bone; he wahi iwi ewaewa ia. *Anat.* 7.

I-WI-PI-LI, *s.* The double or united bones of the arm or leg.

2. A stalk of grass.

I-WI-POO, *s.* The skull bone. *Lunk.* 9:53.

I-WI-PO-NA, *s.* A joint; the bones of a person separated from each other and all jumbled together; hai pu ka *iwipona* i ka uwe. See IWI and PONA.

I-WI-PU-HA-KA, *s.* The bones of the loins.

I-WI-PU-NI-U, *s.* The skull bone.

I-BE-KA, *s.* Name of an animal; the ibex. *Sol.* 5:19.

O.

O, the fourth letter of the Hawaiian alphabet. It is the easiest sounded, next to *a,* of all the letters. Its sound is mostly that of the long English *o* in *note, bone,* &c. There is a difference in some words among Hawaiians as to the quantity; some say *mahope,* others say *mahoppy.* The first is the more correct.

O. This letter is prefixed to nouns, both common and proper, as well as to pronouns, to render them emphatic or definite. This *o* should be carefully distinguished from *o* the preposition. It may be called the *o emphatic.* It is used in particular-izing one or more persons or things from others. The *o emphatic* stands only before the auiku-mu or *nominative* case. *Gram.* § 53.

O, *prep.* Of; belonging to; ka hale *o* ke alii; the house *of* the chief; it is synonymous with ko; as, *ko ke alii hale,* the chief's house; but the words require to be differently disposed. In a few words it is interchangeable with *a.* See A *prep.* As, ka pane ana *o* ka waha, and ka pane ana *a* ka waha, the opening *of* the month.

O, *s,* A place, but indefinitely; mai *o* a *o,* from there to there; throughout. *Puk.* 27:18. From one side to the other; *io* a *io* ae, this way or that way; here or there.

More generally used adverbially; as,

O, *adv.* Yonder; there; ma *o* aku, beyond; mai *o* a *o,* from here to there, or from yonder to yonder, i. e., *everywhere.* It takes the several prepositions *no, ko, i, ma, mai. Gram.* § 165, 2d.

O is sometimes prefixed to the imperative mood instead of *e;* as, *o* hele oe, go thou, instead of *e* hele oe; *o* hoi oukou i na la ekolu, return ye for three days. In this case, for the sake of euphony, the *o* may take a *u* after it; as, *ou* hoi olua, return ye two.

O, *conj.* Lest. This is one form of the subjunctive mood; as, mai ai oukou *o* make, eat not *lest* ye die; also. *Nah.* 14:42.

O, *v.* To pierce, as with a sharp instrument; to dot into; to prick; to stab. SYN. with hou and ou. See OU.

2. To thrust; to thrust through; to gore, as a bullock. *Puk.* 21:28. A o iho la kekahi i ka polulu, some one *pierced* him with a long spear. See OO. PASS. To be pierced with a spear; mai *oia* ke kanaka i ka ihe. *Oia,* passive of *o,* to plunge under water, as a canoe or surf-board.

3. To extend or reach out, as the hand or finger; o ka mea e ae mai, e *o* mai lakou i ko lakou lima, those who assent, let them *stretch out* their hands; to stretch out the hand to take a thing. *Kin.* 8:9.

4. To stretch out the hand to trouble or afflict. *Puk.* 8:2.

5. To dip, as the fingers in a fluid. *Oihk.* 4:6. *Hoo*, for *hoo-o.* To stretch out, as the hand. *Puk.* 14:27. To thrust in the hand or finger into an orifice. *Anat.* 45.

O, *v.* To call for a thing desired. *Sol.* 2:3.

2. To answer to a call. *Ier.* 7:13. To answer to one's name when called; aohe i o mai, he *answered* not.

O, *s. Art.,* ke. An instrument to pierce with; any sharp pointed instrument; a fork; a sharp stick; ke o bipi, an ox goad. *Lunk.* 3:30. Ke o manamana kolu, a three-pronged fork. 1 *Sam.* 2:13.

2. The effect for the cause; a sharp pain in the body; a stitch in the side, as if pierced by a sharp instrument; a keen darting pain in the side of the chest.

O, *s.* Provision for a journey; traveling food. *Puk.* 12:39. E hoomakaukau oukou i o no oukou, prepare *food* for yourselves (for your journey); provision for a voyage; ke kalua iho la no ia o ke o holo i ka moana, that was the preparing the *provision* to go on the ocean.

O, *s.* The sprit of a snail.

O, *s.* The sound of a small bell; a tinkling sound. See OE.

O-A, *v.* To burst over, as a swollen stream.

2. To exceed; to go beyond; to pass over the point intended.

3. To shout, as a multitude of voices.

4. To roll, as a stone over a hill, or toss it over.

5. To change conversation.

O-A, *v.* To gag; to heave, as one sick at the stomach.

2. To split, as a board or log. See OOE, OWA and OAOA.

O-A, *v.* To be bereaved of children; to have lost one's children.

2. To be bereaved of parents; to become orphans.

O-A, *adj.* Bereaved; reduced to orphanage, as parents of children, or children of parents; aole pono na keiki oa makua ole, uncomfortable are children *bereaved* of parents.

O-A, *s.* A species of wood resembling mahogany.

O-A, *s.* A rafter of a house.

2. The timbers in the sides of a ship.

3. Name of the five parallel lines on which music is written.

O-A-AA, *s.* The name of large threads in cloth.

2. Similar appearances in bad potatoes when cooked.

O-AE-AE, *adj.* A little watery; not solid; oaeae ke kalo.

O-A-O-A (o-wa-o-wa), *adj.* Split; shattered; cracked, as wood; he laau oaoa. See OA 2.

O-A-O-A, *s.* The sound of water bubbling, as in a spring, or as water running out of the neck of a calabash.

O-A-O-A, *v.* To gurgle, as water purling or running unevenly, as through the neck of a calabash; oaoa ka wai o ka huewai; oaoa ka nuku o ka huewai pueo.

O-A-O-A. Ua oaoa au; ua oaoa ae loko ou; ua oaoa ka ilio.

O-A-O-A, *adj.* Calm; serene; joyful.

O-A-O-A-KA, *v.* To glitter; to glisten; to spangle.

O-A-O-A-KA, *s.* Name of a shell fish of the sea.

O-AU, *pers. pron.* 1st pers. sing. See AU. I; the o is emphatic, and sounded quickly with the following a, it becomes w, as wau; when the o is a little more heard, it becomes owau; hence the several forms:

1. *Au,* I, simple form.

2. *Oau,* I, with o emphatic.

3. *Wau,* I, the o and a sounded quickly together—w.

4. *Owau,* I, the third form again emphatic—owau. See these several forms in their places.

O-AU, *v.* To mew, as a cat. See OWAU.

O-AU (oa-o-au), *s.* The name of a species of fish; he oopu oau, he oaoau, he oluheluhe.

O-A-HI, *s.* Name of a kind of stone used in polishing canoes and wooden calabashes.

O-A-KA, *v.* To open suddenly; to open, as the mouth in the beginning of a speech; ua hoaka ae la oia e olelo aku ia lakou.

2. To open, as the eyes.

3. To open, as a book, a door, &c. FIG. To open the mouth, i. e., to have made a promise or vowed a vow. *Lunk.* 11:35, 36.

O-A-KA, *s.* The opening of the mouth to speak; ka oaka ana o ka waha, ka ekemu ana. *Sol.* 8:6.

2. The reflection of the sun on any luminous body.

3. A glimpse, glance or flashing of light; he oaka ana ae o ka uila, the flashing of lightning.

O-A-KA-A-KA, *s.* Repeated glancing;

flashing, &c. See OAOAKA.

O-A-KU-A, *s.* Name of the 14th day of the month. See AKUA 2.

O-A-LA, *v.* To toss up and whirl over and over.

2. To cast or throw away.

3. To rear, pitch and kick up, as an unbroken horse; *oala* ka lio, he lio holo ino me ka *oala* mai a hope.

O-A-LA, *s.* A tossing or brandishing, as a cane in the hand.

O-A-LA, *adj.* Name of a weapon or club thrown in fighting in war; o ka poe ike i ka laau *oala*, pa aku i ka newa.

O-A-LA, *s.* The name of a species of fish.

O-A-MA, *s.* Name of a kind of fish.

O-A-NEI, *adv.* Is it there? is it yonder?

O-A-PO-KO-LE, *s.* See OA, lines in music, and POKOLE, short. In *music*, a leger-line.

O-E, *pers. pron.*, second pers. sing. Thou; you; like *au*, it often takes *o* emphatic, as *ooe*; ooe no kau i manao ai, *you* thought of yourself; e noho *oe* me ka makaukau, do *you* sit ready.

O-E, *v.* See O. To prick; to probe; ke *oe* aku nei ia ia oukou me ka laau oioi, he *pricks* you with a sharp stick; to pick up, as with anything sharp.

O-E,
O-E-O-E, } *v.* To grate harshly, as one thing rubbing against another.

2. To whiz, as a ball or grape-shot through the air.

3. To make an indistinct continued sound; heaha la keia mea e *oeoe* ae nei? What is this thing that whizzes by us so?

4. To murmur, as a purling brook or running water.

O-E,
O-E-O-E, } *s.* A continued indistinct sound, as an axe upon a grindstone; as a pen drawn hard upon paper.

2. The continued sound of the surf; the sound of a ship passing through the water; the sound of an army marching at a distance. SYN. with nehe, pawewe, kamumu.

O-E,
O-E-O-E, } *s.* An inverted cone.

2. Epithet of a man who walks genteelly; superiority in some respects; kukulu ka *oe*, spoken of one riding or running swiftly on foot.

3. Epithet of a beautiful woman.

4. A lengthening; a stretching out of the neck. *Isa.* 3:16, 5. A monument; a pillar or sign of something.

O-E,
O-E-O-E, } *adj.* Long; applied to the neck of a person or thing; *oeoe* hoi ka a-i, he maikai no nae, *long* are their necks, but still they are handsome; *oeoe* ka

a-i o ka manu nene, long is the neck of the goose.

2. Applied to a sail; he pea *oeoe*, he kiekie, a long, high sail; applied to a house; hale *oeoe*; kukulu hou i hale *oeoe* a kapu.

O'-E,
O-E-O-E, } *s.* A drumming and singing together; ke *oe* omua, he wahi pahu kapu e ku ana iloko o omua, kauo aku la o Wakea ia Papa ma ke *o'e* omua.

O-E-O-E, *s.* A species of fish.

O-E-O-E-O, *adj.* Of different heights, some taller, some shorter.

O-E-O-E-WE, *adj.* Moving; fluttering, as a leaf in the wind; o oe ia e ka lau *oeoewe*, lau kapalili, thou art it, thou *moving* leaf, leaf fluttering.

O-E-HA, *adj.* See OHAA. Broken or bent, as an arm or leg.

O-E-NO, *adj.* See AHUOENO. *Laieik.* 112. Kauai mats.

O-I, *v.* To project out or over; to go beyond; exceed; generally with *mamua*. *Ioan.* 13:16.

2. To be more in any way; to be more excellent; to be greater naturally or morally; to be better. *Puk.* 1:9. To be excessive in some condition; as, ua *oi* paa loa, aole e hemo, it is very firmly fixed, it will not be moved.

3. To limp; to walk stiffly.

4. To approach; to draw near to, as in speaking to one. *Kin.* 44:18.

5. *Hoo.* To go beyond a prescribed limit. *Luk.* 3:13. Opposed to *hoemi*. *Kanl.* 13:1. Ua *hooi* aku oe i ka lono, thou *exceedest* the report. *2 Oihl.* 9:6.

6. To be sharp, as a knife, hatchet or spade. *Hal.* 45:5.

7. To sharpen; to set on edge, as the teeth. *Ezek.* 18:2. To sharpen, as a knife, on a steel or whetstone. See KEPA. *Oikepa*, a sharp instrument.

O-I, *s.* Excess; superiority; greatness. *Kanl.* 7:7.

2. An uneven number; difference in numbers, as in subtraction.

3. The sharp edge or point of a weapon; hence,

4. Offensive or defensive weapons; arms. *Luk.* 11:22. The sharp points of broken glass bottles; ua maikai ka omole mawaho; aka, ina e naha ka omole, ua piha loa oloko i ka *oi.*

5. The name of a small tree.

6. In *music*, a sharp.

O-I, *adj.* First; most excellent; greater; the best.

2. Sharp; full of sharp points; sharp, as a knife; ka hoana *oi*, the sharp hone; ke apuapu *oi*, the sharp file.

3. Poor; thin in flesh, that is, having sharp features.

O-I, } *adv.* While; whilst; during
O-I-AI, }   some time when a thing was doing; e hele i ka malamalama, *oi* kau ke ea i ke kino; *oi* huli wale lakou ia ia, *while* they sought for him in vain; while yet. 2 *Sam.* 3:35.

O-IA, *pers. pron.*, third pers. sing. He, she, or it; the *o* is emphatic. See IA. *Gram.* § 53 and 54, 3. Oia no wau, I am *he*; o ka laau hua ole, *oia* kana e oki aku, the branch not fruitful, *that* he cuts off; it is not so often used for things as for persons; *oia* iho no, he by himself. 1 *Nal.* 18:6.

O-I-A, *v.* To continue; to endure; to remain the same; *oia* mau no ia, it is always the same; he *oia* ka mea hawawa i ka heenalu, hai ka papa, the awkward person *always* breaks the board in riding on the surf. *Hoo.* To consent; to affirm; to assent; to confess; to admit a truth or fact; to profess. *Kanl.* 26:3. To avouch. *Kanl.* 26:17, 18. NOTE.—The ideas of being, existence, continuance, firmness and truth are from the same root, and has the same form as the third pers. sing. of the pronoun, and supply in some measure the place of the substantive verb. See *Gram.* § 136, 1st.

O-I-A, *s.* Yes; verity; truth; also *hoo*, same.

O-I-A, *adv.* Yes; it is so; a strong affirmative.

O-I-A, *s.* A species of fish.

O-I-AI, *adv.* While; whilst, &c. See OI. Oiai e ola ana kakou i keia manawa, *while* we are living at the present time.

O-IA-I-O, *s.* Oia, truth, and *io*, real.

1. Truth; verity; what is true; uprightness.

2. *Hoo.* A pledge; a thing given in pledge for another; a pawn. *Kin.* 38:20.

OI-A-I-O, *v. Hoo.* To declare to be true; to affirm; to verify; to prove. 1 *Nal.* 8:26.

2. To confess as an article of belief; to acknowledge; to trust in. *Kanl.* 1:32.

OI-A-I-O, *adv.* Truly; verily; of a truth. *Ioan.* 3:3. A strong asseveration of truth.

OI-A-IO, *adj.* True; not false; he *oiaio* maoli kana mau hana, aole keekee iki.

OI-A-NA, *int.* Indeed! truly! *Laieik.* 8.

OI-A-NA, } *v. imp.* Let it be seen; let
OI-A-NE, }   it appear; show it me, &c. SYN. with inane. Oiane kau palapala, show your book; sometimes written *oiana*. SYN.

also with hoike. E *oiane* oe i kau olele.

OI-O, *s.* Name of a species of fish.

2. Name of a kind of stone used in polishing canoes.

3. Name of a species of small bird.

O-IO, *s.* A company or troop of ghosts; he huakai uhane; the same in respect of ghosts as *huakai* is in respect of men.

O-I-O, *s.* A long bundle of salt or fish; he *oio* paakai; he *io* kekahi inoa; also called *io*.

2. The name of a fish that burrows in the sand; o ka *oio* ka ia noho ma ke one.

O-IO, *s.* O, fork, and *io*, flesh. A flesh hook; a flesh fork. *Puk.* 38:3.

OI-OI, *v.* To rest from fatigue, particularly the fatigue of walking. *Nah.* 10:33.

2. To move sideways; to turn the side to one. *Puk.* 20:15.

3. *Hoo.* To shoot out the lips, as in scorn.

OI-OI, *s.* Something sharp; excessive. FIG. A trial.

OI-OI, *adj.* Sharp; full of sharp points; mea *oioi*, pricks; sharp things.

2. Forward; presuming.

O-IO-IO, *v.* To pass and repass by numbers in quick succession.

OI-O-I-NA, *s.* See OIOI, to rest. A resting; a resting place for travelers, where is found some accommodations more than usual; a pile of stones; a tree; a bush, &c. *Kin.* 42:27.

OI-OI-KU, *v.* To struggle; to contend with some difficulty, as traveling in deep mud; *oioiku* ka hele ana o ka mea nui. See OIKU.

OI-HAA, *s.* A person with crooked limbs, but not so much as to hinder from business. See OHAA.

OI-HA-NA, *s.* Oi, principal, and *hana*, work.

1. A special duty or business; the work peculiar to one; an occupation; a trade. *Oih.* 18:3.

2. Duty; employment. *Kin.* 47:3. Service.

3. An observance; custom; ministry; labor; calling; office.

4. One's tools; instruments or apparatus for any business. *Puk.* 27:3. Na kapu kahiko a me na *oihana* wahahee, the ancient kapus and the false customs, i. e., customs founded on false notions; na *oihana* lapuwale, foolish customs; ke hoike mai nei na kumu a kakou i keia *oihana* o na aina naauao.

5. The name of the book of Acts in the New Testament.

OI-HA-NA-A-LII, *s.* Oihana and *alii*, king. A history of the acts of kings; name of the books in the Old Testament called Chronicles. 2 *Nal.* 13:8.

Oi-ha-na-ka-hu-na, *s.* *Oihana* and *kahuna*, priest.

1. Priesthood; the exercise of the priest's office. *Nah.* 18:1.

2. Name of the book *Leviticus.*

O-i-ki-pu-a-ho-la, *s.* The name of a pestilence in the time of Waia.

O-i-ki-i-ki, *s.* Name of the fifth month.

O-i-ki-ki, *s.* Name of a month; same as *ikiki.*

Oi-ku, *v.* To struggle, as one walking in deep mud. See **Oioiku.**

Oi-ku-wa, *s.* Name of the tenth month.

O-i-li, *v.* Kindred with *wili.* To twist; to roll up.

2. To roll up a cloth, kapa or paper.

3. To untwist; to spring back, as a bundle, when it gets loose; e opeope ia wahi mea a paa, o *oili* aku ia mea, hoka kakou. See **Wili.**

4. To feel uneasy; to be agitated with fear.

5. To faint; to be discomposed; to be agitated with strong emotions. *Mele Sol.* 5:6.

6. To ascend; to mount up, as an object seen at a distance; *oili* ka hale kula o Lahainaluna ke nana mai i ka moana; to rise in the mind, as a thought; *oili* mai la keia manao hou iloko o'u, this new idea came up into me.

7. To project; to extend beyond; similar to *kela;* e *oili* ae ana ka holo ana; ka *oili* ae no ia hele ana iwaho; o ka *oili* ae mawaho o ka upena holo ana.

O-i-li, *s.* The region of the heart; the seat of fear; lele ka *oili,* a fright; the seat of judgment; conscience; ka mea maloko e hoapono ana, a e hoahewa ana. *Kamak.* Lele ka *oili* o ka lani; lele i ka lani o ka *oili;* o ka lani, oia ka mea e lele ana me he koki la ia, me he hokulele la.

O-i-li, *s.* Name of a small fish; also *uwiwi.*

O-i-li, *adj.* Ke keiki *oili* wale, an untimely birth. *Kekah.* 6:3. Ka manu *oili* leo lea o ke kakahiaka, the bird of the morning *unfolding* a lovely voice.

O-i-li-la-pa, *s.* Name of a species of fish.

O-i-li-le-pa, *s.* Name of a species of small fish in the ocean resembling, but a little larger than the uwiwi. NOTE.—Perhaps this is the same as the foregoing.

O-i-li-lu-a, *v.* To go before; to project one thing before another. See **Hookela.**

O-i-li-pu-le-lo, *v.* *Oilipulelo* ke ahi o ka maile; to send lighted fire brands down a pali in the night, formerly a sport for chiefs.

O-i-li-wa-le, *adj.* Relating to an untimely birth; prematurely unfolded. *Kekah.* 6:3.

O-i-lo, *s.* He nahelehele liilii loa, e *oilo* ae ana ilalo; grass and other vegetables when it first springs up.

O-i-lo, *s.* Name of a species of fish; he *oilo* puhi.

2. The springing up or first shooting of plants and vegetables.

O-i-lu-a, *adj.* Oi, edge, point, and *lua,* double. Double edged; two edged, as a sword; same as *makalua.*

O-i-wi, *s.* See **Iwi,** *s.* The substantial part of a thing; that which gives character or adds ornament; the upper naked person of a well built man; o hele a hoike aku i ko *oiwi* i ke kumu; maikai ka *oiwi* o mea, kihi peahi lua, maikai ka *oiwi* ke nana aku, pakaka.

> Nani ka *oiwi* o Hilo i ka lehua
> Ke kui la i ke one i Waiolama
> Nani ke kino o ia laau, he laau.

O-o, *v.* To ripen; to become ripe, as fruit. *Ios.* 3:15.

2. Applied to men; he kanaka *oo* loa, a full grown man; he kanaka elemakule, ua *oo.*

3. To come to maturity, as children grown up to manhood.

O-o, *v.* See **O,** to pierce, dot into, &c. To crowd or cram into, as tobacco into a pipe; e *oo* iho i ka ipubaka i paa ai ka ipubaka ke puhi aku; e nounou.

2. To crowd herbs, &c., of an inflammatory nature into the vagina of a female to procure abortion.

3. To pierce with a sharp instrument the foetus in the womb; *oo* no lakou i na keiki, ua nui na kamalii i make pela. See **Aomilo.** He nui wale na wahine i *oo* i ka lakou mau keiki i ka manawa e hapai ai.

4. To commit infanticide generally, of which the Hawaiians had a variety of methods.

5. To stab or pierce, as with a spear; *oo* iho la laua i ko Keeaumoku kua i ka pahoa, they two *stabbed* the back of Keeaumoku with a pahoa.

O-o, *s.* Name of the process by which a child was killed in the womb.

O-o, *s.* The instrument anciently used by Hawaiians in cultivating the ground. Originally it was made of some hard wood

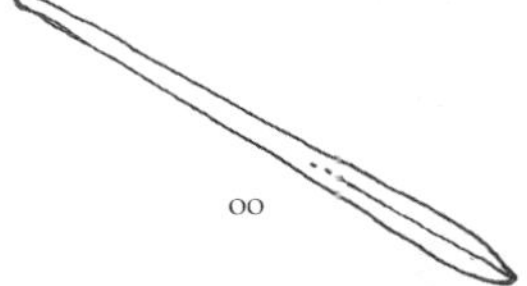

flattened and sharpened at one end so as

to dig with. The kinds of wood were the alahee, ulei, kauila, the uhiuhi, &c. Iron since its introduction has taken the place of these kinds of woods.

O-o, *s.* Name of a species of bird living in the mountains in the daytime and flies to the sea at night; a small brown bird, web-footed.

O-o, *s.* Name of a species of bird found in great numbers on Hawaii; the feathers were much valued by the chiefs for ornamenting their persons.

O-o, *s.* Name of a large fly brush.

O-o, *adj.* Ripe; mature, as fruit. *Ier.* 24:2.

2. Applied also to full grown young people; ai *oo* mua, first ripe fruit. *Puk.* 22:29.

O-o-A-HI, *s.* Oo and *ahi,* fire. A fire shovel. 2 *Oihl.* 4:11. O ka mea ike i ka *ooahi* o Naalono; lele ka papala *ooahi* o ka pali.

O-o-E, *pers. pron.,* second pers. sing, *o* emphatic. See *Gram.* § 131. Thou; you. See OE. In the following cases it seems to be used in the auipili; *ooe* ke kukulu ana o keia hale; *ooe* ka humu ana a keia pea. Ooe is used often in *Laieikawai* for *ou,* of thee; nawai ke kama *ooe. Laieik.* 176.

O-OE, *v.* To split, as a log or a board; *ooe* aku la ia me ka laau no ka menemene i ka lalau aku me ka lima.

O-OI, *v.* To be sharp; pointed; *ooi* na kakalaioa, the kakalaioa are sharp; *ooi* na puakala, the puakalas are sharp. See OI.

O-OI, *s.* Roughness; anything with sharp protuberances; ua like ka *ooi* me ke kalakala.

O-OI, *adj.* Sharp; prickly. *Ios.* 23:13. Mea *ooi,* sharp things; briers; *Lunk.* 8:7. Nahele *ooi,* thorns. 2 *Sam.* 23:6. Mea *ooi,* sting of a wasp or asp. *Hoik.* 9:10.

O-o-o, *v.* To crow, as a cock. *Mat.* 26:74, 75. SYN. with kani.

O-o-o, *s.* Any small vessel for containing water to drink; he *ooo* no ka wai, he kioo, kiahaaha.

O-o-o, *v.* To shrink away.

2. To be very careful of one's person or property.

3. To be parsimonious.

O-OU, *v.* To call aloud; to cry after one to make him hear; ua *oou* aku la au ia ia i lohe mai ai, aole oia alawa mai. *Kam.*

O-o-HAO, *s.* Oo and *hao,* iron. The iron oo. See OO. Applied lately to the plow for tilling the soil.

O-o-HOU, *s.* Oo and *hou,* new. The name given to the plow as an instrument for tilling the soil; the *new oo,* i. e., the plow.

O-o-HU, *v.* To bend over, as the shoulders of a carpenter or any mechanic from the constancy of work; *oohu* ke kua o ke kanaka no ke kulou mau i ka hana; hanana, kuaoohu; ua *oohu* ke kua, he is stoop-shouldered.

O-o-HU, *s.* A stoop-shouldered man.

2. The swell of the sea rolling down from the north part of Hawaii; when it comes from the south point, it is called *kahela.*

O-o-HU, *adj.* Crooking; bending outward.

O-o-KI, *v.* The 5th conj. of *oki.* To cut off; to lop, as the branch of a tree. *Mar.* 11:8. To cut off, as a rope.

2. To cut up, as wood for fuel; ke *ooki* nei au i ka wahie; *ooki* ae la lakou i ke kaula o ka waapa, they cut off the rope of the boat.

3. To cut off, as the limb of a person. *Lunk.* 1:6.

4. To divorce, as a married person; ke *ooki* nei au i kuu wahine no ka hewa; *ooki* i ka piko la, e ka hoahanau, a speech of one friend to another when they are at variance and can not agree.

O-o-LA, *s.* A blister on the foot; a stone bruise on the bottom of the foot.

O-o-LA-PU, *s.* A blister; the rising or swelling up of clothes in a tub of water.

O-o-LE-A, *v.* See Oo, the instrument formerly made of hard wood, and LEA, an intensive, much, very, &c. To be hard; severe; cruel in treatment; to strengthen; to make firm, as bones do the animal system. *Anat.* 1.

2. *Physically,* hard; unyielding.

3. *Morally,* rough; selfish in manners.

4. *Hoo.* To harden; to render obdurate, either naturally or morally; to harden, as the neck, i. e., to be obstinate. 2 *Nal.* 17:14. Mai *hoolea* i ka hana ana, e hana no me ka oluolu.

5. To be stout; strong; confident, as in using words. *Mal.* 3:13. To harden; make bold; fearless, as the face. *Ezek.* 3:8.

O-o-LEA, *s. Physically,* strength; confidence; hardness; severity. *Oihk.* 25:46.

2. *Morally,* surety; stern justice. *Rom.* 11:22. Opposed to *lokomaikai.*

3. Strength; place of confidence. *Hal.* 18:2. Ka ikaika, ka nawaliwali ole, ka paakiki.

O-o-LEA, *adj.* Hard; compact; unyielding.

2. Stiff; forward; obstinate. *Kanl.* 31:27. Untractable; disobedient; *hoo*, same; hookahi malama hookupu dala *oolea*, on the first month they collect *hard* money as taxes.

O-O-LE-KU-KA-HI, *s.* The name of the seventh day of the month.

O-O-LE-KU-KA-HI, *s.* Ka hiku o na la o ka malama; eha oia mau la i kapaia ia mau inoa, o ka *walu*, o ka *aiwa*, a o ka *umi*.

O-O-LE-KU-KO-LU, *s.* The ninth day of the month.

O-O-LE-KU-LU-A, *s.* The name of the eighth day of the month.

O-O-LE-PAU, *s.* The tenth day of the month.

O-O-LO-HU-A, *s.* The fruit of the popolo.

O-O-LO-KU, *v.* *Olo*, flexible, movable, and *ku*, to rise.
1. To be in a state like the sea when the current and wind are opposite; to act like a chopped sea.
2. To be stormy or tempestuous, as the sea; kupikipiki io.
3. Applied to the mind; to be troubled; agitated.

O-O-LO-KU, *s.* The raging of the sea; ka *ooloku* ana o ke kai i ka ino.

O-O-LO-KU, *adj.* Boisterous; stormy, as the sea.

O-O-LO-LA, *s.* Name of a species of fish.

O-O-LO-LI, *adj.* Contracted or narrow, as a place pinched up; as toes within tight shoes.

O-O-LO-LII, *adj.* See OLO and LII, small. Thin; narrow; narrow, as a road; ma ke ala *oololii* aole nahelehele. See OLOLI. *Ololii* is the more correct orthography.

O-O-LO-PU, *s.* A mouthful of food or water; he *oolopu* ai, he poolopu wai. *Moo-olelo Haw.* p. 114.

O-O-LO-PU, *adj.* Swelled full; distended, as a sail, a tumor, &c.

O-O-MA, *s.* An open spout; the nose of a pitcher; a pitcher itself.
2. A gouge; a person with a sharp nose.

O-O-MA, *adj.* Open, as the mouth of a person; as the nose of a pitcher; he kiaha *ooma* wai, a pitcher. *Luk.* 22:10. The flare of a bonnet, &c.; epithet given by Hawaiians to the bonnets of the first missionaries' wives; he papale *ooma* ka!

O-O-NUI, *s.* Name of a species of fish.

O-O-PA, *v.* To be lame; to limp for lameness. 2 *Sam.* 4:4.

O-O-PA, *s.* A lame person. *Mat.* 11:15; *Oihk.* 21:18.

O-O-PA, *adj.* Lame, as by walking; lame, as an arm with hard labor; lame,

having lost a foot; lame, as a cripple; lame naturally; he wawae *oopa*, hapakue.

O-O-PA-LAU, *s.* *Oo*, the name of the Hawaiian digger, to which is added from the English the word *palau* (plow). Hence, a plow for cultivating the ground; he *oopalau* ka oo a ka bipi e kauo ai. See OO-HAO and OOHOU.

O-O-PA-LAU, *v.* To plow; to guide a plow. 1 *Nal.* 19:19.

O-O-PU, *s.* Name of a species of small fish living in fresh water rivers and ponds.

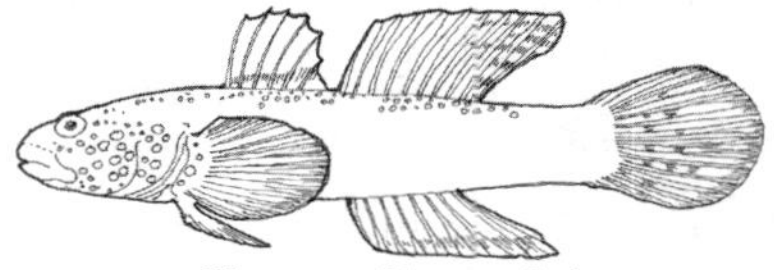

oopu, Hawaiian Shrimp Goby variety

O-O-PU-HA-PUU, *s.* Name of a fish which is caught far out at sea.

O-O-PU-HU-E, *s.* A species of fish with a rough skin, which is poisonous, if eaten.
2. A name of the bitter calabash.

O-O-PU-KAI, *s.* A species of oopu living in the sea. See OOPU.

O-O-PU-LU-UA, *adj.* The liver of an animal served up with other things as a sauce; he ake puaa, he ake *oopuluua*.

O-O-PU-POO-PAA, *s.* Another species of oopu, similar, if not the same as *oopukai*.

OU, *pers. pron.*, second pers. sing., gen. of *oe*. Thine; yours; belonging to you. Sometimes it is used for *kou*, thy; thine; as, me *ou* poe kanaka, instead of me *kou* poe, &c.; *ou* mau kamalii, thy children. *Gram.* § 132, 1.

OU is sometimes used for *o* in the imperative; as, *ou* hele oukou. *Mat.* 2:8; *Neh.* 8:5. See *Gram.* § 192, last sentence. The *o* of this imperative is often written *ou*.

O'U, *pers. pron.*, first pers. sing., genitive of *au*. My; mine; of me; belonging to me. *Gram.* § 124, 1.

O-U, *v.* To lean the breast on a piece of wood in order to float; to ascend upon, as a float.

O-U, *s.* A float. See MCUO.

OU, *v.* To steal.
2. To break off the top of a plant, bud or leaf.
3. To commit a small offense; e *ou* ka muou o ka wa iki; e *ou* ka muou o ka baka.

OU, *v.* To hide away; to escape punishment for a crime; aole wahi e *ou* ai ka poe hewa i keia manawa, ua paa i ke kanawai;

he *ou* nei ka poe hewa i kahi papa popo.

Ou, *v.* See O, verb, and HOU. To pierce or puncture, as with a sharp instrument; e *ou,* e hooeha i ka puupuu i ke poo, to lance or pierce the swelling on the head.

Ou, *s.* Name of a species of bird on the mountains; o ka ou, ua like ia me ka moa opiopio; he omaomao kona hulu.

O-u-a, *v.* To stretch out.

O-u-a-ka, *v.* To be open; to be full of holes. See OWAKA and OAKA.

O-u-o-u, *s.* A sharp quick sound, as of the kapa mallet; kani *ouou* ke kani ana a ka ie kuku.

2. The sound of a drum when struck; e kani *ouou* ana ka leo o ka pahu; ke kani o ka *ouou* kuamuamu, the sound of the sharp voice of railing.

Ou-ou, *v.* To be full of hard lumps, as poi not well pounded; he *ouou* ka ai, he hakuhaku puupuu.

Ou-ou, *s.* The name of a small bird.

Ou-ou, *adj.* Thin; feeble; he puka-puka, he kunono.

Ou-o-le, *s.* Firmness; fearlessness. See OU, to hide away.

O-uo-uo, *adj.* Growing thriftily, as plants; no stinting; mahakea kupu lau *ououo* ole.

Ou-ho-lo-ai, *s.* A kind of mamaki kapa which is dyed or painted different colors on each side.

Ou-kou, *pers. pron.,* second pers. plural. Ye; you.

O-u-li, *s.* A change in the appearance of a thing.

2. Character; kind; description; applied to many things; he *ouli* okoa; ua maopopo ka *ouli* o ka poe hana hewa, ma ka lakou hana ana.

3. A sign; a token of the approach of a storm or calamity; an omen; a sign in the heavens.

4. Form; change; meaning of a word.

5. A sign of something expected; an earnest or pledge; e lawe i ka *ouli* ao, me ka *ouli* hana i pono ai oe i ka maka o kau poe haumana.

6. A sign or signal of divine authority. *Puk.* 4:28.

7. A wonder, i. e., a thing wondered at. *Isa.* 8:18. A token of some evil. *Isa.* 44:25. In *grammar,* mood or mode; as, *ouli hai,* indicative mood.

O-u-li, *s.* Name of the god of those who prayed people to death; ka inoa o ke akua o ka poe anaana.

Ou-mu-a-mu-a, *s.* See MUAMUA. The name of the foremost soldier or the front rank in battle.

O-u-nau-na, *s.* The name of a four-footed animal in the sea.

O-u-pe, } *v.* To vex; to trouble; **O-u-pe-ou-pe,** } to put to hazard; to ill fate; e *oupe* mai kuu akua ia oe.

2. To be limber or weak, as the point of a pen; *oupe* ka maka o ka hulu.

3. To make limber or bend, as a stick.

4. To cause to fall, or to put down. 2 *Oihl.* 25:8. See OKUPE.

Ou-wa, *s.* Auhea kakou a pau loa e o'u poe hoa *ouwa* mau la wela nei la, where are we all, my fellow young cocks of these hot days; also *oua.* See MOAOUA.

Ou-wa, *s.* A person living with strangers till he becomes as one of the people, but still does not feel at home.

Ou-ra-na-ta-na, *s. Eng.* The orangoutang.

O-ha, *s.* The small sprigs of kalo that grow on the sides of the older roots; the suckers which are transplanted.

2. A branch from a stock. *Isa.* 53:2. A sucker from the root of a plant or tree. *Isa.* 11:1. FIG. *Ier.* 23:5.

3. A stick for ensnaring birds; he laau kapili manu.

O-ha, *s.* A salutation between the sexes; rather a call, as halloo! to attract attention, and when the peson looks round, then beckons.

O-ha, *v.* To salute, as a man a woman, or *vice versa;* to call to one at some distance, and when he looks, then beckons to him.

O-ha, *adj.* Sick from grief or care.

O-haa, *s.* The name of a fish; also *oeha;* ke opae *ohaa.*

O-haa, *adj.* He wawae *ohaa;* a person with crooked or distorted limbs.

O-hai, *s.* A flowering shrub resembling a locust.

O-hai-kau, *s.* Name given to a sledge obtained from Captain Cook which was worshipped.

O-ha-o, *s.* A swelling of the body from sickness; ka *ohao* o ka ilio, the *swelling* of the dog.

O-hao, *v.* To weed; to cultivate; to dress land.

O-hao, *adj.* Swelled or dropsical; ka opu *ohao;* puffed up; swelled full, as the bowels with wind or water. See OHAOHAO.

O-hao, *s.* Name of a rope to tie dogs with.

O-hao, *v.* To tie, as a rope or string; to bend on; applied mostly to dogs; e *ohao* i ka ilio a paa.

O-ha-o-ha, *s.* The fond recollection of a friend; joy; great desire; strong affection.

O-ha-o-ha, *adj.* Thriftily, as oha shoots;

like ohas; ulu *ohaoha* na laau kanu, the trees planted grow *thriftily*.

O-HAO-HAO, *v.* See OHAO. To swell, as the belly or body; to be full, as with much eating; ua hookuku, ua nopu.

2. To rise up, as a thought in the mind. See OHAO.

O-HAO-HAO, *adj.* Puffed up; swelled full, as the bowels with wind or water; he *ohaohao* ka opu, he ekeeke ke lomi iho.

O-HAO-HAO-LA, *s.* A false speech; a lie; a contradiction from what one has said before; na olelo au i lohe ai he *ohaohala* wale no ia, aole i like pu me kau i olelo ai, *ohaohaola*, ohalahala.

O-HAO-HA-LA, *adv.* Thrifty; rank, as vegetables. See OHAHA and OHAOHA.

O-HAO-HA-LA, *s.* A pleasant delightful sound.

O-HA-HA, *adj.* Plump; rank; thrifty; flourishing; referring to vegetables. *Kin.* 41:5. Ka ulu maikai ana o ka mea kanu.

O-HA-HA, *s.* Name of a plant, arborescent *lobelia*; a vine growing on trees; a parasitical plant.

O-HA-HA, *adj.* Swelled; puffed up; enlarged. See HAHA.

O-HA-KA, *v.* Ua *ohaka*, ua pololi; to be disconnected, but near together; to have a crack between.

O-HA-KA, *adj.* Open; not joined; not fitted together; he mao *ohaka*, he mao hakaka.

O-HA-KA-LAI, *s. Oha* and *kalai*. A stick to rub or polish with, as a file or other instrument.

O-HA-KU-LAI, *v. Oha*, a shoot, and *kulai*, to push over. To bend off the young kalo from the old to give it room to grow.

O-HA-KU-LAI, *s.* A hard protuberance on the joints of the human body, as the knees, hips, ankles, &c.; also called *haupuu*.

2. A protuberance in the flesh.

O-HA-LA, *adj.* Green; young; not ripe.

O-HA-LAU, *s.* The soft tops and blossoms of kalo leaves made into a luau; often made where kalo grows plentifully.

O-HA-NA, *s.* A family. 2 *Sam.* 9:1. A brood of birds. *Kanl.* 22:6. A litter, as of puppies or pigs; an offspring; a tribe. *Ios.* 14:1, 2, 3. All the young of one animal; ka *ohana* moa, ka *ohana* ilio, &c.; *ohana* uuku, an endearing appellation for little children; *ohana* hipa, a flock of sheep.

O-HA-NA, *adj.* Of or relating to a family; he mohai *ohana*, a family sacrifice. 1 *Sam.* 20:29.

O-HA-NA, *s.* A family of parents, children and servants living together; o ke kakae no ia o ka lepo o Lahainaluna me he *ohana* moa la.

O-HE, *s.* Art., ke. The bamboo; the outside was formerly used for knives on account of its hardness; a reed generally. 2 *Nal.* 18:21.

2. A measuring reed. *Hoik.* 21:15. Ohe kani, a flute; *ohe* nana, a spyglass; puna *ohe*, a spoon made of bamboo.

3. Name of a forest tree; timber soft, like kukui, white, good for making kukuluaeo.

O-HE, *s.* A bundle. See OHI.

O-HE, *s. Art.* ka. Name of a musical instrument of the flute kind; hookahi au mea malama, o ka *ohe* a kaua; aia malama pono oe i ka *ohe. Laieik.* 122. He *ohe* mana. *Ib.*

O-HE-A, *adv. inter.*, the genitive case of *hea*. Of where? of what place? *Gram.* § 160.

O-HEA, *v.* To weed; to hoe. See OHEU.

O-HE-A, *s.* An arrow not well fitted; a matter of play for children; he pua lele ole, he pua *ohea*.

O-HE-A, *adj.* Lazy after eating; tired of work; no inclination to work; he molowa, hoihoi ole, *ohea* i ka la.

O-HEA-HEA, *adj.* Warm; tasteless, as warm water; he wai *oheahea*, he wai mama.

O-HE-A-LA, *s. Ohe* and *ala*, sweet. Sweet cane; a vegetable offered in sacrifice. *Isa.* 43:24. Sweet calamus. *Puk.* 30:23.

O-HEE, *s.* O, to pierce, and *hee*, squid. To take squid by spearing; i ka *ohee* lakou, they are spearing squid.

O-HE-O-HE, *adj.* Half erect, not flat or horizontal, but as a steep roof of a house; ku *oheohe*, a kulu ole.

O-HE-O-HE, *s.* The bamboo; a reed generally. See OHE.

O-HE-U, *v.* To weed or hoe, as potatoes; to dig over a garden.

O-HE-U, } *v.* See HEU. To come
O-HE-U-HEU, } out, as the beard of a young man; *oheuheu*, ua *oheu* ae no hoi kou puukole, make kuu makua.

O-HE-HA, *adj.* Slow; lazy in work. See HEHA, molowa.

O-HE-KA-PA-LA, *s. Ohe*, bamboo, and *kapala*, to print. A piece of bamboo carved for the purpose of printing kapa; he *ohe* kakau.

ohe kapala

O-HE-KE, *adj.* Fearful; bashful; modest; humble; he *oheke* wale ko ke kuaaina kanaka, the country people are modest and diffident; he *oheke* ole kanaka wahi alii, the people about the chief are without modesty.

O-HE-LO,
O-HE-LO-HE-LO, } *s.* A species of small fruit of a reddish color; the Hawaiian whortleberry. See HELO.

ohelo

O-HE-LO-HE-LO, *adj.* Having the color of the *ohelo*, i. e., a light red; he hainaka *ohelohelo*, he silika *ohelohelo*.

O-HE-LO-PA-PA, *s.* A strawberry.

O-HE-MO, *adj.* Weaned; broken off, as from sucking; as a child from the breast. See HEMO. He ukuhi *ohemo* na keiki.

O-HE-MO, *v.* To discharge freely from the bowels, as in a dysentery.

O-HE-MO-HE-MO, *adj.* Faint; languid; weak; omino, alalohe, nawaliwali.

O-HE-NA-NA, *s.* *Ohe*, bamboo, and *nana*, to see, look. A spyglass. See OHE.

O-HE-WA, *v.* O, to pierce, and *hewa*, wrong. To make a false stab at a person or thing.

O-HE-WA-HE-WA, *adj.* Far gone with sickness; dead drunk; dim-sighted; *ohewahewa* mai la na maka, the eyes do not see plainly; not able to see from intense light or other cause; liable to mistake what is seen. See HOOHEWAHEWA.

O-HI, *v.* To gather up, as things scattered; to glean. *Kanl.* 24:21. To collect together; *Nah.* 11:32.

2. To collect, as fruit; to gather in a harvest. *Oihk.* 19:9, 10.

3. To pluck, as fruit, and carry away; to collect together, as property; ua *ohiia* ka waiwai; to collect; to sweep in, as in collecting the spoil of a conquered enemy.

4. To carry away by force; equivalent to *hao*; aohe pu oloko o ka pa, ua pau i ka *ohiia* e na kanaka mawaho, there was no gun in the fort, they were all *taken* away by the people without.

5. To choose out. *Sam.* 17:40.

6. To receive; to be taken into the care or friendship of one; *ohi* mai o Liholiho i poe punahele nana; pau ae la ke kui i ka *ohiia* i makau, all the nails were collected for fish-hooks.

7. To receive, as the interest on money.

8. To take up and protect, as an orphan. *Hal.* 27:10.

O-HI, *s.* A collecting, as of money or property, implying difficulty; the collecting the fruits of a harvest. 2 *Oihl.* 31:5. The collecting, as debts.

2. A bundle or collection of something; as, he *ohi* wauke, he *ohi* kalo, a *bundle* of wauke, a *bundle* of kalo.

O-HI, *s.* For *ohe*, bamboo. *Laieik.* 22. A misprint perhaps.

O-HI, *adj.* False; deceitful; waha *ohi*, a lying mouth; he wahahee; he puaa *ohi*, a female hog that bears no pigs; he alii *ohi*, oia ke alii nana e ae ke kapa moe. NOTE.—Another native says that *ohi* is the appellation given to a female animal upon the first bearing of young. See *Isa.* 7:21. After two or three productions she is called *kumulau*.

O-HI-A, *s.* A contraction for *ohiia*. A forcing; constraining; compelling. 2 *Kor.* 9:5.

O-HI-A, *s.* Name of a species of large tree, the timber used for various purposes, but especially for making gods. See other species below.

2. The name of a class of gods under the general name of *akuanoho*.

O-HI-A, *s.* A deciduous fruit somewhat resembling the apple.

O-HIA-AI, *s.* Name of the tree that bears the ohia fruit; ohia apane, the ohia with red blossoms.

O-HIA-HA, *s.* Another species of the ohia tree; hili *ohiaha* a hooluu.

O-HIA-LE-HU-A, *s.* *Ohia* and *lehua*, name of a blossom of certain trees. Another species of the ohia, bearing beautiful blossoms. See LEHUA.

ohia lehua

O-HI-E, *adj.* Wicked; perverse. See HIE or HIEHIE, and OHIPUA.

O-HI-O, *s.* A hahai i ka *ohio*, a me ka *ohio* unuunu.

O-HI-O, *s.* The thinking; the reflection of the mind upon a beloved but absent object.
2. The undulating motion of the air over a smooth plain in a hot day.

O-HI-O, *v.* To stir and loosen the ground around a vegetable.

O-HI-O-HI, *s.* See OHI. Falsehood; deceitful talk; boasting; bragging; *ohiohi* pukupuku.

O-HI-O-HI, *s.* The small straight branches of trees; *ohiohi* ke kupu o ka laau; *ohiohi* ke kupu ana ae.

O-HI-O-HI, *v.* To have substances of various colors united, or a substance of various shades of color, as mahogany timber, curl-maple, curly koa, &c.
2. To be very beautiful; pleasing to look at; handsome.

O-HI-O-HI-O, *v.* See HIO. To stagger or reel, as one intoxicated; to be slightly intoxicated, so as to produce the desire of sleep.
2. To do a thing but slightly.
3. To shut the door lest loafers should come in.

O-HI-O-HI-O, *s.* The dizziness of slight intoxication.

O-HI-U, *v.* To thatch in a particular manner.

O-HI-U-HI-U, *s.* Name of a species of fish found at Kawaihae; at other places they are called *uhu.*

O-HI-KAU, *v.* To mistake; to make an error in speaking; *ohikau* wale aku no. See OHIPUA.

O-HI-KAU, *s.* A mistake; a blunder in speaking.

O-HI-KI, *s.* Name of a particular manner of thatching; ua *ohiki* ka maka i ka laau; ua *ohikiia* ka laau i ka ai i ka wawae.
2. Name of a species of small crab or sand spider.

O-HI-KI, *v.* To shell, as one shells beans; e *ohiki* a hoihoi aku i ka pulupulu.
2. To put in; to cram down; e *ohiki* iloko.
3. To pry up, as a stone.
4. To lance or open, as an abscess.

O-HI-KI-HI-KI, *v.* To persevere, as when one expects a favor by asking.
2. To pick, as the teeth; *ohikihiki* i ka niho a pilo.

O-HI-LO, *s.* Name of the first day of the month among Hawaiians; same as *hilo.*

O-HI-NA, *v.* Ohi and ana. To have one's property swept away for debt; *ohina* aupapa, same as pau ka waiwai.

O-HI-NU, *v.* To roast, as meat. *Isa.* 44:16. To hang up and turn round by the fire for roasting; to roast over or before a fire; ua *ohinuia* i ka uwahi.

O-HI-NU, *s.* The piece of meat roasted as above, or a piece for roasting. 1 *Sam.* 2:15; *Isa.* 44:16.

Ka ohinu lele uwahi manu e
O ka manu al leleu.

2. The name of the stick which turns while the meat is roasting.

O-HI-NU-HI-NU, *v.* See OHINU. To roast much or often.
2. To be parched and dried, as the skin or as roast meat; ua *ohinuhinu* ka ili, ua upepehu.
3. To be smooth and shining, as a swelled skin; hence,
4. To be sick.

O-HI-PA, *v.* To vow; to take a vow.
2. To perform a vow.
3. To speak that which is false. See HOOHIPA.

O-HI-PU-A, *adj.* Wicked; naughty; perverse; he *ohipua* ka olelo; careless or negligent in speaking, whether truth or falsehood.

O-HO, *v.* To cry out; more often *hooho*; to exclaim, cry out, as many voices; to cry out, exclaim, as a single voice; *hooho* ae la ia leo nui, a pane mai la ia me ka *hooho* ana, auwe! pau! See HOOHO. To cry out, as a flock of birds on being frightened; *oho* ae la ka auna manu i ka ilio.

O-HO, *s.* The hair of the head. *Mat.* 5:36. Or human hair; *oho* hina, gray hair. *Kin.* 42:38. See LAUOHO.
2. The leaves of the cocoanut trees from their resemblance to hair; wehe ke kaiaulu i ke *oho* o ka niu, the strong wind loosens the leaves of the cocoanuts.

O-HO-A-KA, *s.* The name of the second day of the month; same as *hoaka.*

O-HO-KU, *s.* Also the name of the second day of the month.

O-HO-KU, *s.* The name of the fifteenth day of the month, that is, the day that succeeds the day of the full moon.

O-HO-KUI, *s.* Oho, hair, and *kui,* to join together. A wig, made awkwardly, formerly worn in war. *Kum. Haw.* 10.

O-HO-LI, *v.* See HOLI. To question for information.

O-HO-MA, *adj.* Destitute; without conveniences; ua ku au i ka pa *ohoma,* a ua kokoke mai kona la.

O-HU, *s.* A fog; a mist; a cloud. *Puk.* 24:16. Smoke; vapor. *Iob.* 36:27. Ka *ohu* e uhi ana i ke kuahiwi, the *light cloud* that covers the mountains. SYN. with awa, fine rain; also noe, spray.

2. The breath of a person in a cold morning; o ka *ohu* no ia o ke kanaka. See MAHU.

O-HU, *v.* To roll up, as the sea that does not break. *Laieik.* 91. To swell high, as water; *ohu* iluna ka wai; ua piha a *ohu* iluna ke kai.

O-HU, *s.* A roller or swell of water that does not break.

2. Name of a place raised up for any purpose. See OHUKU and AHUA.

O-HU-A, *s.* The family part of a household, as children, servants, domestics, sojourners, &c.; the master and mistress are not generally included. *Kin.* 12:5. Ka *ohua* ia o Hinahele me Kuula.

2. Applied to the passengers on a vessel.

O-HU-A, *v.* To glide; to slip off, as the glancing of the arrow in throwing the arrow; ua *ohua* kau ka ana i ka pua.

O-HU-A, *s.* Name of the young of the fish called manini. See MAKALIIOHUA.

O-HU-A, *s.* Name of the thirteenth day of the month; properly *hua*.

O-HU-A-LI-KO, *s.* A species of fish like the manini.

O-HU-A-LI-MU-KA-LA, *s.* A species of small fish.

O-HU-A-LI-PO-A, *s.* A species of small fish.

O-HU-A-PAA-WE-LA, *s.* A species of fish.

O-HU-A-PA-LE-MO, *s.* A species of small fish. *Laieik.* 12.

O-HU-I, *v.* To twist round, as in pulling out a tooth.

2. To snatch or rescue, as in pulling a child from the flames.

3. To pick or pull out a sliver from the flesh.

O-HU-I-HU-I, *v.* To twist round and draw out, as a tooth; *ohuihui* i ka niho; *ohuihui* i ka naio, to pull up the naio (sandal-wood.) See OHUI.

O-HU-O-HU, *s.* A myrtle wreath worn around the neck.

2. A blackish kind of kapa.

O-HU-O-HU, *adj.* Large; heavy; burdened; *ohuohu* o mea i hele mai la; *ohuohu* o mea i ka lei.

O-HU-O-HU, *v.* To dress in uniform.

2. To decorate, as a room; to dress out, as a ship; to put on wreaths, &c.

O-HU-KU, *s.* A small, flat elevation; a platform.

2. A protuberance; a round or blunt protuberance of earth, stones or other material. SYN. with puu, hua, ahua, wawa, &c.

O-HU-KU, *v.* To stick out; to be prominent in some part; ua *ohuku* ke poo.

O-HU-LE, *v.* To be or become bald-headed. *Isa.* 15:2. Lae *ohule*. *Oihk.* 13:40, 41. *Hoo.* To make the head bald. *Ezek.* 29:15. To make one's self bald. *Oihk.* 21:5. Ka lauoho ole o ke poo, oia ka *ohule*.

O-HU-LE, *s.* A bald-headed person. 2 *Nal.* 2:23.

2. Baldness itself. *Mik.* 1:16. *Ohule* pahukani i ke aluia.

O-HU-LE, *adj.* Bald; bald-headed.

O-HU-LU, *s.* Potatoes of the second growth; old sprouted potatoes; ka uala kahiko.

O-HU-LU, *adj.* A person that sails or goes on the ocean; he kanaka *ohulu* no ka moana.

O-HU-MU, *v.* To complain of or find fault with the conduct of some person or of something done. *Neh.* 5:1. To complain secretly or privately.

2. To confer privately concerning an absent person, either with a good or bad design.

3. To confer clandestinely; to murmur.

4. To speak against one. *Puk.* 16:7. To complain of persons. *Ios.* 9:18. To conspire against one; to grumble secretly; to be discontented.

5. To congratulate one's self; to think in one's own mind; to lay out or plan anything secretly within one's self. 2 *Sam.* 13:32.

O-HU-MU, *s.* A murmuring or complaining. *Puk.* 16:12.

2. A secret conference or council. *Kin.* 49:6. He *ohumu* kipi, a conspiracy. *Ezek.* 22:25. *Ohumu* wale, a grumbling; a complaint without cause.

O-HU-NA, *s.* Name of the eleventh day of the month. See HUNA.

O-HU-NA, *s.* A species of very small fish.

O-HU-NE, *s.* A species of very small fish.

O-HU-NE, *s.* A disease of the skin; the itch; mai puupuu liilii.

O-KA, *v.* To set a decoy; to ensnare; to place a bird in such a position as to catch or tempt another.

O-KA, *v.* To move the lips, as in speaking, but without sound; e *oka* wale ana no ka waha, the mouth only was moving.

2. To blow the nose.

O-KA, *v.* To be small; few in number or quantity; aohe *oka* mai o ka bipi, there were not a few of cattle. See OKANA.

O-KA, *s.* Dregs; crumbs; small pieces of things, as saw-dust, filings, &c.; *oka* palaoa, chaff. *Hal.* 83:13. The refuse or worthless part of a thing. *Isa.* 1:25.

2. An offensive smell; he pilopilo, he wai no loko o ka *oka* awa; he wai *oka* no ke kukui.

O-KA, *s.* A top made of a small gourd.

O-KA, *s. Eng.* An oak tree or wood. *Kin.* 12:6. Laau *oka*, an oak grove or tree.

O-KA, *adj.* Small; fine; little; kaula *oka*, a rope made of any fine substance, as tow or pulu. *Lunk.* 16:9.

O-KAA, *v.* To spin, as a top. See KAA.

O-KAA, *s.* A top; ka niu *okaa*.

O-KAI, *s.* A butterfly.

2. A large company following one; a crowd moving from place to place. SYN. with huakai. *Okai* lua ka hele a kanaka, kakai lua ka hele a kanaka.

3. Kekahi aoao o ka waha o ka upena malolo.

4. Ka *okai* o ke kulina lalani.

O-KAI, *adv.* Of or belonging to the sea (the opposite of *ouka*); towards the sea.

O-KA-O-KA, *v.* See OKA, 13th conj. To reduce to powder; to beat small. 2 *Sam.* 22:43. To be broken up fine. *Ios.* 9:5. To break into small pieces; to shiver. *Dan.* 2:35—7:7. With *liilii*, to be utterly destroyed. *Dan.* 8:25.

O-KA-O-KA, *s.* Dust; small particles, &c. See OKA. *Puk.* 32:20. Fine dust; dregs. *Hal.* 75:9. An intensive; he *oka-oka* liilii me he oka la.

O-KA-O-KA, *s.* An offensive smell; *oka-oka* pilopilo me he oka la. See OKA 2.

O-KA-O-KAI, *s.* Sickness; a heaving of the stomach before vomiting; sickness of the stomach from a bad smell.

2. Sweet, unfermented poi; he poi mananalo.

O-KA-HAI, *adj.* Insipid; unpalatable. See HUKAI and HUKAHUKAI.

O-KA-KA, *s.* A name given to foreigners in former times.

2. In after times the name was transferred to a company of substantial business men belonging to Kamehameha I.

O-KA-KAI, *s.* See OKAI 2. A crowd of persons moving about after a chief.

O-KA-KA-LA, *s.* A shivering; the sensation of cold from the application of a cold substance, as water, &c.

2. A cold tremor from fear, from sudden danger.

3. A chill; a shivering.

4. The name of a rough kind of cloth; ka lole *okalakala* ulaula.

O-KA-KA-LA, *v.* To stand up stiffly and

roughly, like the bristles of a hog; as the hair of one in great fear. See KALA.

O-KA-KA-LA, *adj.* Cold; chilly.

O-KA-LA, *s.* Name of a species of fish.

O-KA-LA, *v.* To bristle up with anger. See KALA, to be rough.

O-KA-LA, *s.* Numbness or a disease (maele) of the head, as if the hair stood on end; akahi no ka *okala* o ko'u poo.

O-KA-LA-KA-LA, *v.* To be astonished; to shudder; to quake. SYN. with kunahihi.

2. To be boisterous or raging, as the wind; to rage with anger.

3. To be intent, or strongly desirous of doing a thing. *Laieik.* 39.

O-KA-LE-KA-LE, *s.* Name of a red fish.

O-KA-NA, *s.* A district or division of country containing several ahupuaas; o Kona, a o Kohala a me Hamakua, akolu *okana*; he mau *okana* iwaena o ka moku. See KALANA.

2. A division of food in dividing it out.

O-KA-NA, *adv.* A contraction of *oka* and *ana*. *Oka*, to be small, few, and *ana*, the participial termination. See *Gram.* § 34. Generally preceded by *aole*; as, aole *okana* mai ka nui, not small the quantity or number, i. e., a great deal; not a little or a few; aole *okana* mai na la o kona mau makahiki. *Kekah.* 6:3. The days of his years are very many; aole *okana* mai o kona waiwai, there is no end of his wealth; aohe *okana* mai o kona hewa, there is no bound to his wickedness; aole *okana* mai ka olioli. *Oih.* 20:12. They were not a little joyful, i. e., a good deal. NOTE.—It is a word used in strong expressions or in exaggerated descriptions.

O-KA-TO-BA, *s. Eng.* Name of a month; October.

O-KE, *v.* See KE and HOOKE. To urge upon. *Hoo.* To press upon; to pursue hard after.

2. To crowd together to hear or see a thing.

O-KE, *s.* Epithet of a person who goes from house to house quickly; he kanaka mama i ka hele kau hale, *oke* i kela hale i keia hale, *oke* wahahee; talkative.

O-KE, *adj.* Rotten; torn; good for nothing; *okeoke*.

O-KE-A, *s.* A kind of gravel or sand; the white sand of the sea. NOTE.—It is the name for sand on Oahu.

O-KE-A-PI-LI-MAI, *s.* Name of that class of persons who have no houses of their own, and thus attach themselves to those who have for the sake of a house. They were also called *unupehiiole*.

O-KE-A, *adj.* Hot, as stones heated to whiteness; he *okea* ka imu, ahulu.

O-KEE, *v.* To turn round, as the wind; to change.

2. To eddy, as water; *okee* mai ke kaomi.

O-KEE, *s.* A changing of direction, as the wind; an eddy, as in water.

O-KE-O-KE, *adj.* Talkative. See OKE. Paapaaina, popopo.

O-KE-NA, *s.* Name of a plant used in coloring.

O-KE-NA, *adj.* Yellow.

O-KI, *v.* To cut off; to cut in two, as any substance; as, *oki* laau, *oki* pohaku.

2. To end or finish any talk or business. *Kin.* 11:8.

3. To cut up root and branch; to destroy in any way.

4. To stop; put an end to; e *oki* i ke kamailio, to cease talking. *Kin.* 17:22.

5. To cut off; to separate from privileges; to punish. *Oihk.* 7:20.

6. To cut grain, as a harvest. *Kanl.* 24:19.

7. To cut off one's head.

8. To cut off food, as a famine; *oki* loa iho la ka aina i ka wi, the land is utterly destroyed by famine; to take possession of; to be subjected to the influence of, as intoxication; inu iho la ke Alii me kona Kuhina, a *oki* mai la ka ona a ka awa. *Laieik.* 34. Ina he kaikamahine, e *okiia* ka piko ma ka hale, ina he keikikane, ma ka heiau e *oki* ai ka piko o ua keiki la. NOTE.—This verb takes *ua* before the imperative mood; as, *ua oki,* stop; *ua oki* pela, stop there. *Hoo.* To stop; to cease; to end; to cut short; to terminate; to defer a decision; the opposite of *hoomaka,* to begin; to cause to stop; cease. *Puk.* 5:4. To cut and gather in, as a harvest. *Oihk.* 19:9. To cut off; destroy. 2 *Nal.* 23:5. NOTE.—*Oki* loa and *hooki* loa imply a destructive process according to the nature of the case; as, *oki* loa ka hana i ka paumaele; *oki* loa ka waiwai i ka popopo; hence,

O-KI, *v.* To be miserable; destitute; hungry; in want of all comforts.

O-KI-A, *v.* Passive of *oki* for *okiia.* To be cut off, &c. *Hos.* 8:4.

O-KI-O-KI, *v.* See OKI. To cut frequently; to cut into small pieces.

2. To reap and gather in, as a harvest. *Oihk.* 23:10.

3. To divide into small pieces. *Oihk.* 1:12. To cut into small pieces. *Lunk.* 19:29.

4. To divide out land among chiefs or people; *okioki* na 'lii a me na kanaka i ka

aina o Hawaii; to cut up; destroy, &c.

O-KI-O-KI, *adj.* Cutting; dividing, &c; oia ka moku i loaa mai ai ka pahi *okioki,* that was the vessel from which was obtained the *cutting* knives.

O-KI-LO, *s.* Afar off; at a distance; a space between two places.

O-KI-LO, *v.* See KILO. To look earnestly for something; to watch for; *okilo* ia, to look into the water for squid; to look for fish, as a fisherman.

O-KI-LOA, *s.* A destruction; a cutting up; a breaking down. *Ier.* 44:39. See OKI, note.

O-KI-LOA, *v.* To be dirty; filthy; polluted; to be dirty all over.

2. To be defeated in one's purpose; to try in vain. *Laieik.* 64.

O-KI-NA, *s. Oki* and *ana,* a finishing.

2. The cutting off of wood or cloth.

3. *Modernly,* the *finis* or ending of a book.

O-KI-POE-POE, *v. Oki,* to cut, and *poepoe,* around; circularly. To circumcise; to be circumcised. *Kin.* 17:10. Used also with *omaka,* to circumcise. *Puk.* 4:25. See the substantive below.

O-KI-POE-POE, *s.* See the verb. A cutting around; circumcision. NOTE.—This is a new coined word, used in the Hawaiian translations of Scripture for circumcision; the Hawaiian word was *kahi,* to cut, and *omaka,* the foreskin. The Hawaiian expression for circumcision anciently was *kahi omaka,* slitted. See OMAKA. *Okipoepoe,* oia ke oki ana i ka omaka; he kahe ana o ka ule o na kamalii ma Hawaii i ka manawa aku nei. See KAHE, to cut longitudinally.

O-KO-A, *v.* To be another; to be unlike in some respects; ua *okoa* ke kanaka waiwai, ua *okoa* ke kanaka ilihune, the rich man *was one thing,* the poor man *was another,* i. e., very different.

2. To be different from another thing; to be a different person or thing.

3. To be besides; over and above; not reckoned in. 1 *Nal.* 10:15.

4. To be unlike in appearance; ua *okoa* ke ano o na helehelena o na kanaka, ua *okoa* na holoholona, *different* from each other are the countenances of men, *different* are those of beasts.

5. *Hoo.* To cause a difference; *hookoa* mai kau hana i ka makou.

6. To set aside; to put off to another time; to defer.

O-KO-A, *s.* The totality of a thing; the whole. *Ezek.* 15:5.

O-KO-A, *adj.* Different; another; separate; distinct from; unlike.

   2. A whole as distinct from a part.

   3. Whole as distinguished from broken; he waa *okoa* ia, i. e., a canoe not broken; he waa nahaha ole *okoa*, a canoe not broken at all, whole; he malama *okoa*, a whole month. *Nah.* 11:20. He mea *okoa*, another thing.

O-KO-A, *adv.* Wholly; entirely. 1 *Nal.* 11:6. Altogether; the all of a thing; e kau *okoa*, to put all. *Oihk.* 8:27.

O-KO-O-KO, *s.* A blaze; anything red hot, as the iron from a blacksmith's forge; as stones thrown out of the volcano; a fiery redness. *Laieik.* 176.

   2. Any one in a dazzling dress.

   3. The zeal of a soldier pressing boldly into battle.

O-KO-O-KO, *v.* To burn, as the sensation of the itch; okooko ka maneo; or the erysipelas.

O-KO-O-KO, *adv.* Ragingly; heatedly, &c.

O-KO-HE, *v.* To begin to heal, as a sore; ua *okohe* kahi eha; to begin to granulate, as a wound; also applied to the bark of trees growing again.

O-KO-HE-KO-HE, *v.* To begin to heal. See OKOHE.

O-KO-HE-KO-HE, *s.* A small kind of mussel attached to wood that has been taken from a ship or from salt water.

O-KO-HO-LA, *adj.* O, to pierce, stab, &c., and *kohola*, a whale. Whale piercing; o ka nui o an moku i ku mai, oia na moku *okohola*, the greater number of ships which anchor here are *whale-stabbing* ships, or simply *whaleships*.

O-KO-KO, *v.* To be red like blood; to be red with heat. See KOKO.

O-KO-KO, *s.* A heat so intense as to be red. *Dan.* 3:22. A red heat.

O-KO-KO, *adj.* Boiling, as lava; lambent, as flame.

O-KO-LE, *s.* O and *kole*, raw.

   1. The anus; kahi malalo e hemo ai ka honowa.

   2. The posteriors; o ke oi iho la no ia o ka *okole*, me he *okole* wahine la, i. e., a very shameful thing. See KOLE.

O-KO-LE-HAO, *s.* The name given to an iron try-pot, brought ashore and made into a still.

   2. The vulgar but expressive name given to liquor which natives and some foreigners distill from ki root; so called from the name of the pot above mentioned.

O-KO-LE-E-MI-E-MI, *s.* Name of a species of fish. See next *art.*

O-KO-LE-HA-WE-LE, *s.* Name of a species of fish; same as above.

O-KO-LE-KE, *s.* A kind of namu; a species of language got up for vile purposes; eia kahi hewa hou, o na olelo hou, o ke kake, o ka nehiwa, o ka *okoleke*. *Lam. Haw.* 13:4, 1.

O-KO-LE-MA-KI-KI, *s.* Name of a plant with small leaves, which grows thick like the koali.

O-KO-LO, *adj.* Slippery, where one is liable to fall; loi ale no i ke alia *okolo*.

O-KO-MO, *v.* To calk a ship or vessel; ka poe haole e *okomo* ana i ka ropi ma ka aoao o ka moku, the foreigners were *calking* (driving in the rope) on the sides of the ship.

O-KU, *v.* To show a thing to one secretly, lest another should see it and demand it.

   2. To set a bird near a snare to catch or tempt another; e hooku aku i ke poo, e *oku* aku i ka lima.

O-KU, *s.* A giving secretly that no one else may know.

O-KU-O-KU, *v.* *Hoo.* See OKU, *v.*

O-KU-O-KU, *v.* To rise up, as the bow of a canoe or ship by the waves in a storm.

   2. To rear and pitch, as an unbroken horse; holo *okuoku* ka lio pupu.

O-KUU, *v.* To sit up because one has no place or conveniences for lying down; to sit up, as one on the deck of a vessel when the water dashes over, because it is better than to lie down; the idea is to keep the head up.

   2. To sit in a meditating posture with the head reclined.

   3. To sit with a covering over the shoulders, and arms across the breast, as if cold.

O-KUU, *s.* Name of a great pestilence which swept over the islands while Kamehameha I. was living on Oahu about 1807. Great multitudes were swept off. The name *okuu* was given to it because the people *okuu* wale aku no i ka uhane, i. e., dismissed freely their souls and died. See KUU, to let go.

O-KU-HE-KU-HE, *s.* Name of a species of fish.

O-KU-KU, *v.* To erect; to turn up, as the head when one is swimming; to raise up, as the head of a fish above water.

   2. To think; to reflect, as when one is unexpectedly accused of a wrong.

O-KU-KU, *s.* Name of a species of fish, the ahuluhulu.

O-KU-KU-LI, *v.* To be satisfied; full, as

with food or drink; to have enough.

O-KU-LI-KU-LI, *v.* To be fat; rich; sweet tasted, as high seasoned food. See KUHIKUHI.

O-KU-LI-KU-LI, *v.* To eat of sweet things till one is sick.

O-KU-LU, *s.* Name of the sixteenth day of the month. See KULU.

O-KU-MU-LAU, *s.* See KUMULAU. A leaf or sprout that grows out of the root or stump.

O-KU-PE, *v.* To sprain the ankle; to stumble. *Heb.* 12:13; *Rom.* 11:11.

O-KU-PU, } *v.* To rise up and
O-KU-PU-KU-PU, } cover with dark shades, as clouds; especially applied to those out at sea.

O-LA, *s.* A recovery from sickness; a state of health after sickness; an escape from any danger or threatened calamity.

2. A living, that is, the means of life, food; e pii ana au i ke *ola*, I am going up (the hill) for life, i. e., to procure food.

3. Life; the period of one's life; living; while one lives.

4. Life; salvation; deliverance from spiritual death. NOTE.—This last (4) definition is a modern one introduced with the Christian system, and is often used in the Hawaiian Bible along with definitions 1st, 2d and 3d.

O-LA, *v.* To be saved from danger; to live after being in danger of death; to recover from sickness; to get well; i mai la o Kamehameha, ina e *ola* keia mai ana o'u; to enjoy an escape from any evil.

2. To live upon, or by means of a thing without which one would die; *ola* no hoi na iwi, proverbial expression: poverty (bones) shall be supplied, prosperity shall flourish. *Laieik.* 124. See IWI 7.

3. *Hoo.* To cause to live, i. e., to save one, or to save alive. *Ios.* 6:25. To cause to escape, as one in danger; to deliver from. *Puk.* 14:30. To heal, as a disease.

4. To save, i. e., cause to escape from future misery. See note under the noun for the new modern idea of the word.

O-LA, *adj.* Alive; escaped; living in opposition to *dead*; o kou alii make no, a me kou alii *ola*.

O-LA, } *v.* The sense from the
O-LA-O-LA, } sound.

1. To gaggle; to gargle water in the throat.

2. To snore.

O-LAE-LAE, *s.* A bitter calabash, having

bitter meat and seeds.

O-LAI, *s.* *Art.* ke. An earthquake. 1 *Nal.* 19:11. He haalulu honua.

2. A piece of pumice-stone, used in polishing canoes.

O-LAI-LA, *adv.* The auipili of *laila*, there. *Gram.* § 165, 2. Of there; of that place.

O-LAO, *v.* To hoe up weeds, as in a garden; to hoe up weeds and hill up the earth around vegetables. SYN. with oheu.

O-LA-O-LA, *s.* An ebullition, or bubbling up of water.

O-LA-O-LA, *v.* To gargle, &c. See OLA.

2. To bubble, as water entering a calabash and the air coming out.

3. To snore in sleep; *olaola* ka ihu me he puaa la.

O-LA-O-LA, *s.* An ebullition; a bubbling up of water, as from a spring.

O-LAO-LAO, *v.* See OLAO. To weed; dig round, as a plant. *Isa.* 5:6. To dig with an oo or spade.

O-LA-HO-NU-A, *adv.* Thoroughly; entirely; altogether; o ka hoomaka ana, ua like no ia me ke ao ana i *olahonua* i ka palapala; i *olahonua*, i pau ka noho hemahema ana. See HONUA, *adv.*

O-LA-HU-A, *s.* The fruit of the popolo; a species of berry; he olelo hoomahua a ka *olahua* ka mai, loaa hua.

O-LA-LA, *v.* To dry; to wither; to warm by the fire until withered, as green leaves; a loaa mai ka lau hala, alaila, *olala* ma ke ahi.

2. To grow lean, as a fleshy person; to pine away. *Ezek.* 33:10.

3. To be lean in flesh; the opposite of *kaha*. *Isa.* 17:4. See LALA.

O-LA-LA, *adj.* Lean; poor in flesh; applied to animals.

2. Small; stinted; applied to vegetables.

O-LA-LAU, *adj.* Silent; dumb; out of one's mind; olula, pupule.

O-LA-LA-LAE, *v.* See the foregoing. To be out of one's mind; pupule.

O-LA-LE, *s.* Name of a species of fish.

O-LA-LI (o-la-li-la-li), *adj.* Bright; shining; glistening.

O-LA-LO, *adv.* The auipili of *lalo*. Of or pertaining to what is below or under. *Gram.* § 161.

O-LA-NI, *v.* To dry or roast by the fire; e ala'e oe, e *olani* i wahi baka no kaua, get up and dry the tobacco leaves for us two; e *olani* iho hoi ha.

O-LA-PA, *s.* Name of a tree in the mountains.

O-LA-PA, *v.* To be moved, as the stomach; to rumble, as the bowels; applied to the stomach or bowels; e *olapa*, e nahu.

2. To flash, as lightning; *olapa* ka uwila. *Laieik.* 163.

3. To move, as a muscle or bone. *Anat.* 19.

O-LA-PA-LA-PA, *s.* A ridge between two ravines.

2. The rough protuberances of a precipice.

3. A rough place; pii i na *olapalapa* wai, a he anu.

O-LA-PA-LA-PA, *adj.* Rough; uneven, as the surface of the ground; full of ravines.

2. Full of corners or projections.

O-LA-PA-NAI, *v.* *Ola*, alive, and *panai*, to redeem. *Hoo.* To save by a substitute; to redeem. *Puk.* 13:5. O ka poe i *hoolapanaiia*, the redeemed ones. *Isa.* 35:9. Syn. with kuai hoolaia. *Isa.* 35:10.

O-LA-PU, *v.* To raise a blister.

2. To act deceitfully, treacherously, foolishly; e hokai, e hoolapu.

3. To catch fish with the hands as the oopu is caught; to stir up water with the hands; *olapu* i ka wai i ka lepo; properly *holapu.*

O-LE, *s.* The eye tooth.

2. Name of a kind of fish.

3. A pau na kui eha, a pau na *ole* eha, a ma ia ao ae o Huna ia la. *Ole* applies to four days in the month, so called because it was unsafe to go to sea on account of high surf, as the tides would be high.

O-LE, *v.* To be not; to cease to exist. 1 *Sam.* 2:31. To pass away. *Iob.* 24:24. A e *ole* loa hoi, and to be no more. *Hal.* 39:14. Aole e *ole*. *Luk.* 21:9. A ua *ole* ia, and it is gone. *Hal.* 103:16.

2. To not, or not to do a thing, with an infinitive. *Rom.* 8:32.

3. *Hoo.* To deny; refuse; make void; abrogate.

4. To answer, or plead *not guilty* to a charge.

5. To refuse; forbid; rebuke. Note.— *Ole* often has the form of a verb, when it serves only to express negation.

O-LE, *s.* Nothingness; vanity; in vain. *Oihk.* 26:20. Aole ka *ole*, without fail; the not; the negative; ka *ole*, no existence. *Ezek.* 12:19.

2. The want; the lack; the destitution of a thing; make ia no ka *ole* o ka ai, he died for the *not* (want) of food. *Iob.* 4:11.

3. *Hoo.* A denial; a want of truth; inability; nothingness.

O-LE, *adv.* A negative; no; not; nor; a particle of deprivation like *un* and *less* in English. See Aole. *Aole* is used *before* a noun or verb, and *ole* after it.

O-LE, *v.* To speak through the throat or through a trumpet.

O-LE, *s.* A speaking-trumpet.

2. A kind of large sea shell.

O-LE-A, *adj.* Shining; hot; olea ka la; of sound, loud; piercing; olea ke kani; same perhaps as *oolea.*

O-LE-O-LE, *s.* Name of a board set on posts with notches on it to hang calabashes on.

O-LE-O-LE, *v.* *Hoo.* To deny; to deny a charge repeatedly.

O-LE-O-LE, *v.* To talk thickly and indistinctly, as one very angry and scolding.

2. To grin like an idol; *oleole* mai ka waha o na 'kua kii o na heiau; *oleole* no ka waha o ka wahine nuku.

3. To make notches in anything; to dovetail two pieces together.

O-LE-O-LE, *adv.* Indistinctly, as a sound; inarticulate; kani *oleole* ka waha o ka uila.

O-LEO-LEO, *v.* To act as one angry; to rage, as the ocean; *oleoleo* la i ka moana kau mai ana.

2. To be uneven, as waves; to rise and fall.

3. To be in confusion. See Hoo.

O-LE-HA, *v.* To fix the eyes; to set them in a squinting manner. See Leha. *Oleha* na maka i ka pololi.

O-LE-HA, *s.* Name of a play or game in which the eyes are set.

2. A setting or fixing of the eyes, as in death; o ka *oleha* make, make ae no ia.

O-LE-HA-LE-HA, *s.* The dazzling or blinding of the eyes by an intense light of the sun; ka *olehaleha* o na maka i ka la.

O-LE-HA-LE-HA, *adj.* Dazzling; blinding to the eyes on account of intense light.

O-LE-KU-KA-HI, *s.* Name of the seventh day of the month.

O-LE-KU-LU-A, *s.* Name of the eighth day of the month.

O-LE-KU-KO-LU, *s.* Name of the ninth day of the month.

O-LE-LO, *v.* See Leo, voice, and Lelo, the tongue. To speak; to say (it implies a more formal or longer speech than *i* or *hai*); to converse.

2. To teach; to call; to invite, as to a feast. *Ioan.* 2:12.

3. To give a name. *Isa.* 56:7. E *olelo* hooweliweli, to threaten. *Oih.* 4:17. E *olelo* hooino, to curse. *Nal.* 22:17. E *olelo* hoomaikai, to bless; e *olelo* hoonani, to glorify; e *olelo* pohihi, to speak mystically, darkly.

Ioan. 16:25. Opposite to *olelo akaka. Ioan.* 16:20.

O-LE-LO, *s.* A word; a speech; language.

2. Counsel; plan; promise; an address; he mau *olelo* umi, the ten commandments. *Puk.* 34:28. Kana *olelo,* his word, i. e., that which one has spoken; kona *olelo,* what is said about him; kahi e *olelo* ai, an oracle; a place to utter an oracle. 1 *Nal.* 6:19, 20.

O-LE-LO, *adv.* Pane *olelo,* to speak a word; to answer a word. 2 *Sam.* 3:11.

O-LE-LOA, *adv. Ole,* not, and *loa,* an intensive. Not at all; by no means; entirely destitute; without thought.

O-LE-LO-AO, *v. Olelo,* to speak, and *ao,* to teach. To give counsel; advice in state affairs. 2 *Oihl.* 22:3. *Oleloao* mai o Vanekouva ia Kamehameha e hooki i ke kaua, Vancouver *advised* Kamehameha to cease going to war.

O-LE-LO-AO, *s.* Counsel; advice in important matters. 2 *Sam.* 15:31.

O-LE-LO-HOO-HE-WA, *s.* An accusation; a charge of wrong against one.

2. The act of speaking against others.

3. Backbiting.

O-LE-LO-HOO-PO-MAI-KAI, *s.* A promise; a promise of a blessing. 1 *Nal.* 2:24.

O-LE-LO-HOO-PO-NO, *s.* Righteousness. *Iob.* 29:14.

O-LE-LO-KU-PAA, *s. Olelo* and *ku,* to stand, and *paa,* fast. An ordinance; an established decision. 1 *Sam.* 30:20. A legal decree; judgment. *Puk.* 15:25.

O-LE-LO-MAI-KAI, *s. Olelo,* word, and *maikai,* good. The gospel; the preaching of the gospel.

O-LE-LO-NA-NE, *s. Olelo,* a word, and *nane,* a riddle. A proverb. *Kanl.* 28:37. A riddle; parable; enigma. *Mat.* 13:3.

O-LE-LO-PAA, *s. Olelo* and *paa,* fast. A precept; a command. *Hal.* 119:87.

O-LE-LO-PAI-PAI, *s. Olelo,* word, and *paipai,* to stir up. An exhortation. *Mal.* 2:1.

O-LE-MU, *v.* To banish one from his place; to cast off; *olemu* hue, kole ka aina paipai.

O-LE-MU-KAA, *s.* See LEMU and KAA, to roll. LIT. The rolling thigh; epithet of a man who often moves from place to place, who gathers no property and never becomes kuonoono, quietly settled; "the rolling stone gathers no moss."

O-LE-NA, *s.* See LENA, yellow. Name of a plant; the turmeric, the root of which is used in dyeing yellow; it also forms an ingredient in curry; it resembles the awa-puhi; also a yellow color, from the root.

O-LE-NA (o-le-na-le-na), *adj.* Yellow, from the plant. See above. Coloring yellow.

O-LE-PA, *v.* To cast about; to scatter round; to be turned up or over; ua *olepa* ke kaupaku o ka hale. See LEPA, a small flag floating in the wind.

O-LE-PA, *s.* Odor; odoriferous; he mea ala.

2. A clam; a kind of flat cockle.

O-LE-PAU, *s.* The tenth day of the month.

O-LE-PA-LE-PA, *v.* See LEPA. To flap, flutter or wave in the wind.

2. To be blown in different directions by the wind, as a sail; *olepalepa* ka pea.

O-LE-PE, *s.* The name of a kind of fish resembling the pipi. *Anat.* 6.

O-LE-PE, *v.* To turn, as a door on a hinge; to turn one way and another, as the helm of a ship.

O-LE-PE-LE-PE, *v.* The opening frequently of a door or window shutter; ka wehe pinepine i ka puka.

O-LE-PE-LE-PE, *adj.* Partially closed up, as a window; puka *olepelepe,* a lattice window. *Mel. Sol.* 2:9. The term applied to window shutters.

O-LE-PO-LE-PO, *adj.* See LEPO. Out of order, as the bowels.

O-LE-WA, *v.* See LEWA. To be unfixed; not firm; to be movable; changeable.

2. To be soft; flowing; applied to poi.

3. To be unstable; liable to be overturned, as a law; ua *olewa* ke kanawai o ka aina haunaele, the law is liable to be overturned in a land of disorder; aneane *olewa* io ke kanawai, the law is nearly nullified.

O-LE-WA, *adj.* Fickle; changeable; swinging; applied to one who often changes his place of residence.

2. Not firmly established; of partial application, as a law; ineffectual; ua *olewa* io ke kanawai minamina ino; he hee, mau-mau ole, paa ole.

O-LI (o-li-o-li), *v.* To sing; to sing with a joyful heart; to be glad; to exult; to rejoice. *Puk.* 18:9. E *oli* i ka oli, to sing a song. *Lunk.* 5:12. *Hoo.* To cause joy; exultation, &c.

O-LI (oli-o-li), *s.* Joy; exultation; gladness; delight; pleasure.

2. A song. *Laieik.* 69. A singing. *Hal.* 96:1. Ka *olioli* nui o na mea a pau i ka hoihoi ana mai o ke aupuni.

O-LI-O-LI, *adv.* Joyfully; cheerfully. *Hal.* 96:2.

O-LI-LI, *adj.* Withered; stinted; not fully grown; applied to fruit.

O-LI-NA, *v.* To play; e lealea, e walea.

O-LI-NA, *adj.* Of or pertaining to play; aha *olina*, a meeting for play.

O-LI-NO, *v.* To shine brightly; to shine with splendor.

O-LI-NO-LI-NO, *v.* See OLINO.

O-LI-NO-LI-NO, *s.* Brightness; splendor; glory. 2 *Sam.* 22:13.

2. Such intense brightness as to dazzle and bewilder the sight; ka ohewahewa ana o ka maka i ka malamalama.

O-LI-NO-LI-NO, *adj.* Where the intense light of the sun has shined; hence,

2. Parched; dry, as land; lepo *olinolino.* *Isa.* 35:7.

O-LI-VA (o-li-ve), *s.* *Eng.* An olive tree.

O-LI-VA (o-li-ve), *adj.* Olive; belonging to an olive; lau *oliva.* *Kin.* 8:11. He laau *oliva*, an olive tree.

O-LO, *v.* To rub, as on a grater; to rub, as kalo or cocoanut on a rough stone to grate it fine.

2. To rub up and down, as the motion of a saw, particularly of a whip-saw.

3. To roll with fat, as the flanks and hips of a very fat animal; hence,

4. To saw. 1 *Nal.* 7:9.

O-LO, *v.* To be loud, as a sound; to make a loud sound, as of many voices.

2. To sound, as a voice of wailing; to make a doleful noise. *Ier.* 7:29. E *olo* no wau i ka pihe; e *olo* pihe ana, moaning; bemoaning one's self. *Ier.* 31:18.

O-LO, *s.* See OLO, to rub up and down. A saw, from its motion; also pahi olo, a saw.

2. A double or fleshy skin; the moving flesh of a fat animal.

3. The swing-gobble of a turkey.

4. A very thick surf-board made of the wiliwili tree. *Laieik.* 90.

O-LO, *s.* A loud wailing; a lamentation, makena. See PIHE.

O-LO-A, *s.* Mulberry bark soaked until soft in water.

2. The name of small white kapas formerly put over the gods while the prayer was said, thus: i puaa, i niu, i maia, i *oloa.*

3. A gift made to a child at the time or soon after it was born. See KOPILI; see *Laieik.* 101.

O-LO-A-LU, *s.* A place where the property of a chief was stored up; he *oloalu* o ke alu o kahi e waiho ai ke kapa o na 'lii.

2. The sound of many voices at once, of many horns blowing at once, of many cocks crowing together, &c.

O-LO-A-LU, *v.* To seize or grasp, as several persons at the same thing; ke aluka ana o ke kani ana o ka moa; ke *oloalu* ana o na kanaka e hao e aluka.

2. To dodge, where many things are flying thickly; *oloalu* i ka ihe ke nui loa.

O-LO-I, *v.* To rub, as the stone rubs kalo as well as pounds it.

2. To run upon or over, as a vessel runs over or upon a canoe, or a cart over a man, or anything drawn over a man.

3. To run aground, as a canoe, or on to a stone; *oloi* ae la ka waa i ka pohaku.

O-LO-O-LO, *v.* See OLO. To hang loosely, as fat under the chin or on the calf of the leg.

2. To vibrate or swing, as a saw. *Isa.* 10:15.

3. To fall behind; to loiter.

4. To lose favor with one.

5. To be denied that which was before freely given. See OLOOLO below.

O-LO-O-LO, *s.* The calf of the leg, from the flexibility of the muscle.

2. A bundle done up loosely; a loose bundle of poi.

> O ka puhi o ke ale ia a hu
> Ka *oloolo* o ka hee o kai uli la,
> Lehu ka *hooloolo* o ka alaala.

O-LO-O-LO, *v.* See OLO. To make a great sound of wailing, or as many wailing together.

2. To roar or rush, as the sound of water; mai *hooloolo* oukou e ku auanei i ke au; o ka mea e *hooloolo* ana ia ia e ku oia i ke au; *oloolo* na kahawai ku ka pihea i kai, the brooks roar like the roaring of the sea. NOTE.—It is not easy to see the connection between *olo—oloolo* to sound, as the voice of wailing, and *olo—oloolo* to swing, vibrate, &c., unless the latter be the radical meaning, and the voice of wailing be so expressed on account of the vibratory motion of the voice in mourning and wailing.

O-LO-O-LO, *s.* A sound like many horns blown at once.

O-LO-O-LO-KA, *v.* See OLO. To shake, as the limbs of a fat person; *olooloka* na wawae nunui maikai. See OLOKA.

O-LO-O-LO-NA, *s.* See OLONA. The cords or ligaments that bind together the bones and muscles of the animal system.

2. Duty; office of one; service.

3. Baggage, or any kind of property to be taken when one removes; e nana ana oia i ka *oloolona* nui e pono ole ai keia manomano kanaka.

O-LO-U, *v.* See ALAU. To strike, as the knuckles on anything hard; to make a rapping noise.

O-LO-HA-NA, *s.* *Eng.* *All hands*; the name given to Mr. John Young.

O-LO-HE, *v.* To turn pale in the face from fear or pain. *Ier.* 30:6.

O-LO-HE, *s.* The epithet of a man that is a robber and skillful at the lua.

2. Ke akua o Kamaomao.

3. Skillful, as one able to direct or oversee the work of others; applied *morally* also to universal skill.

O-LO-HE, *adj.* Rigid; immovable with fear; he kanaka *olohe* uwi paa i ka makau ia.

2. Sick, as a woman in child birth; he mai *olohe* keiki ia no na wahine.

3. Bare; destitute of verdure; ka lua *olohe* o ke alialia, he lua olohelohe.

4. Bare; free from hair on the body, chin, eyebrows, &c.

O-LO-HE-LO-HE, *v.* See OLOHE. To be destitute; empty. *Kin.* 1:2.

2. To be destitute of; to be naked; without clothing. *Ioan.* 21:7. *Olohelohe* ke kuemaka; ua *olohelohe* ka aina, destitute of verdure.

O-LO-HE-LO-HE, *s.* Nakedness; destitution of clothing or covering. *Hoik.* 3:18.

O-LO-HE-LO-HE, *adj.* Destitute; naked; bare of vegetation, as a barren field.

O-LO-HI-O, *v.* See OHIO.

O-LO-HU, *s.* Name of a stone to roll in a kind of play. See ULU.

O-LO-HUA, *s.* A berry somewhat like the whortleberry, the fruit of the popolo.

O-LO-KA, *v.* See OLO. To shake, as the soft limbs of a fat person when walking; *oloka* na wawae. See OLOOLOKA.

O-LO-KAA, *v.* *Olo* and *kaa*, to roll.

1. To roll; to roll over and over, as a stone. *Mat.* 28:2. To roll away; to roll to a place; to roll off, as a burden; to take away, as a reproach. *Ios.* 5:9. *Olokaa* lakou i ka pohaku mai luna a i lalo.

2. To roll off upon another; to transfer, as a debt; ua *olokaa* aku au i ko'u aie a pau, I have paid off (rolled) all my debt.

O-LO-KE, *adj.* Clamorous and incoherent, as the constant talk of one deranged; *oloke* ka waha. See PIOLOKE.

O-LO-KEA, *v.* *Olo* and *kea*, cross ways. To cross; to vex; to thwart one in his plans; e kau *olokea*, to throw together criss-cross, as sticks of wood.

O-LO-KEA, *adj.* A heap of bones thrown together promiscuously.

2. A cross or gibbet. *Eset.* 5:14.

3. A kind of ladder, such as is made by tying sticks horizontally on erect poles.

4. The frame on which the people climbed and stood in putting up a house.

O-LO-KEA, *s.* In the form of a cross, or several crosses; laau *olokea*.

2. Applied to the disposition; cross; fretful; disobliging.

O-LO-KE-LE, *s.* The name of a stream or valley on Kauai.

O-LO-KI-KI, *v.* To loosen, as a board.

O-LO-LA, *s.* A species of the mullet when small.

O-LO-LI, *v.* *Olo* and *li* for *lii*, small, little, &c. To be narrow. *Isa.* 28:20. To be contracted, as a path. *Mat.* 7:14.

O-LO-LI, *adj.* Narrow; contracted; difficult. 1 *Nal.* 6:4.

O-LO-LI-LO-LI, *v.* To be tough, water soaked, like kalo. See LOLILOLI.

O-LO-LO, *v.* *Olo*, to rub, the 9th conj. of *olo*. To rub with the hand; to polish. SYN. with anai.

O-LO-LO, *adj.* Uneven, like a bundle jutting out at the corners.

O-LO-ME-A, *s.* A species of tree; same as *waimea*; *olomea* i paio aina e mai la; used in producing fire by friction.

O-LO-ME-A, *s.* The name of a striped hog; ina i onionio ka hulu o ka puaa ma ka loa, he *olomea* ia puaa.

O-LO-ME-HA-NI, *s.* A place where dirt and filth are thrown.

O-LO-MI-O, *v.* To contract, as the toe of a shoe; to pucker up, as the mouth of an eel; to corrugate, as the skin of a healing wound; *olomio* iki ka hele a ke aloha; palanehe ia i hele aku nei.

O-LO-MI-O, *adj.* Smooth and tapering; verging to a point, but with a smooth surface; meomeo, nuku puhi, olomuo, olomua.

O-LO-MU-A, *s.* *Olo* and *mua*, the front; fore part. The foreskin. *Ier.* 4:4. *Olomua* kahi omaka o ka ule; ka omaka. 2 *Sam.* 3:14.

O-LO-MU-O, *s.* *Olo*, to rub, and *muo*, to open, as a bud.

1. The bud of a blossom before it blooms; ka maka o ka pua aole i pohole.

2. The prepuce that is cut off in circumcision; ka *olomuo* o kahi omaka.

O-LO-NA, *s.* A shrub, the bark of which dressed resembles bleached hemp or flax, and is made into small cords.

2. The name of the cord itself; hence,

3. Flax; hemp; linen. *Puk.* 9:31.

4. A cord; tendon of a muscle of animals or men. *Kol.* 2:19. A muscle. *Sol.* 3:8. *Olona* hao, an iron sinew. *Isa.* 48:4. The hamstring of an animal. *Kin.* 32:32. In

surgery, a ligament. *Anat.* 1:24.

O-LO-NA, *adj.* Flaxen; pertaining to linen. *Ier.* 13:1. Ka lole *olona* maikai; he ie nani *olona*; ua aahuia i ka lole *olona* aiai keokeo. *Hoik.* 15:6.

O-LO-PA, *v.* To break up or break to pieces; similar to *ulupa.*

O-LO-PE, *s.* A house fallen down and persons in it.

2. A house broken up without people.

O-LO-PE-LO-PE, *s.* A species of small shrimp found in kalo patches.

O-LO-PU, *v.* To hold in the mouth without swallowing; *olopu* ae la kona kapa i ka makani. *Hoo.* Hoolopu ae la oia i ka pea i ka makani.

O-LO-PU, *s.* Hooinu iho la oia i ke keiki i ka *olopu* wai; a mouthful, as of food or drink; hookahi *olopu* ai a me ke kiaha wai, one mouthful of food and a cup of water.

O-LO-PU-A, *adj.* Ulili nae *olopua. Laieik.* 142.

O-LO-WAE, *s.* The fat, the movable flesh on the calf of the leg; wawae he mau *olowae.*

O-LO-WA-LU, *s.* See OLOALU. O ke *olowalu* o ke kapu o ke alii; kahi e kau ai ke kapa o ke oloalu.

O-LO-WA-LU-PUU, *s.* Name of a place where many hillocks stand near each other. See also KINIKINIPUU.

O-LU, *v.* To feel comfortably; to be agreeable; to have the sensation of satisfaction.

2. To please; to be pleased; to regard with favor.

3. To be cool, as with a salubrious breeze; *olu* ka wai ke luu aku; *olu* ka makani ke pa mai koaniani; *olu* Lahainaluna i ka makani maaa.

O-LU, *s.* The vibrations or springing motion of the rafters of a house made by the wind. See UPAIPAI.

2. An arch; a bending of timber in a house; a bending or yielding without breaking.

3. The squirming contortions of a worm on a fish-hook. See HOLU, PIO, &c.

O-LU, *adj.* Cool; refreshing. *Lunk.* 5:28. Comfortable; easy; pleasant to the sight; benign; contented.

2. Clear; pleasant, as the voice; o ka *olu* o ka leo ka mea i akaka ai kona manao, the clearness of the voice makes clear the thought.

3. Limber, so as to bend in all directions without breaking. See OLU, *s.*

O-LU, *s.* A cool breeze; he koaniani.

2. Coolness; a refreshing sensation.

O-LU, *adj.* Epithet of certain kinds of fish or shells; as, ka papai *olu*; ka ulu *olu*; he wahi leho *olu.*

O-LU-A, *pers. pron.*, second pers. dual. You two. *Gram.* § 132, 2d.

O-LU-AU, *s.* Name of a ceremony in the worship of Kanaloa; ua kapaia keia hana he *oluau.*

O-LU-E-KE-LOA-HOO-KAA-MO-E-NA, *s.* Epithet of a person who fanned the chief while he slept; o ka mea kahili i ko ke alii wahi moe ai, he *oluekeloahookaamoena* ia.

O-LU-O-LU, *v.* See OLU. To be comfortable; to be gratified; to be contented; satisfied. *Luk.* 3:14.

2. *Hoo.* To comfort; to please; to console; to please one; to render a thing agreeable.

3. To treat kindly; to be favorable; to comfort one; to cheer. *Kanl.* 24:5. Ua *oluolu* ka noho i ke kau o na 'lii maikai, it is pleasant to live in the reign of good chiefs.

O-LU-O-LU, *adj.* Cool; refreshing; agreeable, &c. See OLU. O ka makani *oluolu*, oia ka mea e pale ai i ka wela o ka la.

2. Large and fat, as a fat and weak man; kanaka *oluolu*, an easy, good-natured man.

O-LU-HE-LU-HE, *s.* A species of fish of the oopu kind; he oopu oau, he oaoau, he *oluheluhe.*

O-LU-LE-LU-LE, *adj.* See LULE, to shake. Large; fat, so as to have the fat shake in walking; applied to men.

O-LU-LE-LU-LEA, *adj.* For *oluleluleia.* Large; fat, &c. See the foregoing.

O-LU-LO, *s.* A person cast away.

2. A statue; a figure.

3. Food that has become sour and rotten, as melons.

4. A long water calabash.

O-LU-LO, *adj.* Cast away; shipwrecked; he kanaka *olulo* i make ka waa i ka moana.

O-LU-LO-LU-LO, *adj.* Large; fat; shaking with fat, as a man. See OLULELULE.

O-LU-LU, *s.* A person of portly habits, but lax in joints. See OLU.

O-LU-NA, *adv.* The auipili of *luna.* Of or belonging to what is upward or above. See *Gram.* § 161. See LUNA.

O-LU-PI, *s.* The falling down, as a child; an upsetting; he kaekae ka *olupi* mai ka wai i olu ka puu.

O-MA, *v.* To solicit silently a favor; to hint a desire for a favor.

2. To open the mouth, as a child about to suck; ke *oma* ae nei ka pahi i ka maunu;

o ke *oma* aku no ia e lalau ia ia.

3. To strike with the hands on the surf-board.

O-MA, *s.* The space between two armies where the sacrifices were offered.

2. The preparations previous to war.

3. Name of the man first killed in a battle.

O-MA, *s.* An oven; a baking place; in modern times, a bake pan; ku wale iho no ia hale i ke *oma*; e uhao i ka puaa i ke *oma* i moa maikai.

O-MA, *s.* The highest officer of the king; Kalanimoku was Kaahumanu's *oma*; Kinau was the *oma* of Kauikeaouli.

O-MA, *s.* A small adz or koi.

O-MAI, *adj.* Soft; flexible; limber.

O-MAI, *s.* See O and MAI. To answer to a call; *omai* ke alii nono ia inoa.

O-MAI-MAI, *adj.* See MAI, sick, weak. Weak; void of strength; sick.

O-MAO, *s.* A bunch of food.

2. The cover or wrapper of the food.

3. A round bundle, as of food; sharp above and round below; ka *omao* ai, or *ai omao*.

O-MAO, *s.* Name of a species of small bird; it resembles the *ou* only; its feathers are dark colored.

O-MAO, *adj.* Green; greenish in color; he manu *omao*; he leho *omao*.

O-MAO, *s.* A child always crying; he *omao* la ka uwe o ke keiki, o ka *omao* wale no ia e uwe ai.

O-MA-O-MA, *v.* To solicit silently a favor. See OMA.

O-MA-O-MA, *v.* To be afraid to speak to one for fear of giving offense; ua *omaoma* aku no ka waha e pane aku ia ia, hilahila mai no hoi au. See OMA.

O-MA-O-MA, *s.* The bosom; the breast. See UMAUMA. O ka waha o ka puhi la *oma-oma*.

O-MAO-MAO, *adj.* Green, as grass or vegetation.

2. Blue, as the sky.

Ua *omaomao* ka lani, ua kahaea luna,
Ua pipi ka maka o na hoku.

O-MAO-MAO, *v.* To be or appear green, as vegetation; ua *omaomao* na nahelehele i ka uliuli o na mauu o ke kula, ua puia make i ka nani.

O-MAO-MAO, *s.* Name of a precious stone; an emerald, from its green color. *Hoik.* 21:20.

O-MAU, *v.* To gird, bind or tie on, as a sword; i ka wa i hele ai lakou i ke kaua, *omau* no lakou i ka pahi. *Lunk.* 3:16. To

sheath, put up, as a sword.

2. To tuck in, as the outer edge of a pau to fasten it; e *omau* iho a paa ka lole.

3. To sew; to stitch together; to baste cloth.

O-MAU, *s.* A tucking in of the edge of a pau, which is tucked in under to fasten it on the body.

2. A sheath, as for a sword.

3. *Omau* i ke ala paa ole i ka *omauia*, in the path not hard by frequent use (perhaps.)

4. A pining sickness. *Isa.* 38:12. English translation, a piece cut off; a fragment; a thread, &c. *Heb.* Ka paa maopopo ole, ka *omau* wale iho. The idea seems to be, something unfixed; insecure; something firm in appearance, but liable to give way; temporary.

5. Name of a species of fish-hook.

O-MA-KA, *s.* The fountain head of a stream.

2. The springing up of vegetables. See MAKA, the eye, the bud, &c.

3. The nipples of a female. *Ezek.* 23:3. *Omaka* waiu, the breast. *Kanik.* 4:3.

4. The foreskin in males that was cut off in circumcision. *Kanl.* 10:16. NOTE.—Circumcision was formerly practiced among Hawaiians.

5. Ka *omaka* wai o ka niu; ka *omaka*, ka omua ke poo; ua halu ka *omaka* wai i kai, ua lepo ka *omaka* wai i kinohi. See OLOMUA.

6. The name of a fish.

O-MA-LE-MA-LE, *s.* A species of fish; the same as the *male*; the young of the uhu.

O-MA-LI, *v.* To be weakly in body; sickly; ua *omali* ke kino, he mai paaoao.

O-MA-LI, *adj.* Weak; feeble with sickness.

2. Unripe; wilted, as fruit; he ipu *omali* oo ole, an unripe, soft melon.

O-MA-LI, *s.* Weakness of body; infirmity of the system; ka *omali*, ka nawaliwali, ka paaoao.

O-MA-LI-O, *adj.* Broad; extended; flat, as flat land. See KAHUAOMALIO.

O-MA-LU-MA-LU, *adj.* Cloudy and dark, as when the sun does not break out at all. See MALU.

O-ME-O, *v.* Ua *omeo* ae ka puka ana. See OPUU.

O-ME-O-ME-O, *adj.* Ulaula, meomeo; Red; blushing, as people; yellow, as ripe fruit: orange, musk-melon, &c.

O-ME-GA, *s.* Gr. The name of the last letter of the Greek alphabet, the great O; hence,

2. The last, ka welau, in opposition to *kumu*; an epithet of Jesus Christ. *Hoik.* 21:6.

O-ME-RA, *s.* *Heb.* A dry measure; an *omer*. *Puk.* 16:16.

O-MI, *v.* To wither; to droop, as vegetables; not to grow or vegetate; e ulu ole o ke kanu ana, he loi *homi*.

2. To droop; lose flesh, as a person. See HOMI.

O-MI, *adj.* Withering, as a tree with few roots; he kukui aa ole *omi*. See HOMI and HOOMIMI.

O-MI-O-MI, *v.* See OMI. To wither; to lose flesh; to droop; applied to men or plants; to stop growing. See OMIOMI.

O-MI-KO, *s.* Lean and unproductive soil.

O-MI-KO, *adj.* Unfruitful, as ground that yields nothing.

2. Stinted in growth, as vegetables; he loi *omiko*.

O-MI-LI-MI-LU, *s.* See PAOPAO, the name of a fish.

O-MI-LO, *v.* See MILO. To spin; to twist, as a rope; to spin, as thread. See HILO. To twist with the thumb and finger; also in drilling a small hole.

2. To produce abortion.

O-MI-LO, *s.* The name of a medicine used in procuring abortion; he laau lapaau; applied to the operation or to the medicine used in procuring abortion.

O-MI-LO-MI-LO, *v.* To destroy or cause the death of an unborn infant; ina i ike oe he kaikamahine, e *omilomilo* ae au. *Laieik.* 11.

O-MI-MI, *v.* To droop; to wither, as a plant.

2. To lose flesh as a person; ua *omimi* ka ulu ana o keia laau.

O-MI-MI, *s.* A fading; a decaying; a withering of animal or vegetable life.

2. That which is of small or slow growth.

O-MI-NO, *v.* To wither; to droop. See OMI.

O-MI-NO, *s.* A stinted person; a sickly, crying child.

O-MI-NO, *adj.* Stinted; sickly, as a child; he keiki *omino*, uwe wale; withered; without flesh; small, uuku, io ole.

O-MO, *v.* To suck, as a child. *Luk.* 22:29.

2. To draw up, as a pump.

3. To cleave together, as if by sucking.

4. To evaporate, as water, and pass into the clouds; ua *omoia* ke kai e ka wela, a lilo ia i mau ao.

O-MO, *adj.* Sucking; keiki *omo* waiu, a sucking child. *Nah.* 11:12. He mea *omo* waiu, a suckling. 1 *Sam.* 22:19. He mea *omo*, a thing that sucks, i. e., a child.

O-MO, *s.* A cover to a calabash or pot.

2. The name given to a long, narrow kind of adz; koi *omo*.

O-MOO-MOO, *v.* O ka lepo i *omoomooia*, a hahauia, oia kekahi hale; an oval adobie; any long, oval shaped body, as balls of pia.

O-MOO-NOO, *s.* He lapa, he kualapa, he moo.

O-MO-HA, *s.* A figure used in printing kapa.

O-MO-HA-LU, *s.* Name of the twelfth day of the month; properly *mohalu*.

O-MO-KI, *v.* To stop up with a cork, bung or stopper, &c.; ua paa i ka *omokiia* i ka pani.

O-MO-KI, *s.* A cork; a stopper of a bottle; a bung of a cask; the stopper of a calabash, &c.

O-MO-KI, *v.* To jump from a high place into deep water, a sport for children; *omoki* lua ka wai o ke keiki akamai i ka lelekawa. See UMOKI.

O-MO-KO-KO, *s.* *Omo*, to suck, and *koko*, blood. A horse leech; a blood-sucker. *Sol.* 30:15.

O-MO-LE, *adj.* Round and smooth; he huewai *omole*; hence

O-MO-LE, *s.* A glass bottle; a bottle; a cruse. *Nal.* 17:14. A phial; a polished cane; a large, fat, smooth hog; he puaa nui keia, he *omole* nei ka hulu.

O-MO-LE-A, *s.* A species of tree.

O-MO-LE-O-MO-LE, } *adj.* Round and
O-MO-LE-MO-LE, } smooth. See OMOLE.

O-MO-LI-U, *v.* *Omo*, to suck, and *liu*, bilge water. To absorb or discharge bilge water from a canoe or ship; to pump water from a ship.

O-MO-LI-U, *s.* *Omo* and *liu*. A ship pump. NOTE.—The word *pauma* has been introduced from the English pump. See PAUMA.

O-MO-MO, *v.* See OMO, to suck. To put the end of a thing into the mouth to wet it; a *omomo* ko ke kanaka waha i ua pua la.

O-MU-A, *v.* To tie up the wound of the foreskin when cut off in circumcision.

2. To tie a string around the fore end of the pua or cane top to make a papua for playing that game; e *omua* ke kumu o ka pua i ke kaula.

O-MU-A-MU-A, *s.* The bulb of a flower before it blossoms; *omuamua* pua.

O-MU-E, } *adj.* Sweet scented;
O-MU-E-MU-E, } odoriferous.

O-MU-O, *s.* See OMUA above. *Omuo* pua.

O-MU-O-MU-O, *s.* The upper and youngest leaves of the sugar-cane, ki, &c.; as, *omuomuo* ko; *omuomuo* ki; the huli of the kalo makua. See MUO, a bud.

O-MU-O-MU-O-PU-A, *v.* Muo and *pua*, a flower. To swell out, as the bud of a flower.

O-MUU, *v.* To begin to grow, as a vegetable. See OMUA and OMUO.

O-MU-KU, *v.* See PAHUPAHU. *Kamak.* To cut short; to cut off.

O-NA, *v.* To be drunk; to be intoxicated. 1 *Sam.* 25:36. Ua waiwai loa ia haole, ua *ona*, spoken sarcastically; to be under the influence of intoxicating drinks.

   2. To be delighted or ravished; i *ona* mau mai kona aloha iloko ou. *Sol.* 5:19.

   3. *Hoo.* To make one drunk.

O-NA, *s.* A state of intoxication, as produced by alcohol, tobacco and awa.

   2. Dizziness of the head.

   3. A kind of nettling or pricking of the skin, attended with some pimples.

O-NA, *adj.* Drunk; intoxicated.

O-NA, *pers. pron.*, the auipili of *ia.* Of him; of her, of it; his; hers; its; rarely in the neuter gender; belonging to him, &c. Gram. § 137-139.

O-NA-O-NA, *adj.* Weary; fatigued; faint, as from traveling.

   2. Faint; dizzy, from weakness or want of food; poniuniu.

   3. Applied to food; unpalatable; ono ole; wai *onaona*, bad tasted water; hue-wai *onaona*, bad smelling calabash.

O-NA-O-NA, *adj.* Beautiful; graceful; pretty faced; he mau maka *onaona*, he maikai, he nani; ka wehiwehi i ka *onaona* i ke ala; beautiful; applied to the eyes and face; rosy cheeks.

O-NA-O-NA, *s.* A pleasant, odoriferous smell, as of a rose; aka e hai aku i ke ala ame ke *onaona*, ame ka pukue o ka naauao; *onaona* ala, a pleasant smell; me ka honi ala *onaona*, alaila hoi ka makani ala *onaona*, e nu ana ma ke kaena nei; maluna o ka *onaona* ala launa.

O-NAU-NA, *v.* To come around, as fishes when a baited hook is let down.

O-NA-U-NA, *adj.* Neat; graceful; pretty.

O-NA-HA, *v.* To curve or bend round, as a semi-circle or a half bounding line; *onaha* na kihi o ka mahina, the points of the moon *bend round.*

   2. To spread or crook, as the legs; applied to one whose legs or knees spread wide apart; used in hailiili.

O-NA-HA, *adj.* Crooked; bending, as an aged person; he wahine *onaha* Kalepeamoa; crooked, as one's legs; wawae *onaha.*

O-NA-HA, *adv.* Crookedly; in a bent position; ke waiho *onaha* mai la ka lima, the arm lies half bent. See NAHA, broken.

O-NA-HA-NA-HA, *v.* This word is used in all the senses of *onaha* above; as, *onahanaha* na kihi o ka mahina, &c.; he kanaka wawae *onahanaha* ke hele mai, &c.

O-NA-HA-NA-HA, *s.* The halo of the moon (doubtful.)

O-NA-HA-NA-HA-IA-UA, *v.* See above. *Onahanahaiaua* ke kihi o ka moku; ponahanaha ka moku me ka aina.

O-NA-LU-NA-LU, *adj.* Having a high surf, as the sea; *onalunalu* ke kai. See NALU.

O-NA-NA, *s.* Name of the third month of the year; more properly *Nana.*

O-NA-NA, *adj.* Perhaps a contraction of *ona* and *ana*, partially intoxicated. Weak; awkward; unskillful; he kanaka *onana*, ikaika ole hemahema.

O-NA-WA-LI, *adj.* See NAWALI. Weak; not strong; awkward; nawaliwali.

O-NA-WA-LI, *s.* An unripe, bitter melon or squash; he ipu awaawa oo ole.

O-NE, *s.* The sand; ke *one* o kahakai, the sand of the beach; ke *one* i Mahinahina; ke lele la ke *one* i Maoholaia.

O-NE, *v.* To be sandy; to have sand in plenty; ua *one* Kaupo, ua ka ka ai i ka lua.

O-NE-A, *s.* One, sand, and *a*, burning. (So called by Hawaiians when they first saw gunpowder.) LIT. Burning sand, that is, gunpowder; ke *onea* ka pauda, ka mea e lele ai ka poka; ua pau na kanaka i ke *onea* o ka haole. See PAUDA (powder,) which has since been introduced.

O-NE-A, *adj.* Destitute; all gone; vacant.

O-NE-A-NE-A, *s.* An open country; a desolate place where nothing grows; ka ulu ole na mea kanu.

O-NEA-NEA, *v.* To appear open and clear; to lie in fair sight, as a hill or mountain.

   2. To be desolate; waste; unfruitful, as a tract of country.

O-NEA-NEA, *adj.* Left alone; clear of verdure, as land; desolate; unfruitful; waste, as land; mahakea, nahelehele ole. See NEONEO.

O-NEI, *adv.*, the auipili of *nei.* Of this; of here; of this person; opposite of *olaila*, that there. NOTE.—Though often printed as one word, o *nei* are really two words.

O-NE-O-NE, *v.* To be broken; cracked,

as a melon, so the meat may run out.

O-NE-O-NE, *v.* The flowing out of the meat of a melon.

2. The cracks through which it flows out.

O-NE-O-NE, *adj.* Soft; flowing; fine; dwindled to nothing, &c.; pepehi i na kanaka a oneone.

O-NE-U-LA, *adj.* Great; extended; vast.

O-NE-HA-NAU, *s.* One, sand, and *hanau*, born. The place of one's birth; native-born place; one's native country where he and his ancestors lived; e ike auanei i ko kakou onehanau, we shall soon see our native-born place.

O-NE-LAU-E-NA, *s.* Some imaginary land or country where the god Kane lived or came from; he aina i ke onelauena a Kane, he aina i Kahiki, aia ilaila ke onelauena; he aina momona ke ano.

O-NI, *v.* To move; to stir, but to move only through a small space; aole e hiki ke oni i ka nawaliwali, he was not able to *move* from weakness; to turn the body in a restless mood. 2 *Sam.* 20:12.

2. To ascend with a zigzag motion, as a kite; lele ka lupe iluna o ka lewa oni ae ana.

3. To stretch out, as land into the sea.

4. To swim or move about in the sea. *Oihk.* 11:10.

5. To move on in a steady course of life; e oni wale no oukou i kuu pono a, continue to move on in my course. *Kauoha a Kam.*

6. To move, as a sign of life, in opposition to *moe malie*, a sign of death.

7. To move from one position to another; ua oni kela mai kona kala a hiki ma keia kala, he moved from his end of the house to this end.

8. To move about; to be busy; diligent; to move to and fro; e oni ana no ia me ke kulapa ana; e naku, e lapa, &c.

O-NI, *adj.* Uneasy; restless, as in pain.

O-NI, *s.* Uneasiness; a shifting from place to place; epithet of a living being, the moving. *Ezek.* 47:9.

O-NI-O, *s.* Cloth printed, especially in spots; the printed figures on calico.

O-NI-O, *adj.* Spotted; printed, like calico or kapa.

O-NI-O-NI, *v.* See ONI. To dodge; to move back and forth, as the ears of a horse; onioni no na pepeiao, moe imua a moe ihope; ua onioni ka lupe me he ao la, the kite *floats* like a cloud.

O-NI-O-NI-O, *adj.* See ONIO. Striped; spotted, as a cloth; as animals. *Kin.* 30:32. Variegated, as with colors; humuhumu

onionio, broidered work. *Puk.* 28:39. *Hoo.* Kapa hoonionio, broidered work. *Ezek.* 16:10.

O-NI-O-NI-O, *v.* To be spotted; ua onionio kikokiko ka leopadi.

2. *Hoo.* To embroider; to work figures on cloth. *Puk.* 28:39.

O-NI-U, *v.* To spin, as a top made of a cocoanut; hoka i oniuia kona lae.

O-NI-U, *s.* A top for spinning; a plaything for children, generally made of a cocoanut.

O-NI-HI-NI-HI, See ONINIHI.

O-NI-HO-NI-HO, *s.* Name of a species of fish.

O-NI-KA, *s.* Gr. Onyx; name of a precious stone. *Kin.* 2:12.

2. Also, a spice. *Puk.* 30:34.

O-NI-KI, *adj.* Flat; smooth, as a surface.

O-NI-KI-NI-KI. I ka pawa haahaa onikiniki.

O-NI-NA-NI-NA, *adj.* Fat; plump, as the cheeks of a man. See UNINANINA.

O-NI-NI, *v.* To blow very softly, as the beginning of a breeze.

2. To excite or stir up waves in a calm; to cause a ripple on the surface of water.

O-NI-NI, *s.* A very slight breeze of air like that which occasions a ripple after a calm; he wahi onini iki mai; applied only to a gentle wind when it covers the sea with ripples; onini loa mai na hua; he onini makani; the first beginning of a sea breeze; a puff of wind. *Isa.* 57:13.

2. The word is applied to one of imperfect vision when trying to read; onini ke kanaka i ka ili wai.

O-NI-NI, *v.* To close of shut the eyes on account of too strong light; ua onini na maka i ka malamalama, ua kahuli ka onohi, ua ano e ka maka.

O-NI-NI, *adj.* The state of one almost dead; he lelehu, he kapakahi, he kuhikee, he kokoke make loa.

O-NI-NI, *s.* A kind of surf-board.

O-NI-NI-HI, *s.* Young kalo; the tops of kalo. See PAUANIHI.

O-NI-NO-NI-NO, *v.* To be dazzling like the sun; ua oninonino na maka i ka la; to blind the eyes by a dazzling light. See OLINOLINO.

O-NI-NO-NI-NO, *adj.* Dazzling; dim-sighted through a strong light.

O-NI-PAA, *v.* Oni and *paa*, fast.

1. To be fixed; firmly bound together. *Hal.* 111:8. To be steadfast. *Hal.* 140:11. To be immovable.

2. To be persevering. *Sol.* 10:24. Ua

onipaa loa ke aupuni o ka Mesia. *Hoo.* To establish firmly. *Ier.* 42:10.

O-NI-PAA, *adj.* Firm; strong; fixed; immovable; he nauwe ole, he kulanalana ole; he hale *onipaa* a paa loa.

O-NO, *v.* To be or become sweet; to relish, as food; to have a like or relish for sweet food. *Kin.* 27:4. To have a sweet taste.

2. To be sweet, that is, good to eat; eatable. *Kin.* 3:6.

3. To desire greatly to taste or eat a thing; *ono* iho la kekahi mau kanaka i ka ia.

4. To be savory; ua *ono*, ua mikomiko, ua onoono.

5. *Morally*, to have a relish for virtue.

O-NO, *v.* To disrelish food, as a sick child or person without appetite. *Hoo.* Hooioi, hoono, hoonoono.

O-NO, *s.* Sweetness; that which is pleasant to the taste either in eating or drinking; ka *ono* o ka puu i ka ai ana a i ka inu ana.

O-NO, *adj.* Sweet; palatable; relishable; ala *ono*, a sweet savor. *Oihk.* 1:9. He kanaka hua *ono* oe. *Proverb.*

O-NO, *s.* Name of a very large species of fish, the parents of the opelu; o ke ano makua o ka opelu; computed at one-sixth of the whole.

O-NO, *adj.* The ordinal of six; the sixth; used with the article. *Gram.* 115:4. Aono, *eono*, six.

O-NO-O-NO, *adj.* Palatable; hence, pleasant; comfortable.

O-NOU, *v.* To entice; to allure; generrally for a bad purpose.

2. To give a thing deceitfully; to give away, as one's daughter in marriage for a selfish purpose.

3. To give the products of a land to another, not to the owner.

4. To secrete by craft; to turn aside from what is right.

5. To push against one, as if to push him down; to do things in a hurry.

6. To persuade one to leave his proper station for an improper one.

7. To change employment.

O-NOU, *s.* An enticement; a false giving; a seduction; an enticing, alluring, &c., of one. *Laieik.* 198. O ka *onou* wale ana o na makua i ke keiki, the enticing of parents their children (to vice.)

O-NOU, *s.* The name of a small bird; o ka *onou* he manu eleele ia.

O-NOU, *adj.* Seductive; alluring; deceitful, &c.

O-NOU-NOU, *v.* See ONOU above. To entice; seduce; persuade. NOTE.—This form is frequentative of *onou*, and used in all its senses.

O-NO-HI, *s.* The center of the eye; ka *onohi* o ka maka. *Zek.* 2:8.

2. The eye-ball; the apple of the eye; kii *onohi*, the little image in the eye; so haku *onohi*; hence,

3. The center of a thing; the excess of a thing; applied to darkness. *Sol.* 20:20. I. e., the profundity of darkness; ke *onohi* o ka pouli, where darkness is concentrated.

4. It is applied to light or heat; o ka *onohi* o ka umu ahi enaena, the *center* of a raging, fiery oven; ka waenakonu o ka lapalapa ahi, the center of a flame of fire; o ke *onohi* o ka la, the center of the sun; ke Alii e moe mai ana i ka *onohi* pono o ka la. *Laieik.* 176. He ao *onohi* opua kiikau.

O-NO-HI, *s.* Ike aku la oia e ku ana ka *onohi* iluna pono o Maunalei. *Laieik.* 25.

O-NO-HI-AI-A, *s.* Onohi and *aia*, bad, &c. A watery or sore eye.

O-NO-HI-U-LA, *s.* A deep red; a species of red color.

O-NO-HI-NO-HI, *v.* Ua *onohinohi* ka maka o ka hoku.

O-NU, *v.* To swell; to enlarge; to spring. See PEHU, to rise up, as a swelling.

O-NU, *s.* A swelling; a wen on the neck or head; anything growing up and increasing.

O-NU-HE-NU-HE-A, *adj.* Fat; very fat; shaking fat; applied to men when bloated very much.

O-PA, *v.* To press; squeeze, as the head of a child. *Anat.* 6.

O-PA, *adj.* See OOPA. Lame; fatigued; wearied.

O-PA, *adj.* Huikau, laiki, kulipee.

O-PA, *s.* A limping, walking, as one sore or disabled; ke kulipu, ka huikau, ka laiki.

O-PAE, *s.* A very small fish; a shrimp; a crab.

O-PAE-O-HAA, *s.* A species of small fish, but a little larger than the opae.

O-PAI-PAI, *v.* To shake; to bend in and out, as the rafters of a house; *opaipai* ka mauna, the mountain *trembles*. *Laieik.* 163.

O-PA-O-PA, *adj.* See OPA. Wearied; fatigued; lame from walking. See OOPA.

O-PA-HA, *s.* A house, the rafter of which have been broken.

2. A thin, shrunk up face.

O-PA-HA, *v.* To be bent in; as the roof of a (grass) house partly fallen in.

2. To sink down; to be depressed; to fall in; au *opaha* ka hale, ua hina, ua hilala, a ua poli aku iloko.

O-PA-HA, *adj.* Bent in; indented; pressed down.

O-PA-KA, *adj.* Having regular sides, as a square or octagon.

2. Having hewn or flat sides, as a square piece of timber; e kalai a *opaka*, the timber is hewed; na kalai *opakapaka*, the timber is hewed on all sides.

O-PA-KA, *v.* To hew smoothly; to hew and leave no knots; e kalai a e hoopau i ke ino.

O-PA-KA, *s.* A ravine on the side of a mountain.

2. The geometrical figure; a prism. *Anahon.*

O-PA-KA-PA-KA, *adj.* Hewed on all sides; made flat or square.

O-PA-KA-PA-KA, *s.* Name of a species of red fish.

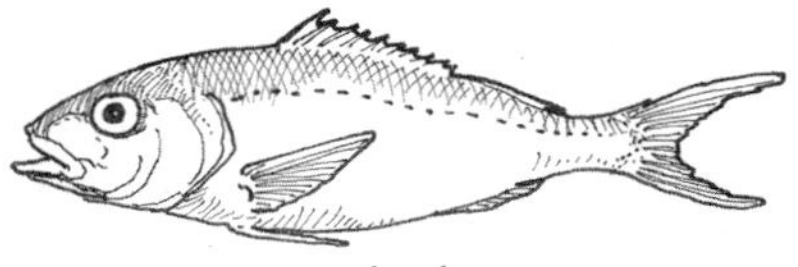
opakapaka

O-PA-LA, *s.* Refuse litter, such as old straw, leaves of trees, dried grass, or anything worthless which may be burnt or blown away by the wind. *Hal.* 1:4. Light rubbish; different things mixed together.

2. FIG. The rabble; people without character; aole i lilo kanaka i ka hewa me Poki, he mau *opala* wale no ka i lilo me ia, the people did not turn to wickedness with Poki, some of the *chaff* (unstable men) only went with him.

O-PA-LA, *adj.* Dirty; filthy; bad; unpleasant; ua lemua *opala*, a long, disagreeable rain.

O-PA-LI-PA-LI, *s.* A small or low pali; a place of low palis.

O-PA-PA, *s.* Proper name of the wife of Akea or Wakea; they are represented as the ancestors of the Hawaiian race. NOTE.—The *o* is no part of the word, it is only *o* emphatic, yet it is sometimes so written. See PAPA.

O-PE, *v.* To tie up in a bundle; to bundle up for carrying away. *Puk.* 12:34.

O-PE, *s.* A bundle; a long bundle; a bundle made up for carrying; *ope* papa, *ope* lole.

O-PE-A, *v.* To be turned or to lean to one side.

2. To turn off, as when land is taken away, perhaps for a fault, perhaps not; ua laweia ka aina, *opeaia* ke kanaka.

3. To drive one away; hakaka laua, a *opeaia* o mea e mea.

4. To bind one's hands behind his back; *opeaia* kona mau lima; to cross; to tie crosswise; to treat ill.

5. To abuse or treat one evil without reason.

6. To judge unrighteously. *Sol.* 18:5.

7. To treat the gods with contempt and risk the consequences. See PEA.

8. To throw over one, as a kapa, or as a child over the shoulder.

O-PE-A, *s.* A cross, as sticks crossed. See PEA and KEA. The cross stick which holds up the outer and upper end of a sail.

O-PE-A, *s.* Used probably for *opeia*, what is bound up; a testicle.

O-PE-A, *adj.* Villainous; perverse; not trusty.

O-PEA-PEA, *s.* A bat, an animal between fowls and quadrupeds. *Kanl.* 14:18. So called from the shape of the wings being similar to the ancient sails (*pea*) of their canoes.

O-PEA-PEA, *s.* A species of shell fish.

2. Kalo lately planted, from the shape of the young leaves.

O-PE-O-PE, *v.* See OPE. To tie up tightly or frequently, as a bundle.

2. To tie and hang up against the side of a house for preservation.

3. To fold up, as clothes. *Iohn.* 20:7.

4. FIG. To bind up, as knowledge. *Isa.* 8:16. *Opeope* ke akamai a waiho malie iloko o ke kanaka noonoo, wisdom is bundled up and laid away quietly in the man's mind.

O-PE-LE, *v.* To rest securely or quietly in a place; noa ke akua kapu ka *opele*.

O-PE-LE-PE-LE, *s.* A flat, weak calabash, partly broken; also, a frail water calabash.

O-PE-LU, *s.* Name of a species of fish; mackerel; *opelu* ka okoa ia iho ka moku.

2. The name of one of the two fish which accompanied Pili when he came to the islands; *aku* was the name of the other. *D. Malo.* 4:13.

O-PE-LU-NU-I-KAU-HAA-LI-LO, *s.* The son of Pele and Kamapuaa, who became a god.

O-PI, *v.* To fold up, as kapa or cloth. See OPE.

2. To sink in, as the mouth when the teeth are gone.

O-PI, *s.* The folds in cloth or kapa; the

depressions made by folding kapa or cloth; akepakepa mai la no ia ma ke *opi* a pau.

O-PI-O, *adj.* Young; juvenile, as a person. 2 *Sam.* 18:29. As an animal; bipi kane opio. *Nah.* 28:19.

O-PI-O-PI, *v.* See OPI. To fold up, as a garment or kapa. 2 *Nal.* 2:8.

2. To put in order; opiopi lua ka auwae me he waha kao la.

O-PI-O-PI-O, *v.* See OPIO. To be young; tender, as a plant or tree; as a child or animal. 1 *Sam.* 1:24.

O-PI-O-PI-O, *adj.* Young, as a person or animal; immature; unripe. *Puk.* 24:5. Applied to persons; opposed to *kahiko.* Ios. 6:21. Applied to fruits; uala opiopio; recent; new; late; as, he mai *opiopio*, a new or recent disease; junior; a son of a father of the same name.

O-PI-HI, *s.* A species of shell fish.

2. A stamp in native cloth.

O-PI-HI-PI-HI, *s.* A particular kind of mat, not the finest kind, though pretty fine.

O-PI-KA-NA-LA-NI, *s.* Used in poetry for something laid up far off; hele ana i Opikananuu i *Opikanalani.*

O-PI-KA-NA-NUU, *s.* See the above. Hele ana i *Opikananuu* i Opikanalani.

O-PI-KI, *v.* To bend over, as in nodding on going to sleep; to bend up, as the legs; to come together, as a trap. See UPIKI.

O-PI-KO, *s.* A species of grass; a species of tree; he kopiko.

O-PI-KO-PI-KO, *s.* Name of a disease; he mai *opikopiko* i ano e ka ili e like me ka pala, ulaulu a keokeo; ke *opikopiko* o ka ili, ina e hoopiliia ka hee, ola i ka ili, ua *opikopiko* ka ili.

O-PI-KO-PI-KO, *s.* Anxiety; concern; solicitude; depression of spirits in view of danger.

O-PI-KO-PI-KO, *v.* To be anxious about an event; to be concerned about some impending danger.

2. To be troubled, as the sea in a storm.

O-PI-LI, *v.* To draw up; contract, as one with the cramp or with cold weather; opili loa iho no ka nui loa o ka ua.

2. To be cold; to shiver with the cold.

3. To draw up or compose one's self on a bed. *Kin.* 49:33.

4. FIG. Ua *opili* ka maka i ka anu i ka wai, nolaila loaa ole ka manao, haalulu a make no hoi.

5. To bend or contract, as the knees in kneeling; oi noho kukuli a *opili* ae na wawae i ka anu i lalo o ka lepo. *Kin.* 49:33.

Opili la o poeleele o opu kalakala
Ua iku, he kua nui kua loa,
He kua noho i ka iuiu.—*He wahi pule.*

O-PI-LI, *s.* A cold; a shivering; a contraction of the limbs and muscles through cold or with the cramp.

2. The cramp itself.

O-PI-LI, *adj.* Stiff with wet and cold; benumbed.

O-PI-LO, *v.* To break out afresh, as an old sore.

2. To have a relapse in the recovery of a disease; to bring back a sickness; mai hele oe i ka auau, o *opilo* ko mai i ka wai. See PILO.

O-PI-LO, *s.* A person who is often sick and has become thin in flesh, is said to be a kanaka *opilo.*

O-PI-LO-PI-LO, *adj.* Dirty; muddy; miry, as a soft, slumpy road; ua nui na wahi *opilopilo* ma ke alanui o Makiki, ua pohopoho loa ka wawae i kahi ino i ka lepo.

2. Dirty; bad smelling, as stagnant water; corrupt; he *opilopilo* no keia opu puaa.

O-PI-LO-PI-LO, *v.* To be dirty; bad smelling, &c.; ke *opilopilo* nei no ka wawae i ka honowa. See PILOPILO and PILO.

O-PO, See in HAUOPO. *Opo*, in good order; even; plainly done.

O-PO-HO-KA-NO, *adj.* Stingy; close; not willing to part with anything good; o ka poe lakou opohokano, he kukuiolelo wale no ia, aole e ai ana.

O-PU, *v.* To expand, as an opening flower. See OPUU.

2. To grow, as a fetus. *Hal.* 139:16.

3. To swell up; to be full, as the belly of a fat person; opu mai ka opu.

4. To rise up, as water; opu ka wai.

5. To live idly; lazily; ke *opu* wale ae nei no, ka noho wale; noho wale iho no, loaa ole.

6. To sit with the knees gathered up.

7. To leap off or over, as a horse; e *opu* aku mao.

O-PU, *s.* A protuberance with an enclosure, as the belly, stomach, bladder, &c.; as, *opu* o ke kai, the heart, belly (midst) of the sea; the crop of a bird. *Oihk.* 1:16. The maw of animals. *Kanl.* 18:3. The womb. *Lunk.* 16:17. A round, liver-like substance in the hog and other animals.

2. The name of a heap upon which a god stands; a bunch or bundle of small wood, grass, weeds, &c.; a hill or bunch of kalo growing together. See OPUU.

3. The disposition of a person; state of mind. See the compounds OPUAO, OPUINO,

OPUKOPEKOPE, &c. *Opu* is here SYN. with *naau*. NOTE.—The Hawaiians suppose the seat of thought, intelligence, &c., and also the seat of moral powers, as the choice and practice of good and evil, to be seated in the small intestines; hence, *naau* or *opu* (the small intestines) is used for what we should call the *heart*, i. e., the seat of the moral powers. See NAAUAO, NAAUPO, NAAUINO, compared with *opuao, opuino*, &c. See NAAU.

O-PU, *adj*. Skillful at diving into the water, so as not to spatter; *opu ia wahi kanaka; opu* i na kea ka pau ai ole, fisherman's phrase.

O-PU-A, *s*. Narrow pointed clouds hanging in the horizon; clouds of a singular shape arising out of the sea; *opua* kea, *opua* eleele.

   2. A bunch; a collection, as of bushes, leaves, &c.; he *opua* hao wale keia no ka aina; ke *opua* puakala. See OPU.

O-PU-A, *s*. The name of a class of gods among the poe akua noho.

O-PU-A, *adj*. Existing or hanging in bunches or clusters; ao *opua*, clouds collected; kahi e puka mai ai na ao *opua* mai ka moana.

O-PU-AO, *adj*. *Opu*, belly, and *ao*, enlightened. Wise hearted; knowing; intelligent; similar to *naauao*, but less used.

O-PU-AO, *s*. Knowledge; intelligence; one instructed; he naauao, he noonoo, he noiau.

O-PU-A-HA-O. No ke komo ana a *opuahao* ke kanaka a make.

O-PU-A-HU-A-WA, *s*. See OPU, a bunch, and AHUAWA, a species of strong rush, A bunch of grass, small sticks, &c., tied up in a bundle with ahuawa string.

O-PU-A-KEA, *s*. Clearness; whiteness; that which shines brightly.

O-PU-A-KEA, *v*. To appear, as a white cloud.

   Ua *opuakea* alalai kanukanu
   Huna i ka meheu naawe alanui a ka puukolu
   Ka makole maawe ala a ka Poukua.

O-PU-A-KII, *s*. The clouds in the morning or evening when they take imaging shapes of things; he ao *opuakiikii*.

O-PU-I-NO-I-NO, *s*. *Opu* and *ino*. An evil disposition; malice. 1 *Pet*. 2:1. Wickedness; depravity; seeking evil against one.

O-PU-I-NO-I-NO, *adj*. Evilly disposed; malevolent.

O-PU-O-HAI, *s*. *Opu*, a bunch, and *ohai*, a shrub. A bundle of grass; a bundle of the ohai shrubs.

O-PU-O-HAO, *s*. Name of a disease in which the abdomen becomes enlarged and hard, while the limbs are enervated; the dropsy; ka opu me ka nanaia alikiliki lalo o ka lemu.

O-PU-O-PU, *v*. To rise up; to swell. See OPU. To be swelled full, as one having eaten heartily.

   2. To fill, as the belly of a hungry man; to be full, as a water calabash with water.

O-PUU, *v*. To bud, as a tree or plant; to shoot forth buds. *Kin*. 40:10.

   2. To bud, i. e., to set fruit. *Mat*. 13:26.

   3. To shoot out, as the branch of a tree. *Mar*. 4:32.

   4. *Hoo*. To cause to grow. *Ezek*. 29:21.

   Ua *opuu* ae kuahiwi i ka ili o ke kai,
   Ua omeo ae ka puka ana.

O-PUU, *s*. A bud. *Nah*. 17:23. The germ of a vegetable; a tuft; a cluster; a bunch of corn. *Kin*. 41:5. An ear or bunch of wheat or barley. *Rut*. 2:2.

   2. A protuberance. See PUU.

   3. A whale's tooth; ka *opuu* niho okohola; *opuu* makamua, first green ears. *Oihk*. 2:14. Ka *opuu* maia, a bunch of bananas.

   4. The spur of a very young cock; ka *opuu* ana'e o ke kalakala o ka moa.

   5. A conical hill; hency, in *geometry*, a cone. *Ana. Hon*. 29.

O-PUU, *s*. Swelling highly, as a very high surf before it breaks; ohu mai la he wahi nalu *opuu*. *Laieik*. 91.

O-PUU-PUU, *adj*. See PUU. Rough; not smooth, as a rough road; the opposite of *laumania*; the same as *apuupuu*; uneven; hilly; bulging or swelling out; opposite to *upoho*; convex. *Anat*. 6.

O-PUU-PUU, *s*. Ma ke kule, ma ka papakole, ma ke kuekue, ma ke *opuupuu*.

   2. Name of a species of fish.

O-PU-HAO, *s*. *Opu* and *hao*. A swelled belly or stomach; i kona ai ana i ka *opuhao*; penu no ia i ke kai me ka *opuhao*; dropsy of the belly, ascites. See OPUOHAO.

O-PU-HEA, *adj*. *Opu* and *hea*. Lazy; inactive; not enterprising or industrious.

O-PU-HU-E, *s*. *Opu*, belly, and *hue*, a calabash. Name of a species of fish, speckled, said to be poisonous if eaten; the fish swells up with air and floats on the sea.

O-PU-KAE-MO-A. *Kam. voc*. keu, keukeu. To condemn one's friend.

O-PU-KEA, *s*. See KOKEA, *Kam*.

O-PU-KEE-MO-A, *s*. An evil disposition; an inclination to badness; also *naaukee-moa*.

O-PU-KO-PE-KO-PE, *adj*. *Opu*, disposition, and *kopekope*, morose. Evilly disposed; malevolent.

O-PU-LE, *s.* A species of fish full of spots; ua paapu i ke kakau.

O-PU-LE-PU-LE, *adj.* Spotted; light and shade; he kinohinohi.

Opulepule ke aka ilalo, kikokiko i na aka,
Paapu i na aka e like me Lahainaluna i ka po mahina,
No ka paa i na lala ulu ame na lau o ka maia
Ame ka wauke, mahina *opulepule* o Lele (Lahaina.)

Spotted, as the feathers of the nene; he hulu *opulepule* ko ka nene.

O-PU-MA-KA-NI, *s.* *Opu*, belly, and *makani*, wind. A bellows; a balloon.

O-PU-MI-MI, *s.* *Opu* and *mimi*, urine. The bladder; the container of urine.

O-PU-NA-HE-LE-HE-LE, *s.* *Opu* and *nahelehele*, a thicket. Ua pee i ka *opunahelehele*, he hid himself in the belly of the forest, i. e., in the *thick forest.*

O-PU-NI-NI, *v.* To compel attendance; to force compliance.

O-PU-NUI, *adj.* *Opu* and *nui.* Epithet of a large bellied man; ina aole lio, make loa na 'lii *opunui* i ka maloeloe, if there are no horses, the big-bellied chiefs will die with fatigue (of traveling.)

O-PU-PA-LA-OA, *s.* *Opuu*, whale's tooth, and *palaoa.* An ornament made of a whale's tooth. See OPUU.

O-WA, *s.* The word given and constantly used by Kukuaokalalau for seizing his prey.

O-WA, *v.* To be split, as a board. See OA.

O-WAA-WAA, *adj.* Hilly; full of knolls; land full of knobs.

O-WAA-WAA, *s.* Thick, heavy clouds; clouds portending a storm; ina i poipu ka lani me ka *owaawaa*, he hakuma ia.

O-WAE, *v.* See WAE. To crack, as a thing breaking; to tremble; to crack, as dry ground.

O-WAI, *pron. int.* Who? what person? It refers mostly to persons. NOTE.—The *o* is the *o* emphatic, and not an essential part of the word. See *Gram.* § 53 and 123.

O-WA-O-WA, *v.* See OWA. To be full of cracks, as rotten wood; to be broken up.

O-WAI-KU, *s.* Name of a pain in the chest, or breast of men or women; he mai, he nae *owaiku.*

O-WA-O-WA-KA, *s.* A species of shell fish of the clam kind.

O-WAU, *pron.,* first pers. sing. I. See AU, OAU, and WAU. *Gram.* § 53 and 123.

O-WAU, *v.* To answer I, in obedience to a call or a question; owai ka mea papale ie o oukou? *owau* aku la no hoi au, *owau?* who among you has a straw hat? I ied to him I, that is, I answered I.

O-WAU, *s.* A cat; so called from her noise; *uwau* is perhaps the right word.

O-WAU, *s.* Name of a species of fish found in the rivers; he okuhekuhe, he akupa.

O-WA-HO, *comp. prep.,* the auipili of *waho.* Of or belonging to the outside. *Ioan.* 7:24. Out of; external. *Gram.* § 161.

O-WA-KA, *adj.* Open; spread open, as a flower. See OAKA. Open, as the mouth for speaking.

O-WA-KA, *v.* To open, as a flower; mohola; ua hamama, ua *owaka* ka pua o ka laau. See OAKA.

O-WA-KA-WA-KA, *s.* The breaking or opening of daylight; o ka wehe ana o ke alaula ame ka malamalama o ke kakahiaka.

O-WA-KA-WA-KA, *v.* To be somewhat light, as the light of the moon. See WAKA-WAKA.

O-WA-LA, *v.* To toss forward with both hands.

2. To throw, as a horse his rider.

3. To brandish, as a spear.

4. To throw about one's hands.

O-WA-LI, *adj.* Weak; infirm; flexible. See NAWALI and WALI.

O-WA-WA, *s.* A ditch; a furrow; e hana *owawa*, e auwaha. See AWAWA, KAHAWAI, &c.

O-WE-O-WE-NE, *s.* Small kalo, &c. See OWEWENE.

O-WE-HE-WE-HE, *s.* See WEHE, to open. A definite period of time in the morning; a i ka *owehewehe* ana o ka alaula. *Laieik.* 30.

O-WE-LA, *s.* The time when the sun is hot and no rain; vegetation dries up.

2. Hard work on land by several people to get it worked.

3. Land burnt over; scorched in the sun.

4. Anything held near the fire so as to be scorched. See WELA.

O-WE-NE, *s.* Small kalo; lulumi i ka lepo, a popoi i ka mauu, a mahope loaa kahi *owene.*

O-WE-WE-NE, *s.* Small kalo, as the finishing of a patch of food; perhaps better written *oweowene.*

O-WI, *s.* The name of a small shrub, a nuisance to farmers.

O-WI-LI, *v.* To roll up; to twist; to fold up, as the hands.

    2. To roll together, as a roll of paper that has been opened. *Isa.* 34:5.

    3. To twist a thing to make it crooked. See OILI.

O-WI-LI, *s.* A roll, as of cloth or of paper; a skein of thread; a roll of a mat; he *owili* palapala, the roll of a book. *Ier.*

36:2. Koi *owili,* a koi made gouge-like for working the inside of canoes.

O-WI-LI, *s.* Name of a very thick surf-board made of wiliwili.

O-RE-NA, *s.* *Heb.* Name of a tree. *Isa.* 44:14. English translation, an ash.

O-SE-FE-RA-GA, *s.* Name of a bird in *Oihk.* 11:13.

O-SE-PE-RA, *s.* The ospray; name of a bird in *Oihk.* 11:13.

O-SE-TE-RI-KA, *s.* *Eng.* An ostrich. *Iob.* 30:29.

U.

U, the fifth letter of the Hawaiian alphabet. It represents generally the sound of the English *oo,* as in *too, coo, fool,* &c.; but when preceded by *i,* it sometimes has the sound of the English *u* or *yu;* as, waiu, *waiyu;* iuka, *yuka.*

U, *v.* To protrude; to rise on the toes; to prepare to stand up; to draw out, as a pencil from a case.

    2. To weep. *Mat.* 5:4. To grieve; to mourn. *Hal.* 38:6. E *u* hele, to go about mourning; to mourn for, i. e., desire earn-estly; i kekahi manao o'u e *u* nei, e ao kakou i ka leo o ka himeni.

    3. To drip or drizzle, as water; to ooze or leak slowly, as water from a kalo patch or from the crevices of rock; e kahe ae.

U, *v.* To be tinctured or impregnated with anything; as, ua *u* ka pipi i ka paa-kai; ua *u* ke kapa i ka mea hooluu; *u* ke kapa i ka ua.

U, *s.* The breast of a female. *Ezek.* 23:8.

U, *s.* Grief; sorrow; expression of af-fection; like me ke aloha, ame ka *u,* ame ka uwe ana.

    2. The breast. *Luk.* 23:29. The pap; the udder; hence, with *wai,* milk, i. e., *waiu.* LIT. Breast water.

    3. Unwillingness; not disposed to do.

U-A, *v.* See Gr. *uo,* Malay *ujan,* to wet; to rain. To rain; *ua* iho la ka *ua,* he *ua* nui loa. LIT. The rain *rained,* it was a very great rain.

    2. *Hoo.* To send or give rain; to cause to rain. *Kin.* 7:4.

U-A, *s.* Rain; water falling from the clouds. 1 *Sam.* 12:17, 18. Rains were di-vided by Hawaiians into *ua loa,* long rains; *ua poko,* short rains; *ua hea.*

U-A, *adj.* Vain; useless; to no profit.

U-A, *adv.* In vain; to no purpose; ma nao no ka poe kahiko ua luhi *ua* ka lakou hana ana.

U-A, *pron. dem. adj.* *Ua* before a noun, and *la* or *nei* after it, forms a strong de-monstrative adjective pronoun; this; that; as *la* or *nei* is used. It refers to some noun that has just been mentioned. *Ua* kanaka *nei, this* man (just spoken of); hiolo *ua* mau hale *la, those* houses (just mentioned) have fallen down. *Gram.* § 152.

U-A prefixed to verbs, marks the fourth form of the preter tense. *Gram.* § 187.

U-A-A-U-LA, *adj.* Bad smelling; filthy. See AAUA.

U-AI, *v.* See UWAI. To open or shut, as a door.

    2. To extend; hoonee. See HUAI.

U-AI, *s.* A door for stopping an en-trance. See UWAI.

U-AO, *v.* See UWAO. To interfere; to procure peace between contending par-ties; to intercede; interpose; reconcile; a na kekahi alii manuwa Amerika i *uao;* to take one's part.

U-AO, *v.* To mew, as a cat. See below.

U-AO, *s.* A cat, from the noise. See also OWAU and UWAU.

U-AU, *s.* A leather bag.

    2. A species of bird that dives in the water.

U-AU, *adj.* Tough, as kalo. See UAUA.

U-A-U-A, *adj.* Poor; naked; destitute.

U-A-U-A, *s.* Pride; haughtiness; acting the spendthrift.

    2. The name of a kapa or pau colored yellow; ina i hooluu ia ka pau i ka olena, he *uaua* ia.

U-A-UA, *adj.* Proud; haughty; arrogant; vain.

U-A-UA, *adj.* Strong; tight; fast; unbroken.

2. Tough, as some kinds of kalo; paa, paakiki.

U-AU-A, *s.* A noise; a confused noise, as of an army or multitude; the noise of wailing; he olopihe.

U-A-U-A-LA, *s.* A strong smell of decaying food; the smell of rotten potatoes; wekoweko.

U-AU-KE-WAI, *s.* The name of a large bird the size of a turkey; breast and wings white, back black.

U-A-HAU, *v.* To imbed in; to lay in, as brick or stone in mortar. See UHAU, *Anat.* 19.

U-A-HI, *s.* U, ooze or milk, and *ahi*, fire, that is, smoke. A cloud; a vaporous appearance. See UWAHI. NOTE.—*Uahi* is undoubtedly the better orthography.

U-A-HI-WAI, *v.* E kulu ana. See WA-WAI. To be desirous of some evil; to lust after; to be greedy for.

U-A-HO-A, *adj.* Hard, as an unfeeling person; unkind; ungenerous; passionate.

U-A-KA-HA, *s.* Stiffness; applied to the neck.

U-A-KO-KO, *s.* See KOIULA, *Kam.*, PU-NOHU, &c. A cloud standing erect and having different colors, somewhat like the rainbow.

U-A-LA, *s.* See U and ALA, sweet. The sweet potato.

2. The large muscles of the upper arm. *Anat.* 18.

3. A name of a certain kind of leho, a sea shell. Sometimes written *uwala.*

U-A-LA-AU (u-wa-la-au), *v.* See WA-LAAU. To cry out; to make a great noise; to cry out in a confused manner, as a great multitude. *Isa.* 22:2.

U-A-LA-AU (u-wa-la-au), *s.* An outcry; a loud noise in conversation; a confused noise.

U-A-LA-KA-HI-KI, *s.* *Uala*, potato, and *kahiki*, foreign. A foreign or Irish potato.

U-A-LA-PI-LAU, *s.* *Uala*, potato; and *pi-lau*, strong scented. A turnip; a radish.

U-A-LE-HA, *adj.* Lazy. See HOOPALALEHA.

U-A-LE-HE, *v.* To strip one of his property; to dispossess one; hemo.

U-A-LO, *v.* To cry; to call out; to complain; to call for help. *Hal.* 4:1. See UOLO.

U-A-LO, *s.* A complaining; a crying to one for help.

U-A-NA, *adv.* *Ua*, sign of the perfect tense, and *na*, quiet, enough, &c. See NA, *v.* It is enough; it is sufficient; a plenty.

U-A-NA-OA, *v.* *Ua* as above, and *na*, satisfied, and *oa*, sick. To have no relish for food.

U-A-NA-OA, *adj.* Wanting an appetite; disrelishing food.

U-A-NEI, *adv.* Adverb of time future; it refers to something to be done or something to take place hereafter, but at no great distance of time; soon; by and by; hereafter. The full form is *auanei*; it is contracted by dropping the initial *a*, after a word ending in *a. Dan.* 1:10.

U-A-NII, *adj.* Too salt; miko loa.

U-E, *v.* To weep; to cry; to cry in an audible manner.

2. To sigh; to have inward anguish; to be afflicted.

3. To have pity upon.

4. To salute; to love.

5. To cry to one for relief in distress.

6. To enter a complaint. See UWE.

U-E, *v.* To hitch or shove along a little; to shake. See NAUE. *Hoo.* To cause a movement or shaking.

U-E, *s.* The wrenching of a stick; the turning of a screw.

U-E, *s.* A kind of mat made without trimming the lauhala.

U-E-UE, *v.* See UE, to shake. Neko-neko, nikuniku, pilupilu. *Hoo.* To cause to shake; to shake violently; hooewaewa ma ka nuku, me ka hoonaueue ae.

U-E-UE-KO, *s.* A bad smell; a stench. See WEWEKO.

U-E-UE-KO, *adj.* Filthy; unpleasant to the smell.

U-E-PA, *s.* *Eng.* A wafer; better written *wepa*; better still, *wefa.*

U-E-WA-LE, *s.* *Ue*, to cry, and *wale*, without cause. A coward.

U-I, *v.* To ask a question; *ui* iho la au penei, ahea ka nui o na haumana? to inquire of; ua *uiia* mai oe e ke alii e olelo aku, thou art asked by the chief to speak.

2. To milk; to squeeze out milk. See KOWI.

3. To wring out, as washed clothes.

4. To creak or squeak, as new shoes in walking.

5. To grate, as the teeth.

U-I, *s.* A question; a series of questions; a catechism; an interrogation; he *ui* no na haumana o ke kulanui, a *question* for the scholars of the high school.

U-I, *s.* A youth; a young person; youth generally; strength. *Kin.* 49:3.

U-I, *adj.* Young; strong; well proportioned; applied to young and vigorous men. *Rut.* 2:9.

UI-IO, *v.* To question; to interrogate. See UI.

U-I-U-I, *v.* To squeak, as new shoes; to gnash the teeth. See UI.

U-I-U-I, *s.* Arrow-root. See PIA.

2. A beer made of the ki root.

3. The fermented juice of the sugar-cane. See UIUIA.

U-I-U-WI, *s.* A tooth; a small, young tooth.

UI-U-IA, *s.* A kind of beer made of cane juice.

UI-UI-KI, *v.* To shine, as a light through a small aperture; to shine through a small aperture into a dark room.

2. To glimmer feebly; ua *uiuiki* iki mai kahi malamalama iki ma Hawaii nei.

UI-UI-KI, *s.* A small hole through which light may shine; he puku uuku, he wahi hakahaka uuku, i puka mai ka malamalama o na hoku liilii loa, i ike powehiwehiia.

UI-UI-KO, *s.* An unpleasant smell. See UEUEKO.

UI-UI-WI, *s.* The name of a species of fish; the oili.

UI-HAA, *adj.* Weary with a long distance.

2. Idle, i. e., without work; burdened with work, but desiring it.

U-I-KI, *s.* See UIUIKI. A small aperture; he hakahaka.

UI-KI, *s. Eng.* The wick of a lamp or candle. *Mat.* 12:20. Better written *wiki*.

UI-LA, *s.* Lightning. *Zek.* 10:1. Ke ahi e holo ikaika ana iloko o na ao ua.

UI-LA-NI, *v.* To struggle ineffectually to get away from a person; to struggle in vain to get out of difficulty; *uilani* ae la makou; mehea la e hemo ae ai? we are struggling ineffectually; by what means shall we break away? The word is also used in a moral sense; aole anei he *uilani?* is he not *in difficulty? Laieik.* 206.

UI-LA-NI, *s.* Pride; haughtiness; self exhortation.

U-I-LI, *v.* To steer, as a canoe.

U-I-NA, *v. Ui* and *ana.* See UI 4.

1. To crack; to snap, as a whip.

2. To crack, as a rope or string of a lei. *Laieik.* 145.

3. To break, as a piece of wood. NOTE.— It is the noise made by the breaking, and not the breaking that makes the *uina.*

U-I-NA, *s.* See UINA, *v.* A report of a pistol; the noise of a gun; the cracking of the fingers; a guttural break in pronunciation between two vowels.

U-O (u-wo), *v.* To cry out; to bellow, as a bull; to roar, as a lion; e *uo* no ka liona i kona leo me ka ikaika loa.

U-O, *v.* Ka *uo* ana i ka lei, ke kui ana me ka manai, a *uo* aku i ke kaula; to fasten by tying or braiding for a certain purpose; to splice two ends of rope.

U-O, *s.* The jingling of money.

U-O, *s.* Ka *uo*, ka aeae, ka wali, ka uouo; the soft fluidity of poi mixed thin with water and clear of lumps.

U-O, *adj.* Ka poi *uo*, ka ai uouo; soft; paste like; fluid, as soft poi.

U-O, *adj.* Quality of a species of ohia; ka ohia *uo*, uouolea iuka.

U-O-A, *s.* Name of a species of fish.

UO-U-O, *adj.* See UO, soft. Soft; paste like, as poi wet with water; clear; fine; without lumps.

UO-UO, *adj.* See UO, to cry out. Roaring; crying; having a strong voice; he kanaka *uouo* o Kamehameha.

UO-UO-LEA, *s.* A species of ohia; ka ohia uo, *uouolea* iuka.

UO-KI, *v.* Contraction of *ua oki*; used in the imperative mood; stop; cease; be done; leave off. See OKI.

U-O-LO, *v.* To call upon one; to call upon; to complain. *Hal.* 4:1. See UALO.

U-U, *s.* Masturbation; onanism; ulehole.

U-U, *v.* To practice onanism; e ulehole.

2. To pull off or pluck, as a flower; e hele oukou e *uu* mai i pua kilioopu. *Laieik.* 192. To strip with the hand, as leaves.

3. To hoist, as a sail; e *uu* ae i ko kakou pea; ua *uuia* kahi pea, a koe no kekahi.

4. To draw out, as india rubber; to pull out, as a pencil from its case, &c.

U-U, *v.* To groan; to be in a suffering state. *Puk.* 6:5.

U-U, *s.* A stammering; an impediment in speech.

U-U, *adj.* Stammering; speaking hesitatingly and indistinctly.

U-U, *s.* A species of fish of a red color.

U-U-I-NA, *v.* To be brittle; to break, as glass.

2. To crack the joints of the fingers.

3. To squeak, as shoes. See UI, UIUI, and PAPAINA.

4. To crepitate or grate, as the two ends of a broken bone; more properly applied

to the joints of the backbone when pressed; kamumumu.

U-U-U, *v.* See Uu. To stammer; to be impeded in speaking, as one affected with the palsy.

2. To strip frequently, as in stripping off leaves.

U-U-U, *adj.* Hoarse; stammering; unable to speak intelligibly. *Isa.* 32:4.

U-U-HAI, *s.* The door or door frame of a house. See UHAI.

U-U-KU, *v.* See Uku, a genus of small insects. To be small; little; few.

2. To diminish in size.

3. To make or be few in number. *Ios.* 7:3. O kela mai ka mea e *uuku* ai na kanaka o ia wa, that sickness was what *reduced the number* of people at that period.

4. *Hoo.* To reduce; to make few. *Nah.* 26:54. To make few; applied to words. *Kekah.* 5:2.

U-U-KU, *s.* A little man; a dwarf; a diminutive person.

U-U-KU, *adj.* Little; small; diminutive; few.

U-U-LU-HA-KU, *v.* To stir up poi as a lazy man, hence the poi will be lumpy.

U-U-LU-KAI, *adj.* Large, fleshy and weak, as a fat man.

2. Full or hanging, as the cheeks of one who is somewhat ill or fat; uhekeheke, upehupehu.

U-U-LU-KAI, *v.* To be large and fleshy, but weak.

U-LU-HA-KU, *adj.* Weary; lame with walking or carrying a burden.

U-U-MA, *v.* To pinch the skin with the hand; uma.

U-U-MI, *v.* See Umi. To choke; to throttle; to strangle; ua uumiia ke keiki e ka wahine kolohe; e kaawe, e kinai.

2. To make great exertions.

3. To restrain, suppress, as the passions; to mortify. *Kol.* 3:5. To refrain from weeping when deeply affected. *Kin.* 43:31. To restrain, hold in, as compassion. *Isa.* 63:15.

4. To keep to one's self, as a saying or a speech; *uumi* i ke aloha, to refuse to love. 1 *Ioan.* 3:17. *Uumi* i ka manao, to refrain from speaking, i. e., to choke the thought. A *uumi* ia Kiwalao me ka lei o manu ma kona lima, he choked Kiwalao with the wreath of a bird's feathers on his arm. See UMI.

U-U-MI, *s.* A choking; killing, as of infants; o ke *uumi* kamalii kekahi hewa kahiko o keia aina. See UMI.

U-U-MU-I-KU. I ka elehei, i ka *uumuiku.*

See MUMUIKU.

U-U-PE-KU-PE-KU, *s.* I ka *uupekupeku* a ka noheo; that which is unequal in length, some long and some short; the practice of defilement and pollution of the sexes; applied to persons of known lewdness.

U-U-WA, *adj.* Slippery; smooth; pau na iwi i kekahi mea lahilahi *uuwa,* oia ka wahi o ka iwi. *Anat.* 4.

U-U-WAI, *adj.* He wawai, he pipiwai. *Uu* for *uuku,* and *wai,* water. A very little water.

U-HA, *v.* To belch up wind.

2. To hawk up mucus; to hawk, as a means of raising phlegm from the throat or lungs. See PUHA.

3. To swell; to distend, as the stomach.

4. To squander; to misspend; to waste; to misuse property. See UHAUHA.

U-HA, *s.* The thigh; the thigh of a person. *Lunk.* 3:16.

2. The ham of a hog.

3. The lap of a woman. 2 *Nal.* 4:20. *Uha* hoali, the heave shoulder. *Oihk.* 7:34.

4. The enlarged intestine near the anus of beasts; the alimentary canal.

U-HA, *adj.* Slipping away; not easily held, as a cunning rogue.

2. Greedy; craving; eating often.

U-HAE, *v.* To tear; to rend, as a garment. *Oihk.* 10:6. Ua *uhaeia* ka lole, ua *uhaeia* ka moena. See HAE and HAEHAE.

U-HAI, *v.* See Hai. To break in two, as a stick; to break, as a bone. *Nah.* 24:8. To break, as the neck. *Puk.* 13:13.

2. To break, as a covenant. *Kanl.* 31:16. To break, as a law; ua *uhai* ke kanawai; to disregard as an agreement; to break away, as from a yoke or bondage.

3. To jerk or pull out; to tear out or off by force, as a branch from a tree.

4. To pound up or break to pieces, as with a rod; to break off, as a horn. *Dan.* 8:8.

5. To follow; chase; pursue. *Laieik.* 71. To overrun; to treat with contempt. See HAHAI.

6. To speak to; to say to one; ke *uhai* mai nei ka naaupo ia makou e hoohalikeia ka mea naaupo me ka mea naauao.

U-HAI, *s.* E hilinai ana no ia maluna o ka *uhai;* the door shutter of a room or house; e pane mai i *uhai.*

U-HAI, *s.* The door, or properly the door frame of a house; ke kikihi o ka hale.

U-HAI-A-HO-LO, *v.* *Uhai* and *holo,* to run. LIT. To break away and run; to run, as in a race; to fly; to hasten after a thing; ke *uhaiaholo* nei na kanaka ma ka waiwai, me ke kukini nui ma ia aoao me he mau elele na ke alii o ka lewa.

U-HAI-A-HO-LO, *s.* A swift running; an eager pursuit after a thing.

U-HAO, *v.* See HAO. To put into; to fill; to put into, as into a bag. *Kin.* 44:1. Or into a basket or other container; ua *uhaoia* ka ai iloko o ka umeke; i ka manawa e *uhao* ai i ka poka i ka pu. See HAHAO.

U-HAO, *s.* The line of lean flesh each side, but outside of the backbone; the lean flesh inside is called *ioliu*; na io e moe lua ana maloko o ke ka o ka puaa a pili aku i ke kuamoo. See IOLIU.

U-HAU, *v.* To pile together; to build up, as the walls of a city. 2 *Oihl.* 32:5.

2. To put in, as clothes into a chest; to pack. See UHAO.

3. To lay brick or stone into the walls of a house or city. *Neh.* 3:2.

4. To pile one thing on another.

5. To whip; to scourge; ke *uhauia* la ke kua o ke kanaka i ke kaula; to strike; to smite. *Oih.* 12:23.

6. To pinch; to afflict; to press.

U-HAU, *s.* A whip to strike with. *Nahum.* 3:2.

U-HAU-A, *s.* The stones; the testicles of the male. *Iob.* 40:17.

U-HA-U-HA, *v.* See UHA 4. To live in a wasteful manner; to squander property.

2. To live in every indulgence of passion; a noho *uhauha* ke alii me ka inu rama ame ka aie, the king lived in a *reveling manner*, drinking rum and going into debt.

U-HA-U-HA, *adj.* Riotous; gluttonous; reveling.

2. Tough; applied to kalo. See UAUA.

U-HA-U-HA, *s.* Moral madness; folly. *Kekah.* 1:17.

U-HAU-HAU, *v.* See UHAU. To crowd on; to press forward.

U-HAU-HAU, *s.* Weakness; tremulous, as of old age.

U-HAU-HAU, *adj.* Weak; tremulous; tottering with age; fearful.

U-HAU-HA-LA-LE, *adj.* Large, fat and unwieldy, as a very fat person; also weak.

U-HAU-HU-I, *s.* Name of a religious ceremony in the pule anaana; same as *auhauhui.*

U-HAU-HU-MU, *v.* *Uhau* and *humu*, to unite. To lay stones smoothly in a wall.

U-HAU-LA, *v.* To waste; to be prodigal of; e hoomauna.

U-HA-KA-KAU, *s.* The office of one of the king's attendants.

U-HA-KI, *v.* See UHAI, *k* inserted. To break, as a stick or staff. *Isa.* 14:5. To break, as the bones. *Isa.* 38:13.

2. To break, as a covenant. *Ier.* 11:10.

U-HA-KI, *adj.* Broken, as some brittle substance; hu ulu *uhaki*; he kuapuu, i. e., a broken or humpbacked person.

U-HA-KU, *v.* To put together; to bundle up; to roll together.

U-HA-LE-HE, *s.* A vulgar word used by children; similar to *wahahee*; he *uhalehe* oe.

U-HA-LE-HE, *adj.* Broad; wide, as a hole; *uhalehe* ka waha; *uhalehe* ka puka.

U-HA-LE-NA, *adj.* Lazy; full by over eating.

U-HA-LO-A, *s.* Name of a small shrub growing in dry places, used in making scars on the skin something like blisters.

U-HA-LU, *adj.* Hungry; weak from hunger; destitute.

U-HA-LU-HA-LU, *adj.* Applied to the visage; gazing; staring.

2. Water-soaked; tough, as kalo.

U-HA-LU-LA, *adj.* Lazy; slow; weak; cowardly.

U-HA-LU-LA, *s.* Weakness; laziness; cowardice.

U-HA-MU-A, *s.* *Uha* and *mua*, first, fore. The shoulder of an animal. *Ezek.* 24:4.

U-HA-NE, *s.* See HANE and HANEHANE in the meles. The soul; the spirit of a person. *Oihk.* 5:1. He mea ninau i na uhane ino, a consulter of evil spirits. *Kanl.* 18:11. He kino wailua.

2. The ghost or spirit of a deceased person.

3. The Spirit; applied to the third person of the Trinity. *Ioan.* 1:32. Uhane Hemolele, The Holy Spirit. NOTE.—Hawaiians supposed that men had two souls each; that one died with the body, the other lived on either visible or invisible as might be, but had no more connection with the person deceased than his shadow. These ghosts could talk, cry, complain, whisper, &c. There were those who were supposed to be skillful in entrapping or catching them.

U-HA-NE, *adj.* Spiritual. 1 *Kor.* 15:44. Partaking of the spirit or soul.

U-HA-NE, *adv.* Me ka hoi *uhane* aku hoi i Kauai. *Laieik.* 95. Their flesh eaten by the birds, they would return as to their souls only to Kauai.

U-HA-NUI, *adj.* Weak; feeble; having little physical strength; not able to bear a great weight; he mea *uhanui* ke kanaka ikaika ole.

U-HEA, *s.* The cover of a pot. NOTE.— This may be an erroneous orthography for *uhia*, a contraction of *uhiia*, covered.

U-HE-U-HE, *adj.* Offended. See UHELEHE.

U-HE-U-LE, *s.* A word used in vilifying and reproaching another.

U-HE-KE, *adj.* Languid; weak; imbecile.

U-HE-KE-HE-KE, *adj.* Full; plump; applied to the cheeks; papalina *uhekeheke*.

2. Large, fleshy and weak, as a fat man.

U-HE-LE, *v.* To bark; to peel bark from a tree or banana.

U-HE-LE-HE, *adj.* Offended.

U-HE-MO, *v.* See HEMO. To break off; to separate into parts.

2. To divorce, as man and wife; alaila, kuha aku la o Wakea i ko Papa mau maka a *uhemo* iho la laua, then Wakea spat in Papa's face and they two were *divorced*.

U-HE-NE, } *v.* See HENEHENE, to
U-HE-NE-HE-NE, } mock. To use vile and lascivious language between the sexes.

U-HI, *v.* To cover over a thing so as to hide it; to cover or hide, as the water covers what is in the bottom of the sea. *Puk.* 15:10.

2. To cover, i. e., spread over the country, as an army. *Nah.* 22:5. To cover; to hide, as a sin, i. e., to forgive it. *Neh.* 4:5.

3. *Hoo.* To veil; to cover with a veil, as the face. *Kin.* 24:65.

4. To spread over a cover; to conceal, as a cloud. *Kin.* 9:14. *Uhi* uha mai ka pele o ka lua ahi, *uhi* mai ka leo o ke ahi o ka pele.

5. To be smothered, as the voice of one by the voices of many; ua *uhiia* kona leo e ka haukamumu. *Laieik.* 22.

U-HI, *s.* A covering; a veil. *Puk.* 26:14.

2. A fence; a protection.

U-HI, *s.* A yam, a vegetable; grows in the ground.

U-HI, *s.* Name of a small shell fish.

U-HI-A-PA-NA, *v.* See PAKUIKUI, *Kam.*

U-HI-U-HI, *v.* To thatch a house poorly with banana leaves; he ako paa ole.

U-HI-U-HI, *s.* Name of a timber tree on Kauai; wood a dark red color, very durable, very hard.

U-HI-KI-NO, *s.* *Uhi*, to cover, and *kino*, the body. A covering for the body; a shield. *Hal.* 35:2.

U-HI-NA, *s.* A net for taking fish.

U-HI-NI, *s.* An insect something like a grasshopper; the word has been used in the Bible for grasshopper. *Nah.* 13:33. For locust. *Puk.* 10:14. Mai ai oe i ka *uhini*; by a change of letters. See UNIHI.

Uhini huluhulu, a canker worm. *Nahum.* 3:15. *Uhini* hulu ole, the palmer worm. *Ioel.* 1:4. *Uhini* opio hulu ole. *Ioel.* 2:25.

U-HI-NI, *adj.* Thin; slender; small; almost broken; puahilo.

U-HI-NI-PAA-WE-LA, *s.* The parent of the uhini; *uhinipaawela*, oia ka uhini makua.

U-HI-NI-PI-LI, *s.* The leg and arm bones bound up together; he akua *uhinipili*; they were worshipped in that condition. See UNIHIPILI.

U-HI-NI-PU-A, *s.* See UHINI. The young uhini before it has wings; oia ka uhini liilii aole eheu.

U-HI-NU, *v.* To take advantage of a man's ignorance in a bargain; to deceive in that way.

U-HI-PAA, *v.* *Uhi*, to cover, and *paa*, fast. To cover up entirely so as to be out of sight, as a cloud or fog. *Laieik.* 16.

U-HOI, *v.* See HOI, to return. To return from following one; to turn back. 2 *Sam.* 2:26.

2. To unite together; to live and sleep together, as a man and wife once separated.

U-HO-LA, *v.* See HOLA. To unfold; to spread out, as the wings of a bird.

2. To spread down, as a mat.

3. To spread out or smooth, as a cloth that has been ruffled up.

4. To wrap up, as to wrap up one in bed clothes; to spread out, as a net. *Hal.* 140:5.

5. FIG. Applied to the mind; to calm; to soothe; to prepare for hearing a message, good or bad.

6. To open, as the mind; to enlighten. See HOHOLA and HOLAHOLA.

U-HO-LE, *v.* See HOLE. To skin; to strip off the skin of an animal; to peel the bark from a tree; to peel off the skin, as a banana; e maihi.

U-HU, *v.* To groan from pain; to complain of suffering.

2. To complain of an injury done to one.

3. To think hard of; mai *uhu* nui wale oe i ka hoi i kou wahi iho, do not *think* too hard of going back to your own place.

4. To bolt, as a horse.

5. *Hoo.* Mai *hoouhu* aku oe i ka holo o ka lio; to groan; to cough. See KANIUHU.

U-HU, *s.* A cry of grief; grief; hard feeling; no keia olelo a ua haole la, o ka *uhu* koke ae la no ia e holo.

2. The groaning of persons.

3. The grunting of hogs; kani *uhu*, a deep groan.

4. Name of a fish the size of a salmon.

U-HU, *adj.* Wasteful; improvident.

U-HU-AO, *v.* To rush; to struggle.

U-HU-E-LA, *s.* A species of red fish.

U-HU-E-LE-E-LE, *s.* A species of fish.

U-HU-U-HU, *v.* See UHU. To neigh, as a horse. *Ier.* 5:8. To bray, as an ass.

  2. To cough frequently.

  3. *Hoo.* To cause a neighing or groaning, &c.

  4. To hem; to hawk, as in clearing the throat.

U-HU-U-HU, *s.* A neighing, as of a horse. *Ier.* 8:16. A frequent coughing; he kunukunu.

U-HU-HA-LA-HA-LA, *s.* Name of a fish.

U-HU-KI, *v.* To pull up, as grass or weeds; to root up, as weeds or small trees. *Ier.* 11:19.

  2. To root up, destroy, as a people. *Amos.* 9:15. See HUKI, to pull; draw.

  3. To rob; to take violently what is another's.

U-HU-KI-WA-LE, *s.* A seizing and taking away what is another's; a robbery.

U-HU-PA-KA-LI, *s.* *Uhu,* a fish, and *pakali,* to deceive so as to catch. The fish used as a decoy in catching other fish; oia ka uhu e hoowalewale ai, e kaana mai ai na uhu e a hei i ka upena. See UHU, fish.

U-HU-PI-KO-U-LA, *s.* Name of a fish; a kind of fish and a way of catching it. See UHU, fish.

U-KA, *s.* The shore; the country inland; opposed to *kai.*

U-KA, *v.* To send; to convey; mostly with *hoo;* to send, as a letter. 2 *Sam.* 11:14. To send, convey, as money or goods. 2 *Oihl.* 16:3.

  2. To bring upon one, as evil. *Ios.* 23:15.

  3. To consume; to destroy; to devour.

  4. To cast up; to make a road. *Isa.* 57:14.

  5. To add to; to make more of. 1 *Nal.* 12:11.

  6. To commence an attack, as in a battle; ekolu paha la e kaua ai; alaila *hoouka* nui.

  7. To throw upon, as goods or property on board a vessel.

U-KA, *v.* To address in calling a hog; i kuu manao, aole manao o ka puaa; ina e olelo aku ke kahu, e i aku ia me neia, *uka—uka—*u mai ka puaa. See UHU, *s.*

U-KAE, *adj.* Dirty; filthy; hoggish.

U-KA-U-KA, *v.* *Hoo.* To throw or pile upon, as baggage on a vessel or canoe.

  2. To gormandize; to eat as long as one can; ka ai nui ana a ono ka puu.

U-KAU-KAI, *adj.* For *ukauka ai.* Large, fat and feeble.

U-KA-HE-WA, *v.* *Uka,* to make an attempt, and *hewa,* wrong. To make an attempt and miss; to attempt and not perform.

U-KA-KA, *s.* The female of the bird oo.

U-KA-LE-KA-LE, *adj.* Deceitful lying. See HOOKALEKALE. He kanaka *ukalekale,* aole oiaio.

U-KA-LI, *v.* To follow after; to follow, as people in a train of a chief; hahai, a *ukali* i ke alii.

  2. To accompany one; to go with. *Sol.* 7:22.

  3. To be sent after as a package. 2 *Sam.* 11:8.

U-KA-LI, *adj.* The younger; the smaller; applied to shot sent from the gun at the same time with the ball; called poka *ukali* because they follow after the ball; called also *pokii,* the younger brothers (of the ball.)

  2. Following, i. e., accompanying; attending upon; ma na waa *ukali* o ke alii. *Laieik.* 112.

U-KA-LI, *s.* Name of the planet Mercury; so called from its following close after the sun.

U-KA-LI, *adv.* After; behind, like one following after; hele *ukali* hou, they went following after. *Laieik.* 72.

U-KA-NA, *s.* See UKA and ANA. A sending; something sent.

  2. Property or something to be conveyed to another place.

  3. Baggage on or to be put on a canoe or vessel.

  4. Any movable property. *Kin.* 46:6. A bundle; one's substance. *Ios.* 14:4.

  5. The calabashes, remnants of food, &c., after a family has eaten. *Laieik.* 86.

U-KE, *v.* To strike, as the cloth mallet; to tick, as a watch. See PUKE and KOELE.

U-KE-KE, *s.* Name of an ancient pulsatile musical instrument among the Hawaiians; a harp. 1 *Sam.* 10:5. Ka *ukeke* hahau.

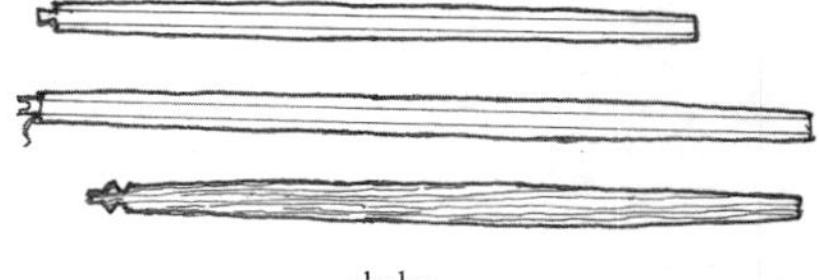

ukeke

U-KE-KE, *s.* A shuddering; a chill. See HAUKEKE, anu, lia.

U-KE-KE, ⎫ *s.* A species of bird.
U-KE-KE-KE, ⎭

U-KE-LE, *v.* To be muddy; slippery. See KELE.

U-KE-LE-KE-LE, *adj.* Muddy; miry; slippery from mud, as a road. See KELE, mud; mire.

U-KI, *s.* A plant or shrub, sometimes used in thatching houses; there are three kinds; the leaves of these bushes could be used only in temporary shelters; kamala *uki*, he hana wikiwiki; kamala *uki* kau hana ana was jestingly said when one thatched badly, leaving holes, as in a shelter made quickly; applied in this sense to all thatching.

2. Name of the grass inside of the house, as the pili was outside.

U-KI, *v.* To provoke; to do that which irritates one; used mostly with *hoo*, or in the frequentative form, as *ukiuki.*

U-KI, *s.* Name of a kind of grass.

U-KI, *adj.* Partaking of the quality of *uki*; as kamala *uki*, a shanty covered with *uki* leaves; unsubstantial; applied also to cloth, as lole *uki*, blue cloth. 2 *Oihl.* 3:14.

U-KI, *v.* To have a strong offensive smell; to smell unpleasantly. See UKIUKI, *adj.*

U-KI-U, ⎫ *s.* The shell of the kukui
U-KI-U-KI-U, ⎭ nut; ka ili a kukui.

U-KI-U, ⎫ *s.* The name of a north
U-KI-U-KI-U, ⎭ wind; similar to the *hoo-lua*; he makani kiu.

U-KI-U-KI, *v.* To be offended; to be vexed; provoked; to be very angry. *Neh.* 4:1.

2. To treat with contempt; to be in anger at one. *Kanl.* 19:6. To be displeased. 2 *Sam.* 6:8.

3. To scold; to be indignant; to treat vindictively; to hate. *Kin.* 50:15. Ua like ka *ukiuki* me ka inaina; *ukiuki* iho la ia no kona nele ana i ka aina ole, he was *very angry* for being deprived of land. *Hoo—na.* The same meaning.

U-KI-U-KI, *v.* To be gently in motion, or to have a little strength, as waves; *ukiu-ki* ka aleale ane. *Aniani, aheahe, nahe,* &c., *ukiuki* and *malanai* are strong in the order in which they are here placed, *malanai* being the strongest.

U-KI-U-KI, *s.* Contempt; anger; rage; envy; disaffection; wrath. *Kanl.* 29:27. FIG. with ninini. *Ezek.* 20:13, 21.

U-KI-U-KI, *adj.* Papa *ukiuki* ka makani, a strong blowing wind.

2. Strong smelling; offensive; he *ukiuki* ka waha o ka mea puhi baka; pilopilo.

U-KI-HI, *adj.* Sores at the corners of the mouth.

2. Well spoken, as a fluent person in speaking; he waha *ukihi*, hoopololei, mikomiko ka waha.

U-KI-KE, *s.* Name of an ancient musical instrument; a kind of jewsharp. See UKEKE.

U-KI-KI, *s.* Name of a species of fish.

U-KO, *s.* An offering which one carried with him before Wakea when he died. Human sacrifices were offered for this purpose; he *uko* keia oihana a ke kahuna—a moa ae la ka puaa *uko.*

U-KO-KO-LE, *adj.* Sore; inflamed; applied to a partial inflammation of the eye. See KOLE.

U-KO-LE, *s.* Name of a species of fish.

U-KO-LE-KO-LE, *adj.* Reddened or inflamed, as the eye; he *ukolekole* ka maka.

U-KU, *v.* To pay; to remunerate; to pay, as a fine. *Puk.* 21:30. To pay a tax or debt.

2. To compensate either good or bad, according to what has been previously done. *Puk.* 34:7. SYN. with hoopai.

3. To reward; require or demand punishment for an offense.

4. To bring evil upon one, as a punishment.

5. PASS. To be punished; to be paid, as wages; e *uku* hewa, to punish; e *uku* maikai, to reward.

6. *Hoo.* To reward; to pay for a benefit. 2 *Sam.* 19:36. To lay a fine upon one. *Kanl.* 22:19.

U-KU, *s.* Wages or reward for work done. *Nah.* 18:31.

2. Fine for a misdemeanor; *uku* hoopai, punishment for a crime. *Laieik.* 212. Tax or tribute to a ruler.

3. A pledge for a dept. *Kanl.* 24:6. A pledge for a thing lent. *Kanl.* 24:10.

4. He *uku* mare, a dowry. *Puk.* 21:10.

5. A price for a privilege; a he *uku* no kou kokoke aku, a *price* for your approach. *Laieik.* 99.

U-KU, *s.* Name of a genus of small insects; *uku* poo, a head louse; *uku* kapa, a body louse; *uku* pepa, the book insect; *uku* lele, a flea, &c. The root is probably *uku*, to be little or small. See uuku.

U-KU, *s.* A species of fish.

U-KU-I, *s.* A reward. See UKU.

U-KU-U-KU, *adj.* Very small; little.

U-KU-HI, *v.* To pour, as water into a

cask; to fill a vessel with any fluid. *Ios.* 9:13. *Ukuhi* iho la a piha na pahu, they poured into the casks till full.

2. To get or obtain water; i holo mai e *ukuhi* wai a loaa ka ai i ola, they come here to obtain water (LIT. To pour water in) and to get provisions.

3. To wean, as a child from the breast. *Kin.* 21:8. Equivalent to *haalele waiu*; hooki i ka ai waiu ana o ke keiki; keiki i *ukuhiia*, a weaned child. *Hal.* 131:2.

U-KU-HOO-PA-NEE, *s.* *Uku*, pay, and *hoopanee*, to put off; i. e., interest on money lent; usury. *Isa.* 24:2.

U-KU-KA-PA, *s.* *Uku*, louse, and *kapa*, garment. A kapa louse; a body louse; he uku no ke kino o ke kanaka.

U-KU-KU-HI, *v.* To put or pour into, as liquid into a vessel. See UKUHI. E kiaha-aha.

U-KU-LE-LE, *s.* *Uku* and *lele*, to jump. A flea. 1 *Sam.* 24:15.

U-KU-PA-NAI, *s.* *Uku*, pay, and *panai*, to redeem. A pledge for a payment. *Puk.* 22:26. Security for a person or thing. *Oih.* 17:9.

U-KU-PE-PA, *s.* *Uku* and *pepa* (Eng.), paper. The insect that eats paper or books.

U-KU-POO, *s.* *Uku*, louse, and *poo*, the head. A head louse.

U-LA, *s.* *Ula*, red. A lobster, from its color; he ia iwi mawaho; also,

2. A species of fish; also written *ulaula*.

U-LA,
U-LA-U-LA, } *v.* To be or appear red, as the end of a blaze of fire, or of a lamp; to be red. *Isa.* 63:2.

U-LA,
U-LA-U-LA, } *s.* Redness; a scarlet color. *Puk.* 25:4. Red, *v.* 5; ua like ka *ulaula* me ka weo; name of a red fish. See ULA.

U-LA,
U-LA-U-LA, } *adj.* Red, as a blaze seen in the night; purple; kanaka *ula*.

U-LA-O-KO-KO, *adj.* *Ula* and *koko*, blood. Red, as fire, or anything painted bright red; red, as blood, or blood red. NOTE.— Sometimes the last a falls out in speaking, thus, *ula—koko*.

U-LAE, *s.* A species of fish.

U-LAI-A, *v.* To live in solitude, as a hermit, on account of disappointment.

U-LA-U-LA, *s.* See ULA above. Ka weoweo, ke kolekole; the redness of the flesh when the skin is rubbed off.

U-LA-U-LA, *adj.* See ULA above. He helohelo; slight red; reddish.

U-LA-U-LA, *s.* Name of a species of fish.

U-LAU-LAI-LA, *s.* Name of a child illegitimately born of a chief and a common woman.

U-LA-U-LA-KE-A-HI, *s.* *Ulaula*, red, and *ke ahi*, the fire.

1. The name given to liquor when first distilled, from its color; also,

2. A name applied to the god who presided over the business of distillation; no *Ulaulakeahi* ke kiaha mua o ka rama, for *Ulaulakeahi* the first cup (distilled) of rum.

U-LA-HIO-HIO, *adj.* *Ula* and *ioio*. The *h* is probably euphonic. Really red. See ULAOKOKO of the same meaning.

U-LA-HI-WA, *adj.* *Ula*, red, and *hiwa*, black. Purple; dark red.

U-LA-LA, *v.* To act insanely; to be out of one's right mind.

U-LA-LA, *s.* Insanity; madness. *Kekah.* 9:13.

2. A crazy person.

U-LA-LA, *adj.* Crazy; demented; out of one's senses.

U-LA-LE-LE, *s.* A favorite; one highly esteemed.

U-LA-NA, *v.* To weave; to plait; to braid; to intertwine, as vines. *Puk.* 28:32. To wreathe; to weave. 2 *Nal.* 25:17. E *ulana* moena, to braid or weave a mat.

U-LA-NA, *adj.* Lying still or calm, as the surface of water unruffled by wind.

2. Idle; unemployed; lulana, heha, molowa.

U-LA-NA, *adj.* Iwi *ulana*. *Kam.*, B. 2, p. 7, 3. The prophecy or expression of the kilokilo when looking upon a person in good health, meaning he will soon die.

U-LA-PAA, *s.* *Ula*, red, and *paa*, fast; concealed. The ossa vagina of females.

U-LE, *v.* To hang; to swing; to project.

U-LE, *s.* The penis; the genital of men and male animals; o ka *ule* no paha ke mene; haha ia i ka *ule* o Kanekii.

2. A tenon for a mortice.

3. The pointed part of the post which enters the crotch of the rafter.

U-LEI, *s.* Name of a tree, the timber very hard; from this tree instruments were made for cultivating the earth, as the oo, &c.

U-LEI, *v.* To open; to uncover; to separate; helei, uwehe, wehe.

U-LEI, *s.* An opening; uncovering; ka helei, ka uwehe.

U-LE-U-LE, *s.* A sty on the edge of the eyelid, ka *uleule* o ka maka.

U-LE-U-LE, *adj.* See ULE. Pendulous; hanging down; projecting out.

U-LE-U-LE-LE, *v.* To ride on horseback; kaukaulelewaihui. See POLEHELEHE.

U-LE-HE-LE-HE, *adj.* Not bound tight; applied to a bundle; paa ole.

U-LE-HI-LO, *s.* The gonorrhea; same as *waiki.*

U-LE-HO-LE, *v.* Ule and *hole,* to peel. To practice onanism or masturbation.

U-LE-HO-LE, *s.* Onanism; masturbation, &c.

U-LE-KA-HI, *s.* Ule and *kahi,* to cut. A name for circumcision.

U-LE-PAA, *s.* Epithet of a man who has not known a woman; the same as *puupaa* applied to a woman.

U-LE-PE, *v.* To stand erect, as the comb of a cock. See LEPE. To stand erect, as the hair when one is cold.
2. To be rough.

U-LE-PU-AA, *s.* Ule and *puaa,* a hog. The name given by Hawaiians to a screw auger, gimlet, or any instrument of that class.

U-LI, *adj.* Blue; cerulean blue; green, as a meadow; whatever is green among vegetables. *Puk.* 9:22. Pertaining to a dark or dusty color; *uli* ka wai o ka niu.

U-LI, *s.* The blue sky; ka poe nana *uli* o ke alii, the foretellers of the weather. *Laieik.* 36.

U-LI, *s.* The name of a god to which a prayer was addressed in the pule anaana.

U-LI, *s.* A canoe steerer for the king's canoes; one of the king's special servants.

U-LI, *v.* To steer a canoe or ship. See HOEULI.

U-LI, *v.* To gurgle; to make such a noise as when water is poured out of a calabash or a cocoanut; e neneke; *uli* ka wai o ka niu.

U-LI, *s.* Name of a species of kalo.
2. Name of a species of fan leaf cocoanut; ka *uli,* ka loulu, ka hawane.

U-LI, *s.* The personal appearance or fitness of a person for any duty; applied particularly to runners as they appeared to the poe kilokilo; e nana no ka poe nana *uli,* e like me ke kukini.

U-LI-E-O, *s.* See ULI. The appearance of a person as fit or unfit for a duty or office, including his mental fitness; hele mai ka poe akamai e nana i ka *ulieo* o kekahi kukini.

U-LI-U-LI, *adj.* See ULI. Blue. *Puk.* 25:4. Green. *Kanl.* 12:2. Dark colored. *Iob.* 6:16. Black. *Mel. Sol.* 5:11. Ka moana *uliuli*; ka lole *uliuli.*

U-LI-U-LI, *s.* Green things; verdure; a pasture. *Ioel.* 1:19.

U-LI-HI, *s.* An advanced state of old age; feebleness; loss of hair; want of strength.

U-LI-HI-LI-HI, *adj.* He mea *ulihilihi*; a running, as a low vine like the kowali.

U-LI-KA, *adj.* Wet; soft to the touch.

U-LI-KA-LI-KA, *v.* Ninanina, linalina; to adhere to, like wax or any gluey substance; like mud or clay; like kalo that is loliloli.

U-LI-KA-LI-KA, *adj.* Sticky; adhesive, as mud; he lepo *ulikalika.*

U-LI-LI, *s.* A species of bird.
2. A small kind of gourd used for a top to play with; also called *uliuliu.*
3. A kind of bamboo flute; he ohi hookanikani.
4. A religious ceremony in the pule anaana, the same as *auhauhui.*
5. The name of a hula; he *ulili* kahi hula.

U-LI-LI, *v.* Ke *ulili* anapu nei i kuu manawa. *Laieik.* 118. To exhibit the tremulous motion of the hot sunlight upon a flat, smooth surface.

U-LI-LI, *s.* A ladder.
2. A whistle made of bamboo, in which fire was put and blowed upon.

U-LI-LI, *adj.* Ladder like; ala *ulili,* a ladder. See ALAHAKA.

U-LI-NA, *adj.* See LINA. Soft, as the flesh of a fat person; full fleshed; plump.
2. Soft and tough, as clayey ground.

U-LI-NA-LI-NA, *adj.* Fat; plump; soft to the touch; tough; adhesive, as cold clayey ground. See LINALINA and UAUA.

U-LO-NO, *v.* To cry, as in distress; to make a complaint; to cry, as one in prayer or in suffering. *Hal.* 30:2.

U-LO-NO, *s.* A cry of distress; the voice of crying. *Hal.* 9:12. He leo pule.

U-LU, *v.* To grow, as a plant. *Isa.* 53:2.
2. To increase in any way; to grow, as a disease in the skin. *Oihk.* 13:39.
3. To become strong or excessive, as in anger, with *puni. Puk.* 32:22. To grow or increase, as good or evil in a community.
4. To grow up, as men. *Iob.* 31:18.
5. To grow in size and strength, as an infant. 1 *Pet.* 2:2.
6. To be extensively known, as a report.
7. To have spiritual possession, either good or bad; to be inspired; in this sense, mostly in the passive; as, *uluia* or *uluhia. Mat.* 8:16. To influence the affections.
8. To poke the hot stones out of the hole in which food is to be baked in order to put in food; e *ulu* kakou i ka umu, to

throw out the stones of the oven when hot. See ULUUMU.

9. To stick fast, as meat or bones between the teeth of the eater.

10. *Hoo.* To cause to spring up, as seed sown. FIG. O ko'u makemake nui, e *hooulu* i ka hana ana ma ka pono, my great desire is to *increase* in good works.

U-LU, *s.* Name of a tree; the breadfruit; the fruit good for food, the timber for building, for canoes, &c.

2. Name of a stone used in a play. At Maui and Oahu this stone was called *olohu.* See OLOHU.

3. Name of the game where the said stone was used.

4. Name of an oven for baking food. See UMU.

U-LU, *adj.* Of or belonging to what grows, as fruit. FIG. *Ier.* 2:3.

2. Wet. See PULU. *Ulu* ka palapala i ka ua.

U-LU-A, *s.* Name of a large kind of fish.

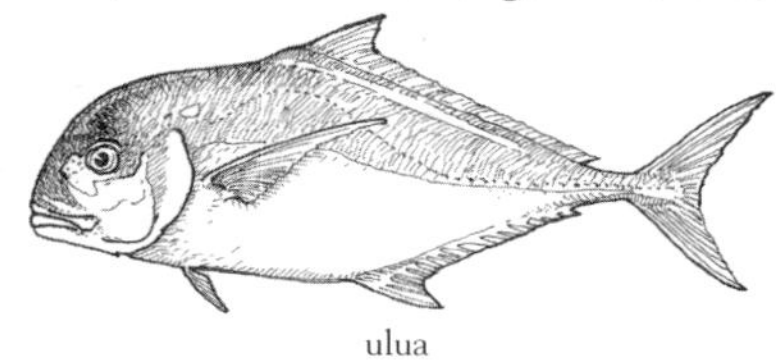

ulua

2. A kind of vegetable forbidden to women to eat; ina i ai ka wahine i ka niu paha, he maia paha, he *ulua* paha, make ia.

U-LU-A, *v.* To assemble together, as men; ua *ulua* mai kakou ma keia wahi.

U-LU-A, *s.* For *uluia.* See ULU. A collection; a gathering together; an assembly.

2. A forest or garden of breadfruit trees; ka haha ulu, ka hopuhopu ana i ke kanaka e pepehi a make.

U-LU-A, *s.* Name of the sacrifice obtained by the kapopo.

U-LU-A-O-A, *v.* To gather in great numbers, as people; to come together irregularly; to make confusion in an assembly.

U-LU-A-O-A, *s.* Confusion; want of regularity in an assembly of men. 1 *Kor.* 14:33.

U-LU-A-O-A, *adj.* Gathered together, as people; confused and noisy.

U-LU-AU-NUI, *s.* The name of a wind off Hilo; *uluaunui,* he makani pono ole ke ku ma ke awa o Hilo, a bad wind for coming to anchor in the harbor of Hilo; the north wind, attended with rain.

U-LU-A-HE-WA.

U-LU-A-LA-NA, *v. Ulu* and *alana,* an offering. To offer upon an altar; to go up upon an altar. See ALANA.

U-LU-A-MO-HAI, *s.* The name of a fish.

U-LU-EO, *s.* Name of a tree; timber very durable, even more so than uhiuhi.

U-LU-IA, *v.* See ULU. *Uluia* is the passive. To be possessed by a spirit; to be inspired; more often written with *h* inserted, *uluhia.* See ULUHIA below.

U-LU-O-A, *s.* He puoa; standing erect; standing uprightly.

U-LU-U-LU, *v.* To grow up; to grow thick &c. See ULU.

2. *Hoo.* To cause to grow up.

3. To excite; to stir up; to provoke to anger. See NAULU.

U-LU-U-LU, *v.* To work or turn about in the mouth, as a person eating sugarcane; *uluulu* no ma ka waha.

2. *Hoo.* To gather together. *Kin.* 29:8. To collect, as things scattered; to lay up; to assemble, as a people. *Nah.* 11:16.

3. To lift up; to carry; to convey to a higher place; e kau ae iluna i ke kapa.

U-LU-U-LU, *s.* A gathering; an assembly of people for any purpose. *Hoo.* A convocation, &c. *Oihk.* 23:3.

U-LU-U-LU, *s.* Name of a species of fish net; upena *uluulu.*

U-LU-U-LU, *v.* To lift up one's dress on passing over water or mud.

U-LU-U-LU, *adj.* O ka hana me ka ikaika, me ka hele *uluulu* ame ka hele kipalale; laboring strongly; with energy.

U-LU-U-MU, *s.* The stick by which the stones are thrown out of an oven when heated. See ULU and UMU.

U-LU-HAI-HAI, *s.* See ULUKU. The feeling of the mind under the influence of fear with uncertainty as to the result, mixed with strong desire, &c.

U-LU-HA-OA, *adj.* Thick, as rough jagged rocks among grass and bushes; *uluhaoa* enaena maloko o ka nahele.

U-LU-HA-LA, *s.* A forest or thicket of hala trees; ka *uluhala* o Polou.

U-LU-HEE, *s.* A species of plant or shrub.

U-LU-HI-A, *v.* See ULU and ULUIA above. *Uluhia, h* inserted, to be possessed by a spirit; to be influenced or under the direction of some spirit without the person. *Mat.* 4:24.

U-LU-HU-A, *v. Ulu,* to grow, and *hua,* envy.

1. To trouble; to give concern.

2. To be tired with one's company; to be weary of one's visit.

3. To be vexed or troubled with any matter. *Laieik.* 78. To be weary with doing or repeating a thing. *Ier.* 15:6.

4. To be weary with life. *Iob.* 10:1.

5. *Hoo.* To cause grief or trouble. *Sol.* 10:1. To be much vexed. *Ezek.* 22:5.

U-LU-HU-A, *s.* Discouragement; want of confidence; disappointment; self displeasure. 1 *Nal.* 20:43.

U-LU-HU-A, *adj.* Displeased; angry; discontented; disaffected.

U-LU-KA-HI-KI, *s.* *Ulu* and *kahiki*, foreign. A foreign breadfruit tree, i. e., the fig tree, from the resemblance of its leaves.

U-LU-KU, *v.* *Ulu* and *ku*, to stand.

1. To have a strong desire to perform anything.

2. To be restless at night or to lie sleepless.

3. To be troubled; restless, as the sea; kupikio; same as *hiaa*.

U-LU-KU, *s.* Restless; sleepless; desiring strongly to possess or to obtain a thing.

> Ka *uluku* uluhaihai
> Komia e uia koia.—*Mele.*

U-LU-LA, *s.* Name of a bird translated *owl*. *Kanl.* 14:15.

U-LU-LA-AU, *s.* *Ulu*, to grow, and *laau*, tree.

1. A thicket of trees; a wood.

2. A habitation of wild beasts. *Ios.* 17:18. He *ululaau*! ua nei ae la iloko o ke kai, it is a *forest*! it has moved into the sea; the exclamation of Hawaiians on first seeing the ships of Captain Cook.

U-LU-LE-LE, *s.* A favorite; one highly esteemed.

U-LU-LU, *v.* To rejoice; to be gay; to be cheerful; e hoohoihoi, e hooolioli.

2. *Hoo.* To pretend to be what one is not.

3. To flatter the gods; to be a favorite.

U-LU-LU, *s.* A rejoicing; gladness; self satisfaction; being on good terms with the gods.

U-LU-LU, *s.* Name of a small fish net which was sunk deep in the water and entangled the fish.

U-LU-LU, *adj.* Rough; not smooth; ka huluhulu, ka manumanu.

U-LU-MAI-KA, *s.* The name of a game.

2. Name of the stone used in playing the game. See ULU; also MAIKA. NOTE.—Since the introduction of bowling-alleys, *ulumaika* has been applied to the game of bowls.

U-LU-MA-HI-E-HI-E, *v.* See HOOMAHIE. To appear or affect an extra appearance in dress or in personal behavior, as we say like one possessed.

U-LU-MA-NO, *s.* Name of a violent wind which blows from the south and other quarters, in the night only, on the west side of Hawaii. Kamehameha ma were once wrecked by it off Nawawa; a whole village was burnt to light them ashore.

U-LU-MO-KU, *s.* A collection or fleet of ships; a navy; applied to the arrival of whaleships.

U-LU-NA, *v.* To support the head; to bolster up, as a weak person.

2. To sleep upon, as a pillow; to make a pillow of. *Kin.* 28:18.

3. To tie up a bundle for a pillow; e pela *uluna*, to make a pillow. See PELA.

U-LU-NA, *s.* A pillow. *Kin.* 28:11. Kuhi makou ua kau ke poo i ka *uluna*, we thought we had laid our heads upon the *pillow*.

uluna

2. The upper part of the shoulders where they unite with the neck. See HOKUA.

U-LU-NA-HE-LE, *s.* Ma na kuamoo ame na *ulunahele* ame na loko; a growing luxuriantly, like fruit in a good soil.

U-LU-PA, *v.* To break into pieces. 1 *Sam.* 2:10. To dash into atoms. *Hal.* 2:9.

2. To beat fine. *Isa.* 27:9. E wawahi, e hoopau.

U-LU-PA, *s.* A breaking to pieces; a breaking up fine.

U-LU-PAA, *s.* The state of virginity. See ULEPAA.

U-LU-PE, *v.* To be wet; to be cold.

U-LU-PII, *v.* To be wet and cold from rain; to be shivering from cold and wet.

U-LU-PII, *adj.* Wet and cold from rain; shivering.

U-LU-PU-NI, *v.* To be or to wax hot, as one in anger. *Puk.* 32:19. See ULU 3. To swell, as in anger. See PUNI.

U-LU-WA-LE, *v.* *Ulu*, to grow, and *wale*, of itself. To grow wild; to grow without cultivation.

U-LU-WE-HI-WE-HI, *s*, *Ulu*, a thicket, and *wehiwehi*, thick; tangled, as vegetables.

1. An overgrowth of verdure; the thick intertwined leaves of a forest.

2. A general name for thick vines in a forest; ka nahelehele nui a maluna i ka lau o na laau.

U-MA, *v.* To screw; to press, as a vice; to grasp or hold.

2. To pry, as a lever.

3. To wrestle; to throw down in wrestling.

4. To throw over from an upright position; e hoohina, e kulai.

U-MA, *s.* A vice; a pressure; a pushing over or down; a kind of wrestling to try strength.

2. The name of a game; o kekahi lealea o ka *uma*.

U-MAU-MA, *s.* The breast; the bosom. *Puk.* 4:6. The breast, i. e., the meat of the breast. *Puk.* 29:26. *Umauma* hoali, wave breast. *Nah.* 18:18. *Umauma* luli, wave breast. *Oihk.* 7:34. Kahi mawaena o na waiu.

U-MAU-MA, *adj.* Of or belonging to the breast; he pale *umauma*, a breast plate. 1 *Sam.* 17:5.

U-MAU-MA-LEI, *s.* A name of a species of fish.

U-MA-LEI, *s.* Name of a disease in the chest.

2. Name of a species of fish.

U-MA-LU, *s.* The brow of a hill; he *umalu* o ka pali.

U-ME, *v.* To pull; to pull after one; to draw out, as a drawer of a bureau.

2. To lengthen, as a sound.

3. FIG. To incline one to go after another. *Mel. Sol.* 1:4.

U-ME, *s.* A drawing out; a pulling; a lengthening out, as a sound.

2. A name given to the character ⌢ hold in *music*.

3. A kind of lascivious play in the night; he lealea o ka *ume* i ka po.

4. The grass and thatching on the corners and ridges of a house.

U-ME, *adj.* Mea *ume*, something drawing; attractive. FIG. Mea *ume*, the mistress of a lover; hele aku o Hauiliki a i ka mea *ume*. *Laieik.* 114. See No. 3 of the preceding.

U-ME-U-ME, *v.* See UMI. To pull; to hook; to draw.

2. To struggle, as two persons for the same thing. See PAUMEUME.

U-ME-U-ME, *s.* Name of a game.

2. E kalai ia na moo a pau i ka *umeumeia*.

U-ME-KE, *s.* A poi calabash; full form, *umekepoi*. See next.

U-ME-KE-PO-I, *s.* A poi calabash full of food, much valued by Hawaiians; o ke aloha ka mea i oi aku ka maikai mamua o ka *umekepoi* ame ka ipukaia.

U-MI, *adj.* The number ten; ka *umi*, the tenth.

U-MI, *v.* To be ten in number. *Kin.* 18:32.

U-MI, *v.* To lengthen out the breath. See UME. To suppress the breath.

2. To choke; to strangle; to press upon one so as to stifle him.

3. To crowd in; thrust down.

4. To seize hold of the neck, as if to choke. *Mat.* 18:28.

5. To suppress a rising emotion.

6. To kill, as an infant in the practice of infanticide. See UMIKEIKI and UMIKAMALII.

7. *Hoo.* To cause to choke; strangle, &c.

U-MI, *adj.* Strangled; pressed; killed; mea *umi* wale. *Oih.* 15:20.

U-MII, *s.* A kind of disease or pain in the side attending disease.

U-MI-U-MI, *v.* The 13th conj. of *umi.* To choke; to strangle; to kill. 2 *Sam.* 10:4.

U-MI-U-MI, *s.* The beard; hair on the chin; ka huluhulu o ka auwae.

2. A kind of moss which fastens the nahawele, a kind of shell fish, to the rocks.

U-MI-U-MI, *adj.* Thick; large, as the branches of trees; na lala *umiumi.* *Isa.* 16:8.

U-MI-HAU, *s.* Name of a strong east wind which blows all before it.

2. The name of the last hog sacrificed when on the point of going into battle; ua kapaia keia puaa he puaa *umihau*.

U-MI-KA-MA-LII, } *s. Umi* and *kamalii*, a
U-MI-KE-I-KI, } child. The practice of infanticide, mostly by pressing or choking to death. NOTE.—The infant was generally killed by choking or pressing on its first presentation; but if the mother had great affection for it, it was buried alive in the ground. *Umikamalii*, oia ke kinai ana i ke keiki a make iloko o ka opu o ka makuahine. Nui na hewa o ka wa kahiko, o ka *umikamalii*, many were the errors of ancient times, *infanticide*.

U-MI-KI, *v.* To pinch with all the fingers.

2. To scratch; to bruise; e wawalu, e wau, e uwau.

U-MI-KI, *s.* A pinching; a scratching of the skin; e awalu ana me ka hoopohole i ka ili; ka waluwalu.

U-MI-KI, *s.* A large gourd.

U-MI-WA-LE, *s.* *Umi*, to choke, and *wale*. The seizing of a person by the throat; a killing by strangulation.

U-MO-KI, *s.* A stopple of a calabash; a cork of a bottle; a bung of a barrel. See OMOKE. He *umoki* pu, the wad of a gun.

U-MO-KI, *v.* To stop up, as with a stopple or bung.

U-MU, *v.* To bake, as in an oven; to dig; to heat; to cover up; to do all that belonged to the process of baking food under ground. See IMU.

2. To collect; to place together; to leave together, as in making an oven.

U-MU, *s.* An oven. *Oihk.* 2:4. A place for baking food; a furnace. *Neh.* 3:11. *Umu* hooheehee, a furnace for melting metals. *Ezek.* 22:20.

U-MU-A-HI, *s.* LIT. A fire oven; a furnace. *Kin.* 15:17.

U-MU-A-KU-A, *adj.* Unfriendly; unsocial; niggardly.

U-MU-LE-PO, *s.* *Umu* and *lepo*, earth. A furnace for trying metals.

U-NA, *v.* To send one, as on business. *Hoo.* The same; to commission to go. *Nah.* 13:17.

2. To send to one with a demand. *Ios.* 2:3.

3. To exercise authority over one in sending.

U-NA, *s.* A sending, especially sending one on business; o ke kena e holo i kahiki e imi waiwai.

U-NA, *adj.* Sore or stiff from hard work; tired; weak; fatigued; exhausted. *Lunk.* 4:21.

2. Dull; stupid; drunk.

3. Tired or weary, as a man sitting still. See UNAUNA same.

U-NA, *v.* To be weary; fatigued from labor. NOTE.—This word is probably the same as *una*, to send, as sending on business may cause fatigue.

U-NA, *s.* Weariness; fatigue, &c.

U-NA, *s.* The shell of the turtle or tortoise.

U-NA,   ⎱ *v.* To pry up, as a stone;
U-NA-U-NA, ⎰   to loosen by prying; more properly *une*. See UNE.

U-NA-O-A, *s.* The barnacle on the outer plank of a ship.

U-NA-U-NA, *v.* To send. See UNA. *Hoo.* To send on repeated errands. *Sol.* 10:26. To send new orders frequently.

2. To exercise authority over. *Mat.* 20:25.

U-NA-U-NA, *adj.* Tired; weak; exhausted. See UNA, to be weary; dull; stupid.

U-NA-U-NA-HE, ⎱ *adj.* Soft; melodious,
U-NA-HE,   ⎰   as the voice; he leo *unahe*.

2. Thin; soft, as kapa; he *unahenahe* ke kapa.

U-NA-U-NA-HI, ⎱ *v.* To scale, as a fish;
U-NA-HI,   ⎰   to scratch off the scales; e hoopau i ka *unahi* o ka ia mawaho.

U-NA-HI, *s.* The scales of a fish. *Oihk.* 11:9. Scaly things; *unahi* laau; ka ili oolea i ka ia mawaho.

U-NA-HI, *adj.* Scaly; hard; 1 *Sam.* 17:5. Thin; flexible, like a scale.

U-NE, *v.* To pry, as a stone with a lever; to bear down, as with a lever; to edge on; to pry up out of the dirt, as a stone; to loosen.

U-NE, *s.* A lever for prying with; a prying; a lifting up.

2. The action or quality of a lever. *Anat.* 1.

U-NE-A, *s.* Indolence; indifference; stupidity.

U-NE-U-NE, *v.* See UNE. To pry up; to loosen, as a stone; to remove or turn over, as stones. *Kekah.* 10:9.

2. To disturb, harass or vex one; o ka hookolokolo hewa, e *uneune* ana ia ame ka imihala.

U-NE-U-NE-A, *adj.* Sickish at the stomach; having no relish for food.

U-NE-LU-NE-LU, *adj.* Fat; soft; pliable. See NOLUNOLU. *Unelunelu* kau haehae ana.

U-NI-HI, *s.* A species of grasshopper. See UHINI. He mea eheu liilii me he pinao la, a little winged thing like the dragonfly; he mea lele.

U-NI-HI, *adj.* Small; thin; spindle legged; hence,

2. Weak; without strength.

U-NI-HI-PI-LI, *s.* The leg and arm bones of a person. See UHINIPILI. He kanaka mai loa a hiki ole ke hele mawaho; ua *unihipili* leo, aole hiki ke pane mai, having a feeble voice, not able to speak; ua uuku ka leo. *Unihipili* was one name of the class of gods called akuanoho; aumakua was another; they were the departed spirits of deceased persons.

U-NI-HI-PI-LI, *adj.* The qualities of some gods; na akua *unihipili*, ame na akua mano.

U-NI-NA-NI-NA, *adj.* Plump; fat; applied to the cheeks of a person. See ONINANA and ULINALINA.

U-NO-A, *adj.* Raw; uncooked.

U-NOO, *adj.* Not well cooked, as food; applied to vegetable food; when applied to meat, it is *kolekole;* but this last is sometimes applied to food; *unoo* ka ai, *unoo* ka malakeke.

U-NO-U-NO, *v.* To be red; inflamed, as the eyes. See also NOUNOU.

U-NU, *s.* A place of worship; a temple; he heiau, he luakini.

U-NU, *s.* A coward.

2. Small stones or chips of stones for propping up and sustaining large ones.

3. A prop or wedge. See MAKIA.

4. The small stones used to fasten the posts of a house when erected in the ground.

5. Any small stones.

U-NU, *v.* To drink; same as *inu; unu* awa, to drink awa.

U-NU, *v.* To make up into a round heap; to shorten.

U-NU, *adj.* Made round; heaped up, &c.

U-NU, *v.* To prop up; to help hold up; e *unu* iki ae paha ka pono, to help a little perhaps will be well; to shove back or retract, as the skin in amputation.

U-NU-A, *v.* To put or thrust into, as a spear into a man.

2. To breathe into a bamboo.

3. To put in and tread down, as feathers or pulu into a cask in order to put in more; e *unua* iho i ka hulu, alaila hahao hou; ua *unuaia* ka wawae.

U-NU-U-NU, *v.* To prop up. See UNU. Hoo. E *hoounuunuia.*

U-NU-U-NU, *s.* Something gathered into heaps; applied to soldiers who are cowardly and shrink from fighting; alaila, o aku imua me he *unuuna* la ke ano.

U-NU-U-NU, *adj.* Piled up, as several ohias in one hand; ame ka ohia *unuunu* ma ka lima.

U-NU-HI, *v.* To draw out in various ways.

2. To take, as a ring from a finger. *Kin.* 41:42.

3. To take out, as the hand from one's bosom. *Puk.* 4:6.

4. To draw out; unsheathe, as a sword. *Puk.* 15:9.

5. To let fall from a bundle. *Rut.* 2:16.

6. To draw out, as from a ditch.

7. To take away a part; to subtract, as in arithmetic.

8. To translate from one language to another; i *unuhiia* mai ka olelo Hawaii a i ka olelo Beritania. See NUHI.

U-NU-HI, *adj.* Perfect; good; skillful;

wise; he hemolele, he maikai, he akamai, he naauao.

U-NU-NA, *s.* A pillow; something for another to rest on. See ULUNA.

U-NU-NU, *s.* Young ohia timber used in making gods.

2. A stick erected as sign of kapu.

3. Name of a wind or sea breeze at Puuloa.

U-NU-NU, *v.* To pull or scrape off the hair of a dog or hog preparatory to cooking. NOTE.—It was done by laying the animal on a fire.

U-NU-PE-HI-I-O-LE, *s.* Name of a class of persons who adhered to others for the sake of a house.

U-PA, *v.* To act, as the jaws in eating; to open and shut, as the mouth in eating or speaking.

2. To devour with greediness.

3. To chew, as food, i. e., the action of the jaws in chewing.

U-PA, *s.* Any instrument that opens and shuts after the manner of shears, scissors, a compass, bellows, &c.; a carpenter's compass. *Isa.* 44:13. The action of the material heart in receiving and sending out blood. *Anat.* 44. NOTE.— Cutting instruments were formerly made of shark's teeth. See the compounds of the *upa* class.

U-PA, *adj.* Strong, as a man who does a great deal of work or rows fast in a canoe.

U-PAA, *v.* O hele e ke kama e *upaa* me ka pipine.

U-PA-A-HI, *s. Upa* and *ahi,* fire. Tongs. *Puk.* 25:38.

U-PAI, *adj.* Long; tall; slender; loihi, piopio.

U-PAI-PAI, *v.* To bend, as the rafters of a house in a strong wind. See OPAIPAI.

U-PAI-PAI, *s.* The bending or vibration of the rafters of a house in a wind.

U-PA-U-PA, *v.* See UPA. To open or act, as the mouth in speaking or in prayer; e *upaupa* ana i ka waha me he mea pule la.

U-PA-U-PAI, *v.* To hover, as an owl or other bird just before darting on its prey; to remain suspended in the air, as an owl; e *upaupai* i na eheu; e peahiahi.

U-PA-KO-LI-KU-KU-I, *s. Upa* and *koli* and *kukui.* Snuffers. *Puk.* 25:38.

U-PA-MA-KA-NI, *s. Upa* and *makani,* wind. Bellows. *Ier.* 6:29.

U-PA-LU, *v.* To be young; beautiful; comely.

Ua *upalu* wale i ke oho o ke kupukupu
Pepe ka maka o ka ahihi ka makahelei o
Malaila—e.—*Mele.*

U-PA-LU, *adj.* Beautiful; splendid; lovely.

U-PA-PA-LU, *s.* Name of a species of fish.

U-PE, *s.* The mucus or secretion of the nose; petuita; a ua kaumaha nui au i na waimaka ame ka *upe* o na makaainana a pau. Mai makamaka wahine i ka *upe* ke ola. *Haw. Prov.*

U-PE, *s.* A living with quietness and propriety after having been mischievous and wicked; ka *upe*, opepe, hoolulelule; e *upe* ana i na malua nui o Hawaii.

U-PE-HU-PE-HU, *v.* To be swollen; enlarged. See PEHU.

U-PE-HU-PE-HU, *adj.* Large; fleshy, but weak, as a fat man. See PEHU.

U-PE-NA, *s.* A net for taking fish; a snare for catching birds; e malama i ka *upena* nanana, take heed to the spider's web; *upena* papale oho, net work. *Isa.* 3:18. Fig. Anything for entrapping one in evil; ua makau au i ka upena o ka make, I am afraid of the snares of death.

2. The cord of which fish nets were made; ke aho i hooliloia i *upena*.

> Ka *upena* kuu kanaka a Lono,
> Ka *upena* mahae e make ai ka luhia
> Ka lalakea, ka mano ka mano ai a ka lani.

U-PE-NA-MA-KI-NI, *s.* Ka *upenamakini* a ka poe kii ai ia ke ahi a ka po, e kinai au e pio—e.

U-PE-NA-NA-NA-NA, *s.* *Upena* and *nanana*, spider. The web of the nanana, a certain kind of spider. See NANANA.

U-PE-PE, *v.* To be flattened down; crushed.

2. Applied to the mind; to be broken spirited; to be humble; to act awkwardly, like a backwoodsman.

U-PE-PE, *adj.* Weak; feeble, as a person sick; dry; without sweetness, as sugar cane; applied also to kalo; kapae ke kea *upepe* o ka hei—e.

U-PE-PE-HU, *adj.* Swollen, as the flesh of a person. See PEHU.

U-PI, *v.* To sound, as water when squeezed out of a sponge.

U-PI, *s.* The noise made by walking when the shoes are full of water.

U-PI-U-PI, *v.* The frequentative of *upi.*

U-PI-KI, *v.* To shut suddenly together, as the jaws of a steel trap; to entrap.

U-PI-KI, *s.* A trap. *Isa.* 8:14. A snare; anything deceitful; a treachery. *Puk.* 34:12.

U-PI-KI-LI-MA, *s.* A handcuff.

U-PI-KI-PI-KI, *adj.* Shutting up; folding together, as a foreign fan; he mea *upiki-*

piki, he peahi maikai no.

U-PO, *v.* To desire strongly; to lust after; to covet. See IPO and UPU.

U-POI, *v.* To sink, as in water; to sink deep.

2. To move, as a bird moves its wings; to cover with the wing. *Isa.* 10:14.

3. To break over, as the surge forming the surf; to spread or cover over, as any large covering. *Laieik.* 104.

4. To bring one's legs together, as when there is need of concealing; applied to men or women when discovered without a pau or malo on. See POI and POPOI.

U-PO-HO, *v.* To be flattened down or fallen in, as the roof of a house; to be concave, as a surface. *Anat.* 6. See OPAHA.

U-PO-PO, *v.* To strike together, as the hollow palms of the hands, making a hollow sound; e halehale, e poopoo.

U-PU, *v.* To desire strongly; to be strongly attached to a person. *Laieik.* 136. To lust; to covet. See UPO.

2. To be long, as one who goes to another place to make a long visit; aoe *upu* aku nei au, ke hoi mai nei no.

3. To swear or vow; hoohiki; to vow, as when a man vows not to eat the food of his land till he catches a certain fish, or vows that the child then born shall eat the sugar-cane that is then planting; ua *upu* ke kanaka i kana ai a loaa ka ia.

U-PU-U-PU, *s.* The desire to see a person after separation of some time; ka *upu-upu* ole aku. See HOO.

U-PU-U-PU, *v.* See UPU. To be not long; not to pass a long time; to be not long after a certain event. *Laieik.* 106.

U-PU-KA, *s.* A gate; the various forms are, *puka, aipuka, ipuka, upuka* and *kanipuka*. See the first in its place.

U-PU-PA, *s.* The name of an unclean bird in *Kanl.* 14:18; the lapwing; also *Oihk.* 11:19.

U-WA, *v.* To cry out; to exclaim aloud; to shout, as the voice of a multitude. *Oih.* 12:22.

2. To cry out together; to make an uproar; to be in commotion. *Laieik.* 91.

U-WA, *s.* An outcry; the sound of many voices in confusion; hakaka iho la lakou me ka *uwa* nui.

2. A joyful shouting. 2 *Oihl.* 15:14.

U-WAI, *v.* To open or shut, as a door. See UAI.

U-WAI, *s.* A door, &c. See UAI.

U-WAO, *v.* To intercede in behalf of

contending parties. *Heb.* 7:25. To make peace.

2. To intercede in behalf of the guilty. *Ier.* 7:16. To reconcile. See UAO.

U-WAO, *s.* A peace-maker. *Mat.* 5:9. An intercessor.

U-WAO, *adj.* Peace-making; mea *uwao,* an intercessor. *Gal.* 3:20.

U-WAU, *s.* A species of bird; a kind of water fowl.

U-WAU, *v.* To scratch the skin; to pinch with the fingers. See UMIKI.

U-WAU, *s.* A cat, from her noise. See OWAU.

U-WAU-WA, *v.* See UWA. To cry out in a clamorous manner. *Mar.* 15:14.

U-WAU-WA, *s.* A frequent shouting, as a disordered multitude; a noise of revelry. *Puk.* 32:17.

U-WAU-WA, *v.* To be tight; fast; hard; e linalina, e moku ole, e paa.

U-WA-HI, *s.* U and *ahi,* fire. Smoke. *Puk.* 19:18. See UAHI. Ao *uwahi,* a vaporous cloud; a fog, &c.; *uwahi* umuhao, the smoke of a furnace. *Ios.* 8:20.

U-WA-KA, *v.* See OAKA. To open, as a door; to open, as the mouth to speak.

U-WA-LA, *s.* Name of a certain kind of the leho, a sea-shell.

U-WA-LA, *s.* See UALA. U and *ala,* sweet or odoriferous.

1. The sweet potato.
2. The large muscles of the upper arm.

U-WA-LA-AU, *v.* To make a noise, as a multitude. *Puk.* 33:17. See WALAAU.

U-WA-LA-AU, *s.* A tumultuous noise; a great confused noise; a shout. See WALAAU. NOTE.—*Uwalaau* is a noise made by the mouths of men; it applies also to birds sitting together in a frequented place called kula manu; other noises are called *koele, halulu,* &c.

U-WA-LO, *v.* See UALO. To cry out; to call aloud. See UWALAAU and UALO. To call upon one in a way of entreaty. *Laieik.* 71.

U-WA-LU, *v.* To scratch, as a cat. See UWAU. To pinch with the fingers; to pucker up.

U-WA-NA-AO, *v.* See WANAAO. To dawn, as the first light of morning.

U-WA-NA-AO, *s.* The dawning of daylight. See WANAAO.

U-WA-TI, *s.* Eng. See WATI. A watch; a time-piece.

U-WE, *v.* See UE. To weep; to mourn; to cry for help for one's self or others. *Nah.* 11:18. To mourn. *Kin.* 32:2.

2. To cry in behalf of one, i. e., to pray for him. *Puk.* 8:8.

3. To bewail; to lament for. *Oihk.* 10:16.

4. To cry out for pain; pepehi iho la na kanaka, a *uwe* ae la ua mau haole la no ka eha, the men (natives) struck them, and those foreigners *cried out* for pain.

5. To salute, as friends. *Mat.* 5:47. To bid good-by at parting. *Oih.* 18:18.

6. To bray, as an ass. *Iob.* 6:5. To low, as an ox. *Iob.* 6:5.

U-WE, *adj.* That which pertains to mourning or lamentation. *Puk.* 32:18.

U-WE, *s.* A movement. See UE, to hitch. A jerking movement; he *uwe,* he mea e lele ana ma ka lewa.

U-WE, *v.* See UE. To jerk; to shake; to move; to hitch along; mostly found in the compounds nawe, naue, &c.

U-WEU-WE, *v.* Hoo. To move a little without moving much; to pretend to move or leave one's place without doing it.

U-WE-HE, *v.* See WEHE. To open; to untie; to uncover.

U-WE-KA, *s.* Epithet of a very crying child; applied to a crying child; kani hoi kela wahi *uweka*; kani papala maia la hoi ua *uweka* nei.

U-WE-KA-WE-KA, *adj.* Troublesome; crying; dirty, as a child.

U-WE-KE, *v.* To open; to open wide, as a door. Hoo. To cause to be opened. See WEHE.

U-WE-KO, *v.* See WEKO. Bad smelling, as food; to smell like soured food; as rotten potatoes, &c.

U-WE-KO, *s.* The smell of rotten potatoes or other food.

U-WE-KO-WE-KO, *s.* A strong reeking smell of decaying vegetables; ka uauala, ka pilopilo.

U-WE-NE, *v.* To break wind slightly.

U-WE-NE-WE-NE, *adj.* Hoo. Dirty in one's habits; stinking.

U-WI, *v.* See UI, to wring; to squeeze. To wring, as water from clothes. *Lunk.* 6:38

2. To gnash or grind with the teeth. *Hal.* 112:10.

3. To wring, i. e., to squeeze, as in milking an animal. *Isa.* 66:11.

4. E *uwi* i ka poo, to wring off the neck. *Oihk.* 1:15.

U-WI-A, *v.* For *uwiia,* the pass. of *uwi.* To break; to injure; to upset; e nahae, e hulipu.

U-WI-A, *s.* An injury done by rubbing or dashing against.

O ua make paha keia
E *uwia* wale ia nei—a.

U-WI-U-WI-A (ui-ui-a), *v*. To rub or dash one against another; to assemble thickly together.

2. To make or create a shade.

U-WI-U-WI-KI, *s*. Place of small holes; full of small holes, through which anything can go.

U-WI-KI, *v*. To be full of small holes, through which light may pass; e hakahaka liilii.

U-WI-KI-WI-KI, *v*. To shine, as light through small apertures.

U-WI-LA, *s*. See UILA. Lightning. *Ier.* 10:13.

U-WI-LI, *v*. To mix together, as grass and mud in making adobies.

U-WI-NI-HE-PA, *s*. A brick; so called from Captain Winship, who brought the first bricks to the islands.

U-WI-WI, *s*. A species of small fish. See OILI.

U-WO, *v*. See UO. To cry out; to proclaim as the watch in the night, "all's well."

2. To bellow, as cattle.

3. To roar, as a ravenous beast; as a lion. *Lunk.* 14:5.

U-WO, *s*. A crying out; a bellowing of cattle. 1 *Sam.* 15:14. A roaring of beasts.

U-WO, *s*. See UO. Food well pounded; soft and flowing to the touch.

U-WO, *adj*. See UO. Soft; well pounded, as poi.

U-WO, *s*. See UO. To drive or expel something from a hollow substance; e kui, e manai, e uo i ka lei i ke kaula.

U-WO-U-WO, *s*. Name of a species of ohia on the hills.

U-RI-MA, *s*. *Heb*. The urim worn by the Jewish high priest. *Puk.* 28:30.

H.

H, the sixth letter of the Hawaiian alphabet. It represents, as in English, the sound of an aspirate. It is frequently euphonic, particularly between the verb and its passive termination *ia*; as, *maluhia* instead of *maluia*. In this case it is sometimes changed for *l*; as, *kaulia* for *kauia*. See *Gram.* § 48.

HA. A particle expressing strong affirmation, stronger than *no*; as, oia hoi *ha*, so it is *indeed*; truly; certainly; indeed; i mai ia, ua hewa *ha* oe, he said you are *indeed* guilty; e hele hoi *ha* wau, I will *surely* go. *Puk.* 2:7.

HA is often prefixed to the original root of a word, or inserted when it takes the causative *hoo*; as, *inu*, to drink; *hoohainu*, to give drink; *like*, to be like; *hoohalike*, to resemble. It is also often prefixed to the roots of words without any apparent modification of the sense; in other words, the sense is variously modified; as, *hauli*, a dark color. See uli, blue, &c. *Lalo*, down; *halalo*, to turn the eyes and head down, to think, reflect.

HA is also used in reciting meles in the middle of a line as *a, o, e*, &c., are at the end for the voice to rest upon while cantillating, as he ana *ha* nui keia no ke auhee la, where *ha* has no meaning except as the voice protracts the syllable.

HA, *num. adj*. The number four; generally prefixed by *a* or *e*. See AHA and EHA. *Ha* seems to be the original word for the numeral four; as wawae *ha*, four feet. It becomes an ordinal by prefixing the article; as *ka ha*, the fourth. *Mat.* 14:25. I ka *ha* o ka la, the fourth day; i ka *ha* o ka makahiki. *Oihk.* 19:25.

HA, *s*. See the foregoing. On fours; by fours; e hele ana ma na *ha*, going on four (feet.) *Oihk.* 11:20, 21.

HA, *v*. To breathe; to breathe with some exertion; to utter a strong breath; different from *hanu*, to breathe naturally. *Iob.* 15:30. It is connected with *hanu* in *Kin.* 7:15.

2. FIG. To breathe revenge. *Oih.* 9:1.

3. To breathe upon; *ha* ke Akua i ka lewa, God breathed into the open space. *Mele of Kekupuohi*. To breathe out; to expire.

HA, *s*. A breathing; a strong breathing.

2. A strong forced breath, as of anger. *Iob.* 4:9.

3. The expression of anger. 2 *Tes.* 2:8.

4. FIG. Light; transitory, as a breath or breathing. *Hal.* 62:9.

HA, *s*. In *music*, name of the fourth note from the key.

HA, *s*. The lower end of kalo tops or

leaves when cut off from the root; the same also of cane tops; the lower part of that which is cut off.

2. The stem of a kalo leaf or of sugar-cane.

3. The outside leaves of the kalo when outside leaves are killed with cold or drought; ua maloo ka *ha,* ua pala ke kumu; *ha* ko, *ha* kalo, *ha* maia.

HA, *s.* A trough for water to run through; a water pipe; in modern times, a lead or iron pipe through which water flows. See HAWAI.

HA, *v.* To dance; *ha* ana, a dancing; more generally written *haa,* which see.

HA, *s.* A species of wood; ohia *ha* or *haa.*

HAA, *v.* To dance; connected among Hawaiians with singing. 1 *Sam.* 18:6. As an act of worship formerly among the Jews. 2 *Sam.* 6:14.

HAA, *s.* A dance; a dancing, as in idol-atrous worship. *Puk.* 32:19.

HAA, *s.* Name of a shrub or tree.

HAA, *adj.* Short; low; humble; gen-erally doubled, *haahaa,* which see; ohi kukui o kanuukea ka *haa.*

HAA is often used in some works for the causative prefix instead of *hoo;* oftener found in the Tahitian dialect.

HA-A-A, *v.* To acknowledge one as a friend; to treat with hospitality; to ex-hibit affection for; to love.

HA-A-A, *adj.* Friendly; kind; hospitable.

HA-AE, *s.* Saliva or spittle, especially the saliva when worked up in the mouth into foam; hence,

2. The name of a beer made of the sugar-cane when fermented and foaming. The beer was intoxicating.

HA-AE, *v.* To drizzle; to drip; to slab-ber at the mouth.

HAA-I-KAI-KA, *v.* To revile; to grin.

HA-AO, *s.* A multitude following.

HA-AO, *adj.* Driving, as rain with wind; epithet of a rain of Auaulele; ua *haao.*

    Kuu haku i ka ua *haao*—e—
    My lord in the driving rain.
    Ka lele la ka ua mauka o Auaulele;
    The rain flies quickly upland of Auaulele.
    Lele ka ua, lele pu no me ka makani.
    The rain flies,—flies with the wind.

HAA-HAA, *v.* See HAA. To be low; humble.

2. To live quietly; e noho malie.

3. *Hoo.* To make low; to humble; to abase. *Ezek.* 8:21. Applied to those who are proud. *Isa.* 2:17.

4. To subdue; to put down. *Kanl.* 8:2.

HAA-HAA, *adj.* Low; short, as a man.

2. FIG. Humble; meek; sorry; cast down. 2 *Cor.* 7:6. See HAA, *adj.,* above.

HAA-HEO, *v.* See HEO. *Haa* is the caus-ative for *hoo.* Gram. § 212, 3d. See Tahi-tian Dict., art. *haa.* To strut; to exhibit pride in dress or movement.

HAA-HEO, *s.* Pride; haughtiness. See HEO. *Oihk.* 26:19. He *haaheo,* he mea anei ia e pono nona iho? *haughtiness,* is that a thing to benefit himself?

HAA-HEO, *adj.* Proud; lofty; haughty; magnificent; applied mostly to persons.

HAA-KEA, *s.* A species of fruit; in *Isa.* 5:7 it is translated in English by *wild grapes;* a species of weed; in *Iob.* 31:40 translated *cockle.*

2. The fruit of a shrub, of which beads are made, something like grapes; the name of the plant is *akia.*

HAA-KEI, *v.* *Haa,* causative, and *kei.* See KEI. To be proud; high minded; vain-glorious; to be puffed up.

HAA-KEI, *s.* Causing pride.

2. A proud person: a scoffer; a con-temptible person; o ka haaheo, he mea paha ia e make ai no ka poe *haakei,* pride, that is a thing perhaps to kill the *scoffer.*

3. Pride; haughtiness.

HAA-KEI, *adj.* Proud; assuming the dress and character of another.

2. Scoffing; scorning. *Hal.* 1:1.

HAA-KE-KE, *v.* *Haa,* causative; also *hoo* and *keke.* See KEKE and KE. To strive; to cause strife; contention; to be angry; to scold.

HAA-KEI-KEI, *v.* See KEI and HAAKEI. To vaunt in pride; to be insolent.

HAA-KO-AE, *Haa,* causative, and *koae.*

1. Name of a species of bird that is white. See KOAE.

2. A high precipice.

HAA-KOI, *v.* *Haa,* causative, and *koi,* to force; urge.

1. To practice onanism; applied to one alone. See PUAUU.

2. FIG. To labor hard and obtain nothing.

HAA-KOI, *s.* The practice of onanism.

HAA-KOI-KOI, *v.* *Haa,* causative, and *koi.* To practice venery, like dogs or hogs.

HAA-KOO-KOO-WA-LE, *v.* *Haa* for *hoo,* and *kookoo.* See HAKOKO, to wrestle. A wrest-ling; a striving in the exercise of wrestling.

HAA-KO-HI, *v.* *Haa,* causative, and *kohi,* to hinder; hold back.

1. To cause a restraint; to choke.

2. To have or endure strong labor pains,

as a female; to be in strong labor. *Kin.* 35:16.

3. To travail in child-birth. *Gal.* 4:19.

HAA-KO-HI, *s.* Labor pains.

HAA-KO-KO-HI, *v.* The 7th conj. of *kohi*, *haa* for *hoo*; intensive.

1. To have or suffer hard labor pains.

2. To draw one thing out of another with difficulty.

HAA-KO-KO-HI, *s.* Strong labor pains of a female. 1 *Tes.* 5:3.

HAA-KO-KO-HI, *adj.* Suffering from strong labor pains. *Hal.* 48:6.

HAA-KU-A-LI-KI, *s.* Name of an office among the followers of the king.

HAA-KU-E, *s.* Name of the person who swings the fly brush over the chief when he sleeps; o ka mea nana e kahili i ko ke alii wahi e moe ai, he *haakue* ia.

HA-A-LE, *v.* Contraction for *haa*, causative, and *ale*, a wave or swell of water.

1. To cause to be full; to swell up, as water.

2. To be deep; to overflow; to rise high; *haale* ka wai, the water rises.

HAA-LE-LE, *v. Haa* and *lele*, to fly.

1. To cause to fly, that is, to forsake; to give up, as a man his wife; as a child its parents.

2. To leave off; forsake, as a job of work before it is finished.

3. To reject; cast off. The following is often used in the same sense, though really as follows:

HAA-LE-LEA, *v.* Pass. of the foregoing with the *i* dropped. *Gram.* § 211. To be left; to be thrown away; to be cast off, &c.

HAA-LE-LEA, *s.* That which is thrown away or forsaken.

2. Name of a process in making gods.

3. The name of the man sacrificed on cutting down a tree to make a god.

HA-A-LI, *v.* To spread out or spread down, as a cloth; generally written

HA-A-LII, *v.* See HAALI. To spread out; to spread down, as a mat, kapa, paper, &c. See LII. *Isa.* 37:14.

HA-A-LI-A-LI, *s.* The lips of a fish, or the cheeks of a fish.

HA-A-LI-A-LI, *v.* To catch by the neck, as a fish.

2. Used *figuratively*, and applied to men.

HAA-LI-LI. See HOOLILI.

HAA-LI-LI, *v.* See HAALII. To spread; to spread out, &c.

HAA-LI-LO, *adv.* Kani *haalilo*, nu ka hinihini.

HAA-LOU, *v. Haa* and *lou*, to bend in sorrow.

1. To cause to bend in sorrow.

2. To sigh; to weep in affliction or grief.

HAA-LOU-LOU, *v.* See foregoing. To be dejected; grieved; sorrowful.

HAA-LOU-LOU, *adj.* Cast down in mind; dejected; sad.

HAA-LU-LU, *v. Haa*, causative, and *lulu*, to shake.

1. To cause a trembling; to shake; to tremble.

2. To be troubled, or to tremble with fear.

3. To be out of joints, as bones.

4. To be in great disorder; to be in a state of trepidation.

HAA-LU-LU, *s.* A trembling; a trepidation. *Puk.* 15:15.

2. A shaking, as the earth in an earthquake. 2 *Sam.* 2:8.

HAA-MA, *v.* To begin to ripen, as ohias, oranges, &c., but not get soft. See HOOAMA.

HA-A-NO, *v.* To boast; to exalt; to extol. See next word. See HOANO.

HAA-NOI, *s.* Boasting language; olelo haanou.

HAA-NOU, *v. Haa*, causative, and *nou*, a puff of wind. See NOU.

1. To be pleased or gratified with the admiration of another.

2. To be puffed up with flattery.

3. To be inflated with pride; akena.

HAA-NOU, *adj.* Boasting; olelo *haanou*, boasting language.

HAA-NUI, *v. Haa* and *nui*, great.

1. To praise greatly; to extol; to boast. *Sol.* 20:4.

2. To exaggerate; to triumph. 2 *Sam.* 1:20. SYN. with akena and haanoi.

3. To speak great words. 2 *Pet.* 2:18. To magnify one's self. *Dan.* 18:11.

HAA-NUI, *s.* The boasting of something received or favor obtained.

2. A boaster; one who brags.

HAA-PU, *v.* To desire strongly; to yearn for.

HAA-PU, *adj.* Na hana naauao *haapu*, the strongly desired labors of learning.

HAA-PU-KA, *v. Haa* and *puka*, to cheat. To gather up; to scrape together the good and the bad, anything and everything for property. *Sol.* 13:11.

HAA-PU-KU, *v.* To unite several children or other friends in one's affection; pilikia iho la oloko, *haapuku* mai la ka manao ana.

HA-A-WA, *s.* Name of a tree; also written

hoawa.

HAA-WE, *v.* *Ha* for *haa,* and *awe,* to carry. To carry on the back; to put upon the back or shoulders for carrying. SYN. with waha. See AWE and LAWE.

HAA-WE, *s.* A burden. *Isa.* 58:6. A pack carried on the back. *Lunk.* 11:46.

HAA-WE-A-WE, *s.* The growth of potatoes from some being left when the crop was dug; ka haupuupu, ka okupu.

HAA-WI, *v.* *Ha* for *ho* or *hoo.* See HOAWI and AWI, a root which has not yet been found.

   1. To give; to grant to another.

   2. To help; to assist.

   3. To offer or propose for a thing.

   4. To commend to one's care; *haawi aie,* usury. *Kanl.* 23:20. *Haawi lilo ole,* to lend. *Kanl.* 24:10. To give; with *nani,* to ascribe praise. *Isa.* 42:8.

HAA-WI-NA, *s.* *Haawi* and *ana,* a participial termination.

   1. A giving; a giving out; hence,

   2. A portion; something given; a gift; a part assigned to one. *Rom.* 11:29.

   3. In *school,* a lesson appointed to be learned.

   4. A present from one. SYN. with makana.

   5. A gift, that is, ability to do a thing. 1 *Kor.* 12:4.

HAE, *s.* See HAEHAE. Something torn, as a piece of kapa or cloth. The Hawaiian signals were formerly made of torn kapa; hence, in modern times,

   2. A flag; ensign; banner; colors. *Hal.* 20:5. The flag of a ship, &c.; ke kia, ame ka pea, ame ka *hae,* the masts, the sail, and the *flag.* See LEPA.

HAE, *adv.* A word expressive of deep affection for another; as, aloha hoi *hae,* from the deep yearning, breaking or tearing of the heart. See HAEHAE below.

HAE, *s.* A species of wood.

HAE, *v.* To bark, as a dog. *Isa.* 56:10.

HAE, *adj.* Wild; tearing; furious; ferocious; cross; he ilio hihiu *hae,* a ferocious wild dog; applied to a wolf.

   2. The growling or snarling of a cross dog.

HAE, *v.* To tear in pieces; to rend, as a savage beast. See NAHAE. Often used in the double form.

HA-EI, *v.* To look; to peep; to look slily. See KIEI and HALO.

HAE-HAE, *v.* See HAE. To tear or rend, as cloth or a garment. *Kin.* 44:13. With *aahu. Ios.* 7:6.

   2. To tear in pieces, as a savage beast does

a person. *Kin.* 37:33. To tear, as a garment, through grief or indignation. *Nah.* 14:6.

   3. To rend, as the mountains in a hurricane. 1 *Nal.* 19:11,4. See HAE, *adv.,* above.

   4. To be moved with compassion; to sympathize with one. *Kanl.* 28:32. *Haehae na maka, haehae ke aloha.*

HAE-HAE, *s.* Strong affection for one.

   2. A strong desire for a thing, as a starving man for food.

HAE-HAE, *s.* Name of two yards pertaining to a particular house of Lono.

HAE-HAE-IA, *adj.* Torn; injured. *Kin.* 31:39. Rent. *Ios.* 9:4.

HA-E-HU, *v.* To grow thriftily and large, as a tree or plant, potatoes or kalo.

HAE-KAI-KAI, *v.* To grin.

HA-E-LE, *v.* To go or come as *mai* or *aku* is used. SYN. with hele. See HELE. But requires a dual or plural subject. *Nah.* 4:5; *Nah.* 9:17.

HAI, *v.* Often SYN. with hae. See above. To break, as a bargain or covenant. 2 *Nal.* 18:12.

   2. To break open; separate, as the lips that are about to speak.

   3. To speak of; to mention. *Puk.* 23:13.

   4. To tell; declare; confess; relate. *Puk.* 18:8. Ke *hai* ole, not to tell; to keep secret. *Ios.* 2:14.

   5. To break off; to stop doing a thing; as, aole *hai* ke hoihoi aku, he does not *cease* (begging) though sent away. NOTE.—The *ha* of this word is sometimes doubled, then it has the form of *hahai,* to follow, but its signification is to break away or tear away; as, *haihaiia* ka lepa a ua poe kahuna la, the ensign of those priests *was broken* away.

HAI, *v.* To put or place in, as in a box; *hai* aku i ke alii o lakou iloko, then they *put* their chief inside.

HAI, *s.* A broken place; hence,

   2. A joint of a limb; ka hai a mawe, the elbow joint.

HAI, *pron.* or *adj.* Gram. § 15, 14:3. Another; another person; no *hai,* for another; ia *hai,* to another. *Neh.* 5:5. Hookahi no makamaka, o oe no, aole o *hai,* one only friend, thou art he, there is no *other.*

HA-I, *v.* To be vain; proud.

HAI, *s.* Name of the god of the poe kuku kapa.

   2. A sacrifice at the altar.

HAI, *s.* Name of a particular form of gathering dead bodies slain in war.

HAI-A, *s.* An assemblage; a number, especially of persons; it is used as a prefix to other words.

Hai-na, *s.* *Hai,* to speak, and *ana.* A speaking; a declaration.

Hai-ai, *v.* To do over again.

2. To tie up a bundle of food anew; to tie up, as fagots.

3. To cook over again.

Hai-ao, *s.* *Hai,* sacrifice, and *ao,* day. A sacrifice offered in the daytime in distinction from *haipo,* a night sacrifice.

Hai-a-o, *s.* A modern word; *hai,* to declare, and *ao,* to teach. A sermon; a public declaration of religious truth.

Hai-amu, *v.*

Hai-a-no, *s.* Grammatical term; *hai,* to declare, and *ano,* the meaning or quality. An adjective.

Hai-a-wa-hi-ne, *s.* See **Haia,** a company, and **Wahine,** woman. The united assemblage of a number of wives of one man exclusive of the favorite one among several.

2. A wife of secondary quality; not a favorite wife. *2 Sam.* 13:3. A concubine. *Lunk.* 19:1. A kept mistress.

Hai-a-wa-hi-ne, *v.* To multiply wives; as, nani kona *haiawahine* ana, wonderful his multiplying wives.

Hai-e-a, *s.* A species of fish.

Hai-i-noa, *s.* *Hai,* to declare, and *inoa,* name. In *grammar,* the word declaring the name; a noun or substantive.

Hai-o-u-li, *v.* *Hai,* to declare, and *ouli,* the sky. To prognosticate; to declare future events from observing the heavens.

Hai-o-u-li, *s.* A prognostication from observing the sky. *Isa.* 47:13. Kindred with kilolani and kilokilo hoku.

Hai-o-la, *s.* *Hai,* to declare, and *ola,* life; salvation.

1. One who preaches or declares there is salvation for men.

2. The declaration of such a fact.

Hai-o-le, *adj.* *Hai,* to break, and *ole,* not. Bold; hard; impudent; unpacified; stubborn.

Hai-o-le-lo, *s.* *Hai,* to declare, and *olelo,* word.

1. A preaching; a declaration of the word (of God). *1 Cor.* 1:21.

2. To make a speech or an address. *Laieik.* 115.

Hai-u-la, *s.* The red or yellow appearance of the dust raised by a whirlwind; the same to some extent in a waterspout.

Hai-hai, *v.* To follow; to pursue; to chase. See **Hahai.**

2. To run a race.

Hai-hai, *v.* See **Hai,** to break. To break; to break in pieces; to break, as a yoke. *Kin.* 27:40. To break off, as the branch of a tree. *Rom.* 11:17. To crush, as a flower. *Laieik.* 142.

2. To break, as a law or command. *Nah.* 15:31.

3. *Hoo.* To tease; to vex; to make one cross; to provoke.

4. To go through the process of separating the flesh from the bones of a dead person; to dissect; ua *haihai* o Kamehameha, alaila hoi mai o Liholiho mai Kawaihae mai.

Hai-hai, *adj.* See **Haihai,** to break. Brittle; easily broken.

Hai-hai, *s.* A state of brittleness; liability to break. *Anat.* 2.

Hai-hai, *s.* See **Hai,** to break. A breach, or breaking of a law.

Hai-hai, *adj.* Proud; vaunting; lascivious.

Hai-hai, *v.* To show one's self haughty, strutting, lascivious.

2. To feign one's self out of his senses in order to escape death from one upon whom he has practiced sorcery.

Hai-hai, *v.* See **Hai,** to speak. To consult or talk together, as two or more persons on business.

Hai-hai-a, *adj.* See **Aia.** *Ai* repeated to give intensity and *h* inserted. Wicked; unreasonable; vile. *2 Tes.* 3:2. Profane. *Heb.* 12:16. Ungodly. *1 Tim.* 1:9.

Hai-hai-a, *s.* Ungodliness. *2 Tim.* 2:16.

Hai-hai-a, *v.* To court the favor of the gods, or rather perhaps to use various arts, as by getting herbs and medicines and offerings to prevent the gods from hearing another's prayers.

Hai-ha-na, *v.* *Hai,* to declare, and *hana,* to do, i. e., to declare something done. In *grammar,* a verb; a modern word.

Hai-kai-ka, *v.* To mock by making wry faces; to make another word by the transposition of letters.

Hai-kai-ka, *adj.* Grinning; expressing anger; he *haikaika* kona maka ame kona waha.

Hai-ka-la, *s.* Name of a fatal disease of which *waiiki* was the medicine.

Hai-ka-la-mu-ku, *s.* Name of a disease equally fatal with the above, in which the same medicine was used.

Hai-ki, *adj.* *Ha* and *iki,* small. See **Iki.**

1. Narrow, as a passage; pinched; scanty.

2. Suffering for want of food.

HA-I-KI, *v.* To be pinched for want; to be pinched with hunger. *Mar.* 2:25. To be desolate; bereaved. *Laieik.* 142.

HA-I-KI-A-KA, *v.* To grin; to make wry faces. See HAIKAIKA.

HAI-LA-WE, *v.* To exchange, as in bartter; to give one piece of property for another.

HAI-LE-A, *adj.* See LOEA. Ingenuity; skill in doing a thing.

HAI-LE-PO, *v. Hai,* to break forth, and *lepo,* dirt.
    1. To evacuate the bowels.
    2. To be sick with the disease called *hailepo.*

HAI-LE-PO, *s.* A name of a disease or sickness in former times.
    2. Name of a large living creature of the sea. See HEHIMANU and HAHALUA. It was forbidden to women to eat under penalty of death.

HAI-LE-PO, *v.* Na maka o kekahi poe e *hailepo* ana, nolaila no ka *hailepo* ame ka olelo ihaiha.

HA-I-LI, *s. Ha* and *ili,* skin; surface.
    1. A spirit; a ghost.
    2. The impression of something fondly remembered; halialia wale mai no ke aloha, hoanoano wale mai no me he *haili* la e kau iho ana maluna, love brought the fond remembrance, it brought solemnity as if a *spirit* rested on him; lele ke aka o ka manao, leleiaka i ka lani; lele ae la ka *haili* o ka ia nui iluna.

HA-I-LI, *v.* To cry out suddenly; to give an alarm.
    2. To gasp; to pant for breath. See AILI.

HA-I-LI, *s.* A temple.

HAI-LI-A, *v.* To be frightened; to start suddenly from fear.

HA-I-LI-A-KA, *s.* See HAILI and AKA, shadow. A ghost; a spirit. See HAILI.

HA-I-LI-I-LI, *v.* Root probably *hai,* to speak, and *ili* (see ILI, hoo 7), to use profane language.
    1. To revile the gods; to swear profanely; to curse.
    2. To speak disrespectfully of one. *Puk.* 21:17.
    3. To reproach; to blackguard; to revile. *Ier.* 15:10.

HA-I-LI-I-LI, *s.* Cursing; profane language; he hoino.

HAI-LI-LI, *v.* To have the feelings of sorrow and affection on the death of one very dear; ua make *hailili* e.

HAI-LI-MA, *s. Hai* and *lima,* the break

of the arm, i. e., the elbow. In *measure,* the distance of the elbow to the end of the fingers; half a yard or a cubit. *Ezek.* 6:3.

HAI-LO-AA, *s. Hai* and *loaa,* to obtain.
    1. A key or answer to a question; a declaration of what one has found out.
    2. The name of a little book called a key to an algebra.
    3. A key or clue to intricate propositions.

HAI-LO-NA, *v.* To cast or draw lots. *Oih.* 1:28. To distribute by lot.
    2. To certify by actions that something will be done.
    3. To make a signal for some purpose.
    4. In modern times, to play at dice. See HOAILONA.

HAI-LO-NA, *s.* A mark, sign, character representing a thing, as a letter representing a sound; an arithmetical sign, &c.
    2. A lot in casting lots. *Neh.* 6:55, 56. Whatever is used in casting lots. *Oih.* 1:28.

HAI-LO-NO, *v. Hai* and *lono,* the news. To tell the news; to spread a report; aohe a *hailono* iki. 2 *Oihl.* 20:24. i. e., none at all (escaped) to tell the news.

HAI-LU-KU, *v. Hai* and *luku,* to slaughter. To stone. *Puk.* 17:4. To stone to death. *Oih.* 7:59. To pelt with stones; okena ae la ke alii e *hailuku* i ua poe la, the king sent word to stone to death those persons; e hoonou, e hooulua, e ahuku.

HAI-LU-KU, *s.* A stoning to death; killing one by stoning him.

HAI-MA-LU-LU, *adj.* Soft; effeminate; deliberate at work; weak in body or person; *haimalulu* i ka ua a ka naulu, *weakened* by the rain of the mist.

HAI-MA-NA-WA, *s.* Name of a species of white kapa rather thin.
    2. Name of the school book used at Lahainaluna in teaching chronology.

HAI-NA, *v.* A verb formed from the contracted *hai ana.* See HAI. To tell; to relate; to declare; to speak.
    2. To break, as a command; as a law. See HAI 1.
    3. To break, as a stick; hence,
    4. To reject; to destroy; to take no care of, as one sick. NOTE.—The ideas of speaking, declaring, &c., seem to be nearly connected in Hawaiian with breaking.

HAI-NA, *s.* A speaking; a declaration; a conversation.
    2. A breaking, as of a stick or other thing; a breaking of a law.

HAI-NA, *v.* To abuse; to be stingy of

food; to withhold food from those who deserve it.

Hai-na, *adj.* Cruel; unmerciful; hard hearted.

Hai-no-le, *v.* See Kinaunau, *Kam.*

Hai-na-ka, *s.* Eng. A handkerchief; a napkin. *Puk.* 28:4. Also spelled *hainika.*

Hai-na-ki, *s.* The name of a prayer on gathering in the property tax for the chief.

Ha-i-nu, *v.* See Inu. *Hoo.* To give drink to one; to cause to drink. *Kin.* 29:3. Note.—The syllable *ha* is often inserted between the causative *hoo* and the verb. See Ha.

Hai-po, *s. Hai,* a sacrifice, and *po,* night. Name of a sacrifice offered in the night in distinction from *haiao.*

Ha-i-pu, *s. Ha,* the but-end of a leaf, and *ipu,* a gourd. The stem of a gourd leaf used in medicine.

Hai-pu-le, *v. Hai,* to speak, and *pule,* to pray.
  1. To speak or say a prayer to the gods.
  2. To worship visibly.
  3. To exhibit the character of a worshipper; to practice religious rites. 1 *Nal.* 8:28. Ina e makemake oe e *haipule,* if you wish to practice religious duties.
  4. To consecrate a temple; to prescribe the forms of religion; nana (na ke alii) e *haipule* na heiau poo kanaka, oia hoi na luakini.

Hai-pu-le, *s.* A devotee; one addicted to worship; a pious person; a saint. *Epes.* 1:1.
  2. Piety; profession of religion; outward worship. *Iak.* 1:26.

Hai-pu-le, *adj.* Pious; devout; religious; religiously disposed; a ike mai o Vanekouva he alii *haipule* o Kamehameha, &c., when Vancouver saw that Kamehameha was religiously disposed, &c.

Hai-wa-le, *adj. Hai,* of another. Another's only.

Ha-o, *v.* To rob; to despoil. *Mat.* 12:29. To strip one of property; to plunder. *Lunk.* 2:14.
  2. To kill and plunder. 1 *Sam.* 27:10.
  3. To strip one of his garment. *Kin.* 37:23. To take by little and little; to collect together.

Hao ka Koolau, pau na mea aloha,
Koolau was robbed of all endeared things.
Ahu iho ka pua wahawaha i Wailua,
The despised blossoms were collected together at Wailua.

Note.—It was formerly the practice of the chiefs to punish offenders for all offenses less than death, by stripping them entirely of their property; this practice continued until the people had a written code of laws.

Ha-o, *v.* To put less things into a greater; to put into; to take up and put into; to take up by handfuls.
  2. To shovel dirt. See Haohao below.

Ha-o, *v.* To wonder at; to be astonished; mostly *haohao.*

Ha-o, *s.* A robber; a plunderer. *Lunk.* 2:14.

Ha-o, *s.* Name of any hard substance, as iron, the horn or hoof of a beast.
  2. The name of a species of wood; name of a tree.

Ha-o, *adj.* Strained tightly; hence, hard, &c.; in the phrases *hao* na kepa, the spurs are *iron,* applied to a horse running swiftly; also, *hao* na polena, the bowlines are *iron,* applied to a swift sailing ship; *hao* ka lima, applied to one working hard.

Ha-o, *adj.* Thin; poor in flesh; wiwi, emi iho ke kino a olala.

Ha-o-a, *adj.* Hot; burning hot, as the sun; wela loa; e na hoa o ka la nui *haoa* o ua kula nei, e imi mua kakou i ka pono o ka naau, O companions of the great burning sun of the high school, &c.
  2. Suffering pain; severe affliction from the pain of burning.
  3. The fear of being burnt.

Ha-o-a, *s.* The fierce burning heat of summer. *Laieik.* 119.
  2. The pungent bitter matter vomited from the stomach; sourness; sourness of the stomach; heart-burn. *Anat.* 53.

Ha-o-a, *v.* Pass. of *hao* instead of *haoia.* To be taken, as by an enemy; to be taken by violence; to be given up, as to an enemy.
  2. To take, as an ensign in war. 1 *Sam.* 4:11.

Ha-oa-pu-hi, *s.* Among *fishermen,* name of the stick used instead of a hook in catching eels.

Ha-oe, *v.* To be uneven, as points of a substance; to rise one above another; *haoe* ka ale o Hopoe i ka ino, the waves of Hopoe stand up, are erect in the storm. See Ha without the *hoo.*

Ha-oe-oe, *v.* See before. To make a rushing noise, as wind upon the trees; *haoeoe* ka ohia, he ua nui ino Kaeleawaawa, loli i ka ua e, the ohia trees give a sound, Kaeleawaawa is in a great storm, it bends to the great rain.

Ha-oe-oe, *adj.* Uneven, as points which stick up, or as waves of the sea; *haoeoe* na ale o ke kai.

2. Applied also to men running where some are before and some behind; *haoeoe na kanaka e holo mai la.*

HAO-HAO, *v.* To doubt; to discredit; to distrust a statement.

2. To be troubled in accounting for an event; to be restless; sleepless at night; *haohao hoi keia po o'u, aole wau i moe iki. Laieik.* 198.

3. To marvel; to wonder. *Isa.* 63:5. To be astonished. *Isa.* 52:14.

4. To be in doubt respecting one's character. *Gal.* 4:20. *Haohao hewa,* to think or design evil.

5. To seek for; to hunt after; to search.

HAO-HAO, *v.* To distribute; to give equally to many; *e haawi like me ka puunawe.*

HAO-HAO, *v.* To dip up with the hands; to measure by handfuls.

HAO-HAO, *s.* Disappointment; doubt; uncertainty. *Laieik.* 105.

HAO-HAO, *adj.* Soft; immature, as fruit; as a soft cocoanut.

HAO-HAO-A, *s.* Places so covered with broken lava that one cannot walk on them; *kapu ma ka haoa ka haohaoa lani.*

HAO-HAO-A-LA-NI, *s.* The reverence and affection formerly felt by the people for their chiefs; *he kuhau lalapa o ke kapu la.*

HAO-HAO-NA, *v.* To spring up in the mind, as love for a friend.

2. To have the recollection of a person by one who is separated from him.

HAO-KA-NU, *v. Hao* and *kanu,* to bury. To plant; to plant or bury a thing with earth brought from another place.

HAO-KI-LOU, *s. Hao,* iron, and *kilou,* hook. An iron hook.

HA-O-LE, *adj.* White; he keokeo; *ina i keokeo ka hulu o ka puaa a puni, he haole ia puaa; he puaa haole.*

HA-O-LE, *s.* See the above derivation. A person with a white skin; hence, a foreigner; but Hawaiians say *haole eleele* for a negro.

2. A person from a foreign country; an alien. NOTE.—The foreigners who arrived first at the islands were white persons.

HAO-MA-NA-MA-NA, *s. Hao,* iron, and *manamana,* divided. A gridiron; so called by natives from the divided irons.

HAO-NA, *s.* Name of some calabashes for food when first cooked.

HAO-WA-HA, *s. Hao,* iron, and *waha,* mouth. The iron of the mouth, that is, a bridle bit. *Hal.* 32:9.

HAO-WA-LE, *s. Hao,* to rob, and *wale,* without cause. Robbery; a taking another's without right.

HAU, *s.* Name of the land breeze that blows at night; hence, any cool breeze; *he hau kekahi makani mauka mai, ua manao ia mai loko mai o ke kuahiwi kela makani.* NOTE.—This word has several forms. It usually takes *ke* for its article instead of *ka*; but the *ke* is sometimes united with it, and then it becomes *kehau.* This however requires a new article, which would be *ke,* ke *kehau*; but this article also sometimes adheres to the noun, and thus requires a new article still; hence the different forms of the word: *hau, kehau,* and *kekehau,* all of which take corresponding articles.

HAU, *s.* The general name of snow, ice, frost, cold dew, &c.; *i hoomanawanui ai hoi kaua i ka hau huihui o ke kakahiaka,* when we two also persevered in the cold *frost* of the morning; *hau paa,* hoar frost. *Puk.* 16:14. In the same verse *hau* is rendered dew; snow. *Nah.* 12:10.

2. The rough bristles of a hog when angry; *huhu ka puaa, ku ka hau;* hence,

3. Anger; applied figuratively to men.

4. Name of a species of soft porous stone.

HAU, *s.* Name of a tree or large bush; the bark was sometimes beaten into a fine species of kapa called *kapa hau. Laieik.* 112.

2. A kind of dance used for lascivious purposes, accompanied by singing.

HAU, *v.* To swallow; to gulp down, as the smoke of tobacco.

2. To inhale; to snuff up, as the wind. *Ier.* 2:24.

3. To snort, as a horse. *Ier.* 8:16.

HAU-A, *v.* To whip; to apply stripes to one; to chastise. *Sol.* 19:18. See HAHAU.

HAU-A, *s.* A whipping; a stripe; a chastisement. *Sol.* 19:29.

HAU-A-PU, *s.* A yearning; a strong feeling for one. See HAULPU.

HAU-E-KA, *v. Hau* and *eka,* filthy. To be defiled; to be filthy; unclean.

HAU-E-LI, *s. Hau,* frost, snow, ice, and *eli,* to dig. Name of the native Glauber salts which are dug up out of caverns in the rocks on the Island of Hawaii.

HAU-I, *s.* The title or epithet of a chief, as noble, a descendant of kings, &c.; *o Haui ka lani, ke alii kiekie, he kumu alii.*

HAU-OI-AO, *s.* A kind of fish net.

HAU-O-KI, *s.* Name of a medicine given to women in labor, similar to slippery elm.

HAU-O-KI, *s.* A kind of palsy or perhaps stiffness of the limbs, as when one is chilled with cold; having been long in the water.

HAU-O-LE, *adj.* *Hau,* frost, dew, &c., and *ole,* not. Without dew, as a barren place.

HAU-O-LI, *v.* *Hau* and *oli,* to sing. See OLI. To sing; to rejoice. 2 *Sam.* 1:20. To express joy by singing; to be joyous. *Hoo.* To cause joy; to make glad. *Hal.* 86:4.

HAU-O-LI, *s.* Joy; rejoicing; gladness.

HAU-O-LI, *adj.* Joyous; glad.

HAU-O-LI-O-LI, *v.* Intensive form. To take delight in; to rejoice in. *Hal.* 119:77.

HAU-O-MA-LO-LO, *s.* Name of a species of fish net.

HAU-O-PO, *v.* To lay in good order, as stones in a wall; to stand evenly; he wahi i nini, i kumanoia a maikai.

HAU-O-PO, *s.* What is put together in good order; a good, well finished work.

HAU-U-PU, *s.* Deep affection for one; a yearning over a beloved object. See HAU-APU and HAUPU.

HAU-HAU, *v.* To lay stones in a wall; to build with stones.

HAU-HAU, *v.* To strike; to smite; to beat. See HAHAU.

HAU-HAU, *adj.* See HAU, cold, &c. Cool, as where the heat is separated from a thing.

HAU-HAU-NA, *adj.* Strong smelling; offensive to the smell. See HAUNA.

HAU-HI-LI, *v.* To bind up; to tie up, as a bundle; e *hauhili* a paa, bind it up tightly. See HILI.

HAU-HI-LI, *s.* Carelessness in doing a thing; no ka mikioi o ka hana, aole no ka *hauhili,* for the niceness of the work, not for the slovenliness.

HAU-HI-LI, *adj.* Diverging from the straight path; blundering; false; not to be depended on for truth.

2. Crooked or blind, as a path in the bushes. See HILI.

HAU-KA, *s.* In *gambling,* when one wins he says *hauka;* a foreign word perhaps.

HAU-KAE, *v.* See HOOKAE. To deface; to blot out; to squander; to behave shamefully.

2. To do a thing carelessly; ina e hauhili a *haukae* ka oukou hana, if you do your work in a slovenly and careless manner.

3. To be filthy; dirty in appearance.

HAU-KAE, *s.* Filthiness; carelessness; also,

2. A mean fellow; a babbler; a trifling talker. *Oih.* 17:18.

HAU-KAE, *adj.* Slovenly done; foul; unclean; impure; wicked.

HAU-KAI, *v.* See HAUKAE, *v.,* above. To erase, blot out and destroy.

HAU-KAI, *adj.* See HAUKAE, *adj.* Careless; unprepared.

HAU-KAU, *s.* The state of the sea in a chopped sea something like the kai kupikio, very difficult to urge a canoe through it.

HA-U-KA-U-KA, *s.* See UKAUKA 2, to eat. A ringworm.

HAU-KA-MU-MU, *s.* *Hau* and *kamumu,* a rustling sound.

1. The confused noise of a multitude; ua uhiia kona leo e ka *haukamumu* leo o ka aha, his voice was drowned by the *confused noises* of the multitude. *Laieik.* 22.

2. The low or indistinct conversation of two persons. *Laieik.* 80.

HAU-KE, *v.* To hunt, as for prey; to fall upon; to catch; e *hauke* uku, to hunt lice in one's head.

HAU-KE, *s.* The act of hunting lice; ka haule ana i ka uku poo.

HAU-KE, *s.* The sea-egg. See HAUKEUKE.

HAU-KEA, *s.* *Hau,* snow, and *kea,* white. The white snow; the whiteness of snow in cold countries; ka *haukea* o Maunakea.

HA-U-KE-U-KE, *v.* To shiver much and intensely with the cold.

HA-U-KE-U-KE, *s.* The name of a small sea animal.

HA-U-KE-U-KE, *s.* Name of a shell fish that has many prongs two or three inches long.

haukeuke

HA-U-KE-U-KE, *s.* Name of a small insect that adheres to the skin of persons, similar to the ane; *haukeuke,* he ane, he mea e pili ana ma ka ili o ke kanaka, ua like me ke kane.

HAU-KE-KE, *v.* To shiver with the cold; to be contracted with cold, as the muscles; *haukeke* mai ana ka lehelehe, minomino na lima, eleele ka lihilihi, the lips *quivered* with the cold, the hands were wrinkled, dark were the eyebrows; to be in pain with the cold. *Iob.* 33:19.

HAU-KE-KE, *s.* A shivering with the cold.

HAU-KE-KE, *adj.* Cold; shivering with cold.

HA-U-LA-U-LA, *v.* See ULA, red. To be

a little red; a *haulaula* ka waha i ka laau.

HAU-LA-LA-PA, *s.* The high ascending blaze of a large fire. See LAPALAPAAHI. E ku *haulalapa*, e lapalapa.

HAU-LA-NI, *v.* To root, as a hog; to plunge, as a canoe.

2. To be restless in one's grasp; to squirm; e oni; to try to free one's self when held fast.

HAU-LA-NI, *adj.* Uneasy; seeking freedom from restraint; restive; he mauli *haulani*.

HA-U-LE, *v.* To fall; to fall from a perpendicular state; to stumble; to fall down.

2. To come upon one, as a new set of feelings; to come to or arrive at a place; to encamp; a *haule* lakou i Kailua.

3. To loosen; to let go; to unfold.

4. To become void; to lack; to fail; to be wanting; to fall dead.

5. To overturn; to destroy; to seek after; to fall upon for destruction.

6. To fail in coming to pass or to be fulfilled, as a promise. *Ios.* 21:45. To fall, as one to fail in his moral or religious character. *Heb.* 6:6.

7. *Hoo.* To cause to fall; with *ua*, as rain, i. e., to cause to rain. 1 *Nal.* 18:1.

8. To throw one's self down on to a thing. 1 *Sam.* 31:4. To cause to fall, i. e., destroy, as an army. *Ezek.* 32:12. To be rendered void, as a law.

HA-U-LE, *adj.* A thing lost; dropped. *Oihk.* 6:3. Kekahi mea *haule*.

HAU-LE-NA, *s.* Contracted from *haule ana*. A falling, that is, whatever falls; a gleaning. *Oihk.* 19:9.

HA-U-LI, *s.* See ULI. Anything of a dark color; the dark shadow of an object; dark clouds; the deep blue sky.

2. FIG. A stain upon a person's character; ka *hauli* o ka mea hewa ole, e nalowale ia, the stain upon a person's character without fault will soon vanish.

HA-U-LI, *adj.* Dark; swarthy; tawny; shadowing; darkish; shady.

2. Cool, having lost warmth.

HAU-LII-LII, *v.* *Hau*, iron, and *liilii*, little. A factitious word got up by Hawaiian cooks, and means, to broil on the gridiron; they call the gridiron *hauliilii*, i. e., *little irons*; with some, SYN. with hoomakaukau, to get ready.

HA-U-LI-U-LI, *v.* The intensive of *hauli*. To be dark, &c.

2. To be in a slight state of commotion; applied to the rippling of the sea when the wind just begins to blow.

HA-U-LI-U-LI, *s.* Name of a species of fish.

HAU-MA-KA-I-O-LE, *s.* Epithet of an advanced state of old age, when the eyes are dim, the steps totter, and the breath short.

HAU-MA-NA, *v.* To be or act, as a scholar.

2. *Hoo.* To teach, as one teaches scholars; to make scholars or learners of persons.

3. To teach them some art, or convey to them some knowledge they had not before.

4. To instruct, as a scholar or apprentice in any art or handicraft.

HAU-MA-NA, *s.* A scholar; an apprentice; a disciple. *Mat.* 10:1.

HAU-MA-NU-MA-NU, *adj.* Full of holes, cracks or crevices. See MANU.

HAU-ME-A, *s.* Name of the mother of Kekauakahi, the war god.

HAU-MI-A, *v.* To defile; to pollute; to be either morally, physically or ceremonially unclean. *Hoo.* To defile naturally, morally. *Kin.* 34:2. Or ceremonially, to stain; defile. *Iol.* 3:5.

HAU-MI-A, *s.* Contagion; ceremonial defilement from contact or contiguity to dead bodies.

2. *Morally*, from various wicked practices.

3. Things forbidden under penalty of death, stronger than *kapu*; uncleanness, &c. *Oihk.* 15:2, 3. Defilement. *Gal.* 5:19.

HAU-MI-A, *adj.* Unclean; impure.

2. That which defileth. *Oihk.* 5:2.

HAU-NA, *s.* The strong offensive smell of meat.

HAU-NA, *adj.* Strong smelling; offensive to the smell.

HAU-NA, *s.* The striking of the hand or other substance in playing the kilu; a i ka umi o ka *hauna* kilu, a laua. *Laieik.* 114.

HAU-NA-E-LE, *v.* To flee in war; to suffer the consequences of such flight; that is, to forsake houses, homes, and the general loss of all comforts.

2. To be in confusion, as in a mob or general disobedience to laws. *Puk.* 32:25.

3. To be in doubt or perplexity of mind.

4. *Hoo.* To stir up the people; to make popular disturbance in a government. *Puk.* 32:25. NOTE.—The English translation *nele* and *hoonele* in this verse is preferable.

HAU-NA-E-LE, *s.* The excitement and disturbance of war.

2. Any popular commotion or disturbance. 1 *Sam.* 4:14.

Hau-na-ma, *s.* A strong offensive smell, but less so than hauna; he wahi pilau uuku. See Hauna.

Ha-u-pa, *v.* To eat much; to swell up, as the stomach from eating too much.

2. To be greedy in eating.

3. To act, as the jaws in eating fast. See Upa.

Hau-pee-pee, *v.* To play hide and seek; e peepee akua; to play hide and seek, as children.

Hau-pee-pee, *s.* The play of children, hide and seek.

Hau-pia, *v.* To mix together (pia) arrowroot and cocoanut and bake it; to cook arrow-root and cocoanut together.

Hau-pia, *s.* The substances of arrowroot and cocoanut mixed together and baked for food.

Hau-po, *s.* The lower end of the breast bone; the place where the ribs unite.

2. The thorax. See Houpo.

Ha-u-pu, *v.* To excite; to stir up, as the affections or passions.

2. To suffer with anxiety; to be much excited or moved; ua *haupu* honua ae la ka makaula, the prophet was much *excited.* *Laieik.* 157.

3. To rise up suddenly in the mind, as a thought.

4. To stir up one to recollection; alaila, e *haupu* ia lakou me ka homanao.

Ha-u-pu, *s.* The sudden excitement of the passions. Note.—This word was used in a moral philosophy for conscience, or the internal monitor; o ka mea i nanea palaka ka *haupu*, alaila aole e ole kona hewa. Afterwards *lunamanao* was used.

Hau-puu, *s.* Any hard bunch or protuberance on the joints or limbs.

Ha-u-pu-u-pu.

Hau-puu-puu, *s.* A hard protuberance on the joints, as on the fingers or wrists. See Haupuu.

Hau-puu-puu, *adj.* Swollen, as the ground by frost; uneven, as with bunches of hail, or with heaps of salt in the salt-pits.

Hau-wa-la-au, *v.* To gabble where all talk and none hear.

2. To get into confusion, as an assembly disagreeing in opinion; alaila *hauwalaau* loa ae la ka lehulehu, then the multitude fell into great confusion. See Walaau.

Hau-wa-la-wa-la-au, *s.* See the foregoing. Noise, as of many talking or bawling at once without cause or meaning.

2. Mere gabbling without cause; make ka alii o Nunu ma Koolau, kahaha kahi poe, i mai kanaka, he *hauwalawalaau* wale no, when the chief Nunu died at Koolau, some were astonished, but the people said there was nothing but a *great talk.* See Walaau.

Hau-wa-na-oa, *v.* To extend; to stretch out. See Wanaoa.

Hau-wa-wa, *v.* To talk in vain, confusedly or in disorder. See Wawa.

Hau-wa-wa, *s.* Confusion; disorder, as a multitude talking at once.

Ha-ha, *v.* See Ha. To breathe hard; to pant for breath, as in great haste.

2. To feel of; to move the hand over a thing. *Kin.* 27:12, 21.

3. To feel, as a blind person; to grope; to feel, as if searching for something. *Isa.* 59:10.

4. *Hoo.* To manipulate; to manufacture; *hoohaha* paakai, to manufacture or make salt.

5. To strut; to act the fop; to walk about like a cock turkey.

Ha-ha, *s.* *Hoo.* A swelling or puffing up.

Ha-ha, *s.* The inside of kalo tops used for food; the whole top is called *huli.* See Ha.

Ha-ha, *s.* A sort of wooden net used for catching the oopu, a freshwater fish, from brooks.

2. The board on which fishermen place their nets.

3. Name of a tree.

Ha-hae, *v.* See Hae. To rend; to tear, as a garment.

2. To break; to separate into parts; to split, as lauhala, lengthways.

Ha-hai, *v.* To follow; to pursue. *Puk.* 14:4. To chase; to follow literally.

2. To follow one's example; ua *hahai* nui na kanaka a pau mamuli o na 'lii e noho ai, all men generally *followed* after the chiefs for the time being.

3. To break; to break to pieces; to break, as a law. See Hae and Hahae.

Ha-hai, *v.* See Hai, to speak. To tell; to talk about; e *hahai* ana no lakou i na moeuhane, they were *telling* their dreams. *Laieik.* 143.

Ha-hai, *s.* A breaking; a disjoining; a separating. See Hae.

Ha-hai, *s.* Name of a disease on the upper part of the thigh or groin, occasioned by impure connections and habits.

Ha-hao, *v.* See Hao. To put or thrust in. *Oihk.* 10:1. To cram down.

2. To put into, as a person into prison. *Oih.* 16:24.

3. To throw or cast wood into a fire.

4. To put into a particular place; to put, as money into a purse; to put, as into a basket. *Mat.* 13:48.

5. To put into one's head; to suggest to the mind; to put words into one's mouth. 2 *Sam.* 14:19.

HA-HAU, *v.* See **HAUA.** To whip; to strike with a cane, stick, rod, or sword.

2. To scourge; to chasten. *Puk.* 5:14. *Hahauia* kona kua i ke kaula e ka haole, his back was *whipped* with a rope by a foreigner.

3. To inflict plagues. *Puk.* 32:35. To smite with blindness. 2 *Nal.* 6:18.

4. *Hahau* ai, to thrash, as grain.

5. To hew stones. 2 *Nal.* 22:6.

HA-HAU, *s.* That which is put or laid upon, as a burden, or punishment; stripes.

HA-HAU-A, *v.* See **HAHAU** above. To scourge; to whip; to strike.

HA-HAU-HU-I, *s.* Name of a religious ceremony in the pule hoopiopio; same as *uhauhui.*

HA-HA-HI, *v.* The frequentative or 5th conj. of *hahi.* To tread upon. *Hal.* 91:13. To trample down. Isa. 63:3. Root *hahi.* See also **HEHI** and **EHI.**

HA-HA-KU, *v.* The 5th conj. of *haku.* To tie together in a bunch; to tie up, as feathers in a fly-brush.

2. To fold up; to put in order. See **HAKU.**

HA-HA-LE, *v.* To flatten down; to sink in.

2. To be hungry. See **HALEHALE;** also **OPAHA.**

HA-HA-LU, *v.* To be internally defective, as wood worm-eaten or rotten inside.

2. **FIG.** Applied to a hungry man. See the root **HALU.**

HA-HA-LU, *adj.* Rotten or defective inwardly; applied to wood, kalo, potatoes, &c., that are decayed inwardly.

2. Applied also to one hungry; ua *hahalu,* ua pololi ka opu.

HA-HA-LU, *s.* Name of a species of fish.

HA-HA-LU-A, *s.* Name of a species of fish, forbidden to women to eat under penalty of death; also, name of a sea animal similar to or the same as ihimanu and hihimanu.

HA-HA-NA, *v.* See the root **HANA,** to work. To be warm; applied to the heat of the sun.

2. To be warm from hard work.

3. To cook popolo, laulea, akeakea, &c., with hot stones.

HA-HA-NA, *s.* Warmth; a genial heat.

HA-HA-NA, *adj.* Very warm, as the heat of the sun, the weather, or the effect of labor.

HA-HA-HA-NA, *v.* See the root **HANA,** and *Gram.* § 225. To cause to work; to do; to do frequently; pela laua i *hahahana* ai.

HA-HA-NO, *v.* To use the syringe; to give an injection. See **HANO.**

HA-HA-PAA-KAI, *s.* See **HAHA** and **PAA-KAI,** salt. A salt bed; a place where salt is made by evaporation of the sun. See **HAHA** 4, hoo.

HA-HEI, *v.* To follow; to push with the shoulder; e pahu pu ma ka hokua; he puaa *hahei,* a pushing or fighting hog.

HA-HEI, *adj.* Fat; plump; full, as the flesh on a healthy shoulder; also *hehei.*

HA-HEO, *v.* To be proud, especially of dress or equipage; to put on airs of superiority. See **HEO.**

HA-HEO, *adj.* Proud; proud of dress or anything gaudy.

2. Haughty in manner.

HA-HI, *v.* To tread upon; to trample down; to tread out, as grain. 1 *Tim.* 5:18. To stamp with the feet. *Ezek.* 6:11. To tread or trample upon. See **EHI** and **HEHI.**

HA-HI, *s.* A treading upon; a trampling down; an overturning.

HA-HI-HA-HI, *v.* Freq. of the foregoing. To tread or trample upon frequently.

HA-HI-LI, *s.* Name of a species of fish.

HA-HO, *v.* To become poor in flesh; to fail; to want strength; e wiwi iho ma ke kino.

HA-HU, *s.* Having taken so much drastic medicine that nothing is left in the bowels.

HA-HU-A-LO, *s.* The tail fin of a fish. See **HUELO.**

HA-KA, *v.* To stare at. **FIG.** *Hal.* 22:17.

2. To look earnestly at a person or thing for evil. *Hal.* 10:8.

3. To set one's eyes upon a thing with desire. *Dan.* 10:15. Often connected with *pono* as an intensive. *Oih.* 1:10. **SYN.** with nana, and sometimes with maka.

4. A *haka* mai na moa ma ka lani.

HA-KA, *s.* A hole; a breach, as in a side of a house; hence,

2. A ladder, i. e., the cross sticks and spaces between.

3. An artificial hen-roost; hanaia i *haka* no ua moa la e kau ai.

4. A building not tightly enclosed, having many open places.

HA-KA, *adj.* Full of holes or crevices; many spaces.

Ha-ka, v. To quarrel; to spar; to dispute; to contend. See Hakaka.

Ha-kae, v. Probably for *haka ae*. To be unsound; to be weak; frail; applied to a person out of health; applied to other things deficient in strength.

Ha-ka-o, v. To go naked; to walk about destitute of clothing.

Ha-ka-o-le-lo, v. *Haka*, to quarrel, and *olelo*, word. To lay blame upon one; to accuse falsely.

Ha-ka-o-le-lo, s. Name of one whom a chief employs to report the errors of the people; the epithet of parents in governing their children, having the right to sustain and govern them.

Ha-kau, v. To look slim and tall, as a person whose flesh is wasted from his limbs.

Ha-kau, adj. Slim; tall; poor in flesh.

Ha-kau, v. To fight together, as two cocks; to practice cock-fighting.

Ha-kau, v. See Haka. To fight; to contend.

Ha-ka-ha, v. To delay; to detain.

Ha-ka-ha-ka, v. See Haka. To be full of holes; unsound; cellular; to be hollow, as a bone. *Anat.* 4. To be empty.

2. *Hoo.* Fig. To be open; to be penetrable, as the ear to sound, i. e., to listen. *Isa.* 48:8. E *hoohakahaka* i ka pepeiao i wahi e komo ai ka olelo.

Ha-ka-ha-ka, s. That which is full of holes or open spaces.

2. Fig. Want; deficiency; loss.

3. Empty room; place unoccupied; me or ma ka *hakahaka*, in the place of. *Eset.* 2:4. He *hakahaka* ka naau for pololi, hunger. *Isa.* 29:8. One in the place of another. 1 *Nal.* 1:30, 35.

Ha-ka-he-le, v. To walk with measured steps, as one weak. See Akahele.

Ha-ka-ka, v. See Haka. To quarrel; to contend; to fight. 2 *Sam.* 14:6. But often only in words. *Kin.* 26:20. To debate.

2. *Hoo.* To set at variance; to cause strife; e *hoohakaka* ana i na bipi.

Ha-ka-ka, s. A fighting; a quarrel; a contention; a controversy. *Mik.* 6:2.

Ha-ka-kae, v. To rend; to tear; to separate into parts. See Haka and Kae.

Ha-ka-kai, v. To be swelled. See Ku-hakakai.

Ha-ka-kau, v. *Haka*, ladder, and *kau*, set up.

1. To be suspended, as on a haka.

2. To stand with a slender footing, as on the edge of a canoe looking for squid; ke *hakakau* la ke kanaka me he kioea la, the man stands like a kioea (a long-legged bird.)

Ha-ka-kau, s. A place to hang things upon.

2. A thin, spare, tall man.

Ha-ka-kau-lu-na, s. Name of the stools on which double canoes were placed when out of water; also *ake*.

Ha-ka-kau-pi-li, v. To stand intent upon any sound, like a thief.

2. To be ready to fly from the approach of any one; e kau me he iwa la i ka lai, e lele aheahe malie ana.

> Ke *hakakaupili* me he iwa la i ka lai,
> Ke aka lele au a ka la hiki ole,
> Ola ka maka ia Kohala pali uka.

Ha-ka-ke, v. To stand on stilts; to stand, as a spider on long legs.

2. To stand huddled or crowded together.

Ha-ka-ku, s. A frame for drying fish for the chiefs which are kapu.

Ha-ka-la, s. The gable end of a house. See Kala. Aia mahea ia? aia ma ka *hakala* o ka hale.

Ha-ka-li-a, v. *Hakaia*, the *l* inserted. *Gram.* § 48. To be hard; difficult to accomplish. *Kin.* 18:14.

2. To be dilatory; slow in doing a thing; ua *hakalia* ka amo ana o ka maka, *slow* was the winking of the eyes.

3. *Hoo.* To defer or put off doing. *Kekah.* 5:4.

Ha-ka-li-a, s. A difficulty in doing a thing; meeting with obstacles; a detention; he hewa nui, o keia *hakalia* o lakou, the great error was this slowness of them. See explanations in the next.

Ha-ka-li-a, adj. Long in doing a thing; dilatory; slow; taking too much time; also,

2. Careless; unthinking; holo makou me ka hoopiipii mau ana'ame ka *hakalia*.

Ha-ka-li-na.

Ha-ka-lu-nu, s. Extreme old age when one is no longer able to walk; hele o mea akauka *hakalunu*.

Ha-ka-mo-a, s. *Haka*, to quarrel, and *moa*, a fowl. Cock-fighting; the name of a game practiced in former times; o ka *hakamoa* kekahi mea makemake nui e na 'lii.

Ha-ka-ne-ne, v. To be swelled; puffed up; e maimai, e ukeke.

Ha-ka-ne-le, adj. Thin; spare in flesh; ua *hakanele* oe i ko oukou hiki ana mai; applied to man and beast.

Ha-ka-po-no, v. See Haka. To look earnestly at; to look steadfastly; to direct the eyes upon. 2 *Nal.* 8:11.

2. To stare or gaze at; to be amazed; to see something to be wondered at. *Isa.* 13:8. NOTE.—These two words are often written separately as well as together, and then *pono* is used as an intensive adverb.

HA-KE, *s.* See HOO. To resist; stand against. See KE and HOOKEE. To displace; put aside; put away.

HA-KE-A, *adj.* See KEA, white. Pale, as one sick.

HA-KE-LO, }
HA-KE-LO-KE-LO, } *adj.* Hanging down, in swelling or pendulous bunches, as the mucus from the nose of a child; applied to swellings of internal parts, as the uterus; *hakelo* or *hakelokelo* ka hupe.

HA-KI, *v.* See HAI, *k* inserted. To break, as a piece of wood; to break, as with the hands. *Hal.* 18:34. To break, as a bone. *Hal.* 34:20. PASS. *Hakia* for *hakiia,* to be broken. *Oihk.* 26:26. FIG. Applied to the punishment of wicked men. *Iob.* 24:20. To break, as the teeth, that is, one's power crushed. NOTE.—The word applies mostly only to such things as are somewhat brittle.

HA-KI, *adj.* That which is easily broken; *haki* wale, brittle.

HA-KI-A, Pass. of *haki.* See above.

HA-KI-A, *s.* A pin; a nail. SYN. with makia and kakia.

HA-KII, }
HA-KII-KII, } *v.* To tie fast; to make fast by tying. See NAKII.

HA-KI-U, *v.* See KIU. To spy out; to look at; to examine; alaila, *hakiu* like iho la lakou i ka mea a lakou i iini ai.

HA-KI-HA-KI, *v.* 13th conj. of *haki.* To break in pieces, as wood; to break frequently. *Hal.* 76:3.

HA-KI-LO, *v.* To observe narrowly; to watch closely and attentively.

2. To look at what one is about to do. *Luk.* 14:1. To watch one's actions or conduct, generally to find occasion, or with some evil design. *Mar.* 3:2.

3. To eaves-drop or listen secretly, expecting something bad; ua *hakilo* aku au ia mea ma e ohumu ana.

4. To act the spy. See the root KILO. To watch, as a thief does if anyone sees him.

HA-KI-NA, *s.* Contraction for *haki ana,* a breaking. A piece broken off; a piece of a thing; a remnant; *hakina* ai, a piece of food. *Ioh.* 6:12. A part; a portion, &c.

HA-KI-NA-O-LE-LO, *s.* Used for syllable in the music Gamut.

HA-KO, *v.* To be dignified in one's bearing; to appear honorable; to be noble in form; ua *hako* kona helehelena, ma kona mau maka.

HA-KO, *s.* The leaf of the sugar-cane; wakawaka o Mano e moku ae ka *hako.*

HA-KOI, *v.* To dash, as water against water.

2. To be agitated, as water carried in a dish unsteadily; *hakoi* ka wai.

3. To be unsettled, as one's thoughts when in trouble.

HA-KOI, *adj.* Heavy; weighty, as luggage, &c.; kaumaha, koikoi; heavy; burdensome.

2. FIG. Heavy, as the heart.

HA-KOI, *s.* An action productive in children of paraphimosis.

HA-KOI-KOI, *v.* To rise or swell up, as water.

2. FIG. Ma ka haale o ka manao e pii iluna me he wai la e *hakoikoi* iloko o ka manawa, through the overflow of thoughts rising up like water, the affections flow within.

HA-KO-HA-KO, *adj.* See HAKO. Portly; dignified in appearance; noble in person.

HA-KO-KO, }
HA-KOO-KOO, } *v.* To wrestle; to contend with another to cause him to fall. *Kin.* 32:24. FIG. *Epes.* 6:12. NOTE.—Hawaiians write the word in both the forms. The last syllables are equally long and accented.

HA-KO-KO, }
HA-KOO-KOO, } *s.* A wrestling; contention of strength between two persons to cause each other to fall; eia kekahi lealea, o ka *hakookoo,* here is one pastime, *wrestling.*

HA-KO-NA, *adj.* Scorched or dried black, as breadfruit which hangs on the trees long after the season is over, when one side becomes parched and black with the sun; he *hakona* ka hua ulu.

2. It applies also to the side lying long on the dirt; the other side is *kua paa.*

HA-KO-NA-KO-NA, *adj.* Rough; dark; clouded; uneven.

HA-KU, *v.* To dispose of things in order; to put in order.

2. To arrange or tie feathers in a kahili; to make a wreath or lei; e *haku* i ka lei; e *haku* oe i lehua. *Laieik.* 146.

3. To put words in order, as in poetry; to compose a song.

4. To rule over people, i. e., to put and keep them in order; to act, as a lord over men.

5. By a change of letters, *haku* for *kahu,* to bake fish with hot stones.

6. FIG. The forming of a new affection in the mind; ka manawa i *haku* ai ke aloha

ma ka naau.

7. *Hoo.* To rule over; to direct others. *Oihk.* 25:43. *Haku* mele, a composer of songs, i. e., a poet; nana ia i *haku*, he composed it.

Ha-ku, *s.* A lord; a master; an overseer; a ruler. *Oihk.* 21:4.

2. A hard lump of anything; the tongue of a bell; a padlock; a hard bunch in the flesh; the ball of the eye; *haku* onohi; the name of several species of hard stones formerly used in working stone adzes; ua kapaia kela mau pohaku, he *haku* ka koi ka inoa.

Ha-ku-ai-na, *s.* *Haku,* lord, and *aina,* land. A land-holder, i. e., one who manages the land and the people on it under the chief or owner.

Ha-ku-a-kea, *s.* A phrase in praise of Lono; a lord of extensive power; papa ka *hakuakea* o Lono.

Ha-ku-a-pa, } *v.* *Haku* and *apa* and *epa,*
Ha-ku-e-pa, } false. To speak falsely; to speak to the hurt of one; to detract.

Ha-ku-a-pa, } *s.* A false speaker; a de-
Ha-ku-e-pa, } tractor.

2. A false report; evil speaking. 1 *Pet.* 3:16.

Ha-ku-e, *s.* A species of sea-egg with many prongs.

2. The prongs of such fish. See HAKUI.

Ha-ku-e-ku-e, *s.* The prongs of the hakue.

2. The ringworm. See HAUHAUKA.

Ha-ku-e-pa, *s.* See HAKUAPA.

Ha-ku-i, *v.* See KUI, to sound out. To reflect sound, as an echo.

2. To sound in every direction, as thunder rumbling through the heavens; e kani mahope o kekahi kani ana me he kihili la; to reverberate.

Ha-ku-i, *v.* To be sickish or a little sick at the stomach; hoopailua.

2. To make attempts at vomiting, as one sick at the stomach; *hakui* wale mai no, aole luai mai, he was merely sick at the stomach, he did not vomit.

3. To flutter; to palpitate, as the heart.

4. To shoot, as pain in the chest; *hakui* maloko o ka houpo; e apo ka oili.

Ha-ku-i, *v.* To roast blood in cooking; *hakui* koko.

Ha-ku-i, *s.* The blood of hogs when roasted for eating.

Ha-ku-i, *s.* The horn of the sea-egg. See HAKUE, which is probably the more correct orthography.

Ha-ku-ia, *adj.* See HAKU. Bound; braided; wreathed together, &c. *Laieik.* 112.

Ha-ku-i-ku-i, *v.* To crack, as breaking timber; to sound; to make the noise of breaking timber.

Ha-ku-o-hi-a, *s.* The lord of the ohia trees.

2. The ohia tree of which an idol was to be made; a i ka la i pii aku ai i ka *hakuohia* make kekahi kanaka, i mea e mana ai ua kii ohia la, on the day they went up for an *ohia tree* some man would die, to give efficacy to the idol. NOTE.—The species of ohia used was the *ohiaapane. Hakuohia* the same as *kiiohia.*

Ha-ku-o-le-lo, *v.* *Haku* and *olelo,* to put words together. To accuse falsely; to detract; to slander.

Ha-ku-o-le-lo, *s.* A false accuser; a detractor.

Ha-ku-o-ne, *s.* *Haku,* lump, and *one,* sand. Name of a small division of land, similar to or smaller than a koele cultivated for the chief. See KUAKUA.

Ha-ku-o-no-hi, *s.* *Haku,* a hard lump, and *onohi,* the eye-ball. The apple of the eye; the little image in the eye. See KIIONOHI.

Ha-ku-ha-ku, *v.* See HAKU, to put together. To fold up, as kapa; to put in order; to arrange.

Ha-ku-ha-ku, *adj.* Full of hard lumps; lumpy.

Ha-ku-ha-le, *s.* *Haku,* master, and *hale,* house. The master or owner of a house. *Puk.* 22:8.

Ha-ku-ha-na, *s.* A word applied to the appearance or motion of the clouds; he ao *hakuhana.*

Ha-ku-kai, *v.* *Haku,* lumpy, and *kai,* sea. To be in perturbation, as the sea; to be stormy. See OOLUKU.

Ha-ku-ko-i, *v.* See HAKUKAI.

Ha-ku-ko-le, *v.* To blackguard; to reproach in filthy language.

Ha-ku-ko-le, *s.* A blackguard; a vile person.

Ha-ku-ma, *s.* A thick cloud; one threatening a storm.

Ha-ku-ma-ku-ma, *v.* To lower; to frown; to look threatening, as clouds portending a storm. *Mat.* 16:3.

2. To be rough or pitted, as from the scars of the small-pox; *hakumakuma* ka ili.

3. To be thick together; to be thick, as a board. See KUMAKUMA.

Ha-ku-ma-ku-ma, *adj.* Lowering, as clouds threatening a storm.

2. Pitted, as the skin with disease.

3. Thick, set close together.

HA-KU-ME-LE, *v. Haku*, to compose, and *mele*, a song; poetry. To compose or make poetry.

HA-KU-ME-LE, *s.* A poet; one skilled as a poet; a composer of songs. *Nah.* 21:27; *Oih.* 17:28.

HA-KU-PE, See KUPEHE.

HA-KU-PE-HE, *v.* See LOLOHI. To speak carefully as to truth and propriety; to roll, as a ship with but little wind.

HA-KU-WA-HI-NE, *s. Haku*, a lord, and *wahine*, a female. A female master, i. e., a mistress; the wife of a chief or noble. *Gal.* 4:22.

HA-LA, *v.* To miss the object aimed at. *Lunk.* 20:16. Nou mai la ia, a *hala* ka pohaku; nou hou mai la ia a *hala* hou no; a i ke kolu o ka nou ana, pa aku la; he threw and the stone *missed*; he threw again and *missed* again; the third time he threw he hit.

2. To be gone; to pass away; to pass over.

3. To proceed; to pass onward; to go beyond. *Nah.* 22:18. To pass away, as time.

4. *Hoo.* To miss the object; to cause to err; to be guilty or blame-worthy.

5. To depart from a command, or act in opposition. *Kanl.* 1:43. To err in opinion; to disobey; to object to a request or command; to refuse obedience. *Eset.* 3:3. To transgress. *Nah.* 14:4.

HA-LA, *s.* A trespass; a sin; an offense; a transgression.

2. A matter of offense. *Kanl.* 9:21.

3. A law case; e imi *hala*, to seek occasion against. *Lunk.* 14:4. Lawe *hala*, a sinner; *hala* ole, without sin; without cause. *Puk.* 34:7.

HA-LA, *adj.* Sinful; wicked; kanaka *hala*, a sinner; one often breaking some law.

HA-LA, *adv.* Sinfully; in a state of sin; hanau *hala*, born a sinner.

HA-LA, *adv.* (Referring to space passed over) onward; throughout; even to; up to; he pa pohaku a *hala* i ka lani, a stone wall (reaching) *clear up* to heaven. *Kanl.* 1:28. Also *a hala*, clear up to. *Kanl.* 9:1.

HA-LA, *s.* The pandanus tree.

2. The pine-apple.

3. A species of fish.

HA-LAI, *s.* The lulling of a strong wind; a calm. See LAI and LAE.

HA-LA-IO, *adv.* The *l* is probably substituted for *n*. Well done! clever! brave!

HA-LA-I-WI, *s.* See HALAWI, to scrutinize. Looking earnestly at a thing with a desire to obtain or possess it; *halaiwi* me ka manao e lawe malu.

HA-LA-O, *v.* To feel pain, as the eye with some mote in it; to have pain in the eye from a mote; *halao* ana i kuu maka.

HA-LA-O, *s.* Pain in the eye from some small mote. See LAO. A small particle of something moving in the eye.

HA-LA-OA, *v.* To project; to stretch out; to extend upwards, as the mast of a ship; to project, as the horns of the sea-egg.

HA-LA-OA, *adj.* Projecting; standing up.

HA-LAO-LAO, *v.* To be small; thin in flesh; poor, as small stunted weeds or brush on poor land.

HA-LAO-LAO, *adj.* Small; stunted; poor; thin.

HA-LAU, *v.* To be long; to extend; to stretch out.

HA-LAU, *s.* A long house with the end in front; used mostly for canoes.

2. Name of a hen that has had chickens.

HA-LA-HA-LA, *v.* See HALA. To turn aside; to go astray; mostly used in the causative *hoo*.

2. To object to one; to decline a proposition; to find fault with one's words or conduct; aole *hoohalahala* kekahi o lakou, not one of them found fault.

HA-LA-HA-LA, *adj.* Bitter; sour; brackish; ko *halahala*, sour or fermented cane.

HA-LA-HA-LA, *s.* Name of a species of fish; the uhu. See UHUHALAHALA.

HA-LA-HA-LA-WAI, *adv.* Slippery; wet, as a road; running; ua kelekele *halahalawai* i ka ua.

2. Wet, as a sore eye.

HA-LA-HI, *v.* To miss, as anything thrown at another.

2. To dodge any missile.

3. To fly near to one, as a stone or other missile thrown.

4. To hum while passing through the air.

HA-LA-HI, *s.* A hissing or whizzing of any projectile passing through the air.

HA-LA-HU-LA, *s.* Name of a particular aha used in preparing for war.

HA-LA-KAU, *v.* To place one thing on top of another.

2. To lean over; e haukau.

HA-LA-KE-A, *s.* The name of a kapa when dyed with the niu.

2. The name of upright posts inside of houses; o na *halakea*, oia na kia e ku ana maloko o ka hale.

HA-LA-LA, *adj.* Long and curving, as hog's tushes; *halala* ka niho o ka puaa kahiko.

2. Applied also to men exposing them-

selves.

3. A large bunch of bananas.

HA-LA-LO, *v.* *Ha* and *lalo*, downward.

1. To take hold of with the arms under, as in taking up a child or anything else.

2. To drop the head downward, as in deep thought.

3. To begin to think. 2 *Oihl.* 20:3. To think within one's self; pela kuu *halalo* ana ia'u iho, so I *thought* within myself.

4. To think or reflect on the moral actions of others. *Kekah.* 8:9.

5. To look earnestly at a thing near or far off; to think closely.

6. To look internally; *halalo* iho la no au a loaa no.

7. To search closely or look for a thing with effort.

HA-LA-LO, *v.* To administer an injection. See HAHANO.

HA-LA-LOA, *s.* The name of a species of fish.

HA-LA-NA, *v.* *Ha* and *lana*, to float.

1. To overflow, as water over the banks of a river, or over a levee or low land. *Amos* 9:5.

2. To float on the surface of the water.

3. To be overflowed, i. e., to be drowned.

4. Hoo. To flood; to overflow with a flood. *Isa.* 54:9.

HA-LA-NA-LA-NA, *v.* See HALANA. To overflow; to flow thick and fast, as the tears of one weeping; nolaila i *halanalana* ai lakou me ka haloiloi i ko lakou waimaka; to shed tears.

HA-LA-PA, *v.* In a *prayer*, to bring to pass; to pray that a thing hoped for may be granted; *halapa* i ke mauli kukala ia hale hau.

HA-LA-WAI, *v.* To meet, as two persons; to meet, as two lines in an angle.

2. To assemble, as persons for business or for public worship.

3. *Hoo.* To cause to meet with, i. e., to find. *Kin.* 27:20.

4. To come to one for assistance. *Hal.* 59:4.

HA-LA-WAI, *s.* A meeting; a place of meeting; the place of union between the heavens and the earth; the space between them; same as *lewa* and *hookui*. See HOOKUI. *D. Malo* 5:5.

2. A meeting or assembly of people for business or public worship.

HA-LA-WAI, *adj.* Of or pertaining to meeting; hale *halawai*, a house for a public meeting.

HA-LA-PE-PE, *s.* A tree; the hala tree, a species of the pandanus; he laau ano like me ka hala.

HA-LA-PI-A, *s.* The white hala; hala keokeo.

HA-LA-WI, *v.* See HALAIWI. To scrutinize; to look critically at.

HA-LE, *s.* A house; a habitation; a dwelling place; mostly for men.

2. A sheltered and inclosed place for any purpose. NOTE.—In ancient times every man was supposed to have six different houses of some size.

1. The *heiau*, house of worship where the idols were kept.

2. The *mua*, the eating house for the husband, and distinct from the eating house of the woman. Husband and wife never ate together. The *mua* was kapu to the wife.

3. The *noa*, the separate house of the wife, but free for the husband to enter. The woman ate in the hale *noa*.

4. Hale *aina*, the eating house of the wife.

5. The *kua*, the house where the wife beat out kapa.

6. Hale *pea*, the house of separation for the wife during the periods of her infirmity. They had other houses and for other purposes, but these were considered necessary fixtures for every person in respectable standing. See the above words in their places.

HA-LE-AI-NA, *s.* *Hale* and *aina*. See AINA. The eating house for the woman; one of the houses anciently used to eat in; the *mua* was the eating house of the man. See HALE.

HA-LE-A-KA-LA, *s.* House of the sun; name of the high mountain on East Maui.

HA-LE-A-LII, *s.* *Hale* and *alii*. A chief's house; a palace. 1 *Oihl.* 29:19. *Halealii* palaoa, an ivory palace. *Hal.* 45:8.

HA-LE-O-NE, *s.* A place made by men for a temporary residence; sand or soft dirt made into a house; kukulu lakou i *haleone*, ua kapaia he hale puone; more properly *puu one*, a sand pile.

HA-LE-O-PE-O-PE, *s.* *Hale* and *opeope*, to fold up, as clothes. The name of the house where the chief's wardrobe was kept.

HA-LE-U, *v.* To comb; to clear out; to purify; to cleanse.

HA-LE-U-MA, *s.* See HELEUMA.

HA-LE-U-MU, *s.* *Hale* and *umu*, an oven. Name of Lono's house.

HA-LE-HAU, *s.* *Hale*, house, and *hau*, the hau tree. A house built of hau timber for the use of the gods.

Ha-le-ha-la-wai, s. *Hale* and *halawai*, to meet; assemble. A meeting house; a synagogue; a place of meeting.

Ha-le-ha-le, v. To sink down; to fall in; to flat down, as the roof of an old house.

Ha-le-ha-le, s. A place deep down; a pit; *halehale* poipu, deep under the surf. *Laieik.* 133.

Ha-le-ha-le, adj. Deep down, as a pit dug; deep, as a cavern.

Ha-le-hei-au, s. *Hale* and *heiau.* See Heiau. One of the houses of an establishment. See Hale.

Ha-le-hoo-lu-hi, s. *Hale* and *luhi.* A house of bondage; hence,
2. Fig. Slavery. *Lunk.* 6:8. A place of bondage. *Puk.* 13:3.

Ha-le-hoo-ki-pa, s. *Hale* and *kipa.* See Kipa, to turn in and lodge with one. A lodging house; a house for strangers. See Halekipa.

Ha-le-kaa, s. *Hale* and *kaa,* to roll.
1. Any carriage with a top or covering.
2. A chariot. *Puk.* 14:7.

Ha-le-kau-a, s. *Hale* and *kaua,* war. A fort; a tower; a fortification. Lunk. 9:51, 52.

Ha-le-ka-hi-ko-kau-a, s. *Hale, kahiko,* armor, and *kaua,* war. An armory; a place for storing or keeping arms.

Ha-le-ka-ma-la, s. *Hale* and *kamala,* a temporary shed.
1. A house quickly and slightly built.
2. A temporary shed; a booth; a tabernacle. *Mar.* 9:5.

Ha-le-ki-a, s. *Hale* and *kia,* a post; a pillar. A portico to a house; a verandah supported by pillars. 1 *Nal.* 7:6.

Ha-le-ki-ai, s. *Hale* and *kiai,* to watch. A watch tower; a tower. *Lunk.* 8:9.

Ha-le-ki-pa, s. *Hale* and *kipa,* to lodge a traveler. An inn; a lodging house. *Puk.* 4:24.

Ha-le-ko-ko, s. Name of the house where the hoalii slept; ua kapaia ka *hale-koko* o ka hoalii. See Hoalii.

Ha-le-ku-a, s. *Hale* and *kua.* One of the houses of a residence. See Kua.

Ha-le-ku-ku, s. *Hale* and *kuku,* to beat kapa. Name of the house occupied by the woman in beating out kapa. See Kua under hale.

Ha-le-ku-la, s. *Hale* and *kula* (Eng.), school. A schoolhouse.

Ha-le-ku-pa-pa-u, s. *Hale* and *kupapau,* a dead body; corpse. A tomb; a sepulchre. 2 *Sam.* 19:37. A grave. 1 *Nal.* 13:22.

Ha-le-la-au, s. *Hale* and *laau,* wood; timber. A wood house, in distinction from a grass covered house.

Ha-le-la-na, s. *Hale* and *lana,* to float. A floating house; applied to Noah's ark.

Ha-le-la-na-la-na, s. See Halelana above.

Ha-le-la-la-la-au, s. *Hale, lala,* a branch, and *laau,* tree. A house made of branches of trees or other slight materials; a booth; a shanty. *Oihk.* 23:42.

Ha-le-le-lo, s. Caves supposed to be in the ocean.

Ha-le-le-po, s. *Hale* and *lepo,* dirt; earth. A mud house; a house built of adobies or sun-dried brick.

Ha-le-le-wa, s. *Hale* and *lewa,* swinging. A portable house; a tent. *Ios.* 22:4.

Ha-le-lo-le, s. *Hale* and *lole,* cloth. A cloth house, i. e., a tent. Syn. with hale-lewa. 2 Sam. 7:6. Poe humuhumu *hale-lole. Oih.* 18:3.

Ha-le-lu, s. Heb. A psalm; na *halelu,* the psalms of David.

Ha-le-lu, v. Heb. To sing praise to God. *Ier.* 31:7.

Ha-le-lu, adv. E mele *halelu* aku ia ia, to sing praises. 1 *Oih.* 16:9.

Ha-le-lu-a, s. *Hale* and *lua,* a pit. A tomb; a sepulchre; a grave. 1 *Sam.* 2:6.

Ha-le-lu-a-paa-hao, s. *Hale* and *lua,* pit, and *paa* and *hao,* iron. A prison house. See Halepaahao.

Ha-le-lu-ia, v. Heb. imperat. Praise the Lord.

Ha-le-ma-lu, s. *Hale* and *malu,* cool; shady. A shaded house; a shed.

Ha-le-ma-lu-ma-lu, s. Same as above. *Kin.* 49:14.

Ha-le-mo-e, s. *Hale* and *moe,* to sleep. A sleeping house; one of the houses of a Hawaiian house-holder. See Moe.

Ha-le-mu-a, s. See Hale. Name of one of several houses of a house-holder in former times; the house where the husband ate his food.

Ha-le-na-le, s. Clear moonlight.

Ha-le-pa-a-ni, s. *Hale* and *paani,* to play. A play-house; a theater.

Ha-le-paa-hao, s. *Hale* and *paa,* fast, and *hao,* iron. A house of confinement; a prison house.

Ha-le-pa-hu, s. *Hale* and *pahu,* a box. Name of a particular house in the war ceremony.

Ha-le-pa-paa, s. *Hale* and *papaa,* secure. A store-house. *Kin.* 41:56.

Ha-le-pa-kui, s. *Hale* and *pakui,* to splice. A fortified house; a tower. *Kin.*

11:4. A pyramid.

HA-LE-PE-A, *s. Hale* and *pea*, filthy and unclean. See under HALE. A house where the menstruous women formerly were obliged to remain. *Laieik.* 171. NOTE.— The people might go to each woman's house, but the priests could not.

HA-LE-PI-O, *s. Hale* and *pio*, an arch. A particular kind of a house.

HA-LE-PO-HA-KU, *s. Hale* and *pohaku*, stone. A house built of stone; a stone house.

HA-LE-PO-KI, *s.* The name of the heiau where the bones of the king were deposited.

HA-LE-PU-KAU-A, *s. Hale*, *pu*, a gun, and *kaua*, war. A fort; a tower; a house of defense; a castle.

HA-LE-PU-LE, *s. Hale* and *pule*, to pray. A prayer house; a house of worship; a meeting house.

HA-LE-PU-NA, *s. Hale* and *puna*, lime. A house plastered with lime.

HA-LE-PU-PU, } *s. Hale* and *pupupu*,
HA-LE-PU-PU-PU, } poor; frail. A temporary, frail house. *Isa.* 1:8.

HA-LI, *v.* To bear; to carry; to convey; *hali* mai, to bring; *hali* aku, to take or carry away.

2. To bear, as a burden. *Nah.* 10:17.

3. To carry, as a child. *Kanl.* 1:31.

4. To carry, as an armor bearer. 1 *Sam.* 31:4.

5. FIG. To bear the sin of others. *Oihk.* 10:17.

HA-LI, *s.* Contraction of *halii*. That which is spread down, as a mat, a carpet, a cloth spread out.

HA-LI-A, *v.* Pass. of *hali* for *haliia*. To be carried; borne, &c.

HA-LI-A, *v.* To have a fond recollection of a person or thing. *Laieik.* 116. See next.

HA-LI-A, *s.* A symptom; a premonition; the first beginning of a feeling; ke kau e mai nei ia'u ka *halia* o ka makau, ame ka weliweli. *Laieik.* 180.

HA-LI-A-LI-A, *v.* To have a recollection of a friend; e *halialia* ana no nae ke aloha ia'u ma na wahi a kaua i ao ai.

2. To become intent, as the mind, or fixed, as thoughts which keep one wakeful.

3. To spring up, as thoughts or affections in the mind; *halialia* ke aloha. See LIA.

HA-LI-A-LI-A, *s.* The rising of a fond recollection of a person or friend in the mind; ke kau mai nei ka *halialia* aloha ia lakou; malaila no ka *halialia* aloha ana, there was the beloved recollection. *Laieik.* 34.

HA-LI-A-LI-A, *adj.* Beloved; cherished;

remembered with affection; ka manao *halialia* a'u i ka manao i ke ao, I have a fond remembrance of the desire for instruction.

HA-LII, *v.* To spread out and lay down, as a sheet or mat.

2. To spread upon or over, as a garment; to spread or cover over, as snow over the tops of the mountains. *Laieik.* 112.

3. To spread out, as grass or hay.

4. To expose to view as something that had been concealed. *Ios.* 7:23.

5. To spread, as grain upon a cloth. 2 *Sam.* 17:19. To spread over, as a sheet.

HA-LII, *s.* The out or under side of leaves of certain plants; the under or dried leaves of plants; laele.

HA-LII-KU-LI, *v.* To be hard; disobedient; stubborn.

2. To be thick.

HA-LII-LII, *v.* See HALII. To spread out or over frequently.

HA-LII-PI-LI, *v.* To spread over a region, as a shower, like the spreading of a mat; *haliipili* i ke kula o Lele, the shower extends over the plain of Lahaina.

HA-LI-U, *v.* To turn towards or from, as *mai* or *aku* is used.

2. To turn one's attention to a thing; to turn round to look.

3. To turn the ear; to listen.

4. To turn aside from the following one. 2 *Sam.* 2:21, 22.

5. To turn from a direct road. *Kanl.* 1:40. With *pepeiao*, to listen.

6. To turn towards one with love and respect; manao iho la au e *haliu* ae i ka Haku, I determined to turn to the Lord.

7. *Hoo.* To cause to turn, as the attention or care. 1 *Nal.* 8:58.

HA-LI-U, *s.* What the fundament is wiped with; a word which Kamehameha applied to Keoua when he threatened to join kings against him.

HA-LI-HA-LI, *v.* The frequentative of *hali*. To convey frequently; to bring; to carry. *Nah.* 11:14.

HA-LI-KE, *v.* To liken; to resemble; to be like.

2. To give equally; to equalize in disposing of things.

3. *Hoo.* With *me*, to compare; to do as one does; to resemble some one in conduct. 1 *Nal.* 14:8. See LIKE. NOTE.—*Like* is the root, *ha* is euphonic. *Gram.* § 48 and 211, 2.

HA-LI-NA, *s. Hali* and *ana*. A bearing or carrying; hence,

2. A bearing, or personal appearance; form; more generally *halinalina*. See LINA.

HA-LI-NA-LI-NA, *s.* See HALINA. Resemblance or similar appearance; he helehelena like.

HA-LO, *v.* To turn; to look; to look at; a *halo* aku la au mahope; to sweep round.

2. To spread out, as the hands in the act of swimming. *Isa.* 25:11.

3. To look out; to peep; to look slily or shy.

4. To rub, grind or polish.

HA-LO, *s.* The motion of the fins of a fish in swimming; the motion of the side fins of a shark; the motion of rubbing or polishing.

HA-LO-A-LO-A, *v.* To be rough or uneven, as with stones.

HA-LO-A-LO-A, *s.* Roughness.

HA-LO-I,
HA-LO-I-LO-I, } *v.* To be about to weep; to have that deep feeling that exists just before the tears flow.

2. To shed or pour out tears.

3. To wipe the eyes when weeping; to wipe the tears of grief; me ka *haloiloi* i ko lakou waimaka no ke aloha. See HALOKO-LOKO.

HA-LO-I-LO-I, *s.* The state of feeling just as one is about to weep; deep internal feeling.

HA-LO-I-LO-I, *adj.* Weeping; shedding tears; ka maka *haloiloi* o ka ohia, the *weeping* eyes of the ohia.

HA-LO-KE, *v.* To rub against each other, as the ends of broken bones. *Anat.* 26.

HA-LO-KE, *adj.* Sprained or broken, as a limb.

HA-LO-KO, *s.* A puddle of water standing after a rain; a small pool of water.

HA-LO-KO-LO-KO, *v.* To stand in pools, as water after a rain; hence,

2. To be about to weep; to have deep affliction. See HALOI.

HA-LO-KO-LO-KO, *s.* Small pools of water after a rain.

2. Drops of tears as they flow from the eyes.

HA-LO-KO-WAI, *s.* A pool of water; a small lake; o na waipuna huihui, o na *halokowai*.

HA-LO-KU, *v.* To bubble up, as when a heavy rain falls into water; *haloku* ka ia o Kuluhaipo.

2. To disturb the surface of smooth water, as when many small fish come to the surface.

HA-LO-LA-NI, *s.* The flight of a bird that sails round and round with but little motion of the wings; lele ka pinao o *Halolani*, lele i ka lani.

HA-LO-LI-I-LI, *adj.* Lazy; idle; useless, as a canoe made in the mountains, and there lies and rots; o Mano kapu o ke ka-ele *haloliili*.

2. Applied to lazy, useless persons.

HA-LU,
HA-LU-HA-LU, } *v.* To be thin; lean, as a person poor in flesh.

2. To be hungry for food.

3. To be greedy after what is another's; to confiscate property, as chiefs in ancient times.

HA-LU-A, *v.* To lie in wait for one. 1 *Sam.* 22:13. *Hoo.* To lie in wait in order to kill or injure one. *Ier.* 9:8.

HA-LU-A, *s.* A ripple on the water; the rising up of water by the wind; he nao kuku.

2. A streak, stripe or seam, as of a stocking.

HA-LU-A, *adj.* Striped; seamed; streaked; he lole *halua*; he kil ka *halua*.

HA-LU-A-LU-A, *v.* See LUALUA, soft; flexible.

1. To be soft; flexible.

2. To be weak.

HA-LU-A-LU-A, *s.* Softness; weakness; flexibility.

HA-LU-A-PO, *v.* *Halua* and *po*, night.

1. To lie in wait in darkness.

2. *Hoo.* To waylay; to lurk for one; to lie in wait for a person with a design to kill him. See HALUA.

HA-LU-A-POU, *v.* To plant out bananas.

HA-LU-I,
HA-LU-LI, } *v.* See LULI. To turn; to twist; to shake.

HA-LU-KU, *v.* To wallow in the mire, as a hog. 2 *Pet.* 2:22.

2. To lap water, as a dog; e kope i ka wai me he ilio la.

3. To use the paddle in rowing.

HA-LU-KU-LU-KU, *v.* To fall, as a heavy shower with a heavy sound; to drip, as water in a shower-bath.

HA-LU-LA, *v.* To become calm, as wind after blowing.

HA-LU-LA, *s.* A calm; stillness, as the sea without wind.

HA-LU-LE-LU-LE, *v.* *Ha* and *lule*, to be shaken. To be weak; yielding; to be flexible.

HA-LU-LU, *v.* To roar; to rage; to roar, as thunder; as the sound of a heavy wind; to roar, as the sea. *Isa.* 5:30. *Halulu* aku la ka pohaku i ke kahakai, the rock thundered off to the sea shore; *halulu* ana o laua ma ka puka o ka hale, *shook* violently the door of the house.

HA-LU-LU, *s.* A noise of a chariot and

horsemen rushing to battle. 2 *Nal.* 7:6. The noise of rushing water. *Hal.* 42:7. The sound of thunder or wind. *Ioh.* 3:8. *Halulu* hekili. *Hoik.* 6:1.

HA-LU-LU, *s.* The name of a fabulous bird in ancient times killed by the chief Waukulenuiaiku; o *halulu*, o ka mani kani halau.

HA-LU-NA, *v.* To summon men to work.

2. To breathe hard, as when the nose is filled with mucus.

3. To snore.

HA-MA, *v.* To open, as the mouth.

HA-MAU, *v. imper.* Silence; hush; be still. *Lunk.* 18:19. Alaila, hea mai la ia makou, i mai la, *hamau* kakou, then he called to us and said; let us be still.

HA-MAU, *v.* With the imperative form *e hamau*, to keep silence as an act of worship. *Zep.* 1:7.

HA-MAU, *adj.* Silent, as a person who refrains from speaking. *Sol.* 10:19. Restraining speech.

HA-MAU, *adv.* Silently. *Sol.* 11:12.

HA-MAU, *s.* A species of the ohia tree.

HA-MA-KU-A, *s.* The name of two districts of land; one on the north-eastern side of Hawaii, and the other on the north-eastern side of Maui.

HA-MA-KUU, *v.* To raise up and stand erect, as the hair with the fingers, &c.

HA-MA-MA, *v.* The 9th conjugation of the verb *hama.* To open wide, as a door; to open, as the mouth. See HAMA.

2. To gape, as the earth. *Nah.* 16:30, 32.

3. To open, as a door, box or book.

4. *Hoo.* To cause to open; to open wide. *Hal.* 35:21. FIG. To cause to open the mouth. *Hal.* 81:10.

HA-MA-MA, *adj.* See HAMA. Open; disclosed.

HA-MA-MA, *adv.* Openly; standing open, as a door. *Ios.* 8:17.

HA-MA-RE, } *s. Eng.* A hammer. *Lunk.*
HA-ME-RE, } 4:21.

HA-ME, *s.* Name of a tree supposed to be very superior for the finest cabinet work.

HA-ME, *s.*

HA-MI-HA, *v.* To make calm, as the surface of the sea.

HA-MO, *v.* To stroke over with the hand; to wash the face; to rub or brush, as in cleaning clothes.

2. To besmear with blood; to plaster with lime; to anoint with oil. *Puk.* 29:2. Or ointment. 2 *Sam.* 12:20.

3. To bend or crook the arm, as in doing

the foregoing things; to crook round; to bend round, as an oval surface.

4. To be exactly circular, as a good calabash; ua *hamo* ka ipu. See *Ana. Hon.* 10.

HA-MO, *adj.* Anointed; plastered; besmeared; ina hele ke kanaka me ke poo *hamo* palolo, if a man went with head *besmeared* with white clay; mea *hamo*, ointment, perfume.

HA-MO-U-LA, *s. Hamo*, rubbed over, and *ula*, red. A kind of kapa colored or stained red; similar to *kuaula*.

HA-MO-HA-MO, *v.* Freq. of *hamo.* To rub; to feel frequently; to touch; to rub the hand over a surface.

HA-MO-HA-MO, *s.* Name of an office executed by one of the servants of the king.

HA-MO-LE, *adj.* Rounded and smooth, as the edge of a board.

2. Small, as the eyes; he maka *hamole.*

HA-MU, *v.* To eat fragments of food; to eat the skin; to pick bones; to scrape up and eat what is left; e ai *hamu.*

HA-MU, *s.* The refuse of food.

HA-MU-I-LI, *s.* The class of persons about a chief; a distinct class of persons with superior privileges.

HA-MU-HA-MU, *v.* To crumble up into fragments.

2. To eat fragments. See HAMU.

HA-MU-MU, *s.* A low indistinct rumbling sound; an indistinct sound of conversation.

HA-MU-MU-MU, *v.* To talk in a low indistinct manner; to whisper. 2 *Sam.* 12:19. To talk in a low voice just above a whisper.

HA-NA, *v.* To do; to work; to cause; used in the most extensive sense; to act; to labor.

2. To make; to do a thing; to affect; to produce. *Rom.* 3:32. To perform a duty; to cause a thing; to build, as an edifice.

3. To form for a particular purpose.

4. To observe a ceremony; to keep a command. *Puk.* 12:47. PASS. To cause to be done, i. e., to become. *Puk.* 15:25.

5. To be or become warm. See this in the compounds HAHANA, MA or MEHANA, HANAHANA, and KOEHANA. NOTE.—*Hana* is qualified by other words; *hana* paa, to bind, imprison. *Luk.* 3:20. *Hana* is often used in a causative sense. *Oih.* 3:12. *Hana* hou, to proceed to do again, or something similar. *Oih.* 5:3. *Hana* make, to destroy; kill. *Rom.* 14:15. *Hana* kanawai, to keep a law. *Hana* is often causative of the following verb. *Isa.* 42:2. *Hana* ino, to do badly. *Hana* kumu ole, to do without

cause. *Hoo*. To cause or compete. *Ezek*. 14:23. To work; to afflict. *Puk*. 1:13. To refresh; to renew.

HA-NA, *s*. Work; labor; duty; office; calling; trade, &c.; *hana* mana, a miracle; *hana* a ka lani, the doing or the work of the chief.

HA-NA, *s*. Name of the white or wauki kapa.

HA-NA, *s*. Name of the middle post of a house; pou *hana*.

HA-NA-A-LE, *v*. To pester; to hector; to rally.

HA-NAE, *v*. To blunder in doing a thing; to labor at trifles.

HA-NAE, *s*. Vain labor; trifling effort; a blunder.

HA-NA-EA, *v*. See HANA. To do; to work; to make a thing.

HA-NAI, *v*. From *hana* and *ai*. To feed; to nourish, as the young.

2. To support, as those in need. 1 *Nal*. 18:4.

3. To feed, as a flock; to feed; to sustain, as a people. *Kanl*. 32:13.

4. To entertain, as strangers; e hookipa i na malahini; *hanai* waiu, to give suck; to suckle, as an infant. *Mat*. 19:24.

5. To act the part of a parent towards an orphan.

HA-NAI, *s*. One fed or sustained by another; a foster child; a ward.

HA-NAI, *adj*. Nourished; fed; applied to the receiver; a servant, &c. *Luk*. 1:54. FIG. Keiki *hanai*, a foster child.

2. Applied to the giver; as, makua *hanai*, a foster parent; he alii *hanai*, &c.

HA-NAI, *v*. To skim along the ground, as a bird.

HA-NAI, *s*. Name of the strings that surround a calabash.

2. Kite strings.

HA-NAI-A-HU-HU, *v*. Hanai, to feed, and *hu*, to swell out.

1. To feed or stuff with food, as a favorite hog or dog.

2. To make a pet of a hog so he will follow everywhere.

3. To feed, as a child or any young animal from birth; he keiki *hanaiahuhu* na'u.

4. To be fed or brought up by hand, as a cosset or any young animal. *Hoo*. The same; ua *hoohanaiahuhu* ka puaa i ka poi.

HA-NAI-A-HU-HU, *adj*. Full fed; plump; swelled out; puaa *hanaiahuhu*, a pet hog well fed.

HA-NA-I-LI, *s*. *Hana* and *ili*, the skin.

A tanner; a manufacturer of leather. *Oih*. 9:43.

HA-NAI-PU, *s*. The feeding of a god with the person who carried him; o ke kanaka nana e amo ke akua ia ia no e hanai aku ai, ua kapaia he *hanaipu*.

HA-NA-OI, *s*. *Hana* and *oi*, sharp. A general name for cutlery, as knives, &c.; such things as are sharp; a unuhi ae i ka *hanaoi*, then he drew out his knife.

HA-NAU, *v*. To come from or be separated, as a young animal from its mother; to be born.

2. More rarely used in an active sense to bear or bring forth, as a mother. *Kin*. 16:1. NOTE.—The translators of the Hawaiian Bible have used the word in the active sense for want of a better term, but Hawaiians seldom do; it mostly expresses the act of separation of the child from the mother; hence in a neuter or passive sense often, *there was born to* or *for* (such a one) so and so. *Kin*. 5:3, and throughout.

3. *Hoo*. To cause to be born, i. e., to beget, as a father.

4. To bring forth, as a mother. *Nah*. 11:12. *Hanau* ana, the being born, i. e., the birth. *Mat*. 1:18.

HA-NAU, *s*. Child-birth.

HA-NAU, *adv*. Hoo. Ka holoi *hoohanau* hou ana, the washing of regeneration. *Tit*. 3:5.

HA-NAU-A-NAU-A, *v*. To whisper. See HAWANAWANA.

HA-NAU-HO-PE, *s*. The second child in relation to the first, or the third in relation to the second, &c., even to the last, according to the connection.

HA-NAU-KA-HI, *s*. *Hanau*, born, and *kahi*, one. The one born, i. e., an only child of parents; the only born. *Sol*. 4:3.

HA-NAU-KA-MA, *adj*. *Hanau* and *kama*, a child. Child bearing; fruitful in children; epithet of a mother having borne many children.

HA-NAU-MUA, *s*. *Hanau* and *mua*, the first; the first born of parents.

1. The first child. See HIAPO and MAKAHIAPO.

2. FIG. Ka *hanaumua* o ka make, the first born of death. *Iob*. 18:3.

HA-NAU-NA, *s*. For *hanau ana*. Is used for relations in general. *Kin*. 47:1. Equivalent to *hoahanau*. See *Kin*. 47:3.

1. A circle of relations of the same family.

2. A succession, as of father, son, grandson, &c.

3. A generation, i. e., people living at the same time. *Kin.* 5:1.

HA-NAU-WA-LEA, See HANAWALEA.

HA-NAU-WA-HA-PAA. See HANAWAHAPAA.

HA-NA-HA-NA, *v.* To be severe; to be hard; to affect evilly; to afflict, as a famine. *Kin.* 47:13.

2. To be fatal; deadly, as sickness.

3. To be warm, as from violent exercise; to be warm, as by the sun or fire. NOTE.— This word is often used by foreigners as an intensive of *hana*, to do quickly or frequently, but Hawaiians never use it in this sense unless in imitation of foreigners. See HANA.

HA-NA-HA-NA, *adj.* Warm; heated, as with exercise or other ways. See HAHANA, MEHANA, &c. See the root HANA.

HA-NA-HA-NA, *adj.* Disagreeable to the smell; offensive; stinking; *hanahana ka ai awaawa.*

HA-NA-HA-NAI, *s.* See PALIPALI. A place near the top of a pali on the ascending side.

HA-NA-HA-NAU-NA, *s. Hana*, a reduplication, and *hanauna*, a generation. A relation; a kindred; relations by friendship.

HA-NA-HA-NAU-NA, *adj.* Cotemporary born; of the same age.

HA-NA-HE-MO, *v. Hana* and *hemo*, to loosen. To loosen; to let go; to untie.

HA-NA-HE-MO, *s.* A feeble state of health; state of weakness.

HA-NA-HI-O, *v. Hana* and *hio*, to lean over.

1. To cause to lean or push over from an upright position.

2. To stagger in walking; to go here and there.

HA-NA-HI-O, *s.* A staggering; a walking crookedly.

HA-NA-HI-HI-U, ⎱ *s. Hana*, a work, and
HA-NA-HI-KI-U, ⎰ *hihiu*, wild. A strange work; a miracle. NOTE.—The last form, *hanahikiu*, was found in a Hawaiian manuscript, but it may be a mistake for *hanahihiu*, therefore both are inserted.

HA-NA-HI-HI, *adj. Hana* and *hihi.* Wild; uncivil; untamed.

2. Branching, as a vine, &c.

HA-NA-HO-KAI, *v. Hana* and *hokai*, to waste. To behave foolishly; to behave carelessly; to act the spendthrift; to do mischief. See HOKAE.

HA-NA-KAI, *v. Hana* and *kai*; same as *hokai*. To erase; to blot out; better written *hanahae.*

HA-NA-MA-NA, *s. Hana* and *mana*, super-natural power. The words are often separated; as, *hana mana.*

1. Something done above or beyond human ability; a work of the gods; hence,

2. Used in the Bible for a miracle. NOTE. Hawaiians supposed there was a class of gods having superhuman power, and next to these were the highest chiefs who were reverenced as gods. Kamehameha was one.

HA-NA-MA-NU-EA, *v.* To blunder; to be careless; to be slow in movement.

HA-NA-NA, *adj.* Crooking inwardly; bending; flowing away.

HA-NA-NA, *v.* See HALANA, a change of *l* for *n.* To flow, as water; to overflow, as a stream its banks; to overflow land.

HA-NA-NAI, *v.* To be lofty; proud.

HA-NA-NAI, *s.* Loftiness; pride.

HA-NA-PAA, *v. Hana* and *paa*, fast; tight. To fasten; to make fast; to tighten. The full form is *hana a paa.*

HA-NA-PE-PE, *v. Hana* and *pepe*, broken fine.

1. To bruise greatly; to crush; to hurt severely. *Hal.* 44:19.

2. FIG. To be pained. *Ezek.* 6:9.

HA-NA-WAI, *v.* Aia *hanawai* kou makuahine. *Laieik.* 171. Twice SYN. with mai. *Ib.*

1. A euphemism for *kahe koko.*

2. To void urine.

HA-NA-PI-LO, ⎫ *adj. Hana* and *pilo*, pu-
HA-NO-PI-LO, ⎬ trid or bad smelling.
HA-NU-PI-LO, ⎭ Hoarse; speaking with a low hoarse voice, as with a cold or sore throat. See these words in their places.

HA-NA-WA-LE, *v. Hana* and *wale*, only.

1. To do for the sake of doing; to do something without reward, i. e., gratuitously.

2. To work without design as to the end.

3. To labor in vain.

4. To do or say a thing in sport.

HA-NA-WA-LE, *s.* A gratuitous work; a benefaction.

HA-NA-WA-HA-PAA, *s.* A boisterous, noisy person.

HA-NA-WA-HA-PAA, *adj.* Obstreperous; full of noise in talk.

HA-NA-WA-LEA, *v. Hana* and *walea*, satisfaction.

1. To live, act or do as one pleases.

2. To be satisfied with one's self or one's condition.

3. To be contented.

HA-NA-WA-LEA, *s.* Self satisfaction; contentment; quietness.

HA-NA-WA-NA-WA, *v.* Hawanawana by inversion of letters, which see. To whisper.

HA-NE, *s.* He nui ka *hane* ma kekahi alii; irregularity (perhaps) in living. See HANEHANE.

HA-NEA, *v.* To have no appetite.

2. To be indolent; inefficient; stupid.

HA-NEA, *s.* Having no appetite; loss of strength; indolence.

HA-NEE, *v.* *Ha* and *nee*, to slip; slide along.

1. To fall flat, as a decayed house; to flat down; to tumble down, as a stone wall.

2. To slip or slide down, as an avalanche; ua kapaia o Kaholo mahope o ka *hanee* ana o ka pali, it (the place) was called Kaholo (the moved) after the sliding down of the pali. See NEE.

HA-NEE-NEE, *v.* Intensive of the above. To hitch along; me he oopa la *haneenee* ae la ka nee, as a lame man *hitches along* his pace.

HA-NE-HA-NE, *v.* To cry; to wail, as the ghosts of the dead were supposed to do.

HA-NE-HA-NE, *s.* The wailing or crying of the spirits; hoopihaia i na leo wawalo o ka *hanehane*, me ka leo uwe; (the air) was filled with the voices of lamentation, and crying out and the sound of wailing.

HA-NE-NE, *v.* To blackguard; to use vulgar, filthy language.

HA-NE-NE, *s.* Low, vulgar, filthy language; blackguardism.

HA-NE-RE, *num. adj. Eng.* A hundred.

HA-NI, *v.* To step lightly; to walk softly.

2. To graze or just to touch in passing, as a canoe does a rock.

3. To pass quickly through the air with a humming noise.

HA-NI-U, *s.* *Ha*, but-end or stem of a leaf, and *niu*, cocoanut. The thick large heavy end of a cocoanut leaf used in beating the sides of kalo patches.

HA-NI-HA-NI, *v.* To make first or slight advances in tempting to adultery. *Hoo.* The same.

HA-NI-LE, *v.* To prepare for company; to receive company.

HA-NI-NA, *s.* A pau, an ancient woman's garment colored with olena or turmeric.

HA-NI-NA, *v.* See HOO and HANIHANI. No right; no portion; no part in a thing.

HA-NI-NI, *v.* See NINI and NININI. To overflow; to run out, as water from a vessel full of liquid; to spill.

2. To pour out, as water. 2 *Sam.* 14:14. To pour down, as a powerful rain. *Isa.* 45:8.

3. To be gone; to disappear. *Ier.* 49:7.

HA-NO, *s.* The asthma; a cough; a wheezing with the breath; a cough, a sig-nal or one's presence. *Laieik.* 146. Ia wa no kani aku la ka *hano*, then he emitted a cough. *Ib.*

2. A syringe for giving injections; a squirt-gun. See HAHANO.

HA-NO, *v.* To use, as a syringe; to inject.

HA-NO, **HA-NU,** *v.* To breathe naturally, as a well person. *Hoo.* The same.

HA-NO, **HA-NU,** *s.* The breath; the power of breathing. *Oih.* 17:25. The natural breath.

HA-NO, *adj.* Desolate; lonely, as a place uninhabited; silent; still.

HA-NO-A-LE-WA, *s.* A temple; a place for sacrifice.

2. The oven of the temple; he heiau, he luakini.

HA-NOU, *v.* *Hano*, to breath, and *u*, pain; grief; To pant; to breathe with difficulty.

HA-NOU, *s.* A hard or difficult breathing; the asthma.

HA-NO-HA-NO, **HA-NU-HA-NU,** *v.* To honor; to exalt; to triumph.

2. To be rich; to have the honor that wealth gives.

3. *Hoo.* To raise to honor, glory, &c.

4. To exercise authority or dominion. *Hal.* 91:15.

HA-NO-HA-NO, *s.* Glory; honor; pomp; splendor; excellency; especially such as arises from wealth.

2. Wealth; the privileges of wealth.

HA-NO-HA-NO, *adj.* Glorious; honored; grave; sober; dignified. 1 *Tim.* 3:4, 11. Also,

2. Proud; haughty.

HA-NO-NA, *v.* To drag a long fishing line towards shore; to lie along stretched out, as a long line.

HA-NO-NA-NO-NA, *s.* An artificial pond made, but in letting in the water it will not hold.

2. A kahawai that overflows with water but the rain stops and the stream is dry; he hanonono, he panonono.

HA-NO-NO-NO, *adj.* Cracked; full of holes; hakahaka, pukapuka.

HA-NO-PI-LO, *v.* To be hoarse; to speak in a deep-toned voice; to speak, as one without a palate. See HANAPILO.

HA-NO-PI-LO, *adj.* Hoarse; speaking with a deep-toned voice.

HA-NU, *v.* See HANO. To breathe; to emit air from the lungs. *Laieik.* 104.

2. To beat; to throb, as the pulse.

3. To act with energy.

4. To be so exceedingly angry that one cannot stand still, that he runs one way then another, ranting, scolding and threatening all that come in his way.

5. *Hoo.* To breathe furiously or angrily. *Puk.* 15:8.

HA-NU, *s.* The breathing; the natural breath.

2. Breath; spirit. FIG. 2 *Oihl.* 9:4. *Hanu wale,* mere existence without enjoyment; vanity. *Iob.* 7:16.

3. Breath, i. e., anything evanescent; vanity. *Hal.* 39:5, 11.

HA-NU, *adj.* Na mea *hanu,* the breathing things, i. e., people. *Ios.* 10:40.

HA-NUI, *s. Ha* and *nui,* great. The but-end of the stem of a cocoanut leaf.

HA-NUI, *s.* Name of a species of fish.

HA-NU-HA-NU, *v.* To smell; to smell, as a dog following the track of his master; e imi ma ka *hanuhanu* ana ka ka ilio e loaa ai ka hookapuhi.

HA-NU-NU, *v.* To bend over; to be stoop-shouldered. See OOHU.

HA-NU-NU, *adj.* Stooping; bending over, as a stoop-shouldered person.

HA-NU-PI-LO, *v.* See HANUPILO and HANAPILO.

HA-NU-A, *v.* To be low; level; plane; flat; to lie flat. See HONUA.

HA-NU-A, *adj.* Level; plane; flat.

HA-NUU, *s.* Stairs; steps for ascending; uneven places. See NUU.

HA-NUU, *adj.* Rising by steps; ala *hanuu. Puk.* 20:23.

HA-NUU-NUU, *v.* See HANUU. To ascend, as upon stairs; to go up stairs.

2. To lay one thing on the top of another.

3. To be uneven, as stairs; as protuberances on a plane.

HA-NUU-NUU, *s.* Stairs; steps, &c.

2. Uneven; irregular places on a plane. See HANUU and NUU.

3. Irregular flashes of flame; also,

4. Vibrations of sound.

HA-NUU-NUU, *adv.* Irregularly; not smooth; unequally; ina i ulaula *hanuunuu* ke ao, if the clouds be *unequally* red.

HA-NU-HA-NU, *s.* Name of a pastime among the ancient Hawaiians; kekahi lealea o ka *hanuhanu.*

HA-NU-NA-NU-NA, *s.* The rising of fumes from the stomach to the nose, as in drinking soda-water, or after eating highly fermented food, as new risen poi.

2. The hard breathing from the stoppage of the nose.

HA-NU-PA, *s. Ha* and *nupa,* deep mud. A deep muddy pit; a dark hole.

HA-NU-PAA, *s. Hanu* and *paa,* tight. A cold or catarrh.

HA-NU-PAU, *s. Hanu,* to breathe, and *pau,* to finish. The gasping of a dying person; the giving up of the spirit; he *hanupau* ka make.

HA-NU-PA-NU-PA, *v. Ha* and *nupa,* soft; muddy. To be muddy; soft; to find it difficult to walk from slipperiness. See HANUPA.

HA-NU-PA-NU-PA, *adj.* Slippery; muddy, as a road bad from deep mud; unsteady, as by walking in a bad road; allowing the feet to sink in, as a sandy or very dirty road.

HA-NU-PI-LO, *v.* See HANAPILO and HANOPILO.

HA-PA, *v.* To diminish; to make less; to decrease; to be partly done, as a job of work.

HA-PA, *s.* An indefinite part of a thing; a few; a small part.

HA-PAI, *v.* To lift up; to elevate; to take up; to carry.

2. To raise the hands, as in taking an oath. *Kin.* 14:22.

3. To honor; to praise; to exalt for past deeds; to recompense. *Eset.* 6:6.

4. With *pu,* to assist one in his business; to act together.

5. To take up, that is, commence, as a speech. *Nah.* 23:7.

6. To conceive, as a female; to become pregnant. *Oihk.* 12:2. *Hoo.* To conceive. FIG. *Nah.* 11:12.

HA-PAI, *adj.* Having conceived; pregnant, as a female; kou *hapai* ana, thy conception. *Kin.* 3:16. *Hapai* ana, the conception (of females.)

HA-PAI-A-NA, *s.* See HAPAI above.

HA-PAU-EA, *s. Ha,* breath, *pau,* all, and *ea,* life.

1. Short breath; applied to invalids and aged persons.

2. Weakness; feebleness.

HA-PA-U-MI, *s. Hapa,* part, and *umi,* ten. A tenth part; a tenth. *Kin.* 14:20. NOTE.—This word has been used erroneously by Hawaiians to mean a small coin, six and a quarter cents, which is not a *hapaumi* of any known coin; *hapaumi* is ten cents, or one-tenth of a dollar; *hapawalu* is one-eighth of a dollar, or twelve and a half cents; *hapaha* is one-fourth of a dollar, and *hapalua* is one-half of a dollar.

HA-PAU-PAU, *adj.* Besmeared; dirty;

obscured, as glass, furniture, &c.; ua *hapaupau* ke aniani, ua *hapaupau* ka papa, e holoi ae.

HA-PA-HA, *s.* *Hapa*, part, and *ha*, four. A fourth part of a thing. *Nah.* 23:10. A quarter; *specifically*, the sum of twenty-five cents, or a quarter of a dollar.

HA-PA-HA-PAI, *v.* See HAPAI and HOO-LEILEI. To lift or toss up, as a child.

HA-PA-KO-LU, *s.* *Hapa* and *kolu*, three. A third part of a thing.

HA-PA-KU-E, *v.* To be twisted in the legs and feet; to be deformed; to be crippled.

2. To stammer or be slow in speech, as an aged person; ma ka olelo a na elemakule, ua lohi ke kamailio ana, *hapakue* ka waha i ka olelo.

HA-PA-KU-E, *adj.* Crooked; deformed; crippled.

2. Stammering; hesitating in speech.

HA-PA-KU-I, *v.* To stammer. See HAPAKUE.

HA-PA-LA, *v.* See PALA. To defile externally; to disfigure; to besmear.

2. To daub; to paint; to plaster with lime. *Kanl.* 27:2.

3. FIG. To be satiated, i. e., stained, as with blood. *Isa.* 34:6.

4. To be soft, as kalo killed with cold or drought; ua *hapala* ke kalo, ua pala ke kumu.

HA-PA-LE, *s.* A shovel or trowel.

HA-PA-LI-MA, *s.* *Hapa*, part, and *lima*, five. One-fifth; a fifth part of a thing. *Kin.* 41:34.

HA-PA-LU-A, *s.* *Hapa*, part, and *lua*, two. One-half; a half part. *Puk.* 24:6. This word is used specifically for half a dollar as *hapaha* is for twenty-five cents.

HA-PA-PA, *s.* A stratum of rock covered with thin earth; a stony place.

2. Earth covered with stones.

HA-PA-PA, *adj.* Shallow, as earth above the rock; shallow; not deeply planted, as seed; o kahi *hapapa* i ulu ole a mae koke.

HA-PA-PA-PA, *s.* and *adj.* Very shallow, &c. See above.

HA-PA-WA-LE, *s.* *Hapa* and *wale*, only. Only a part; a few; a small portion.

HA-PA-WA-LU, *s.* *Hapa* and *walu*, eight. The eighth; the eighth part of a thing; *specifically*, the sum of twelve and a half cents.

HA-PE, *adj.* Wrong; incorrect.

HA-POU, *s.* Name of a soft porous kind of stones.

HA-PO-PO, *adj.* Dim-sighted; almost blind; blear eyed, as one who cannot see clearly; *hapopo* ka maka.

HA-POU-POU, *adj.* Blurred; darkened or whitened over, as the eye; e like me poaeae; *hapoupou* ka maka. See HAPOPO.

HA-PU, *s.* Name of a vegetable eaten in time of famine.

HA-PU-EE, *s.* Name of a species of fish.

HA-PUU, *v.* To be many; to be multitudinous; to abound in plenty; thick together.

HA-PUU, *adj.* Many; abounding; plenteous.

HA-PUU, *s.* Name of a species of large fern; the root is eatable in time of famine. See KAHAPUU.

2. Name of a species of fish.

HA-PUU-PUU, *v.* To be undecided as to what one has said; to be not plain as to the meaning of something said; ua *hapuupuu* kana olelo, aole akaka; ke *hapuupuu* nei ka manao, mahope paha akaka.

HA-PUU-PUU, *adj.* See HAPUU, many. To be numerous; *hapuupuu* ke lelo o Hilo i ka ua.

HA-PUU-PUU, *s.* Name of a species of fish. See HAPUU.

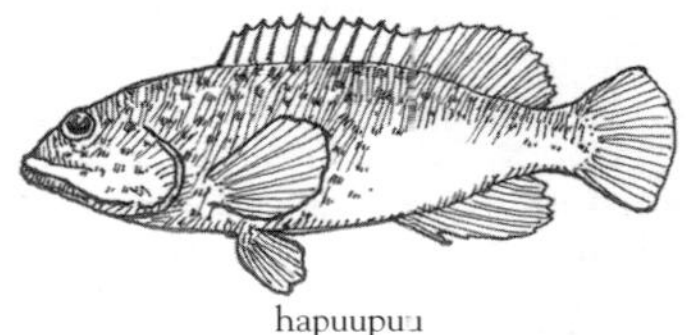

HA-PU-KA-O-HI-O-HI, *v.* To speak foolishly; to talk nonsense; ma ka *hapukaohiohi* ana paha a ka waha me ka poe Kauai la.

HA-PU-KA-O-HI-O-HI, *s.* Foolish, nonsensical talk.

HA-PU-KA, } *v.* To gather up everything;
HA-PU-KU, } to collect together indiscriminately good and bad; to scrape together.

2. To be crowded together, as thoughts in the mind; pilikia iho la oloko, *hapuku*, *hapuku* mai la ka manao ana.

HA-PU-NA, *s.* A dirty puddle of water. See KIO, HALOKOWAI, &c.

HA-WA, *v.* To be daubed with excrements; to be defiled; to be in a pitiable state.

HA-WAE, *s.* The white sea-egg.

HA-WAE-KAI-NUI, *adj.* Awkward, as in diving and spattering the water much; *hawaekainui* ke kanaka i ka luu.

HA-WAE-WAE, *s.* A species of small lobster.

HA-WAI, *v.* To pour water on an oven when heated to generate steam.

HA-WAI, *v.* To pour or dash water on to

an oven to increase the steam; i hale pa-lima, hale *hawai* ma ka la hookahi.

HA-WAI, *adj.* Pertaining to the place or business of steaming food in an oven.

HA-WAI, *s.* A pipe for conveying water; a lead pipe, hose, &c.

HA-WAI-I, *s.* Name of the largest island of the Hawaiian group, and gives name to the group. From time immemorial the people have called themselves "ko Hawaii," and the islands "ka pae aina o Hawaii," "na moku Hawaii," &c.

HA-WAI-I-A-KEA, *s.* Broad or large Hawaii; i kane na ke kaikamahine alii o *Hawaiiakea. Laieik.* 168.

HA-WA-HA-WA, *adj.* Filthy; dirty; especially with such dirt as sticks to one. See HAWA.

HA-WA-LE, *s.* Lying; deceitful; no confidence in.

HA-WA-LI,
HA-WA-LI-WA-LI, } *s.* A place where vegetation grows around a salt pond.

2. A kind of slimy, sticky fish.

HA-WA-NA, *v.* To whisper; to speak in the ear; to speak in a low voice.

HA-WA-NA-WA-NA, *v.* To whisper, &c. See HAWANA. A huki iho la ia ia, e *hawanawana* i kona pepeiao, he pulled him towards him to *whisper* in his ear; to consult against one. *Hal.* 41:7.

HA-WA-NA-WA-NA, *s.* Whispering; low talk in the ear; soft conversation.

HA-WA-NE, *s.* The name of the palm cocoanut.

2. The fruit of the tree otherwise called *loulu*; the fruit is eatable; its leaf made into hats.

HA-WA-WA, *v.* See HAWA. To be awkward; foolish; ignorant; not to know how to do things.

HA-WA-WA, *s.* Awkwardness; ignorance; without skill or energy to obtain it.

HA-WA-WA, *adj.* Awkward; unapt; unskillful; ignorant; rude; weak in knowledge. *Rom.* 1:21. Mea *hawawa*, a silly person. *Iob.* 5:2.

HA-WE-LE, *v.* To lengthen; to lengthen by tying on a piece; e loloa ae; hence,

2. To tie or lash on with a cord or string.

3. To bind or secure by tying; to fasten by tying.

4. To bind on, as shoes or sandals. *Ios.* 9:5. To tie or fasten on, as a sword. 1 *Sam.* 25:13. As the cover of a vessel. *Nah.* 19:15. As armor generally. *Kanl.* 1:45.

5. To shoe; to put on shoes. *Epes.* 6:15.

HA-WE-LE, *s.* A tying on; a binding on.

HA-WE-NA, *s.* A substance similar to chalk; chalk.

2. Hoariness; the whitishness of gray hair; a hoary or gray head; hapala ia i ka *hawena*, daubed with whitishness.

3. Applied to a gray headed man who has but little wisdom.

HA-WE-WE, *v.* To make a monotonous rustling sound, as one moving his feet, drumming with his fingers, &c.; nehe, neneke. See UE and UEUE.

HA-WE-WE, *s.* A rustling indistinct sound; a slight rumbling sound.

HA-DA-SA, *s.* H*eb.* The myrtle tree. *Isa.* 41:19.

HA-DA-SA, *adj.* Lala *hadasa*, myrtle branches. *Neh.* 8:15.

HA-RE, *s. Eng.* Name of an unclean animal; a hare. *Oihk.* 11:6.

HE, *art.* The indefinite article, answering somewhat to English *a* or *an*. For its various uses, see *Gram.* § 66, 111, Rule 6th, Syntax, &c.

HE, *s.* A grave; a place where one person is buried. *Kin.* 35:20. A sepulchre; he lua kupapau.

2. A dividing line or boundary between lands.

HE, *s.* Name of the little worm that eats the leaves of the cocoanut and the palm leaf pandanus.

HE, *s.* Name of a weapon used in war; hawane, he laau hanaia i *he* kaua.

HE, *v.* To roar, as a strong wind, such as roars down the ravines; he leo o ka makani kauaula ka'u i *he* iho nei, ke nee nei i na kahawai.

HE-A, *v.* To call; to give an appelation. SYN. with kapa. *Ioan.* 13:13. To call to one; to call one.

2. To choose; to appoint.

3. To sing or recite a mele; ina ku ke kanaka i ka *hea* mele ana, if any man stand up for *reciting* a mele. See KAHEA.

HE-A, *s.* A call; a calling out; a cry.

HE-A, *adv. int.* Which? what? when? where? referring to place, *where*; ka hale *hea*? what or which house? ka manawa *hea*? when? what time? &c.; it is declined like a noun. See *Gram.* § 160 and 165. It takes also other prefixes; as, *auhea? pehea?* &c.

HE-A, *v.* To eat up entirely; to leave nothing uneaten. NOTE.—This was applied to the last hog that was sacrificed on the eighth day at the dedication of a heiau. The hog itself was called *puaa hea*, as it was to be entirely eaten up. Should any person refuse to eat of it on this occasion, he would be immediately sacrificed; or if any part of the hog should be left after all had eaten, they would all die by some dreadful judgment.

HE-A, *v.* To be red or sore, as inflamed eyes; to be stained or colored red.

HE-A, *s.* Sore eyes; inflamed eyes.

HE-A, *adj.* He ua *hea.* See UA, *s.* A cold rain. See KONAHEA, cold rain. See KONA.

HE-A. Used as a suffix to various words, as paapu*hea,* meaning perhaps heavy or smoky.

HE-AU, *s.* Name of the place where fishermen set the basket in catching fish; the place was artificially built; alaila kukulu hou i mau *heau*—ma ka hema o ka mokupuni, me ke kukulu *heau* no.

HE-A-HA, *adv. int. He* and *aha.* LIT. A what? what? why?

HE-A-HA, *v.* To what; to ask what; *heaha* mai la kekahi, *heaha* ia? a certain person whatted (asked what) is it? *Gram.* § 37. See AHA.

HE-A-HE-A, *v.* See HEA. To call; to call frequently; to call out; to call for help with earnestness.

HEA-HEA, *v.* See HEA, *v.*, to be red. To imprint with spots; to stain, especially with red colors; to be smeared, as with red dirt.

HEA-HEA-IA, *s.* A calling; a voice of calling; aole nae i loaa ka *heaheaia* mai. *Laieik.* 91.

HEA-HEA-HEA, *adj.* See HEAHEA. Warm, &c.; bald.

HE-A-HI-O, *adj.* Lazy; loitering behind.

HE-A-NA, *s.* The dead body or corpse of one or more slain in battle. *Kanl.* 28:26. A carcass of any dead animal. *Mat.* 24:28. See HE, a grave.

HEE, *v.* To melt; to change from a solid to a liquid substance; to run, as a liquid; to flow, as blood or water.

2. To slip or glide along; to melt away; to play on the surf-board. *Laieik.* 91. See HEENALU.

3. To flee through fear; ke kaua ana, o ka poe i *hee,* makau lakou; to flee; to be dispersed in battle. *Kin.* 14:10.

4. To melt; applied FIG. to the heart; to be fearful; cowardly. *Kanl.* 20:8.

5. To be disappointed. *Isa.* 28:16. To dip up and pour out water; to skim off the scum, as cream, &c. See AUHEE.

6. *Imperatively, hee* aku paha, be off; go about your business; contraction perhaps for *hele.*

HEE, *s.* A flowing, as of blood or other liquid.

2. A flight, as of a routed army.

3. A bloody issue, catamenia; he *hee* koko ka wahine; *heeholua,* to slide on the holua, a pastime among the ancients; *heenalu,* a playing on the surf-board.

HEE, *s.* The squid, from his slippery qualities.

2. The rope that supports the mast; a stay.

HE-E-HE, *v.* To bleat, as a goat.

HEE-HEE, *v.* The 13th conj. of *hee.* To flow or melt away; to disappear; to become liquid; to flee in battle; to dip up water with a cup. *Hoa.* To melt away, as an army; hence, to flee; to run.

2. A word used in enforcing the highest kapus.

HEE-HEE, *s.* A boil; a sore emitting matter. See HEHE. Root *hee.*

2. An avalanche or pali slidden down; earth or dirt fallen down from a steep side hill.

HE-E-HI-A, *v.* To be filled with awe; to tremble with fear. See EEHIA.

HEE-HO-LU-A, *v. Hee* and *holua,* a machine something like a sled upon which the ancients slid down hill; a pastime among the ancient Hawaiians. See HOLUA.

HEE-KEE, *s.* Name of a species of fish.

HEE-KO-KO, *s. Hee* and *koko,* blood. A flowing of blood; any great flow of blood; *specifically,* the catamenia. *Oihk.* 15:25.

HEE-MA-KO-KO, *s.* Name of a species of large squid found in the ocean, not eatable; he hee nui loa ia ma ka moana, he mea ai ole ia.

HEE-MA-KO-LE, *s.* Squid that has been cured with salt, and is red.

HEE-NA-LU, *v. Hee* and *nalu,* the surf. To slide down the surf; to play on the surf-board. See below.

HEE-NA-LU, *s. Hee* and *nalu,* the surf. A playing on the surf, a pastime among the ancients; the name of their play on the surf.

HEE-NE-HU, *s.* The name of a species of small fish; he uahuki *heenehu* na ka lawaia.

HEE-PU-LOA, *s.* A fish of the squid genus.

HEE-WA-LE, *v. Hee* and *wale,* only. To melt easily; to flee, as a coward in time of danger.

HEI, *s.* A net; a snare for entangling

and taking an animal; applied to men. *Sol.* 29:5.

2. A draught of fish. *Luke* 5:4.

3. Game caught in hunting.

4. A cat's cradle. *Bal.*

HEI, *v.* To entangle, as in a net. *Habak.* 1:15.

2. FIG. To be insnared or entangled with difficulty. 1 *Tim.* 3:7.

3. To catch and entangle one by the neck or legs; i mea e *hei* ai ka a-i, ka wawae paha.

4. *Hoo.* To catch in a net. FIG. *Luke* 5:10. To entrap, entangle, &c.; ua makau au i ka mea kii mai ia'u e *hoohei* aku, I am afraid of him who shall come to *entrap* me.

HEI, *s.* The form of hanging greens about the house of the gods to render the sacrifices acceptable; i mea e hoohiwahiwa aku.

2. A wreath of green leaves. FIG. An ornament; o ke akamai o ka makuakane, e lilo no ia i *hei* na ke keiki, the wisdom of the father, it shall become a *wreath* for the child.

HEI, *s.* The name of the pawpaw tree; also called *mili.*

2. Also the name of the fruit.

HEI-AU, *s.* A small secret room in the large temple.

2. A large temple of idolatry among Hawaiians; a temple for the worship of one or more of the gods; e kukulu oe i mau *heiau* no na akua, no Ku, no Lono, no Kane ame Kanaloa, build thou some *temples* for the gods, for Ku, for Lono, for Kane and Kanaloa.

3. The *heiau* was one of the six houses of every man's regular establishment—the house for the god; eono hale o na kanaka, he *heiau*, oia kekahi, men had six houses, the *heiau* (temple) was one.

4. In the Bible, a high place of worship. 2 *Nal.* 12:14; *Isa.* 15:2.

HEI-E, *s.* A servant to a prophet who reported his declarations.

HEI-HEI, *v.* To run, as in a race; to run a race. *Hal.* 19:5.

HEI-HEI-HO-LU-A, *s.* A race with the hoolua; a sliding down hill on a hoolua.

HEI-HEI-NA-LU, *s. Hehei* and *nalu*, surf. A riding the surf in the way of a race between two or more persons; an ancient pastime.

HEI-HEI-WAA, *s.* A race between two or more canoes; practiced much in former times.

HE-O, *adj.* Proud; haughty; used mostly with the causative *haa.* See HAAHEO

and HOOHEO.

HE-O, *s.* The semen masculinum; e olu ka puu, i olu ka *heo?*

HE-O, } *v.* To be in haste, as an assem-
HE-OO, } bly to disperse.

2. To be in haste to go, as one afraid or not welcome.

3. To be in doubt what way to go.

HE-O-HE-O, *s.* The glans penis; applied to men and to some animals; within the prepuce; loaa ka *heoheo.*

HE-U, *s.* Down or fine hair.

2. A youngster; a young man, from his down or first beard; kuu kane o ka wa *heu* ole, my husband from the time of *youth* (without a beard.) *Laieik.* 204.

3. The quicksilver on the back of a looking-glass; holoi lakou i ka *heu* o ka aniani, they washed off the quicksilver of the glass.

4. The work first done, the speech first made, the first movement in an affair.

HE-U, *v.* To begin to grow, as the beard; he kanaka opiopio wale no, akahi no a *heu.*

HE-U, *adj.* The first shooting of beards in boys; he keiki *heu*, a child bearded.

HE'U, } *v.* With a sharp break in
HE'U-HE'U, } pronouncing, to sing, as birds; to sound, as the voice of birds; to sound, as the voice of spirits with sweet sounds.

HE-U-HE-U, *v.* See HEU above.

HE-U-KAE, *v.* To split, as a cane.

2. To treat one badly; to use harshly.

3. To act the villain. See HAUKAE.

HE-U-MI-KI, *adj.* Good.

HE-HA, *adj.* Lazy; indolent; slow in work; opu *heha. Tit.* 1:12. Translated *slow bellies.* SYN. with ulana. Molowa i ka hana, manaka.

HE-HE, *v.* See HEE. To run or flow out, as an ulcer or the contents of a boil.

2. *Hoo.* To melt or cause to become liquid, as metals by heat. See HEEHEE.

HE-HE, *v.* To laugh; to mock; to deride.

HE-HE, *s.* A swelling ulcerated on the skin.

HE-HE, *s.* The upper calabash of a drum.

HE-HE, *adj.* Ulcerous; belonging to a boil; mai *hehe. Kanl.* 28:27.

2. Molten; that which has been cast.

HE-HEE, *v.* To melt, as metals; to liquefy any solid substance. 1 *Pet.* 3:12.

2. FIG. To soften, as the heart; to make fearful. *Puk.* 15:15.

3. *Hoo.* To melt and cast into any figure. *Puk.* 25:12. To cause to be soft; unstable; e lewa.

4. To flow; to run, as a liquid metal; he pohaku i *hoohehee* wale ia no. See HEE.

HE-HEE, *s.* With *mai*, a running sore. *Oihk.* 13:18.

HE-HEE, *adj.* *Hoo.* Liquid; thin; flowing; melting. *Sol.* 17:3.

HE-HE-HEE, *v.* See *Gram.* § 225. A poetical form of the verb *hee*, to flow away, i. e., to fade, as the colors of calico; *hehehee* i ka wai, to fade by washing.

HE-HEI, *v.* See HEI. To entangle in a net, as fish or birds in a snare.

HE-HE-O, *v.* E peeaniki, e koheo, e pueo. *Kamak.*

HE-HE-LO, *v.* To be like the helo or ohelo, a reddish brown; hence,

2. To be good looking; grand; proud.

HE-HE-NA, *v.* To be mad; crazy; insane. *Ier.* 25:16.

HE-HE-NA, *s.* A madness. *Kanl.* 28:28.

2. A mad person; hana iho la e like me na *hehena* ame na holoholona, they acted like *madmen* and brutes. 2 *Nal.* 9:11. See EHENA.

HE-HE-NA, *adj.* Insane; crazy; delirious; raving mad. 1 *Sam.* 21:13, 14.

HE-HI, *v.* To tread upon. *Kanl.* 1:36. To trample down. See EHI. With *kapuai.* *Kanl.* 11:24.

2. To put the foot upon, a symbol of subjection. *Ios.* 10:24.

3. To trample upon, i. e., disobey or disregard, as a law; *hehi* na mea a pau maluna o ke kanawai o ka aina, everybody *trampled upon* the law of the land; *hehi* berita, to trample upon or disregard a covenant. *Lunk.* 2:20.

4. To loathe, as a full person his food. *Sol.* 27:7.

HE-HI, *s.* A treading; a place for treading; kahi *hehi* palaoa, a thrashing floor where grain was trodden out. *Nah.* 15:20.

HE-HO, *s.* A cob; a corn cob.

HE-HU, *v.* To pull up by the roots; to root up. 1 *Nal.* 14:15.

2. FIG. To root out, as a people; malia paha i *hehuia* makou i poe nana e kuhikuhi i na iwi o ka poe kahiko, perhaps we shall be *rooted up* as those who shall point to the bones (land-marks) of the ancients.

3. To pull up for transplanting; to transplant.

4. To carry manure for the good of a transplanted tree.

HE-HU, *v.* To summon to work or to war; to warn out.

HE-HU, *s.* A tree pulled up for transplantation.

2. Mist; steam; vapor; spray from the sea. See EHU and HEHUKAI.

3. Name of a medicine.

HE-HU-KAI, *s.* See EHU. *Hehu* and *kai*, the sea. The spray of the sea.

HE-HU-NA-KAI, *s.* *He* and *huna*, small particle and *kai*, sea. The spray of the sea.

HE-KA, **HE-KA-HE-KA,** } *adj.* Sore; red, as inflamed eyes; eyelids turned out by inflammation.

HE-KAU, *v.* To tie with a rope.

2. To make fast, as in anchoring a boat or cask, by tying to stones or rocks under water. *Laieik.* 124. Aole e lilo, ua *hekauia.*

HE-KAU, *s.* A large strong rope for fastening boats, canoes, &c.

HE-KAU, *adj.* Epithet of a large strong rope; he kaula *hekau*; strong; firm.

HE-KE, *s.* A nail or pin to hang things on.

2. One thing up over another; a sail drawn up over another sail.

HE-KE, *adj.* Fallen, as the countenance with shame.

2. Faded; wilted, as a plant.

3. Angry; cross; reluctant.

HE-KE-HE-KE, *adj.* Weak; faint; destitute of energy.

HE-KE-KE, *adj.* Hakeke, leilei, pokole.

HE-KI-LI, *s.* Art. ke. *Puk.* 9:33; *Puk.* 20:15. Thunder; a voice from the clouds.

2. Anything terrible, raging, terrific; uhi paapu mai la oia i na *hekili* o ke kuko ino. *Laieik.* 196.

HE-KI-LI, *v.* To thunder. *Hal.* 29:3. *Hoo.* To cause to thunder. 2 *Sam.* 22:14.

HE-KU-NI, *s.* A steward.

HE-KU-PAU, *s.* *He*, a grave, and *kupapau*, a dead body. A grave; a place for depositing a corpse. *Nah.* 19:16.

HE-LA, **HE-LA-HE-LA,** } *adj.* Redness of the corner of the eye; partial blindness; o ka paholehole o ka ili, *helahela* ino ka poe i hana pela.

HE-LE, *v.* To move in any way to a large or small minute distance; the quality of the motion is expressed by other words.

2. To walk; to go; to move.

3. To act; to exhibit moral conduct. 1 *Kor.* 3:3.

4. To stretch, as a string or rope.

5. *Hoo.* To cause one to go or pass on. *Ezek.* 16:21. To desire or pretend to go on; to depart; aole nae e pono ia laua e *hoohele* wale i na pohaku *hoohele*; *hele* kue, to go against, as an enemy. *Lunk.* 1:10. *Hele* wale, to be or to walk about naked. See

HELEWALE. *Hele* e, to go before; ke *hele* aku nei ke keiki, the child grows, i. e., increases in stature; *hele* liilii, helelei, to scatter; to separate. See the compounds.

HE-LE, *s.* A noose; a snare for catching birds. See PAHELE.

2. A going; a passing on; a journey; a course.

HE-LE-A, *v.* To put a noose around the head of a shark; i *helea* ka o kai o ka lani.

HE-LEI, *adj.* Inflamed; opened, as the eye, so as to turn the lid out; he maka *helei*, an inflamed eye.

HE-LEI, *v.* To open or spread open, as the legs; to straddle. See KUHELEI. A specific word, and rather indelicate.

2. To say *no* by a signal, that is, by pulling down one corner of the eye slily.

HE-LE-U, *s.* A vulgar word for the welu used in wiping the fundament.

HE-LE-U-MA, *s.* *Hele*, to move, and *uma*, to grasp.

1. The stone anciently used as an anchor to hold a canoe.

2. In modern times, an anchor of a vessel; aole i kuu ka *heleuma* o ka moku, the *anchor* of the ship was not let down. FIG. *Heb.* 6:19.

HE-LE-HE-LE, *v.* See HELE. To go through; hence, to cut up; to divide asunder, as with a knife or shears. See MAHELE.

HE-LE-HE-LE-NA, *s.* The external appearance of a person, his form, contour; especially the face of a person. *Iak.* 1:23. With *maka*, the appearance of the face. *Dan.* 10:6. *Helehelena* o ka poino, *face* of sadness. *Laieik.* 142.

HE-LE-HO-NU-A, *v.* *Hele* and *honua*, preceding; going before. To precede; to go before; to do previously.

HE-LE-HO-NU-A, *v.* *Hele*, a noose or snare, and *honua*, *adv.* To tie; to bind; to entangle; to catch in a snare or net.

HE-LE-KI-KA-HA, *v.* *Hele* and *kikaha*.

1. To act in ignorance of what is doing; to walk in obscurity.

2. To wander a long way off; a proverbial expression, mai noho a *helekikaha* aku, act not without object. See KIKAHA.

HE-LE-KI-KI, *v.* *Hele* and *kiki*. See KIKI. To act hastily; to do quickly; to go in a hurry.

HE-LE-LEI, *v.* *Hele* and *lei*, to throw away.

1. To scatter, as any small articles; to spill, as water.

2. To distill, as dew, i. e., to fall upon one, as music or a speech. *Kanl.* 32:2.

3. To slaver with one's spittle. 1 *Sam.* 21:13.

4. To scatter, i. e., to fall, as seed sown. *Mat.* 13:4. *Hoo.* To cast or throw away, &c.

HE-LE-LEI, *adj.* Scattered; drooping or falling, as tears; halawai oia me kana keiki me ka waimaka *helelei*, she met with her son with *flowing* tears.

2. Broken or crumbled, so as to separate. *Ios.* 9:12. Crumbling, as dirt; he lepo *helelei*.

HE-LE-PE-LA, *v. imperat.* *Hele* and *pela*, thus; so.

1. Be gone; be off; get out; go just as you are; often more full; thus, *e hele loa pela*, get you gone clear away.

2. *Hoo.* To cast out; to throw away; to drive off.

HE-LE-WA-LE, *v.* *Hele* and *wale*, in the condition one is in naturally. See WALE.

1. To go about destitute of clothing; to be naked.

2. To be poor; destitute of comforts. See ILIHUNE.

3. To go or be anywhere without any fixed purpose; *helewale* mai nei au, I happened to come along here. NOTE.—The words are often written separately.

HE-LI-U, *v.* To face about; a military term. See HALIU.

HE-LO, *s.* Name of a species of whortleberry, of a reddish brown color; generally written *ohelo*; hence

HE-LO-HE-LO, *adj.* Red as the ohelo berry; reddish brown.

HE-LO-HE-LO, *v.* To be red like the ohelo.

HE-LU, *v.* To scratch the earth, as a hen; to dig potatoes with the fingers; to paw the ground, as an angry bull.

2. To count; to number; to compute; to reckon up the sum of numbers. *Puk.* 30:12.

3. To reckon in favor of one or against him; to impute. *Oihk.* 7:18.

4. To tell; to relate; to recount some past transaction. 2 *Nal.* 8:4.

HE-LU, *s.* The seeds of the puakala.

2. Shot used in shooting birds.

HE-LU, *adv.* Reciting or proclaiming the virtues of a deceased person; alaila, uwe *helu* mai la ia, penei, a uwe *helu* iho la. *Laieik.* 50.

HE-LU-AI, *s.* The office of a person engaged in the play of kilu; a lalau mai ka *heluai* i ke kilu.

HE-LU-IA, *adj.* Pass. of *helu*. That which is counted or reckoned in. *Nah.* 7:2.

HE-LU-IA'NA, *s.* See HELU. *Heluia* and

ana, a number; a numbering. The being numbered. 1 *Oihl.* 27:1.

HE-LU-HE-LU, *v.* To read; to con over and over; to read in or from a book.

2. To recount; to make mention of some past transaction. 2 *Nal.* 23:2.

HE-LU-NA, *s.* *Helu* and *ana.* Gram. § 34.

1. A numbering, counting, &c.; hence,

2. A number, i. e., the result of counting. *Hoik.* 13:18. Ua like ka *heluna* o kona mau niho me ko ka lio, the *number* of his teeth is like that of a horse.

HE-LU-HO-I-KE, *s.* *Helu* and *hoike*, to show. An arithmeticon, a frame with strings of counters, used as an aid in solving questions in arithmetic; a modern word.

HE-MA, *adj.* Left; applied to two opposite things; as, lima *hema*, the *left* hand, in distinction from lima *akau*, the *right* hand; welau *hema* (in *geography*), the *south* pole; opposed to welau akau, the *north* pole; kanaka lima *hema*, a left-handed man. *Lunk.* 3:15. NOTE.—In marking the cardinal points of the compass, a Hawaiian will place himself back to the east and his face to the west; hence, his right indicates the north and his left the south.

HE-MA-HE-MA, *adj.* See HEMA. Left-handed; hence,

2. Awkward, as a left-handed man; unskillful; inexpert.

3. *Hoo.* Dull of apprehension; ignorant. *Rom.* 1:31.

4. Wanting; lacking; destitute. *Oihk.* 22:23.

HE-MA-HE-MA, *v.* See HEMA. To be destitute of; to want. *Kanl.* 15:8. I makaukau ko oukou hoi ana, aole e *hemahema*, that you may be supplied on your return and not be *destitute*.

2. *Hoo.* To make destitute; to deprive of; pehea kakou e *hoohemahema* nei i ko kakou ola? how are we *depriving* ourselves of our living?

HE-MA-HE-MA, *s.* Want; need; necessity.

HE-MO, *v.* To loosen; to untie, as a rope; to cast off.

2. To come out; move away; depart; to turn off, as a tenant; to dispossess of one's land.

3. To loosen, i. e., to sail, as a vessel; to set sail.

4. To break loose from a restraint or confinement; to break over a boundary. *Puk.* 19:21.

5. To break off a habit; to wean, as a child; i *hemo* ke keiki i ka waiu, let the child be *broken off* from the milk, i. e., weaned.

6. *Hoo.* To loosen, &c.; to put away, i. e., divorce, as married persons; he wahine i *hoohemoia.* See OKI and HOOKI.

HE-MO, *s.* A loosening; a separation of things once united; ua like ka *hemo* me ka makili.

HE-MO, *adj.* Loose; separating.

HE-MO-E, *adj.* *Hemo* and *e*, strangely, i. e., very much. Faint; hungry; gasping; near dissolution of soul and body; dying; *hemoe* ke aho, the breath is *very loose.* See E, *adj.*

HE-MO-HE-MO, *v.* Freq. of *hemo*. To loosen often or very much.

2. To be weak from fear; to be unfastened.

3. *Hoo.* To take away; to separate; to take off. *Puk.* 14:25.

HE-MO-HE-MO, *s.* A separating; a going off; a loosening.

HE-MO-LE-A-LE-A, *v.* *Hemo* and *lea*, joy; cheerfulness. To consent cheerfully to one's going for, or doing a thing; to bid him God speed; ka ae pono ia aku; ka hele ana aku me ka pono.

HE-MO-LE-LE, *v.* *Hemo*, to loosen, and *lele*, to jump or fly off; to be separate from some other thing; hence,

1. In a *natural sense* (the defect of a thing is spposed to have been separated), to be complete; perfect; fully finished.

2. In a *moral sense*, to break or separate from what is wrong or evil. *Kanl.* 26:19. In this passage the *lele* is evidently used as the intensive of *hemo*, i. e., to be entirely separated. *Oihk.* 19:2.

3. To be perfect; lacking nothing; completed, as a work. 1 *Ioan.* 2:5. Also in a moral sense. *Kol.* 4:12.

4. To be perfect in moral rectitude. 1 *Nal.* 8:61. To be holy; perfect. 1 *Pet.* 1:15.

5. *Hoo.* To perfect; to finish. *Ezek.* 27:4.

HE-MO-LE-LE, *s.* The perfection of a thing.

2. Virtue; holiness. *Oih.* 3:12. A separation from what is evil; goodness; a state of glory.

HE-MO-LE-LE, *adj.* Perfect; faultless; holy; complete. *Hal.* 139:22.

HE-MU, *v.* To scare or drive away, as fowls, pigs, &c.

HE-NA, *s.* The hollow of the thigh. *Kin.* 32:25. The buttock; the nakedness of a person. *Isa.* 47:3. The place of the kauha intestine. *Anat.* 52. The mons veneris.

He-na-he-na, *v.* See Henehene.

He-na-lu, *v.* See Heenalu.

He-ne, *s.* A bundle, as of potatoes or other things done up for carrying. See Kihene.

He-ne, *v.* To laugh at; to mock; to deride. See Henehene.

He-ne-he-ne, *v.* To laugh in derision; to mock; to treat a person or thing with contempt.

2. To cast off and forsake as worthless or contemptible.

3. To be secretly pleased when another falls; applied to wicked men when a good man falls into sin. *Sol.* 25:10. With the passive *heneheneia*, to be the subject of ridicule. 1 *Nal.* 9:7.

4. *Hoo.* To laugh scornfully; to reproach. *Isa.* 37:22. E *henehene* mai ka make ia lakou, death mocks them.

He-ne-he-ne-ia, *s.* Mockery; contempt. 2 *Oihl.* 29:8. Superciliousness; haughtiness.

He-ne-he-ne, *adj.* Disdainful; foolish; insipid; aka, i ka poe hewa, he mea *henehene* ia e lakou ka nani o ke Akua.

He-ni-po-a, *adj.* See Nipoa. Feeble; debilitated; weak.

He-nu, *v.* To anoint, &c. See Hinu.

He-nu-he-nu, *v.* See Hinuhinu. To be smooth; to be polished.

2. To be shining.

He-nu-he-nu, *adj.* Shining; glittering; polished.

He-pa, *s.* A shaking of the limbs; the palsy; a sitting in silence.

He-pa, *adj.* Mischievous; false; lazy; nani ke kanaka *hepa*.

He-pa-he-pa, *adj.* A person so diseased that he cannot help himself; applied to the palsy.

He-pa-no-a, *adj.* See Panoa. Dry and parched, as land.

He-pu-e, *s.* See Pue. A pushing on or along; the rapid flow of a current.

He-wa, *v.* To be wrong; to be in the wrong; to act or to be in error.

2. To sin, i. e., to go contrary to right; to transgress. *Isa.* 43:27. To be viciously inclined.

3. *Hoo.* To accuse; to find fault with; to complain. See ahewa.

4. To condemn; to reprove.

5. To be under a curse; to be accursed. *Kin.* 3:17.

He-wa, *s.* Error; wrong; sin; vice; often connected with *ino* and *hala. Puk.* 34:7.

2. The fruit or consequence of sin, i. e.,

punishment; overthrow. *Lunk.* 20:41. He mau *hewa* lele wale, little vices that spring up of themselves and are not punished.

He-wa, *adj.* Wrong; improper; sinful; wicked.

He-wa, *adv.* Erroneously; wrongfully; hele *hewa*, to go wrong; to miss the right way. Fig. To commit sin.

He-wa-he-wa, *v.* See Hewa, to be wrong. To make a mistake; to commit an error; mostly used in the causative.

2. *Hoo.* To forget one's appearance or name.

3. To mistake one person for another.

4. To be deranged in mind; to be silent and unsociable through alienation of mind.

He-wa-he-wa, *s.* A mistake of one person or thing for another.

2. Derangement of mind from sickness.

3. Sudden silence.

He-wa-he-wa, *adj.* Crazy; unsound in mind; mad. *Ier.* 29:26.

He-be-do-ma, *s.* Gr. A term or space of seven days; a week; a space of seven years. *Kin.* 29:37.

He-be-ra, *s.* Heb. A Hebrew; a man of the Hebrew race. *Kin.* 14:13. One of the descendants of Abraham; mostly used as an adjective.

He-be-ra, *adj.* Hebrew; pertaining to the Hebrew people. *Puk.* 21:2. Also pertaining to the Hebrew language. *Luk.* 33:38.

He-re-e-ke-la, *s.* Eng. Herschel; the planet of that name. See *Astronomia.*

Hi, *v.* To droop; to be weak.

2. To flow away, as the contents of the bowels in a dysentery; to purge.

3. To blow out with force any liquid from the mouth.

Hi, *s.* A flowing away; a purging, as in dysentery.

2. The name of the disease called dysentery; he *hi* ka mai.

3. A hissing sound, as the rapid flow of a liquid; *hikoko*, a bloody flux. *Oih.* 28:8. See Hikoko.

Hi-a, *v.* To rub two sticks one upon another to obtain fire. See Aulima and Aunahi. E hana i ke ahi me ka aunahi, a maluna iho ka aulima, alaila kuolo me ka anai ana i mea e a i ke ahi.

2. To reflect; to think.

3. To run about as wild; to strut about.

4. To entangle; to catch, as in a net; eha ai i ka upena.

Hi-a, *s.* A reflecting; the act of thinking.

2. The person who catches or entangles fish in a net.

Hɪ-a, *adj.* Roving; unsteady; also entangled.

Hɪ-a, The passive termination of many verbs instead of *ia*; as, *pauhia* for *pauia*. *Gram.* § 48.

Hɪ-a-a, *v.* To lie awake; to be sleepless; restless while attempting or wishing to sleep; e *hiaa* ana no kona aloha, he was *wakeful* on account of his love. *Laieik.* 205. See **Uluku** 2.

2. To be absent from one, as sleep; to be sleepless, as one troubled in mind. *Dan.* 2:1.

Hɪ-a-a, *adj.* Sleepless; desiring to sleep, but cannot.

Hɪ-a-ai, *s.* Strong desire; a desire which keeps one awake during the time of sleep; applied to the mind; o ka *hiaai* o ka naau.

Hɪ-a-hɪ-a, *v.* See **Hie** and **Hiehie.** To be honorable; to be honored; noble; to be respected.

Hɪ-a-hɪ-a, *v.* See **Hia,** to rub two sticks for fire. To obtain fire by rubbing two sticks.

Hɪ-a-hɪ-a, *s.* Goodness; honor; nobility.

Hɪ-a-hɪ-a, *adj.* Fading; transitory; soon done.

Hɪ-a-ka, *v.* To recite legends or fabulous stories. See **Hiiaka.**

Hɪ-a-ka, *s.* The recitation of legends.

2. A particular kind of mele or song.

3. The company of gods belonging to Pele; among the class called akuanoho.

Hɪ-a-ku, *s.* Name of a place in the sea beyond the kaiuli, and inside the kohola.

2. The name of the fish caught in such a place.

Hɪ-a-la, *v.* Hoo. *Lam. Haw.* 16:4, 3. To be greedy of food; to eat largely of all kinds of food.

Hɪ-a-mo-e, *v.* *Hi*, to droop, *a*, until, and *moe*, to prostrate.

1. To lie asleep; to sleep; to fall asleep.

2. Fɪɢ. To rest in sleep; e *hiamoe* i ka make, to sleep in death, i. e., to be dead. 1 *Nal.* 15:8. To die. *Kanl.* 31:16.

3. To fall prostrate, as if asleep. *Dan.* 8:18.

Hɪ-a-mo-e, *s.* Sleep; deep sound sleep; rest in sleep. Sʏɴ. with moe. *Sol.* 6:10.

2. *Hiamoe,* the sloth, an animal of South America.

Hɪ-a-po, *s.* The first born of parents. See **Makahiapo.** *Panina,* the youngest child, or *mulihope*; first of several children. *Neh.* 10:36. In opposition to *mulihope*; me

ka leo o na keiki *hiapo,* aole me ka leo o na keiki mulihope.

2. The first born of animals as well as of men. *Puk.* 12:12. *Hiapo* is also opposed to *muli* or *muli loa. Ios.* 6:26.

Hɪ-e, *v.* To be good; excellent; grand; used mostly in compounds.

Hɪ-e-hɪ-e, *v.* To be excellent or good in appearance; maikai loa ke nana aku.

2. *Hoo.* To show a splendid appearance; hence,

3. To be proud; self dignified; haughty.

4. To be regardless of others; to act shamelessly or unseemly. 1 *Kor.* 13:5.

Hɪ-e-hɪ-e, *s.* *Hoo.* Dignity in appearance; honor.

2. Pride; haughtiness; overbearing conduct.

Hɪ-e-hɪ-e, *adj.* Neat; tidy; good; lively.

2. Proud; haughty; o na mea *hoohiehie* ame na mea lealea.

Hɪ-e-na, *s.* *Eng.* A hyena. *Lam. Haw.* 22:1, 2; *Ier.* 12:9. Noᴛᴇ.—This last reference is not *hyena* in English.

Hɪ-e-na, *s.* Name of a species of stone, soft and porous.

Hɪɪ, *v.* To lift up; to bear upon the hips and support with the arms, as a child; to hold, as a child on the knees. *Isa.* 66:12. To carry in the arms and on the bosom; ike ae la oia i ke kaikamahine e *hiiia* mai ana. *Laieik.* 10. To nurse; to tend, as a child. *Kanik.* 2:22.

Hɪɪ-a-ka, *s.* A general name of the gods of volcanoes. See **Hiaka.** O *Hiiaka* ke akua i hookahe mai i ke koko ma ke poo o kona kahu.

Hɪɪ-kau, *v.* See **Hikau.** To throw, as a stone at a person or thing; *hiikau* aku la na kanaka i ka pohaku, the men *threw* stones at them; similar to *nou*.

Hɪɪ-ka-la, *s.* Name of a species of fishhook.

Hɪɪ-la-ni, *v.* *Hii*, to lift up, and *lani*, on high.

1. To nurse or take care of, as an infant chief.

2. To exalt; to praise; to admire. See **Hoolani** and **Hoonani.** *Hal.* 117:1.

3. To admire and obey, as a servant does his master.

Hɪɪ-la-ni, *s.* Praise; exaltation; deference paid to one dignified.

Hɪɪ-pa-ka, *v.* Aole no ia e *hiipaka* o ka wahine ke kane waiwai.

Hɪɪ-po-i, *v.* *Hii* and *poi*, to protect.

1. To tend and feed, as a young child.

2. To feed and defend, as a chief does his people. *Oih.* 13:18.

3. To take in the arms, as a child. *Mar.* 7:36. To carry in the bosom, as a child. *Nah.* 11:12.

4. To take care of and provide for generally; spoken of God's care of men; ke *hiipoi* mai nei ke Akua ia kakou.

Hii-puu-puu. See **Hipuupuu.**

Hi-o, *v.* To lean over; to slant; to incline from a perpendicular; hence,

2. To be one-sided; to swing to and fro.

3. To lean upon; to trust in. *Isa.* 30:12.

4. To wander. *Hoo.* To cause to wander. *Ier.* 48:12. Mea *hoohio*, a wanderer.

Hi-o, *s.* A slanting wind, i. e., a wind down a hill.

2. The inside corner of a (grass) house, i. e., slanting two ways.

3. A howling confused noise.

4. The comb of a cock.

5. Eructatio ventris.

Hi-o, *adj.* Leaning; oblique; kaha *hio*; any line which is not parallel, nor perpendicular, nor horizontal, is *hio*. *Ana Hon.* 4.

Hi-o-o-le, *s.* With stability; firmness. LIT. Without leaning; me ka haipule mau i ke Akua me ka *hioole*.

Hi-o-hi-o, *v.* To draw the breath into the mouth, as one eating a hot potato; hence,

2. To eat in a hurry.

Hi-o-hi-o, *s.* Name of a species of fish-hook.

Hi-o-hi-o, *adj.* Bright red; ula *hiohio*.

Hi-o-la-ni, *v.* To lie stretched out with laziness; to sit at ease, as a chief; to be in a posture of thought; e pio na wawae, e lele pio.

Hi-o-hi-o-na, *s.* *Hio* and *ana*, the leaning. The features of a person; his peculiar gait; the form, external appearance. *Isa.* 52:14. Face; presence. SYN. with helehelena.

Hi-o-lo, *v.* *Hi*, flowing, and *olo*, to vibrate.

1. To tumble down, as a wall. *Ios.* 6:20. To fall over, as a house.

2. To stumble or fall down, as a horse.

3. To roll away, i. e., pass away in forgetfulness; i ole e *hioloia* kona inoa.

4. To become useless or void.

5. *Hoo.* To throw down; to overthrow; to destroy, as a fortification. *2 Nal.* 25:10.

6. To make void; to set aside, as a law. *Rom.* 3:31.

Hi-o-lo, *s.* A tumbling down; a sliding away; a falling over.

Hi-o-na, *s.* Personal appearance; face, countenance, &c. See **Hiohiona.** *Anat.* 5.

Hi-u, *v.* To seize; to grasp hold of, as a rope.

2. To throw a stone with violence.

3. To be wild; untamed, as an animal.

4. To cry, as a sailor does in pulling a rope; hence,

5. To haul down a ship for repairs.

6. To practice sorcery.

7. To move the *hiu* (see the *s.*) in playing konane, a game.

Hi-u, *s.* The tail of a fish, but not SYN. with huelo.

2. The practice of sorcery.

3. The name of the counter or iliili used in playing konane or konene; ina he *hiu*, a he aneo paha, a he lalani, a he punikihi paha, aia no i ko laua mau lunamanao.

Hi-u-a, *adj.* He mea ula *hiua*; name of a game played on a board of four squares.

Hi-u-hi-u, *v.* See **Hiu.** To practice sorcery.

2. To play the game konane.

Hi-u-ma-lo-lo, *s.* *Hiu* and *malolo*, the flying-fish. The tail of the flying-fish.

Hi-u-wai, *s.* The name of the ceremony of bathing in cold water in the worship of some of the gods.

Hi-hi, *v.* To branch or spread out, as vines, or as the limbs of a tree; to grow thick together; ka pikopiko, ua *hihi*; hihi pea ka lewa. *Laieik.* 168.

2. To be satisfied; to have enough.

Hi-hi, *s.* The running, spreading out, the entwining or creeping of vines, or a thick growth of vegetation.

2. A cause of entangling; an offense; a cause of offense. NOTE.—This last sense mostly in the form *hihia*.

Hi-hi, *adj.* Thick together, as grass; as vines; as men.

Hi-hi-a, *v.* That is, *hihiia*, pass. of *hihi*. To be perplexed; entangled, either physically or morally.

2. To be in a state of difficulty or perplexity.

3. To be lost by going astray; to turn this way and that for relief.

4. To be offended.

5. *Hoo.* To entangle; to be the cause of trouble. *Puk.* 10:7.

6. To be entangled; to be led astray; to be the cause of evil to one.

7. To entrap one in his speech; to be offended.

Hi-hi-a, *s.* A difficulty; a thing perplexed; a cause of trouble.

2. A thicket of forest; ka *hihia* paa o ka nahele. *Laieik.* 94.

HI-HI-A, *adj.* Difficult; perplexing; troublesome.

HI-HI-A-LOU, *s.* Name of a plant with small yellow flowers.

HI-HI-A-WAI, *s.* The name of a plant sometimes eaten for food.

2. The name of a species of fish.

HI-HI-O, *v.* See HIO. To sleep; to fall asleep.

2. To dream; e paa ka maka a ike ka uhane, to shut the eyes and see with the soul, that is, to have a vision. *Hoik.* 1:10.

3. To fall asleep again after waking.

4. To sleep soundly.

5. To blow; to rush violently, as a strong wind. See PUAHIOHIO.

HI-HI-O, *s.* A vision. *Kin.* 15:1. A dream.

HI-HI-U, *v.* See HIU 3. To be wild; untamed, as an animal; to be wild and savage, as men.

2. To mistake in speaking, as one untaught.

HI-HI-U, *adj.* Wild; untamed; strange; unfriendly; unsocial; often applied to animals that have been once tamed, but have become wild. *Hihiu* is the opposite of *laka*, tame. Na holoholona *hihiu* ame na holoholona laka; he ilio *hihiu* hae, a wolf.

HI-HI-KA-E-KA, *v.* To tangle up, as a rope or string; to tangle, as the hair; ua hihia na mea a pau, ua *hihikaeka* ma ka leo mana; to tangle or perplex one in speaking.

HI-HI-MA-NU, *s.* Name of a large, broad, soft living creature found in the sea; it was forbidden to women to eat under penalty of death. See IHIMANU.

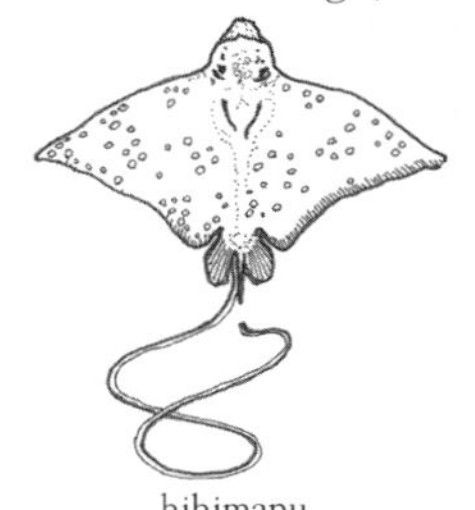
hihimanu

HI-HI-WAI, *s.* The name of a four-footed animal living in the sea.

HI-KAU, *v.* To throw stones at one. See HIIKAU. *Hikau* is perhaps the best orthography.

HI-KA-U-HI, *adv.* To no purpose; of no use, &c.; aia ko'u waa *hikauhi* ma Molokai; *hikauhi* oe a holo e ka moku; hele a *hikauhi.*

HI-KA-KA, *v.* To stagger; to reel in walking, as a drunken man. *Isa.* 19:14. To stagger, as a man carrying a heavy burden.

2. To wander; to go astray. *Isa.* 47:15.

3. *Hoo.* To cause to stagger, i. e., to walk in darkness. *Iob.* 12:25.

HI-KA-KA, *adj.* Staggering; walking unsteadily.

HI-KA-KA, *adj.* Bent round; curved; crooked.

HI-KA-PA-LA-LE, *s.* A word used in the kaki or namu, unintelligible except to those taught.

HI-KI, *v.* To come to; to arrive at, as connected with *mai* or *aku.*

2. To be able to do a thing; to acomplish a purpose; to prevail. *Hiki* is often used with other verbs as a kind of helping verb. *Gram.* § 171.

3. *Hoo.* To cause to come; to bring forth; to produce. *Puk.* 8:3.

4. To take an oath; to affirm a thing or an event as true.

5. To call or give a name to. *Mat.* 22:43, 45. To name or speak of with approbation. *Epes.* 5:3.

6. To mention in one's prayers. *Pilem.* 4.

7. To vow; to consecrate; to set apart; to promise a thing especially to a god; to set apart as sacred. 1 *Sam.* 1:11. *Hoohiki ino,* to desecrate; to treat with contempt; *hoohiki* wahahee, to swear falsely; to take a false oath. See HOOHIKI, *s. Hiki* wale, to happen; to come by chance.

HI-KI-A-LO-A-LO, *adj.* The rising and coming to the zenith, as the full moon; i ka mahina *hikialoalo.*

HI-KI-E-E, *v.* To approach to; to draw near.

2. To bridge over a stream.

HI-KI-E-E, *s.* An approach of one; a coming near to.

2. A bridge over a stream.

3. A raised platform for sleeping; a sort of bedstead or couch; a place for a bed. *Puk.* 17:28.

HI-KII, *v.* To tie; to fasten by tying; to bind, as a person. *Kin.* 22:9. To bind, as a prisoner; to tie, as a rope or cord to anything. *Ios.* 2:18 and 21. See NAKII. To bind on, as a sandal; to tie up, as a purse.

HI-KII, *s.* A binding; a tying; a fastening.

HI-KII-KII, *v.* See HIKII. To tie; to bind strongly. *Mat.* 27:2.

HI-KI-KU, *s. Hiki* and *ku,* to rise. The place of the sun's rising; *poetically,* the east. See HIKINA.

Hi-ki-le-le, *v. Hiki* and *lele*, to jump; to fly.

1. To wake suddenly from sleep. *Isa.* 29:8. To wake with affright.

2. To jump or start suddenly from surprise or fear.

3. To do a thing suddenly and in haste; to be weak with fear from any event. *Kin.* 42:28.

4. *Hoo.* To wake up a person from sleep. *Isa.* 29:8.

5. To come by surprise, as one army upon another. *Ios.* 11:7.

Hi-ki-le-le, *s.* A sudden coming upon; a rising up quickly; a sudden fright.

Hi-ki-le-le, *adv. Hoo.* Quickly; suddenly. *Isa.* 47:11.

Hi-ki-mo-e, *Hiki* and *moe*, to lie down. Poetical name of the west; place of (the sun's) lying down.

Hi-ki-na, *s. Hiki* and *ana*, participial termination. The full form is ka *hiki ana* (a ka la), the coming (of the sun), i. e., the east; the place of the sun's rising. *Hal.* 50:1.

Hi-ki-na, *adj.* The eastern; ma ka aoao *hikina* o Hawaii, on the eastern side of Hawaii.

Hi-ki-na, *adv.* Eastwardly. 1 *Nal.* 17:3.

Hi-ki-wa-we, *v. Hiki* and *wawe*, quick. To do quickly; to be quick or smart in doing a thing. *Hoo.* To cause quickness; to make dispatch.

Hi-ki-wa-we, *adv.* Quickly; speedily; without delay.

Hi-ki-wa-le, *adv. Hiki* and *wale*, merely. What has happened; come by chance; without design.

Hi-ki-wi, *v.* See Kiwi. To crook; to bend.

Hi-ko-ko, *s. Hi* and *koko*, blood. A flowing of blood; specifically applied to a disease of the anus called emerods. *Kanl.* 28:27. A dysentery; a bloody flux.

Hi-ko-ni, *s.* Name of a servant marked in the forehead; o ka poe kauwa i hoailonaia ma ka lae, ua kapaia he kauwa *hikoni.*

Hi-ku, *adj.* The seventh in order; i ka *hiku* o ka malama. *Oihk.* 16:29; *Gram.* § 115, 2, 4. As a cardinal, seven.

Hi-ku-hi-ku, *s.* A noise; confusion by many voices.

Hi-la, *v.* Not yet found in this single form. See the double forms and Hoo.

Hi-lai, *adj.* A word used in the prayers of the ancients, meaning not very clear. See Lanahilai.

Hi-la-hi-la, *v.* To be ashamed; to be put in confusion; to be ashamed of. 2 *Nal.* 2:17.

2. *Hoo.* To cause shame; to make ashamed.

3. To have that quick agitation which arises from shame; confusion, suffusion of the face.

Hi-la-hi-la, *s.* Shame; a blushing of the face; confusion attendant on shame.

Hi-la-hi-la, *adj.* Ashamed.

Hi-la-hi-la, *adv.* Shamefully.

Hi-la-la, *v.* To bend; to crook; to bend from a straight line. See Hikiwi.

Hi-le-a, *adj.* Lazy; indolent; doing nothing.

Hi-li, *v.* To braid; to plait, as a wreath; to braid, as the hair. 1 *Pet.* 3:3. To string, as kukui nuts; e *hili* kukui.

2. To turn over and over, as in braiding; to twist; to spin; to tie on, as Hawaiians formerly tied or braided their kois on to the handles.

3. To deviate from the path in traveling; to wander here and there. *Sol.* 15:22. To miss one's way.

4. To droop; to flag. See Milo and Wili.

5. To smite, as with a sword or the hand.

Hi-li, *s.* A general name for barks used in dyeing; as, *hili* kolea, *hili* koa, &c.

2. A black dye for coloring kapas made of kolea bark.

3. The principle of tanning in koa and other barks.

Hi-li, *adj.* Turning; wandering aside.

Hi-li-au, *v. Hili* and *au*, current. To wander; to go astray morally; to do wrong; he ikaika *hiliau*, strong to do evil.

Hi-li-e-e, *s.* A shrub having a powerful stimulant corrosive bark. See Ilihee.

Hi-li-ou, *s.* A square braid of eight straws.

2. A sickness of the bowels; sickness of the stomach; fullness of the stomach.

Hi-li-u, *s.* The voice of a shell or trumpet; the sound of one blowing a wind instrument.

Hi-li-hi-li, *v.* See Hili, coloring barks. To color or dye red, or any dark color.

Hi-li-hi-li, *adj.* Red or brown in color; shaded; dark.

Hi-li-hi-li-ho-nu, *adj.* Rich; wealthy.

Hi-li-kau, *v.* To accuse much, and falsely; to say and unsay.

Hi-li-kau, *adj.* Tripping in one's walk; stumbling.

2. Varying in one's story; e lauwili, e lalau.

3. Walking cross-legged.

Hi-li-na-e-hu, *s.* The name of a Hawaiian month; the tenth month of the Hawaiian calendar.

Hi-li-nai, *v.* *Hili* and *nai*, to strive for.
1. To lean upon; to lean against. *Lunk.* 16:26.
2. To trust in; to have confidence in one's word. 2 *Nal.* 18:19, 20.

Hi-li-nai, *s.* Trust; confidence; a leaning against or upon.
2. What is leaned upon, as a table; a bed or place for reclining.

Hi-li-na-ma, *s.* Name of the ninth month among Hawaiians.

Hi-li-ne-hu, *s.* Name of the eleventh Hawaiian month.

Hi-li-no-hu, *s.* The name of the eighth month.

Hi-lo, *v.* To twist, as a string on the thigh; to twist with the thumb and fingers.
2. To spin; to turn, as in twisting. See Hili, Milo, Wili, &c.

Hi-lo, *s.* The name of the first night in which the new moon can be seen, as it is like a twisted thread; o *hilo* ka po mua no ka puahilo ana o ka mahina.
2. An issue; a running sore. *Oihk.* 15:2, 3.

Hi-lo, *adj.* Spun; twisted. *Puk.* 26:1. Iwi hilo. *Anat.* 16.

Hi-lo-hi-lo, *v.* See Hilo, *v.* To wander here and there in telling a story; to lengthen a speech by mentioning little circumstances.
2. To make nice oratorical language.

Hi-lo-hi-lo, *s.* The sweet juice of the ki root, especially when there is but little and very sweet.

Hi-lu, *s.* Name of a species of fish, spotted, variegated with colors.

Hi-lu, *adj.* Still; quiet; reserved; dignified; a word of commendation; *hilu* ka noho ana o mea.
2. Neat; elegant; powerful; magnificent.

Hi-lu-hi-lu, *s.* See Hilu. The excellent; the glorious; the powerful.

Hi-lu-hi-lu, *adj.* Excellent; nice; beautiful.

Hi-me-ni, *s.* *Eng.* from *Gr.* A hymn; a song in sacred worship; a mele in praise of Iehova. 2 *Oihl.* 29:28.

Hi-me-ni, *v.* *Eng.* from *Gr.* To hymn; to sing a hymn.

Hi-na, *v.* To lean from an upright position.
2. To fall; to fall down, as a house.
3. To fall morally, as a person from a state of uprightness; to relapse or decline from a state of rectitude.
4. To offend; to be offended. *Ioan.* 16:1.
5. *Hoo.* To slant over; to throw down, as a person. *Luk.* 4:35.

Hi-na, *s.* A leaning; a falling; a causing to fall; a stumbling.

Hi-na, *s.* *Heb.* A hin, a Hebrew measure. *Puk.* 29:40.

Hi-na, *s.* Name of a goddess. See Hinahele below.

Hi-na, *adj.* Gray; hoary; applied to the head; oho *hina*. *Kin.* 44:29. Gray, as the beard; he umiumi *hina*.

Hi-na-a-le, *s.* A species of small fish.

Hi-na-a-lo, } *s.* The blossoms of the
Hi-na-lo, } hala fruit; the leaves which inclose the hala fruit.

Hi-na-a-lo, } *adj.* Aromatic; fragrant,
Hi-na-lo, } as the fruit and blossoms of the hala tree.

Hi-nai, *s.* A container braided out of the ie and other materials; a basket. *Oihk.* 8:2.

Hi-nai-a-e-le-e-le, *s.* Name of the seventh Hawaiian month.

Hi-nai-po-e-po-e, *s.* A round basket; a basket braided around a calabash; hinaihooluuluu.

Hi-na-he-le, *s.* Often called simply *Hina*; the goddess of fishes, mother of Aiaiakuula; *Hinahele* laua o Kuula na 'kua lawaia, mai Hawaii a Niihau.

Hi-na-hi-na, *adj.* Gray; grayish.
2. Withered, as fruit ready to fall.

Hi-na-ku-lai-na, *v.* See Hina and Kulaina, to push over. To partially fall down.

Hi-na-ku-lu-i-ua, *s.* *Hina*, goddess, *kulu*, to drop, as rain, and *ua*, rain. The goddess of rain; has two sisters, viz.: Hinakealii and Hookuipaele.

Hi-na-le-a, *s.* A species of fish.

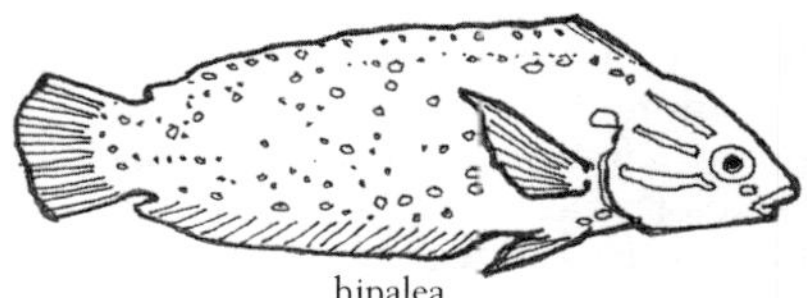

hinalea

Hi-na-le-a, *adj.* Applied to a basket for catching fish; hinai *hinalea*.

Hi-na-le-a, *v.* To blow from aft, as wind favorable for sailing.

Hi-na-lii, *adj.* *Hina*, gray, and *lii*, very little. Very little gray, as the hair; whitish.

Hi-na-lii, *s.* The name of a person (chief) in whose time there occurred a universal deluge or kai a ka *Hinalii*; hence *kaiakahinalii* is at present used for the flood of Noah. *Kin.* 6:17. See also ke kai a ka *Hulumanu.*

Hi-na-lo, *s.* The leaves inclosing the hala fruit. See HINAALO.

2. The flowers of the hala tree.

Hi-na-mo-e, *s.* *Hina,* to fall, and *moe,* to lie down. A place of death; often applied to the volcano.

Hi-na-na, *s.* Name of a very small fish, the young of the oopu.

Hi-na-we-na-we, *adj.* Thin; spindling; slender. See UNIHI.

Hi-ne, *adj.* Strutting; proud of one's appearance.

Hi-ni, *v.* To be small; thin; feeble.

Hi-ni-hi-ni, *s.* See HINI. Speaking in a small, thin voice; a whispering; hanehane.

Hi-ni-hi-ni, *adj.* See HINI and UHINI. Thin; slender; pointed.

Hi-ni-po-a, *adj.* See HENIPOA and NI-POA. Heavy, as the eyes when drowsy or very sleepy; he maluhiluhi.

Hi-nu, *v.* To anoint; to besmear, as with oil or grease.

2. To be smooth; shining.

3. To slip; to slide easily.

4. To anoint. See KAHINU.

Hi-nu, *s.* Ointment; substance for besmearing; momona, mea poni, &c.

Hi-nu, *adj.* Smooth; greasy; polished; dazzling with brightness; anointed.

Hi-nu-hi-nu, *v.* See HINU. To shine as if anointed with oil. *Hal.* 104:15. To glisten; to be bright; to sparkle.

Hi-nu-hi-nu, *adj.* Bright; shining; splendid, as red cloth; glittering, as polished stones. 1 *Oihl.* 29:2.

Hi-pa, *s.* A little bundle.

2. A blunder in speaking; the use of words out of their ordinary meaning.

3. *Hoo.* A falsehood.

Hi-pa, *v.* To blunder in speaking. *Hoo.* To falsify.

Hi-pa, *adj.* *Hoo.* He olelo *hoohipa,* a kind of mele.

Hi-pa, *s.* *Eng.* Sheep. *Ioan.* 10:2, 3.

Hi-pa-hi-pa, *v.* To be joyful; to express gladness.

Hi-pa-ka-ne, *s.* *Hipa,* sheep, and *kane,* male. A ram. *Kin.* 15:9. Ili *hipakane,* a ram skin. *Puk.* 25:5, *Gram.* § 95. FIG. *Hipakane wawahi,* a battering ram. *Ezek.* 4:2.

Hi-pa-ke-i-ki, *s.* *Hipa,* sheep, and *keiki,* the little one. A lamb. *Oih.* 8:32. See KEIKIHIPA. NOTE.—The word lamb is rendered in Hawaiian by both forms, *hipa-*

keiki and *keikihipa.*

Hi-pa-pa-la-le, *s.* See PAPALALE. A speaking with readiness and correctness, without a tone, and not through the nose; o ka hana maiau *hipapalale* ole, noiau papalale ole.

Hi-po-po-ta-mu, *s.* *Gr.* The river-horse. *Iob.* 40:15. The hippopotamus.

Hi-pu,　} *v.* To tie in knots, as the string
Hi-puu,　} of a bundle or bag.

Hi-pu,　} *s.* A knot; a fastening; any-
Hi-puu,　} thing tied. FIG. E wehe oe i ka *hipu* naaupo, o make auanei oe.

2. A bag for carrying small things in, as money; a purse. *Sol.* 1:14.

3. *Hipuu* kala, in the English translation, a crisping pin. *Isa.* 3:22.

Hi-puu, *adj.* Knotty, as a string tied up in knots; tied fast; applied to men, mischievous.

Hi-puu-puu, *v.* See HIPUU. To tie up in knots; hence, to tie up in a bundle.

2. To tie fast; to gird around, as with a sash; aole kakou i like me na kanaka kiai alii a *hipuupuu* kahi malo, we are not the men who guard the king, *belted up* with sashes.

Hi-puu-puu, *s.* What is tied up in knots or made fast.

Hi-puu-puu, *adj.* See HIPUU. Tied; fastened; knotty, as tied in knots; he *hipuupuu* kahi malo o kahi alii, the malos of some chiefs were tied up in knots.

Hi-pu-ka, *s.* A kind of snare for catching birds; ka *hipuka* no na manu hihiu; kau aku la ia i ka *hipuka* pahele.

Hi-wa, *adj.* Black; clear black; applied mostly to that which was used in sacrifice to the gods, as a black hog; ina i eleele a puni ka hulu, he *hiwa* pa ia puaa; a black cocoanut, a black kapa, &c., and always considered valuable; hence,

2. Dear; valued; beloved; precious; he puaa *hiwa,* he niu *hiwa,* he awa *hiwa.*

Hi-wa, *v.* To be of a black color, such as was considered precious or valuable in sacrifice; to be of a clear or pure black.

Hi-wa, *s.* Any black article supposed to be acceptable to the gods as an offering; hence,

2. A precious valuable article.

3. Applied to persons; keiki *hiwa,* a dear child.

Hi-waa-waa, *adj.* See MOMONA. Large; fat, as a large fleshy person; applied only to persons.

Hi-wa-hi-wa, *v.* See HIWA, *adj.* To be

greatly loved; mostly with *hoo*.

2. To be pleased with; to be satisfied with, as a god with an offering; to be acceptable to; e *hoohiwahiwa* kakou i ka hana, let us make the work acceptable.

3. To pet; to treat a child, a servant or an animal with delicacy. *Sol.* 29:21.

HI-WA-HI-WA, *s.* A person or thing greatly beloved; applied mostly to animals or children; a pet; a beloved one. *Kanl.* 33:12. The beloved one. *Luk.* 23:35.

HI-WA-HI-WA, *adj.* See HIWA. Thick; dense; black, as a cloud; glossy black.

2. Acceptable; desired by any one.

3. Very precious; greatly esteemed. 1 *Tes.* 2:8. Greatly beloved. *Isa.* 5:1.

4. Meek; docile; he keiki *hiwahiwa* ia.

HI-WI, *v.* To diminish, as a swelling; to flatten down, as a protuberance; ua *hiwi* mai. See the compounds POOHIWI and KUA-HIWI.

HI-WI, *s.* The flat or depressed summit of a protuberance.

HO, *v.* To transfer, i. e., to bring here or carry away, according as it is followed by *mai* or *aku.* See MAI and AKU. *Gram.* § 233 and 234. As, *ho* mai, bring here; *ho* aku, carry away.

2. To bring; to present. 1 *Sam.* 17:10. To give or put away, as money at interest. *Hal.* 15:5.

3. To carry or cause to be conveyed; to transport; to remove.

4. To produce; to bring forward, as food on to the table. *Kin.* 43:31.

HO, *v.* To cry out in a clamorous manner.

2. *Hoo.* To cause the voice to be raised; to raise the voice to a high pitch.

3. To speak together, as in voting *viva voce*; to proclaim; to shout acclamation of approval. *Puk.* 24:3.

4. To shout in triumph. *Ios.* 6:5. *Hooho* olioli, to triumph over one. *Hal.* 41:11.

5. To cry out for fear; to cry out in distress. *Nah.* 14:1.

6. To wheeze; to breathe hard as in the asthma; to snort; to blow, as a horse. See HOOHO in its place.

HO, *s.* The asthma; the lowing of cattle, &c.

2. *Eng.* A farming utensil; a hoe; the colter of a plow. 1 *Sam.* 13:20.

HO. This syllable (see the two articles above) has a meaning of its own, and as such may enter into compound words; but very often, as will appear, it is a contraction of *hoo.* (See HOO.) The contraction is made before all the letters, but mostly where the word commences with some of the vowels, especially with the letter *o.*

HO-A, *s.* A companion; a fellow; a friend; an assistant. It is found in many compounds; as, *hoapio*, a fellow prisoner; *hoamoe*, a bed-fellow; *hoahele*, a traveling companion, &c.

HO-A, *v.* To strike on the head with a stick.

2. To beat, as kapa with a stick on a stone.

3. To strike, as in fighting.

4. To drive, as cattle.

HO-A, *v.* To tie; to secure by tying; to bind; to wind round, as a rope or string; to rig up, as a canoe; a ma ka ka wa e *hoa* ai ka waa, he kapu ka *hoa* ana. See A and HOHOA. Alaila, *hoaia* ka pou me ka lohelau.

HO-A, *v. Ho* for *hoo*, and *a*, to burn.

1. To kindle a fire; to burn, i. e., to cause to blaze; to make a light. *Laieik.* 77. To rage, as a flame of love; ua *hoaia* ke ahi, enaena o ke aloha wela, the raging fire of hot love blazed forth. *Laieik.* 204.

2. To comb or dress the hair or the head.

3. To cast or throw away; e hookuke; hence,

4. To commit mischief, as a child.

HO-A, *s.* A tying; a binding.

HO-A, *adj.* Unsteady; movable. See HIA, *adj.*

HO-AA, *v.* See HO for HOO, and AA, to blaze. To kindle; to cause to burn.

2. To stare; to look about in doubt. See AA, to be bold.

3. To mistake; to blunder; to go astray.

4. To challenge; to dare; to provoke.

HO-AA, *s.* A mistake; a blunder; an error.

2. The kindling, i. e., small pieces of fuel used in kindling a fire.

HO-A-AI, *s. Hoa*, companion, and *ai*, to eat. An eating companion; a guest. 1 *Nal.* 1:41.

HO-A-AI-NA, *s. Hoa* and *aina*, land.

1. A person to whom the hakuaina or konohiki commits the care of his land.

2. The husbandman; a tiller of the ground.

HO-A-A-HI, *s. Ho* for *hoo*, *a*, to burn, and *ahi*, fire. Fire kindlings; the materials for causing a fire to burn; e imi mua oe ia no ka *hoaahi* ana.

HO-A-A-HI, *v. Ho* for *hoo*, and *aahu*, to clothe. To clothe; to put on a garment; to give kapa or clothes to one. *Mat.* 25:36.

Ho-A-A-LO-HA, *s*. *Hoa*, companion, and *aloha*, to love. A friend. *Ioan*. 3:29. A beloved companion; ia wa, ua lilo ko Hawaii nei i poe *hoaaloha* no na misionari, at that time the Hawaiians became *friends* to the missionaries.

Ho-AA-MA-KA, *v*. *Ho* for *hoo*, *aa*, bold, and *maka*, eye. To beg for a thing by looking wishfully at it.

Ho-A-A-NO, *v*. A factitious word; *ho* for *hoo*, *aa*, to dare, and *no*, a particle of affirmation, indeed; truly; hence, to have confidence in one's self; to brag; to express bravery.

Ho-A-A-NO, *adj*. See the verb. Forward; presumptuous; defying punishment.

2. Proud; daring; obstinate; self confident.

Ho-A-A-PU, *v*. *Ho* for *hoo*, and *aapu*, to warp; bend up. To make a cup of the hollow of the hand; e *hoaapu* ae i kou poho lima, make the palm of your hand into a cup.

Ho-AE, *v*. See Ho, *v*., and *ae*, verbal directive. *Gram*. § 233, 5th. To move sideways; to turn a little. NOTE.—The *ae* is no part of the verb.

2. To raise up; to cause to ascend; to go up.

Ho-A-E-A, *v*. *Ho* for *hoo*, and *aea*, to wander about. To pretend to wander; to make as though one was a wanderer or vagabond in order to accomplish a particular object.

Ho-AI, *v*. *Ho* for *hoo*, and *ai*, food.

1. To stir up; to mix; to make poi thin with water that it may be fit for eating.

2. To unite two things together, as by stretching or sewing kapas together.

3. To be singular in one's conduct or deportment.

Ho-AI, *s*. The union of things sewed together; ka hoopili ana ma na hookuina.

2. In *anatomy*, a suture; a joining; *hoai* manawa, coronal suture; *hoai* kaupaku, sagittal; *hoai* kala, lambdoidal; *hoai* maha, temporal suture, &c.

Ho-AI-AI, *v*. *Ho* for *hoo*, and *aiai*, to be white.

1. To be clear; white; shining.

2. To cause to be white, &c., i. e., to whiten; to clear off rust or dirt from a substance that it may shine.

3. To be clear, as the unclouded moon; to be shining, as a light.

4. To be proud; to be lifted up with pride.

Ho-AI-AI, *s*. See the foregoing. A soft clear white light; a pure light; *abstract*, whiteness.

Ho-AI-AI, *adj*. White; clear; shining.

Ho-AI-KA-NE, *v*. *Ho* for *hoo*, *ai* and *kane*. See AIKANE.

1. To commit the sin against nature; to commit sodomy; applied to either sex.

2. To be an intimate friend of the same sex, i. e., to give and receive favors from one of the same sex. *Laieik*. 81.

3. To act the part of an aikane or intimate friend.

4. To make friends, as two persons about to fight. *Laieik*. 47.

Ho-AI-KA-NE, *s*. A friend on terms of reciprocity.

2. The house where such friends reside or meet.

Ho-AI-KO-LA, *v*. *Ho* for *hoo*. See AIKOLA, AKOLA and NAIKOLA.

1. To express triumph over one with contempt for him; to cause contemptuous treatment; to triumph over one with expressions of vanity and contempt.

2. To blackguard; to triumph over another's ills; to reproach; ua *hoaikola* mai o Palu ia oe; to rejoice or triumph over. *Isa*. 14:8.

3. To perplex; to bring one into difficulty.

4. To desire to have one put to death.

Ho-AI-KO-LA, *s*. A sneer; a sneering expression of approval.

2. A contemptuous cheering, calling one *good fellow*, *well done*, &c.; in an *ironical* sense, ku no ka akaiki o lakou ame ko lakou *hoaikola* ana, their chuckling and their *false cheering* hit us.

Ho-AI-LO-NA, *v*. See HAILONA. To sound the depth of water, i. e., to throw the lead.

2. To mark; to set a mark upon one.

3. To cast lots for a thing. *Oihk*. 16:8. In modern times, to play at dice.

Ho-AI-LO-NA, *s*. See the verb. A mark; a signal; a sign of something different from what it appears to be.

2. A sign or forerunner of something coming to pass or expected. *Oih*. 2:19.

3. A part representing the whole. *Oihk*. 2:2.

4. Something whose real signification is different from the appearance. *Ios*. 4:7.

5. A sign; a pledge; a distinguishing mark. *Puk*. 3:12. A signet. *Puk*. 28:11.

6. A target; a mark to shoot at. 1 *Sam*. 20:20.

7. A lot cast, as in casting lots; ma ka *hoailona*, by lot. *Lunk*. 20:9.

8. A scepter; a badge of authority. *Heb*. 1:9. See next word.

Ho-ai-lo-na-mo-i, *s.* See Hoailona above, and Moi, sovereignty. A scepter; a badge or emblem of regal authority. *Hal.* 45:6.

Ho-a-i-mu, *v. Ho* for *hoo, a,* to burn, and *imu,* oven. To kindle a fire in the oven; to heat the oven.

Ho-a-i-po-o-la, *v.* See Aipoola and Puupoola. To gulp up wind from the stomach after eating heartily.

Ho-ai-pu-ka-ha-le,
Ho-a-kai-pu-ka-ha-le,
Ho-a-ka-ku,
Ho-a-ka-ka-kai, *s.* In Hawaiian *pathology,* the names of a class of diseases, all fatal; the *waiiki* the only remedy used.

Ho-ai-puu-puu, *v. Ho* for *hoo,* and *aipuupuu,* which see. To act the aipuupuu; to serve out provisions; to distribute food.

Ho-ao, *v. Ho* for *hoo,* and *ao,* to try.

1. To try the qualities of a thing; to taste; to tempt; to make trial; assay; to begin. *Laieik.* 184.

2. To cohabit after marriage; to make public a marriage contract after the ancient manner.

3. To prove; to put to the test. *2 Oihl.* 9:1.

4. To undertake; to attempt. *Eset.* 9:23.

5. To hang up; e kaulai.

Ho-ao, *s.* See the verb. Marriage after the ancient custom of the islands.

2. The taste of any eatable. *Nah.* 11:8.

3. A temptation; a trial. *Kanl.* 4:32.

Ho-ao, *adj.* The night of the day called Huna; mamua o ka po *hoao* o na alii, i ka po o Huna.

Ho-a-o-le-lo, *s. Hoa,* companion, and *olelo,* word. A companion in conversation; one consulted on business; a counsellor; o lakou no ko Kamehameha mau *hoaolelo* no kela mea keia mea nui o ke aupuni, those were Kamehameha's *counsellors* concerning every important matter of the kingdom.

Ho-a-pu-i-no-i-no, *s. Hoa* and *opuino,* evilly disposed. A companion in crime; one alike evilly disposed with another.

Ho-au, *v. Ho* for *hoo,* and *au,* to swim.

1. To move gently a little; to dodge.

2. To bring forward and present on the altar of the gods.

3. To offer a sacrifice; to courtesy.

Ho-au, *v.* To strike; to beat with a stick.

2. To wash clothes, as Hawaiians wash clothes by beating them. See Hoauau.

Ho-au-au, *v. Ho* for *hoo,* and *au,* to swim, or *auau,* to wash. To wash the body; to bathe; to cleanse away filth by bathing.

Ho-au-au, *s.* See the verb. A washing; a cleansing by the use of water.

Ho-au-au, *v. Ho* for *hoo,* and *auau.* See Auau 4. To excite; to stir up; to hurry; to quicken one to do a thing.

Ho-au-au, *s.* Quickness in doing a thing; haste.

2. Name of a snare used in catching birds, like kipuka, pahele, ahele, &c.

Ho-au-au-wa-ha, *v. Ho* for *hoo, auau* for *au,* and *waha.* See Auwaha. To make a ditch; to plow a furrow.

Ho-au-ae-puu,
Ho-au-wae-puu, *v. Ho* for *hoo,* and *auae,* to be lazy. To be lazy; indolent; inactive; to spend time to no profit.

Ho-au-ae-puu, *s.* See Auae. Indolence; loitering; inactive; disposed to treat with contempt.

Ho-au-hee, *v. Ho* for *hoo,* and *auhee.* See Hee, to flee. To cause to flee, as an army; to rout; to put to flight.

Ho-au-hee-hee, *v.* See above. To converse of things generally.

Ho-au-lii, *adj.* Nice; well dressed; straight as a stick; skilful; mikioi, palawaiki, hoakamai.

Ho-au-mo-e, *v. Ho* for *hoo,* and *aumoe,* to sleep.

1. To sleep with; to lie in one's bosom.

2. To fondle; to cherish in the bosom, as a child or a pet.

Ho-au-mo-e, *s.* A cherishing; a fondling, as a child or a pet animal; fondness; attachment.

Ho-au-na, *v. Ho* for *hoo,* and *auna,* a flock. To collect together, as a flock of birds.

Ho-a-u-na, *s. Hoa,* companion, and *una,* to send. A companion of a messenger; one who accompanies a messenger.

Ho-au-hu-lu, *v.* To converse. See Ho-auheehee.

Ho-a-ha, *v. Ho* for *hoo,* and *aha,* a cord. To make or braid together the strings for a calabash; to tie up a calabash; e *hoaha* i ka ipu.

Ho-a-ha-a-ha, *v.* To sit cross-legged, à la Turk, in eating.

2. To be proud; high-minded; he kanaka *hoahaaha.*

3. To be bent up; stunted; crooked out of shape.

Ho-a-ha-na, *s. Hoa,* companion, and *hana,* to work. A fellow laborer in any kind of business. *1 Kor.* 3:9.

Ho-a-ha-nau, *s. Hoa,* companion, and *hanau,* to be born. A companion by birth;

a kindred; some blood relation; a relative; a brother in an extensive sense. 1 *Oihl.* 9:25. In a modern sense, a fellow professor of religion.

HO-A-HA-NAU-NA, *s.* *Hoa,* companion, and *hanauna,* relations. Relatives of one's own clan, tribe or nation. *Gal.* 1:14. See HANAUNA.

HO-A-HA-AI-NA, *v.* *Ho* for *hoo, aha,* collection, and *aina,* to eat. To cause a collection for eating; to make a feast.

HO-A-HA-AI-NA, *s.* *Ho* for *hoa* (one *a* dropped), and *ahaaina,* a feast. A fellow feaster; one at the same feast.

HO-A-HE-LE, *s.* *Hoa* and *hele,* to go. A fellow traveler. *Ios.* 14:8.

HO-A-HE-WA, } *v.* See AHEWA and
HOO-A-HE-WA, } HEWA. A finding or pronouncing guilty of a crime or wrong; to condemn.

HO-A-HI-A-HI, *v.* *Ho* for *hoo,* and *ahiahi,* evening. To darken; to obscure; to cause a thing to be obscure in vision; to be neither clear nor dark.

HO-A-HO, *v.* *Ho* for *hoo,* and *aho,* breath.
1. To give breath, i. e., deliverance from immediate danger; to put one in safety from danger.
2. To be quick; to hasten; to do quickly.
3. To kindle a fire.

HO-A-HO, *v.* *Ho* and *aho,* a string.
1. To make or twist strings for a house.
2. To tie aho on to a building. See AHO.

HO-A-HO, *s.* Quickness; rapidity.
2. One who has escaped a place of protection.

HO-A-HO-A, *v.* See HOA, to strike. The freq. conj. of hoa. To strike or smite frequently.
2. To break fuel, as Hawaiians did before they had axes.
3. To cause the hair to stand erect; e hookuku ae i ka lauoho iluna.

HO-A-HO-A, *s.* A striking, smiting, &c.
2. The name of the mallet with which kapa (the wauki) was beaten.

HO-A-HO-A-A-KA, *v.* To cause a fire to burn; to make a blaze; to make a shining light.

HO-A-HO-A-A-KA, *s.* A burning fire; a blaze; a bright light.

HO-A-HOO-LAU-KA-NA-KA, *s.* *Hoa,* friend, *hoo,* causative, *lau,* the number 400, *kanaka,* men.
1. A friend of the increase of men; one friendly to the multitude.
2. The multitude itself; aloha oe e kuu

hoahoolaukanaka o kahi kanaka ole, good morning my *friend of the people* where there are none.

HO-A-HOO-I-LI-NA, *s.* *Hoa,* companion, *hoo,* causative, and *ilina,* an inheritance. A fellow heir to an inheritance.

HO-A-HU, *v.* *Ho* for *hoo,* and *ahu,* a collection of things.
1. To cause a collection or gathering together.
2. To lay up, as goods for future use. *Mat.* 6:26.
3. To collect articles; to lay up in heaps.
4. To lay up against one, as anger; e *hoahu* ana i ka huhu maluna o kela poe.

HO-A-HU, *v.* To esteem lightly; to despise; to contemn; to dislike; to be dissatisfied with.

HO-A-HU, *s.* An assemblage of things; a collection.
2. A collecting, as of property; a gathering together.
3. Dislike; contempt for a thing.

HO-A-HU, *adj.* Disagreeable; unsatisfactory.

HO-A-KA, *v.* To lift up; to lift up, as a spear in fighting. 2 *Sam.* 23:18.
2. To drive away; to frighten.
3. To open; to open the mouth in speaking. See OAKA. *Hoik.* 13:6.
4. To glitter; to shine; to be splendid. *Nahum.* 2:3.

HO-A-KA, *v.* *Ho* for *hoo,* and *aka,* to laugh. To cause one to laugh; to laugh; to be pleased.

HO-A-KA, *s.* A name of one of the kapu days; to second day of the moon.
2. The crescent of the new moon; the hollow of the new moon.
3. The arch or lintel over a door. *Puk.* 12:7.
4. In *speaking,* a defense; an apology.

HO-A-KA, *s.* Brightness; shining; a glittering; a flaming torch. *Nahum.* 2:3. Glory, as of a people, i. e., their liberty; freedom.

HO-A-KAA, } *v.* To covet; to desire
HO-A-KA-A-KA, } earnestly.

HO-A-KA-A-KA, *v.* *Ho* for *hoo,* and *aka,* to laugh.
1. To cause laughter; to cause one to laugh.
2. To laugh at; to mock; to reproach.

HO-A-KAU-A, *s.* *Hoa,* companion, and *kaua,* war.
1. A fellow soldier.
2. One against whom a soldier is fighting; an antagonist; hoapaio.

Ho-a-kau-wa, *s.* *Hoa,* companion, and *kauwa,* a servant. A fellow servant. *Hoik.* 19:10.

Ho-a-ka-ka, *v.* *Ho* for *hoo,* and *akaka,* clear; explicit. To make plain; clear to render explicit; to explain; to interpret.

Ho-a-ka-ka, *s.* An explanation; an opening of what is intricate.

Ho-a-ka-ka-ia, *adj.* Expressed; stated proved; rendered explicit; approved. *Oih.* 2:22.

Ho-a-ka-ka-kai, *s.* Name of a disease generally fatal.

Ho-a-ka-ke-a, *s.* *Hoaka* and *kea,* a cross. The arch over a door; a lintel.

Ho-a-ka-ku, *v.* *Ho* for *hoo,* and *akaku,* a vision. To have a vision with the eyes open. See AKAKU.

Ho-a-ka-ku, *s.* A vision.

Ho-a-ka-ku, *s.* Name of a fatal disease; an internal disease.

Ho-a-ka-la-ka-la, *s.* A bracelet made of hog's teeth.

Ho-a-ke-a, *v.* *Ho* for *hoo,* and *akea,* broad. To make broad or wide; to cause enlargement; hence, to deliver from difficulty.

Ho-a-ke-a-ia, *s.* Enlargement; escape; deliverance. *Eset.* 4:14.

Ho-a-ki, *v.* To withhold from the landlord his due; *hoaki i ka hakuaina.*

Ho-a-ko-a, *s.* *Hoa,* companion, and *koa,* soldier. A fellow soldier; one under the same leader. *Pilip.* 2:25. See HOAKAUA.

Ho-a-ko-a-ko-a, *v.* *Ho* for *hoo,* and *akoakoa,* to assemble.

1. To assemble; to come together, as men.

2. To collect, as things generally. See AKOAKOA.

Ho-a-ku-ka, } *s.* *Hoa,* companion,
Ho-a-ku-ka-ku-ka, } and *kuka,* to consult. A fellow counsellor; an adviser. *Rom.* 11:34.

Ho-a-la, *v.* *Ho* for *hoo,* and *ala,* to rise up.

1. To raise up from a prostrate position.

2. To awake from sleep; to cause one to awake.

3. To raise up; to excite; to stir up; applied to the mind.

4. To rouse one to action.

Ho-a-la-a-la, *v.* The intensive of the foregoing.

Ho-a-lau-na, *s.* *Hoa,* companion, and *launa,* friendly. A companion on intimate terms; an intimate friend always near. 2 *Sam.* 15:37. One in the habit of rendering

kind offices; a neighbor. *Puk.* 12:4.

Ho-a-la-kaa, *v.* *Ho* for *hoo,* *ala,* road, and *kaa,* to roll. To cause to roll; to roll along a road.

Ho-a-la-la, *v.* *Ho* for *hoo,* and *alala,* to cry out. See ALALA. To make one cry out, as the alala.

Ho-a-la-la-hi-a, *v.* To stir one asleep so as to wake him; to punch; to touch; to shake so as to waken one; *hoalalahia aku ua kane hele loa nei au la.*

Ho-a-la-wa-ia, *s.* *Hoa,* companion, and *lawaia,* a fisherman. A fellow fisherman; a fishing companion.

Ho-a-la-we-ha-na, *s.* *Hoa,* companion, *lawe,* to bear, and *hana,* work. A fellow laborer; a fellow workman; a helper; an assistant. *Ezer.* 5:3. See LAWEHANA.

Ho-a-la-we-pu, *s.* *Hoa* and *lawe,* to carry, and *pu,* together. One who works with another; a partner in labor. *Pilem.* 17.

Ho-a-le-a-le, *v.* *Ho* for *hoo,* and *ale,* a wave. To make or cause waves in water; to stir up, as water. See ALEALE.

Ho-a-li, *v.* To shake; to wave an offering made to the gods; to swing; to move to and fro. *Puk.* 29:24. To wave, as an offering. *Nah.* 5:26.

2. To offer, as a sacrifice. *Nah.* 8:21.

3. To stir up, as ashes.

Ho-a-li, *adj.* That which may be waved. *Puk.* 29:24. Mohai *hoali,* a wave-offering.

Ho-a-li-a-li, *v.* See HOALI 2. To offer frequently to the gods.

Ho-a-li-a-li, *v.* *Ho* for *hoo,* and *aliali,* to whiten. To make white, as snow or paper.

Ho-a-lii, *adj.* *Ho* for *hoo,* and *alii,* chief; king. Causing a royal appearance; imitating royalty; royal; kingly; kapa *hoalii,* clothing of tapestry. *Sol.* 31:22.

Ho-a-lii, *s.* *Hoa,* companion, and *alii,* chief. A contraction for *hoaalii* or *hoa'lii.* The companion of the king or high chief; *kukuluia i hale kamala no ka hoalii,* a moe no ka *hoalii* ma ua hale la.

Ho-a-lo, *v.* *Ho* for *hoo,* and *alo,* to dodge.

1. To shun or avoid; to escape from. 1 *Pet.* 3:11. To pass over or by. *Isa.* 46:27.

2. To skip over, as in counting, ka hana i kekahi la, ka noho wale i kekahi la, to work one day, to do nothing one day. See ALO.

Ho-a-lo, *s.* A man that works, then ceases, then works by spells.

Ho-a-lo-a-lo, *v.* See HOALO. To dodge or pass by frequently.

Ho-a-lo-aa, *s.* *Hoa,* companion, and

loaa, to obtain.

1. A fellow receiver; a partaker with one. 1 *Pet.* 5:1.

2. One who receives as much as another; ka loaa like.

Ho-a-lo-ha, *s.* A contraction for *hoa-aloha*. A friend; a beloved companion; one on friendly terms. See Hoaaloha.

Ho-a-lo-ha, } *v.* Ho for *hoo*, and
Ho-a-lo-ha-lo-ha, } *aloha*, to love.

1. To love; to fondle; to cherish.

2. To give thanks for something received. 1 *Kor.* 11:24.

3. To make suit to; to pay respects to. *Iob.* 11:19. To apply to for a favor. *Laieik.* 72.

Ho-a-ho-a-lo-ha-lo-ha, *s.* Poetic: *hoa*, companion, and *aloha*, love. Those who converse often together, who are chief friends and love each other.

Ho-a-lu, *v.* Ho for *hoo*, and *alu*, flexible.

1. To be flexible; to loosen; to hang down.

2. To bow down; to make low; to be humble; to courtesy. See Alu.

Ho-a-lu, *s.* Flexibility; pliableness; humility; a bending down.

Ho-a-lu, *adj.* Yielding; bending; loose; hanging down.

Ho-a-lu-a-lu, *v.* See Hoalu and Alu. To be soft; flexible; yielding.

2. To bow down; to be humble.

Ho-a-lu-a-lu, *s.* Softness; a yielding to any pressure; humility.

Ho-a-lu-a-lu, *adj.* Hanging loosely; bending down; yielding.

Ho-a-lu-hi, *s.* *Hoa*, companion, and *luhi*, fatigue from labor. A companion or fellow laborer in any work or business, whether there be much or little fatigue; eia keia, e o'u *hoaluhi*.

Ho-a-ma, *v.* To begin to ripen, as ohias and other fruit, but not yet soft.

Ho-a-na, *s.* A hone; a whetstone; a grindstone.

2. He *hoana* e paa ai ka waa, a *polishing stone* for finishing a canoe.

Ho-a-na, *v.* To rub, as with a stone; to grind, as with a grindstone. See Anai. But *hookala* is more often used for grinding, i. e., for sharpening tools.

2. To make believe; to make pretense.

Ho-a-na, *s.* The name of a species of fish, large and singularly abrupt behind, as if cut off in the middle; the diodon.

Ho-a-na-a-na-puu, } *v.* See Hoana, to
Ho-a-na-puu, } grind. To twist; to bend; to undulate, as the air.

2. To throw up in heaps.

Ho-a-na-a-na-puu, } *s.* A crooking; a
Ho-a-na-puu, } bending; an undulating motion; protuberances. See Anapuu.

Ho-a-na-e, *v.* To lay up; to stow away for future use. 1 *Pet.* 1:4.

2. To set aside; to reserve. *Iud.* 6. To lay aside, i. e., to conceal. Note.—In *Oihk.* 8:12 hoana is printed for *hoano*, to sanctify, to consecrate, and in some senses *hoana* is similar in meaning to *hoano*.

Ho-a-na-hu-a, *v.* Ho for *hoo*, and *ana-hua*, stooping; bending. To stoop; to bend over, as a tall, slim man who walks stoop-shouldered. See Anahua and Kanahua.

Ho-a-na-hu-a, *s.* A tall, slim, stoop-shouldered man.

2. Anything like a humpbacked person. See Kanahua.

Ho-a-na-kaa, *v.* *Hoana*, grindstone, and *kaa*, to turn. To turn a grindstone; to grind or sharpen, as an edged tool.

Ho-a-na-kaa, *s.* A grindstone. See Hoana.

Ho-a-na-pa, *v.* Ho for *hoo*, and *anapa*, to flash; to shine.

1. To exhibit a flashing light; to cause sudden reflected light, as from a mirror.

2. To flash, as lightning; to glitter. See Anapa.

Ho-a-na-pa, *s.* Light from reflection; a bright flashing light, like lightning; any reflected or sudden light.

Ho-a-na-pau, *v.* To turn, as on hinges.

2. To bend, as a flexible piece of timber; to form a curve. See Anapau.

Ho-a-na-pau, *s.* See Anapau. A turning; a place of turning; a hinge joint; a bending; a crook.

Ho-a-na-puu, *v.* See Hoanaanapuu above. To crook, as a piece of timber; to be uneven, as a rope of unequal size; to project; to make an angle. See Anapuu.

Ho-a-na-puu, *s.* A crook; a bending; a protuberance.

Ho-a-no, *v.* Ho for *hoo*, and *ano*, form.

1. To reverence in the highest degree. *Mat.* 6:9. To hallow. *Oihk.* 10:3. To be holy. *Oihk.* 11:45.

2. To set apart; to consecrate; to lay up, as a sacred deposit; to put by; to keep back. See Hoanae.

3. *Hoano e*, to set apart for a particular purpose, either good or bad; to keep back; to conceal; to embezzle property.

4. To dare; to venture.

5. To be proud; to be full of self confi-

dence. *Rom.* 2:17.

6. To change one's appearance; to appear what one is not; to disguise. 2 *Sam.* 28:8.

HO-A-NO, *s.* See the verb. Pride; self confidence; a high, daring spirit. See HOA-ANO and AANO. Boasting of one's bravery. See HAANO.

HO-A-NO, *adj.* Sacred. *Puk.* 3:5. Devoted to sacred uses. *Oihk.* 5:15, 16. Consecrated.

HO-A-NO-HO, *s.* Hoa, companion, and *noho*, to dwell. A neighbor; one who resides with or near by another. *Ios.* 20:5.

HO-A-PAI-O, *s.* Hoa, companion, and *paio*, to contend. An antagonist; a fellow wrestler or fellow fighter. 1 *Sam.* 2:16.

HO-A-PA-O-NI-O-NI, *s.* Hoa, companion, and *paonioni*, to struggle. A fellow contender. See PAONIONI.

HO-A-PA-PU-A, *s.* Hoa, companion, and *papua*, to throw arrows. One who plays with or bets with another in the game of papua.

HO-A-PI, *v.* See HOAKI.

HO-A-PI-O, *s.* Hoa, fellow, and *pio*, prisoner. A fellow prisoner. *Pilem.* 23.

HO-A-PI-LI, *s.* Hoa, companion, and *pili*, to adhere. One who attaches himself to a chief and goes with him constantly; a friend. *Hal.* 15:3. An attaché. NOTE.— This was the name given to the late Governor of Maui, from his attachment to Kamehameha I. His original name was Ulumaheihei.

HO-A-PI-PI, *v.* To be united together, as two canoes, but not like a double-canoe; he waa aole i *hoapipiia*, he waa hookahi.

HO-A-PO-NO, *v.* Ho for *hoo*, and *apono*, to approve. To pronounce blameless; to approve; to find not guilty on trial.

HO-A-PO-NO, *adj.* Approved as not in error; right.

HO-A-WA, *v.* Ho for *hoo*, and *awa*, bitter.

1. To cause bitterness; to make bitter to the taste.

2. FIG. To be hard; to be cruel; to oppress; more often *hoawaawa*.

HO-A-WA, *s.* Name of a tree or shrub.

HO-A-WAA, *s.* The tackling or rigging up of a canoe, tying on the ako, &c.; o ka aha, he mea *hoawaa* ia, a e holo ai.

HO-A-WA-A-WA, *v.* Ho for *hoo*, and *awaawa*. See AWA.

1. To be bitter to the taste; to make bitter; to cause bitterness.

2. To be hard; to be cruel; to embitter one's life; to curse.

HO-A-WA-A-WA, *s.* Bitterness to the taste. FIG. Hardship.

HO-A-WA-A-WA, *adj.* Bitter to the taste; severe; cruel; hard.

HO-A-WA-A-WA, *s.* Bitterness; sourness; badness.

2. A rising in the stomach from sourness or other causes.

HO-A-WA-HI-A, *v.* For *hoawaia*, passive. To be bitter; to cause bitterness; to cause sadness, sorrow, suffering. See AWA and AWAHIA.

HO-A-WA-WA, *v.* Ho for *hoo*, and *awawa*, a ditch. To make a ditch or furrow. See AWAWA.

HO-A-WE, *v.* Ho for *hoo*, and *awe*, to carry on the back. To carry on the back, as a child or a person. See AWE and LAWE.

HO-A-WE, *s.* Ho and *awe*, a burden. A burden; a weight carried on the back.

HO-A-WE-A-WE, *s.* Anything made small or diminished.

HO-A-WE-A-WE-A, *v.* To discolor; to be colored a reddish brown, like red that is faded.

HO-A-WE-A-WE-A, *s.* A reddish color; an indistinct color, like the sea at times.

HO-A-WE-A-WE-A, *adj.* Faded; discolored.

I kikohukohu *hoaweawea* a ke kai.—*Mele.*

HO-E, *s.* A paddle for a canoe; an oar for a boat.

HO-E-U-LI, *s.* A rudder.

HO-E-HA, *v.* Ho for *hoo*, and *eha*, pain. To cause pain; to give pain.

hoe

HO-E-HA-E-HA, *v.* Ho for *hoo*, and *ehaeha*, the reduplication of *eha*. To give pain, bodily or mentally; to vex; to harass; to get one into perplexity; to oppress.

HO-E-HA-E-HA, *s.* Pain; distress, either of body or mind; vexation; perplexity.

HO-E-HA-E-HA, *adj.* Painful; distressing; difficult; troublesome.

HO-E-HO-E, *s.* See HOE. The shoulderblade, from its resemblance to a canoe paddle; ka iwi ma ke kumu o ka iwi uluna.

HO-E-HO-E, *v.* See HOE, a paddle. To row a canoe or boat here and there.

HO-E-HO-E, *s.* A wind instrument among Hawaiians somewhat resembling the flute.

HO-E-HO-E-NA, *v.* See HOEHOE above and ANA. To play softly on the hoehoe;

hence,

2. To be joyful. See HOENE.

3. To bore; to pierce through in boring; e *hoehoena* iloko o ka pepeiao.

HO-E-HO-E-NE, *v.* To be poor; destitute; sick.

HO-E-HU, *v. Ho* for *hoo,* and *ehu,* to scare away.

1. To drive or frighten away; e *hoehu* i ka puaa e ku mai nei, *drive away* the pig standing here.

2. To do a thing quickly.

HO-E-LE-E-LE, *v. Ho* for *hoo,* and *eleele,* dark. To make black; to darken.

HO-E-LE-I-KI, *s.* Robbery; a lying in wait to rob one; deceit; treachery.

HO-E-LO, *v.* To urge on; to push along; to cram down; e ohiki iloko.

2. To kindle up, as a flame; o ke ahi nana e *hoelo* wela.

HO-E-LO, *adj.* Urging; throwing in.

HO-E-LO-E-LO, *v.* To press on; to urge forward.

HO-E-MI, *v. Ho* for *hoo,* and *emi,* to lessen.

1. To cause a diminution; to lessen.

2. To shrink; to become blunt, as an edged tool.

3. To return backwards; to fall behind.

4. To drive back; to put down.

HO-E-MI-E-MI, *v.* See HOEMI. To shrink back, as the mind; to doubt; to hesitate.

HO-E-MU, *v. Ho* for *hoo,* and *emu,* to throw away. To cast away; to banish; to send away; to drive off; to drive off as one drives off hogs.

HO-E-NA, *v. Ho* for *hoo,* and *ena,* to rage, as fire.

1. To cause to burn, to glow with heat.

2. To be in anger; to exhibit a high degree of anger. See ENA.

HO-E-NA-E-NA, *v.* To glow, as stones red hot in a fire. See ENA.

HO-E-NE, *v.* To sing; to be joyful; to play well on an instrument.

HO-E-NE, *s.* Pleasure; enjoyment; o ka *hoene* ku o ka uwe a ka lani.

HO-E-NE, *v.* To give an injection; e halalo; to administer medicine.

HO-E-NE, *s.* A syringe.

HO-E-NO, *v. Ho* for *hoo,* and *eno,* to be wild. To run as wild; to be scary, as an animal once tame, but has become wild. See AHIU.

HO-E-PA, *v. Ho* for *hoo,* and *epa,* to deceive. To deceive; to cheat; to act basely in everything. See EPA.

HO-E-PA-E-PA, *v.* Freq. of the foregoing.

To act out a general bad character; to steal; to cheat; to slander, &c. See EPA.

HO-E-WA, *v. Ho* for *hoo,* and *ewa,* to turn aside. To be one-sided; to lean over; to sway to and fro like an old grass house in the wind.

HO-E-WAA, *v. Hoe,* paddle, and *waa,* canoe. To row or paddle a canoe.

HO-E-WAA, *s.* An oarsman; one who rows a boat or paddles a canoe. *Laieik.* 35.

HO-I, *v.* To return; to go back; with *hou,* to return again; *imperatively,* e *hoi,* and o *hoi,* go back; return.

HO-I, *adv.* Also; besides; moreover; indeed; an intensive word; *no hoi,* also; besides.

HOI, *s.* The name of a vine bearing a bulbous root, eaten in time of scarcity, acrid to the taste.

HOI, *s.* The name of a state of marriage among chiefs.

HO-I-I, *v. Ho* for *hoo,* and *ii,* parsimonious.

1. To save; to gather together little things.

2. To be close; parsimonious; pinching in a bargain.

3. To squeeze or work out of another some little favor.

4. To be hard upon; to oppress; applied to begging for charitable purposes; o ka hookohukohu ame ka *hoii* a kanaka no ke Akua. See II and KAII 3.

HO-I-I, *s.* Stinginess; closeness in dealing; hard and cruel oppression upon the weak and poor.

HO-I-I-MA-KA, *v. Ho* for *hoo, ii,* to be hard, and *maka,* face.

1. To forbid or discountenance iniquity openly, but favor it secretly in practice.

2. To play the hypocrite. See HOII.

HO-I-O, *s.* A species of plant, the tender leaves of which are used for herbs.

HO-I-O-LE, *v. Ho* for *hoo,* and *iole,* a mouse. To cause to rush upon; to seize, as a cat does a mouse; to hold fast.

2. To force; to compel.

HO-I-O-MO, *v. Ho* for *hoo,* and *iomo,* to fall into the water without spattering. To bung up; to stop, as with a cork or bung.

HO-I-U, *v. Ho* for *hoo,* and *iu,* to lay a kapu.

1. To lay a kapu upon a person, place or thing; to consecrate such person, place or thing to a particular purpose.

2. To create fear, as fear was connected with this kapu.

3. To be afraid. See IU.

Ho-i-u, *s.* Fear; trembling; anxiety.

Ho-i-hi, *adj.* Afar off; at a very great distance. See LOIHI.

Ho-i-ho-i, *v.* See HOI. Used *actively*, to return a thing to its former place; to restore; to bring back. 2 *Sam.* 19:10, 11.

    2. To send back; to dismiss.

    3. To change one thing for another.

    4. To return; to restore, as a rebellious people to their allegiance. 1 *Nal.* 12:21.

    5. To return an answer; e *hoihoi* i ka olelo. *Iob.* 35:4.

Ho-i-ho-i, *v.* In a *neuter sense*, to return; to go back; used for *hoi.*

Ho-i-ho-i, *v.* To be pleased; to rejoice; to be joyful.

    2. *Hoo.* To refresh; to assist; to give pleasure. 2 *Tim.* 1:16. To be greatly consoled. *Heb.* 6:18.

    3. To reprove. 2 *Tim.* 4:2.

Ho-i-ho-i, *s.* Joy; gladness; good feeling; rejoicing; cheerfulness. *Rom.* 12:8. Gratification in a thing. *Neh.* 4:6. Me ka *hoihoi,* me ka hauoli ame ka manao lana, with *good feeling,* with joy and with hope.

Ho-i-ho-i, *adj.* Glad; joyful; gratified; well pleased.

Ho-i-hou, *v.* Hoi, to return, and *hou,* again. To return again.

Ho-i-hou, *s.* In *music,* name of the character signifying a repeat.

Ho-i-ho-pe, *v.* Hoi, to return, and *hope,* backwards. To go back after an advance; to return to former practices after a reformation; to revolt, as one taken captive; to turn back. *Ier.* 6:28.

Ho-i-ke, *v.* Ho for *hoo,* and *ike,* to know.

    1. To cause to know; to make known.

    2. To show; to make a display; e unihi, e puka iwaho; to put outside for appearance; to exhibit; to explain, as a language.

Ho-i-ke, *s.* That which shows or is shown; an exhibition, as of a school; a witness of an event; a witness in a court of justice. SYN. with ikemaka, also hoikemaka, an eye-witness. *Pilip.* 1:8.

Ho-i-ke, *adj.* Exhibiting; showing; making plain.

Ho-i-ke, *adv.* Openly; visibly; clearly.

Ho-i-ke-a-na, *s.* A showing; exhibiting.

    2. The name of the last book in the Bible, *Revelations.*

Ho-i-ke-i-ke, *v.* Ho for *hoo,* and *ike,* to know. To know, more particularly than *hoike;* to make known clearly; to communicate knowledge; to point out truths or facts.

Ho-i-li, *v.* Ho for *hoo,* and *ili,* to strike; to hit.

    1. To cause to bring or to come upon one.

    2. To place upon, i. e., to put on board a ship.

    3. To strike upon, as a ship upon a rock; to go ashore; to strand.

    4. To fall to one, as property from a parent; to inherit. See ILI.

Ho-i-li-i-li, *v.* Ho for *hoo,* and *iliili,* to collect.

    1. To collect together, as things of any kind in one place.

    2. To lay up; to heap together.

Ho-i-lo, *s.* The season of the year answering to winter in more northern latitudes.

    2. Winter, the stormy season, from the interruption of regular trade winds. *Hoilo* is used in opposition to *kau,* the hot or summer season. The word is also written *hooilo.*

Ho-i-lo, *adj.* Wintry; pertaining to winter. *Ier.* 36:22.

Ho-i-lo-i-lo, *v.* To guess before hand; to predict something future; *especially,* to predict evil; to tell one when he was sick that he would die; i *hoiloilo* mai o mea ia'u e make, a ua ola; to give up a sick person to die as incurable.

Ho-i-li-hu-ne, *v.* Ho for *hoo,* and *ili-hune,* poor; destitute.

    1. To make one poor; to deprive one of his property.

    2. To be humble; lowly. See ILIHUNE.

Ho-i-li-ko-le, *v.* Ho for *hoo,* and *ilikole,* raw skin. Like the foregoing, only more strong. To make very poor; to deprive of all comforts. See ILIKOLE.

Ho-i-mi, *v.* Ho for *hoo,* and *imi,* to seek. To search diligently.

Ho-i-nai-na, *v.* Ho for *hoo,* and *inaina,* anger. To cause hatred; to stir up anger; to provoke one to anger.

Ho-i-na-i-na, *v.* See INA. To ease off; to hang down; to crook.

Ho-i-no, *v.* Ho for *hoo,* and *ino,* bad.

    1. To curse one. 1 *Sam.* 17:43. To vex; to harass; to harm; to injure; to cause reproach.

    2. To make filthy; to defile. See INO.

Ho-i-no, *s.* Reproach; contempt. 1 *Sam.* 17:26.

Ho-i-no, *adj.* Berena *hoino,* bread of affliction. *Kanl.* 16:3.

Ho-i-no, *adv.* Mai olelo *hoino,* do not revile. *Puk.* 22:28.

Ho-i-no-ia, *s.* That which is contemptible; a reproach; contempt. *Kin.* 30:23.

HO-I-NO-I-NO, *v. Ho* for *hoo,* and *inoino* (see INO), to deface. To disfigure; to sadden; to disguise, as the face by austerity. *Mat.* 6:16.

HO-I-NU, *v. Ho* for *hoo,* and *inu,* to drink. To give drink; to cause one to drink; generally written *hohainu.*

HO-I-PO, } *v. Ho* for *hoo,* and *ipo,*
HO-I-PO-I-PO, } a paramour. To commit fornication or adultery secretly.

HO-I-WI, *v. Ho* for *hoo,* and *iwi,* crooked. See IWI, *adj.* To turn the eye-ball from its natural position; to turn the eyes aside; to squint; to be cross-eyed.

HOO. This word is the causative prefix to verbs; as, *malu,* to shade, *hoomalu,* to cause a shade, to overshadow; *pono,* good, right, *hoopono,* to correct, to make right; *akea,* to be broad, *hooakea* or *hoakea,* to cause to be broad, i. e., to extend, enlarge, &c. See *Gram.* § 33 and § 212, and the conjugations 7, 8, 11, 12, 15 and 16.

This prefix, though originally adapted to the verb, continues its influence though the verb with its causative prefix becomes a noun, adjective or adverb. Ua hele oia i ka *hoike,* he has gone to the *exhibition;* he kanaka *hoopunipuni,* a man *causing deception,* i. e., a *deceitful* man; olelo *hooino* iho la, he spoke *causing reproach,* i. e., he spoke reproachfully. Before words whose first letter is a vowel, the last *o* of the *hoo* frequently coalesces with the vowel of the word following, particularly before *a, e* and *o;* as, *hoano* for *hooano; hoole* for *hooole,* &c. (See the preceding pages from the word *hoaa* to *hoo.*) Some words have *haa* for their causative prefix instead of *hoo;* as, *haaheo* for *hooheo* (from *heo,* pride), to be haughty. This form seems to come from the Tahitian dialect. A few words take both forms for their causative, as *hoonui* and *haanui,* from *nui,* to be large. *Hoawi,* to give, is used for *hooawi,* but *haawi* is used oftener than either.

Strictly speaking, *hoo* in a dictionary should not begin a verb, but verbs having this prefix should be set in their places, and their meanings be modified by the *hoo* as it occurs; as, ike, to know, &c., *hoo.* or *ho.,* to cause to know, to show, to exhibit; *ikeia,* to be known, *hoo.,* to be made known, to be shown; *ikeike,* to know clearly, *hoo.,* to make known clearly or frequently, &c.; but a large class of words have been found beginning with the causative prefix *hoo,* whose roots are not known or have not come to light, or are out of use. It is true, such a root might be assumed as being in existence or having once existed, as Greek Lexicographers often assume an obsolete theme; but there would be much danger in Hawaiian of getting the wrong word: hence, we know not where to put such roots unless we retain the *hoo* for the beginning of the word. This occasions some repetition, but it is hoped it will not be a serious inconvenience. The following words beginning with *hoo* are such as were first found in that form and whose root was not known. They are now retained in that form because many are other parts of speech than verbs. Where the words beginning with *hoo* have been defined under their roots, the definitions here will be very short and the reader referred to the root.

HO-O, *v. Ho* for *hoo,* and *o,* to pierce. See the verb O. To pierce; to stab; to cause to enter; to thrust or put in.

2. To furnish; to supply. *Iob.* 38:36.

3. To stretch out; to extend, as the hand to do a thing.

HO-O, *v.* To cause to enter; to put one's hand in his pocket; *hoo* iho la i ka poi, kukulu iwaho.

HOO-A, *v.* To break; to break up, as fuel; to break to pieces.

2. To vomit; to be sick at the stomach. See HOOWA.

HOO-A, *s.* A breaking up; a separating.

HOO-AA, } *v.* The *o* and *a* coalescing
HOO-WAA, } give the sound of *w. Gram.* § 13:7, note.

1. To dig up, as a trench; to dig, as with an oo or spade.

2. To wander about without friends; to be destitute.

HOO-AE, *v.* See AE, to break kapu. To break, as a law or kapu; to transgress.

HOO-AI-KA-NE, *v.* See AIKANE. To make friends.

HOO-AI-PUU-PUU, *v.* See AIPUUPUU. To make or constitute one an aipuupuu or waiting servant; to act as a servant, particularly at waiting on the table.

HOO-AU-AU, *v.* See AUAU, to wash. To wash the body; to bathe.

HOO-AU-A-NA, } *v.* See AUANA, to wander. To cause to wander; to scatter; to disperse, as a conquering army disperses the enemy. PASS. To be dispersed.

HOO-AU-WA-NA, }

HOO-AU-HEE, *v.* See HEE and AUHEE,

to run, as from an enemy. To disperse in battle; to put to flight.

2. To pillage a conquered people.

3. FIG. To be destitute; to be stripped of everything as those formerly conquered were; hence,

4. To be poor; to be destitute of every comfort and resource.

HOO-AU-WA-HA, *v.* See AUWAHA and AUAUWAHA. To plow; to make a long ditch; to dig a furrow.

HOO-AU-WA-HA-WA-HA, *v.* Freq. of *hoo-auwaha* above.

HOO-AU-WA-NA, *v.* See AUWANA. To disperse, as a dog disperses a flock of goats, or as a conqueror disperses his enemies.

HOO-A-HA, *v.* So written for *hoowaha.* To make a dig a trench, ditch or furrow. See WAHA.

2. To covet; to seize upon without permission.

HOO-A-HA-A-HA, *v.* To sit cross-legged.

HOO-A-HE-WA, *v.* See HOAHEWA. To pronounce one guilty; to condemn.

HOO-A-HI, *v.* See AHI, fire. To set fire to; to set on fire.

2. FIG. To fire up; to be angry for a supposed offense; to be troubled with jealous feelings.

3. To peck or dig into, as a bird with its bill.

HOO-A-HO, *v.* See AHO, sticks for thatching on. See also HOAHO. To put the aho on a house; to tie on small sticks to hold the thatching of a house.

HOO-A-HU, *v.* See AHU, to collect. To gather together; to collect; to heap up.

2. To put down; to leave.

HOO-A-HU, *adj.* Gathered; collected; laid up.

2. Dissatisfied, as with work imperfectly done.

HOO-A-KA, } *v.* See AKA and AKA-
HOO-A-KA-A-KA, } AKA. To cause to laugh; to make one laugh.

HOO-A-KA, } *v.* See AKAKA, clear. To
HOO-A-KA-KA, } explain; to make clear what is intricate; to make perspicuous; to expound.

HOO-A-KA-MAI, *v.* See AKAMAI, skillful. To make wise; to be skillful at any art or business; to be intelligent.

2. To make a pretense of wisdom; to be proud of one's attainments.

HOO-A-KE-A, *v.* See AKEA, broad. To enlarge; to spread out; to widen; to make broad.

HOO-A-LA-LA, *v.* See ALALA and HOA-LALA. To cry out, as the alala; to make one cry.

HOO-A-LE-A-LE, *v.* See ALE, a wave, and ALEALE. To stir round soft poi with the fingers, as in eating poi; hence,

2. To eat poi. SYN. with miki.

3. To make the sea into waves.

HOO-A-LI-A, *v.* See ALIA. To hinder; mai *hooalia* mai oe; to stand in the way of another.

2. To cause one to stop doing a thing.

3. To wait; to procrastinate.

HOO-A-LII, *v.* See ALII, chief. To make a chief; to establish one in office.

HOO-A-LO-HA, *v.* See ALOHA, to love. To cause to love; to make one's self friends.

HOO-A-LO-HA-LO-HA, *v.* See ALOHA, to love. To take pleasure in; to give thanks; to bless.

HOO-A-LU-A-LU, *v.* See ALUALU, loose. To cause to loosen or slacken, as a rope; to make one's clothes loose.

HOO-A-MO, *v.* See AMO, to carry. To cause one to carry or bear a burden.

HOO-A-NA-E, *v.* See HOANOE. To set aside; to set apart for a particular use.

HOO-A-NI, *s.* A rumbling; a movement of wind in the bowels.

HOO-A-NO-A-NO, *v.* See HOANO. To be solemn, as with the idea that an invisible spirit was present.

2. To solemnize the mind, as for worship, or as in the presence of a spirit; *hooano-ano* wale mai no me he haili la e kau iho ana maluna.

HOO-A-PO-NO, *v.* See PONO and HOA-PONO. To pronounce not guilty, i. e., to justify.

HOO-E-A, *v.* See EA, to rise up. To lift up; to elevate.

HOO-E-A-E, *v.* To read with a tone.

HOO-EU, } *v.* See EU and EUEU. To
HOO-EU-EU, } animate; to encourage; to excite.

HOO-E-LE-E-LE, *v.* See ELE and ELEELE. To make black; to blacken, like the gathering of clouds before a storm.

HOO-E-MI, *v.* See EMI. To draw back; to diminish in size or number; to lessen; to humble.

HOO-I-A, *v.* For *hoooia.* See OIA, *v.* To prove; to confirm; to make evident; to confirm the truth of a thing.

HO-OI-OI, *adj.* See OIOI. Assuming; forward; desirous of appearing conspicuous; vain; conceited.

Hoo-ia-i-o, *v.* *Hooia* and *io*, really. To prove, &c.; to substantiate as a fact.

Hoo-ia-i-o, *s.* A pledge for something promised. *Kin.* 38:20.

Hoo-i-e-i-e, *v.* See Ieie, *adj.* To be proud; vainglorious; light minded; foppish.
2. To be quarrelsome.

Hoo-i-e-i-e, *adj.* Proud; vain; light minded. See above.

Hoo-i-i-ka, *v.* Freq. of *ika.* See Hooika.

Hoo-i-o, *v.* See Hooia above. To prove; to confirm.
2. To think much of one's self; mai ao i na mea hewa—i ka *hooio*, i ka hookiekie.

Hoo-i-ha-i-ha, *v.* See Iha. To draw tightly, as a rope; to be intent.

Hoo-i-ho, *v.* See Iho, to descend. To cause to descend; to go down; e *hooiho* ana ka waa i Oahu.

Hoo-i-ho-i-ho, *v.* Freq. of *iho*, *v.* To go down.

Hoo-i-ho-na, *s.* See Hooiho and Ana. A road leading down hill; a descending.

Hoo-i-ka, *v.* See Ika, to float ashore. To go ashore from a boat or canoe; to put ashore, as from a canoe; to throw on a bank from any water.

Hoo-i-kai-ka, *v.* See Ikaika, strong. To make strong; in a *reciprocal sense*, to make one's self strong.
2. To strengthen; to encourage; to animate.

Hoo-i-ke, *v.* See Ike and Hoike. To show; to make known; to exhibit; to enlighten.

Hoo-i-ki, *v.* See Iki, little. To make small; to diminish; to hold back.

Hoo-i-li, *v.* See Ili, to strike. To hit upon; to put upon, as to put on board a ship; to place upon, as upon the shoulders.

Hoo-i-li, *adj.* Articles of supply, as for family use; he nui no ka maona ma ke kuaaina, he maona *hooili*; something to eat and lay aside.

Hoo-i-li-i-li, *v.* See Li and Iliili, to collect. To collect in store; to gather together; to gather in heaps.

Hoo-i-li-na, *s.* See Ilina, burying place. An inheritance; property falling to one from the death of a person.
2. An heir; an inheritor of the property of a deceased person. *Kin.* 15:3, 4.
3. A burying place.

Hoo-i-lo, *s.* The name of the rainy or wintry months, in distinction from *kau*, the summer season; also *hoilo*.

Hoo-i-lo-i-lo, *v.* See Hoiloilo. To guess correctly; to predict; to tell beforehand; especially to predict evil.
2. To rejoice.

Hoo-i-nu, *v.* See Inu. To give drink to; to cause to drink; generally written *hoohainu*. For the *ha*, see *Gram.* § 48.

Hoo-i-nai-na, *v.* See Ina, *v.*, and Hoinaina.

Hoo-i-po, *v.* See Ipo, a mistress. To woo; to court; to solicit the affections of one; applied either to men or women.
2. To cohabit secretly; to keep a mistress.

Hoo-i-po-i-po, *v.* Freq. of the foregoing.

Hoo-oi-oi, *adj.* See Hooioi. Assuming; desirous of appearing at the head; conceited; vain. *Isa.* 3:16.

Hoo-o-lu-o-lu, *v.* See Oluolu and Hooluolu. To comfort; to console one in affliction and pain; to give to body or mind; to please.

Hoo-u-a, *v.* See Ua, rain. To cause it to rain; to give or cause rain.

Hoo-u-aa, or Hoo-u-waa, *adj.* Open; free to enter, as a harbor; e komo no na moku manuwa iloko o na awa a pau i *hoouaaia*.

Hoo-u-a-u-a, *v.* To be tight; strong; to draw along.

Hoo-u-a-hi, *v.* See Uahi, smoke. To cause smoke, steam or vapor; to burst forth, like steam.

Hoo-u-e, } *v.* See Ue and Uwe. To
Hoo-u-we, } cause one to cry; to cry out for pain or grief.

Hoo-u-e-u-e, *v.* Intensive of *hooue* above. To cry out; to sob; to sigh; to grieve; to mourn; to cry long; to wail.

Hoo-ue-ue, *v.* See Ueue, to shake. To cause a shaking; to bend; to crook; to move along a little.

Hoo-u-ha, *v.* To draw tightly.

Hoo-u-ha-u-ha, *v.* To fatigue; to tire.

Hoo-u-ha-lu, *v.* To bring out; to unfold.

Hoo-u-he-ne-he-ne, *v.* See Henehene. To laugh secretly at one; to mock ironically.

Hoo-u-hi, *v.* See Uhi, to cover up. To overspread; to cover up; to wrap up; to put out of sight by covering up.

Hoo-u-hi-u-hi, *v.* See Uhi as above. To cover up; to conceal in various ways; to cover over; to hide from view.

Hoo-u-hu-hi, *v.* To trouble; to vex.

Hoo-u-ka, *v.* See Uka, to send; convey. To put or lay upon, as to lade a horse or other animal; to put on board a canoe or vessel; to freight; to send property by ship.

2. To attack, as an enemy; to make an attack; to rush upon, as in battle.

Hoo-u-ka, *adj.* La *hoouka,* day of battle; day of attack. *Iob.* 38:23.

Hoo-u-ka-u-ka, *v.* Frequent. of *hoouka.*

Hoo-u-ka-li, *v.* See Ukali, to follow. To cause to follow; to follow after; to accompany by following.

Hoo-u-ka-na, *v.* See Ukana, goods to be carried along. To bundle up or pack movable goods.

Hoo-u-ki, *v.* See Uki, Ukiuki and Na-uki. To provoke; to do that which will offend.

Hoo-u-ki-u-ki, *v.* See Uki. To cause one to be offended; to insult.

Hoo-u-ku, *v.* See Uku, reward. To pay or discharge a debt; to pay a fine; to punish or reward; hoopai.

Hoo-u-ku, *v.* See Uku. A recompense; payment; doing justice. *Isa.* 35:4.

Hoo-u-lau-lau-a-ka, *v.* To enjoy, as the union of the sexes.

Hoo-u-le, *v.* See Ule, to hang down. To cause to hang; to swing.

Hoo-u-le-u-le, *v.* See Ule. To swing; to hang pendulous; to ease off; to crook or turn down.

Hoo-u-li, *v.* See Uli, to be dark colored. To make black; to darken; to be green, as the sea; as a forest.

Hoo-u-li-u-li, *v.* Intensive of the above.

Hoo-u-lu, *v.* See Ulu, to grow, as a vegetable. To cause to grow, as seeds planted; to sprout; to increase in size, as fruit.

2. To lift up; to release, as something fast; ma kahi e paa ai ka waa, e *hooulu* no kekahi kanaka i ka waa.

Hoo-u-lu-a, *v.* See Ulua, to assemble. To collect; to assemble together, as men; to collect together, as things.

Hoo-u-lu-a, *v.* To sing in order to encourage men to work.

Hoo-u-lu-u-lu, *v.* See Ulu and Ulu-ulu, to collect together. To collect together, as men or things; to assemble in one place.

Hoo-u-lu-u-lu-wa,   } *v. Ulu,* to collect,
Hoo-u-lu-u-lu-waa, }   and *waa,* canoe. To collect many canoes together in one place.

Hoo-u-lu-hu-a, *v.* See Uluhua. To give trouble; to weary; to vex; to oppress; to wear out the patience of one; mai *hoouluhua* i ke keiki.

Hoo-u-lu-lu, *v.* E *hooululu* akua, to make pretensions of being a god, or having a god in one.

Hoo-u-lu-ma-hi-e-hi-e, *v.* See Ulumahie.

Hoo-u-mi-ki, *v.* See Umiki, a gourd. To swell out round and full, as a large gourd.

Hoo-u-mi-ki-mi-ki, *v.* Intensive of the above.

Hoo-u-na, *v.* See Una, to send. To cause one to go on business; to send on an errand.

Hoo-u-na-u-na, *v.* Intensive of *una.* To send frequently.

2. To perform some part in the hoopio-pio or anaana.

3. To ask or urge one to do a thing; aole o'u manao e *hoounauna* aku ia olua. *Laieik.* 21.

Hoo-u-ne, *v.* See Une, to pry up. To pry up, as with a lever; to lift by prying.

Hoo-u-ne-u-ne, *v.* Frequentative of *hoo-une.* To pry up.

2. To deceive.

Hoo-u-noo, *v.* See Unoo, not well cooked. To be not sufficiently cooked; hence,

2. To be raw; to be red, as raw meat.

Hoo-u-no-u-noo, *v.* Freq. of the above.

Hoo-u-pu-u-pu, *v.* See Upu, to desire. To desire strongly; to covet; to lust after.

Hoo-u-wa, *v.* See Uwa, to shout. To cause to cry out; to shout; to be clamorous.

Hoo-u-wa-u-wa, *v.* Intensive of the above.

Hoo-u-wa-hi, *v.* See Uwahi. Lit. *Uahi.* To rise up, as a column of smoke.

Hoo-u-we, *v.* See Uwe, to cry. To cause to cry; to make one cry.

Hoo-u-we-ke, *v.* To open. See Wehe.

Hoo-u-we-we, *v.* See Hooueue. To be fickle; to move about; to shake.

Hoo-u-we-u-we, *v.* To sound, as a bell; to sound, as a musical instrument.

Hoo-u-we-ne,   } *v.* To speak in a
Hoo-u-we-ne-we-ne, }   small shrill voice, like a weak dying person.

Hoo-u-wi-u-wi, *v.* See Uwi, to wring; to twist. To wring; to squeeze; to twist.

Hoo-u-wi-u-wi, *s.* The name of a shade tree; he laau malumalu.

Hoo-u-wi-ki, *v.* See Uwi. To squeak, as new shoes; to grind the teeth.

2. To cause to shine through small holes. See Uwiki.

Hoo-u-wi-u-wi-ki, *s.* See foregoing 2. Very small holes.

Hoo-haa, *v.* See Haa, low; short. To cause to be low; to humble; to be unlike another; e *hoohaa,* e ano e.

Hoo-haa, *v.* To be deceitful; to get one's living by cheating.

2. To be lazy; to live in a careless manner.

Hoo-haa-haa, *v.* See Haa, short, and Haahaa. To make low; to humble; to abase; to make humble.

Hoo-haa-haa, *adv.* Humbly; modestly. *Rom.* 12:3.

Hoo-haa-nu-i, *v.* See Haanui. *Haa,* causative, and *nui,* to be great. To boast; to swell in glorying; to multiply words; to speak unintelligibly.

Hoo-haa-lu-lu, *v.* See Haalulu, i. e., Haa, prefix, and lulu, to shake. To shake; to tremble, as one in great fear. Note.—It appears from this and other words that the causative prefix *haa* is more ancient than *hoo,* for we have here *lulu,* to shake, and *haalulu* as a causative form, and this seems to have been incorporated with the word: since, however, the more modern causative *hoo* has been prefixed, thus the word has two causatives.

Hoo-hae, *v.* See Hae, wild. To be wild; savage; to provoke to anger.

Hoo-hae-hae, *v.* See Haehae. To make one angry; to provoke; to tease; to vex; to trouble.

Hoo-hai, *v.* See Hai, proud. To be proud; to strut about; to look down upon others.

Hoo-hai-hai, *v.* Intensive of the foregoing. See Haihai. To be proud; vain.

Hoo-ha-i-li, *v.* See Haili. To be of a dark color; to be dark; dim to the sight.

2. To take the appearance of a spirit.

3. To be transformed, as one taking a new form.

Hoo-ha-i-nu, *v.* See Inu and Hainu. To give drink to; to cause one to drink; to quench one's thirst by drinking.

Hoo-hao-hao, *v.* See Haohao, to search. To seek; to cause a search after a thing; to hunt after.

Hoo-hau-o-li, *v.* See Hauoli, joy. To cause joy; to rejoice.

Hoo-hau-hi-li, *v.* See Hili, to wander, and Hauhili. To cause a blundering in speaking; to talk foolishly without regard to truth.

Hoo-hau-kae, *v.* See Haukae, a sloven. To be a sloven, or to act in a slovenly manner; to be base in one's conduct.

Hoo-hau-mi-a, *v.* See Haumia, filthy. To defile; to pollute; to cause to be unclean; to contaminate; to deface; to disfigure.

Hoo-hau-na, *v.* To deceive; to entice; to insnare.

2. To clasp around.

3. To seize with the hands, as something difficult to hold.

Hoo-hau-na, *v.* To stuff the vagina in order to produce abortion.

Hoo-hau-na-e-le, *v.* See Haunaele. To cause a disturbance; to get up a riot; to do mischief in a mass.

Hoo-ha-u-wa-u-wa, *v.* See Uwa and Uwauwa, to gabble. To talk all together; to make confusion by a multitude talking all at once.

Hoo-ha-ha, *v.* See Haha, to strut. To be obstinate; opinionated.

2. To be proud; high minded; to strut; to act the dandy; to strut, as a cock turkey; he kanaka hoohaha, *hookano,* haaheo, noho wale, aole hana; he *hoohaha* kana hele ana; to strut as a person of consequence. *Ier.* 48:29.

3. To beat down; to pound; to make hard, as the bottom of a salt pond.

Hoo-ha-ha, *adj.* Covered up; shaded; overshadowed, as by clouds; ina i poipu ka lani, a aneane makani ole, he *hoohaha* ia.

Hoo-ha-hai, *v.* See Hahai, to follow. To pursue; to chase; to follow after.

Hoo-ha-hau, *v.* To make believe; to pretend to be what one is not; to put on the dress and appearance of another; e hoano, e hoohaili.

Hoo-ha-hu, *v.* To make even; smooth; level.

Hoo-ha-hu-ha-hu, *v.*

Hoo-ha-ka, *v.* See Haka, full of holes. To be open; to be full of openings, cracks or spaces.

Hoo-ha-ka-ha-ka, *v.* See Haka. To open; to be full of holes or cracks.

2. Fig. To open, as the ear; to give attention to what is said.

Hoo-ha-ka-li-a, *v.* See Hakalia. To detain; to delay; to lengthen out the time.

Hoo-ha-ka-nu, *v.* See Hakanu. To be speechless; silent; unsocial.

Hoo-ha-ke, *v.* See Hake. To break, as a boil; to thrust; to push; to cram in.

Hoo-ha-ki, *v.* See Haki, to break. To cause to break; to break, as a stick or a bone. See the foregoing.

Hoo-ha-ko-i, *v.* See Hakoi. To cause water to dash wave against wave, or against the sides of a vessel.

2. To be agitated, as water in a dish unsteadily carried.

3. To swell and rise up, as water.

4. To be agitated, as the mind.

HOO-HA-LA, *v.* See HALA, to miss; to pass on. To cause to miss the mark; to dodge; to turn aside.

2. To transgress; to go beyond. *Nah.* 14:41.

3. To pass by the house of a friend; mai *hoohala* oe ia ia, do not miss him, i. e., in throwing a spear at a man.

HOO-HA-LA-HA-LA, *v.* See HALA and HALAHALA. To refuse assent to the terms of a bargain; to break off a bargain; to be displeased with the proposed conditions of another; to break a promise.

2. To turn aside; not to listen to what one says.

3. To find fault with a proposal or offer.

HOO-HA-LA-HA-LA-WA-LE, *s.* A complaint without cause; an unreasonable objection to a proposal.

HOO-HA-LA-LA, *v.* See HOOHALA above and LA, day. LIT. To cause the day to pass away.

1. To pass off the time; to spend the day.

2. To endure for the present day; applied to sick persons; ua pono kou mai? *Ans.* Aole, he *hoohalala* wale no, no ka make. Applied to the hungry; he ai anei ka oukou? Aole, he *hoohalala* wale no— he kamau ea. Applied also when one has but a little food, just enough for the day.

HOO-HA-LE, *v.* See HALE, house. To rest in a house; to stay in a house; to receive one into a house; to lodge; to solicit one to be a host or friend. See HOAIKANE.

HOO-HA-LE-HA-LE, *v.* Intensive of the foregoing. To sink down, as the stomach when hungry, or like a house roof fallen in.

2. To be hungry; to suffer with hunger.

HOO-HA-LE-KI-PA, *v.* See HALEKIPA. To entertain, as a guest; to receive into one's house, as a friend.

HOO-HA-LE-PA-PAA, *v.* See HALEPAPAA. To shut up one in a tight house; to inclose; to secure by putting in a tight house; to store; to put in a store-house.

HOO-HA-LI, *v.* See HALI, to carry. To cause to bear; to carry.

2. To transfer to another person or to another place.

3. To carry the words of one to another; to put words together.

HOO-HA-LIA, *v.* To stir up, as anger; *hoohalia* mai i ka inaina.

HOO-HA-LI-HA-LI, *v.* Intensive of *hali.* To carry or bear, as a burden; to carry frequently.

HOO-HA-LI-KE, *v.* See LIKE and HALIKE. To cause to be alike; to resemble; to make similar.

HOO-HA-LI-KE-LI-KE, *v.* Freq. of the foregoing. See HALIKE. To make alike; to divide equally; to equalize.

HOO-HA-LI-KE-LI-KE, *s.* A resemblance; likeness; a similarity.

HOO-HA-LU, *v.* See HALU. To be or become poor or thin in flesh.

HOO-HA-LU-A, *v.* To watch an opportunity for mischief; to lie in wait. *Ios.* 8:4. Either to kill or rob.

2. To act as a spy; to go secretly to do a thing; to rob; to watch for an opportunity to see or speak to a person. *Laieik.* 77.

HOO-HA-LU-A, *s.* An ambush; an ambuscade. *Ios.* 8:2. Poe *hoohalua,* liers in wait. *Lunk.* 9:25.

HOO-HA-LU-HA-LU, *v.* Freq. of *hoohalu.* See HALU and HAHALU. To be poor in flesh; to be thin; to be hungry.

HOO-HA-LU-LU, *v.* See HALULU. To cause a roaring like thunder, or a heavy wind; to rage; to make a rumbling sound.

HOO-HA-MO, *v.* See HAMO, to rub. To cause a rubbing, as with the hand; to besmear, as with oil.

HOO-HA-MO-HA-MO, *v.* See the above. To feel with the hand frequently; to rub over; to anoint.

HOO-HA-NA, *v.* See HANA, to work. To cause to work; to do service for another; to compel to work, as a slave; to encourage to work.

HOO-HA-NAU, *v.* See HANAU, to bring forth young. To cause to bring forth, as a female. NOTE.—The word was mostly used in connection with the application of medicines designed to effect premature parturition.

2. In modern times *hoohanau* has been used in the sense to beget or cause to be born; not used by Hawaiians themselves in this sense.

HOO-HA-NI, *v.* See HANI, to approach. To come near to so as just to touch; to pass softly by.

HOO-HA-NI-NA, *v.* See HOOHANIHANI. Also, to turn a little so as to allow one to pass in a narrow road.

HOO-HA-NI-HA-NI, *v.* Freq. of *hoohani.* To tempt slightly to adultery; to make gentle advances.

HOO-HA-NI-NI, *v.* See HANINI and NINI, to spill. To pour or run out, as water from a vessel; to cause to flow, as water; also, as tears; ua *hoohaniniia* na mapuna wai-maka, the fountains of tears overflowed. *Laieik.* 203.

Hoo-ha-no, *v.* See Hano, to be still; undisturbed. To honor; to exalt; to be vain; to be haughty; to be self-glorious.

Hoo-ha-no-ha-no, *v.* See Hano. To exalt one's self above others; to conduct haughtily; to raise one to honor.

Hoo-ha-nu-a, *v.* See Hanua, plane; level. To live independently; to have enough; to be supplied.

2. To be level; plane, as low level ground. See Honua.

Hoo-ha-nu-ha-nu, *v.* See Hanu, to breathe. To cause to breathe frequently; to draw the breath in and out.

2. To resuscitate; to revive from fainting.

3. To snuff up, as the wind.

Hoo-ha-pai, *v.* See Hapai, to lift or raise up. To conceive, as a female; parallel with *hoohanau.* Nah. 11:12. Note.— *Hoohanau* and *hoohapai* are both factitious words and of modern date, and are not after Hawaiian idiom, as the Hawaiian has no words properly signifying *to conceive* as a mother, or to *beget* as a father; at least no such words have yet been discovered.

Hoo-hee, *v.* See Hee, to melt; to flow. To cause to melt; to flow, as a liquid.

2. To cause to flee; to put to flight; to rout, as an army. See Auhee.

Hoo-hee-hee, *v.* Freq. of *hoohee.* Also, to make angry; to vex; to be wild.

Hoo-hee-wa-le, *v.* To melt easily; to run into liquid.

2. To flee or run away; to act the coward. See Hohe.

Hoo-he-hee, *v.* See Hee, to melt. To melt away; to run, as a liquid; to liquify, as any hard substance.

Hoo-hei, *v.* See Hei, a snare or net. To set a net or snare; to be entangled in a snare.

2. To beset with difficulties.

Hoo-hei-hei, *v.* To sound or strike on the drum.

Hoo-hei-hei, *s.* A drum; a playing on the drum.

Hoo-he-o, *v.* See Heo, pride. To be proud; vaunting; lofty.

Hoo-he-he-o, *v.* See Heo. To swell out; to be large, as a woman with a large pau.

Hoo-he-u, *v.* See Heu, a beginning. To open a speech; to commence a talk.

Hoo-he-he-lo, *v.* See Hehelo. To be proud; to be proud of one's appearance or

dress; to be deceitful.

Hoo-he-ki-li, *v.* See Hekili, thunder. To cause it to thunder.

Hoo-he-le, *adj.* See Hele, to move. Movable; moving.

Hoo-he-le-he-le, *v.* See Hele and Mahele, to divide. To go between; to divide; to separate by cutting, as cutting cloth with shears.

Hoo-he-le-lei, *v.* See Helelei, to scatter. To scatter, as in sowing grain; to throw away.

Hoo-he-ma-he-ma, *v.* See Hema, left (hand.) To be unfurnished; unprepared; not ready.

2. To be wanting in some important quality or thing.

3. To cause a destitution; to deprive of.

4. To dislike and take no care of; applied to all things not desired.

5. To set no value upon; *hoohemahema i ka waiwai, waiho wale a lilo ia hai.*

Hoo-he-mo, *v.* See Hemo, to loosen. To make loose; to loosen; to set at liberty.

Hoo-he-mo-he-mo, *v.* Freq. of the above. To make loose.

Hoo-he-mu, *v.* See Hemu, to drive away. To scare away; to frighten; to drive off, as hens, pigs or other animals.

Hoo-he-na, *v.* See Hena, thigh. To see, feel or handle the thigh; to take off one's clothes.

Hoo-he-na-he-na, *v.* Intensive of the foregoing. To act lasciviously; to uncover one's nakedness; to dress so as to show the hena.

Hoo-ne-ne, *v.* See Hene, mockery. To cause mockery; to show contempt.

Hoo-he-ne-he-ne, *v.* See the foregoing. To cause laughter at another's expense or feelings; to mock; to vilify.

Hoo-he-pa, *v.* See Hepa, to be silent. To be mischievous; to be careless; to imitate another.

Hoo-he-pa-he-pa, *v.* See Hoohepa. To talk improperly, as imitating the talk of foreigners.

2. To mispronounce words or misconstruct language; *e hookahuli i ka olelo.*

Hoo-he-wa, *v.* See Hewa, wrong; error. To condemn; to convict of crime or misdemeanor; to accuse one of crime; to punish. See Ahewa.

Hoo-he-wa-he-wa, *v.* See Hoohewa, to cause to do or be in error. To forget; to mistake; to forget the name of a person.

2. To mistake one person for another;

to be doubtful with regard to a thing.

3. To be slightly deranged; to be delirious; but not so strong as *hehena* or *pupule*.

HOO-HE-WA-WA-LE, *v.* See HOOHEWA and WALE, gratuitously. To condemn without cause; to oppress; to injure. NOTE.— This word is often divided into two words in writing, and perhaps should always be.

HOO-HI, *v.* To open; to dissolve; to act as a cathartic; e hoomama.

HOO-HI-A-HI-A, *v.* To be good; honorable; noble in aspect and deportment.

2. To have the outward appearance of a gentleman without the substance.

3. To be proud and vain. See HOOMAHIE.

HOO-HI-A-LA, *v,* To eat with greediness; to cram down food; to swallow, as one insatiate.

2. In a *moral sense*, to swallow down iniquity; no ka mea, ke *hoohiala* ae nei oukou i ka hewa iloko o oukou iho.

HOO-HI-A-LA-AI, *v. Hoohiala* and *ai*, food.

1. To stuff with food.

2. FIG. To be intent on evil; e hana mau ma ka hewa.

HOO-HI-A-MOE, *v.* See HIAMOE, to sleep. To cause one to sleep.

2. To be lazy; to be weary; to be dull.

HOO-HI-A-PO, *v.* See HIAPO. To be constituted as first born; to have the privileges of a first born.

HOO-HI-E, *v.* See HIE, excellent. To make or cause to be excellent; to be grand to look at.

2. To be proud; to be haughty; to carry a high head.

HOO-HI-E-HI-E, *v.* See HIEHIE, pride, &c. To show a proud behavior; to act proudly.

HOO-HII, *v.* See HII, to carry a child. To lift up, as a child in the arms to carry.

HOO-HI-O, *v.* See HIO, to lean. To cause to lean or slant from a perpendicular; to bend over.

2. To stagger in walking.

HOO-HI-O-LO, *v.* See HIOLO, to fall down To overthrow; to cause to roll down or away; to throw down; to demolish.

HOO-HI-U, *v.* See HIU, strong; fierce. To be wild; to be fierce; to be untamed.

2. To be unfriendly; to be unsociable.

3. To fear; to be afraid.

HOO-HI-HI, *v.* See HIHI, to entangle. To cause entanglement; to get entangled in any way.

2. To desire to get what is another's.

HOO-HI-HI, *adj.* Offensive; injurious.

HOO-HI-HI-A, *v.* See HIHIA, entangle-

ment. To get one into difficulty; to entrap; to hold fast.

HOO-HI-HI-U, *v.* See HOOHIU above. To cause fear; to be fearful; to make afraid; hence, to make or be wild; to be untamed.

HOO-HI-KA-KA, *v.* See HIKAKA, to stagger. To lean this way and that, as a rickety grass house; to lean over.

2. To stagger in walking, like a drunken man.

HOO-HI-KI, *v.* See HIKI, to come to. To arrive at a place, especially at a place designated.

2. To vow; to swear to a fact; to adjure on oath.

3. To swear at; to reproach; to revile; mostly with *ino*.

HOO-HI-KI, *s.* A vow; a promise; a prayer; in swearing. *Oihk.* 5:1. *Hoohiki wahahee,* a false swearing. *Oihk.* 6:3.

HOO-HI-KI-HI-KI, *v.* To bear or carry frequently; to carry a little at a time.

HOO-HI-KI-LE-LE, *v.* See HIKILELE, to startle. To startle one; to cause one to jump; to startle with affright; to wake one suddenly, as from sleep.

HOO-HI-LA, *v.* See HILA. To cause shame; to be ashamed.

HOO-HI-LA-HI-LA, *v.* See HILAHILA. To be timid; modest; fearful, as a bashful person; hence, to be affected with shame; to make ashamed; to act with modesty; to put one to shame, by his own superiority. *Laieik.* 138. E *hoohilahila* aku ai ia Laieikawai.

HOO-HI-LA-HI-LA, *adj.* Bashful; modest, as a backwoodsman; he hoolua nui ke kuaaina, he *hoohilahila.*

HOO-HI-LA-LA, *v.* See HILALA, to bend; to crook. To bend, as the slim branches of a tree with the wind; to curve; to bend round, as a hook.

HOO-HI-LI, *v.* See HILI, to wander. To wander from the right path; to wander; to go here and there without object.

HOO-HI-LI-HI-LI, *v.* See HILI. To cause to wander often.

2. To besmear with blood; to defile with blood.

HOO-HI-LI-U.

HOO-HI-LO, *v.* See HILO, to twist. To cause to twist; to spin or twist, as a cord.

HOO-HI-LU, *v.* See HILU, to be glorious. To exalt; to praise; to dignify.

HOO-HI-LU-HI-LU, *v.* See the foregoing. To exalt; to praise; to honor; to dignify.

HOO-HI-PA, *v.* See HIPA. To vow; to

perform a vow.

2. To speak falsely.

HOO-HI-PA, *s.* Affection; attachment.

HOO-HI-PA-HI-PA, *v.* To blunder in speaking; to speak falsely.

HOO-HI-PUU, *v.* See HIPUU, a little bag or bundle for carrying provisions. To make up into a bundle; to bundle up for carrying.

HOO-HI-WA-HI-WA, *v.* See HIWA, black; acceptable to the gods. To be acceptable to the gods; to be dear; to be greatly beloved; to honor; to treat as beloved or precious.

HOO-HO, *v.* See HO, to cry out. To shout or cry out, as a single person; to call after one.

2. To exclaim with many voices; holo ka moku makai, hele na kanaka mauka e *hooho* hele ai, the ship went on the sea, the men went on shore with vociferation.

3. To make the low noise of a horse.

HOO-HO, *s.* A shout; an exclamation of joy; to triumph. 1 *Tes.* 4:16.

HOO-HO-A, *v.* See HOA, to drive cattle. To challenge; to dare one to fight; to provoke to anger.

HOO-HO-A-HO-A, *v.* Frequentative of the above.

HOO-HO-HO, *v.* To force out; to emit wind.

HOO-HO-HO-NO, *v.* See HOHONO, strong smelling. To give or cause a strong offensive smell, like tar, sulphur and decaying fish.

HOO-HO-KA, *v.* See HOKA, disappointed. To cause a mistake or error; to disappoint one.

HOO-HO-KA-HO-KA, *v.* To make frequent mistakes or blunders; to be disappointed.

HOO-HO-LE-PAA-HAA, *v.* To preserve for another.

HOO-HO-LI, *v.* See HOLI, to do first. To come out, as the first beard of a young man.

2. To make one's first effort to do a thing. See HOOHEU.

HOO-HO-LO, *v.* See HOLO, to run. To cause to run; to run along a road.

2. To move in various ways; to sail; to set sail, as a vessel; to ride on horseback.

3. To thrust the hand into, as into the bosom; to stretch out the hand, as in gesturing.

4. To agree, as a deliberate assembly; to pass, as a vote; to confirm an assertion.

HOO-HO-LO, *s.* A rider on a horse; a horseman; more generally united with *lio*; as,

HOO-HO-LO-LI-O, *s.* A horseman; cavalry.

HOO-HO-LO-MO-KU, *v.* *Holo* and *moku*, ship. To sail or to direct the sailing of a ship; applied either to the master or men.

HOO-HO-LO-MO-KU, *s.* *Holo* and *moku*, a vessel. One who sails or causes a ship to sail.

HOO-HO-LU, *v.* See HOLU, to bend. To bend; to arch; to crook; to be flexible.

HOO-HO-LU-HO-LU, *v.* See HOLU, to bend. To bend, as a flexible piece of timber; to bend, as a stick.

HOO-HU, *v.* See HU, to rise. To cause to rise; to well, as leaven.

2. To bake in an oven.

3. To start up suddenly.

4. To run along the bank of a kalo patch.

5. To detect; to discover.

HOO-HU-A, *v.* See HUA, fruit. To cause to swell, as a bud; to produce fruit, as a tree; to bring forth, as a female.

2. To tease or vex by begging; to resort often to one for favors.

3. To persevere in, as in any habit; ke *hoohua* nei ke noi a na kanaka i kela mea i keia mea; *hoohua* kanaka i ka inu rama, men persevere in drinking rum.

HOO-HU-A, *v.* Perhaps *hoohuwa*, to lengthen out the time. To persevere long; to continue in a practice; to retain a habit, good or bad, especially the latter.

HOO-HU-AE, *v.* See HU. To cause to overflow; to have more than enough; to allow to escape.

HOO-HU-A-HU-A, *v.* See HUA, to swell. To cause to enlarge; to increase; to grow in size. See MAHUAHUA.

HOO-HU-A-HU-A-LAU, *v.* To question in sport or derision, the person questioned being ignorant of the design.

2. To puzzle with captious questions; to throw difficulties in the way of explanation; to talk strangely.

3. To make one's self strange; to pretend not to be acquainted.

HOO-HU-A-HU-A-LAU, *adj.* Puzzling; captious; olelo *hoohuahualau*, insidious questioning.

HOO-HU-A-HU-A-LAU, *v.* To question with belief or with unbelief; o ka poe hoomaloka, *hoohuahualau* mai i ke akua noho, the unbelieving *question* the existence of the resident gods.

HOO-HU-A-HU-A-A-NA-LAU, *v.* To question captiously, &c. See above.

HOO-HU-A-KA, *v.* To smoke tobacco constantly.

HOO-HU-A-KE-EO, *v.* See HUA, jealousy, and KAEO or KEEO. To be evilly disposed;

to cherish a bad disposition.

2. To reject a proffered gift; to turn away with disdain; to be displeased.

3. To consent against one's will; to consent in anger.

HOO-HU-A-KE-EO, *s.* Pride; disdain; contempt for one.

HOO-HU-A-LI, *v.* See HUALI, to glitter. To shine with brightness; to glitter with a pure white.

2. To make pure; to cleanse; hence, to be shining.

HOO-HU-E-LO, *v.* See HUELO, the tail of an animal. To lengthen out; to make small by drawing out in length.

HOO-HU-I, *v.* See HUI, to unite. To cause a union between two or more things; to add to; to add on; to annex.

HOO-HU-OE, *v.* To wonder.

HOO-HU-I-PO, *v.* To go in the night without a light.

HOO-HU-OI, *v.* See HUOI, jealousy. To be jealous; to feel jealous towards another for some real or supposed advantage; ina i noho lakou me kekahi alii, *hoohuoi* kekahi alii, if they had lived with a particular chief, another chief would have been jealous.

2. To allow to touch; to permit to blow upon, as the wind. *Laieik.* 17.

HOO-HU-OI, *s.* Jealousy; o ka *hoohuoi* o na kanaka ame na 'lii i na misionari, the *jealousy* of the people and chiefs respecting the missionaries.

HOO-HU-OI, *adj.* Causing jealousy; distrusting one's faithfulness; he mea *hoohuoi* ia Halaaniani ka nalo ana o Laieikawai. See *Laieik.* 128.

HOO-HU-HU, *v.* See HU and HUHU, anger. To make angry; to provoke; to be very angry.

HOO-HU-HU-KI, *v.* To act as a man and his wife when they quarrel and she sets out to leave her husband and he catches her and they have a tussle, that is, to *hoohuhuki*; e hoonanai, e hookano.

HOO-HU-LA, *v.* To destroy; to finish up; to punish; to tremble for fear.

HOO-HU-LEI, *v. Eng.* To cry out hurra (hu-re)! to ride rapidly on a horse and cry out hurra!

HOO-HU-LI, *v.* See HULI, to turn. To turn; to change; to cause an overturn; to express in another manner the same thing.

HOO-HU-LI-HU-LI, *v.* See HULI above. To change; to turn; to put in order; to overturn; to mix up.

HOO-HU-NA, *v.* See HUNA, to conceal.

To hide; to secrete; to conceal.

HOO-HU-NA-HU-NA, *v.* See above. To hide frequently or thoroughly.

HOO-HU-NE, *v.* See HUNE, to tease. To tease; to beg often; to ask something from another; to entreat a favor; to persist in, as in a bad habit.

HOO-KA, *v.* See KA, to dash; to strike. To dash; to strike; to cause to kill.

HOO-KAA, *v.* See KAA, to roll. To pay out money; to pay a debt.

2. To roll; to cause to roll, as a wheel.

3. To turn over often in bed; to toss in distress or sickness.

4. To throw over or down a precipice, i. e., to roll down it.

HOO-KAA, *s.* See above. The payment of a debt.

2. The rolling of a wheel.

3. A throwing anything down a precipice.

HOO-KAA-O-KO-A, } *v. Kaa* and *okoa,*
HOO-KAA-KO-A, } other; different. The first orthography is preferable. To make a difference; to place one side; to separate; to abstain from; to let alone. See HOOKAOKAO.

HOO-KAA-KAA, *v.* See KAAKAA, to open. To open, as the eyes; to cause to open; to cause one to see by opening the eyes.

2. To cause to roll, i. e., to ride in a carriage. See KAA, a wheel.

HOO-KA-A-NA, *v.* To make tame or gentle; to follow after one.

HOO-KAA-WA-LE, *v.* See KAA and WALE, only. To roll off; to separate; to make a space between.

2. To divide off; to cause a division.

HOO-KA-WI-LI, *v.* See KAA and WILI, to twist. To cause to turn or writhe, as in pain; hence, to be in severe pain.

HOO-KAE, *v.* See KAE, to rub out. To hate; to dislike; to treat contemptuously; to reject.

2. To blot out; to kill; to destroy; to take away life; ina i *hookae* mai ke Akua i ke ola o ke kino, if God should take away the life of the body.

HOO-KAE-KAE, *v.* To daub over; to paint badly; to defile; to pollute, as food, books, mats, &c.; mai *hookaekae* i ka moena, don't dirty the mats.

HOO-KA-E-O, *v.* See KAEO and KEEO, to be quick tempered. To stir up anger in one; to provoke; to show an evil disposition.

HOO-KA-E-O-E-O, *v.* Intensive of the foregoing.

Hoo-KAI, *v.* See KAI, to displace. To waste; to destroy; to put away.

Hoo-KAI-I, *v.* To harden.

2. To be hard in a bargain; to be close; to be stingy.

Hoo-KA-O-KA-O, *v.* See KAOKAO. To put one's self forward; to be prominent among many others; makemake no oia e *hookao-kao* ia ia. *Laieik.* 91.

Hoo-KAU, *v.* See KAU, to hang or put up. To put up upon; to go up; to place one thing upon another; e *hookau* hiamoe, to fall asleep. *Laieik.* 143.

Hoo-KAU-A-HE, *v. Kau* and *ahe*, light, gentle, as a light breeze. To fly softly or gently, like a kite.

Hoo-KAU-HU-A, *s.* See KAUHUA. The forming or growing state of the young in the womb. *Anat.* 2.

Hoo-KAU-KAU, *v.* See KAU, to put upon. To put up; to ascend upon; to cause to arise; to lift up a thing, as a child in putting him on a horse.

2. To gather, as clouds before a rain.

Hoo-KAU-KAU, *s.* See above. The gathering of clouds before a rain regarded as a sign of foul weather.

Hoo-KAU-LA-NA, *v.* See KAULANA, to be renowned. To make a person or event known as famous; to send abroad a report concerning a person or thing; to make famous.

Hoo-KAU-LU-A, *v.* See KAULUA, to be slack. To procrastinate; to delay; to detain; to be slow in obeying a command.

2. To be in doubt; to hesitate about doing a thing; to postpone a work.

Hoo-KAU-KAU-LU-A, *v.* See the foregoing. To wait; to procrastinate.

Hoo-KAU-MA-HA, *v.* See KAUMAHA. To lay a burden upon one; to be hard upon; to trouble; to oppress.

Hoo-KAU-WA, *v.* See KAUWA, a servant. To make a servant of; to cause one to serve or to be a servant; to act in the capacity of a servant.

Hoo-KAU-WA-KU-A-PAA, *v.* See KAUWA and KUAPAA, to make one's back rough. To serve with rigor; to act under, and live in hard bondage.

Hoo-KAU-WA-KU-A-PAA, *s.* Hard service; cruel bondage.

Hoo-KAU-WO-WO, *v.* See KAUOWO and KAUWOWO, to branch out and spread, as vines. To cause to grow and increase, as vines or vegetables of rapid growth; to grow thriftily, as vines or plants.

2. To cause to multiply, as a people.

Hoo-KA-HA, *v.* See KAHA, to seize. To extort property from another; to cheat.

2. To seize upon what is another's.

3. To take property with the owner's knowledge, but without his consent.

Hoo-KA-HA, *s.* An extortioner; one who strips people of their property. *Luk.* 18:11. *Hookaha* is the result of *kuko, lia, iini,* &c.

Hoo-KA-HA-KA-HA, *v.* To put on many clothes, as children; to make a great show.

2. To make a great heap of kapas on which to sit or be carried, as in former times.

3. To make a display; to exhibit finery.

Hoo-KA-HA-KA-HA, *s.* A display; an exhibition; a celebration; hana iho la ia i *hookahakaha* no kana poe wahine, he made an *exhibition* of his wives.

Hoo-KA-HA-KA-HA, *adj.* Superb; fine; nice; making a display as a dandy.

Hoo-KA-HE, *v.* See KAHE, to spill water. To water; to cause water to flow over land; to cause to flow, as a liquid; to irrigate.

Hoo-KA-HE, *s.* A flowing, as of blood.

Hoo-KA-HE-A, *v.* See HEA and KAHEA, to call out. To cause to cry out; to call; to raise the voice in calling.

Hoo-KA-HEE, *v.* See HEE and KAHEE, to slip or slide off. To cause to slip away; to slip off; to flow off.

Hoo-KA-HE-KA-HE, *v.* Freq. of *hookahe.* To water, as land; to cause to flow, as water; to wet; to drain, as land.

Hoo-KA-HE-LA, *v.* See KAHELA, to bend round; to curve. To come along, as the swell of the sea when it comes along the western coast of Hawaii from the south; to flow along, as a high swell of the sea.

Hoo-KA-HE-LA-HE-LA, *v.* See KAHELA and KUHELA. To bend round; to curve, as passing round a cape.

Hoo-KA-HI, *v.* See KAHI, one. To be or cause to be one; to divide by individuals.

2. To make one, i. e., to resemble; to be similar or like something else. 2 *Oihl.* 18:12. E imi kakou ma ka mea e *hookahi* ai ka manao ana, let us seek to unite our *thoughts into one.*

3. To attend to one thing; to make one out of many.

Hoo-KA-HI, *s.* A oneness; a unity; a being only one.

Hoo-KA-HI, *adj.* One; only one, in distinction from many.

Hoo-KA-HI, *art.* One of the semi-definite articles; a; an; one; only one. *Gram.* § 63, 65, 3.

Hoo-ka-hi-ka-hi, _v._ See Kahi, to rub; to comb. To anoint; to daub over.

2. To rub; to polish.

3. To comb.

Hoo-ka-hi-o-hi-o, _v._ See Hio, to lean over. To cause to lean over a little.

2. To be a little intoxicated so as to stagger some.

Hoo-ka-hi-ko, _v._ See Kahiko, to be old. To return to conversation and manners of ancient times; to talk of former times; to imitate ancient manners.

Hoo-ka-hi-ka-hi-ko, _v._ Frequentative of the above.

Hoo-ka-ho-kai, _v._ To mix together two ingredients, as flour and water, spittle and earth.

Hoo-ka-hu-li, _v._ See Huli and Kahuli, to turn; to change. To change the outward form of a thing; to turn over; to turn upside down; to overthrow.

Hoo-ka-hu-li-hu-li, _v._ Frequentative of the above.

Hoo-ka-hu-na, _v._ See Kahuna, a professional man. To act in any profession; to act the artisan, the priest, the doctor, &c.

Hoo-ka-hu-na-hu-na, _v._ See Huna, a small particle. To be little, small or fine. See Hunahuna.

Hoo-ka-ka, _v._ See Ka, to dash; strike. To break up, as wood for fuel (anciently Hawaiians had no axes for cutting fuel.)

2. To strike against; to dash; to break up fine.

Hoo-ka-kaa, _v._ See Kaa, wheel. To turn, as a wheel; to turn round.

Hoo-ka-kaa, _s._ The dark involving of clouds before a storm; the rolling together of clouds; a thick atmosphere before a storm.

Hoo-ka-ka-ha, _v._ See Kaha, to write; to scratch. To strike; to dash against.

2. To pierce, as on coming in contact like two cocks in fighting; to strike with spurs, as a cock.

3. To scratch; to make marks.

Hoo-ka-ka-he-le, _v._ E hoopopololei, e hooinainau, e hookawowo.

Hoo-ka-ke-ka-ke, _v._ To wipe or wash imperfectly or slovenly, as a table or dishes; in washing clothes when one daubs on soap and hardly washes it off, it is said, he _hookakekake_ hau hana ana, aole pau ka lepo.

2. To mix medicine with food in order to take it.

3. To daub or paint over carelessly, as in coloring a map.

4. To blot over.

Hoo-ka-ke-ka-ke, _adj._ Muddy; dirty; pehea ia wahi, maikai anei? Aole, he _hookakekake_ wale no.

Hoo-ka-ka-la, _v._ See Kala, rough. To make rough; to have many protuberances; to be rough with sharp points.

2. To sharpen; to grind on a stone.

Hoo-ka-ka-le, _v._ To make soft or spongy; to be soft; to be flexible, like the comb of a cock.

Hoo-ka-ka-ni, _v._ To have the itch; to be sore. See Meau.

Hoo-ka-la, _v._ See Kala, rough. To sharpen; to grind, i. e., to rub on a stone for sharpening; to grind, as a tool.

Hoo-ka-la-ha-la, _v._ See Kalahala, to pardon sin. To cause to pardon sin; to make an atonement. _Nah._ 16.

Hoo-ka-la-ku-pu-a, _v._ To lie in wait; to ambuscade for the purpose of robbery; to act the part of spies.

2. To entrap one in his words.

3. To observe or watch slyly as one plots mischief.

Hoo-ka-lae, _v._ See Kalae, clear sky. To clear off, as clouds after a rain; to open, as the clouds that the sky may appear; to be clear, as the sky.

Hoo-ka-lai, _v._ See Kalai, to hew. To cause to hew; to cut, as wood or stones into some shape.

Hoo-ka-la-ka-lai, _v._ See the above. To cut off; to smooth, as the inside of a canoe.

Hoo-ka-la-li, _v._ See Kalali. To go quickly and straightforward.

Hoo-ka-le-ka-le, _adj._ Lying; deceitful; treacherous.

Hoo-ka-li, _v._ See Kali, to delay. To cause to wait; to wait; to delay; to wait for something.

Hoo-ka-li-lo-li-lo, _v._ See Kalilo. To draw near to death; to have the last symptoms of death; to die.

Hoo-ka-lu-hi, _v._ To bend; to vibrate, as a leaf in the wind.

2. To ogle; to bend and twist, as a fop or a vain woman; e _hookaluhi_ waiokila.

Hoo-ka-ma, _v._ See Kama, a child. To adopt, as a child; to make the child of another one's own.

Hoo-ka-ma, _s._ An adopted child.

Hoo-ka-ma-hao, _v._ See Kamahao. To be or do something wonderful; to be transformed; to take a new form, especially a more splendid one.

Hoo-ka-ma-ka, _adj._ As a prostitute, living in a state of prostitution; he *hooka-maka* kekahi mea nui ma kahi alii. NOTE.—This may be an erroneous orthography for *hookamakama.*

HOO-KA-MA-KA-MA, *v.* See KAMAKAMA. To prostitute one's wife or daughter for pay; to prostitute one's self for money; to make one a prostitute; to behave lasciviously.

HOO-KA-MA-KA-MA-KA, *v.* See HOOMAKA, to begin. To prepare the way for doing a thing; to begin to do a thing.

HOO-KA-MA-LA-NI, *v.* See KAMALANI. To make one a favorite, especially one that appears unworthy to everyone else except the chief; to treat, as a doting parent a disobedient or mischievous child; to lavish favors on a bad child.

HOO-KA-MA-NI, *v.* To have a very good external appearance, as any substance, but internally worthless.

2. Applied to persons, to be deceitful; to act the hypocrite; to make hypocritical pretensions; to be a worthless person under a pleasant exterior.

HOO-KA-MA-NI, *s.* A hypocrite.

2. Hypocrisy; guile. *Hal.* 32:2.

HOO-KA-MA-NI-HA, *v.* See KAMANIHA, to be rude. To be rude; to be rough; to be wild; to be unsocial.

HOO-KA-NA-HAI, *v.* See KANAHAI, to decrease. To be small; to be stinted; to make small; to make less; to reduce in size; to humble somewhat. See next word.

HOO-KA-NA-HAU, *v.* To be small; to be depressed; to make less.

HOO-KA-NA-OE, *v.* To push forward; to urge on; to quicken; to hasten in doing a thing. See KAHANE.

HOO-KA-NA-HE, *v.* To drive or urge forward; to accelerate movement; to hurry; to quicken.

HOO-KA-NA-HU-A, *v.* See KANAHUA, crooked; stoop-shouldered. To bend upwards, as a crooked rafter.

2. To rise above water, as a whale's back.

3. To bend; to crook; to be humpbacked.

HOO-KA-NA-KA, *v.* See KANAKA, a man. To be or act like a man; to be brave; to be manly; to act the part of a brave man.

HOO-KA-NA-KA-MA-KU-A, *s.* See KANAKA-MAKUA. The state of being mature, as a young person of either sex; being grown up. *Laieik.* 28.

HOO-KA-NA-KA-NA-IE, *v.* To quicken; to hasten; to urge on. See HOOKANAHE.

HOO-KA-NA-LE-O, *v.* To try hard to walk straightly, as one who wishes to disguise his drunkenness.

HOO-KA-NA-LU-A, *v.* See KANALUA, to be in doubt. To be in doubt; to hesitate; to be fearful.

2. To stalk about in a proud swinging manner.

HOO-KA-NA-WAI, *v.* See KANAWAI, law, &c. To be enraged at; to set off from one in anger; to dislike one who has been a friend; *hookanawai* aku la ia i kona wahi i hele ai, aole e hele hou; *hookanawai* aku la i na makamaka.

HOO-KA-NE, *v.* To make a special friend of a man; applied only to a woman.

2. To keep a lodging house.

HOO-KA-NI, *v.* See KANI, to make a musical sound. To sing; to sing for joy; to make a musical sound.

2. To ring a bell; to play on an instrument of music.

HOO-KA-NI-KA-NI, *v.* See the foregoing. To play the ukeke; to strike on anything to make a sound.

2. To sing often.

3. To make a noise, as a multitude of voices and instruments preparatory to a mokomoko or boxing match; a noho malie na kanaka, alaila, *hookanikani* pihe mai, penei.

HOO-KA-NI-PI-HE, *v.* To make a great noise, as in an assembly for the hula and other assemblies; alaila, *hookanipihe* mai kela aoao o ka aha.

HOO-KA-NO, *v.* See KANO, to be proud. To be proud; to be lofty in demeanor; to be haughty.

2. To abstain from; to let alone; to spare; to treat with affection.

HOO-KA-NO, *s.* See KANO. Haughtiness; pride; self sufficiency.

HOO-KA-PAE, *v.* See KAPAE, to pervert. To turn off; to push aside; to parry off; to render ineffectual, as an argument.

2. To conceal under one's kapa.

HOO-KA-PE-KE, *v.* See KAPEKE, to be out of joint. To unloose; to uncover; to send forth.

2. To lay aside, as property; to conceal.

3. To take off; to remove, as the cover of a calabash; *hookapeke* i ka waiwai, to lay aside property; *hookapeke* i ka poi, to take off the cover; *hookapeke* i ka waa, to conceal the canoe.

HOO-KA-PE-KE, *s.* Putting on a dress and yet being exposed, an incentive to lewdness; eia kekahi mea e moekolohe ai, o ka hoohiehie a o ka *hookapeke.*

HOO-KA-PE-KE-PE-KE, *v.* See above and KAPEKEPEKE.

HOO-KA-PU, *v.* See KAPU, prohibition. To prohibit; to forbid; to put under an interdict.

2. To consecrate; to make sacred; to set aside for a particular use.

HOO-KA-PU-KA-PU, *v.* See KAPU. Intensive and frequentative of the foregoing.

HOO-KA-PU-HI, *v.* To take care, as the kahu or nurse of a chief's child; applied only to chiefs. NOTE.—This is said to be a word peculiar to Oahu.

HOO-KA-PU-HI, *s.* A nurse of a king's or a chief's child; e na haumana, ame na kumu, ame na *hookapuhi,* ame na kahu.

2. The kahu of an animal, as the master or owner of a dog; e imi ma ka hanuhanu ana ka ka ilio e loaa'i ka *hookapuhi,* to seek like the dog's smelling to find the *master.*

HOO-KA-WI-LI, *v.* See KAAWILI and KAWILI, to twist. To twist; to turn.

HOO-KA-WO-WO, *v.* See KAWOWO 5, to roar. To make a slight rumbling noise, as by moving the feet, drumming with the fingers, &c.; to rustle, as leaves in the wind; to roar, as a waterfall.

HOO-KE, *v.* See KE, to force; to compel. To crowd together, as at the door of a house (as formerly); to elbow; to edge on by degrees.

2. To get possession in a foreign country without permission; applied to many foreigners who have crowded themselves in; to push aside any person or thing that is in the way.

3. To get one into difficulty; to struggle against opposition.

4. To abstain from; to let alone; to leave untouched.

5. To blow the nose.

HOO-KE, *s.* A struggling against difficulty; an urging on.

HOO-KE-AI, *v. Hooke* and *ai,* food. To abstain from food; to fast.

HOO-KE-E-O, *v.* See KEEO, to be angry. To be quickly angry; to be wrathful; to be quick tempered.

HOO-KEE-KEE, *v.* See KEKEE, crooked. To make crooked; to crook; to bend.

2. To do wrong; to pervert right.

HOO-KEI, *v.* To set one's self above others literally; to take a higher seat; *morally,* to be proud; to be self exalted; alaila, *hookei* iho la ke kahuna nui nana i kai ka aha.

HOO-KEI-KEI, *v.* See KEI, to glory; to boast. To honor one's self; to be proud of one's skill at any business; to be vainglorious; to think much of one's self.

HOO-KE-O, *v.* See KEO, white. To make white; to whiten.

HOO-KE-O, *s.* A long calabash.

HOO-KE-O-KE-O, *v.* See KEO, white. To cause whiteness; to be white.

HOO-KE-U, *v.* See KEU, a remainder. To have over and above; to have or make a remainder.

HOO-KE-HA, *v.* See KEHA 3, to be puffed up. To be puffed up; to be proud; to be self glorious.

HOO-KE-HA-KE-HA, *v.* See above and KEHA. To be proud; to be high minded; to imitate a chief in manners and dignity.

HOO-KE-KEE, *v.* See KEEKEE, crooked. To crook; to bend; to pervert; to spurn; to make crooked.

HOO-KE-KEE, *adj.* Crooked; warped; bent, naturally or morally.

2. Displeased; offended at any neglect.

HOO-KE-LA, *v.* See KELA, to extend beyond. To exceed; to go beyond; to be higher; to be more.

HOO-KE-LA, *s.* The name of a month.

HOO-KE-LE, *v.* See KELE, to slip; to slide along. To sail, as the master of a ship or canoe.

2. To direct or steer a ship or canoe; to hold the helm.

3. To praise; to extol.

HOO-KE-LE, *s.* A steerer of a canoe. *Laieik.* 45. See HOOKELEWAA.

HOO-KE-LE-KE-LE, *v.* See KELE, to slip, &c. To slip or slide easily.

2. To sail about for pleasure in a canoe or boat.

3. To bathe a child near dead with famine.

4. To scatter water; to wet mats; e *hookelekele* i ka moena.

HOO-KE-LE-WAA, *s.* The helmsman of a canoe.

HOO-KE-PA, *v.* See KEPA, to snatch at. To snap or snatch at with the teeth; to prick like a spur.

HOO-KI, *v.* See KI, to shoot, and HOOKIKI. To spill; to drop.

2. To shoot a gun.

HOO-KI-E, *v.* See KIE, high. To lift up; to be high. See KIEKIE.

HOO-KI-EI, *v.* See KIEI, to look sharply. To cause to peep; to look slyly at.

HOO-KI-E-KI-E, *v.* See KIE and KIEKIE, to be high. To elevate; to lift up.

2. To be proud; to be high minded; to lord it over another.

Hoo-ki-e-ki-e, *s.* Pride; haughtiness; overbearing conduct. *Nah.* 15:30.

Hoo-kii, *v.* See Kii, to go after. To cause to go for a thing; to cause to fetch; to go after; to take hold of; to seize.

Hoo-kii, *v.* To grow thin in flesh; to dissolve; to disappear. *Ier.* 34:4.

Hoo-kii, *s.* Thinness of flesh; consumption. *Kanl.* 28:22. Leanness. *Hal.* 106:15.

Hoo-kii, *adj.* Thin; lean in flesh.

2. Close; parsimonious.

Hoo-kii-kii, *v.* To swell out, as the breast; as the stomach; to rise up.

Hoo-ki-o, *v.* See Kio, a pool; a puddle. To spread out; to enlarge.

2. To assemble together, as water in a lake or pond.

Hoo-kio-kio, *v.* See Kiokio, to play on a pipe. To pipe; to play on, as a fife; to play on any wind instrument.

Hoo-ki-he, *v.* See Kihe, to sneeze. To cause to sneeze. *2 Nal.* 4:35.

Hoo-ki-hi, *v.* To defend off; to reproach; to persecute; to put one under a law.

Hoo-ki-kii, *v.* See Hookiikii above.

Hoo-ki-hi-ki-hi, *v.* See Kihi, corner; edge, &c. To branch out; to make many corners; to make the sides of a figure irregular.

Hoo-ki-ki, *v.* See Hooki, to spill. To spill; to drop, as water; to squirt or throw water, as a fire-engine.

Hoo-ki-ki-na, *v.* See Kina and Kikina, to send one on an errand. To send on an errand with dispatch; to command; to order; to hurry.

2. To scold; to be angry.

3. To leave suddenly, as in a great hurry.

Hoo-ki-ki-no, *v.* See Kino, body, and Hookino. To make or cause a body; to embody.

Hoo-ki-lo, *v.* See Kilo and Hakilo, to look earnestly. To spy; to eavesdrop or overhear; to act as a spy upon those who do wrong; e *hookilo* i ka hewa.

2. To watch, as one who is doing wrong; to watch slily.

Hoo-ki-lo, *v.* To grow thin and spare; to waste away, as one in the consumption; *hookilo* kino ole, wiwi.

Hoo-ki-mo, *v.* See Kimo, to strike. To seize; to catch up; to grasp, as the hand does a stone.

Hoo-ki-mo-ki-mo, *v.* To be oppressed; to be weighed down; to be weary; to be near fainting.

Hoo-ki-na, *v.* See Kina, to urge on. To make one heavy or sad; to oppress; to make weary; to put one burden on after another; to add one command after another.

2. To urge one to do a thing; to compel to do it; malia i *hookina* ai kuu kane ia'u i ka inu awa, perhaps my husband will compel me to drink awa. *Laieik.* 208.

3. To pour down fast, as rain.

Hoo-ki-na-ki-na, *v.* Frequentative of *kina.*

Hoo-ki-no, *v.* See Kino, body. To embody; to give body, form or solidity to a thing; to take a shape; *hookino* ai ka honua, he gave the earth a body or shape. See Hookikino.

Hoo-ki-pa, *v.* See Kipa, to turn aside. To turn in to lodge.

2. To entertain with hospitality; to invite to enter one's house.

Hoo-ki-pa, *adj.* Disposed to entertain strangers; kanaka *hookipa,* a man liberal in entertaining strangers; wahine *hookipa.* *Ios.* 2:1.

Hoo-ki-pi, *adj.* See Kipi, rebel. Rebelliously; treacherously. *Kanl.* 13:6.

Hoo-ki-wi, *v.* See Kiwi, to crook. To crook or bend, as a horn.

2. To pull along; to fall down.

Hoo-ki-wi-ki-wi, *v.* See Kiwi above. To pull along; to seize hold of; to fatigue.

2. To hook on to; to crook.

Hoo-ko, *v.* See Ko, to fulfill. To fulfill; to carry out, as a contract; to fulfill, as an agreement or promise.

Hoo-ko-a, *v.* See Koa, a soldier. To act the soldier; to be brave; to be strong; to be fearless.

Hoo-ko-a, *v.* For *hoookoa.* See Okoa, another. To make another.

2. To divide; to distinguish; to separate.

3. To whirl; to turn round.

4. To put off; to postpone.

Hoo-ko-e, *v.* See Koe, remainder. To cause some to remain; to be over and above; to be left after some are taken; to reserve; to set aside.

Hoo-ko-e-ko-e, *v.* See Koekoe, cold. To cause to be cold; to be cold and wet; to be chilly.

Hoo-ko-e-ne, *v.* See Koene, shelter; rest. To cause rest; to cause quietness; to be free from trouble.

Hoo-ko-i, *v.* See Koi, to urge on; to compel. To speak in a rough harsh voice; to make rough or harsh; to urge; to drive on.

Hoo-ko-i-ko-i, *v.* See KOIKOI, heaviness; weight. To make heavy literally or morally; to oppress; to treat with rigor.

Hoo-ko-i-ko-i, *s.* A bearing of a burden; the act of making one sad; putting one in circumstances very disagreeable and grievous to be borne.

Hoo-ko-i-ko-i-pu-a-hi-o-le, *v.* To make great pretensions of forbidding iniquity, and at the same time to practice it secretly. NOTE.—This is a new coined word adapted to modern times.

Hoo-ko-i-ne, *v.* See KOINE, to hasten. To be calm, as the mind; to be at rest; to be quiet.

Hoo-ko-ho-ko-la, *v.* To rejoice at the overthrow of one's enemy; to be glad at his discomfiture. See HOONAIKOLA and AIKOLA.

Hoo-ko-hu, *v.* See KOHU, to agree; to be alike. To resemble; *hookohu ke keiki a Daniela i kona makua*; to cause a resemblance; to make a likeness; to set apart for one's self.

Hoo-ko-hu, *s.* A favorite or chosen one; one appointed first to a post of duty. *Laieik.* 104.

Hoo-ko-hu-ko-hu, *v.* See the foregoing. To ask with forwardness.
2. To affect resemblance; to be assuming.
3. To make advances to a woman with a view to have her for a wife.
4. To agree together.

Hoo-ko-ko, *v.* See KOKO, blood. To spill, as a liquid; to flow, as blood.

Hoo-ko-ko-hi, *v.* To be black and threatening, as clouds; to lower.

Hoo-ko-ko-hi, *adj.* Running low; black; thick; threatening, as clouds; *he ao hookokohi*, a thick black cloud.

Hoo-ko-ko-ke, *v.* See KOKOKE, near either in time or place; to cause to draw near; to approach.

Hoo-ko-ko-le, *v.* See KOLE, raw; uncooked. To remain uncooked; unfinished.

Hoo-ko-ko-lo, *v.* See KOLO, to crawl. To cause one to crawl or creep.
2. To stoop or bend down.

Hoo-ko-ko-no-ie, *v.* To be at rest; to be quiet.
2. To stir up; to provoke.

Hoo-ko-la, *v.* See AKOLA and AIKOLA, to triumph. To rejoice at the ills of another; to express such joy.

Hoo-ko-la-ko-la, *v.* To rouse up the sexual passions.

Hoo-ko-le, *v.* See KOLE, raw, as flesh.

To make red, as raw meat; to look red; to make raw flesh.

Hoo-ko-le-ko-le, *v.* See above. To make raw or red, as raw or fresh meat.

Hoo-ko-li-li, *v.* See KOLILI. To flutter in the wind.

Hoo-ko-lo, *v.* See KOLO, to creep; to crawl. To cause to creep or crawl along; to walk bent over; to crouch.
2. To approach one with the intention of entering into conversation with him.
3. To draw near to a chief to inform against one.
4. To approach humbly to ask a favor. NOTE.—In ancient times all persons sent for by a chief as suspected or accused of an offense, and all who came to a chief to ask a favor, approached him on their hands and knees, crawling from a distance.

Hoo-ko-lo-ko-lo, *v.* Intensive of the above. To call to account.
2. To question with the design of eliciting some fact; to investigate by questioning.
3. To try an accused person; to hold a court.

Hoo-ko-lo-nu-ha, *v.* *Hookolo* and *nuha*, to sit doubled up in silence. To sit bent over in sullen silence; not to reply when spoken to; *aole ou kanaka hookolonuha e like*, you have no man sullen like him.

Hoo-ko-lo-nu-ha, *adj.* See KOLO and NUHA, silent. Sullen; silent; refusing to speak. See example above.

Hoo-ko-mo, *v.* See KOMO, to enter; to sink down. To cause to enter in various ways; to enter an aperture; to enter the door of a house; to sink down into, as into water.

Hoo-ko-mo-ko-mo, *v.* See KOMO and KOMOKOMO, to enter. To cause to enter frequently.
2. To be supplied, as with food; to be satiated with eating.
3. To play at a game called komokomo.

Hoo-ko-na, *v.* See KONA, to be strong. To be brave; to dare; to be hard upon.

Hoo-ko-ni, *v.* See KONI, to taste; to try. To try; to experience; to make plain.
2. To ask or try a little by way of begging or making a bargain; to tempt.

Hoo-ko-ni-ni, *v.* See KONINI, to revive from fainting. To cause to shoot up or grow like a plant.
2. To swell, as a bud.
3. To convalesce, as a sick person.

Hoo-ko-no, *v.* See KONO, to invite. To invite; to lead along.

Hoo-ko-no-ko-no, *v.* See Kono, to invite; to urge. To set on; to urge, as dogs to fight.

2. To entice so as to force one to do wickedly.

3. To stir up or excite feeling in one.

4. To send frequently to hurry one on; to be induced to do a thing. *Laieik.* 128.

Hoo-ko-no-ko-no, *s.* A setting on, as dogs to fight; a getting up a difficulty between persons that they may fight and kill each other.

Hoo-ku, *v.* See Ku, to stand. To cause to stand; to stand erect; to stick up in a perpendicular position.

2. To decline; to withhold; to refuse; to be unwilling.

3. To hold water with the paddles when the canoe is sailing.

Hoo-ku-a, *v.* To fail in one's strength, as after much and long effort one's spirits and strength begin to fail.

Hoo-ku-a-mi-a-mi, *v.* See Kuamiami, the motion of a hinge. To make motions, perhaps indelicate ones, like a hinge.

Hoo-ku-a-nu-i, *v.* See Kua, back, and Nui, large. To cause the back to swell; to make one work hard; to be severe; to increase; to enlarge, as a swelling.

Hoo-ku-a-ke-e-o, *v.* See Hoohuakeeo. To act contrary to; to go to an extreme in anything because of anger, as when a little is asked and a great deal is thrown to him in anger.

Hoo-ku-e, *v.* See Kue, to resist. To cause to resist; to oppose; to make opposition.

Hoo-ku-e-ku-e, *v.* See the above. To excite anger; to stir up opposition; to grin with a frown.

Hoo-ku-e-ku-e-ma-ka-nu-i, *v.* See above with Makanui, great face. To grin most horridly with range or anger.

Hoo-ku-e-ne, *v.* See Kuene, to measure. To take the measure for laying out a building; to measure; to lay out.

Hoo-ku-e-ku-e-ne, *v.* See Kuene. To make way.

2. To wait on one.

3. To move back and forth, as a fan in fanning.

4. To cool one with a fan.

Hoo-ku-e-wa, *v.* See Kuewa, to wander. To wander about, as a vagabond; to go here and there without object; to be friendless.

Hoo-ku-i, *v.* See Kui, to join. To stitch together, as with a needle; to stitch together, as the five kapas for a pau or sleeping kapas.

2. To pierce, as in sewing cloth or kapa.

3. To join together, as letters in making a word, i. e., to spell.

4. To meet together.

Hoo-ku-i, *s.* A joining or connecting; o kahi mawaena o ka lani ame ka honua, ua kapaia he lewa, he *hookui* ame ka halawai.

Hoo-ku-i-ka-hi, *v.* See Kuikahi, to unite in one. To unite in one; to agree together.

2. To make a treaty of peace and friendship.

Hoo-ku-i-ku-i, *v.* See Kui, to unite. To unite; to join together; to put words together, as in a dictionary.

2. To collect in one mass.

3. To unite by sewing, as cloth; e *hookuikui* i ka manai, a uo i ke kaula a lawa.

4. To resemble; to be like.

Hoo-ku-i-ku-i, *s.* Something united or put together; a sentence; a collection of words.

Hoo-ku-i-na, *s.* A uniting; a joining; a seam in a garment; he *hookuina* ami, a hinge joint. *Anat.* 18.

Hoo-ku-o-e, *v.* To cause to be or act the vagabond; to wander about without business or care; to live in poverty; to be worthless.

Hoo-ku-oi, *v.* See Oi 3. To limp; to walk with unequal steps.

Hoo-ku-oo, *v.* See Kuoo, to stand ready. To stand ready; to be prepared for any business or event; to be in readiness for a call.

2. To assume great gravity for the sake of deception.

Hoo-ku-o-ha, *s.* A disease from the illicit intercourse of the sexes. See Kuoha.

Hoo-ku-o-ko-a, *v.* See Kuokoa, to stand aside. To cause to stand aside; to put one by himself; to make another.

Hoo-ku-o-lo, *v.* See Kuolo, to shake; to tremble. To shake; to be unsteady, as with the palsy; to have the palsy.

Hoo-ku-o-ni, *v.* See Kuoni, to move gently. To move a little; to move slightly or easily; to walk slowly; to lag behind.

Hoo-ku-o-no, *v.* See Kuono, a bay or gulf. To sink in, as the eye in sickness; to sink down; to indent, as the land on the sea shore and cause a bay.

Hoo-ku-o-no-o-no, *v.* See Kuonoono, a sufficiency. To be supplied; to have sufficiency.

2. To be quiet; to remain quiet a long time; to be well established.

3. To put in order; to keep in order.

Hoo-ku-o-no-o-no, *s.* Persons living at ease having a competency of the means of living; aole hune nui o ka poe *hookuono-ono*, he lako lakou.

Hoo-kuu, *v.* See Kuu, to loosen. To let go; to dismiss; to send away; to release; to let down.

Hoo-kuu, *adj.* Let down; loosened; dismissed.

Hoo-kuu-kuu, *v.* Freq. of above. To let down, as a rope; to subside, or cause to retire.

Hoo-ku-hi, *v.* See Kuhi, to think. To cause to guess; to suppose; to think.

Hoo-ku-hi-hi, *v.* To entangle; to cause to entangle. See Kahihi.

Hoo-ku-hi-ku-hi, *v.* Freq. of *hookuhi*. To guess; to think; to be uncertain.

Hoo-ku-ho, *v.* See Kuho, the sound of a stone falling perpendicularly in the water. To sound short and quick, as a stone falling perpendicularly in the water.

2. To cough; to cough up from the throat.

Hoo-ku-ke, *v.* See Kuke, to drive off. To throw away; to banish; to drive off.

Hoo-ku-ku, *v.* See Kuku, stuffed with food. To eat to uncomfortable fullness; to stuff with food.

2. To have a sufficiency; to eat enough.

3. To eat food voraciously; applied to many eating together; applied to one person it is *hoonuu*.

4. To try or fit on, as a garment.

Hoo-ku-ku, *s.* Fullness of food; over eating.

Hoo-ku-ku, *adj.* Full, as with food; satiated.

2. Fitted; having a resemblance.

3. See Ku, to stand. A standing up, as in the practice of boxing. *Laieik.* 46.

Hoo-ku-ku-li, *v.* See Kuli, the knee. To cause to kneel; to kneel down.

Hoo-ku-la-na-la-na, *v.* See Kulana-lana, to walk weakly. To walk or stand unsteadily.

2. To stumble; to recede back.

Hoo-ku-li, *v.* See Kuli, to be deaf. To turn away from hearing; to refuse to hear.

2. To disregard one's advice or instruction.

3. To bribe to disobedience.

4. To give one's property for an evil purpose.

Hoo-ku-li, *adj.* Silently; made to say nothing by a bribe, in the phrase *moe hoo-kuli*.

Hoo-ku-lou, *v.* See Kulou, to bow. To bow down; to cower; to sit cowering.

2. To cast the eyes downward.

Hoo-ku-lou-ku-lou, *v.* To bend over, as in sorrow or in pain.

Hoo-ku-lou-lou, *v.* To bend over, &c. See above.

Hoo-ku-lu-ku-lu, *v.* See Kulu, to drop. To leak; to fall in drops; to drip; to sprinkle with water.

Hoo-ku-ma-kai-a, *v.* To cause an ambuscade; to betray; to accuse an innocent person.

Hoo-ku-ma-ki-na, *v.* To cause to wail, as persons for the dead.

Hoo-ku-mu, *v.* See Kumu, foundation. To settle; to root; to establish; to appoint to a particular business or office; to lay a foundation.

Hoo-ku-nai-na, *v.* To make a conquest; to conquer; to show an exterminating spirit.

Hoo-ku-na-na, *v.* See Hookulana, *n* substituted for *l*. To step sideways; to stumble in walking.

2. To hesitate in speaking; to be undecided.

Hoo-ku-nou, *v.* See Kunou and Kulou. Lit. To stand bent. To bow, as the head; to nod, as the head; to wag the head, or shake it in derision; to bow; to bend over.

Hoo-ku-nu, *v.* See Kunu, to cough. To cause to cough; to make one cough; to hack and cough. See Hookuho.

Hoo-ku-pa, *v.* See Kupa. To dig out; to cut; to hew, as in digging out a canoe.

Hoo-ku-pa, *v. Eng.* To be or work like a cooper; to act the cooper.

Hoo-ku-paa, *v.* See Kupaa, to stand fast. To cause to stand fast; to confirm, as an agreement; to make perpetual, as a promise or covenant.

Hoo-ku-pa-ku-pa, *v.* See Hookupa. To cut; to carve; to pare; to dig.

Hoo-ku-pe, *v.* To turn, as one's ankle or foot in walking; hence, causing a stumbling.

Hoo-ku-pu, *v.* See Kupu, to spring up. To cause to grow up, as a vegetable; to spring up, as a seed.

2. To pay or gather a tax; to pay a tax or tribute.

3. To accomplish; to perform.

4. To give freely; to make a present to one.

Hoo-ku-pu, *s*. A tax; a taxation; a tribute to one in higher standing; a present; a gift; a gratification.

Hoo-ku-pu, *adj*. Liable to taxation; mea *hookupu*, a tributary. *Kanl.* 20:11. Taxed; laid under tribute. *Lunk.* 1:30.

Hoo-ku-we-ku-we, }
Hoo-ku-e-ku-e, } *v*. See Kuekue, the knuckle or elbow joint. To elbow; to jog with the elbow; to push.

Hoo-la, *v*. To withhold openly; to be parsimonious.

Hoo-la, *s*. A kapa or Hawaiian cloth; applied mostly to single kapas; but on Kauai, used instead of the word kapa generally.
2. A remnant; a piece.

Hoo-la, *v*. For *hooola*. See Ola, to recover from sickness. To have ease after pain; to recover from sickness.
2. To save from danger; to cure a disease.
3. To deliver or free from death.

Hoo-la, *s*. Used for *hooola*. Safety after danger; deliverance from peril; salvation as of a people. *Puk.* 14:13.

Hoo-laa, *v*. See Laa, to consecrate. To consecrate; to hallow; to set apart for a particular purpose, especially for religious purposes.

Hoo-laa-laa, *v*. For *hoolala*. See Lala, a branch; a limb. To branch out, as the limbs of trees.

Hoo-la-au, *v*. To ask, as a child for food.
2. To swell up, as the stomach.

Hoo-lae-ho-nu-a, *v*. See Lae, the forehead, and Honua, entirely. To bow or carry the face low, as one affecting great solemnity.

Hoo-lae-lae, *v*. See Laelae, clear. To be clear; to shine; to be bright, as an unclouded sky.

Hoo-lai, *v*. See Lai, to be still. To appease; to quiet, as a mob; to be quiet; to be still.

Hoo-o-la-o-la, *v*. For *hooolaola*. See Olaola, the sound of the throat in drinking. To gurgle, as water when drinking.

Hoo-la-o-a, }
Hoo-la-o-wa, } *v*. To tie up, as small sticks for fuel.

Hoo-la-o-a, *s*. A hook for catching eels.

Hoo-lao-lao, *v*. See Laolao, a bundle. To do up in bundles; to tie up, as a bundle for carrying; to tie a string around.

Hoo-lau, *v*. See Lau, many; the number 400. To make numerous; to make company for one.
2. To take away the solitude of a place.

Hoo-lau-a-ka-ne-a, *v*. To hide; to conceal; to go or put away out of sight; to deceive.

Hoo-lau-lau, *v*. See Hoolaolao and Laulau. To tie up a bundle.

Hoo-lau-le-a, *v*. See Laulea, to be on friendly terms with. To appease; to calm one angry; to satisfy an injured party; to reconcile.

Hoo-lau-na, *s*. See Launa, friendly. To be on good terms with one; to act the part of a friend.

Hoo-lau-wi-li, *v*. See Lauwili, to turn; to be fickle. To cause to twist; to take many positions or shaped.
2. To go round and round in speaking; to use many words in saying little.
3. To be inconstant or fickle in doing a thing.

Hoo-la-ha, *v*. See Laha, to spread out. To spread out; to widen; to spread abroad, i. e., to publish extensively, as news; to cause to become of general interest.

Hoo-la-ha-la-ha, *v*. To bear; to carry, as on a double-canoe or peleleu.

Hoo-la-ha-la-hai, *v*. See Lahai and Lalahai, to hover over. To hover over, as a bird; to flap the wings without making any advance, as an owl.
2. To float in the air, as a kite.

Hoo-la-ho-la-ho, *v*. See Laho, the testicles. To rub the testicles; to practice onanism.

Hoo-la-hu-i, *v*. See Lahui, to prohibit. To cause to be consecrated; to be made kapu; to forbid the doing of a thing.

Hoo-la-ka, *v*. See Laka, tame, as an animal. To tame; to domesticate, as an animal; to take away wildness by quiet friendly treatment.

Hoo-la-ka-la-ka, *v*. See above. To make tame, &c.

Hoo-la-ko, *v*. See Lako, a sufficiency. To supply; to cause a supply; to be furnished; to supply for an emergency; to prepare; to get ready.

Hoo-la-ko-la-ko, *v*. Freq. of the above.

Hoo-la-la, *v*. See Lala and Hoolaalaa, to branch out. To branch out, as the branches of a tree; to divide off different ways.
2. To lay the foundation of a work; to commence a job.

Hoo-la-la, *s*. A stick once crooked that has been made straight; he hau hana ka inoa o ia wahi i ka *hoolalaia*.

Hoo-la-la, *v*. To begin or commence

a work or business.

Hoo-la-la, *v.* To move aside out of the course, as one sailing in the surf turns off and goes somewhere else.

Hoo-la-la-hai, *v.* See Lahai and Hoo-lahalahai.

Hoo-la-le, *v.* See Lale, to urge on. To stir up; to hasten the doing of a thing; to excite to action; to get ready quickly for an event.

Hoo-la-la-au, *v.* To stop up a path; to plant or cause bushes to grow.

Hoo-la-le-la-le, *v.* See Hoolale. To get ready quickly; to put in order in a hurry, as a house when a visitor comes un-expectedly; to hasten generally.

Hoo-la-na, *v.* See Lana, to float; to hope. To cause to float; to be light; to float upon, as upon water.

2. To offer, as a sacrifice.

3. To listen with attention; e *hoolana i ka pepeiao.*

Hoo-la-na, *s.* Indifference in regard to morals and moral principles; aole e pili nui kekahi mau hewa iloko o ka pono, o ka hookaulana, o ka *hoolana,* &c.

Hoo-la-na-la-na, *v.* See Lana and Lanalana. To cause to be light; to float, &c.

Hoo-la-na-ki-la, *v.* See Lanakila, to overcome. To cause to triumph.

Hoo-la-ni-la-ni, *v.* To exalt; to praise.

2. To enjoy the privileges of a chief.

3. To take deceitfully (as Puniai did from Kauwa.)

Hoo-la-pa-la-pa, *v.* See Lapa, a ridge, and Lapalapa. To spin round, as a top.

2. To roll, as the wheel of a plow.

3. To boil; to bubble up, as boiling water; to fry.

4. To blaze, as a blazing fire.

Hoo-la-pa-nai, *v.* For *hooolapanai.* See Hoola, to save, and Panai, to redeem. To save one by redeeming; to buy one's liberty who is in bondage; to redeem.

Hoo-la-pa-nai, *s.* A redeemer. *Isa.* 41:14; *Hal.* 78:35.

Hoo-la-pee, *v.* See Lapee, to bend over. To bend up; to double over; to swell up.

Hoo-la-puu, *v.* See Lapuu, to bend up. See also Lapee. To bend over; to arch; to crook; to recede from a straight line.

Hoo-la-wa, *v.* See Lawa, sufficiency; enough. To finish; to make means suit the intended purpose; to accomplish a purpose.

2. To have enough; to be supplied.

Hoo-la-wa-la-wa, *v.* To finish alike. See above.

Hoo-la-we, *v.* See Lawe, to carry. To draw out; to carry from one place to another; to cause to bear or carry; to take away.

Hoo-la-we-la-we, *v.* See the foregoing. To carry frequently; to get things together; to make ready; to wait on, as a servant; to do this and that.

Hoo-la-we-ha-la, *v.* To seek occasion against one; to find something for ground of accusation.

Hoo-la-we-ha-la, *s.* Treachery; seeking evil of one; a desire to detract from one's reputation.

Hoo-le, *v.* For *hooole.* See Ole, no; not. To deny; to be unwilling.

2. To contradict; to refuse assent; to withhold.

Hoo-le-a, *v.* See Lea, to be pleased with. To praise; to extol; to sing praise to.

Hoo-le-a, *s.* Praise; the object of praise. *Kanl.* 10:21.

Hoo-le-a-le-a, *v.* See Lea, to please. To amuse; to sport with; to sing in order to attract attention.

2. To soothe; to assuage; to alleviate sorrow or pain.

Hoo-le-a-le-a, *adj.* Anything pleasing; soothing, as music. *Laieik.* 79.

Hoo-lei, *v.* See Lei, to cast; to throw. To cast or throw away; to reject; to drop carelessly.

Hoo-lei-lei, *v.* See the above. To cast or throw away often.

Hoo-lei-loa, *v.* See Hoolei and Loa, long; also Hooloa. To extend or straighten the body; to straighten out; to make straight.

2. To stretch out the arm or extend it straight.

3. To stretch out the lower limbs.

Hoo-lei-na, *s.* For *hooleiana.* That which is cast or thrown away; refuse matter. *Dan.* 3:29. See Hoolena and Hoolina.

Hoo-lei-wa-le, *v. Hoolei* and *wale.* To throw away as useless or worthless.

Hoo-le-o-le-o, *v.* To rise and fall, as the waves of the ocean.

2. To go about in confusion, as men running hither and thither.

3. To be uneven; up and down, as a wrinkled mat or floor.

Hoo-le-he-le-hei, *v.* See Lehei, to jump from a high position. To fly in an imperfect manner, as an unfledged bird.

2. To jump from a high position.

3. To dive into the water from a height. See Lehai.

Hoo-le-he-le-he-kii, *v.* To be disappointed; to be baffled.

Hoo-le-le, *v.* See Lele, to fly. To let fly, as a bird from its cage.

2. To fix up in the air; to flutter in the wind.

3. To flutter, as a bird from fear; ua *hooleleia* ka oili, she was afraid, her heart fluttered. *Laieik.* 205.

Hoo-le-le-hu, *v.* See Lelehu 3, to be sleepy. To be sleepy; to writhe, as in the pangs of death.

2. To turn sideways.

Hoo-le-ma-na, *v. Hoole*, to deny, and *mana*, power; authority. To deny one's power or authority, as the people in Liholiho's time denied the authority of the priests and the ancient gods; as the Jews also denied the authority of Jesus Christ.

Hoo-le-na, *s.* See Hooleina. That which is thrown away, &c.

Hoo-le-pe, *v.* See Lepe, the comb of a cock. To be scalloped out, as the comb of a cock; to be cut out.

Hoo-le-pu-le, *v.* See Hoole, to deny, and Pule, prayer; religion. To deny one's authority to act as priest, as the people did after Liholiho had broken the kapu. See Hoolemana above.

Hoo-le-wa, *v.* See Lewa, to swing. To cause to swing; to vibrate; to float in the air.

2. To lift up and carry, as between two persons; to carry in a manele or palanquin.

3. To bear or carry a corpse at a funeral procession.

4. To hang pendulous; to hang down, as a flag without a breeze.

Hoo-le-wa, *s.* A bearing; a carrying; a floating in the air.

2. The act of bearing a corpse at a funeral; hence,

3. A funeral procession.

Hoo-le-wa-le-wa, *v.* See Lewa. To suspend; to swing back and forth.

Hoo-le-wa-le-wa, *adj.* Moving; flying, as clouds that fly low; ina e kokoke mai ke ao, he ao *hoolewalewa.*

Hoo-li-o-li, *v.* For *hooolioli.* To cause to rejoice; to make glad; to be cheerful; to be joyous.

2. To be dazzling with brightness. See Oli.

Hoo-li-o-li-o, *v.* To dazzle with brightness.

Hoo-li-u-li-u, *v.* See Liuliu, a long time. To cause time to be long; to lengthen out time.

2. To stay or delay a long time in a place.

3. To get ready; to prepare to do a thing.

Hoo-li-ha-li-ha, *v.* To cause fear; to be afraid; to be fearful.

Hoo-li-ke, *v.* See Like, to be like. To make alike; to make equal; to liken one thing to another; to make a resemblance.

2. To divide equally.

Hoo-li-ke-li-ke, *v.* Intensive of the above.

Hoo-li-li, *v.* See Lili, jealously. To partially close the eyes on account of a bright light.

2. To contract the sight of the eye; to make a wry face.

3. To make one jealous; to cause jealousy.

4. To question with pertness; to appear consequential; to be dignified.

5. To set up for or assume what does not belong to one; *hoolili* ko Oahu e hookolokolo i ko Lahaina.

Hoo-li-li, *v.* To undulate, as the air under a hot sun; to undulate, as the surface of water by the skipping of fishes.

Hoo-li-li, *s.* The name of the place where the opelu are found.

2. The putting on of airs; a feeling of one's importance; the act of creating jealousy in another.

Hoo-li-li, *adj.* Firm; hard; bold; dignified; important.

Hoo-li-lo, *v.* See Lilo, to pass from one to another. To cause a transfer; to change from one to another; to be lost; to deliver from one to another.

Hoo-li-ma-li-ma, *v.* See Lima, hand. To make a bargain; to hire; to buy or sell.

Hoo-li-ma-li-ma, *s.* A person hired to work. *Iob.* 7:2.

Hoo-li-na, *v.* See Hooleina and Hoolena.

Hoo-li-na-li-na, *v.* See Lina and Linalina, to be tough. To be tough and hard, like wax or gum.

2. To be smoothed or polished.

Hoo-lo-a, *v.* See Loa, long. To stretch out or extend the arms or legs after being bent. Lit. To make long. Note.—*Hooloa* is said to be a Kauai word for *hooleiloa.*

Hoo-lo-i-hi, *v.* See Loihi, long. To lengthen out; to prolong.

Hoo-lou, *v.* See Lou, a hook. To hook; to pull with a hook; to draw tight; to bind on; to insert, as one thing into another.

Hoo-lou-lou, *v.* To bend over; to stoop in grief or sorrow; to cry; to weep; to be afflicted.

Hoo-lo-ua, *v.* See Lou and Loua, a hook. To hook; to pull with a hook; to pull; to bind on.

Hoo-lo-ha-lo-ha, *v.* See Loha and Aloha, to love. To be sick; to be weak; to fade; to fail through weakness.

2. To hang down, as a withering leaf.

3. To cherish; to fondle; to caress.

Hoo-lo-he, *v.* See Lohe, to hear. To cause to hear; to turn the attention; to listen; to regard; to obey.

Hoo-lo-he-lo-he, *v.* To give ear; to pay attention.

Hoo-lo-hi, *v.* See Lohi, to be slow. To make slow; to delay; to detain.

Hoo-lo-hi-lo-hi, *v.* To procrastinate; to postpone.

Hoo-lo-ko, *v.* To insinuate; to suggest as a sport.

2. To send; to order away.

3. To dance; to play; to rejoice.

Hoo-lo-la, *v.* To be dull; to be stupid; to be indolent; to be unable to accomplish anything; to neglect.

Hoo-lo-la-lo-la, *v.* Freq. of *hoolola.*

Hoo-lo-le, *v.* See Lole, skin of an animal. To turn; to change; to turn outside in.

2. To skin, as an animal. See also Loli.

Hoo-lo-li, *v.* See Loli, to change. To change; to alter; to renew; to take a new form.

2. To change one thing for another.

Hoo-lo-li-lo-li, *v.* See Loli. To rectify; to change; to reform.

Hoo-lo-lo-he, *v.* See Lohe. To be sour and to act roughly.

2. To be harsh in one's speech and behavior.

3. To refuse compliance with one's invitation; to refuse all approaches; to be disobedient. *Laieik.* 65.

Hoo-lo-no, *v.* See Lono, kindred with *lohe.* To regard; to listen to; to obey; to keep.

Hoo-lu-a, *v.* See Lua, two; twice. To do twice; to repeat; to do over again.

2. *Specifically*, to bake over; to cook twice.

3. To stop up a pathway that had been common.

Hoo-lu-a, *s.* The name of the strong north wind; he ua kahi *hoolua*, a he ua ole kahi *hoolua*, some strong winds have rain, others not.

2. The name of the rain accompanying the north wind; he ua *hoolua*, he ua nui no ia.

Hoo-lu-a, *adj.* Strong; rough; muscular; he *hoolua* nui ke kuaaina, he hoopepehu.

Hoo-lu-ai, *v.* See Luai, to vomit. To vomit; to cast out of the stomach.

2. Fig. To cast out, as a people; to drive off.

Hoo-lu-ai-e-le, *v.* To be deceitful; e hoopunipuni; to go here and there; to move about often.

Hoo-lu-a-lu-ai, *v.* See Luai, vomit. To raise the cud, as ruminating animals; to raise again. *Kanl.* 14:6.

2. To use means to provoke vomiting; a *hoolualuai* aku la, a pau loa ka awa i ka luaiia. *Laieik.* 208.

Hoo-lu-e, *v.* See Lue, to overthrow. To overthrow; to cast down; to cause to slide away; to hang down.

2. To bring forth many young, as a woman that has borne many children; as a hen that hatches many chickens.

Hoo-lu-e-lu-e, *v.* To cast down; to loosen; to throw away; to be loose, as a garment.

Hoo-lu-e-lu-e, *s.* A gown; a loose dress; a flowing robe, so called from its looseness.

Hoo-lu-e-lu-e, *adj.* Hanging low and loosely.

Hoo-lu-i, *v.* To overturn the decision of a council.

Hoo-lu-o-lu, *v.* For *hoooluolu.* See Olu and Oluolu, to please; to comfort. To make easy; to quiet; to comfort; to be cool.

Hoo-luu, *v.* See Luu, to dive in the water. To plunge in a liquid; hence, to dye; to color.

Hoo-luu-i-li, *v.* See Hooluu and Ili, a skin or hide. To tan hides.

Hoo-luu-i-li, *s.* A tanner of skins or hides. *Oih.* 9:43. Note.—A later edition has *hanaili* instead of *hooluu'li.*

Hoo-luu-luu, *v.* See Luu, to dive. To fish for the fish called hinalea; to dive and take fish in a basket.

Hoo-luu-luu, *s.* The act of taking or catching fish in a basket.

Hoo-luu-luu, *adj.* Applied to a fish basket; hinai *hooluuluu.*

Hoo-luu-paa-kai, *s.* Ike i ka ulana moena ame ka *hooluupaakai.*

Hoo-lu-he, *v.* To be proud; to act haughtily.

2. To wither, as a leaf; to be weak; to hang down.

Hoo-lu-he-lu-he, *v.* To hang loosely; to be flexible with weakness.

Hoo-lu-hi, *v.* See Luhi, fatigue. To make weary; to oppress; to make one work hard; to overbear.

Hoo-LU-HI-HE-WA, *v.* *Hooluhi* and *hewa*, wrongfully. To oppress; to harass; to burden wrongfully. *Hal.* 9:9.

Hoo-LU-HI-LU-HI, *v.* Freq. of *luhi.* To force one to do many kinds of much hard work.

Hoo-LU-LE, *v.* See Lule, often Syn. with luli, to turn; to shake. To turn; to turn round; to change.

2. To shake, as flesh with fatness; to be loose.

Hoo-LU-LE-LU-LE, *v.* To cause a trembling or shaking.

Hoo-LU-LE-LU-LE, *s.* A trembling; the state of old age.

Hoo-LU-LI, *v.* See Luli, to vibrate; to shake. See Lule above. To rock; to vibrate; to cause a motion back and forth.

Hoo-LU-LI-LU-LI, *v.* See Luli, to rock, roll, &c. To stir up; to awake one out of sleep; to disturb one's quiet; to rock, as a child in a cradle; to agitate.

Hoo-LU-LU, *v.* See Lulu, quiet; calm. To lie quietly and still in the water, as a ship in a harbor; to be calm.

Hoo-LU-LU-HI, *v.* See Luhi, weary with labor. To cause the eyes to be heavy with sleep; to be drowsy; to be sleepy.

Hoo-LU-LU-HI, *s.* The heavy and dark clouds gathering before a storm; thickening atmosphere before a storm.

Hoo-LU-NA, *v.* See Luna, an officer; an overseer. To be or act as an officer; to be in authority over others.

2. To stir up or order men to their duties; to act the luna.

Hoo-LU-NI, *adj.* See Hooluli. Weak; shaky; applied to persons or things where there is weakness.

Hoo-MA, *v.* See Ma, to fade; to wilt. To cause to fade; to wilt, as a flower; to perish.

2. To strike with the hands or paddle, as a man on a surf-board.

Hoo-MAA, *v.* See Maa, to accustom. To accustom; to practice; to exercise by practice.

2. To be ready for any business by having experience in it.

Hoo-MA-AU, *v.* See Maau, to trouble. To defend off; to take an oath; to make a law.

2. To persecute; to injure maliciously; to offend; to hate; to dislike.

3. To follow from affection.

4. To go from place to place.

5. To be indifferent; to neglect.

Hoo-MA-AU, *s.* A tempting; a trial as to one's constancy. *Laieik.* 102.

Hoo-MA-AU-E-A, *v.* See Maau and Ea.

To work lazily; to leave one's work unfinished.

Hoo-MA-A-KA-A-KA, *v.* See Akaaka, to laugh. To cause laughter; to make sport; to play a trick; to say that which is not true.

Hoo-MA-A-LE-A, *v.* See Maalea, cunning. To act wisely; to act craftily; to act deceitfully; to be lazy.

Hoo-MA-A-LI, *v.* See Ali, a scar. To make the trace of a thing, as the wake of a ship; to make a faint track of a person walking; to make a slight road; to appear, as the scar of a wound.

Hoo-MA-A-LI-LI, *v.* See Malili and Maalili, to assuage; to cool. To assuage heat; to cool; to pacify, as anger.

Hoo-MAA-MAA, *v.* See Maa, to accustom. To accustom one to work; to teach one to work; to be furnished; to be ready for business.

Hoo-MA-A-WE, *v.* See Maawe, a small indefinite part. To divide out in small quantities.

Hoo-MA-A-WE-A-WE, *v.* Frequentative of the foregoing.

Hoo-MAE, *v.* See Hooma and Mae, to wilt; to fade. To cause to wilt, as a leaf; to wither; to dry, as a vegetable; to blast; to fade, as colored cloth; to hang down, as a wilting vegetable.

Hoo-MA-E-A-E-A, *v.* To disregard; to turn a deaf ear to; to refuse to listen. See ·Hoonalulu.

Hoo-MAE-E-LE, *v.* See Maeele. To pity; to have one's sympathy excited; ua *hoomaeeleia* ka naau o ko lakou kaikunane i ke aloha. *Laieik.* 74.

Hoo-MA-E-HA, *v.* To date; to provoke; to be boisterous.

Hoo-MAE-MAE, *v.* See Mae, to fade. To wilt, as a leaf; to fade, as the colors of cloth; to dry up.

2. To cleanse; to purify; to clear away filth or stench.

Hoo-MA-E-WA, *v.* See Maewa, to mock. To mock; to mimic; to reproach; to provoke.

Hoo-MA-E-WA-E-WA, *v.* See the above. To reproach; to sneer at; to ridicule.

Hoo-MAI, *v.* See Mai, sickness, and Mae. To cause sickness; to be weak; to be out of health.

Hoo-MA-IO, *v.* See Ma, to fade, and Io, flesh. To grow thin in flesh; to have little flesh on the bones.

Hoo-MA-IO-IO, *v.* To peep like a chicken. See Ioio.

2. To mar; to spoil

3. To cut up; to make marks.

HOO-MA-I-HA-I-HA, *v.* See MAIHA, to be energetic. To draw firmly, as a rope; to be intent upon, as the mind; to pursue eagerly.

HOO-MAI-KA, *v.* To be strong; to be intent upon.

HOO-MAI-KAI, *v.* See MAIKAI, handsome; good. To make good; to correct; to make handsome.

2. To bless; to ascribe goodness to one; to make prosperous.

HOO-MAI-KAI, *s.* See above. Thanksgiving. *Oihk.* 7:15. Honor. *Kanl.* 26:19. A blessing. *Kanl.* 33:1. Favor; respect; admiration. *Eset.* 2:15.

HOO-MAI-KAI-IA, *s.* Honor; outward respect paid to a superior. *Mat.* 1:6.

HOO-MAI-KAI-KA, *v.* See HOOMAIKA. To be strong; to draw firmly.

HOO-MAI-LA-NI, *v.* To tend, as a child; to take care of; to honor.

2. To treat mildly when one is discouraged.

HOO-MAI-MAI, *v.* See MAI, sickness. To pretend to be sick; ua *hoomaimai* ae la oia, a nolaila. Ua hala ia po. *Laieik.* 209.

HOO-MA-I-NO, *v.* See INO, badness. To make sad; to treat with severity.

HOO-MA-I-NO-I-NO, *v.* See MAINOINO, to suffer affliction. To afflict; to treat with severity; to slander; to deride.

HOO-MA-O-A, *v.* See MAOA, pain; lameness. To have lameness in the hip joint; to be weak in the muscles of the thigh.

HOO-MA-OE, ⎱ *v.* See MAOE and MAOI,
HOO-MA-OI, ⎰   forward; bold. To be impertinent; to speak or ask for a thing; to give a hint of one's desire.

HOO-MAO-MAO, *v.* To darken; to make a black or blue color. See OMAOMAO.

HOO-MA-O-NA, *v.* See MAONA, satisfied with food. To feed to satiety; to fill with food; to be satisfied with eating.

HOO-MA-U, *v.* See MAU and MAUU, wet; moist. To moisten; to wet, as with dew; to soak.

2. To be cool; to be agreeable; to be refreshing.

HOO-MAU, *v.* See MAU, to repeat. To be constant; to be immovable; to perpetuate; to make fast, as an anchor in sand or rocks; to keep perpetually in action; to persevere; to go forward; *hoomau* aku la laua i ka hele. *Laieik.* 101.

HOO-MAU, *adj.* Irreconcilable; opposite in natures, as fire and water; as virtue and vice.

HOO-MAU-A-KA-LA, *v.* To be lazy; to spend the day; to be indolent; to go about doing nothing.

2. To accuse falsely; to laugh with scorn. *Luk.* 8:53.

HOO-MAU-AE, *v.* To be lazy; to be idle.

2. To lay or place one thing on top of another. See MAUAE.

HOO-MAU-IA, *adj.* Continual; perpetual. *Nah.* 4:7. See HOOMAU.

HOO-MAU-IU-IU, *v.* To become sore again; to oppress more.

HOO-MAU-HA-LA, *v.* See HOOMAU, to perpetuate, and HALA, offense. To keep long enmity against one; to retain long the memory of an offense; to seek revenge long after an offense.

HOO-MAU-HA-LA, *s.* An old grudge; cherished revenge. *Laieik.* 69.

HOO-MAU-LE-HO, *v.* See HOOMAU and LEHO, a callous bunch. To cause one to work hard; to oppress; to make one work all day and every day without wages.

HOO-MAU-NAU-NA, *v.* See MAUNAUNA and MAUNA. To waste, as property; to spend uselessly; to consume; to destroy without regard to expense.

HOO-MAU-NAU-NA, *s.* Waste; useless destruction of property. *Mat.* 26:28.

HOO-MA-HA, *v.* See MAHA, rest. To cause to rest from fatigue or pain; to cease from exertion.

HOO-MA-HA-HA, *v.* See HAHA, the inside of kalo tops. To throw the small refuse kalo roots on the side of the kalo patch.

HOO-MA-HA-LA, *v.* To loosen; to unravel; to clear up or vindicate one's character.

HOO-MA-HA-NA, *v.* See MAHANA, warm, also MEHANA. To cause to be warm; to warm by the fire or by the sun.

HOO-MA-HA-NA-HA-NA, *v.* Freq. of above.

HOO-MA-HA-NA-HA-NA, *s.* Name of one of the last kapus; kakali iho la oia i pau ka *hoomahanahana*, a neenee aku.

HOO-MA-HI-E, *v.* See HIE, pride, and HOOHIE. To be excellent; to be grand; to be noble in appearance.

2. To be proud; to have a high look.

HOO-MA-HO-LA, *v.* See MAHOLA, to open as a flower. To spread out smoothly, as clothes or kapa. See HOLA.

2. To open; to spread open; to expand, as a flower.

HOO-MA-HO-LA-HO-LA, *v.* Freq. of the foregoing. NOTE.—The different forms *mahola* and *mohala* have the same meaning.

HOO-MA-HU, *v.* See MAHU, steam;

vapor. To steam; to burst forth like steam.

Hoo-ma-hu-a, *v*. To watch; to lie in wait; to act as a spy secretly; to mock; to deride.

2. To hide one's self; to conceal from view; to dodge behind something.

Hoo-ma-hu-a, *v*. To increase; to grow in size; to swell out; more often used in the double form, as

Hoo-ma-hu-a-hu-a, *v*. See Mahua and Hua, to grow. To increase; to enlarge; to grow big.

Hoo-ma-hu-a-ka-la, *v*. To jeer at; to treat with contempt.

Hoo-ma-hu-i, *v*. See Mahui, to follow after. To follow after; to imitate; to listen to one's counsel or advice; to imitate one's example.

Hoo-ma-hu-ka, *v*. See Mahuka, to run away. To counsel or advise one to run away; to assist one to leave a place or business secretly; to hide one's self to avoid work.

Hoo-ma-hu-wa, *v*. To be blind, especially with one eye.

Hoo-ma-ka, *v*. To begin; to commence a work; to set forth a new thing; to commence, as a course of evil. *Laieik.* 191.

2. To be wild; to be untamed; to be evilly disposed.

Hoo-ma-ka, *s*. The fresh blade of a plant; the first leaf of a tree. *Mar.* 4:28.

Hoo-ma-ka-a-ki-u, *v*. See Makakiu, watchful eye. To spy out; to act the part of a spy; to watch with jealousy. Note.— This is rather a phrase than a word, *to commence to watch. Halelu* 10:8.

Hoo-ma-ka-e, *v*. To look at with disdain; to stand aloof from; to be at enmity with; to look askance or be angry at.

Hoo-ma-ka-i, *v*. See Makai, a policeman. To be bold; to be fearless; to be assuming.

2. To act the sheriff; to be a policeman.

3. To be stingy; to be close; to be hard to deal with.

Hoo-ma-ka-u, *v*. See Makau, fear. To cause one to fear; to make afraid; to frighten.

Hoo-ma-kau-au-a, *v*. To hang or fasten up, as clothes to dry.

Hoo-ma-ka-u-ka-u, *v*. Freq. of *makau*. To make afraid; to try to scare; e lilo ana oe i mea e *hoomakaukau* ia ai ma na alanui, thou shalt become an example causing fear by the road sides. *Laieik.* 212.

Hoo-ma-kau-kau, *v*. See Makaukau, ready; prepared. To make ready; to prepare; to get in readiness for business or for a coming event.

Hoo-ma-kau-lii, *s*. One who feigns friendship and eats with one while he watches his opportunity to injure him; one acting with cunning and duplicity.

2. Strong desire for and corresponding effort to obtain a thing.

Hoo-ma-kau-lii, *v*. To be thorough going; to persevere; to hold out; to have a strong desire for a thing; e hoomanawanui a loaa mai; he kanaka *hoomakaulii* haku, a nolaila e malama pono i ka waiwai; he *hoomakaulii* ma ka manao i ke Akua.

Hoo-ma-ka-ki, *v*. To beg; to ask.

2. To design revenge; to meditate mischief.

Hoo-ma-ka-ki-u, *v*. See Hoomaka and Kiu, to spy. To watch with a jealous eye; to lie in wait to do evil.

Hoo-ma-ka-ki-u, *adj*. Jealous; suspicious; watchful through jealousy.

Hoo-ma-ka-ma-ka, *v*. See Makamaka, a friend. To be on terms of intimacy; to make friends for the sake of profit or convenience.

Hoo-ma-ka-la, *v*. See Makala, to loosen. To cause to open a little, as a door; to loosen; to untie. See Kala. To loosen, as in taking off one's garment.

Hoo-ma-ka-na-he-le-he-le, *v*. See Hoomaka and Nahele, land grown up to bushes. To go astray in the bush; to get out of the road.

Hoo-ma-ke, *v*. See Make, death. To cause death; to kill.

2. To wish to die; to fast.

3. To put in a state of privation; to cause thinness of flesh.

4. To put one's self where he would appear to be lost; mai hoopae oe (i ka aina), e *hoomake* oe i kou nalu, go not ashore, *plunge under* your surf.

Hoo-ma-ke-a-ka, *v*. See Aka, to laugh. To excite laughter; to exercise wit.

Hoo-ma-ke-a-ka, *adj*. Exciting laughter; witty; he olelo *hoomakeaka*.

Hoo-ma-kee, *v*. To be greedy after property; to scrape together; to lust after property.

Hoo-ma-ke-he-wa, *v*. To accuse falsely; to do a thing in vain.

Hoo-ma-ke-ma-ke, *v*. See Makemake. To desire; to wish for.

Hoo-ma-ke-na, *v*. See Makena. To cause mourning; to cause sorrow; to cause grief.

Hoo-ma-ki-u, *v.* See Kiu, to spy. To watch with a design to surprise; to watch for an opportunity to do mischief.

Hoo-ma-ko-a, *v.* To walk, talk or act bravely; to act as an officer among soldiers; e hookoa, e hookalali.

Hoo-ma-koi, *v.* To be hard; to be stingy; to be close; to be regardless of others.

Hoo-ma-kou, *v.* See Makou, to be red, as the eyes. To make red; to be blood shot, as the eyes from being long in salt water.

Hoo-ma-ko-le, *v.* See Kole and Makole, red, as raw flesh. To be raw, as flesh; to be red, as inflamed eyes.

Hoo-ma-ko-li, *v.* See Koli, to trim; to cut short. To cut short; to make small; to render fine.

Hoo-ma-ko-ma-ko, *adj.* The epithet of a cloud; he ao *hoomakomako*, a large cloud, perhaps.

Hoo-ma-ku, *v.* To increase; to grow large; to grow thickly.

Hoo-ma-ku-a, *v.* To grow; to enlarge; to become thick or many.

Hoo-ma-ku-e, *v.* To burden one; to vex; to trouble; to be angry at; to frown at.

Hoo-ma-ku-e, *s.* An angry look; a frowning at; a stirring up of displeasure.

Hoo-ma-ku-e-ku-e, *v.* To frown; to frown at one.

Hoo-ma-ku-ma-ku, *v.* See Hoomaku. To increase; to enlarge; to grow fat; to be heavy, as a fat person or animal.

Hoo-ma-lae, *v.* See Malae, to be calm. To put on a pleasant countenance; to assume the appearance of friendship when the heart is disaffected; to hide an evil design by assuming pleasantry.

Hoo-ma-la-e-a, *v.* To be calm; to be quiet; to settle down in quietness; applied to the presence of one who was reproached when absent.

Hoo-ma-lae-lae, *v.* See Laelae, clear, as the sky. To enlighten; to make clear and pleasant; to calm.

Hoo-ma-lai-le-na, *v.* See Malailena, bitterness. To make bitter; to embitter.

Hoo-ma-la-o, *v.* To act the idler; to be a vagabond; to go about from place to place doing nothing.

Hoo-ma-lau, *v.* See Malau, to reject good advice. To be unbelieving; to be ungodly; to be irreverent towards sacred things.

Hoo-ma-lau-e-a, *v.* To be lazy; to be indolent. See Malao.

Hoo-ma-la-hi-a, *v.* Pass. for *malaia*, to be bitter. To make bitter; to be bitter.

Hoo-ma-la-ma-la-ma, *v.* See Lama, a torch. To enlighten; to shine upon.

Hoo-ma-la-na, *v.* To throw away, as refuse matter.
   2. To be disrespected.
   3. To take care of.
   4. To be large; to swell, as a dead body.

Hoo-ma-la-na-la-na, *v.* Freq. of above.

Hoo-ma-le-a, *v.* See Malea and Maalea, wise; crafty. To deal wisely; to be crafty; to act wisely or prudently.

Hoo-ma-li-e, *v.* See Malie, calm; quiet. To hush, as a tumult; to clear off, as the sky after a storm.

Hoo-ma-li-e-li-e, *v.* To appease, as a ruffled mind; to soothe; to calm, as anger; to treat kindly.

Hoo-ma-li-hi-ni, *v.* See Malihini, a stranger. To make one's self a stranger; to become a stranger; to be foreign to one.

Hoo-ma-li-ko, *v.* To discredit.

Hoo-ma-li-ma-li, *v.* See Malimali, to flatter. To flatter; to secure one's favor by flattery.

Hoo-ma-loo, *v.* See Maloo, parched; dry. To cause to dry up, as water; to wither, as a tree or flower; to make anything dry.

Hoo-ma-lo-hi-lo-hi, *v.* See Lohi, to be slow. To be fatigued, as by traveling; to be lame. See Maluhiluhi.

Hoo-ma-lo-ka, *v.* See Maloka, to be sluggish; to be stupid. To be dull; to be stupid in mind; to disregard any important truth; to be unbelieving; to disobey the command of a chief.

Hoo-ma-lo-lo, *s.* The name of the day before the la kapu; hence under the christian system, the *la hoomalolo* is Saturday, i. e., the day before the Sabbath.

Hoo-ma-lu, *v.* See Malu, a shade, peace, &c. To rule over, especially in a peaceful way; to govern quietly; to make peace.

Hoo-ma-lu, *adj.* Making or causing peace between differing parties; mohai *hoomalu*, a peace-offering. *Puk.* 20:21.

Hoo-ma-lu-le, *v.* To change from one form to another; to metamorphose, as a caterpillar into a butterfly.

Hoo-ma-lu-ma-lu, *adj.* Overshadowing; shading, as clouds that run low; he ao *hoomalumalu*.

Hoo-ma-na, *v.* See Mana, superhuman power. To ascribe divine honors; to worship; to cause one to have regal authority.

Hoo-ma-nao, *v.* See Manao, to think.

To turn the mind upon; to call to mind; to cause to consider; to remember that which is past.

Hoo-ma-nao-nao, *v.* See **Manaonao,** to lament. To call up the past with sorrow; to think or reflect on the past.

Hoo-ma-nao-nao, *s.* A reflection on the past; sorrow for the past.

Hoo-ma-na-kii, *v.* See **Hoomana** above and **Kii,** an idol. To worship idols; to worship any god except Jehovah.

Hoo-ma-na-kii, *s.* The practice of worshipping idols; idolatry; called *figuratively* in Scripture, whoredom. 2 *Nal.* 9:22. Also vanity; a vain service; idolatry. 2 *Nal.* 17:15.

Hoo-ma-na-lo, *v.* See **Manalo,** sweet; free from taint. To purify; to sweeten anything from salt or any unpleasant taste or smell.

Hoo-ma-na-wa-le-a, *v.* See **Manawa-lea,** alms. To appease by a gift; to give alms to the poor; to relieve the distressed.

Hoo-ma-ne-a, *v.* See **Manea.** To render callous; to harden; he mea ia na ke kalaimoku e *hoomanea* i kanaka i haalele ole i ke alii.

Hoo-ma-ne-o-ne-o, *v.* See **Maneo,** to itch. To scratch where it itches; to tickle.

Hoo-ma-no, *v.* See **Mano,** a shark. To act the shark; to be greedy.

2. To be continually at; to persevere in, as one in begging.

3. To tease with importunity.

Hoo-ma-wae-na, *v.* To come into the midst of a company of people or things; a i ka au hou ana o ka mea i komo i ka pua, *hoomawaena* mai oia.

Hoo-me-a, *v.* See **Mea,** to trouble; to effect. To cause something; to do something; to make pretense; to deceive; to disappoint; to make trouble.

Hoo-me-ha, *v.* See **Meha,** to live alone. To stay at home from work; to cease from work. NOTE.—Formerly *hoomeha* was applied to a la kapu, but is now used as synonymous with la hoomalolo, the day before the Sabbath, i. e., Saturday.

Hoo-me-ha, *adj.* Preparing for the Sabbath. See **Hoomalolo.**

Hoo-me-le, *v.* See **Mele,** a song. To cause or make a song; to sing a mele; to be joyous; to rejoice.

Hoo-me-ne-me-ne, *v.* See **Mene,** to have pity. To be dear to one; to have compassion upon; to pity; to treat tenderly, as a beloved one.

Hoo-mi-ho, *v.* To build by laying one thing on top of another.

Hoo-mo-a, *v.* See **Moa,** cooked. To cause to be cooked; to be thoroughly baked.

Hoo-mo-ae, *v.* To tear or snatch away; to steal.

Hoo-mo-a-ka-ka, *v.* See **Akaka,** clear to the mind. To cause to be very plain to the mind; to make one understand what may be intricate; to explain. See **Hoakaka.**

Hoo-mo-a-la-a-la, *v.* See **Moalaala,** to rise up to go. To be busy about; to go from house to house; to be forward; to be impertinent.

Hoo-mo-a-na, *v.* As if *hoomoena.* To spread down mats for staying overnight; hence,

2. To encamp, as travelers; to encamp, as soldiers. See also **Moana.**

Hoo-mo-a-na, *adj.* Encamped; kahi *hoomoana,* a camping place; a camp. *Oihk.* 16:28.

Hoo-mo-e, *v.* See **Moe,** to lie down. To cause to lie down; to prostrate in adoration.

2. To speak of one's sleeping with another, that is, of marrying together. *Laieik.* 66.

3. To lie down to rest; to rest one's self by lying down.

Hoo-mo-e-mo-e, *v.* To cause to lie down.

2. To hush or put to sleep.

Hoo-moo, *v.* To continue or persevere in laying taxes upon the people; to follow up a pursuit; ame ka *hoomoo* o na puu waiwai, to urge or force people to give their property for such purposes as the rulers need; e kaukolo, e hookoikoi.

Hoo-mo-u-ki-u-ki, *v.* See **Ukiuki,** hot and bad smelling. To cause an offensive smell; to reek with offensive smells, like an old and dirty ship, or like the breath of a tobacco smoker; to be warm or stifled for want of pure air.

Hoo-mo-ha-la, *v.* To open; to unfold or blossom, as a flower.

2. To spread, as a kapa or sheet. See **Hoomahola** by a change of syllables.

3. To have a little hope, as one disappointed; ua *hoomohalaia* kona naau kanalua. *Laieik.* 93.

4. To unfold, as one's inward desire; to rage, as lust. *Laieik.* 196.

Hoo-mo-ha-lu, *v.* See **Mohalu,** to be at ease. To entertain in one's house; to invite to one's house.

2. To lie at ease; to rest securely.

3. To break; to crack. See next word.

Hoo-mo-ha-lu-ha-lu, *v.* To crack; to break, as the auamo or stick on which things are carried on the shoulders of men.

Hoo-mo-ho-la, *v.* See MOHOLA and HO-HOLA. To spread out widely; to unfold, as the growing of a plant.

Hoo-mo-ho-le, *v.* See HOLE, to peel. To peel; to strip the skin from an animal; to peel the bark from a tree. See UHOLE.

Hoo-mo-ko, *v.* This is probably for *hookomo*, or it may mean, to cut short. A *hoomoko* ka wai ma na pae.

Hoo-mo-ku, *v.* To cause a division; to cut and divide, as a land.

Hoo-mo-ku, *s.* A cutting or a dividing, &c.

Hoo-mo-le, *v.* See MOLE, smooth. To be shorn close; to be cut smooth.

2. To cause to linger; to be slow; to be behind.

3. To refuse; to be unwilling.

Hoo-mo-le-mo-le, *v.* Intensive of the above.

Hoo-mo-lo-wa, *v.* See MOLOWA, inactive. To be indifferent about a thing; to be indisposed to do a thing, especially to work; hence,

2. To be lazy; to be idle.

Hoo-mo-mo-le, *v.* See HOOMOLE above. To be smooth.

Hoo-mu, *v.* See MU, to shut the lips. To sit silent; to be speechless; to make no reply; to refuse to answer. See MU-MULE, like the English to be mum.

Hoo-muu, *v.* To cause a collection; to heap together.

2. To gormandize.

Hoo-mu-e, *v.* To be bad tasted to the palate; to be offensive to the taste; to be bitter; to be brackish.

Hoo-mu-e-mu-e, *v.* Freq. of the above.

Hoo-mu-hu, *v.* To collect together. See MUMUHU.

2. To make a low humming sound.

Hoo-mu-ka, *v.* See MUKA, tasteless; insipid. To be tasteless; to be insipid; ono ole.

Hoo-mu-ka-mu-ka, *v.* To be insipid; to be tasteless.

Hoo-mu-mu, *v.* See MU. To hold in the mouth without swallowing.

2. To hold the mouth silent from speaking.

Hoo-mu-mu-hu, *v.* See MUHU, to hum. To collect; to assemble together, as men; to gather together, as other things.

2. To make a low indistinct noise; to sound like an indistinct low hum.

Hoo-mu-mu-ku, *v.* See MUKU, to cut short. To cut short; to cut too short; to break off. See MUMUKU.

Hoo-mu-mu-le, *v.* See MUMULE, to be dumb. To be silent; to be dumb.

2. To be out of one's mind; to be crazy; to be insane.

Hoo-mu-mu-lu, *v.* To collect together in great numbers; to be thick together, as swarms of flies.

Hoo-na, *v.* See NA, to be quiet. To cause ease; to give quiet from pain.

2. To obtain a refuge from danger.

3. To search or look for a place. See NANA.

Hoo-nae, *v.* See NAE, to breathe hard. To breathe hard; to puff like one traveling fast up hill; to be fatigued.

Hoo-nae-nae, *v.* Freq. of the above.

Hoo-na-e-le, *v.* See NAELE. To cause to be thick, as mud; to be muddy.

2. To break open; to crack, as dried mud.

Hoo-na-i-ki, *v.* To persecute.

Hoo-nai-ko-la, *v.* See AIKOLA and HO-AIKOLA. To cause to triumph over an enemy; to rejoice at a victory.

2. To treat with contempt, as a conquered one.

Hoo-nai-nai, *v.* See HOONAE, to pant. To sob; to breathe hard.

Hoo-na-ue, *v.* See NAUE, to vibrate. To cause to rock; to reel to and fro; to shake, as the earth in an earthquake.

2. To move a little; to shove along. See NAWE and NAUWE.

Hoo-na-ue-ue, *v.* Freq. of above. To rock; to shake to and fro.

Hoo-na-u-ki, *v.* See UKI and NAUKI. To fret; to provoke; to make one angry.

Hoo-na-u-ki-u-ki, *v.* See above. To provoke; to make angry.

Hoo-na-u-lu, *v.* See NAULU, to vex. To vex; to provoke. *Kanl.* 9:22. To vex. 1 *Sam.* 1:6.

Hoo-na-ha, *v.* See NAHA, to crack or break, as glass. To break or crack, as glass.

2. To cause to operate, as a cathartic.

Hoo-na-he-na-he, *v.* See NAHE, thin; soft. To be low; to be flat; to be thin; to be humble.

Hoo-na-hi-li, *v.* See NAHILI, to be awkward; to be slow. To lengthen out; to make long, as a road by going a circuitous route, or by losing one's way.

2. To hesitate; to linger.

Hoo-na-ho-a, *v.* See NAHOA, strong; bold. To be hard; to be strong; to be bold, as a soldier.

2. To turn a deaf ear; to refuse to listen. See HOONEHOA.

HOO-NA-HO-NA-HO, *v.* See NAHONAHO, to be deep. To be set deep in the head, as the eyes; to be deep, as a pit.

HOO-NA-HU, *v.* See NAHU, to bite; to gripe. To snap, as corn parching; to crack, as a pistol; to make a report, as fire-arms.

HOO-NA-HU-NA-HU, *v.* See the above. To snap at, as a dog.

2. To be in labor pains.

3. To be seized by sudden pain.

HOO-NA-KE-LE, *v.* See NAKELE, soft; slippery. To make boggy, as land; to be soft and shaky, as a miry place.

HOO-NA-KOA, *v.* See KOA, a soldier. To be bold; to be brave; to act the soldier; to be fearless; to be daring.

HOO-NA-KU-I, *v.* See KUI, to sound abroad. To make a rumbling noise; to tremble.

2. To spread out, as a sound from a place.

HOO-NA-KO-LO, *v.* See KOLO, to crawl, and NAKOLO. To run along; to spread, as ink on paper.

HOO-NA-KU-LU, *v.* To cause to fall in drops, as rain; as perspiration. *Laieik.* 118.

HOO-NA-KU-LU-KU-LU, *v.* See KULU, to drop. To drop down, as rain; to drip from the clouds, as rain. *Isa.* 45:8.

HOO-NA-LO, *v.* See NALO, to disappear. To be lost; to vanish; to be out of sight; with *wale*, to be forgotten.

HOO-NA-LO-NA-LO, *v.* Freq. of the above.

HOO-NA-LU, *v.* See NALU, the surf. To cause a swell of the sea on shore; to rise, as the surf; to act, as the sea when the wind and tide are contrary.

HOO-NA-LU-LU, *v.* To turn a deaf ear; to refuse to listen; to disregard. See HOO-MAEAEA.

HOO-NA-MU-NA-MU, *v.* See NAMU, to speak rapidly. To speak in an unintelligible manner.

2. To find fault behind one.

HOO-NA-NAA, *v.* To enrage.

HOO-NA-NA-AU, *v.* See NANA and LANA, to float, and AU, tide; current. To cause to float on the surface of water; to swim standing or erect; to float here and there as the current goes.

HOO-NA-NA, *v.* See NA and NANA, to hush; to quiet, as a child. To calm; to quiet, as a child; to hush up a difficulty; to ease a pain; to comfort; to console.

HOO-NA-NA, *adj.* See NANA, to bark; to growl. Angry; cross; reluctant.

HOO-NA-NA-U-HA, *v.* To be strong; to be hard; to be tight; to drag; to draw.

HOO-NA-NA-HI-LI, *v.* See NAHILI, slow; lagging. To go in a crooked manner; to wander about; to mistake the road.

HOO-NA-NA-HO, *v.* See NANAHO, deep down. To be deep.

2. To be strong; to be tight.

HOO-NA-NA-HU, *v.* See NAHU, to bite, and NANAHU and LANAHU, a coal of fire. To char, as wood; to make coal; to burn wood to charcoal.

2. To bite; to sting like a burn.

HOO-NA-NA-KA, *v.* See NAKA and NA-NAKA, a crack; a crevice. To be full of cracks, openings or chinks.

2. To be unstable; not firm, as a bog.

HOO-NA-NA-KI, *v.* See NANAKI and NA-KII, to tie; to fasten. To bind; to tie up.

HOO-NA-NE, *v.* See NANE, a riddle. To put forth a riddle; to propose something mysterious for explication.

HOO-NA-NE-A, *v.* See NANEA, easy; quiet. To be easy; to be contented; to be satisfied with one's self; to be indifferent to the future.

HOO-NA-NI, *v.* See NANI, also LANI, beautiful; glorious. To glorify; to praise; to exalt; to honor.

HOO-NA-NI-NA-NI, *v.* Intensive of the above. To be proud; to be vainglorious; to be haughty; to be arrogant.

2. To act the spendthrift; to waste property.

HOO-NA-NU-E, *v.* See NANUE, to swell up. To tremble; to shake. See NAUE.

HOO-NA-PAI, *v.* See NAPAI, to bend in. To crook; to bend; to arch.

HOO-NA-PE, *v.* See NAPE, bending; flexible. To bend; to crook; to bend, as an elastic stick.

HOO-NA-PE-LE, *v.* See NAPELE, to hurt; to wound. To make a wound on the head; to swell, as the effect of a wound; to swell out, as the belly.

2. To be soft and yielding, as a boggy, miry place; to shake, as a bog; to soften, as the food in the stomach; o ka opu, oia kahi e *hoonapele* ai i ka ai, the stomach is the place to soften the food. *Anat.* 51.

HOO-NA-PE-LE-PE-LE, *v.* Intensive of the above.

HOO-NA-PO-LO, *v.* To straighten; to make straight.

HOO-NA-WA-LE, *v.* See NA and HOONA with WALE. To comfort; to attempt to quiet without effort.

Hoo-na-wa-li, *v.* See Nawali, weak; feeble. To be weakly; to be sickly; to have little strength.

2. To totter when one walks; to be thin; to be flexible.

Hoo-na-wa-li-wa-li, *v.* Intensive of the above.

Hoo-na-we-le, *v.* See Nawele, fine; small; thin. To make very little; to be fine, like the threads of a spider's web; to spin, as a spider its web.

Hoo-ne, *v.* To tease; to fret; to ask for food, as a child.

Hoo-ne, *s.* Name of a soft porous stone.

Hoo-ne-a, *v.* See Nea, to desolate. To make desolate; to sweep off all; to destroy wholly. See Neo and Neoneo.

Hoo-ne-a-ne-a, *v.* To take all away; to dispossess one of everything; to take all the fruits of one's land.

Hoo-nee, *v.* See Nee, to move. To move; to shove along; to rub against.

Hoo-nee-nee, *v.* See Nee, to move along. To push along; to move frequently; to shake.

Hoo-nei, *v.* See Nei, to move. To move, as people in a tumult; to move, as trees by the wind.

Hoo-nei-nei, *v.* See Nei and Hoonei. To crowd one upon another; to move along, urged by others.

Hoo-ne-o, *v.* See Neo, to be silent. To make silence; to hush; to be still.

2. To be silent from loneliness or desolation.

3. To be in a wild, lonely place.

Hoo-ne-o-ne-o, *v.* See the above. To hush to stillness; to be still.

2. To be still or quiet for want of people.

Hoo-ne-ho-a, *v.* See Hoonahoa. To be severe; to be bold; to act the soldier; to be brave.

Hoo-ne-le, *v.* See Nele, destitute. To deprive one of something; to make destitute; to deprive of.

Hoo-ne-mo, *v.* See Nemo, to smooth over. To be polished; to be made smooth; to be nice and good.

Hoo-ne-mo-ne-mo, *v.* To make smooth; to polish.

Hoo-ne-ne, *v.* To chirp, as a cricket; to sing, as a cricket.

Hoo-ne-ne, *v.* Ka leo o ka ewaewa iki e *hoonene* ana. *Laieik.* 149.

Hoo-ne-ne, *s.* The voice of a cricket.

Hoo-ni-au, *v.* To go away and leave one's company secretly, generally for some evil purpose; a no keia mea (ka ikea ana o ke kahoaka o Laieikawai), *hooniau* aku la ka Makaula i ka pule ana. *Laieik.* 26.

Hoo-ni-au, *v.* See Niau, to sail genteelly. To copy or follow those whose conduct is upright; to do rightly.

Hoo-ni-a-ni-a, *v.* See Nia, baldheaded. To make smooth or fair the outside; to be smooth, as a baldhead.

2. Fig. To make fair pretenses.

3. To blame or accuse falsely. See Niania.

Hoo-ni-a-ni-ao, *v.* To ask questions often and frequently; to question; hooniele.

Hoo-ni-o-ni-o-lo, *v.* See Nioniolo, correct; straight. To be morally straight; to be upright; to be correct in practice.

2. To be correct in principle; to have right views.

3. To go without carrying anything, while others perhaps are heavily loaded; kaumaha lakou, a he *hoonioniolo* kana hele ana. He kanaka haaheo ka!

Hoo-ni-o-ni-o-lo, *s.* Straightness; that which is correct; upright; me ka *hoonioniolo* o ka manao kekahi, some with correctness of opinion.

Hoo-ni-ho, *v.* See Niho, to indent; to set in. To lay stones in a wall; to lay stones in the wall of an embankment, as the lower side of a road, that is, to insert stones into a bank like teeth in the gums. See Niho, tooth.

Hoo-ni-ho, *s.* Stones inserted in a bank; a stone wall or hedge.

Hoo-ni-hi-ni-hi, *v.* See Nihinihi. To be full of ridges; to diminish upward.

2. To take slender hold of a thing, as from fear of filth.

3. To eat sparingly; e ai *hoonihinihi*.

Hoo-ni-na, *v.* See Nina and Lina, soft to the touch. To be soft to the touch.

2. To be wet and tough, as cold land.

3. To be weak and feeble, as one recovering from sickness; pili i ka mea ua ola, aole ola loa.

4. Not to have full cheeks, as one sickly. See Papalina.

Hoo-ni-na-ni-na, *v.* Freq. of the above. See Ninanina and Linalina.

Hoo-no, *v.* For *hoohoro.* See Hono, to mend, as a garment or a fish net. To join together, as in mending a net; to unite, as in tying sticks together.

Hoo-no, *v.* To think; to look at attentively; to be sharp upon.

Hoo-no-a, *v.* See Noa, the cessation of

a kapu. To cause to cease, as the force of a kapu; to put an end to a kapu.

Hoo-no-a, *v.* To keep continually burning, as a fire; e hoomau i ke ahi; to burn continually, as a volcano.

Hoo-no-e, *v.* See Noe, mist; fine rain. To make thin or small, like a head with few hairs; to be small, like fine rain.

Hoo-no-e-no-e, *v.* See Noenoe, mist. To make small or fine, as small dots on paper.

2. To attend, as the mind to little things.

Hoo-noi, *v.* See Noi, to beg. To beg; to ask something of another.

Hoo-noo-noo, *v.* See Noonoo, to think. To cause to think upon; to remember; to consider; to reflect upon.

Ho-o-no-o-no, *v.* For *hooonoono.* See Ono, ready. To be ready; to be prompt; to be mature; to act the man.

Ho-o-no-o-no, *s.* Promptness; readiness; having a supply. See Kuonoono.

Hoo-nou, *v.* See Nou, to throw a stone. To throw a stone; to pelt with stones; to throw, as missiles.

2. To loosen; to send forth.

Hoo-no-hi, *v.* To cause to be red; to be of a reddish color.

Hoo-no-hi-no-hi, *v.* To shine with brightness; to be red.

2. To have a different form.

Hoo-no-ho, *v.* See Noho, to put down; to place. To set in order; to place rightly; to regulate.

Hoo-no-ho, *s.* The name of a species of fish-hook.

Hoo-no-ho-no-ho, *v.* To settle; to establish; to collect together; to arrange.

Hoo-no-ho-no-ho, *s.* In the phrase *hoonohonoho* akua, the act of setting up or worshiping the poe akua noho; hana ino nui ia kekahi poe *hoonohonoho* akua, a mahuka lakou ma kahi e aku.

Hoo-no-ho-no-lo.

Hoo-no-hu, *v.* To let down, as the sails of a ship.

Hoo-no-ke, *v.* See Noke, to be energetic. To work energetically and perseveringly; to be acute in searching for the means to secure an end; to act with energy and intelligence.

Hoo-no-le, *v.* Used perhaps for *none,* to snore.

Hoo-no-ni, *v.* To joggle; to rustle; to disturb.

Hoo-no-no-lo, *v.* To chirp like a bird; to warble; to sing.

2. To coo like a dove.

3. To growl, as a dog.

4. To grunt like a hog.

5. To snort, as a horse.

Hoo-nu-a, *v.* To tread upon continually; to do over and over again; to act with energy and perseverance.

Hoo-nu-a, *s.* A treading; vigorous exercise.

Hoo-nu-a-nu-a, *v.* To be ennobled; to be honored; to be rich.

Hoo-nu-i, *v.* See Nui, to be great. To cause to enlarge; to grow big; to increase.

2. Fig. To boast; to brag. See Haanui.

Hoo-nu-i-nu-i, *v.* Intensive of the above.

Hoo-nuu, *v.* See Nuu and Anuu, a raised place. To be greedy in eating; to eat to great fullness; to gormandize; applied to a single person. See Hookuku. Hence,

2. To swell; to rise up, as one's stomach from great eating.

3. To begrudge the food another eats.

Hoo-nuu, *s.* Greediness after food; a voracious appetite; a seizing food with eagerness.

Hoo-nuu, *adj.* Greedy after food.

Hoo-nu-ha, *v.* See Nuha, silent; taciturn. To be idle; to be lazy; to be indisposed to do anything.

2. To sit still, as a person unable to walk.

3. To be disabled.

Hoo-nu-ha-nu-ha, *v.* Intensive of the above.

Hoo-nu-ha-nu-ha, *s.* A palsied person; one disabled from palsy.

Hoo-pa, *v.* See Pa, to touch. To cause to touch; to take hold of; to hit; to strike.

Hoo-paa, *v.* See Paa, fast; tight. To make fast; to bind; to keep tight; to detain.

2. To tie or fasten a thing; to make tight.

3. To stop one's speech; to be silent; you have said enough. *Laieik.* 65.

Hoo-paa-ki-ki, *v.* See Paakiki, hard morally and physically. To hold fast to one's opinion; to be obstinate; to be unyielding.

2. To have no respect to other's feelings, person or property.

3. To be hard in the treatment of others; to be hard hearted.

Hoo-paa-ki-ki, *s.* Stubbornness; disobedience. 1 *Sam.* 15:23.

Hoo-paa-paa, *v.* See Paapaa, to dispute. To be hard upon others; hence,

2. To dispute pertinaciously; to contend; to quarrel; to have a mental contest.

Hoo-pae, *v.* See Pae, to go ashore. To

cause to arrive at land; to go ashore from a canoe, boat or vessel.

2. To float ashore, as anything at sea.

3. To throw up on a bank of a kalo patch.

Hoo-pae-e, *v.* See Pae, to misunderstand. To hear indistinctly through some noise; to misunderstand what is said; to be partially deaf.

Hoo-pa-ee, *s.* A desire and an effort to obtain another's property; a species of robbery.

Hoo-pa-e-le, *v.* See Paele, to be dirty. To besmear; to defile; to make dirty; to blacken. *Figuratively*, to disturb with other thoughts and reflections. *Laieik.* 142.

Hoo-pae-pae, *v.* See Hoopae above. To be driven or dashed on shore by the surf; to ride ashore through the surf.

Hoo-pae-pae, *v.* See Pae, to sound. To make a loud boisterous noise in conversation; to talk with a loud voice so that everybody can hear.

Hoo-pa-e-wa, *s.* See Paewa. Crookedness in dealing; so dealing as to get the advantage; also, in *conversation*, a perversion of truth or an erroneous statement. It is often connected with robbery and murder.

Hoo-pai, *v.* See Pai, to strike. To strike back; to revenge; to treat one as he treats us.

2. To pay back; to punish; to punish according to law.

3. To stir up; to excite; to reward either good or evil.

Hoo-pai, *s.* An avenger; ka *hoopai* koko, an avenger of blood. *Kanl.* 19:6.

Hoo-pai-ho, *v.* To make a significant gesture by putting the thumb between the fingers.

2. To give a warning with the hand.

3. To tempt, or to kuamuamu; eia na olelo hou e hewa ai, o ke kake, o ka olelo Kauai, o ka *hoopaiho* lima.

4. To rub the skin from the arm; to skin.

5. To make crooked. Note.—This word is said to be peculiar to Kauai.

Hoo-pa-i-ki, *v.* See Pa, to touch, and Iki, little. To touch lightly or softly; to move gently; to move a very little.

Hoo-pai-lu-a, *v.* See Pailua, nausea. To be sick at the stomach; to nauseate.

2. To dislike greatly; to be displeased with.

Hoo-pai-lu-a, *s.* Sickness at the stomach; disgust; loathing.

2. A disgusting sight; an abomination.

Hoo-pau, *v.* See Pau, all. To make an end of a thing; to finish; to complete a work; to cease to work.

2. To devour; to consume all.

Hoo-pa-u, *v.* See Pa-u, a woman's garment. To put or gird on the pa-u; to bind on one, as a loose garment; to tie around.

Hoo-pau-a-ka, *v.* See Pauaka, to be weary. To work without wages or reward; to be compelled to work gratis; to oppress with hard labor; to work here and there.

Hoo-pau-li-na-li-na, *v.* See Lina, soft; yielding. To work lazily or carelessly because of little or no pay.

Hoo-pau-ma-e-le, *v.* See Paumaele, to defile. To cause defilement or pollution; to daub over; to foul; to dirty.

Hoo-pau-ma-ko, *v.* See Paumako, heaviness of eyes. To have great affection for; to weep over one from grief; to be sad at the loss of a friend or anything valuable.

Hoo-pau-ma-na-wa, *v.* To waste time; to play the child after one has grown up; to act foolishly; to live idly.

Hoo-pau-pau, *v.* See Hoopaumaele. To defile; to make filthy; to render vile; polluted.

Hoo-pau-pau-a-ho, *v.* See Hoopau and Aho, breath. To be nearly out of breath; to pant; to breathe hard.

2. Fig. To be weary in doing a thing; to be discouraged.

Hoo-pa-hee, *v.* See Pahee, to slip. To slip; to slide; to fall prostrate; to fall down; to slide, as the feet in a slippery place.

Hoo-pa-hee-hee, *v.* Intensive of above.

Hoo-pa-he-le, *v.* See Pahele, to insnare. To insnare; to take or catch with a snare.

Hoo-pa-he-mo, *v.* See Hemo and Pahemo, to loosen. To loosen; to slip off, as an axe from the helve.

Hoo-pa-ho-le, *v.* See Pahole, to peel off. To peel; to pull off, as the skin of a banana.

2. To rub; to polish.

3. To do a thing with indifference.

Hoo-pa-hu, *v.* See Pahu, to mock; to push away. To mock; to deride; to treat with contempt.

2. To defend off; to push away.

3. To snap, as parching corn.

4. To beat the pahu or drum.

5. To frighten, as one who carries the report of death or calamities.

Hoo-pa-hu-a, *v.* To strengthen; to confirm.

2. To sail in a zigzag manner; to beat

against the wind.

3. To dance.

HOO-PA-HU-PA-HU, v. See PAHU. To snap, as corn in the fire; to crack or make a report, as a pistol.

2. To beat the drum.

3. To do a thing very quickly or rapidly.

HOO-PA-HU-PA-HU, s. A drumming or thrumming on a pahu or drum; a thumping; aole wau i moe iki, i ka *hoopahupahu* wale ia no a ao wale. *Laieik.* 198.

HOO-PA-KA-UA-A-KA, v. See AKA, to laugh. To cause one to laugh; to create laughter; to make sport.

HOO-PA-KA-KA, v. See PAKAKA, to be smooth. To make smooth; to swell up, as a swelling of the skin; hence,

2. To be smooth and shining; to swell, as the belly so as to be smooth.

3. To glide smoothly, as over a surface.

HOO-PA-KA-KE, v. See KAKE and PAKAKE. To practice the kake.

2. To talk unintelligibly except to those instructed in a kind of mystical language.

3. To talk like a foreigner without learning his language.

HOO-PA-KE, v. See PAKE, to push away. To partition off; to guard; to defend; to push away; to allow to escape.

HOO-PA-KE-LE, v. See PAKELE, to escape. To cause to escape from; to deliver; to save one from danger.

HOO-PA-KE-LO, v. See PAKELO, to slip out of. See PAKELE. To slip out of the grasp of a person or thing, as a fish from the hands.

2. To inject; to give an enema.

HOO-PA-KI, v. See PAKI and PAKE, to resist; to push away. To be hard against; to resist; to push; to crowd out, as an egg about to hatch; to swell out; to urge through any opposing substance.

HOO-PA-KI-O, v. See PAKIO, to drop continually, as rain. To cause to rain frequently; to drop down rain continually.

HOO-PA-KI-KI, v. See PAKIKI and PAA-KIKI, very hard. To resist; to set against; to stir up; to excite.

2. To harden; to be or act obstinately.

3. To skim stones on the surface of the water.

HOO-PA-KO-LE, v. See PAKOLE and PO-KOLE, to be short. To curb in; to restrain; to shorten; to make short.

HOO-PA-KU-PA-KU, v. To be brisk at work; to work quickly, without laziness.

HOO-PA-LA, v. See PALA, mellow; soft.

To make soft; to ripen soft, as dead-ripe fruit.

2. To stain; to daub; to smutch; to plaster.

HOO-PA-LAU, v. To engage to marry, as a man and woman; to make an agreement of marriage.

2. To betroth, as parents a daughter; to make a matrimonial alliance.

HOO-PA-LAU, adj. Betrothed; engaged in marriage, as a woman to a man.

HOO-PA-LAU, v. See PALAU, to lie; to deceive. To lie; to deceive; to act treacherously.

HOO-PA-LA-HA-LA-HA, v. See LAHA, to extend. To spread out; to make broad; to widen.

HOO-PA-LA-HE-A, v. See PALAHEA, dirty. To defile; to daub over; to stain; to make dirty.

HOO-PA-LA-HEE, v. See PALAHEE, to shrink from duty. To be lazy; to be unoccupied.

HOO-PA-LA-HU-LI, v. To turn upside down; to turn over and over.

2. To be lazy; to be unoccupied.

HOO-PA-LA-LE, v. See PALALE, to be slovenly. To speak with another voice; to disguise the voice; to stammer; to vociferate.

HOO-PA-LA-LE-HA, v. See PALALEHA, slothful. To be slothful; to be idle; to be careless.

HOO-PA-LA-LE-HE, v. To be idle; to waste time; to be inactive.

HOO-PA-LA-NI, v. To cause a strong offensive smell, as that of tar, sulphur, &c.

HOO-PA-LE, v. See PALE, to ward off. To drive off from; to defend off when attacked; to separate from.

2. To be or act the defendant in court.

HOO-PA-LE-LA, v. See PALELA, idle; lazy. To be indisposed to work; to be idle; to be lazy.

HOO-PA-LE-MO, v. See PALEMO, to sink in water. To plunge; to cause to sink in water.

HOO-PA-LE-PA-LE, v. See PALE and HOO-PALE. To separate; to ward off; to loosen.

HOO-PA-LO, v. See PALO, to live idly. To sit speechless, as one watching others; to sit silent and quiet, but with sly and wicked thoughts or intentions.

HOO-PA-LU, v. See PALU, to lick or lap water. To lick or lap water with the tongue, as a dog.

2. To run out the tongue to taste.

3. To paint or daub over; to blot; to paint, as in painting a map.

Hoo-pa-lua, v. To put two things together, as two letters in reading.

Hoo-pa-lu-hee, v. See Paluhee, to soften. To make soft; to cook soft; to cause to flow.

Hoo-pa-lu-pa-lu, v. See Palu, soft; gentle. To soften; to be soft or tender, as a sick person; to be young and tender; to be weak and flexible.

Hoo-pa-ne, v. See Pane, to speak in reply. To reply back and forth in conversation; to make a reply to what has been said.

Hoo-pa-nee, v. See Panee, to postpone. To put off; to push out of place; to postpone doing a thing; to delay.

Hoo-pa-nee, adj. Put off; postponed; delayed; uku hoopanee, interest on a debt.

Hoo-pa-ne-pa-ne, v. See Pane and Hoo-pane above. To speak and reply; to answer each other, as people in conversation.

Hoo-pa-ni-o-ni-o, v. See Panio, to spot; to paint. To spot; to print, as in printing kapa; to variegate.

Hoo-pa-ni-ni-o, v. See above. To variegate with colors; to put different colors on a thing; e wai kilikiloia, e panionio.

Hoo-pa-no-a, v. See Panoa, wild dry land. To be dry, hard and rocky, as a barren dry place.

Hoo-pa-no-pa-no, v. See Panopano and Papano, thick; black; glossy. To make thick and black, as a cloud; to be thick, glossy black.
2. To regulate.

Hoo-pa-pa, v. Pa doubled. See Pa, to touch. To touch; to feel; to take hold of; to examine.
2. To communicate with each other, as husband and wife.
3. To be intimate with another person's wife or husband.

Hoo-pa-pa, v. See Papa, a row; a rank. To place in rows or ranks, as soldiers; to lay in rank one above another; to pack in order, as clothes in a trunk.

Hoo-pa-pa, s. A shelf made by placing sticks across the corner of a room.
2. The condition of a female with a board tied on to her abdomen to secure her conception; a e hoomaemae i kona hanau keiki.

Hoo-pa-pa, v. For hoopaapaa. To quarrel; to contend; to dispute; to scold.

Hoo-pa-paa, v. To burn; to scorch in the fire, as food burnt black.

Hoo-pa-pai, v. See Papai, to strike with the open hand. To move softly or gently; to move lightly.
2. To touch or strike softly.

Hoo-pa-pau, v. See Papau, to be intent. To be all engaged in a thing; to be wholly taken up with it.
2. To be in earnest in a work or in an affair; to have great anxiety about a thing.
3. To persevere.

Hoo-pa-pau, s. Engagedness; devotedness; earnestness and perseverance in a pursuit.

Hoo-pau-ha, v. To exert one's self greatly, as in carrying a very heavy load; to be strong; to be energetic.

Hoo-pa-pa-li-ma, v. See Papa and Lima, to touch hands. To touch, join or shake hands as confirmatory of a previous agreement. Note.—This was an ancient practice among Hawaiians.

Hoo-pe, v. See Pe, to anoint. To anoint with what is perfumed; hence, to perfume.

Hoo-pe, adj. Perfumed; anointed with perfumed substances.

Hoo-pe, v. See Pepe, mashed; bruised. To break up; to break fine; to scatter abroad; to roll over anything; to mash it.

Hoo-pe-a, v. See Pea, to make a cross; to oppose. To accuse or punish an innocent person; to bring one into difficulty; to deal falsely or unjustly.

Hoo-pee-pee, v. To conceal one's self; to go off out of sight through shame or diffidence.
2. To deceive one; to get him into difficulty. See Hoopea above.

Hoo-pe-hu-pe-hu, adj. Full; large; spreading, as clouds; he ao hoopehupehu.

Hoo-pe-pe, v. See Pepe, soft; pliable. To be downcast or ashamed; to be not bold; not confident.

Hoo-pe-pe-hu, adj. Strong; muscular; energetic; he hoolua nui ke kuaaina, he hoopepehu.

Hoo-pe-pe-lu, v. See Pelu, to bend over. To cause to bend or double over.
2. To be in doubt; to be doubtful which way to go.
3. To talk double, here and there; e lauwili, e olelo pelupelu.

Hoo-pi, v. See Pi, to be stingy. To be hard; to be close; to be stingy.
2. To be sour; to be unsociable.

Hoo-pi, s. The name of such persons as were economical in regard to food and took care of it in distinction from the wasteful; o ka poe mahiai malama i ka ai, ua kapaia ua poe la, he hoopi aole o lakou wi.

Hoo-PI, *v.* To follow; to attend.

Hoo-PII, *v.* See PII, to ascend. To cause to ascend; to go up; to appear; to protrude above; ua *hoopiiia* ka huelo o ua moo nui nei. *Laieik.* 103.

  2. To inform the chief of the fault of a person.

  3. To complain to one in authority of one in error or fault.

  4. To accuse before a court of justice.

  5. To ask a favor.

Hoo-PII-NA, *s.* See PIINA. The ascent of a hill; a path or road leading up a hill.

Hoo-PII-PII, *v.* See PII, to go up. To ascend; to go up.

  2. To beat against the wind; to sail in a zigzag manner.

  3. To raise the cud, as ruminating animals.

  4. To cause to flow upward, as water out of a spring.

Hoo-PI-O, *v.* See PIO, to extinguish. To put out; to extinguish, as a fire or light.

  2. To bend, as a stick; to make an arch; to bend over.

  3. To humble; to reduce to servitude; to make a prisoner of; to conquer.

Hoo-PI-O-PI-O, *v.* To practice sorcery, a part of which was the *auhauhui* and *hiu.* See ANAANA.

  2. To pray in the practice of sorcery.

  3. To perform other ceremonies with medicines, &c., in order to kill. NOTE.— The god to whom the prayer was made was called Pua.

Hoo-PI-O-LO-O-LO, *v.* To be in trouble, as the mind.

  2. To feed a sick person with the fruit of the noni which makes one sick.

Hoo-PI-HA, *v.* See PIHA, full, as a container. To cause to fill; to fill full, as a container; to put into a vessel until it runs over.

  2. To overflow its banks, as a stream.

Hoo-PI-HA-PI-HA, *v.* See PIHA. To cause to be full; to overflow; to abound.

  2. To swell up, as the stomach from disease.

  3. To be full, as cloth gathered and plaited into a ruffle; hence,

  4. To be full and flowing, as a ruffle.

Hoo-PI-KI-KI, *v.* To be too short; to shorten.

Hoo-PI-LI, *v.* See PILI, to adhere to. To adhere to; to stick to; to cling to.

  2. To put together the parts of a thing.

  3. To attach one's self to another; to ad-

here to a person, as a servant or retainer; no ka *hoopili* mea ai i loaa mai ka ai ia lakou.

Hoo-PI-LI-KI-A, *v.* See PILIKIA, crowded close. To get one into difficulty; to lead one into straits; to cause one to be in want.

Hoo-PI-LI-MEA-AI, *v.* To attach one's self to a chief or rich person for the sake of a living; to be a retainer, especially where not much service is required; to serve merely for a living.

Hoo-PI-LI-MEA-AI, *s.* A person serving another merely for his living.

Hoo-PI-LI-PI-LI, *v.* See PILI and PIPILI, to adhere to. To put together two or more things into one; to cause them to adhere closely.

  2. To live together in close friendship, as two intimate friends.

  3. To put in opposition; to bring into difficulty.

Hoo-PI-NA-NA, *v.* To swim standing upright; to float, as a log perpendicularly.

  2. To rise and pitch, as a vessel in a storm.

Hoo-PI-PI-KA, *v.* To go here and there; to stagger.

  2. To wander; to go into an inclosure.

  3. To go wrong in advance.

Hoo-PO, *v.* See PO, night; dark. To act in the dark. FIG. To do ignorantly.

  2. To give without discretion; to act foolishly without intelligence; e hoonaaupo, e hoonalowale.

  3. To absent one's self slily, as if in the dark; i kekahi manawa, ike ia mai lakou i ka pule, a i kekahi manawa, *hoopo* loa aku, sometimes they appear at worship, at other times they make themselves *dark.*

  4. To keep out of one's sight.

  5. To be willingly blind or ignorant.

Hoo-PO-E, *v.* See POEPOE, round. To cut off short; to cut off square, as pieces of sugar-cane or pieces of wood.

  2. To cut the hair alike all over the head.

  3. To make globular.

Hoo-PO-E-PO-E, *v.* See HOOPOE above. To make round; to collect into a ball.

  2. To shorten endways.

  3. To cut off, as a section of a log for a cart wheel.

Hoo-PO-I, *v.* See POI, to examine by torture. To cause to be awake; to excite; to stir up.

  2. To examine by torture or threats.

Hoo-PO-I-PO-I, *v.* Freq. of foregoing. To smother, as a fire; to extinguish.

Hoo-po-i-na, *v.* See Poina, to forget. To cause to forget; to be unmindful; to be indifferent as to business or knowledge; to be thoughtless.

Hoo-po-i-no, *v.* See Poino, to be in distress. To be illfated; to be unlucky; to be in distress.

2. To be filthy; to be unclean.

Hoo-poo, *v.* See Poo, the head. To go ahead; to go forward; not to retrograde.

2. To be brave; to hold fast.

Hoo-poo-poo, *v.* See Poopoo, deep. To be deep; to dig deep; to sink down.

Hoo-po-u-li, *v.* See Pouli, darkness. To darken; to make dark.

2. To blind.

Hoo-pou-pou, *v.* See Poupou, short, particularly of stature. To shorten; to make or be short.

2. *Morally,* to be low; to be humble.

Hoo-po-ha, *v.* See Poha, to burst; to break. To cause to break or burst forth, as a sound.

2. To burst, as the contents of a boil; to overflow.

3. To flow away.

Hoo-po-hae, *v.* See Pohae. To cause to tear; to tear open.

Hoo-po-ha-ku, *v.* See Pohaku, a stone; a rock. To become a stone or rock; to harden; to become as a rock or stone; to be very hard.

Hoo-po-ha-la, *v.* See Pohala, to recover from sickness. To rest; to be quiet; to recover from sickness.

2. To prevent or dissuade one from giving his consent to a bargain or proposition.

3. To object to; to speak against.

Hoo-po-ha-la, *s.* A pretense; a specious course of conduct.

Hoo-po-ha-lu, *v.* To make a hole or crevice; to split; to crack; to burst forth; to swell up, as a wound; to be large.

Hoo-po-he-o-he-o, *v.* To make a head on the end of a stick or other substance, as in making the neck on the top of a rafter on a native house; e kalai ia luna o na oa, a uuku, a *hoopoheoheo* ia ko luna o na oa.

Hoo-po-ka-kaa, *v.* See Pokakaa, the wheel of a pulley. To turn, as the wheel of a pulley; to cause to roll, as a wheel.

2. Fig. To go over and over again with the same story, as a verbose speaker.

Hoo-po-ko-le, *v.* See Pokole and Pakole, short. To shorten; to cut short; to curtail the length of a thing.

Hoo-po-ko-po-ko, *v.* See Poko, short.

To make short; to curb in; to cut short.

Hoo-po-la-po-la, *v.* See Polapola, to sprout. To push or urge on.

2. To revive or come to, as one sick.

3. To sprout; to push out, as a bud; to quicken; to hasten on.

Hoo-po-lo-lei, *v.* See Pololei, straight. To make straight; to straighten; to correct; to make corrections; to put to rights.

Hoo-po-lo-li, *v.* See Pololi, hunger. To cause hunger; to fast; to eat no food.

Hoo-po-lu-lu-hi, *v.* See Poluluhi, dark; foggy. To cover the sky with dark storm clouds; to thicken and darken, as clouds before a storm.

Hoo-po-lu-lu-hi, *s.* The dark gathering of clouds before a storm.

Hoo-po-mai-kai, *v.* See Pomaikai, fortunate. To make one fortunate; to be fortunate in obtaining what one wishes; to be blessed.

Hoo-po-na-lo-na-lo, *v.* See Nalo and Ponalonalo, to obscure. To appear dimly as scarcely discernible; to be obscure to the sight; to be vanishing.

Hoo-po-ni-u-ni-u, *v.* See Poniu, vertigo. To have a dizziness of the head.

Hoo-po-ni-ni-u, *v.* See above and Poniu, dizziness. To be dizzy; to have the sensation of a turning of the head; to turn or whirl like a top.

Hoo-po-ni-po-ni, *v.* See Poni, purple color. To be of a black or deep blue color.

2. To have a mixture of colors; to be purple.

Hoo-po-no, *v.* See Pono, good; right. To rectify; to put in order; to make correct; to do rightly.

Hoo-po-no-po-no, *v.* See Hoopono. To rule over; to be a superintendent.

2. To put in order; to regulate; to correct what is erroneous.

Hoo-po-po-lo-lu, *v.* See Hookakahele. To be weak in body; to be unstrung, as the nerves and muscles.

Hoo-pu, *v.* See Pu or Puu, to contract into a bunch. To sit shrugged up in one's kapa or blanket; to shiver with the cold; to sit crumped up in a bunch.

Hoo-pu, *s.* For *hanapu.* A mediator for peace or war.

Hoo-pu-a-hi, *v.* See Hookohukohu and Puahiahi. To dress one's self up finely.

Hoo-pu-ai, *v.* See Puai, to flow, as blood. To vomit; to cast out; to boil up, as a spring.

Hoo-pu-a-ke-a, *v.* To appear at a distance as beautiful, desirable.

Hoo-pu-a-ke-a, *s.* A white cloud, or any beautiful distant object.

Hoo-pu-a-pu-ai, *v.* See Puai, to flow. To gurgle, as one drinking from a calabash; to boil up, as a spring.

Hoo-pu-i-pu-i, *v.* See Puipui, fat. To become large, fat and fleshy, as the body.

Hoo-pu-i-wa, *v.* See Puiwa, to start suddenly. To be suddenly scared; to frighten one; to be overtaken; to be seized by; ua *hoopuiwaia* ke alii kane e ke kuko ino. *Laieik.* 37.

Hoo-pu-o-pu-o, *v.* To be deep.

2. To spread abroad, as the ocean.

3. To spread out, as all the sails of a ship.

Hoo-puu, *v.* See Puu, a heap. To collect together; to collect in heaps; to lay up in store.

2. To fill up, as the belly with wind; to fill, as the heart with resentment; *hoopuu* ae la ka'u ia ia i kana hoahewa ana ia'u.

3. To make ridiculous gestures or faces in ridicule of others. See Hoopuukahua and Hoomaloka.

Hoo-puu, *s.* A fullness of resentment of one against another; e kuu aku i kou *hoopuu* i pau, let loose all your resentment.

Hoo-pu-u-a, *v.* See Puua, to be choked. To push away; to treat with dislike.

2. To be choked; to have hard labor, as a female.

Hoo-puu-ka-hu-a, *v.* See Hoopuu above. To make ridiculous faces and gestures to the disparagement of others.

Hoo-puu-puu, *v.* See Hoopuu. To lay in heaps; to collect.

Hoo-pu-ha-la-lu, *v.* See Palalu, the snorting of a horse. To imitate the neighing of a horse; to snort like a horse.

Hoo-pu-ha-lu, *v.* To spend time lazily.

2. To explain language so as to mean nothing.

3. To object to; to refuse consent to.

4. To magnify an offense.

Hoo-pu-ha-lu, *s.* One that acts underhanded; a hypocrite.

Hoo-pu-ha-lu-ha-lu, *v.* To be tough and watery inside; to be inwardly unsound; to be of poor quality.

Hoo-pu-ha-nu, *v.* See Puhanu. To rest a little; to breathe soft and easy.

Hoo-pu-ho-lo-ho-lo, *v.* To warm by the fire; to cook.

Hoo-pu-ka, *v.* See Puka, an opening. To cause to pass through an orifice, as through a doorway or through a hole in a fence, &c.

2. To make a substance full of holes or chinks.

3. To appear in sight, as a ship at a distance.

4. To emerge to light, as from darkness.

5. To publish, as a newspaper.

Hoo-pu-ka-ku, *v.* To adhere to another and not to one's proper lord; ka! kupaianaha, no'u aku kuu aina, a *hoopukaku* oe i kou waiwai mamuli o ke alii.

Hoo-pu-ka-pu-ka, *v.* See Puka. To push forward; to make prominent.

2. To charge interest or per cent. on goods.

3. To answer or reply back and forth; to show one's skill in answering again; to contradict, as two who are obstinate in conversation.

Hoo-o-pu-ku-mo-a, *v.* See Opu and Kumoa, to be sour. To be evilly disposed; to be envious.

2. To be greedy after property.

3. To be sour and selfish in disposition.

Hoo-o-pu-ku-mo-a, *adj.* Hard-hearted; close-fisted; selfish.

Hoo-pu-la-pu-la, *v.* See Pula and Pulapula, the tops of sugar-cane. To plant in order to increase vegetables; to propagate by planting; to begin to plant a new kind of vegetable.

Hoo-pu-la-le-la-le, *v.* See Lale and Pulale, to hurry; to scare fish. To hurry; to hasten; to make a stir in doing a thing.

2. To encourage strongly.

Hoo-pu-le-le-hu-a, *v.* See Pulelehua, a butterfly. To blow away, as small bits of paper.

2. To act the butterfly; to flutter about, as vain dressy persons.

3. To talk much with little sense.

Hoo-pu-lou, *v.* See Pulou, to veil the head. To cover the head with a kapa.

2. To sit bending the head down so as to keep warm.

Hoo-pu-lu, *v.* To deceive; to act treacherously; to get the advantage of one by deceit.

Hoo-pu-lu, *v.* To manure; *hoopulu* loi.

Hoo-pu-lu-pu-lu, *v.* To cause a stench; to make an offensive smell.

2. To deceive.

3. To protest against.

Hoo-pu-lu-pu-lu, *adj.* Strong smelling; stinking.

2. Deceitful; hypocritical.

Hoo-pu-ma-ha-na, } *v.* See Pumehana.
Hoo-pu-me-ha-na, } To warm, as by fire; to warm by covering with clothes; to warm up, as food.

Hoo-pu-na-he-le, *v.* See Punahele, a favorite. To make a favorite of one; to treat one as a favorite; applied mostly to chiefs who were inclined to treat one or more of their people as favorites.

Hoo-pu-na-he-lu, *v.* See Punahelu, mould, spiders' webs, &c. To grow mouldy or musty; to grow old.

Hoo-pu-na-lu-a, *v.* See Punalua. To have, as a man, another woman equally beloved as his wife; to have, as a woman, another man equally beloved as her husband.

Hoo-pu-na-na, *v.* See Punana, to sit on, as a nest. To sit like a fowl on eggs to hatch them.

2. To hatch eggs by warming them.

3. To brood or cherish, as a fowl her young.

4. To warm, as a person by the fire.

Hoo-pu-ni, *v.* See Puni, to surround. To come around; to surround.

2. To get the advantage of; to deceive; to beguile.

3. To be charmed with; to desire much, as the desire of the sexes. *Laieik.* 38.

Hoo-pu-ni-pu-ni, *v.* See Hoopuni above. To get around one, i. e., to deceive; hence, to lie; to speak falsely.

Hoo-pu-ni-pu-ni, *s.* Deceit; treachery; falsehood.

Hoo-pu-ni-pu-ni, *adj.* Deceitful; causing deceit; treacherous.

Hoo-pu-no-no-hu, *v.* See Punohu, to ascend, as smoke. To enlarge; to spread out, as a sail on a mast; to rise up, as a thick smoke when there is no wind.

Hoo-pu-no-ni, *v.* See Noni, a plant. To be or to make of a reddish color; to be brown.

Hoo-pu-no-no, *v.* See Punono, to dress gorgeously. To be noble; to dress gorgeously.

2. To have red eyes.

Hoo-pu-pu, *v.* See Pupu, a bunch, as of grass or leaves. To collect together; to heap up. See Hoopuu.

2. To be uncomfortably filled with food. See Hookuku.

3. To hinder; to be unwilling; to refuse; to hold fast.

4. To cleave to one's home when driven or invited away.

5. To breathe quick and short, as an aged person; hence,

6. To be feeble and tottering; to walk like an aged person.

7. To dispute; to converse roughly.

Hoo-pu-pu, *s.* For *hoopuupuu.* See Puupuu. A collection of things; a gathering up.

2. An old person, from his walking in a stumbling, irregular manner.

Hoo-pu-pu-ka, *v.* See Puka and Pupuka, worthless; full of holes. To speak contemptibly.

2. To act disgracefully.

3. To be ugly to look at.

Hoo-pu-pu-le, *v.* See Pupule, crazy. To make one crazy; to be out of one's wits; to be insane.

Hoo-pu-wa-pu-wa, *v.* See Puwa, to ascend, as smoke. To hang suspended, as a flag, or as smoke or clouds in the air.

2. To act proudly, as above others.

3. To glitter with brightness.

Hoo-wa, *v.* To cause to vomit; to make sick at the stomach; to flow off.

Hoo-waa, *v.* To dig a trench; to set out, as plants where many are planted together.

Hoo-wai, *v.* To move so as to make room.

Hoo-wai-ho, *v.* See Waiho, to lay down. To leave exposed, as a woman her shame; *eia kekahi mea e moekolohe ai, o ka hoowaiho.*

Hoo-wai-ho-wa-le, *v.* To sit in a state of nudity; to expose one's shame. See Hoowaiho.

Hoo-wai-wai, *v.* See Waiwai, property. To make rich; to have a supply; to be abundantly provided for; hence,

2. To be honorable.

Hoo-wa-ha, *v.* To covet; to seize; to take with the knowledge, but without the consent of the owner. See Hookaha.

Hoo-wa-ha, *adj.* Having a disposition to take another's property; greedy; he *hoowaha,* he alunu, he hao wale no.

Hoo-wa-ha-wa-ha, *v.* See Waha. To make mouths at; to treat with contempt; to ridicule; to hate; to dislike.

Hoo-wa-hi, *v.* See Wahi, to break, and Wawahi, to break up. To grind or break to pieces.

Hoo-wa-hi-ne, *v.* See Wahine, woman. To make special friendship with a woman; applied only to men.

2. To imitate, as a man, the manners of a woman.

Hoo-wa-hu, *v.* See Hoowaha above. To

rob; to take by force.

Hoo-wa-hu-a, *v.* See Wahua, a snare; a trap. To insnare; to entrap.

Hoo-wa-le-hau, *v.* See Walehua. To distill; to flow from the nose, as mucous.

Hoo-wa-le-wa-le, *v.* See Walewale, to deceive. To deceive; to insnare; to plot mischief.

Hoo-wa-le-wa-le, *s.* The deceiver; the tempter.

Hoo-wa-le-wa-le-na-he-sa, *v.* To exercise enchantment. *Kanl.* 18:11.

Hoo-we-hi-we-hi, *v.* See Wehi, a wreath. To gather a bunch of flowers for ornament.

  2. To fix up ornaments for a person.

Hoo-we-la, *v.* See Wela, heat. To burn; to cause to be burned or scorched.

  2. To cook in the fire.

Hoo-we-la-we-la, *v.* See Wela, to burn. To burn up; to consume.

  2. To be lost out of sight.

Hoo-we-li-we-li, *s.* Causing fear; a threatening of one or keeping him in fear in order to secure obedience or to extort property.

Hoo-we-li-we-li, *adj.* See Weliweli. Fearful; threatening; having the quality of exciting fear; he ao *hooweliweli*, a threatening cloud.

  2. Exciting fear for the sake of obtaining property.

Hoo-wi-u-wi-u, *v.* To cause to be entangled; to entangle, as a kite.

  2. To daub or besmear one with any filthy substance.

Hoo-wi-ki, *v.* To open a little; to make a small aperture; not so much as *hoohakahaka*.

Hoo-wi-ki-wi-ki, *v.* See Wiki, quick. To hasten; to hurry; to do a thing quickly.

Hoo-wi-li, *v.* See Wili, to twist. To bind or tie up, as a bundle; to fasten tightly by tying; to tie around.

Hoo-wi-li-moo, *s.* The name of a certain aha; also *hulahula*.

Hoo-wi-li-wi-li, *v.* See Wili, to bind. To bind or tie up tightly; to tie up in bundles.

  2. To make afraid. See Weliweli.

Hoo-wi-li-wi-li, *v.* To move here and there irregularly.

  2. To move, as clouds with contrary winds.

  3. To cause darkness or obscurity by the commingling of dark clouds.

Hou, *v.* To stab; to pierce. 1 *Sam.* 31:4. To run through the body, as with a spear. *Puk.* 19:13.

  2. To exert one's self in casting a spear or javelin. 1 *Sam.* 18:11.

  3. To dip, as a pen into an inkstand; *hou aku la i ka hulu i ka inika*; to dip into a liquid. *Rut.* 2:14. To moisten or soak in water.

  4. To thrust, as the hand into a hole.

  5. To stretch out, as the hand; to draw out; to extend.

  6. To search for something, as the mind; *hou* wale aku la ka manao i o, i o, e ake e loaa; i. e., to reach after.

Hou, *v.* See Hou, new. To be new; to be fresh; to be recent. *Iob.* 29:20.

  2. To repeat; to do over again. *Kanik. Ier.* 3:23. To do again as before. *Lunk.* 20:31.

  3. To breathe short; to pant.

Hou, *adj.* New; recent; lately done.

Hou, *adv.* Again; recently; anew; afresh.

Hou, *s.* Sweat; perspiration. *Luk.* 22:44.

  2. The asthma; shortness of breath.

Hou, *s.* Name of a species of fish.

Hou-hou, *v.* To be blunt; to be obtuse; to be dull, as an instrument.

  2. To be persevering; to continue doing a thing.

  3. To thrust through; to drill; to bore; to pierce. 1 *Tim.* 6:10.

Ho-u-lu-u-lu, *v.* For *hoouluulu*. See Ulu, to grow. To collect together; to assemble, as people.

  2. To bring together things scattered.

Hou-u-lu-u-lu, *s.* An assembly; a convocation. *Oihk.* 23:24.

Ho-u-lu-u-lu-a-ku-a, *v.* See Ulu 6 and Akua, god. To set up one's self for a god; to make pretensions of being a god.

  2. To make or appoint gods.

Ho-u-me-ke, *v.* For *hooumeke*. See Umeke, a poi calabash. To swell in growing like the calabash gourd; to swell, as fruit in growing.

  2. To have enough; to be supplied with comforts.

Ho-u-pe-pe, *v.* See Pepe, crushed; bruised. To be modest; to be bashful; to act as a backwoodsman; to be diffident; to be crushed, as the mind.

Ho-u-po, *s.* The thorax; the region of the material heart. *Laieik.* 45.

  2. A palpitation or fluttering of the heart.

  3. The action of the region of the mind; lelele ka *houpo* i ka olioli, the mind (or heart) leaped for joy.

  4. The heart. *Isa.* 60:5. See Haupu.

Ho-u-po-le-wa-le-wa, *v.* See Houpo above and Lewalewa, movable. To flat down, as the stomach of a hungry person.

2. To be hungry; to be dizzy for want of food.

3. To be light or empty, as the stomach.

Ho-u-po-le-wa-le-wa, *s.* A hungry, empty stomach.

2. Faintness for want of food.

Ho-u-pu-u-pu, *v.* For *hooupuupu.* See Upu, to desire strongly. To tell lies, as in giving a false alarm, or in accusing another in order to clear himself of suspicion.

Ho-u-we-ke, *v.* For *hoouweke.* See Uweke, to open wide. To open; to open, as a door; to open, as the mouth; to open wide. See Wehe.

Ho-ha-na, *v.* To grasp; to seize hold of with the hand; to hold fast; e puili.

Ho-ha-na, *s.* A measure, both hands full, used in giving out food, small fish, &c.; a small measure box or calabash.

Ho-he, *v.* Probably for *hoohee.* To be afraid; to flee. *Neh.* 6:11. To flee from fear. *Sol.* 28:1. To be overcome or routed; aole e *hohe* ka ilo ma ka lua ahi, e ai mai no.

Ho-he, *s.* Fear; terror.

2. A coward.

Ho-he, *adj.* Fearful; timorous.

Ho-he-he, *adj.* Faint-hearted; weak.

Ho-he-wa-le, *s.* A fleeing without cause; cowardice.

Ho-ho, *v.* See Ho, to breathe. To snore; to breathe hard; to gurgle, as one breathing through water in the throat.

2. To snort, as a horse; alaila, *hoho* mai ka lio.

3. To cry out; to shout after. See Hooho.

Ho-ho, *s.* Snow; the spray of water from a cataract.

2. The distant sound of a small cataract.

Ho-ho, *v.* To sink down, as a canoe in the water.

2. To leap or slide down, as one from a pali.

3. To jet, as water into a canoe where there is a hole; ke *hoho* mai la ka liu.

Ho-ho-a, *v.* See Hoa, to strike. To strike repeatedly on the head with a stick.

2. To beat kapa after coloring that it may be soft; *hohoa* kapa, to beat kapa with a stick on a stone.

3. To strike, as in fighting.

4. To smooth kapa out by beating; applied to the first process in beating.

Ho-ho-a, *s.* A cane; a staff; a war club, an instrument for knocking down an adversary. See Pahoa.

Ho-ho-hoi, *v.* See Hoi, to return. To return again. *Gram.* § 209.

Ho-ho-ka, *v.* See Hoka. To be ashamed.

Ho-ho-la, *v.* See Hola, to spread out. To unfold and spread down, as a mat; to spread out, as a kapa or garment; *hohola* i ke kapa. *Kanl.* 22:17.

2. To spread out, i. e., to smooth a cloth that has been ruffled.

3. To spread out, as a net. *Sol.* 29:5.

4. To spread up, i. e., to make up, as a bed. *Sol.* 7:16.

5. To spread or stretch out, as the visible heavens. *Iob.* 9:8. To spread out, as the clouds. *Iob.* 36:29.

6. To stretch out, as the hand. *Kin.* 48:14. To spread out, as the wings of a bird. *Kanl.* 32:11.

7. To spread over, as darkness or dark clouds. Note.—*Hohola* applied to the mind signifies

8. To calm; to soothe; to prepare to hear or receive information.

9. To open; to enlighten the mind.

10. To set forth; to manifest.

11. To make a gesture or stretch out one's hand in speaking. See Uhola and Mahola.

Ho-ho-la, *adj.* Open; opened; unsealed; me ka palapala i *hoholaia,* with an open letter. *Neh.* 6:5.

Ho-ho-le, *v.* See Hole, to skin; to peel. To peel off the skin, as a banana; to skin, as an animal.

2. To peel; to rub; to file off.

Ho-ho-lo, *v.* See Holo, to run; to sail. To run; to sail; to glide swiftly.

2. Pass. To be driven swiftly by the wind. *Iak.* 3:4.

3. To put out one's hand to take a thing. *Lunk.* 15:15. See Hohola 6.

Ho-ho-ma, *v.* See Homa, lean. To be poor in flesh; to be lean.

Ho-ho-ma, *adj.* Reduced in flesh; poor; lean.

Ho-ho-no, *v.* To smell strongly, as tar or burning sulphur; to cause a strong offensive smell.

Ho-ho-no, *s.* A strong offensive smell; a stench; the smell of anything. *Dan.* 3:27.

Ho-ho-nu, *v.* To be deep, as water; deep down, as a pit.

2. To be full, i. e., deep, as the sea at full tide.

Ho-ho-nu, *s.* The deep, i. e., the sea; the depth. *Puk.* 15:5.

Ho-ho-nu, *adj.* Deep, as a pit; as a

well. *Ioan.* 4:11.

HO-HO-PA, *adj.* Long, thin, slender or spare, as a man; he kanaka *hohopa*, a thin slender man.

HO-HU-LE, *adj.* See OHULE, bald. Bald, as the head; baldheaded.

HO-KA, *v.* To squeeze; to press; to take hold of; to gather up.

2. To search or look after; to examine into.

3. To strike; to attack.

4. To be destitute; to perish; to be destroyed. *Hal.* 9:18.

5. To fail; to be disappointed. *Hal.* 22:5. To fail; to forsake. 1 *Oihl.* 28:20.

6. To be ashamed through a failure. *Rom.* 9:33. Mai *hoka* au imua ona, e ole ka ekemu ana o ka waha.

7. *Hoo.* To put to shame. *Hal.* 44:7. To be disappointed; to be mocked. *Mat.* 2:16.

HO-KA, *s.* A mistake in understanding one's words.

2. A blunder; carelessness in doing a thing.

HO-KA, *adj.* Destitute; poor.

2. Blundering; careless.

HO-KAA, *v.* For *hookaa.* See KAA. To cause to roll.

HO-KA-A-WA, Mai hele i ahuawa, *hoka-awa*; aka, pakele ae nei paha au i keia la.

HO-KAE, *v.* For *hookae.* See KAE, to rub or blot out. To seize hold of awkwardly; to blunder in doing a thing.

2. To erase; to blot out.

3. To smite; to kill. 2 *Sam.* 6:7.

HO-KAI, *v.* For *hookai.* See KAI, *hoo.* To drive; to drive away; to banish; to dash, as a melon on the ground and break it.

2. To disregard; to squander; to misspend.

3. To turn upside down; to destroy; to blot out. *Kanl.* 7:24. To destroy utterly. *Kanl.* 25:19.

4. To put away; to do mischief generally; mea *hokai*, a destroyer. *Mat.* 3:11.

HO-KAI, *adj.* Unprepared.

HO-KAI, *adv.* Disorderly; mischievously; wickedly. 2 *Tes.* 3:6.

HO-KA-HO-KA, *v.* See HOKA before. To feel demeaned; to be ashamed; *hokahoka* wale iho no ka mea haku ole, he is ashamed of himself who has no master.

HO-KA-HO-KAI, *v.* See HOKAI 3. To stir up; to mix, as two ingredients. *Ioan.* 9:6.

HO-KA-LA-LU. *Hokalulu* na holoholona ia mau malama.

HO-KA-LE, *s.* A hard concretion in the flesh; a kernel; he mau wahi anoano ma ke kumu pepeiao, a malalo o ke a lalo.

HO-KA-LI, *s.* The loss of appetite.

HO-KA-LI, *adj.* Thin in flesh; meager.

HO-KE-O, *s.* The lower of two gourds which compose the drum.

2. He *hulilau*, a calabash to put clothes in when traveling on a canoe.

HO-KI, *s.* *Eng.* An ass; a mule. *Nah.* 16:15. *Hoki* keiki, a young ass. NOTE.— *Hoki* is the Hawaiian pronunciation of the English word *horse*, which was first used, but afterward *lio* was applied to a horse, and *hoki* was applied to the ass and the mule.

HO-KII, *v.* See KII, also HOOKII. To dissolve; to pine away, as a diseased person. *Isa.* 34:4. To pine away, as with the consumption.

HO-KII, *s.* The phthisic. *Isa.* 10:18. A consumption; a pining sickness. *Oihk.* 26:16.

HO-KII, *adj.* Lean, low or thin in flesh.

HO-KI-O, *v.* For *hookio.* To play the pipe; to whistle.

HO-KI-O, *s.* A pipe; a whistle; some musical wind instrument played with the mouth. 1 *Sam.* 10:5.

HO-KI-O-KI-O, *v.* For *hookiokio.* To pipe; to play on the pipe.

HO-KI-O-KI-O, *s.* An ancient wind instrument among Hawaiians, the pipe; among the Hebrews. *Isa.* 5:12.

HO-KI-LO, *v.* To be sick and famished away.

HO-KO, *v.* To imitate.

HO-KO, *s.* The fleshy movable part of a fat person or animal.

2. The buttock; applied to men and fat animals.

3. The inside of the thighs; ua pili na *hoko*, or ua hui na *hoko* on account of fatness.

4. The under part of the thigh.

HO-KO, HO-KO-HO-KO, } *adj.* Large; fat; rolling; applied to the thighs of men, women and fat animals.

HO-KU, *s.* The asthma. See HOKII.

HO-KU, *adj.* Thin in flesh; meager. See HOKII.

HO-KU, *s.* The name of the fifteenth day of the month.

HO-KU, *s.* A star; *hoku* lele, a comet; ka poe *hoku* o ke kaei, the planets. 2 *Nal.* 33:5. The twinkling orbs of heaven.

HO-KU, *s.* A word; a thought; something rising in the mind; he wahi *hoku* iki ko'u no keia mea.

HO-KU-A, *s.* The lower and back part

of the neck where it joins the shoulders. *Kin.* 49:15.

2. The back between the shoulders. *Puk.* 12:34.

3. A division of men at work; a party; a company where a number of men are divided into several companies, one of them is called a *hokua*.

HO-KU-A-EA, *s.* *Hoku*, star, and *aea*, wandering. A moving or wandering star; i. e., a planet.

HO-KU-AO, *s.* *Hoku* and *ao*, light. The morning star; the bright star; the planet Venus when it is the morning star. See also HOKULOA.

HO-KU-A-MO-A-MO, *s.* *Hoku* and *amoamo*, to wink. The twinkling or winking of the stars.

2. The motion of the winking of the eyes. See next word.

HO-KU-I-MO-I-MO, *s.* *Hoku* and *imoimo*, to wink. Same as above.

HO-KU-HE-LE, *s.* *Hoku* and *hele*, to move. A planet. See HOKUAEA.

HO-KU-HOO-KE-LE-WAA, *s.* *Hoku*, star, *hookele*, to steer, and *waa*, canoe. Name of a star, the appearance of which was the signal for sailing on a voyage; a i ka wanaao, i ka puka ana o ka *hokuhookelewaa*, at the dawn of the morning, at the appearance of the *star. Laieik.* 36.

2. The name of a star that appeared just before the birth of a high chief.

HO-KU-HO-KU, *v.* To breathe hard; to wheeze as one stuffed with food.

HO-KU-HO-KU, *adj.* See HOKU, asthma. Having the colic.

2. Filled with anger or unpleasant sensations; *hokuhoku* au iloko—e ake e hele a hookolokolo.

HO-KU-LE-LE, *s.* *Hoku* and *lele*, to fly. A meteor.

HO-KU-LO-A, *s.* *Hoku* and *loa*, great. The morning star. See HOKUAO, also MANANALO.

HO-KU-PU-HI-BA-KA, *s.* *Hoku* and *puhibaka*, tobacco smoking. A comet. See the next word.

HO-KU-WE-LO-WE-LO, *s.* *Hoku* and *welowelo*, a tail. A comet from its tail of light. A comet is also called by Hawaiians *hokupuhibaka*, tobacco-smoking star; also *hokuhuelo-loihi*, long-tailed star.

HO-LA, *s.* The name of the root and stalk of the auhuhu, a poisonous and intoxicating plant, the bark of which was used in poisoning or intoxicating fish so they could be caught. See AUHOLA and AUHUHU.

2. The name of the system of fishing when they were to be caught by poisoning.

HO-LA, *v.* To poison or intoxicate fish with the hola or auhuhu.

HO-LA, *v.* To open; a *hola* ia ka waha a palahalaha; to spread out. See HOHOLA and UHOLA.

HO-LA-O, *v.* To pass by; to run on.

HO-LAU, *s.* A collection or multitude of people assembled.

2. One person together with a collection of fowls, or other animals.

HO-LA-HO-LA, *v.* See HOLA above. To poison or intoxicate fish.

HO-LA-HO-LA, *v.* See HOLA, to spread out. To spread out; to smooth; to smooth, as a kapa or cloth; to make up, as a bed. *Oih.* 9:34.

2. Applied to the mind, to calm; to soothe; to open; to enlighten. See HOHOLA and UHOLA.

HO-LA-PA, *s.* For *hoolapa*. See LAPA, a ridge. The act of rising or boiling up; the swelling or rising of a blister.

HO-LA-PU, *v.* To stir up; to mix water and dirt; to make water dark colored by putting in dirt.

HO-LE, *v.* To curse.

2. To peel off; to skin; to flay.

3. To rasp; to file; to rub off.

4. To scratch or break the bark of a tree or skin of the flesh.

5. To notch the end of a spear; to make grooves, as in a kapa beater; *hole* ie.

HO-LE, *s.* A bruise; a scratch or break in the skin. See POHOLE.

HO-LEI, *v.* To open; to gape open, as the eyelids, or as the labia feminarum.

HO-LEI, *s.* Name of a tree used (bark and root) to color yellow.

HO-LE-I-E, *v.* *Hole*, to peel, and *ie*, a vine. To peel the bark from the ie used in basket making.

HO-LE-I-E, *s.* See above. The name of those who prepared the *ie* for braiding or weaving.

2. Those who in connection with preparing the *ie*, also pounded kapa; a me ka poe *holeie* kuku kapa.

HO-LE-HO-LE, *v.* See HOLE, to peel. To peel; to strip off, as the skin from the flesh; as the flesh from the bones; *holehole* iho la lakou i na iwi o Lono, they *skinned* the bones of Lono (Captain Cook), that is, separated the bones from the flesh.

2. To separate one thing from another.

Ho-li, *v.* To commence or start first; to go forward.

2. To beg earnestly, in such a manner as that one cannot be denied.

Ho-li, *s.* The first appearance of a thing, as the first coming out of the beard of a young man.

Ho-lo, *v.* To go fast; to move generally, like *hele.*

1. To travel in any way, i. e., to run or ride or sail.

2. To put or thrust in, as the hand into the bosom.

3. To flee away; to go swiftly.

4. To run, as the thought, i. e., to decree; to decide. *Ioan.* 9:22.

5. *Hoo.* To ride on horseback, or on a camel. 1 *Sam.* 30:17.

6. To cause to ride, i. e., to carry in any vehicle, as a carriage. 1 *Oihl.* 13:7.

7. To slip; to cause to slide down, as an avalanche.

8. To stretch out, as the hand for taking anything; to reach forth, as the hand. *Lunk.* 3:21.

9. *Hooholo* manao, to take counsel; to consult. *Isa.* 30:1. See No. 4.

10. To promise; to agree with; to pass, as the sentence of a judge.

11. To decide by vote of a deliberate body; ua *hooholo*, it was voted; it passed; it was decreed. NOTE.—The common formula is, *ua holo ka manao*, the thought goes, or a shorter form is, *ua holo*, it runs, i. e., the vote is carried.

Ho-lo, *s.* A running; a racing; a going; a moving.

2. A bundle; *holo* ai, a bundle of food.

Ho-lo, *adj.* Running; moving; sailing; racing; he lio *holo*, he moku *holo*.

Ho-lo-aa, *v. Holo* and *aa*, the small roots of trees. Hence, to make a mistake; to run here and there; to go wrong; to blunder. See HOAA.

Ho-lo-aa, *adj.* Destitute of property or of friends.

Ho-lo-ai, *s.* See HOLO, bundle, and AI, food. A bundle of baked kalo.

2. A wrapper to carry food in.

Ho-loi, *v.* To wash with water, as clothes; to separate the dirt from a thing.

2. To scrape or clean the dirt from the feet.

3. To brush clothes; to wipe; to cleanse.

4. To blot out, as a writing. 2 *Nal.* 21:13.

5. To clean in any way; *holoi* a maloo, to wipe clean. *Ioan.* 13:5.

Ho-loi, *adj.* Washed; cleansed by washing or wiping.

Ho-lo-u-ka, *v.* Makani uka, wind from behind; he kio, pali wauaka ma ke kua, makani *holouka.*

Ho-lo-ho-lo, *v.* See HOLO. To walk; to walk about. *Kin.* 3:8.

2. To sail or run to and fro. *Jer.* 5:1. To go about from place to place. *Luk.* 13:33.

3. *Hoo.* To cause to ride, &c. *Kanl.* 32:13. NOTE.—This double form, *holoholo*, has most of the senses that are attached to *holo.*

Ho-lo-ho-lo, *s.* The name of a game among the ancient Hawaiians.

Ho-lo-ho-lo-o-le-lo, *v.* See HOLO and OLELO, talk. To slander; to tell tales to the disadvantage of another; to propagate false reports.

Ho-lo-ho-lo-o-le-lo, *s.* A tale bearer. *Oihk.* 19:16. A tattler. 1 *Tim.* 5:13. NOTE. This is often written in two words.

Ho-lo-ho-loi, *v.* See HOLOI. To rub with pressure and quick motion; to rub off dirt; to rub down smooth.

Ho-lo-ho-lo-ka-ke, *adj.* Ke ai *holoholo-kakeia* la e ka makani.

Ho-lo-ho-lo-ke, *v.* See HOLOKE, to rub against. To strike upon; to light upon easily; to touch; to rest upon, as the ends of a rainbow. *Laieik.* 16.

Ho-lo-ho-lo-li-o, *s.* See HOLO and LIO, a horse. A rider on a horse; a horseman; cavalry. 2 *Oihl.* 1:14.

Ho-lo-ho-lo-mo-ku, *s.* See HOLO, to sail, and MOKU, ship. A sailor; one who rides in a ship.

Ho-lo-ho-lo-na, *s.* See HOLOHOLO and ANA, a running about. A four-footed beast; generally applied to domestic animals, but often to wild ones.

Ho-lo-ho-lo-pi-na-au, *s.* The Hawaiian name of the planet Mars.

Ho-lo-hu-a, *v.* Ua *holohua* ka manao.

Ho-lo-kaa, *v. Holo* and *kaa*, a chariot. To ride majestically. *Hal.* 45:4.

Ho-lo-kai, *s. Holo* and *kai*, sea. One who rides on the sea; a seaman; na *holokai*, seafaring men. *Ezek.* 26:17.

Ho-lo-ka-hi-ki, *s. Holo* and *kahiki*, a foreign country. Epithet of a Hawaiian sailor who has visited foreign countries; ua tausani paha na *holokahiki* no Hawaii aku, there were thousands perhaps of sailors from Hawaii; o Lehua ka inoa o ka *holokahiki* nana i hoolike iwaena o Vanekouva ame Kamehameha, Lehua was the name of the *sailor to foreign countries* who interpreted between Vancouver and Kame-hameha.

Ho-lo-ke, *v.* *Holo* and *ke,* to strike against. To run or rub against some opposing object.

2. To be stopped short, as the mind in a course of thought or investigation; a *holoke* ka noonoo, a kukapikiio ka manao ke loaa ole.

Ho-lo-ke-lo-ke, *v.* To creak; to crepitate or grate, as the two ends of a broken bone against each other.

Ho-lo-ki-ki, *v.* *Holo,* to run, and *kiki,* intensive. To run or sail swiftly; to run headlong.

Ho-lo-ko-ha-na, *v.* *Holo,* to go, and *kohana,* destitute of clothes. To go about naked; to be destitute of clothes, not even a malo.

Ho-lo-ku, *s.* Some kind of a garment; a long flowing garment. *Hal.* 109:29. A cloak. *Isa.* 59:17.

Ho-lo-ku-ku, *v.* *Holo* and *kuku,* to stop short. To trot, as a horse.

2. To ride roughly or uneasily.

Ho-lo-la, *v.* The *la* is a particle. Ke *holo la* oe e manao ua hoka makou, you, O thought, have supposed that we are ashamed.

Ho-lo-li-o, *s.* *Holo,* to ride, and *lio,* horse. A rider of a horse. *Isa.* 36:8. Hoo. A horseman; a rider on a horse. *Puk.* 14:9.

Ho-lo-lu-a, *v.* *Holo* and *lua,* double. To go or move two ways; to go both ways, like the crab; as the muhee, the papai, &c.

Ho-lo-lu-a, *adj.* Creeping or running both ways, like the crab; aole e like me kou manao ka muhee, ka *hololua.*

Ho-lo-mo-ku, *v.* *Holo* and *moku,* ship. To sail on a ship.

2. To rush along, as a torrent.

Ho-lo-mo-ku, *s.* A sailor; a seaman; ka halepule no ka poe *holomoku* ma Honolulu; he mau mea *holomoku,* seamen. 1 *Nal.* 9:27.

2. A rushing, as of water; an overwhelming; applied to the wicked. 2 *Sam.* 22:5.

Ho-lo-na, *s.* In *music,* a close; the end of a tune.

Ho-lo-pa-a-ni, *v.* *Holo,* to run, and *paani,* to play. To run and play like children.

2. To sail about for pleasure.

Ho-lo-pa-pa, *v.* To rule; to control; to overcome; to prevail over; used where one man conquers several others.

Ho-lo-pa-pa, *s.* *Holo* and *papa,* a board. A shelf made of sticks in the corner of a room where kapas and other articles were laid.

2. A raft for floating logs, boards, stones, &c. 1 *Oihl.* 2:16.

3. A bridge over a small stream.

4. An arch over a space.

Ho-lo-wa, *s.* *Holowa* kaa, certain engines for throwing missiles in war. 2 *Oihl.* 26:15.

Ho-lo-waa, *s.* *Holo* and *waa,* canoe. A box; a chest; a trunk; a coffin; a cradle.

2. A species of fishing net.

3. A trough; a watering trough. *Puk.* 2:16.

Ho-lo-wa-le, *v.* *Holo,* to run, and *wale,* freely. To flee without cause or danger; to act the coward.

2. To go about destitute of clothing, i. e., in a state of nature.

Ho-lo-wa-le, *s.* A coward; one fleeing without cause.

Ho-lu, *v.* To bend, as an elastic stick; to arch over.

Ho-lu, *s.* A broad axe; a hoe; an adze; *koiholu,* an adze.

2. The depth of the sea; the deep ocean; the flood tide.

Ho-lu-a, *v.* To glide down on a sledge; to play the *holua.*

Ho-lu-a, *s.* A smooth path on a side hill for sliding down.

2. The name of the sled or sledge for sliding downhill. NOTE.—To play with the *holua* was an ancient pastime among Hawaiians.

3. The name of the strong north wind, generally in the winter.

Ho-lu-ho-lu, *v.* See HOLU, *v.* To bend; to be flexible.

Ho-lu-ho-lu, *adj.* Ductile; elastic; springy, as a sword blade.

Ho-lu-lu, *v.* To oppress.

Ho-ma, *v.* To be poor; to be thin in flesh; to make one's self poor.

2. To be disappointed; to be baffled in one's efforts to do a thing.

Ho-ma, *adj.* Thin in flesh; poor; hollow; applied to the cheeks.

2. Disappointed; baffled.

Ho-ma-ho-ma, *v.* See HOMA. To be destitute; to be bereaved.

2. To be thin; to be poor.

Ho-mai, *v.* See HO for HOO, and MAI, a verbal directive, used mostly in the imperative. LIT. Cause to be this way; hand this way; give this way; bring here. *Rut.* 3:15. *Homai* i wahi wai inu na'u, *give me here* some water to drink.

Ho-me, *s.* *Eng.* Home; place of one's

family and residence.

Ho-me-ra, *s. Heb.* A homer, a Jewish liquid or dry measure.

Ho-me-ta, *s. Heb.* A snail. *Oihk.* 11:30.

Ho-mi, *adj.* See Omi. Withered; sick; unfruitful, as a plant; sick, as a person.

Ho-mi-ho-mi, *v.* See Omiomi. To spring up, as a seed planted, but with feeble strength and produce nothing.

Ho-ne, *v.* See Ne. To be saucy; to be playful; to be trickish; to tease one; to run upon.

2. To prick; to enter, as a sharp thing; me he wahi kuikele la ia e *hone* nei iloko o ka manao, like a needle it *pierces* into the thought.

Ho-ne, *s.* Mischief; a trick; teasing; he mea hookanikani o ka moku.

Ho-ne-a, *s.* Dirt; the matter in the intestines not voided. *Lunk.* 3:22. See Honowa.

Ho-ne-ho-ne, *v.* See Hone. To be trickish; to be mischievous.

Ho-ne-ho-ne, *adj.* Playing tricks; teasing; fretting; not letting one alone.

Ho-ne-ko-a, *v.* See Hone and Koa, to be bold. To rail; to be saucy.

Ho-ne-ko-a, *adj.* Impudent; undaunted; not afraid.

Ho-ni, *v.* To beg earnestly. See Holi.

Ho-ni, *v.* To touch; to apply a combustible article to the fire. *Lunk.* 16:9.

2. To smell, as an odor. *Kin.* 8:21. To smell any perfume; to snuff, as a candle.

3. To feel the influence of, as the roots of trees do the water. *Iob.* 14:9.

4. To salute by touching noses (the ordinary way of saluting among Hawaiians); *honi* iho la i ka ihu. *Laieik.* 203.

5. To kiss; to salute by kissing. *Kin.* 27:26, 27. To embrace on parting; applied to various forms of salutation, as good-by, shaking hands, &c.

Ho-ni, *s.* A salutation; a kiss. *Mele Sol.* 1:2.

2. A touch as of a match to a combustible.

3. A shaking of hands at parting, &c.

4. Commanding a complimentary salutation to one; e haawi i ko'u *honi* ala aloha ia lakou, give them my sweet loving *kiss*, i. e., affectionate salutation.

Ho-ni-na-ni-na, *adj.* See Oninanina and Uninanina. Fat; plump; round, as a fleshy person.

Ho-no, *v.* To stitch; to sew up; to mend, as a garment or a net. *Mat.* 4:21.

2. To join; to unite together by sewing or stitching.

Ho-no, *s.* A stitching; a sewing; a joining together; ka *hono* o na aina o Maui, the *uniting* of the lands of Maui.

2. The back of the neck.

3. The name of a kapu when every man must hold his hands in a particular posture.

4. The name of a place where the wind meets some obstruction and is reflected back; oia kahi *hono* e hoi mai ai ka nui o ka makani.

Ho-no-a, *s.* See Honowa.

Ho-no-ai, *s.* See Hono and Ai, the neck. The back of the neck.

Ho-no-ai, *s.* See Honowai below. A uniting; a bringing together and causing a new relationship; mostly brought about by marriage; as, makua *honoai*, a parent by marriage, or a parent-in-law; makua *honoai* kane, a father-in-law; makua *honoai* wahine, a mother-in-law. Note.—The orthography *honoai* is better than *honowai*. See also the word Hunoai.

Ho-no-ho-no, *s.* Name of a weed, very thrifty in growth and very hard to kill.

Ho-no-ho-no, *adj.* Bad smelling. See Hohono.

Ho-no-kaa, *s.* A water course.

Ho-no-ke-a-na, *s.* Name of a species of soft porous stone.

Ho-no-le, *v.* See Hone. To be mischievous; to be trickish; to be saucy.

Ho-no-pu, *s.* A hai e ka lua i *honopu.* See Lumilumi, burnt; scorched, as the ground by the great heat of the sun.

Ho-no-wa, *s.* See Honea and Honoa. The matter contained in the intestines.

2. Excrements; human fæces; used mostly in reference to chiefs. Note.—This is the proper and polite name of excrements.

Ho-no-wai, *s.* A uniting; a bringing together and causing a new relationship; mostly brought about marriage; as, makua *honoai*, a parent by marriage, or a parent-in-law; makua *honoai* kane, a father-in-law; makua *honoai* wahine, a mother-in-law. Note.—The orthography *honoai* is better than *honowai*. See also the word Hunoai.

Ho-nu, *s.* The turtle; a terrapin; more generally applied to the sea turtle; a tortoise. *Oihk.* 11:29. Note.—The *honu* was formerly forbidden to women to eat in the times of the kapu under penalty of death.

Ho-nu-a, *s.* Flat land; land of an even or level surface, in distinction from hills and mountains.

2. In *geography*, the earth generally, including sea and mountains.

3. A foundation; a resting place.

4. The bottom of a deep place, as of the sea or a pit; wahi *honua* ole, bottomless.

Ho-NU-A, *adj.* Preceding; going before hand; olelo *honua*, the foregoing description; pule *honua*, the former religion; i kau kauoha *honua* ana, your charge just given. *Laieik.* 20. Ke makau *honua* e mai nei no. *Laieik.* 180.

Ho-NU-A, *adv.* Gratuitously; without cause; naturally; ua aloha *honua* anei na kanaka kekahi i kekahi? do men *naturally* love each other? No ka pono a ke Akua i waiho *honua* mai ai, for the righteousness which God had *freely* manifested; o ka hoomaka ana, ua like no ia me ke ao ana, i ola *honua* i ka palapala; thoroughly; entirely. *Lunk.* 20:25. Altogether. 1 *Nal.* 11:13.

Ho-NU-HO-NU, *v.* See **HONU**, terrapin. To play the terrapin; a play where people crawled on all fours like terrapins.

Ho-PA-LA, *v.* Ho for *hoo*, and *pala*, soft. To paint; to daub; to besmear.

2. To blame one who is innocent.

Ho-PA-LA-PA-LA, *v.* Ho for *hoo*, and *palapala*, to write; to paint. To cause to write badly; to scrawl in making letters with a pen; to daub with a pen.

Ho-PA-PAU, *s.* Sorrow; grief of a husband or wife for the death of a companion.

Ho-PE, *s.* The end or beginning of a thing; the termination of an extremity; the finishing result or termination of a course of conduct.

2. A place; stead; office; successor in a place.

3. The finishing; the close of a period of time.

4. A particular age or time. *Heb.* 9:26, in this age of the world.

5. The time of one's death; the end of life.

6. The end, i. e., the consequence or result of an action; ma neia *hope* aku, from this *time* on; ma ia hope iho, after that *time*; *hope* ole, endless. *Iob.* 22:5.

Ho-PE, *adj.* Ending; last; na olelo *hope*, the *last* words; mea *hope* ole, without *result*, i. e., without *profit*.

Ho-PE, *adv.* Adv. declinable. *Gram.* § 165, 2 class. Behind; after, &c. See the different cases.

Ho-PE-NA, *s.* *Hope* and *na* for *ana*. The ending; the bringing to a close.

2. The end; the hindmost, as the rear of

an army. *Ios.* 10:19.

3. The end of a series of events. *Ezek.* 7:2, 3.

Ho-PE-PE, *v.* *Ho* for *hoo*, and *pepe*, to mash fine. To cause to crush, as any substance.

2. FIG. To overbear, as the mind; to humble. See **HOUPEPE.**

Ho-PE-PE, *adj.* Humble; depressed; downtrodden, as the people of a hard, cruel chief; o ko ke kuaaina noho ana, he *hopepe*, he hopohopo, he wiwo wale me ka makau; he *hopepe* ke ano o na kuaaina.

Ho-PE-POO, *s.* See **HOPE** and **POO**, the head. The back part of the head.

Ho-PI-LO, *v.* See **OPILO**. To relapse after a partial recovery from sickness.

2. To be often sick.

Ho-PI-LO-LE, *adv.* To eat slowly and carefully, as a sick person. See **NIOLE.**

Ho-PO, *v.* To fear; to be afraid; to shrink back through fear.

Ho-PO-HO-PO, *v.* See **HOPO**. To fear much; to be agitated by fear; to dread; to be troubled by fear. *Kanl.* 1:2.

Ho-PO-HO-PO, *s.* Fear; dread; the feeling of fear.

Ho-PO-HO-PO, *adj.* Fearful; afraid; having the sense of fear.

Ho-PU, *v.* To seize upon, as something escaping; to grasp; to catch.

2. To take, as a prisoner; to apprehend, as a criminal. *Lunk.* 21:21. To hold fast, as something caught.

Ho-PU, *s.* A taking; a seizing; a catching of one.

Ho-PU-E, *s.* The name of a tree, the bark of which is used like the olona, and made into strings, cords, &c.

Ho-PU-HO-PU, *v.* See **HOPU**. To seize; to grasp frequently; to hold fast firmly.

Ho-PU-HO-PU-AU-KE-LA.

Ho-PU-HO-PU-A-LU-LU, *v.* See **HOPUHOPU** and **LULU**, to tremble. To do something in a state of trepidation.

2. To prepare in haste, as a room or a house when company unexpectedly arrives.

3. To catch quickly and shake; to do quickly; to make haste.

Ho-PU-HO-PU-A-LU-LU, *s.* Quickness; dispatch; a sudden effort to do a thing.

Ho-PU-PU, *v.* For *hoopuupuu.* See **PUU** and **PUUPUU**. To be filled or puffed up with wind, as the bowels, or as a bladder; *hopupu* ka opu; *hopupu* ka naau i ka inaina, *filled* with anger; kai! ka *hopupu* loko i ke aloha, wonderful! he is internally *full* of love.

Ho-RA, *s. Lat.* An hour; a particular time; a measure of time.

Ho-SA-NA, *interj. Heb.* An exclamation of praise to God. *Mat.* 21:19.

Ho-SA-NA, *s.* Exultation; praise.

Hu, *v.* To rise or swell up, as leaven or new poi; to effervesce.

2. To swell and rise up, as water in a pot.

3. To rise up, as a thought; *hu* mai keia manao iloko o'u, this thought *swelled* up in me.

4. To overflow; to run over the banks, as a river. *Isa.* 8:7.

5. To burst out, spoken of affection. 1 *Nal.* 3:26. Or a flow of passion (hence *huhu.*)

6. To shed or pour out, as tears. *Iob.* 16:20. *Hu* ka uhane, to have compassion. *Isa.* 58:10.

7. To ooze out silently.

8. To circulate, as the story of a murder.

9. To miss one's way; to deviate from a direct path.

10. To come, i. e., to heave in sight; to make its appearance, as a ship at a distance.

11. To be unstable; to be inconstant. *Kin.* 49:4.

12. To whistle, as the wind through the rigging of a ship.

13. *Hoo.* To meditate; to indite, as a song. *Hal.* 45:1.

Hu, *s.* That which causes rising, leaven.

2. A class of the common people, nearly SYN. with makaainana; e ka *hu*, e na makaainana, &c. *Laieik.* 21. O ka poe hemahema a naaupo, ua kapaia lakou he *hu* ka inoa, he makaainana kahi inoa.

3. A noise; a rustling, as the wind among trees. *Laieik.* 104.

4. A top; *hu* kani, a humming-top.

Hu, *adj.* Fermenting, as beer or new wine.

2. Leavened, as bread; mea *hu*, anything leavened. *Puk.* 34:25. Berena *hu* ole, unleavened bread. *Ios.* 5:11.

Hu-A, *v.* See HUWA. To be envious of another; to feel jealous of another; to envy; to hate.

2. To quarrel with; to be angry with; to be much addicted to evil.

Hu-A, *s.* Envy; jealousy; an envious disposition; making unfounded complaints against another.

Hu-A, *adj.* See HUWA. Envious; jealous of success in another; quick to find fault.

Hu-A, *v.* To sprout; to bud; to bear fruit, as a tree or vegetable.

2. To grow or increase in size, as fruit;

to increase, as a people. *Oihk.* 26:9.

3. To swell up, as the foam of water. See HUAHUA.

4. *Hua* with *huaolelo*, to speak; to utter; to produce words. *Kin.* 49:21.

5. *Hoo.* To produce fruit.

6. To increase, as a people. *Kin.* 1:28. To be fruitful, as a race. *Kin.* 9:1.

Hu-A, *s.* The swelling, growing and maturity of vegetables; name of the moon when perfectly full; the name of that night is *akua.*

2. Fruit; offspring; production of animals or vegetables. *Kin.* 46:7.

3. A fruit produced; an egg; a kidney, &c. *Hua* oo, ripe fruit; *hua* maka, fresh fruit. *Oihk.* 23:14.

4. The effect, product or consequence of an action; ka naaupo, he *hua* ia na ka ino, ignorance is the *result* (fruit) of evil practices.

5. A summary of one's wishes; a short sentence; e waiho mai oe i hua na makou, leave for us some *short expression*; a word, an idea (said to Kamehameha I. when dying.)

6. A letter of the alphabet; ma ka *hua* o ke kanawai, i. e., *literally*; *hua* kena, an order; a word of command; no keia *hua* kena a kana wahine. *Laieik.* 198.

7. Fruit in several senses; as, *hua* o ke kino, children; *hua* o ka aina, increase of the fruits of the land, i. e., means of living; *hua* o na holoholona, flocks, herds, &c.; *hua* ala, spices.

8. A flowing; a going out from; froth; foam, as of one in a fit.

9. A flowing robe; a train. *Isa.* 6:1. *Hua* lole, the skirts of a garment. *Ier.* 13:22, 26.

10. Seed, as of grain for sowing. *Kin.* 47:23.

11. The human testicles. *Oihk.* 21:20.

Hu-A, *adj.* Iwi *hua. Anat.* 6.

Hu-A, *s.* A flowing. See No. 8 above. The trail of a pa-u; the trail of a garment; the tucks at the bottom of a gown.

2. The snapper of a whip.

Hu-AA, *v.* To pry up.

Hu-AA, *v.* To be displeased at importunity or intercession.

2. To be small; to be stinted in growing, as fruit.

Hu-A-A-E-LO, *s. Hua*, egg, and *aelo*, rotten. A rotten egg.

Hu-A-A-E-LO, *adj.* Empty; deficient; rotten.

Hu-a-ai, *s. Hua,* egg, and *ai,* to eat. An egg that may or can be eaten, or an egg for eating.

2. Grain; fruit for food. *Mat.* 3:12.

3. A kind of wind; *huaai* malili. *Kanl.* 28:22.

Hu-a-ai, } *v.* To dig up something cov-
Hu-ai, } ered in the ground; to open, i. e., dig up, as opening a native oven and take out what is baked; *huai* oia i kana umu iho, he *uncovered* his own oven.

2. To open, as a grave; to disinter. *Ezek.* 37:12.

3. To open, as a reservoir of winds; to cause the wind to blow; *huai* mai la Kahiki i ko ipu makani, Kahiki thou *didst open* thy wind-box.

4. To open upwards, as the lid of a chest.

5. To suck or draw up water in drinking, as a beast. *Iob.* 40:23.

6. *Hoo.* To bring a wind; to cause it to blow. *Kin.* 8:1.

7. To turn or dig up the ground. *Iob.* 28:5.

Hu-a-a-le, *s.* A pill; a medicine in the form of a little ball, to be swallowed whole.

Hu-ae, *v.* To rise up against; to resist; to defend off. *Hoo.* To cause to resist, &c.

Hu-a-e-lo, *v.* See *Hua,* egg, and *Elo,* wet, as a kapa; hence, rotten; worthless. See also *Huaaelo.* To be or become useless, worthless or in vain; e malama hoi, o *huaelo* ka luhi o ka hoikaika ana, beware, lest the weariness in perseverance *be in vain.*

Hu-a-o-le, *adj.* LIT. Without fruit. Epithet of a person without character, no reputation.

Hu-a-o-le-lo, *s.* See *Hua,* a letter, and *Olelo,* speech. A word in distinction from a speech; in *grammar,* a word in distinction from a syllable; the words of a song. *Kanl.* 31:30.

Hu-a-ha-u-le, *adj. Hua,* seed, and *haule,* to drop; to fall. LIT. Seed fallen; prematurely born; hence, friendless; without support; no means of living; set loose from any chief or parent.

Hu-a-ha-u-le, *s.* See the foregoing. One prematurely born; an orphan. *Hal.* 109:12.

Hu-a-ha-u-le-la-ni, *s.* The name of a species of sweet potato.

Hu-a-ha-u-le-wa-le, *s.* Name of certain leaves of the potato.

2. The name of the potato itself.

Hu-a-he-ki-li, *s. Hua,* egg, and *hekili,* thunder. LIT. A thunder egg.

1. A hail stone; hail. *Puk.* 9:18, 22. NOTE.—It generally thunders during the hail storms on the mountains of Hawaii, hence the supposition that hail was produced by thunder.

2. The name of a plant used in medicine.

Hu-a-hu-a, *v.* See *Hua* and *Huahuwa* below. To foam; to froth at the mouth, as one in a fit. *Luk.* 9:39. To froth, as the sea in dashing ashore. *Iuda.* 13.

2. To turn away in disgust; to hate; to envy. *Kin.* 26:14. *Huahua* mai la na punahele mua. *Laieik.* 31.

Hu-a-hu-a, *s.* See *Huahua* above. Foam or froth, as of the sea or anything causing froth.

2. A bunch or kernel in the flesh, as in hogs or other animals; especially applied where many *huahuas* are growing together.

3. Small swellings about the eye, the forehead and neck.

4. See *Hua,* to be envious. An evil eye; looking with disdain upon another; envy.

Hu-a-hu-ae, *v.* To open and shut with violence.

Hu-a-hu-a-a-na-lau, *v.* See *Huahua-lau,* also *Hoohuahualau.*

Hu-a-hu-ai, *v.* See *Huai.* To boil up, as water in a spring.

2. To break up; to break forth, as water. *Nah.* 21:17.

3. To open frequently that liquid may flow.

4. To tear or break the skin.

Hu-a-hu-ai, *s.* See *Huai.* A violent boiling; a frequent opening.

Hu-a-hu-a-hu-a-lau, *v.* To question with a design to entangle; to put one to the torture.

Hu-a-hu-a-kai, *s.* A sponge. *Mar.* 15:36.

Hu-a-hu-a-lau, *v.* To tempt; to try to deceive; to puzzle or try one with questions; to question captiously. *Hoo.* To make one's self strange to another; to pretend not to know one. *Kin.* 42:7. To talk temptingly or deceitfully. 3 *Ioane* 10.

Hu-a-hu-a-lau, *s. Hoo.* A deceiving; an endeavor to insnare one; a temptation for one to say something he would not.

Hu-a-hu-a-na-la, *s.* The same as *huahualau.*

Hu-a-hu-a-na-na, *s. Huahua,* froth, and *nana* for *lana,* to float. LIT. Floating froth. A reproaching; making use of reproachful epithets; calling one an ignorant nothing.

Hu-a-hu-wa, *s.* See *Huahua.* Envy.

Gal. 5:26; *Pilip.* 1:15. But *huahua* is the common orthography.

Hu-a-ka, *adj.* Clear as crystal; clear as pure water, &c.; bright; white; shining.

Hu-a-kai, *v.* *Hua*, foam, and *kai*, sea. To foam and froth, as the sea; hence,

2. To boil or be agitated violently.

3. To travel in large companies, as in caravans. See KAIHUAKAI.

Hu-a-kai, *s.* See HUA and KAI. The foam of the sea.

2. A sponge. See HUAHUAKAI.

3. A large company traveling together. *Kin.* 32:21.

Hu-a-kai-he-le, *s.* See HUAKAI above and HELE, to go. A great number of persons traveling together; a caravansera; a troop. *Iob.* 6:18.

Hu-a-ka-pu, *s.* *Hua*, foam, froth, and *kapu*. The rich property about the chiefs and kapu to the people, was called *hua-kapu*, forbidden froth.

Hu-a-ke, *adj.* Full; plump, as a healthy man; well proportioned, as a good modeled canoe.

Hu-a-ke-e-o, *s.* *Hua* and *keeo*, displeasure; anger. Hardness of heart; stubbornness.

Hu-a-ke-e-o, *adj.* See the foregoing. *Hoo.* Hard-hearted; stubborn; stubbornly bent on wickedness; i mai la me ka olelo *hoohuakeeo*, he said to me *in stubbornness*; he *hoohuakeeo* mamuli o ka hewa, *hard-hearted* in wickedness.

Hu-a-ke-u, ⎱ *adj.* (In a *good sense*) fear-
Hu-a-ku, ⎰ less; bold; he kanaka *huaku*, wiwo ole; he olelo *huaku* ma ka pono, a speech *fearless* for the right. (In a *bad sense*) bold; impudent.

Hu-a-ke-o, *v.* See HUAKEEO above.

Hu-a-ki-ne-to, *s.* Gr. A hyacinth, name of a precious stone. *Hoik.* 21:20.

Hu-a-ku-ku-i, *s.* Name of schools of fish that show their heads above water, as the anai.

Hu-a-ku-ku-i, *s.* *Hua* and *kukui*, the name of the candle-nut tree. A kukui nut; the fruit of the kukui tree.

Hu-a-la-ke, *v.* To tie; to bind up. SYN. with nakiki.

Hu-a-la-ke, *v.* To swell out; to be large; to be round; to be full.

Hu-a-la-la, *adj.* Applied to surfaces, circular; oval; ili *hualala*, an oval surface; spherical; curved; equally arched, as the rainbow. *Ana. Hon.* 10.

Hu-a-la-lai, *s.* Name of a mountain on the western side of Hawaii.

Hu-a-le-le, *s.* *Hua*, seed, and *lele*, to fly. The seeds of the plant laulele.

2. A term expressive of hernia.

Hu-a-li, *v.* To be bright, as polished metal; to be clean; to glitter with whiteness or purity, as a garment. *Mat.* 28:3. *Hoo.* To furbish or burnish. *Ezek.* 21:10.

2. To strike.

3. To commence a kapu of a particular kind.

Hu-a-li, *adj.* Bright; clean, as a substance polished; bright; polished. *2 Oihl.* 4:16. Pure whiteness; lole *huali*, very white cloth; shining.

2. In a *moral sense*, pure; undefiled; morally good; applied to the heart. *2 Pet.* 3:1.

3. Glittering, as a sword. *Kanl.* 32:41.

4. *Hoo.* Keleawe i *hoohualiia*, polished brass. *Ezek.* 8:2.

Hu-a-lii, *adj.* *Hua*, seed, and *lii*, little. Small; diminutive.

Hu-a-li-li, *s.* The second crop of fruits, trees or vegetables, or degenerated fruit; ka *hualili*, huamaili o Kohala.

Hu-a-lo-le, *s.* See HUA and LOLE, cloth. The skirts of a garment. *Kanik. Ier.* 1:9.

Hu-a-lu, *adj.* Small; diminutive. See HUALII.

Hu-a-me-le, *s.* *Hua*, letter, and *mele*, to sing. The notes in music; a modern term.

Hu-a-mo-a, *s.* *Hua*, egg, and *moa*, a fowl. A hen's egg.

2. The name of the round bone that enters the socket of the hip. *Kin.* 32:25; *Anat.* 16.

Hu-a-no-ni, *s.* *Hua*, fruit, and *noni*, a shrub. The fruit or the apples of the noni; he kaua *huanoni* kekahi, some fought with *noni apples*.

Hu-a-pa-la-o-a, *s.* *Hua*, seed, and *palaoa*, Eng. (flour), bread. The seed of bread, i. e., wheat. *Puk.* 22:6.

Hu-a-pa-la-o-a-e-le-e-le, *s.* See HUA-PALAOA above, and ELEELE, dark colored. Hence, rye, as distinct from wheat.

Hu-a-poo, *s.* The side of the head.

Hu-a-wai-na, *s.* *Hua*, fruit, and *waina*, grape. A grape; *collectively*, grapes; the fruit of the vine. *Oihk.* 19:10. *Huawaina* pala mua, the first ripe grapes. *Nah.* 13:20.

Hu-a-ba-le, *s.* *Hua*, fruit, and *bale* (*Eng.*), barley. The grain of barley, or simply barley. *Rut.* 2:17, 23.

Hu-a-fi-ku, *s.* *Hua* and *fiku* (*Eng.*), fig. A fig; a bunch of figs. *2 Sam.* 16:1.

Hu-e, *v.* To look slily at a thing; to glance with the eye.

 2. To steal; to take secretly what is another's; *hue* ae la kekahi kanaka i ka apa lole kukaenalo, a certain man *stole* a piece of unbleached cotton cloth. See Aihue.

Hu-e, *v.* See Hu and E. To cause to flow out; to unload, as a ship.

Hu-e, *s.* A thief; one who steals.

Hu-e, *v.* To dig; to throw out dirt, as in digging a pit.

Hu-e, *adj.* Thievish; disposed to steal. *Kanl.* 24:7. Kanaka *hue.*

Hu-e, *s.* A gourd; a water calabash; *hue* ili, a skin bottle.

Hu-e-ie, *s.* *Hue* and *ie*, a vine used in basket making. A demijohn, from its case or covering.

Hu-e-u, *s.* A bold fearless man; one who excites to action, good or bad; soldier like; he kanaka koa; *hueu* oe i ke kolohe, you are *bold* in mischief; a bold energetic man in action; hooeu.

Hu-e-u-ai-na, *adj.* *Hueu* and *aina*, eating. Bold and rapid in eating.

Hu-e-i-li, *s.* *Hue*, calabash, and *ili*, skin. A skin bottle, such as the Asiatics used for containing liquids. *Ios.* 9:4.

Hu-e-hu, *v.* To shiver, as with cold.

Hu-e-hu, *s.* The strong (cold) blowing wind.

Hu-e-hu, *adj.* Chilled; cold.

Hu-e-hu-e, *s.* The name of the water on Hualalai where the last volcano broke out.

Hu-e-hu-e, *v.* See Hue, *v.* To throw up; to raise up; to loosen; to open.

Hu-e-hu-e, *adj.* Spreading over; growing thickly like thrifty vines, as the koali (convolvulus.)

 2. Spreading over like rain; he ua *huehueia* no Uli.

Hu-e-hu-e-lo, *s.* See Huelo. The tail end of a thing; the last of it; nolaila, ke hai aku nei au i keia wahi *huehuelo* manao, wherefore, I declare this *tail end* of a thought (last idea); loaa mai o ka *huehuelo* wale no, aole o ke kino pu kekahi, I obtained the *tail* only, not the body with it.

Hu-e-ka-hi, *adj.* One alone; a single child of a family.

Hu-e-lo, *s.* The tail of a beast or reptile; ke kahili o na holoholona ma ka hope, the fly-brush at the extremity of animals; *huelo* awa, a sting. 1 *Kor.* 15:55. Mai noho a makamaka ilio, i ka *huelo* ka ike, be not friends with the dog, for the *tail* will show it; the tail. *Puk.* 4:4. The rump. *Puk.* 29:22.

 2. Fig. An inferior in opposition to poo, a superior. *Kanl.* 28:13.

Hu-e-lo-e-lo, *adj.* Tail like; having appendages like tails.

Hu-e-ne, *s.* Name of a sickness causing panting; want of breath.

Hu-e-wai, *s.* *Hue*, calabash, and *wai*, water. A water calabash, in distinction from calabashes used for other purposes; a large gourd; any kind of bottle used to contain water.

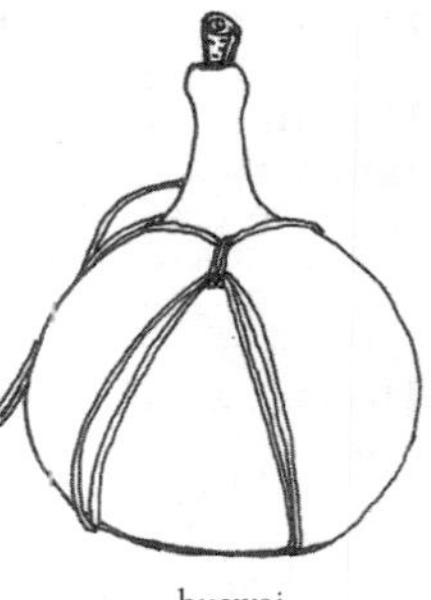

Hu-e-wai-na, *s.* See Hue and Waina (*Eng.*), wine. A bottle for wine; a bottle filled with wine. 2 *Sam.* 16:1.

Hu-i, *v.* To mix; to unite together, as different things; to unite, as an aha with the spectators; hence, *hui* ka aha, to *break up* the assembly. *Laieik.* 47.

 2. To add one thing to another. *Kin.* 28:9.

 3. To assemble together, as people for business.

 4. To agree in opinion; to have a union of thought; ua *hui* pu ka manao.

 5. To bend; to turn one way then another, as the voice in rising and falling in reading music.

 6. To ache; to be in pain.

 7. *Hoo.* To add one thing to another; to connect. *Luk.* 3:20.

 8. To unite, as in a treaty; to make affinity. 1 *Nal.* 3:1.

 9. To collect together, as men.

 10. To meet; to mingle; to come together, as waters.

 11. To meet, as persons long separated.

Hu-i, *s.* A uniting; an assembling.

 2. A cluster or collection of things; as, *hui* maia, a bunch of bananas; *hui* kalo, a kalo hill; *hui* waina, a cluster of grapes; *hui* niu, a cluster of cocoanuts.

 3. The flippers of the sea-turtle.

 4. The small uniting sticks in a thatched house, parallel with the posts and rafters and between them.

 5. Bodily pain; rheumatic pain; niho *hui*, the toothache.

 6. The name of the prayer on the morning after the anaana. See Huihui.

Hu-i, } *adj.* Cool; cold; chilly, as
Hu-i-hu-i, } the morning air from the
mountain; i hoomanawanui ai hoi kaua i
ka hau *huihui* o ke kakahiaka; cold, as
cold water. *Mat.* 10:42.

Hu-i-o-pa-pa, *s.* The name of a prayer
used in or near the luakini; a ma ia ahiahi
no haule ka *huiopapa.*

Hu-i-u-na, *s.* Perhaps for *huiana.* A
seam; a uniting by sewing together.

Hu-i-hu-i, *s.* A bunch; a cluster of
things, as stars.
   2. A constellation. *Isa.* 13:10.
   3. A bunch; applied to kalo. See Hui 2.
   4. The name of the seven stars. See
Huhui.

Hu-i-hu-i, *adj.* Cold; chilly. See Hui
above.
   2. Mixed; manifold; much; many containing the idea of union; aloha *huihui,*
much love.

Hu-i-kai, *v.* To mix or jumble together
things dissimilar; to make discordant compounds; to put several stories into one.

Hu-i-kau, *v.* See Huikai above. To turn
topsy-turvy; to mix up irregularly; to
throw things together without order.
   2. To accuse much and falsely; to vary
in narration; to cross one's own track in
a story.

Hu-i-kau, *s.* Confusion; without order;
irregularity.

Hu-i-kau, *adj.* Stumbling in walking;
without order; varying in one's story; put
together irregularly. See Opa.

Hu-i-ka-hi, *adj.* Lit. United in one.
Bound up; girded, as a man with a malo,
or a woman with a pa-u.

Hu-i-ka-hi, *s.* Name of a short malo.

Hu-i-ka-la, *v. Hui* and *kala,* to loosen;
to forgive. To cleanse, as a disease; to purify.
   2. To be purified. *Puk.* 29:23.
   3. To sanctify one's self. *Oihk.* 20:7.
   4. To cleanse morally. *Kin.* 35:2.
   5. To cleanse ceremonially. *Neh.* 12:30.
Huikala ole, unholy. 2 *Tim.* 3:2.
   6. *Hoo.* To cleanse; to purify; to sanctify. *Heb.* 9:13.

Hu-i-ka-la, *adj.* Cleansing; purifying;
wai *huikala,* water of purification. *Nah.* 19:9.

Hu-i-la, *v.* See Uila. To flash, as burning powder; to give a sudden light; haule
i ka papu, e *huila* na pu e.

Hu-i-la, *s. Eng.* A wheel. *Puk.* 14:25.
Syn. with pokakaa. *Ezek.* 1:16.

Hu-i-na, *s. Hui* and *ana,* a uniting. A
number; the sum of several numbers. 2

Sam. 24:9. E hookui i ka *huina,* to add up
the sum. *Nah.* 1:49.
   2. The point where two lines meet, an
angle; the place where two roads meet; a
corner, as of a house, fence, &c.
   3. In *music,* a close of a tune.
   4. In *geometry, huina* is the general name
for angle, qualified by such terms as designate the various kinds of angles.

Hu-i-na-oi, *s. Huina* and *oi,* sharp
pointed. An acute angle. *Ana. Hon.* 8.

Hu-i-na-ha, *s. Huina* and *ha,* four. A
quadrilateral or four-sided figure. *Ana.
Hon.* 14. Note.—Under the name *huinaha*
are the following: *huinahalike,* a square;
huinahaloa, a rectangular parallelogram;
huinahahio, four equal sides but oblique
angles; *huinahahioloihi,* an oblique parallelogram; *huinahakaulike,* a square or parallelogram; *huinahalualike,* a four-sided
figure which has two parallel sides only;
huinahalikeole, a four-sided figure where
all the sides are unequal.

Hu-i-na-he-lu, *s. Huina* and *helu,* to
count; to number. A number; the sum
of several numbers; *huinahelu* okoa, the
whole number, *Nah.* 14:29. See Heluna.

Hu-i-na-ko-lu, *s. Huina* and *kolu,* three.
The general name for triangle; thus, *hui-
nakolulike,* an equilateral triangle; *huinakolu elua aoao like,* an isosceles triangle;
huinakolu aoao like ole, an irregular triangle; *huinakolu kupono,* a right angled
triangle; *huinakolu peleleu,* an obtuse angled triangle; *huinakolu oi,* an acute angled triangle.

Hu-i-na-ku-po-no, *s.* A right angle.

Hu-i-na-la-au-la-na, *s. Huina,* a uniting, *laau,* timber, and *lana,* to float. A
union of floating timbers; a raft. 1 *Nal.* 5:9.

Hu-i-na-li-ma, *s. Huina,* angle, and
lima, five. In *geometry,* a five-sided figure;
huina ono, a six-sided figure; *huina hiku,* a
seven-sided figure; *huina walu,* an eight-
sided figure, &c.

Hu-i-na-pe-le-leu, *s.* An obtuse angle.

Hu-i-na-wai, *s. Huina,* a meeting or
union, and *wai,* water. A meeting or collection of waters; a pool. *Puk.* 7:19.

Hu-i-na-wai-na, *s. Hui,* bunch, and
waina, grapes. A cluster of grapes.

Hu-i-ni, *v.* To end in a sharp point, as
the top of a high mast. See Winiwini.

Hu-i-ni, *adj.* Having sharp points like
needles.

Hu-i-pa, *s.* Name of a species of stone
out of which the maika stones were made.

Hu-i-pa, *s. Eng.* A whip.

Hu-i-pu, *v. Hui,* to unite, and *pu,* together. To mix together; to come together; to unite; to assemble, as persons.

Hu-i-ta, *s. Eng.* Wheat. 1 *Kor.* 15:37; *Puk.* 29:2.

Hu-oi, *v. Hu,* to swell up, and *oi,* to exceed. To have an overflow of passion. *Hoo.* To feel or express jealousy; to have ill feelings towards one.

Hu-oi, *s. Hoo.* Evil surmising respecting another. 1 *Tim.* 6:4.

Hu-o-le, *adj. Hu,* leaven, and *ole,* none. Without leaven; unleavened; berena *hu-ole,* unleavened bread. *Puk.* 34:18.

Hu-o-no-o-no-o-le, *adj. Hu,* rising up, *onoono,* comfortable, satisfied, and ole, not. Unsteady; not fixed; unsatisfied. See KU-ONOONO.

Hu-ha, *adj.* Something said; a report, but no certainty as to the truth; he wahi olelo i maopopo ole, he lohe laulahea.

Hu-ha, *s.* A large fleshy person, but weak, indolent and lazy, either man, woman or child.

Hu-ho-nu-a, *v. Hu,* to rise, and *honua,* land. To pray that the land or country might be overturned; *huhonua i mana kai ka wai e.*

Hu-hu, *s.* The name of a worm, a moth-like animal that eats cloth. *Isa.* 51:8.

2. A worm or bug that bores into wood, rendering it full of holes.

Hu-hu, *adj.* Rotten, as a calabash; worm-eaten, as wood.

Hu-hu, *v.* See HU, to rise up; to swell. To be angry; to express angry feelings by scolding, storming, cursing, &c. *Hoo.* To provoke anger; to offend. *Puk.* 23:21. To be crabbed; to be churlish. 1 *Sam.* 25:3.

Hu-hu, *s.* Anger; wrath; displeasure.

Hu-hu, *adj.* Angry; offended; provoked.

Hu-hu-i, *s.* See HUI. *Hu* doubled. A bunch; a collection of things, generally qualified by a following word; as, *huhui palaoa,* a head of wheat. Mat. 12:1. *Huhui mau,* a bundle of grass; *huhui maia,* a bunch of bananas; huhui (hoku understood), the pleiades or seven stars. *Iob.* 38:31. The constellations of stars. *Isa.* 13:10. See HUIHUI.

Hu-hu-i-he-lu, *s. Huhui* and *helu,* arithmetic. Logarithms; the tables of logarithms; ina e imi au maloko o ka *huhui-helu,* if I should compute by *logarithms.*

Hu-hu-i-ka-lo, *s. Huhui,* bunch, and *kalo.* A bunch of kalo.

Hu-hu-i-wai-na, *s. Huhui,* cluster, and *waina,* grapes. A cluster of grapes. *Kanl.* 32:32.

Hu-hu-hu, *adj.* See HUHU, *adj.,* above. Rotten; worm-eaten, &c.

Hu-hu-hu-e, *v.* See HUE, to steal. A frequentative. To steal frequently; to carry off at many times secretly.

Hu-hu-hu-la, *v.* See HULA, to dance. A frequentative. To dance and sing; to dance much and often.

Hu-hu-hu-la, *v.* See HULA. To dance and sing and play, as at a hula; e pae, e hula, e like pu.

Hu-hu-hu-lei, *v.* To ride rapidly with a dress fluttering in the wind; to dance with kapas fluttering.

Hu-hu-hu-li, *v.* See HULI, to turn. To turn often; to turn, as many persons.

Hu-hu-hu-na, *v.* See HUNA, to conceal. To hide often or much; to conceal.

Hu-hu-hu-ne, *v.* See HUNE, poor; destitute of property. To be poor; to be stripped of all property.

Hu-hu-ki, *v.* See HUKI, to pull. To draw frequently; to pull out, as in drawing cuts. *Laieik.* 72. To pull along.

2. To dry up, as water; hoomaloo.

3. To cut down, as a tree; e kua aku.

Hu-ku-ku, *adj.* Full of holes; puka-puka, popopo. See HUHU and HUHUHU.

Hu-hu-la, *v.* See HULAHULA. To sing, dance and practice the forms of the hula.

Hu-hu-li, *v.* See HULI, to turn. To turn; to turn up; to search; to look here and there.

Hu-hu-lu-i-i, *v. Hulu,* hair, and *ii,* mould like. To stand up, as the comb of a cock; to stand up, as bristles; to stand erect, as the hair on the flesh when one is wet and cold.

2. To be wet and cold; to shiver with cold.

Hu-hu-lu-i-i, *adj.* Made rough and ugly, as the hairs or feathers of an animal in water.

Hu-hu-lu-lo-lo-a, *v. Hulu,* hair, and *loa,* long. To let the hair grow long.

Hu-hu-ne, *v.* See HUNE, to tease. To set a trap for one; to entice; to lay a bait.

Hu-hu-ni, *s.* The sickness of hogs.

Hu-hu-pau-la-au, *s.* A slanderer; a backbiter.

Hu-ka, *v.* To call hogs; to call to one, as in calling hogs.

Hu-ka, *s.* A term used in calling hogs.

2. Advice; information.

3. Name of an herb similar to balm.

4. A vulgar word of contempt; hele a

piha, *huka* pala, &c.

HU-KAA, *s.* A general name for pitch, resin or gum from a tree; any substance of a resinous nature.

2. A species of tree; an oak perhaps. *Isa.* 1:29. The turpentine tree perhaps.

HU-KAI, *s.* Water slightly brackish; drinkable.

HU-KAI-LO-LO-A, *s.* Epithet of a person who always lives with one particular chief; a no ma *hukailoloa*, o ke kanaka i noho me ke alii hookahi, aole i noho me ke alii e.

HU-KA-HU-KAI, *adj.* Insipid; tasteless; unpalatable; not relishable.

HU-KE-KI, *adj.* Cold; shivering with the cold.

HU-KI, *v.* To draw; to pull; to draw, as with a rope. *Ioan.* 4:7.

2. To raise; to lift up, as a person by the hand.

3. To put up upon, as one substance on another.

4. To brace or prop up.

5. To cook soft; to soften, as vegetables cooked, or meat undergoing decomposition. See KAHUKI.

HU-KI-HEE, *s. Huki*, to pull, and *hee*, to slip. A gliding along; a passing over, as over a bridge.

2. A bridge for passing smoothly over a stream. See PUNEE.

HU-KI-HE-LEI, *s.* The skin about the eye drawn aside and the eye diseased.

HU-KI-HU-KI, *v.* Freq. of *huki*. To draw or pull frequently. *Puk.* 2:16. To draw out; to pull upwards; to brace against.

HU-KI-KI, *v.* To be wet; to be cold on account of wet; to shiver with the cold. See HUKEKI and OPILI.

HU-KI-KI, *adj.* Small; pointed; dwarfish.

HU-KI-KI, *s.* Name of a species of fish.

HU-KI-WAI, *v.* To draw water, as from a well.

HU-KI-WAI, *s.* One whose business it is to draw and fetch water. *Kanl.* 29:10.

HU-KU, *s.* A heap of dirt or rubbish; a protuberance in any way. See OHUKU.

HU-KU, *adj.* Prominent; projecting, as the forehead; he *huku* ka lae, he has a *projecting* forehead. See OHUKU.

HU-KU-HI, *v.* See HUKI. To pull by force.

HU-KU-LII, *v. Huku*, branch, and *lii*, little. To be very small; to be little; to be dwarfish.

HU-KU-LII, *adj.* Small; little; dwarfish.

HU-LA, *v.* To pry up with a lever.

2. To transplant, as a tree; to plant out, as a young tree.

3. To cut off the tops of plants.

4. To bend over, as a tree; to push over any upright thing; to fall over upon.

5. To shake or tremble for fear of injury from another.

6. To trample and make a beaten path; to tread down; to trample upon.

7. To shake; to dance; to play an instrument and dance; to sing and dance. 2 *Sam.* 6:21. The same as *haa* and *lele* in verses 14:16. Alaila, *hula* iho la kahi poe alii ame kanaka, then *danced* certain of the chiefs and people.

8. To play on an instrument.

9. To sing; to sing and dance together.

10. To make sport. *Lunk.* 16:25.

11. To palpitate, as the heart; to throb, as an artery.

12. To move from place to place.

13. To bore a hole; e *hula* a puka, to bore and pierce through.

HU-LA, HU-LA-HU-LA, *s.* Music; dancing; singing, &c.

2. A play in which numbers dance and a few sing and drum.

3. A dance; a carousal; the action of dancing. *Puk.* 15:20.

4. A dance; a dancing, an expression of joy. *Kanik. Ier.* 5:15. NOTE.—The name of the *hula* god was Lakakane.

HU-LA, HU-LA-HU-LA, *s.* A swelling; a protuberance under the arm or on the thigh; he o ka mai mamua, a mahope *hula* mao a mao, a ma kela wahi ma keia wahi o ke kino, pela i *hulahula* ai.

2. A twitching, as of the eye; an involuntary muscular motion.

HU-LA, HU-LA-A-NA, *v.* To swim past a cliff that projects into the sea and interrupts the passage along the beach.

HU-LA-A-NA, *s.* A place where one must swim to pass a precipice that projects into the sea. *Laieik.* 73.

HU-LA-HU-LA, *s.* The name of a good or favorable aha. See AHA, the name of a prayer formerly very sacred.

2. Ka mea e hoopuka ai i ka leipoo.

HU-LA-HU-LA, *v.* To twitch often, as the eye; to twitch, as involuntary spasmodic motion.

HU-LA-LE, *adj.* Wet; muddy, &c. See HULALI.

HU-LA-LI, HU-LA-LI-LA-LI, *v.* To be muddy; to be slippery, as the ground on account of rain; *hulalilali* ke ala, pakika i ka ua.

2. To have a gloss; to glitter; to shine.

3. To shine, i. e., to reflect light, as a glass window at a distance; ka *hulalilali* a na puka aniani.

Hu-la-li, *s.* A shining surface; a reflector of light, as a white shining kapa; he mea e ka *hulali*, ia manawa. *Laieik.* 121.

Hu-la-ni, *v.* *Hu*, to rise, and *lani*, heaven. To praise; to exalt. See LELEPAILANI.

Hu-lei, *v.* To place on high; to put up on a precipice; to be lifted up, as a female's dress by the wind.

Hu-lei-a, *s.* Name of a species of soft stone.

Hu-le-hu-lei, *v.* See HUHUHULEI. To go up and down, as children on a see-saw.

Hu-li, *v.* To turn generally in any way; to turn over and about.

2. To change; to turn over, as the leaves of a book; to search here and there for a thing. *Kin.* 31:37.

3. E *huli* i ka naau, to give attention to a thing.

4. To turn to or towards one.

5. To roll over and over; to roll over or away, as a stone. *Ioan.* 20:1.

6. E *huli* i ka manao, to change the mind or opinion; hence, to repent and change the life.

7. To seek, i. e., to hunt after, as a wild beast. *Oihk.* 17:13.

8. To turn; to change one's course in traveling. *Kanl.* 2:8.

9. *Hoo.* E hoohuli e i kanaka, to pervert the people; to overturn; to upset, as any system of government or society.

10. To turn, i. e., to persuade one to change his course. 2 *Kor.* 5:11. See KAHULI.

Hu-li, *s.* A searching; a seeking; a turning over.

2. The name of kalo tops for planting. See HULIKALO.

Hu-li-a-ma-hi, *v.* To overflow, as a river; to be full of water. *Hal.* 78:2. *Huliamahi* na moku, to overflow the islands. *Laieik.* 175.

2. In a *figurative sense* quite often; as, kaua *huliamahi*.

Hu-li-hu-li, *v.* See HULI. To turn over frequently; to search after. *Iob.* 13:9.

Hu-li-ka-lo, *s.* See HULI, *s.* The tops of kalo for planting by which the kalo is propagated.

Hu-li-lau, *s.* A calabash for carrying clothes in a canoe. See HOKEO.

E noho no oe e Kaohana
Me na *hulilau* a kaua.—*Mele.*

Hu-li-li, *v.* To be cold; to shiver with the cold; to be contracted with the cold. See HUHULUII.

Hu-li-li, *adj.* Shivering, as with wet and cold.

Hu-li-li, *v.* See ULILI. To burn, as the fire; to be warm.

2. To undulate, as the air under a hot sun; to undulate, as the surface of water by the skipping of fishes.

3. To lay sticks across, as in covering a pit; e *hulili* aku i ka laau, alaila kanu i ka laau.

Hu-li-li, *s.* A fluttering blaze; the vibrations of the air under a hot sun.

2. The rolling up, as the swell of the surf before it breaks.

3. A garrison; a fort. 2 *Oihl.* 27:4. A strong place.

4. A ladder; a bridge. See ALAHAKA.

Hu-li-mo-ku, *adv.* *Huli*, to search, and *moku*, island. To search the island; that is, everywhere, all about, every place.

Hu-li-na, *v.* To be soft to the touch; to be weak. See LINA and ULINA.

Hu-li-na, *s.* *Huli* and *ana*. A turning; a turning place.

Hu-li-na-a-lo, *s.* *Hulina*, turning, and *alo*, front. A place over against; one place opposite to another. *Mar.* 13:3.

Hu-li-lu-a, *adj.* *Huli*, to turn, and *lua*, two; double. Turning two ways; blowing two ways, as the wind.

2. Changing from one thing to another, as the thoughts.

> Me he makani *hulilua* la,
> Huli ka manao—hele ka noonoo.—*Mele.*
> Like a shifting wind,
> The mind changes—thought moves.

Hu-li-pu, *v.* To turn together; to wring, as wet clothes; to press together.

Hu-lo, *v.* and *int.* *Eng.* To shout; to cry aloud; to cry out huzza! hurra!

Hu-lu, *v.* To be disobedient; to disregard one's commands; not to pay attention. See ENUHA.

Hu-lu, *s.* A feather of a bird. *Oihk.* 1:16. A quill.

2. A bristle of a hog; the hair of the body; *hulu* kuemaka, the eyebrows. *Oihk.* 14:9.

3. Wool; a fleece from a sheep. *Kanl.* 18:4.

4. Name of a kind of fish-hook.

Hu-lu, *adj.* Sluggish, as the mind; disobedient.

Hu-lu-a-nai, *s.* See HULU, bristles, and ANAI, to rub. A brush for painting; especially for whitewashing.

Hu-lu-i, *v.* To draw together, as a fish net when full of fish.

Huluiia mai kuu lani kuu alii—e—he.—*Mele.*

HU-LU-I-I-WI, *s.* *Hulu*, feather, and *iiwi*, a small red bird. A feathered cloak made or adorned with the feathers of the iiwi.

Eia ka lani ka hahai *huluiiwi.*—*Mele.*

HU-LU-O-O, *s.* *Hulu*, feather, and *oo*, the name of a bird. The feathers of the oo; o ka hulu mamo, ua oi aku ia mamua o ka *huluoo.*

HU-LU-HI-PA, *s.* *Hulu*, wool, and *hipa* (*Eng.*), sheep. Wool (LIT. Hair of sheep); a fleece of wool. 1 *Sam.* 25:7.

HU-LU-HU-LU, *s.* See HULU. Cotton; a fleece blanket; a fleece of wool. *Lunk.* 6:37. The hair of an animal; feathers, &c.

HU-LU-HU-LU, *adj.* Hairy; covered with hair, feathers, wool, &c.

HU-LU-MA-MO, *s.* *Hulu* and *mamo*, a yellow bird. The feathers of the mamo with which war cloaks and royal robes were adorned.

HU-LU-MA-NU, *s.* *Hulu* and *manu*, a bird. A bird-feather. NOTE.—Birds' feathers were highly valued in former times; o ka *hulumanu* ka mea i manao nui ia, he waiwai ia.

HU-LU-MA-NU, *s.* LIT. A bird's feather. Name of a class of men around a chief, very great favorites; a favorite of the chief. See the foregoing.

HU-MA, *s.* Name of the star Aquila.

HU-MA-MA, *s.* Name of the cluster of three stars in a row in the constellation of Aquila.

HU-ME, *v.* To bind around the loins, as a malo; to gird on, as a sash. *Ier.* 13:12. Ina *hume* ke kanaka i ko ke alii malo, e make no ia, if a person should bind on a chief's malo, the penalty would be death. *Haw. Hist.*

HU-ME-MA-LO-MAI-KAI, *s.* Wearing an ornamental malo, i. e., imitating a chief; acting the fop or dandy.

HU-MU, *v.* To sew cloth; to fasten together by sewing.

HU-MU-U-LA, *s.* Name of very hard stones out of which the ancient kois were made.

HU-MU-HU-MU, *v.* Freq. of *humu*. To sew; to stitch; to fasten by sewing. *Puk.* 18:6.

HU-MU-HU-MU, *adj.* Mea *humuhumu* rope ano e, needle-work; embroidery. *Puk.* 35:37.

HU-MU-HU-MU, *s.* A sewing; a stitching; a fastening together.

 2. A species of fish.

 3. A dark spot or mole on the cheek.

HU-MU-HU-MU-HI-U-KO-LE,
HU-MU-HU-MU-MEE-MEE, } *s.*
HU-MU-HU-MU-NU-KU-NU-KU-A-PU-AA,
See HUMUHUMU 2, a fish. Different species of the humuhumu kind.

HU-MU-NA, *s.* *Humu* and *ana*. A sewing; a seam. See KUIUNA.

HU-NA, *v.* To hide; to conceal; to keep from the sight or knowledge of another. *Kin.* 26:15.

 2. To keep back truth in speaking. 1 *Sam.* 3:17.

 3. To hide, as a trap or snare.

 4. To hide; to conceal; with *maka*, to hide the face, i. e., to turn from *Kanl.* 32:20.

 5. To conceal, i. e., to disguise one's self. 2 *Oihl.* 18:29.

 6. To protect; to defend. *Hal.* 64:2.

 7. *Hoo.* To conceal, as knowledge or wisdom. *Iob.* 17:4.

HU-NA, *v.* To be small; to be little; to be reduced fine, as powder.

HU-NA, *s.* That which is concealed; kahi *huna*, the private members of the body. *Oihk.* 18:6, 7. Wahi *huna*, same. *Puk.* 20:23.

HU-NA, *s.* A small part of anything. *Luk.* 16:17. A particle of dust; a crumb of food or other substance. 2 *Oihl.* 1:9. See HUNA, to be little. See other words below with their qualities.

HU-NA, *s.* A name of a day of the month; i ka po i o *Huna. Laieik.* 112.

HU-NA-A-HI, *s.* *Huna* and *ahi*, fire. A spark of fire. *Isa.* 1:31.

HU-NA-O-LO-NA, *s.* *Huna* and *olona*, a shrub, the bark of which resembles flax. Tow, the refuse of flax. *Isa.* 1:31.

HU-NA-HU-NA, *s.* See HUNA above. Crumbs, as of food.

 2. Fine rain; spray; fine dust; maluna o na *hunahuna* lepo a pau ma ka honua.

 3. Little particles of knowledge; o na *hunahuna* o ka naauao, oia ka i loaa mai ia'u, the *little parts* of knowledge, that is what I have received; eia ke ano o ka *hunahuna*, he wahi mea uuku loa ia.

HU-NA-HU-NA, *v.* See HUNA, to conceal. To steal away and hide; to conceal one's self.

HU-NA-KAI, *s.* *Huna* and *kai*, sea. The fine spray of the sea.

HU-NA-KAU-A, *s.* *Huna* and *kaua*, war. The individuals of a war-host. *Ios.* 10:5.

HU-NA-KE-LE, *v.* To bury a corpse secretly, as in former times, so that no one might know where it was and thus steal it; to bury one without any mark by which the place might be known.

HU-NA-KE-LE, *s.* A place where only one body is buried secretly; a burying place for only one. See the above.

HU-NA-LE-PO, *s.* *Huna* and *lepo*, dust. Dust; very small particles of matter. *Nah.* 23:10.

HU-NA-LE-WA, *s.* The van of an army; the front ranks; the opposite of *hunapaa*; o ka poe mamua, he poe uuku ia, ua kapaia lakou he *hunalewa*.

HU-NA-PAA, *s.* The rear of an army, in distinction from *hunalewa*, the front. *Ios.* 6:9.

HU-NA-WAI, *s.* *Huna* and *wai*, water. A particle of water.

HU-NE, *v.* To tease; to persevere in entreaty.
2. To be trickish. *Hoo.* The same.

HU-NE, *v.* To be poor; to be destitute; to be impoverished. *Lunk.* 6:6. To be in want. *Hoo.* To impoverish; to strip one of property. *Lunk.* 14:15.

HU-NE, *adj.* Destitute of property; naked; poor; applied to persons.

HU-NE, *s.* A poor man; e ola auanei ka *hune*, the *poor man* will soon recover.

HU-NE-HU-NE, *v.* See HUNE, to be trickish. To entrap one; to deceive; to play a trick on.

HU-NO-AI, *s.* A parent-in-law, either father or mother, according to the designating terms *kane* or *wahine*. See HONOAI.

HU-NO-AI-KA-NE, *s.* A father-in-law.

HU-NO-AI-WA-HI-NE, *s.* A mother-in-law.

HU-NO-NA, *s.* A child-in-law.

HU-NO-NA-KA-NE, *s.* A son-in-law.

HU-NO-NA-WA-HI-NE, *s.* A daughter-in-law.

HU-PE, *s.* The mucus from the nose, snot. See KAKELO.

HU-PE-KO-HO-LA, *s.* See HUPE above and KOHOLA, whale. A kind of slimy substance found in the ocean (probably a living creature); so called because supposed to be from the nose of the whale.

HU-PI, *v.* To pull or draw. See HUKI.

HU-PO, *v.* To be ignorant; to be wild; to be savage; to be in mental darkness.

HU-PO, *adj.* Savage; ignorant; barbarous; dark; idiot like. *Hal.* 119:130. He nui ka poe *hupo* loa ma kuaaina.

HU-PO-KA-RI-TO, *s.* Gr. A hypocrite. NOTE.—This word was formerly used by the translators of the New Testament for hypocrite, but lately *hookamani* has taken its place.

HU-PU, *adj.* Angry. See HUHU.

HU-PU-NA, *s.* A collection, as of water in a hollow place.

HU-PU-NA-WAI, *s.* *Hupuna* and *wai*, water. Standing water; a collection of water.

HU-PU-PU, *s.* Name of the worm that eats hard bread.

HU-WA, *s.* See HUA. Envy. 1 *Tim.* 6:4.

HU-WE-LO, *s.* See HUELO. The tail of a beast.

HU-SO-PA, *s.* Gr. Eng. Hyssop, an herb. *Oihk.* 14:4.

HU-SO-PA, *adj.* Pupu *husopa*, a bunch of hyssop; lala *husopa*, same.

K.

K, the seventh letter of the Hawaiian alphabet. Its sound varies somewhat from the English *k* sound to that of the *t*, according as the enunciation is made at the end of the tongue or near the root. It is difficult to make Hawaiians perceive the difference between the English sounds of *k* and *t*. The natives on the Island of Hawaii generally pronounce the letter with the palate, that is, give it the *k* sound, while the natives of the Island of Kauai pronounce it with the end of the tongue, that is, pronounce it as *t*.

KA in the beginning of a speech is used to call attention.

KA, *int.* An exclamation of surprise, wonder, disappointment or disgust; also,

similar to hark, hush; often repeated. See KAHAHA.

KA! KA! *int.* Enough; sufficient; stop.

KA in different parts of a sentence, contains something like an assertion with disapprobation; used also on the discovery of a mistake. 1 *Sam.* 23:12. It is used on expressing opposition of sentiment. *Puk.* 32:17. After a verb it implies oblique absurdity, something unaccountable. *Luke* 23:35. When the contrary takes place from what was expected or attempted. *Isa.* 14:14, 15. He kau malie ka la, o ka honua *ka* ke kaa nei! it is the sun is it that stands still, the earth *forsooth*, that rolls! Ka contains the idea of some supposed error, or something wrongly done or thought. *Oih.* 11:3.

KA, *art.* The definite article, *the.* Before nouns beginning with the letter k, it is changed into ke instead of ka. See KE. See *Gram.* § 59, 60, 61. *Ka* as an article often represents not only the article but the noun supposed to belong to it, or it may have *mea* or some other word understood (like, in another sense, the English *what,* as an antecedent and a relative); as, o ka aila *ka* (mea) iloko o kona lima, the oil the (thing) which, *that which* was in his hand. *Oihk.* 17:11. O ke koko *ka* (mea) i hana i kalahala, the blood the (thing) it makes atonement; that is, the thing which *makes*; o ka pono wale no *ka* i oi mamua o ka hewa, righteousness only is the thing (that which) excels wickedness. *Ka* also as an article stands for *ka mea,* and *ka mea nana,* the person who, or the thing which. See the following passages: John 12:2, 49; Mat. 18:23; Mar. 9:7. See also Grammar, Syntax, Rule 6, Note 3.

KA, *prep.* Having the general sense, of; belonging to; it marks the relation of possession and is used before nouns and pronouns; it is similar in meaning to the preposition *a,* but used in a different part of the sentence. See Grammar § 105, 4. *Ka* (also *ko*) before nouns is similar in meaning to the apostrophic *s* in English, and signifies the *thing* or the *things belonging* to those nouns; as, ka ke alii, *belonging* to the chief; *ka* laua, *that of* them two. See Grammar § 105, 4.

KA, *v.* To bail water, as from a canoe; e *ka* oe i ka liu.

2. To strike; to dash; to overthrow. *Puk.* 15:4.

3. To strike, as to strike fire with flint and steel; *ka* ahi. See KAKA. To block or split off a piece of hard stone for the purpose of making a stone adze in ancient times; o ka poe ka koi *ka* poe i manao nui ia; hele no ka poe *ka* koi e imi i na pohaku paa e pono ai ke hana i koi; *ka* makau, to fabricate a bone into a fish-hook.

4. To finish or end a thing; to rest; to escape from pursuit; to flee away; ua *ka* ilaila kuu po auhee.

5. To radiate; to go out from the center, as light from the sun; as cinders from a red hot iron; to braid or knit, as a fish net (o ka poe *ka* upena) from a center point.

6. To go out every way, as from a center. *Kin.* 3:24. See KAA.

7. To curse; to express anger at one by wishing evil from God; a low kind of swearing.

8. To doom; to pass sentence; *ka* ola, *ka* make, to *doom* to life, to *doom* to death (according to the pleasure of the gods.)

9. To catch birds in a snare.

10. *Hoo.* To destroy; cause to perish.

11. To be disappointed; put to confusion; to be made ashamed.

12. A nolaila e aho hoi ke *ka* i ka nele lua. *Laieik.* 197.

KA, *s.* A dish to bail water with.

2. A striking against; a collision.

3. A vine, the branches of which spread and run.

KAA, *v.* To radiate. See KA 5. To go out, as rays of light from the sun; as cinders from a red hot iron; to turn every way, as bones in a socket joint. *Anat.* 18.

KAA, *v.* To roll, as a wheel; e olo *kaa*; to travel about from place to place; often with *puni.*

2. To operate; to take effect, as an emetic or cathartic.

3. To pass off or out from; to go out from the presence of one.

4. To fall away; to leave one party to join another. 1 *Oihl.* 12:19. See KAANA.

5. To remove; to change one's place; to be transferred to another. *Nah.* 36:9. To cause to be done; to be gone; ua *kaa* na peelua, the worms (peeluas) are done, i. e., the time for them is past. *Isa.* 10:25.

6. To be sick; to suffer pain in sickness; to lie or be confined with long sickness. *Isa.* 51:20.

7. To mourn, as in the loss of relatives; *kaa* kumakena na wahine i na kane i kela la i keia la, wives *were sick* with weeping for their husbands every day.

8. To pay a debt; e emo *kaa* koke ae no ka aie a ke alii, very soon *will be paid* the debt of the chief; to postpone; to put off; to put aside. *Oih.* 5:34.

9. *Hoo.* To roll off; to remove.

KAA, *s.* A tradition; a legend. See KAAO.

2. A cross; same as *kea.*

3. Anything that rolls or turns, as a top, a wheel of a carriage, a carriage itself, a cart, wagon or chariot. *Kin.* 46:5. *Kaa* i uhiia, a covered wagon. *Nah.* 7:3. A grindstone.

4. The branch of a vine.

5. A name given to all kinds of foreign timber, except oak.

6. A strand of a cord; a rope; the string that fastens a fish-hook to the line.

7. A path to walk in. *Hal.* 6:11.

8. A shrub.

KAA, *adv.* Gone; absent; no more.

KA-AA, *num. adj.* The number forty. This perhaps is a mistake for *kaau.*

KAA-A-LA-A-LA, *adj.* Hard, as the healthy body of a growing infant; a *kaaalaala ke keiki e hanai i ka ai.*

KA-AI, *v.* To bind or tie round; to gird on, as an oriental dress; to tie on, as a fillet on the head, or a girdle around the waist. See KAEI. Paai o haho aku i ke *kaai.*

KA-AI, *s.* The girdle around the loins of the gods, put round by the chief, made of vines; e lawe ia mai no ko ke alii kane akua *kaai.*

KA-AO, *s.* A legend; a tale of ancient times. See KAA above. A traditionary story; a fable. 1 *Tim.* 4:7. A history in the manner of a story. 2 *Oihl.* 13:22. Aole i oleloia ma na *kaao* kahiko o ko o nei poe kanaka, it is not spoken of in the ancient *legends* of this people.

KA-AO, *v.* To be calm in some places while the wind blows on one side or in some parts; kaao ae la ka makani; to be smooth, as the sea in a calm, but not a dead calm; i ua po nei e *kaao* ana no o ianei ia makou. *Laieik.* 30.

KA-AO, *s.* A multitude (doubtful.)

2. The name or the quality ascribed to the fruit of the hala tree when nearly ripe.

KA-AO-E, *s.* A poor man; one destitute of property; a wanderer; a vagabond. See KAAOWE.

KA-AO-E, *adj.* Wandering; vagabond like; he hele wale, he kuewa.

KAA-O-KI, *v.* To end; to cut short; to put an end to; to beautify; to finish off, as a canoe.

KAA-O-KO-A, *v.* Kaa and *okoa.* To spare; to let alone; not to employ. *Hoo.* Same. *Sol.* 13:24. See KAOKOA. To abstain from a person or thing. *Oih.* 15:20. To withdraw from.

KAA-O-KO-A, *adj.* Separate from; left by itself.

KA-A-O-NA, *s.* The name of the second month of the year.

2. A bundle of anything hung up to smoke or dry; applied to fish, sugar-cane, &c.; that which is smoked red or brown.

KA-A-O-NA, *adj.* Red or reddish brown; me he pua *kaaona* la, like a blossom dried reddish.

KA-A-O-WE, *s.* See KAAOE. A person that owns no land; o ka poe aina ole, he *kaaowe* ia.

KA-AU, *num. adj.* The number forty; applied in counting fish; *kaau* ia.

KA-AU-AU-PUU, *s.* Name of a species of soft porous stone.

KA-A-HA, *s.* A stick or rod having at one end a bunch of leaves with kapa fastened, and held by the priest while offering sacrifice on the heiau.

KA-A-HA, *s.* The name of a long fish.

KA-A-HA-A-HA, *v.* To grow; to increase in size and solidity.

KA-A-HE, *v.* To be feeble; to be near dying; pehea o Auhea? Aole akaka ka pono—ke *kaahe* ae la. See AHE, a slight breathing.

KAA-HA-LE, *s.* A wheel carriage with a covered top. LIT. A house-cart.

KAA-HE-LE, *v.* *Kaa* and *hele,* to go. To travel about; to visit different parts of the country; to go here and there.

kaahale

Nah. 13:32. To pass over or through a country. *Lunk.* 11:29. To travel from place to place. *Mat.* 10:23.

KAA-KAA, *v.* Kaa, to roll. To open, as the eyes; to look upon; to have re-spect to; to watch over. 2 *Oihl.* 6:20. *Hoo.* To cause to open, as the eyes. *Kin.* 21:19.

KAA-KAA-HI-KI, *v.* To go to a place of safety; to feel secure in a place.

KAA-KAA-LI-NA, *adj.* See LENA. Tough; stringy; not soft or pulpy; applied to bananas.

KAA-KAA-WI-LI, *v.* See KAA. *Hoo.* To turn frequently; to writhe in agony; hoo-*kaakaawili* iho la oia no kona ehaeha, he *writhed much,* being in great pain.

KAA-KAU-A, *s.* A chariot; a war carriage. *Lunk.* 4:15.

KAA-KAU-A, *v.* Kaa, to keep off, and *kaua.* To prevent or keep off war.

KAA-KAU-A, *s. and adj.* Name of a class of chiefs consulted by the king in times of difficulty; he alii *kaakaua,* he alii akamai i ke *kaakaua;* koho oia i kekahi poe kanaka akamai i ke kakaolelo, ame ke *kaakaua,* i mau hoaolelo nona; one skillful in managing war operations; o ka mea akamai i ke kaua, he *kaakaua* ia. *Kaakaua* also refers to the maneuvers of the armies in time of battle.

KAA-KA-LO-LO, *v.* A *kaakalolo* o ko laua noho ana.

KAA-KO-LU, *adj.* Three-fold; three-stranded, as a rope. *Kekah.* 4:12.

KAA-KU-A, *s.* A headache with dizziness and weakness.

KAA-KU-A, *adv.* Kukini, alaila, pili nui lakou, pili hihia, pili *kaakua*.

KAA-KU-MU, *adj.* Dull; blunt, as a tool; not sharp; koi *kaakumu*, a dull koi or adze.

KA-A-LA, *s.* The name of a mountain on the Island of Oahu.
   2. The name of a porous species of stone; he pukapuka e like me kaala.

KA-A-LA, *s.* A widow or a widower.
   2. The name of some art anciently taught among the chiefs; he nui ka poe ao i ke kaka laau me ke *kaala*.
   3. The name of an instrument used in war.

KAA-LA-LO, *v.* To talk crookedly by way of flattery; to flatter; to crouch in order to gain some point; to act meanly to secure some object.

KAA-LE-LE, *v.* To make a reeling motion, as a feeble person attempting to lean on a staff; to reel.

KAA-LE-LE-WA, *s.* *Kaa*, to roll, and *lewa*, to swing. Clouds which are driven or float swiftly through the air. See KAA and LEWA.

KAA-LE-LE-WA, *adj.* Flying; driven with the wind.

KAA-LU-NA, *v.* E moe me ke kaa o ke poo i *kaaluna* me ka lolii ana i ke kapa a paa. See KEHA.

KAA-MAU-KOI, *s.* A fishing pole; an angling rod.

KAA-MA-LOO, *v.* *Kaa* and *maloo*, dry. To wipe dry; to wring dry, as a cloth.

KAA-MA-LU-NA, *v.* *Kaa* and *maluna*, above. To take the oversight of business; to exercise an office over others.

KAA-ME-HAI, *v.* To backbite; to slander.

KAA-ME-HAI, *s.* Detraction; slander.

KAA-ME-HOU, *s.* The tying on of a fish-hook to the string.

KAA-MO-LA, *v.* *Kaa* and *mola*, to turn. To turn round; to be not firm; not steadfast.

KAA-MO-LA, *adj.* Turning round; changing; not steadfast.

KA-A-NA, *v.* To make alike; to resemble.
   2. To bring over to one's party or purpose; to proselyte. *Mat.* 23:15.
   3. To fall away from one party to another. 1 *Oihl.* 12:19. See KAA.
   4. To make; to gain.
   5. To deceive; to entrap; to outwit.
   6. To compare, i. e., to resemble; to make like; to be mingled in with others; ua *kaana*

ka iho (kapa) me ka hewa; ua *kaana* mai ka bipi hihiu maloko o ka bipi laka a laua, the wild cattle *were mixed* with the tame.

KA-A-NI-AU, *adj.* Broken; past away, as a kapu; noa ke kapu; he kapu ka laua, noa ke kapu, the kapus of the long gods and the short gods are no more—noa.

KAA-NI-NI, *v.* To be agitated; to be in a flutter.
   2. To run in agitation, as a child wishing to go with its parent who has started before, or to be agitated as a child afraid to be washed in cold water; *kaanini* ke keiki i ka wai.

KAA-NO-I, *s.* Desire; kuko.

KAA-PA-HU, *v.* To cut off; to cut in pieces. See APAHU.

KAA-PA-LA-OA, *s.* A modern word. *Kaa*, wheel, and *palaoa*, flour. A flour mill; a grinding of flour.
   2. A thrashing instrument. *Isa.* 41:15.

KAA-PA-LA-OA, *v.* To grind; to make flour. *Iob.* 31:10.

KAA-PE, *adj.* Disobedient to orders.

KAA-PE-HA, *s.* A name given to the oil plant on Hawaii.
   2. The name of a large sized person—also of great influence.

KAA-PE-KA, *s.* A person of a large size; a large bodied person, like a chief.

KAA-PU-NI, *v.* *Kaa* and *puni*, around. To go or roll around; to go round from place to place; to circumambulate; in *law*, he lunakanawai *kaapuni*, a circuit judge.

KAA-PU-NI, *adj.* Going or traveling about, or from place to place.

KA-A-WA, *s.* A large dish or hollow place worn by water in a rock.

KAA-WA-LE, *v.* *Kaa* and *wale*, only. To separate, as persons or things; to separate, as friends.
   2. To separate, as two things that adhere; to open.
   3. *Hoo.* To separate one thing from another; to divide between; to create a vacancy.
   4. To start in surprise; to be frightened.

KAA-WA-LE, *s.* A separation; a space between two or more things; an empty space.

KAA-WA-LE, *adj.* Separate from; free; empty, as space; empty, as a house; state of being unchanged; convenient; fit; wa *kaawale*, spare time.

KA-A-WE, *v.* To tie any flexible thing tightly around the throat; to choke by tying the throat.
   2. To suspend; to hang up; generally

by the neck; to strangle with a cord. *Ios.*
10:26. *Kaawe ia ia iho a make,* to commit
suicide. *Mat.* 27:5. NOTE.—*Kaawe* rather
applies to suicide; *li,* to a public execution
by hanging.

KA-A-WE, *s.* A suspension; a strangling,
i. e., death. *Iob.* 7:15.

2. A neckhandkerchief; a cravat; *o ke
kaawe kekahi mea e nani ai ka a-i kanaka,*
the *cravat* is what adorns the neck of a man.

KA-A-WE-A-WE, *s.* Oppression of the
chest; sickness of the stomach; a disease
of the neck and chest.

KAA-WE-LA, *s.* The name of one of the
planets, Venus, the evening star.

KAA-WI-LI, *v. Kaa* and *wili,* to twist.
To writhe; to writhe in pain.

2. To mix together, as different ingredients; *mea kaawili laau,* an apothecary.
Puk. 37:29.

3. To knead, as bread. *Ier.* 7:18.

4. *Hoo.* To torture; to cause to writhe
in pain; to give pain to. *Ier.* 4:19.

5. To tear; to rage, as a foul spirit. *Mar.*
1:26.

KAA-WI-LI, *s.* A pain; a torture; a
writhing pain.

2. A mixture of things.

3. A school of fish; *kaawili iheihe, kaawili auau, kaawili pukiki.*

KA-E, *v.* To rub out, as a mark; to blot
out; to erase.

2. To kill; to take away. *Hoo.* To blot
out; to destroy; to kill instantly; to smite.
1 *Oihl.* 13:10.

3. To make desolate. *Oihk.* 26:31.

KAE, *s.* The brink, border or edge of a
thing; the exterior of the anus; the side, as
of a precipice, wood, lake, &c. *Puk.* 25:25.
The brim of a vessel or container. 1 *Nal.*
7:23. The inner bark, as of wauke;
kae wauke.

KAE, *v.* To have a border or brim. *Hoo.*
To hold on the brink or border; to protect.

KAE, *v.* To spurn; to turn a deaf ear;
to refuse to listen; to answer foolishly.

2. To try a kalo patch, to know if it is
ripe enough to eat; *e kae i ka loi.*

KAE, *s.* Contempt; a refusal to hear
advice.

2. A name of an office in the king's train.

KA-EA, *v.* To have no appetite; to lose
the appetite for food. See KANEA and KUA-
NEA. To be indolent; to be lazy.

KA-EA, *s.* The loss of appetite; no relish for food; *o ke kaea pu wale no ia. Laieik.*
142.

KA-EA, *adj.* Having no appetite. See
MANAWAHUA.

KA-E-E, *s.* The name of a fruit which
resembles a bean, used as a cathartic.

2. Joy; gladness, as at the arrival of a
friend.

KA-EE, *adj.* Hard or stiff, as new kapa.

KA-E-E, *v.* To dry up, as water in the
sun or by heat. See KAE, to rub out. He
wahi wai, aole i *kaee* i ka la.

KA-E-E-E, *adj.* Stiff; ragged. See KAEE
above. *Kaeee* kela, i ka onohi o kuu maka.

KA-E-E-LE, *s.* The body of a canoe.

KA-E-E-LO, *s.* The name of a kind of
food, perhaps of Borabora origin.

KA-EE-PA-O-O, *s.* Name of a species of
fish net.

KA-EI, *v.* To gird on; to bind on, as a
belt around the body; *e apo ma ka opu.*

2. To put on, as armor; to gird on, as
an official or extra garment. 1 *Sam.* 2:18.

3. To put on, as a mourning dress or a
loose garment. *Kin.* 37:34.

KA-EI, *s.* A belt; a girdle; a sash. *Puk.*
28:4. Ke apo ma ka opu.

2. In *geography* and *astronomy,* a zone of
the earth or heavens; *na hoku o ke kaei,*
the planets. 2 *Nal.* 23:5.

KA-EI-POO, *s.* A turban; a diadem. *Iob.*
29:13.

KA-E-O, *s.* Anger or excitement against
what is wrong; anger at sin. See KEEO.

KA-E-O, *adj.* Full, as a calabash with
food; *he aloha ie ka ipu kaeo.*

KA-EU-EU, *v.* To be the largest, as of
two ropes or pieces of wood joined together;
to be big; to excel.

KA-EU-EU, *s.* Joy; delight; gratification; excitement. See EUEU.

KA-E-KA, *v.* To be entangled, as a rope
or string; *e hihia, e lauwili.*

KA-E-KA, *adv.* Rolled and twisted up;
entangled; *e wili kaeka.*

KAE-KAE, *v.* To be smooth and plump;
without protuberances.

KAE-KAE, *adj.* Young, fresh and smooth,
as an unmarried woman who is much
desired; hence, applied to a small woman.

2. Applied to a canoe, new; smooth;
without knots, &c.; *he waa kaekae;* also, i
mai no ia, *he kihei pili nau, he kaekae ka
olupi.*

KAE-KAE, *adj.* Soft; mellow; soft, as a
cooked potato.

2. Light in traveling.

KAE-KAE, *s.* See KAE. The narrow edge
of a rule.

KAE-KAE, *adv.* See KAE, border. Having many edges; by borders; on the borders.

KA-E-KE, *v.* To beat the drum. See HOO-EKEEKE.

KA-E-KE, *s.* Drum beating; the skill of drumming; he poe akamai i ke *kaeke*. *Laieik*. 112.

KA-E-KE-E-KE, *v.* To beat or play the drum, as in ancient times; e pai pahu, e hookanikani.

KA-E-KE-E-KE, *s.* A kind of drum made of the cocoanut tree.

2. The art of drumming; oia ka wa i laha mai ai ke *kaekeeke*.

KA-E-LA, *s.* A beam, brace or cross-piece. See KAOLA.

KA-E-LA, *adj.* Half full; partly filled; unfinished. See KAELEWAA.

KA-E-LE, *v.* To increase in number; to be a great number; *kaele* ua make, *kaele* ua ia, *kaele* ua kanaka.

KA-E-LE, *v.* To be partially filled, as a calabash with fish or food, leaving some empty space at the top.

KA-E-LE-LOI, *s.* The sound of the drum in ancient times; the roll of the drum; kaekeeke.

KA-E-LE-WAA, *s.* An unfinished boat or canoe. See KAELA. He waa i kapili ole ia i ka laau.

2. The bottom of a canoe.

KA-E-LO, *s.* The name of that month of the year nearly corresponding with our January.

KA-E-NA, *s.* A room in a house. *Mar*. 14:15. A cabin in a ship; a drawer of a bureau; a closet of a room. See KEENA.

KA-E-NA, *v.* To boast; to glory; to brag, 1 *Oihl*. 16:10. To make pretenses; to boast of what one has done. 2 *Oihl*. 28:19. To be self-conceited; auhea la ka mea nui i *kaena* ai oukou ia oukou iho? where is the great thing for which you boast yourselves? See KAEENA.

KA-E-NA, *s.* High mindedness; pride; self-exaltation.

KA-E-NA, *adj.* Excelling; going before; self-opinionated.

KA-E-NA, *adv.* With certainty; surely; without error, &c.; no ko'u ike i ka maikai, ko'u mea no ia i olelo *kaena* ai, from my knowledge of beauty, I can speak *with confidence*.

KA-E-NA-KOI, *s.* A low blackguard word; e hele oe a i *kaenakoi*.

KAI, *v.* To lift up on the hands and carry; to lift up the foot and walk, as an infant in beginning to walk, or as one recovering from sickness; to step amiss, as a child; generally connected with *hina*; as, *kai* aku la ke keiki a hina iho la.

2. To lead; to guide; to direct; *kai* aku i ke kaa, to drive a cart. 2 *Sam*. 6:3. To direct the ceremonies of the luakini; ke kai ana o ka aha. SYN. with oihana.

3. To lead, direct or bring to a place. *Kin*. 2:19.

4. To lead into or entice, as fish into a net, or any animal into a trap or snare.

5. To bring; to take in hand; to do with; to pull up, as kalo.

6. To shove along; to move; to go a journey; to travel slowly.

7. To bring, i. e., to lead; to transfer, as a people from one place to another. *Kanl*. 7:1.

8. *Hoo*. To separate or part asunder, as a cracked part of a canoe; ua *kai* ka pili o ka waa; or as a door so swelled as not to shut; ua *kai* na pili o ka pani; to displace; to put away. *Heb*. 10:9.

9. To take away by robbery; to misspend; to squander. *Luk*. 15:30. To reject; to disregard. See HOKAI.

KAI, *s.* The sea; sea water; a flood; *kai* hooee, an overflowing flood. *Dan*. 9:26. Hence,

2. Brine; a gravy of roast meat; broth. *Lunk*. 6:20.

3. The surf of the sea; *kai* ula, the red sea; *kai* piha, the full sea or flood tide; *kai* make, the dead sea or ebb tide; *kai* koo, a very high surf, &c. See these compounds.

4. A current in the sea; he *kai* i Hawaii, a current towards Hawaii.

5. A traveling guard.

KAI, *s.* See verb, No. 4. A net for fish; a snare for birds; a lasso for cattle, &c.

KAI, *s.* The toothache; a pain in the teeth.

KAI, *adj.* Insipid, as food; having no appetite; the state of a person so suffering affliction as to have no desire for food.

KAI, *adv.* A long time; *kai* ka hana loa ia oe, *very long* the time you were doing it; e hana loa *kai* ka loihi, it is long to do, *how very* long. See KAI, *int*.

KAI, *int*. How; how much; how great. 2 *Sam*. 1:19. *Kai* ka nani! O how glorious! 2 *Sam*. 6:20. *Kai* ka hemolele! how excellent! *Hal*. 8:1. Renowned; wonderful; kai ka luhi, what a weariness. *Mat*. 1:13.

KAI-AU, *s.* A place a little ways out in the sea, beyond the kuaau; also called *ho-*

honu.

KAI-A-U-LU, *s.* The kilohana; the out side; the best; the figured one of a set of kapas, i. e., *figuratively,* something rather remarkable in appearance.

2. An overhanging cloud.

3. The space on top of a pali.

4. A high elevated post.

KAI-A-U-LU, *s.* Name of a strong wind off Waianae on Oahu.

KAI-A-HU-A-KAI, *v. Kai* and *huakai.* To lead a large traveling company. See HUAKAI.

KAI-A-HU-A-KAI, *s.* A large company traveling together. See HUAKAI.

KAI-A-HU-LU, *v. Kai,* sea, and *hulu,* hairy. To be in a foam, as the sea agitated greatly by the winds; to act, as the sea when current and wind are contrary.

KAI-A-HU-LU, *s.* The sea in great agitation, so as to be white.

KAI-A-KA-HI-NA-LII, *s. Kai,* sea, and *Hinalii,* name of a chief of Hawaii. See HINALII. The name of a great flood in ancient times which by tradition covered the whole earth, i. e., the Hawaiian Islands. See the story in D. Malo's work. Hence this is the word used for Noah's flood. *Kin.* 6:17.

KAI-A-KA-HU-LU-MA-NU, *s. Kai,* sea, and *hulumanu,* a favorite of the king. The name of the flood yet to come, as the foregoing is the name of the flood that is past.

KAI-A-LII, *s.* Name of a species of hard rock out of which hatchets were made.

KAI-A-LI-LE, *v.* To be indolent, lazy or indifferent; to treat with contempt any effort to be otherwise.

KAI-A-LI-LE, *adj.* Indolent; lazy; contemptuous.

KAI-A-LI-LE, *adj.* Unskillful; awkward; inexpert; aole e loaa keia mea o ka manao, i ka mea *kaialile* lomalomaaihalale.

KAI-A-NO-A, *s.* The name of a kind of fish-hook.

KAI-A-PO, *s.* A rising or high tide; i ka pii ana o ke kai, ua kapaia he kaipii, he kainui, he *kaiapo* kahi inoa.

KAI-E-A, *s. Kai,* sea, and *ea,* to rise. A rising tide; a swelling of the sea; a spreading over the land.

KAI-EE, *s. Kai,* sea, and *ee,* to come up. See KAIEA above.

KAI-E-E, *s.* The name of a the purgative bean.

KAI-E-LO, *s.* Water of the cocoanut mixed with other ingredients.

KAI-E-MI, *s. Kai* and *emi,* to lessen. A decreasing or falling tide. See KAIMAKE.

KAI-E-NA, *v.* To be self-opinionated; to boast; to glory; to make pretenses. See KAENA.

KAI-E-WA, *v. Kai* and *ewa,* crooked. To be led astray; to be tossed about.

2. To live as it happens, sometimes well off, sometimes in poverty, exalted or depressed.

KAI-E-WE, *s. Kai,* to lead, and *ewe,* the navel string. A company following a chief; ka huakai, ke *kaiewe* o ka lani.

KAI-I, *v.* To walk buttoned up tightly; to strut; to be vain.

2. To turn away; to refuse to listen to one's request.

3. To be stingy; to be close-fisted. See HOII.

4. To tie up the throat; to choke.

KA-II, *s.* A kind of net for taking fish.

KAI-II, *s.* Name of a vegetable growing on the mountains, eaten as food in time of famine.

KA-I-O, *s.* The name of a bird like the pueo or owl.

KAI-OE, *s.* The name of a plant or tree; he pua laau no ke *kaioe,* the tree blossom of the *kaioe.*

KA-IO-IO, *adv.* Ulu *kaioio* ka nahelehele.

KA-IO-O-LE-LE-PA, *adj.* O Kalani *kaioolelepa* ka alapa pii moo o Ku.

KAI-O-HU-A, *s.* Name of a place a little way out in the sea; same as *poana.*

KAI-O-KI-LO-HEE, *s.* Name of a place in the sea; same as *kaiau.*

KA-IO-LE-KAA, *s.* The name of a famine in former times.

KAI-O-LE-NA, *s. Kai,* liquid, and *olena,* yellow. Yellow coloring matter.

KAI-O-LE-NA, *v.* To cleanse; to purify; e huikala, e hoomaemae.

KAI-O-LO-A, *s.* The name of a ceremony of tying the malo on to the god; it was done by the women of the chief.

KAI-O-PE-LU, *s.* A place in the sea. SYN. with kaiuli.

KAI-O-PO-KE-O, *s.* Name of a long prayer at the dedication of a heiau.

KAI-U-A, *v.* To repeat over and over, as one does when drunk; *kaiua* ka olelo; he olelo kuawili; e *kaiua* ka hookahe i ka wai, continue to water the ground.

KAI-U-LA, *s. Kai* and *ula,* red. The Red Sea. *Puk.* 13:18. The sea that separates Africa from Asia.

KAI-U-LA-LA, *s.* Far out at sea; out of sight of land.

KAI-U-LI, *s. Kai,* sea, and *uli,* blue. The

dark blue sea; hence, the deep sea; the name of the sea beyond the kohola; also called *kailuhee.*

KAI-U-LU, *s.* The name of the sea at full tide. See KAINUI and KAIPIHA.

KAI-U-WE, *v.* Ka poe i *kaiuwe* pinepine.

KAI-HEE-NA-LU, *s.* Name of a place on or near a reef, like *kohola.*

KAI-HE-HEE, *s.* Name of an ancient kapu of the chiefs, connected with death; also called *lumalumaia.*

KAI-HE-HE-NA, *s. Kai* and *hehena,* mad. The raging sea. The following epithets of the sea are found in a prayer of Keanini: kaikane, kaiwahine, kaipupule, kaihehena, kaiulaula, kaipiliakee—e.

KAI-HE-LE, *s.* The laying of stones, as in a pavement, one beside another; a i ke *kaihele* ana o na pohaku, oia no ka mea i kau i ka pohaku.

KAI-HE-LE-KU, *s.* The name of the sea beyond the poana, i. e., the second space beyond where the surf breaks; also called *kaipapau.*

KA-I-HI, *v.* To spin round like a top; to be dizzy.

2. To withhold what is another's; to keep back what is forfeited in a game.

KA-I-HI, *s.* Dizziness; a sense of turning in the head.

2. The name of a species of fish net; he upena *kaihi.*

KAI-HOI, *s. Kai* and *hoi,* to return. A falling or low tide.

KAI-HO-HO-NU, *s. Kai* and *hohonu,* deep. High tide; full sea; deep water.

KAI-HU-A, *s.* High tide; high water. See KAIKI.

KAI-KA, *s.* The border of a cultivated plat; the border of a kalo patch.

KAI-KAI, *v.* See KAI. To lift up, as the hand. *Nah.* 20:11. To lift or raise up, as the eyes to heaven. SYN. with leha. To lift up or raise, as the voice in complaint; *kaikai* i ka leo. *Nah.* 14:1.

2. To take up; to bear; to carry upon. *Kin.* 7:17. To carry off; *kaikai* no laua i ka pahu a hiki ma ka hakae.

3. To take off, as a burden; to carry away, to lift, as a weight. *Isa.* 40:15.

4. To carry tenderly, as a child. *Puk.* 19:4.

5. To promote; to exalt; to favor, as a king a subject. *Eset.* 3:1.

6. To be led or urged on, as by strong desire or lust; a na keia kuko, *kaikai* kino hou ia mai la. *Laieik.* 196.

KAI-KAI, *adj.* That which is lifted up or heaved. *Puk.* 29:27. Uha mua o ka mohai *kaikai,* heave shoulder. *Nah.* 6:20.

KAI-KAI-A-PO-LA, *s.* The tail of a kite; e ka mea e pono ai ka lupe, o na laau liilii ame ke kaula, ame ka welu, ame ke *kaikaiapola,* ame ke aho.

KAI-KAI-NA, *s.* The younger of two brothers or sisters; used by a brother when speaking of a brother, or a sister of a sister. But if a brother speak of a sister, or a sister of a brother, it is *kaikunane.*

KAI-KA-O-WA, } *v. imper.* Seize; take;
KAI-KO-WA, } follow; the word given by Kekuaokalani for seizing boys, fish &c., that were not his own.

KAI-KA-HI, *adj.* Few; scarce; unfrequent; here and there one. See KAKAIKAHI.

KAI-KA-MA-HI-NE, *s.* A daughter; a female descendant. *Kin.* 20:12. NOTE.—According to analogy this word for daughter should be *keikiwahine,* like *keikikane,* but Hawaiians do not use it so.

KAI-KE-A, *s.* The fat of hogs or other animals. *Puk.* 29:13. FIG. *Isa.* 34:6.

2. The sap of a tree, the outside white, wood resembling in color the fat of animals.

KAI-KI, *s.* High water; high tide.

KAI-KO, *s.* A constable; a policeman. See MAKAI.

KAI-KOA-KOA, *s.* The watery fluid of the bowels.

KAI-KO-E-KE, *s.* A brother-in-law; a sister-in-law; generally designated by *kane* or *wahine.*

KAI-KO-E-LE, *s.* A very shallow sea in a calm, too shallow for a canoe; he kai kui opihi, he malia paha.

KAI-KO-I, *s.* A species of kalo; he kalo.

KAI-KOO, *s.* A high surf of the sea; a raging swell of the sea.

KAI-KOO, *v.* To roll in; to rage, as a high surf; *kaikoo* ke kai. *Laieik.* 165.

KAI-KO-WA, *v.* See KAIKAOWA above.

KAI-KU, *s.* A middle tide, not high nor low. See KAIMAU.

KAI-KU-A, *s.* A countryman; a backwoodsman.

KAI-KUA-A-NA, *s.* The elder of two brothers or sisters; used by a brother when speaking of a brother, or by a sister when speaking of a sister; but when a brother speaks of an elder sister, it is *kaikuwahine.* When a sister speaks of an elder brother it is *kaikunane.*

KAI-KU-O-NO, *s. Kai,* sea, and *kuono,* a bay. A gulf; a creek; an inlet of water into the land. *Isa.* 11:15.

Kai-ku-na-ne, *s.* The brother of a sister. *Kin.* 20:5.

Kai-ku-wa-hi-ne, *s.* The sister of a brother. *Kin.* 12:13.

Kai-la-na-hu-a-hi, *s. Kai* and *lanahuahi* (same as *nanahuahi*), a coal of fire. Very dark or black water of the ocean.

Ka-i-li, *v.* To snatch; to take away; to take by force; to take away, as one's pleasure and joy. *Ioan.* 16:22. To take away one's right. *Kin.* 31:31. To spoil or rob one's glory. *Kol.* 2:15.
 2. To give up; to depart, as the spirit of a dying person; *kaili* ke aho, to catch for the breath. See Aili. To breathe the last. *Kin.* 35:18.

Ka-i-li, *s.* Name of a fish net from its use, to take away.

Ka-i-li, *adj.* Waiwai *kaili,* spoil. *Ezek.* 7:21. Manu *kaili* wale, a ravenous bird. *Ezek.* 39:4.

Ka-i-li, *s.* He mea *kaili,* extortion; a taking by force.

Ka-i-li, *s.* The act of taking fish with a hook. See Aili.

Ka-i-li, *s.* The name of the great feather god of Kamehameha.

Ka-i-li-i-li, *v.* To take and carry here and there.

Ka-i-li-i-li, *s.* A narrow valley near the top of Waialeale on Kauai, a resting place for kings and queens in ancient times.

Kai-li-ke, *v. Kai* and *like,* alike. To divide equally between a number of persons. *Luk.* 22:17.

Kai-li-ko-li-ko, *s. Kai,* gravy, and *liko,* oily. Fat gravy; the oily part of fat.
 2. The appearance of oil poured upon water. See Liko.

Kai-li-ko-li-ko, *adj.* Fat or greasy; applied to gravy.

Kai-li-po-li-po, *s. Kai* and *lipolipo,* blue or black. Epithet of the deep sea, as dark blue or black.

Ka-i-li-po-ni, *s.* A disease in which one falls down dead; something like apoplexy; he *kailiponi* ka make.

Ka-i-li-wa-le, *v. Kaili* and *wale.* See Wale. To take without regard to right or to consequences; to take by force. 1 *Sam.* 2:16.
 2. To rob; to plunder. *Oihk.* 19:13.

Ka-i-li-wa-le, *s.* Seizing the property of another; a plunder; a robbery.

Kai-lu-hee, *s.* Name of a place in the sea; same as *kaiuli,* blue water.

Kai-mau, *s.* Middle tide, neither high nor low. See Kaiku.

Kai-ma-ha-mo-e, *s. Kai,* gravy, and *mahamoe,* a fish. The gravy made for the fish mahamoe.
 2. The fat or grease of that fish.

Kai-ma-ke, *s. Kai* and *make,* dead. Low water; ebb tide.
 2. A calm sea; no wind; still water; in *geography,* name of the Dead Sea.

Kai-ma-loo, *s. Kai* and *maloo,* dry. Low tide; ebb tide, when many places on the sea shore are dry, or the coral and reef are bare.

Kai-ma-lo-lo, *s. Kai* and *malolo,* resting; quiet. A shallow place of the sea near the shore where the sea is at rest.
 2. A place where the sea is green and shallow; place of soundings.

Kai-mo-ku, *s.* Middle tide, i. e., when the tide begins to recede. See Kaimau.

Ka-i-na, *v.* See Kai, to take, and Ana. To take; to seize, as a fit; as the influence of a wicked spirit. *Mar.* 9:18.
 2. To seize, as a prisoner; to lead away to trial; ua uku i ke dala, ua hana, ua paa i ka hao, ua *kaina* aku imua o na lunakanawai.

Kai-na, *v.* To move slowly and softly, as a weak person trying to walk.

Kai-na, *s.* A younger of two brothers or two sisters; hence, a thing that is after or second to another; pokii *kaina,* the very younger.

Kai-na, *s.* A sitting to practice sorcery; the practice of sorcery.

Kai-no, } *v.* (Impersonal.) I thought;
Kai-no-a, } just as if; *kaino* he oiaio, aole ka! I thought it was true, but it is not; alaila, e i aku au ia oukou, ka! *kainoia,* alia e hoole.

Kai-nu-i, *s.* High sea; high tide.

Kai-nu-nu-ki, *adj. Kai* and *nunuki.* Irregular ebbing and flowing, as the sea.

Kai-pa-ea-ea, *s.* A calm, smooth sea; same as *pohu.*

Kai-pa-pau, *s.* A shallow place in the sea, the same as the *poana,* or *kaiohua.*

Kai-pii, *s.* A rising or full tide. See Kaipiha and Kainui.

Kai-pi-ha, *s. Kai* and *piha,* full. A high sea; high tide.

Kai-pu, *s.* Same as *kainui* and *kaipiha* above.

Kai-puu, *v.* To divide out into parts or portions. See Puu.

Kai-puu, *s.* A division or portion; more commonly written *puu.*

Ka-i-wi-poo, *s. Ka,* article, *iwi,* bone, and *poo,* the head. The skull bone; the name of the place where Jesus Christ was crucified. *Ioan.* 19:17.

KAI-U-LU, *s.* Wehe ke *kaiulu* i ke oho o ka niu.

KA-O, *interj.* The article *ka* and *o*. Similar to kahana; *kao* mai, make kela kanaka; it expresses surprise.

KA-O, *v.* To cry out as above; *kao* mai la o mea, somebody cries out with astonishment.

KA-O, *v.* To intercede; to mediate; to separate contending parties; to prevent one from accusing or slandering another. See UWAO. Ua *kao* mai oe ia'u.

KA-O, *s.* A peace-maker; an intercessor.

KA-O, *s.* A goat; *kao* hele, a scape-goat. *Oihk.* 16:15.

KA-O, *s.* A legend; a tradition. See KAAO.

KA-O, *s.* A dart; a javelin; a rocket.

KA-O, *v.* To throw or cast, as a dart or javelin.

KA-OO, *v.* To bind; to tighten; to be in a press of people; to be in straits.

2. To punch, as a man does his own breast in the colic, with a stick or his hand.

KA-OO, *s.* Being in straits; suffering pain.

2. A multitude; applied to animals.

3. Also, a traveling company; same as *huakaihele.*

KA-O-HI, *v.* To fix; to establish.

2. To abide; to continue to adhere firmly to a thing or course of conduct; to be steadfast.

3. To keep; to retain; to keep back. *Laieik.* 176. To restrain.

4. To invite to stay when one is about to go away or further on. *Luk.* 24:29.

5. To keep, i. e., to pay regard to a law or command.

6. To restrain one from doing a thing by friendly advice.

7. To compel or urge. 2 *Oihl.* 21:11. *Kaohi* na 'lii ia ia e noho, aole oia i ae mai, the chiefs urged him to stay, but he did not consent; e *kaohi* i kou wawae, to refrain the foot from wandering. *Ier.* 14:10. To restrain; to hold back. *Hal.* 19:13.

8. To keep as a promise. 1 *Nal.* 8:24.

9. To choose. *Isa.* 7:15.

10. To save; to screen, as a guilty person from punishment. *Ezek.* 13:19.

KA-O-HI-HI-U, *s.* *Kao*, goat, and *hihiu*, wild. The gazelle or wild goat.

KA-O-KAA, *s.* Name of a play and a former pastime.

KA-O-KA-NA-KA, *s.* *Kao*, goat, and *ka-naka*, man. Name of an animal to be found in the desolations of Babylon; a satyr. *Isa.* 13:21.

KAO-KAO, *v.* To be prominent; to project.

2. To be red.

3. To be hard to the touch.

KAO-KAO, *s.* The first dropping of a shower; the fore part of a cloud; ke *kao-kao* ae, e ua iuka o Kaumana.

2. Hardness; redness; prominence.

3. The venereal disease.

KA-O-KO-A, *v.* *Ka* and *okoa*, different. To be whole; to be undivided.

2. *Hoo.* To separate from. 1 *Sam.* 21:4. To abstain from a thing; to separate one's self from moral evil; e hookaawale ia ou-kou iho i na mea haumia.

3. To stand aloof from; to let alone.

4. To make one's self conspicuous; to be eminent.

KA-O-KO-A, *adj.* Whole; unmutilated; he ia *kaokoa*, okioki ole, mai ke poo a ka hiu, a fish *whole*, uncut from head to tail.

KA-O-KO-A, *s.* The being separate; aloof (from wrong-doing); o ke *kaokoa*, he hewa ole, he hihia ole, he oluolu, he maikai.

2. A man who leaves his proper haku and serves another, or pays his food and presents to another.

KA-O-LA, *s.* A stick or beam laid across a house from rafter to rafter to strengthen it; a beam; the beam of a house. *Kekah.* 10:18.

2. A bar for a door; a bar across the gate of a city. 1 *Sam.* 20:7.

3. FIG. Na *kaola* o ka po, the *bars* of night. *Iob.* 17:16.

KA-O-LA-HAU, *s.* *Kaola* and *hau*, iron. An iron bar. *Sol.* 18:19.

KA-O-LE-LE, *s.* *Kao*, dart, and *lele*, to fly. A dart; a javelin; a sky-rocket. See KAO.

KA-O-LO, *s.* The descent of a hill or pali; the going down a hill. See KAKAI-PALI, also OLO.

KA-O-MI, *v.* To press down, as with a lever; to bear down upon a thing.

2. To press; to squeeze out, as wine. *Lunk.* 6:11.

3. FIG. To press, as the breasts; a euphemism for *moekolohe. Ezek.* 23:3.

4. To crush; to humble one; e hoohaahaa.

KA-O-MI, *s.* Name of a wind; the northeast trade wind on the east side of Lanai, and about Maui. SYN. with moae. Loaa makou i kekahi makani ikaika, he *kaomi* ka inoa.

KA-O-MI-WAI-NA, *s.* A wine press. *Mat.* 21:33.

KA-O-NA, *s.* The name of a Hawaiian

month.

KA-O-PA, *s.* A painful stiffness or rheumatic affection of the limbs, which makes it difficult for one to stand or walk. See OPA, *adj.*, and OOPA.

KA-O-PA, *adj.* Lame; stiff; rheumatic; kanaka *kaopa.*

KAU, *v.* In an *active sense*, to hang; to hang up; to suspend, as an article to be out of the way; to crucify or hang, as a criminal. *Kin.* 40:22.

2. To hang, tie or gird on, as a sword; *kau* i ka pahi kaua. *Puk.* 32:27.

3. To put upon or place a thing in some designated place; to put in an elevated situation; to mount a horse; to go on board a ship or canoe.

4. To overhang, as the heavens over the earth.

5. To fall upon; to embrace affectionately, with *ai. Kin.* 46:29.

6. To put upon one, as a heavy burden. *Nah.* 11:11.

7. To set or fix the boundaries of a land or country.

8. To put down, as words on paper. See KAKAU. To write; to dot; hence,

9. To give publicity to a thing; to promulgate, as a law; i *kau* aku oukou i kanawai maikai, that you may establish good laws.

10. To set before one, as food.

11. To tempt, as in taking birds with a snare.

12. In a *neuter sense*, to light down upon, as a bird; as the spirit or divine influence upon one. *Nah.* 11:26.

13. To come down upon one unexpectedly.

14. *Kau* pono kona maka, to set or direct one's face or desire.

15. To rest upon; to stretch out or over.

16. To come upon one, as a suffering or calamity.

17. To rehearse in the hearing of another that he may learn.

18. A *kau* ka hamere ma kekahi lima, he took the hammer in one hand. *Lunk.* 4:21. To lay or place the hand upon one for evil.

19. *Hoo.* To set against; to resist. *Lunk.* 7:22.

20. To appoint against; to come upon. *Ier.* 15:3.

21. To bring upon; to cause to fall upon.

22. To rest; to place. *Kanl.* 7:23.

23. *Kau* aku i kau hale, to go about from house to house; to go about idly. See definition 11.

KAU, *s.* Season. *Kin.* 1:14.

2. The summer or warm season, in distinction from *hooilo*, the winter months. NOTE.—The Hawaiians had but two seasons in a year, viz.: the *kau* summer, and *hooilo* winter; hence,

3. A period of time when one lives. *Eset.* 1:1. A Specified time. *Lunk.* 10:8. A i ke *kau* i ke alii, ia Kamehameha, in the life time of Kamehameha.

4. A time for a particular purpose.

5. Time of indefinite length; *kau* ai, a fruitful season; *kau* wi, a time of famine.

6. Midnight; so called from the game called *puhenehene*, in which were five puu or places to conceal the noa: the first called *kihi*, second *pili*, third *kau*, fourth *pilipuka* (i. e., applied to night, 3 o'clock, A. M.), fifth *kihipuka. Dr. Baldwin.*

KAU, *s.* A place; *kau* kanaka laha ole, place where men go not; *kau* kanaka, a place where men live; *kau* kanaka ole ai, where there are no people.

KAU, *s.* A canoe; *kaukahi*, a single canoe; *kaulua*, a double-canoe.

KAU, *adj.* A setting of the sun; a resting; mai ka la hiki a ka la *kau*, from the rising to the *setting* sun. *D. Malo* 5:11.

2. A sitting place, as a roost for fowls; kau ka moa i ke *kau*, the fowl sits upon its *roost.*

KAU, *s.* Name of puukapu in the game of noa.

KAU, *pers. pro.* An oblique case of *oe*, second person. Of thee; of thine. *Gram.* § 132, 133. Also a prefix pronoun, thy; thine. *Gram.* § 149, 150.

KA'U, *pers. pro.* An oblique case of *au.* Of me; mine; belonging to me. *Gram.* § 124, 1. Also a prefix pronoun, my; mine; of me. *Gram.* § 150.

KAU-A, *v.* To war; to fight, as two armies.

2. To make war upon or against. *Kin.* 14:2.

3. To fight for. *Puk.* 14:14.

4. *Hoo.* To cause to fight.

5. To serve as the conquered serve the conqueror; hence, with a stronger pronunciation, *kauwa*, a servant.

KAU-A, *s.* A war; a battle; an army drawn up for battle. 2 *Nal.* 28:5. Poe *kaua*, a host; an army. *Puk.* 14:24.

KA-U-A, *v.* To hesitate about doing a thing after an engagement; to be in doubt about fulfilling a promise; to beg off; hoohala.

2. To invite to stay. See KAOHI. Aole o maua mea nana e *kaua* mai, a liuliu ko maua noho kuewa ana, there is no reason

why we two *should stay* and lengthen out the time of our sojourning.

Ka-ua, *pro. dual.* We two; you and I. *Gram.* § 124, 3.

Kau-ai, *s.* Name of one of the Hawaiian group of islands; ma ka hapukaohiohi ana paha a ka waha me he hoe *Kauai* la.

Kau-ai-ka-na-na, *v.* To sleep in the day time for pleasure or comfort; to take a siesta.

Kau-au-la, *s.* A kind of soft porous stone.

Kau-a-u-la, *s.* A strong wind from the mountains, occasioned by the breaking over of the trade winds; often destructive at Lahaina.

Kau-a-u-la, *adj.* Strong; raging; furious; applied to the tradewinds when they break over the hills back of Lahaina; he leo o ka makani kauaula ka'u i lohe iho nei.

Kau-a-hau-a, *s.* Ua pau i ke *kauahauaia* na kanaka a pau i ka hana.

Kau-a-ho-a, *s.* Coarse grained; a sour disposition; not easily pleased.

Kau-a-ka, *s.* A person crazy, noisy with constant muscular motion.

Kaua-lae-paa-kau-ana, *s.* The most offensive of language; when used, instant fighting is the consequence.

Kau-a-lau, *s.* The plantain, a vegetable like the banana.

Kau-a-lii, *s.* A low chief, not a high one. See KAUKAUALII.

Kau-a-li-o, *s. Kaua,* war, and *lio,* a horse. A warrior on horseback; cavalry, in distinction from infantry. 1 *Sam.* 13:5.

Kau-a-lu-pe, *v.* To carry, as a man wounded in battle, without much care.

Kau-a-mai, *v.* To invite, &c. See KAUA.
2. The *mai* is simply a verbal directive.

Kau-a-pai-o, *s.* A combat where there is striking back and forth.

Ka-u-e, *v.* To be in fear.

Kau-ea, *adj.* Having no appetite.

Kau-e-ke-ke, *adj.* Short, as a coat or gown; lean, as a man.

Kau-i-la, *v.* To offer sacrifice at the close of a kapu.

Kau-i-la, *s.* Name of a species of hard reddish wood resembling mahogany.
2. He oa no Puukapele.
3. Puhi *kauila.*
4. He kapu *kauila.*
5. I kahi a lakou i pee ai a noa ke *kauila.*

Kau-i-la-hu-lu-hu-lu, *s.* The name of a prayer at the heiau.

Kau-o, } *v.* To draw or drag along;
Kau-wo, }   to haul, as a load. *Kanl.* 21:3. To draw morally, i. e., to endure; to incline to do a thing.
2. To conduct, as a prisoner.
3. To pray for a special blessing or favor; applied to the worship at the time of makahiki.

Kau-o, } *s.* Seed; offspring; increase;
Kau-wo, }   fruit of marriage. If Naheinaena had had a son, the old chiefs would say "ua loaa ke *kauo.*" *D. Malo.* Hence, a supporter; a sustainer.

Kau-o, *s.* The yellow part or yolk of an egg; *kauo* moa; *kauo* ke akua hulu.

Kau-o, *adj.* Drawing; pulling; dragging along; bipi *kauo,* a laboring ox. *Oihk.* 7:23.

Kau-o-e, *s.* Name of an office in the king's train.

Kau-o-uo, } *v.* To increase or grow
Kau-wo-wo, } rapidly, as vines; to spread
Ka-wo-wo, } over, as vines or other running vegetation that grows thriftily and covers the ground.
2. To increase rapidly, as a people or race; applied to the peopling of Hawaii from the first man.

    O *kauouo* i lani a paakani lea,
    Puapua, huahua mai la ka la manuia.

Kau-o-ha, *v.* To give a dying charge; to make a bequest or a parting charge. *Isa.* 38:1. Hence, to make a will. NOTE.— Ancient wills, of course, were verbal; now, by law, they must be written.
2. To give a charge on any subject; to command; to put in charge or trust, as one dying or going away; *kauoha* ae la oia (o Kamehameha) ia Kauikeaouli e noho i alii no Hawaii nei, he (Kamehameba) *gave in charge* to Kauikeaouli to reign as king over the Hawaiian Islands.
3. To commit into the hands of another. 1 *Pet.* 4:19.
4. To give orders concerning a person or thing. *Kin.* 12:20.
5. To commit to paper, i. e., to write down; nolaila, ke *kauoha* aku nei au i ko'u manao ma keia palapala, i ike oe i ko'u manao.

Kau-o-ha, *s.* A will, verbal or written; a command; a charge; a dying request.
2. A covenant; a commission; a judicial decision.
3. A determination; a decree.
4. Beggary.

Kau-o-ka-hi-ki, *s.* Name of a species of ohia; o ka ohia nui ke *kauokahiki* i kai, oia ka laau o ka lananuu; out of this same timber the god was made for the heiau.

KAU-O-KUU, *s.* The name of a sickness or pestilence which formerly spread over the Islands; ua kapaia ka inoa o kela mai (ahulau) he *kauokuu*, the name of that sickness was *kauokuu*.

KAU-O-LA-NI, *v.* To express admiration of a chief or his deeds.

2. To express admiration generally.

KAU-O-LU-PE, *v. Kauo* and *lupe*, kite. To draw; to pull this way and that, as a kite pulls the string of him who holds it.

KAU-O-WAA, *s. Kauo*, to drag, and *waa*, canoe. The work or business of drawing down canoes from the mountain when finished or partly so.

KAU-HA, *s.* The rectum, the third of the large intestines. *Anat.* 52.

KAU-HAU, *v.* To strike with a whip or stick; to throw a stone at, &c.

KAU-HA-KA-KE, *adj.* Short, &c. See KAUHEKEKE and KAUEKEKE.

KAU-HA-LE, *s. Kau*, place and *hale*, house. A small cluster of houses; a village. *Puk.* 8:5.

2. A house or residence of a person.

3. A place where a house has been, or where one is designed to be.

KAU-HE-KE-KE, } *adj.* Short, as a coat
KAU-HE-KE-KEI, } or gown. See KAUEKEKE.

KA-U-HI-U-HI, *s.* Name of a forest tree, timber used for the boards of the holua and for oos for tilling the ground.

KAU-HI-LO, *v.* To fasten with a rope the sticks of a building while in the course of erection; he aho mai waho mai o ka hale i ka manawa e *kauhilo* ai; alaila, *kauhilo* ia ka hale a pau.

KAU-HO-LA, *s.* Some disease of the neck and chest.

KAU-HO-LA, *v.* To open; to expand; to unfold, as a kapa folded up; as a flower in blooming.

KAU-HO-LO, *v.* To wish and try to condemn one.

2. To try to bring one to terms or obey orders.

3. To send after, and try to get one back who has gone.

KAU-HO-LO-PA-PA, *s.* Name of a person who knows himself to be a chief by birth but others know it not, and he refuses to hang his clothes among those of other people; ua kapaia aku ia he alii *kauholopapa*, no ka mea, ma ka holopapa i ikeia ai kona alii ana.

KAU-HUA, *v.* To conceive; to become pregnant.

2. To swell out, as one with child.

3. *Hoo.* To conceive; to be full of. *Hal.* 7:14. To be full morally of evil.

4. To put down in letters; to reduce to writing; no ko oukou kaikaina hanane mahoe i *hookauhua* ia (i keia manao) i ka malama o Augate: *hookauhua* paha auanei kakou iloko o ka hewa.

KAU-HUA, *s.* The swelling out of pregnant females.

2. The longing of pregnant women, especially the sickness of stomach.

3. The state of pregnancy; ua *kauhua*, ua ko, ua hapai.

4. The act of writing down words or thoughts.

KAU-HU-HU, *s.* A ridge or edge of a precipice.

2. The pole running lengthways of the house to which the tops of the rafters are fastened; a ridge pole.

3. The shark that was formerly worshiped.

KAU-KAI, *v.* To wait for an event to happen, or for any change in affairs; *kaukai* aku nei ka pono, it is better to wait awhile. *Laieik.* 67.

KAU-KAU, *v.* To set or fix, as a snare or net for birds. See KAU. *Hal.* 141:9.

2. To take counsel; to revolve in one's mind. *Hal.* 13:2.

3. To speak to one, especially to chide; to speak reproachfully; e nuku; to address one, as a petitioner, and in a way of complaint. *Laieik.* 71.

4. To explain; to make clear, i pohihi ole.

KAU-KAU, *s.* An appeal to one's sense of justice or compassion. *Laieik.* 76.

KAU-KAU, *s. Kaukau* is said to be a corruption of a Chinese word, and signifies to eat, to drink. It is used by foreigners in conversing with natives, and by natives conversing with foreigners.

KAU-KAU, *s.* A heap of stones made into a rude altar.

2. A snare so placed or fixed as to catch birds.

3. The name of a disease, the piles (mostly used in Oahu.)

4. The snaring or taking of fish; *kaukau* ulua.

5. What is clear, explicit in expression, without doubt.

KAU-KAU-A-LII, *s.* The name of a class of chiefs below the king; a prince. *Dan.*

1:3. O na 'lii malalo o ke alii nui. NOTE.—
The poe *kaukaualii* were generally the descendants of chiefs where the father was a
high chief and the mother a low chief, or
no chief at all.

KAU-KAU-LE-LE, *adj.* Nimble; active;
jumping.

KAU-KA-HI, *s.* *Kau*, canoe, and *kahi*, one.
A single canoe. See KAU. Ma ke kaulua
o Keopuolani, a ma ke *kaukahi* o Hoapili,
he waa aole i hoapipi ia, he waa hookahi.

2. *Figuratively*, a oneness; a perseverance; steadiness in doing a thing; ma ka
kaukahi kana hana ana, aole ma ka lauwili.

KAU-KA-LI, *v.* To wait for. See KALI.
Aole hoi kakou i haalele aku o ke kuku ame
ka wahahee *kaukali*.

KAU-KA-LI, *adj.* See example above.

KAU-KA-MA, *s.* *Eng.* A cucumber. *Nah.*
11:5. Na *kaukama* ulu wale, wild gourds.
2 *Nal.* 4:39.

KAU-KA-MA, *adj.* See KAMA. He kane
kama. *Kamak.*

KAU-KA-NA-WAI, *v.* *Kau*, to appoint, and
kanawai, law. To establish or appoint, as
a law; as a king or legislature.

KAU-KA-NA-WAI, *s.* One that makes
laws; a lawgiver. *Kin.* 49:10.

KAU-KA-NI or **TAU-SA-NI,** *s.* A thousand.

KAU-KO-KO, *v.* An ancient word not
much used. To string or hand on strings,
as a load to be carried on the mamake.

KAU-KO-LO, *v.* To chase, as a fowl; to
follow; to pursue.

2. To persevere in asking a favor until
obtained; e hoomoo, e hookoikoi.

3. To run and spread out, as the roots of
a tree just under the surface of the ground.

KAU-KO-LO, *s.* The small roots of a tree
spreading and running every way.

KAU-KU-KUI, *adj.* Of or belonging to a
candlestick or lamp. *Luk.* 8:16.

KAU-LA, *s.* A rope; a strong cord; a cord
or tendon in the animal system. *Anat.* 25.

2. *Kaula* uila, a chain of lightning.

3. A bow string. *Hal.* 11:2.

4. A line in a book or written document.
Isa. 28:10.

5. A stick laid across the rafters of a
house or the top of the posts, after the
manner of a beam; more properly written
kaola. See kaola.

6. In *geometry*, the chord of an arc of a
circle. *Anahonua* 28.

7. A lash, i. e., the wound of a lash in
whipping; a stripe. 2 *Kor.* 11:24.

KAU-LA, *s.* A prophet; one who preaches

or announces future events. *Oih.* 3:24.

KAU-LAE-LAE, *v.* To put up something
plainly to be seen; to exhibit clearly; to
make plain. See LAELAE.

KAU-LAI, *v.* To put up in the sun to
dry; kapili ma ka poi, a pili ka welu ma
ka laau, *kaulai* aku i ka la a maloo; to
hang up, as clothes to dry.

2. To lay aside for use. *Nah.* 11:32.

3. To hang up. *Puk.* 26:13.

4. To spread out in the sun. *Ier.* 8:2.

KAU-LAI, *s.* The act of drying what is
wet; things so put up to dry.

KAU-LA-HAO, *s.* *Kaula*, rope, and *hao*,
iron. A chain; a cable; a chain of any size.

KAU-LA-LEI, *s.* A bunch; thick together,
as a bunch of grapes.

KAU-LA-LU-A-HI-NE, *s.* The name of a
rope for binding a mat on to a canoe; o ke
kaulaluahine e moe ana ma ka aoao o ka
waa, oia ka mea e paa ai ka ahu. See AHU,
a mat.

KAU-LA-NA, *v.* To be or become famous
or renowned; to be celebrated for some
quality; ua *kaulana* aku keia wahi no ka
naauao, this place is *famous* for intelligence; a *kaulana* aku i na aina e, to be
renowned even to foreign lands.

2. *Hoo.* To publish; to spread abroad, as
news; to publish evil reports. *Kanl.* 22:14.

3. To make famous or renowned either
for good or evil.

KAU-LA-NA, *s.* Fame; report; renown.
Ios. 9:9.

2. Government of an island; he *kaulana*
o ka aina.

KAU-LA-NA, *adj.* Universally known,
noted or remarkable for some quality; celebrated; notable.

KAU-LA-NA-AA, *s.* A resting place on
the road. See OIOINA.

KAU-LA-NA-O-LE-LO, *s.* Formerly used
synonymous with hooilinaolelo. He kauoha, i. e., the will of a deceased person.

KAU-LA-WA-HA, *v.* *Kaula*, rope, and
waha, mouth. To bridle; to rein in; to
restrain, as a horse. FIG. Applied to the
tongue. *Iak.* 1:26.

KAU-LA-WA-HA, *s.* A mouth rope, i. e.,
a bridle. *Iak.* 3:2.

KAU-LA-WA-HI-NE, *s.* *Kaula*, prophet,
and *wahine*. A prophetess. *Puk.* 15:20.

KAU-LEI, *v.* To be insecure; e kauwale
iho iluna, aole mapopo o ka paa; to trust
to what will not benefit.

2. To be deceived in our opinion of a
thing.

3. To be too short for the purpose designed; *kaulei ka naau*, to be deceitful (perhaps.) *Kum. Haw.*, B. 2, p. 26.

KAU-LEI, *adj.* Not firmly established; deceptive; without secure foundation; applied to men seeking happiness in life and failing.

KAU-LE-O, *v.* To exhort; to urge or request one to do a thing; to enjoin, as a duty. *Pil.* 8.

2. To charge; to command one to say or do something to or for another. 1 *Nal.* 5:8.

KAU-LEI-LEI, *v.* See KAULEI.

KAU-LE-LE, *v. Kau* and *lele*, to be separated. See LELE. To add something on; to enlarge; to be or do something besides what was proposed, as in making a bargain; to add more so as to satisfy.

2. To spread over; to make abundant; to increase; manao iho la au, e *kaulele* aku i ko'u aloha maluna ou.

KAU-LE-LE, *s.* An addition made to something; an enlargement; that which is added to complete the bargain.

KAU-LE-LE, *adj.* Over and above; added on; enlarged; very great; he aloha *kaulele* ia oe e ka hoaluhi.

KAU-LE-LE, *adv.* With addition; excessively; ke aloha *kaulele* aku nei au ia oe.

KAU-LE-LE, *s.* A rocket.

KAU-LE-LE, *adj.* Flying. See LELE. That which is set a flying; hoike oia i ke ahi *kaulele*, he exhibited sky-rockets.

KAU-LI-A, *v.* Pass. of *kau* for *kauia*. *Gram.* § 48. Sometimes written *kauhia*.

1. To be hung up; to be suspended. *Kanl.* 21:23. Hence,

2. To kill; to slay. *Ios.* 10:26.

KAU-LI-KE, *v. Kau* and *like*, alike. To balance or hang even.

2. To make alike; to make no distinction; to be just; to be equal; to be right. *Ezek.* 18:28. SYN. with ewaewa ole.

3. To be just as good; to be as well as; ua pololei, ua *kaulike* keia mea me ka naauao.

4. In *law*, to deal in equity or righteously; to decree, decide or do that which is just, equitable and right without regarding the letter of the statute law.

KAU-LI-KE, *s.* Justice; uprightness; no partiality.

KAU-LI-KE, *adj.* Just; equitable.

2. In *geometry*, parallel, as lines; kaha *kaulike*, parallel lines. *Anahon.* 4.

KAU-LII-LII, *v. Kau* and *liilii*, little. To divide out in small quantities; to make distributions on a small scale.

KAU-LO-LO-A, *v.* To ask frequently for a thing; to tease in order to obtain a thing requested; a loaa i kekahi kanaka ke koi hao, a lohe ke alii, alaila *kauloloaia* aku la, a lilo mai la.

2. To speak to one (a chief) often as to an offense.

KAU-LUA, *s.* To be slack; to be remiss in fulfilling a promise; to delay the time of doing a thing. *Hoo.* To wait; to delay; to procrastinate; also *hookaukaulua*; to put off; to postpone. 2 *Pet.* 3:9. To linger in doing a thing. *Kin.* 19:16. To stay a long time in a place. 2 *Nal.* 15:20.

KAU-LUA, *v. Kau* and *lua*, two. To put two together; to yoke or harness together, as two animals. *Kanl.* 22:10.

KAU-LUA, *s.* The name of several things where two are put or used together; *kaulua*, a double-canoe; bipi *kaulua*, a yoke of oxen. 1 *Sam.* 11:7. *Kaulua* lio, a span of horses. 2 *Nal.* 7:14.

KAU-LUA, *s.* The name of the second month; the fourth month of the summer season.

KAU-LU-A-LI-O, *s.* See KAULUA above.

KA-U-LU-MA-LOO, *s.* The dry growth, the name of a famine.

KAU-MA-HA, *v.* To be heavy, as any substance.

2. To be weary with carrying a heavy burden.

3. To suffer oppression from rigorous service.

4. To be weary for want of sleep.

5. Applied to the mind, to be downcast in mind; to be heavy-hearted; to be sad; to be sorry; to be grieved. *Kin.* 40:6.

6. *Hoo.* To make heavy; to oppress; to treat one with rigor.

7. To afflict; to make one suffer unnecessarily; to be afflicted. *Oihk.* 23:27.

KAU-MA-HA, *v.* To offer in sacrifice; to kill a victim for sacrifice; to offer a gift upon an altar. *Puk.* 3:18.

KAU-MA-HA, *s.* Weight, as of a burden; weariness; heaviness; depression of spirits; nui ke *kaumaha* o kona naau no ko lakou luku wale ana, he was very *sorrowful* at such a slaughter of men.

KAU-MA-HA, *s.* A sacrifice; a service rendered to God.

KAU-MA-HA, *adj.* Heavy loaded, as a person or a beast of burden; burdensome; applied to the mind, painful. *Hoo.* Hard bearing. *Puk.* 23:1.

KAU-MA-KAI-O-LE, *s.* An epithet of old

age. See NIHOKAHI, one tooth.

KAU-MA-KAI-O-LE, *v. Kau* and *makai*, to look, and ole, not. Not able to see or to see clearly; applied to old age. Generally *haumakaiole.*

KAU-MI-HAU, *v.* To appoint a kapu by the priest; men were separated from their wives, and a hog was baked, hence the name to bake a hog; a *kaumihau* ana ma ka la kaua.

KAU-MOO, *v.* To be inactive because of ignorance or uncertainty how to act; to be in doubt what to do, and hence, to do nothing; aole makou i mahi i ka aina, *kaumoo* wale no, i ke akaka ole.

KAU-MO-KU, } *v.* To cut short; to cut
KAU-MU-KU, } off; to shorten; to be unfit for the purpose desired.

KAU-NA, *s.* Four; the composite number four. *Oih.* 12:4. See Grammar § 116, 5.

KAU-NA-KO-MA, *s. Kauna,* four, and *koma* (*Eng.*), a comma. The four commas " " used in quoting another's words.

KAU-NE, *v.* To be slow; to be dilatory; to walk or move leisurely; to cause delay.

KAU-NE, *s.* Delay; slowness in doing a thing; lagging behind.

KAU-NEI-NEI, *v.* To cut off; to shorten; not to be sufficient; to be unsteady; to be unfinished. See KAULEI.

KAU-NO-A, *s.* A slender worm which when it comes upon a tree or herb, there is a universal withering; ua kau mai ke *kaunoa.*

2. The dodder, a parasitic plant.

KAU-NO-O-A, *s.* See KAUNOA 2. A species of vine which grows without a root.

KA-U-NU, *v.* To make angry; to provoke; to express the feeling of jealousy.

KA-U-NU-A-NA-LAU, *s.* Name of a large bird on Hawaii.

KAU-PAO-NA, } *v.* To weigh, as with
KAU-PAU-NA, } scales or steelyards; to weigh out, as goods or money; i. e., to pay out. *Isa.* 55:2. To weigh morally, as the deeds of men. 1 *Sam.* 2:3. As one's life and character. *Dan.* 5:27.

KAU-PAO-NA, } *s.* Scales for weighing;
KAU-PAU-NA, } steelyards or other instruments for weighing. *Hoik.* 6:5.

2. The weight of a thing. *Oihk.* 26:26.

KAU-PA-KU, *s. Kau* and *paku*, a partition. The upper ridge pole of a house, dividing the house properly so called and the bonnet or cap of the house. *Isa.* 22:1.

KAU-PA-KU, *v.* To put on the bonnet or thatch the ridge of a house; alaila, *kau-paku* a paa, pau ia hana.

KAU-PA-LE, *v. Kau* and *pale*, to defend off. To separate, i. e., to put a mark or sign of partition; to cause a division. *Isa.* 59:2. To stand between; to set or put, as an obstruction or division. *Hal.* 104:9. To raise a slight partition between, so as to stop a child. *Hoo.* To fence or partition off. FIG. To fence off, i. e., resist temptation to evil; *hookaupale* aku ia hewa.

KAU-PA-LE, *s.* Something coming between two things to separate them, either sensibly or imaginary; a boundary line between two lands; a partition in a house; a dam, &c.

KAU-PE, *v.* To put down; to put low; to humble; to crush. See PE.

KAU-PI-LI, *v.* Used in a mele as follows:

> *Kaupili* alo ula o Maheha,
> O ke kanaka no kuhe i ka wai.

KAU-PI-LI, *s.* To unite, as man and wife; to love one another, as two persons.

KAU-POO-HI-WI, *v. Kau* and *poohiwi,* the shoulder. To put or place on the shoulder; to shoulder, as something heavy; as firearms.

KAU-POO-HI-WI, *adj.* What is placed on the shoulder; applied to a musket; ua mahuahua iki ae na pu *kaupoohiwi,* the number of muskets (shoulder-guns) was a little increased.

KAU-PO-U-NA, *s.* Another orthography for *kaupaona,* but seldom used. See KAU-PAONA. Steelyards and scales for weighing.

KA-U-PU, *s.* Name of a large black bird the size of a turkey, found mostly on Nihoa and Kaula.

KAU-PU-A, *s.* An elevated cloud of singular appearance.

2. Name of an ancient pastime.

KAU-WA, *v.* See KAUA, *v.,* 5. A servant; in the most general sense, one who serves or does the business or labors for another.

1. Any subject of a king or chief.

2. A household or domestic servant.

3. A slave; a menial servant; *kauwa lepo,* an order of men who sacrificed themselves on the death of a chief.

KAU-WA, *v.* To serve; to do the will of another. *Hoo.* To serve another, as a people serve a king; to serve, as a master; to be in a state of bondage. *Puk.* 14:12.

KAU-WAI, *v.* To pour out, as water; to lead along, as a small stream; to pour into; to fill with water.

KAU-WAU, *s.* The sickness of dogs; sickness of all kinds.

KAU-WA-HI, *art.* Some; something; some place; any one place or thing. See KAU, place.

KAU-WA-HI, *s.* Some; some part; a part of a thing. *Isa.* 44:16. A parcel indefinitely large. *Kin.* 33:19. *Kauwahi o ke koko,* some of the blood. NOTE.—*Kauwahi* as a substantive rarely takes the article, except when it refers to place. *Mat.* 25:8. It has always the idea of a partitive.

KAU-WA-KA-NE, *s. Kauwa* and *kane,* male. A man or male servant. *Kanl.* 5:18.

KAU-WA-LU-PE, *v. Kauwa* and *lupe,* kite. To carry; applied to persons who have a friend in danger from others, some taking him by the arms, some by the legs and other parts to carry him off.

KAU-WA-WA-HI-NE, *s. Kauwa* and *wahine,* female. A maid servant. *Puk.* 20:14.

KAU-WE-LU, *v.* To put up some signal that the year has past and that a new year is begun; ma ka malama o Ikuwa e *kauwelu* ai ka makahiki.

KAU-WE-WE, *s.* A covering, or what is put on top of an imu or oven in baking food.

2. A ruffle for the neck, not for the bosom, that is *pihapiha.*

KAU-WI-LA, *v.* To appoint as a day of consecrating a heiau; o kekahi akua o Kauikauila; e hoomakaukau no ka la e *kauwila* ai ka heiau. *Laieik.* 164.

KAU-WI-LA, *s.* Another orthography for *kauila.* See KAUILA. A species of hard reddish wood found on Kauai, used for war spears, kapa mallets, &c.

KAU-WI-LA, *adj.* A day or time under a kapu; a kokoke i ka la *kauwila. Laieik.* 164.

KAU-WI-LI, *v.* To mingle in with other things.

2. To gather on to a moving thing, as people join on to a traveling party.

KAU-WO, *v.* To pull; to draw, &c. See KAUO.

KAU-WO-HA, *v.* To give a charge, &c. See KAUOHA.

KAU-WO-WO, *v.* To increase; to grow thriftily. See KAUOUO.

KA-HA, *v.* To scratch; to make marks; to write; to make marks indefinitely.

2. To cut; to hew, as timber.

3. To cut open, as a fish or animal; to rip open, as the belly of a person. *Amos* 1:13.

4. To turn about and go away; to go off; to set out to go. *Laieik.* 67.

5. *Hoo.* To seize; to take with one's knowledge, but without his consent; to rob; to take what is another's. See HOO-

KAHA, an extortion. See MAKAHA.

KA-HA, *v.* To stand sideways; to stand up on the edge like the comb of a cock; to tread water; to swim standing up. *Laieik.* 92.

2. To land or be thrown on the shore from the surf without a surf-board.

3. FIG. To press the land on the back, as when one lands on shore in the surf; e *kaha* i ka nalu; hence the proverbial expression, ua *kaha* aku la ka nalu o kuu aina, means (LIT. The surf has pressed upon my land) to have a famine for land, i. e., to press, to squeeze the people for food.

KA-HA, *s.* A scratch; a mark; a letter.

2. In *mathematics,* a line.

3. A strip of barren land on the sea shore; hence,

4. Barren land anywhere where upland kalo will not grow, but the people depend on another place.

5. The channel of a small stream. See KAHAWAI and KAHAKAI.

KA-HA, *s.* A kind of paper or cloth.

2. The crack of a whip; the report of a pistol.

3. Robbery; plunder; rapine; oppression.

KA-HA, *v.* To be fat; to be plump; to be full, as a well-fed animal. *Kin.* 41:2.

KA-HA, *s.* Largeness; fatness; plumpness; aohe io o ke *kaha.*

KA-HA-A-KU-A, *s. Kaha,* marks, and *akua,* god. A track of a god in a desert place.

KA-HA-A-PO, *s. Kaha,* marks, and *apo,* hoop. LIT. An embracing mark.

1. The circumference; he umi kapuai ke *kahaapo* o kekahi, ten feet is the circumference of some.

2. In *grammar,* brackets [ ].

KA-HA-E-A, *v.* See OMAOMAO. To extend over the heavens as a cloud, variegated, black, white, blue, &c.; ua *kahaea* luna, ua hoopono i ka maka o ka opua.

Ua omaomao ka lani, ua *kahaea* luna,
Ua pipi ka maka o na hoku.

KA-HA-E-A, *s.* The name of a disease, the thrush; the scald head; then goes over the body and is called *kahaea.*

2. The name of a god.

KA-HA-E-A, *s.* A singular appearance of the sky in the morning: a sign of rain; he *kahaea* ia, he aouli ua ia.

KA-HAI, *v.* To gird; to bind on a girdle.

2. To decrease, as a noise; to cease; to come to and to be quiet. See KANAHAI.

KA-HAI, *s.* A girdle; a belt; a fillet.

2. Quietness; stillness after a clamor.

KA-HAU, *v.* To abate, as the wind; pehea ka makani? Ua *kahau* iki mai, aole ikaika: e holo kakou.

2. To be diminished, as sickness; ua *kahau* iki mai kou mai, ua pale ka nui.

3. To abate, as a stream of water; *kahau* ka wai, kokoke pau.

KA-HAU, *s.* The name of a play or pastime; he *kahau* kahi hana.

KA-HA-U-LA, *adj.* See AIKAHAULA and MOEKAHAULA.

KA-HA-U-LE, *v.* *Kaha,* to cut, and *ule,* penis. To circumcise. See KAHEULE.

KA-HA-HA', *int.* An expression of wonder, surprise or displeasure. NOTE.—Hawaiians in the use of this word express a great variety of shades of meaning, according to the pronunciation, tone of voice, &c.

KA-HA-HA', *v.* To wonder or be surprised at a thing; to be astonished at the sight of a thing or at an idea expressed by one; to marvel; to hiss at; to treat with contempt; to be in doubt or perplexity of what one sees or hears and know not how to account for; to think a thing strange. 1 *Pet.* 4:4. NOTE.—This word is used with *manao* or *naau* to express wonder.

KA-HA-HA-IA, *s.* A wonder; an object of wonder or astonishment to the beholder, as something unaccountable. *Kanl.* 28:3.

KA-HA-HA-NAI, *s.* *Kaha* and *hanai,* the name of the strings that surround a calabash; hence, in geometry, the radius of a circle. *Anahon.* 23.

KA-HA-HUI, *s.* *Kaha,* a mark, and *hui,* to unite. In *music,* a brace.

KA-HA-KAI, *s.* *Kaha,* mark, and *kai,* sea. The sea shore. *Kin.* 49:13.

2. The sand of the sea beach.

3. The name of the region of country bordering on the sea.

KA-HA-KA-HA, *v.* The 13th conj. of *kaha,* to mark, &c. To mark or scratch frequently. 1 *Sam.* 21:13. To write upon paper or a slate. *Puk.* 31:18. To engrave on stone or copper; to write in the sand or upon the ground; aole anei e *kahakaha* ko kakou naau i kekahi hena o kele kanaka? To cut off; to divide frequently.

KA-HA-KA-HA, *s.* *Hoo.* A display; a show of dress; a parade, &c. See HOOKAHAKAHA.

KA-HA-KA-HA, *s.* An engraving; a writing. *Puk.* 28:21.

KA-HA-KA-HA-NA, *s.* The clothes in which a corpse is dressed; grave clothes. *Ioan.* 11:44.

KA-HA-KE-LE-A-WE, *s.* *Kaha,* to cut, and *keleawe,* copper. A cutting of copper; an engraving; ka mea a ka poe *kahakeleawe* i hanai'i.

KA-HA-KU-HI, *s.* *Kaha,* mark, and *kuhi,* to point out. In *grammar,* any letter, mark or character directing the reader to the margin or bottom of the page.

KA-HA-KI-KI, *v.* To pour down violently, as rain.

KA-HA-LA, *s.* Name of a species of fish.

KA-HA-LA-HA-LA, *s.* He *kahalahala,* ua palai.

KA-HA-LA-WAI, *s.* The mixing of two unlike substances so as to make a third unlike, as paints of different colors.

KA-HA-LE-LE-LE-PO, *s.* The name of a famine in former times.

KA-HA-LI-LI, *v.* To struggle.

KA-HA-LO-A, *s.* The name of a stone brought before a priest in a certain pule anaana.

KA-HA-NA, *s.* The name of a valley on Kauai.

KA-HA-NI-A, *v.* N inserted for *l.* To be shaven; to be cut close; to be made smooth, as a shaven head; *kahania* ke poo o ka ohule.

KA-HA-PI-LI, *s.* *Kaha,* a mark, and *pili,* to touch. In *geometry,* a tangent of a circle. *Anahon.* 23.

KA-HA-PO-AI, *s.* *Kaha,* a mark, and *poai,* to surround. In *geometry,* the line of a circle; the circumference of a circle.

KA-HA-POO-HI-WI, *s.* *Kaha,* fat, and *poohiwi,* shoulder. The fat or muscle on the shoulder-blade or over it.

KA-HA-PUU, *s.* Name of a plant of the fern species growing on the mountains, eaten in time of famine for food. See HAPUU.

KA-HA-WAI, *s.* *Kaha,* a small stream and *wai,* water. A brook; a rivulet; a water course; a cascade; a stream with frequent rapids; any small stream. *Kanl.* 8:7.

KA-HE, *v.* To spill; to pour out, as water or blood.

2. To run, as water; to flow, as a stream or river.

3. To flow, i. e., to abound in any substance. *Nah.* 14:8.

4. To drop; to trickle, as tears. *Ezek.* 24:16.

5. To flow, as froth from the mouth of a person in a fit.

6. To flow, as blood from a wound.

7. *Hoo.* To cause to flow or run, as a liquid, i. e., to water, as a land; to shed or cause to flow, as blood in murder. *Kin.* 37:22.

8. To cause to flow back, as the sea. *Puk.* 14:21.

* * * * * O keaka,
O na pue o Kaikua ku i ka maka ili,
Hanini, ninilani e luai e ao
E *kahe* e kakahi mai auanei
Ka omaka wai kapu o Lono.

KA-HE, *v.* To cut or slit longitudinally; to cut off; with omaka, to circumcise after the Hawaiian manner; to castrate; to shave. See KAHI.
2. To bind round the waist; to gird.
3. To begin to wither, as leaves eaten by a worm.

KA-HE, *s.* Hoo. A flowing; a flowing of blood; he poko ma kauwahi, he la ma kauwahi, he hauoki ma kauwahi, he kahe ma kauwahi.

KA-HE-A, *v.* See HEA, to call. To call any one for any purpose. *Oihk.* 1:1.
2. To cry to one for help; to call upon one, as in prayer. *Puk.* 14:15.
3. To speak; to call aloud.
4. To cry out, as in pain.

KA-HE-A, *v.* To be dirty; to be foul; to be corrupt. See PALAHEA.

KA-HE-A, *adj.* Foul; filthy.

KA-HE-A-WAI, *v.* To flow; to be soft; to run like water.
2. To be multitudinous.

KA-HEE, *v.* See HEE, to slip; to slide. To slip flowers along from the needle or manai to the string in making wreaths.

KA-HEI, *v.* To tie round, as a girdle or belt; to gird on. See KAEI.

KA-HEI, *s.* A belt; a band around the belly of a person.
2. A sack passing over the shoulders, as a soldier's belt.
3. A cloth for preserving goods.

KA-HE-U, *v.* To clean weeds, as in a garden; to put a garden in order; to stir up the dirt, pull up the weeds, grass, &c. See HEU.

KA-HE-U-LE, *v.* *Kahe*, to cut, and *ule*, the penis. To circumcise. See KAHE.

KA-HE-U-MI-U-MI, *s.* *Kahe*, to cut, and *umiumi*, beard. A beard cutter, i. e., a razor.

KA-HE-HI, *v.* To slip; to mistake; to slip off.

KA-HE-KA, *s.* Na io paakai liu o na *kaheka.*

KA-HE-KO-KO, *s.* *Kahe*, to flow, and *koko*, blood. *Literally*, the shedding of blood; ua *kahekoko* i ka nahua e ke anu.

KA-HE-LA, *s.* The name of the swell of the sea when it comes along the western shore of Hawaii from the south.

KA-HE-LA, *v.* To move along, as the kahela above mentioned.

Kahela ka nalu o ka pae lauhala,

Hoo aiai ke kaiko o Maliu—e.

KA-HE-LA-HE-LA, *v.* To lie spread out, as a person asleep, his limbs extended and spread apart. See KAHELA.

Kuhela, kahelahela ka lae o Lele.

KA-HE-LE, *s.* LIT. The going. A braiding; a wreathing, as of vines; a platting of leaves.
2. The name of the common adze.

KA-HE-NA-WAI, *s.* LIT. *Kahe-na-wai*, flowing of water. A water brook; running water.

KA-HE-WA, *v.* To miss; to make an attempt but not succeed; to try and to be foiled.

KA-HI, *v.* To rub gently with the thumb and finger.
2. To comb, as the hair. NOTE.—The idea is from the *motion* of rubbing, polishing, sawing, &c.
3. To cut; to shave, as the beard. 2 *Sam.* 10:4.
4. To cut, that is, to tear; to lacerate. *Lunk.* 8:7. See KAHE, to cut, &c. Mea *kahi* umiumi, a barber.
5. To cut, as the hair. *Lunk.* 16:17. From the old manner of sawing off the hair with bamboo knives.
6. To slit open, i. e., cut longitudinally; *kahi* i ka opu, *kahe* i ka omaka. See KAHE. NOTE.—The feeble sound of *e* and *i* so much resemble each other that both orthographies are used, i. e., *kahe* and *kahi*, to cut, though the latter is preferable.

KA-HI, *s.* A place; some definite place spoken of or understood; it does not admit of the definite article; often SYN. with wahi. *Kahi* kuai, a market place, or simply a market; ma *kahi* e aku, at another place; *kahi* kakakaka o ko'u kina, the beaten place of my offense; *kahi* hoana, a holy place; a sanctuary. *Nah.* 3:28.

KA-HI, *art. Gram.* § 65. One; some one; some; it takes the article *ke—kekahi*, which see. Some; a part; a portion; o ka ia *kahi* na ke akua, some fish for the god. See HOOKAHI.

KA-HI-AU, *v.* To give away lavishly and inconsiderately.

KA-HI-AU, *adj.* Lavish of gifts; wasting of property by indiscriminate giving; he kanaka *kahiau*. See KIHIKAU.

KA-HI-O, *adj.* Proud.

KA-HI-O-LO-NA, *adj.* Of cutting or peeling olona; ma ka hale *kahiolona*, at the house for cutting olona. *Laieik.* 206.

KA-HI-U-MI-U-MI, *v.* *Kahi* and *umiumi*, beard. To shave off the beard.

Ka-hi-u-mi-u-mi, *s.* A beard cutter, i. e., a barber. See **Kaheumiumi.**

Ka-hi-hi, *v.* See **Hihi.** To entangle; to choke, as weeds do plants. *Mat.* 13:7.

2. To sue one at law; to cause one to be entangled with a law or kapu. *Mat.* 5:40.

3. To entangle one by accusing him; to tell false stories; to slander.

4. To block up an entrance; ua *kahihi* ka puka o ka hale e ka upena nanana, the door of the house was stopped with a spider's web.

Ka-hi-hi, *s.* Entanglement; perplexity.

Ka-hi-ka-hi, *v.* To scratch out, as writing with a knife.

Ka-hi-ka-ka-ka-ka, *s.* A nau no e hookomo iho ma kahikakakaka o ko'u kina. *Kahi* here is probably the noun, and *kakakaka* the adjective.

Ka-hi-ka-le-na, *v.* To finish; to dispose of before another is aware, as if a part of a family should eat up the food while part were absent; a e anai mai *kahikalena* ku i kapa—hai ka mea haku ole; pau loa, aohe mea koe.

Ka-hi-ki, *s.* It takes no article. The general name of any foreign country; hai mai la oia i na 'lii i kona holo i *kahiki,* he told the chiefs of his sailing to a foreign country; hence, *holokahiki* means any Hawaiian who has been to a foreign land.

Ka-hi-ko, *s.* The name of the first man upon the Hawaiian Islands according to some genealogies; ua hou ia mai, ma ka mookuauhau i kapaia *Ololo,* he kane ia kanaka mua loa, o *Kahiko* kona inoa, it is said again, in the genealogy called *Ololo,* that the very first inhabitant was a male, whose name was *Kahiko.* The question here discussed is whether the first person on the Islands was a man or woman. *D. Malo,* chap. 3, 4.

Ka-hi-ko, *v.* To be or become old; to fade, as a flower or leaf; ua kahiko e, to become old prematurely; to be ancient.

Ka-hi-ko, *adj.* Old; ancient; that which is long past; poe kahiko, the ancients; the old people; wa kahiko, old time.

Ka-hi-ko, *s.* An elderly person; an old man; elua mau mea kahiko, e kipakuia'na, e hele pela, two old men, they were being driven away. Syn. with poohina. *Iob.* 15:10.

Ka-hi-ko, *v.* To put on or dress in superb clothing; to put on splendid apparel for appearance sake; to be clothed splendidly. *Mat.* 6:29.

2. To deck or put on ornaments, as an Eastern bride. *Isa.* 61:10.

3. To adorn with royal robes, as ancient kings in their armor. *Laieik.* 112. To go in full armor, as a soldier equipped. *Kanl.* 3:18.

4. To be armed for battle.

5. To show honor; to dignify by honorable treatment. 1 *Kor.* 12:23.

Ka-hi-ko, *s.* A splendid dress; the dress and ornaments, as of an Eastern bridegroom. *Isa.* 61:10.

2. The priestly robes of Aaron. *Puk.* 29:21. Na *kahiko* laa, the consecrated garments.

3. Armor; defensive weapons; military dress. *Epes.* 6:13.

4. The furniture of a house, especially handsome costly furniture; e hookupu paha no ko lakou waiwai, ko lakou *kahiko* o ka hale.

Ka-hi-ko-kau-a, *adj.* Hale *kahikokaua,* house for armory. *Isa.* 22:8.

Ka-hi-ko-hi-ko, *v.* To be very aged; to be well versed in ancient affairs; to speak in the language of ancient times; to follow ancient customs.

Ka-hi-ko-lu, *s.* Three in one; the Trinity; used only in the Scriptural sense; the Godhead, Father, Son and Holy Spirit.

Ka-hi-ko-lu, *adj.* Three-fold; three in one.

Ka-hi-li, *s.* See **Hili,** to plat; to twist. A brush generally, but especially a flybrush, made of feathers bound on to a stick.

2. *Emphatically,* the large brushes used by the chiefs; they were used as badges of royalty on all public occasions.

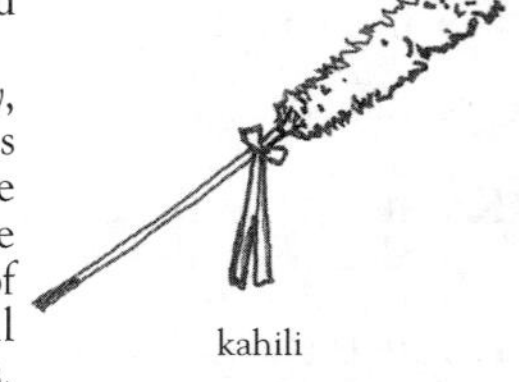

kahili

Ka-hi-li, *v.* To brush; to sweep, as with a broom; to sweep, as a house. *Mat.* 12:44. To wipe.

2. To sweep away, as the wind blows away light substances; hence,

3. To destroy.

4. To change; to be changeable.

Ka-hi-li-hi-li, *v.* To scatter away; to brush off, as small dust or light substances.

Ka-hi-mo-e, *s.* *Kahi,* place, and *moe,* to sleep. A sleeping place; a bedstead.

Ka-hi-na, *v.* See **Hina,** to fall. To fall before one; to be victim at one's intrigue or displeasure.

2. To supplant; to take the advantage

of one. *Kin.* 27:36.

KA-HI-NA-LII, *s.* Proper name of a celebrated chief in whose days was the flood; hence, kaiakahinalii, the flood. See also HINALII with the article dropped.

KA-HI-NU, *v.* See HINU. To rub over with oil; to anoint. *Kanl.* 28:40.

2. To rub over or anoint, as a sacrifice, with a brush large in the middle.

3. To rub or grease the runners of a sled or holua which was formerly used. See HOLUA.

4. To roast, as meat. *Kanl.* 16:7.

KA-HO-A, *v.* To appease one who may be angry with us; to exhort an evil person to be good, to do right, &c.

KA-HO-A-HO-A, *v.* To be still; to behave quietly; to do no evil.

KA-HO-A-KA, *s.* The spirit or soul of a person still living, supposed to be seen by priests; nona ia *kahoaka* e hihia nei, he uhane, he haili, he uhane kakaola.

KA-HOI, *v.* To hinder; to keep back.

KA-HOO-KU-I, *s.* A union; a joining; a uniting. See KUI and HOOKUI.

KA-HO-HO, *v.* To cry out or after one. See HOOHO.

KA-HO-HO, *s.* A crying out; a shouting; a calling.

KA-HO-KAI, *v.* To mix up.

2. *Hoo.* To mix two ingredients, as earth and water; to mix up, as in making bread.

KA-HO-LO, *v.* To work rapidly at any business.

2. To row quickly.

3. To jostle; to be moved or put out of place; e omau, e holo luna.

KA-HO-LO, *adj.* Movable; unfixed; unsteady.

KA-HU, *v.* To bake in the ground as Hawaiians do; to cook food.

2. To kindle or make a fire; to burn, as lime in a pit; to burn, as brick. *Kin.* 11:3. To burn; to consume. *Ezek.* 39:9. SYN. with puhi. *Kahu* umu, to bake in an oven; a contracted form is *kahumu*. See below.

KA-HU, *s.* An honored or upper servant; a guardian or nurse for children. *Rut.* 4:16. Hence, a feeder; a keeper; a provider; *kahu* hipa, a shepherd.

KA-HU, *v.* To be or act as a servant. *Hoo.* To act the part of a servant; to have or take the care of persons or property; spoken of a king, to take care of his people. 1 *Nal.* 12:7.

KA-HU-A, *s.* The prepared foundation of a house, i. e., the ground cleared off and leveled down on which to set up a building;

ua maikai ke *kahua* o kekahi hale, the place (for the foundation) of the house is good.

2. A place of encampment for a company of travelers or an army; an open space proper for an encampment; a camp ground; *kahua* kaua, a camp. 2 *Sam.* 1:2. *Kahua* hehi palaoa, a thrashing floor. *Nah.* 18:27. *Kahua* mokomoko, a place where people assembled to wrestle. *Laieik.* 42.

KA-HU-A, *s.* Wrath; anger. See HUA, envy; jealousy.

KA-HU-A, *v.* To designate; to point out; to direct.

KA-HU-AI, *v.* *Kahu*, to bake, and *ai*, food. To bake kalo in the ground.

KA-HU-AI, *s.* A baker; one who prepares the food. *Kin.* 40:2.

KA-HU-AI, *v.* Pass. part. of *kahu*. That which is or has been burnt.

KA-HU-AI-NA, *s.* *Kahu* and *aina*, land. The head man of a land.

KA-HU-A-O-LE, *s.* *Kahua*, foundation, and *ole*, not. A good for nothing person; one useless.

KA-HU-A-O-MA-LIO, *s.* *Kahua*, foundation, and *malio*, the first dawn of morning light. *Literally*, the source of light and comfort.

2. *Figuratively*, the source of life's enjoyments, such as food, fish, mats and all the fruits of the land.

KA-HU-A-HA-LE, *s.* *Kahua* and *hale*, a house. The foundation of a house. See KAHUA. A town; a village; a cluster of houses.

KA-HU-A-HA-NE-NE, *s.* *Kahua* and *hanene*, low; vulgar. A place used for pleasure and vile purposes.

KA-HU-A-HI, *s.* *Kahu*, servant, and *ahi*, fire. One who has the care of the fire; a fire builder.

KA-HU-A-HI, *v.* To build a fire.

KA-HU-A-HOO-U-KA, *s.* *Kahua* and *hoo-uka*, to attack. A battle ground; a place selected for the contest of two armies.

KA-HU-A-HU-A, *s.* One engaged about the altar; one who has charge of the gods; a priest.

KA-HU-A-KAU-A, *s.* *Kahua* and *kaua*, war. A field of battle.

KA-HU-A-KO-I, *s.* A species of pastime formerly on the kahua with the koi; he kahu e kukele mai ai.

KA-HU-A-LE-A, *s.* Name of the place where people assembled for play or gaming or other pastime.

KA-HU-A-MAI-KA, *s.* The path made for

playing at maika. See MAIKA.

KA-HU-I-LA-O-KA-LA-NI, s. The lightning flash of heaven; one of the names of Kalai-pahoa, supposed to be a god from a foreign country, who entered the nioi, a tree on Lanai and Molokai, hence the tree was called by his name; it is very poisonous.

KA-HU-U-MU, v. To bake food in an oven; to cook food generally. See KAHU and UMU, oven.

KA-HU-U-MU, s. One who cooks or bakes food.

KA-HU-HI-PA, s. Kahu and hipa, sheep. A shepherd. Ioan. 10:11.

KA-HU-KA-HU, v. To offer a sacrifice to the gods; to sacrifice; to worship the god of fishermen, to the aumakua.

KA-HU-KA-HU, s. The sacrifice offered to the gods.

KA-HU-KI, v. To corrupt; to rot; to putrefy, as a dead body. See PALAKAHUKI.

KA-HU-KI, s. Corruption; putrefaction, especially of animal bodies.

KA-HU-KU-LA, s. Kahu and kula, school. A school committee; one having charge of schools.

KA-HU-LI, v. See HULI. To change; to turn over; to upset.
2. To overturn; to confound, as a language.
3. Hoo. To overturn; to overthrow; to pervert. Tit. 1:14. Hookahuli i ka pono, to pervert judgment. 1 Sam. 8:3.
4. To overthrow, as a city. Kin. 19:25.
5. To change; to confound; to confuse, as a language. Kin. 11:7.

KA-HU-LI, s. A change; an overthrow; an overturning.
2. Uprightness; correctness.
3. The singing or sounds of what Hawaiians suppose to be snails. Laieik. 149.
4. The snails themselves.

KA-HU-LI-O, s. Kahu and lio, a horse. One who tends or feeds a horse.

KA-HU-LI-HU-LI, v. See KAHULI and HULI. To be overturned; to be changed; to be tossed about frequently, as a ship in a storm; to rock; to wave; to stand in a tottering manner. See LULI.

KA-HU-LU-I, adj. Broad and well planned and built, as the foundation of a house; ina he kahua akea, a malaelae, he kahului ke kaua kupono ma ia kahua.

KA-HU-MO-KU, s. Kahu and moku, a ship. A mate of a ship; specifically, the second mate.

KA-HU-MU, s. Something relative to mahiai or farming.

KA-HU-MU, v. A contraction of kahu and umu. To bake in an oven; to bake, as kalo. Oihk. 26:26.

KA-HU-NA, s. Kahu and ana, a cooking. Hence, a general name applied to such persons as have a trade, an art, or who practice some profession; some qualifying term is generally added; as, kahuna lapaau, a physician; kahuna pule, a priest; kahuna kalai laau, a carpenter; kahuna kala, a silversmith; kahuna kalai, an engraver. Puk. 38:23. NOTE.—Generally in Hawaiian antiquities, the word kahuna without any qualifying term, refers to the priest or the person who offered sacrifices. Puk. 18:1. O ka mea pule i ka ke alii heiau, he kahuna pule ia. See the above and others in their own places.

KA-HU-NA, v. To exercise a profession; to work at one's appropriate business.
2. Specifically, to be or act the priest. Lunk. 18:19.
3. To sprinkle salt on a sacrifice; e kapi i ka paakai i awaawa ole. See KAHUNAHUNA.
4. Hoo. To sanctify or set apart to the priests' office. Puk. 28:41.

KA-HU-NA-AO, s. Kahuna, and ao, to teach. A preacher; a pulpit teacher; one whose business it is to impart knowledge to men.

KA-HU-NA-A-NA-NA, s. Kahuna and ana-ana, sorcery. One who uses divination or sorcery. Kanl. 18:10.

KA-HU-NA-HAI, s. Kahuna and hai, to speak. One who speaks or declares publicly; a preacher. 2 Tim. 1:11. The full form is kahunahai olelo.

KA-HU-NA-HOO-PIO-PIO, s. Kahuna and hoopiopio, to practice sorcery. A priest or one who practices sorcery in connection with his priest's office.

KA-HU-NA-HU-NA, v. To sprinkle; to sprinkle a little salt upon meat; to sprinkle salt or water in small quantities; e kapi awaawa ole i ka paakai. See KAHUNA 2.

KA-HU-NA-HU-NA, s. See HUNA and HU-NAHUNA, small particles, &c. Small particles of any substance, as small bits of food, fine dust.
2. A fog; a mist, &c.

KA-HU-NA-KA-LAI, s. Kahuna and kalai, to hew. One who hews out canoes; a carpenter generally.

KA-HU-NA-KII, s. There are several forms of this term; as, kahuna o na kii, kahuna pule kii aoao. The director and guide of the high chief or king in things relating to war; ma ka wa e kaua ai, o ke *kahunakii* ka mea alakai mua i ke alii nui ma kana oihana.

KA-HU-NA-LA-PA-AU, *s.* *Kahuna* and *la-paau*, to heal. A physician; a doctor of medicine.

KA-HU-NA-PE-LE, *s.* *Kahuna* and *pele.* The priest or priestess of Pele.

2. The worshipers of Pele.

KA-HU-NA-PU-LE, *s.* *Kahuna* and *pule,* prayer. A priest; one who publicly officiates in the exercises of religion.

KA-HU-PU-AA, *s.* *Kahu* and *puaa,* swine. One who tends or feeds swine; a swine herd. *Mat.* 8:33.

KA-HU-WAI, *s.* *Kahu* and *wai,* water. One who has the charge or oversight of the division of water.

KA-HU-WAI, *s.* A brook or stream of water. See KAHAWAI.

KA-HU-BA-KA, *s.* *Kahu* and *baka* (*Eng.*), tobacco. A servant of the chiefs who has charge of their tobacco, lights their pipes, smokes a little himself, and presents it to his master.

KA-HU-BI-PI, *s.* *Kahu* and *bipi,* an ox or cow. A keeper of cattle; a herdsman. *Kin.* 13:7, 8.

KA-KA, *v.* *Ka,* to strike; to dash. To beat; to whip.

2. To cut and split or break wood (this was anciently done, not with an axe, but by striking sticks against stones or rocks.)

3. To wash, as dirty clothes (this is done by Hawaiians by beating them.)

4. To strike, as fire with flint and steel; *ka* or *kaka* ahi.

5. To thrash, as grain. *Rut.* 2:17.

6. To rip open. *2 Nal.* 18:12.

7. To dip or bail out water. See KA.

KA-KA, *v.* To be odorous or sweet-scented; to smell agreeably.

KA-KA, *s.* Fruits that grow in clusters, as grapes; much fruit in one place.

KA-KA, *s.* A bird; a species of duck; he manu nene.

KA-KAA, *v.* See KAA, to roll. To roll; to turn this way and that.

2. To stare or gaze with wonder; to strain the eyes with looking.

3. To turn aside from; to deviate from a right line; to sail in a zigzag manner.

4. To squint.

KA-KAA, *adj.* Rolling.

2. Watery; sore eyed.

KA-KAA, *s.* A watery or sore eye.

KA-KAE, *v.* To run; to be spry; to be quick.

KA-KAE, *adj.* Spry; lively, as a child in walking.

KA-KAI, *v.* See KAI, to lead. To go along in company; *kakai* ka aha i muli honua, the company followed all together; to travel together as a huakai or caravan; *kakai* lua ka hele a kanaka.

2. To follow, as chickens do a hen.

3. To follow one after another, as in Indian file.

4. To look carefully around, as with an evil design.

5. To gird on to the loins, as a sword.

6. To pray, as in ancient times at a great kapu occasion; *kakai* ka aha a loaa hoi.

7. To copulate, as the different sexes.

8. *Hoo.* To look after; to see to; aka, aole e pau i ka *hookakai* aku.

KA-KAI, *s.* A company traveling together.

2. A family, including servants, dependents, &c.

3. A litter, as of animals.

4. A cloud that hangs low near the ground; he makani auanei, ke kau mai la ke *kakai* o Waimea.

5. Name of some of the strings used in tying up a calabash.

KA-KAI-A-PO-LA, *s.* The tail of a kite; alaila, nakinaki na kaula hanai ame ke *ka-kaiapola* ame ke aho. See KAIKAIAPOLA.

KA-KAI-E-LE, } *v.* To be slow; to be
KA-KAI-HI-LI, } sluggish; to lag behind.

KA-KA-O-KO, *adj.* Dull; slow; crooked.

KA-KAI-KA-HI, *v.* To be few; to be scarce; to be seldom occurring; hence, to be precious. 1 *Sam.* 3:1.

KA-KAI-KA-HI, *adj.* Few; scarce; here and there one; a small number.

KA-KAI-PAU-DA, *s.* *Eng.* A cartridge box; also *kapepauda.*

KA-KA-O-LA, *s.* The spirit or soul of a living person as seen or pretended to be seen by the kahuna kilokilo or juggling priest. If many spirits were seen in company they were called *oio.* The ghost of a single deceased person was called *kinowai-lua,* which see.

KA-KAI-PA-LI, *s.* See KAKAI, a going. A going down a pali.

2. The descent of a pali.

KA-KA-O-LE-LO, *s.* *Kaka* and *olelo,* word. A counsellor; an adviser; a lawgiver; a scribe; one skilled in language; kekahi poe kanaka akamai i ke *kakaolelo,* certain men skillful in judgment.

KA-KAU, *v.* See KAU. To write; to

mark with a pen or pencil; to make letters.

2. To write upon; to print or paint on kapa, as in former times; to put down for remembrance. *Nah.* 33:2.

3. To describe; to mark out; to designate; to divide out into parcels, as land. *Ios.* 18:6, 8.

KA-KAU, *s.* A writing, i. e., anything written.

2. The act of writing, hence,

3. A taking, i. e., writing down the names of persons who are to pay tribute. *Luk.* 2:1.

KA-KAU-A-LII.

KA-KAU-O-LE-LO, *s.* *Kakau* and *olelo*, word. A person whose business it is to keep or write a record.

2. A scribe; a clerk; a secretary. 2 *Sam.* 8:17.

KA-KAU-HA, *v.* To stretch out, as the arm with muscular energy; to exert great strength; hence,

2. To oppress; to be hard or cruel to those who are subject.

3. To bring under bondage; to cause one to groan through hard service.

4. *Hoo.* To oppress; to harass; to impose burdens upon.

5. To stretch out the hand to punish. *Puk.* 7:5. Hookaumaha iho la me ka *hookakauha* maluna o kanaka, he oppressed and imposed upon the people.

KA-KAU-HA, *adj.* Stretched out, i. e., strong; powerful; stiff; *kakauha* kuu puu, my neck is stiff; strained, as a large rope; as the muscles of the arm in exerting strength; *kakauha* ka lima; energetic. *Puk.* 6:6. Hard; severe; exacting.

KA-KAU-KA-HA, *v.* To print, paint or mark, as on the skin. *Oihk.* 19:28.

KA-KAU-MOO-O-LE-LO, *s.* *Kakau* and *moo-olelo*, a connected story. A record. 2 *Sam.* 20:24.

KA-KA-HA, *s.* Name of a shallow place out in the sea.

KA-KA-HE, *v.* See KAHE, to flow. To flow; to overflow; to run, as a liquid; to melt; to flow, as a melted substance. 2 *Pet.* 3:12.

KA-KA-HE, *s.* A flowing brook; a flowing or dripping of water.

KA-KA-HE-A-WAI, *s.* A brook; a flowing stream. See KAHAWAI.

KA-KA-HE-LE, *v.* *Kaka* and *hele*, to go. To go quickly; to move quick; to be in a hurry.

KA-KA-HE, *v.* An error perhaps in writing for *kakahi.* To break; to dispel; ua *kakahe* ae i ka manawa pono e hana'i, he broke in upon the proper time to work.

KA-KA-HI, *s.* An iron hoop. See KAKAKI.

KA-KA-HI-A-KA, *s.* *Kakahi* and *aka*, shade. LIT. Breaking the shade (of night), i. e., morning; *kakahiaka* nui, early in the morning. *Puk.* 8:16.

KA-KA-HI-A-KA, *v.* To be or become morning.

KA-KA-HI-KI, *adj.* Conversing a long time to no purpose; waste of time in vain talk. See MAILEKAHIKI.

KA-KA-HI-LI, *s.* Long conversation about many things without much profit.

KA-KA-HOU, *adj.* Just planted.

KA-KA-HOU, *v.* E kakaola, q. v.

KA-KA-KA, *s.* A bow for shooting arrows; a cross-bow. 1 *Oihl.* 12:2.

KA-KA-KA, *v.* To crook; to arch; to bend, as a bow.

KA-KA-KAU, *v.* To write, as a law. 2 *Oihl.* 31:3.

KA-KA-KA-KA, *adj.* Small cracks or open spaces in any substance; a nau no e hooko-mo iho ma kahi *kakakaka* o ko'u kino.

KA-KA-KE, *s.* A species of potato. See KAKE.

KA-KA-KI, *s.* See KAKAHI. An iron hoop; iron from a hoop, i. e., hoop iron; hookahi puaa, hookahi pauku *kakaki*, one hog for one piece of iron hoop. *Mooolelo Hawaii.*

KA-KA-KII, *v.* To blunder in speaking; to speak without regard to truth; to be careless of what one says.

KA-KA-KII, *s.* Carelessness in speaking; falsehood.

KA-KA-KI-HI, *v.* To step lightly; to step softly; to go quickly; to run lightly.

KA-KA-LA, *v.* To be rough with sharp points; to be craggy; to be sharp, as a needle, pin, &c.

KA-KA-LA, *s.* The breaking of the surf.

2. Anything sharp pointed; small and sharp, like a needle.

3. The spur of a cock. See KALA, to sharpen.

4. A species of worm that destroys potatoes and other vegetables; same as *pelua* and *pelue.*

KA-KA-LA, *adj.* Sharp; sharp pointed; rough with sharp points.

KA-KA-LA-AU, *s.* Name of some art taught among the chiefs in ancient times; he nui ka poe ao i ke kupololu ame ke *kakalaau*, me ke kaala.

KA-KA-LA-IO, *v.* To stand erect, as the hair of one frightened.

2. To shudder with fear.

3. To have the sensation of cold; to be

rough, as the skin affected with cold. See OKALA.

KA-KA-LAI-O-A, *s.* A thorny vine with pods very prickly, seeds globular, very hard, shining; a thorn. *Kin.* 3:18. Guillandina Bonduc.

KA-KA-LAI-O-A, *adj.* Thorny; composed of thorns.

KA-KA-LAI-O-A, *v.* To stand erect, as the hair; to be stiff; to be sharp pointed.
2. To be angry. See KAKALA.

KA-KA-LA-NA, *v.* To cry out; to call aloud.

KA-KA-LA-WE-LA, *v.* *Kakala* and *wela*, to burn. To make a scar by burning; to sear.
2. To have the color and appearance of a seared or scarred skin.

KA-KA-LA-WE-LA, *s.* A scar from burning; the smooth, brown, hard surface of the skin after being seared.

KA-KA-LE, *v.* To be thin; to be watery; to be nearly liquid, as thin poi; to be mixed with water.
2. To be movable; to be flexible; to be shaky. See KALE.

KA-KA-LE, *adj.* Thin; greatly diluted with water, as thin poi; he ai *kakale*.

KA-KA-LI, *v.* See KALI. To wait for some person or thing to come or be done; to expect. *Isa.* 64:4. To continue waiting for something.
2. To be detained.

KA-KA-LI, *adv.* Waitingly; in a waiting posture; in wait. *Ier.* 3:2.

KA-KA-LU-LE, *s.* Wandering; repetitious in conversation; *kakalule* ma ke kamailio ana.

KA-KA-NA, *v.* To speak sneeringly or contemptuously; to hurt one's feelings by sneering language.

KA-KA-NA, *s.* Contemptuous language; reproach; vilification.

KA-KA-NA-KA-NA, *s.* A species of grass.
2. A species of sea-weed; limu *kakanakana*; a slippery or smooth limu.

KA-KA-NI, *s.* A blast or blight on vegetables.
2. A small insect which lives on the outside of fruit, leaves, &c.
3. The itch; little round pimples on the flesh.

KA-KA-PA, *s.* A small strip of land adjoining another's large land; ina he *kapapa* o ka loi, i hookahi lalani o ua *kakapa* ai la.

KA-KA-PA-HI, *v.* *Kaka*, to strike, and *pahi*, knife; sword. To fence; to use the sword in fencing.

KA-KA-PA-HI, *s.* A fencing; the sword exercise.

KA-KA-WA-HI-E, *s.* The name of a bird; he *kakawahie* kahi manu.

KA-KA-WE-LE-WE-LE, *s.* Something unknown at present, but looked for in future; a i loaa hoi *kakawelewele* pono iki no ia manawa.

KA-KE, *s.* A kind of artificial language; it is used both in speaking and writing; it is designed as a secret kind of communicating thoughts, and understood only by the initiated. In writing it is made by transposing the letters of words and by giving words new meanings; it is used mostly, if not always, for vile, lascivious purposes.

KA-KE, *s.* A species of potato. See KAKAKE.

KA-KE-KA-KE, *v.* To change; to intermix.
2. *Hoo.* To mix up.
3. To be heavy; to be water soaked, as kalo.

KA-KE-KO, *adj.* Powerful; strong.

KA-KE-LE, *v.* See KELE. To slip; to slide, as on a muddy road.
2. To glide on the surface of the water; to sail about for pleasure.
3. To besmear, as the skin with oil.
4. To do that which will please one.

KA-KE-LE, *s.* A rubbing over the surface of the body; an anointing the skin of a person.

KA-KE-PAU-DA, *s.* *Eng.* A cartridge box. See KAKAIPAUDA.

KA-KI, *adj.* Cross; petulant; angry.

KA-KI-A, *s.* A nail; a pin; a wedge. See MAKIA.

KA-KI-A, *v.* To wedge or fasten up tightly; to fasten in a particular place or situation with a nail, pin or wedge.

KA-KI-O, *s.* The itch; the itching pustules of the skin. *Kanl.* 28:27. The same as *maiau*.

KA-KI-NI, *s.* A garment made to cover the foot and leg; a stocking.

KA-KI-NI, *adj.* *Eng.* Twelve in number; a dozen.

KA-KI-WI, *v.* See KIWI, to crook. To bend; to crook, as a horn.
2. To bend the body, as in bowing; to nod, as one going to sleep.
3. To press down upon; to crush flat.
4. To slap; to strike suddenly.

KA-KI-WI, *adj.* Crooked; bent; pahi *kakiwi*, a crooked sword; a crooked knife; a sickle. *Hoik.* 14:4.

KA-KO', } *v.* To bind up; to gird on, as
KA-KOO, } one's loose garment with a sash; to bind around. 1 *Sam.* 2:4.
2. FIG. To give strength. *Hal.* 18:39.

KA-KOO, *s*. A sash; a girdle. *Isa*. 11:5.

KA-KOU, *pers. pron*., first person plural. We; spoken of more than two, including the speaker and the persons addressed. *Gram*. § 124, 125 and 130.

KA-KO-LU, *adj*. Three-stranded; three-fold; *kakolu* ke kaula.

KA-KO-NA, *v*. See ALAI. To stop; to hinder anything in its progress; kakona ke ahi haule wale iho no.

KA-KO-NA-KO-NA, *s*. Name of a species of grass.

KA-KU, *s*. The name of a long fish. See KUPALA.

KA-KU-A, *v*. To bind or fasten on, as a pa-u.

2. To tie on, as a kihei. 2 *Sam*. 20:8. To put round, as a cincture or girdle. See KAKOO.

KA-KU-A, *v*. To ascribe power to the gods; to magnify; to offer sacrifice to the gods.

KA-KU-A, *s*. The worship of the gods, ascribing to them power; worship.

KA-KU-AI, *v*. To worship the gods; to pray in a particular manner.

KA-KU-AI, *s*. The constant daily sacrifice offered at every meal. NOTE.—The offerings were mostly of bananas.

KA-LA, *v*. To loosen; to untie, as a string or rope; to let loose, as an animal. *Mar*. 11.2.

2. To unloose; to put off, as clothes from a person; to undress; to put off, as armor. 1 *Sam*. 17:39.

3. To open halfway, as a door or book.

4. To absolve from a contract.

5. To put away; to take away, i. e., to forgive sin or a crime; to pardon. *Puk*. 34:7.

6. To forgive, as a debt; to release one from payment. *Mat*. 18:27.

7. To spare; to save from punishment. 2 *Sam*. 21:7.

8. *Hoo*. To whet; to grind or sharpen on a grindstone or hone. *Kanl*. 32:41.

9. To run out the tongue, as a serpent; to sharpen the tongue, i. e., to speak against or injure one. *Ios*. 10:21.

10. To sharpen, as a sword. *Hal*. 7:12.

KA-LA, *v*. To proclaim, as a public person the will of his sovereign; to cry, as a public crier.

2. To proclaim; to send for; to invite. *Oihk*. 23:2.

3. To publish; to make known. 2 *Sam*. 1:20.

4. *Hoo*. To cause to be proclaimed. *Puk*. 36:6

KA-LA, *s*. A person whose business it was to summon people and chiefs together in time of war, in a great assembly, with lights and torches, &c.; a public crier.

2. A substitute; one in the place of another. *Kin*. 22:13.

3. The ends of a house, in distinction from the sides.

4. The name of a species of fish; also species of bird.

5. *Kala* (English) the Hawaiian pronunciation of dollar; hence, silver; silver coin generally.

KA-LA, *adv*. Spoken of time; used only in the negative *aole*; as, *aole e kala*, long ago; long since; not very lately; not just now; a good while ago; *aole e kala* ka noho ana o na haole maanei, it is a good while that foreigners have lived here, i. e., their coming here is not lately.

KA-LA-AU, *v*. *Kala*, to call, and *au*. See WALAAU. To call; to call aloud.

KA-LA-AU, *s*. The striking of one stick upon another, as a part of the music in a hula; he *kalaau* ka hula nui a na 'lii e hana ai.

KA-LAE, *s*. Clearness; whiteness. *Puk*. 24:10.

2. A clear pure atmosphere; a calm. See LAE and LAELAE. *Laieik*. 25.

KA-LAE, *adj*. Clear; pure; white; calm; pleasant.

KA-LA-E-A, *s*. Roughness; rudeness in speaking; harshness.

KA-LA-E-A, *adv*. Roughly; harshly; angrily; applied to speaking. *Oihl*. 10:13. He olelo *kalaea* wale no ka Hakau ia Umi, Hakau spake only *rough words* to Umi.

KA-LAI, *v*. To hew; to cut. *Kanl*. 10:1. *Kalai* laau, to hew wood; *kalai* pohaku, to hew stones.

2. To pare; to cut; to grave; to carve out, i. e., to divide out, as one's portion; *kalai* laau, a hewer of wood. *Ios*. 9:20. *Kalai* pohaku, a stone cutter. *Isa*. 22:16.

KA-LAI, *adj*. Hewed; cut; carved.

KA-LAI-AI-NA, *v*. *Kalai*, to divide, and *aina*, land. To manage or direct the affairs of the land, i. e., the resources.

KA-LAI-AI-NA, *s*. The name of the office of the Minister of the Interior.

2. Political economy.

KA-LAI-IA, *part*. of *kalai*. Engraved; cut. *Puk*. 20:4.

KA-LAI-I-NO, *v*. *Kalai*, to carve out, and *ino*, wickedness. To concoct mischief; to devise a plan of evil again another. See AIAHULU.

KA-LA-I-HI, *adj*. Proud; exalted on account of one's office or nearness to a chief; ame ka leo *kalaihi* o na kumu.

KA-LAI-MO-KU, *s.* One who is concerned in managing the affairs of the moku, i. e., island.

2. One whose advice is valued in managing a people; o ka mea akamai i ke kakaolelo no ke aupuni, he *kalaimoku* ia.

KA-LAI-PO-HA-KU, *s.* *Kalai* and *pohaku,* a stone. A stone cutter. 2 *Sam.* 5:11.

KA-LAU, *v.* To thatch with leaves or potato vines; to work inefficiently.

KA-LAU-AE, *v.* To be indifferent to work; to be lazy; to be indisposed to work; to work without satisfaction.

KA-LAU-AE, *adj.* Indisposed to work; lazy; loitering.

KA-LAU-NU-I-O-HU-A, *s.* Name of an ancient king of Hawaii who lived in a time of universal famine which came on account of drought.

KA-LA-HA-LA, *v.* *Kala,* to pardon, and *hala,* guilt. To loose or absolve one from guilt or sin; to pardon sin.

2. To take away the ground of an offense, or to answer for it.

3. *Hoo.* To make an atonement. *Puk.* 29:36.

KA-LA-HA-LA, *s.* The taking away of guilt; an atonement. *Oihk.* 4:20.

2. That which takes away sin; that which absolves sin; a redeemer.

KA-LA-HA-LE, *adv.* *Kala* and *hale,* the end of a house. Like the end of a house, i. e., perpendicular, or nearly so; o na wahi kiekie *kalahale* ana ma kahi aoao, he pali ia.

KA-LA-HE-WA-HE-WA, *v.* To settle or bestow one's property, as a crazy man; eia ka'u, eia kau until it is all gone.

KA-LA-HU-A, *s.* The ceremony of chief women being allowed to eat fish after a kapu; ai no hoi na wahine a pau i ka ia hou mai, ua kapaia keia hana ana he *kalahua.*

KA-LA-KA-KA, *v.* To be craggy; to be rough; to be harsh.

KA-LA-KA-KA, *adj.* Rough; scraggy; thorny; knotty.

KA-LA-KA-LA, *adj.* Rough; sharp, as a rasp; as saw teeth.

KA-LA-KA-LA, *adv.* Roughly; harshly. *Sol.* 18:23.

KA-LA-KA-LAI, *v.* See KALAI. To hew; to cut; to carve, as in wood. 1 *Nal.* 6:18.

KA-LA-KI-NI, *s.* *Kala,* money, and *kini* for *tini,* tin, i. e., silver or new money as we say *silver dollars;* kau kuai ana i ka wahine o Maui i ke *kalakini,* your buying

a woman of Maui with *silver dollars.*

KA-LA-KU-A, *s.* *Kala,* roughness, and *kua,* back. The fin on the back of a fish; the same as *kuala.*

KA-LA-KU-PU-A, *v.* To lie in wait for one; to entrap one in his words.

2. To act the spy; to pounce upon secretly, as a cat does upon a mouse. *Hoo.* The same.

KA-LA-LAU, *s.* The name of a place on Kauai.

KA-LA-LAU, *v.* To call, as one person to another; napelepele *kalalau* owali i ka makani.

KA-LA-LE-A, *s.* Height; what is high up.

2. Pride; haughtiness, as in men.

3. The name of a fish of the eel kind on the mountain Kalalea; oia ka ia ino ma ke Kalalea.

KA-LA-LE-A, *s.* Name of a mountain on Kauai. *Laieik.* 13.

2. Prominent and long, as the nose of a person; a long prominent nose; *kalalea* ka ihu o kekahi haole.

KA-LA-LE-A, *adj.* Distorted, as the face of an angry man; maka *kalalea.*

KA-LA-LI, *v.* To walk stiffly or proudly; to walk like a soldier marching.

KA-LA-LI, *adj.* Quick and straightforward; applied to motion; *kalali* ka holo o ka moku; *kalali* ka hele o ke kanaka mama.

KA-LA-MA-U-LA, *s.* Name of a species of stone out of which maika stones were made.

KA-LA-MA-LO, *s.* A sort of grass with a furzed top.

KA-LA-MA-NI-A, *s.* *Kala* and *mania,* smooth. The smooth end of a house; a steep smooth hill; a pali.

KA-LA-MO, *s.* Eng. Calamus. *Mel. Sol.* 4:14.

KA-LA-MO-E, *s.* A species of fish like the kala, but bluish.

KA-LA-MO-KU, *s.* A kind of fish of the awa kind, but large; awa *kalamoku.*

KA-LA-NA, *s.* The name early given by Hawaiians to white writing paper; he pono anei keia manao o na kumu ao a pau o keia *kalana?*

2. The name of a division of an island next less than moku, and SYN. with okana in some places.

KA-LA-NA, *v.* To sift; to strain, as through a cloth, &c. See KANANA.

KA-LA-NA, *s.* See the above. A sieve; a strainer.

KA-LA-NAE, *v.* To persevere; to hold on to a job; to persevere against difficulties; he hana ikaika, aole e hoonawaliwali, aole he hoomolowa, aole he *kalanae.*

KA-LA-NAE, s. Perseverance; acting in the face of difficulties.

KA-LA-NE-O, v. To hide; to conceal; to go secretly. *Hoo.* The same.

KA-LA-NI-A, adj. Smooth, as the sea without a wave. See ALANIA.

KA-LA-NI-U-LI, s. The blue sky; the upper visible heavens. See KAPAPALANI.

KA-LA-NI-PAA, s. The broad blue sky; the fixed, strong firmament. See KAPAPA-LANI.

KA-LA-WA, v. To move off one side and partly round; ua *kalawa* ae la ma ke kua o ka hale; to move a little sideways and in a circular motion.

KA-LA-WA, s. A place where a bend in the road comes again to a straight line.

2. Shooting pains in the side, neck, &c.

KA-LA-WAI, v. To go round; to go about; to surround; like *poai.*

KA-LA-WA-IA, s. The occupation of a fisherman; the act of taking fish. NOTE.—The *ka* of this word is the article, or else the word takes no article. The word is written and pronounced by Hawaiians as though *ka* was an integral part of the word. See LAWAIA and LOWAIA.

KA-LA-WA-KU-A, v. See KALAWA above and KUA, the back. To move sideways and round the back side.

KA-LA-WA-LA-WA, adv. He maona *kala-walawa* kahi alii. This is probably an error for *kawalawala,* seldom; here and there one.

KA-LE, v. To be thin and watery, like very thin poi. See KAKALE and KALEKALE.

KA-LE, adj. Thin and watery; very nearly liquid poi so mixed with water; he ai *kale.*

KA-LE-A, v. To go into the windpipe, as water or other liquid when it goes the wrong way; to choke; to cough; to strangle, as in swallowing a liquid.

KA-LE-A, s. Some kind of disease; ina i haalele i ka baka, a puhi aku, o ke *kalea* no ia, a nui ke kunu; a choking; a coughing.

KA-LE-O-KU-MUU, s. Name of a place near the summit of Waialeale on Kauai.

KA-LE-KA-LE, adj. See KALE above. Thin; watery, &c.; soft; nearly fluid.

KA-LE-KE-DO-NA, s. Gr. A chalcedony, the name of a precious stone. *Hoik.* 21:19.

KA-LE-LE, v. To lean upon, as upon a cane or staff. 2 *Sam.* 1:6.

2. To press upon gently.

3. To be propped up; to lean, as the head on the hand.

KA-LE-LE, s. A stay; a railing; any-thing like the arm of a chair. 2 *Oihl.* 9:18.

KA-LE-LEI, v. To appear beautiful, as a beautiful woman.

2. To yield obedience, as a scholar to the precepts of his teacher; a papapu mai mamuli o ke kumu, o *kalelei* mai no ia i ka maka.

KA-LE-LE-KU, v. See KALELE. To press gently; to bear on softly.

KA-LE-LE-MU-KU, v. To lean on the stern of a vessel with haughtiness; to lean upon the side of a canoe.

KA-LE-LE-WA, adj. See KAALELEWA. Flying; floating, as clouds; ao *kalelewa.* 1 *Tes.* 4:17.

KA-LE-LE-WA, v. To float, as a vessel not at anchor; to stand off and on, as a vessel; aole nae i ku ka moku, *kalelewa* wale no, the vessel, however, did not anchor, it only *lay off and on.* See LEWA and KAALELEWA.

KA-LE-NA, v. See LENA. To stretch out for drying, as a hide; to spread out, as a cloth.

KA-LE-PA, v. To peddle; to hawk about goods; to sell from place to place.

2. To vend merchandise, as a shop-keeper (this is a modern use.) NOTE.—*Kalepa* was formerly used on Hawaii, *maauauwa* on Oahu, and *piele* on Kauai for peddling. See MAAUAUWA and PIELE.

KA-LE-PA, s. One who brings things to market; in modern times, a merchant. 1 *Nal.* 10:15.

KA-LE-PA, adj. Trading; peddling; he mau moku *kalepa* kekahi, some were *trading* ships. NOTE.—It is the custom of Hawaiians when they have poi or other articles to sell, to hoist a small flag (lepa); hence *kalepa,* to sell; to make market. See LEPA and LEPALEPA.

KA-LE-PA-LE-PA, v. To flap, as the sails of a ship; to flap in the wind, as a flag or ensign. See KILEPA and LEPALEPA.

KA-LE-WA, v. See LEWA. To float; to be floating, as any substance in the air.

2. To sail here and there on the water; to lie off and on, as a vessel.

3. To carry a weight suspended on a pole between two persons.

4. To be unsettled; to move often from place to place.

KA-LE-WA, s. A swing; a pendulous machine for moving back and forward, like *kowali.*

2. A place near or in the luakini where the king and a few people were separated from the multitude.

KA-LE-WA, *adj.* Hanging; swinging, as a weight on a pole; flying, as clouds; lying off and on, as a ship.

KA-LI, *v.* To wait; to tarry; to stay. *Puk.* 12:39.

2. To sojourn with one.

3. To wait for something; to lie in wait.

4. To hesitate in speaking.

5. To expect; to look for.

6. To gird; to tie; to fasten on.

7. *Hoo.* To waste away with disease.

KA-LI, *s.* The edge, as of a board, leaf, &c.

2. Disease; sickness, i. e., a waiting for death.

3. A word of contempt; o oe *kali.* See KALIPILAU.

4. Slowness; hesitancy of speech. *Puk.* 4:10.

KA-LI-A-LI, *s.* A tree or plant used as a medicine.

KA-LI-A-WE, *s.* Brass; copper, &c. See KELEAWE.

KA-LII, *s.* Name of the ceremony when the high chief lands from a voyage with his people and his god.

KA-LI-KA-LI, *v.* See KALI, to wait. To be a little behind; not quite up even with something else.

2. To be not quite full; to lack something.

KA-LI-KE-A, *s.* *Kali,* edge, and *kea,* white. A white border or fringe; white on the edge or border. See KUAKALIKEA.

KA-LI-KU-LU-I, *s.* The union of several strings of the meat of the kukui nut made into a flambeau; he *kalikukui* i aulamaia.

KA-LI-LO, *s.* A fatal disease or sickness, like *mai make;* a sickness so great that death only remains; he mai lilo wale aku no koe.

KA-LI-LO-LI-LO, *v.* To be about to pass away, that is, to die; to be so in the last stages of life as to be impossible to live. See KALILO and LILO.

KA-LI-NA, *s.* *Kali* and *ana,* a remaining. Old potato vines that have done bearing.

2. Potatoes of the second growth.

3. A garden of potatoes where the old refuse potatoes and vines only remain.

KA-LI-PI-LAU, *s.* See KALI, disease, and PILAU, offensive to the smell. A word of contempt or blackguardism, used to provoke; *kalipilau* oe; one that intercedes would say to the speaker, e, oe *kali.*

KA-LO, *s.* The well known vegetable of the Hawaiian Islands; a species of the *arum esculentum;* it is cultivated in artificial water beds, and also on high mellow upland soil; it is made into food by baking and pounding into hard paste; after fermenting and slightly souring; it is diluted with water, then called poi, and eaten with the fingers. NOTE.— The origin of the *kalo* plant is thus described in Hawaiian Mythology

kalo, Elepaio variety

(see *Mooolelo Hawaii* by Dibble, p. 37): ulu mai la ua alualu la, a lilo i *kalo,* the fetus grew (when it was buried) and became a *kalo.*

KA-LO, *s.* One of the class of gods called akua noho; Opua ame *Kalo* kekahi akua makau ia.

KA-LO-A-KU-KA-HI, *s.* A name of a day of the month; also kanaloakukahi.

KA-LO-A-KU-LU-A, *s.* Name of a day of the month.

KA-LO-A-PAU, *s.* Name of a day of the month.

KA-LO-HA, *s.* The name of a species of rush. See KALUHA.

KA-LO-HE, *s.* See KOLOHE. Violence; mischief; evil. *Laieik.* 104.

KA-LO-HI, *s.* See LOHI, to be slow. A hindrance; a delay; e pono paha e kapa hou ia kona inoa o *kalohi* mahope o ka lohi ana o na moku malaila, viz.: the southwest side of Lanai.

KA-LO-KA-LO, *v.* To pray to the gods; to supplicate favors.

2. (In a *modern christian sense*) to call upon God; to ask for assistance; aka, e *kalokalo* aku kakou i ke Akua, a nana e lileuli lelewae, but let us call upon God, and he will blot out and wash away (our sins); e hoi a *kalokalo* aku i ka mea nani hiwahiwa o ka lanikolu.

KA-LO-LE, *s.* Straight smooth hair, like the Chinese; e like me ko na Pake.

2. Name of an office in the king's train.

KA-LO-LE, *adj.* Slick; smooth, as some kinds of cloth.

2. Straight and smooth, as hair; he huluhulu *kalole* ko ka lio, he piipii inoino ko ke kamelo.

KA-LO-LE, *v.* To turn the tone of the voice; to change one's voice so as not to be known.

KA-LO-LO, *s.* A name given to the first liquor that runs off in distillation; the last running is called kawae. See OKOLEHAO.

KA-LU, *s.* The falling of ripe fruit; also,

2. The falling of dried leaves.

3. The yielding; a bending before the wind.

KA-LU-A, *v.* *Ka* and *lua,* a pit. To bury; to hide under ground.

2. To bake, as animal or vegetable food. NOTE.—This was always done in an oven under ground, i. e., it was buried.

3. To kill, dress and cook an animal for food, embracing the whole process.

4. To burn brick or lime; the latter was always burnt in a covered pit.

KA-LU-A, *s.* The name of a month answering to February; ka malama o Feberuari, o *Kalua* ka inoa i ka olelo Hawaii, the month of February is called *Kalua* in the Hawaiian language.

KA-LU-A, *s.* See LUA, a pit. A deep place; a pit; a deep ravine.

2. A descending or down-hill road. See KAOLO and IHONA.

KA-LU-A, *adj.* Double; two-stranded, as a rope; *kalua* ke kaula.

KA-LU-A-LU-A, *adj.* Rough, as a road; rough; uneven, as land.

KA-LU-A-NUU-NO-HO-NI-O-NI-O, *s.* Name of one of the gods in the luakini.

KA-LU-HA, } *s.* A kind of sea grass
KA-LU-HA-LU-HA, } or rush of which strings are made; kaula kaluha. Iob. 41:2.

2. A general name for all kinds of grass and rushes which grow in water.

KA-LU-HI, *v.* See HOOKALUHI. To yield; to bend; to fall, as ripe fruit or withered leaves.

KA-LU-KA-LU, *s.* A vegetable growing like the kaluha, chiefly at Kapaa on Kauai.

2. A very thin gauze like kapa; pale *kalukalu.* Isa. 3:19. Translated in English muffler; *kalukalu* nui, a mantle.

KA-MA, *s.* The first husband of a wife; he kane mua o ka wahine, he kaukama.

2. Children generally, i. e., male and female children; the second generation in a family.

3. *Specifically,* children adopted into the family of another; *kama* ole, childless.

4. *Hoo.* Adoption; the act of receiving or being received, as a child into the family of another; ka *hookamaia,* adoption. *Rom.* 9:4.

KA-MA, *v.* To lead or direct.

2. To bind or tie up, as a bundle. See KAMAKAMA.

3. *Hoo.* To adopt, as a child; to take

another's child as one's own. This has been a very common practice among Hawaiians of all grades from time immemorial.

KA-MA, *adj.* *Hoo.* The state of being a child by adoption; keiki *hookama,* an adopted child.

KA-MA, *s.* A cavern; a fissure in a rock.

KA-MAA, *s.* Sandals; shoes, i. e., shoes for the bottom of the feet.

2. Kapa or other material bound round the feet and legs when traveling on places of scoria or other rough places. *Puk.* 12:11.

KA-MAA, *v.* *Hoo.* To shoe; to furnish with shoes or sandals. *Ezek.* 16:10.

KA-MA-A-HA, See the compound MOLO-KAMAAHA.

KA-MA-AI-NA, *s.* *Kama,* child, and *aina,* land. LIT. A child of the land. A native born in any place and continuing to live in that place. *Oihk.* 18:25.

2. One belonging to a land and transferred with the land, from one landholder to another.

3. The present residents in a place; a citizen. *Oih.* 21:39.

4. FIG. The indwelling of evil in the heart; he *kamaaina* kahiko loa ka hewa ma ka naau, mai ka hoomaka o Satana ka hakuaina o ka po. See KUPA.

KA-MAA-LO-A, *s.* See MAALOA.

KA-MAA-LO-I-HI, *s.* *Kamaa* and *loihi,* long. LIT. Long shoes. Shoes with legs, i. e., boots.

KA-MA-EU, *s.* *Kama,* child, and *eu,* mischievous. A mischievous, vicious child.

2. A vicious, lying, deceitful person.

KA-MA-E-HU, *s.* Strength; energy; ku *kamaehu,* to stand firmly.

KA-MAI, *v.* To play the whoremonger for hire.

KA-MAI-O-A, *s.* He kapipine i huiia me ke *kamaioa.*

KA-MAI-KA-HU-LI-WAA-PU, } *s.* Different
KA-MAI-KA-HU-LI-PU, } names of the
KA-MAI-HU-LI-WAA, } god who aided in floating upset canoes; their jurisdiction extended over all the islands.

KA-MA-I-KI, *s.* *Kama* and *iki,* little. The oldest or first born; the most endeared or best beloved; an expression of endearment, as *my precious child.* Mar. 2:5.

KA-MA-I-LI-O, *v.* To converse; to exchange ideas colloquially; to confer together; to consult; to talk with. *Ios.* 22:15.

KA-MA-I-LI-O, *s.* Conversation; consultation.

KA-MAU, *v.* To remain a long time; to

persevere in any state or business in which one is.

2. To hold on or continue in a business with no certainty as to the result.

3. To hang by a trifle, as a heavy body by a small string; to be long sick and eat but little.

4. To be unfixed; to be insecure; paa pono ole.

5. To strain; to persevere; to take a long breath.

6. To trump, as with a trump card; *kamau* i kela ai, trump that trick.

KA-MAU, *s.* Endurance; perseverance, especially in uncertainty.

2. Name of a kind of kalo.

KA-MAU, *s.* A friend of one on account of relationship, i. e., a friend as well as a relation.

KA-MAU, *adj.* Fast adhering; constant, as a friend or beloved relative.

KA-MAU-E-A, *v.* See KAMAU and EA, breath. To hold on for the present; just to live; to eat but little; to live on till the breath leaves.

KA-MA-HAO, *adj.* See KAMA and HAO, to wonder. Wonderful; astonishing; surprising; unheard of; incomprehensible; ke ku ana mai o keia mea *kamahao*, the standing of this *wonderful* thing; *kamahao* aina, a wonderful thing in the land.

KA-MA-HO-E-HO-PE, *s.* The name of a month, September; also *Hilina*.

KA-MA-HO-E-MU-A, *s.* The name of a month, August; also *Hilinehu*.

KA-MA-HO-I, *adj.* Glorious; all over splendid; he puni nani; beautiful; he alii *kamahoi*, a glorious chief.

KA-MA-KAU, *s.* *Ka*, to block out, and *makau*, fish-hook. The art of manufacturing the bones of men or animals into fish-hooks; o ke kanaka akamai i ke *kamakau*, he kanaka waiwai ia.

KA-MA-KA-HI, *s.* *Kama* and *kahi*, one. An only child. *Mel. Sol.* 6:9.

KA-MA-KA-LEI-O-KU, *s.* Name of a god made of the tree called koalaukane, a species of koa; he was Keawe's god.

O ka haku maka o Kalananuu
O *Kamakaleioku* kalai aku Hooneenuu
Ke ana a Kalaukani
Kani kuhele ka ua i kaupaku o ka hale o moe—a.

KA-MA-KA-MA, *v.* See KAMA. To bind; to tie; to make fast; to bind up, as a bundle; to bind on.

KA-MA-KA-MA, *v.* To practice prostitution; to live a life of lasciviousness. *Hoo.* The same.

KA-MA-KA-MA, *s.* *Hoo.* A prostitute.

KA-MA-KA-MA-KA, *s.* A speech; a prayer; the asking of a favor.

2. The covering materials of an oven; a cover for an oven.

KA-MA-KA-MA-I-LI-O, *v.* To converse; to talk together familiarly; otherwise SYN. with kamailio. *Hal.* 119 46.

KA-MA-KA-NE, *s.* *Kama*, child, and *kane*, male. A male child.

KA-MA-KE-NA, *s.* Sorrow; the eyes heavy with sorrow; great sorrow. See MAKENA.

KA-MA-KII, *v.* To be idle; to be wandering about doing nothing.

KA-MA-KII, *adj.* Going about idle; lazy.

KA-MA-KII-LO-HI-LO-HI, *s.* A kapu worship for the chief.

KA-MA-KI-NI, *s.* A kapu worship for the chief. See above.

KA-MA-KO-NA-KA-HI-KU-LA-NI, *s.* Without love; without affection for one. See MAKONA, want of reciprocity between persons, parents and children, people and chiefs.

KA-MA-KUU, *s.* A setting up of the hair of the head; setting the jib of a vessel; the assembling of persons and horses to ride.

KA-MA-LA, *v.* To thatch with the leaves of the uhi for a temporary house.

KA-MA-LA, *s.* A booth; a temporary house; a stall for cattle. *Kin.* 33:17. Hale *kamala.* 2 *Oihl.* 8:13.

KA-MA-LA, *adj.* Temporary, as the covering of a house or shelter.

KA-MA-LA-NI, *s.* *Kama*, child, and *lani*, chief. The child of a chief, i. e., a favorite or petted child. SYN. with punahele.

KA-MA-LA-NI, *v.* To treat one as a favorite. *Hoo.* The same; also, to favor; to gratify; e hoopunahele, e hoohiwahiwa.

KA-MA-LE-NA, *s.* The name of a pa-u or other kapa dyed with the root of the olena or turmeric.

KA-MA-LII, *s.* *Kama*, child, and *lii*, little. Children, either male or female.

2. Dear friends; the young people of a family.

3. A word of endearment, used both in the singular and plural.

KA-MA-LO-LE, *v.* To reject; to forsake one thing and seek another, as food, kapa, women, &c.

KA-MA-LU, *v.* See MALU, secretly. To do secretly; to steal; ua *kamaluia* kuu puaa e mea, my hog has been stolen by somebody.

2. To prohibit; to forbid; ua *kamalu* mai o mea ia makou, aole make hana.

KA-MA-MA-KI, s. See MAMAKI.

KA-MA-NA, s. *Eng.* See KAMENA below. A carpenter. *Mar.* 6:3.

KA-MA-NI, s. The name of a tree, producing beautiful wood and leaves; hence, what is fair and beautiful outside; hence, *hoo.* A hypocrite; hypocrisy. *Mat.* 15:7.

KA-MA-NI, v. To appear to be what one is not; to dissemble.
2. *Hoo.* To feign; to dissemble; to pretend; to profess to be what one is not.
3. To deal falsely. *Oihk.* 19:11.
4. To disguise one's self. 1 *Nal.* 14:2.

KA-MA-NI, *adj.* Feigned; hypocritical.

KA-MA-NI, *adv.* Beautiful outside; pleasingly in exhibition without corresponding substance; ano nani kino *kamani* iho la ko Hawaii nei ia manawa.

KA-MA-NI-U-LA, s. Name of a timber like the koa growing in various places.

KA-MA-NI-HA, v. To be rude; to be wild; to be unsocial. *Hoo.* Same.

KA-MA-NO, s. *Eng.* The name of a fish, a salmon.

KA-MA-NO-MA-NO, s. A bitter gourd with a bitter shell outside.

KA-MA-PU-AA, s. *Kama,* child, and *puaa,* hog. LIT. The son of a hog. The name of a fabled kupua or wizard, half man, half hog. He was the son of Hina and Kahiki-ula, and grandson of Kaunuaniho. *Kamapuaa* was the husband of Pele, and their child's name was Opeluhoolili. He was worshiped as a god.

KA-MA-PU-KA, v. To beg; to ask favors; to get from another.
2. To glory; to boast; to praise; to extol. *Hoo.* The same.

KA-MA-PU-KA, s. A beggar.

KA-MA-WA-HI-NE, s. *Kama* and *wahine,* female. A female child.

KA-ME-HAI, *adj.* Baiting; giving something to a priest to obtain his favor.
2. Lasciviously mischievous, as a young boy; he mau keiki *kamehai. Hae. Haw.*

KA-ME-LE-O-NA, s. *Eng.* The chameleon.
2. The mole. *Oihk.* 11:3.

KA-ME-LO, s. *Eng.* A camel, an unclean animal among the Jews. *Oihk.* 11:4.

KA-ME-LO-PA-DI, s. *Eng.* A camelopard.

KA-ME-NA, s. *Eng.* A carpenter. *Zek.* 1:20. See KAMANA.

KA-MO-KU-MO-KU, v. To move, as the bowels in a diarrhea, at intervals.

KA-MO-LA, v. To be slackly twisted, as a string; to be tied.

KA-MO-LE, s. Name of a plant growing around kalo patches having a yellow blossom; jussiæa.

KA-MU-MU, } s. A rumbling indis-
KA-MU-MU-MU, } tinct noise of something doing.
2. The noise and action of a person eating meat baked to a crisp, or cartilaginous meat.
3. The rumbling of wagons or chariots; ke *kamumu* o na kaa.
4. The sound of many footsteps; ke *kamumu* o na wawae. 1 *Nal.* 18:41.
5. The roar of a great rain at a distance. 1 *Nal.* 18:41.
6. The rustling of wings. *Ezek.* 3:12. The sound of wheels; the sound of going. *Ezek.* 3:13. The sound of horsemen. *Ezek.* 26:10.

KA-NA, *pron.* An oblique case of the personal pronoun, third person singular of *ia.* His; hers; its (seldom used in the neuter.) Ka is a preposition, of. More often it signifies possession, where in English the apostrophic s would be used. See Grammar § 137, 138 and 139.

KA-NA, *pron.* A possessive adjective pronoun; it has the same meaning of possession as the above, but is used in connection with some noun expressed or understood. *Gram.* § 149, 150.

KA-NA, s. Name of a man who formerly resided at Hilo, said to have been four hundred fathoms high; he stepped over the hill of Haupu on Molokai and slipped down; he also fought with Keolaewanuiakamau. See the story.

KA-NA, v. To dislike; to despise; to treat in an angry manner. See KONAKONA.

KA-NA, v. To see; to appear; to get a sight of; to obtain what one wished; i nana aku i ka hana i ka hale o ke alii, aole i *kana* mai, o ko'u hilahila no ia mea, I went to see the house of the chief, I did not *see* it (get sight of), I was ashamed.

KA-NA, s. The outside of the neck; similar to *kaniai.*

KA-NAE, s. *Ka* and *nae,* hard breathing. Hence, fear; a holding the breath from fear.

KA-NAE-NAE, v. To observe; to watch.
2. To pray to the gods; to offer sacrifice to the gods; e *kanaenae* i ke akua.
3. To appear angry.

KA-NAE-NAE, s. A sacrifice; an offering to the gods; a propitiatory sacrifice. *Laieik.* 27.

KA-NAE-NAE, *adj.* Propitiating; appeasing; eia ka mohai *kanaenae* ia oe e ke akua, here is a peace-offering to thee O god; he hale *kanaenae* no ka lani e ola, a house offered to the god in sacrifice for the chief that he may live.

Ka-nai, *s.* Name of a place in the sea where the water lies smooth and calm like a road; o kahi o ke kai e moe ana me he alanui la, he *kanai* ia.

Ka-na-ha, *v.* To be forty. *Kin.* 18:29; *Oih.* 4:22. See HA, No. 4.

Ka-na-ha, *num. adj.* Forty in number; used for forty in counting ropes, cord, bundles of food and property generally, but in counting kapas *iako* is used. See IAKO.

Ka-na-hae, ⎱ *v.* To decrease; to dimin-
Ka-na-hai, ⎰ ish; to cease; to leave off; ua *kanahae* ka wela o ke kuni, the heat of the burning has ceased; *kanahai* ka ue, the wailing has ceased; *kanahai* anei ka inu rama? Aole. See KANAKAI.

Ka-na-ho, *v.* To be moved; to pant from hard exercise; to cause one to shake; to tremble.

2. To take refuse from fear; to be safe under the protection of another.

Ka-na-ho, *s.* A refuge; a place of protection.

2. One who has escaped from danger.

3. A coming with eager expectations.

Ka-na-hu-a, *v.* To walk bending forward; to walk in a proud swinging manner; to walk as a stoop-shouldered person; to be crooked in one's person.

Ka-na-ka, *s.* A man; one of the human species; one of the genus *homo*; the general name of men, women and children of all classes, in distinction from other animals.

2. A common man, in distinction from alii or chief.

3. People generally; persons; mankind.

4. In a *vulgar, low sense* as sometimes used by foreigners, a Hawaiian, a native, in distinction from a foreigner.

5. Own; self; person; aka, i makau ia kakou *kanaka* iho, but they feared us our *own persons*; *kanaka* e, another man, i. e., a stranger. *Puk.* 12:19.

Ka-na-ka, *s.* The end of the outrigger of a canoe.

Ka-na-ka, *v.* To be or dwell as men; a e *kanaka* ole auanei. *Zek.* 9:5. Hookohukohu, a *kanaka* iho la kekahi poe no ke Akua.

2. *Hoo.* To act the man, i. e., to act courageously or firmly. 1 *Sam.* 4:9.

3. To observe rectitude of conduct. 1 *Kor.* 16:13. To show one's self a man, i. e., of common sense; not a fool; not silly. *Isa.* 46:8.

4. To act faithfully, firmly, courageously, and not faint-heartedly. 2 *Oihl.* 15:7.

Ka-na-ka, *adj.* Manly; firmly; stable; ame ko lakou ano *kanaka* no ke Akua.

Ka-na-kai, *v.* To cease; to decrease; to leave off. See KANAHAI.

Ka-na-ka-ma-ku-a, *s. Kanaka* and *makua*, parent. The state of mature age, whether one has children or not, i. e., one mature of person, full grown. *Ioan.* 9:21.

2. A man of bodily strength; a man by way of eminence. 1 *Nal.* 2:2.

3. One who acts the part of a master of a household; a provider.

Ka-na-ka-no, *int. Kanaka* and *no*, emphatic, indeed! really! A phrase expressing applause or approbation, well done! noble! fine! manly!

Ka-na-ko-lu, *num. adj.* Three tens; the number thirty.

Ka-na-le-o, *v. Hoo.* To make efforts to be regular and self-possessed when intoxicated; to try to walk straightly when partially drunk.

Ka-na-lo-a, See KUKANALOA.

Ka-na-lo-a, *s.* The name of a small fish.

Ka-na-lo-a-ku-ka-hi, *s.* Name of a day of the month. See also KALOAKUKAHI.

Ka-na-lu, *s.* The name of the priests of Ku who served at the luakini; ua kapaia na kahuna o ia aoao na kahuna o *Kanalu*, no ka mea o *Kanalu* ke kahuna mua.

Ka-na-lu-a, *v.* To be in doubt; to hesitate between two things; to be in doubt how to act in a certain case; to be in doubt how to account for an event; to have in suspense; to hang in doubt. *Kanl.* 28:66. *Hoo.* To put, make or cause one to be in doubt. *Ioan.* 10:24. See KUIHEE.

Ka-na-lu-a, *s.* Doubt; uncertainty what to think or how to act.

Ka-na-lu-a, *adj.* Wavering; fickle-minded; fearful of a result.

Ka-na-lu-a, *num. adj.* Two tens; twenty; elua umi, umi lua. *Kamk.*

Ka-na-na, *v.* See KALANA. To sift, as flour; to winnow, as grain. *Rut.* 3:2.

2. To strain; to pour through a strainer, &c., with a view to separate the good from the poor.

3. To sift, i. e., to try one's moral character. *Luk.* 22:31.

Ka-na-na, *s.* A sieve; a strainer. *Amos* 9:9.

2. White paper for writing; ua makaukau ia ka hulu, ka inika ame ke *kanana*.

Ka-na-na-na, *v.* See KANANA. To separate what is evil from the good.

KA-NA-NU-HA, *v.* To be dull in listening to a story; to sit in sullen silence, giving no reply; to be dull in learning; to have a want of apprehension; to be stubborn or surly. *Hoo.* The same.

KA-NA-NU-HA, *adj. Hoo.* Dull; stupid; slow. *Heb.* 5:11. Slow or dull at answering.

KA-NA-PI, *v.* To snap, as a gun; kani *kanapi* ka pu.

KA-NA-PI, *s.* The Hawaiian orthography for centipede, a creeping animal.

KA-NA-PU, *v.* To bend upwards; as, ua *kanapu* ke oa.

KA-NA-WAI, *s. Ka,* preposition, of, belonging, relating to, &c., *na,* sign of the plural, and *wai,* water. LIT. What belongs to the waters, i. e., rights of water. N.B.— The ancient system of regulations for water courses contained almost everything the ancient Hawaiians formerly had in common in the shape of laws; hence the name *Kanawai* has in more modern times been given to laws in general.
   1. A law; an edict; a command of a chief.
   2. Still more modern, a legislative enactment.

KA-NA-WAI, *v.* To put under law; to forbid a thing to be done; aole nae makou i *kanawai* i ka puhi baka no ka ilihune, we did not, however, forbid (put under law) the smoking tobacco.

KA-NA-WAI-LU-A, *s. Kanawai* and *lua,* double. *Deuteronomy,* the name of the fourth book of the Scriptures, i. e., a repetition of the laws by Moses.

KA-NA-WA-O, *s.* A hard, heavy stone from some water brook, used in war with a sling; a sling stone.
   2. Name of the small fresh water fish found back in the mountains.
   3. Name of a fruit found on a tree in the mountains.

KA-NA-WI, *v.* To be poor; to be thin in flesh.

KA-NE, *s.* The male of the animal species; opposite to *wahine.*
   2. A husband; he *kane* mea wahine, a husband having a wife; *kane* hou, a man lately married; a bridegroom; also, *kane* mare, a bridegroom.
   3. The name of a stone god.
   4. White spots on the flesh.
   5. The god of living water; he akua nana ka wai ola.
   6. The name of certain gods, Kane and Kanaloa.
   7. The name of a small insect. See ANE.

   8. Name of a day of the month; ma ia ao ae, o *Kane* ia la.

KA-NE, *v.* To be or act the part of a husband. 1 *Tim.* 3:2.

KA-NE-A, *v.* To have no appetite for food; to be sickish; to loathe food.
   2. To be slow and dumpish about work.

KA-NE-A, *s.* The loss of appetite; sickishness; without strength; without inclination to do anything.

KA-NE-A, *adj.* Stiff; lazy; inactive.

KA-NE-A-PU-A, *s.* A younger brother of Kane and Kanaloa; they were all left on Lanai.

KA-NE-I-A-HU-E-A, *s.* One that blunders in managing a canoe by night, or traveling by day.

KA-NE-I-KA-PU-A-LE-NA, *s.* The god of Kawelo, son of Mahunalii and Malei.

KA-NE-KI, *v.* To be near to trouble; to be near to overflowing, as a river; ua hele ka wai a *kaneki* wale o ka pua.

KA-NE-KU-PU-A, *s.* The name of a mock fight on the arrival of a high chief; ua kapaia keia kaua ihe ana he *kanekupua.*

KA-NE-MA-KE, *adj. Kane,* husband, and *make,* dead. Epithet of a woman whose husband is dead; a widowed woman. 1 *Nal.* 17:9.

KA-NE-MA-KU-A, *s.* The god of the fishermen who caught the malolo in a net.

KA-NE-MA-RE, *s.* See KANE. A married man; a bridegroom. *Isa.* 62:5.

KA-NE-NU-I-A-KE-A, *s.* A general name of a class of gods; the individuals in the class are as follows: Kanekii, Kanehakia, Kanelele, Kaneikamakaukau, Kanekohala, Kaneikaalei, Kaneikokea, Kanepaina, Kanepohakaa, Kanemakua, Kaneholopali, Kaneikapualena, Kaneikapuahakea.

KA-NE-PAI-NA, *s.* A living thing like a fish, worshiped as a god.

KA-NE-PO-LU, *s.* Name of a chief on the Island of Oahu, killed by falling from a pali one or two feet high; make o *Kanepolu* i ka pali uuku.

KA-NE-PU-AA, *s.* Name of the god of husbandry; ke nuhu nei, alia i oki ka aina a ka hewahewa a heu. See KOWAA.

KA-NE-GA-RU,   *s.* Name of an animal
KA-NE-GA-ROO,   found in New Holland; a kangaroo.

KA-NI, *v.* To make a sound more or less musical; to hum, as a tune.
   2. To strike, as a clock; *kani* wale ka wati me ka hookani ole ia aku e ka lima kanaka.
   3. To sound, as a trumpet. *Puk.* 19:13.
   4. To explode, as a pistol.

5. To crack, as a whip.

6. To rumble, as thunder.

7. To squeak, as shoes.

8. To crow, as a cock; ke kani mai nei ka moa.

9. *Hoo.* To sing; to praise; to play on an instrument of music. 1 *Sam.* 16:18, 23.

10. To cry out, as a multitude; to exclaim; *hookani aku la na kanaka penei,* the people exclaimed thus.

11. To be unpleasantly affected, as the ears at hearing bad news. 1 *Sam.* 3:11. Na mea *kani,* musical instruments.

KA-NI, *s.* A singing; a ringing sound; a report, as of a gun; the sound of a trumpet, or of musical instruments.

KA-NI, *adj.* Sounding; singing; squeaking; making a noise.

KA-NI-A-AU, *v.* To mourn; to grieve for the loss of a husband or wife.

2. To wander about in sorrow; to go from place to place in despondency.

3. To be greatly afflicted, so that the sight of objects bringing the deceased to mind would be distressing.

KA-NI-A-AU, *s.* A mourning for the loss of a wife or husband; deep seated grief; solemn mourning.

KA-NI-A-I, *s. Kani* and *a-i,* neck. The throat. *Hal.* 5:9.

2. The protuberance at the end of the windpipe; also,

3. The windpipe itself.

KA-NI-AU-KA-NI, *s.* The name of Kamehameha's return from Oahu to Hawaii; ua kapa kela hoi ana o *kaniaukani.*

KA-NI-A-HI-A, *v.* To weep immoderately and lament for one absent, as a man for a beloved wife.

KA-NI-I-E, *adj.* Hard in distinction from soft; oolea, nahoa.

KA-NI-U,   } *v.* To be full of hard lumps.
KA-NI-U-U, }   2. To have a sharp, quick sound.

KA-NI-U,   } *s.* A groaning; an expression of grief, trouble or pain.
KA-NI-U-U, } See KANIUHU.

KA-NI-U-HU, *v. Kani* and *uhu,* to complain. To complain of pain of body; to groan with pain or grief.

2. To coo or mourn like a dove. *Isa.* 59:11.

3. To mourn, as in affliction. *Neh.* 1:4.

4. To sigh on account of oppression. *Puk.* 2:23.

5. To be sad; to be sorrowful.

KA-NI-U-HU, *s.* Sorrow; sighing; complaint. *Hal.* 142:2. Groaning; trouble; sorrow. *Isa.* 30:6. Groaning from oppression. *Lunk.* 2:18. Noho no lakou me ke *kaniuhu* ole iloko o lakou iho, they live without *complaint* within themselves.

KA-NI-U-HU, *adj.* Sighing; sorrowing on account of oppression or wrong.

KA-NI-U-LI, *v.* To put out the lip.

KA-NI-HI-A, *adv.* Suffering from love or affection for another; e noho *kanihia* aloha ae ana au ia oe.

KA-NI-KAU, *v.* To mourn for the loss of friends; to lament; to bewail, as for the dead. *Kin.* 23:3.

2. To compose a dirge, or to sing one extemporaneously. 2 *Sam.* 3:33. To compose an elegy for one. 2 *Sam.* 1:17. See KUMAKENA.

KA-NI-KAU, *s.* A dirge; a mourning song; mourning; lamentation. *Ezek.* 19:1.

KA-NI-KAU, *adj.* Mourning; hale *kanikau. Kekah.* 7:2, 4.

KA-NI-KA-NI, *v.* Freq. of *kani,* to make a sound. To tinkle, as a small bell. *Isa.* 3:16. To sound, as any sharp noise; to cry out with a shout, *kanikani* pihe aku la ka aha, "ka wahine maikai, e!" the woman is beautiful! *Laieik.* 165.

2. To play on a musical instrument. *Hoo.* The same.

KA-NI-KA-NI, *s.* The sound of any tinkling instrument.

2. A jack-knife, from the sound of opening and shutting; a unuhi ae i ka hanaoi ame ke *kanikani*; also, a case knife.

3. The name of a famine.

KA-NI-KA-NI, *adj. Hoo.* Sounding; giving or causing a sound.

KA-NI-KOO,   } *s.* Epithet of an old
KA-NI-KOO-KO, } man; an old man, so old
KA-NI-KOO-KOO, } that he cannot walk without a staff. See KOO, a cane.

2. The state of old age.

KA-NI-KO-HA, *v. Kani,* to sing, and *koha,* to crack. To cackle like the *ao,* a bird of the mountains.

KA-NI-LI-HU-A, *s.* A mist like rain; small misty rain with wind.

KA-NI-MOO-PU-NA, *s. Kani* and *moopuna,* a grand child. That state of old age when one has many grand children.

KA-NI-NI, *s.* A state of convalescence; state of recovering from sickness.

2. A covering; a screen; a shade to keep off the sun.

KA-NI-PU-KA, *s.* A gate; a door. See PUKA.

KA-NI-WA-HI-E, *adj.* Hard; difficult; intractable; anything paakiki.

KA-NI-WA-WAE, *adj.* Of or belonging to

a foot soldier; na kanaka *kaniwawae*, foot soldiers. 1 *Oihl.* 19:18.

Ka-ni-wa-wae, *s.* A foot soldier; infantry. 2 *Sam.* 10:6.

Ka-no, *v.* To be proud; to be haughty.

2. *Hoo.* To exhibit pride; to show a lofty independence; to act proudly. 1 *Tim.* 6:4.

3. To be always eating.

4. To spare; to treat with affection.

Ka-no, *s. Hoo.* Pride; arrogance. *Hal.* 10:2. Haughtiness; impudence; disobedience. *Ezek.* 3:7.

Ka-no, *s.* The name of the two bones of the lower arm; hence,

2. A cubit in measure.

3. The body of a tree in distinction from its branches.

4. The handle of an axe, oo, hoe, shovel, &c.; *kano* oo. See KUAU.

5. The running vines of a grape vine, gourd, melon, &c.

6. A notch made in a tree, &c., where birds may light in order to catch them.

Ka-no, *v.* See KANO, *s.*, the bones of the arms. To grasp in one's arms, as in wrestling; e *kanoia* i kekahi me kona ikaika iho.

Ka-no-a, *s.* A round spot of land lower than the surrounding land. See PANOA.

Ka-no-a, *adv.* Externally; outside; applied to the dish containing awa; e poepoe *kanoa*, e hae *kanoa*.

Ka-no-e-no-e, *v.* See NOE and NOENOE, the north-east trade winds. To blow strongly; applied to the trade winds; ke *kanoenoe* mai nei no ka makani.

Ka-no-ka-no, *v.* See KANO. To be high; to be lofty; to be majestic.

Ka-no-ka-no, *adj.* High; independent in feeling; proud; great.

Ka-no-no, *v.* To ring, as a bell; to sound; to make a noise by striking against a sonorous body, as a clock hammer.

2. To snore. See NONO.

Ka-no-no, *s.* A ringing sound; a snoring. See NONO.

2. A red fowl; he moa ula hiua.

Ka-no-wa, *s.* See KANOA.

Ka-nu, *v.* To bury, as a corpse. 1 *Sam.* 25:1. To cover up in the earth.

2. To plant, as seed; to plant out a vegetable. *Hal.* 80:15. To transplant.

3. To hide in the earth.

Ka-nu', *v.* To be silent; to be stubborn.

Ka-nu, *s.* A burial; a planting; a putting out of sight in the earth.

Ka-nu, *adj.* Mea *kanu*, seed or a vegetable for planting; laau *kanu*, a tree for planting.

Ka-nu-e-e-i-na, *v.* See EEINA. To fix and smooth down, as the wet ruffled feathers of a fowl.

Ka-nu-lu, } *adj.* Change of *l* for *n.*
Ka-nu-nu, } Heavy, as a sound; oppressively heavy, as a deep heavy voice or sound.

Ka-nu-lu, } *s.* See above. An excell-
Ka-nu-nu, } ing; an increasing; a growing larger.

Ka-nu-nu, *v.* To have a heavy deep sound, as the voice of a person with a cold. *Anat.* 6.

Ka-nu-pa-pa-hu-wi-li.

Ka-pa, *v.* To call; to name; to give a name to. *Kin.* 3:2. To give an appellation.

2. To designate; to stigmatize.

3. To gather up in the hands and squeeze, as awa dregs; e *kapa* mai oe i kuu wahi awa.

Ka-pa, *s.* A bank; a shore; the side of a river, pond or lake; the side of a kalo patch; the side of a wood or land; the side of a road. SYN. with aoao.

2. A name given to the labium of a female; both labia together are called *kapakapa*.

Ka-pa, *s.* A kind of eel that makes havoc among all kinds of fish. See PUHI-KAPA. Hence Kamehameha was called Puhikapa, because victorious over all.

Ka-pa, *s.* The cloth beaten from the bark of the wauki or paper mulberry, also from the mamaki and other trees; hence,

2. Cloth of any kind; clothes generally; *kapa* komo, a coat; a dress.

Ka-pa, *adj.* A rustling; a rattling, as large drops of rain; he ua *kapa* nui. See PAKAPAKA.

Ka-paa-i-lu-na, *s.* The arch of heaven above supposed to be firm and strong.

2. Any place in the air or above the earth; o kahi e pili ana i ka lani ua kapaia o *kapaailuna.* D. *Malo.*

Ka-paa-i-la-lo, *s.* Ka *paaolalo* was supposed to be the opposite of *paaoluna*, but was under the earth ;but it applies to any place on the earth in distinction from heaven; o kahi e pili ana i ka honua, ua kapaia o *kapaailalo.* D. *Malo.*

Ka-pa-au, *s.* Name of the place of the god in the heiau, and where offerings were laid. See NUU.

Ka-pae, *v.* To pervert; to turn aside; to make crooked morally, i. e., to turn aside from moral rectitude. 1 *Nal.* 9:6.

2. To turn aside from the direct road in traveling. *Kanl.* 2:27.

3. To turn aside from following one. 2

Sam. 2:19.

4. To turn aside from obedience to law. *Kanl.* 9:12.

5. To turn a thing from its designed use or object. NOTE.—It was often applied when a commander in battle ordered a soldier to throw a spear at one of the opposite party who was the soldier's friend; the soldier would throw his spear under his arm or some place where it would do no hurt, and yet would pretend to obey; he would thus be said to kapae the spear. The word was much used formerly as applied to the management of a chief's property, a species of embezzling.

6. To change the meaning of a word from its common acceptation.

7. To pretend not to understand what is said.

8. To set aside, as an officer or ruler; to dethrone. *Oih.* 13:2. To suspend from the church.

9. *Hoo.* To cause to turn aside, &c.

KA-PAE, s. The act of turning aside anything from its proper use, or from moral rectitude.

KA-PAI, v. To pound gently with the fist, as on one's flesh to promote circulation. See PAI.

2. To anoint the body with ointment. See KAKELE.

3. To break up wood for fuel. See KAKA.

KA-PAI, adj. He popo *kapai*, a ball for lomiing or rubbing the sick.

KA-PA-O-A, s. The name of a plant, the root of which was used to dye kapa and scent it.

KA-PA-O-KA, s. The Polynesian pronunciation of Sabaota—Sabaoth; *Heb.*, armies. Supposed to be introduced from the Society Islands.

KA-PAU-U, v. To catch fish in a net by turning it this way and that; to cause fish to enter a net.

KA-PAU-U, s. A moving of a net in taking fish.

KA-PAU-U, v. To flutter, as an ensign or flag in the wind; *kapauu* ka lani, ua hehehili ka lani.

KA-PA-HAI, s. The seashore; ku i *kapahai* ka mea haku ole.

KA-PA-KAI, v. To look quietly at another taking property without the order of a chief.

KA-PA-KA-HI, adj. *Kapa*, side, and *kahi*, one. One-sided; uneven; crooked; partial to one party to the injury of another;

lawe *kapakahi*, to act with partiality.

KA-PA-KA-HI, v. To act partially; to put out of square; to turn aside.

KA-PA-KA-PA, v. To be lame in the hip joint.

2. To call by an assumed or fictitious name. See KAPA, v.

KA-PA-KA-PA, adj. Fictitious, assumed, as one's name; he inoa *kapakapa*; an assumed name for purposes of concealment.

KA-PA-KA-PA, s. See KAPA. The labia of females; kahi huluhulu.

2. The crotch of men; he mai *kapkapa* uha i ka manawa e hele loihi ai.

KA-PA-KE-U, v. To deny; to refuse; to reject; to quarrel; to dispute; to be angry; to distort the countenance.

KA-PA-KA-KEU, v. See KAPAKEU.

KA-PA-KO-MO, s. *Kapa* and *komo*, to enter in, i. e., to put on. A garment for putting off and on. *Kin.* 37:3.

KA-PA-KU-I-NA, s. *Kapa* and *kui*, to stitch. The five kapas sewed together for a set of sleeping kapas.

KA-PA-LA, v. See PALA, to daub. To blot; to daub; to strike or blot out.

2. To stain; to spot; to paint or print kapa or cloth. See PALAPALA.

KA-PA-LA, s. A writing; a printing; a stamping.

KA-PA-LA, s. The name of a plant, the leaves eaten for food in scarcity.

KA-PA-LA-AU, s. The place of sunsetting; kokoke ka la e hiki i *kapalaau*, the sun will soon reach the setting place.

KA-PA-LAU, s. The leaves with which the dead body of a chief was bound up previous to burial.

KA-PA-LA-LU, adv. Badly; awkwardly; without skill; *kapalalu* ka pu.

KA-PA-LI-LI, v. To shake rapidly; to vibrate, as a reed or leaf in the wind; to vibrate, as the tongue in pronouncing the letter r.

2. To trepidate, as the heart either by fear or joy; *kapalili* ka houpo. *Hoo.* To be in fear; to tremble.

KA-PA-LI-LI, s. A trembling or palpitation, as of the heart; the vibration of the tongue in pronouncing the French r.

KA-PA-LU-LU, v. To move; to tremble; to shake; to make a tremulous or buzzing sound.

KA-PA-LU-LU, s. A tremulous sound, as a fly buzzing in the ear.

KA-PA-NA-HA, adj. Crazy.

KA-PA-PA, v. To sprawl about, as one

having fallen down in the dark feels about; hina wale i ke ala *kapapa*.

KA-PA-PAU-LU-A, *s.* A human sacrifice; a ma kekahi kanaka i ke *kapapaulua* ana.

KA-PA-PA-KU, *s.* Some unknown place in the center of the earth.

KA-PA-PA-LA-NI, *s.* The broad sky; the firmament. See KALANIPAA.

KA-PA-PE-A, *s. Kapa* and *pea*, filthy. A kapa or dress which a menstruous woman wore, and left when she returned to the family. See also *Isa.* 64:6.

KA-PA-WA, *s.* A border or edge of a garment. See LIKI and PAWA.

KA-PE-A, *v.* To lay hold of; to seize, as a criminal.

2. To acuse falsely. See HOOPEA and PEA.

3. To collect charges of evil without cause against a good man.

KA-PE-A-PE-A, *v.* See the foregoing. To watch closely; to seek occasion; to entangle one.

KA-PE-HE, *v.* See KUPEHE.

KA-PE-HE, *s.* A companion; an assistant; a fellow; an associate.

KA-PE-KE, *v.* To be out of joint, as a limb; to limp, as a lame person. *Kin.* 32:35, 31. To misstep. *Hal.* 37:31.

2. To miss in attempting to do a thing; to mistake; to disjoint.

3. To be colored, as a malo of one color on one side, and another color on the opposite side; he malo *kapeke*; hence, the name for that species of malo.

4. *Hoo.* I *hookapekeia* me ka holei, that it (kapa) may be colored on one side with the holei; e pake, e hamama, e waiho wale.

KA-PE-KEI, *v.* To drive, as fish into a net.

KA-PE-KEU, *v.* To quarrel; to scold; to disagree; to be on unfriendly terms.

KA-PE-KE-PE-KE, *v.* See KAPEKE. To be unsettled in mind or opinion; to be in doubt. 1 *Nal.* 18:21. To be inconstant; to be fickle.

2. To go in a crooked manner.

3. To stand unsteadily; to tottle; to roll; to be about to fall.

4. To fasten or put up a thing superficially; ua paa *kapekepeke* no, aole i paa pono.

KA-PE-KE-PE-KE, *s.* Inconstancy; doubt; fickleness; hesitancy.

KA-PE-KE-PE-KE, *adj.* Unsteady; hesitating; doubtful; unlike at different times.

KA-PE-KE-PE-KE, *adv.* Doubtfully; irresolutely; unsteadily. 2 *Pet.* 3:16.

KA-PE-KU, } *v.* To splash or spatter in the water, as peo-
KA-PE-KU-PE-KU, } ter in the water, as people do to drive fish into a net; to spatter, as a fish does when suddenly frightened.

KA-PE-LE-LE-U, *s.* See PELELEU. The name of Kamehameha's voyage when he went to take possession of his kingdom; so called from the kind of canoes he went in; ua kapaia kela hele ana o *kapeleleu*, the voyage was called *kapeleleu*.

KA-PE-NA, *s. Eng.* A captain or master of a ship; i kapaia'ku ai *Kapena* Kuke o Lono.

2. A captain; a military officer.

3. A carpenter; but Hawaiians lately write *kamena* for carpenter.

KA-PI, } *v.* To sprinkle with salt; to
KA-PII, } preserve with salt; to season with salt. *Mar.* 9:49.

2. To sprinkle with water. *Isa.* 52:15. To pour out water.

3. To sprinkle, as with ashes. *Ier.* 25:34.

4. To apply to; to put to, as one thing to another. *Lunk.* 7:6. See PIPI.

KA-PII, *s.* Name of an office among the king's retinue.

KA-PI-O, *v.* To be arched; he pio kolea. See PIO.

KA-PI-HI, *adj.* One-sided.

KA-PI-KI, *s.* A kind of poi.

2. *Eng.* The Hawaiian pronunciation for the word cabbage, hence, a cabbage or head of cabbage.

KA-PI-LI, *v.* See PILI. To join or unite together in various ways.

2. To fit different substances together.

3. To put or fit together, as the different parts of a house or ship or other work of the kind. 2 *Oihl.* 3:1. *Kapili* laau, to work at carpenter's business; *kapili* moku, to build a ship; ua popopo ke kia moku, hoi hou oia e *kapili*, the mast of the ship was rotten, he returned to *repair* it.

4. To repair or mend what is broken. *Neh.* 2:8.

5. To plaster; to besmear.

KA-PI-LI-A-LO, *s.* Some unknown land, where the people were unknown of what kind; he pilikau, he kanaka ano e.

KA-PI-LI-KU-A, *s.* See above. An imaginary country not known where nor the character of the people; he kanaka pili makua, ma ke kaao ana e loaa mai ai.

KA-PI-LI-MA-NU, *s.* See KAPILI and MANU, a bird. The art of catching birds with bird lime (pilali, &c.); i ko'u pii ana iuka i ke *kapilimanu*.

KA-PI-LI-MO-KU, *v.* See KAPILI. To build,

but especially to calk ships.

KA-PI-LI-MO-KU, *s.* The art of ship building.

2. A ship builder or a ship calker. *Ezek.* 37:9.

KA-PI-LI-PI-LI, *v.* See KAPILI. To fit one thing to another; to join two things so as to make one; to unite.

2. To set, as precious stones. *Puk.* 35:33.

3. To fix blame on another; to complain of another.

4. To excuse one's self.

KA-PI-PI, *v.* See KAPI and PIPI. To sprinkle, as salt; to sprinkle, as blood or water. *Puk.* 24:6.

KA-PI-PI-NE, *s.* A word of uncertain meaning brought from some of the western islands; i aku ke kama *kapipine,* he *kapipine* ohuiia me ke kamaioa.

KA-PO, *s.* A sister of Kalaipahoa, a fabled goddess from abroad who entered some kind of a tree and rendered it poisonous. See KALAIPAHOA.

KA-POO, *v.* To enter into, as a spirit; *kapoo* ka uhane o ke Akua iloko.

2. To sink, as in water; *kapoo* i ke kai.

3. To set, as the sun; i ke *kapoo* ana o ka la, hele au; kamailio iho la makou a *kapoo* ka la.

4. To sink into, as the foot in soft mud. See NAPOO.

KA-POO, *s.* Sunken in; the armpit; the same applied to a fowl.

KA-POO-POO, *v.* See KAPOO. To descend; to go down.

KA-PA-LA, *v.* To bind up in a wrapper; to fold up in a kapa; e wahi, e kupola.

KA-PO-LA-PI-LAU, *s.* Any limb sore, bad smelling and swathed with kapa or rags is called a *kapolapilau.* See KAPOLA.

KA-PU, *s.* A general name of the system of religion that existed formerly on the Hawaiian Islands, and which was grounded upon numerous restrictions or prohibitions, keeping the common people in obedience to the chiefs and priests; but many of the *kapus* extended to the chiefs themselves. The word signifies,

1. Prohibited; forbidden.

2. Sacred; devoted to certain purposes. *Nah.* 6:7.

3. A consecration; a separation. (See Hawaiian History and D. Malo on *kapus.*) Eha na po *kapu* ma ka malama hookahi, there were four *tabu* nights (days) in a month; 1st, *kapuku,* 2d, *kapuhua,* 3d, *kapukaloa,* 4th, *kapukane.*

KA-PU, *v.* To set apart; to prohibit from use; to make sacred or holy.

2. *Hoo.* To devote to a special purpose.

Puk. 23:3. To consecrate; to set apart as sacred. *Ios.* 20:7, 8. *Hookapu* ae la o Wakea i kekahi ia, Wakea tabued certain fish.

3. To put on airs of distance or separation from others, airs of self-importance. See HOOIHIIHI.

KA-PU, *adj.* Prohibited; forbidden; hence,

2. Sacred; consecrated; holy; devoted.

KA-PU, *s.* A place of fire; a stove; a gun lock. See KAPUAHI.

KA-PU-AI, } *s.* The sole or bottom of
KA-PU-WAI, } the foot. *Ios.* 1:3.

2. The track of one's foot; a foot-print; a foot-step.

3. A foot in measure (modern use); *kapuwai* manamana, the paw of an animal. *Oihk.* 11:27. NOTE.—The Hawaiians have no word for *foot* in distinction from wawae, leg; but *wawae* includes often both foot and leg; so *lima* signifies *arm* including the hand, but no specific word for *hand.*

KA-PU-A-HI, *s.* See KAPU, place, and AHI, fire. A fire place.

2. The pan of a musket or gun.

3. A censer for sacrifice.

4. One who attends upon an oven or bakes.

5. The place itself of baking; an oven.

KA-PU-A-HI-HAO, *s. Kapuahi* and *hao,* iron. An iron stove; an iron furnace.

2. FIG. The place or circumstances of affliction. *Kanl.* 4:20.

KA-PU-A-MO-E, *s.* The name of a kapu when everybody was required to prostrate themselves when the chief passed; he alii niaupio no, he *kapuamoe* no kona.

KA-PU-A-NO-HO, *s.* A kapu requiring the people all to sit when the king's calabash or other utensil was carried by; he alii nui, he niaupio no, he *kapuanoho* nae kona. See above.

KA-PU-A-PU-A, *s.* A kind of plantain or banana.

KA-PU-O, *s.* A kapu in honor of the god Kaili.

KA-PU-HI, *s.* A master of an animal; a nurse of a child; a provider. See HOOKAPUHI.

KA-PU-HI-LI, *s.* Name of a species of fish.

KA-PU-KA-PU, *s.* See KAPU. Honor; praise; dignity; separation from what is common.

KA-PU-KA-PU, *v. Hoo.* To put on airs of self-consequence; to ape dignity; a *kapukapu* no hoi me ou mau kaikuahine. *Laieik.* 99.

KA-PU-KA-PU-LA-NI, *v.* To frown or repel one by sour looks; to be distant and ill-natured; *kapukapulani* ka maka.

KA-PU-KA-WAI, *v.* To be handsome; to be noble.

KA-PU-LE, *v.* To be hung up, as a bunch of bananas until the skin turns black in spots; ua *kapule* ala mea wale i ka ua.

KA-PU-LU, *v.* To be unfaithful in business; to be careless; to be slovenly.

KA-PU-LU, *adj.* Work slovenly done; dirty; filthy; foolish; sottish. *Ier.* 4:22.

KA-PU-LU-PU-LU, *v.* See KAPULU. To work lazily; to act in a shiftless manner.

KA-PU-NI, *s.* See PUNI. The circumference of a thing; a surrounding; a circuit.

2. The name of a chief who was born, grew up, became old and died in the same place.

KA-PU-NI, *adj.* Overspreading; widely diffused; he ua *kapuni*, a rain over all the islands.

KA-PU-WAI, *s.* See KAPU, place, and WAI, water. A bathing tub.

2. A foot-step. See KAPUAI.

KA-PU-WO-HI, *s.* A kapu less than a kapu niaupio, i. e., a relaxation of the kapu niaupio; o ke alii *kupuwohi*, aole oia ame kona lawe kahili; o Kamehameha I. he *kapuwohi* kona.

KA-WA, *s.* A precipice down which a suicide plunges; a lele aku i ka make me he kio *kawa* la. See LELEKAWA.

2. A manner of playing.

3. A person who goes behind or follows after another.

KA-WA, *s.* A deep pool of water with a precipice overhanging it, from which to dive.

KA-WA, *v.* To strike secretly; to pierce one in the dark; to assassinate.

2. To overtake and shoot ahead of one.

3. E pulepe.

4. To shoot or fall down. See LELEKAWA.

5. To rain heavily; to flow freely, as perspiration upon the skin.

KA-WAA, *s.* The voice of a bird on Molakai which seems to say, "i *kawaa*, e holo, ua nui ke kai o ke aumoe."

KA-WAA, *s.* The name of a species of fish net; he upena *kawaa*.

KA-WAE, *v.* To bring up the foot, as in sitting cross-legged on a mat.

2. To draw one to you with the foot.

3. To trip one with the foot.

4. To put the arm over one's shoulder, or the foot over another; to bring the legs across.

5. To bind on, as a girdle.

KA-WAE-WAE, *s.* Name of a kind of stone used in polishing canoes.

KA-WAI, *s.* The name of the coloring matter or residuum when water is poured on the second time.

2. The name of the partially colored water itself.

3. The liquor obtained from cane, &c., after most of the intoxicating matter is extracted; aohe ikaika o keia rama, he *kawai* wale no, there is no strength in this rum, it is nearly all water.

KA-WAI-KA-MA-MA, *v.* See LOPIO and NIO. To soften down, as the rigor of work; to make easier to do; to modify one's character for the better.

KA-WAU, *v.* To be wet and cold; to be damp.

2. To keep back; to detain.

KA-WAU, *s.* Dampness.

2. Distemper among dogs resembling the itch.

3. A seed used in deceiving fish.

4. The block on which kapa is pounded. See KUA.

5. A species of tree, used somewhat for canoes and other things.

KA-WAU-KE, *s.* See WAUKE.

KA-WA-HA, *v.* To be hollow, as a log or pillar. *Puk.* 38:7; *Ier.* 52:21.

KA-WA-HA, *adj.* Vacant, as a space; hollow. *Puk.* 27:8. Hollow, as an arch. *Puk.* 28:11.

KA-WA-KA-WA, *s.* The name of a species of fish.

KA-WA-KA-WA, *v.* See KAWA. To be wet with water or rain.

KA-WA-KA-WA, *adj.* Wet; damp with fine rain.

KA-WA-KA-WAU, *v.* To be wet and cold.

2. To be wet with perspiration, as the body or bed where one sleeps.

KA-WA-KA-WAU, *adj.* Damp, as mats or grass. See KAWAU.

KA-WA-LA-WA-LA, *v.* To speak in an unintelligible manner.

KA-WA-LA-WA-LA, *adj.* Few; scattering; here and there one, as persons; few and scattering, as houses in the country; hence, *kauhale kawalawala*, the country in distinction from a village.

KA-WA-LA-WA-LA, *s.* Fewness; scarcity.

KA-WE-A, *s.* A species of fish.

KA-WE-LAU, *s.* See WELAU. The extremity of a thing; the top of a bank; the top of a precipice.

KA-WE-LE, *v.* To work slowly or moderately, as at rowing a canoe, or at cultivating the soil; *kawele* wale aku no.

KA-WE-LE, *adj.* Slow; lingering, as a disease; o ka hookuli ka mea e *kawele* nei ia poe.

KA-WE-LE, *s.* *Eng.* A towel; a napkin; a wiping cloth.

KA-WE-LE-A, *s.* See WELEA. A species of fish.

KA-WE-LE-WE-LE, *v.* See KAWELE, *v.* To work slowly or moderately.

KA-WE-LE-WE-LE, *s.* The name of certain short ropes about a canoe; he mau wahi kaula ma ka pu o ka waa.

2. The beard.

KA-WE-LO, *s.* Name of a species of fish.

KA-WE-WE, *v.* To cover kalo with mats in the oven when about to bake.

2. To clatter, as in the movement of plates or slates; to make a rustling noise. *Ezek.* 37:7.

3. To be dry; to be unfruitful, as potatoes without water.

KA-WE-WE-LE, *s.* The person at the end of a long rope where many persons are drawing a heavy substance; o Kama ke akua i *kawewele.*

KA-WI, *v.* See UI and KOWI. To press; to squeeze, as grapes or any substance in order to extract the juice.

KA-WI-LI, *v.* See WILI. To mix together different ingredients, as flour and water in making bread; to stir up together.

2. To be changeable or variable. See LAUWILI.

3. *Hoo.* To mix together; to knead bread. *Nah.* 15:4.

4. To tear; to rend; to vex; to harass. See KAAWILI.

KA-WI-LI, *s.* The art of catching birds with bird lime, &c.; pela no oia i papa aku ai i ka poe *kawili* manu oo, so also he forbid those who caught full grown birds.

KA-WI-LI-KA-E-KA, *v.* *Kawili* and *kaeka,* to entangle. To entangle; to go this way and that; to involve; to go over and over again.

KA-WI-LI-MA-NU, *s.* See KAWILI and MANU, a bird. A method of catching birds with bird lime; he lawaia manu.

KA-WI-LI-WI-LI, *s.* Name of a tree, the timber of which was very much used for surf-boards and the amas or outriggers of canoes; erythrina corallodendron. See WILIWILI.

KA-WO-WO, *v.* To grow thriftily, as vines which branch out and run luxuriantly every way.

2. To grow; to increase; to spread out. *Ier.* 23:3.

3. To increase, as a prosperous people. *Ier.* 29:6.

4. To make a rustling noise; to rattle. See KAWEWE above.

5. To roar; to rage; to sound heavily.

KA-WO-WO, *s.* A plant growing thriftily. *Mel. Sol.* 4:13.

2. Plants; running vines, &c.; a sucker; a scion.

3. A continued rustling or rushing noise; the noise of a waterfall.

KA-BA, *s.* *Heb.* A cab, a Hebrew dry measure, nearly three pints. 2 *Nal.* 6:25.

KA-SI-A, *s.* *Eng.* Cassia, an odoriferous herb. *Hal.* 45:8.

KA-TA-RA-KE-TE, *s.* *Heb.* A cormorant, name of an unclean bird. *Kanl.* 14:17.

KE, *def. art.* The. See KA, *art.* This form of the article (*ke*) is used before all nouns beginning with the letter *k*. A few nouns beginning with the letter *p* have *ke* also for their article, and a still smaller number beginning with the letter *m*. Nouns whose first letter is *a* have both *ka* and *ke* for their article; that is, some nouns take one and some the other, but no one noun, without a radical change of meaning, takes both forms of the article. Nouns beginning with *o*, like *a*, take both forms of the article. Before all other letters, whether vowels or consonants, ka is the form of the article. See Grammar § 59, 60.

KE, *particle,* before a verb and *nei* after it, marks the present tense of the indicative mood; but *ke* with the subjunctive mood marks the future tense. After the verbs *hiki,* always, and *pono* generally (both used as auxiliary verbs), *ke* is used before the infinitive instead of *e*. *Gram.* § 203.

KE, *interj.* An exclamation of surprise, indeed! 1 *Kor.* 15:36. See KA. *Ke* is often used in beginning a reply to what one has said, and expresses astonishment at what had been advanced; sometimes disgust and the greatest contempt; e manao ino me ka henehene.

KE, *v.* Mostly with *hoo.* To force; to compel; to urge on. *Lunk.* 1:34.

2. To be intent upon; to press forward; to go ahead in any affair; *hooke* loa mai la o Keoua me ka manao e lawe i ko Kamehameha mau okana nona, Keoua *was intent* upon the idea of taking Kamehameha's districts for his own.

3. To thrust; to push or drive at. *Hal.* 118:13.

4. To obstruct one as he goes along; to get a person or persons into difficulty; to struggle against; to be troubled. 2 *Kor.* 4:8.

5. To crowd together at a door or about a person; to assault one's house; to press upon.

6. With *ai*, food, to push away, as food without eating; to abstain from food; hence,

7. To fast. 2 *Sam.* 12:16. NOTE.—Voluntary fasting among Hawaiians requires the exercise of some force.

KE-A, *s.* A cross; the form of a cross, viz.: one post upright, the other transverse. See AMANA.

KE-A, *s.* A tightness of the chest attended with difficulty of breathing; nearly synonymous with pani.

KE-A, } *adj.* White. See KEO. Pel-
KE-A-KE-A, } lucid, clear.

KE-A, *v.* To shoot or throw arrows of sugar-cane. See KEAPUA.

KE-A, *s.* Two different places in the thorax; the *kea paa* was above, the *kea hakahaka* below; elua *kea*, o ke *kea* paa ame ke *kea* hakahaka.

KE-A, *s.* The name of a play of children with arrows of cane.

2. The name of a mountain on Hawaii—*Maunakea*, white mountain.

3. The name of the rain or mist at Hana and at Koolau on Maui.

4. The name of the semen of males, from the color. See KEAKEA below and KEA, *adj.*

5. The name of the male unmasculated hog; ina i kahe ole ia, he *kea* ia puaa.

6. The name of an office in the king's train.

KE-A, *v.* To hinder; to object to. See KE, *v.*, and KEAKEA below.

KE-AA-WA-I-LE-IA, *s.* Name of a species of fish-hook.

KE-AI, *v.* See KE above and AI, food. *Hoo.* To thrust away food; to fast.

KE-AO, *s.* A legend; a tale of ancient adventures. See KAAO.

KE-A-HA-KA-HA-KA, *s.* *Kea* and *hakahaka*, empty. The part of the body in men and beasts which embraces the abdomen, as *keapaa* does the chest.

KE-A-KE-A, *v.* See KEA, to hinder. To hinder. 1 *Sam.* 14:6. To stand in the way of.

2. To object to that which would be to the advantage of another.

3. To keep back; to restrain one from doing a thing. *Nah.* 24:11. To prohibit; to resist. *Oih.* 13:10.

KE-A-KE-A, *adj.* See KEA, cross, above. In the form of several crosses, as sticks under a piece of timber to carry it; a *keakea* a amo aku.

KE-A-KE-A, *s.* See KEA 4 above. The semen masculinum; the semen of all males. See KEKEA.

KE-A-KE-A-LA-NI, *s.* The name of an ancient chief woman, supreme over all the islands, a woman of good character (haipule loa), from whom was descended Keawe.

KE-A-KU, *s.* Name of a cave on the eastern side of the valley of Kailiili, which see.

KE-A-KU-A-LA-PU, the ghost god, and KE-KUPUOHI, the bamboo plant, *s.* The names of two red coats which Vancouver gave to Kamehameha I.

KE-A-LI-A, *s.* A place where the salt water is brought or caused to flow inland, the sea then shut out and the water evaporated, leaving the salt, which may be gathered up. See ALIAPAAKAI.

KE-A-MAU-MAU, *s.* See AMAUMAU.

KE-A-PAA, *s.* The chest of the human body, that is, the whole body included within the ribs, in opposition to *keahakahaka*, the abdomen.

2. The same also in relation to beasts.

KE-A-PUA, *v.* See KEA, to shoot, and PUA, the blossom of the sugar-cane; hence, an arrow. To throw or shoot arrows of the sugar-cane. NOTE.—This was and is now a favorite play of children; formerly it was a game among men.

KE-A-WA-KOO, *s.* The name of a stone idol near the top of Mauna Waialeale on Kauai.

KE-A-WE, *s.* A name frequently heard among Hawaiians either by itself or compounded with other words; it signifies the *bearer*.

KE-A-WE-NUI-KAU-O-HI-LO, *s.* One of the class of gods called akua noho.

KE-E, *v.* To bend; to crook; to bulge out; to oppose. See KUE. Ka puu a Kana i *kee* ai a hiolo iho. See KEEKEE.

KE-E, *s.* Crookedness; want of uprightness in conduct; wrong doing; mai hai aku i ke *kee* o ko kakou aina; aka, e hai aku i ke ala ame ke onaona ame ka peekue o ka naauao.

KE-E, *adj.* Crooked. See the verb.

KE-E-O, *v.* To be angry; to be indignant at what is wrong.

2. To perform the office of executioner.

3. To be suddenly excited; to rage. See KAEO.

KE-E-O, *s.* Dissatisfaction; displeasure; anger.

KE-E-HA-NA, *s.* *Kee* and *ana*, *h* inserted. See KEE. The bottom or sole of the foot;

kapuai.

2. A place for the bottom of the foot, or a place to rest a thing on.

3. Ground stamped upon or trodden by the foot.

4. A footstool; a place to put the feet upon.

5. A prop; a supporter; keehanawawae. *Isa.* 66:1. See KEHANA.

6. A place for the feet, i. e., a floor. 1 *Nal.* 6:16. A pavement. *Ezek.* 4:17.

KE-E-HA-NA-WA-WAE, *s.* A footstool, &c. See the foregoing.

KE-E-HI, *v.* To kick; to stamp with the foot.

2. To lift up the foot against one, i. e., to resist.

3. To kick at; to despise. 1 *Sam.* 2:29.

4. To rebel. *Kanl.* 32:15.

5. To strike or hit upon, as a beam of light; i ka manawa e *keehi* iho ai na kukuna o ka la i ka piko o na mauna, when the rays of the sun *shall hit* the top of the mountains.

KE-E-HI, *s.* The stirrup of a saddle.

KE-E-HI-LAE, *adj.* Proud; haughty; disdainful.

KE-E-HI-NA, } *s.* A different or-
KE-E-HI-NA-WA-WAE, } thography for *keehana* and *keehanawawae.* A footstool, &c. See above.

KE-E-KE-E, *v.* See KEE and KEKEE. To crook; to bend.

2. To pervert. *Hoo.* The same. *Kanl.* 27:19.

KE-E-KE-E-NU-KU, *v. Keekee* and *nuku,* to scold. To rise up, as two persons in order to fight, and after scolding at each other awhile, separate without fighting.

KE-E-LA, } *adj.* Great, as a noise; great,
KE-E-LE, } as a land; large; excelling; very great; *keele* kou aloha.

KE-E-LE, *v.* To be very great, as a trouble or perplexity; *keele* ka pioo ana o ka mai a ola.

KE-E-LE-Ā-WAA, *adj.* Having frequent ditches or gullies; *keeleawaa* ke ala.

KE-E-MO-A, *v.* To be sour; to be crabbed; to be ill-natured.

2. *Hoo.* To be greedy; to be covetous.

KE-E-MO-A, *adj.* Having lost one's affection or attachment for another and looks at him with indifference. See NAAUKEEMOA.

KE-E-NA, *s.* A room; an apartment in a house. 1 *Nal.* 6:6.

2. A drawer of a bureau; *keena* kapu, a sanctuary. *Puk.* 25:8.

3. A partition of a room.

KEI, *int.* An expression of wonder; wonderful! glorious! excellent! stupendous!

KE-I, *v.* To praise; to extol; to boast; to glory.

2. *Haa.* To be lifted up with honor or pride.

KE-I, *s.* A boasting; glorying; pride; high-mindedness.

2. The name of a species of hard rock out of which kois were made.

KE-I-A, *adj. pron. Ke,* article, and *ia,* he, she or it. This, referring to something present or just said; this person; this thing. *Gram.* § 152.

KE-I-KE-I, *v.* Intensive of *kei.* To glory; to boast; to be proud.

KE-I-KI, *s. Ke,* article, and *iki,* little, small, i. e., the little one. The *ke* has now become assimilated to the word *iki* and takes another article.

1. A child, male or female.

2. The offspring of one, whether a child or grown person.

3. A descendant of any number of degrees.

4. The young of animals or vegetables; *keiki* maia.

KE-I-KI, *v.* To have or obtain a child. *Kin.* 30:3.

2. To be or become a child. *Rom.* 8:16. Properly *hookeiki.*

KE-I-KI-A-LA-ME-A, *s.* Name of a fatal disease; kawaiiki was used as the remedy.

KE-I-KI-HI-A-PO, *s. Keiki* and *hiapo,* first born. The first born of a family.

KE-I-KI-HI-PA, *s. Keiki* and *hipa* (*Eng.*), sheep. A lamb. *Oihk.* 4:35.

KE-I-KI-HO-KI, *s. Keiki* and *hoki,* an ass. The young of an ass. *Kin.* 49:11.

KE-I-KI-KA-O, *s. Keiki* and *kao,* goat. A kid. *Oihk.* 4:23.

KE-I-KI-KA-NE, *s. Keiki* and *kane,* male. A son; a male child.

KE-I-KI-PA-PA, *s. Keiki* and *papa,* an ancestor. A resident; a descendant; one who among many others, is a descendant of some great man, who lived perhaps several generations back; but it is on the condition that said descendants continue to reside on the ground where their ancestor did.

2. A native born in distinction from *kanaka e,* or *malihini. Ios.* 8:33.

KE-I-KI-WAI-U, *s. Keiki* and *waiu,* milk. Any young suckling; a sucking child; an infant. *Kanl.* 32:25.

KE-I-KI-BI-PI, *s. Keiki* and *bipi,* an ox or cow. A calf. 1 *Nal.* 12:28.

KE-I-KI-BI-PI-KA-NE, *s. Keikibipi* and *kane,* male. A young bullock; a grown male calf. *Nah.* 7:15.

KE-I-NA, *s.* The number four; more

generally written *kauna*. See KAUNA.

KE-O, *s.* A comb.

KE-O, *adj.* White; clear; glistening white. See KEA.

KE-O, }
KE-O-KE-O, } *adj.* Proud; haughty; carrying one's self haughtily.

   2. White, as paper or cloth; white, as fruit that is ripe. *Hoo.* Whitened; made white.

KE-O-KE-O, *v.* See KEO, white. To whiten; to become white.

   2. *Hoo.* To whiten; to cause to glisten with whiteness. *Mark.* 9:3. *Keokeo* olinolino, glistening white.

KE-O-LO-E-WA, *s.* Name of one of the class of gods called akua noho.

KE-U, }
KE-U-KE-U, } *v.* To be more; to have a remainder.

   2. To excel; to run over; to hang out; to project like a hog's tush.

   3. *Hoo.* To do over and above; to do more than is required; to exceed. *Puk.* 30:15. Opposite to *hooemi.* NOTE.—This word is used in counting or in specifying a general amount, with something over, thus: pa kauna a *keu*, four each and *something over*, or four and some *besides*; pa umi a *keu*, ten and *upwards*; pa kanaha a *keu*, forty and *more*; pau lau a *keu*, four hundred and *over*; the fraction over the definite sum is not specified.

KE-U, *s.* What is over and above; in *arithmetic*, a remainder.

KE-U, *adj.* Remaining; over and above; besides. *Lunk.* 2:8.

KE-U, *adv.* A *keu*, and over.

KE-UE-UE, }
KE-UE-WE, } *v.* *Ke*, to push, and *ue*, to move. To push against; to oppose one; to treat harshly.

KE-U, }
KE-U-KE-U, } *v.* To contradict; to scold; to find fault; to show a bad disposition; to be morose.

KE-U, }
KE-U-KE-U, } *s.* Surliness; pettishness; anger.

KE-U, }
KE-U-KE-U, } *adj.* Very angry; cross.

KE-U, }
KE-U-KE-U, } *s.* The voice of a bird, the alae; the singing voice of the alae; ina e lohe oe i ke *keu* a ka alae. *Laieik.* 149.

KE-HA, *v.* To snap with the teeth, as when a dog seizes an animal and tears out a mouthful.

   2. To extend; to lengthen out, as time.

   3. To be puffed up with pride.

   4. To sing or repeat a song.

KE-HA, *v.* To lean the head on one's hand and lean over sideways; e moe me ke kaa o ke poo i ka a luna me ka lolii ana i ke kapa a paa.

KE-HAU, *s.* See HAU. The gentle land breeze at night on the west side of Hawaii.

   2. The mountain breeze in the morning anywhere; e o'u poe hoa o ka la wela o Lahainaluna ame ke *kehau* anu o ke kakahiakanui.

   3. A mist; a cold, fine rain floating in the air, mostly in the mountainous regions.

KE-HAU, *adj.* Frosty; rainy, &c.; hoahele, hoa o ke anu *kehau* o ke kakahiaka.

KE-HA-KE-HA, *v.* See KEHA 3. To be proud; to be haughty; to be arrogant; to be wasteful.

KE-HA-KE-HA, *s.* Wastefulness; pride; arrogance.

KE-HA-KE-HA, *adj.* Swaggering; lofty; proud. *Isa.* 2:12.

KE-HA-LU-HA, *v.* See KEHA 4. To sing or repeat a song.

KE-HA-NA-WA-WAE, *s.* See KEEHANA and WAWAE, leg. A footstool.

KE-HA-PA, *v.* To be less or fewer than was expected; to be not enough.

KE-HE-NE, *s.* The name of a place where offals or filth is thrown; a kind of Tophet like the Gehenna of the Scriptures.

   2. A basket.

   3. A fire; a volcano.

KE-HI-NA, *s.* See KEEHANA and KEEHINA. A place for putting the feet; a footstool.

KE-HU, *s.* A contraction perhaps of *ka ehu*, the steam.

   2. An unnatural puffing or distention of the abdomen, as from over-eating.

KE-KAU-HA, *adj.* Stretched out; straight and stiff. SYN. with kakauha.

KE-KA-HI, *adj. pron., art.* See KAHI. One; some; some one; certain. Gram. § 63, § 65, 2.

KE-KA-HU-NA, *s.* *Ke*, article, the, and *kahuna*, priest. The preacher; the name of a book in the Scriptures, *Ecclesiastes*.

KE-KA-LO-A-KA-MA-KA-MA-KA, *s.* Name of a prayer in ancient worship.

KE-KA-NA-LII, *s.* Food that grows very slowly; vegetables that are a long time small.

KE-KE, *v.* The intensive of *ke*. To strive together; to contend.

   2. To scold; to be angry at; to provoke.

   3. To skin; to pull off the skin; to show the teeth, as a cross dog.

   4. *Hoo.* To press hard upon, i. e., to be intent upon; to carry a point. *Kin.* 19:9. Mai *hookeke* i ko kakou hele ana.

KE-KE, *v. imp.* A word used to children in charging them to cover up their private parts.

Ke-ke, *s.* Name of a species of bird. See AKEKE.

2. Name of a fish.

3. Displeasure; scolding; angry expressions.

Ke-ke-a, *s.* The semen of all males; semen virile. See KEAKEA.

Ke-kee, *v.* See KEKE and KE. To be crooked; to be twisted; to be out of shape.

2. To pervert; to turn to another purpose. *Puk.* 23:8.

3. *Hoo.* To do contrary to the rule of right. *Kanl.* 27:19.

Ke-kee, *s.* Name of a kind of fish which swims near the surface of the water.

Ke-kee, *adj.* Crooked; twisted; incorrect; contrary to the rule of right; twisted out of shape; cross; petulant.

Ke-kee, *adv.* Crookedly; erroneously; hana *kekee,* to do unrighteously. *Oihk.* 19:35.

Ke-ke-ka-ha, *v.* To make a show; to be wondered at.

2. To contend, as two cocks when one is beaten and shrinks away; *kekekaha* ae la i ke kula o Puopelu.

Ke-ke-ko, *v.* See KEKO. To be small; of small and low stature, whether men or women; e keko, e ihukoki, e kokikoki.

Ke-ke-ne, *v.* To be jealous of; to envy.

Ke-ke-ne, *adj.* Envious; jealous; i aku la au, no ke aha? no ka opu *kekene* o Moo, I said what for? for the *envious disposition* of Moo.

Ke-ke-we, *adj.* Swelled; full, as the belly, *kekewe* ka opu.

Ke-ki, *s.* The name of a bush or small tree whose fruit is eaten in time of scarcity.

Ke-ki, *s.* O *keki* no ame ka uhane.

Ke-ko, *s.* A little short man; hence, a monkey. 2 *Oihl.* 9:21. He kanaka poupou inoino, kokikoki ka ihu me ka maka.

Ke-ko-ke-ko, *adj.* Pertaining to a small man or woman; short; little; keko, ihu kumene, kokikoki.

Ke-ku-i-e-lu-a, *s.* Name of an instrument used in war.

Ke-ku-pu-o-hi, *s.* Name of a red coat which Vancouver gave to Kamehameha I. See KEAKUALAPU.

Ke-la, *adj. pron.* From *ke,* the, and *la,* there. That; that person; that thing; that fellow (more emphatic and definite than *ia*); he; she; it. It is used in opposition to *keia,* this; it is used when the noun to which it refers has just before been used. *Gram.* § 152.

Ke-la, *v.* To exceed; to go beyond. 1

Nal. 10:7.

2. To project out beyond another thing.

3. To be more. *Ier.* 7:26.

4. To cause to exceed; to be more. *Hal.* 119:98. E *hookela* i ke aloha, to love more. *Mat.* 10:37.

Ke-la, *adj.* Excelling; going beyond; preceding; great above another.

Ke-la-ke-la, *v.* The intensive of *kela.* *Hoo.* To boast; to brag. *Hal.* 10:3. To enlarge one's desires; to prefer one to another; to act with partiality. 1 *Tim.* 5:21.

Ke-le, *v.* To slip; to slide; to glide easily.

2. To sink in the sea or in the mud.

3. To be entangled at the bottom of the sea when diving.

4. To sail far out to sea, as a canoe; e *kele* wale ana ka waa mawaho.

5. *Hoo.* To steer a ship or canoe; hiki ia ia ma kona ike ke hookele moku; eia ka pule:

A *kele* akiu, kelekele akiu.

Ke-le, *s.* Mud; mire; the fat of animals; grease or whatever induces slipperiness.

2. *Hoo.* The steersman of a canoe or ship; the director of a boat or ship.

Ke-le, *adj.* Reached or arrived at by sailing; he moku *kele* i ka waa, an island reached by a canoe. *Moolelo Hawaii* 7:3.

Ke-le-a-we, *s.* Brass; copper; tin; polished steel. *Puk.* 25:3. *Keleawe* melemele, yellow copper, i. e., brass.

Ke-le-a-we, *adj.* Pertaining to copper, brass, tin, &c. *Ios.* 6:24.

Ke-le-ke-le, *v.* See KELE. To sail about in a boat for pleasure; to glide easily here and there. *Hoo.* The same; also, to ride the surf in a canoe.

Ke-le-ke-le, *s.* Fat; grease. *Puk.* 29:22. Fatness. *Hal.* 109:24.

2. Fat meat in opposition to io, the lean meat of an animal.

3. The fat part of a hog; fat meat generally.

4. Mud; mire; *kelekele* ke ala, the road is slippery.

Ke-le-ke-le, *adj.* Fat; plump; slippery, as a muddy road.

Ke-le-wai, *s.* Name of a species of kapa, from its color; ina i kalua pu ole me ka palaa, oia ke kapa *kelewai.*

Ke-le-ro, *s.* Gr. A lot in casting lots.

Ke-lo, *int.* With a prolonged sound. *Eng.* The Hawaiian English cry of *sail ho!*

Ke-lou, *s.* A fishing hook; a hook of any kind. See LOU.

Ke-mau, *s.* Name of a plant on the mountains, eaten in time of scarcity by the people.

KE-MA-KE-MA, *s.* A wish; a desire; a rejoicing. NOTE.—This is merely the word *makemake* with the syllables transposed, and probably belongs to the *kake.*

KE-MO-A, *v.* To be angry.

KE-NA, *v.* To command; to order to be done; to give orders; to compel. *Neh.* 5:12; *Laieik.* 176.

2. To send to, as an officer on business; *kena* aku la o Kamehameha i kona poe kanaka e imi i ka laau ala, Kamehameha *sent* his men to look for sandal-wood.

3. To give orders in case of emergency.

KE-NA, *v.* To drink; to slake thirst. *Hoo.* To give or furnish drink. *Hal.* 107:9.

KE-NA, *v.* To be weary; to suffer under hard labor; to grieve.

KE-NA, *adj. pron.,* for *kela,* n for *l.* He; she; that person; aohe kekahi la kula e like me *kena* olelo, there was not a single day's school as he said.

KE-NA, *s.* Hard labor; wearisome service.

2. Depression of mind under unmitigated toil.

3. The feelings of a parent towards a child that refuses his instructions; weariness, anger and love all combined.

KE-NA, *adj.* Weary; heavy; sad; sorrowful.

KE-NA-KE-NA, *v.* See KENA above. To mourn. *2 Kor.* 5:2. To weep; to groan; to suffer inconvenience; to be bitter.

KE-NA-KE-NA, *v.* Freq. of *kena,* to send. To send frequently.

KE-NE-TA, *s. Eng.* A cent, the hundredth part of a dollar.

KE-NI, *v.* To walk very softly, so as to make no noise with the feet.

KE-NI-KE-NI, *v.* To furnish a supply; to have enough.

KE-PA, *v.* To snap, as with the teeth; to chank the teeth, as a boar.

2. To turn; to turn back upon. *Mat.* 7:6.

3. To scrape, as dirt from a stone or board.

KE-PA, *s.* Corruption of English spur. A spur; so named from its use or motion on the heel; he kui e hooeha ai i ka lio ma na aoao.

2. The fruit of a tree used in seasoning food.

KE-PA, *adj.* Of or belonging to the fruit *kepa*; hua *kepa. Kekah.* 12:5.

KE-PAU, *s.* A general name of substances fusible by heat, as tar, pitch, rosin, lead, pewter, &c.

2. The name given to Hawaiians to printer's types; o ke *kepau* i paiia'i ka manao o ke kanaka, the *types* by which the thoughts of men are printed.

KE-PAU-PO-KA, *s. Kepau* and *poka,* a ball or bullet. Lead; a mass of lead. *Ezek.* 22:18.

KE-PA-KE-PA, *v.* To crack or snap, as with a whip; *kepakepa* iho la kekahi pu i ke mele me ka hoolealea mai.

KE-PI-A, *s.* The matter about one's face who has sore running eyes; applied also to oil that stands and gets partially dry.

KE-PO-DA, *s.* Name of an unclean bird in *Isa.* 34:11.

KE-PU-E, *s.* The name of a species of hard stone out of which kois were made.

KE-PU-KA, *v.* See PUKA. To play curious tricks.

KE-PU-KA, *s.* A curious or wizard art; a sleight of hand trick; a trick of legerdemain.

KE-WA, *s.* Something far absent, but with which one hopes to meet or be united with in future; a future point of time; ua ai i ke awa i ke *kewa.*

KE-WAI, *s.* Wind from a place of rain; a mist connected with rain some distance off; pili ke *kewai,* kuhaluka ka mauna.

2. The moisture which settles on mats and walls inside of a house from the dampness; applied sometimes to a wind with a little rain.

KE-WAI, *adj.* Spoiled; rotten, as an egg.

KE-WA-KE-WAI, *v.* To be addled, as an egg; to be spoiled.

KE-WE, *adj.* Contorted; twisted out of meaning, as words; incorrect.

KE-WI-KE-WI, *s.* The horns, as of the new moon. See KIWI.

KE-DE-RA, *s. Eng.* A cedar tree; cedar wood.

KE-DE-RA, *adj. Eng.* Pertaining to cedar; laau *kedera,* cedar timber. *2 Sam.* 5:11.

KE-RA-TI-O, *adj. Gr.* Hua *keratio,* a vegetable mentioned in Luke 15:16; a shuck or shell of a vegetable.

KE-RO-KO, *s. Gr.* Saffon. *Mel. Sol.* 4:14.

KE-RO-KO-DI-LE, *s. Gr.* and *Eng.* A crocodile. *Iob.* 41:1.

KE-RU-BA, *s. Heb.* A cherub.

KE-RU-BI-MA, *s. Heb.* The plural of *keruba.*

KE-RU-SO-LU-TO, *s. Gr.* A chrysolite, the name of a precious stone. *Hoik.* 21:20.

KE-RU-SO-PE-RA, } *s. Gr.* A chryso-
KE-RU-SO-PE-RA-SO, } prasus, a precious stone. *Hoik.* 21:20.

KI, *s. Eng.* The key of a lock. *Lunk.* 3:25.

2. The lock itself. *Neh.* 3:3.

3. The trigger of a gun.

KI, *v.* Modern. To pull the trigger (*ki*) of a gun; hence, to shoot a gun; alaila *ki* mai la na haole i koe i ka pu; to discharge fire-arms; ina e ae oe i kuu lio, e *ki* koke aku au ia oe i ka pu, a make oe.

2. To squirt water, as with a syringe.

3. To sift; to strain.

4. To make fine by separating the coarse.

5. To blow from the mouth into the sea, as fishermen blow from the mouth a kind of oily nut chewed up in order to quiet the surface of the sea, so that they can look deep down into the water.

KI, *s.* The name of a plant having a saccharine root, the leaves of which are used for wrapping up bundles of food; the leaves are used also as food for cattle and for thatching; dracæna terminalis.

KI, *s.* Name of a small bird; he *ki* kahi manu, he manu uuku.

KI, *adj.* Close; parsimonious; kanaka *ki.* See PI.

KI-A, *s.* A pillar or inner post of a house which supports the ridge.

2. A pillar or post set up for any purpose. *Puk.* 26:32.

3. The mast of a ship or any vessel.

4. A standing idol; he *kia* hoailona, a standing image of worship; *kia* ao, a pillar of cloud; *kia* ahi, pillar of fire. *Puk.* 13:21.

KI-A, *v.* To drive by knocking, as with a hammer.

2. To drive, as a nail or spike; to nail; to spike.

3. To run against or push another.

4. To catch birds or fish; *kia* manu, a bird catcher. See the substantive.

KI-A, *s.* One who entraps or catches birds or fish; *kia* manu, a bird catcher. *Laieik.* 106.

2. The name of the material used like kepau or pilali in catching birds.

KI-A, *s.* A spike or nail for fastening boards or timbers.

KI-A-AI-NA, *s.* Kia, pillar, and *aina*, land. LIT. The pillar or support of the land. A governor; a governor of an island; a ruler.

KI-A-AO, *s.* Kia, pillar and *ao*, cloud. A pillar of cloud or cloud pillar. *Puk.* 13:21.

KI-A-A-HI, *s.* Kia, pillar, and *ahi*, fire. A pillar of fire; a fire pillar. *Puk.* 13:21.

KI-AI, *v.* To watch over; to guard; to take charge of; to look out for; to act the part of, or to do the duty of a guard.

2. To wait for; to expect; to think; poe *kiai*, guards.

KI-AI, *s.* A guard; a watchman. 1 *Sam.* 14:16.

2. The time of a watch. *Hal.* 90:4.

KI-AI-PO, *s.* Kiai, watch, and *po*, night. A night watch. *Neh.* 4:22.

KI-AI-POO, *s.* Kiai, watch, and *poo*, the head. A head guard; a title of the person who guarded the king for the time being; ua kapaia ua kanaka la, *kiaipoo*, that person (who guarded the king) was called *kiaipoo*.

KI-AI-PU-KA, *s.* Kiai, guard, and *puka*, a door or gate. A porter; a guard at a gate. *Ioan.* 10:3.

KI-AU-AU, *v.* To smooth; to smooth down; to take wrinkles out of kapa or clothes.

2. To walk lightly; e mama i ka hele ana; e mele pale waa.

KI-A-HA, *s.* A drinking dish; a cup; a mug; a tumbler; *kiaha* ooma, a pitcher; also, a basin. *Puk.* 12:22.

KI-A-HA-A-HA, *v.* See KIAHA. To pour water, as out of a container.

2. To drink out of a cup.

KI-A-HA-MA-NU, *s.* Name of a small kind of fish found in fresh water, in streams, ponds, &c.; called also *nawao.*

KI-A-KA-HI, *s.* Kia, mast, and *kahi*, one. A one-masted vessel; a sloop.

2. Firmness of purpose; adharance to a fixed plan; constancy.

KI-A-KA-HI, *adj.* With one accord; agreeing; noho *kiakahi* ma ka pono; alike; in unison; applied to opinion or action. See KUIKAHI.

KI-A-KO-LU, *s.* Kia, mast, and *kolu*, three. The name given to a ship for having three masts; he *kiakolu*, a three-masted thing, i. e., a ship.

KI-A-LO, *v.* To dig out, as the eye. See POALO. To twist out, as a tooth; to reach after, as in drawing something to one.

KI-A-LO, *s.* A digging out; a wrenching or twisting off.

KI-A-LO-A, *s.* A small, long, beautiful canoe.

2. A fisherman belonging to such a canoe.

3. A long fishing line.

KI-A-LU-A, *s.* Kia, mast, and *lua*, two. A brig or schooner from having only two masts; he moku *kialua*, a vessel of *two* masts.

KI-A-PA, *s.* A bark, in distinction from a ship.

KI-A-WE, *s.* The name of a tree; also, the name of the fruit.

KI-A-WE-U-LA, *s.* A species of red; applied to the clouds; ina he ulaula ke ao, ua ula ia, he *kiaweula.*

KI-E, *v.* To be high; to be lifted up;

more often doubled, kiekie.

KI-E-E, } *v.* To look into; to scrutinize;
KI-EI, } to peep at; oi imi aku i ka manao, oi huli aku, oi halalo aku, a *kiei* aku,
a nana iho; a *kiei* malalo o ka papale o na
haole, they *peeped* under the bonnets of the
foreigners (women.)

2. To look at one by stretching the head
around or over something; to look over in
order to see anything.

3. To look slily; e nana malu.

4. To watch the conduct of one; ke *kiei*
mai nei no ia i ka poe uhai kanawai.

5. To look at a particular object; *kiei*
aku la au makai a mauka, a holo aku la au.

6. To look through a door or crevice to
see something. *Laieik.* 174.

7. To be moved with joy or fear. *Hal.*
68:16.

KI-E-KE, *s.* See EKE. A bag; a pocket;
a satchel; a bag for carrying provisions.
Luk. 10:4. *Kieke* kahuhipa, a shepherd's
bag. 1 *Sam.* 17:40.

KI-E-KI-E, *v.* See KIE. To be lofty; to
be high.

2. To be lifted up; to be raised high, as
a material object.

3. To be high, as the mind; to be proud;
to be self-exalted; to think one's self above
or better than others.

4. *Hoo.* To be exalted; to be lifted up,
as with pride. *Nah.* 16:3.

5. To exalt one's self; to think much of
one's self.

6. To raise one to a higher station. *Eset.* 3:1.

7. To promote; to signalize one's self.

8. To raise or lift up the voice in a cry.

KI-E-KI-E, *s.* A height; a high place;
ke *kiekie*, the high one, i. e., God; ua like
ke *kiekie* me ka loa, the height is like the
length.

KI-E-KI-E, *adj.* High; lofty; exalted;
separated; holy.

KI-E-KI-E-NA, *s.* *Kiekie* and *ana.* Being
high; rising high. See PALIPALI.

KI-E-LE, *s.* The name of an odoriferous
shrub or tree; he laau aala. Some say it was
brought from a foreign country, but the
word is found in two ancient meles at least.

 He *kiele* ka alau niu
 No Hana lau aala ai na 'lii.—*Mele.*

 O ka lau o ke *kiele* i aala;
 E ka lani ai mai ai mae
 Aala no mai ka lau a ke kumu.—*Mele.*

KI-E-LE, *v.* To emit a fragrant odor; o
ka lau o ke kaa i *kiele* i aala, the leaf of the
kaa sent forth odor.

KI-E-LEI, *v.* To squat; to sit on the hams.

KI-E-LEI, *s.* The name of a kind of hula;
he *kielei* kekahi hula.

KII, *v.* To go after a thing; to go for
the purpose of bringing something; to
fetch. 1 *Nal.* 12:3.

2. To come to one; to approach; to meet.

3. To send for a person or thing; to send
away.

4. To take from another; to procure for
one. *Kin.* 34:4.

5. To require of one. *Ezek.* 3:18, 20.

6. *Hoo.* To pine away, as in the consumption; to cause to grow thin in flesh.

7. To starve; to suffer starvation.

8. To mourn; to suffer. *Hal.* 88:9.

9. To make thin, i. e., to deprive of; i
hoonele a i *hookiia* oukou i ka ike.

KII, *s.* An image; a picture; i ko lakou ike ana i ke *kii* o ko lakou mau hale;
an idol; a statue; *kii* kalaiia, a graven
image. *Puk.* 20:4. *Kii* palapalaia, a picture. *Nah.* 33:52. *Kii* hooheeheeia, a molten or cast image. *Nah.* 33:52. *Kii* akua,
images of gods for worship. 1 *Nal.* 14:23.
He laau ke *kii* no na kanaka ame na 'lii,
the common people and the chiefs have
idols of wood; *kii* ku, a standing image.
Oihk. 26:1. *Kii* pohaku, an image of stone;
kii onohi, pupil of the eye.

KII-A-KU-A, *s.* See the foregoing. An
image representing a god.

KII-HE-LEI, *v.* See HELEI. To stand with
the legs wide apart; to straddle; ua ku *kiihelei*
oia ma kela aoao a ma keia aoao o ke awa.

KII-HE-LEI, *adv.* Branching apart; strad-
dling. See the verb.

KII-HOO-HEE-HEE-IA, *s.* See KII above.
A molten or cast image.

KII-KAU, *adj.* Pertaining to clouds divided into strips black or white; he ao
onohi opua *kiikau.*

KII-KA-LAI-IA, *s.* See KII, *s.*, and KALAI,
to hew. A carved idol; a graven image.
Kanl. 5:8.

KII-KE-A, *s.* A medicine used to relieve
pain; it is a kind of bark.

KII-KII, *v.* To swell; to enlarge, as the
abdomen of pregnant women; to be full
from over-eating.

2. To paint the hair over the forehead
white.

KII-KU, *s.* *Kii* and *ku*, to stand. A standing image or idol.

KII-MA-NA-NA, *v.* To enlarge; to swell;
as the belly god.

KII-PA-LA-PA-LA, *s.* *Kii* and *palapala,*

writing. A picture; a portrait; a picture for worship. *Nah.* 33:52.

KII-PO-HA-KU, *s.* *Kii* and *pohaku*, stone. A stone idol. See EHO.

KII-NA, *v.* *Kii* and *ana*, a sending. To send after or call for persons; to go for a person or thing; to fetch; to bring something. *Eset.* 3:12. NOTE.—It is used often in a passive sense. *Kiina mai la e na kahu ma ke kaulua, he was sent for* by his guardians on a double-canoe.

KII-PU-A, *adj.* Going about, as a person without business, more or less mischievous; nahili, lalau, lohiau, hanamanuea.

KI-O, *v.* To break wind; ua hanai oia i kana mau keiki, a pau ke aho, no ke *kio* ana o na keiki.
2. To blow on a pipe.
3. To blow on a leaf across the lips, the vibration of which produces a sound.

KI-O, *s.* An excrement.
2. A pond or puddle of water, especially if filthy. See KIOWAI and HALOKOWAI.
3. A cistern; a pool; a water sluice.
4. The dregs, lees or settlings of liquor.
5. A part of a potato which branches off from the main root.
6. A process; a projection; a bunch on a large body.
7. A bubo, a disease connected with lewdness.

KI-O, *adj.* Practicing in a military school, as the chiefs in former times had mock fights for practice; he kaua paani, he kaua lealea, he kaua *kio*, &c.; he kaua pahukala kahi inoa.

KI-O-A-HI, *s.* *Kio* and *ahi*, fire. A fiery pit; a place of torment; hell; a poino mau ka poe hewa i ke *kioahi* a ka po mau loa.

KI-O-E, *v.* To skim off the scum of a liquid, or to skim the cream from milk; to dip up water, as with a ladle.

KI-O-E, *s.* The name of a small surfboard; he papa heenalu liilii.

KI-O-E-A, *s.* The name of a bird having long legs, found on Molokai and in other places.
2. The voice of a bird on Molokai (the *kioea* probably); kani mai la ua manu la, penei: "*kioea, kioea*, lawekeo, lawelawekeo."
3. Name of a cape where the bird lives; ua kapaia kela lae mahope o kekahi manu olaila, he *kioea.*

KI-O-E-A, *v.* To be long; to extend; to stretch out.
2. To be lifted up; to stand high, as on long legs (see the noun); ua like ke kiekie me ke *kioea.*
3. To be set confusedly together, as many things of different kinds.

KI-O-E-O-E, *adj.* A contract of *kiaoeoe.* Long; tall, as the mast of a ship. See OEOE.
2. Flat; extended.

KI-O-KI, *adj.* Fat; plump; muscular; rolling, as the flesh of fat animals.

KI-O-KI-O, *v.* See KIO. To play on a pipe or other wind instrument. *Hoo.* The same, to play on the pipe or flute. 1 *Nal.* 1:40.

KI-O-KI-O, *s.* See KIO. A pond of water; a puddle where hogs may wallow.

KI-O-KI-O, *s.* Name of a musical instrument; also, with *hoo*, the names of instrument players; poe *hookiokio*, players on instruments. *Hal.* 87:7.
2. A file (from the noise), or any material to polish with.

KI-O-KI-O, *s.* Anything variegated, as cloth; as spots in the sea, some places calm and some ruffled; variegated; unequal in appearance.

KI-O-KI-O, *adj.* *Hoo.* Of or belonging to a pipe.

KI-O-KI-O-KI, *adj.* See KIOKI. Plump, fat with rolling muscle; muscular; applied to young strong men's shoulders.

KI-O-LA, *v.* To lay down a substance for inspection. *Laieik.* 193.
2. To overthrow; to cast down. *Puk.* 15:1. To reject, as a people for their moral worthlessness. *Oihk.* 20:23.
3. To throw away as worthless or improper to be kept. *Neh.* 13:8.

KI-O-LA-O-LA, *v.* See KIOLA. To throw or cast frequently, as stones or other missiles.

KI-O-LE-A, *v.* *Ki* and *olea*, hard; severe. To sit on a high seat; to sit unsafely; to sit uncomfortably.

KI-O-LE-A, *s.* A high seat; an exalted station.
2. A rickety seat on an elevated place; hence,
3. FIG. An unsafe state or condition for one.

KI-O-LEI, *v.* To squat on the hams; to sit on a seat with the feet drawn up.

KI-O-LE-NA, *v.* *Kio* and *lena*, to iron clothes. To spread out to dry, as kapa; to whiten in the sun.

KI-O-LE-NA, *s.* A place for coloring kapa.

KI-O-LE-PO, *s.* *Kio*, a pool, and *lepo*, dirt. A puddle; a place of filth; a collection of mud, water and filth. 2 *Pet.* 2:22.

KI-O-LO-A, *s.* A very small canoe in which only one man can sail; holo aku la ia ma kona waa *kioloa* i ka lawaia luhee.

2. A long fishing line for taking fish in deep water.

KI-O-NA, *s. Kio* and *ana.* A place for throwing excrements; he wahi hoolei honowa; a dung hill. *Hal.* 113:7. A privy or back-house.

2. The fundament.

KI-O-NA, *adj.* Of or belonging to excrements. *2 Nal.* 10:27.

KI-O-NA-HA, *v.* See ONAHA, to crook; to bend. To bend or curve outward; to fall over a defense; to bend up and over.

KI-O-PE, *v.* See OOPA, lame. To be lame in the legs; to limp. See KAOPA.

KI-O-PO-I, *s. Kio* and *poi,* food. A poi calabash.

KI-O-WE-A, *s.* See KIOEA.

KI-O-WAI, *s. Kio,* collection, and *wai,* water. A collection of water; a puddle; standing water.

2. A place of pouring out water; a water sluice. *Kin.* 7:11.

3. A fountain. *Mel. Sol.* 4:12. SYN. with punawai.

KI-O-WA-O, *s.* The name of the mist or cloud almost always settled on the hills of Oahu.

KI-U, *v.* To spy; to act the part of a spy by watching another's conduct or movements; e kiu malu, to spy secretly.

2. To spy out, as a country. *Lunk.* 18:2.

3. To look at with mischievous intent.

KI-U, *s.* A spy. *Kin.* 42:9. I kou hoi ana, ea, mai hoolike ia oe me na *kiu;* hoouna mai la oia i poe *kiu,* he sent forward a company of *spies;* ki mai ua poe kanaka *kiu* la i ka lakou pu, that company of *spymen* fired their guns.

2. A hook; a fish-hook.

3. The name of a strong wind at Honuaula, Maui, occasioned by the trades breaking over the mountains.

4. The north-west wind at Hana, Kaupo, &c., and very similar to a *hoolua.*

KI-U-HOO-PU-LU, *v. Kiu,* to spy, and *hoopulu,* to flatter; to deceive by flattery. To act with cunning in order to entrap one; e hana maalea e punihei ai.

KI-U-HOO-PU-LU, *s.* The business or action of a person sent as a spy; cunning practice.

KI-HA, *v.* To sneeze.

KI-HA, *s.* See the foregoing. The movements or convulsions in the act of sneezing. *Iob.* 41:18.

KI-HAE, *v.* To fade; to decay; to corrupt, as dead vegetables or animals; *kihae*

oho o ka lau ki o Luakaka.

2. To be inspired or possessed of some god.

3. To become a god and go above.

KI-HAE-HAE, *v.* To tear to pieces; to rend into small parts. See HAEHAE.

KI-HAU, *v.* To eat a meal when there is but little to eat; to eat sparingly.

KI-HA-MU, *v. Ki* and *hamu,* to eat fragments. To eat proudly or daintily; to taste this and that, as though tasteless.

KI-HA-PA, *v.* To be half clothed; to have only a kihei over one shoulder; to have only one-half the head shaved.

KI-HA-PAI, *s.* A small division of land next less than a *pauku.*

2. A cultivated patch of ground, a garden, a potato patch, a field, a small farm, &c., belonging to the people in distinction from the chief's, which was called *koele.*

3. A particular department in business or office. NOTE.—Formerly the ceremonies of religion were divided into several departments; it was the business of one to keep the altar in order, of another to offer the sacrifice, &c.; these different departments or offices were called *kihapais.*

KI-HA-WA-HI-NE, *s.* The name of the lizard god; it was classed among the poe akua noho. It is said to have been applied also to certain fish, the *hilu* and others.

KI-HE, *v.* See KIHA. To sneeze. *2 Nal.* 4:35. To snore; to breathe hard.

2. To have the nose filled with mucus.

3. To dive down, as the bow of a vessel in a heavy sea.

4. To dive, as one dives under the surf; to roll or dive, as a porpoise.

KI-HE, *v.* See KIHAE, to wilt. To fade; to wilt, as a plant.

2. To be weak; to faint, as a person.

3. To become a demi-god.

KI-HEE, *v.* To blow; to blow or strike upon, as the wind.

2. To wheeze; to cough up phlegm; e kunu me ka hookahe ana i ka hupe.

KI-HEI, *s.* Name of the garment formerly worn by Hawaiian men; a loose garment of kapa thrown over one shoulder and tied in a knot; it was thrown off at work.

KI-HE-HE, *v.* To be or become deified; to pass or live invisibly in the air.

KI-HE-KI-HE, *v.* See KIHE. To pant or struggle for breath; to cough severely.

KI-HE-LE, *v.* To scratch or tear, as briers or anything crooked.

KI-HE-LEI, *v.* See HELEI. To stand with the legs spread apart; to straddle. See

KUKIHELEI.

KI-HE-NE, *s.* A bundle, as of potatoes done up for carrying.

KI-HI, *s.* The outside corner or projection of a thing. *Kin.* 47:21. The apex of an angle.

2. The edge of a garment.

3. The border or outside of a land or country. *Oihk.* 19:9.

4. The extremity of a thing; ke *kihi* o ka pepeiao, the *tip* of the ear. *Oihk.* 8:23. Ke *kihi* o ka aahu, the *border* of a garment. *Nah.* 15:38. The corner, as of a board; the sharp point of a leaf.

5. The commencement of evening, when darkness begins, as, ke *kihi* o ka po. See KAU 6.

KI-HI, *s.* The name of a variety of sweet potatoes, the ancient potato of Hawaii; uala paa.

KI-HI-KAU, *v.* To give lavishly and until all is gone; i ke *kihikau* au, a ua pau. See KAHIAU.

KI-HI-KI-HI, *v.* To bend, as a curved surface; to hollow out, as sails in the wind.

2. To branch off from the main body.

KI-HI-KI-HI, *s.* The curving of the horns of the moon; that is, the extremities are the *kihikihi.*

2. The curve of the wings of a bird.

3. The broad part of an ancient cocked up hat, as the brim was turned up and made sharp corners; ua *kihikihi* ke poo, curved are their heads, viz.: the officers of Captain Cook's ships with their cocked hats on.

KI-HI-KI-HI, *s.* The name of a species of fish.

KI-HI-LOA, *adj.* Crooked; blundering; wandering, &c.

KI-HI-MO-E, *s.* Name of a puu kapu in playing the game of noa.

KI-HI-PO-HI-WI, *s.* *Kihi,* corner, and *pohiwi,* shoulder. Generally used as synonymous with *pohiwi,* the shoulder, but really the corners, points or sides of the shoulders.

KI-HI-PU-KA, *s.* Name of one of the five puu kapus in playing the game of noa.

KI-HO-E, *v.* To shift from place to place.

KI-HO-LO, *s.* The name of a large kind of hook formerly made of wood, used to catch the shark and other large fish.

KI-HO-NU-A, *s.* The side or bank of a water-course.

KI-KA, *adj.* Strong; energetic, as a magistrate in applying the law to transgressors.

KI-KA-O-LA, *s.* *Ki* (*Eng.*), key, and *ka-ola,* a bar or cross-beam. The bar of a city gate. *Ier.* 51:30.

KI-KAU, *v.* To give freely; to bestow favors upon others with good will.

KI-KA-HA, *adv.* Passing by a former friend; not recognizing one with whom he was formerly acquainted; e wawau, e hele loa ma ke alanui, e aloha ole.

KI-KA-KA-HA, *v.* See KAKA, *v.* To pitch into; to dash against; to rush together, as two cocks when fighting.

KI-KA-KA-LA, *v.* To spur; to strike with the spurs, as fighting-cocks.

2. In *fishing for squid,* to draw up with a hook.

KI-KA-LA, *s.* The hollow of the back between the hips.

2. The name of the bone called coccyx.

3. The hip; ke kikala ame ka uha. *Lunk.* 15:8.

4. The buttocks; the posteriors. 2 *Sam.* 10:4.

KI-KA-LA-PAI, *s.* The hips of a person sunk, not well formed; papai, pananai.

KI-KA-MA, *s.* The white kapa made from the wauke.

KI-KA-MU, *v.* Persons for a time sociable, then to sit silent for some cause.

2. The gathering of small fish around a baited hook, but do not bite.

KI-KA-KA-PU, *s.* Name of a species of fish, white and round, with black spots.

KI-KA-NA-LEI, *v.* To squat on one's feet.

2. To stop or stay for a short time.

KI-KE, *v.* To break or strike, as with a hammer; to break, as a stone; to crack, as a nut upon a stone.

2. To speak by turns, as in a dialogue.

3. To divide into two or more equal parts.

4. To reason; to confer together. *Isa.* 1:18.

KI-KE, *v.* To sneeze. See KIHE.

KI-KEE-KEE, *v.* See KEE and KEEKEE. To crook; to bend; to move crookedly.

KI-KEE-KEE, *adj.* Crooked; zigzag, as a path; ke *kikeekee* ke ala; not straight.

2. In a *moral sense* wrong; perverted; erroneous; mai hele oe ma ke ala *kikeekee* o ka aina o kaua, o kuia auanei oe a hina; aka, e hele oe ma ke ala pololei, go not in the *crooked* path of our land, lest ere long you stumble and fall, but go in the straight path.

3. *Kikeekee* is the opposite of *pololei.*

KI-KEE-KEE, *s.* A winding or crooked path.

KI-KE-KE', *v.* See KIKE, to break. To knock, as at a door for entrance. *Lunk.* 19:22.

2 To strike frequently upon, as in cracking a nut.

KI-KE-NE-NEI, *v.* See NEINEI. To draw

in; to contract.

2. To draw or lift up; to throw or cast up; to put upon something.

KI-KE-NE-NEI, *adj*. Too short; changing one's place.

KI-KE-PA, *v*. To fix or place a thing in a one-sided manner; to lean over on one side; to cover one side of the head.

KI-KE-PA, *s*. The hair of the head turned over one side as though the head was one-sided; a sash over one shoulder.

KI-KE-PA-KE-PA, *v*. See the above. To put on a dress irregularly; to dress fantastically.

2. To cut the hair of the head fantastically.

3. To adorn the person differently from the fashion.

4. To disfigure one's self, as in ancient times when a chief died, the people knocked out their teeth, lacerated their bodies, &c.

KI-KI, *v*. A frequentative and intensive of *ki*, to shoot or squirt. To spurt, as water pressed through a small orifice.

2. To eject black matter, as the squid.

3. To practice masturbation.

4. To flow swiftly, as water from the bottom of a full barrel.

5. To do a thing with vehemence; to run very swiftly; to fly furiously at, as one cock at another, or as a hen in defense of her young. NOTE.—*Kiki* is used as an intensive adverb in various senses. See below.

KI-KI, *v*. To paint the face or hair white with lime or with clay (palolo.)

KI-KI, *s*. Bundles done up for carrying on a stick, of which a man carries two.

2. A rough kind of basket.

3. The rushing or striking of a cock with his spurs; also, the action of a hen in defense of her chickens.

4. The swinging or slamming of the door of a house.

5. The leaves used in tying up bundles of potatoes or other things.

6. The name of a bird, usually caught with a net.

KI-KI, *adv*. Quickly; suddenly; violently; in a hurry. *Ios.* 7:22. NOTE.—*Kiki* is often used as adverb of intensity after verbs of action or condition, and signifies very, exceedingly, &c.; as holo *kiki*, he ran *swiftly*; paa *kiki*, *very* tight; hele *kiki* aku la, i ike ole o Papa ia ia, he went *hastily* that Papa might not see him.

KI-KI-AO, *s*. A sudden gust of wind; a squall; a strong wind.

KI-KI-A-LO, *v*. To move quickly; to hasten; to be in a hurry.

2. To catch fish in a net.

KI-KII, *v*. See KII. To slumber.

2. To touch or strike softly.

3. To move quickly, gently or softly.

KI-KI-O, *v*. See KIO. To void stool; to discharge fæces.

KI-KI-HI, *adj*. See KIHI. Having corners like a cocked up hat; ua kapaia'ku e makou, o ka papale he poo *kikihi*; anything having many corners; aole like me ke poo *kikihi* a Kane; he poo *kikihi*, a half-mooned, cocked up or military hat.

KI-KI-HI, *s*. A sailing about in a canoe with a sail, or walking about quickly.

2. The brim of a broad-brimmed hat turned up.

KI-KI-HI, *s*. A door frame.

2. The side posts of a door; the door itself.

KI-KI-KI, *adj*. Very hot; oppressively hot, as a tight room filled with people; *kikiki* ka wela a ka la.

KI-KI-KO, *v*. See KIKO, to make a point, dot, &c. To print; to tattoo the skin; to make marks or letters on the skin.

KI-KI-KO, *adj*. Dotted; spotted, as on paper, kapa or the skin.

KI-KI-LO, *s*. Some place or thing afar off. See OKILO.

KI-KI-LO, *adv*. Afar off; at a great distance.

KI-KI-MO, *v*. See KIMO. To bow or bend over the head in front; to fall, as the head in front when one is going to sleep in a sitting posture; to nod with drowsiness.

KI-KI-NA, *v*. Intensive of *kina*, to urge, drive, &c. To send with speed.

2. To hurry one in doing a thing.

3. To act as if in anger.

4. *Hoo*. To command with earnestness; to compel or drive one to do a thing; to hasten; to urge on that a thing may be done quickly. *Puk.* 11:1. *Hookikina* aku no lakou i na kanaka, they *hurried on* the men (to work.)

KI-KI-NA, *s*. A hurrying time or season; kokoke pau ke *kikina* nui ma Honolulu nei, kawalawala loa na moku i koe iloko o ke awa. *Hoo.* Hard driving or urging people to do anything; o ka *hookikina* ana paha ka mea i make ai, the *severe driving*, perhaps, was the cause of his death.

KI-KI-PA, *v*. See KIPA, to turn aside. To turn in, i. e., to call upon one.

2. To go frequently or often to a neighbor's.

3. To make a circuit to avoid one.

4. To turn aside from a straight road, or from one's regular business.

KI-KI-WI, *v*. See KIWI, to bend. To bend

or bow the head; to nod from drowsiness.

2. To bend over; to bow down.

3. To be very faint and weary from hard fatigue.

Ki-ki-wi, *adj*. Bent and rounded at the point like a duck's bill.

Ki-ko, *v*. To reach after; to stretch out the hand to take a thing.

2. To pluck; to pull off, as fruit from a tree.

3. To pick up, as a fowl does its food.

4. To peck or break the shell, as a chicken in hatching.

5. To mark on a roll opposite one's name for absence.

Ki-ko, *s*. A small spot, dot or point.

2. A spot on the skin.

3. The figure marked on the skin in tattooing.

4. The general name given by Hawaiians to the marks used in punctuation.

5. The dot or mark made as a sign of absence in a school roll.

6. The cock of a pistol.

Ki-ko, *adj*. Striped; spotted; speckled.

Ki-ko-a, *v*. Pass. for *kikoia*. *Gram*. § 211. To be picked up; to be marked, &c. *Mat*. 13:4. *Kikoa na lae o na kane ame na wahine*, the foreheads of men and women were marked or dotted.

Ki-ko-i, *v*. To do a little here and there; to hip-skip; to do things irregularly.

2. To be bold; to reprove indiscriminately.

3. To interrupt the attention of a hearer.

4. To supersede; to forestall.

Ki-koo, *v*. See Kiko. To stretch out the hand to take something, or to do something. *Puk*. 17:11.

2. To stretch or spread out the wings, as a bird about to fly.

3. To extend the hand in making a gesture.

4. *Kikoo* for *kakoo*, to gird; to tie on; to strengthen. *Hal*. 18:32.

Ki-koo, *s*. An arm or weapon of some kind; a bow. 1 *Sam*. 2:4. He kaka, he mea e pana'i ka pua; a bow, a thing to shoot arrows.

2. A span; a measure made by the thumb and fore finger. *Oihl*. 41:5. Aha *kikoo* i koe o ko ia la maikai ia ia nei, that person is four *points* less handsome than this.

3. A line across the arc of a circle; the chord of an arc. *Anahon*. 23.

4. The bend bow was called *kikoo* in shooting; *kikoo* kakaka, a bow. *Hos*. 2:20.

Ki-koo-koo, *v*. To reach as far as one can for a thing; to stand on tip-toe and reach as high as one can.

Ki-ko-o-la, *v*. To huddle together; to put together confusedly; to fill a container without any order.

Ki-ko-o-la, *adj*. Carelessly performed; entangled; topsy-turvy; mixed together confusedly.

Ki-ko-hoo-ma-ha, *s*. *Kiko*, point, and *hoomaha*, causing rest. The name of the points or characters used in writing which indicate pauses or rests for the voice in reading, as comma, semicolon, period, &c.

Ki-ko-hu, *v*. See Kohu. To spot; to make a spot with coloring matter.

Ki-ko-hu-ko-hu, *v*. See above and Kohu. To daub; to dirty; to defile, as a clean garment; to spot; to make unclean; to spatter, as ink in writing.

Ki-ko-hu-ko-hu, *s*. A dirty place on a garment; defilement; spots of impurity. Fig. 2 *Pet*. 2:13. A blemish; an imperfection. Syn. with palahee.

Ki-ko-ka-hi, *s*. *Kiko* and *kahi*, one; one point. A period; a pause in reading.

Ki-ko-ka-la, *s*. *Kiko*, point, and *ka la*, the sun. The spot or place of the sun; near the time of the sun's rising.

Ki-ko-ki-ko, *v*. To nibble, as fish at the bait.

Ki-ko-ki-ko, *adj*. Spotted; speckled; of different colors. *Kin*. 30:39. Striped; having spots of different colors.

Ki-ko-ki-ko-i, *v*. See Kikoi. To skip about, as in working in one place and then in another; applied to reading or teaching the alphabet, to read skipping about; kuhikuhi lelele, to point here and there.

Ki-ko-ki-ko-i, *adj*. Here and there; irregular, hip-skip, &c.

Ki-ko-ko-ma, *s*. *Kiko*, point, and *koma* (*Eng*.), comma. A semicolon, a sign of a pause in reading. See Kikohoomaha.

Ki-ko-la, *v*. Contraction of *kikoola*. To place together in confusion; to huddle together without order.

Ki-ko-la, *adj*. Mixed up; entangled; without order.

Ki-ko-lu-ko, *adj*. *Kiko*, a dot, and *luko*. Spotted; speckled; dotted.

Ki-ko-moe, *s*. *Kiko* and *moe*, to lie down. A hyphen (-), the name of one of the points in written or printed language.

Ki-ko-ni, *v*. To smooth off and finish a canoe after it is dug out.

2. To prepare and make soft the wauki for making kapa; ka wauki i *kikoniia* a palupalu maikai.

3. To pierce or lance a swelling on the

head.

4. To rap one gently on the forehead, as with the knuckles of the hand.

Kɪ-ko-nɪ, *s.* The art or trade of finishing off canoes after they are dug out and shaped.

Kɪ-ko-nɪ-a, *s.* The stork. *Kanl.* 14:18. The name of an unclean bird.

Kɪ-ko-nɪ-ko-nɪ, *adj.* Having hard lumps on the head; ke *kikonikoni* ana i ke poo.

Kɪ-ko-nɪ-nau, *s.* *Kiko,* point, and *ninau,* question. The name of the interrogation point (?.)

Kɪ-ko-pu-ɪ-wa, *s.* *Kiko,* point, and *pu-iwa,* surprise. The name of the point expressing surprise or wonder (!.)

Kɪ-ko-wae-na, *s.* *Kiko,* point, and *wa-ena,* the middle. The center of a circle. *Anahon.* 22.

Kɪ-la, *adj.* Strong; stout; able.

Kɪ-la, *s.* *Eng.* Steel; a flint-steel for striking fire.

2. A general name for chisels; ka hao ma ka maka o ke koi, the iron at the edge of the adze; ka hoaka o na *kila* o na hale koa, the flashing of *steel* of the chariots. *Nah.* 2:3.

Kɪ-la-ha, *s.* See Laha, to spread out. An enlarging; a swelling up; ke *kilaha* o ka opu.

Kɪ-la-kɪ-la, *v.* *Kilakila* ia e ku mai la, long may she (Laieikawai) stand there, as we say, long live the king. To express admiration of one's person. *Laieik.* 165.

Kɪ-la-kɪ-la, *adj.* Great; long; strong; stout; brave; applied to a person.

Kɪ-la-kɪ-la, *s.* Height; grandeur; magnificence; applied to a mountain.

Kɪ-le-a, *s.* The name of a small but prominent hill; a hillock; mai pii au i puu *kilea,* i ka hoolehelehe.

Kɪ-le-o, *s.* The pistil of the flowers of plants.

2. The palate of the human mouth. *Iob.* 34:3. He ike aku i ka pu i kani no i ke *kileo.*

3. The roof of the mouth. *Iob.* 29:10.

4. The stopper of the lungs.

5. The trigger of a gun.

Kɪ-le-pa, *v.* See Lepa, a small flag. To float in the wind, as a kapa or a piece of cloth fastened to a stick.

Kɪ-le-pa-le-pa, *v.* See Kilepa, Kale-palepa and Lepa. To flap or flutter in the wind, as an ensign or flag; to flap in the wind, as a sail.

Kɪ-le-pa-le-pa, *s.* The fluttering or floating of a flag or colors. *Laieik.* 26.

Kɪ-lɪ, *v.* To rain fine rain; to rain but little; to wet.

Kɪ-lɪ, *s.* A kind of shrub or grass.

Kɪ-lɪ-o-o-pu, *s.* Name of a species of grass. *Laieik.* 192.

2. Name of a wind at Waihee, Maui.

Kɪ-lɪ-hau, *v.* To fall gently, as a soft shower; to diminish, as the termination of a shower.

2. To be meek; to be mild; to act gently.

3. To eat modestly and but little. See Kɪlɪka.

Kɪ-lɪ-he-he, *v.* To sneeze; to snore; to breathe hard. See Kɪhe.

Kɪ-lɪ-hu-na, *v.* To be scattered into small pieces like fine rain. See Lelehuna.

Kɪ-lɪ-ka, *v.* To fall in few drops, as rain; to decrease, as rain; to grow small.

2. To eat sparingly. See Kɪlɪhau 3.

Kɪ-lɪ-ka, *s.* *Eng.* Silk. *Sol.* 31:22.

Kɪ-lɪ-ka, *adj.* Silken; lole *kilika,* silk cloth.

Kɪ-lɪ-kaa, *v.* See Kɪlɪka above. To diminish or to be near ceasing, as rain.

Kɪ-lɪ-kɪ-lɪ-hau, *v.* See Kɪlɪhau. To fall, as mist or fine rain; to sprinkle slightly, as rain.

2. To sprinkle, as a little salt; aole ua, ke *kilikilihau* wale mai la no.

3. To blow gently, as the wind; *kilikili-hau* ka makani.

Kɪ-lɪ-kɪ-lɪ-hau, *adj.* Diminishing; softening; ceasing.

Kɪ-lɪ-kɪ-lɪ-hu-na, *s.* See Huna, small particles of dust, rain, &c. Syn. with the foregoing. A small particle of dust, fine rain, &c.

Kɪ-lɪ-poɪ-poɪ, *v.* To strike the hollow hands together, causing a sound.

Kɪ-lo, *v.* To look earnestly at a thing.

2. To look at and watch the stars.

3. To prognosticate events by looking at the stars; to foretell what the weather will be.

4. To act as a sorcerer.

5. To be or act as a judge between man and man.

Kɪ-lo, *s.* A star-gazer; o ka mea nana lani, he *kilo* lani no ia.

2. A predictor of future events from the observation of the stars, from the barking of dogs, the crowing of cocks, &c.

3. An astrologer; a magician. *Kin.* 41:8. A soothsayer; an enchanter. *Kanl.* 18:10.

4. A judge; a prophet; o Kahiko ke alii pono, a akamai ia, he kahuna ame ke *kilo,* Kahiko was a good king, he was wise, he was a priest and a *prophet.*

Kɪ-lo, *s.* A kind of looking-glass.

Kɪ-lo-ɪa, *v.* *Kilo,* to look at, and *ia,*

fish. To look as a fisherman looks into the water for fish; heaha kana e hana la? e *kiloia* ana.

KI-LO, *adv.* Used sometimes improperly for *lilo*; iuka kilo for iuka *lilo*.

KI-LOU, *s.* See LOU, to bend. A hook. 2 *Oihl.* 4:16.

KI-LOU, *v.* To hook; to fasten on to, as with a hook; to catch with a hook; to take fish with a hook. *Ezek.* 29:4.

KI-LOU, *s.* A still, quiet place; a place of no noise; a place favorable for sleep.

KI-LO-HA-NA, *s.* The outside kapa of a pa-u, which was of the best material and the most beautifully printed.

2. The very best as contrasted with that which was poorer; ka mea maikai loa i huipuia me na mea ino.

3. A hillock or heap of stones used as a resting place; he puu hoomaha.

KI-LO-HA-NA, *adj.* Fine; beautiful; excellent; best.

KI-LO-HEE, *s.* Squid looking; name of a place in the sea beyond the kuaau and synonymous with hohonu, a place where fishermen look for squid.

KI-LO-HI, *v.* To look at one's self, his person, his features, his dress, &c., with admiration; to be proud of one's dress or person.

2. To act with self-complacency.

3. To be vain; to exhibit vanity in any way.

4. To scrutinize, as one's character; to examine; to observe.

KI-LO-HI, *s.* Pride; vanity; a high opinion of one's self.

KI-LO-HI, *adj.* Proud; self-opinionated.

KI-LO-KI-LO, *v.* See KILO. To act the kilo, i. e., to tell fortunes by magic; to act the sorcerer.

2. To examine carefully.

3. To guess concerning future events; to predict; to tell beforehand what the weather will be. *Mat.* 16:3. E koho honua wale no me ka manao wahahee.

KI-LO-KI-LO, *s.* A guessing at the future; a predicting; a watching the singular appearance of clouds.

2. An enchantment. *Nah.* 23:23. A diviner. 1 *Sam.* 6:2.

KI-LO-KI-LO, *adj.* Practicing enchantment; divining; fortune telling.

KI-LO-KI-LO-U-HA-NE, *s.* Kilo and *uhane*, the spirit. To foretell the condition of one's soul as being safe or near death, as living or as about to suffer; a species of necromancy based upon falsehood, much practiced in former times.

KI-LO-KI-LO-HO-KU, *s.* See KILOKILO and HOKU, a star. An astrologer; a star-gazer.

KI-LO-KI-LO-LA-NI, *s.* See KILOLANI. An astrologer. *Dan.* 2:27.

KI-LO-LA-NI, *s.* Kilo and *lani*, heaven. One who looks at the stars; a star-gazer; an astrologer. *Isa.* 47:13. One who pretends to predict the future by watching the stars.

KI-LO-MA-KA-NI, *s.* Kilo and *makani*, wind. One who prognosticates the future by observing the winds.

KI-LO-WA-HI-NE, *s.* Kilo and *wahine*, a woman. A prophetess; a sorceress. Isa. 57:3.

KI-LU, *s.* The name of a small gourd or calabash for putting in small, choice things.

2. A kind of small gourd used at play; o ke *kilu*, he ipu no ia i kalai kapakahi ia ma kahi o ke au; a game attended with gambling and licentiousness.

3. The name of the play itself; he paani ino o ke *kilu* i ka po. *Laieik.* 114. O ke *kilu* ka mea e olioli ai na mea akamai i ke mele. NOTE.—*Kilu* was a play for grown people, *puheoheo* for children. See PUHEOHEO.

KI-LU, *v.* To play at the pastime called *kilu*; a ma ka wa e *kilu* ai.

KI-LU-A, *s.* See LUA, double; deceitful. A liar; a deceiver; a falsifier.

2. In the *abstract*, a lie; a deceit; a falsehood.

KI-ME-BA-LA, *s.* Gr. A cymbal. 2 *Sam.* 6:5.

KI-MO, *v.* To strike, as with a stone; a stick or a sword; to thrust with a stick.

2. To pound, bruise or mash, as in pounding poi.

3. To seize something while in motion.

4. To go headlong or headfirst, as down a pali; *kimo* e mai ke poo a make loa.

5. To strike, as with a stick in choosing the puu in playing at puhenehene where the noa is.

6. To bend over or forward, as in making a bow.

7. To nod, as with drowsiness.

KI-MO, *s.* The name of a former game or play, described as follows: ka pai ana i kekahi pohaku me ka hoolei ana i ka pohaku liilii iluna me ka apo ana e me ka pohaku nui me ka lima i kekahi pohaku uuku.

2. Name of a play for children.

KI-MO-KI-MO, *v.* To hew, shave or smooth off the inside of a canoe. NOTE.—This was done with a koi or small adze, with many repeated strokes.

2. To pound up fish for bait in taking other fish.

KI-MO-MO, *v.* See KIMO, to strike. To strike; to pound; to bruise; to break, &c.

KI-MO-PO, *v.* *Kimo*, to strike, and *po*, night. To kill in the dark; to assassinate; to rob in the night; to lie in wait to kill; to do a thing in the dark and in secret; a po hio, *kimopo* iho la na kanaka, during that night men *committed* assassinations.

KI-MO-PO, *s.* Secret rebellions; assassinations.

   2. He *poe kimo*, assassins; persons of rebellious disposition.

   3. Night robbers and plunderers; ma ka papu (ma Kauai) ke *kimopo* ana.

KI-MO-POO, *v.* See KIMO 6 and *poo*, the head. To bow down; to bend the head forward; e kulou ilalo mamua ke poo.

KI-NA, *v.* To drive on; to urge; to oppress.

   2. *Hoo.* To command; to order; to urge strongly. See KIKINA.

KI-NA, *s.* A blemish, as in a person or body of an animal. *Kanl.* 15:21.

   2. Sin; error; wickedness; *kina* ole, without fault; sinless.

   3. Any troublesome untoward event or circumstance that prevents the realization of one's hopes; ma na aina kula he hoomanawa nui ka hana no na *kina*, he poko, he la, he hauoki, he pulua ame kahi mau *kina* e ae.

KI-NA, *adj.* Sinful; wicked; bad; erroneous; defiled.

   2. Having a blemish, as an animal; hipa kane *kina* ole, a ram unblemished.

KI-NA, *adv.* *Hoo.* An intensive. Bad; much; very. *Isa.* 23:5.

KI-NAI, *v.* To quench; to extinguish, as fire. *Oihk.* 6:12.

   2. To put out a light; ua *kinai* loa ia ka malamalama.

   3. To extinguish, as life; to kill by strangling, striking or piercing, as *oo keiki*.

   4. To make bitter with bitter ingredients.

   5. To kill by poisonous medicines.

KI-NAI-NA, *s.* *Kinai* and *ana.* The putting out of life; the end of life.

   2. The end of a road, or where it vanishes.

   3. A mourning for the life, or loss of one dead.

KI-NAU, *s.* Name of a species of fish.

   2. The name of a god.

   3. The name of a species of a small white eel living in the sand.

KI-NAU-NAU, *v.* To grumble secretly; to complain to one's self on account of not having one's expectations realized.

   2. To scold; to threaten; to breathe vengeance.

   3. To be full of evil; to be internally vile.

   4. To complain of another; to find fault.

KI-NA-KI-NA, *v.* See KINA 2. To call to one in anger; to call loudly after one; to hurry one.

KI-NA-NA, *s.* A hen, especially one that has hatched chickens.

KI-NA-NA-HA-LE, *s.* A house; a residence for people; especially a crooked-sided house.

KI-NA-NA-PE, *adj.* Crammed full; filled; stuffed, as with food.

KI-NE-MO-NA, *s.* *Eng.* Cinnamon, the odoriferous bark of a tree. *Mel. Sol.* 4:14.

KI-NI, *s.* The number 40,000.

   2. Any number indefinitely great.

   3. A retinue of persons; a train following a chief, as in former times. 1 *Nal.* 10:2.

   4. Kinsfolks; relations, &c.

   5. *Eng.* Tin; as, *pa kini*, a tin plate; so written instead of *pa tini*.

KI-NI, *s.* Hawaiian orthography for *gini*, gin, a distilled foreign intoxicating liquor.

KI-NI-HO-LO, *s.* *Kini* and *holo*, to run. The name of a particular game of ball, similar to base ball.

KI-NI-KI-NI, *s.* A multitude; a number indefinitely large. *Hal.* 139:18.

KI-NI-KI-NI, *adj.* Numerous; multitudinous; very many; me he hale puka *kini-kini* la, like a house with *many* windows.

KI-NI-KI-NI-PUU, *s.* The name of many puus or hillocks standing near each other. See OLOWALUPUU.

KI-NI-LAU, *s.* Name of a multitude or school of fish in the sea.

KI-NI-PO-PO, *v.* *Kini* and *popo*, a globular substance. To play at ball in the various different games.

KI-NI-PO-PO, *s.* Playing at ball; a general term for all the games of ball-playing.

KI-NO, *s.* The body of a person or other substance as distinguished from the limbs or other appendages.

   2. The body of a person in distinction from *uhane*, the soul; okoa ke kino, okoa ka uhane.

   3. A person; an individual; one's self; kuhi oia me kona *kino* iho, he thought with *himself*.

   4. The body; the substance; the principal part of a thing; he keokeo ke *kino* o ko'u kapa.

   5. A stalk of grass; the body of a tree; that which is the substantial part of mat-

ter. See OIWI.

6. In *grammar*, person; as, kino kahi, first person; kino lua, &c.

KI-NO, *v*. *Hoo*. To take a body; to take shape; to embody, as a shapeless mass; *hookino* ka honua, the earth took shape (from chaos.) *Mel. of Creation*.

KI-NO-A-KA-LAU, *s*. *Kino* and *akalau*, a spirit or ghost. The spirit or ghost of a person not yet dead. See WAILUA, AKALAU, and KINOWAILUA. NOTE.—There were persons formerly, mostly priests, who pretended to see the ghosts or souls or spirits of others while still living, and would inform the living persons that they had seen their spirits, and that it was a sign of some great calamity about to befall them; this the priests did to extort something valuable from them. I aku la kela (ke kahuna), ua ike au, he hele ino ana kou *kinoakalau*, he (the priest) said, I have seen your spirit going about in sadness; i aku la au, heaha ka pono? I said, what is proper to be done? I aku la kela, he ilio keokeo paha, he kapa keokeo, he hee, he kala, he weke, he (the priest) said, a white dog perhaps, or a white kapa, or a squid, or a kala (a fish), or a weke (also a fish.) One or more of these was required by the priest that he might appease the ghost, and escape death.

KI-NO-HI, ⎫ *s*. The beginning; the first
KI-NO-HOU, ⎭ of a series.

2. Primitive; the first in time.

3. The beginning of the world.

4. The name of the first book of the Bible, *Genesis*, from the first word. *Note*.—*Kinohi* never takes the article.

KI-NO-HOU, *adv*. At first; before. 1 *Nal.* 20:9.

KI-NO-HI-NO-HI, *adj*. Printed, as calico; spotted; kikokiko, onio.

KI-NO-MA-KE, *s*. *Kino* and *make*, dead. A dead body. *Oihk.* 5:2. A corpse of a man or animal. See KUPAPAU.

KI-NO-PU, *s*. The effluvia or smell or strong scent of tobacco; o ka poe a pau i lawe i ke *kinopu*, ua okiia ka lakou mau ipu.

KI-NO-WAI-LU-A, *s*. *Kino* and *wailua*, a ghost. A poetical name for a spirit or ghost of one seen while living, distinct from and in a different place from his body. See KINOAKALAU and KAKAOLA.

KI-NO-RA, *s*. *Heb*. Name of a musical instrument. *Hal.* 57:8.

KI-PA, *v*. To turn from the direct path.

2. To turn in and lodge; to put up or stay with one. *Kin.* 38:1.

3. With ae, to turn from. *Kanl.* 28:14. To turn aside. *Puk.* 3:3.

4. To stay; to abide; to live; to dwell. 2 *Sam.* 14:24. To dwell in a certain place; to go and come with familiarity at one's house; e hookanaka ia kaua o *kipa* hewa ke aloha i ka ilio, i ka huelo ka ike; a kipa i na hale o Keopoulani, they *stayed* in the houses of Keopuolani.

5. To water land artificially, directing the streams here and there.

6. *Hoo*. To receive into one's house; to lodge; to entertain, as a guest; to receive morally. *Ioan.* 1:5.

7. To be a lodger or guest at another's house.

KI-PA, *s*. Kindness; hospitality; access to one.

2. *Hoo*. An entrance upon any business.

3. The name of a medicine given to madmen; same as *pipa*.

KI-PA, *adj*. Friendly; kind; hospitable.

KI-PAE-PAE, *s*. Stone steps for entering a house.

2. A pavement. 2 *Oihl.* 7:3. See PAEPAE and KIPAIPAI.

KI-PAI, *v*. To drive off or expel, as dogs or chickens belonging to others; ke *kipai* ana i ka mea e hoomalu ana i kana mau keiki.

KI-PAI, *s*. The driving away or expulsion of animals that do not belong to one.

KI-PAI-PAI, *s*. See KIPAEPAE. A pavement, i. e., a road paved with stones, fern trunks or the like. See KIPAPA.

KI-PAI-PAI, *v*. To pave a road, as with stones or other materials.

KI-PAO-PAO, *v*. See PAOPAO. To strike; to pound, as with a hammer; to beat; to bruise.

2. To pelt with stones. See KIPOPO.

KI-PA-KU, *v*. To drive away forcibly; to expel or turn out of a house or place of residence. *Kin.* 3:23.

2. To put away, as a wife. *Mat.* 1:19. To cast out; to turn off. *Ioan.* 6:37.

3. To put away, as property unlawfully obtained. *Ios.* 7:31.

KI-PA-KU, *s*. A banishment; an expulsion.

KI-PA-LA-LE, *s*. A rushing; a hurry; a rapid flow, as a swollen stream of water; i na *kipalale* a na waiahulu, by the *rushing* of muddy water.

KI-PA-LA-LE, *adj*. See LALE, to hurry. What is done quickly and expeditiously; ka hana me ka ikaika, me ka hele alualu ame ka hele *kipalale*; what is swollen and enlarged, as a rushing stream.

KI-PA-PA, *v.* To pave; to lay a pavement of stones. *Mel. Sol.* 3:10. See KIPAE-PAE and KIPAIPAI.

2. To balance on the top of the surf; to turn sideways, as on a surf-board in the surf.

3. To be thick together.

4. To lay with flat stones or boards, as a road or bridge.

5. To protect and support when another condemns.

KI-PA-PA, *s.* The topping off of a wall; the filling up of a hole with stones.

2. *Kipapa* pohaku, a pavement.

3. A back-load of anything; a burden; same as *haawe*.

KI-PA-PAU, *v.* To descend from a high place to a place below.

KI-PA-PA-LA-LE, *s.* See KAPALALE. A balancing of two heavy burdens on a stick that they may be easy to carry.

KI-PA-PA-PO-HA-KU, *s.* *Kipapa* and *pohaku*, a stone. A stone pavement. *Ioan.* 19:13.

KI-PA-WA-LE, *v.* *Kipa* and *wale*, gratuitously. To go and sit unbidden in another's house.

2. To enter another's premises with dishonest intentions.

3. To seize and take another's property.

KI-PA-WA-LE, *s.* The coming upon and taking another's property without right.

2. The name of a species of sweet potato.

KI-PE, *v.* To bribe; to offer secretly a reward for some wrong doing; to give something secretly to screen one from justice; e haawi malu i ka waiwai i mea e pakele ai.

KI-PE, *v.* To stone; to pelt with stones; to pelt or strike, as hail or rain in a storm.

KI-PE, *s.* A reward; an inducement to do what otherwise one would not do because evil; a bribe; a gift; *Kanl.* 10:17.

2. Property given to screen from punishment; he waiwai e haawi malu ia e pakele ai ka hihia ma ke kanawai, o lilo i ka hoohewaia.

3. One who practices bribery. *Iob.* 15:34.

KI-PE, *adj.* Tending to bribery; inducing one to commit bribery. *Puk.* 23:8.

KI-PEA,   } *v.* See PEA. To cross one
KI-PEA-PEA, }   stick with another; to build a shanty or temporary shed for a shelter, as from the rays of the sun; to erect a secret place where one may hide.

KI-PE-HI, *v.* See PEHI, to pelt with stones. To throw clubs or stones; *kipehi* aku la ia i ua wahi manu la, a pa aku la kona wawae a hai. See KIPE.

KI-PE-PA, *v.* To bite or snatch, as with the teeth.

KI-PI, *v.* To resist lawful authority; to rebel; to revolt.

2. To withhold allegiance; *kipi* hou iho la o Kanekoa a kaua me Keoua.

3. To act contrary to one in authority. *Kanl.* 9:7.

4. *Hoo.* To stir up rebellion.

5. To kill or murder one's chief.

KI-PI, *s.* A rebel.

2. Rebellion, opposition and resistance to lawful authority. *Kanl.* 31:27.

3. A breaking up or overturning a government; he ku e, he pepehi a he mokuahana.

KI-PI, *adj.* Seditious; rebellious. *Hoo.* Rebellious; exciting to rebellion.

KI-PI, *adv.* *Hoo.* Rebelliously; seditiously. *Kanl.* 13:6.

KI-PI-KI-PI, *v.* Frequentative and intensive of *kipi.* To stir up sedition; to fight.

2. To excite to rebellion.

3. To fight, as in a melee; e hakaka maluna, malalo, e paio me ka inoino.

4. To dig and hill up, as in hoeing potatoes; to dig a hole.

5. *Hoo.* To gather together for rebellion. *Isa.* 54:15.

KI-PI-KI-PI, *s.* Commotion; tumult, as people in a state of revolt; he poe *kipikipi*, rebels.

2. A striker; a boxer; one given to striking. 1 *Tim.* 3:3.

KI-PI-KI-PI, *adj.* Rebellious; acting in frequent rebellions.

KI-PI-KU-A, *s.* The Hawaiian name for pickaxe.

KI-PO, *v.* To break; to break open, as a box or chest; e hoonaha, e wawahi; alaila, *kipo* iho la i ka pahu i ka pohaku.

KI-PO-I-PO-I, *adj.* Concealing one's own errors; hiding one's own faults; kanaka wahine i ka awa *kipoipoi.*

KI-POU, *v.* See POU, post of a house set in the ground. To drive down, as a stake in the ground.

2. To stand leaning, as the post of a thatched house; to bend over.

KI-PO-LA, *v.* See POLA. To warm, as a sick person in order to favor the operation of medicine.

2. To wrap up a hen or turkey or fish in order to carry to market.

KI-PO-LA, *s.* The wrapper fastened around any substance for carrying to market, as fowls, fish, &c.

Ki-po-la-po-la, *v.* To warm a sick person; to apply whatever will tend to warm a sick person.

Ki-po-lo, *s.* A prayer desiring the death of an enemy; he hua pule.

Ki-po-na, *s.* Variable places in the sea, some calm, some ruffled; hiki i na *kipona* ino o Kohala.

Ki-po-na, *v.* To be variable, as spots in the sea in a calm. See Kiponapona.

Ki-po-na-po-na, *v.* To be variegated, as the sea, sometimes calm, sometimes rough; e kiokioki e like me ke kai i kekahi manawa malie, e kipona.

Ki-po-po, *v.* See Kipo. To strike; to hit; to break.

Ki-po-da, *s.* *Heb.* Name of an animal mentioned in *Isa.* 14:23; the bittern or porcupine.

Ki-pu, *v.* To turn the paddle, as in setting a canoe back; *kipu* iho la lakou i na hoe, they *turned back* the paddles, that is, rowed backwards; to turn away; ka huahua i ke *kipu*. *Hoo.* The same.

2. To fold tightly around one, as a large kapa.

3. To keep back, as a shower appearing to approach, but does not come.

Ki-puu-puu, *s.* The thought that arises in one's mind when he hears that another has slandered or spoken evil of him; an internal pain; a disturbance of mind.

Ki-pu-ka, *s.* A snare for taking birds. *Kekah.* 9:12. A sliding noose.

2. Something variable; a change; variety.

3. An opening; a calm place in a high sea.

Ki-pu-ka-pu-ka, *adj.* Full of openings or kipukas.

Ki-pu-lu, *v.* To apply manure to the soil to enrich it; to do to the ground whatever will cause vegetables to grow.

2. *Hoo.* To cause to enrich, as the ground; to manure.

Ki-pu-lu, *s.* Manure; dung, &c. 1 *Nal.* 14:10.

Ki-pu-lu, *adj.* *Hoo.* Enriching; making fruitful; ka ua noe anu *hookipulu* lehua o na pali.

Ki-pu-ni, *v.* To gird on; to wrap around, as a coat or cloak around the body; e *kipuni* i ka aahu.

2. Fig. E *kipuniia* makou i ka pono, i ke aloha, &c., we are encircled with righteousness, with love, &c.

Ki-pu-pu, *v.* See Kipu. To set an oar back little by little.

2. *Hoo.* To brace back the oar little by

little.

3. To be hindered or impeded in some way.

4. To draw back or refuse to go when invited or ordered, or pulled by the arm, as a wife by her husband. See Hoopupu 3.

Ki-waa, *s.* The name of a very large bird.

Ki-waa-waa, *s.* A rough kind of kapa used for various purposes, but of a rough texture; a coarse kapa; he huna hoopulu kuku na ka wahine; he pa-u manoanoa.

Ki-waa-waa, *adj.* Broad-shouldered; stout, as a strong man.

Ki-wa-wa, *s.* Wauki partly beaten into kapa; the thick kapa matter when partly beaten out, or ready for beating. See Kiwaawaa above.

Ki-wi, *v.* To turn from a natural shape or position.

2. To fall or tumble down.

3. To pull along, as a fish that is fast to a hook, i. e., to bend the line out of its natural place.

4. To bend or to be crooked.

5. To bend forward or sideways, as a sleepy person; to nod.

6. To turn a little one side or edgeways.

7. To walk crookedly; he *kiwi* ka hele ana.

Ki-wi, *s.* The horn of an ox or cow, from their crookedness. *Kanl.* 33:17. *Kiwi hipa,* a ram's horn. *Ios.* 6:5. Any hooked thing; a crooked horn; a sickle.

2. A pulling here and there, as a fish caught with the hook in his mouth.

Ki-wi, *adj.* Sideways; lateral.

Ki-wi-ki-wi, *v.* See Kiwi. To turn; to bend; to nod, &c. See Kakiwi and Kikiwi. *Hoo.* To pull frequently at a hook with a fish on it; hopu mai la ke kanaka iwaho, *hookiwikiwi* iho la, a hemo ae la.

Ki-da, *s.* *Heb.* Cassia. *Puk.* 30:24.

Ko, *adj. pron.* Contraction of *kou.* Thy; thine; of thee. *Gram.* § 132.

Ko, *prep.* Of; the sign of possession or property, answering often to the apostrophic s in English, thus *ko na,* of him, of her, of it, that is, his, hers or its (seldom however in the neuter); *ko kakou,* of us, that is, our, ours; *ko lakou,* of them, theirs, &c. It has the same meaning as *o,* but is placed in another part of the sentence. *Ko* is used also before nouns proper and common in the same way. Sometimes *ko* and *o* are both used; as, *ko o nei poe kanaka, of,* or what belongs to the people *here,* or the *o* may be taken as a noun of place. *Gram.*

§ 69, 1, 2, 3.

KO, *v.* To accomplish; to fulfill; to bring to pass, as a promise or a prophecy. *Lunk.* 13:17. To fulfill, as an agreement; opposite to *haule*, to fail. *Ios.* 23:14. To fulfill, as a threat; to be avenged. *Ier.* 5:29. To obtain; to conquer; to overpower.

2. To win in a bet; olioli iho la ka poe i *ko*, so those who *won* in a race rejoiced; to prevail, as one party over another. *Luk.* 23:23. To obtain what one has sought after; to succeed in a search. *Laieik.* 63.

3. To proceed from, as a child from a parent; to beget, as a father. *Ier.* 16:3.

4. To conceive, as a female; to become pregnant; e hapai, e piha. *Kin.* 16:4.

5. To draw or drag, as with a rope; e kauo, e huki. 2 *Sam.* 17:13.

6. *Hoo.* To fulfill an engagement. *Laieik.* 109. To perform what has been spoken. *Nah.* 23:19.

7. To put a law in force; e *hooko* i ke kanawai. 2 *Sam.* 8:15. That is, cause to fulfill the law.

KO, *adj.* Drawn; dragged, &c.

KO, *s.* Sugar-cane; hence, sugar; molasses.

2. In *music*, the second ascending note.

KO-A, *v.* To be dry; to be without moisture; maloo, mauu ole.

2. To be unfruitful; to bear no fruit, as a plant or tree; e hua ole mai i ka hua.

3. To speak unwittingly; to speak in jest; not meaning exactly what one says.

4. To miss; to make a mistake in speaking; e olelo kikoola; to throw words carelessly together without thought.

5. To be bold; to be courageous; to act the soldier; e ikaika oe, e koa hoi, mai makau.

6. *Hoo.* To be valiant; to act valiantly. *Ier.* 9:3.

KO-A, *s.* A barren, fruitless plant or tree.

2. A soldier; *plural*, soldiers; an army; a multitude.

3. The horned coral; the same as *akoakoa*; the coral rock; *koa* ahi and *koa* opelu, places among the coral rocks where the fishes ahi and opelu are found; o ke *koa* a lakou e lawaia ai, the *coral* is where they fished; he puu *koa*, a clump of coral rocks.

4. A mean beggar.

5. The name of a large tree growing on the mountains, good for furniture, of which canoes are made and instruments of war.

6. A mistake in speaking or acting; doing what was not designed.

7. In *geography*, a sound; a strait; a channel; waha koa, a strait. See KOWA.

8. A broad, prominent forehead.

KO-A, *adj.* Brave; bold, as a soldier.

2. Dry; without moisture.

3. Unfruitful, as a plant or tree.

4. Unsteady; irregular in habit.

KO-A, *adv.* Boldly; without fear; e olelo *koa*, speak boldly.

KO-A-A, *v.* See KOA. To be dry; to lack moisture; hence,

2. To be unfruitful, as plants in dry ground.

KO-A-A, *s.* The name of an unfruitful plant; aole hua, he *koaa*; he uala hua ole ke *koaa*.

KO-AE, *adj.* White; of a whitish color; bright.

KO-AE, *s.* The name of a species of white bird which is found about precipices.

2. The name of a species of red fish.

KO-A-E-A, *adj.* Dry; unfruitful; bearing no fruit. See KOAA.

KO-AI, *v.* To wind round; to tie about; to creep round like a circling vine; to gird round, as a pa-u, or girdle upon the body; e *koai* i ka pa-u. See KAEI and KOALI.

KO-AI-AI, *v.* See KOAI. To move round the hand; to stir, as one does tea.

KO-A-I-E, *s.* Name of a species of timber growing inland; wood hard; used for house posts and for making shark hooks.

KO-A-KA, *v.* To be continually changing one's residence; to go here and there.

2. To marry wives and go and leave them.

3. To act the debauchee.

KO-A-KA, *s.* A debauchee; one who marries wives and puts them away again; he moekolohe pinepine.

2. *Eng.* The Hawaiian pronunciation for quarter, i. e., a quarter (of a dollar.)

3. Name of the place where a retreating wave meets one coming in, in shallow water. See PUAO.

KO-A-KA, *adj.* See KOAA. Valiant; brave; applied to men. 1 *Sam.* 14:52. He keiki *koaka* nae (Halaaniani.) *Laieik.* 128.

KO-A-KE-A, *s.* *Koa*, coral, and *kea*, white. The white coral of the ocean.

KO-A-KO-A, *v.* To live in one place; not to move or rove about from one place to another; not to visit here and there. See KUPENE. *Hoo.* Same.

KO-A-KO-A, *adj.* Furnished; supplied; having what is necessary for comfort. See KUONOONO. Kuonoono *koakoa* ka noho ana.

2. Brave; bold; daring; impudent; he olelo *koakoa* ko kekahi alii kanaka; the opposite of *hopepe* and *oheke*. See KOA,

brave; soldier-like.

Ko-a-ko-a, *s.* Generally written *akoakoa*. See Koa and Akoakoa. The coral of the ocean; the coral rock.

Ko-a-ko-a-na, *adj.* Applied to a person once lazy and indolent, but changed in his habits, and now has a house and comforts and is collecting valuables; i ka waha wikiwiki *koakoana* ole.

Ko-a-ku-mu-o-le, *s.* A tree of that name mauka of Kahihikolo; the tree was devoted to Kamapuaa.

Ko-a-la, *v.* To roast over coals of fire; to broil on the coals. *Luk.* 24:42. To cook on the fire; *properly*, to lay on the coals.

2. To leave or have a remainder; to grow less and less; to be over and above.

Ko-a-la, *adj.* Cooked; broiled on the coals.

Ko-a-la, *s.* The uterus; the placenta of females; he puu koko i paa maloko o ka wahine hanau.

Ko-a-la-a-la, *s.* Breakfast. *Rich.* Koalaala ma ka hewa.

Ko-a-lau-ka-ne, *s.* A particular kind of koa; the name of the wood or tree of which gods were made.

Ko-a-li, *s.* The plant convolvulus; he mea hihi kolo.

Ko-a-li, *v.* See Koai. To creep around; to twine about, as a vine; to run and grow thickly together, as the convolvulus.

Ko-a-na, *adj.* Clear, as water when the dirt has settled to the bottom.

Ko-a-na, *v.* To remain; to be over and above. See Koala 2.

Ko-a-na, *s.* A small part or piece of anything; a fragment; a particle; ka maawe o ka papale a o ka moena.

2. A bladder; the container of urine. *Anat.* 15. *Koana* mimi; he wahi e waiho ai ka mimi.

Ko-a-na-a-wa, *v.* See Miala and Mahaoi. To treat one hardly to whom he has given property to take care of; to be hard upon one.

Ko-a-ni-a-ni, *v.* To blow; to breeze, as a fresh breeze; ke *koaniani* mai nei ka makani. See Aniani.

2. To blow softly or gently, creating coolness.

3. To make or cause a breeze, as with a fan; e *koaniani* me ka peahi.

Ko-a-ni-a-ni, *s.* A soft cooling wind.

2. A place cooled by a gentle breeze.

3. The blowing of a cool breeze; he peahi *koaniani*.

Ko-a-pa-ka, *adj.* Valiant; brave; successful, as a combatant.

Ko-a-pa-ki, *s.* A soldier well cared for; an active soldier.

2. A tree thoroughly manured.

Ko-a-we-o-we-o, *s.* Name of a species of cane, joints striped white and red.

Ko-e, *v.* To remain; to be over and above; not quite all.

2. *Hoo.* To cause to remain; to save from destruction; to leave; to let remain. *Puk.* 16:19. To spare; to save; to reserve. 2 *Sam.* 8:4.

3. To fulfill; to accomplish, as a promise. 1 *Nal.* 8:24.

4. To allow or permit to remain. *Oihk.* 7:15. Aole i *koe* ke aho, no courage remained, i. e., it was despair. *Ios.* 2:11.

Ko-e, *v.* To spit; to discharge phlegm; e kuha iho.

2. To divide off; to separate; e mahele.

Ko-e, *s.* The remainder; what is left; an excess; an overplus; more; a surplus. See Koena.

2. The angle worm.

Ko-e, *adj.* Remaining; enduring.

Ko-e-a, *v.* To be dry; to be hard, as earth dried in the sun.

2. To refuse a favor; to be unkind; i ole makou e aaka a *koea* iho, that we may not be stubborn and *refuse*.

3. To divide off; to cut off; to separate.

Ko-e-a, *s.* A person inclined to indolence; indisposed to yield to the wish of another.

Ko-e-a, *adj.* Disobedient to orders; self-willed; taciturn; lazy indolent; indisposed to go when ordered.

Ko-e-ha-e-ha, *s.* For *koeaea.* See Koea. One who is hard, unobliging or morose.

Ko-e-ha-e-ha, *adj.* Hot; uncomfortable by reason of heat; sultry; *koehaeha* ia wahi i ka la.

Ko-e-ha-na, *s.* A footstool. See Kuhana.

Ko-e-ha-na, *adj.* Warm; applied to weather; mehana, welawela.

Ko-e-ha-na, *s.* Warmth; heat, as of the sun; ka wela o ka la.

Ko-e-ho-nu-a, *s.* *Koe* and *honua,* adverb. A remainder; a remnant; as when a piece of work is almost done, the unfinished part is the *koehonua.*

2. A mele composed on the name of a chief; he mele lahi.

Ko-e-ko-e, *v.* To be wet and cold; to be cold from being wet.

2. To scratch out, as writing with a knife.

KO-E-KO-E, *s.* Dampness; cold; chilliness; i ke anuanu ame ke *koekoe* o ua wahi nei la.

KO-E-KO-E, *adj.* Chilly from being wet; chilled; cold.

KO-E-LE, *s.* A small division of land less than a *kihapai*; hence, a field planted by the tenants for the hakauaina or landlord; a garden belonging to the chief, but cultivated by his people.

2. A slight knocking or pounding; the sound of the kapa mallet at a distance.

3. The ticking of a watch.

4. A tall man.

5. Equality in numbers or strength.

6. A union of two things.

KO-E-LE, *v.* To strike; to beat; to tick, as a clock.

KO-E-LE, *adj.* Dry, as the ground; maloo; dry, as bones; *koele* na iwi o Hua ma i ka la, *dry* are the bones of Hua and his company in the sun. NOTE.—Hua was a chief whose people and himself died traveling in the sun.

KO-E-LE-E-LE, *v.* To make a sound frequently by striking; to sound often; kanikani.

2. To be dry, as a place without rain and under the heat of the sun; *koeleele* aku o Ikua.

KO-E-LE-E-LE, *adj.* Contentious; quarrelsome, as a man and his wife; strong for fighting; much disposed to fight.

KO-E-LE-LU-A, *v.* See KOELE 5. To be equal in numbers or strength.

KO-E-LE-PA-LAU, *s.* A pudding made of potatoes and cocoanut.

KO-E-LI, *s.* *Ko* and *eli*, to dig. The sugar-cane planted or put under ground; he ko malalo o ka lepo no Halalii.

KO-E-LO, *s.* See KOWELO and WELO. That which hangs fastened at the top, as a signal, colors, a streamer, &c.

KO-E-LO-E-A, *adj.* Some character of the wind; pa mai la ka makani o *koeloea*.

KO-E-LO-E-LO, *v.* See KOELO. To stream off, as the tail of a comet; to float, as an ensign; to flap in the wind.

KO-E-NA, *s.* Contracted from *koe* and *ana*. The remainder; an overplus; a remnant of something larger or more numerous; hence,

2. The ruins of anything. *Ios.* 10:20.

KO-E-NE, *v.* To take shelter in some safe place or under some one's protection; to feel safe or secure from harm.

KO-I, *v.* To use force with one, either physical or moral.

2. To urge; to entreat one to do or not to do a thing; to compel by entreaty.

3. To tempt; to be led to do a thing. *Kanl.* 4:19. *Koi* ae la lakou ia ia (ia Liholiho) e aie, they *urged* him (Liholiho) to go in debt.

4. To drive; to urge with violence; to compel by force; to insist on a thing; to practice any athletic exercise; e *koi* mau a mama i ka holo.

5. To ask or invite one to go in company with him.

6. To take aside to ask a favor.

7. To carry a bundle on the shoulders of two men on a stick between them.

8. To drive or force in, as a nail or spike into wood; to force one thing into another.

9. To flow or rush like rushing water over a dam or any obstruction.

10. To put in the stick or vine on which kukui nuts are strung; e *koi* i ke kukui.

KO-I, *s.* A compulsion; an urging, &c.

2. A small adze; *koi* lipi, a hatchet.

3. A projecting forehead, i. e., a sharp face; he lae *koi* kou, an insulting expression.

4. The name of a species of kalo.

koi

5. The name of a play; a sort of race in sliding; ina i ao i ka pahee, ame ka hooholo moa, ame ke *koi*; he mau ikaika pili waiwai.

6. The name of a splinter of bamboo on which kukui nuts are strung.

7. An indolent person wanting energy or decision in action.

KO-I, *adj.* Shrill; sharp; fine, as a voice on a high key.

KO-IA, *pron. pers.* *Ko*, preposition, and *ia*, third pers. sing. pron. The ancient but regular form of the auiiki of *ia*. Of him; his; ka welau wale no o *koia* la lima, the end only of his finger.

KO-I-EI-EI, *s.* See KOI, *v.*, 8. A rapid current sucking in and carrying off everything.

2. The things thus swept away.

3. The name of a play.

KO-I-EI-EI, *v.* To rest; to be quiet; to be still.

KO-I-E-LE, *v.* See KOI, to force. To

drive; to force; to push on; to urge.

2. To overflow; to rush here and there, as overflowing water; to drive on, but in the wrong road.

Ko-II, *v.* To diminish; to grow less, as water flowing a long distance; *koii* ka wai.

Ko-II, *adj.* Fresh; vigorous; green; flourishing, as young healthy plants.

Ko-II, *s.* A reproachful epithet; sneering language.

Ko-IU-IU, *v.* See IUIU. To be afar off; to be high up; to be at a great distance. See POIUIU.

Ko-IU-IU, *adj.* What is far off; very distant; at a great height.

Ko-I-U-LA, *v.* To rise or ascend, as smoke; to float in the air; to ascend, as a cloud.

Ko-I-U-LA, *s.* A rising smoke; a floating cloud.

Ko-I-HO-LU, *s.* See KOI and HOLU, to bend. An adze, i. e., a bent axe.

Ko-I-KA-HI, *s.* *Koi* and *kahi*, to cut. A plane for planing boards or timber. *Isa.* 44:13.

Ko-I-KO-I, *v.* See KOI. To urge; to be hard upon; to be heavy.

2. To carry a heavy burden on a stick in two bundles.

3. To ask; to entreat with perseverance.

4. *Hoo.* To compel; to exercise authority over.

5. To bear down upon; to treat with rigor or violence.

Ko-I-KO-I, *s.* Substance; strength; spirit.

2. Honor; substance. *Iob.* 21:7.

3. Weight; heaviness; solidity; riches.

4. *Hoo.* Rigor; severity. *Puk.* 1:13.

Ko-I-KO-I, *adj.* Heavy; weighty. *Sol.* 27:3.

2. Substantial; honorable; valiant, as persons of integrity. *2 Sam.* 23:19.

3. Applied to words or speech, full of meaning; emphatic; also, rough; inconsiderate; olelo *koikoi,* a rough speech. *Kin.* 4:2, 7. Poe *koikoi,* honorable persons. *Ios.* 14:1.

4. *Hoo.* Oppressive; hard; cruel. *Zek.* 10:4.

Ko-I-LI, *v.* To set; to go down, as the moon; to set (apparently), as the moon on the surface of the sea when going down; ke kau ana o ka mahina maluna o ka ili o ke kai i ka manawa e napoo aku ai.

Ko-I-LI-PI, *s.* *Koi* and *lipi,* sharp; tapering. An axe; an instrument for hewing stones. *Puk.* 20:22. A hatchet. *Kanl.* 19:5. Any tool. *Kanl.* 27:5.

Ko-I-NA, *s.* See KOI, to force. A pressure; a compulsion; a forcing.

Ko-I-NE, *v.* To hasten; to be quick; to hurry on.

Ko-O, *v.* To support; to prop up; to establish; to sustain in any position or purpose. *Hal.* 112:8. To brace one's self.

2. To push off, as with an oar or setting pole.

3. To help; to assist. *Isa.* 63:5.

4. To prop or brace up anything liable to fall; to uphold. SYN. with kokua.

5. To uncoil, as a rope or string when wound up; to slacken, as a rope that is drawn too tight.

6. To struggle hard, as in rowing a canoe against the wind.

7. To be loose; to be separate; to fall off.

8. *Hoo.* To loosen; to unbind; to make or cause to be vacant; aole no oe e *hookoo* iki aku i kau wahi.

Ko-O, *s.* A prop; a brace for holding anything up.

2. Some part of a canoe; e lalau ae kou lima i ka hoe, ame ke ka liu, ame ke *koo.*

3. A vacant place; eia no kahi *koo* iki. Aohe wahi *koo* iki o ka la, spoken of one who has no leisure.

Koo, *adv.* Equivalent to *fold,* as how many fold? *Koolua,* two-fold; *kokookolu,* three-fold; *koo* or *kowalu,* eight-fold, &c.

Ko-OU, *adj.* Wet with sea water; cold; damp; chilly from moisture of clothes; moist, also, as mats, house, &c. See KOU.

Koo-KA-PU, *v.* To forbid strictly on pain of death; *kookapuia* ae la ka puaa ame ka neulelo. See HOOKAPU.

Koo-KOO, *s.* A staff; a cane for supporting a weak person; *kookoo* hao, an iron rod; a rod; a shepherd's crook. *Oihk.* 27:32. FIG. A stay; a staff; a supporter; that is, means of livelihood. *Isa.* 3:1.

Koo-KO-OU, *adj.* See KOOU. Damp; wet; *kookoou* me he kapa pulu la.

Koo-KOO-HAO, *s.* *Kookoo,* staff, and *hao,* iron. An iron staff; a rod of iron. *Hal.* 2:9.

Koo-KOO-LAU, *s.* A very small tree or bush; a little tree for planting.

Koo-KOO-LU-A, *s.* See KOKOOLUA.

Koo-KU, *v.* To swell; to enlarge; to puff up, as a ruffle.

Koo-KU, *s.* A swelling of land on the side of a mountain; ma ke *kooku* o ke kuahiwi.

2. Name of a road or path leading up hill. See PIINA.

Ko-O-LA, *v.* See KOLA.

Ko-O-LA, *s.* The tail of a cock; me ke *koola* no ka moa kane.

Koo-LAU, *s.* The name of districts on

the north sides of two or three islands.

Ko-o-li-li, *s.* The quivering motion of an arrow as it flies through the air.

2. The twinkling of the eyelids.

3. The undulating motion of the atmosphere near the earth under the direct rays of the sun.

Koo-lu-a, *s.* See Koo 2 and Lua, two. A canoe with only two persons; elua wale no ma ka waa.

Koo-mo-a, *s.* *Koo* and *moa*, a fowl. The long feathers in a cock's tail.

Koo-mo-a, *adj.* Long tailed; waving like the tail feathers of a cock; long and bent like a cutlass.

Ko-o-nei, *pron.* Oblique case of *nei*. *Gram.* § 105, 3. Of this here. *Oih.* 26:23. *Koonei* kanaka, the people of here; this people; the people of this region.

Ko-o-na, *s.* See Koena. A remnant; the remainder of water in a calabash; the little water that remains in a calabash.

Ko-u, *v.* To look; to look about; to look here and there; e nana, e imi i o i o.

2. *Hoo.* To have a sufficiency; to be supplied with the necessaries of life.

Ko-u, *adj.* Moist; wet; damp; chilly from moisture; moist, as dry bread brought to a moist place. See Koou.

Kou, *s.* The name of a large shade tree growing mostly near the sea beach; timber good for many purposes, especially for cups, bowls, dishes, &c.; takes a polish.

Kou, *adj. pron.* Thy; thine; of thee; of you; of yours; an oblique case of *oe*. *Gram.* § 132 and 133, 3d. See Kau. Note. It has the diphthongal sound.

Ko'u, *adj. pron.*, first person. My; mine; of me; an oblique case of *au* or *wau*, and formed like the foregoing. See Grammar § 124, 1st, and § 126, 3d. *Ko'u* is distinguished from *kou* by a slight break in the pronunciation between the preposition *ko* and the *u* and indicated in writing by an apostrophe. It is doubtless a contraction of *ko ou*.

Ko'u,
Ko'u-ko, } *v.* To cluck, as a hen.

Ko-u-ko-u, *s.* The noise of a mouse.

Kou-kou, *adj.* Moist, as a healthy skin when somewhat cold; *koukou* ka ili; moist; damp; chilly, as a kapa or house.

Kou-kou, *adj.* Heavy, as a canoe or anything which sinks in the water instead of floating lightly. See Koikoi.

Ko-u-la, *s.* *Ko*, sugar-cane, and *ula*, red. A variety of sugar-cane, which is of a reddish color.

Ko-u-ga, *s.* *Eng.* The name of an animal, the cougar.

Ko-ha, *s.* The cracking of a whip; a report of a pistol; a sudden squeak, and a smaller sound than *poha*. See Poha.

Ko-ha, *adj.* Cracking; sounding with a sudden noise.

Ko-ha-ha, *adj.* Large; increased in size; swelled up; plump, as a fat animal; swelled; puffed up, as a swelled limb. See Haha.

Ko-ha-ka, *s.* A vicious pronunciation for *koaka* or *kuaka* for *kuata* (*Eng.*), quarter. A quarter (of a dollar); Hawaiian, *hapaha*.

Ko-ha-la, *s.* The name of the northern district of Hawaii.

Ko-ha-na, *v.* *Hoo.* To make bare; to strip naked. *Ier.* 49:10. To be destitute of covering.

Ko-ha-na, *s.* Nakedness; an utter destitution of clothing; hele wale, aole kapa.

Ko-ha-na, *adj.* Naked; destitute of clothing; not even a malo.

Ko-ha-na, *adv.* Nakedly; holo *kohana*, fled in nakedness. *Oih.* 19:16. Ku *kohana*, to stand nakedly, i. e., to be in nakedness. *Isa.* 58:7.

Ko-ha-na-ha-na, *v.* *Ko* and *hanahana*, to be warm. To be hot; to be warm; to burn. See Hanahana.

Ko-he, *s.* A sickness; the name of a disease.

2. Vagina feminarum.

Ko-he, *v.* To detain. See Kohi.

Ko-he-a, *s.* A warm day; pleasant, agreeable weather.

2. A loose flowing garment.

Ko-he-a-ka, *s.* A disease of females, attended with pain or difficulty in passing urine.

Ko-he-o, *v.* To walk about, as a hen with her wings loose or partially spread open; me ka upaupa ana o na eheu.

2. To fly up on something; e lele a kau maluna.

Ko-he-o-he-o, *s.* A mixture containing a deadly poison; he mea awaawa e make ai.

2. A medicine of the sorcerer to kill with.

Ko-he-o-he-o, *adj.* Deadly; causing death, as a deadly poisonous drug; apu *koheoheo*, the poisonous cup, the contents of which were made up of several poisonous ingredients, designed for self-murder or for the execution of criminals by the order of a chief, the person presenting the cup saying, *he wahi mea ola ia*.

Ko-he-o-he-o, *s.* A kind of play among children, as swinging a rope to be jumped over.

2. Name of a certain stick or buoy to float a fish-hook.

3. An instrument to assist in mourning or wailing along with other sounds; he mea kanikani pihe me ka uwalaau.

KO-HE-O-HE-O, *adj.* The epithet of a frock coat, not a jacket, not a dress coat; he lole *koheoheo*.

KO-HE-KO-HE, *s.* Name of a small rush or grass growing in kalo patches.

2. A kind of shell fish that grows to the sides of plank of a ship at sea, but different from the *okohekohe*.

KO-HE-KO-HE-A, *v.* See KOHEA. To be clear, as the sky; to be serene; without clouds; to be calm; to be warm; to be agreeable.

KO-HE-KO-HE-PA-PA, *s.* A sore and ulcerated throat; an eating sore.

KO-HE-LE-MU, *v.* See KOHE and LEMU, the under part of the thigh. To stand or sit still; to be inactive.

2. Not to do what is bidden.

KO-HE-LE-MU, *adj.* Dull; inattentive; disobedient; inactive.

KO-HE-LU-A, *s.* The name of a species of fish-hook.

KO-HE-LU-A-PAA, *s.* Name of a kind of fish-hook.

KO-HE-NA-LO, *s.* Name of a species of stone.

KO-HI, *v.* To dig; to make a hole or cavity in the ground; to dig, as a well. *Puk.* 7:24. To dig in the ground. *Isa.* 5:2. SYN. with eli.

2. To take up; to separate, as the kalo from the huli.

3. To prevent; to hinder; to hold back.

4. *Haa.* To travail in birth; to endure the pains of child-birth. *Gal.* 4:19.

KO-HI, *s.* Hoo. The first or commencing pains of child-birth. See HAAKOKOHI. The throes of child-birth pains.

2. A fat piece of pork; a piece of fat.

3. A swinging off or outside.

KO-HI-A, *v.* To rub gently with the thumb and fingers.

2. To be stingy; to be close; to be hard; to crowd on to one.

KO-HI-AI, *v. Kohi,* to dig, and *ai,* food. To dig food from the ground, as potatoes.

2. To watch; to guard; to keep.

KO-HI-KO-HI, *v.* See KOHI 2. To separate food, the worthless from the good.

2. To separate the good from the bad fish after a great haul.

KO-HI-KO-HI, *s.* The act of separating or sorting out the good from the bad fish after a large haul.

KO-HI-KO-HI-KA-PA-LA-LA, *s.* A heaping up of sand in ridges and heaps which has been dug up.

2. A pastime only to make one dirty; he hana lealea e hawahawa ai.

KO-HI-KU, *v.* To waste and destroy food in time of war.

KO-HO, *v.* To choose generally; to select without regard to number.

2. To choose one of two persons; to make choice among two or more objects. *Ios.* 24:15, 22.

3. To choose one of two or more uncertain things.

4. To choose, i. e., to determine; to decree; to name out.

5. To interpret a riddle or parable.

6. To guess; to guess, as a riddle. *Lunk.* 14:12.

7. To ask for a chosen or specified object.

KO-HO-HO-NU-A, *v.* See KOHO 7 above and HONUA, entirely; only. To ask for; to beg, as for land, fish or any definite object desired; *kohohonua* i ka aina, he begged for land; *kohohonua* i ke akua i waiwai, he asked the god for property.

KO-HO-KO, *s.* A disease in utero.

KO-HO-KO-HO, *v.* A frequentative of *koho.* To choose frequently.

2. To cast lots for a thing.

3. To guess in uncertainty.

4. To acquiesce concerning a thing which is in great obscurity.

5. To unriddle, i. e., to solve a riddle.

6. To choose some one; to draw near; to attach one's self to another.

KO-HO-LA, *s.* A reef; a dry place in the sea a little way from the main land.

2. A place of very shallow water some distance from the shore like Kalia on Oahu; also some places still more shallow or dry, as at Kona on Molokai.

3. A whale from his spouting water, raising up water like a reef. NOTE.—The flesh of the whale was forbidden to women under the kapu system. Something like the surf as it breaks on the outer reef.

4. The name of the first law which a chief promulgates; a very strict law.

KO-HO-LU-A, *s.* A hard polished bone used in piercing unborn infants. FIG. He papa *koholua* oi ke alii.

KO-HO-MU-A, *s. Koho,* to choose, and *mua,* first. A first choice, and one greatly desired.

Ko-hu, *v.* To agree together; to dwell in harmony.

2. To take or receive color from one, i. e., to resemble physically or morally; ua *kohu* i ka makuahine, he takes his color from his mother, i. e., *physically*, the color of the skin, or *figuratively*, her character.

3. To be ennobled; to be honored; to be beautiful; to appear noble, like a chief

4. *Hoo.* To follow after; to take the type of one, i. e., to be like him; e *hookohu* io kakou i na oihana i hoomakaia'i.

Ko-hu, *s.* The sap or milk of plants or vegetables, particularly if colored, and such as may be drawn or expressed from the juice of vegetables. *Nah.* 6:3. Hence,

2. Ink or any fixed coloring matter for printing or coloring kapas or cloth; pale ink.

3. The fixing or permanency of the color.

4. *Hoo.* A screen; a covering; a pretense. 1 *Tes.* 2:5.

5. Resemblance; likeness.

Ko-hu, *adj.* Agreeable; suitable; fit; convenient; becoming. 2 *Tim.* 2:9. Alike; similar; he maka *kohu* haole keia.

Ko-hu-ko-hu, *v.* See KOHU, to agree. *Hoo.* To be harmonious in opinion; to agree together; *hookohukohu,* a kanaka iho la kekahi poe no ke Akua, a certain company *agreed together* and acted like men towards God.

2. To exhibit; to make a show or display. *Kol.* 2:23. To have the form of something, but not the reality. 2 *Tim.* 3:5.

Ko-hu-ko-hu, *adj.* Noble; honorable; dignified. See KOHU 3.

2. Rushing, as water, or as a multitude.

3. Jealous.

Ko-ka, *v.* To stuff anything, as paper into the mouth.

Ko-ka, *adj.* Dry, as land; dry; barren; hard, as dry soil.

Ko-kaa, *s.* Lean meat; meat on which there is no fat.

Ko-ka-he, *s.* A false assertion; a lie; an untruth.

Ko-ka-ko-ka, *v.* Intensive of *koka*. To put paper into the mouth; to stuff the mouth full.

Ko-ka-la, *s. Ko* and *kala*, a fish. The sharp thorns on the back of the fish kala.

2. A white thorny fish.

Ko-ke, *v.* To be near; not far off; to be nigh, either in time or place.

2. To be near, as in friendship; e launa mai, e pilikana.

3. To come near or strike together, as two or more things. See UKE and PUKE.

4. To guess; e koho i kana puu noa ma kahi e, a e haawi aku ka puu ana i *koke* ai na ka mea nana i huna.

5. To draw near; to be friendly to one.

Ko-ke, *adj.* Quick; soon (in time); near; not far off (in space.)

Ko-ke, *adv.* Quickly; straightway; immediately; quickly, as in moving from place to place.

Ko-ke-a, *s. Ko,* Sugar-cane, and *kea,* white. The white cane; he opukea, he ainakea.

Ko-ke-a-no, *adj.* Silent; deserted; uninhabited.

Ko-ke-ko-ka, *v.* To punish or strike one for an offense real or imaginary.

Ko-ki, *adj.* Short-nosed; snub-nosed, like a monkey; kekokeko, keko, ihu kumene, kokikoki.

Ko-ki, *s.* The extremity; the end of a tree; a very high place.

Ko-ki-o, *s.* A shrub; a tree.

Ko-ki-o, *v. imp.* Stop; don't go with; spoken in contempt.

Ko-ki-ki, *s.* A bending branch of a tree; the highest top of a tree, especially a bending twig or branch; a place where a branch divides off.

Ko-ki-ko-ki, *s.* See KOKI.

Ko-ko, *v.* To feel; to squeeze; to press, as in lomilomi.

2. To set a broken bone; to replace a bone.

3. To go about from place to place without object.

4. To pull this way and that; to pull or drag along; to tie up the koko or strings of a calabash. See KOKO, *s.,* 3. To push; to jostle, as in a crowd.

5. To be inconstant; to be fickle.

6. To fill; to fulfill; to fill up a specified time. *Iob.* 39:2. See KO, *v.*

Ko-ko, *s.* Blood; the red flow in the arteries and veins of animals; *koko* hala ole, innocent blood. 2 *Nal.* 24:4.

2. A species of shrub or bush used for fuel.

3. The netting or net work of strings around a calabash.

4. A rising up; an extension; ke kilaha o ka opu.

5. A noise or cry of a cock when a hen announces that she has laid her egg; to cackle, as a hen.

6. *Koko* is sometimes used by Hawaiians in modern times for *cocoa* or *chocolate*;

also written *kokoa*, which is better.

Ko-ko, *s.* The strings braided for carrying a calabash; alaila, hanaia kekahi *koko* hakahaka; a pau na kanaka eha ma na kihi eha o ua *koko* la.

Ko-ko, *adj.* Falling rain where the light shines through it and it appears reddish; e ku ana ka punohu i ka moana, ame ka ua *koko. Laieik.* 25.

Ko-ko-a, *s.* A modern word. Chocolate. See the above, 6.

Ko-ko-e, *v.* To divide; to separate into parts; to divide out.

2. To cut with a sharp instrument. 1 *Nal.* 18:28.

3. To be in advance or ahead of another; to hasten forward; to set or fix one's eyes upon; *kokoe* aku la na maka, i ka ike i kona enemi. *Laieik.* 120.

4. To strike, injure or disfigure the eyes of one when angry.

5. *Hoo.* To scratch or dig at one's eyes in order to injure them; mai *hookokoe* i na maka a ka mea i alohaia, o ku ia oe ia ala hookahi.

Ko-ko-i, *v.* See KOI. To spurt; to eject, as water; to cast out suddenly.

Ko-koo, *adv.* Connected with any numeral, it expresses as many fold or as many persons as the numeral expresses; as, *kokoo* lua, two together, or two-fold; *kokoo* kolu, three in company; *kokoo* ono, six together, or six-fold, and so on to ten.

Ko-ko-o-u, *adj.* Cold; damp in the house, as in a valley where much rain falls; muddy and damp.

Ko-koo-hi-a, *adv. int.* How many? how many fold? Asked in reference to the number of persons or things together. See KOKOO above.

Ko-koo-ko-lu, *adv.* See KOKOO above. It answers the question *kokoohia?* how many times? how many? Three-fold; three times; a firm of three; three together. *Luk.* 12:52.

Ko-koo-lu-a, *adv.* See KOKOO. Answering the question *kokoohia?* two-fold; two times; two persons.

Ko-koo-lu-a, *s.* A staff; a cane; hence, a second; an assistant; a helper; a companion; a union of two; two-fold; two together. *Luk.* 12:52.

Ko-ko-hi, *v.* See KOHI, to dig. To dig up; to separate the kalo from the huli.

2. To give thoughtlessly until all is gone, and perhaps has promised another.

Ko-ko-hi, *s. Haa.* The strong pains of a woman in child-birth.

2. The sadness of fear felt in time of a storm.

3. The storm cloud itself. See HAAKOHI and HAAKOKOHI.

Ko-ko-hi-ku, *v.* To do evil to a land; to pull up the food and throw it away; hele mai la ia, a *kokohiku* i na kalo o Waipio.

Ko-ko-hu, *v.* See KOHU. To spot; to mark; to daub.

2. To have a form; to take the garb or assume the manners of another.

Ko-ko-hu-a-wai-na, *s. Koko,* blood, and *huawaina,* grape. The blood or juice of the grape, i. e., pure wine. *Kanl.* 32:14.

Ko-ko-ke, *v.* See KOKE. To be near to; to favor; to approach. *Hal.* 34:18. *Hoo.* To be on friendly terms with; to be attached to one; to meet with.

Ko-ko-ke, *adv.* Near to; close by; e hele *kokoke* mai, draw near. *Kanl.* 4:11. NOTE.— The adverb is mostly *koke*, which see.

Ko-ko-ki, *adj.* See KOKI. High; extended, as the end or top of a thing.

Ko-ko-ko, *adj.* See KOKO, blood. Like a person with his blood up; raging with anger; ready for murder or any deed.

Ko-ko-ko, *s.* The act of eating fish or other meat with the blood.

Ko-ko-koo-ha, *s.* Very small potatoes with red veins.

2. Water-soaked potatoes.

Ko-ko-ko-he, *adj.* Kindly; friendly; pleasantly, as peaceable neighbors; he noho pono, he oluolu.

Ko-ko-le, *s.* Small kalo stinted with weeds.

Ko-ko-lo, *v.* See KOLO. To go on the hands and knees; to crawl.

2. To walk with the back bent, as a hump-backed person.

3. To creep in growing, as a vine. *Hal.* 80:9.

Ko-ko-mo, *s.* See KOMO. A sinking canoe; a going down, or entering in.

Ko-ko-mo, *adj.* Sinking; entering in.

Ko-ko-ni, *v.* See KONI. To throb; to beat, as the pulse.

2. To be in pain; to suffer in distress; e *kokoni* ka aha ia ia hea o Lono.

Ko-ko-no-i-e, *v.* See KONO and IE, to insult. Hoo. To stir up; to excite; to provoke.

Ko-ko-pe, *v.* See KOPE. To defend off; to push away; to shovel, as dirt.

Ko-ko-pu-na, *s.* Menstrual blood from one who is purely a *virgo intacta.*

Ko-ko-we, *v.* To run swiftly; to be light.

Ko-ku-a, *v.* *Ko*, a brace, and *kua*, the back. To back or brace up, as a falling house.

2. To assist in business or an undertaking.

3. To help; to help forward; to help one who is poor or in distress.

4. To bind or tie on, as a pa-u or a garment. See KAKUA.

5. To cut; to hew; to grave.

6. In *deliberative bodies*, to second a motion.

Ko-ku-a, *s.* Help; assistance; what is given in charity; entertainment: hospitality; epithet of the Holy Spirit. *Ioan.* 14:26. The Comforter.

Ko-ku-li, *s.* That which is soft and yellow in the ear; ear wax.

Ko-la, *s.* See KOOLA. The tail feathers of a cock.

2. *Kola* is written for *kohola*, the whale; nui na lawaia i kii i na ia a pau, koe nae ke *kola*.

Ko-la, *v.* To spread out; to grow; to enlarge; to be thick together; to extend beyond, as the tail of a cock.

2. To be excited, as the animal passions.

Ko-la, *adj.* Unripe; used in reference to bananas put into the ground which do not ripen.

Ko-lai-la, *adj.* The auiiki of *laila*. *Gram.* § 65, 2. There; that which belongs to that place, person or thing. *Sol.* 28:2.

Ko-la-hi, *s.* *Ko*, sugar-cane, and *lahi*, a species of white cane. White sugar-cane.

Ko-la-ko-la, *v.* See KOLA, to spread out. To cause a spreading out; to spring up; to raise up.

Ko-la-ne, *v.* To be clear, as the moon; to be explicit, as a statement.

Ko-la-ni, *s.* Name of a species of hula; he *kolani* kekahi hula.

Ko-le, *v.* To be red, like raw meat; to be inflamed, as the eyes; as a wound; to be raw, as flesh with the skin off.

2. To shave the hair of the head closely.

3. To cause one to be naked; e hooolo-helohe.

Ko-le, *s.* Redness; inflamed eyes, &c.

2. Name of a fish.

Ko-le, *adj.* Raw, as meat not fully cooked.

2. Inflamed; red; as an inflamed wound.

3. Used *adverbially*, you are denied; you are nothing, as in the sentence *kolekole* kou maka, i. e., the corner of your eye is red or pulu; down! you see that you are up a stump. See also KOLEKOLEMAKA.

Ko-le-a, *v.* To make a friend of one; to form a friendship quickly and without object; e hoomakamaka wale aku no; to be on very friendly terms with one for the present.

Ko-le-a, *s.* A parent-in-law, that is, a father-in-law, makuakane *kolea*, or a mother-in-law, makuawahine *kolea*; he kane hou na ka makuahine, he wahine hou na ka makuakane.

2. The name of a small fish.

3. The name of a fowl of the duck genus.

4. The name of a tree having a very astringent bark, which is red and used in coloring black; the wood reddish and used for boards.

Ko-le-a-le-a, *s.* See LEA and LEALEA, to please. The action of hushing or stilling children when they cry.

Ko-le-ko-le, *v.* See KOLE. To be raw; not cooked, as meat.

Ko-le-ko-le, *s.* Red earth; the red clay found in different places; he alaea, he lepo ulaula.

Ko-le-ko-le, *adj.* Reddish; raw, as meat half cooked; red; flushed with red; uncooked in the oven.

Ko-le-ko-le-a, *s.* See KOLEA 2. Name of a species of fish.

Ko-le-ko-le-ma-ka, *adv.* See KOLE, *adj.*

Ko-li, *v.* To pare; to shave off little by little; to whittle.

2. E *koli* i ke oho, to shave or cut the hair. *Ier.* 16:6.

3. E *koli* i ke kukui, to trim the lamp. *Puk.* 30:7.

4. E *koli* i ke kila, to chamfer or work with a chisel. *Puk.* 32:4.

5. To sharpen, as a pen with a knife; to trim off the outside, as the fringe of a cloth.

Ko-li, *s.* Something moving through the air; a meteor; ahi *koli*, a jack o lantern; he mea e lele ana ma ka lewa, me he akua lele la, he oili.

2. The name of a tree; also called *aila*.

Ko-lii, *v.* See KOLI, *v.* To diminish; to taper off; to grow less.

2. To be greasy.

Ko-lii, *s.* A name given to the castor-oil plant, from *kolii*, to be greasy. See above.

2. The dazzling of the eyes by looking at the sun.

3. The partial blindness of the eyes by looking at any dazzling substance.

4. The dancing undulating appearance of any large smooth surface shone upon by the sun in a hot day.

5. The name of a particular prayer used in ancient times.

Ko-li-u-li-u, *s.* See LIULIU. An imaginary sound heard or supposed to be heard from afar; a whisper from some other world; something from afar; inu wai *koliuliu* o Hilo; something seen afar off, as a person, but so far as not to distinguish anything particularly.

Ko-li-ko-li, *v.* See KOLI. To cut off frequently; to cut off; to cut short; to trim.

Ko-li-ko-li-ko, *v.* See LIKO. To swell out; to enlarge.

2. To be fat; to have the appearance of grease floating on the surface of water.

Ko-li-li, *v.* To drop or leak out, as from a cork.

2. To flutter, as a flag in the wind. *Hoo.* To wave, as a flag in one's hand; e *hookolili* ana i ka welau o ka maile. *Laieik.* 120.

3. To rush out, as pent up water; to flow swiftly, as water from a deep cistern.

Ko-li-li-u, *adj.* Dimly seen, as fine print by a person of defective vision; ka ia ano *koliliu*, ka hele ana e ka lani. See KOLIULIU.

Ko-lo, *v.* To creep on all fours, as an infant.

2. To crawl, as a worm; to grope, as a blind man.

3. To crouch; to stoop, as an inferior to a superior.

4. To grow or run, as a lateral branch of a vine. *Kin.* 49:52.

5. To creep, run or penetrate, as the fine roots of a tree or plant into the earth; *kolo lea ke aa malalo*, to take root downward. 2 *Nal.* 19:30.

6. To urge, as in asking a favor; to persevere till one obtains the thing asked for.

7. To drive; to row swiftly, as a boat of a war ship.

8. *Hoo.* Hookolo i ka nui manu o kakou. NOTE.—In former times no common person was allowed to approach a high chief to ask a favor or deprecate his displeasure except on his hands and knees. See KOLO. Also, when one was called to account for some delinquency, he was expected to come into the presence of the chief on all fours, and lie prostrate until ordered to look up; hence, in modern times, *hookolokolo*, to call to account; to have a trial; to try judicially. See HOOKOLU and HOOKOLOKOLO.

Ko-lo-a, *v.* To pull; to drag along. See KOKO and KAUO.

Ko-lo-a, *s.* A duck; *specifically*, a muscovy duck.

2. *Literally*, long cane. This fact of long cane is said to have given a name to a dis-

trict on Kauai.

Ko-lo-au, *v.* To stretch out the neck; to be weak; to be fatigued; e loa ka a-i, e maloeloe, e auau, e hookaluhi waiokila.

Ko-lo-a-ha, *s.* A species of potato with fine roots and watery inside.

Ko-lo-a-puu-puu, *s.* The name of a wind; he wa kipuupuu.

Ko-lo-he, *v.* To be mischievous; to act dishonestly; to render one's self obnoxious to the feelings of others.

2. To defile; to pollute.

3. *Hoo.* To trick; to defraud; to cheat.

Ko-lo-he, *s.* Mischief; evil; that which is bad in conduct.

2. Pollution; defilement.

Ko-lo-he, *adj.* Roguish; troublesome; mischievous; polluting; vile; moe *kolohe*, adultery; fornication.

Ko-lo-he, *adv.* Mischievously; badly; vilely.

Ko-lo-ki-o, *s.* Name of a person who catches by a long rod and bird-lime; *kolokio manu* o Kaile ka uka nahele o Laa.

Ko-lo-ko-li-o, *s.* A calling or catching of birds; a taking of birds mauka of Laa and Pakahi.

Ko-lo-ko, *prep.* Ko and *loko.* An oblique case of *loko.* That which belongs within; the inside or inner parts of a thing.

Ko-lo-ko-lo, *v.* See KOLO. To crawl towards one to give an account of himself.

2. To call chickens, turkeys, dogs, &c.

3. To be vexed, as a woman with her husband.

4. *Hoo.* To call to account; to examine, as an accused person.

5. To decide respecting an accused person; to judge.

6. In modern times, to reckon with one; to look over his account; to keep an account with one. 2 *Nal.* 12:16.

7. To make inquiry into a matter. *Eset.* 2:23. NOTE.—Since the promulgation of written laws and the establishment of courts of justice, *hookolokolo* is used in connection with legal investigations; to try, &c., as in a court of justice.

Ko-lo-ko-lo, *s.* The loud rumbling at the close of a peal of thunder.

2. *Hoo.* A trial; a legal investigation; a judgment; a legal decision.

Ko-lo-ko-lo, *adj.* Relating to a judgment, trial or decision.

Ko-lo-ko-lo-hai, *s.* A chief or a common person whose character is respected for probity and virtuous conduct; a term of respect; nona ka lala kau *kolokolohai.*

KO-LO-KO-LO-NA-HI, *s.* See NAHI. A light soft breeze; a very gentle wind.

KO-LO-LI-O, *s.* A very strong wind at sea, such as would swamp canoes.

2. A strong rushing of water, as of a powerful torrent.

3. A breeze on one side or between two other winds.

KO-LO-LI-O-I-KI, *s.* A gentle current; a light flow of water in a stream.

KO-LO-LU, *adj.* Deformed; irregular in structure, as a deformed child; the word applies to the body and mind.

KO-LO-NA, *s. Eng.* The name of a pause in reading; a colon; thus (:).

KO-LO-NA-HE, *s.* A gentle, pleasant breeze; he makani e aniani mai ana.

KO-LO-NA-HE, *adj.* Gentle; mild; peaceful; blowing softly; fanning, as a gentle breeze.

KO-LO-PU, *adj.* Full; well fed; well proportioned throughout; full fleshed.

KO-LO-PU-A, *adj.* Smooth, easy breathing; breathing without constraint; i ka nae *kolopua. Laieik.* 142.

KO-LO-PU-PU, *adj. Kolo,* to crawl, and *pupu,* roughly. Old; lean; withered, as a very aged person.

KO-LO-PU-PU, *s.* An aged infirm person; an advanced stage of old and infirm age. 2 *Oihl.* 36:17.

KO-LU, *s. Eng.* The Hawaiian orthography for glue; e like me he *kolu* la ka linalina, like *glue* is the adhesiveness.

KO-LU, *num. adj.* The simple form for the number three; with the article, ke *kolu,* the third. The common forms are *akolu* and *ekolu.*

KO-LU-A, *v. Ko* and *lua,* a pit. To bury, i. e., to bake; to cook. See KALUA. NOTE.— The Hawaiians made their ovens under ground.

2. To put into a pit; to hide.

KO-LU-A, *s.* The act of burying, i. e., of putting into an oven under ground. See KALUA.

KO-LU-I-LU-I, *v.* To strike upon the ear indistinctly, as a sound.

KO-LU-LU, *v.* To be or act as a guard or defense; to parry off; to defend from evil; e paku, e alai.

KO-LU-NA, *comp. prep.* The auiiki of *luna,* above. *Gram.* § 161. Of or belonging to that which is above. *Ezek.* 40:13.

KO-MA, *s. Eng.* A comma, the shortest pause in reading (,).

KO-MA-KO, *s.* The Hawaiian orthography for tomato, an edible fruit; the Hawaiians generally call the fruit of the tomato *ohia.*

KO-MA-LA, *adj.* Pleasant.

KO-MA-LI, *adj.* Bright, as moonlight.

KO-MA-LU-NA, *s. Koma* and *luna,* above. The sign called apostrophe, as ka'u, no'u, ke 'lii, &c., and signifies that a letter has been dropped.

KO-ME, *adj. Heb.,* rushes. The Egyptian papyrus; bulrushes. *Puk.* 2:3; *Isa.* 18:2. He waa *kome,* a bulrush canoe.

KO-ME, *v.* To push away; to make room for something; e hookaawale.

KO-ME-KO-ME, *v.* To hold back; to grudge in giving, as a wife when her husband is disposed to give, or as a husband when the wife is disposed to give.

KO-MI, *s.* See KAOMI and KOWI. To press together; to bear down; to press down into a small space.

2. To rub down smooth, as ruffled kapa; to rub or press, as a folded paper; i ka hau *komi* o ke kakahiaka.

KO-MI-KO-MI, *v.* To press; to urge on; to urge on one to labor.

2. To be little or to attend to trifles in dealing.

3. To be stingy; to be close; to urge for the last mite.

KO-MI-KO-MI, *adj.* Put away; secreted; stolen.

KO-MO, *v.* To enter; to go in, as into a house.

2. To put in, as the hand into a calabash in eating poi; to dip; to rinse, but not so strong as *holoi.*

3. To sink or to go under water, as a canoe.

4. To put on clothes. NOTE.—To put on clothes in Hawaiian idiom is to enter into them.

5. *Hoo.* To insert, as a ring on the finger, i. e., the finger enters the ring. *Kin.* 41:42.

6. To put on, as a hat or crown; that is, the head enters the hat.

7. To enter, as into another's country.

8. To cause to enter, as joy into one's heart.

9. To put on, as a dress, i. e., to go into it. *Oihk.* 8:7.

10. To fill full, as a canoe or ship; hence,

11. To sink, as a canoe or ship heavy loaded.

KO-MO, *s.* The name of anything that enters; a tenon. *Puk.* 26:17. The handle of a hoe, &c.

2. Anything that is entered; a finger-ring; a thimble, &c.

3. The filling up of any empty space; ka piha o ka mea hakahaka.

Ko-mo, *adj*. That which relates to putting in, filling or inserting.

Ko-mo-a, *s*. See KOOMOA. The tail feathers of a cock.

Ko-mo-ai-na, *v*. *Komo* and *aina*, land. To enter upon an inheritance; to take possession of a land.

Ko-mo-ha-le, *v*. *Komo* and *hale*, house. To dedicate a house (after which it was proper to use it); to enter a new house as a habitation.

Ko-mo-ha-na, *s*. *Komo* and *hana*, h inserted for *ana*. An entering in, as the sun in setting appeared to Hawaiians to enter into the sea; the sinking or going down of the sun.

2. The west, the place where the sun enters the sea. See KOMO, to sink.

Ko-mo-ha-na, *adj*. Western; pertaining to the west. *Puk*. 10:19.

Ko-mo-ko-mo, *v*. See KOMO. To insert on; to gird on; to try; to fit on, as a garment upon a person.

2. *Hoo*. To hold one spell bound; to bewitch; to possess, as an evil spirit.

Ko-mo-ko-mo, *s*. The act of fitting a garment to a person until it fits well.

2. A disease, epilepsy; a demoniacal possession perhaps.

3. The name of a play or game.

Ko-mo-li-ma, *s*. *Komo* and *lima*, the hand. A finger-ring; a thimble.

2. The hoop of a barrel; he mea e hoopuni ana mawaho o ka pahu.

3. A stocking; he kakini; a thing which the foot enters.

Ko-mo-lo-le, *v*. *Komo* and *lole*, cloth; clothes. To dress; to put on clothes.

2. To fit a dress to a person.

Ko-mo-lo-le, *s*. Apparel; a change of clothes or raiment.

Ko-mo-na, *s*. *Eng*. A common person in distinction from a lord; he poe i kohoia e na makaainana e komo ma ka ahaolelo alii.

Ko-mo-wa-le, *s*. *Komo* and *wale*, gratuitously. To enter and reside in a house unbidden.

2. To wander out of the way.

Ko-mo-wa-le, *s*. Epithet of a person going here and there where he pleases; a privileged character.

Ko-na, *s*. A name of the south-west wind; also, the south wind.

2. Pleasant or good weather; also, the name of the rain accompanying a south wind; he ua *kona*, he ua nui loa ia. See names of various species of *konas* below, as konahea, konalani, &c.

3. Name of a division of an island belonging to several islands, as Hawaii, Oahu, Kauai and Molokai, mostly on the west or south-west sides of the islands.

Ko-na, *adj. pron*. The *auiiki* or an oblique case of ia, the third person singular of the pronouns. His; hers; its, &c. *Gram*. § 139 and 150.

Ko-na, *v*. To be strong; to be rigid; to be obdurate; to be unyielding.

2. To pass or rush through, as the air from the lungs; he ea e *kona* ana a e puka mai iwaho.

Ko-na, *adj*. Strong; fierce; angry; blustering, from the fact that Kona winds are so.

Ko-na, *v*. To despise; to dislike; to disregard; to contemn.

Ko-na-hau, *v*. To abate heat; to cool, as the atmosphere; as a hot room.

Ko-na-hau, *v*. To be fat, as an animal; to be greasy; to be sick of grease or fatness.

2. To bend forward in walking, as a tall man. See KANAHUA.

Ko-na-he-a, *s*. A species of the rains called kona; a cold rain.

Ko-na-hi-li-mai-a, *s*. Name of a species of rain on the mountains.

Ko-na-hu-a, *s*. The inside fat of animals. *Anat*. 53. The fat of hogs, &c; a kidney. *Puk*. 29:13.

Ko-na-hu-a, *adj*. Fat; fleshy, as an animal; as a man. *Lunk*. 3:17.

Ko-na-ko-na, *v*. To be rough; to be uneven; to be dark colored.

2. To be undesired; not to like.

3. To despise; to be displeased with; to treat with contempt.

Ko-na-ko-na, *s*. Dislike; disregard.

Ko-na-ko-na, *adj*. Undesirable; contemptible.

2. Strong; not easily tired or exhausted.

Ko-na-ko-ne-a, *v*. To be restored to health after sickness; to receive strength after weakness.

Ko-na-ku, *s*. A class of the kona rains; a heavy rain. See KONA, rain.

Ko-na-la-ni, *s*. A species of the rains called kona; a fine rain.

Ko-na-le, *adj*. Bright; clear; unobscured; white.

2. Quiet; still, like moonshine in a calm still night. *Mel. Sol.* 6:10. Aiai e like me ka mahina i ka po malie loa; he mahina konane—*konale.*

KO-NA-LE-LE-WA, *s.* Name of a species of fish.

KO-NA-MO-E, *s.* A class of the kona rains; a cold rain.

KO-NA-NE, *s.* Name of a game like checkers; a species of punipeke; he mea hana lealea e like me ka punipeke; the stones are placed in squares black and white, then one removes one and the other jumps, as in checkers; ua lilo oe ia'u i ke *konaneia,* you are mine by the game *konane. Laieik.* 59.

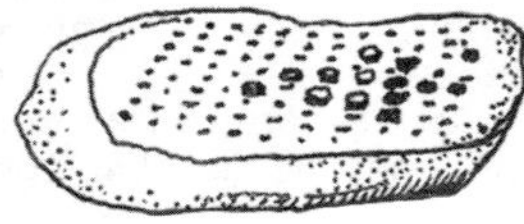

konane

KO-NA-NE, *adj.* See KONALE above. Na po mahina *konane,* bright moonlight nights. *Laieik.* 181.

KO-NE, *s.* Eng. A cony; a species of hare. *Kanl.* 14:7.

KO-NE-KO-NE-A, *v.* To be shaved smooth, as the head; to be made bald or smooth, as the forehead.

2. To be hard and dry.

3. To be strong, as a person without disease.

4. To be restored from sickness; to be recovered from disease. See KONAKONEA.

KO-NE-KO-NE-A, *adj.* Restored; recovered again from sickness.

2. Shaven, as the head; made bald.

KO-NE-NE, *v.* To move or jump, as one moves his iliili, or jumps in the play konane; to take up quickly.

2. To be very dry.

KO-NE-NE-LE, } *v.* To be quick; to go
KO-NE-NE-NE, } quickly; to hasten.

2. Applied sometimes to one who has been sick and is recovering; to be strong; to be well, &c.

3. To be hard and stiff, as a garment (kapa) wet and dried again. See KONEKONEA.

KO-NE-RI-SA, *s.* Name of a foreign bird.

KO-NI, *v.* To try; to taste; to make proof of by tasting.

2. To try, as one's constancy or affection.

3. To throb, as the pulse; to be in pain of body or mind; to be jealous; to suffer from apprehension or fear.

4. *Hoo.* To try the quality of a thing by experiment; *hookoni* hele aku la lakou i kahi e ono ai ka wai, they went along *tasting* till they found sweet water.

KO-NI, *s.* The beating or throbbing of the pulse or heart. See API.

2. The thumping, as on a melon to try its ripeness.

3. A trial of strength or ability; make-make na kamalii i ka hele no ke koni o ka wawae.

KO-NI, *adj.* Beating; throbbing; painful.

KO-NI-A, *adj.* Disobedient.

KO-NI-KO-NI, *v.* To throb fast or frequently, as the pulse.

2. To nibble, as a fish at a hook.

3. To snatch away a little at a time.

KO-NI-KO-NI, *adj.* Ardent; active; busy; feeling deeply; he aloha huihui *konikoni* ana iloko o'u.

KO-NI-NI, *v.* See KONI. To revive after fainting.

2. To be convalescent.

3. To grow up, as a plant; to spring up, as a shoot.

KO-NI-NI, *adj.* Convalescent; getting well from sickness.

KO-NI-NI-U, *s.* See NIU and NINIU. Dizziness; vertigo. See PONINIU.

KO-NO, *v.* To lead one along to any place. *Nah.* 22:41.

2. To take along, as a servant. *Kin.* 22:3.

3. To invite, as a guest; to take in company. *2 Sam.* 13:23.

4. To imitate; to go along slowly, as foot travelers; e *kono* mau ana i ka lae kahakai. *Laieik.* 157.

5. To take, as one's wife in company. 1 *Kor.* 9:5.

6. *Hoo.* To hasten; to hurry; to send away.

7. To set on, as dogs; to set one against another. See KONOKONO.

KO-NO-HI-KI, *s.* The head man of an ahupuaa.

2. A person who has charge of a land with others under him; o ka mea ai aina, he *konohiki* ia.

KO-NO-KO-NA, *v.* To despise; to be displeased with. See KONAKONA.

KO-NO-KO-NO, *v.* See KONO. To urge on; to excite, &c.

2. *Hoo.* To set on each other, as dogs.

3. To make one angry with another by persuasion; to stir up discord. *Sol.* 6:14.

4. To excite to commotion; to stir up popular feeling; *hookonokono* mai ia (o

Satana) i keia mau mea ia kakou e hana, Satan stirs us up that we should do these things.

5. To persuade to go, as on business; *hookonokono* aku o Liliha ia Kalama; o kii a hoi mai, Liliha persuaded Kalama (saying) go for him and return.

KO-NU, *s.* The center; the central point; the middle, especially with *waena*. See WAENAKONU. NOTE.—*Konu* is used to render *waena* more emphatic and definite, as the *middle point*; the *very center* of a place or thing.

KO-NU-I, ⎤ *v.* To strike upon, as the
KO-MU-I, ⎦ rays of the sun; to be very hot. See NOU.

KO-NU-WAE-NA, *adv.* See KONU above. In the midst.

KO-PA, *s.* A shrub, the fruit of which is made into beads.

KO-PA, *s. Eng.* The Hawaiian pronunciation for soap; kula *kopa* lole, the fuller's field. *Isa.* 7:3. See also SOPA.

KO-PA-LA-NI.

KO-PE, *v.* To shovel, as dirt; to paw; to scratch.

2. To defend off; to parry, as a blow; to turn aside from.

KO-PE, *s.* A shovel; a spade; a scoop for lading flour; any instrument of the kind. *Nah.* 4:14.

KO-PE-A-HI, *s. Kope* and *ahi*, fire. A fire shovel. 2 *Nal.* 25:14.

KO-PE-KO-PE, *adj.* Morose; silent; taciturn; ill-natured.

KO-PE-LA, *s.* Name of a shrub or tree.

KO-PE-LE-HU, *s. Kope* and *lehu*, ashes. A fire shovel. See KOPEAHI above.

KO-PE-NA, *s.* He moonihoawa.

KO-PE-RA, *s. Heb.* Camphire. *Mel. Sol.* 1:14.

KO-PI, ⎤ *v.* To salt, as fish or meat; to
KO-PII, ⎦ sprinkle on salt; to preserve in salt.

KO-PI-KO, *s.* A kind of grass.

2. The name of a shrub. See OPIKO.

KO-PI-KO, *s.* The name of a tree, the timber used for kuas in making kapa; it is also used for fuel.

KO-PI-LI, *s.* A gift presented to a child at its birth.

2. The name of a small white kapa put on the idols. See OLOA.

3. A species of wauki.

4. The wauki bark pounded thin; ikoiko ia a lahilahi.

KO-PI-LI-NUI, *s.* The name of a day when the altars and sacrifices were dressed out with white kapa; ua kapaia ua la la he la *kopilinui* no ke kopili ana o ka lananuumamao.

KO-PI-NA, *s. Eng.* perhaps. A coping on the top of a building. 1 *Nal.* 7:9.

KO-PI-PI, *v.* See KOPI. To sprinkle, as water or salt. *Heb.* 9:19. Also, to sprinkle, as a perfume. *Sol.* 7:17. See PIPI.

KO-PO-LE, *s.* A method of cooking fish by wrapping them in leaves and roasting them.

KO-PU-KE-A.

KO-WA, *v.* To separate; to divide between two things.

KO-WA, *s.* See KOA and WA, a space. A vacant space between two things, as

1. The spaces between the fingers or toes.

2. A strip or space of water between two lands; hence, the channel of a harbor.

3. A strait or sound.

KO-WAA, *s.* A rope or string for drawing or dragging a canoe or other things; he ili hau, he mea *kowaa* ia; he akua kowaa o Kanepuaa, a furrow-making god was Kanepuaa. See KANEPUAA.

KO-WAA, *v.* To drag; to draw; to move a thing by drawing.

KO-WAU, *s.* The testicles. See HUA.

KO-WA-HA, *s.* A species of wauki. See KOPILI. Eia kona laau, o ka popolo ame ke *kowaha*.

KO-WA-KO-WAU. See KOKOOU.

KO-WA-LI, *v.* To swing to and fro, as a rope for children to jump over.

KO-WA-LI, *s.* A kind of play for children; swinging a rope. There were two kinds of *kowali*.

2. Name of a certain stick or buoy on which to float a fish-hook.

3. The name of a running vine; a convolvulus; also written *koali*.

KO-WA-LI-PE-HU, *s.* A species of convolvulus with a white flower.

KO-WE-LO, *v. Ko* and *welo*, to float in the wind. To drag or trail behind, as the trail of a garment.

2. To stream or float in the wind, as colors or an ensign. See koelo.

KO-WI, *v.* To press; to squeeze together. *Kin.* 40:11.

2. To wring out, as water. *Hal.* 73:10. See KAWI and UI.

KO-RA, *s. Heb.* A cor, a dry measure. 2 *Oihl.* 2:10.

KO-RA-KA, *s. Gr.* A raven. *Kin.* 8:7. An unclean bird. *Oihk.* 11:15.

Ko-re-ba-na, *s.* *Gr.* Corban; a gift; consecrated property. *Mar.* 7:11.

Ko-re-ne-ta, *s.* *Eng.* A cornet, a musical instrument. 1 *Oihl.* 15:28.

Ko-re-ni-sa, *s.* Name of a bird in *Kanl.* 14:13; the glede; a kite.

Ko-ri-a-na, *s.* *Eng.* Coriander; the seed of the coriander. *Puk.* 16:31.

Ko-ri-ne-ta, *s.* See Koreneta above.

Ko-ro-na, *s.* *Eng.* A crown; the official head dress of a king or queen. *Ezek.* 21:26. Syn. with leialii.

Ku, *v.* Note.—This word has two distinct meanings and yet they run into each other; as, first, *ku* to rise up; second, *ku* to stand.

1. To arise; to rise up, as from a sitting posture. *Ioan.* 11:29. To stand erect.

2. To rise, as war. 1 *Oihl.* 20:4. To rise up to do a thing or for a specified purpose. *Ioan.* 1:2.

3. To stand against; to resist; to act contrary to.

4. *Hoo.* To excite; to stir up, as an insurrection.

5. To raise up, as an eminent person. *Kanl.* 18:15, 18.

6. To raise up; to propagate. *Kanl.* 25:7.

Ku, *v.* To stand, i. e., to stop still; to let down, as an anchor (generally written *kuu*); *ku* iho la makou ia nei, we anchored (stood, stopped) at this place; to stand against or opposite to.

2. To hit; to strike against; to pierce, as a spear; a *ku* oia i ka poe panapua.

3. To hit, as the foot in walking; to stumble. *Rom.* 9:32.

4. To stand, as a ship, i. e., to come to anchor.

5. *Hoo.* To cause to stand, i. e., to hold up; to stretch out, as the hand. 1 *Nal.* 8:22.

6. To be placed or set in a state or condition. *Iob.* 20:4.

7. To fit; to be like; to resemble; to agree with; ua *ku* ke keiki i ka makua, the child *resembles* the parent; aole e *ku* i ke kanawai, it is not according to law.

8. To fit, as a garment. The following are miscellaneous uses:

9. With *pono*, to be opposite to; holo mai la lakou a *ku* pono i Honaunau, they sailed till *opposite* to Honaunau.

10. *Ku* e, to resist; to oppose.

11. Ka *hooku* ole i ka hala, not condemned.

12. *Ku* i ka wa, to stand in a space (between two parties); hence, to be free; to be uncommitted. 1 *Kor.* 9:1.

13. *Ku* o ka hao, to be fitted of iron, i. e., to be bound with iron. *Mat.* 8:28.

14. To be suitable; to be proper; to be fit. *Luk.* 3:8.

15. To extend; to reach from one place to another; ua ku ko'u pilau mai Hawaii a Kauai, my evil influence (ill savor) *has reached* from Hawaii to Kauai.

16. To come to one, as a report or information; *ku* mai ia Poliahu ka ike no Aiwohikupua mau hana.

Ku, *s.* A portion of land which does not pass with all the land from one to another, but is fixed; lilo ka aina i *ku*. Lit. The land has become *fixed*.

2. The name of a month.

Ku, *adj.* Right; fit; proper; put in order; berena *ku* lalani, the *show* bread. *Puk.* 35:13.

Ku-a, *v.* To strike in a horizontal direction; hence,

1. To cut or hew down, as a tree with an axe; alaila *kua* laau ala o Kalanimoku, then Kalanimoku *cut down* sandal-wood.

2. To hew, as wood or stones. *Kanl.* 7:5. To cut out, as stone from a quarry; ke *kua* pohaku oe; to cut, as coral; hele aku la makou e *kua* puna.

3. To overthrow; to destroy (cut down), as an idol. *Oihk.* 26:30.

4. To throw or cast away; to put away; e kipaku.

Ku-a, *s.* The back of a person or animal in distinction from the face. *Puk.* 33:23. He kahi mahope o ke poo o ke kanaka, a o ka holoholona.

2. The top of a ridge or high land.

3. The hewed stick, block or wood on which kapa is beaten.

4. The anvil of a blacksmith, from its similarity to the kapa block (a modern application.) *Isa.* 41:7.

5. The name of one of the six houses of an ancient Hawaiian residence; he hale *kua*, oia kekahi. See Hale.

6. The name of a species of fish.

7. The front side of a place; ma ke alo o keia aina, he *kua* o ka moku ia. *D. Malo* 3:23.

Ku-a-ai-na, *s.* *Kua* and *aina*, land. The back country; up the mountain where there are no chiefs; the country in distinction from a village or city. *Mar.* 6:56.

2. The inhabitants or people of the back country; o ka poe i noho ma ke kua o ka mokupuni, ua kapaia he *kuaaina*, he inoa hooino nae ia.

3. Ignorant, uninstructed people; the ignoble; the back-woods people. 1 *Kor.* 1:28. The inhabitants of a back country. *Oih.* 4:13. Ka poe makaainana, na wahi kokoke ole mai i kahi alii.

KU-A-AI-NA, *adj.* Of or pertaining to the upland country; rude; away from refined society.

KU-A-AU, *s. Kua*, back, and *au*, current; surf. A bare reef; ke kohola; a dry place within the sea; he wahi maloo; a very shallow place in the sea; papau o ke kai.

KU-A-A-HA, *s.* Name of a place where the gods were worshiped; he wahi e hoomana ai i ke akua.

2. Name of a cup used in worshiping the gods, i. e., the poe aumakua; he ipu aumakua, he ipu i hana ia i ka aaha a paa.

KU-A-A-NA, *s.* Epithet of a relationship signifying the older of two children of the same sex; as, *kai-kuaana*, the older of two brothers or of two sisters, each to each; ka hoahanau mua ma ka hanau ana.

KU-AI, *v.* To rub one thing against another; to grind by rubbing one surface against another; to rub or stir round, as flour in sifting it.

2. To barter one thing for another. NOTE. This was the ancient idea of selling and buying, as Hawaiians formerly had no common circulating medium.

3. To traffic or exchange one commodity for another; after coin began to circulate, *kuai* lilo mai signified to buy, and *kuai* lilo aku, to sell. *Puk.* 21:16. At present, the phrase is contracted into kuai mai, to buy, and *kuai* aku, to sell; ina i make kahi kanaka, a *kuai* ia oia i ke akua kii.

KU-AI, *adj.* Of or belonging to trade; he hale *kuai*, a house for sale, or a house where sales are made, i. e., a store; waiwai *kuai*, goods or property for sale.

KU-AI-A-KO, *s.* The place where the akos are bound on to the canoe, both before and behind; mai *kuaiako* mua, a *kuaiako* hope o ka waa. *Laieik.* 17.

KAU-AI-O-LE, } *s.* The upper ridge pole
KU-AI-I-O-LE, } of a house; ka laau maluna iho o kauhuhu ma kaupaku.

KU-A-I-O, *s.* The side or border of a kalo patch; the border of a cultivated plot; the separating line between two fields. See KUAAUNA.

KU-AI-HOO-O-LA, *v. Kuai*, to buy, and *hooola*, to save alive. See OLA. To redeem; to save from death. *Hoik.* 14:3, 4.

KU-AI-HU, *adv.* Over and over.

KU-A-I-LO, *v.* To declare or explain some enigma or mysterious expression; e hai mai i ka nane nalowale loa, loaa ole i ka imiia.

KU-A-I-NO, *v.* To turn back to an evil course after having forsaken it.

KU-AO, *adj.* Cloud-standing; a cloud standing in an upright position.

KU-AU, *s.* The stick or mallet with which the kapa is beaten out.

2. The handle of an oo; *kuau* oo; the handle of a hoe. See KANO.

3. The handle of a knife, file, auger, &c.

KU-A-U-A, *s.* Contraction for *ka ua ua*, frequent rains. The season of rains; ame ka hekili iloko o ke *kuaua. Laieik.* 181.

2. A fertilizing rain; *kuaua* mua, the former rain; *kuaua* hope, the latter rain. *Hos.* 6:3.

KU-A-U-A-HO-PE, *s.* The latter rain. See KUAUA above.

KU-A-U-A-MU-A, *s.* The first or former rain. See KUAUA above.

KU-AU-HA, *v.* To council; to advise.

KU-AU-HAU, *v. Ku* and *auhau*, to tax. To be recorded in genealogy, in history or tradition; o na kupuna mua o ko Hawaii nei i *kuauhauia*, the first ancestors of Hawaii which are *noted in genealogy*. LIT. Genealogized. Also *Heb.* 7:6.

2. To have the knowledge of genealogies; to know the path of the descent of chiefs; e ike i ke kuamoo kupuna alii mai kahiko mai.

KU-AU-HAU, *s.* A genealogy; a pedigree. 1 *Tim.* 1:4. Mai manao kakou he pololei loa keia *kuauhau*, let us not think that this *genealogy* is strictly correct. *Neh.* 7:5.

2. A person skilled in genealogy or tradition; a historian. *Kin.* 5:1. He mea ike-ike kuamoo alii.

KU-AU-HAU, *adj.* Relating to what is registered or retained as historical; palapala *kuauhau*, a genealogical register.

2. Honorable; distinguished.

KU-A-U-LA, *s.* Red thick kapa; red bark.

KU-AU-KA-HI, *s. Kuau* and *kahi*, one. The principal or single rain during the summer months; ka ua hookahi o ka makalii.

KU-A-U-KA, *s. Kua*, a god, and *uka*, inland. The name of the gods of the mountains in opposition to *kuakai*, gods on the sea shore.

KU-A-U-NA, *s.* The bank of a stream; the side or border of a kalo patch. See KUAIO. Ke hele nei makou ma na *kuauna* poho, we are traveling at present on the borders of kalo patches liable to sink in.

KU-AU-PAA, s. Name of a bundle of pololu carried by the chief on going into battle.

KU-A-HA-U-A, v. To call out all the people, as a chief; to call together on business; to assemble all the people.

KU-A-HA-U-A, adj. Proclaiming; calling together, as the people of a chief; mamuli o ka olelo *kuahaua*, according to proclamation. *Laieik.* 162.

KU-A-HA-NA, s. The name of a god who killed men.

KU-A-HE-A, s. A region on the side of a mountain below the kuamauna and where small trees grow.

KU-A-HI-LO, v. See HILOHILO. To ramble in telling a story; to make a long story.

KU-A-HI-LO-HI-LO, v. To talk without coming to the point.

KU-A-HI-NE, s. A sister of a brother; e kuu lani, eia ko *kuahine*, o Kahalaomapuana, ka mea au e aloha nui nei. *Laieik.* 176.

KU-A-HI-WI, s. *Kua*, back, and *hiwi*, summit. The top or summit of a mountain. *Nah.* 3:1. Hence,

2. A mountain of the highest class.

3. Mountains or a mountainous country.

4. A single mountain. 2 *Oihl.* 2:2.

KU-A-HA, s. An altar for sacrifice. *Kin.* 8:20. *Kuaha* okoa, a whole altar. 1 *Nal.* 6:22. He wahi e hoomoa ai na mohai.

KU-A-HU-A, v. *Kua*, back, and *ahua*, a raised place. To bend upward, as the back; to rise above water, as a whale's back.

KU-A-HU-I, s. Sticks tied temporarily on to the frame of a house while building; he aho mawaho o ka hale i ka manawa e kauhilo ai.

KU-A-HU-LU, s. Name of a vegetable eaten in time of famine.

KU-A-KA-HI, s. The third generation of a series, that is, the third from the parent. *Puk.* 20:5. Thus, first, the parent, makua; second, the child, keiki; third, the grandchild, kuakahi; moopuna *kuakahi*, a grandchild; he keiki na kana keiki aku.

KU-A-KA-HI, adj. Name of a place indefinitely known, or rather not known, but considered to be far off; oi noho kou uhane ma puu *Kuakahi*.

KU-A-KA-HI-KI, s. *Kua*, back and *kahiki*, a foreign country. Something afar off in another land, or done long ago so as to be forgotten; i *kuakahiki* ka pule; kahi nalowale loihi loa paha.

KU-A-KA-LA, s. See LU. A medicine mixed up with some liquid and taken as a purgative; the name of the plant is *naule*.

KU-A-KA-LI-KE-A, s. *Kua*, back, and *kalikea*, border; fringe. White on the back, border or edge.

KU-A-KE-A, v. To be white as chalk; as salt on or about salt ponds; ua hele a *kuakea* i ka paakai.

KU-A-KE-A-HU, s. An unseen imaginary place at a great distance off.

2. The poe kuaaina that live far off from the metropolis; a hala loa kou uhane ma *kuakeahu*.

KU-A-KE-AO, s. See the foregoing.

KU-A-KI, v. To feel sad at the loss of a bet in gambling; *kuaki* paha, pili oia i kona waiwai a pau loa, a ilihune, a pupule maoli kahi poe i ka minamina nui.

KU-A-KO-KO, s. Pain; distress, as of a woman in child-birth. FIG. *Isa.* 13:8. He *kuakoko* nei ka wahine, o ka mea ikaika loa no ia, a hiki mai ke *kuakoko* hanau.

KU-A-KO-KO, v. To travail; the have the pains of child-birth. *Isa.* 23:4.

KU-A-KO-KO, adj. Of or belonging to child-birth. *Isa.* 21:3.

KU-A-KO-LO.

KU-A-KO-LU, s. The fifth in a series of generations; a great grandchild; he kupuna *kaukolu*. See KUAKAHI.

KU-A-KU, adj. Ironically spoken.

KU-A-KU-A, v. See KUA, to cut down, as a tree; to cut; to hew out, as a canoe; o ke koi keia e *kuakua* ana i ka waa.

KU-A-KU-A, s. A section or piece of a fish net; *kuakua* upena.

2. A small section of land like a koele or hakuone.

KU-A-KU-A-KU, s. A kalo patch.

KU-A-KU-AI, v. See KUAI, to rub. To rub with pressure; to polish; to grind.

KU-A-KU-PI, s. A sore on the back.

KU-A-LA, s. The fore fin on the back of a fish.

2. A sharp and cutting bone on the side of a certain fish near the tail.

3. Hard kalo; heavy food.

4. Increase; interest; usury. *Ezek.* 18:8. Interest on money; a word derived from *kuwala*, a somerset; turning over and over. See KUWALA.

KU-A-LA, v. To set a cask on its head.

2. To take or exact usury; to pay over and above.

KU-A-LA, adj. Pertaining to usury. *Oihk.* 25:36. Uku *kuala*, usury. *Neh.* 5:7.

KU-A-LA, adv. Usuriously; giving upon usury. *Ezek.* 18:8.

KU-A-LAU, s. A strong wind; a gale of

wind; wind and rain upon the ocean; he ua me ka makani ma ka moana.

Ku-a-la-au, *s.* *Kua,* to hew, and *laau,* wood. A hewer of wood. *Kanl.* 29:10.

Ku-a-lau-wi-li, *v.* See LAUWILI. To be circuitous in conversation; to wander here and there in one's talk.

Ku-a-la-kai, *s.* The name of a species of fish.

Ku-a-la-kai, *s.* The eating of fresh fish pounded up finely and mixed with other things. NOTE.—The malolo was the fish frequently served up in this way.

Ku-a-la-kai, *s.* A swelling up of the cheeks, perhaps the abdomen, from rich eating, perhaps from disease.

Ku-a-la-na, *v.* To be idle; to be indifferent to all business; to wander about without object; to sit uninterested with nothing to engage attention, as one who does not understand the conversation; lilo oukou i ka olelo haole a *kualana* makou; to sit idle, as one lazy (malowa) on a canoe instead of paddling.

Ku-a-la-na, *s.* Indolence; laziness; fatigue; nui ka poe *kualana* e noho aina ole ana; o ke kanaka hoopili wale he *kualana* ia, he who joins himself to another without work is a lazy fellow.

2. A man who roves about without a chief or haku or any support or any one to depend on.

Ku-a-la-na, *adj.* Lazy; not disposed to work; o ka noho a ka ohua *kualana.*

2. Fatigued, as a man by paddling a canoe and lays down his paddle.

3. Not sinking; floating; komo ole, lana.

Ku-a-la-na-pu-hi, *s.* The office of the person who kept the flies off from the king when he slept; o ka mea kahili i ko ke alii wahi e moe ai, he *kualanapuhi* ka inoa.

Ku-a-la-pa, *v.* To stretch out, as a head-land; to project, as a cape. See LAPA.

Ku-a-la-pa, *s.* A ridge of land between two ravines. See LAPA, *s.*

Ku-a-la-pe-hu, *s.* Name of an office among the king's train.

Ku-a-le-he-le-he, *v.* To converse with many words; to talk fluently; aka, o keia pae aina i *kualehelehe* a Binamu.

Ku-a-le-na, *v.* See LENA. To stretch or spread out in order to free from wrinkles.

Ku-a-li-a-li, *adj.* White, as lime; as white paper and other things.

Ku-a-li, *v.* To whiten; to make white.

Ku-a-lii-lii, *v.* *Kua* and *liilii,* small; little. To abate; to slacken; to decrease

in heat.

Ku-a-lo-no, *s.* *Kua* and *lono,* to hear. The space on the top of a mountain; a place of silence, i. e., of hearing.

2. A knoll, small hill or protuberance on the top of a mountain.

Ku-a-lu-a, *s.* The fourth in descent; a great grandchild; he moopuna, he keiki na kana keiki; the fourth generation. *Puk.* 34:7.

Ku-a-lu-a, *adj.* Repeating; doing a thing twice. *Mar.* 14:30, 72.

Ku-a-lu-a, *adv.* Twice; the second time.

Ku-a-mau-na, *s.* *Kua,* back, and *mauna,* a mountain. A protuberance or hillock on the side of a mountain.

Ku-a-ma-ha, *s.* The side of the head; the bones back of the ear.

Ku-a-ma-ka, *s.* To cut down, as a tree with the edge of an axe.

Ku-a-ma-ka-ni, *adj.* Not sinking; floating; without constraint; free, as the wind; inconstant; komo ole, lana, *kuamakani.* See KUALANA.

Ku-a-mi-a-mi, *v.* See AMI, a hinge. To make a motion like the working of hinges.

2. To express the intercourse of the sexes.

3. To laugh at; to mock; to express contempt.

Ku-a-mi-a-mi, *s.* The motion of a turning hinge.

2. Any motion imitating that of a hinge.

3. The motion of sexual intercourse.

4. A term of reproach. See AMIAMI.

Ku-a-moo, *s.* *Kua,* back, and *moo,* a lizard. The backbone of a man or animal.

2. A road of frequented path. NOTE.— This was the word used formerly on the Island of Hawaii for path or road; the word *alanui* is now general; a road or highway. *Lunk.* 21:19.

3. FIG. A way; custom. SYN. with aoao. *Mat.* 10:15. Obedience to law. *Mar.* 1:3.

Ku-a-moo, *s.* The name of some place on the bottom of a canoe; alaila kalai ia na aoao ame ke *kuamoo* malalo.

Ku-a-moo, *adj.* Of or pertaining to the backbone; iwi *kuamoo. Oihk.* 3:9.

Ku-a-mo-a-mo, *v.* To curse the gods; to curse generally. *Oihk.* 19:14.

2. To blaspheme; to reproach; to swear; to quarrel. *Oihk.* 20:9.

Ku-a-moo-o-le-lo, *s.* See KUAMOO 3 and OLELO, speech. A style of speaking; a dialect.

Ku-a-mu-a-mu, *v.* See AMU and AMU-AMU. To blaspheme, curse, &c. SYN. with kuamoamo above.

Ku-a-mu-a-mu, *s.* Blasphemy; a reviling of sacred things by word; reproachful language. *Kanl.* 28:37.

2. The name of a play or dance.

KU-A-NA, *s.* A shower.

2. *Ku* and *ana.* A standing; being in an erect posture; ma ke *kuana* a ke kanaka.

KU-A-NA-KA, *s.* *Kua* and *naka,* not solid. An extensive disease up and down the back resembling *kuapuhi,* but longer.

2. Name of a kind of coral formation; the coral used in polishing.

3. Name of a species of fish.

KU-A-NA-LU, *s.* The outside of the surf towards the sea just before it breaks; ike-ia'ku ekolu oukou e ku mai ana ma *kuanalu. Laieik.* 130.

KU-A-NE-A, *s.* See KANEA, laziness, &c. Dry barren land; unprofitable land.

2. An awkward ignorant person.

3. A reproach; a laughing stock.

4. Loss of appetite; loss of strength.

KU-A-NOO, *v.* *Kua* and *noo,* to think. A place on the top of a mountain; a place for thinking or meditation.

KU-A-NU-I, *adj.* *Kua,* back, and *nui,* great. Big-backed, i. e., awkward, in doing something more or besides what was required, and thus spoiling what he tried to do; or doing a thing in his own way in opposition to the will of him for whom he works.

2. Obstinate; self-willed; he alii *kuanui,* a chief that will have his own way; aole *kuanui* o Parao, he hewa maoli no.

KU-A-PA, *s.* A crab of the species *paiea,* but with a hard shell.

KU-A-PAA, *v.* *Kua,* back, and *paa,* hard. To harden the back, i. e., to be hard upon one; to oppress.

2. To press or urge one to evil; e ala, e hele mai i kahi e *kuapaa* ole ai na uhane i ka hewa.

3. *Hoo.* To make one's back tough or callous with hard labor, as by carrying burdens and other hard work.

4. To have or exercise great patience under hard labor or cruel treatment.

KU-A-PAA, *s.* A name given to breadfruit which remains on the trees long after the season is over and is parched on the side next the sun.

2. The name of a worm that eats vegetables.

3. Name of a species of fish.

4. A coral reef or rock showing itself above water, though sometimes water may be over it.

KU-A-PAA, *adj.* Hard; severe; slavish.

2. Laborious; hurried with work; kauwa *kuapaa,* a slave.

3. Parched on one side; he ulu *kuapaa.*

KU-A-PA-PA, *v.* *Kua,* to cut down, and *papa,* a board. To hew out boards or plank. NOTE.—This was the former way of making boards, one log made but one board.

KU-A-PA-PA, *v.* To unite or be united, as people under one chief.

2. To be at peace; to live quietly; hele mai ia nei, *kuapapa* o ko kakou noho pu ana, we came here (Lahainaluna), *peaceful* has been our living together.

KU-A-PA-PA, *s.* Peace; quietness; rest from turbulance or anarchy.

KU-A-PA-PA, *adj.* Peaceful; quiet; resting in confidence.

KU-A-PA-PA-NU-I, *v.* See KUAPAPA and NUI, great. To enjoy quietness and satisfaction under the same ruler; to be free from the turmoils of war. *Lunk.* 3:11, 30.

2. To be at ease; to live quietly, as without much care, and out of the bustle of business.

3. To be quiet, as the effect of a virtuous life. *Isa.* 32:17.

KU-A-PA-PA-NU-I, *s.* Real substantial peace and quiet in a government.

2. Peace following a treaty of mutual benefits.

KU-A-PO-I, *s.* The name of the board on the front part of a canoe.

2. The knee pan; moe pono ka iwi ihu maluna o ka ihu e like me ke *kuapoi* maluna o ka waa.

3. Name of a bone in the arm or hand. *Anat.* 21.

KU-A-PO-I, *v.* *Kua,* back, and *poi,* to cover. To be full fledged, as birds or any kind of fowls; applied to young birds when almost fully grown; *kuapoi* na manu, the birds are fully fledged.

KU-A-PO-LA-O, *s.* Name of a small pile of waiwai collected for the king.

KU-A-PU-I-WI, *adj.* Long residence in a place. See KULAIWI.

KU-A-PUU, *s.* *Kua,* back, and *puu,* a protuberance. A hump or crooked-backed person. *Oihk.* 21:20.

KU-A-PU-HI, *s.* *Kua,* back, and *puhi,* to burst. A sore back; a boil on the back.

KU-A-WE-HI, *s.* A kind of disease in the back, or a sign of disease on the back.

2. A worm that has a black back.

KU-A-WI-LI, *v.* *Kua* and *wili,* to twist. To repeat over and over again without meaning; to wander from the point in speaking; to use foolish repetitions in speaking. *Mat.* 6:7.

KU-A-WI-LI, *s.* The name of a prayer used at the dedication of the highest order of heiaus and continued all day.

2. Indirectness, repetitions and irregular in work.

KU-E, *v.* *Ku*, to stand, and *e*, opposite. To be opposed; to be contrary; to be strange.

2. To act contrary to authority; to oppose the civil government.

3. *Hoo.* To set against; to oppose. *Ier.* 21:10. To cause to oppose. *Kanl.* 2:30.

4. To oppose, as the bow of a canoe to the wind. NOTE.—*Kue* has been written as one word and as two, in which case the *e* is an adverb;. Thus, *ku e*, to stand against, i. e., be opposite to.

KU-E, *s.* Opposition; strife; commotion.

2. The crooked side timbers in a ship; he laau wae kekee.

3. Any object with an angle.

4. Name of a species of fish-hook.

KU-E-A, *v.* A contraction of *kuewa*. To wander about; to have no home. See KUEWA.

KU-E-A, *s.* A wanderer; a friendless man.

KU-E-E, *v.* *Ku*, to stand, and *ee*, with a meaning stronger than *e*. See KUE above. To disagree; to contend in words.

2. To do contrary to; to oppose.

3. To rise up against; to attack.

4. To bicker; to quarrel, as a man and his wife. See KUKUE.

KU-E-E, *s.* Disagreement; dissension; opposition of sentiment.

KU-EE-O-HU-A, *s.* A species of fish net.

KU-E-O, *adj.* Unsteady; going here and there; a vagabond. See KUEWA.

KU-E-HU, *v.* *Ku* and *ehu*, to drive away. To stir up; to make turbid, as water; to shut off, as water running over land.

2. To shake the dust from a mat.

3. To let go; to cast away, as a thing not desired.

4. To hold up; to present, as a signal for something; a *kuehu* ae la oia i ka lepa o kona aahu. *Laieik.* 22.

KU-E-HU-E-HU, *v.* Freq. of *kuehu*. To cast or throw dust or dirt.

2. To toss up and down.

KU-E-KAA, *v.* See PANOANOA. To return, as the current or tide and sweep everything away; to cast or turn one out of house and home and all he has.

KU-E-KU-E, *s.* See KUE, *s.*, 3. A joint; a protuberance; the knuckles; the wrist

bones; ka puupuu o ka hailima; the elbow, &c.; qualified by some other word.

KU-E-KU-E-HU, *v.* To rub hard. See KUEHO.

KU-E-KU-E-O, *v.* To stir or move slightly, as one supposed to be dead.

KU-E-KU-E-LI-MA, *s.* The elbow.

KU-E-KU-E-WA-WAE, *s.* The heel. *Kin.* 3:15. The ankle joints.

KU-E-KU-E-NE, *v.* See KUENE, to lay out a building. To act the part of a steward; to serve out food.

KU-E-KU-E-NI, *v.* To shake; to tremble; to move; to struggle.

KU-E-LU, *v.* To loosen; to cast down.

KU-E-MA-KA, *s.* *Kue* and *maka*, face. The eyebrows.

2. The brow of a hill.

KU-E-MA-KA-PA-LI, *s.* See KUEMAKA and PALI, a precipice. The brow of a hill.

KU-E-MI, *v.* *Ku* and *emi*, to shrink back. To stand or retreat, as from something feared.

KU-E-NE, *v.* To measure for the purpose of laying out the foundation of a house.

2. To frame; to lay out, as the frame of a building.

3. To set up; to put in order, as seats for a multitude; to set up the posts of a house.

4. To care for and divide out, as a steward does to a cook; to act the steward; ke hooko nei oia, ke *kuene* nei; e lana'e ka pepeiao ke *kueneia* nei.

KU-E-NE, *s.* A steward; a treasurer. *Isa.* 22:15.

2. A small quantity of anything; a fraction, as half a glass of rum or water, &c.; he wahi *kuene* ai uuku, a little food.

3. Detraction; slander; false speaking against another.

KU-E-NE-HA-LE, *s.* *Kuene* and *hale*, a house. The knowledge of putting up a house and in the practice of several trades.

2. One skilled in framing and finishing a house; o ka ike i ka mahiai, o ka ike i ka lawaia, o ka ike i ke *kuenehale*, ame ke kaupaku.

KU-E-WA, *v.* To wander about; to be unstable.

2. To be friendless; to wander about without a home. *Kin.* 21:14.

KU-E-WA, *s.* One who has no place to live, no friends; a fugitive; a vagabond; connected with aea. *Kin.* 4:12.

KU-I, *v.* To stick together; to join.

2. To stitch or sew together. *Kin.* 3:7. E kui lehua, to braid lehua blossoms into

a wreath. *Laieik.* 145.

3. *Hoo.* To splice; to join on; to add or attach one thing to another. *Iob.* 34:37.

4. To add or sum up, as numbers. *Nah.* 1:49.

5. To employ; to use, as the tongue, especially in slander. *Hal.* 50:19.

KU-I, *v.* To pound with the end of a thing; to pound with a hammer or mallet; to knock out, as the teeth; mai *kui* wale i na niho a hemo.

2. To pound, as poi, a *kui* i kana ai, and he pounded his food.

3. To beat out, as metals. *Puk.* 39:3.

4. To pound up; to break fine. *Kanl.* 9:21.

5. To smite; to injure; to smite with the hand. 2 *Oihl.* 18:23.

6. To smite, as the conscience. 1 *Sam.* 24:6.

7. To buffet or smite as a punishment. 1 *Pet.* 2:20. *Kui* a wali, to beat to pieces. *Isa.* 3:15.

8. To smite, as hail. *Puk.* 9:28.

KU-I, *v.* To sound, as thunder; *kui* iho la ka hekili maluna.

2. To sound abroad; to sound or spread abroad, as fame or report; kui aku la ka lono. 1 *Oihl.* 14:17. To be heard, as a report.

3. *Hoo.* To roar, as the wind; ke *hookui* la ka makani i kela aoao i keia aoao, a puka mai auanei.

4. To resist; to oppose; to put in disorder.

KU-I, *s.* A general name for small pointed instruments; he mea oioi ma ka maka; a nail; a pin; an awl; a spike; a goad. *Puk.* 21:6. The double teeth; na niho nui ma ka nao, maloko o ke a. NOTE. *Kui* mostly has some qualifying term added to designate what particular thing it is; as, *kuihao*, a nail; *kuikele*, a needle; *kuikeleawe*, a brass or copper nail, &c.

KU-IA, *v.* The passive participle of *ku.* Hit; fitted; stumbled; not sharp; blunt; doing over and over again; meeting.

KU-I-A, *s.* Name of an instrument used in war.

KU-I-AI, *s.* *Kui*, to pound, and *ai*, food. The act of pounding poi or food.

KU-I-AU-MO-E, *s.* The name given by those about the chief to those below them in privilege, though better persons; o ka poe i komo ma ke *kuiaumoe*, o ka poe lakou o pohokano, he kukuiolelo wale no ia.

KU-I-A-LU-A, *s.* The name of some art taught in former times; he nui ka poe i ao i ke kaala me ke *kuialua.*

KU-I-EE, *v.* *Kui* and *ee*, the armpit. To secure or carry under the arm; to fold up and put under the arm.

KU-I-E-LU-A, *s.* The name of an ancient game; same perhaps as *kuialua.*

KU-I-HAO, *v.* *Kui*, to pound, and *hao*, iron. To forge; to work iron, as a blacksmith.

KU-I-HAO, *s.* See above. An iron spike; a nail.

2. A blacksmith; an armorer.

KU-I-HAO, *adj.* Pertaining to a blacksmith.

KU-I-HE, } *v.* *Ku*, to stand, and *hee*, to
KU-I-HEE, } slide. To go forward, then retreat; applied to the mind; hence,

2. To doubt; to hesitate; to be unbelieving; to hesitate to obey or believe a statement; alaila, *kuihe* iho la kela no ke aloha i na makua, then she *hesitated* on account of love to her parents. See KANALUA.

KU-I-HEE, *adj.* Doubting; hesitating; advancing and retreating.

KU-I-HE-WA, *v.* *Kui*, to strike, and *kewa*, wrong. To strike or hit by mistake.

KU-I-KA-HI, *v.* *Kui*, to unite, and *kahi*, one. To have things and interests united in one.

2. To make peace or to be at peace; ua *kuikahi* ke aupuni, the kingdom is in a state of peace.

3. To make or to be conducive to peace; he mea anei ia e *kuikahi* ai? is that a thing to make peace? *Kuikahi* like, peace; quietness. *Hoik.* 6:4. I *kuikahi* ai ka ainoa o ke aupuni, that the breaking kapu might be peaceably done throughout the kingdom.

4. *Hoo.* To make peace, as contending parties. 2 *Sam.* 3:12. To enter into a treaty of peace after a war. 2 *Sam.* 10:19. To make peace; to unite on terms of amity. *Epes.* 2:15.

KU-I-KA-HI, *s.* A union of sentiment or feeling.

2. A state of peace; satisfaction.

3. A covenant; a treaty. 1 *Sam.* 18:3.

4. A treaty of peace and amity.

KU-I-KA-HI, *adj.* Peaceful; quiet; olelo *kuikahi*, a league; a covenant; a treaty; *Ios.* 9:6, 7.

KU-I-KA-HI, *adv.* Together; in common; peacefully.

KU-I-KA-WA, *adj.* *Ku*, to stand, *i*, preposition, in, *ka*, the, and *wa*, space. LIT. To stand in the space. A phrase signifying independence; not attached to either side. It is applied to persons concerning whom it is doubtful to what chief they belong, or to whose authority they are amenable; or as in English, *he is on the fence*, that is, on neither side; hence,

1. Free; not bound to any chief.

2. Not subject to any one's control; not in bondage. NOTE.—This phrase is sometimes written in one word as above, and sometimes in four, as *ku i ka wa*. 1 *Kor.* 9:1.

KU-I-KE, *v.* For *ku i ka ike.* To know or think alike; to agree.

2. To be understood; e haawi e paa i ka lima ke *kuike* e mamua o ka olelo, to give the hand in confirmation, provided the agreement be previously understood.

KU-I-KE, *v. Kui* and *ke*, to push away. To smooth off a place; to leave nothing rough.

2. To destroy men, as in war until not one is left; ua *kuikeia* a pau loa, it is all smoothed over; *kuike* i ka auhau nui, i na kamalii ame na mea a pau, they were heavily taxed, children and everything else.

KU-I-KE-LE, *s. Kui*, pin, and *kele*, slippery. A needle; a sewing needle.

KU-I-KE-PA, *s.* The name of the work of making the god named Lonomakua.

KU-I-KU-I, *v.* Intensive of *kui*, to strike. To strike often; to beat; to smite or buffet, as a person. *Isa.* 58:4. To box; to exercise for a boxing match.

2. To take up arms against any one, i. e., to unite against; e hele kuiee.

3. To pelt; to throw at; to beat against.

4. To fasten together, as the parts of a building.

5. *Hoo.* To put together; to form; hence, to feign; to pretend; *Neh.* 6:8.

KU-I-KU-I, *s.* Name of a medicine, compounded or made into a drink from the sap or gum of the koko tree.

KU-I-KU-I, *adj.* Striking or blowing strongly, as the wind; he makani *kuikui*; more frequently *pakuikui.* See AKUIKUI.

2. Pounded; bruised; wauki *kuikui*, pounded wauki.

3. United; fastened. See the verb.

4. He upena *kuikui*, a net well woven, i. e., fastened.

KU-I-KU-I-WA-LE, *s.* A pounding or bruising to death; an ancient method of killing.

KU-I-LA, *s.* The name of a kind of foreign cloth; he lole hinuhinu paa loa.

KU-I-LI, *s.* The name of a prayer which lasted all night.

KU-I-LU-A, *v. Kui*, to add, and *lua*, two; double. To add on; to double by adding to a thing; e *kuilua*, e *kuilua* mai i ka pono ia lakou, add on, increase the goodness to them, i. e., increase continually in goodness.

KU-I-NA, *s. Kui* and *ana*, a uniting. A sewing, that is, a set of sleeping kapas, generally five, sewed together, answering the purpose of sheets.

2. A seam; a place where pieces of kapa or cloth were united.

3. In modern times, a sheet.

KU-I-NE-HE, *adj. Kui*, to strike, and *nehe*, a rustling sound; O ka lani *kuinehe* uwe, the heaven *uttering* sorrowful sounds.

KU-I-PA-LU, *v. Kui*, to break, and *palu*, soft or fine. To bruise or pound fine, i. e., soft.

2. To break up; to break fine. 2 *Oihl.* 31:1. To break down; to demolish, as idol gods. 2 *Oihl.* 4:3. *Kuipaluia* na akua kii.

3. To beat or bruise, as a cruel man does his wife.

KU-I-PA-LU, *adj.* Broken fine; bruised; pounded.

KU-I-PE, *v. Kui*, to beat, and *pe*, crushed flat. The full form is *kui a pe.* To beat down; to bend over flat; i *kuipeia* e ka makani a paa.

KU-I-PE-HI, *v.* To be in doubt; to hesitate in acting; to go with hesitancy; to distrust one's friendship or offer.

KU-I-PE-HI, *s.* Hesitancy; distrust; making objections. *Oih.* 10:29.

KU-O, *v. Hoo.* To desire to do a thing, but from some cause he does not do it.

KU-O, *v.* To cry with a loud voice; to lift up the voice in weeping for joy; e aloha nui mai me ka uwe.

KU-OI, *v. Ku* and *oi*, to limp. To move slowly, as a vessel with little wind.

2. To rock or reel to and fro, as a vessel in a calm.

3. To reel or stagger, as fowl drenched in water.

4. To stagger, as a person unable to walk through weakness.

KU-O-I-LI, *v. Ku* and *oili*, to ascend. To walk a steep road up hill.

KU-O-I-LI, *adj.* Steep, as a road up hill.

KU-OO, *v. Ku*, To stand, and *oo*, ready; prepared. To stand ready; to be prepared for any event; *especially*, to be prepared against evil. 1 *Pet.* 1:13.

2. To be fearless; to be intent on carrying a point.

3. To be sober, i. e., unexcited; to be calm; to be fully awake to circumstances. 1 *Pet.* 4:7.

KU-OO, *adj.* Fearless; ready; prompt in action; vigilant.

KU-OU, *v. Ku*, to stand, and *ou*, to rest the head on anything. To incline the head; to bend the head forward, as in bowing. See KUNOU.

KU-OU-E-LE-NA, *adj.* Standing firmly

and constantly by the chief at all times; o ke paupau akoa o ke paupau *kuoulena.*

Ku-o-ha, *s.* Name of a prayer used for causing a man to love his wife and a wife to love her husband.

Ku-o-ho, *s.* Name of a shell fish.

Ku-o-ko-a, *v. Ku,* to stand, and *okoa,* another. To stand aside by one's self.

2. To stand aloof from assisting or injuring another.

3. To cast off the authority of a king or ruler; to rebel.

4. *Hoo.* To set free; to deliver from the power of another.

Ku-o-ko-a, *adj.* Standing aloof or separate from; existing in independence of anything else.

Ku-o-la, *v. Ku* and *ola.* To stand alive and safe; to escape some great danger.

Ku-o-ku-o-lo, *v.* The intensive of *kuolo.* To make a vibrating motion, as in rubbing or polishing; to rub; to polish, as in scouring a utensil.

Ku-o-lo, *v.* To make a vibrating motion; to rub; to polish; to scour; to scratch.

2. To shake, as a fluid in a bottle or cask.

3. To tremble, as the voice.

Ku-o-lo, *s.* A small sort of drum; a timbrel. *Hal.* 92:3. The hula drum; he ipu hula; he hula paipu.

Ku-o-lo-hi-a, *s.* Name of a species of grass.

Ku-o-lo-ka-ni, *s.* See Kuolo above and Kani, to sound. An ancient musical instrument among Hawaiians, used at hulas and on other occasions of amusement and dissipation; a timbrel. *Puk.* 15:20. Translated *psalteries* in 2 *Oihl.* 9:11.

Ku-o-lo-ku, *v.* See Kuolo. To sing like a bird.

Ku-o-lo-ku, *s.* The voice or song of a singing bird; *kuoloku* ka leo o ka manu kani leo.

Ku-o-lo-no, *s.* The general name of hillocks or protuberances on the tops of the mountains; a o na puu maluna pono iho o ke kuahiwi, e ku lalani ana, a ku hookahi paha, ua kapaia'ku ia he *kuolono.*

Ku-o-ni, *v. Ku* and *oni,* to move. To walk gently or softly; to move lightly; to fall back or behind another on account of a slow movement.

Ku-o-no, *s.* A corner, as of a room; applied only to the inside. See Hio. But *kihi* is the corner outside of the house.

2. In *geography,* a bay; a gulf; a recess of the sea into the land. See Kaikuono.

He wahi kai e poopoo ana iloko o ka aina.

3. The part of a house (inside) opposite to the door.

Ku-o-no-o-no, *v.* To be comfortably settled; to be well furnished with things for comfort and convenience; to be above want.

Ku-o-no-o-no, *s.* An inheritance; a settlement.

2. A settled place, i. e., a place of rest. 1 *Nal.* 8:13.

Ku-o-no-o-no, *adj.* Well furnished; supplied; *kuonoono* ole, unsteady; unsettled. *Kuonoono* is applied to a woman skillful in pounding kapa and in braiding mats, &c. See Loea.

Kuu, *adj. pron.* It is used for *ko, ko'u* and *ka'u,* my, mine, what belongs to me. Note.—*Kuu* is often synonymous with ko'u and ka'u, but as these apply to different things, and the speaker was at a loss which to use, it was proper, i. e., grammatical to use *kuu;* thus, Hawaiians say *ka'u* keiki, ko'u hale, but not *ko'u* keiki or *ka'u* hale; but it is correct enough to say *kuu* keiki and *kuu* hale. *Gram.* § 150, 4.

Kuu, *v.* To let go; to loosen; to release; to slacken, as a rope that is too tight; to let down, as by a rope; to let down from the shoulder. *Kin.* 24:18.

2. To dismiss or send away, as on an errand; to send away, as a messenger; to allow to come. *Lunk.* 13:8.

3. To put down, as one in authority; to dethrone.

4. To pay out, as a rope or cable in casting anchor.

5. To loose, i. e., to cast, as a net into the water for fish; to take fish in a net, i. e., to let down the net for them; to become calm, as the mind after intense anxiety; to be assuaged. *Laieik.* 77.

6. To give liberty; to suffer or permit to be done.

7. To cause to do; to suffer to be done. *Kanl.* 18:10.

8. E *kuu* i ka uhane, to give up the ghost; to die. *Kin.* 35:29.

9. To fail; to give up; to cease to help. *Kanl.* 31:6, 8.

10. *Hoo.* To excuse; to let go; to send away, as a multitude. *Puk.* 3:18.

11. To lead out of an inclosure; to deliver from difficulty; to set free from; e hoomaha, pau ka nae make.

Kuu, *s.* A releasing; a letting go.

2. The act of taking fish in a net. Note. This idea is more from letting down the

net than from insnaring the fish. See the verb 5.

KUU, *s.* The name of a species of fish net; he upena *kuu.*

KUU-A-LA, *v.* See KUALA.

KUU-E, *v.* The *e* gives intensity to the verb. To release, as one from his sufferings; to have one's difficulties pass away; *kuue* ka luhi, pau ka pilikia.

KUU-KA-NAE, *s.* *Kuu*, release, and *kanae*, the breathing. A free breathing, i. e., free from fear; safe; palekana.

KUU-KUU, *v.* The frequentative of *kuu.* To let down; to let go; also, *hoo.*, to let down. *Oih.* 9:25. Alaila, *kuukuu* lakou i kii malolo.

KUU-KUU, *s.* The name of a game. *Hoo.* The same.

2. A species of spider, commonly called Grandfather Longlegs.

3. Name of another species of short-legged spider.

KUU-KU-LI, *v.* To sit on the heels with the knees on the ground.

KUU-LA, *s.* The name of the god of fishermen from Hawaii to Kauai. Hina was his wife and the goddess of fishermen. When the people prayed to *Kuula* and he would not give them fish, they then prayed to Hina to intercede with her husband.

KUU-LA-LA, *v.* To be beside one's self; to be out of one's right mind; e pupule, e hehena; to go here and there; to be lawless.

KUU-LA-LA, *s.* Great ignorance; stupidity; a want of common sense views; no ke *kuulala* loa o ko onei poe kahiko i na olelo lalau.

2. Wantonness; effeminacy; lasciviousness.

KUU-LA-LA, *adj.* Wanton; lascivious. *Iak.* 5:5.

2. Insane; out of reason; lilo loa ma kona makemake iho; unrestrained from following one's own inclinations; ua nana na kanaka, aole he *kuulala* loa e like me mamua, men looked to him, he was not so much out of his senses as before.

KUU-LU-LU, *v.* To be cold; to be contracted with cold; to shiver with the cold.

KUU-LU-LU, *adj.* Cold; shivering with cold; chilled; hence,

2. Fearful or abashed; *kuululu* na kahu ia oe i ke kahuna.

KUU-NA, *s.* *Kuu* and *ana.* A descending; passing down. See KUU. A hereditary disease; he mai na na kupuna, a disease from their grand-parents.

KUU-NA, *adj.* Hereditary; descending or derived from parents to children, as some diseases; he mai *kuuna* ia no lakou, theirs is a *hereditary* disease. FIG. Ma ka manao *kuuna* o oukou, according to your *traditionary* opinions; na uhane i ka hewa *kuuna*, traditionary vices.

KU-HA, *v.* To spit; to spit upon. *Nah.* 12:14. To eject saliva from the mouth.

KU-HA, *s.* Saliva; spittle; water from the mouth. 1 *Sam.* 21:13.

KU-HA, *adj.* Pertaining to saliva.

KU-HA-I-KI, *adj.* *Ku* and *haiki*, narrow. Narrow; contracted; too small or narrow.

2. Straightened in mind; concerned greatly in mind.

KU-HAO, *v.* *Ku*, to stand, and *hao*, iron. To stand as iron; to stand alone; to be singular in a good sense; to acknowledge God before wicked men; to obey God rather than follow our own opinions or those of others; to stand alone morally; to stand alone; applied to a letter of a book standing by itself; it applies also to men.

KU-HAO, *adj.* Standing firmly and acting alone; he ua *kuhao*, rain from a single cloud or without a cloud.

KU-HAU-HAU, *v.* *Ku* and *uhauhau*, weak. To be weak; to totter with age. See UHAU-HAU.

KU-HA-KA-KAI, *v.* *Ku* and *hakakai*, to be swelled. To be swelled out, as one fat or full fleshed.

2. To be swelled with disease; hence,

3. To be weak; to be sickly.

KU-HA-KU-HA, *v.* Freq. of *kuha.* To spit upon frequently.

KU-HA-LA-HA-LA, *v.* See HOOHALAHALA. To break off from a bargain; to grumble at another's prosperity; to find fault with.

2. To envy one his prosperity or wealth and procure his death by the pule anaana; i opuinoino ia mai no ka hanohano.

KU-HA-LU-KA, *adj.* Many; numerous; huddled together; going in great companies; pili i ke kewai *kuhaluka* ka mauna.

KU-HA-NA-O-LE, *v.* *Ku* and *hana*, work, and *ole*, not. To be lazy; to be idle; to do nothing.

KU-HA-NA-O-LE, *adj.* Lazy; idle.

KU-HA-PA, *v.* *Ku*, to fit, and *hapa*, partly. To be incorrect, or correct only in part in speaking.

KU-HA-PA-HA-PA, *v.* See KUHAPA. To be frequently incorrect in speaking.

2. To make blunders often.

3. To be not trusty.

4. To be various at different times.

Ku-he, *s.* A change of color in the skin in consequence of being long in the water, as purple, blue, brown, &c.

2. The name of a species of fish.

Ku-he-a, *v.* *Ku* and *hea,* to call. To call; to cry aloud; to call for one; to make a noise; to call out. See KAHEA.

Ku-he-a, *s.* A hunter, as of birds; *kuhea* manu; one who imitates the whistling call of birds, and then calls them into his snare; a fowler. *Sol.* 6:5.

Ku-he-a, *adj.* Calling; insnaring, as of birds; makaala ke kanaka *kuhea* manu, watchful the man who *insnares* birds; noisy; boisterous.

Ku-he-ku-he, *s.* Freq. of *kuhe.* Changeable as to colors, as black, green, blue, thick dark.

Ku-he-la, *v.* To rise and move along, as the swell of the sea; to pass along standing or rising high, as a high swell of the sea; to rise, as a high surf. See KAHELA and KAHELAHELA.

Ku-he-la, *s.* The high unbroken swell of the sea as it moves along.

Ku-he-le-lo-a, *v.* *Ku,* to rise, *hele,* to go, and *loa,* any distance. To be sent off from one's house and land and neighborhood.

2. To wander about from place to place. See WAILANA.

Ku-he-le-lo-a, *s.* A person banished and sent off to live where he can, stripped of everything.

2. A banishment.

Ku-he-le-lo-a, *adj.* Of or belonging to a state of banishment.

Ku-he-le-mai, *s.* *Ku,* to rise, *hele,* to move, and *mai,* this way. The name given to a kind of play used in gambling; he koi, he hooleilei.

Ku-he-pa, *v.* *Ku* and *hepa,* false. To be untrustworthy; to be uncertain what one will do, as a servant or neighbor.

2. To break a bargain without paying well.

Ku-he-pa-he-pa, *adj.* Doubtful; different from what was expected; aole ike maopopo; having an imperfect knowledge of a thing.

Ku-he-wa, *adj.* *Ku,* to hit, and *hewa,* wrong. Coming suddenly; seizing upon, as a disease; striking unexpectedly, as the wind; he mai *kuhewa,* he makani *kuhewa.*

Ku-hi, *v.* To think; to suppose; to imagine. *Sol.* 17:28. *Kuhi* lakou he loko-ino ko na kanaka o Hawaii, they thought the people of Hawaii of bad disposition.

2. To point out; to point at with the finger.

3. To give an appellation.

4. To cast up to one.

5. To judge; mai *kuhi* hewa oukou, do not mistake; do not judge erroneously.

Ku-hi, *s.* A gesturing with the hand to regulate singing, time, &c.; the use of the baton or hand in directing music; a na lakou (ka poe hula) e ao i ke *kuhi* a paa ke *kuhi* o ua mau mele la.

Ku-hi-a-la-e-a, *adj.* Epithet of a certain priest of Lono; he kahuna *kuhialaea* kona inoa.

Ku-hi-a-no, *s.* *Kuhi,* to point out, and *ano,* the meaning. In Hawaiian *grammar,* a pronoun; *kuhiano* pili kanaka, a personal pronoun; *kuhiano* pili inoa, a pronoun relating to things.

Ku-hi-he-wa, *v.* See KUHI and HEWA, wrong. To mistake; to judge erroneously; to err; to have a wrong opinion.

Ku-hi-he-wa, *s.* An error in judgment or opinion.

Ku-hi-ku-hi, *v.* Freq. of *kuhi.* To show; to point out. *Kanl.* 1:33.

2. To designate; to point out; to direct one to a particular place.

3. To teach; to make signs with the hand; to point the finger; to direct by the hand; *kuhikuhi* heiau, to direct the ceremonies of the temple service.

4. To ask by signs.

Ku-hi-ku-hi, *v.* To be fat; to be rich with fatness, as food.

2. To be sweet of pleasant to the taste, as high-seasoned food.

Ku-hi-ku-hi, *adj.* Sweet, as sugar; fat, as the fat of a well fed animal; sickish with fatness; momona, liliha.

Ku-hi-ku-hi-ni-a, *adj.* Pleasant to the taste; delicious; applied to food. See KU-HINIA.

Ku-hi-ku-hi-puu-o-ne, *s.* Name of a class of priests in ancient times who were consulted and gave advice concerning the building of luakinis, especially the location.

Ku-hi-la-ni, *adj.* Proud; haughty; high minded; looking up.

Ku-hi-li, *v.* To blunder; to mistake. See HILI, to wander.

Ku-hi-li, *adj.* Mixed with coloring matter, as wauki before it is pounded and thus colored in the bark; ka onohi ula me he wauki *kuhili* la.

Ku-hi-na, *v.* To bear the commands or execute the orders of the chief.

Ku-hi-na, *s.* One that carries the orders and executes the command of the king or highest chief; the highest officer next the king; Kalanimoku was the *kuhina* of Kamehameha.

2. An officer of the king's guard. 2 *Sam.* 23:23.

Ku-hi-ni-a, *v.* To eat to the full; to be satiated with food; hence, to be fat; to be round; to be plump; to be sickishly fat; to be greasy.

Ku-hi-ni-a, *s.* The fat of hogs.

2. Sweetness or richness in connection with food.

3. The unpleasant sensation after eating too much or too rich food.

Ku-hi-ni-a, *adj.* Fat; rich; sweet; spoken of food.

Ku-hi-pa, *v.* Not to know or understand clearly; to mistake one person for another.

Ku-hi-pa-hi-pa, *v.* To be not understood, as one's speech or plans; to surmise; to guess; to think in distinction from knowing certainly. See Kuhepa.

Ku-hi-wa, *v.* To be under a kapu; to be subject to a chief and under his control, in distinction from the freedom of the people; ua omea ia (ka aina) he *kuhiwa*.

Ku-ho, *s.* The falling of a stone into the water.

2. The sound of such stone as it strikes perpendicularly into the water.

Ku-hou-a-na, *s.* *Ku*, to rise, *hou*, again, and *ana*, participial termination. A rising anew; a rising again; a resurrection.

Ku-hou-poo, *v.* See Kuho and Poo, the head. To dive head-first, as a man into the water.

Ku-ho-ho, *s.* A deep ravine; a high precipice.

Ku-ho-ku-ho, *v.* To fall or plunge into a wave. See Kuho.

Ku-ho-nu, *s.* A species of crab-fish.

Ku-hu-a, *adj.* Hard; thick, as a liquid; as paste or bad ink; scarcely flowing; firm; constant.

Ku-hu-ku-hu-a, *adj.* Hard; thick, as liquid. See Kuhua.

Ku-hu-ku-ku, *adj.* Epithet of a dove, from its noise; manu *kuhukuku*, a dove. *Kin.* 15:9.

Ku-hu-ku-ku, *s.* A dove. *Mel. Sol.* 2:12.

Ku-ka, *v.* To think with one's self; to revolve in one's own mind. *Neh.* 5:7.

2. To consult together, as persons, i.e, to consider how a thing is to be done.

3. To consider deliberately; to think; to decide a question. 2 *Sam.* 24:13.

4. To choose out; to appoint to a certain business.

5. To reckon; to compute; *Oihk.* 25:50.

6. To consult together, as a council of state; *kuka* iho la lakou no ke kaua ana, they consulted together respecting the war; *kuka* hewa, to think or devise mischief.

Ku-ka, *s.* A council for transacting business; a caucus meeting preparatory to business.

2. A reasoning on a subject; an inquiry; *kuka* olelo, a consultation.

3. (Corrupt from English.) A surtout.

Ku-kaa, *s.* See Kaa, to roll. A roll; a bundle of cloth or kapa; a large bundle; hookahi punahele, hookahi *kukaa*, each intimate friend, one *bundle* (piece) of cloth.

Ku-kaa, *v.* *Ku* and *kaa*, to roll. To roll up, as a bundle of kapa or cloth; to make a heap; to swell up; e pehu.

Ku-ka-ao-ao, *v.* To be opposed to one; to injure, as by slander; *kukaaoao* mai nei o mea ia'u.

Ku-kaa-wa-le, *v.* *Ku*, to stand, and *kaawale*, alone; apart. To stand by one's self; to stand alone.

Ku-kaa-wa-le, *adj.* Standing off; separate; alone.

Ku-ka-a-we, *adj.* Safe.

Ku-kae, *s.* Excrements; dirt; filth; he honoa.

Ku-ka-e-a, *s.* A great discharge of fæces; hence, strength.

Ku-kae-u-li, *s.* *Kukae* and *uli*, blue. The black or blue liquor in the hee or squid; the soft matter of the squid used for bait.

Ku-kae-u-wau, *s.* A groaning or moaning animal found on the mountains.

Ku-kae-ko-lo-a, *s.* Name of a species of grass found at Koloa.

Ku-kae-lo-li, *v.* See Kukae and Loli, to dirty. To spot; to stain.

Ku-kae-na, *s.* *Ku* and *kaena*, wrath. Anger; rage; unappeasable wrath.

Ku-kae-na-lo, *s.* *Kukae* and *nalo*, a fly. A name given by Hawaiians to unbleached or brown cotton cloth.

2. Beeswax; he kepau e hoohele ai i na lopi humuhumu.

Ku-kae-pe-le, *s.* *Kukae* and *pele*, sulphur. LIT. The excrements of Pele, i. e., sulphur; brimstone; also, matches.

Ku-kae-po-po-lo, *s.* Name of a person whose father was a chief and his mother not. See Kulu.

Ku-kae-pu-e-o, *s.* Name of a species of grass.

2. A species of sea-weed.

Ku-kai, *v.* To cheat in various ways.

2. To go back at the beginning and say the same thing over again.

3. To do the same in reading; ua *kukai* i na hua.

4. To plant or set up wauki by the sea; e kukulu i ka wauki i ke kai.

5. To replace; to redeem. See Panae.

Ku-kai, *s.* The name of a rope fastening together two fish nets. See Aea.

Ku-kai-o-le-lo, *s.* A thing put in the place of another; a substitute; particles or connecting words. See Kukai above.

2. Words often repeated. See Kaiua.

Ku-kai-o-le-lo, *v.* To repeat over and over.

Ku-ka-i-hu, *int.* Ku, to set up, ka, the, and *ihu*, nose. To turn up the nose; a phrase signifying contempt.

Ku-kai-ka-hi, *v.* Ku and *kaikahi*, one alone. To stand by one's self; to stand alone.

Ku-kai-ka-hi, *adj.* Standing alone; being by one's self.

Ku-kai-ke-a, *adj.* Kukai and *kea*, white. Faded, as cloth; pale, as a sickly person.

2. Ceasing to interest, as the same words, thoughts or story often repeated; *kukai-kea* ka olelo i ka lohe pinepine.

Ku-ka-i-li-mo-ku, *s.* Name of a feather god.

Ku-ka-oo, *s.* Name of the god of husbandmen.

Ku-ka-u-la, *s.* Name of a species of fish caught with a hook.

Ku-ka-ha, *v.* Ku, to stand, and *kaha*, to turn away. To stand bent sideways; e ku ewa ae ma ke kua.

Ku-ka-he-u, *v.* To stand up, as the bristles of a hog when angry; applied to men when the face is flushed with anger; *kukaheu*, okala ka heu o ka moe.

Ku-ka-he-ka-he, *v.* To relate falsely.

2. To become a great talker with jests and laughter.

3. To tell a great many stories or anecdotes; e lilo loa ma ke kamailio ana me ka lealea; e hai waha aku i na olelo he nui wale.

Ku-ka-he-ka-he, *s.* An incredible story; a lie; an untrue story.

Ku-ka-hi, *s.* Name of a day of the month or of the moon.

Ku-ka-hu-a, *adj.* Thick; fat; soft, as a fat animal.

Ku-ka-kai-ka-hi, *v.* See Kukaikahi.

Ku-ka-ka-lai-o-a, *s.* Ku, like, and *ka-kalaioa*, a rough prickly shrub. Wildness; rudeness; resembling the kakalaioa.

Ku-ka-lai-o-a, *adj.* Wild; rough; rude; untamed; bristling up.

2. The sensation on the application of cold water. See Aalaioa.

Ku-ka-ku-ka, *v.* See Kuka, to think. To think; to reflect.

2. To hold a consultation. 1 *Nal.* 12:6. To consult together how to manage a difficult matter. *Luk.* 19:30.

3. With naau or *iho*, to consult or think within one's self; to muse; to think. *Luk.* 3:15.

4. To devise good or evil. *Ezek.* 11:2.

Ku-ka-ku-kai, *v.* To go over and over again. See Kukai.

Ku-ka-la, *v.* Ku, to stand, and *kala*, to call out. To proclaim publicly. *Ezra.* 8:21. To publish extensively; ina e *kukalaia* keia kanawai ma kekahi kulanakauhale, a ma kahi aina paha, o ka la i *kukalaia'i*, oia ka la; to proclaim, as a public crier. 2 *Oihl.* 20:3.

2. To cry or sell goods, as an auctioneer.

Ku-ka-la, *adj.* Of or pertaining to a public proclamation.

2. Belonging to a crier or auctioneer.

Ku-ka-lu-hi, *v.* To rest after labor, toil and care. After Kamehameha conquered the Islands, he exclaimed, ua *kukaluhi*; so a man weary with carrying a burden, when freed from it, exclaims, *kukaluhi*. Note.— The *ku* is probably for *kuu*, to let down, *ka*, article, and *luhi*, pain from fatigue.

Ku-ka-moo, *v.* Kuka, to consult, and *moo*, lizard. To use enchantment. *Oihk.* 19:26.

Ku-ka-na-lo-a, *adj.* Some property or kind of banana; he mai *kukanaloa*.

Ku-ka-no-no, *v.* See Kanono. To rise up and spread, as a great smoke; to make a great smoke.

Ku-ka-pa-ka-hi, *v.* Ku, to stand, and *kapakahi*, sideways. To stand bent over; to stand leaning sideways.

Ku-ka-pa-la-ni, *s.* The name of a fish, to which a chief was likened.

Ku-ka-pu, *adj.* A person never sick in youth, but taken sick when grown up.

2. Applied to a young female obedient and kind to her parents; he wahine *kukapu*.

Ku-ka-wo-wo, *v.* See Kawowo. To proceed with speed.

2. To pray with great earnestness and strength.

3. To speak correctly and very earnestly.

Ku-ka-wo-wo, *s.* The gurgling of water

when poured into the bung hole of a cask; ke kani ana o ka wai iloko o ka pahu i ka manawa e ukuhi ai.

Ku-ke, *v.* *Ku* and *ke*, to drive off. To drive or force away.

2. To hunch or push off, i. e., to give a hint with the elbow to go.

3. *Hoo.* To cast out; to expel; to drive away. *Nah.* 32:21.

4. To be angry at.

Ku-ke, *s.* A thin kind of adze, chisel shaped.

Ku-ke, *s.* *Eng.* A cook.

Ku-ke-ku-ke, *v.* The intensive of *kuke*. To drive away; to expel with energy.

Ku-ke-ku, *v.* To bluster; to rage.

Ku-ke-ku, *s.* The scattering of dust before the wind; the violent blustering of the waves of the sea.

Ku-ke-le, *v.* *Ku* and *kele*, to slip; to slide. To slip easily; to glide about, as a boat in smooth water for pleasure.

2. To tremble.

3. To be muddy; to be slippery, as a bad road.

Ku-ke-le, *s.* A trembling; a slipping; a sliding of the feet in walking.

Ku-ki-a, *v.* *Ku* and *kia*, a pillar. To set up a pillar or post; to raise up a mast.

2. To be trusty; to be confidential; to be attentive.

3. To be unable to sleep, as one in trouble or distressed in mind.

Ku-ki-a, *adj.* Attentive; confidential; trustworthy.

2. Not able to sleep through trouble or anxiety of mind.

Ku-ki-he-lei, *v.* To stand with the legs spread open or apart; to straddle open.

Ku-ki-ni, *v.* To run, as in a race; to run swiftly. *Ier.* 12:5.

2. To run round from place to place on an express.

3. To hasten; to hurry on; to go anywhere.

4. To run on an errand for mischief.

5. *Hoo.* To cause to run a race; a ikeia na mea mama, e *hookukini* ia laua.

Ku-ki-ni, *s.* A runner in a race; a post; a messenger. 2 *Oihl.* 30:6. Syn. with elele, messenger. *Sol.* 13:17. He mea mama i ka holo.

2. A runner in a race; one who contends with another in a race course. 1 *Kor.* 9:24. Note.—The *kukini* was formerly an officer of government, whose duty it was to carry orders to different parts of the island, and

such were held in estimation according to their fleetness; wae mai oia (o Kamehameha) i mau *kukini* nana, he chose some runners for himself.

Ku-ki-ni, *adv.* In the manner of a race; e holo *kukini*, to run, as in a race.

Ku-ko, *v.* To desire strongly; to lust after; to set the mind and desire upon; to covet. *Puk.* 20:14. To expect; to cherish evil in the heart; e lia, e manao ino maloko; *kuko* no i ke kaua ame ka make o Kaahumanu, he *greatly desired* war and the death of Kaahumanu. *Kuko* in reference to idolatry, to go after; to yield to other gods. *Lunk.* 8:27.

Ku-ko, *s.* Strong desire; lust. *Puk.* 15:9. *Kuko* hewa, lust; *kuko* umi ole, unrestrained desire; incontinent. 2 *Tim.* 3:3.

Ku-ko, *adj.* Lusting; kanaka *kuko*.

Ku-ko-ae-a-ha-wai, *s.* The full flowing of water in a water course with mud and dirt; a pau ia, *kukoaeahawai* ma ia la hookahi no.

Ku-ko-e-ae, *s.* Name of a heiau; hoolaleia ka laau o ka heiau hou, he *kukoeae* ua heiau la.

Ku-ko-ha-na, *v.* *Ku* and *kohana*, naked. To strip off one's clothes; to be naked. *Isa.* 32:11. To go about without clothing; e hele aole kapa e uhi ana ia ia iho.

Ku-ko-hoo-nui, *s.* *Kuko* and *hoonui*, to increase. The desire of hoarding up; covetousness; ka uluku me ka hiaa; sleepless with desire.

Ku-ko-lu, *s.* The name of a day of the month.

Ku-ko-na, *s.* Sourness of disposition; easily put out and made angry.

Ku-ko-na, *adj.* A ike aku la ia Hinai ka malama e hele ana me ka maka *kukona*. *Laieik.* 203.

Ku-ko-nu-ko-nu, *s.* A great increase of rain; being wet or soaked with rain; great moisture.

Ku-ku, *v.* See Ku, to strike; to hit. To strike; to beat, as in pounding kapa; ua *kukuia* ke kua me ka pulu kapa i ka hale.

2. See Ku, to stand. To be or to stand perpendicularly, as a precipice; to stand before one; ua hele mai nei e *kuku* i mua ou.

3. To rise up, as a thought in the mind; nolaila, *kuku* mai la kahi manao iloko o'u.

4. To sweep; to brush away, as dirt.

5. To be high; to excel; to be eminent.

6. *Hoo.* To be filled, as with food; to surfeit. *Sol.* 25:16.

Ku-ku, *s.* The operation of beating out

kapa.

2. A rising or standing up; nana aku la oia i ke *kuku* o na opua, he saw the long clouds *standing erect. Laieik.* 48.

3. The name of an unclean bird. *Oihk.* 11:16. *Eng.* The cuckoo.

4. The thorn bush.

5. A small pricker that fastens readily upon clothes.

KU-KU, *adj.* Standing thickly together, as trees; laau *kuku*, a thicket. 1 *Sam.* 13:6.

2. Having many sharp points; laau *kuku*, thorns; prickly bushes. *Nah.* 1:10.

3. Standing erect; rising up.

KU-KU-A, *s.* A crab-fish.

KU-KU-AU, *s.* The name of a four-footed animal in the sea.

KU-KU-A-HI, *adj.* High, as a house.

KU-KU-E, *s.* A lame person; one deformed or somewhat twisted. See HAPAKUE.

KU-KU-EE, *v.* See KUKE. To contend with; to oppose; to bicker; to quarrel, as two persons.

KU-KU-I, *v.* See KUI, to publish. To publish; to spread, as a report; to make famous.

2. See PAKUI. To splice or piece out so as to lengthen, as a stick or rope.

KU-KU-I, *s.* The name of a tree and nut; the nut was formerly used to burn for lights; the tree produces also the gum pilali; the body of the tree was sometimes

kukui

made into canoes; the bark of the root was used in coloring canoes black.

2. A lamp. 1 *Sam.* 3:3. A candle; a light or torch; a lighter. *Kin.* 1:15.

KU-KU-I-A-HI, *s.* Lamps of fire. *Dan.* 10:6.

KU-KU-I-O-LE-LO, *s.* A company of people full of talk and noise at night when they should be asleep; o ka poe o lakou opohokano, he *kukuiolelo* wale no ia, aole e ai ana.

KU-KU-I-WA-NA-AO, *s.* Name of the people about the chief who talk and sing and tell stories all night; o ka poe noho me ke alii ma ke *kukuiwanaao*, he poe lakou no makou.

KU-KU-HE, *v.* To be dark colored; to be black or blue. See AKUHE.

KU-KU-HI, *v.* See UKUHI. To pour water into a calabash or barrel; to fill with water.

KU-KU-KAA-A-LAI-O-A, *v.* To bristle up; to be wild; to act as an untamed animal; as a wild boar.

KU-KU-KU, *s.* The rising of anger.

2. Whatever is full of holes, i. e., of little value.

3. Sickness; weakness.

4. The disease called the piles.

5. Strong steam.

6. A name given to the soap plant of the Hawaiian Islands.

KU-KU-KU, *v.* A reduplication of *ku*, to stand. To stand uprightly; to stand together; to sit together; to sleep together.

KU-KU-KU-KU, *s.* The name of a bird; a turtle. *Ier.* 8:7.

KU-KU-LA, *v.* From the English; *kula*, school. To have school, that is, to attend school; to go through the excercises of school; alaila, *kukula* iho la kakou i kakahiaka nui, then we *attended school* early in the morning.

KU-KU-LE, *s.* A beautiful blossom; the beautiful opening of the petals of a flower; the opening of a flower.

2. A kind of disease; an indisposition to move; applied to persons, to animals and to fowls.

KU-KU-LE, *v.* To be dumpish; to be loth to move, as in some kinds of disease.

KU-KU-LI, *v.* See KULI, the knee. To kneel; to bow the knee. *Kin.* 41:43. To kneel in reverence. *Isa.* 45:23. *Kukuli* hoomaikai, to kneel in prayer; to worship.

2. To crouch; to lie down, as a beast. *Nah.* 24:9.

3. *Hoo.* To cause to kneel down, as a camel. *Kin.* 24:11. To stand on the knees.

KU-KU-LI, *s.* The joint of the knee. See KULI.

2. An unpleasant sensation of the stomach produced by food.

KU-KU-LU, *v.* To set up on end; to erect, as a tent. *Puk.* 40:2. To make fast in a perpendicular position.

2. To set up, as the frame of a native house. *Puk.* 26:30. To build, as a house.

3. To stand up together, as a multitude. *Oihk.* 9:5, To stand up for one, i. e., to speak words in his favor. *Iob.* 4:4.

4. To set up, as an idol. 2 *Oihl.* 25:14.

5. To stick up, as a stake.

6. With *hale, figuratively,* to perpetuate a family. *Kanl.* 25:9. *Kukulu* i ka olelo,

to reason.

7. See KULU. To cause to flow, as water; to scatter; to be unstable.

8. *Hoo.* FIG. To be established in the christian faith. *Kol.* 2:7.

KU-KU-LU, *s.* The place where the sky apparently meets the horizon; *kukulu* eha, the four cardinal points of the compass, i. e., everywhere ; na *kukulu* o ka honua, the points or ends of the earth. *Isa.* 45:22. The border or edge of a country; ka pea kapu o *kukulu* o Tahiti. *Laieik.* 167.

2. A pillar; a post. *2 Sam.* 18:18.

KU-KU-LU-A-E-O, *s.* The name of a bird with long legs.

2. A person walking on stilts.

3. The name of the stilts; he ohe kahi laau hana ia i mea *kukuluaeo.*

KU-KU-LU-A-KAU, *s. Kukulu,* point, and *akau,* north. The north, that is, the north point. *Kanl.* 2:3.

KU-KU-LU-HE-MA, *s. Kukulu,* point, and *hema,* left; the south. The south; the south point. *Ios.* 13:4.

KU-KU-LU-PA-PA, *v. Kukulu,* to build, and *papa,* a board. To erect a temporary shed or house.

KU-KU-MA, *s.* A whitish crab of the species *paiea.*

KU-KU-NA, *s.* The rays of the sun or any luminous body.

2. The radii of a circle; the spokes of a wheel.

3. The end posts of a native house which verge towards the center.

4. The side posts of a door, i. e., of an ancient Hawaiian house.

5. The gate post; eha *kukuna* i kukuluia no ka pa; well posts; a elua *kukuna* i kukuluia no ka punawai.

KU-KU-NI, *v.* See KUNI, to kindle; to burn. To kindle, as a fire. *Hal.* 18:8. To burn, as a sacrifice. *2 Oihl.* 13:11. To kindle a fire generally.

KU-KU-NI, *adj.* Burning; very hot; feverish; *kukuni* keia la, this day has a fever, i. e., it is very warm. See KUNI and WELA.

KU-KU-NI, *s.* The prayer of a sorcerer; he pule anaana.

KU-KU-NU, *s.* A door post; a side post of a door; the end of a house. See KUKUNA.

KU-LA, *s.* The country in rear of the sea shore; the open country back from the sea. LIT. The name of the region of a mountain near its base, next below the *pahee;* it is a region where houses may be built and people live. It extends to the region called *kahakai,* or sea shore.

2. Any open uncultivated land. *Kin.* 3:1.

3. A field for cultivation. *Nah.* 16:14.

4. Uncultivated land in the neighborhood of a city, i. e., suburbs. *Nah.* 35:3, 4.

5. A field; a pasture.

6. A place in a tree or trees where for the sake of flowers, perhaps, birds assemble and sit; he *kula* manu paha keia e walaau nei.

7. The name of the ancient god who could overleap fences and mountains, perch on straws, converse with all the other gods, &c., &c.

8. The name of a species of fish caught in a basket; hinai *kula.*

KU-LA, *v.* See above. To be in, or to have perpetual solitude, as to live in uncultivated and uninhabited places; e paa mai ka meha o ka la, e uhi mai ka malu.

KU-LA, *s.* Eng. A school; a place of instruction; ua kukulu ia keia *kula* i wahi e imi ai i ka naauao.

2. *Kula* is often written incorrectly for *gula,* gold.

KU-LA, *adj.* Eng. for *gula.* Golden; made of gold.

KU-LAI, *v.* To push over from an upright position.

2. To knock down; to overthrow.

3. To move, as the tail of an animal. *Iob.* 40:17.

4. To dash in pieces; to kill. *Isa.* 13:18.

5. *Hoo.* To thrust at. *Nah.* 35:20.

6. To cause to fall, i. e., to bring upon. *Isa.* 37:7.

KU-LAI, *s.* A knocking down of a person with a view to kill him; a running over one; a thrusting at one to kill him.

KU-LAI-A, *s.* A feast day; a day in commemoration of some event.

KU-LAI-NA, *v.* See KULAI above. To overthrow; to cast down. *2 Kor.* 4:9. To be overthrown; to cast down, as a transgressor in judgement. *Ier.* 6:15. To start and spring from his hiding place, as a man when he is discovered. *Hoo.* To overthrow. *Iob.* 18:7. To break down, as a forest. *Zek.* 11:2.

KU-LAI-NA-KA-WA.

KU-LA-I-WI, *s.* Long residence in a place. See KUAPUIWI.

KU-LA-KU-LA, *s.* Name of a play like nine-pins.

KU-LA-KU-LAI, *v.* To wrestle; to scuffle. See KULAI.

2. The name of a game; *kulakulai* ma ke kai.

KU-LA-KU-LAI, *s.* A wrestling; a scuffling; a throwing another down.

Ku-la-la, *s.* See Ku and Lala, branch. A vine.

Ku-la-la-ni, *v.* *Ku,* to stand, and *lalani,* a row. To be or to stand in a row; to be equal each to each; he *kulalani* wale no ka onionio, the spots stand in straight lines.

Ku-la-la-ni, *adj.* Standing in rows; standing for presentation. *Mar.* 2:26.

Ku-la-na, *s.* *Ku* and *lana,* to float. A place where many things are collected together, as a village, a garden; a meeting or collection of persons; e hele ana oukou i hea? E hele ana i o, i ke *kulana* pule, i. e., to a meeting which is held only once at a place or occasionally.

2. The sea in a calm immediately after a high wind, or the state of the sea when wind and current are opposite. See Oloku. *Kulana* nalu, a place in the sea where the surf rises high and thick, i. e., where the high surfs follow each other in quick succession.

3. A market place.

4. Name of new food from foreign countries; he mea ai hou no na aina e mai.

Ku-la-na, *v.* *Ku* and *lana,* to float. To pitch backwards or sideways, as one sitting in a chair and nodding.

2. To nod, as a person partially asleep; to bend the neck in nodding. See Kakiwi. To reel, as a drunken man. See Naue and Kunou.

Ku-la-na, *s.* A place in a hulili or fortification where the men stand to throw their spears.

2. The sides of a house; na *kulana* o ka hale.

Ku-la-na, *adj.* Nodding; bending the neck; he poo *kulana* ka kela wahine. See Kunewa.

Ku-la-na-ha-le, *s.* See Kulana, *s.,* and Hale, house. A village. 1 *Oihl.* 9:25. A cluster of houses; a town; a city; ma ko kakou noho ana ma keia *kulanahale,* ma Lahainaluna nei, by our living at this *village,* at Lahainaluna; more generally written *kulanakauhale.*

Ku-la-na-hee-na-lu, *s.* *Kulana* and *heenalu,* to swim on the surf-board. The place or village where a good surf came in that the people might have the pleasure of riding on the surf. Note.—A good surf from the sea was considered an important appendage to a village.

Ku-la-na-kau-ha-le, *s.* See Kulana-hale. A large town, village or city; also,

often synonymous with kulanaheenalu, as the terms were interchangeable.

Ku-la-na-la-na, *v.* *Ku* and *lanalana.* See Lana, to float. To be moved; to be agitated with fear. Lit. To stand trembling; to be disturbed in mind.

2. To act upon uncertainties; to be troubled. *Hal.* 15:5.

3. To be removed from its place.

4. To stumble. *Isa.* 63:13. To walk in a stumbling manner. *Isa.* 59:10.

5. To reel, as one drunk.

Ku-la-na-la-na, *s.* A false step; a stumbling. *Hal.* 121:3.

Ku-la-ni-ha-koi, *s.* *Ku,* to stand, *lani,* high up, and *hakoi,* heavy. What is above or on high; a supposed place in the heavens from which the waters of rain came; the windows of heaven. *Isa.* 24:18. Ina i nui ke ao eleele ma ua poipu la, ua manao ia aia maloko olaila o *Kulanihakoi,* nolaila mai ka hekili, ka uila, ka makani, ka ua, ka ino nui.

Ku-la-pa, *s.* See Lapa, a ridge. A stretching out; a rubbing against something; a rising or swelling up.

2. A hill or small mound on which kalo is planted.

Ku-le, *v.* To seize or take another's; to give one trouble in dispossessing another of his own. See Kulekule.

Ku-le, *s.* The name of a fish which burrows in the sand; he *kule* ka inoa o ka ia noho ma ke one.

Ku-le-a, *adj.* Successful; competent; able.

Ku-le-a-na, *s.* A part, portion or right in a thing. *Oihk.* 7:33.

2. A right of property which pertains to an individual.

3. A friend; a portion belonging to a friend.

4. One's appropriate business; hookahi o kaua makamaka, o ka imi naauao, oia hoi ko kaua kuleana e noho ai ma keia kulana-kauhale. Note.—In modern times, *kuleana* often refers to a small land claim inside another's land, that is, a reserved right in favor of some claimant; the original term was synonymous with lihi, an attached piece of land which another was allowed to cultivate and had some claim to.

Ku-le-a-na, *v.* To stir up; to excite, as the ripples or waves of water. *Laieik.* 15.

Ku-lei-u-la, *s.* An expression of admiration for one's chief, as clothed with rainbow-colored kapas; o ke *kuleiula* au o ke alii.

Ku-le-hu, *v.* See Pulehu. To roast in

the fire or hot ashes; to roast partially.

Ku-le-ku-le, *v.* To be ousted from house to house, or from place to place.

2. To trample often where one ought not, as a horse; *kulekule* ko'u kapa ia lakou, my kapa is *trampled on* by them.

Ku-le-ku-le, *adj.* Unsettled; unfurnished; lacking in conveniences; the opposite of *kuonoono* and *koakoa*; noho wale aku no lakou aole *kulekule*.

Ku-le-le, *v.* *Ku* and *lele*, to fly. To drive or scatter away, as some light or small thing; to drive away, as a puff of wind; *kulele* ka makani.

Ku-le-le-i-wi, *adj.* Making false steps; stumbling, as an aged person; hence,

2. To do awkwardly or badly.

Ku-le-le-u-la, *adj.* *Kulele* and *ula.* Bending; arching, as the rainbow.

Ku-le-pe, *v.* To hew out roughly, as timber.

2. To make a hole in the ground; *kulepe* ekuia a awaawaa.

3. To split open, as a fish.

4. To blow, as the wind in the middle of a channel; *kulepe* lele ka hauli.

Ku-le-pe, *s.* The wind blowing in the middle of a channel.

Ku-li, *v.* To be stunned with noise; to be deafened; not able to hear.

2. *Hoo.* To turn a deaf ear; to refuse to hear.

3. To be disobedient; to be stubborn in disobedience.

4. To be silent.

Ku-li, *v.* To give or pay something as a reward for adultery or fornication.

Ku-li, *s.* A reward given to a female for adultery or fornication.

Ku-li, *s.* Deafness; inattention to duty.

2. A deaf person. *Puk.* 4:11. One unable from deafness to join in conversation.

Ku-li, *adj.* Deaf. *Isa.* 35:5. Ka pono *kuli. Hal.* 58:1.

Ku-li, *s.* The knee. *Isa.* 35:3. See KUKULI.

Ku-li-a, *s.* A young handsome person desired and sought after; a beauty.

Ku-li-a, *v.* For *kuia, l* inserted. Used *imperatively*, stand up; be present; present yourself; *kulia* kou ikaika, let your strength come out. *Laieik.* 104.

Ku-li-a-na, *s.* The desire of a gift or present to be made to one.

Ku-li-u, *s.* A person quick to be very angry; one quick and violent tempered; one given to seek quick revenge.

Ku-li-hi-a-moe, *v.* *Kuli* and *hiamoe*, to sleep. To doze; not to hear through drowsiness.

Ku-li-hi-li-hi, *v.* *Ku* and *lihilihi*, side; edge. See LIHI. To be caught or hooked on the side or slightly, as a fish; to seize on some feeble part.

Ku-li-ku-li, *v.* See KULI. To stun with noise; to be confused with noise so that one cannot think.

2. Used *imperatively*, hush; be still; keep silence; referring to what another says.

Ku-li-na, *v.* *Kuli* and *ana*, being deaf. To hear partially or indistinctly; less than *lohe.* SYN. with mahui.

Ku-li-na, *s.* See KURINA.

Ku-li-pee, *v.* *Kuli*, knee, and *pee*, to run and hide. To be lame; to be fatigued; to be topsy-turvy; to be confused; to be sick; to be weak; to be feeble.

Ku-li-po-li-po, *adj.* Deep water, as in pools on the mountains; dark, as deep water. See NIPONIPO.

Ku-lo, *v.* To continue doing a thing; to persevere; to wait long.

Ku-lo-a, *v.* *Ku*, to stand, and *loa*, long. To wait some time; to wait till food is ripe; to procrastinate; e hooloihi ai i ka manawa e waiho ai; to continue doing a thing; ke *kuloa* mau ana i ke ao a i ka po.

Ku-lo-a, *v.* For *hokuloa.* The morning star.

Ku-lo-i-hi, *v.* *Ku* and *loihi*, long. To protract the time; to be long about a thing.

Ku-lou, *v.* *Ku* and *lou*, to bend, as a hook. To bow the head; to bend forward.

2. To stoop in order to look down.

3. To bow with respect to another.

4. To reverence; to bow in worshipping. *Puk.* 12:27. *Kulou* lakou ilalo me ka hoomana, they bent forward as in worship.

5. To bow down with grief. See LOULOU. With *maka*, to be cast down; to be disappointed. *Neh.* 6:16.

6. *Hoo.* To lament; to grieve. *Kan.* 2:8. To subdue, as an enemy, i. e., to cause to submit. *2 Sam.* 22:40.

Ku-lou-poo, *v.* *Kulou* and *poo*, the head. To dive into the water with the head down, i. e., head foremost.

2. To turn, as a somerset.

3. To leap down a precipice.

Ku-lo-ko, *adj.* Fighting, as one chief against another in civil war; a mahope iho o ko lakou kaua *kuloko* ana.

Ku-lo-ku-lo-ku, *v.* To stand in pools or puddles of water. See HALOKOLOKO.

Ku-lo-la-lo-la, *v.* *Ku* and *lola*, paralyzed. To be stiffened; to be paralyzed.

2. To act as an idiot in drooling or slabbering.

3. To be weak or imbecile; to be slow and awkward. See KULOMALOMA.

KU-LO-LA-LO-LA, *adj.* Stiff, as the limbs; not obeying the desire.

2. To be feeble in body and mind.

KU-LO-LI, *s.* Name of a species of wauki on Hawaii at Palilua.

2. A person who has no wife nor children is called *kuloli.*

KU-LO-LI-A, *v.* *Kulo* and *lia* for *ia.* To dash against; to shake; to tremble.

KU-LO-LI-A, *adj.* Wandering; going from place to place without object; lazy.

KU-LO-LO, *s.* A pudding made of kalo and cocoanut, or of breadfruit and cocoanut; imi oia i *kulolo*, he mea ono loa ia ai.

KU-LO-LO-HI-LI, *v.* To be long in doing a thing; to be very slow; to converse or tell a story with many episodes and much unnecessary matter; to lengthen out, as a story.

KU-LO-MA-LO-MA, *v.* *Ku* and *loma*, slow; awkward. To do a thing very slowly and awkwardly; to act as one partially paralyzed.

KU-LO-MA-LO-MA, *s.* Dullness; awkwardness; stupidity; inexpertness.

KU-LO-NO, *adv.* Ascending to a great height; a e pii *kulono* i ke alo o ka lani.

KU-LO-NO, *s.* Small holes in the bottom of a calabash or other vessel where the water may drop through. See KUNONO.

KU-LU, *v.* To drop, as water; *kulu* ka lani, the heavens dropped water, that is, it rained. *Lunk.* 5:4. To drop, as tears; na waimaka o kela mea keia mea e *kulu* i lalo; to distill from. *Mel. Sol.* 5:5. Hence,

2. To leak, as the roof of a house.

3. To flow, as water.

4. To fall down; to tumble over.

5. To be asleep; to dream; to be in a trance.

6. To be in a pleasant frame of mind.

7. To be near or quite midnight; ua *kulu* ka po; ua *kulu* ke aumoe.

8. To be near night; kokoke po ka la.

KU-LU, *s.* A drop of water or other liquid.

2. The dropping of water.

3. The name of a disease.

4. The name of a tree.

5. The name of a day of the month; the first night in which the moon is dark or cannot be seen.

KU-LU-A, *s.* The name of a day of the month or of the moon.

2. The union of two things; a pair of twins.

KU-LU-A, *v.* To flow down; to run, as water. See KULU.

2. To water, as land; to give drink, as to an animal.

3. To flow along, as in singing or reciting poetry.

4. To sing, as a song.

5. The name of a person whose father is a chief and his mother not; ina he alii ka makuakane, a he alii ole ka makuahine, ua kapaia ka laua keiki he *kulua*, a he waiki kahi inoa, he kukaepopolo kahi inoa; o ke ano o ia mau olelo, he alii akaka ole.

KU-LU-I, *s.* The name of a tree.

KU-LU-I-HI-A-MO-E, *v.* *Kulu*, *i* inserted, and *hiamoe*, to sleep. To doze; to fall into sleep. See KULUHIAMOE.

KU-LU-I-KI, *v.* *Kulu*, to sleep, and *iki*, little. To be partially asleep; to doze.

2. To endure; to persevere; to be constant.

3. To enter in; to soak in, as water.

4. To eat daintily or sparingly.

KU-LU-HI-A-MO-E, *v.* See KULU and HIAMOE, to sleep. To sleep; to be in a trance; to dream. See KULUIHIAMOE and KULUIKI.

KU-LU-KA-HI-O-HI-O, *adj.* *Kulu* and *hio*, to lean over. To be partially drunk; to reel to and fro.

KU-LU-KU-LU, *v.* See KULU, to sleep. To sleep; to dream; to be in a trance.

2. To be sociable and interesting in conversation.

3. *Hoo.* See KULU, to drop. To distill; to drop silently, as a mist from the clouds.

KU-LU-MA, *v.* To see often; to be well acquainted with, as with a person often seen; to know well.

2. To do frequently; to know certainly by frequent intelligence; aole paha kakou i *kuluma* ia ia, akahi no a ike, we are not *well acquainted* with him, we have seen him but once; aole kakou i *kuluma* i ka ike ana, we are not *perfect in knowledge.* NOTE. *Kuluma* is opposite to *kulina*, partially deaf.

KU-MA, *adj.* Pitted; rough, as the skin from scars of sores; set thick together; dark colored, as clouds. See KUMAKUMA.

KU-MA, *s.* *Kuma* is a word used for *standing in company with.* See KU, to stand, and MA, implying some persons not mentioned. See MA. Hence, it implies *an addition to, an enlarging.* It is found in the compounds of numerals above ten; thus, *umi*, ten; *kuma*, increased or standing with *kahi*, one, that is *eleven*; the second *ma* may be used for euphony's sake for me, with. *Gram.* § 115, 4.

Ku-ma-ka, *v. Ku*, to set, and *maka*, the eye. To know certainly; to apprehend fully; e ike maopopo, e ike lea. See KULUMA.

Ku-ma-ka, *adj.* Thoroughly understood; fully known.

Ku-ma-ka-ia, *v.* To betray; to ambuscade.

2. To accuse an innocent person.

3. To allure; to entice to sin; to offend against one. *Hal.* 73:15.

4. To revile; to reproach.

Ku-ma-ka-ia, *s.* A traitor; one who is apparently friendly, but is in reality an enemy.

Ku-ma-ka-le-hu-a, *v. Ku*, to put, place, *ma*, at, on, *ka*, article, the, and *lehua*, the lehua tree. To hang, as a bunch of bananas, a hog, or a man (a transgressor) as sacrifices upon the tree which was to be used in building a heiau. NOTE.—Such tree was generally a *lehua*; hence the term.

Ku-ma-ka-le-hu-a, *s.* The action of putting or hanging bananas, or a hog, or a man, as sacrifices upon the tree which was to be used in building a heiau.

Ku-ma-ka-pa, *v.* To live in another place.

Ku-ma-ke-na, *v.* To mourn; to wail; to lament for the dead. 1 *Tes.* 4:13. To grieve; to be in distress for the loss of a relative or friend; e uwe aloha me ke kanikau. FIG. *Ier.* 4:28.

Ku-ma-ke-na, *s.* A mourning; a lamentation for the dead when great multitudes raised their voices in lamentation.

2. The general mourning that followed the death of the king or high chief, when the people wailed, knocked out their teeth, lacerated their bodies, and at last fell into universal prostitution; nui na hewa o ka wa kahiko, o ke *kumakena* kekahi, many were the vices of ancient times, *kumakena* was one.

3. A mourning or sorrow for the loss of property, house, goods, &c., and the distress that followed; no ka pilikia o ka noho ana. See KANIKAU.

Ku-ma-ke-na, *adj.* Mourning; hale *kumakena*, house of mourning.

Ku-ma-ku-ma, *adj.* See KUMA, rough, as the surface of akoakoa or coral. Rough or pitted, as the skin of a person after having the small-pox.

Ku-ma-no, *v.* To set in good order, as in laying stones.

Ku-ma-no, *s.* The head of a watercourse; a fountain; a brook or stream of water; he poowai, he pu, he manowai.

Ku-me-ne, *adj.* Dull; blunt. See MENE. He keko ihu *kumene*, a monkey with a blunt short nose.

Ku-me-ba-la, *s.* Gr. A cymbal; a musical instrument. 1 *Kor.* 13:1. *Kumebala* walaau.

Ku-mi-mi, *s.* The small sprouts that shoot from the root of the sugar-cane, after the stalk is broken off.

2. The name of a species of shell fish, poisonous to eat; it resembles the papai; *kumimi*, he papai, he mea make ke ai, he awaawa.

Ku-mi-no, *s.* Gr. Cumin, an herb. *Isa.* 28:25.

Ku-moo-a-lii, *s.* A race or line of kings; a dynasty; o ke alii, nana no e mau ai ka noho alii ana o na 'lii, a e mau ai hoi ke *kumooalii*, aole e pau i ka hokai ia.

Ku-mo-mo-le, *v. Ku* and *momole*, smooth. See MOLE. To be straight up and down, as a smooth pali; to be smooth and steep, as a pali that cannot be climbed.

Ku-mu, *s.* The bottom or foundation of a thing, as the bottom of a tree or plant, but not the roots; as, *kumu* laau, the *bottom* of a tree; *kumu* maia, banana stumps for planting; the stump of a tree; the stalk or stem of plants; the but end of a log, &c.; hence,

2. The beginning of a thing, as work or business.

3. The foundation, that is, the producing cause.

4. An example; a pattern; a copy; *kumu* hoohalike, a pattern; a model. *Puk.* 25:9. A socket. *Puk.* 26:19.

5. A fountain of water.

6. The price of a thing, or the property to be given for a valuable.

7. The property to be paid for hire. NOTE.—Formerly all trade among Hawaiians consisted of barter, and the price of a thing was not a *cash price*, but one article became the kumu of another if it could be exchanged for it.

8. A shoal of fish; a flock; a herd; *kumu* puaa, a herd of swine; *kumu* hipa, a flock of sheep.

9. Civil power; legal authority. NOTE. The word *mana*, out of its ancient and legitimate meaning, has lately been used for *power* or *legal authority*.

10. A teacher; an instructor from the

highest to the lowest class, including the ministers of religion.

(11. A cough; a hard breathing; a pestilence; he mai ahulau, he mai *kumu*, he aheahe; this is a vicious pronunciation for *kunu*. See KUNU.) *Kumu* ole, without cause. *Ioan.* 15:25. *Kumu* mua, elements of things. 2 *Pet.* 3:10.

12. A species of fish of a red color, forbidden to women to eat by the ancient kapus.

KU-MU, *v.* To begin or commence a work; to make an experiment.

2. *Hoo.* To found; to lay a foundation.

KU-MU-AO, *s.* *Kumu* and *ao*, to teach. An intensive and giving definitiveness to *kumu.* A teacher; an instructor.

KU-MU-A-LA-KAI, *s.* *Kumu* and *alakai*, to lead; to guide. A leading teacher; a school teacher directing to higher pursuits.

KU-MU-E-A, *s.* *Kumu* and *ea*, tortoise shell. The *ea* or tortoise shell on the handle of a fly-brush.

KU-MU-I-PU-KU-KU-I, *s.* *Kumu* and *ipu*, cup, and *kukui*, torch. A candlestick; a lamp. *Puk.* 25:34.

KU-MU-O-HAI, *s.* See KUMU and OHAI, a large flowering shrub or tree. The bush or body of the ohai tree.

KU-MU-O-NE, *s.* Name of a stone out of which maika stones were made.

KU-MUU, *s.* The name of a kind of fish.

KU-MU-HA, *s.* The bottom of the intestines; the rectum.

KU-MU-HE-LE, *s.* Something connected with the intestines. See NIHINIHI.

KU-MU-HI-PA, *s.* *Kumu* and *hipa*, sheep. A flock of sheep. *Mik.* 5:7.

KU-MU-HOO-HA-LI-KE-IA, *s.* A pattern of a thing. *Heb.* 8:5.

KU-MU-HOO-LA, *s.* *Kumu* and *hoola*, to save from danger. A ransom; a price paid for deliverance from death. *Mat.* 20:28.

KU-MU-HOO-LA-HA, *s.* *Kumu* and *hoolaha*, to spread abroad. Seed; applied to animals; means of propagation. *Kin.* 7:3.

KU-MU-HOO-LI-KE, *s.* A pattern; a copy.

KU-MU-HOU, *s.* *Kumu*, teacher, and *hou*, new. LIT. A new teacher. An epithet of the Holy Spirit. *Ioan.* 14:16, 17.

KU-MU-KU-AI, *s.* *Kumu* and *kuai*, to buy. The thing paid for an article in barter.

2. In modern times, the price of an aritcle in cash or barter. *Kanl.* 33:19. See Note under *kumu*, 7.

KU-MU-KUI, *s.* A teacher of boxing; a fencing master. *Laieik.* 44.

KU-MU-KU-MU, *v.* To be short, as the remnant of what is cut off.

2. To be cut short or shaved close, leaving the stumps or kumus, i. e., the roots or stumps of hair or beard when shaved.

3. To make blunt, dull or short.

KU-MU-KU-MU, *s.* The stumps or roots of what is cut off; the short hairs with the roots left after dressing a hog; the roots or stumps of the beard after shaving; the short stumps left after breaking off weeds instead of pulling them up.

KU-MU-LAU, *s.* *Kumu* and *lau*, a leaf. That which propagates or brings forth often; a producer; a breeder.

1. A vegetable that produces much, as the stump of a tree that throws out many sprouts; so of other vegetables producing their own kind.

2. A female, man or beast that produces many offspring. LIT. The bringers forth, as a hen that has hatched more than once, a sow that produces pigs often, &c.

3. FIG. Applied to chiefs, because they nourished or fed men.

4. Also, *figuratively*, a fruitful source of evil or good, generally the former; ua lilo kekahi o ua mau hewa la i *kumulau* hoolaha no ka hewa, some of those vices became the *principal* source of spreading evil.

5. The leaf or sprout that grows out of the root or stump.

KU-MU-LE-O-ME-LE, *s.* *Kumu* and *leo*, voice, and *mele*, a song. The rules of music.

KU-MU-MA-O-MA-O, *s.* The name of an easterly wind at Oahu.

2. The name of a kind of stone from which maika stones were made.

KU-MU-MU, *v.* To be blunt; to be obtuse. See KUMUKUMU.

2.To have the qualities of something broken or cut off.

3. To be dull, as a tool.

KU-MU-MU, *adj.* Dull; blunt; obtuse; dull, as an edged tool. See MUMU.

KU-MU-MU-MU, *s.* Cartilage; something between bone and meat. See PILALI.

KU-MU-PAA, *v.* *Kumu* and *paa*, fast. To have a fast foundation. *Hoo.* To establish; to confirm. *Hal.* 99:4.

KU-MU-PAA, *s.* *Kumu* and *paa*, complete. The sum in distinction from its parts; the principal in distinction from the interest.

KU-MU-PA-KO-LI, *s.* *Kumu* and *pa-ko-li*, three of the syllables used in solmization in practicing vocal music. The staff or five lines on which music is written. See PAKOLI.

KU-MU-PE-PEI-AO, *s.* The name of a process just behind the ear.

KU-MU-PU-AA, *s.* *Kumu* and *puaa*, a pig. A flock or herd of swine. *Mat.* 8:30.

KU-MU-WAI, *s.* *Kumu* and *wai*, water. A water spring; a fountain; the head of a water course or stream.

KU-MU-WAI-NA, *s.* *Kumu* and *waina* (*Eng.*), wine. A grape vine. *Ioan.* 15:1.

KU-MU-BI-PI, *s.* *Kumu* and *bipi* (*Eng.*), beef; cattle. A herd of neat cattle. *Ioel.* 1:18.

KU-NA, *s.* A dangerous sore; a species of itch difficult to cure.

2. A species of fish; something living in fresh water; he *kuna* ka mea noho o ka wai; he puhi no ka aina; a land eel.

KU-NAE, *v.* *Ku* and *nae*, to pant. To stand firmly against opposition, that is, to stand and breathe, but to stand.

KU-NAE-NAE, *v.* See KUNAE. To stand alone; to stand unmoved.

KU-NAI-NA, *v.* To push over; to push from an upright position; to overthrow. *Hoo.* To conquer; to overcome.

KU-NAI-NA, *adj.* Pushed over; thrown down; laid prostrate.

KU-NA-HE-LU, *v.* To be strong smelling; to have an unpleasant odor.

2. To be mouldy; to smell of mould and age. See PUNAHELU.

KU-NA-HI-HI, *v.* *Ku*, to stand, and *hihi*, thick together. To have the hair standing erect, as a wild man; to stand shivering with the cold; to stand erect, as the hair; to be rough, rude or wild; to shudder; to have the sensation of cold water applied. See OKALA.

KU-NA-HI-HI, *s.* Ferocity; wildness in appearance; a standing up of the hair.

KU-NA-HI-HI, *adj.* Shivering; ferocious; wild; fierce; bristling up; applied to words, ka olelo ikaika ame ke *kunahihi*, strong language with *fierceness*.

2. Growing; standing up; hence, mouldy.

KU-NA-HU-A, *v.* To bend forward in walking, as a tall man. See KANAHUA.

KU-NA-KU-NA, *s.* *Ku* and *na* for *ana*. A standing; the things standing up, i. e., the side posts of a door; lapauila.

KU-NA-KU-NA, *s.* A sore; a kind of itch; a species of disease.

KU-NA-NA, *v.* *Ku* and *nana* for *lana*, to float. To step awry; to stumble sideways; to stand tottering. See KULANA. To be moved; to be agitated; to stumble.

KU-NA-NA, *s.* A garden; a place cleared away for building a house; a house lot; a cultivated plat of ground. See KULANA.

KU-NA-NA, *s.* A goat.

KU-NA-NA-HA-LE, *s.* See KULANAHALE. A number of houses near together.

2. A place where a house may be built.

3. A place where a house once stood.

KU-NA-NE, *s.* A game played on a board with black and white stones.

2. The relationship of a brother to a sister, generally with the prefix *kai*; as, *kai-kunane*, the brother of a sister.

KU-NE-KI, *v.* To be full; to overflow; to be over and above; to be crowded thick together, as people.

KU-NE-KI, *s.* A crowd of people together; the condition, the inconvenience of a crowd; a fullness; an overflowing.

KU-NE-WA, *v.* To be in a deep sleep; to sleep soundly.

2. To close the eyes in sleep.

3. To be weary; to be fatigued. See NEWA.

KU-NE-WA, *s.* Sleep; heaviness for want of sleep; fatigue.

KU-NE-WA-NE-WA, *v.* See KUNEWA and NEWA. To be sound asleep.

2. To be weary; to be overcome with sleep.

3. To fall asleep.

4. To stagger like a drunken man; to reel. *Hal.* 10:27. SYN. with hikaka.

5. To go or to wander out of the way through intoxication. *Isa.* 28:7. Hence,

6. To be drunk.

KU-NE-WA-NE-WA, *s.* Sound sleep.

2. A heavy weariness.

3. A staggering through weakness for want of food; e hoomanawanui i alo ai kaua i ka pololi ame ka hune, i ke anuanu koekoe ame ke *kunewanewa*.

KU-NI, *v.* To kindle, as a fire. *Oihk.* 10:6. To light, as a lamp.

2. To blaze up and burn, as a fire; to consume. *Oihk.* 1:9.

3. To burn, as a sacrifice. *Oihk.* 4:19.

4. To burn, as a fever.

5. To touch off, as a cannon.

6. To scorch or burn, as with a blaze of fire.

KU-NI, *s.* A fever; the ague and faver.

2. The heat of the sun.

3. The burning of lime; *kuni* hao, the branding of cattle.

4. The name of a prayer connected with sorcery and with praying people to death.

5. The practice of sorcery; the same as *anaana*.

KU-NI-A, *v.* To be disobedient; not to yield to one's wishes; to be close. See KOMA.

Ku-ni-a-hi, *v.* *Kuni,* to kindle, and *ahi,* fire. To touch fire to a gun or cannon.

Ku-ni-a-hi, *adj.* Firing; noise by firing a gun; kani ka pu *kuniahi,* the cannon sounded.

Ku-ni-hi, *v.* *Ku,* to stand, and *nihi,* to turn edgeways. To turn a thing edgeways; to set up on edge; to lay on one side; to stand up prominently as a ridge of hair on the head left uncut.

Ku-ni-hi-ni-hi, *v.* See Ku and Nihi. To stand up, as a pali that cannot be climbed.

Ku-ni-hi-ni-hi, *s.* A pali so smooth and steep as not to be climbed; a steep ridge.

2. A tuft of hair left on the head after cutting.

3. The ridge of a war cap or helmet.

Ku-ni-ni-hi, *v.* *Ku* and *ninihi* or *nihi.* To stand up edgeways. See Kunihi. To stand, as a ridge of hair on the head, or as a military hat.

Ku-ni-ni-hi, *s.* A tuft or ridge of hair left on the top of the head from the front backwards after cutting.

2. A military hat.

3. A helmet. See Kunihinihi.

Ku-ni-po-ni-po, *adj.* Weak; languid, &c. See Kulipolipo.

Ku-no, *v.* *Ku,* to stand, and *no,* affirmative particle. To stand firmly or securely.

Ku-nou, *v.* See Kulou. To make signs for one to do a thing. *Oih.* 21:10.

2. To bow gently or slightly with respect to one.

3. To recognize one as an acquaintance or friend by a bow or nodding of the head.

4. To nod or beckon with the head in order to communicate something secretly. *Laieik.* 17. To hint to one by a motion of the head.

5. E aea kahi ai me he manu kolea la e ae ana.

Ku-nou-ku-nou, *v.* Freq. of *kunou.* To bow often; to nod the head in derision. *Ier.* 18:16. *Hoo.* To bow or wag the head in scorn. *Mar.* 15:29.

Ku-nou-nou, *s.* The name of a species of fish.

kunounou, wahine

Ku-no-ku-no-ku, *v.* To stand, as standing water in puddles. See Kulokuloku.

2. To stir up; to trouble, as water; to make into waves.

3. To be about to weep.

Ku-no-ni, *v.* To shake gently, as a gentle shake of the head.

Ku-no-no, *adj.* Red; bright red, as blood; like *uluhiwa,* dark red: purple.

Ku-no-no, *adj.* Full of small holes, as a calabash that lets out the water.

2. Weak; feeble; without strength.

Ku-no-no, *s.* Small or fine holes in any container, as a calabash.

2. A small idea; a little thought; he wahi *kunono* manao iki no nae.

Ku-no-no-pa, *v.* See Kunono, weak. To be helpless, as a person with the palsy; to be weak.

2. To lean over, as a tall man.

Ku-nu, *v.* To blow gently or softly, as the wind.

2. To have a cough; to cough.

3. To lay meat on the embers to roast; hence,

4. To roast meat on the coals.

Ku-nu, *s.* See Kumu. A soft gentle wind; a cough; a pestilence; he mai ahulau.

Ku-nu-ku-nu, *v.* To do a thing with an evil intent; to cherish secret anger.

2. To groan; to complain, as an oppressed people. *Iob.* 24:12.

Ku-nu-ku-nu, *s.* Anger at the haku for his requiring too much labor; anger laid up and cherished in the mind ("nursing one's wrath to keep it warm." *Burns.*) E noi aku ia ia me ka hoowahawaha ole ame ke *kunukunu* ole; ua noho ia i keia wahi me ka hoomanawanui ame ke *kunukunu* ole.

Ku-nu-na, *adj.*

Ku-pa, *v.* To dig out; to dig a trench.

2. To clean off or dig out the inside of a canoe; a *kupa* ia oloko o ka waa.

3. *Eng.* To act as a cooper.

Ku-pa, *v.* To be at home; to enjoy one's place of residence; ua *kupa* lakou ma ko lakou aina iho.

Ku-pa, *s.* One native-born in a place; a long resident or native of a place; he kamaaina kahiko; *kupa* ai au, a native-born who eats (enjoys) the land; *au,* poetic for aina.

2. Name of a species of worm or caterpillar. See Peelua.

3. The name of a sea-shell; he leho.

4. *Eng.* Hawaiian pronunciation for soup.

Ku-paa, *v.* *Ku,* to stand, and *paa,* fast. To stand fast or firmly, as a material object.

2. To stand fast morally; to continue constant, as a person intent upon his purpose; e hoomanawanui.

3. FIG. To confirm; to prove true, as a promise or covenant. *Rom.* 9:11. To confirm, as an agreement. *2 Nal.* 23:3. *Hoo.* To confirm; to establish. *2 Oihl.* 7:18.

KU-PAA, *adj.* Unmovable; constant, as a memorial pillar.

2. Unshaken in mind or purpose.

3. Firm; strong, as an arm; fixed, as a plan; olelo *kupaa*, an ordinance; a covenant; a statute. *Puk.* 21:1.

KU-PAA, *adv.* Fully; thoroughly; firmly. Kanl. 1:36.

KU-PAI, *v.* To send away by water; *imperatively*, get away; be off.

KU-PAI-A-NA-HA, *adj.* Wonderful; unaccountable; strange, as a story or the relation of an event good or bad; it is used as an intensive. See KUPANAHA.

KU-PA-O-A, *s.* An odorous plant used to scent kapa.

2. FIG. What gives character to the life; o ke *kupaoa* ia e hoope ai i na uhane, that is the *plant* which gives scent to souls, i. e., their *peculiar character*.

kupaoa

3. Name of a species of porous stone.

KU-PAU, *s.* A name of several of the days of the month.

KU-PAU, *adj.* Going back; fearful; shrinking.

KU-PA-KA, *v.* To writhe; to twist; to bend this way and that; to move one way then another.

2. To be borne down or overwhelmed with sadness. *Isa.* 21:3.

3. To be in great perplexity and sleepless anxiety; to be fearful; to shrink from doing a thing; *kupaka* ae la aole e hiki.

4. To throw the limbs about, as in great pain.

KU-PA-KA, *s.* A writhing; a bending this way and that; a tearing; a treating with violence.

KU-PA-KA-KI, *adv.* Awkwardly, as anything done in a hurry or in consternation.

KU-PA-KU-PA, *v.* See KUPA. To work digging a trench.

2. To work hewing out a canoe; to work off, as with an adze.

KU-PA-LA, *s.* The name of a vegetable, the root eaten in time of scarcity.

2. The name of a species of long fish; he kaku.

KU-PA-LA-HA, *s.* The name of a class of Kamehameha's heiaus.

KU-PA-LII, *v.* To be little; to be dwarfish; to be diminutive.

KU-PA-LII, *s.* The name of a plant.

2. A small man or woman; a dwarf.

KU-PA-LII, *adj.* Small; dwarfish; diminutive, as a dwarfish person.

KU-PA-LII-AI-AU, *s.* A person who has lived many years, or to old age.

KU-PA-LO-LOI, *v.* To drum with the fingers on the drum or pahu at a hula or other gathering; *kupaloloi* ka leo o ka pahu e kani i Mauoni.

KU-PA-LU, *v.* To stuff with food; to give a person or animal as much as he can eat.

2. To fatten; to nourish; to feed highly. *Dan.* 1:5. Hence,

3. To make a favorite of one.

4. To pound and beat out, as kapa.

KU-PA-LU-IA, *s.* A fatling; a well-fed animal. *Mat.* 22:4.

2. A taming, as of fish by feeding; ka hoohauna ana i laka mai ka ia.

KU-PA-LU-I-A, *adj.* Fatted; well fed.

KU-PA-NA-HA, *v.* To be wonderful. *Hoo.* To exhibit some extraordinary trait of character. *Hal.* 31:21.

KU-PA-NA-HA, *s.* A wonder; a strange event. See KUPAIANAHA.

KU-PA-NA-HA, *adj.* Wonderful; strange; illiberal; close.

KU-PA-NA-HA, *adv.* Wondrously; unaccountably. *Kanl.* 28:59.

KU-PA-PAU, *s.* A dead body; a corpse; a deceased person; lawe aku la lakou i ke *kupapau* o Lono, the people carried away the *dead body* of Captain Cook; eia ke kauoha a ke *kupapau* ia'u, here is the last charge of the *deceased* to me.

KU-PA-PAU, *adj.* Of or belonging to a dead body; hale *kupapau*, a tomb.

KU-PA-PAU-LA, *v.* To stand with the side to the wind, as a house; to blow directly on, as the wind; to have the wind in front or ahead.

KU-PA-PA-KU, *s.* A place deep down in the ground; olalo o *kupapaku*.

KU-PA-PA-LA-NI, *s.* A chief. FIG. Likened to a fish.

KU-PE, *v.* To manage or direct a canoe, as the man with the steering paddle; to direct the bow of a boat or canoe; e hoo-pololei ae i ka ihu.

2. To shovel dirt; to use a shovel or spade. See KOPE.

KU-PE, *s.* The name of a rim of a canoe before and behind.

2. A fetter. See KUPEE.

KU-PEE, *v.* To bind with fetters; to fasten with fetters.

2. To bind; to tie fast.

3. To ornament the wrist or arm with bracelets; to put ornaments on the arm.

KU-PEE, *s.* An ornament, generally of a string of shells (pupuhoaka.) *Kin.* 24:22. *Kupee* gula.

2. A bracelet. *Puk.* 35:22. *Kupee* lima.

3. A fetter. See KUPE. 2 *Nal.* 25:7. *Kupee* keleawe, a fetter of brass. *Lunk.* 16:21. Laau *kupee,* stocks. *Ier.* 20:2.

KU-PE-U-LU, *s.* An old broken worn out canoe, without sail or other conveniences.

2. A canoe with a large ihu; ina nui ka ihu, he *kupeulu* kahi inoa.

KU-PE-U-LU, *adj.* Old; worn out, as a canoe; pehea ko oukou waa? he wahi waa *kupeulu* no hoi, how is your canoe? it is even a canoe *worn out.*

KU-PE-HE, *s.* A going softly, as a person; a moving, as a weak person; hakupe, he *kupehe.*

KU-PE-HI, *v.* See PEHI. To throw at; to pelt; to cast stones at; e hoolei i ka pohaku.

KU-PE-KI-A, *s.* The fear of evil.

KU-PE-LE, *v.* To bruise, as fruit to soften it; to soften; to pound up, as kalo.

2. To feed full or till surfeited, as a parent does a child or a pet dog; e *kupele* i ka ilio.

KU-PE-LE, *v.* To mix up or work over poi the day after it is made. See HOOWALI. Huli ka waha (ka waa) iluna, alaila *kupele* maloko.

2. To dig out the inside of a canoe.

KU-PE-LE, *s.* The name of a medicine given to soften the pou two or three days before the waiki or poepoe.

KU-PE-LE-LEU, *v.* *Ku* and *peleleu,* a short wide canoe. To stand in a broad or spreading posture, as one who blocks up the door or a narrow passage.

2. To be broad, as one with spreading or bulky baggage on his back; heaha kau e *kupeleleu* nei? what are you doing standing so big here?

KU-PE-NE, *v.* To live steadily in one place, instead of roving about, visiting, &c. *Hoo.* The same.

KU-PE-NU, *v.* To dip into coloring matter. *Kin.* 37:31. To stain by immersion; to dip, as into blood or any liquid. *Kanl.* 33:37. To plunge into a ditch. *Iob.* 9:31.

2. To smooth, as a ruffled kapa; to press down.

KU-PE-NU-PE-NU, *v.* The frequentative of the foregoing.

KU-PI-KI-O, *v.* *Ku* and *pikio,* to stand up, as water. See PEKI. To rage; to be in commotion, as water agitated by the wind.

2: To rage or be in commotion, as an angry multitude.

3. To be troubled, as the mind. *Iob.* 30:27.

KU-PI-KI-PI-KI-O, *v.* See the foregoing. To be in commotion generally.

2. To rage, as the sea when wind and current are opposite.

3. To be furious; to be agitated, as a people in a popular tumult. *Hal.* 2:1.

4. To be agitated, as the mind.

5. *Hoo.* To cause a storm; to make boisterous; to rage, as the elements. *Isa.* 51:15.

KU-PI-KI-PI-KI-O, *s.* The agitation of water when the surface is thrown out of its level; the commotion of the waves of the sea in a storm.

2. The raging of a multitude.

3. The agitation of the mind. *Iak.* 1:6.

KU-PI-KI-PI-KI-O, *adj.* Troubled; raging, as kai *kupikipikio. Isa.* 57:20.

KU-PI-LI-KII, *v.* See PILIKIA. To stand close together so as to crowd.

KU-PI-NAI, *v.* *Ku* and *pinai,* thick together. To mourn; to wail; to make a great and confused noise, as of wailing.

2. To go from house to house or from place to place.

3. To be thronged with the numbers of people; to stand thickly together, as people in a crowd.

4. To reverberate, as a sound; to echo back a sound.

KU-PI-NAI, *s.* A great crying; a general or universal lamentation where multitudes are wailing together.

2. The echo of a mourning or lamentation.

3. An echo; a reverberation of sound, as from a pali.

4. A great and confused noise of people.

KU-PI-NAI, *adj.* Noisy, confused with noise; aloha na hoa *kupinai,* wawa hanehane o ua hale nei (hale kula.)

KU-PI-NA-PI-NAI, *v.* To come and stand thick together, as people day after day.

KU-PI-PI, *v.* *Ku,* to stand, and *pipi,* thick

together. To stand thick together, as a multitude; to be confused.

KU-PI-PI, s. Name of a species of fish.

KU-PI-PI, adj. Close together; thick, as people standing together.

KU-PO, s. Name of a species of fish net; he upena *kupo*.

KU-POE-POE, v. *Ku*, to fit, and *poepoe*, round. To be fitted round, i. e., well furnished, as one wearing much kapa.

2. To have much property; to be fully furnished.

KU-POU, v. To bend or bow forward, as in drowsing, or if one hits his foot and stumbles forward; a *kupou* iho la kona poo ma ka waha o ka ipu. *Laieik.* 211.

KU-PO-U-LI, v. To be darkened; to be benumbed; *kupouli* ka naau i ka ona i ka baka.

KU-POU-POU, s. A species of fish; a long fish.

KU-PO-HU, s. *Ku* and *pohu*, calm. A calm; the state of the sea when there is no wind.

KU-PO-LA, v. See KAPOLA. To roll up, as a bundle; to tie up together.

2. To wither and roll up, as the under or dead leaves of bananas.

KU-PO-LO-LU, s. The striking or stabbing one with a pololu; he nui ka poe ao i ka lono maka ihe, me ke *kupololu*.

KU-PO-NO, v. *Ku* and *pono*, right. To be or to act uprightly; to be just; to be true. *Hoo.* To stand upright, i. e., to stand firmly; to establish; to hold up; to be just; to be upright.

KU-PO-NO, adj. In *geometry*, upright; perpendicular; kaha *kupono*, a perpendicular line. *Anahon.* 4.

2. Morally upright. 2 *Nal.* 20:3. Honest; conscientious. *Oihk.* 13:37.

KU-PU, v. To sprout; to spring up; to grow, as vegetation; to shoot out buds; to open out, as leaves or blossoms.

2. To grow large; to increase.

3. FIG. To grow up or increase, as evil. *Kanl.* 29:17.

4. *Hoo.* To pay, as a tax; to collect taxes; hookaumahaia na makaainana e *hookupu* i kela mea waiwai i keia mea waiwai, the common people were burdened by *being taxed* on all sorts of property.

KU-PU, s. A vegetable; a thing sprouted up.

2. A tax. *Hoo.* A tax; a tribute to a ruler. *Ezr.* 6:8.

3. One whose ancestors were born where he himself was and vice versa.

4. One who is mischievous or lawless. *Laieik.* 104. He *kupu* oe, hookahi no mea i kolohe i ka'u. See EU.

KU-PU, adj. Thick, as paste.

2. *Hoo. Hookupu* hapaumi, a little tax. *Kanl.* 26:12.

KU-PU-A, s. A sorcerer. *Isa.* 8:19. A witch. *Kanl.* 18:11. A wizard. *Puk.* 22:18.

2. A person of extraordinary powers of body or mind; one able to do what others cannot; o Aiwohikupua keia, ke *kupua* kaulana a puni na moku. *Laieik.* 100. NOTE.—Sorcerers, wizards and witches are frequently spoken of in Hawaiian antiquities—in their kaaos and meles—as things that existed and were fully believed in.

KU-PU-A, adj. See KUPU above. Thick, as paste.

KU-PU-E-U, s. A person who excels in doing good or in doing mischief; ma ke ahiahi o ua la hoouka kaua nei o na *kupueu*. *Laieik.* 109.

KU-PU-O-HI, v. *Kupu*, to shoot up, and *ohi*, bamboo. To grow up quickly, as a vegetable of quick growth.

2. To grow quickly, as a child that has grown to maturity early.

KU-PU-O-HI, adj. Quick growing; early mature, as men or plants.

KU-PUU, s. See KUPU and AIKUPUU.

KU-PU-KU-PU, s. A vegetable; what springs up from the ground.

2. A species of ground pine.

3. An odoriferous plant.

KU-PU-KU-PU-U-LA, s. A plant used to scarify the skin.

KU-PU-LII, s. *Kupu* and *lii*, little. A small man, but not properly *aa* , a dwarf; it applies to slowness of growth in men, animals and vegetables.

2. A monkey.

KU-PU-NA, s. A grand parent, either father or mother.

2. A father of two or more generations back.

3. A forefather or ancestor indefinitely.

4. A patriarch. *Kin.* 17:5. No na *kupuna* mua o ko Hawaii nei, concerning the first fathers (ancestors) of the Hawaiian race.

KU-PU-NA-KA-NE, s. *Kupuna* and *kane*, male. A grandfather. *Kin.* 32:9. An ancestor of several generations back; o Kukanaloa ke *kupunakane* o kekahi poe o Hawaii nei.

KU-PU-NA-WA-HI-NE, s. *Kupuna* and *wahine*, female. A grandmother, &c. See the foregoing.

KU-PU-NI, *v.* *Ku,* to stand, and *puni,* around. To stand around; to surround, as an enemy. *Ier.* 1:17.

KU-WA, *s.* The name of a prayer made when a person finished a new house by trimming the grass from over the door; *kuwa* ka inoa oia pule; also a prayer when a canoe was finished.

KU-WAI, *v.* To rub in a circular manner.

KU-WA-LA, *v.* See KUALA. To turn over, as a man or other substance.

2. To add to price agreed on, as for delay in payment.

3. To take something else in pay in lieu if the thing agreed on is not sufficient; *kuwala* i ka waiwai e, i ka puaa paha ke lawa ole ka wahie.

KU-WA-LA, *s.* A somerset; a turning over and over, from which is derived the word for interest. See KUALA.

KU-WA-LA, *adj.* Usurious; taking usury. *Puk.* 22:25. SYN. with uku hoopane.

KU-WA-LA-POO, *v.* See KULOUPOO.

KU-WA-LA-WA-LA, *v.* To bend; to yield, as grass or any flexible thing to a flowing stream of water, but which being elastic, bends back again, causing the motion called *kuwalawala; kuwalawala* ka hala ame ka ohia; *kuwalawala* ka pono.

KU-BI-TA, *s. Eng.* A cubit in measure; eighteen inches. *Kin.* 6:15. Iwi *kubita,* he iwi hailima e pili pu ana me ka ili kano, one of the bones of the forearm joined to the wrist. *Anat.* 19.

KU-RI-NA, *s. Eng.* Corn; corn meal.

KRIS-TI-A-NO, *s. Gr.* A christian; a follower of Jesus Christ. *Oih.* 11:26.

L.

LA, name of the eighth letter of the Hawaiian alphabet. It represents the sound of a liquid as in other languages; hence it is easily assimilated to such of the other liquids as are similarly pronounced, viz.: *n* and the smooth American *r* in foreign words. Thus, *nanai* for *lanai;* on the contrary *lanahu* is used for *nanahu,* &c. *L* is inserted sometimes, for the sake of euphony, between a verb and its passive termination *ia;* as, *kaulia* for *kauia; manaolia* for *manaoia.* The letter *h* is used in a similar manner. See H and Grammar § 48.

The name of the letter *la* instead of *el* is required by a law of the language, viz.: that every syllable must end with a vowel sound.

LA, a particle following verbs, mostly in some preterit tense, and generally connected with either *mai, aku, iho* or *ae. Gram.* § 239 and 240. It is also used with nouns and adverbs and seems to have a slight reference to place; similar, but not so marked or strong as the French *la.*

LA, *s.* The sun; he mea e malamalama ai i ke ao, ke alii o ka malamalama, that which gives light to day, the king of light.

2. Day or light, in distinction from *po,* darkness.

3. A particular or appointed day; *la kalahala,* day of atonement. *Oihk.* 23:27. A particular day of the month or year.

4. The effects of the heat of the sun, i. e., a drought; ka *la* nui, a great drought; heat; warmth. Stifling heat is *ikiiki.*

LA, *s.* The name of an ancient sail for canoes; o ka pea o ko lakou waa i ka wa kahiko, he *la* ka inoa o ia pea.

LA, *adj.* Like the sun; sunny, that is, warm; haalele o Poleahu i kona kapa hau, lalau like lakou i ke kapa *la. Laieik.* 113.

LAA, *v.* To be holy; to be set apart for holy purposes; e hookaawale i na waiwai i hoanoia. *Puk.* 30:29.

2. To be devoted to any person; to be consecrated to a particular use or purpose, generally religious; to be under or bound by an oath. *Laieik.* 38. By a kiss. *Laieik.* 126.

3. To be devoted to destruction or death. *Ios.* 6:17. A ike mai la na ilamuku o Liloa ua *laa* keia keiki no ka ae ana ma kahi kapu, and the sheriffs of Liloa saw that the child *was devoted* (had forfeited his life) on account of his climbing over a kapu place (fence.)

4. To be defiled; to become impure by mixing one plant with another of a different kind. *Kanl.* 22:9.

5. *Hoo.* To sanctify; to be sanctified; to be devoted; to be set apart as sacred, or for sacred purposes. *Puk.* 13:2. To make sacred or holy; to revere; to dedicate, as a temple or image. *Dan.* 3:2. To devote. *Oihl.* 18:11.

LAA, *adj.* Sacred; devoted, i. e., given up or set apart to sacred purposes; hence, holy; mea *laa,* a consecrated or holy one. *Puk.* 16:23. He lahui kanaka *laa,* a consecrated nation. *Puk.* 19:6.

2. Accursed; devoted to destruction. *Ios.* 6:18. (See the verb in the same verse.)

LAA, *adv.* Also; together with others; so; like *pela*; besides all this; oia mea a pau e *laa* me keia, all that thing *together* with this; o ka launa nui aku i ka wahine e, e *laa* me ka wahine i ke kane e. See ELAA.

LAA, *s.* Width; breadth. SYN. with laula.

LA-AU, *s.* A general name for what grew out of the ground; o na mea e ulu ana ma ka honua ua kapaia he *laau*.

    1. Wood; trees; timber; but not often fire-wood, which is *wahie*.

    2. A forest; a thicket of trees; ka mea ulu ma na kuahiwi.

    3. FIG. Strength; firmness; hardness.

    4. *Laau* palupalu, herbs; tender vegetables. *Mat.* 13:32.

    5. Medicine; that which is taken in case of sickness. NOTE.—The ancient Hawaiian medicines were numerous, and consisted mostly of mixtures of leaves of trees, barks, roots, &c., and some were exceedingly nauseous, and others very acrid; but the physicians depended more on their enchantments, their invocations to the gods, the sacrifices offered, or the prices paid, than on the virtue of their medicines.

LA-AU-A, *adj.* See LAA, devoted. Devoted to destruction, as for having broken kapu.

LA-AU-A-LA, *s. Laau*, wood, and *ala*, odoriferous. Sandal-wood, an odoriferous wood formerly in great abundance in the mountainous regions.

LA-AU-A-NA, *s. Laau*, wood, and *ana*, participial termination. A ruling; making a mark by a rule or piece of wood. NOTE. This is a modern word.

LA-AU-I-KI-AI, *s. Laau*, wood, *iki*, little, and *ai*, to eat. A general name for herbs. *Rom.* 14:2.

LA-AU-O-OI,   *s. Laau*, bush, and *oioi*,
LA-AU-OI-OI,   sharp; full of sharp points. A bramble bush. *Isa.* 34:13.

LA-AU-O-LI-VA, *s. Laau* and *oliva* (Gr.), olive. An olive tree. *Kanl.* 6:11.

LA-AU-O-WE, *v.* To make a noise with the feet; to drum with the fingers; to make a shuffling noise. See LAUOWAE.

LA-AU-HOO-PII, *s. Laau*, medicine, and *hoopii*, to cause to ascend. An emetic.

LA-AU-KAA, *s. Laau*, tree, and *kaa*, pine. A fir tree. *Zek.* 11:2. An oak tree. *Kin.* 35:4.

LA-AU-KE-A, *s. Laau* and *kea*, a cross. A cross of wood.

LA-AU-KI, *s. Laau*, timber, and *ki* (Eng.),

key. A bar for a gate.

LA-AU-KI-A, *s. Laau* and *kia*, a sticky mixture. A mixture used as bird-lime in catching birds; he laau a hoopili ai i ka manu me he kepau la.

LA-AU-KU, *s. Laau* and *ku*, to stand. A side post of a door, from its erect position. 1 *Nal.* 6:31. A post of a house; an upright post. *Ezek.* 45:19.

LA-AU-KU-KA-HI,   *s.* The names of par-
LA-AU-KU-LU-A,   ticular days in the an-
LA-AU-KU-PAU,   cient month.

LA-AU-KU-PEE, *s. Laau* and *kupee*, a fetter. Stocks, fetters, &c., for criminals; any instrument of confining a person.

LA-AU-LA, *s.* A division of the year.

LA-AU-LA-LO, *s. Laau* and *lalo*, down. The boom of a vessel, from its horizontal position, in distinction from *kia* or *laauku*.

LA-AU-LA-PA-AU, *s. Laau*, medicine, and *lapaau*, to heal, cure, &c. Medicine, i. e., herbs, roots or other compounds for the relief of diseases. *Ier.* 46:11.

LA-AU-LI, *s.* The name of an ancient god who made laws that were not to be broken; ka inoa o ka mea nana i kau na kanawai paa, o Kanelaauli.

LA-A-U-LU, *s. La*, day, *au*, season, and *ulu*, to grow. A time when vegetables spring or grow fast in distinction from *laamake*.

LA-AU-LU-AI, *s. Laau*, medicine, and *luai*, to vomit. An emetic. See LAAUPII and LAAUHOOPII.

LA-AU-MA-KAI, *s. Laau*, wood, and *makai*, constable. The signal or badge of a constable under the first code of laws; it was a square piece of wood five or six inches in length, each side an inch, one-third of the length was turned for a handle; this the constable carried with him as a designation of his office.

LA-AU-MO-E, *s. Laau*, medicine, and *moe*, to sleep. Medicine causing sleep; an opiate.

LA-AU-NA-HA, *s. Laau*, medicine, and *naha*, to operate, as a cathartic. A cathartic medicine.

LA-AU-PA, *s. Laau*, medicine, and *pa*, barren. An ancient drug given to produce abortion, or rather perhaps to prevent fecundation; nolaila, inu nui na wahine i ka *laaupa* i hapai ole lakou. He laau hanau keiki ole.

LA-AU-PAU, *s.* Name of a day of the month. See LAAUKUPAU

LA-AU-PA-LAU, *s.* The name of an instrument of offense used in war, a long club;

ihe, pololu, *laaupalau,* &c.

LA-AU-PII, *s.* *Laau* and *pii,* to ascend. An emetic. See LAAULUAI.

LA-A-HI-A, *v.* *Laa* and *ia,* passive, *h* inserted. See LAA, *adj.,* 2. To be involved in what others do, especially of evil.

2. To be reproached for others' faults on account of living or associating together; inu rama oe, a *laahia* ma ka hewa makou i ka hohonu ia oe.

LA-A-LA-AU, *s.* An herb; a bush; herbs; green things. *Puk.* 3:2. That class of vegetables between trees and grass.

LA-A-MA-KE, *s.* *La,* day, time, and *make,* dead. The time when vegetables generally die or dwindle or grow slowly, like autumn in cooler climates; opposite to *laaulu.*

LA-A-NA, *adj.* See LAA, devoted. Devoted to destruction, as for having broken kapu; e hu *laana.*

LA-A-LO, *s.* The name of kalo tops when dry.

LA-E, *v.* To be light; to be clear, as day; to be shining, as a light. See LAELAE and kindred with *lai.*

LA-E, *s.* Any projecting substance, as a prominent forehead. 1 *Sam.* 17:49. A brow of a hill; a cape of headland. In *geography,* a cape or promontory.

2. A calm; a calm place in the sea, as under a bluff, cape or headland.

LAE-HAO-KE-LA, *s.* *Lae,* forehead, *hao,* horn, and *kela,* projecting. Name given to the unicorn; the unicorn.

LAE-HAO-KE-LA, *adj.* Having one horn in the forehead; he holoholona kiwi hookahi ma ka ihu. Lio *laehaokela. Nah.* 23:22.

LAE-KOI, *s.* *Lae,* forehead, and *koi* sharp; projecting. A sharp or projecting forehead.

LAE-KO-LO-A, *s.* A species of soft porous stone.

LAE-LAE, *v.* See LAE, *v.* To enlighten, i. e., to make visibly clear or plain by means of a light.

2. To make clear or explicit by words, as a statement or assertion.

3. To be free to move; to be unfettered; to be loose; to be separate from another.

LAE-LAE, *adj.* Bright; bright shining, as the sun; e like me ka la *laelae* i ke awakea; pure; clear; serene, as a clear sky. FIG. Pure in sentiment. *Hal.* 19:8.

2. Clear; unobscured to the sight.

3. Clear; distinct, as the meaning of a word or speech.

LAE-LAE, *s.* See LAE. A light; a bright light.

2. Calm, pleasant weather.

LA-E-LE, *s.* The name of kalo tops when partially dry or thrown by as refuse. See LAALO. The litter, as of kalo tops or old kalo leaves; any litter or refuse material.

2. The name of the outside leaves of the loulu, tobacco, &c.; the same as *halii.*

LAE-LU-A, *adj.* *Lae* and *lua,* double. Projecting; sharp; prominent, as a ridge. See MUKOI.

LAE-NI-HI, *s.* Name of a species of fish.

2. A steep, perpendicular forehead.

LAE-PAA, *s.* Name of a servant marked in the forehead. See LAEPUNI.

LAE-PU-NI, *s.* Name of a servant marked in the forehead; o ka poe kauwa i hoailonaia ma ka lae, ua kapaia he kauwa *laepuni.*

LAI, *s.* Used for *lani,* the heavens, especially when the sky is clear and the weather calm; e ke alii wahine o ka *lai. Laieik.* 154.

2. A calm still place in the sea where there is no ripple and the sea is like a looking-glass.

3. Any calm still place; e noho mai a i ka *lai* o Lele.

4. Still, as water; pohu, malie o ka *lai.* See MALINO.

5. Any still, silent place; he wahi mehameha, hakanu.

LA-I, *s.* The leaf of the ki plant. See LAUI and LAUKI.

2. Name of a species of fish.

LAI, *v.* To be calm; to make no noise; to be silent; ua *lai* loa ia po, it was *very still* that night.

2. *Hoo.* To quiet; to appease, as a mob. *Oih.* 19:35.

3. To be quiet, as the elements.

LAI, *adj.* Calm; still; quiet; shining, as the surface of the sea in a calm.

LAI-KI, *v.* To cram; to stuff; to throw together confusedly; to eat too much; to be full, as an over-loaded stomach.

LAI-KI, *s.* Fullness, as of the stomach from over-eating; ua *laiki* ka opu.

LAI-KI, *adj.* Full, as the stomach from eating too much.

LAI-KI, *s.* Hawaiian orthography for *raisi. Eng.* Rice; a vegetable; a species of grain.

LAI-KU, *s.* A calm, either with reference to the atmosphere, without wind, or to the stillness of the ocean, without wave or ripple; he pohu, he malie hinu no ka moana.

LAI-LA, *adv.* Referring to time, then; at that time; referring to place. there; at that place. It almost always takes one of the simple prepositions, *a, i, o, no, ko, ka, ma* or *mai*. See each of the compounds in their places; also, *Gram.* § 68 and § 165, 2d class.

LAI-LAI, *v.* See LAI. To be very calm and clear, as the sun; i ka wa e *lailai* ana ka la maluna o ka aina. *Laieik.* 158.

LAI-NA, *s.* A kind of eruption on the body like shingles.

LA-O, *v.* To spring up, as grass or weeds after a rain.

LA-O, *s.* The leaf of the sugar-cane, especially in its use as formerly in thatching houses. The other names are *lauo, lauko* and *hako.*

2. The name of a species of fish.

3. A mote moving in the eye and causing pain; he pula oni ana iloko o ka maka laolao.

LA-O-A, *v.* To tie up the bones of a person in a bundle; to bundle up.

2. To put a girdle around the body tightly.

3. To choke or strangle, as with a cord around the neck; also written *laowa.* See LAULAU.

LA-O-LA-O, *s.* A bundle of small sticks tied up for fuel.

2. A bundle of anything tied up for carrying.

3. Little sticks put down to help sustain the kuauna or bank of a kalo patch; ka *laolao* nahele kuakua loi.

4. The booming or bass sound of a bell.

5. The pain of the eye suffering from a mote. See LAO 3.

6. An uneasy state of the bowels tending towards colic.

LA-O-WA, *v.* See LAOA above.

LAU, *v.* To feel after a thing.

2. To spread out; to be broad, as a leaf.

3. To be numerous or many. See the noun. Ma keia kula panoa kanaka ole, *lau* kanaka ai, in this dry uninhabited place there are now *many* people.

LAU, *s.* The number 400.

2. The leaf of a tree or plant green or dry. *Oihk.* 26:36. An herb; lau mulemule, bitter herbs.

3. The face of a person, like *helehelena*; *lau* kanaka, persons; where persons live; *lau* kanaka ole, solitary. See LAUKANAKA. *Lau* makani, a stray puff of wind.

4. The end of a pointed substance. SYN. with elau or welau. *Lau* alelo, the tip of the tongue.

LAU-A, *pron. dual.* They two. *Gram.* § 139. Ma *laua o, prep.*, together with; along

with.

LAU-AE, *s.* An aromatic herb.

LAU-AU-A, *s.* A playing at games of chance; gambling. See PILIWAIWAI.

2. Name of the maneuvers in or during a battle; also *kaakaua.*

LAU-A-UA, } *s.* The name of a wind at
LAU-A-WA, } Hana, Maui; makani lauawaawa.

LAU-A-KI, *s.* A body of men working together at the same business.

LAU-A-LA, *s. Lau,* leaf, and *ala,* standing up. Tha name given to kalo leaves before the kalo is pulled or gathered. NOTE. After they are gathered for food they are called *luau.* See LUAU.

LAU-A-LO, *s.* The kalo leaf; the same as *laukalo.*

LAU-A-WA, *s.* The leaf of the kalo when it first shoots out after the huli is planted.

2. The first two leaves or shoots of the huli.

LAU-E-KA, *adj.* Awkward; unskillful in work. See LOPALAUEKA.

LAU-I, *s.* See LAU. The leaf of the ki plant. See LAI and LAUKI.

LAU-I, *adj.* Of or belonging to the ki plant; he pale *laui* kou akua ke hiki i Kailua, a *ti* fence is your god if you come to Kailua, i. e., a frail defense.

LAU-IA, *s.* Name of a species of fish.

LAU-I-LI, *v.* To be fickle; to be inconstant; to be changeable. The better orthography is *lauwili.* See WILI.

LAU-I-PA-LA, *s.* A species of fish.

LAU-O, *s.* See LAU. The leaf of the sugar-cane. See LAO.

LAU-O-E, *s.* The sound of scratching, or walking on anything making a rustling noise.

LAU-OE, *v.* To ascend straightly upwards.

LAU-O-HA, *s.* Any vegetable that grows large and thrifty.

LAU-O-HA, *s.* The sail of a vessel above the spanker.

LAU-O-HAI, *s.* Name of a large bush bearing beautiful flowers; ka lau o luhea o ka ohai i mana.

LAU-O-HA-O-HA, *s.* See LAUOHA above. A thrifty growing vegetable.

LAU-O-HE, *s.* Some material used in polishing wooden calabashes.

LAU-O-HO, *s. Lau* and *oho,* the hair of the human head. The hair of the head. *Nah.* 6:5. Ka hulu o ke poo. NOTE.—The hair of animals is *hulu,* and so is hair on the other parts of the body.

Lau-o-ne, *s.* Any place where the soil is light, mellow and without stones and easy to cultivate.

Lau-o-wae, *v.* To make a rustling noise with the feet or fingers. See Laauowe.

Lau-u-ku-ka-hi, *s.* Name of a day of the month, otherwise called *Laau;* a ma ka la o *Lauukukahi.*

Lau-u-lu, *s. Lau,* leaf, and *ulu,* the breadfruit tree. The leaf of the breadfruit tree.

2. A word heard indistinctly, or an idea so obtained from a speaker as to give an uncertain meaning.

Lau-hau, *s.* Name of a species of fish.

Lau-ha-la, *s. Lau,* leaf, and *hala,* the pandanus. A pandanus leaf.

2. Applied to people as wanderers who come as strangers and stop in a place, and after a time move again. See Aihuawaa.

Lau-he-le, *s.* Name of a vegetable, a small bush; also called *laulele.*

Lau-ho-e, *v.* To paddle together, as several persons paddling a canoe with great strength and resolution; i kahi a kakou e *lauhoe* aku nei.

Lau-hu-a, *s.* Name of a species of fish, small, broad and yellow.

Lau-hu-ki, *s.* The god of those who pounded or manufactured kapa; he akua no ka poe kuku kapa.

2. The office of the person who moistened the kapa during the process of pounding it.

Lau-hu-lu, *s.* The banana leaf.

Lau-kai-a, *s.* The name of a god.

Lau-ka-hi, *s.* Name of a plant, the seeds of which are to infants as a mawai or cathartic to carry off the meconium.

Lau-ka-hi-u, *s. Lau, ka,* article, and *hiu,* the tail of a fish. A long shark, or long-tailed shark (the tail leaf-shaped.)

2. The son of Kuhaimoana.

Lau-ka-na, *adj.* Applied to one who seldom prays in secret; *laukana* kahi mehameha.

Lau-ka-na-ka, *s.* See Lau and Kanaka, people. A place of people; where people live; *laukanaka* ole, a solitary place.

Lau-ka-pa-la-la, *s.* The kalo leaf that grows up from the midst of other kalo leaves sustaining the life of the kalo; he mau maka no Luaipo.

Lau-ka-pa-li-li, *s. Lau* and *kapalili,* to tremble or vibrate quickly. The name of the kalo leaf that first grew on the Hawaiian Islands.

Lau-ke-a, *s.* Name of a hard stone made into kois for its hardness.

Lau-ki, *s. Lau* and *ki.* See Ki. The leaf of the ki plant.

2. The name of a species of fish.

Lau-ki-pa-la, *s.* The name of a yellow colored fish.

2. The leaf of the wiliwili tree.

Lau-ko, *s. Lau* and *ko,* sugar-cane. The leaf of the sugar-cane. See Lao.

Lau-ko-a, *s. Lau* and *koa,* name of a tree. The leaf of the koa tree.

2. The name given to a table knife.

Lau-ko-a, *v.* To be hatched out, as the eggs of any kind of fowls; pehea ka oukou mau hua? Ua *laukoa,* e lele auanei.

Lau-ko-a-i-e, *s. Lau* and *koaie,* a species of timber. *Literally,* a koaie leaf.

2. *Figuratively,* anything which is found only in inland places.

Lau-ko-ha, *adj. Lau* and *koha.* Fledged; feathered, as young birds; he lau laha ole.

Lau-ko-na-ko-na, *v. Lau* and *konakona,* to despise. See Kona. To despise; to contemn; to treat contemptuously.

Lau-ku-a, *v.* To gather together and lay up the good and the bad, or to use what is one's own by right along with what is another's, as by theft or extortion; he *laukua* wale no ko makou.

Lau-ku-a, *adj.* Things put together irregularly or in confusion; applied also to words in a speech; he olelo *laukua,* he olelo hoohihia.

Lau-ku-a, *s.* Things scraped or gathered irregularly together; aia ke aloha o ka *laukua* e laukua wale ai; also, the name of a fish-pond where are many sorts of fish.

Lau-ku-a, *s.* Applied to a person who works industriously at many kinds of work and prospers.

Lau-la, *v.* To be broad; to be wide; to be extended.

Lau-la, *s.* Extension; breadth; width, &c. 1 Nal. 6:3.

Lau-la, *adj.* Broad; wide; he keena *laula,* a wide room.

Lau-lau, *s.* A bundle; a bag, as of money. Kin. 42:35.

2. A wrapper of a bundle; that which surrounds anything. Kin. 42:35.

3. A bundle, as of food done up the second time.

4. A bundle of small wood, or fagots.

5. The netting in which food is carried.

6. A container generally.

Lau-la-ha, *v. Lau* and *laha,* to spread abroad. To be spread abroad, as a noise or report; to be heard extensively; to learn something by report.

LAU-LA-HE-A, *adj.* Something said indistinctly or without clearness; indistinctly heard; he olelo *laulahea.*

LAU-LA-HA-O-LE, *adj.* See LAULAHA and OLE, negative. Kept in; not reported; not spread abroad.

LAU-LA-HI-LA-HI, *adj. Lau* and *lahilahi,* thin. LIT. Thin leaf. Thin, as the leaves of ki leaf or banana. See LALAHI.

LAU-LA-MA, *s.* The lamas or many torches at night.

LAU-LA-WI-LI, *s.* See LAUWILI.

LAU-LE-A, *s. Lau* and *lea,* pleasure; joy. Peace; friendship; satisfaction with a person or thing after having experienced dislike.

LAU-LE-A, *v.* To be on terms of friendship. See LAUNA, i. e., *lau ana.*

2. *Hoo.* To satisfy, as one offended; to reconcile; to become reconciled. *Kin.* 32:20.

3. To obtain favor with one; to make reconciliation.

4. To please; to flatter; to see favor. *Gal.* 1:10. See HOOLEALEA.

LAU-LE-A, *adj.* Peaceful; friendly; pacified.

LAU-LE-LE, *s. Lau* and *lele.* The leaf of a species of turnip.

2. Also the name of the plant.

3. A species of sea-weed into which fish get entangled.

LAU-LE-LE, *s.* Name of a plant self propagated, but eaten for food in time of scarcity; he ilailau, he ananu, he pilapilau.

LAU-LI-MA, *s.* The name of a company of men who worked together on each other's land, or at each other's work.

LAU-LO-A, *s. Lau* and *loa.* LIT. Long leaf. Name of a species of kalo.

LAU-LO-LE, *adj. Lau* and *lole,* cloth; cloth-leafed. An epithet of the mulberry; laau *laulole,* a mulberry tree.

LAU-MA-E-WA, *s. Lau* and *maewa,* to injure; to mock. He palala *laumaewa* kapu no Lono.

LAU-MA-KE, *s. Lau* and *make,* death. A poisonous herb.

2. The barb of a spear; the point of an instrument causing death.

3. The abating or subsiding of water, i. e., a drought.

LAU-MA-NA-MA-NA, *s. Lau* and *manamana,* divided. Applied to that species of potato whose leaves are slim and much divided.

LAU-MA-NI-A, *s. Lau* and *mania,* smooth;

plane. A smooth thin leaf.

2. A straight, smooth even surface of a body.

LAU-MA-NI-A, *adj.* Smooth, straight and even; applied to the surface of bodies. *Isa.* 40:4. Smooth or polished, as glass; ili *laumania,* a plane surface.

LAU-MA-NI-A, *v.* To spread out smoothly and even; to smooth off what is rough. *Hoo.* To level down; to make smooth, as uneven ground. *Isa.* 45:2.

LAU-MA-NI-E, *v.* Another orthography, but the same meaning as *laumania.*

LAU-ME-KI, *v.* To flow slowly, as a stream with very little water.

2. To move very slowly, as a very slow trotting horse.

LAU-MI-LO, *v.* To writhe; to squirm; to turn and twist awry. See LAUWILI. Ua *laumiloia* na uhane, ua make.

LAU-MI-LO, *adj.* Squirming; contorting; mixing up. See LAUWILI. O ka lena o ka puhi *laumilo* i ka pa.

LAU-NA, *v.* For *lau ana,* probably a spreading. To associate with; to be on friendly terms with one; to treat with kindness or attention.

2. To receive in a friendly manner.

3. To be intimate with one; to have an agreement with.

4. *Hoo.* To have fellowship with one. *Gal.* 2:9.

LAU-NA, *adj.* Friendly; social; intimate; with *ole,* unlike; different from; excellent, &c.; i ka hanohano *launa ole* o ke alii kane. *Laieik.* 113.

LAU-NA-HE-LE, *s. Lau* and *nahele,* a thick growth of brush. The leaves or thick growth of a forest; hence,

2. Herbs generally. *Kin.* 1:11. *Launahele* hou, tender herbs. *Kanl.* 32:2.

LAU-PAA-PA-A-NI, *s.* A word used by chiefs in flattering and caressing each other; also a term of exciting pleasure; he *laupaapaani* no me he wahi alii la.

LAU-PAE, *s.* A single branch of a kalo top.

LAU-PAI, *s.* The first two leaves of kalo or huli after planting. See LAUAWA.

LAU-PAU, *s.* A species of fish.

LAU-PA-LA, *s.* A leaf fading and turning brown or red.

2. A person failing in health and considered not to live long.

LAU-PA-LAI, *adj.* Shining; glittering; greasy; hinuhinu, lile.

LAU-PA-PA, *s. Lau* and *papa,* a board. A broad smooth plane.

Lau-wa-hi, *v. Lau* and *wahi*, to gather up leaves. To be greedy of gain; to gather property avariciously.

2. To be eager after food.

3. To be active in indulging lust, as the adulterer.

Lau-wi, *s.* Name of a species of bird, small and yellow; same as the *alauwahio*.

Lau-wi-li, *v. Lau* and *wili*, to turn; to twist, as leaves affected by the wind. To whirl or whiffle about, as the wind.

2. To be unstable, as a fickle-minded person.

3. To be double tongued; to be double minded; to be changeable.

4. To be fickle; to be inconstant; to change one's opinions often.

5. To lay a wager when one has no property.

6. To mix, as different ingredients.

7. To be in great trouble or perplexity.

8. To talk or speak in a round about manner, as one never coming to the point.

Lau-wi-li, *s.* Fickleness in conduct.

2. Carelessness in speaking or pronouncing, with frequent repetitions.

3. The whiffling or sudden changes of the wind.

4. A whirlwind.

5. Fig. Affliction; trouble. See Kuawili. Ua like ka *lauwili* me ke kuawili.

6. *Hoo.* Aole ka *hoolauwili* ma na mea lapuwale.

Lau-wi-li, *adj.* Changeable, like the wind; turning this way and that, like leaves in the wind; hence,

2. Fickle; inconstant. *Kanl.* 32:5. Deceitful. *Hal.* 78:57.

Lau-wi-li-ia, *v.* Passive of *lauwili.* To be in, or suffering affliction. See Lauwili 7.

Lau-wi-li-ia, *s.* Affliction; persecution; distress.

Lau-wi-li-wi-li, *v.* Freq. of *lauwili.* To change often; to be very fickle, &c.

La-ha, *v.* To spread out; to extend laterally; to make broad; to enlarge.

2. To extend; to spread abroad, as a report; aole hoi i *laha* nui ka ai noa ia la, the free eating (i. e., the report of it) did not *extend* greatly on that day.

3. To be distributed far and wide.

4. To be circulated, as a proclamation.

5. To increase; to spread out; to become numerous, as a people. *Kin.* 48:16.

6. *Hoo.* To spread intelligence extensively.

7. To promulgate, as a law or decree among the people. *Luk.* 2:1.

8. To increase greatly; applied to beasts, birds, fish and men.

La-ha, *s.* Name of a calabash broad and flat, but not high; he ipu nou. See Nouu.

La-ha, *adj.* Broad; extended; spread out.

La-hai, *v.* To start up suddenly; to jump; to fly.

2. To hover over; to remain suspended in the air, as a bird. See Lehai.

La-ha-la-ha, *v.* The 13th conj. of *laha.* To spread out much or often.

2. *Hoo.* The same; also, to open, as the wings of a bird in order to fly.

3. To brood over or upon, as a bird upon a nest.

La-ha-la-hai, *v.* See Lahai. The intensive of *lahai.* To hover over; to fly; to light upon, as from a flight. *Hoo.* To flutter over her young, as an eagle. *Kanl.* 32:11. See Lalahai.

La-ha-la-ha-wai, *s.* A broad puddle or pond of water.

La-ha-la-wai, *adv.* Slippery; unpleasant to travel; ua helehele *lahalawai* i ka ua.

La-ha-na, *s. La*, day, and *hana*, to work. A day's work; the work of a day.

La-he-a, *v.* To be soft or rotten, as fruit or flesh. *Hoo.* To smell strong or rancid.

La-hi, *adj.* Thin; flat; opposite to *manoanoa.*

2. He mele *lahi.*

La-hi, *s.* A species of white cane.

La-hia, *v.* To be involved and unjustly condemned with the guilty.

La-hi-la-hi, *adj.* See Lahi. Thin, as paper; gauze like; thin, as beaten gold.

La-ho, *s.* The testes of men or animals. See Kowau and Hua.

La-ho-oo, *adj. Laho* and *oo*, ripe; mature. Hard; stingy; close; applied to persons.

La-hoo-ka-ha-ka-ha, *s. La*, day, and *hookohakaha*, display. A day of exhibition, of display, of fine appearance; he la e hoike ai i ka hanohano; a public day.

La-ho-u-la, *s. Laho* and *ula*, red. A term of reproach; a railing.

La-ho-ko-le, *s. Laho* and *kole*, raw. A blackguard word; an epithet of reproach.

La-ho-li-o, *s. Laho* and *lio*, horse. A name given by Hawaiians to gum elastic or India rubber.

La-ho-pa-ka, *s.* A reproachful epithet; a blackguard word signifying cracked testicles.

2. A stingy man.

La-hu, *adj.* Forbidden; prohibited;

usually applied to food; as, ka ai i *lahuia*, the *forbidden* food; in this, it is equivalend to *kapu*.

La-hu-i, *v.* See Lahu. To prohibit; to forbid; to lay a kapu; to proclaim a law or ordinance.

La-hu-i, *s. La,* day, and *hui,* to unite. A time of coming together; hence, an assemblage; a company; a union of many. See the following words and lahu above.

La-hu-i-ai-na, *s. Lahui* and *aina,* land. The nations of many lands; spoken of collectively, the people of many countries.

La-hu-i-kau-a, *s. Lahui,* assemblage, and *kaua,* war. People assembled for war; warriors; a company of soldiers.

La-hu-i-ka-la, *s. La,* day, and *huikala,* to purify. A day for purification, in ancient religious ceremonies.

La-hu-i-ka-na-ka, *s. Lahui,* collection, and *kanaka,* people. A body of people collectively. *Oihk.* 18:24.

2. The people under one chief or king in distinction from those of another. *Kin.* 10:5. Collective bodies united in one people; a union of men, but under different chiefs; i mea e pono ai no na *lahuikanaka* o ko kakou pae aina; hence,

3. As in modern times, a nation; a people. 1 *Nal.* 18:10.

4. A people without a king; any multitude; he poe, he pae, he puu.

La-ka, *v.* To tame, as a wild animal; to feed to the full. *Hoo.* To bring under, as a ferocious beast; to render docile and obedient; to tame; to domesticate. *Iak.* 3:7.

La-ka, *adj.* Well fed; tame; domesticated; familiar; gentle; not ferocious; the opposite of *hihiu.*

La-ka, *s.* Domesticated or tamed animals.

2. The name of a species of bird, perhaps; kani ka *laka.*

La-ka-ka-ne, *s.* The name of a god; the god of dances; he akua no ka poe hula.

La-ka-la-ka, *v.* See Laka. *Hoo.* To tame; to domesticate; e hoopau i ka noho hihiu ana.

La-ke-e, *v.* To coil up, as a snake or centipede; to double over; to bend, as a flexible substance.

La-ke-e, *adj.* Bent; crooked; doubled over.

La-ke-ke, *s.* The Hawaiian pronunciation of the English jacket. A roundabout.

La-ke-we, *s.* See Lakee. Anything flexible; easily bending.

2. A person leaning or bending from weakness or disease.

La-ko, *v.* To possess what is necessary for any purpose; to be supplied with requisite means of doing a thing; to be supplied with; to have a sufficiency; eia na kanaka i *lako* i kela mau mea; to be fitted out or furnished with what is requisite for use or ornament, as the works of nature; ua *lakoia* ka honua nei i ka mauna, i ka awaawa, i ka pohaku, &c.

2. *Hoo.* To provide a supply for the needy. *Hal.* 146:9. To supply a competency for a living. 1 *Tim.* 5:8. Aole ke alii i ike i na mea i *hoolakoia* nei, the king did not know what things *were provided* here.

3. To be endowed; to be furnished; to be supplied. *Kanl.* 28:11.

4. To supply what is wanting.

La-ko, *s.* A supply; a fullness; a sufficiency.

La-ko, *adj.* Rich; prosperous; completely furnished with every necessary convenience.

La-ko, *s.* For *lauko.* The leaf of the sugar-cane.

La-kou, *pers. pron.* The third person plural of the personal pronouns. They; used mostly of persons. *Gram.* § 122 and § 139, 3.

La-ko-la-ko, *v.* See Lako. To enrich, &c. *Hoo.* To furnish; to provide for, as for family use, or for any occasion. *Mat.* 12:54.

La-ku-a, *v.* See Laukua. To put together words incongruously; to talk foolishly and wisely, properly and improperly at once; ua lauwili, ua hoi hope, ua *lakua,* ua hopu hewa.

La-la, *v.* To begin a piece of work or a job.

2. To draw the outline of a piece of land desired; to mark out the plan or lines of what is to be done.

3. To set a copy for writing, as a teacher.

4. To make straight; to straighten, as a stick or timber that is sprung.

5. See La, sun. To bask in the sunshine.

6. To be hot, as the sun.

La-la, *s.* The limb or branch of a tree; *lala* laau, branches of trees.

2. A limb of the human or animal frame.

3. The shining or glazing of varnish on leather.

4. The four corners of a house.

5. A species of potato bearing its fruit on the leaves. See Alala.

La-la, *adj.* For *laa, l* inserted. See

LAA. Consecrated; set apart for a particular purpose; kala *lala*, money given for pious uses; aole oia i hookoe i kekahi mea me ka *lala* ole, he did not keep back from consecration.

LA-LA-AU, *s.* A grove of bushes. See LAALAAU.

LA-LA-AU, *adj.* Bad; spoiled; rotten; applied to eggs.

LA-LAU, *v.* To extend out, as the hand; to lay one's hand on a thing; e *lalau* wale iho no.
2. To seize; to catch hold of. *Puk.* 4:4. To take out of or from. *Oihk.* 5:12.
3. To undertake on one's own account.
4. To wander; to err; to go out of the right way; hele hewa.
5. To err. *Nah.* 15:22. SYN. with hana hewa naaupo. To mistake; to make a blunder. *Mat.* 22:29. To act carelessly; to be inattentive.
6. To wander about a gossip. 1 *Tim.* 5:13.
7. To take without liberty; e lalau wale.
8. To turn aside from right. 1 *Nal.* 9:9. To err in heart. *Heb.* 3:10. *Lalau* no na lima i ka hewa me ka makau ole, the hands indeed *seized* upon wickedness without fear.

LA-LAU, *s.* A mistake; an error; a blunder. *Iob.* 19:4. *Hoo.* A leading astray; a causing to err (morally.) *Isa.* 3:12.

LA-LAU, *adj.* Seizing; catching up things, as a child; mischievous; wicked; violating good morals; dispersed; scattered.

LA-LAU-HE-WA, *s.* *Lalau* and *hewa*, wrong. The practice or indulgence in sin generally.

LA-LAU-WA-LE, *s.* *Lalau* and *wale*, only. The doing that which is contrary to reason or has no reason; foolishness.

LA-LA-HAI, *v.* See LAHAI and LAHALA-HAI. To hover over, &c.

LA-LA-HA-LA-HA, *v.* To rise and swell and move along, as the surf before it breaks. See HOOKAHELA.

LA-LA-HE-LA, *s.* Idleness; living long in the practice of vice.

LA-LA-HI, *v.* To be thin, &c. See LAHI.

LA-LA-HU, *adj.* *Lala* and *hu*, to rise up. Convex; swelling out, as a bone set crookedly.

LA-LA-KE-A, *s.* A species of fish; a kind of shark.

LA-LA-LA-AU, *s.* *Lala*, branch, limb, and *laau*, tree. A branch or limb of a tree.
2. Herbs; herbage; green bushes, &c. *Isa.* 42:15. See LAALAAU.

LA-LA-MA, *v.* To meddle with one's work, or business, or tools.
2. To feel about the sides of a thatched house, or under the edges of a mat to find some little thing to steal; to pilfer some article of small value.

LA-LA-MA, *s.* A looking here and there for something; a pilfering; a taking secretly.

LA-LA-MA, *adj.* Meddlesome; looking into other people's business.

LA-LA-NA, *v.* To warm, as by a fire. *Mar.* 14:54.

LA-LA-NA, *s.* Name of some small animal or insect, perhaps a species of spider.

LA-LA-NI, *v.* To lead or go along in Indian file; to be put in rows; to stand in rows or ranks.

LA-LA-NI, *s.* A row, as of trees; a rank, as of soldiers; a line or column of words; a row of corn. *Oihk.* 24:6.

LA-LA-NI, *adv.* In rows; by columns; in ranks.

LA-LA-NI-PUU, *s.* Name of hillocks or small hills when they stand in a row; also called *paepuu.*

LA-LA-PA, *v.* To blaze, as a fire. *Hoo.* To burn, as fire in a blaze. See LAPALAPA.

LA-LA-WA-HI, *adj.* Dark colored; black; the deepest, most intense blackness; pouli.

LA-LA-WE, *v.* See LAWE, to take. To take something from another; to take out of.
2. To pinch; to get hold of to remove.
3. To scratch where it itches; to feel the sensation of itching.

LA-LE, *v.* To urge on; to hurry; to stir up; to constrain one to do a thing quickly.
2. *Hoo.* To hasten another forward; to hasten to meet one; to hurry; *hoolale* mai la ka poalima hai manoa ia'u. FIG. E *hoolale* ana i na waimaka o kela mea keia mea.

LA-LE, *s.* Name of a species of bird.

LA-LE-A, *s.* A buoy; a floating guide to one entering a harbor; a beacon to steer by. See MOUO.

LA-LEI, *s.* A bunch or cluster of things, as grapes. See KAULALEI.

LA-LE-LA-LE, *v.* See LALE. To hasten. *Iob.* 31:5. To hurry; to be quick in doing a thing. 1 *Sam.* 25:18. *Hoo.* To hasten another. *Kin.* 19:15. To be forward; to hasten to meet one; to hurry. *Eset.* 3:15.

LA-LE-LA-LE, *s.* Haste; hurry in doing a thing. *Kanl.* 16:3.

LA-LI, *adj.* Greasy, as the face or hands in eating pork; fat; shining with grease.

LA-LII, *v.* To prepare; to make ready.

LA-LII, *adj.* A word distinguishing several kinds of the opule, a species of fish;

as, opule *lalii*, opule *makole*, opule *lauli*, opule *eleele*, &c.

LA-LI-LA-LI, *adj.* Wet; moist with water; wet and cold; koekoe.

LA-LO, *adv.* Down; downwards; usually with the prefixes *i, o, no, ko, ma* and *mai. Gram.* § 165, 2d class. *Lalo* is also found among the compound prepositions. See Grammar § 161. As an adverb, *mai lalo mai*, out from under. 2 *Nal.* 13:5.

LA-LO, *adj.* That which is down; low; base; very low in character; ka poe *lalo* loa. 1 *Kor.* 4:9. Na kanaka *lalo* loa, the basest of men. *Dan.* 4:17. See LUNA, *adv.*

LA-LO-A, *adj.* Lengthy. See LOLOA. He *laloa* no kamalii.

LA-LO-LA-LO, *adj.* See LALO, *adj.* Low down; short; very low.

LA-LO-LA-LO, *adj.* Epithet of a rich influential person, but not a chief; o ke kanaka waiwai a ai aina paha, he alii *lalolalo* ia; a chief by influence and character, but not by birth; aole loaa na 'lii *lalolalo.*

LA-LO-WAI-A, *s.* Ancient history in distinction from modern; an account of events in very ancient times, before Umi.

LA-MA, *s.* The name of a species of forest tree of very hard wood, used in building houses for the gods.

2. A torch; a light by night made of any materials, but mostly from the nuts of the kukui tree; a light. *Lunk.* 7:20. A lamp. 2 *Oihl.* 4:20. Connected with *ipu kukui.* A torch. *Lunk.* 15:5. He pulama, he aulama, he kalikukui i aulamaia.

LA-MA-KU, *s. Lama* and *ku*, to stand. A large torch for giving light in darkness; a torch of kukui nuts; a lamp. *Lunk.* 7:16. Sparks of fire. *Isa.* 50:11. A fire-brand; momoku ahi. NOTE.—The *lamakus* were made by stringing the meats of roasted kukui nuts on a wiry stalk of grass and putting six, eight or ten of these strings together parallel, and binding the whole together with dry banana leaves, the whole forming a cylinder from three to six inches in diameter and from two to four feet in length, and on lighting one end, it produced a large and brilliant light, and also much smoke.

LA-MA-LA-MA, *s.* Many lights; much light. See LAMA. He *lamalama* ke kino o ka mea ai uala.

LA-MU-MA-O-MA-O, *s.* A word used in the ancient prayers praying that a heiau might be built and sacrifices offered; koia ka ohia i kai i laau no ka *lamumaomao* a i laau kii

kekahi.

LA-NA, *v.* To float; to swim on the surface of water. 2 *Nal.* 6:6.

2. *Hoo.* To cause to swim; to bear up, as water does a vessel, that is, to cause to float. *Kin.* 7:17.

3. To float or swim in the air; e *hoolana* kou uhane i ke ao, to cause your soul to *float* into the skies.

4. FIG. With *manao*, to have hope; to be confident; with *manao* dropped, e *hoolana* oukou, be cheerful; be of good courage. *Mat.* 14:27.

LA-NA, *s.* The carriage or bearing of a person; the countenance. *Isa.* 2:11. Hence, *lanahaakei.* See HAAKEI.

LA-NA, *adj.* Buoyant; floating; mama.

LA-NA-AU, *v. Lana*, to float, and *au*, current. To float carelessly in the current. See NANAAU.

LA-NAI, *s.* A bower; a shed; a piazza; a porch. *Ezek.* 40:7. A booth. *Iona* 4:5.

2. Name of one of the Hawaiian Islands west of Maui.

3. A pain or swelling on the back; a humpbacked person. See NANAI. NOTE.— The hump gives name to the island.

LA-NAI-A, *v.* See NANA. to see. To see; to behold; to look.

2. To walk in a wriggling manner with self approbation.

LA-NAI-E-A, *s.* The appearance of a person when dying, sight gone, chin fallen, &c.; pinanai, pinanaiea.

LA-NAU, *v.* To be bitter against; to rail at; to have no friendship for; to act the misanthrope. See NANAU.

LA-NA-HAA-KEI, *s. Lana*, the bearing of a person, and *haakei*, pride. Pride; haughtiness in conduct and treatment of others. *Isa.* 3:16. LIT. Proud bearing.

LA-NA-HU, *s.* A coal; charcoal. *Oihk.* 16:12. Collectively, coals of fire; *lanahu* ahi. 2 *Sam.* 14:7. *Figuratively* for the remnant of life. The word is more properly written *nanahu.*

LA-NA-HU-A, *s.* Some part of a heiau.

LA-NA-HU-A, *adj.* Bent in; crooked; pressed down.

LA-NA-KE-A, *s.* A general weakness of the system; sick; hence,

2. Paleness; whiteness from long sickness; also written *nanakea.*

LA-NA-KI-LA, *v. Lana* and *kila*, strong; able. To be too strong for another party.

2. To come off victorious in a contest; to conquer. *Puk.* 15:21. To prevail over

an opposing party. 1 *Nal.* 16:22.

3. To hold dominion over.

4. *Hoo.* FIG. To be victorious, &c. *Hal.* 98:1. NOTE.—This word applies only to war and not to single combat.

LA-NA-KI-LA, *s.* *Lana* and *kila,* a very strong man. One who is powerful in physical strength; a conqueror; a brave soldier.

LA-NA-KI-LA, *adj.* Conquering; prevailing; overcoming.

LA-NA-LA-NA, *s.* See LANA. A rope with which the ama and the iako of a canoe are tied; ka luikia i ka iako, ame ka *lanalana* i ka ama; also the name of the string with which the ancient kois were tied on to the handles.

2. The name of a large brown spider which stands high on its legs. *Isa.* 59:5.

3. An image; an idol.

LA-NA-LA-NA, *v.* See LANA. To make light; the opposite of heavy; e hoomama; to cause to float; to be buoyant.

LA-NA-NA, *v.* To strain, as a liquid.

LA-NA-NUU, *s.* *Lana* and *nuu,* a step; a rise. A high stage in the frame where the idols of the heiau stood.

2. One of the gods out of the heiau.

LA-NA-NUU-MA-MAO, *s.* See LANANUU 2. Name of one of the gods which stood outside of the heiau; ma ka hikina ka *lananuumamao.*

LA-NI, *s.* The upper air; the sky. *Kin.* 1:15. The visible heavens; kahi i kau nei na hoku; na ao o ka *lani,* the clouds of heaven; na manu o ka *lani,* the fowls of heaven; equivalent to na manu o ka *lewa.*

2. Heaven; a holy place. *Kanl.* 26:15. Anything high up *literally* or by dignity of character; haui ka *lani,* ke alii kiekie.

3. The title of a high chief when addressed by a subject; equivalent to *your highness;* also when spoken of by a subject; as, *e ka lani,* ke hai aku nei au ia oe i na mea a kou makuakane, *your highness,* I declare to you the decisions of your father. See also meles and e ka *lani* o na *lani,* ke ae aku nei wau ma kau noi e kuu *lani. Laieik.* 197. This is like Chinese adulation.

LA-NI, *adj.* Heavenly; pertaining to the sky.

2. Heavenly; ano *lani,* having a heavenly or holy character; o ka imi anei ia i ka pono ano *lani?* is that seeking righteousness of a *heavenly character?*

LA-NI-A, *v.* To warm, as a person warms himself by a fire.

LA-NI-HI-NI-HI, *adj.* See NIHI and NIHI-NIHI. Narrow in opposition to broad; narrow; as a wheel; thin.

LA-NI-KAE, *s.* Name of the people who ate with the chief at sundown; ma ka napoo ana o ka la, o ka poe i komo mai e ai ana me ke alii. ua kapaia he *lanikae.*

LA-NI-KAE, *s.* The name of the kalaimoku when there is only one chief.

LA-NI-KU-A-KAA, *s.* The highest heaven; nothing beyond. *Laieik.* 194.

LA-NI-LA-NI, *v.* See LANI. To be highminded; to act chiefishly.

2. To be proud; to show haughtiness.

3. *Hoo.* To exercise authority. *Mark* 10:42, Same as *hooalii* and *hookiekie.*

LA-NI-PI-LI, *s.* *Lani,* sky, and *pili,* to adhere to. The place where the sky appears to touch the earth. LIT. The touching of sky and earth.

2. The clouds as they appear to touch the horizon.

LA-NI-PI-LI, *adj.* Touching the heavens; he ua *lanipili,* a shower reaching to heaven, i. e., a very heavy shower.

LA-NI-PO, *s.* An expression of admiration at a garden or field where vegetables are thrifty and produce a shade over the ground; o kahihi la *lanipo* o Waiku ka pawa.

LA-NUU, *s.* See LANANUU. Name of one of the gods outside of the heiau; o ka hakumaka o ka *lanuu.*

LA-PA, *s.* A ridge between two depressions; a ridge of land between two ravines. See OLAPA.

2. The steep side of a ravine.

3. A swelling. SYN. with pehu.

4. The name of some parts of the organs of generation in females.

5. The name of an instrument made of bamboo used in infanticide, before or at the birth of a child; he mea hou; a piercing thing; he ohe hapai i ke keiki.

6. A species of red potato.

7. The bamboo on which were cut various figures, used by women in printing kapa.

8. *Ardens femina coitus.* See the verb.

LA-PA, *adj.* Having a flat or square side; e kalai a *lapa,* hew one side.

2. Squared, as a hewed stick of timber; kalai a *lapalapa,* hew all sides *flat* or *square.* NOTE.—Hewing three or four sides of a stick of timber brings out the ridges or corners.

3. Troublesome, as a child in the way; uneasy; disobedient; mischievous.

LA-PA, *v.* To desire sexual intercouse (applied to the female); ia ia e *lapa* kane ai. *Ier.* 2:24.

2. To jump and spring about as a wild colt or a calf that is tied.

LA-PA-AU, *v.* To administer medicine.

2. To heal; to cure. *Ezek.* 34:4. SYN. with hooikaika i ka nawaliwali.

LA-PA-AU, *s.* That which is used in curing diseases, medicine.

LA-PAU-E-A, *s.* The state or condition of old age; the trembling or feebleness or old age.

LA-PAU-I-LA, *s.* The side posts of a door frame. *Isa.* 57:8. He mau kunakuna o ka puka hale. LIT. The spread of a door frame. *Puk.* 12:17.

LA-PA-LA-PA, *v.* See LAPA. To rise or stand up, as water bubbles up in boiling; to protrude upwards; hence,

2. To boil in water; to seethe.

3. To blaze, as a fire in materials highly combustible, i. e., to project or protrude upwards, as a flame; hence, to blaze up, as a fire.

4. *Hoo.* To boil; to cook by boiling.

LA-PA-LA-PA, *s.* A ridge of earth; a sharp ridge between two valleys. *Hal.* 65:10. Generally written *olapalapa*.

2. The blaze of fire; the flame. *Puk.* 3:2. The straight blaze of fire from an altar. *Lunk.* 13:20.

3. The flashing of a flame of fire.

4. The boiling or bubbling of a liquid in a vessel.

5. A square yard for cattle.

6. Timber hewed square or triangular.

7. A square glass bottle.

8. Several hillocks or mounds near each other.

9. The name of a large elegant tree with wide spreading branches; peculiar serrate leaves and light glossy green; found on the sides of Waialeale on Kauai.

LA-PA-LA-PA, *adj.* Flat or square, i. e., where the corners are prominent, either square or triangular.

LA-PA-WAI, *s.* *Lapa* and *wai*, water. The surf or rolling up of water where a cascade pours down.

2. The agitation where two forces of water meet; the meeting of the sea with the waters of a river.

LA-PEE, *v.* To bend over; to double up; to crook. See LAKEE and LAPUU.

LA-PI-KA, *s.* A Hawaiian but vicious orthography for *rabita. Eng.* A rabbit.

LA-PU, *v.* To appear, as a ghost or spirit, especially at night. *Hoo.* To cause a spirit to appear to one.

LA-PU, *s.* An apparition; a ghost; the appearance of the supposed spirit of a deceased person. *Hal.* 88:10. Na mea *lapu*, the ghosts; the dead. *Isa.* 34:14. A o kou inoa, he *Lapu*, a o kau mea e ai ai, o na pulelehua, thy name shall be Ghost (*Lapu*), thy food the butterflies (the judgement against Kaonohiokala for his crimes.)

2. A night monster.

LA-PU, *adj.* Spectral; ghostly; akua *lapu*, a specter; an apparition of a god.

LA-PU-IA, *v.* The passive of *lapu*. To be visited by a ghost; to have seen a ghost.

2. To search for something in the mud or in places of filth.

3. To be possessed of a spirit.

LA-PUU, *v.* See PUU, a heap. To coil up in a circle.

2. To bend or double over; to crook; nanaia iho la, ua *lapuu* ka welau o ke alelo iloko.

3. To hump up; to swell out like a hump-backed person. See HOOKOLO, also PUU.

LA-PUU, *adj.* Bunched or swelled out; o ke aalele lapuu.

LA-PU-LA-PU, *v.* To collect together in little heaps; to pick up, as small sticks for fuel. *Oih.* 28:3. To bind or tie up small substances into bundles or fagots for fuel. See LAOLAO.

2. To feel of; to handle over; to tie up.

LA-PU-WA-LE, *v.* *Lapu*, ghost, and *wale*, only. To be only a ghost; to be not real; to be something not according to appearance; hence,

2. To be disappointed; kii aku o Maewa i ka wai, aole i loaa, hoi mai, a olelo iho la, ka! *lapuwale* i ka wai ole.

3. *Hoo.* To disappoint, as one's expectations. *Hal.* 17:13. To stultify one's wisdom. *Isa.* 44:25. Hence,

4. To act foolishly; e hana ma ka mea ino.

LA-PU-WA-LE, *s.* LIT. A ghost of a thing; nothing substantial.

2. Vanity. *Kekah.* 1:1. That which in appearance or imagination is something, but in reality is nothing; mea *lapuwale*, folly; foolishness; wickedness. *Ios.* 7:15.

LA-PU-WA-LE, *adj.* Foolish; worthless; contemptible. *Iob.* 13:4. Void of truth and reality in action; he mea oiaio ole ma ka hana.

LA-WA, *v.* To work out even to the edge or boundary of a land, i. e., to leave none uncultivated.

2. To fill a container up to the brim; hence,

3. To suffice; to be enough. *Puk.* 36:7.

To satisfy.

4. *Passively*, to be satisfied; to have enough. *Ioh.* 6:7.

5. *Hoo.* To supply what is wanting. 1 *Tes.* 3:10.

6. To fulfill, as a task; to complete, as a job. *Puk.* 5:13.

LA-WA, *s.* The full finishing of a work.

2. The filling up of a vessel or container to the brim.

3. An enough; a sufficiency; a supply.

4. The name of a disease concerning which it is said, paapu ka opu i na iwi aoao.

5. A white fowl; he moa keokeo; such as was offered in sacrifice. *Laieik.* 49.

6. Name of a hook for catching sharks; he *lawa* ka makau mano.

7. The name of an office in the king's train.

LA-WA, *adj.* Sufficient; enough.

2. Full to the brim.

3. White; shining; he moa *lawa*, a white fowl. *Laieik.* 14.

LA-WA-AE-AE, *s.* Name of a white fowl, especially a cock; ka *lawaaeae* ka nono paa.

LA-WA-IA, *v.* *Lawa* for *lawe*, to take, and *ia*, fish. To catch fish, i. e., to exercise the calling of a fisherman, by understanding the places and times of the appearance of different kinds of fish and the art of taking them; in more modern time the word was applied also to the taking of birds. See LAWAIAMANU.

LA-WA-IA, *s.* A fisherman; one skilled in catching fish, and whose occupation it is. *Mat.* 4:18.

2. A fishing; the business of taking fish. *Ier.* 16:16. NOTE.—The art of catching fish was anciently cultivated among Hawaiians to a great extent, and those who followed it as a business became very expert; but the introduction of cattle, goats, &c., has rendered fishing less necessary at present.

3. The cormorant, a bird that feeds on fish; an unclean bird. *Oihk.* 11:17.

LA-WA-IA-MA-NU, *s.* See LAWAIA, *v.*, and MANU, a bird. A hunter and catcher of birds; a fowler. *Hal.* 124:7. NOTE.—Catching birds was formerly practiced to a great extent on the mountainous parts of the islands.

LA-WA-KE-A, *s.* A white cock. See LA-WAAEAE.

2. People who dress in large white flowing kapas; me I ka uwe hoouwe a ka *lawakea*.

LA-WA-KU-A, *v.* *Lawa* and *kua*, back. To bind or tie fast on the back; to bind tightly; to make fast; e lawalawa, e hoa paa loa. See LAWALAWA below.

LA-WA-KU-A-IA, *v.* Passive of *lawakua*. See LAWALAWA 3.

LA-WA-LA-WA, *v.* See LAWA, to hold fast; to bind tightly. To bind, as a grass house or anything in danger of floating or being blown away by the wind; e lawa-lawa i ka hale a paa.

2. To stretch cords from one place to another to fasten something.

3. To bind round and make fast; e lawa-lawa i ka ukana ma ka waa. NOTE.—The force of this word and *lawakua* consists in the completeness with which the fastening is done, as we say, *do it up all snug.*

LA-WA-LU, *v.* To cook meat on the coals inclosed in ki leaves; e koala, e hoomoa me ka laui.

LA-WA-LU, *s.* Meat roasted on the coals bound up in ki leaves.

LA-WA-LU, *adj.* Cooked, as meat or fish. See above. Hoomanao ae la lakou i na wahine a lakou, i na ia *lawalu*, i ka poi, &c., they remembered their wives, their *cooked* fish, their poi, &c.

LA-WE, *v.* The passive is often written *lawea* instead of *laweia*. To take; *particularly*, to take and carry in the hand.

2. To transfer from one place to another.

3. To take away from, or out of.

4. To carry in any way.

5. To take, as a wife, i. e., to marry; e *lawe* i ka wahine. *Nah.* 12:1.

6. *Hoo.* To take out of, a smaller number from a larger, as in subtraction. SYN. with unuhi.

LA-WE-A, *v.* To do well; to do correctly; to be upright in dealing; e hana maikai, e hana pono.

LA-WEA, *v.* Passive of *lawe* for *laweia*. See LAWE.

LA-WE-O-LA, *v.* *Lawe* and *ola*, living. To take alive; to carry alive.

LA-WE-O-LE-LO, *s.* A tale bearer; reporting stories to the injury of others.

LA-WE-HA-LA, *v.* *Lawe* and *hala*, an offense. To carry or bear guilt, i. e., to commit an offense.

2. To sin; to sin against one. *Puk.* 20:17. To transgress, by taking a forbidden object. *Ios.* 7:11. To trespass.

3. *Hoo.* To find occasion against one. *Kin.* 43:18. To cause one to appear guilty.

4. To be overtaken in a fault; e loohia ma na mea ino.

LA-WE-HA-LA, *s.* One bearing sin; an open transgressor of the law.

2. The indulgence of sin; the practice of evil.

3. One that breaks an obligation or covenant; one overtaken in the commission of evil.

4. Abstractly, sin; evil; a sinner; an adversary; an enemy.

5. The person against whom one has sinned.

LA-WE-HA-LA, *adj.* Sin-carrying; sinful; doing that which is forbidden.

LA-WE-HA-NA, *v. Lawe* and *hana*, work. To engage in business; to commence and carry on work; to be ready for any business; to be industriously engaged.

LA-WE-HA-NA, *s.* One that engages in work; a workman; a laborer; one engaged in any set of duties. 1 *Oihl.* 25:1. Hoa *lawehana*, a helper in any business.

LA-WE-KA-HI-LI, *s. Lawe* and *kahili*, the great brush. The badge of royalty.

2. The person who attended the high chief, carried the kahili, and executed his orders. See ILAMUKU, IWIKUAMOO and POELAMUKU.

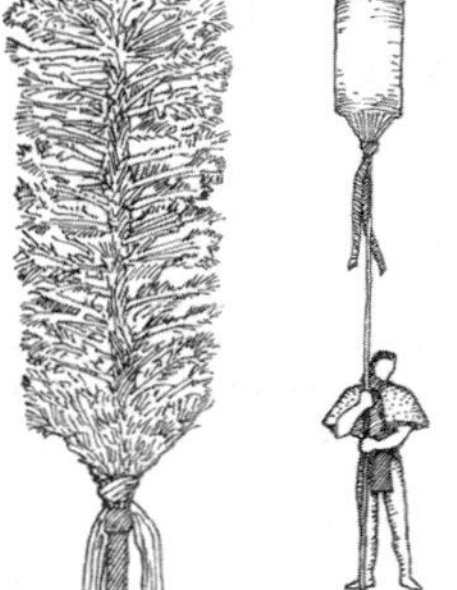
lawekahili

LA-WE-KE-O,
LA-WE-LA-WE-KE-O, } *s.* The song of a species of bird found on Molokai; kani mai la ua manu la, penei: kioea, koiea, *lawekeo, lawelawekeo.*

LA-WE-LA-WE, *v.* Freq. of *lawe.* To take or carry frequently.

2. To wait upon at table, as a servant in attendance.

3. To serve; to perform the duties of a station. *Puk.* 28:1.

4. To minister to one; to serve. *Puk.* 28:3. To be busy; to employ one's self. *Ezek.* 27:16.

5. To handle; to feel of. *Luk.* 24:39. To handle, as in turning the leaves of a book; to handle, as in using musical instruments.

LA-WE-LA-WE, *adj.* Pertaining to work, service or office; ka poe *lawelawe*, servants, waiters, &c.

LA-WE-LA-WE-I-WI, *adj. Lawelawe* and *iwi*, a bone. Skillful in putting things in order; skillful or apt at different kinds of work; *lawelaweiwi* o kana hana ana.

LA-WE-LU-A, *v. Lawe* and *lua*, double. To bind or tie up the second time; hence, to bind tightly; e hawelelua a paa.

2. To act in reference to both sides of the question; to act impartially.

LA-WE-PI-O, *v. Lawe* and *pio*, prisoner. To take captive by a conqueror; to carry off, as a prisoner. *Ier.* 29:14. To carry into captivity.

LA-WE-PI-O-IA, *s.* Part. pass. of *lawepio.* The state of being a prisoner; captivity. *Ier.* 29:14.

LA-WE-WA-LE, *v. Lawe* and *wale*, without reason. To take without leave or right; to extort property from one.

LA-WE-WA-LE, *s.* The taking the property of another; as a chief or head man in former times; not strictly *aihue*, as the *taking* might be with the knowledge of the owner; a distraining property; extortion.

LA-WE-WE, *v.* The 9th conj. of *lawe.* To carry frequently. *Gram.* § 209.

LA-RU, *s.* The cuckoo, mentioned in *Kanl.* 14:15; an unclean bird.

LA-TI-KE, *s.* Nets; lattice work. 1 *Nal.* 7:17.

2. A chapter in architecture perhaps. 2 *Oihl.* 4:12.

LE-A, *v.* To be pleased; to feel comfortable.

2. To delight in; to be pleased with; to take pleasure in a thing; to enjoy; e *lea* auanei au i ka hiamoe, I shall soon *enjoy* sleep.

3. *Hoo.* To praise, especially in song and with musical instruments. 1 *Oihl.* 23:5.

4. To make music; to praise; to rejoice in.

5. *Impersonal,* i *lea* ia oe, if you please; if it pleases you.

LE-A, *s.* Joy; gladness; pleasure; merriment; satisfaction.

LE'A, *s.* Pronounced with a break. Name of sexual gratification.

LE-A, *adj.* Pleasing; delightful; agreeable.

LE-A, *adv.* Pleasantly; agreeably.

2. *Lea* is used as an intensive; thus, perfectly; clearly; thoroughly; very; as, maa *lea*, much accustomed; moa *lea*, *thoroughly* cooked; ike *lea*, *well* known.

LE-A-LE-A, *v.* The intensive of *lea.* To delight in; to be pleased with. *Eset.* 2:4. FIG. To play, as in a game of boxing. *Laieik.* 46.

2. To be merry; to be exhilarated; spoken of the heart. *Lunk.* 16:25.

3. To be satisfied; to be contented. 2 *Nal.* 5:22.

4. *Hoo.* To praise; to rejoice; to sympathize with; to comfort; to make friends with one.

5. To negotiate terms of peace. *Ios.* 11:19.

6. To flatter; to please. *Epes.* 6:6.

LE-A-LE-A, *s.* Gladness; pleasure; joy. See LEA.

LE-A-LE-A, *adj.* Pleasing; agreeable, &c. See LEA.

LEE-NI-HI, *s.* A species of fish, reddish and striped.

LEI, *v.* To put around the neck, as a wreath; to tie on, as one's beads. See the substantive. To put on an ensign or badge, as an officer in battle; ma ka la kaua, *lei* no ke alii i ka niho palaoa.

2. To rise up, as a cloud; to lift up. PASS. To be lifted or raised up, as a cloud. *Nah.* 10:11.

3. *Hoo.* To cast out; to cast off; to fling away from; to reject as useless; to throw or cast down upon the ground. *Puk.* 4:3.

4. To put on one, as a crown; to crown. PASS. To wear, as a crown.

5. To put on shore, as freight from a ship; aole lakou i *hoolei* mua i ka lakou ukana, they did not at first put their goods on shore.

6. To cast out, as out of the mouth; to belch, i. e., to talk profanely. *Hal.* 59:7.

7. To defile; to profane.

8. To lie down; to fall at full length; to stretch out; to cast down.

LEI, *s.* Any ornamental dress for the head or neck.

1. A string of beads; a necklace; a wreath of green leaves or flowers.

2. A crown for the head. See LEIALII. *Lei* bipi, the bow of an ox yoke; the garland for crowning a god.

3. Any external ornamental work. *Puk.* 25:11. NOTE.—The *leis* of Hawaiians were made of a great many materials, but the lauhala nut was the most valued on account of its odoriferous qualities. See LEIHALA.

LEI-A-I, *s.* *Lei* and *a-i*, the neck. A wreath for the neck.

LEI-A-LII, *s.* *Lei* and *alii*, a chief. A crown, i. e., a king's lei. FIG. *Pilip.* 4:1. A diadem. *Isa.* 62:3. See PAPALEALII.

LEI-A-PI-KI,
LEI-A-LI-MA, } *s.* *Lei* with the qualifying words. Different sorts
LEI-PA-PA-HI, } of leis, or leis made from different materials.

LEI-O, *v.* To open the eyes with wildness.

LEI-O, *s.* The opening of the mouth to speak. See LEO.

LEI-O-A, *v.* The passive of *leio* for *leioia.* To be opened, as the eyes with wildness.

LEI-O-HA-NO, *s.* *Leio* for *leo*, and *hano*, hoarse. A voice, as one hoarse or having a cold.

LEI-O-LE, *s.* Name of a kind of soft stone.

LEI-O-WI, *s.* A kind of disease in the chest.

LEI-HA-LA, *s.* *Lei*, wreath, and *hala*, the pandanus. A lei made of the hala fruit, which is odoriferous; he *leihala* oe ma ka a-i o ka poe naauao, thou art a *hala wreath* on the neck of the wise.

LEI-HU-A, *s.* A plant; the globe amaranth; so named from the flowers, which are made into wreaths for the head.

LEI-HU-LU, *s.* A lei or wreath for the neck made of the feathers of the bird mamo; ka lei mamo no Laa.

2. Children beloved of their parents.

LEI-HU-LU-MA-NU, *s.* A wreath of bird's feathers tied to the necks of the gods.

LEI-LEI, *v.* Freq. of *lei.* Hoo. To scatter; to disperse frequently, as dirt. *Isa.* 57:20. To disperse, as a people. *Oihk.* 26:30. To scatter; to throw away. *Mat.* 12:30. Opposite to *hooiliili.*

LEI-LE-HO, *s.* *Lei* and *leho*, a shell. A string of the leholeho.

LEI-LI-MA, *s.* A species of lei; he lei-apiki. See LEIALIMA.

LEI-NA, *s.* For *lei ana.* Hoo. A throwing or casting away.

2. That which is thrown or cast away. *Dan.* 3:29.

LEI-PA-PA-HI, *s.* A kind of lei. See LEI-APIKI.

LE-O, *s.* A voice; a sound, mostly of a person or an animated being; hookahi pane ana a ka waha, he *leo* ia.

2. In *grammar*, a syllable.

3. In *music*, a tone.

4. FIG. The good or bad influence of conduct; o ka *leo* o ka pono ka'u e malama nei; o ka *leo* o ka hewa ka'u e kipaku nei.

5. The meaning or intention of an act. *Puk.* 4:18.

LE-O-UU, *s.* *Leo* and *uu*, to groan; to stammer. An impediment in speech; a stammering.

LE-O-U-WO, *s.* *Leo*, sound, and *uwo*, to bellow. To lowest notes in music; the name of the base notes.

LE-O-HA, *s.* The voice or speech of a person intoxicated.

LE-O-LA-NI, *adj.* High; lofty; tall, as a man; high, as the mast of a ship; he kia *leolani,* he kuahiwi *leolani,* he laau *leolani.*

LE-O-LE-O, *v.* To wail, as for the dead. See UWE.

LE-O-LE-O, *adj.* Tall; high; shooting upwards, as a tree; as a mountain; he kanaka *leoleo,* he laau *leoleo,* he hale *leoleo.* See LEOLANI.

LE-O-LE-O-A, } *v.* To wish evil; to
LE-O-LE-O-WA, } curse; to wish one dead; to make a great noise; to bawl in vociferous manner.

LE-O-LE-O-WA, *adj.* Wishing evil; cursing; he olelo *leoleowa,* an expression consigning one to death. See HOILOILO. He *leoleowa* ia i ko'u manao.

LEO-ME-LE, *s.* *Leo* and *mele,* a song. Musical sounds; music generally.

LE-O-PAA, *s.* *Leo* and *paa,* tight; fast. One whose voice is stopped with a cold.
2. A mute; a deaf person. *Isa.* 35:6.

LE-O-PA-DI, *s.* *Eng.* A leopard. *Ier.* 5:6.

LE-O-WAE-NA, *s.* *Leo* and *waena,* middle. The middle voice in music; a second treble.

LE-O-WA-HI-NE, *s.* *Leo* and *wahine,* a woman. In *music,* the highest voice; the air of a tune.

LE-U-WI, *s.* A word of canoe makers; the fore point of a canoe where the ends of the two boards come together; ina i palahalaha maluna o ka manuihu, he *leuwi* ia waa.

LE-HA, *v.* To turn the eyes different ways without turning the head.
2. To turn the eyes upward or askance.
3. To turn or lift up the eyes. *Kanl.* 4:19.
4. To direct the eyes toward any object; to turn the eyes to look; hence, to look with expectation. *2 Sam.* 22:42. To lift up the eyes, as in prayer. *John* 17:1. To lift up the eyes in admiration. *Dan.* 4:34.

LE-HAI, *v.* To jump; to leap; to jump over a thing, as a wall. *2 Sam.* 22:30. To start up suddenly, as a bird.

LE-HA-LE-HAI, *v.* See LEHAI. To jump on both feet; to jump often; e lelele.

LE-HE, *s.* Name of a shell fish.

LE-HEI, *v.* See LEHAI. To jump from an elevation, as a dog or goat from a wall.
2. To start up suddenly.

LE-HE-LE-HE, *adj.* Fat; plump; in good flesh. See NELUNELU.

LE-HE-LE-HE, *s.* The root *lehe* not found. The lips. *Kanl.* 23:24. I. e., synonymous with *waha*; put for the organs of speech generally.
2. The lip, i. e.. language; manner of speaking. *Kin.* 11:1. SYN. with olelo.
3. *Hoo.* Puukilea i ka hoolehelehe. See KILEA.

LE-HE-LE-HEI, *v.* Freq. of *lehei.* To hop or jump from twig to twig, as a little bird; to take short but frequent flights.

LE-HO, *s.* Name of a species of shell fish.
2. The shell itself.
3. A bunch or knotty swelling on the shoulder or back of a person like the *leho* (the shell of the fish *leho*), caused by long carrying heavy burdens; oia ke alii hilahila no ka *leho* no kona kokua i ke amo ana, he was the chief who was ashamed of the *bunch* (on his shoulder) from carrying burdens. NOTE.—This *leho* was frequently seen on the shoulders of laboring men as late as 1840.

LE-HO, *v.* To have knots or bunches on one's shoulders from carrying heavy burdens; a *leho* kana hokua i ke amo i ka wai ame kela mea keia mea.

LE-HO, *adj.* Swollen hard; as a small callous place on the skin; he kua *leho,* he a-i *leho.*

LE-HO-O-MA-O, *s.* *Leho* and *omao,* green. A species of leho of a green color.

LE-HO-U-LA, *s.* *Leho* and *ula,* red. A species of leho of a red color; a red shell fish.

LE-HO-U-LA, *adj.* See the above. Beautiful; precious; beautiful red; very precious, as the red-shelled leho.

LE-HO-LEI, *s.* A small white shell of the leho species, used for beads.

LE-HO-LE-HO, *s.* See LEILEHO. A small delicate shell fish of the leho kind, whitish, mixed with yellow and gray, used for leis for the wrist or neck; a string of small lehos.

LE-HO-LE-HO, *v.* To string lehos for leis.

LE-HO-LE-HO, *adj.* Knotted; swelled from carrying burdens. See LEHO 3.

LE-HO-PAA, *s.* A species of leho. See LEHO.

LE-HO-PO-U-LI, *s.* A variety of the leho.

LE-HU, *s.* Ashes. *Puk.* 9:8. Ka lepo o ke ahi; ke oka keokeo o ka lanahu.
2. The number 400,000 the highest in the Hawaiian series of numbers.

LE-HU, *v.* To be or become ashes; e puhi aku a *lehu,* to burn to ashes, i. e., to burn up. *2 Pet.* 2:6.

LE-HU-A, *s.* The name of a large rock or small island on the north-east of Niihau, which has a good spring of water and a fine cavern.
2. The name of a species of ohia, otherwise called the *ohia hamau*; metrosideros.

3. The blossom of the ohia and the lehua and the ahihi.

4. Flowers done up in bundles, as among foreign families; he pua lei mai kahiki mai.

5. Name of a species of kalo; also called *lehuakuikawao*.

6. The name of the first man slain in sacrifice on a particular occasion.

7. *Lehua* is used often figuratively for a person highly esteemed; as, kuu *lehua* ala o Koolau, my sweet-scented *lehua* (very dear friend) of Koolau.

LE-HU-A-A-PA-NE, *s.* A species of the ohia ai.

LE-HU-A-HA-MAU, *s.* A species of the ohia ha, on the blossoms of which the birds feed.

LE-HU-A-HI, *s.* *Lehu* and *ahi*, fire. The remnants of fire; ashes. *Iob.* 2:8.

LE-HU-A-KU-I-KA-WAO, *s.* A species of kalo.

LE-HU-U-LA, *s.* Dust and dirt when carried by the wind and appears reddish.

LE-HU-LE-HU, *v.* See LEHU. To grow exceedingly numerous; to become multitudinous. *Hoo.* To increase greatly in number and also in size; to magnify, as a convex glass; he aniani *hoolehulehu* maka ame na kino, a glass *magnifying* the face and the body.

LE-HU-LE-HU, *s.* A multitude; an indefinitely large number. *Kin.* 30:30. With the article *ka*, the multitude; the many. *Mat.* 24:12. A host; a great number; Iehova o na *lehulehu*, Jehovah of *hosts.* 1 *Sam.* 1:3.

LE-HU-LE-HU, *adj.* Many; numerous; ma kona mau ipuka *lehulehu* i komo aku ai ka hewa, through its *many* doors does evil enter in.

LE-HU-LI-U, *adj.* *Lehu* and *liu*, raging; wild. Hot, as stones in an oven heated to a white heat; *lehuliu* ka imu. See AHULIU.

LE-KA, *s.* *Eng.* A leek, an herb. *Nah.* 11:5.

LE-LE, *v.* To fly; to jump; to leap; to fly, as a bird; a ike aku la au i ka *lele* ana o ka manu.

2. To burst forth, as fire in a conflagration.

3. To move, as a meteor through the air.

4. To depart from one, as the spirit of a dying person; *lele* ke aho.

5. To come upon, as an officer upon a criminal; to fly or rush upon one, as an enemy. *Lunk.* 20:37.

6. To land or go ashore from a canoe or ship; a *lele* iuka lakou e makaikai, they *came ashore* to look about.

7. To brandish, as a sword.

8. *Haa.* for *hoo.* To leave; to forsake; to leave one place of residence or business for another.

9. To reject as not fit for use; *lele* liilii, to scatter; to disperse; to scatter entirely.

LE-LE, *s.* An altar for sacrifice; he wahi e kau ai i ka mohai kuni i ke kuahu.

LE-LE-A, *s.* The kapu which the priest imposed upon awa while the chief was drinking it.

LE-LE-A-A-KA, *v.* To hang; to suspend; to carry on the back as one carries a child or a load.

LE-LE-A-I-O-I-O, *s.* Name of the god who inflicted bodily pain, such as *nukee, oopa*, &c.

LE-LE-A-O-A, *s.* The act of sailing rapidly away in a canoe or ship to another land.

LE-LE-A-KA, *s.* The name of the white belt of stars in the heavens; the milky way; he ala waiu. See LELEIONA.

LE-LE-IO, *v.* *Lele* and *io*, really. To die quickly; to die suddenly.

LE-LE-I-O-MO, *v.* *Lele* and *iomo*, to plump into the water from a height. E poni, e omoki.

LE-LEI-O-NA, *s.* A fish; a shark.

2. The milky way. See LELEAKA.

LE-LE-I-NO, *v.* *Lele* and *ino*, bad. To be in an unquiet state, as the stomach from eating some kinds of food; e *leleino* auanei ka ai ma ka opu o ke kanaka.

LE-LE-OI, *v.* To be quick and ready to speak of one's faults; to say more than is true about one, especially of evil.

LE-LE-O-PE-A-PE-A, *s.* *Lele* and *opeapea*, a bat. To flutter, as birds in a fright.

LE-LE-U, *s.* Name of a fruit tree; also, name of the fruit.

2. Name of the bird which eats the *leleu*; o ka manu ai *leleu*.

LE-LE-U-LI, } *v.* To cleanse; to purify.
LE-LE-U-U-LI, }   2. To pardon; a nana no e *leleuli* lelewai mai i ko kakou hewa, 'tis his to *wash* away our sins.

LE-LE-HA, *v.* To be sleepy; to be drowsy; to be lazy; to be stupid. *Hoo.* The same. See LELEHU.

LE-LE-HA-PA-HA, *adj.* *Lele*, to skip over, and *hapaha*, by fours. Counting by fours; skipping four in counting; in *music*, leaping over four places; leaping to the minor fourth.

LE-LE-HOO-HAA-HAA, *s.* The female goddess of Leleaioio. See above.

LE-LE-HOO-LA-HA-LA-HA, *s.* To fly or float over one's head, as a large bird with out-spread wings; e lele i ka imo o ka lani.

LE-LE-HU, *v.* To see with difficulty; to be partially blind.

2. To be almost dead; to be weak; to be faint.

3. To be sleepy or drowsy. See HOOLELEHU.

LE-LE-HU-A, *adj.* Skillful; able to apply the mental powers. See MIKOLELEHUA.

LE-LE-HU-NA, *v.* *Lele* and *huna*, a small particle. To fly into small pieces; to scatter, as fine particles; to become fine, as dust or fine rain; mukiki ka ia lele a ka manu.

LE-LE-HU-NA, *s.* Small, fine rain; he kilihuna; small particles of food.

LE-LE-KA-HA-U-LI, *s.* *Lele* and *hauli*, a black spot. Surprise; admiration; fear; a trembling through fear.

LE-LE-KA-WA, *v.* *Lele* and *kawa*, a precipice. To jump or leap down a precipice (a method of committing suicide.)
2. To jump into the sea from an elevation, a pastime among Hawaiians; e lehaikawa, e hana lealea me ka lele ana mai ka pali mai ilalo o ka wai.

LE-LE-KA-WA, *s.* The act of jumping from a precipice on purpose to destroy life, or of jumping a precipice into the sea as a pastime.
2. The place or precipice where such jumping takes place; hele aku la lakou a hiki ma kahakai, he wahi *lelekawa* ia.

LE-LE-KO-A-LI, *s.* The name of a play.

LE-LE-KO-KE, *adj.* *Lele* and *koke*, quick. Flying quickly in a passion; quick angry; excitable.

LE-LE-KO-LU, *s.* In *music*, a skip of a third; a third.

LE-LE-KO-LU-HA-PA, *s.* In *music*, a minor third.

LE-LE-LE, *v.* Freq. of *lele*. To leap; to jump; to fly frequently. *Isa.* 35:6. See LELE.
2. To light on something above.
3. *Hoo.* To cause to skip or jump. *Hal.* 29:6.
4. To be agitated, as the mind with joy or fear. *Isa.* 60:5.

LE-LE-LE-LE, *v.* See LELE, root doubled. To run off; to run off in haste; to run off frequently or for a trifling offense, as a servant.
2. To forsake frequently, as a man his wife, or a wife her husband; lelelele maua i ke kula o Pele, we two *hastened away* to the plain of Pele.

LE-LE-LE-LE-KO-KE, *v.* See LELE and KOKE, quick. To forsake quickly for a trifling offense. See LELEKOKE.

LE-LE-LE-PO-NI, *s.* *Lele* and *poni*, cold; shivering with cold. A sudden dying; one struck suddenly dead.
2. Anything done suddenly; no time lost; no postponement.

LE-LE-LI-MA-HA-PA, *s.* *Lele* and *lima*, five, and *hapa*, part. In *music*, a minor fifth.

LE-LE-LU-A, *s.* *Lele* and *lua*, two. In *music*, a second.

LE-LE-MA-LAI-O-A, *v.* *Lele* and *malaioa*, small; fine. To scatter or blow away, as small fragments of things; to dust.

LE-LE-LU-PE, *v.* *Lele* and *lupe*, a kite. To fly the kite.

LE-LE-MU, *s.* Weight; heaviness; a burden carried on the hips.

LE-LE-MU, *v.* To be slow; to be sluggish in movement; to be slow in obeying a command.

LE-LE-PAI-LA-NI, *v.* *Lele* and *pai*, to touch, and *lani*, heaven. To praise; to bless; to extol.

LE-LE-PAU, *v.* To trust in; to trust to something. *Hal.* 4:5. To lean upon.
2. To apply the mind; to give heed; to attend to. *Heb.* 2:1. Lelepau i ka manao.
3. To think much of another; e manao nui ia hai.

LE-LE-PA-LI, *v.* *Lele* and *pali*, a precipice. To leap down a precipice, a common way formerly (not entirely forsaken yet) of committing suicide; pehea la ka uhane o ka poe *lelepali?* how is it with the souls of those who *leap the precipice?* See LELEKAWA.

LE-LE-PI-NAU, *s.* The name of a game.

LE-LE-PI-O, *v.* *Lele* and *pio*, an arch. To fly, as a meteor through the sky; to move along, as a comet showing its tail; to appear, as a supernatural sign in the heavens.

LE-LE-PO, *s.* A small flying-fish.

LE-LE-PO-NI, *v.* To be struck suddenly dead; to die suddenly; to die without warning. See LELELEPONI.

LE-LE-PO-NO, *v.* *Lele* and *pono*, right. To live prosperously; to be blessed in one's business; to transact business rightly; to die happily.

LE-LE-PU-NI, *s.* A kind of play with black and white stones on a board; in *music*, the octave.

LE-LE-WA, *s.* See LEWA, pendulous. The private parts; applied to men; the stem of a vessel; a company following a chief.

LE-LE-WA, *v.* See LEWA, to swing. To float in the air or on water; ke *lelewa* nei ka moku.
2. To follow one about, as a company of persons; to follow after; to hang on, as those who followed a chief.

LE-LE-WAI, *v.* To purge; to cleanse; to purify.

LE-LE-WA-LE, *v.* *Lele* and *wale*, without cause. To be or be done spontaneously; to move of one's own accord.

LE-LE-WA-LE, *s.* A falling; a breaking

off; a yielding.

2. A term formerly used to express a good omen; hush; silence, &c.

LE-LE-WA-LO,
LE-LE-WA-WA-LO, } *v. Lele* and *uwalo*, or *ualo*, to call. To call; to call aloud; to call after.

LE-LE-WE-LU-WE-LU, *v. Lele* and *welu*, to rend. To tear in pieces; to rend.

LE-LO, *s.* See ALELO and ELELO. The tongue; *ka hoeuli o ka olelo ma ka waha*, the rudder of speech in the mouth.

2. Persons speaking different languages.

3. The name of a fish.

LE-LO, *adj.* Hung up in the smoke; smoked red.

LE-LO-LE-LO, *adj.* See LELO. Reddish; reddened.

LE-MU, *v.* To be slow; to lag behind; to walk as one weak.

LE-MU, *s.* The under part of the thigh; the buttock.

2. The bottom part of a thing; *kahi malalo o na mea a pau; e eu ka lemu*, stir your stumps; get up from sitting.

LE-MU-KU, *v.* To break off short; to cut short. See MUKU.

LE-MU-LE-MU, *v.* To go hesitatingly; to walk slowly; to step like an aged person. *Hoo.* To be slow; to be slow to come when called.

LE-MU-LE-MU, *s.* Walking slowly and with care and hesitancy. See HOLOPUPU.

LE-NA, *v.* To bend; to strain, as a bow; to make ready to shoot, as with a bow. *Nal.* 22:34, 8.

2. To take sight or aim, as in shooting with a bow; *he poe lena i na kakaka*.

3. To bend or use the tongue for falsehood. *Ier.* 9:3.

4. To pull out straight and iron, as clothes; *e hoomohala a e hoopalahalaha ae*; to stretch out, as cloth or kapa to dry.

5. To squint; to strain the eyes.

LE-NA, *s.* The name of a plant, the root of which is used in coloring yellow.

2. A yellow coloring matter from the *lena*.

3. *Lena* is also used as an ingredient in curry.

4. The name of a sickness; a complaint of the bowels while the skin becomes yellow.

LE-NA,
LE-NA-LE-NA, } *adj.* Yellow; yellowish. 2. Lazy; doing nothing.

LE-NA-TI-LA, *s. Eng.* Lentiles, a kind of food. *Ezek.* 4:9.

LE-PA, *v.* To roll up the eyes.

2. To stand up, as the comb of a cock.

3. To cut a piece of cloth obliquely; *e oki kapakahi*.

LE-PA, *s.* A border, hem or fringe of a garment. *Puk.* 28:33. A skirt or flowing of a garment; *he kihi o ke kapa, he mea e lewalewa ana malalo.* 1 *Sam.* 24:5.

2. An ensign; a flag used in a war canoe; the flag used at the door of a sacred house.

3. Anything standing up edgeways and making a show, as the comb of a cock. NOTE.—The *lepa* was a piece of kapa tied at the end of a stick as a sign or flag and used for various purposes; *i ke kukulu ana a ua poe kahuna la i ko lakou lepa*, on the putting up of those priests their flag; *a hahaiia ka lepa a ua poe kahuna la*, the *flag* of the priests was torn away.

LE-PA-LE-PA, *s.* A torn rag or kapa, viz.: as an ensign fluttering in the wind becomes torn; the torn end or border of a piece of cloth or kapa.

LE-PE, *s.* The comb of a cock; *he kipaku o ka moa kane*.

LE-PE, *adj.* Diagonally; from corner to corner; *e opiopi lepe*, fold from corner to corner.

LE-PEE, *s.* A gash in the flesh; an open wound.

LE-PE-LE-PE-O-HI-NA, *s.* A red animal of the sea, with a shell on one side; *he mea ano ia maloko o ke kai*.

2. A species of miller or butterfly hatched from a worm; *he wahi mea lele ma ka lewa, he peelua i hoomaluleia*.

LE-PE-LU-A, *adj.* Cute; skillful; cunning; maalea.

LE-PE-RA, *adj. Gr.* Leprous; belonging to leprosy; *mai lepera. Oihk.* 13:2.

LE-PE-RA, *v. Gr.* To be or become leprous; *ua lepera. Nah.* 12:10.

LE-PE-RO, *s. Gr.* A person diseased with the leprosy; a leper. *Oihk.* 14:2.

LE-PE-TA, *s. Gr.* A mite; a very small piece of money. *Luk.* 21:2.

LE-PO, *s.* The general name for dirt, dust or defilement of any kind.

1. The dirt; ground; dust; earth; *ka honua malalo o na wawae*.

2. Dung; excrements. *Puk.* 29:14.

3. Clay; *lepo manoanoa.* 1 *Nal.* 7:46.

4. Dust; anything pulverized to dust. 2 *Nal.* 23:6. *Lepo* poho, mud; mire. *Iob.* 8:11.

5. Name of that part of the ocean where it is deep. SYN. with moana. *He moana kahi inoa, he lepo kahi inoa*.

LE-PO, *v.* To be dirty; to be defiled. *Hoo.* To dirty; to defile; to pollute; to make turbid, as water. *Ezek.* 32:2.

LE-PO, *adj.* Dirty; unclean; earthy;

made of earth; he ipu *lepo*, an *earthern* cup; he wai *lepo*, *dirty* water; he kapa *lepo*, a *soiled* garment.

LE-PO-HA-NAI, *s.* *Lepo* and *hanai*, to feed. Dirt or rubbish which is carried to fill a pit or hole; aole paa ka lepo, he *lepohanai* wale no.

LE-PO-KI-A-HA, *s.* Clay prepared for pottery. *Isa.* 45:9.

LE-PO-LE-PO, *adj.* Intensive of *lepo*. Very dirty; turbid, as water. *Sol.* 25:26.

LE-PU, *s.* *Heb.* A hare, an unclean animal mentioned in *Kanl.* 14:7.

LE-WA, *v.* To swing; to float in the air, as clouds; to hang in a swinging manner; to float in mid heaven; e *lewa* wale ana no (ka honua) i ka lani, (the earth) *was floating* freely in mid heaven.

2. To move back and forth like a hinge; e ami.

3. To float on the water.

4. To put a thing up in an unsafe place or in a tottering position where it may easily fall.

5. *Hoo.* To carry on the surface, as to float on water; e *hoolewa* me ka wai.

6. To be carried, as a coffin at a funeral, on the shoulders of men; i ka *hoolewa* ana i ke kupapau.

LE-WA, *s.* The upper regions of the air; the region of the clouds; na ao o ka *lewa*, the clouds of the air.

2. Whatever is suspended or movable.

3. The space where anything may be suspended.

4. The air; the atmosphere; the visible heavens; kahi o ke ea, ka lani; a particular place in the air or atmosphere; ma keia *lewa* o ka lani, in this *part* of the heavens.

5. Persons without home or local attachment. 1 *Pet.* 2:11. Auhea oukou e na kamalii o ka *lewa* mai, ame na kanaka makua o ka *lewa* mai no hoi.

6. A foreign country; mai ka *lewa* mai mai ke kua mai o ka moku; o ke ano o ia mau olelo, ua hele mai lakou mai ka aina e mai, he *lewa* ia; a ma ke alo o keia aina he kua o ka moku ia. *D. Malo* 3:22.

7. Name of that part of the ocean where it is deep. SYN. with moana.

LE-WA, *adj.* Swinging; pendulous floating; unstable; homeless.

LE-WA-LA-NI, *s.* *Lewa* and *lani*, heaven. An indefinite space in the air; a part of the sky; a place belonging to anything above or in the heavens; the opposite or in someway connected with *lewanuu*.

LE-WA-LE-WA, *v.* See LEWA. To float; to dangle; to swing frequently; to move or go often from place to place; hence, to be deceitful.

LE-WA-LE-WA, *adj.* See LEWA. Swinging; unstable; floating.

LE-WA-NUU, *s.* *Lewa* and *nuu*, a high even place. Some indefinite place on earth, generally connected with or opposed to *lewalani*.

LE-WA-WA-LO, *v.* *Lewa* and *ualo*, or *uwalo*, to cry out. To call; to call out; to run calling after another.

LE-GE-O-NA, } *s.* *Gr.* A legion, 10,000;
LE-GI-O-NA, } an indefinitely large number. *Hal.* 91:7.

LE-SE-MA, *s.* *Heb.* A ligure, a precious stone. *Puk.* 36:12.

LE-TA, *s.* *Eng.* A letter; an epistle. *Haw.* He palapala.

LE-VI-A-TA-NA, *s.* *Heb.* A leviathan, a poetical name of a sea animal; the whale perhaps; the crocodile perhaps. *Hal.* 74:14.

LI, *v.* To hang by the neck. *Eset.* 2:23. To strangle by hanging; to hang; to furl, as a sail; eia ko kakou pea e *li*.

2. To see; to observe. *Hal.* 48:5.

3. To fear; to be afraid; to shrink back with dread.

LI, *s.* The chill or shake of an ague fit; the ague. *Kanl.* 28:22. Any sickness connected with the chills; *li* nui, inflammation. *Kanl.* 28:22. In *music*, the third note of the scale; pa, ko, *li*.

LI, *adj.* Trembling, as from cold; shaking, as with an ague fit.

LI-A, *v.* To ponder; to think; to contemplate.

2. To fear; to be afraid; to start suddenly, as a dog in catching a fly.

3. To desire greedily; to lust after; to ponder or run, as the mind on something foolish.

4. To be cold; to shiver with fear or cold; to have the sensation of cold.

LI-A, *s.* A shaking or trembling through fear.

2. Fear or dread, as when one supposes he sees a spirit.

3. A strong desire; a desire to obtain or possess something, like *kuko* and *iini*; restlessness from something on the mind.

4. Thinking intensely upon some subject; the application of the mind upon something; ke kau nui o ka manao ma ka mea e noonoo ana.

5. Cogitations; serious thoughts; a vi-

sion. *Dan.* 2:28 and 4:5.

Li-a, *adj.* Fearful; affrighted.

Li-e, *s.* A goddess of the mountain whose business it was to braid leis; ke ano o (Lia) *Lei* wahine.

Lii, *s.* The primary form for *alii.* A chief; a king; a ruler. See Alii. Note.— The *a* is often dropped and an apostrophe substituted; as, he 'lii, na 'lii. *Gram.* § 47.

Lii, *v. Haa.* To spread out; to spread down, as a mat or kapa; to open and spread out, as a letter. *Isa.* 37:14.

Lii, *s.* The falling off or turning of the hair white in children; he lauoho keokeo i ka manawa kamalii.

Lii, *adj.* Aguish; sick of a fever and ague. See Li.

2. Little; small, &c.; generally doubled, *liilii,* but found single in compounds; as, *kamalii, makalii, moilii,* &c.

Lii-li, *s.* Name of the place where the sacrifices were laid before the altar; a ma ke alo iho o ka lele ka *liili,* malaila e hoo-ahu ai ka mohai.

Lii-lii, *s.* See Lii, *adj.,* 2. Small; little; diminutive; young.

Lii-lii, *adv.* Slightly; in a small manner; piecemeal; little by little. 2 *Oihl.* 21:15. E hana *liilii,* to work by little and little; e hele *liilii,* kau *liilii;* e oki *liilii,* to cut up finely, &c.

Li-o, *s.* A name given to foreign animals generally when first introduced into the islands. See the verb. The word is now mostly applied to the horse; the horse.

2. A species of bird.

3. The collar or tie beam of a house or other building; ka welau o ka lohi o ka *lio.*

Li-o, *v.* See Leio. To open the eyes wide, as a wild affrighted animal.

2. To act wildly or ferociously, as an untamed animal; to bristle up, as a wild hog. See Kukakalaioa.

3. To have great affection for; e paea-uma ka manawa.

4. To utter a sound as the bird *ao* screams as it flies.

Li-o, *adj.* Tight; strained, as a rope.

Li-o-a, *adj.* See Lio above. Wild; untamable; he ano laka ole.

Li-o-li-o, *v.* To draw tight, as a rope, but not extremely tight; to bind or tie on, as a rope or malo.

2. To make tight; to make hard; to make solid.

Li-o-li-o, *s.* The sound or scream which the bird *ao* makes when disturbed, when she bristles like a hen with chickens.

Li-o-li-o, *s.* The name of a small bird.

Li-o-li-o, *adj.* Bright; shining; dazzling.

2. Strained tight, as a rope.

Li-o-na, *s. Eng.* A lion. *Kin.* 49:9.

Li-u, *v.* To leak, as a canoe in the water; to fill with water, as a ship.

2. To season, as with salt; to render palatable, as food; to restore food that has been corrupted.

3. To get ready to do a thing; to be a long time doing a piece of work.

4. To draw out or protract the sound in blowing a conch shell.

Li-u, *s.* Saltness; the savory taste of food.

2. The peculiar property of a thing or that quality by which it is known.

3. The water in the bottom of a canoe or ship; bilge water; aole i pau ka *liu* i ke ka ia, the *bilge water* is not all dipped out.

Li-u, *adj.* Insipid; not seasoned; tasteless, as unripe fruit or unsalted meat.

Li-u, *adv.* Slowly; tardily.

Ala *liu* ka la o Waianae
Wehe ke kaiulu i ke oho o ka niu
Komo okoa iloko o ka hale.

Li-u-a, *s.* To see indistinctly; to know uncertainly; to be in doubt.

2. To be transformed; to be different from what was supposed after being seen clearly. See Niua.

Li-u-a, *s.* A vertigo; a turning of the eyes so as not to see things distinctly.

Li-u-a, *adj.* Dizzy; indistinctness in vision. See Niua. *Liua* na maka i na wahine moekolohe.

Li-u-la, *s.* See Ula. Dark; twilight, i. e., time of indistinct vision. See Liua.

Li-u-li-u, *v.* To get ready for doing a thing. See Liu 3. To prepare, as for a journey; *liuliu* iho la na kanaka o Oahu e holo i ke kaua i Kauai, the people of Oahu *made ready* to go to the war on Kauai; to get ready, i. e., to prepare materials for a building.

2. To be awake; to watch for something; to wait long for an event, but be ready or prepared for it; a mio, a *liuliu* e i ola honua.

3. To procrastinate; to be for a long time future. 2 *Sam.* 7:19. To stay a long time in a place; to delay a return; to tarry long; *liuliu* iki, soon after.

4. To continue long, as a particular season or time; he *liuliu* no na la e pa mai ai, many are the days (the wind) blows.

Li-u-li-u, *s.* A living or staying a long time at another place.

Li-u-li-u, *adj.* Prepared; ready.

2. Saltish; brackish, as water; unfit to drink; insipid; tasteless, &c. See LIU, *adj.*

Li-u-li-u, *adv.* For a long time; during a long time. *Nah.* 9:19. *Hoo. Oih.* 18:2.

Li-ha, *v.* To be sick at the stomach; to nauseate. See LIHALIHA and LILIHA.

Li-ha, *s.* Nausea; sickness at the stomach.

2. A nit; the egg of a head louse.

Li-ha, *adj.* Sick; nauseous; loathing food.

Li-ha-li-ha, *v.* To be sickish, i. e., sick at the stomach. See LIHA and LILIHA.

2. To be fat; to be greasy; to be slippery with grease.

Li-ha-li-ha, *s.* See LIHA. Sickness at the stomach.

2. Sorrow; sighing; mourning, as for the dead.

Li-ha-li-ha, *adj.* Fatty; greasy; slippery with grease.

2. Sick at the stomach; loathing food. See LILIHA.

Li-he, *s.* See LIHA 2. A nit; the egg of a louse.

Li-hi, *v.* To arrive at; to approach to.

2. To come together; to be united, as two pieces of cloth in a garment.

3. To be united in close friendship, as two friends.

Li-hi, *s.* A border or edge of a thing where it unites or is near to another when in contact, as edges of bones. *Anat.* 6. A border, edge or boundary of a land; the seam or place of uniting in a garment.

2. A lot or portion of land marked off. *Isa.* 57:6. *Lihi* wai, a border or edge of water. *Ios.* 3:8. A part or portion. SYN. with kuleana. *Hoik.* 22:19. He *lihi* maikai ka liki o ka hana, a good *fitting* is the tightness of the work.

3. The union or nearness of relationship, i. e., the friendship of relationship; he mea e maopopo ai ke ano hoahanau ana.

4. The bending of an arch upward, as a rainbow.

5. The rainbow itself.

6. With *iki*, a very small portion of a thing; *lihi iki*, a very small piece. SYN. with huna, a small fragment. *Mat.* 5:18, also *Oih.* 8:21. Aole ona wahi *lihi* ike iki i ka ka Haku olelo, he has no knowledge *at all* of the Lord's word.

Li-hi, *adv.* By the edge; by the end; kau *lihi*, laid with the edge or end only resting on, i. e., slightly resting on; he wahi helehelena wale no kana ike *lihi* ana, he *partly* saw the outlines of her counte-

nance. *Laieik.* 33.

Li-hi-lau-na, *v. Lihi* and *launa*, friendly. To go to; to reach or arrive at.

2. To be frequently at, as at a place near; aole ia i *lihilauna* aku ilaila.

Li-hi-li, *v.* See PUHILI. To think of an object, then to desire it strongly, then to make vigorous efforts for it, then to give it up and fail; in a *race*, to run well with a prospect of success, and then turn aside and lose the race.

Li-hi-li-hi, *s.* The eyelids; the eyelashes. *Iob.* 16:16.

2. The eyebrows; he lauoho ma ke kuekue maka.

Li-hi-wai, *s. Lihi* and *wai*, water. The border or edge of a stream of water. See LIHI, *s.*, above.

Li-ho-li-ho, *adj.* Very hot.

Li-ke, *v.* To be like; to resemble as one thing resembles another; to be similar or to have many qualities in common with something else.

2. *Hoo.* To make one thing, in qualities or appearance, resemble another. *Ha* is often inserted for the sake of euphony. *Gram.* § 211, 2d.

3. To do the same with; to make a thing according to instructions; with *me* following, to do as some one else does; i. e., to resemble in conduct; to imitate.

4. To vanish.

Li-ke-li-ke, *v.* The intensive of *like*; also with *hoo.*

Li-ke-li-ke, *adj.* Alike; resembling. *Hoo.* Same. He olelo *hoolikelikeia*, a parable.

Li-ki, *v.* To gird; to tie up tightly; to bind about, as a loose garment. *Oih.* 12:8.

2. To throng; to be troubled to move along on account of a multitude. *Mar.* 5:31.

3. To be stiff, as a limb with spasmodic affection.

4. *Hoo.* To gird on, as a loose garment.

Li-ki, *s.* A boast, or boasting; kanaka *liki*, a braggart.

Li-ki-li-ki, *v.* Intensive of *liki*. To tie up or tie on tightly. See ALIKILIKI.

Li-ki-pa-hu, *s. Liki* and *pahu*, barrel. A tight hoop for a barrel; an iron hoop.

Li-ko, *v.* To swell out round; to be plump; to be full.

2. To be fat, as a fleshy person.

3. To swell; to enlarge, as the growing bud of a vegetable before the leaves spread open, or as the bud of a flower before the petals open.

4. To expand, as an opening flower.

Hal. 129:6.

5. To shine; to glisten like drops of oil poured on to water.

Li-ko, *s.* The swelling, budding, protruding, &c., of a growing plant.

2. The swollen bud just before leaves or flowers appear.

3. The top or growing end of a plant. Fig. A young child, especially of a chief.

4. The appearance of drops of oil on water.

5. The light or shining points in a person's eye; ka *liko,* oia ka muo, ka ao, ka omaka, ka mea e ulu ai ma ka maka.

Li-ko, *adj.* Swelling; growing; opening, as a bud of a tree or a flower; thrifty, as a growing plant.

Li-ko-li-ko, *v.* See Liko. To swell; to grow, &c

2. To shine, as the white point in one's eye.

Li-la, *adj.* Blasted, thin or shriveled up, as a banana; he maia *lila,* aohe io; he *lila* wale no mai ka eka luna a hiki i ka pola.

Li-la-li-la, *adj.* Shrunk up; turned white or gray; blasted, as fruit.

Li-le, *v.* To be thin; to be weak; to be flexible; to be thin and long, as the lines of words across the page of a book, or as a long stave of music.

Li-le, *adj.* Hoo. Weak; thin.

Li-le-li-le, *v.* To shine very brightly, as a lamp. *Iob.* 29:3. To be dazzling, as the rays of the sun. *Hoik.* 1:16.

Li-le-li-le, *adj.* Bright; shining; kahi *lilelile,* a bright spot. *Oihk.* 13:2. Smooth and shining, as the skin of a bald or shaved head.

Li-li, *v.* To be jealous; to be jealous of a husband or wife. *Nah.* 5:14.

2. To hate; to abhor; to be indignant at where jealously is the cause.

3. Fig. To be jealous for the honor of God. *Nah.* 25:13.

4. To dare; to be bold; to magnify one's self; e aa, e koa, e hoaano.

5. To be stiff, as limbs with lameness; ikaika liki o ka wawae, e oopa, e maloeloe.

6. To join together, as letters to make words; same as *hookui.*

7. *Hoo.* To make jealous or to provoke to jealousy. *Kanl.* 32:16. Syn. with hoonaukiuki. *Lili* ae la ino moa, a haka mai na moa ma ka lani.

Li-li, *s.* Jealousy; wrath; displeasure at one.

2. Fig. Zeal for the honor of God. *Nah.* 25:11.

3. Pride; haughtiness; a disregard of other's rights; ka manao ole i ko hai pono.

4. Pain; distress; internal anguish.

5. Weight; heaviness; that which is not able to be lifted up.

Li-li, *adj.* Jealous, as husband and wife of each other; jealous of the honor and esteem of another.

2. Spoken of Jehovah in his feelings towards other gods. *Puk.* 20:5 and 34:14.

3. Proud; haughty; overbearing.

4. Heavy; not easily lifted.

Li-li-a, *s.* Gr. and *Eng.* A lily. *Mel. Sol.* 2:1.

2. Carved work in Solomon's temple in imitation of lilies. 1 *Nal.* 7:22.

Li-li-o, *v.* See Lio and Liolio. To draw tight, as a rope; to stretch so as to make straight; e malo, e moe pololei.

2. To be tight, as the skin of a glutton's stomach after he has eaten; to be drawn tightly or tensely, as the skin of the face; *lilio* i ka puama ana; to be drawn tightly by stretching.

3. To be filled, as a glutton with food.

4. To have the pain or sensation of eating too much; e maona pono ole, e hokuhoku.

5. To go foward quickly without looking to the right or left.

Li-li-o, *s.* A drawing or turning of the eyes so as not to see clearly.

2. A dragging; a lancinating pain.

Li-li-o, *adj.* Tightly drawn, as a rope; full; plump, as one full fed.

Li-li-ha, *v.* See Liha. To be satisfied, as the appetite with food or drink; to be stuffed full.

2. To be supplied with a sufficiency of a thing. *Isa.* 1:11.

3. To be sick at the stomach; to nauseate, as after eating much rich food; to vomit.

4. Fig. To be disgusted at immoral conduct; *liliha* no hoi ke noonoo i ka ino o ko lakou noho ana, it is *sickening* to think of the evil of their living; to feel disgust at any disgusting object.

Li-li-ha, *s.* The fat of hogs.

2. Anything causing sickness at the stomach.

3. The feeling of nausea at the stomach.

4. Anything offensive to good morals.

Li-li-hu-a, *v.* To go prepared; to be furnished for the purpose: to be supplied with what is necessary; *lilihua* na kanaka i ka hele, aole kanaka aa ole.

Li-li-li, *v.* See Lii. To be small; to be little; applied to fruit, withered; stinted.

Li-li-na, *s. Eng.* Linen cloth, i. e., fine

white cloth. FIG. O Kahele oe, e ka *lilina ume naau.*

LI-LI-NO-E, *adj. Lili* (see LII) and *noe,* fine rain. Sprinkling; fine, as rain; he ua *lilinoe,* a fine rain; a mist.

LI-LI-PI, *adj.* See LIPI. Running to an edge or point; pointed; sharp; tapering like the edge of an axe; ua koe *lilipi* akahi puu.

LI-LO, *v.* To transfer or be transferred in various ways.

1. To become another's; to pass into the possession of another; *lilo* mai, to obtain; to possess; *lilo* aku, to be lost; to perish.

2. To turn; to change; to be lost; to be gone indefinitely.

3. *Hoo.* To cause a transfer or change in different ways; to raise one to office; to place one over others as an officer.

4. To give a thing in trust to another; to give absolutely; to consecrate; to dedicate; to devote. *Kanl.* 20:5.

5. To bring under one's dominion or authority.

6. To change from one thing to another.

7. To change from one form or appearance to another, or from one quality to that of another. NOTE.—When *lilo* is followed by an article before the substantive following, it means *to become* another's; as, ua *lilo* ia ke alii, he *has become* the chief's, i. e., from being in other circumstances before, he, she, it or the property of the chief, or is transferred to him. But when the article is dropped from before the noun following *lilo,* it means to *become* another character or thing; as, ua *lilo* ia i alii, he *has become* a chief, i. e., from being a common man, he is transferred to the honors and office of a chief. When no noun follows *lilo,* it means the subject or thing spoken of *is lost* or *gone* absolutely or indefinitely.

LI-LO, *adv.* Out of sight; a great ways off; lost; gone; distant; iuka *lilo,* far inland; kai *lilo,* out of sight at sea; hala iluna *lilo,* gone very high up.

LI-LO-A, *v.* To lie idly and lazily in the house; e lolo a maiele.

LI-LO-E, *v.* To sit reclining on one's back and his feet raised, as one lounging and idle; e pio na wawae, e lele pio, e kiolani.

LI-LO-LI-LO, *v.* See LILO. To be loosened; to be liberated; to spread out freely; to expand; from a bud to become a full opened blossom; to be liberal and free in giving. See MOHALAHALA.

LI-LO-LI-LO, *adj.* Loosened; unbound; broken loose, as a fish once caught by a hook; open-handed; liberal, as one in giving to others.

LI-MA, *s.* The arm; the hand. FIG. Power; a stay; a support. 1 *Nal.* 10:19. *Lima* nui, the thumb. *Puk.* 29:20. *Lima* iki, the little finger. 1 *Nal.* 12:10. NOTE.— The Hawaiians make no distinction between arm and hand, *lima* applies to or includes both; so *wawae* is both leg and foot. See WAWAE.

LI-MA, *adj.* With the article, an ordinal; the fifth. *Gram.* § 110 and § 115, 4th. I ka *lima* o ka makahiki. *Oihk.* 19:25. See ALIMA and ELIMA.

LI-MA-A-KAU, *s. Lima,* hand, *akau,* right. The right arm or hand.

LI-MA-I-KAI-KA, *s. Lima* and *ikaika,* strong. A strong hand or arm. *Figuratively,* force; power; strength. *Ezer.* 4:23.

LI-MA-I-KAI-KA, *v.* To handle roughly; to assult; to throw one down; to force one against his will.

LI-MA-I-KI, *v.* To assassinate; to kill in a secret place; to fall upon, as a robber.

LI-MA-HE-MA, *s. Lima* and *hema,* left. The left hand.

LI-MA-KU-HI, *s. Lima* and *kuhi,* to point out. In *reading books,* the index; the form of a hand ☞.

LI-MA-LAU, *v.* To carry on the hips.

LI-MA-LI-MA, *v.* See LIMA, hand. To handle; to employ the hands. *Hoo.* To hire; to bargain for work to be done; to agree with one concerning wages.

LI-MA-LI-MA, *adj.* Appellation of a prayer when his priest made many gestures with his hands; the ceremony was called hoopii na aha *limalima.*

LI-MA-LI-MA, *adj.* See LIMA. Full of hands; one hired to work. *Hoo.* That which is bargained for or hired. *Ioan.* 10:12.

LI-MA-LI-MA, *s. Hoo.* A hired person. *Ioan.* 10:13.

LI-MA-LI-MA-PI-LAU, *s.* See LIMALIMA, *v.,* and PILAU, dirty. Dirty hands.

LI-MA-NU-I, *s. Lima* and *nui,* great. The thumb.

LI-MI, *v.* To be entangled or be in difficulty in the surf; to be upset in the surf and turned over and over. See LUMAIA.

LI-MI-LI-MI, *v.* Freq. of *limi.* To be turned over and over in the surf; e *limilimiia* e ka nalu.

Li-MU, s. Sea-moss or sea-grass; a general name of every kind of eatable herb that grows in the sea; the Hawaiians also class the *limu* among fish; the varieties are limu-aalaula, limu-ekaha, limu-iliohaa, limu-opai, limuu-laula, limuhi-naula, limuhululio, limuhuna, limukahakala, limukala, limukele, limukiki, limukoko, limulipahapala, limulipalao, limulipalawai, limulipoa, limulipupu, limulipuula, limulipu-upuu, limuloloa, limunanue, limupaakaiea, limupalahalaha, limupalawai, limupipilani.

limu, lipoa variety

Li-MU, v. To turn; to change; to have various appearances. SYN. with ouli.

Li-MU-A, s. A long or constant rain; a constancy of water or wet weather; a constant flowing of water.

Li-MU-A, adj. The quality or action of wet weather, of a long rain.

Li-MU-KA-KA-NA-KA, s. *Limu* and *kakanaka*, a species of grass. A smooth or slippery kind of grass.

Li-MU-LI-MU, adj. Twisting; turning; dissembling; trifling; trickish; the opposite of honest and open in conduct.

Li-MU-LI-MU, s. A twirling; a curling; the whiffling of the wind; the curling of a negro's hair; instability of conduct.

Li-MU-LI-PU-PU, s. A species of limu; he pipilani. See LIMU above.

Li-NA, s. Anything soft and yielding to the touch; *papalina*, the cheek.
2. *Hoo.* Anything soft, tenacious or tough.

Li-NA, adj. Tightly drawn, as a rope. See LIOLIO.

Li-NA-LI-NA, s. See LINA. Tough food, i. e., kalo.
2. Wet, clayey land.
3. Any soft adhesive substance.
4. A drawing together of the skin of a wound; a scar.

Li-NA-LI-NA, v. To stick to; to adhere to, like pilali or shoemaker's wax; to be tough and adhesive, like water-soaked vegetables.

Li-NA-LI-NA, adj. Soft; mucous; adhesive; tough; tightly drawn, as a rope. See LINA. Tough or elastic, as India rubber.

Li-NE-KA, s. *Gr.* The lynx, a four-footed animal.

Li-NO, v. To twist, as a string or rope; to wear; e lili eha aoao.

Li-NO, s. A rope.

Li-NO-HAU, v. To be proud or haughty.

Li-NO-LI-NO, s. Brightness; splendor; so bright as to dazzle the sight and make one blind.

Li-NO-LI-NO, adj. Calm; unruffled, as the sea where there is no wind; hence, reflecting the light of the sun. See MALINO.

Li-NU, adj. Close; hard; ungenerous.

Li-PA-HA, s. He wahi limu. See LIMU, sea-grass.

Li-PI, s. An axe for cutting wood, from its tapering down to an edge.
2. Gluttony; he ai nui ana i ka ai, he pakela ai.

Li-PI, adj. Sharp; tapering down like the edge of an axe.

Li-PI-O-MA,
Li-PI-HO-E-HO-E,
Li-PI-KA-HE-LA,
Li-PI-KU-KE, } s. The names of several species of cutting instruments introduced among Hawaiians in modern times.

Li-PI-LI-PI, s. See LIPI. Anything thin and standing up edgeways, like a sharp ridge of land.

Li-PI-LI-PI, adj. Thin; sharp; tapering; axe shaped. See LILIPI.

Li-PO, s. A deep shady forest.
2. Deep water in the sea; moana *lipo* loa; hence

Li-PO, adj. Blue, black or dark from the depth of a cavern, or from the depth of the sea; deep; bottomless, as the ocean.

Li-PO-LI-PO, s. See LIPO. Great depth of the ocean so as to appear blue or black; ka hohonu, ka moana.

Li-PO-LI-PO, adj. Deep blue or black.
2. Deep down; ocean like; deep; bottomless.

Li-PO-LO-LO-HU-A-ME-A, s. The appearance on looking into very deep water or a deep pit where no bottom is visible; black; dark.

Li-PO-WAO-NA-HE-LE, s. *Lipo* and *waonahele*, thick forest. The darkness and gloom of a thick forest.

Li-PU-PU, s. A species of the limu. See LIMULIPUPU.

Li-WA-LI, adj. Soft; thin; worked up like thin poi.

Li-BA-NO, s. *Gr.* LIT. Lebanon. *Oihl.* 9:29. I. e., frankincense, a gum from Lebanon. *Hoik.* 18:13.

Li-GU-RA, s. *Gr.* A ligure, a precious stone. *Puk.* 28:29.

Li-RA, s. *Gr.* A lyre, a musical instrument; a harp. *Kin.* 4:21.

Lo, s. The fore part of the head.
2. A species of bug, long and with sharp claws.
3. The name of some chiefs who lived on

the mountain Helemano and ate men; he mau alii ai kanaka no uka o Helemano.

Lo. A syllable prefixed to many words, the precise definition of which does not appear, as *lokahi, lomilo, lokea,* &c.

Lo-a, *v.* To extend; to be long; to be indefinitely long as to time, measure or distance.

Lo-a, *s.* Length. 1 *Nal.* 6:2. The whole of any district of land; long space from one place to another; a length of time.

 2. A bank; a raised place; he ahua a.

 3. A receptacle of filth; he nenelu inoino.

 4. An officer who has universal charge of the taxes.

 5. The name of the general tax itself.

Lo-a, *adj.* Long; spoken of time, of space or measure.

Lo-a, *adv.* An intensive word of general application; much; very; exceedingly; it is connected with nouns, adjectives and verbs.

Lo-a-a, *v.* Anomalous. *Gram.* § 232. To obtain; to find; to receive; to have, i. e., to have obtained; to meet with; to happen; to befall; to be overtaken; to be caught; to be seized; to be possessed of. NOTE.—*Loaa* is mostly confined in its meaning to a passive or neuter sense; makau wau i ke kapaia mai he holoholona i ka *loaa* ole e kahi manao, I was afraid of being called a beast for *not being seized* (possessed of) by a thought; that is, for not *having* a thought.

Lo-a-a, *s.* The name of a rough scraggy stone, as a coral rock or a rough slab of lava.

 2. Applied *figuratively* to hard, severe, cruel kapus; e ku i ka *loaa* i ke kapu.

Lo-a-a, *s.* A receiving; an obtaining; a getting; a possessing.

 2. Luck; fortune; success or otherwise; e hoao aku hoi i kau loaa. *Laieik.* 64.

Lo-a-la, *v.* In *poetry*, to praise; to extol; to bless as the people spoke of a chief.

Lo-e, *s.* The end of a fish-hook opposite the point.

Lo-e-a, *s.* Skill; ingenuity in doing a thing; cleverness in planning and executing a project. See HAILEA.

Lo-e-a, *adj.* Skillful; cunning; ingenious at any business. See LOIA.

Lo-e-lo-e, *adj.* Flexible; feeble. See LOE and MALOELOE.

Lo-i, *s.* A water kalo patch; an artificial pond where kalo is cultivated.

Lo-i, *v.* To sneer at or ridicule another's opinion.

Lo-i, *s.* Disapprobation or contempt shown for another's opinion; he hoowahawaha i ko hai manao. See LOILOI. *Loi* is used as a word of contempt, similar to *pupuka.*

Lo-ia, *s.* See LOEA. An ingenious skillful person; one who is handy and expert at any business; applied only to women as *maiau* is to men. See MAIAU.

 2. Skill; ingenuity; experience in business.

Lo-ia, *adj.* Skillful; ingenious; dextrous; applied only to women. See NOEAU and MIKOLOLOHUA.

Lo-i-e, *s.* See LOINA. A rule of conduct; a command; a way of doing things.

Lo-i-e-le, *v.* To be slow in doing a thing; to linger; *loiele* kana hana; heaha keia hana au e *loiele* nei? what are you doing that you should be *so slow?*

Lo-i-e-le, *s.* Slowness in doing a thing; ka! manomano ka *loiele* ia oe, astonishing the *slowness* of you.

Lo-i-e-le, *adj.* Sluggish; dull; slow; awkward.

Lo-i-o, *adj.* Thin; poor; reduced in flesh; spare.

Lo-i-o, *s.* Straightness; a substance, as a stick without crook.

 2. A person reduced in size; thin in flesh.

 3. *Eng.* A lawyer.

Lo-io-io, *s.* The prancing of an untamed horse on attempting to ride him; *loioio* expresses his wild appearance.

 2. The appearance of a person half frightened.

Lo-i-hi, *v.* To be long; to be lengthened out, as space or time; to live long.

 2. To be far off; to be at a great distance.

 3. *Hoo.* To make long; to lengthen out, as time; to procrastinate; to put far off. *Amos* 6:3. To add to the length of time or distance. 2 *Nal.* 20:6.

Lo-i-hi, *s.* Length; distance; length of time.

Lo-i-hi, *adj.* Long; applied to time or distance; also, the measure of anything, as timber, cloth, &c.; kahi *loihi,* a great distance off. NOTE.—This word is sometimes vulgarly pronounced as if written *lokihi.*

Lo-i-lo-i, *v.* See LOI. To ridicule; to contemn or sneer at one's thought or opinion.

Lo-i-na, *s.* A statue; an ordinance; a rule; a command; an act; a device, &c.

 2. The meaning of a word or thing.

 3. A pithy or wise saying.

 4. A sign of some coming event.

Lo-i-na, *adj.* Rulable; according to order after established custom.

LOO, *v.* To overtake; to come upon, as a disease; to come upon, as evil or a judgement; found only in the passive *loohia*.

LOO-HI-A, *v.* For *looia*, passive of *loo*. To be overtaken by anything, as a disease. 1 *Sam.* 5:12. By suffering or misfortune. *Kin.* 44:29. By sadness or grief. *Puk.* 15:14. To come upon, as oppression. *Lunk.* 6:13. To fall upon one, as fear. *Luk.* 8:37. To befall one. *Eset.* 4:7. See LOHIA.

LOO-KA-HI, *v.* *Loo* and *kahi*, one. To be of one mind or accord; to agree together; to think alike. See LOKAHI.

LOO-KA-HI, *adj.* Same; similar; mutual; alike.

LOO-KA-HI, *adv.* With one accord; with unanimity. *Oih.* 4:24.

LOU, *v.* To bend, as a hook; to bend around (hence *kulou*, to stand bent, i. e., bowing down.)

2. To hook; to pull with a hook; to come up with a hook, as a fish.

3. To insert; to fit on, as a ring on the finger. *Kin.* 24:47.

4. *Hoo.* To hook; to pull with a hook. 2 *Oihl.* 33:11. I *hoolouia* i ka makau ke-kahi poe i holo ilalo, some who had sunk down *were hooked* up with fish-hooks.

LOU, *s.* A hook. *Isa.* 37:29. *Lou* io, a flesh hook. *Puk.* 27:3. *Lou* hao, an iron hook; a joining. 1 *Oihl.* 22:3.

2. A pain in the side; a stitch.

3. A perpendicular descent.

LO-U-A, *v.* For *louia*. To crook, as a hook; to be crooked.

2. To pull off with a stick or hook, as oranges or other fruit from a tree.

LO-U-A, *adv.* Quickly; no delay, as the lapse of time, as quick work, &c.; *loua* ole aku nei; ua *loua* ole aku ka hana.

LOU-HAO, *s.* *Lou* and *hao*, iron. An iron hook. See LOU above.

LO-U-HU, *v.* To leap off; to fly away; e lehai aku.

LOU-LA, *adj.* Fast; firm, as a nail that takes firm hold of the wood.

LOU-LOU, *v.* See LOU. To bend over; to bend down.

2. To hold fast, as with a hook; to hook round the fingers and pull, a trial of strength. See LOULOULIMA.

2. *Haa.* To be bowed or bent over with grief; to be deeply affected. 2 *Sam.* 13:33.

3. To weep on account of deep repentance.

LOU-LOU, *adj.* Bending over or around.

2. Bent with pain or grief.

3. Hooked or held fast.

LOU-LOU, *s.* The name of an exercise or play; eia kekahi lealea, o ka *loulou*, here is one exercise, the *loulou*.

LOU-LOU-LI-MA, *v.* See LOULOU, *v.*, and LIMA, the hand. To hook in one's fingers with the fingers of another person and pull.

LO-U-LU, *s.* A tree with wide leaves; the fan-leafed palm tree.

2. The fruit of the *loulu*.

3. An umbrella, especially a Chinese umbrella.

4. A screen from the sun or rain, as the leaf was used for a covering.

5. The name of a species of fish.

LO-U-LU, *adj.* Lala *loulu*, the palm branching tree. 2 *Oihl.* 3:5.

2. Pointed; sharp, like the points at the ends of palm leaves.

LO'U-PA-LI, *s.* A kind of residence for people, like *puha*.

LO-HA, *s.* Love; affection, &c.; the root of the word *aloha*.

2. A plant or branch of a tree growing thriftily.

3. The trimming to the corners and ridge of a thatched house.

4. The art of thatching well.

5. An under head man.

6. A kind of sport of former times, the same as *kilu*; e haele kakou i ka hale *loha* o Mea.

LO-HA, *v.* To fade; to wilt; to wither, as vegetables; e mae.

LO-HA, *adj.* Sullen; dumpish; indisposed to speak or act.

LO-HA-LO-HA, *adj.* Speechless through fear; unable to utter on account of fear or astonishment. See the above.

LO-HA-I, *s.* A lever for raising heavy articles.

2. The name of a disease; a swelling of the face, breast, &c.

3. The lameness of the legs from walking.

LO-HA-I, *adj.* Belonging to a lever for prying up heavy masses; he laau *lohai* moku e upe ana i na malua nui.

LO-HE, *v.* To hear, as the ear a voice or sound.

2. To obey; to follow instructions; to regard.

3. *Hoo.* To give such attention as to understand and practice or obey. *Lunk.* 2:2.

LO-HE-A, *v.* Passive of *lohe* for *loheia*. To be heard, &c.

LO-HE-LAU, *s.* The plate of a house frame on which the rafters are fastened; kauia ka *lohelau* ma ka waha o ka pou.

Lo-he-lau, *adj.* Old; worn out; rotten, as timber, houses, &c.

2. Exhausted; spent, as a man by fasting or hunger or fatigue.

Lo-he-lau, *adj.* Excellent; good; fitting.

Lo-he-lo-he, *v.* To hear indistinctly or incorrectly; scarcely to hear.

Lo-hi, *v.* To linger; to be tardy; a *lohi* aku la maua mahope me ka hele malie, we two *lingered* behind by walking slowly.

2. To wait; to stay; to be slack to do a thing. *Kanl.* 7:10.

3. *Hoo.* To be slow; to be dilatory; to be cautious. *Iak.* 1:19.

Lo-hi, *s.* The name of the sexual organ of a horse; also, the sexual organ of men. See *Ule.* Ka welau o ka *lohi* o ka lio.

Lo-hi, *adj.* Tardy; lingering; slow; feeble.

Lo-hi, *adv.* Tardily; slowly.

Lo-hi-a, *v.* See *Loohia.* To happen to one; to fall upon; to befall, as a calamity or disease. *Mat.* 4:24.

2. To unite; to come together, as two things.

3. To overtake.

Lo-hi-a, *adj.* Overtaken; seized; possessed of, as by a spirit; overcome, as by sleep; overtaken by a fault.

Lo-hi-au, *v.* To be slow in doing a thing; to make blunders; *lohiau* Puna i ke akua wahine.

Lo-hi-lo-hi, *v.* See *Lohi.* To be very slow, &c. *Hoo.* To be tardy; to delay doing a thing; to bear long with one's offenses; to be slow in executing justice; to procrastinate.

Lo-ka, *s.* A state of mind full of doubt about any fact or information; unbelief; disbelief, especially of religious truth.

Lo-ka-hi, *v.* To be alike; to be agreed; i *lokahi* ka ike, a i kuikahi ka manao, that they may *know the same thing,* and agree in opinion; to be of one mind; to be in union or unison. *2 Oihl.* 5:13. *Hoo.* To cause a union; to make a united effort of the moral powers. *Hal.* 86:11.

Lo-ka-hi, *s.* See *Lookahi.* Agreement in mind; unanimity of sentiment; union of feeling; oneness; similarity.

Lo-ka-hi, *adj.* See *Lookahi.* Of the same mind; agreed; of the same opinion. *1 Sam.* 11:7.

Lo-ka-hi, *adv.* Similar; with one accord; with unanimity of sentiment. *Ios.* 9:2.

Lo-ke, *s.* A vicious orthography for rose. *Eng.* A rose.

Lo-ke-a, *s.* A long pointed knife with a white handle; pahi loihi, kumu keokeo.

Lo-ke-a, *adj.* White. See *Kea* and *Keo.*

Lo-ko, *s.* The inner part; that which is within; applied to persons or things.

1. To persons, the internal organs.

2. The moral state or disposition of a person, either good or bad, according to its compounds; as *loko* maikai, *loko* ino, &c.

3. Applied to things, the within; the interior; that which belongs within; the inwards; ia po no, ai no i ka *loko* o ka ilio noa, on that night indeed, they ate the *inwards* of a dog not forbidden; he mau mea e pili ana maloko o ka naau; ia *loko,* the within. *Mat.* 23:26. Note.—The Hawaiians believed that the moral powers or dispositions had their seat in the small intestines. See *Naau.*

Lo-ko, *adj.* Inner; what is within; pahale *loko,* the inner court. *1 Nal.* 6:36.

Lo-ko, *prep.* In; within; inner, &c.; compounded with the simple prepositions o, ko, no, i, ma and mai. *Gram.* § 161. See each in its place. Ia loko is used in *Mat.* 23:26.

Lo-ko, *s.* A pond; a lake; a small collection of water; he wai lana malie i puni i ka aina.

Lo-ko-i-no, *v.* *Loko,* disposition, and *ino,* bad. To act vilely; to deal malevolently; to exhibit a bad disposition.

Lo-ko-i-no, *s.* An evil disposition; destitude of kindness.

Lo-ko-i-no, *adj.* Careless; slothful; unmerciful; unkind; ungenerous.

Lo-ko-i-no-ia, *s.* Cruelty; malevolence. *Lunk.* 9:24.

Lo-ko-ha-i-ki, *adj.* *Loko* and *haiki,* close. Standing thick together; little space between.

2. Parsimonious; close-fisted; hard.

Lo-ko-lo-ko, *v.* See *Loko,* pond. To stand in puddles or pools of water; e halokoloko.

Lo-ko-li-u, *v.* *Loko* and *liu,* insipid. To be insipid; to be without strength; to be bitter.

Lo-ko-li-u, *adj.* Cross; angry; indifferent.

Lo-ko-li-nu, *adj.* *Loko* and *linu,* close. Parsimonious. See *Lokohaiki.*

Lo-ko-mai-kai, *v.* *Loko,* disposition, and *maikai,* good. To feel and act benevolently; to be kindly disposed towards one; to be favorable to one.

Lo-ko-mai-kai, } *s.* Grace; favor; special favor; good will.
Lo-ko-mai-kai-ia, } *Kin.* 39:4.

Lo-ko-mai-kai, *adj.* Merciful. *Puk.* 34:6.

Disposed to do good; generous; obliging; kind.

Lo-ko-wai, *s.* *Loko* and *wai*, water. A fountain. *Sol.* 5:16.

Lo-ku, *v.* To prostitute for pay on a large scale.

Lo-ku, *s.* A sort of pain, ache, distress.

Lo-ku, *adj.* Distressing; painful; fearful; ka leo o ka ua *loko* me ka hekili, the sound of the *severe* rain with the thunder.

Lo-ku-lo-ku, *v.* To suffer pain; e *loku-loku* nei iloko o ka hanaia, to suffer pain in what was done.

Lo-ku-lo-ku, *s.* See Loku. Pain; distress; numbness of limbs.

Lo-ku-lo-ku, *v.* See Lokoloko.

Lo-la, *adj.* Paralyzed; stiff; lame.

2. Idle; neglected; barren, as a fruit tree; emasculated.

Lo-la, *s.* A palsied person; one helpless.

Lo-la-lo-la, *v.* See Lola. Ua *lolalola* lolohili.

Lo-la-mo-e-ha-lau, *v.* Lola and *moe*, to lie down, and *halau*, a long house. To be idle; to be useless, as a person. See Lolo-moehalau.

Lo-le, *v.* To turn inside out; e huli-huli; to unfold to view.

2. To change one's mind. *Hal.* 15:14. To rectify; to arrange; to alter from one thing to another. *Eset.* 9:1.

3. To beat down one's price.

4. To flay; to skin, as an animal. *Oihk.* 1:6. *Lole* i ka ili.

5. To work with one's own hands.

6. To thatch a house smoothly.

7. To be weary, as with traveling; to be lame.

8. To be weak in the knees. *Hoo.* To flay; to take off the skin. *Mik.* 3:3.

Lo-le, *s.* Cloth, particularly foreign cloth; he aa haole.

2. A garment. *Lunk.* 8:25. *Lole* komo, garment; wearing apparel; *lole* hana, garments for particular work. *Puk.* 39:1. *Lole* lauoho, sack cloth. *Hoik.* 6:12.

3. Straight smooth hair, like the Chinese.

Lo-le-a, *adj.* Found in the phrase *lo-lea* keia kala, bad money perhaps; perhaps it is for *loleia*, to be changed.

Lo-le-hau, *v.* To limp; to be weary from walking; to be lame.

Lo-le-ha-na, *s.* Lole and *hana*, work. A working garment. See Lole, *s.*

Lo-le-lau, *s.* Lole and *lau*, leaf. The art of thatching and trimming off a house. See Lole 6.

Lo-le-lo, *v.* To jump; to skip. *Ier.* 48:27. Ua *lolelo* no oe i ka olioli.

Lo-le-lu-a, *v.* Lole and *lua*, twice. To be changeable; to be unstable; to be double minded; *lolelua* ka naau. *Iak.* 1:8. See Naaulua. To act with indecision; to change; to pervert; to cause a change. *Kekah.* 7:7.

2. To be in doubt; to hesitate; to turn back.

Lo-le-lu-a, *s.* Doubt; hesitancy; a changing often of one's opinions or plans; e hana paha, aole paha, aole anei ia he *lole-lua?* to work perhaps, not perhaps, is not that *indecision?*

Lo-le-lu-a, *adj.* Changeable; fickle; double minded. *Sol.* 24:21.

Lo-le-na, *v.* Lole and *ana*, i. e., *lole ana*. To be limber; to be flexible, as cloth.

2. To be inefficient; to be impotent; to be incapacitated.

3. To have lost one's beauty and energy of person.

4. To produce no fruit, as a vegetable.

Lo-le-na, *s.* A person, animal or vegetable slighted for want of beauty and other desirable qualifications; he maia aao; he maia kukanaloa, he mea ku wale iho no; he *lolena*, no ka mea aohe ona kulia; a person despised or not desired by women.

Lo-le-na, *adj.* Weak; faded; withered, as a plant or fruit or a person.

Lo-li, *v.* The definitions of this word run into those of *lole*. To turn over; to change; to alter.

2. *Hoo.* The same. To turn into. *Neh.* 13:2. Also, to change one thing, purpose or plan for another. *Kin.* 50:2. To alter one's design; e hoololi i ka manao. *2 Sam.* 24:16.

3. To make a spot with coloring matter; to daub; to color; e kikohu, e onionio; to color in spots, as was often done with kapa.

Lo-li, *s.* The biche de mer, the name of a species of fish; he ia maka ole; a fish without eyes; a soft limpsy fish without bones. *Anat.* 1.

Lo-li-a, *v.* See Loliia. To turn on one side, then on the other, as a sleepy person.

2. Applied to a new canoe when drawn from the mountains, it turns on one side then the other when drawing; *lolia* ke akua i kaula.

Lo-lii, *v.* To make ready; to prepare before hand; to prepare for an event; no-laila, e *lolii* e oukou iho, therefore *prepare* yourselves before hand.

Lo-lii, *s.* What is thought of before hand; that which is prepared previous to use.

Lo-lii, *adj.* Prepared; ready; furnished.
2. Having very many sides, as a stick of house timber; where there are less sides it is *opaka.*

Lo-li-ia, *v.* To be turned or changed.

Lo-li-lo-li, *v.* See LOLI. To be water soaked or tough, as kalo sometimes is; to be damaged or changed as food; to be unsound. See OLOLILOLI.

Lo-li-lo-li, *adj.* A term applied to water-soaked vegetables, especially to kalo; tough; changed for the worse; applied also to vegetable food.

Lo-li-lu-a, *adj.* See LOLELUA. Changeable; fickle; given to change.

Lo-lo, *v.* To punish; to fine for delinquency.
2. To ordain; to appoint.

Lo-lo, *s.* The brain of a person or animal; *lolo* poo. Anat. 49.
2. The marrow of the bones; *lolo* iwi.
3. The seat of thought; ke kumu o ka manao ma ke poo. NOTE.—This is a modern idea: the ancient Hawaiians supposed the seat of thought to be in the *naau.*
4. The palsy; feebleness or disuse of one's limbs. Mat. 4:24.
5. A person afflicted with the palsy.
6. A person very awkward at doing anything as though he had not the use of his limbs.
7. The sheath that surrounds a young cocoanut.

Lo-lo, *s.* The name of the hog sacrificed on the finishing of a canoe; alaila, *lolo* ka waa, hoomana hou no i ke akua; e hoolohe mai oe i ka maikai o ka *lolo* ana o ka waa.

Lo-lo, *adj.* Palsied; lying helpless.
2. Indolent; lazy.
3. Crazy; insane.
4. Tall; slender, as a man.

Lo-lo, *interj.* An expression of triumph over the ills of another; same as *akola.* See OLOLO.

Lo-lo-a, *v.* See LOA. To be long; to grow or to become long. Dan. 4:33. To go afar off; to be at a great distance.

Lo-lo-a, *s.* Length.

Lo-lo-a, *adj.* See LOA. Long; tall, as a tree; connected with kiekie. Isa. 2:13. Afar off.

Lo-lo-a, *adv.* Afar off; a long time; uhai *loloa,* following a long distance.

Lo-lo-au, *s.* A species of fish.

Lo-lo-he, *v.* See LOHE. The intensive conj. of *lohe,* to hear. To hear quickly; to listen attentively, &c.; but the same word also signifies nearly the opposite; as,
2. Not to hear quickly; to make excuses; to procrastinate obedience; to be sluggish in obeying one's orders; to be heavy; to be dull; to be inattentive. *Hoo.* The same. NOTE.—The second definitions are probably from *lohi,* to be slow.

Lo-lo-he, *adj.* The same in the adjective as in the verb. See above. Hearing quickly; giving ready attention; yielding quick obedience. &c.
2. Slow in hearing; dull; disobedient. *Hoo.* The same.

Lo-lo-hi, *v.* The intensive of *lohi.* To be very tardy or slow; to be very lingering; to lag far behind.

Lo-lo-hi, *s.* One slow from disease, as the palsy or other disease.

Lo-lo-hi, *adj.* Very slow; tardy; lingering behind; dilatory.

Lo-lo-hi-li, *v.* See LOLOA and HILI, to wander. To be far off; to be at a great distance; to stretch out a long way; ua lolalola *lolohili.*

Lo-lo-ki, *adj.* See LOLOHI. Slow; lingering; weak in walking.

Lo-lo-ki-a, *s.* The stem of a cocoanut fruit; the branch that connects the fruit with the tree.

Lo-lo-hu-a, *s.* One skilled in the use of language, especially the ancient language; o ka *lolohua* alii o Kama i ka moku.

Lo-lo-hu-a, *adj.* Indulging or cherishing an evil disposition.

Lo-lo-hu-a-me-a, *s.* The appearance of the verge of the ocean to one in a canoe on the ocean, as it appears green or dark colored.

Lo-lo-hu-a-me-a, *s.* The epithet of a child who speaks correctly and uses language with propriety.

Lo-lo-kaa, *s.* *Lolo,* brain, and *kaa,* to turn. A disease of the head; dizziness affecting the eyes; a dropsy in the head.

Lo-lo-ku, *adv.* Spatteringly, as a heavy rain; as rain drops falling into water, causing a sound and a bubbling up; ue, ue *loloku* mai ana.

Lo-lo-ku-li, *adj.* Sick and deaf, that is, deaf from disease; want of hearing; ko makou pepeiao i mau aa *lolokuli.*

Lo-lo-lo, *v.* To think; to reflect; to reason; to turn over in one's mind.

Lo-lo-lo-a, *s.* *Lolo,* palsy, and *loa,* very. The feeling of an arm or leg when the blood ceases to circulate.

Lo-lo-lo-a, *adj.* Intensive of *loa.* Very long, as to time or measure; na lima *lolo-*

loa, very long arms.

Lo-lo-lo-he, *adj.* See Lolokuli. Deaf; unable to hear from disease or other ways; i loheia e na aa *lololohe;* aka, ina i lilo ke aa *lololohe* i ko makou pepeiao i mau aa lolokuli.

Lo-lo-lo-hu-a, *adv.* See Lolohua above. To pronounce clearly, distinctly and correctly; ke pane *lololohua* mai nei ia.

Lo-lo-lo-lo-hu-a, *adj.* Thinking; wise; skillful; reflecting.

Lo-lo-mo-e-ha-lau, *adj.* See Lolamoe-halau. Idle; useless, &c.

Lo-lo-mo-e-ha-lau, *s.* A man, woman or child who is lazy, indisposed to work; o ke kane palaualelo, molowa, hana ole, oia hoi ka *lolomoehalau.*

Lo-lo-ni-u, *s. Lolo* and *niu,* cocoanut. A canoe made of a cocoanut tree; he waa *loloniu.*

Lo-lo-pai-o, *v.* To be tall and slim, as a man; ua *lolopaio* i ka la.

Lo-lo-pai-o-ea, *s.* A tall slim person with a thin hatchet face.

Lo-lo-pai-o-ea, *v.* To walk unsteadily, as a thin person.

Lo-lo-pi-o, *v. Lolo* for *lele,* and *pio,* an arch. To fly in a curved line; to fly as a meteor; e lele me he akua lele la; me ka welowelo, as a comet; to bend up the legs, as one jumping into the water.

Lo-lo-poo, *s. Lolo,* palsy, and *poo,* head. The marrow of the head; the brain.

2. A disorder of the head.

3. The seat of thought in men. See Lolo.

Lo-lo-pu-a, *s.* The zenith; the point directly over head; eia la i ka *lolopua* o ka lani.

Lo-ma, *v.* To be lazy; to be slow; to be awkward; to be indolent.

Lo-ma, *s.* Slowness; want of skill; awkwardness.

Lo-ma, *adj.* Lazy; awkward; unskillful.

Lo-ma-lo-ma, *v.* The intensive of *loma* in all its definitions.

Lo-ma-lo-ma, *s.* Idleness; indolence; awkwardness.

Lo-ma-lo-ma-ai-ha-la-le, *adj. Loma,* lazy, and *aihalale,* to live on others. Lazy and eating the food of others through idleness; aole e loaa keia mea, o ka naauao, i ka mea manaka, aole hoi i ka mea kaialile *lomalomaaihalale,* this thing, knowledge, cannot be obtained by the easily discouraged nor by the *indolently awkward.*

Lo-mi, *v.* To rub; to press; to squeeze with the hand any one that is in pain or fatigued; to shampoo; hence,

2. Fig. To comfort; to quiet; e *lomi* ana au i ka eha o ko'u naau, I *am comforting* myself for my bad feelings.

3. To crush; to mash fine; e hoowali; e hooaeae.

Lo-mi, *s.* A rubbing, pressing or squeezing of one in pain or sick.

Lo-mi-a, *v.* For *lomiia.* To feel of; to pinch; to squeeze; to press.

Lo-mi-lo, *v.* See Milo, Omilo and Hilo. To spin with the fingers; to twist, as thread; to make ropes, cords, &c.

Lo-mi-lo-mi, *v.* See Lomi. To rub; to squeeze and chafe the limbs of one who is weary or in pain; to shampoo except the bathing.

2. To mitigate or ease pain by so doing.

3. To mend letters in writing, that is, to draw the pen two or three times over the same line to improve its appearance.

4. To feel a thing to ascertain its qualities; *lomilomi* iho la kuu lima i ua pohaku la, he paakiki la! my hand *felt* of that stone, it was hard.

5. To act upon, as the Spirit of God acts upon the heart; i na manawa a pau loa kona (ko ke Akua) *lomilomi* ana mai ia'u, at all times has he (God) *acted upon me.*

Lo-mi-lo-mi, *s.* A rubbing, pressing, &c. See Lomi.

2. The servant whose business it was to take care of the spittle and excrements of the chief.

Lo-na, *s.* The blocks of wood on which double canoes rest when out of water.

2. The name of the wood out of which such blocks were made.

Lo-na, *adj.* Useless; in vain; without advantage; awkward.

2. Straight; direct.

Lo-no, *v.* To hear, as a sound; to hear, as the voice of one calling.

2. To regard, as a command; to keep; to observe; to obey.

3. To hear a report. *Dan.* 11:44.

4. *Hoo.* To cause to hear, &c.; to listen; to regard. *Dan.* 9:10.

Lo-no, *s.* A report; news; a hearing of something new; fame.

2. A report of what one has heard another say. *Kin.* 37:2. News; nui ka maua kamailio ana ia po na na *lono* ame na hana i hanaia, we two had much conversation that night respecting the *news* and what had been done.

3. A rumor; a report. *2 Nal.* 19:7.

4. Fame. 1 *Oihl.* 14:17.

5. Tidings. *Ezek.* 21:7.

6. A remembrance. *Kanl.* 32:26.

7. The name of a day of the month; o kakahiaka ae, o *Lono* ia la.

LO-NO, *s.* He nui ka poe ao i ka *lono* maka ihe.

LO-NO, *s.* Name of one of the four great gods of the Hawaiian Islands; the four were Lono, Ku, Kane and Kanaloa.

LO-NO-A-KI-HI, *s.* Name of the eel god.

LO-NO-HII, *s.* *Lono* and *hii,* to tend a child. A child that is much tended and dandled.

LO-NO-LO-NO-A, *s.* A hearsay; a gossip; tattling; a story without foundation; *lonolonoa* i ka hiki o ka aina.

LO-NU, *v.* To swell; to be large.

2. To be in pain; to groan with pain.

3. To cheat in play; to be trickish.

LO-NU, *s.* A swell; a cheat; a liar; a rogue.

LO-PA, *s.* A man who cultivates land under a common farmer, but owns no lands himself; a tenant; he mahi kihapai malalo aku o ka hoa aina.

LO-PA-HOO-PI-LI-WA-LE, *s.* A low grade of farmers who obtained their living by adhering to the lopas or under farmers.

LO-PA-KU-A-KE-A, *s.* *Lopa* and *kuakea.* A man who cultivates a garden under a lopa; a farmer of a lower grade than even a lopa. *Laieik.* 21.

LO-PA-LAU-E-KA, *s.* *Lopa* and *laueka,* awkward. A man slovenly, awkward and unskillful in his work.

LO-PE,   *s.* *Eng.* from the *Eng.* rope,
LO-PI,   but used by Hawaiians for thread, sewing thread; it should be written *rope* or *ropi. Lunk.* 16:12. He mea e humuhumu ai i ka lole. See ROPE.

LO-PI-O, *v.* See PIO. To bend over, as in nodding or going to sleep.

LO-PU, *s.* The name of the koi (hatchet) offered in sacrifice.

LO-WAI-A, *s.* See LAWAIA. A fisherman.

LO-WAI-A, *v.* See LAWAIA. To catch fish.

LO-GA, *s.* *Heb.* A Hebrew liquid measure, a log. *Oihk.* 14:10.

LO-GOU, *s.* *Gr.* The name of the second person in the Trinity; an appellation of Jesus Christ. *John* 1:1.

LU, *v.* To scatter; to throw away small things, as ashes or sand. *Puk.* 9:8. To drip, as water. *Laieik.* 80.

2. To sow, as grain.

3. To shake; to kick or remove dust from one's feet.

4. To dive or plunge in the water. 2 *Nal.* 5:14. To dive, as in taking a squid.

LU, *s.* That which is thrown away or scattered.

2. That which is shot from a gun; hence, gun shot. from their scattering.

3. The small seeds of the puakala.

4. A kind of medicine; the same as *kuakala;* small seeds beaten up and mixed with some liquid for a purgative; the real name of the plant is *naule.*

LU-A, *v.* To kill by breaking the bones. NOTE.—The *lua* was much practiced in ancient times and is understood now by some old people.

2. To dig a pit; to make a deep hole in the ground.

LU-A, *s.* The art of breaking the bones of a person.

2. The art of noosing men in order to murder them, as was practiced on Kauai.

3. The place where the art of lua was taught.

4. A pit. *Puk.* 21:33. A hole; a grave; a den. *Lunk.* 6:2.

LU-A, *s.* See LUA, *adj.* A second; an equal; an assistant; a copy of a writing. *Kanl.* 17:18.

2. Likeness in quality; aole *lua* e like me ia, there is no *second* like it, i. e., there is nothing like it. See LUAOLE.

3. *Lua* expresses admiration and applies to what is good; lua poli, the endeared bosom of a warm-hearted friend. NOTE.— *Lua* was the watch-word given by Hoapili previous to the last battle on Kauai.

LU-A, *adj.* The number two. See ALUA and ELUA. Two; double; hence,

2. Deceitful; naau *lua,* a deceitful heart; double minded. *Hal.* 12:2.

3. Weak; flexible; feeble; nawaliwali, palupalu.

LU-A, *adv.* Secondly; a second time. *Nah.* 1:9.

LU-A-A-HI, *s.* *Lua,* pit, and *ahi,* fire. *Literally,* the volcano of Kilauea on Hawaii.

2. *Figuratively,* the place of punishment hereafter; hell; o ka hewa ka waa pae i ka *luaahi,* sin is the canoe that lands in *hell;* o ka *luaahi* ke awa o ka make mau loa, *hell* is the harbor or eternal death.

LU-A-A-PA-NA, *v.* To live idly or in pleasure; to live wantonly; e noho lealea me ka akaaka ame ke kamailio lapuwale. Heaha ka oukou e hana nei? Aole, e *luaapana* wale ana no makou. See LUANA.

LU-AI, *v.* To vomit; to cast out of the stomach; to cast forth from the mouth. *Hoik.* 12:15. O ka mea i *luaiia,* aole ia e ai hou iho, that which has been vomited up is not to be eaten again. FIG. Applied to a country, to cast out as a country casts out its people for their crimes. *Oihk.* 18:25.

LU-AI, *s.* Sickness of the stomach

2. A discharge from the stomach.

3. The matter or that which is vomitted up. *2 Pet.* 2:22.

LU-AI-A-KO-KO, *s.* *Luai* and *koko,* blood. A vomiting of blood.

LU-AI-E-LE, *v.* To go about from house to house or from place to place without apparent object; to live without purpose. *Hoo.* To live by deceit.

LU-AI-E-LE-IA, *s.* Laziness; indolence; bad habits; destitution; minamina ino ko'u manao i ka luaiele i keia la, o *luaieleia* e kanaka.

LU-AI-KU, *s.* A word made use of by Kamehameha I. to express his contempt of cowards, meaning Kamehameha *will vomit.*

LU-AI-PE-LE, *s.* *Luai* and *Pele,* the goddess of volcanoes. Brimstone; sulphur. *Kanl.* 29:22.

LU-AI-PO, *s.* The name of an ancient progenitor, before Wakea; his contemporaries were called *he poe ike ole, he poe na-aupo.*

LU-A-O-HA-NE, *s.* *Lua,* pit, and *ohane* for *uhane,* soul. The inner canthus or angle of the eye; the lachrymal duct perhaps.

LU-A-O-LE, *s.* *Lua,* second, and *ole,* no; none. A darling; a nonesuch; an only and dear one. *Hal.* 35:17.

2. Used in a bad sense, *luaole* o ka waha-hee, *no other such* liar; *luaole* o ka ike maka ole, *none his like* in blindness or want of observation.

LU-A-O-NI, *s.* The name of the second man that fell in battle; o ka lua o ke kanaka i make mua mai, he *luaoni* ia.

LU-AU, *s.* The petal of a plant; the leaf of the kalo; boiled herbs. i. e., the young kalo leaves gathered and cooked for food.

2. FIG. A parent; one to whom a child can resort for food; probably so called because a parent is one to whom a child can resort for his food; o kona *luau* (ka makua) no ia.

3. The name of a species of soft porous stone.

LU-AU, *adj.* Full; stuffed; crammed; filled full.

LU-AU-I, *s.* A parent; those whom children call parents or makuas; he makua, he mau makua. NOTE.—*Luaui* united with *makua,* means the *natural parent* as distinct from an *adopted* parent or uncle or aunt.

LU-A-U-HA-NE, *s.* See LUAOHANE above. The inner corner of the eye. *Anat.* 11.

LU-A-HE-LE, *v.* *Lua,* pit, and *hele,* to go. To lead astray from the path of virtue; to seduce.

LU-A-HE-LE, *s.* A leading astray; a deceiving; a speaking evil against a person.

LU-A-HI, *s.* Name of a person or persons captured in battle; name of one whipped in a single fight; i upu aku ai oukou o ka oukou *luahi* ka ike.

LU-A-HI-NE, *s.* *Lua* and *wahine,* woman. A contraction of *luwahine.* An old woman.

LU-A-HO-HO-NU, *s.* *Lua,* pit, and *hohonu,* deep. A deep pit or ditch; the bottomless pit, hell. *Hoik.* 9:1.

LU-A-HU-NA, *s.* *Lua* and *huna,* to hide. A cave or pit in which property was concealed, as in time of war; a concealed or hidden pit.

LU-A-HO-A-NA, *s.* The halo or rainbow appearance around the sun or moon.

LU-A-KA-HA, *v.* To have dwelt long in a place; to have become an inhabitant; to be at home; to be familiar with a location; heaha ka oukou e noho ai maanei? *Ans.* Ka inoa he *luakaha* ko makou noho ana.

LU-A-KA-LAI, *s.* See LUAHOANA. A halo around the sun or moon in cloudy or hazy weather.

LU-A-KA-LAI-LA-NI, *s.* See LUAHOANA and LUAKALAI. A halo, &c.

LU-A-KE-LE, *s.* A sepulchre; a place for depositing the dead.

LU-A-KI-NI, *s.* *Lua,* pit, and *kini,* multitude. A heiau of the largest class; o ka *luakini,* oia ka heiau a ke alii nui e noi aku ai i na 'kua ona.

2. The highest species of house in a heiau where human sacrifices were offered.

3. The worshipers in a temple. *Ier.* 7:4. NOTE.—Since the introduction of the christian religion, the name *luakini* has been given to places of worship dedicated to Jehovah; e hai i ka olelo a ke Akua iloko o ka *luakini* o Iehova.

LU-A-KU-PA-PAU, *s.* *Lua* and *kupapau,* a corpse. A grave; a receptacle of dead bodies; a tomb; a sepulchre. *1 Nal.* 13:30.

LU-A-LO-A, *s.* A species of fish-hook.

LU-A-LU-A, *v.* To be flexible ; to be pliable; to be soft; hence,

2. To be old, as garments; to be much

worn or used. *Heb.* 1:11.

LU-A-LU-A, *s.* A second-hand garment; soft; pliable; flimsy cloth.

2. A rough road; many small ravines crossing it.

3. Rough uneven land.

4. A round net for taking fish; he upena poepoe.

LU-A-LU-A, *adj.* Limber; flexible; flimsy.

LU-A-LU-AI, *v.* *Lua*, twice, and *luai*, to raise from the stomach. To raise the food again from the stomach to the mouth, as ruminating animals.

2. To chew the cud. *Kanl.* 14:6. *Hoo.* The same; to raise and chew the cud.

LU-A-LU-AI, *s.* *Hoo.* The cud; that which is raised from the stomach of an animal to be chewed over again; he mea *hoolualuaiia. Oihk.* 11:3.

LU-A-LU-A-NA, *v.* The intensive of *luana*. To be satisfied; to live comfortably; to seek pleasure; to be merry.

LU-A-ME-KI, *s.* *Lua* and *meki*, so deep as not to see the bottom. A very deep pit; a concealed hole in the ground. *Zek.* 9:11.

LU-A-NA, *v.* To live in idleness or pleasure; to be satisfied with one's self. *Hoo.* The same. Heaha ka oukou e hana nei? Aole, e *luana* wale ana no makou.

LU-A-NA, *adj.* Satisfied; easy; living in pleasure or idleness. See LUALUANA.

LU-A-NUU, *v.* To be dressed out with a large kuina of kapa, as the gods were on important occasions.

2. To stand around, as the gods around the temple.

LU-A-NUU, *s.* The name of two gods in the house of Lono.

LU-A-PAA-HA-O, *s.* *Lua*, pit, and *paahao*, iron fast. A dungeon. *Ier.* 37:16. A place of the lowest prisons. *Puk.* 12:29.

LU-A-PAA-HA-O, *adj.* Appertaining to the lowest prisons or dungeons; hale *luapaahao*. See reference above.

LU-A-PAU, *s.* The bottomless pit in the luakini; hence synonymous with luakini.

2. A yawning or devouring pit.

3. FIG. That which causes ruin or destruction; o ka mai pala, oia ka *luapau* o keia pae aina.

LU-A-PE-LE, *s.* *Lua*, a pit, and *Pele*, the goddess of volcanoes. Hence,

1. A volcano itself.

2. A volcano either now in action or extinct.

3. A puu or hillock on the top of a mountain, especially if it have a cavity on the top.

LU-A-PO, *s.* *Lua* and *po*, night. The grave. *Hal.* 88:3.

LU-A-WAI, *s.* *Lua* and *wai*, water. A well of water. *Kin.* 21:19.

2. A cistern; a pit for water. *Isa.* 36:16. He punawai hohonu.

LU-A-WE-HE-O-LE, *s.* *Lua* and *weheole*, unopened. The unopened or bottomless pit. See LUAPAU.

LU-E, *v.* To loosen that which has been fast; hence,

2. To break up, as any structure.

3. *Hoo.* To overthrow, as a system. *Oih.* 5:39. To destroy, as a house or city.

4. To scatter here and there.

5. To bury up; to overwhelm.

LU-E-A, *s.* See POLUEA. Sleepy; fatigued; the unpleasant sensations on board a ship; *luea* i ka ua.

LU-E-HU, *s.* Name of a species of soft or porous stones; there are many varieties; the term is opposed to *paa* or *pohaku paa*.

LU-E-HU, *adj.* Soft; yielding, &c.

LU-E-LU-E, *v.* Freq. of *lue*. To loosen; to destroy; to break up, &c.

LU-E-LU-E, *adj.* Loose; flowing; long, as a large loose kapa; lole *hooluelue*, a long loose robe. *Eset.* 8:15. He lole e uhi ana mai luna a hala loa ilalo.

LU-E-LU-E, *s.* A long flexible fish net; he upena *luelue*.

LU-I,
LU-I-LU-I, } *v.* See KOLUILUI.

LU-I-KI-A, *s.* A tying or binding up the outrigger of a canoe with taste and firmness; ka poe i aoia i ka hoonanawa, ame ka holo moana, ame ka *luikia* i ka iako.

LU-I-NA, *s.* A resident in a ship; a sailor. *Hoik.* 18:17. Ka poe kanaka hooikaika no ka moku.

LU-O-NI, *s.* The person or chief who delivers one condemned to death and in confinement.

2. The work of salvation as effected by Jesus Christ; this personage was called by Hawaiians *Haku malama.*

LUU, *v.* See LU. To dive; to plunge into the water out of sight.

2. To spill out; to flow rapidly; to rush, as water confined in narrow places.

3. To sow, as seed; to scatter; hence, to overturn; to overthrow. See LU.

4. *Hoo.* To dip into coloring matter; to dye. *Puk.* 25:5. To dye, as a garment in a liquid. *Hoik.* 19:13.

5. To plunge headlong down into the deep.

Luu, *s.* That which may be thrown or scattered, i. e., shot; *luu manu,* duck shot. See **Lu.**

Luu-i-li, *s. Luu* and *ili,* skin. A tanner of skins or hides. *Oih.* 9:43. NOTE.—This word in the reference has been changed to *hanaili.*

Luu-i-na, *s.* See **Luina.** A diving; from this, perhaps, common poor foreigners were called *luina.*

Luu-ha-lo, *v. Luu* and *halo,* to spread out the hands to swim. To make with the hands the motions of swimming.

Luu-ki-a, *s.* Also written *lukia.* He aha waa, he hoana e paa ai ka waa, e *lukia* (luukia) i ka ama me ka iako.

Luu-ki-mo, *v.* To dive; to dive head-foremost for some purpose; *luukimo* iho la ia me ka manao e alualu aku i ua hee la.

Luu-luu, *v.* To be in a tremor from hard exercise or from fear.

2. To shake, as a tree to get the fruit.

3. To droop; to be oppressed with sorrow. *Mat.* 26:37. To be sad; to be dejected; to be troubled in mind. *Ioan.* 13:21.

4. *Hoo.* To be sorrowful; to be cast down.

Luu-luu, *s.* Grief; trouble. *Iob.* 6:2. Depressing fear; pau ka pali, hala ka *luuluu* kaumaha, past the pali, past the heavy fear.

Luu-luu, *adj.* Toilsome; painful. *Iob.* 7:3. Heavy; sorrowful.

Luu-u-la, *v. Luu* and *ula,* red. To color red. *Hoo.* To dye red. *Isa.* 63:1.

Lu-he, *adj.* Proud; exhibiting one's haughtiness; making a show; fat; acting the chief; lula, *luhe,* i ke kaha o Kaunalewa.

Lu-he, *v.* To fade; to wither; to hang down, as a withering plant.

Lu-he-a, *s.* Name of a species of plant; ka lau o *luhea* o ka ohai o mana.

Lu-he-a-na, *v.* To feel comfortable, as a hungry person after eating; e *luheana* e ka malie.

Lu-hee, *v.* To pull up and down the line, as in catching a squid.

Lu-hee, *s.* Name of a species of fish caught with a hook.

2. Name of a quality of stone or rock; eia na pohaku *luhee,* he mau ano e loa ko lakou, here are the *luhee* rocks unlike all others.

Lu-he-le-lei, *v. Lu* for *luu,* and *helelei,* to scatter. To be scattered about here and there, in this place and that, as books, papers or small funiture.

Lu-he-lu-he, *adj.* See **Luhe.** Fat; full; plump; momona, kaha.

Lu-hi, *v.* To be fatigued with labor; to labor severely so as to be oppressed.

2. To labor or suffer with grief; to be weighed down with grief.

3. *Hoo.* To oppress; to be hard on one; to urge one to labor equal to, or more than his physical powers can bear; to weary one with intercession. *Luk.* 18:5.

Lu-hi, *s.* Weariness; fatigue. FIG. A cause of anxiety; one especially beloved; i aku la, e kuu *luhi,* eia ke kane, my *dear one,* here is a husband. *Laieik.* 197.

2. A heavy burden; ka mea e hooluhi ai.

3. Oppression; hard labor. *Isa.* 56:11.

Lu-hi, *adj.* Tiresome; causing weariness; requiring a long time to finish. NOTE. *Luhi* is mostly occasioned by carrying a burden. *Hoo.* Causing hard service or bondage; luna *hooluhi,* an officer who has power to oppress.

Lu-hi-a, *s.* A species of large fish of the shark kind.

Lu-hi-e-hu, *adj.* Soft; cooked soft; pala, moa.

Lu-hi-he-wa, *v. Luhi* and *hewa,* wrong; wicked. To oppress wrongfully. *Hoo.* To cause one to be oppressed; to vex. *Oihk.* 19:33. To be ill treated; to maltreat. *Hal.* 9:9.

Lu-hi-lu-hi, *v.* Freq. of *luhi.* To trouble or burden one often. *Hoo.* To weary one with importunity; to weary one with bad conduct. *Isa.* 43:24. To burden with expenses or taxes. *Isa.* 43:23.

Lu-ka, *s.* An assembly of women for prayer; he aha pule na ka wahine.

Lu-ka-lu-ka, *s.* The appearance of growing, flourishing, thrifty vegetables; also applied to animals; as, puaa *lukaluka.* See **Nukanuka.**

Lu-ka-ma-e-a, *s.* A prayer used by females from the time of Papa; ma ia ao ana ae, *lukamaea,* o olekukahi ia la.

Lu-ki-a, *v.* See **Luukia.**

Lu-ko, *adj.*

Lu-ku, *v.* To make a slaughter, i. e., to kill a multitude, as in a severe battle; to overthrow; to destroy; to slay, as in war. *Oihk.* 26:17.

2. FIG. To smite; to destroy, as with a pestilence. *Nah.* 14:12. To root out or utterly lay waste a people. NOTE.—*Luku* applies mostly to the destruction of a great many at once; to make havoc; to root out. The word is also mostly confined to the first conjugation; it is applied also to an extensive cutting up and destroying of vines

and fig trees. *Hos.* 2:14.

Lu-ku, *s.* Slaughter; a destruction of people on a large scale. *Isa.* 34:6. The rooting out or utter destruction of a people.

Lu-ku, *adj.* Mea *luku,* a destroyer. *Puk.* 12:23.

Lu-ku-a, *v.* Passive for *lukuia.* To be slaughtered; to be scattered; e hoopauia.

Lu-ku-na, *s. Luku,* slaughter, and *ana.* A slaughtering; a destruction of persons; a papauku wale ka *lukuna.*

Lu-la, *v.* To be calm, as when there is no wind; to be smooth, as the sea.

2. To be lazy; to be indolent.

Lu-la, *s.* A calm state of the atmosphere when there is no wind.

2. A diminishing or calming of a storm.

Lu-la, *adj.* Smooth, as the surface of the sea unruffled by the wind.

2. Lazy; careless; indolent; hanging like a flag without wind; *lula,* luhe, i ke kaha o Kaunalewa.

Lu-la-na, *v.* To be calm, as people that have been wailing for a deceased person, they cease wailing and are still; *lulana* aku i ka ae wai liu la.

Lu-le, *v.* To shake, as the flesh of a fat person.

2. To be fat; to have soft flesh. See OLULELULE.

3. *Hoo.* To make one fat or fleshy, i. e., to have one's flesh shake and roll with fatness. NOTE.—In some cases *lule* and its compounds have definitions like *luli,* they are kindred to each other.

Lu-le-lu-le, *v.* See LULE. To be very fat, as a person; to have the flesh soft and rolling.

Lu-le-lu-le, *adj.* Fat; rolling; shaky, as the flesh of a fat person.

Lu-li, *v.* To vibrate; to shake; to shake, as a bush in the wind. *Mat.* 11:7.

2. To vary from one position; to rock; to roll, as a ship with the wind astern; to overturn; to lay down sideways.

3. To be moved from place to place.

4. To be unsteady.

5. *Hoo.* To change, as a law. *Dan.* 6:8. and 12. To shake, as the head in defiance. 2 *Nal.* 19:21. To shake together.

6. To wave as a wave-offering. *Oihk.* 7:30.

Lu-li, *adj.* Unsteady; changeable; shaking; moving to and fro.

Lu-li-lu-li, *v.* See LULI. To shake often; to vibrate; to shake, as in shaking hands.

2. To overturn; to overthrow, as the

shaking of an earthquake.

3. To shake together; to shake down, as corn in a barrel.

4. To shake, as the head in scorn. *Isa.* 37:22.

5. *Hoo.* To rock, as in a cradle; to shake the head in mockery. *Iob.* 16:4.

6. To stir up, i. e., to awaken out of sleep.

Lu-li-lu-li, *adj.* Tottering; standing unsteadily; easily shaken; rocking; not firm.

Lu-lo, *s.* Thick leaves of a tree wreathed or twisted into an ornament for the neck; a wreath for the neck.

Lu-lo, *s.* A vicious orthography for *rula,* a rule.

Lu-lo-ni, *v.* To be in a deep sleep; to sleep soundly. See LULUHI.

Lu-lu, *v.* To shake, as the dust from anything; to shake, as the dust from one's feet. *Mat.* 10:14. To fan; to winnow.

2. To shake, as a cloth. *Neh.* 5:13. To shake, as the fists in defiance. *Laieik.* 46.

3. To sow or scatter, as grain. *Kin.* 26:12.

4. To scatter; to disperse, as a people. *Ezek.* 30:26. To shake; to overthrow. *Puk.* 14:27.

5. To lie quietly or still, as a ship in a harbor.

6. *Haa.* for *hoo.* To tremble; to shake through fear. *Kanl.* 2:25.

7. To be awe struck; to be afraid.

8. To be borne down; to be pressed down, as with a weight. See LULUU.

9. To be calm, as the sea. See No. 5. above. Hence,

10. To flap or flutter, as a sail turned into the wind; *lulu* ka pea.

Lu-lu, *s.* A calm spot at the leeward of an island precipice.

2. A level spot of ground, as the kahua of a house.

3. The play of dice used in backgammon.

4. *Haa.* A trembling.

Lu-lu, *adj.* Sowing; hua *lulu,* seed for sowing. *Oihk.* 11:37.

2. Calm; wahi *lulu,* a place where the wind does not reach.

Lu-lu-ai-e-le, *v.* To be inconstant; to go here and there; to change one's place; e kealia. See LUAIELE.

Lu-lu-ai-na-o-le, *s.* A young person that has been well cared for from a child and has grown up handsome and agreeable.

Lu-lu-a-lii, *s. Lulu,* a shaking or fluttering, as a loose garment, and *alii,* chief; royal. A garment of bird's feathers; a robe of royalty.

Lu-luu, *adj.* Heavy with grief; sleepy; bowed down, as the head. See LUULUU.

Lu-lu-hi, *v.* See LUHI. To be very much fatigued and heavy with sleep. *Mat.* 25:5.

2. To be sleepy; to be in a deep sleep; to sleep soundly. See LULONI.

3. To hang black and heavy, as clouds.

4. *Hoo.* To be harshly treated; to be frequently fatigued with hard labor; to labor as a servant constantly. *Oih.* 7:6.

Lu-lu-hu-a, *s.* *Lulu* and *hua*, seed. A sower of seed. *Mat.* 13:3. *Lulu* anoano, a sower of seed. *Luk.* 12:24.

Lu-lu-lu, *v.* See LULU. To flap, as a sail when the wind is irregular or but little; to be calm, or want of steady wind; *lululu* ka pea.

Lu-lu-mi, *v.* See LUMI. To gather into small compass; to come together, as a rush of people; to press upon one, as in a crowd; to come together in multitudes. *Luk.* 20:33. To rush along irregularly; e uhauha ma ke alanui; to fold up; to press hard, as dirt around kalo; huki i ke kalo nui, *lulumi* i ka lepo, a popoi i ka mauu.

2. To hide; to conceal.

> *Lulumi* malua i ke alo o ka umuloa,
> Kuikui hilo i ke kai a halehua
> I na 'ku no la i Peekoa.

Lu-lu-mi, *s.* A thick crowd of people; a great multitude, particularly if they have come together without order.

Lu-ma, *v.* To kill one by putting his head under water.

Lu-mai, *v.* See LU. To put to death by putting the head under water.

Lu-mai-a, *v.* To be entangled or turned over and over by the surf; e lauwiliia, e limilimi e ka nalu.

Lu-mai-a, *s.* The being overwhelmed, as in a heavy storm, rain pouring down all over one; ua kilu wale i ka *lumaia* e ka ua.

Lu-ma-na-wa-hu-a, *s.* An internal pain; a pain of the bowels.

2. Internal pain for the loss of one's property, like *minamina*.

Lu-mi, *v.* See LULUMI. To come together; to come together, as a rush of people; to rush along, &c. See LULUMI for the various meanings.

Lu-mi-a, *s.* A species of sorcery; he pule anaana.

Lu-mi-lu-mi, *v.* Intensive of *lumi*. See the definitions of *lulumi*.

2. To practice sorcery; to repeat the pule anaana.

Lu-mi-lu-mi, *v.* To act foolishly; to act wickedly; to do slovenly; e hana ino, kapulu, opiopi inoino; to be in a state of drunkenness and debauchery; ua *lumilumiia* laua e ka ona a ka awa. *Laieik.* 203.

> *Lumilumi* a ka poli o aaialoha
> A hai e ka lua i honopu.

Lu-na, *s.* The upper side of anything.

2. The upper; the above.

3. A high place or seat; kahi kiekie.

4. A person who is over others in office or command; hence, an overseer; an officer; a director.

5. A head man of a land who gives orders.

6. A herald; a messenger; one sent on business by a chief; an ambassador.

7. An executive officer of any kind, qualified by the added word. See the examples below.

8. The chief piece in the game konane; paa mua ia'u na *luna* o ka papa konane a maua. *Laieik.* 115.

Lu-na, *adj.* Upper; higher; above; keena *luna*, an upper room. NOTE.—*Luna* as opposed to *lalo*, down, takes its base at the height of a man's head; all above the height of a man's head is said to be *luna*, above, upward, high, according to the thing spoken of; and all below the height of a man's head is said to be *lalo*, down, below, under. See *D. Malo* 6:1. Hence the terms in ascending are, *oluna ae, oluna aku, oluna loa aku, oluna lilo aku, oluna lilo loa, oluna o ke ao*, above the clouds; still higher, *ke aouli, ka laniuli, ka lanipaa.*

Lu-na, *comp. prep.* On; above; higher; over, &c.; found only in the compounds *a, i, o, ko, no, ma* and *mai*. See each in its place, also Grammar § 161.

Lu-na-au-hau, *s.* *Luna*, officer, and *auhau*, a tax. One who collects taxes and has charge of tax money; a tax-gatherer; a publican. *Luk.* 7:34. A master of the tribute. *1 Nal.* 12:18.

Lu-na-a-ha-ai-na, *s.* *Luna* and *ahaaina*, a feast. The master or director of a feast. *Ioan.* 2:8.

Lu-na-o-ha-na, *s.* *Luna* and *hana*, work. An overseer or officer of work. *1 Oihl.* 9:34.

Lu-na-o-le-lo, *s.* *Luna* and *olelo*, speech. An officer of communication; one sent to make proclomation; an apostle. *Oih.* 1:2.

Lu-na-ha-le-ki-ai, *s.* *Luna* and *hale*, house, and *kiai*, to watch. The governor of a fortress. *Isa.* 33:18.

Lu-na-ha-ne-ri, *s.* *Luna* and *haneri* (*Eng.*), a hundred. An officer over a hundred soldiers; a centurion. *Luk.* 7:2, 3.

LU-NA-HOO-LU-HI, *s.* *Luna* and *hooluhi,* to vex; to burden. A task master. *Puk.* 5:6.

LU-NA-KAU-A, *s.* *Luna* and *kaua,* war. A captain in war. *Lunk.* 11:6.

LU-NA-KA-HI-KO, *s.* *Luna* and *kahiko,* old. An elderly man of influence from age, dignity of character, knowledge, &c. *Puk.* 3:16.

LU-NA-KA-NA-LI-MA, *s.* *Luna* and *kanalima,* fifty. A leader of fifty men. *2 Nal.* 1:10.

LU-NA-KA-NA-WAI, *s.* *Luna* and *kanawai,* law. A judge; a magistrate; one who applies the law to delinquents or transgressors.
2. Name of a book of the Old Testament. *Judges.*

LU-NA-KI-A, *s.* *Luna,* over, above, and *kia,* a pillar or post. That which is above or over the kia or pillar; a chapter; the upper part of a column. *1 Nal.* 7:16.

LU-NA-KI-AI, *s.* *Luna* and *kiai,* to watch. A person who oversees or watches over others; a bishop; an overseer. *Pilip.* 1:1.

LU-NA-KI-E-KI-E, *s.* *Luna* and *kiekie,* high. A dignified person; a person high in responsible office; dignity. *Iuda* 8.

LU-NA-KO-A, *s.* *Luna* and *koa,* soldier. A military officer; a captain; a sergeant, &c.

LU-NA-LA-WE, *s.* *Luna* and *lawe,* to take; to carry. An upper servant.

LU-NA-LA-WE-HA-NA, *s.* *Luna* and *lawe,* to take, and *hana,* work. A minister; a chief servant. *Kol.* 1:23.

LU-NA-MA-NAO, *s.* *Luna* and *manao,* thought. The director of one's thoughts; the internal monitor, i. e., conscience; the sense which feels in view of right and wrong; pioloke ka noonoo ana a ka *luna-manao,* the thinking of the *conscience* was troublesome. NOTE.—This is a late coined word introduced into the work on Moral Philosophy and used to some extent in other late books; used with *hoopuiwa.* See *Laieik.* 79.

LU-NA-TAU-SA-NI, *s.* *Luna* and *tausani* (Eng.),a thousand. The captain or officer over a thousand men. *Mar.* 6:21.

LU-NU, *v.* To covet, as the property of others.
2. To extort; to have that feeling that would extort from others. See ALUNU and also (incorrectly pronounced) NUNU.
3. To swathe; to fold or bind up; to roll up, as a bundle of kapa or cloth; to bind up, as an article in kapa.

LU-NU, *adj.* Covetous; stingy; parsimonious; exercising a kind of violence; oppressive; lawless. See ALUNU.
2. Swollen; puffed up.

LU-PA-LU-PA, *s.* The name of a prayer at a luakini; a pule no ke kahuna, he *lupalupa* ka inoa o ia pule.

LU-PE, *s.* A kite.
2. The end of the outrigger of a canoe. See KANAKA.
3. A species of fish.
4. A large creature of the sea. See HIHIMANU.

LU-PE-A-KE-KE, *s.* The name of a bird; the sea eagle.

LU-WA-HI-NE, *v.* To be an old woman. *Rut.* 1:12. See LUAHINE.

LU-WA-HI-NE, *s.* An old woman.
2. A particular class of men under Kamehameha I.: some were chiefs, some were common people.

LU-WA-HI-NE, *adj.* Of or pertaining to an old woman; wa *luwahine,* time of being an old woman.

M.

M is the ninth letter of the Hawaiian alphabet. It is a liquid, and yet it is interchangeable with *k,* a mute; as, *makia, kakia,* &c.

MA. The syllable *ma* is used for several purposes.
1. *Ma* is formative of many nouns, in which case it seems to imply fullness, solidity, addition, &c., to the orignal word.
2. It often carries the idea of accompanying, together, &c. See MALANA, MAMAMAKE, to die together, &c.
3. *Ma* is used in swearing or taking an oath (1 *Sam.* 17:43, 55), and signifies by. See the preposition *ma.*
4. *Ma* is also used sometimes like the emphatic *o* in such phrases as this: *ma* kela mau mea elua, ua loaa paka no i na kanawai.

MA, *prep.* At; by; in; through; unto; by means of; according to, &c. *Gram.* § 67 and § 68, 1. Ma laua o, together with; haalele oia i ka aina o Wailuku *ma laua* o Waihee, he forsook the region of Wailuku *together with that of* Waihee; in this case it is synonymous with *laua me* and *a me.*

MA, *adj.* or a *particle,* which mostly follows proper names of persons, and signifies *an attendant upon*, or *persons belonging to*, or *accompanying*; as, ke alii *ma*, the chief *and his train*; an officer *and his posse*; the master of a family with his children and domestics; Hoapili *ma*, Hoapili and *those known to be about him*. It included persons in all capacities from an equal with the one named to all connected with him, even to his servants. *Nah.* 16:8. NOTE.—It is possible that the double *ma* or *mama* which enters most of the numeral adjectives both cardinal and ordinal above umi or ten, should be referred to this particle.

MA, *v.* To fade, as a leaf or flower; to wilt.

2. To blush, as one ashamed.

3. To wear out, as a person engaged in too much business. *Puk.* 18:18.

4. *Hoo.* To fail; to perish, as a person or thing.

MAA, *v.* To accustom; to be accustomed to do a thing, as a work; to be easy in one's manners; to be polite; to be friendly; e walea, e launa; to be used; to be accustomed; to have practice. *Ier.* 2:24.

2. To accustom one's self; applied to the knowledge of a road often traveled.

3. To gain knowledge by practice.

4. To sling, as a stone; to cast a stone from a sling. *Lunk.* 20:16. To throw or cast away, as a sling does a stone. *Ier.* 10:18.

5. To be small or little, as a substance.

MAA, *s.* A sling. 2 *Oihl.* 26:14. An offensive weapon of war formerly in use among the Hawaiians. 1 *Sam.* 17:40. He kaula hoolele i ka pohaku.

2. A string of a musical instrument; he kaula hookani.

3. Ease of manners; politeness gained by practice.

4. Experience; long use; frequent trial.

5. A going about here and there; ka hele wale i o ia nei.

6. The name of a sea breeze at Lahaina; the same as *aa.*

MAA, *adj.* Accustomed to do a thing. *Ier.* 31:18. Practiced in any business; used to.

2. Offensive in smell; stinking.

MA-A-A, *s.* Name of a sea breeze at Lahaina. See MAA 6 above. Makani *maaa.*

MAA-E-LE-LE, *v.* To be cold; to shiver; to shake with the cold; e anuanu, e haukeke.

MA-A-O, *s.* The name of a fish.

MA-AU, *v.* To entangle; to get one into difficulty; to make a law or lay a kapu in order to entrap people, as in former times; mostly used with

2. *Hoo.* To give one trouble; to afflict without cause; to persecute. *Kanl.* 30:7.

3. To avenge or to take vengeance. *Oihk.* 19:18. SYN. with hoomauhala.

MA-AU, *s. Hoo.* Indifference; neglect of that which is good.

2. Persecution; tribulation; affliction.

3. Willful or needless opposition to one; a going about from house to house, being forward, impertinent, troublesome.

MA-AU, *s.* The name of a weed.

MA-AU-A, *v. Hoo.* To increase; to come upon, as fear; to be afraid.

MA-AU-A, *s.* Anything old or ancient; what is of long standing; epithet of a person who has lived long; old age.

2. A garden; a patch of ground.

MA-AU-A, *adj.* Old; ancient; old, as a person; long ago, as an event.

MA-AU-AU, *s.* A poi calabash.

MA-AU-AU-A, } *v.* To have articles for
MA-AU-AU-WA, } sale; to sell goods; to peddle; to trade; to make market. NOTE. This word was formerly confined to the Island of Oahu; at the other islands it was *piele* and *kalepa.*

MA-AU-AU-A, } *s.* A market man; a
MA-AU-AU-WA, } peddler; one who trades and gets money without work.

MA-AU-AU-A, *adj.* See MAAUA. Old; applied to men; a very indefinite term.

MA-AU-E-A, *adj.* Lazy; manifesting a lazy disposition.

MA-A-U-LA-U-LA, *s.* Maa and *ula*, red. A kind of red earth used in coloring, obtained in some deep ravines.

MA-AU-PO-PO, *adj.* Thick.

MA-A-HE, *v.* See AHE, a light breeze. To make small ; to diminish; to reduce to less size.

MA-A-LA-HI, *v.* To escape from any evil real or imaginary.

2. To be possessed of privileges, as an intelligent person over an ignorant one; nolaila, *maalahi* wale ka poe i imi aku ia oe (ka naauao), aohe nui ka hana.

MA-A-LA-HI, *s.* Nobleness; exultation; ka hanohano.

MA-A-LE-A, *s. Maa*, accustomed, and *lea*, *adv.*, very. Cunning; craft; subtlety, such as is obtained by practice; skill in doing a thing, especially mischief, such as getting the advantage of another. *Luk.* 20:23.

MA-A-LE-A, *adj.* Prudent; having forethought; wise.

2. Cunning; crafty. *Iob.* 15:5.

Ma-a-le-a, *v.* To be wise; to be artful; to be cunning; to use policy.

2. *Hoo.* To act wisely; to act skillfully; &c.

Ma-a-le-a, *adv.* Deceitfully. *Puk.* 21:14. Cunningly; craftily. *Ios.* 9:4.

Ma-a-li, *s.* Some small slender substance; a piece broken off. See MOALI.

Ma-a-li, *adj.* Small; thin; he maawe.

Maa-li-li, *v.* To abate heat in any hot substance. *Anat.* 43.

2. To cool or appease, as anger. *Eset.* 2:1.

3. *Hoo.* To cool; to reduce the temperature; to appease the anger of any one. *Sol.* 16:14.

Maa-li-li, *adj.* Cooled; spoken of what has been hot; lukewarm.

2. Blasted; stunted; spoken of fruit. *Amos* 4:9.

Ma-a-lo, *v.* Ma and *alo*, to pass from one place to another. To pass along by a place or thing. *Kanl.* 2:8.

2. To pass by one. *Iob.* 9:11.

3. To pass through, as a land; to make way through a crowd.

4. To pass away, as one's glory or property. *Dan.* 4:31.

5. To pass by, as a shadow. *Iob.* 4:15.

Maa-lo-a, *s.* The name of a bush or small tree, from the bark of which kapa was made.

Ma-a-lo-a-lo, *v.* See MAALO above. To go frequently or quickly from place to place.

Ma-a-lo-a-lo, *s.* The act of reading by hitching along without being able to read fluently.

Maa-lo-e-lo-e, *v.* See MALOELOE. To be weary; to be tired; to be heavy with sleep.

Maa-maa-le-a, *adj.* The intensive of *maalea.* Very cunning; very crafty; more than ordinarily politic.

Ma-a-ma-a-ma, *v.* For *malamalama,* the *l* dropped as in the Marquesan dialect. Light; the opposite of darkness; ka pau ana o ka manawa po. *Laieik.* 26.

Ma-a-ma-a-ma, *adj.* Light as opposed to dark. See MALAMALAMA.

Ma-a-nei, ⎫

Ma-e-nei, ⎬ *adv.* Ma, preposition, and *anei* or *enei* or *nei*, here. Here;

Ma-nei, ⎭ at this place, in distinction from some other place. LIT. At here. See NEI.

Ma-a-we, *v.* To go along a narrow road; to wind along, as in a crooked path.

2. To be small; to be thin; to be poor in flesh; hence,

3. To be weak or sickly. See AWE, the

strings or tails of a squid.

Ma-a-we, *s.* Ma and *awe.* See AWE-AWE, to be small. A small indefinite part of something; a small substance; a bit of a string or small piece of a rope; a shoe string, &c. *Kin.* 14:23.

2. A print of a footstep; a track; the wake of a ship; he aweawe, me he holo ana na ka moku.

Ma-a-we, *adj.* Small; narrow; thin.

2. Moving in a narrow path; applied to a road or path; hele aku la oia i ke ala *maawe* iki a ke aloha, he has gone in the path little *traveled* by the loved ones.

Ma-a-we-a-we, *s.* Spots; variegated colors on a thing; marks making different shades of colors. See MAAWE and AWE.

Ma-a-we-a-we, *adj.* Spotted; marked; variegated with small changes of color or form.

Ma-a-we-u-la, *s.* Maawe and *ula*, red; brown. A path or road so much trodden as to cause the red or brown earth to appear.

Ma-a-we-lo-lo-a, *s.* Maawe and *loloa*, long. The warp of cloth. *Oihk.* 13:48.

Ma-a-we-po-ko-po-ko, *s.* Maawe and *pokopoko*, short. The filling or woof of cloth. *Oihk.* 13:48.

Mae, *v.* To blast; to wither; to fade.

1. To wither, as the petals of flowers or leaves of vegetables; e loha ka lau o ka laau, e maloo.

2. To roll up, as the leaves of vegetables in drought (kindred with *mai,* sick.) See MA.

3. To pine away, as persons with disease, i. e., to perish. *Hal.* 18:45.

4. To pass away, as a people; to disappear, as a judgment from heaven. *Oihk.* 26:39.

Mae, *s.* See MAI. A species of sickness; a pain in the bowels.

Mae, *adj.* Blasted, as fruit; withered, as a flower or a leaf.

2. Faded, as a color.

3. Sad; sober, as a person disappointed in his expectations.

Ma-e-a, *adj.* Ma and *ea*, strong smelling. Bad smelling; strong; unpleasant to the smell; hauna.

Ma-e-a-e-a, *adj.* Ma and *eaea*, strong smelling. See EA. Turbulent; refractory.

2. Strong in disobedience, as a child that refuses obedience to his parents and runs away; not under restraint.

3. Strong physically; he keiki *maeaea,* a strong child; *maeaea* i ka holo, swift to run; *maeaea* i ka hana, strong for work.

Mae-e-le, *v.* Mae and *ele,* an intensive.

To be void of proper feeling, as a leg or an arm from the want of proper circulation of blood. *Anat.* 49. Ua maeele kona puuwai i ke aloha.

2. To be benumbed; to be insensible to the touch; *maeele* oia no kona kaikuahine opiopio. *Laieik.* 176.

3. *Hoo.* To be touched with sympathy; to have feeling for one. *Laieik.* 74.

MAE-E-LE, *s.* Numbness of any part when the circulation of blood is retarded; ka pilikia loa o na aalolo no ka noho mau ana ma ka aoao hookahi. NOTE.—Hawaiians express a strong internal glow of love for a person by the term *maeele*, equivalent to the external feeling of a limb when the flow of blood has for a time been stopped or retarded and the limb, in common language, is said to be asleep; he mea e ka *maeele* o ke alii wahine i ke aloha. *Laieik.* 205.

2. Hardness and numbness of any part.

3. The sensation of a female during the time of gestation.

MAE-E-LE, *adj.* Benumbed; he *maeele* no ka lima; void of feeling, as a leg or an arm which has its circulation stopped.

2. Filthy; polluted. See PAELE.

MA-E-HA-E-HA, *s.* Ma and *ehaeha*, pain. Twilight; dusk of the evening when it is painful for the eyes to see.

MAE-MAE, *v.* To be pure; to be clean; to be without defilement physically or morally; to be free from any wrong done to another. *Oih.* 20:26.

2. *Hoo.* To cleanse; to make clean; to purify naturally, morally or ceremonially; e hoopau i ka pelapela. *Oihk.* 8:15.

3. To sanctify; to cleanse what has been impure. *Ios.* 7:13.

4. To dry; to put up to dry.

MAE-MAE, *s.* Cleanness; purity, either physical or moral; a separation from what is wrong; a separating between good and evil.

MAE-MAE, *adj.* Clean; pure; free from defilement morally. *Oihk.* 11:44.

2. Glorious; good.

3. Dried; put in a situation to dry.

MA-E-NEI, *adv.* See MAANEI. Ma and *enei* or *nei*. See NEI. Here; in this place. *Nal.* 22:7. Here, i. e., in this life, in distinction from another. *Heb.* 7:8. Ma o ka puka, a *maenei* o ka puka, that side of the door, and this side of the door.

MA-E-NO-E-NO, *v.* Ma and *eno*, to be wild. To be jealous; to entertain jealous thoughts.

MA-E-WA, *v.* Ma and *ewa*, to bend out

of shape. To be tremulous; to be unstable, as any substance unfixed.

2. To be led crookedly; e kaiewa.

3. To be blown here and there; as the spray of the surf by the wind; e hoopuehuia e ka wai.

4. To mock; to revile; to treat with scorn; to make ashamed; to reproach one with some base act of which he is not guilty. *Hoo.* The same.

MA-E-WA-E-WA, *v.* Intensive of *maewa*. To abuse; to mock, &c. *Hoo.* To trouble; to vex; to redicule. 1 *Nal.* 18:27. To abuse; to treat vilely or contemptuously. 1 *Sam.* 31:4. To suffer affliction. *Iak.* 5:10.

MA-E-WA-E-WA, *s.* A reproach; a scorning. See MAEWA.

2. The cutting of the hair irregularly on account of the death of a chief or relative.

MA-E-WA-E-WA, *adj.* Reproaching. *Sol.* 17:5. Scorning.

MAI, *v.* See MAE, to fade, &c. To be or to fall sick. 2 *Sam.* 12:15. To be diseased; to be unwell. *Ioan.* 11:1, 3.

MAI, *v.* Oia kekahi mea e hooheehee ai ka ai, alaila *mai* iho la. *Anat.* 52.

MAI, *s.* Sickness generally; illness; disease; *mai* ahulau, *mai* luku, a pestilence; *mai* eha nui, a painful disease; *mai* pehu, the dropsy.

2. The private parts of men and women; o ka malo, oia ka wawae e paa ai ka *mai*; *mai* wili, the venereal disease or gonorrhea.

MAI, *adj.* Sick; diseased; weak.

MAI, *prep.* From, as from a person, place or thing *spoken of*.

2. Towards a person, place or thing *speaking*, and repeated after the noun when the motion is *towards* the person speaking; otherwise *aku* or *ae* is used; as, *mai* Kauai *mai*, *from* Kauai (here) this way; *mai* Honolulu *aku* a i Kailua, *from* Honolulu *onward* to Kailua. *Gram.* § 75.

MAI, *adv.* An adverb of prohibition; before a verb it is used imperatively for prohibiting; *mai* hele oe, *don't* you go; *mai* hana hou aku, *do* it *not* again. It is often used with *noho a* in a prohibitory sense; as, *mai noho* oukou *a* hana kolohe, *do not* do mischief. See NOHO.

MAI, *adv.* Almost; nearly; near to; exposed to; about to be; *mai* ike ole oe ia'u, you were *near* never seeing me; *mai* make au, I was *almost* dead; mostly used in the beginning of a sentence.

MAI-A, *s.* The plantain, the banana and its different varieties; a fruit kapu for women to eat in ancient times.

MAI-A, *v.* To chew in the mouth; to masticate; to soften for swallowing.

MAI-A, *adj.* Chewed; groud up in the mouth; masticated; hoowaliia.

MAI-AO, *s.* A toe or finger nail; the hoof of a beast; the claws of a bird or animal. See MAIUU.

MAI-AU, *s.* Natural skill; ingenuity; wisdom. *Iob.* 11:6. SYN. with noiau.

2. The itch; same as *kakio*; more correctly written *meau*.

MAI-AU, *adj.* Neat; cleanly.

2. Industrious; constantly employed.

3. Skillful; ingenious; expert at doing various kinds of business.

4. Ready and correct in speaking; o ka hana *maiau*, he hipapalale ole, he noiau, he papalale ole. NOTE.—This epithet applies to men chiefly; the same quality applied to women is *loia*.

MAI-A-KU-KA-NA-LO-A, *s.* Maia and *kukanaloa*, a species of banana. A thin, shriveled or blasted banana. FIG. Any fruit blasted or shriveled up.

MAI-A-HU-LAU, *s.* Mai, sickness, and *ahulau*, pestilence. A general sickness among the people; a pestilence. *Ezek.* 12:16. See AHULAU.

MAI-A-PI-LO, *s.* The name of a shrub or tree.

MAI-E-LE, *s.* A knowledge of the use of words in a language.

2. Skill in using words. See NOILI.

3. Asking questions with skill, so as to puzzle one.

MAI-E-LI, *s.* The name of a thick brush growing on the tops of the mountains. See PUPUKEAWE.

MAI-I, *v.* To sprout or grow, as a plant; to open or spread out; to unfold, as a flower.

MAI-II, *s.* Mai, sickness, and *ii*, heavy. A pain in the back.

2. Fatigue from lying long on one side.

3. The name of a species of fish; same as the *maiko*.

MAI-O, *s.* A sickness reducing the patient's flesh like consumption; consumption; the phthisic; he mai e wiwi ai ke kino a olala.

MAI-O, *s.* A toe or finger nail, &c. See MAIAO above.

MAI-O, *v.* To scratch or mark with the nail or pointed instrument.

MAI-O-IA, *v.* To scratch or mark with a knife or one's nail.

MA-IO-IO, *adj.* Uneven; some short some long, as hair cut unevenly.

MAI-UU, *s.* See MAIAO. A nail of a finger or toe; a hoof of a beast. *Isa.* 5:28. *Maiuu* mahele, a cloven foot. *Kanl.* 14:6. E oki i ka *maiuu*, to pare the nails. *Kanl.* 21:12.

MAI-HA, *v.* Ma and *iha*, to be intent upon. To be energetic; to be intent on doing a thing; to act perseveringly in a cause; to fix the mind upon.

MA-I-HE, *v.* Ma and *ihe*, to peel off. To strip off, as the bark from a tree; to scrape off. See MAIHI.

MAI-HE,
MAI-HE-HE,
MAI-HEE-HEE, *s.* Mai, sickness, and *hee*, to run or flow. A boil; a running sore; a blister. *Puk.* 9:9.

MA-I-HI, *v.* Ma and *ihi*, to peel. To strip off; to peel, as the outside of fruit; to skin, as an animal; to strip off, as the bark of a tree.

MA-I-HI, *adj.* Stripped; peeled; everything outside taken off.

MA-I-HI-I-LI, *v.* Maihi and *ili*, the skin. LIT. To strip off the skin.

2. To strip one of property; to leave one destitute.

3. To lay a tax so as to take all the people have except their persons.

MA-I-HI-LI, *s.* One who strips another of all he has; a skinflint.

MAI-HI-LO, *s.* Mai, sickness, and *hilo*, a running sore. The venereal disease; the gonorrhea. See MAIWILI.

MAI-HO-LE, *s.* Name of a species of fish.

MAI-HU-LI, *s.* Presents made at the birth of a child. See PALALA.

MAI-KA, *v.* To play at the game called *maika*; it consisted in rolling a round smooth stone called ulu or olohu; it was connected with betting.

2. *Hoo.* To exercise at *maika*; e hoomau lewalewa.

3. To exercise violently, as at *maika*.

4. To be fatigued with hard exercise.

MAI-KA, *s.* The name of an ancient play.

2. The name of the stone used in the game of *maika*.

3. Fatigue, pain or weariness from playing *maika*.

4. Fatigue, lameness, &c., from any cause.

MAI-KA, *adj.* Weary; fatigued; lame.

MAI-KAI, *adj.* Externally good; handsome; beautiful; he wahine maka *maikai*, a handsome woman.

2. Morally good; upright; correct; excellent.

3. The sum of external excellence in conduct.

Mai-kai, *s.* Beauty; external excellence of persons or things.

2. Beauty of personal appearance; helehelena *maikai.* *Eset.* 1:11.

3. Goodness; that which is excellent in moral conduct; uprightness.

4. The sum of various external excellencies; ua like ka *maikai* me ka nani, ame ka hemolele, ame ka mimo, ame ka pono, ame ka panakai ole, ame ka auiiholo manu.

Mai-kai, *v.* To be handsome; to be externally good; to be pleasing to the sight.

2. To be of use; to be useful; to benefit; to be good.

3. *Hoo.* To make good; to repair what has been wasted, lost or destroyed. 2 *Oihl.* 24:4. To supply a deficiency; to set things in order; to regulate.

4. To treat kindly; to speak favorably of. *Kin.* 12:15.

5. To bless; to praise, as in worship.

6. *Passively,* to cause to be blessed; to pronounce a blessing upon.

7. To honor; to reverence, as a worthy character. *Puk.* 20:12.

8. To exalt; to extol; to glorify.

Mai-kai-ka, *v.* *Hoo.* The intensive of *maika.* To play hard and long at the game of maika.

2. To be wearied; to be fatigued.

Mai-kai-ka, *adj.* Tired; wearied, as a person from labor or exercise.

Mai-ka-hu-li-pu, *s.* One of the names of the god who assisted in restoring and righting canoes when upset in the ocean. See **Kamaikahulipu.**

Mai-ka-kai, *adj.*

Mai-ke-i-ki, *s.* *Mai,* sickness, and *keiki,* child. Pregnancy; the sickness of pregnancy.

Ma-i-ke-i-ke, *v.* *Ma* and *ikeike,* to know clearly. To declare; to set forth. *Hoo.* The same.

Ma-i-ko,
Ma-i-ko-i-ko, } *s.* A species of fish.

Mai-ko-la, *adj.* Worthless; trifling; used in provoking or irritating language. See **Naikola, Akola** and **Aikola.**

Ma-i-le, *s.* Name of a vine with green odoriferous leaves, of which wreaths are made; alyxia olivæformis.

2. The name of a certain chief woman who lived in former times.

3. The name of a rod used in playing at puhenehene and other games. *Laieik.* 114. See **Mailepuhenehene.**

Ma-i-le-ka-ka-hi-ki, *s.* A shrub whose branches and leaves are odoriferous; he laalaau liilii hohono.

Ma-i-le-pu-he-ne-he-ne, *s.* The rod used in playing at the puhenehene which was struck on a bunch of kapa.

Ma-i-li, *s.* Name of a soft porous stone.

Mai-lo, *v.* Probably contraction of *mai loa.* To be thin or spare, as one wasted away with long sickness; ua hele kona mai a *mailo.*

Mai-lo, *adj.* Thin; spare; wasted away; applied to sick persons; *mailo* ke kanaka.

Mai-lo-i-hi, *s.* *Mai,* sickness, and *loihi,* long. He nonopapa, he piliaiku, he mai papaakai.

Mai-lu-na, *comp. prep.* and *adv.* Mai, from, and *luna,* above. From above. *Isa.* 32:15. The auihele of *luna.* Gram. § 161.

Mai-mai, *v.* Intensive of *mai,* sick. To be sick; to be weak; to be feeble.

2. *Hoo.* To feign sickness; to pretend to be sick. 2 *Sam.* 13:5, 6.

Mai-mai, *s.* Languor; feebleness; somewhat sick; unwell.

Mai-mai, *adj.* Feeble; languid; weak.

Mai-mai, *v.* Formed from *mai* expressing motion towards one. See **Mai,** *prep.* To call one to come; to invite towards one; to call, as in calling chickens; e hea, e kolokolo aku i ka moa; to call fowls. See **Kolokolo.**

Mai-mu-li, *comp. prep.* Mai, from, and *muli,* after. From after, i. e., from following after one; *maimuli* ona aku. *Nah.* 32:15. See Grammar § 161.

Ma-i-no, *v.* Ma and *ino,* to hurt; to injure. To be the cause of evil or injury to one.

2. *Hoo.* To hurt; to afflict; to make miserable by evil treatment.

Ma-i-no-i-no, *v.* The intensive of *maino.* To afflict; to abuse; to bring evil upon.

2. *Hoo.* To suffer from perverse treatment.

3. To torment; to afflict; to trouble; to curse; to be under a curse. *Gal.* 1:8.

4. To strip one of property; to make one ashamed.

5. To betray; to deceive; to persecute.

Ma-i-no-i-no, *s.* A defacing or marring the beauty of a thing, as the countenance. *Isa.* 52:14.

2. *Hoo.* Affliction; persecution.

Ma-i-no-i-no, *adj.* Reproachful; mocking; causing shame. *Hoo.* Despiteful; sneering; contemptuous.

Ma-i-no-i-no, *adv.* Miserably; with much suffering. *Ier.* 16:4. *Hoo.* With great suffering; with severity; severely painful. 2

Pet. 2:6.

Mai-no-ho, *adv. prohib.* See **Mai,** forbidding. Do not (followed by *a* before a verb); *mainoho a hana pela,* do not so. *Mainoho* is sometimes printed in one word, sometimes in two. *Neh.* 8:10, 11.

Mai-pu-ha, *s. Mai,* disease, and *puha,* to burst or break, as a boil. An ulcer; a running sore.

Mai-wae-na, *comp. prep.* From out of; from the midst of. *Gram.* § 161.

Mai-wi-li, *s. Mai,* sickness, and *wili,* to writhe in pain. An incessant pain or sore; a sore constantly running. See **Maihilo.**

Ma-o, *v.* To carry; to bear off; to carry away.

2. To separate; to take to another place; to pass off or away, as a cloud or fog. *Laieik.* 90.

3. To hush up; to quiet; to make an end.

4. To fade, as a decaying plant.

5. To corrupt, as a dead body.

Ma-o, *s.* A kind of shrub used in dyeing kapa.

2. A blossom of that shrub.

3. The name of a species of fish.

4. The name of a great heiau.

5. A moving along; a change of position, as a body of persons. *Laieik.* 49.

Ma-o, *adj.* Separated; quiet, as in a retreat from danger; kuu po *mao* ole makole ka la.

2. Meek; mild; gentle; applied to persons.

3. Applied to colors, green; greenish; also blue. See **Maomao.**

Ma-o, *comp. prep. Ma,* preposition, and *o,* there. LIT. At there. Yonder; there; some place not far off; *mao aku,* beyond; *mao mai,* from *over* there this way. *Gram.* § 161.

Ma-o-a, *v.* To be dry; to be hard; to be cracked, as the skin.

2. To be painful, as a sore made by friction of the skin. See **Maoha.**

Ma-o-a, *s.* A sore caused by the friction of the malo between the legs during a long journey; he mai ma kapakapa, he eha i ka manawa e hele loihi ai; a sore, also, on the legs or feet; maloeloe na wawae, *maoa* na uha mamae.

Ma-o-e-a, *adj.* Tired; weary; lazy.

Ma-oi, *v. Ma* and *oi,* to exceed. To be bold; to be forward with strangers.

2. To assert one's rights with confidence. *2 Kor.* 11:21. To act the soldier.

3. To be intrusive; to be inquisitive respecting forbidden things. *Kol.* 2:18.

Ma-oi, *s.* Boldness; arrogance; forwardness.

Ma-oi, *adj.* Bold; forward; fearless; shameless.

Ma-oi-oi, *v.* See **Ma** and **Oioi,** projecting. To be rough; to be uneven; to be irregular.

Ma-oi-oi, *adj.* Uneven; notched; projecting, as a rough board or one that is split crookedly; zigzag, as a line; aliali, nihomole.

Ma-o-ha, *v.* To rub; to chafe, as the skin; to make a sore.

Ma-o-ha, *adv.* Appearing gray or whitish, as tops of mountains at a distance; kupu *maoha* ke kilakila o na kuahiwi; applied also to a person when he begins to grow gray.

Ma-o-ha, *adj.* Grayish, as the whitish feathers of a black bird; ka iwa, he manu nui ia, he eleele kona hulu, he *maoha* kahi hulu.

2. An affectionate salutation between persons for some time absent.

Ma-o-ki, *s. Ma* and *oki,* to cut, Anything cut up in pieces; pieces cut short.

2. A vulgar and incorrect pronunciation for the word *maoli.*

Ma-o-ki-o-ki, *adj.* Spotted; variegated; having different colors.

Ma-o-li, *s.* A species of banana; the long dark colored plantain; he maia eleele loloa.

Ma-o-li, *adj.* Indigenous in distinction from foreign; native; real in distinction from fictitious; true; genuine.

Ma-o-li, *adv.* Really; truly; without doubt.

2. An intensive added to other epithets to strengthen them; he lio kolohe hana ino *maoli.*

Ma-o-li-a, *adj.* Drawn out and diminished, as an elastic substance, a rope or other thing.

Ma-o-lo-ha, *s.* The ancient name of the strings or net for a calabash, equivalent to the modern word *koko;* ua kapaia o koko a *maoloha* ia koko. See **Koko.**

Ma-o-lu, *adj.* Muddy; sinking down, as in a quagmire; pohopoho, moolu, noolu, nenelu.

Ma-o-ma-o, *adj.* See **Mao.** Green, as vegetation; dark blue. See **Omaomao.**

Ma-o-ma-o, *s.* Green verdure; thick grass and bushes; a forest.

2. A species of fish living near banks and shallow places.

3. Applied to clouds, bluish green; he ao *maomao.*

Ma-o-ma-o-po-ho-le, *s.* The name of a species of fish. See above.

Ma-o-na, *v.* Ma and *ona,* drunk. To be stuffed, as in eating; to be filled, as with food. *Kanl.* 31:20. To eat to satiety; to be satisfied with food.

2. To have one's desire upon an enemy. *Puk.* 15:9.

3. *Hoo.* To fill with food; to satisfy one's self by eating. *Hal.* 103:5.

Ma-o-na, *s.* Fullness; satiety.

Ma-o-na, *adj.* Filled; satisfied; distended, as the stomach with food.

Ma-o-pa-o-pa, *adj.* Ma and *opaopa.* See Opa, lame. Weary from walking; lame; fatigued.

Ma-o-po-po, *v.* Ma and *opo,* clear; plain; even. To be plain; to be clear to the sight or senses.

2. To be clear and explicit to the understanding; to be not doubtful.

3. *Hoo.* To understand clearly; to comprehend the meaning of a word or expression; to have a clear understanding of a thing.

4. To credit; to trust.

5. To appoint, as an evil, i. e., to bring evil or a curse upon one. *Oihk.* 26:16.

6. To appoint or set, as a time; to appoint a concerted signal. *Lunk.* 20:38.

7. To set apart; to designate, as a place for doing a thing.

Ma-o-po-po, *s.* Clearness; that which is explicit, as a natural or moral truth; not liable to mistake.

2. *Hoo.* A clearing up of what is doubtful.

3. An interpretation or an explanation of a foreign language.

Ma-o-po-po, *adj.* Plain; clear to the senses or to the understanding; not doubtful; ready; in a state of preparedness to act.

2. Generous; friendly; obliging; mahamaha, luana.

Ma-o-po-po, *adv.* Clearly; evidently; plainly.

Mau, *v.* To repeat often or frequently, as in counting; to do over and over the same thing; ua *mau* ka ua o Hilo.

2. To continue; to endure; to persevere; e hiki ia oe ka *mau* ana (a gerundive form), you will arrive at *endurance,* i. e., you will be able to *continue.*

3. To continue; to remain perpetually; to be evermore. *Oihk.* 13:28. To have continually. *Ioan.* 12:8. E *mau* i ka hele, to be constantly going.

4. To persevere; to preserve constancy; to flow on ever, as a living stream of water; e kahe *mau,* e pio ole ka wai.

5. *Hoo.* To persevere; to continue in the same state in which one is; ke *hoomau* nei no ia mau mea pono ole, they will *continue to practice* those evil things.

6. To continue in the same place or same business. *Oih.* 1:14.

7. To remain in force, as a law or statute.

Mau, *v.* (A word of this orthography is used in several senses, some of which are nearly opposite, but the pronunciation is slightly changed.) See Mauu.

1. To be dry; to stop flowing, as a liquid. 2 *Nal.* 4:6.

2. To terminate, as the catamenial period.

3. *Hoo.* To fit or tie on, as sandals or shoes. See Hawele.

4. To fill with water; to wet; to soak up, as a sponge.

5. To water; to irrigate land. *Isa.* 27:3.

6. To stock or plant ground with verdure.

7. *Mau* for *mauu.* To moisten; to be moistened or wet; to soak.

Ma-u, *s.* Dampness; moisture; coolness, as the air around a shady moist place. *Hal.* 32:4. See Mauu. Also written *ma'u.*

2. The name of the region on the sides of mountains next below the waoakua; also called *waokanaka,* i. e., where men may live.

3. A species of small bulrush growing in damp places; green grass. See Mauu.

4. Dryness, from No. 1 of the preceding word; the period in each month of the sickness of females, especially the termination of that period; ke hiki i ko lakou wa e *mau* ai.

Mau, *adj.* Statedly occurring; constant; continuous; evermore; never ceasing.

2. From *mauu.* Moist; wet; cool.

3. Obscured by the sun, as the stars in the morning.

4. Ceasing to flow, as the catamenia. *Laieik.* 173.

Mau, *adv.* Frequently; continually; perpetually.

Ma'u, *s.* Name of a plant on the mountains, eaten for food in time of scarcity.

Mau. A sign of the dual or plural number. See Mau, *v.*

1. Two or a couple for the dual.

2. Some, several, a number, as a sign of the plural. Note.—*Mau* did not formerly apply to great number; in modern times the application extends to a larger number. *Gram.* § 85, 86, 90.

Mau-a, *pers. pron. dual.* We two, viz.: those who are speaking, but not including any who are addressed.

Mau-a, *adj.* Large; many.

2. Close; stingy; illiberal; obstinate. See

Makona. He kanaka *maua.*

3. Lame; sore; stiff, as with walking.

Mau-a, *s.* The name of a tree, timber good for boards.

Mau-a, *adv.* See Mau. Often or constantly repeated; loaa mau mai, mau *maua,* hiki pinepine mai.

Mau-aa-li-na, *v.* To be heavy or hard upon, as two men contending; to seize; to force one to do a thing; to use force upon.

Mau-aa-li-na, *adj.* Powerful; conquering; overcoming; strong.

Mau-ae, *v.* To exchange a thing differently from what was first agreed upon.

2. To vary in statement; to say and unsay.

Mau-ae, *s.* A crack or cleft in a rock. *Puk.* 33:22.

Mau-ai, *s.* A space between two boards; a crack; a cleft; perhaps a wrong orthography for *mauae.*

Mau-a-ka-la, *v.* To laugh. *Hoo.* To laugh with scorn or contempt; to deride; to insult.

2. E hoomahuakala. e hoopohala.

Mau-e-le, *v.* To be lazy; to be idle.

2. To waste or spend time in doing nothing.

3. To be indifferent as to future good or evil. See Mauwele.

Mau-e-le, *adj.* Lazy; indolent; going about doing nothing; acting the vagabond.

Mau-i, *s.* Name of one of the Hawaiian Islands.

Mau-i, *s.* Pain from a broken or fractured limb; ka eha, ka haki.

Mau-i, *adj.* Broken; fractured; painful, as a broken limb.

Mau-i, *v.* See Mauu. To moisten; to make wet.

2. To wring the stem of a bunch of bananas to cause it to ripen. *Hoo.* E hoopalapalani, e hoomakaukauea.

Ma-uu, *v.* See Mau. To moisten; to wet. *Sol.* 30:16.

2. To make a noise in swallowing water.

3. To work up the saliva of the mouth into froth.

4. *Hoo.* To make wet; to moisten.

Ma-uu, *s.* The noise made by swallowing a liquid.

2. A general name for green herbs, grass, seeds, rushes, shrubbery, straw, &c. *Kin.* 1:11, 12. *Mauu* uliuli, green herbs. *Hoik.* 8:7. *Mauu* maloo, hay. *Kin.* 24:25. Grass; straw, &c. Note.—Connected with *mauu* is the idea of moisture, greenness and coolness.

3. Coolness as connected with green verdure.

Ma-uu, *adj.* Green; moist; refreshing, as a cool breeze; cool.

Mau-uu-lii-lii, *s.* Earth that is little wet; vegetation that partially grows and covers the ground.

Mau-u-li-po, *s. Mauu* and *lipo,* dark. Dark green verdure, as in a dark forest.

Mau-u-la-i-li, *s.* A poisonous plant used to burn and scarify the skin.

Mau-ha, *adj.* Weary; fatigued; slow; lazy; indolent.

Mau-haa-le-le, *s.* The shadow of death; death shade. See Malukoi.

Mau-haa-le-le-a, *s.* Epithet of the man sacrificed on cutting down the ohia tree to make a god; the man thus sacrificed was a kanaka *mauhaalelea.*

Mau-haa-li-na, *v.* To bore or pierce a hole in a hard rock.

2. To carry a heavy burden on the back until fatigued; expressions for hard slavish work; ke *mauhaalina* ae la mauka o Makeahi.

Mau-ha-la, *v. Mau,* to continue, and *hala,* offense. To keep up a grudge against one; to remember his offense. *Hoo.* To be offended with one; to have a supposed cause of enmity; to lay up or remember the offense of one. 2 *Sam.* 19:19. To bear a grudge. *Oihk.* 19:18. To reserve anger. *Isa.* 3:5.

Mau-ha-la, *s. Hoo.* Envy; revenge; malice. 1 *Kor.* 5:8. Ka manao ino; a bad feeling towards one.

Mau-ka, *s.* The name of a play; ao i ka hana ana i ka *mauka;* e kalai i ka pohaku pono i ka *mauka.*

Ma-u-ka, *adv. Ma,* preposition, and *uka,* inland. Inland, in a direction opposite to the sea; opposite to *makai,* towards the sea.

Mau-koi, *s. Mau* and *koi,* perhaps for *koe,* an angle worm. An angling rod.

Mau-ko-li, *v. Mau* and *koli,* to trim or pare off. To divide out food sparingly each day for one's self or family in a time of famine; also, to divide out water in time of drought.

2. To make an offering stingily or on a small scale to the gods.

3. To live along from day to day when one is expected to die.

4. To be constant; to be persevering; ke *maukoli* nei i ka hana, i ka hele, aohe molowa.

5. To make or to be small or little; to draw out into fineness.

Mau-ko-li, *s.* The worship or sacrifice rendered to the gods.

2. One who worships or sacrifices to the

gods.

3. Any small diminutive thing; he maawe.

MA-U-KU-KU, *s.* *Mau,* grass, and *kuku,* to stand erect. A species of low grass growing on the sand in certain places.

MA-U-LE, *v.* *Ma* and *ule,* to swing. To be weak or faint through great fear or suffering.

2. With *naau,* to faint from hearing strange or exciting news. *Kin.* 45:26.

3. To be dispirited; to lose courage.

4. To be dizzy or weak through dizziness.

5. To be faint through fasting. *Mat.* 15:32.

6. *Hoo.* To consume; to cause to fail. *Isa.* 64:7.

MA-U-LE, *s.* A dispirited state of mind; weakness; faintness. *Oihk.* 26:36. Dizziness.

MA-U-LE, *adj.* Faint; weak; fearful; fainthearted; dizzy; poniuniu.

MA-U-LE-U-LE, *v.* Intensive or *maule.* To be faint for want of food. *Mar.* 8:3.

MAU-LE-HO, *v.* *Mau* and *leho,* a bunch on the shoulder from carrying burdens. To make or continue a hard bunch on the body from hard labor.

2. *Hoo.* To cause one to work hard and continuously.

3. To oppress with hard labor unrequited.

MA-U-LI, *s.* The name of the first day of the new moon.

2. An obscure cloud seen at a distance; he *mauli* ua paha.

3. A shoot, as from the root of a tree or vegetable, as from kalo or banana; *poetically,* from persons, as chiefs; *mauli* au honua, a descendant (of chiefs) from ancient times.

MA-U-LI-A-WA, *v.* *Ma* and *uli,* to gurgle, and *awa,* bitter. To hiccough; to gasp for breath; to be faint; to be dizzy.

MA-U-LI-A-WA, *s.* The hiccough; a gasping for breath; a hard breathing.

MAU-LI-HI-LI-HI, *v.* *Mau* and *lihi,* edge. To hang by the edge, i. e., to be fastened slightly; to adhere, but without tenacity; e pili iki.

MAU-LI-HI-LI-HI, *adj.* Slightly fastened; not strongly put together.

MA-U-LI-NA, *s.* *Ma* and *ulina,* tough. Hard laborious work without pay.

2. Disappointment in not obtaining what one expects.

MAU-LO-E-LO-E, *adj.* Tired; fatigued. See MALOELOE.

MAU-LU-A, *adj.* Hard; difficult; paakiki.

MA-U-LU-U-LU, *adj.* Lame from traveling. See MALOELOE. Stiff and swelled, as the feet and ankles from traveling. See

POANAANA.

MAU-MAE, *s.* The name of a heiau.

MAU-MAU, *v.* See MAU, to be constant. To be firm; to be fixed; to be constant; to be enduring; e *maumau* ole, to be inconstant; ua *maumau* ka hana, the work *endures*; ua *maumau* ka ai, aole he hehee, the food is *hard,* not flowing.

MAU-MAU-A, *v.* To obtain often without reward and without labor, as the chiefs formerly obtained their property

MAU-MAU-A, *s.* The obtaining of property without work; ka loaa o ka waiwai a na 'lii.

MAU-MAU-A, *adj.* Got or obtained often; arrived at; come to; he elemakule loa, ua *maumaua.*

MAU-MAU-AE, *adj.* See MAUAE. Different from what was expected; doubtful; uncertain.

MAU-MA-NA-HA, *s.* The heart-burn (perhaps.)

MAU-NA, *s.* A mountain; the inland regions of an island. NOTE.—On all the islands with which Hawaiians were acquainted, the land rises on all sides from the sea to the central parts of the island; this is called the *mauna.* A high hill, as Maunaloa, Maunakea: names of the two highest mountains on Hawaii.

2. A mountainous region. *Mauna* is the opposite of *awawa.* *Ios.* 9:1.

MAU-NA, *s.* The name of a species of hard stone out of which kois or adzes of the ancients were made.

MAU-NA, *adj.* Large; swelling; extensive; nui, mahuahua; prominent for excellence; *mauna* ili ke keiki, he punahele ia; *mauna* ka ili i ka wauwauia; scratched; marked.

MA-U-NA, *v.* To waste; to dispose of uselessly; i *mauna* aku ai i ka pono kahiko. See MAUNAUNA.

MAU-NAU-NA, *v.* To spend property; to waste; to live without regard to expense. *Hoo.* To waste property; to spend uselessly; mai hiamoe i ke ao, oia ke *hoomaunauna* i na la ame na hora i loaa mai i ke Akua.

MAU-NAU-NA, *s.* A wasting. *Hoo.* No ka *hoomaunauna* i ka waiwai, on account of wasting property.

MAU-NAU-NA, *adj.* Wasteful.

MA-U-NU, *s.* A species of crab used for bait in catching fish.

2. Any bait for taking fish.

3. The writing motions of a fish worm on a hook.

4. Anything belonging to a person, as his kapa, hair, spittle, &c., which another could get, and by means of it, could pray him to death. See mele na Niau.

5. The shedding of bird's feathers; ka manawa *maunu*, the time birds shed their feathers.

MA-U-NU, *v.* Hoo. To moult or shed, as the feathers of birds.

2. To cast off, as some reptiles do the skin.

3. To change from the chrysalis state to that of a new animal; e hoomaheleia ke kino mamua, a lilo ia i kino hou.

MAU-NU-NU, *s.* The name of a sea breeze at Puuloa on Oahu.

MAU-WA-LE, *adj.* Constant; never ending; kuu pilikia *mauwale* ana a kuu haku. *Laieik.* 165.

MAU-WE-LE, *adj.* Lazy; idle, &c. See MAUELE.

MA-HA, *v.* To rest; to rest, as from labor or toil; to give or cause to rest.

2. To enjoy ease and quiet after pain; to be better; to begin to recover from sickness.

3. To be assuaged; to be softened down, as anger. *Lunk.* 8:3.

4. To rest, as a land, i. e., to cease from being the theater of evil. *Oihk.* 26:34.

5. *Hoo.* To give or take rest from labor or fatigue.

6. To relieve from suffering; to comfort; to be satisfied.

7. To ease one's self; to attend to a call of nature. *Kanl.* 23:14.

MA-HA, *v.* To exercise affection towards one; to acknowledge or treat one as a friend; to be complaisant towards one; to love; to cherish.

2. To make a rent or hole in, as in a kapa; to tear in two.

3. To hide a thing away; to steal.

MA-HA, *s.* Rest; repose; respite or relief from pain or sickness; convalescence; relief from any calamity. *Puk.* 8:11. Rest; peace.

2. The wing of an army; the fore fins of a fish.

3. The side of the head; the temple. *Lunk.* 4:21. See MAHAMAHA.

MA-HA, *adj.* Easy; quiet; resting, as from labor; free from pain; ceasing from anger.

MA-HA, *adv.* Hoo. Silently; quietly; at rest. *Isa.* 62:1.

MA-HAE, *s.* Name of a species of fish.

MA-HA-O, *s.* The pith of a tree or vegetable; a soft or decayed place in the center or body of a tree; a hole in a tree. See PUHO and PUHA.

MA-HA-O, *adj.* Defective in the center, as a tree; soft; rotten; hollow; bent in or down, as a decayed grass house.

MA-HA-OE, *adj.* Not ashamed.

MA-HA-OI, *v.* See MAOI and *ha* dropped. *Maoi* is probably the original form of the word. To be bold; to be impertinent.

2. To treat a superior as an equal or with great familiarity.

3. To be forward in asking questions; to be asking begging of a chief frequently.

MA-HA-OI, *s.* Forwardness; immodesty in asking favors; impertinence in addressing a superior; boldness in address; nani ka nui o kuu hilahila, a he mea e hoi ka *mahaoi* loa o kekahi poe o kakou. Ua kapaia aku ia o *Maoi*, no ka *mahaoi* o ka olelo ana.

MA-HA-OI, *adj.* Always asking favors (of chiefs), thus: na'u kela lole; na'u kela palaoa, &c.; and so of all which one desires.

MA-HA-HA, *v.* See HAHA. To be soft; to be tender; to be weak, as a person.

2. To be tender or flexible, as a vegetable.

3. To be soft and tough, as water-soaked vegetables.

MA-HA-HA, *s.* The name of a species of fish, the kala.

2. A species of kalo.

MA-HA-HA, *adj.* Soft and tough.

2. Tender, as a weak person.

3. Soft and mealy, as a baked potato.

MA-HA-KE-A, *s.* An uncultivated piece of land overgrown with weeds and grass; a jungle; a wild place.

MA-HA-KE-A, *adj.* Wild; overgrown with weeds, grass and bushes; nahelehele, weuweu.

MA-HA-LA, } *v.* Ma and *halo*, to look
MA-HA-LO, } out; to turn the eyes upon. To admire; to wonder at; to magnify the goodness or virtues of a person or thing.

2. To be glorious; magnificent to behold.

3. To approve; to praise; to honor; to glorify.

MA-HA-LO, *s.* Wonder; surprise; admiration.

2. Approbation; blessing; honor given to one.

3. The act of blessing or praising God; ua like ka *mahalo* me ka hoonani.

MA-HA-LO, *adj.* Beautiful; glorious; admirable.

MA-HA-MA-HA, *v.* To glow, as with friendly feelings towards one; to expect a meeting with a friend. *Laieik.* 58. To be glad to see an old friend or relative.

MA-HA-MA-HA, *s.* See MAHA. A fondling; the exercise of affection, friendship or hospitality.

2. The temples of the head; the sides of a substance.

3. The gills or fins of a fish. *Kanl.* 14:9. Also the fore fins of a fish.

4. The wings (eheu) of the malolo or fly-ing-fish.

5. The things or appendages which be-long to the wings; na mea maha, na mea eheu.

6. The preputium (paha.)

MA-HA-MA-HA-OO, *s.* A piece cut or broken off; he apahu, he pauku.

MA-HA-ME-A, *s.* A species of fish.

MA-HA-MO-E, *s. Maha* and *moe,* to rest quietly. To appear fat, oily or shining.

2. To be plump or round, as a fruit; to be fat, as an animal. See KOLIKOLIKO.

MA-HA-MO-E, *s.* A species of fish.

MA-HA-MO-E, *adj.* Clear; plain; blue or black.

MA-HA-NA, *v. Ma* and *hana,* work; ex-ercise. To be or become warm, as the rising sun. *Puk.* 16:21.

2. To warm, as one person in contact with another. 1 *Nal.* 1:1, 2.

3. *Hoo.* To warm, i. e., to make warm by the fire or by exercise. See MEHANA.

MA-HA-NA, *s.* A small degree of heat; warmth.

MA-HA-NA, *adj.* Warm, as by the influ-ence of the sun. *Neh.* 7:3. Warm; not yet cooled, as newly baked bread. 1 *Sam.* 21:6.

MA-HA-NA, *s.* For *mana,* a branching out, *ha* inserted. Any substance branch-ing out; anything double; having two branches; hence,

2. A pair of twins; mau mahoe; two things connected; na mea elua, a pair of things.

MA-HA-NA, *adj.* Double; mates; branch-ing out.

MA-HA-NA-HA-NA, *v.* See MAHANA. To warm very much or frequently. *Hoo.* To warm one's self by a fire. *Isa.* 44:15.

MA-HA-NI, *v. Ma* and *hani,* to pass si-lently. To pass easily and silently; to be evanescent; to disappear; to vanish, as a thought; ua *mahani* ka manao.

2. To heal up; to granulate, as a wound so as to disappear.

3. To vanish, as an ulcer when it heals; *mahani* keia wahi, a e poha hou ma kahi e.

MA-HA-WE-LA, *s.* A blue kind of fish.

ME-HE-A, *int. adv. Ma* and *hea,* where. Where? at what place? *Gram.* § 165, 2.

MA-HE-A-LA-NI, *s.* The name of the six-teenth day of the month; the day when the full moon began to lose its roundness. See also MALANI.

MA-HE-U, *v.* See MEHEU.

MA-HE-U, *s.* Name of a porous kind of stone.

MA-HE-HA, *adv. Ma* and *heha,* slow. Slowly; lazily. *Hoo.* Working slowly and lazily but perseveringly; aka, hana *hoo-maheha* ana ame kohu molowa, hoomau no nae i ka hana.

MA-HE-LE, *v. Ma* and *hele,* to go; to move. To divide; to cut in pieces; to di-vide a portion to one, as land.

2. To divide or separate from one an-other, as people. *Kin.* 10:32. To divide into two parts, as an army. 1 *Nal.* 16:21.

3. To divide, as streams of water; as the sea. *Puk.* 14:21.

4. *Hoo.* To cause a division; to separate one thing from another.

MA-HE-LE-HE-LE, *v.* Freq. of *mahele.* To divide into small pieces; to divide fre-quently. *Kin.* 49:7. *Hoo.* Same.

MA-HE-LE-LU-A, *v. Mahele* and *lua,* two. To divide into two parts.

MA-HE-LU, *v. Ma* and *helu,* to scratch the earth. To spread dust over as an arti-ficial soil.

2. To spread loose soft dirt over a kalo patch after the bottom has been pounded hard. See PALUKU.

MA-HI, *v.* To dig the ground for the purpose of planting food; to cultivate land by digging; to dress land; to till, as a field or garden; e *mahi* aku i ke kihapai o ka aina. NOTE.—Clearing off the weeds, grass, &c., is *waele.*

MA-HI, *s.* Cultivation; planting, &c. 1 *Sam.* 8:12.

MA-HI, *adj.* Strong; energetic, as a laboring man; as a fighting-cock; moa *mahi,* a fighting-cock.

MA-HI-AI, *v. Mahi* and *ai,* food. To cul-tivate land; to produce food from the ground; to till the ground.

MA-HI-AI, *s.* A cultivator of the soil; a tiller of the ground; a husbandman.

2. Culture; tillage of the ground.

MA-HI-AI, *adj.* Of or belonging to til-lage; kanaka *mahiai,* a farmer.

MA-HI-E, *v. Ma* and *hie,* shameful. To be proud; to be lofty; to act without re-spect to good manners or morals.

2. *Hoo.* To break over every rule of de-cency; to act shamefully; he mea maikai

no nae ka naauao, *hoomahie* ole.

MA-HI-E-HI-E, *v.* To dye fast colors; to color kapas with clear distinct spots or colors; hence,

2. To dress finely; to be clothed in honorable robes.

MA-HI-I-LI, *v.* *Mahi* and *ili*, the skin. To take or seize the property for the king. NOTE.—This was often done by the unscrupulous officers, who left nothing to the people but their skin.

MA-HI-O-LE, *s.* A war cap; a helmet; an officer's cap. 1 *Sam.* 17:5.

MA-HI-HI, *v.* See IHI. To peel off bark from a tree.

MA-HI-KA-KA, *v.* *Ma* and *hikaka*, to stagger. To crook; to bend; to put out of a straight line.

MA-HI-HI-KI, *v.* To spatter; to flap in the water, as a duck at play.

MA-HI-KI, *v.* To vibrate; to play up and down, as the beam of a scale; hence,

2. To weigh, as in scales.

3. To play up and down, as a lever upon its prop in the center; to pry, as with a lever. *Anat.* 3.

4. To cast out, as an evil spirit; to exorcise.

5. To hop; to jump; to leap.

6. To scatter; to blow away, as with a puff of wind.

7. To lift up; to carry in the arms.

MA-HI-KI, *s.* Thick, tall grass in a damp place; thick, low shrubs or underbrush.

2. The place where tall grass or thick bushes grow.

3. A prop on which a lever rests in prying up a weight.

4. A calabash for water.

MA-HI-KI-HI-KI, *v.* Freq. of *mahiki.* To jump or fly frequently.

2. To vibrate rapidly, as the tongue; e kapalili.

3. To shake, as in an earthquake; to move frequently.

4. To overturn; to upset.

5. To spatter; to flap; to spatter, as ink in writing.

MA-HI-KI-HI-KI, *s.* A sort of thick high grass; the place where such grass grows.

MA-HI-LO-A, *adj.* Distant; afar off.

MA-HI-MA-HI, *s.* A species of fish; the dolphin.

MA-HI-NA, *s.* *Mahi* and *ana*, participial termination, a cultivating. A cultivated patch; a garden.

2. The moon; ka mea e malamalama ai i ka po; hence,

3. A lunar month; *mahina* o hoku, the name of the day of the full moon.

4. The eye of a snail in the end of his horn; he maka pupu.

MA-HI-NA-AI, *s.* *Mahina* and *ai*, food, as if a contraction of *mahi ana i ka ai.* A field, either in a state of cultivation or prepared for it. *Nah.* 24:6.

2. A field, generally of larger size than *kihapai* where food is raised. *Oihk.* 23:22.

3. A cultivated patch; hence,

4. Husbandry itself.

MA-HI-NU, *v.* *Ma* and *hinu*, to anoint. To rub over; to anoint.

MA-HI-WAI-NA, *s.* *Mahi* and *waina*, a grape vine. A vine dresser; a cultivator of grapes. *Ioan.* 15:1.

MA-HO-E, *s.* Two of men or animals born at the same time of one makua; twins. *Mel. Sol.* 7:3; *Kin.* 25:24. See MAHANA 2.

MA-HO-E-HO-E, *adj.* Straight and free from branches, as a tree; pololei, lala ole.

MA-HO-E-HO-PE, *s.* The name of a Hawaiian month.

MA-HO-E-MU-A, *s.* Name of a Hawaiian month.

MA-HO-LA, *v.* *Ma* and *hola*, to spread over. To spread out; to open wide, as a flower in full bloom.

2. To spread out; to unfold, as a kapa to dry. See UHOLA, HOHOLA and KALENA.

MA-HO-LA, *s.* The spreading out and extension of the stomach; me ka mahana, ame ka *mahola* ana o ka opu. *Anat.* 52.

MA-HO-LA, *adj.* Spread open; spread out; extended.

MA-HO-LA, *adj.* In the ancient practice of the kahunas: hee *mahola*, ahi *mahola*; o ka hee *mahola* oia no ka mea e heehee ai ka mai.

MA-HO-LA-HO-LA, *v.* Intensive of *mahola.* To spread out extensively.

MA-HO-LE, *v.* *Ma* and *hole*, to peel off; to skin. To bruise, as the flesh; to hurt; to break up.

Uli aa'i na moku, *mahole* eha ka nahele.

MA-HO-LE-HO-LE, *v.* Intensive of *mahole*, to bruise. To break up; to break or crush into pieces; e inikiniki, e waluwalu.

MA-HO-LE-HO-LE, *s.* A bruise; a hurt; an injury; aole *maholehole* o ke kino a'u i ike ai.

MA-HO-LE-HO-LE, *adj.* See MAHOLE. Bruised and broken to pieces; crushed together.

MA-HO-PE, *adv.* and *comp. prep.* Ma and

hope, the end. Behind; after; afterward. It expresses future time in respect of the time in which an action was performed, though past in respect of the person speaking. *Gram*. § 161.

Ma-hu, *v*. To blow out steam or smoke; to smoke, as a smothered fire; to throw out hot vapor, as from a volcano.

Ma-hu, *s*. Steam; hot vapor; smoke.

Ma-hu, *s*. A man who assimilates his manners and dresses his person like a woman.

2. A hermaphrodite; a eunuch.

Ma-hu, *adj*. Silent; indisposed to conversation; silent, as a deserted place.

Ma-hu-a, *v*. *Ma* and *hua*, envy; jealousy. To be envious. *Hoo*. To mock; to deride; to have in derision. *Hal*. 2:4.

Ma-hu-a, ⎫ *v. Ma* and *hua*, to grow
Ma-hu-a-hu-a, ⎭ or increase. To increase in size or numbers; to grow large.

2. To boast; to brag; to glory over.

3. To grow strong, as a ruler over a people. *Oihl*. 11:9.

4. To increase, as money. *Kanl*. 8:13.

5. *Hoo*. To increase in number, as animals, vegetables or men.

6. To increase; to make more of. *Ezek*. 36:29.

7. To set or employ, as a spy; to act the part of a spy; e hoomakakiu.

Ma-hu-a, ⎫ *s*. Increase; growth;
Ma-hu-a-hu-a, ⎭ a growing. *Puk*. 1:12.
Ma-hu-a, ⎫ *adj*. Increasing; large
Ma-hu-a-hu-a, ⎭ in quantity.

Ma-hu-a-ka-la, *adj*. Contemptuous of good things; disobedient to the gods; wicked.

Ma-hu-e, *v*. To be numerous; to go or move in crowds.

Ma-hu-i, *v. Ma* and *hui*, to join; to unite. To follow the example of one; to imitate him.

2. To imitate, i. e., to be led to do as another does. *Gal*. 2:13. To pattern after. *3 Ioan*. 11. To be an example for another. *1 Pet*. 5:3.

3. To adhere firmly, as to a purpose or habit; e *mahui* i ka hana ino; e *hoomahui* i ka hana ino, to determine on doing evil.

4. To hear a little, as when one hears only partially, or in parts; similar to *kulina*.

5. To go about here and there, as an insane person; to act foolishly and without good sense. NOTE.—The following examples will illustrate definitions 1 and 2: Ma ka like kakou e *hoomahui* ai, *let us follow*

by doing likewise; he pono no ia kakou ke *hoomahui* ma ia hana, it is proper for us to *imitate* that transaction; *hoomahui* na makaainana ma o Kekuokalani la, the common people *followed the example* of Kekuokalani; o ko lakou pono, oia ka kakou e *hoomahui* ai, their good deeds that is what we *should imitate*.

Ma-hu-i, *s*. A kind of sly conduct in a female by which she means to express to one of the other sex her desire.

Ma-hu-i-hu-i, *v*. To learn or understand obscurely; to strike upon the ear indistinctly, as a sound at a distance.

Ma-hu-ka, *v*. To flee away; to escape from. *1 Sam*. 22:7. To flee away secretly. *Kin*. 16:6. To run away, as a servant from his master. *1 Sam*. 25:10. To flee from fear of punishment. *2 Sam*. 13:34.

Ma-hu-ka, *s*. A runaway; one who has escaped.

Ma-hu-ka, *adj*. Escaping; running away secretly; he luina *mahuka*, a runaway sailor.

Ma-hu-lu, *s*. The name common to three gods in the house of Lono.

Ma-hu-ma-hu, *v*. To be silent, as a weak dying man.

Ma-hu-ma-hu, *adj*. See Mahu, silent. Desolate; without inhabitant; silent, as a place deserted.

2. Brittle; not stringy, as kapa that falls easily to pieces.

3. Brittle; not sticky; applied to poi.

Ma-hu-na, *s. Ma* and *huna*, a particle; small; fine. The scaly appearance of the skin after drinking awa; the chapping, cracking or breaking up of the skin; i kona wa i inu ai i ke awa, maikai ka ili, a mahope, *mahuna* ka ili, nakaka, puehuehu, inoino loa kona kino.

2. A species of kapa like the *paipaikukui*.

Ma-hu-ne, *adj. Ma* and *hune*, poor; destitute. Poor; stripped of property; bereft of comforts.

Ma-hu-ne-hu-ne, *adj. Ma* and *hune*. See above. Poor; with nothing but one's person.

Ma-hu-ne-hu-ne, *adv*. Scarcely; nothing left; with difficulty; ola *mahunehune* ae la o Aikake (Isaac Davis) mai ko lakou lima ae, *scarcely* did Isaac Davis escape their hands; i. e., he escaped with nothing but his person.

Ma-ka, *s*. The eye; the organ of sight; aole e ike ka *maka* i kona pula iho, the *eye* does not see its own mote. *Proverb*. The face; the countenance; he *maka* no he *maka*, face to face. *Ezek*. 20:35.

2. The point or edge of an instrument, as a knife or sword; *maka* o ka pahi kaua; the blade of a knife or sword in distinction from the handle. *Lunk.* 3:22.

3. The bud of a plant.

4. The teat or nipple of a female.

5. The presence of one, i. e., his favor or blessing. *Puk.* 33:14, 15. Manao i ka maka, to regard a person. *Kanl.* 10:17.

6. FIG. A guide; a director. *Nah.* 10:31.

7. *Hoo.* A destruction; a slaughter. 1 *Sam.* 5:9.

8. The budding or first shooting of a plant; hence,

9. The beginning or commencement of a work or an action. See HOOMAKA.

10. Name of a very hard stone, out of which maika stones were made.

MA-KA, *v.* Hoo. See above, 8 and 9. To begin; to commence, as a work or job; to commence doing a thing; komo wau i ke kula i *hoomakaia'i* ka naauao, I entered the school that knowledge *might be commenced.* NOTE.—Hoomaka is used as opposed to *hooki.*

MA-KA, *adj.* Raw in opposition to cooked, as raw, uncooked flesh.

2. Fresh, as fresh provisions in distinction from salted.

3. White, as a potato well cooked and dry; moa a *maka.*

MA-KA, *adv.* See MAKA, edge of an instrument. By the edge; with the edge; alaila, ooki *maka* koi hookahi iho ana, then he cut with the *edge* of the adze (koi) one stroke (one bringing down.)

MA-KAA, *s.* A species of fish.

MA-KA-AI-NA, *s.* Ma, at, on, *ka,* the, and *aina,* land. A resident; one belonging to the land and was transferred with it, as in ancient times.

MA-KA-AI-NA-NA, *s.* See MAKAAINA and ANA, being of the land. The laboring class of people in distinction from chiefs; a countryman; a farmer; *collectively,* the common people in distinction from chiefs; o na 'lii ame na *makaainana,* the chiefs and the *common people.*

MA-KAA-O-A, *s.* A species of fish.

MA-KA-A-HA, *s.* A swinging bed; a cot; he wahi moe lole lewa.

2. The outlet of a fish-pond into the sea.

MA-KA-A-HA, *s.* Small pimples; sores; the itch; kakani, meeau.

MA-KA-A-HA, *adj.* Covered with sores; full of pimples, as with the itch; leprous; hookuku, hana, hoao.

MA-KA-A-KAU, *s.* Maka, eye, and *akau,* right. The right eye.

MA-KA-A-KAU, *adj.* Open; clear.

MA-KA-A-KI-U, *v.* Maka and *kiu,* a spy. To spy out secretly; to observe, as a spy. Hoo. To lie in wait for one to kill him.

MA-KA-A-KI-U, *adj.* Spying secretly; watching for evil; lurking after something; going secretly. *Hal.* 10:8. See MAKAKIU.

MA-KA-A-LA, *v.* Maka, eye, and *ala,* awake. To wake; to be awake, i. e., to be watchful; to be aware or on the guard; to look out; to take heed; beware. *Kanl.* 24:8.

2. To look at but not to see by reason of blindness.

MA-KA-A-LA, *s.* Watchfulness; a being on guard.

2. A small faint track made by a person going once; a path scarcely visible; he maawe alanui; a faint path.

MA-KA-A-LA, *adj.* Awake; watchful; vigilant.

MA-KA-A-LU-A, *s.* Maka and *lua,* a hole; a pit. A hole (lua) to plant or set a tree in.

MA-KA-E, *v.* Maka, eye, and *e,* against. To set against; to be opposed to. *Nah.* 3:5.

2. Hoo. To turn away from. 1 *Pet.* 3:12. To slight; to turn off; to treat contemptuously. *Habak.* 3:8.

MA-KAI,   *v.* Maka, eye, and *i,* intensive, real; particularly.
MA-KAI-KAI,   To look at closely; to inspect; to search out. *Puk.* 39:43.

2. To spy or look out; to act the part of a spy. *Ios.* 6:22.

3. To look at from motives of curiosity; to take a view of a place; to examine. SYN. with kiu. *Ios.* 2:1.

4. To look on as a spectator. *Puk.* 3:4.

5. To examine secretly for evil purposes; hookalakupua.

6. To follow; to entrap one; e ukali, e hakilo.

MA-KAI, *s.* A guard; a constable; an officer always found in the king's train; a name given to policemen from the nature of their office. See the verb.

2. Any instrument with a sharp edge; a hatchet; a koi; a needle or an instrument used as a needle in stringing flowers for wreaths; manai.

3. Sourness of mind; stinginess; he pi, he aua.

4. Ka *hoomakai* kohi ole a ka ua.

MA-KAI, *adj.* Guarding; going or acting as a guard; huakai *makai,* a train or people accompanying as a guard. See *Laieik.* 190.

MA-KAI, *adv.* *Ma,* at, and *kai,* sea. At or towards the sea, in opposition to *mauka,* inland. The full form is *makahakai,* at the sea beach.

MA-KA'I, *s.* A person that owns no land; o ka mea aina ole he *maka'i* ka inoa.

MA-KA-IA, *s.* Name of a person punahele of a chief, but turned off and become a punahele of another chief; the two go to war and through the efforts of the *makaia* the second chief conquers the first; ia manawa e ku ai ka *makaia* o Laieikawai. *Laieik.* 150.

MA-KAI-O, *v.* To be frightened and run off, as a wild animal.

MA-KA-I-HU, *s.* The sharp point at the bow of a canoe; e kapiliia na *makaihu.*

MA-KAI-KAI, *v.* See MAKAI, *v.,* above. To look; to examine, &c.

MA-KAI-KAI, *s.* Trouble; grief; evil treatment or treachery from a supposed friend.

MA-KA-I-NO, *v.* *Maka,* eye, and *ino,* bad. To have an evil eye towards one; to lose one's affection for a child or person. *Kanl.* 28:54.

MA-KA-I-WA, *s.* The name of Lono's gods.

MA-KA-I-WI, *s.* The twinkling of the eye, i. e., suddenness; suddenly, as we say, in the twinkling of an eye.

MA-KA-O-KA-O, *s.* *Ma* and *kaokao,* hardness. Hardness; obduracy.

2. A hard substance.

3. That which is much broken up; nakakaka.

MA-KA-O-LE, *s.* *Maka,* eye, and *ole,* the eye teeth; the edge of the eye teeth. Epithet of the oo; an oo.

MA-KAU, *s.* A fish-hook; also a shark hook. SYN. with kiholo.

MA-KAU, *v.* To fear; to be afraid; to dread; to fear in time of danger. *Puk.* 14:31.

makau

2. To have in reverence, as one feared and greatly respected.

3. To tremble; to be agitated through fear.

4. *Hoo.* To cause to fear; to put one in fear. *Neh.* 6:4.

5. To drive or fray away. *Kanl.* 28:26.

MA-KAU, *s.* Fear; dread of evil. *Oihk.* 26:16. *Makau* nui, terror; dread; disquietude of mind.

MA-KAU, *adj.* Fearful; afraid; causing fear or dread.

MA-KAU, *v.* To be ready; to be prepared for an event. *Hoo.* To make ready; to prepare. 2 *Nal.* 9:21. See HOOMAKAUKAU.

MA-KAU, *adj.* Ready; in a state of preparation; prepared; furnished.

MA-KAU-A, *v.* To increase; to grow large.

2. *Hoo.* To vex; to harass; to trouble.

3. To make afraid. See MAKAU, *hoo.*

MA-KAU-AU-A, *adj.* Hung up to dry.

MA-KAU-IA, *s.* Perf. part. of *makau.* Fear; respect. *Puk.* 20:17.

MA-KAU-HA-NO-NA, *s.* The hook that belongs to the hanona or long fishing line.

MA-KA-U-HI, *adj.* *Maka,* eye, and *uhi,* to shade; to cover. Hidden or covered, as the eyes.

MA-KAU-KAU, *v.* Intensive of *makau,* to be ready. See above. To be ready. *Hoo.* To be put in readiness; to make ready; to be prepared for any event.

MA-KAU-KAU, *s.* Readiness; preparation.

MA-KAU-KAU, *adj.* Ready; prepared for an event.

MA-KAU-KII, *adj.* *Makau,* fear, and *kii,* idol. Great fear; dread of the gods.

MA-KAU-LA, *s.* *Ma* and *kaula,* a prophet. A foreteller of future events; a star-gazer; a person supposed to be possessed of some supernatural gifts. *Laieik.* 13. NOTE.— *Kaulas* and *makaulas* were connected generally with high chiefs, forming a part of their council. See their office, *Mooolelo Hawaii,* chap. 31.

MA-KA-U-LI, *adj.* *Maka,* eye, and *uli,* dark green. Dark, black or blue-eyed.

MA-KAU-LI-A, *s.* For *makauia,* *l* inserted. See MAKAU, fear. Fear; qualities inducing fear. *Iob.* 25:2.

MA-KAU-LII, *v.* *Makau,* fear, and *'lii,* a chief. *Hoo.* To take special care of the property of a chief; to be careful that no little thing be lost.

2. To fear, i. e., to serve a chief in order to obtain favors from him; to follow; to adhere to from motives of advantage; i lako o ua kanaka la, o kana *hoomakaulii* ana, that man's *obedience to the chief* is from the favors (lako) he expects; ua *hoomakaulii* anei kakou e malama ia ai? *have we been obedient* in order to be taken care of? Eia ka manao iloko o ua kanaka la, o kana *hoomakaulii* ana, o ka loaa mai ka aina. He

kanaka huhu wale, he poe *hoomakaulii* aina.

MA-KAU-LII, *s.* A very careful person; one saving the property of a chief. *Hoo.* The same.

   2. An accuser; a defamer; a slanderer.

MA-KAU-LII, *adj.* Very careful; saving.

MA-KAU-LI-MO, *adj. Makau,* fear, and *limo* for *limu,* sea grass. Ea makaulimo, the sea turtle fearing the sea grass. NOTE.— The turtle is said to be afraid of the sea grass, as his flippers are easily entangled in it.

MA-KA-U-PE-NA, *s.* The midriff; that which covers the bowels. *Anat.* 51. Ka *makaupena* e uhi ana i ka naau. See NIKI-NIKI. *Oihk.* 3:3.

MA-KA-HA, *s. Maka,* eye, and *ha,* water sluice. An outlet or inlet of a pond where the sea flows in and out.

   2. An inflamed, swelled and running eye; he maka pehu.

   3. The sickness of hogs.

   4. He humu, he paehumu.

MA-KA-HA, *v. Ma* and *kaha,* to extort property. To seize what is another's; to rob; to plunder; to extort property. See HOOKAHA.

MA-KA-HA, *s.* A robbing; a seizing what is another's; robbery; extortion.

MA-KA-HA, *adj.* Robbing; plundering; seizing the property of another.

MA-KA-HA-HI, } *v.* To be filled with won-
MA-KA-HE-HI, } der and delight; to admire; to be astonished and yet pleased; *makahahi* aku la na kanaka i keia mea nui kupanaha, the people *were seized* with wonder at this huge strange thing; ike lakou ua nui ka hao, *makahahi* iho la, they saw there was much iron, *they were astonished.*

   2. To go triumphing or rejoicing.

MA-KA-HA-HI, *s.* Wonder; amazement; astonishment. *Hal.* 22:17.

MA-KA-HA-KAI, *adv. Ma,* at, *kaha* and *kai,* sea beach. At the sea side; on the sea shore.

MA-KA-HA-KA-HA, *s.* The ceasing of rain; the slow dropping of rain.

MA-KA-HA-KA-HA-KA, *s. Maka* and *haka-haka,* full of holes; open. A deep pit or hole; ka poopoo.

MA-KA-HA-LA, *v.* See MAKAHA. To take another's property unjustly.

MA-KA-HA-NI, *v.* See HANI, to step lightly. To go lightly or softly; to touch lightly; just to graze.

MA-KA-HE-HI, *v.* See MAKAHAHI above.

MA-KA-HE-KI-LI, *s. Maka,* eye, and *hekili,* thunder. LIT. The eye of the thunder. A hailstone. See HUAHEKILI.

MA-KA-HE-MA, *s. Maka,* eye, and *hema,* left. The left eye.

MA-KA-HI, *s.* Name of a species of fish.

MA-KA-HI, *adj.* Contraction for *maka* and *akahi,* one. One-eyed; having one eye.

MA-KA-HI-A-MOE, *v. Maka,* eye, and *hia-moe,* to sleep. To fall asleep; to allow one's self to doze. *Hoo.* To give one's self to sleep.

MA-KA-HI-A-MOE, *adj.* Sleepy; dull; stupid.

MA-KA-HI-A-PO, *s. Maka* and *hiapo,* the first born. The first born child. See HIAPO.

MA-KA-HI-O, *adj. Maka* and *hio,* to lean. A leaning this way and that; a motion to and fro.

MA-KA-HI-KI, *s.* The name of the first day of the year.

   2. The commencement of the year.

   3. The space of a year; a year; ka puni o na malama he umikumamalua, a finishing of the twelve-month.

MA-KA-HI-NU, *s.* The unpleasant feelings of a chief when a person goes to him frequently for favors; the natives describe such a person as greasing his forehead with oil; e hamohamo i kona lae me ka aila kukui; he alamakahinu i ke alii.

MA-KA-KII, *s. Maka* and *kii,* an image. A mask.

   2. A lustful eye; a proud look; generally connected with *moekolohe.*

MA-KA-KI-U, *v. Maka* and *kiu,* to spy. To spy; to spy out, as an enemy. *Hoo.* To act the part of a spy on an enemy.

   2. To spy out, as a country. 1 *Oihl.* 19:3.

   3. To lie in wait to kill. See MAKAAKIU.

MA-KA-KO-A, *adj. Maka* and *koa,* a soldier. LIT. A soldier's face. Fierce in countenance. *Kanl.* 28:50.

MA-KA-KO-LE, *s. Maka* and *kole,* raw; sore. Inflammation of the eyes; sore eyes. See MAKOLE.

MA-KA-KO-LE, *adj.* Sore or watery-eyed.

MA-KA-KO-KO-E, *adj. Maka* and *kokoe,* to strike at the eyes. Angry; evil eyed; designing to hurt.

MA-KA-KU-I-KU-I, *v. Maka* and *kui,* to strike; to buffet. To stir up anger in another; to provoke.

   2. To grin at; to scowl at one.

MA-KA-LA, *v. Ma* and *kala,* to loosen. To open what is closed; to separate a little.

   2. To draw out; to extract.

   3. To open a little, as a door; to open, as a book that has clasps on it.

   4. To untie; to loosen; to set at liberty.

   5. To remit, as a debt; to forgive, as an

offense; e *makala* mai i kuu hala, *forgive my offense.* See KALA.

MA-KA-LA, *s.* A loosening; an opening; a separating.

MA-KA-LA, *v.* A contraction for *maka-ala*, to be awake. To watch; to take heed; to beware; to be vigilant.

MA-KA-LA-KA-LA, *v.* Intensive of the foregoing. To hold or keep the eyes open; to be sleepless; makili, *makalakala* i ka hiamoe.

MA-KA-LAU-NA, *s. Maka*, face, and *launa*, an intimate. An intimate acquaintance; one on terms of friendship; ka mea i maa e mamua.

MA-KA-LE-HA, *v. Maka*, eye, and *leha*, to lift up the eyes. To wonder after; to admire. *Hoik.* 13:5.

MA-KA-LE-HA, *s.* A lofty, mischievous eye.

MA-KA-LE-HO, *s. Maka*, eye, and *leho*, the shell of a fish. Haughtiness; lasciviousness. 1 *Pet.* 4:3. Proud behavior.

MA-KA-LI, *v.* To bait a hook; to angle for fish; e *makali* e loaa iki.

MA-KA-LII, *s.* The celestial sign Castor and Pollux.

    2. The seven stars.

    3. The name of a month.

    4. The name of the six summer months collectively.

MA-KA-LII, *s. Maka* and *lii*, small; little. Smallness; littleness; inferiority.

MA-KA-LII, *adj.* Very small; diminutive; very fine.

MA-KA-LII-O-HU-A, *s.* A species of very small fish found in shoals near the shore; also called *ohua*.

    2. A multitude of diminutive creatures of any kind.

MA-KA-LI-O, *adj.* Drawn or strained tightly, as a rope.

MA-KA-LO-A, *s. Maka*, green, fresh, and *loa*, a long time. A kind of rush of which mats are made.

MA-KA-LO-A, *adj.* Always green; always fresh.

MA-KA-LU-A, *s. Maka*, eye, and *lua*, pit. A hole dug for planting upland kalo in; also a hole for planting vines. *Isa.* 5:2.

    2. The socket for the eye-ball. *Anat.* 6.

    3. The name of a certain fish.

MA-KA-LU-A, *adj. Maka* and *lua*, double. Two-faced; two-eyed; epithet of a two-edged sword. *Hoik.* 1:16. See OILUA.

MA-KA-LU-I, *v.* See MAKALUHI. To labor long and perseveringly, then to make a feast.

That feast is called an ahaaina *makalui.*

MA-KA-LU-KU, *v. Maka* and *luku*, slaughter. To turn against one for harm; to be bent on slaughter,

MA-KA-MAE, *adj.* Precious; valuable; much desired; costly; precious, as a stone. 2 *Sam.* 12:30. Precious, as a beloved child or servant. *Isa.* 43:4. Na mea makamae, precious things. *Ezek.* 22:25.

MA-KA-MAE, *s. Maka* and *mae* for *mae-mae*, pure. A darling; a precious one; a beloved one. *Hal.* 22:20.

MA-KA-MA-KA, *s.* A friend; a beloved one; an intimate; one on terms of receiving and giving freely. *Iob.* 2:11. A relative. FIG. Anything to which one is greatly attached; hookahi hoi o kaua *makamaka*, o ka imi naauao, oia hoi ko kaua kuleana i noho ai ma keia kula nui, we two have only one *friend*, that is knowledge seeking, that is the right (reason) of our living at this high school.

MA-KA-MA-KA, *adj.* Good; beautiful; splendid; fresh; new.

MA-KA-MO-MI, *s. Maka* and *momi*, the pearl in the oyster shell. A white speck in the eye by disease.

MA-KA-MU-A, *s. Maka* and *mua*, the first; the beginning. The beginning; the first of things, as a period of time. *Ier.* 26:1.

    2. The first or oldest of a family of children. SYN. with mua. Ka *makamua* o na la, the beginning of days, i. e., the Son of God. *Dan.* 7:9.

MA-KA-MU-A, *adj.* First. *Kin.* 4:20. Primary; beginning; the first of a series, like *mua. Puk.* 12:2. Ua maopopo i ka poe i komo (i ke kula) i ka la *makamua* o Iulai, it was understood by those who entered (the school) on the *first day* of July.

MA-KA-NA, *v.* To give freely or gratuitously; to make a present to one.

MA-KA-NA, *s.* A gift; that which is freely bestowed upon one by another; a present; that which is received gratuitously.

MA-KA-NA, *adj.* Freely given or received, as a present.

MA-KA-NA-A-LO-HA, *s. Makana* and *aloha*, love. A free-will or willing offering. *Puk.* 35:29.

MA-KA-NA-HE-LE, *s.* See the foregoing. A free offering; ka haawi wale ana.

MA-KA-NA-HE-LE, *adj. Ma*, at, *ka*, the, and *nahele*, wild land. Wild; untamed; dwelling in the wilderness.

MA-KA-NAU, *s.* The name of a heiau.

MA-KA-NI, *s.* Wind; a breeze; air in motion.

2. The weather; the general state of the atmosphere.

3. The news; the report of some recent event; the gossip of a neighborhood.

MA-KA-PA, *v.* To be shy; to run away, as an untamed animal; e hoeno mau ia, he meo.

MA-KA-PA, *s.* One who goes about from house to house or goes here and there; he holoholo kauhale.

MA-KA-PAA, *s.* Maka and *paa*, fast. One with closed eyes; a blind person. *Oihk.* 22:22. See MAKAPO.

MA-KA-PAA, *adj.* Closed eyes; without sight; blind. *Ioan.* 5:3.

MA-KA-PAA, *adv.* Blindly; without seeing.

MA-KA-PAI, *adj.* Sore, as the eyes; thus, it applies where one eye has been sore and the disease has gone to the other, and both eyes are sore.

MA-KA-PA-LA, *adj.* Maka and *pala*, soft. Secreting healthy pus, as a sore; e holoi a *makapala*.

2. Ripe or ready to break, as the head of a boil.

MA-KA-PE-HU, *s.* Maka, eye, and *pehu*, swollen. Swelled or inflamed eyes; ola iho la ko'u *makapehu* ia ole.

MA-KA-PE-LA, *s.* Maka and *pela*, foul. Offensively smelling eyes.

MA-KA-PO, *v.* Maka and *po*, night. To be blind naturally; unable to see; to be blind morally. *Puk.* 23:8.

2. *Hoo.* To blind; to make one blind; to smite with blindness. *Kin.* 19:11. See MAKAPAA and MOOWINI.

MA-KA-PO, *s.* Blindness. *Kanl.* 28:28. A blind person. *Puk.* 4:11.

MA-KA-PO, *adj.* Blind; without the sense of sight; moowini.

MA-KA-PO, *adv.* Blindly; in a state of blindness.

MA-KA-PO-U-LI, *v.* Maka and *pouli*, darkness. To faint; to fail for want of strength; to be dizzy; e poniuniu.

MA-KA-PO-U-LI, *s.* The darkness that precedes fainting.

MA-KA-PO-NI-U-NI-U, *v.* Maka and *poniu*, to be dizzy. To faint; to be dizzy or faint for want of food. *Lunk.* 8:4. To be dizzy; hence, to faint.

MA-KA-PO-NI-U-NI-U, *s.* Obscure vision; applied to the eyes, blindness. See POLUA. Applied to the heart, want of courage.

MA-KA-PU-HI, *s.* Name of a species of fish-hook.

MA-KA-PU-LA, *adj.* Maka and *pula*, a mote in the eye. Sore-eyed; blind with one eye; having matter in the corner of the eye.

MA-KA-WAI, *adj.* Maka and *wai*, water. Watery-eyed; near sighted. *Kin.* 29:17.

2. Corrupt; running, as a sore.

3. Large at one end and small at the other.

MA-KA-WA-LU, *v.* Maka and *walu*, to scratch. To scratch like a cat; to rub; to scrape.

2. To go in large companies; to travel by caravans; hele okai.

MA-KA-WA-LU, *s.* A large company; a large army; aole e pono ke kaua uuku ke hana i *makawalu* ame ke kahului, it is not proper for a small army to engage a *large army* in a smooth place.

MA-KA-WE-LA, *s.* Epithet of a servant marked in the forehead; ina i hoailonaia ke kauwa ma ka lae, ua kapaia he kauwa *makawela*.

2. Name of a species of soft porous stone.

MA-KA-WE-LE, *s.* The name of a valley on Kauai which opens into the Waimea valley.

MA-KE, *v.* To die; to perish; to be killed; to suffer, as a calamity.

2. *Hoo.* To put to death; to deaden; to cause to die; to be slain. *Ezek.* 11:6. To mortify; to kill. *Oihk.* 20:4.

MA-KE, *v.* To desire; to wish for; to wish; e manao nui, to think much upon; to desire often; to love.

MA-KE, *v.* Used impersonally. To need; to have necessity; it is necessary; generally a negative; aole *make* kukui, *there is no need* of a lamp.

2. To be proper; to be fit; to be right; aole *make* hookuke ia Kalaiwahi, *it is not proper* to banish Kalaiwahi.

3. To be; to exist; to be present; aole *make* hau maluna iho ou, *let there be* no dew upon thee.

4. To permit; to allow; aole *make* au e haule i ka lima o kanaka, *let me not fall* into the hands of men. 1 *Oihl.* 21:13. Aole *make* hakaka kaua kekahi i kekahi, *let us two not* contend, one with the other. NOTE. In all the examples the meaning of *make* seems to be, *to wish* or *will*, and it may be the obsolete root of *makemake*.

MA-KE is also used impersonally in the sense, *it is agreed, it is a bargain*, &c.; ehia huamoa *make* ka hapawalu? how many hen's eggs *will buy* (will pay for, will be equal to) a rial? Hookahi puu wahie *make* ka pahu aila, one pile of wood *paid for* a cask of oil. *Make* hewa, a bad bargain;

no profit; in vain, &c.

Ma-ke, *s.* Death; the dissolution of soul and body; the state of being dead; as an agent it triumphs over the bodies of men. *Rom.* 6:9. Na *make* wahehee. *Ier.* 2:14.

Ma-ke, *adj.* Dead; hurt; injured; wounded.

Ma-ke, *adv.* E hina *make,* to fall dead; i hina *make* ai, he fell down dead.

 2. Even; nor; besides; neither.

Ma-ke-e, *v.* *Make* and *e,* before. To be jealous.

 2. *Make,* to desire. See verb, Note and E intensive. To desire, as property.

 3. To be greedy after a thing generally; used in reference to hoarding property; ua nui na mea i *makee* i kela mea i keia mea, i ka waiwai, i ka hanohano, a ia mea aku ia mea aku. Ma Hawaii nei, o ka aina kekahi mea a lakou i *makee* ai.

 4. To withhold from others property that is due. *Ezek.* 18:16. *Makee* is synonymous with *puniwaiwai,* but is stronger. See **Alunu.**

 5. To gather or scrape together things of value and of little value to keep them; e hapuku.

Ma-ke-e, *s.* Joined with *waiwai,* covetousness. *Ier.* 22:17. Greediness of gain. *Hal.* 10:3.

 2. Without *waiwai,* a covetous person.

 3. A robber. *Iob.* 5:5.

Ma-kee-waa, *v.* Manao ae la lakou, *makeewaa* ana e make ai o Kamaiole.

Ma-ke-e-wai-wai, *s.* See above in *makee, s.*

Ma-ke-he-wa, *v.* *Make* and *hewa,* wrong. To be or to do to no purpose; to do in vain or to no profit. *Ier.* 2:30.

Ma-ke-he-wa, *adv.* In vain; to no profit; not answering the purpose. *Hal.* 89:47. Vainly, as labor without reward. *Isa.* 49:4.

Ma-ke-kau, *adj.* Angry; irascible; quick in a passion; unfriendly; *makekau* oe, aole ike i kou hoahanau, aole hookipa, ea.

Ma-ke-ke, *s.* *Eng.* Mustard. *Mat.* 13:31. Hua *makeke,* mustard seed.

Ma-ke-le, *s.* A deep place of earth and water; deep mud, but partially hardened or covered with grass so as to be shaky; unstable land. See **Naka.**

Ma-ke-ma-ke, *v.* See **Make,** to desire. To desire much; to wish for; to love.

 2. To rejoice, i. e., to obtain one's desire; to be glad; e hoihoi, e olioli; ua like ka *makemake* me ka hauoli ame ka olioli. **Note.**—*Makemake* is often used by foreigners where other words such as *ake, manao, anoi,* &c., would apply better.

Ma-ke-ma-ke, *s.* A desire; a wish; a want; a thinking much of.

 2. A rejoicing; gladness.

Ma-ke-na, *v.* *Make* and *ana,* a dying. To mourn, that is, to make the sound of mourning; to mourn; to wail, as for the dead; to mourn, as at the death of a relative or friend; to mourn in any manner.

 2. To float in the air, as the sound of mourning. **Note.**—Mourning among Hawaiians was expressed by audible lugubrious tones of the voice.

Ma-ke-na, *s.* A wailing; a mourning or lamentation for the dead; the sound of mourning or wailing. *Kanl.* 26:14. See **Kumakena.**

 2. Sorrow or suffering from habits of intoxication; pau ka *makena* ana o ka poe ona rama, the *sorrows* of those drinking rum were ended.

 3. Sorrow; disappointment. *Laieik.* 66.

Ma-ke-na, *adj.* Mourning; lamenting the death of a friend; wawa *makena,* a noise of lamentation for the dead; kapa *makena,* mourning garments. *Kin.* 38:14.

Ma-ke-na-wai, *s.* *Make* and *na,* plural article, and *wai,* waters. A place where a brook loses itself in the ground.

Ma-ke-wai, *v.* *Make,* to desire, and *wai,* water. To be thirsty; to thirst; to desire to drink. *Lunk.* 4:19.

Ma-ke-wai, *s.* A desire to drink; thirst.

Ma-ke-wai, *adj.* Thirsty; desiring to drink.

Ma-ke-wa-le, *adj.* *Make,* death, and *wale,* without cause. That which has died of itself. *Oihk.* 22:8.

Ma-ki-a, *v.* See **Kakia.** To fasten, as with nails, spikes or pins; to nail; to bolt; to drive a nail. *Lunk.* 4:21.

 2. To tighten or make fast what otherwise would be loose.

 3. Fig. To bind; to make fast, as by a covenant or treaty.

 4. To be at peace with one; to be in a state of peace or quietness; ua makia ka aina.

 5. To lay or mark out the ground for a heiau; *makia* huli ka moku, to turn as the earth, though fast.

Ma-ki-a, *s.* A pin; a bolt; a nail; a wedge; anything used to keep a substance in its place.

 2. Fig. The state of being settled without disturbance; the state of being under treaty.

 3. The measure used in laying out the ground for a heiau.

Ma-ki-au, *s.* A nail of the finger or toe.

See MAIAO.

MA-KI-KA, *s.* *Eng.* The Hawaiian pronunciation for musquito or musketo. A stinging fly; mai noho hoi a aki wale aku e like me na *makika* nahu kolohe. NOTE.— Musketoes were first brought to the islands in 1823. A ship lying in the roads at Lahaina, on being cleared of vermin by smoke, a light breeze brought some musketoes ashore. They are now numerous and troublesome on the leeward sides of all the islands.

MA-KI-KI, *s.* Name of a kind of soft porous stone; maika stones were sometimes made of them.

MA-KI-KO-E, *adj.* Extended; long; flat. See KIOEOE.

MA-KI-LI, *v.* See MIKILI. To open, as the mind; to be conscious of some internal feeling or desire.

2. *Hoo.* To open the mind to receive as well as understand important truths; e *hoomakili* ae kakou i ka maka o ko kakou naau.

MA-KI-LO, *v.* *Ma* and *kilo*, a star-gazer. To look wishfully after a thing.

2. To beg. *Hal.* 37:25. Pololi loa oia, a hele oia ma kauhale e *makilo* ai i ai nana me ka hilahila ole.

3. To go about begging food.

MA-KI-LO, *s.* A beggar.

MA-KI-MA-KI, *s.* Name of a fish; a dolphin.

MA-KI-NI, *v.* To be uneven, as land, some places high, some low; *makini* kona aoao.

MA-KI-NI, *s.* Name of a species of fish.

MA-KI-NI, *adj.* Name of a certain kind of fish net; ka upena *makini* a ka poe kii ai ia ke ahi a ka po.

MA-KO, *adj.* Angry; provoked at others so as to quarrel and fight.

MA-KO-A, *s.* *Ma* and *koa*, a koa tree. A tract of land midway between the shore and interior where koa trees grow.

MA-KO-A, *v.* *Ma* and *koa*, a soldier. To go forward fearlessly; to do courageously.

2. To be hard with people; to be close; to be stingy; to be unkind.

MA-KO-E, *v.* Contraction of *maka*, eye, and *kole*, raw. To have sore or inflamed eyes.

MA-KO-E-A, *adj.* Hard; difficult; paakiki, makona.

MA-KO-I, *adj.* See the foregoing. Hard; severe; uncourteous; hostile.

MA-KO-I-E-LE, *v.* To teeter; to balance, as two children in play; to swing, as a single one on a rope.

MA-KO-I-O-LE, *v.* To restrain breathing; to hold in breath.

MA-KOU, *pers. pron.,* first person plural. We; our company, excluding the persons addressed. *Gram.* § 117:4 and § 129. O ka ea noii ka *makou* ku kahakai.

MA-KOU, *v.* To be red; to be inflamed; to have red or inflamed eyes. See MAKOLE.

2. To be red like the flame of a lamp which has burnt all night.

MA-KOU, *s.* Name of a lamp with a red flame, or a flame that has burnt all night; he poe lakou no *makou*, no ka mea o *makou* ka inoa oia kukui.

2. Name of the kalaimoku where the chiefs are concerned; such a person was esteemed highly.

MA-KO-HI, *s.* A species of red kalo.

MA-KO-KO, *s.* A species of large fish of the squid kind, of a reddish color; it is eaten by whales; *makoko*, he wahi ia nui ano hee, ulaula, he ai na ke kohola.

MA-KO-LE, *s.* Contraction of *maka*, eye, and *kole*, raw; inflamed. Inflamed eyes; the ophthalmia. *Makole* is mostly brought on by swimming long in salt water. See MAKOE.

2. The time when the sun is high or fiercely hot; i. e., from eight o'clock to two or three in the afternoon.

MA-KO-LE-KO-LE, *s.* See the foregoing. Sore, running eyes; red with soreness; he maka helohelo; ohelo eyed, i. e., red like an ohelo.

MA-KO-LI, *adj.* Little of any work done; a little way that any one travels in a day; mohai, loaa iki mai.

MA-KO-LO, *v.* *Ma* and *kolo*, to crawl; to creep. To crawl, as a four-footed animal.

2. To run along; to creep, as a vine.

3. To approach on hands and knees, as the people in former times approached a chief to ask a favor; hence,

4. To ask a favor; to ask a question.

MA-KO-LO-A, *s.* Name of some vegetable out of which mats were made, a kind of small rush; o ka *makoloa* kekahi hanaia i moena.

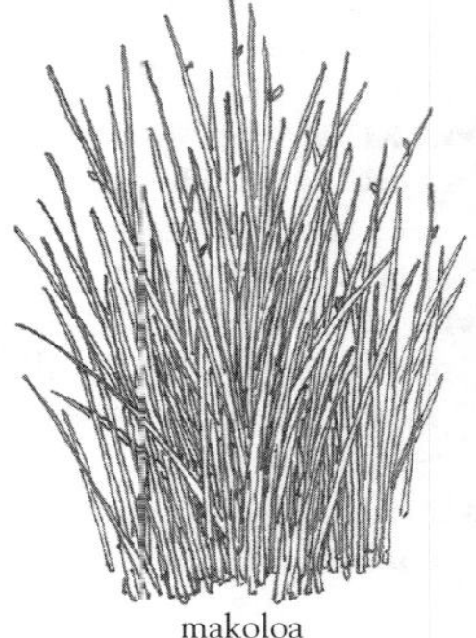

makoloa

MA-KO-LU, *s.* Name of a certain kind of fish.

MA-KO-LU, *adj.* Wide; thick; deep; besmeared thickly with dust. SYN. with manoanoa.

MA-KO-LU-KO-LU, *adj.* Intensive of the foregoing. Thick; deep; thick, as a plank.

MA-KO-MA-KO, *v.* To enlarge; to increase; to be great. See MAKU-MAKU.

MA-KO-MA-KO, *s.* Greatness; great size; largeness.

MA-KO-NA, *s.* An unpeaceful disposition; fretfulness.

MA-KO-NA, *adj.* Implacable; unappeaseable; aloha ole.

MA-KU, *v.* To run and hide; to flee.

MA-KU, *v.* To be full grown; to be full sized.

    2. To be fixed; to be firm; to be hard.

    3. To be large or numerous.

    4. *Hoo.* To dress up in a quantity of kapa with pomp; to make a great show.

MA-KU, *adj.* Full grown; firm; hard.

    2. Stiff or thick, as oil by long standing; *maku* ka aila. See MAKUA below.

MA-KU, *s.* Dregs of a liquid; lees; settlings. *Isa.* 50:17. The mother of vinegar; the lees of wine.

MA-KU-A, *s.* See MAKU, full grown. A parent; a begetter, either a father or mother, i. e., a mature person; applied also to an uncle or aunt.

    2. FIG. A benefactor; a provider; o ko kakou *makua* ma keia wahi, o ka naauao no ia. Aloha ka naauao, ka *makua* hoi o kahi *makua* ole.

MA-KU-A, *adj.* Full grown; of full age; mature; kanaka *mauka*, a full grown man.

MA-KU-A, *v.* See MAKU above, to be large. To enlarge; to grow. *Hoo.* To increase; to be full; to be thick set.

    2. To strengthen; to sustain. *Hal.* 18:35.

    3. To call one father or master; to honor. *Mat.* 23:9.

MA-KU-A-HI-NE, } *s. Makua,* parent,
MA-KU-WA-HI-NE, } and *wahine,* female.
MA-KU-A-WA-HI-NE, } A mother, &c., subject to all the figurative ideas of *makua, s.*

MA-KU-A-HO-NO-AI, } *s. Makua* and *ho-*
MA-KU-A-HO-NO-WAI, } *noai,* to bind together. A parent-in-law, either father or mother as it is followed by *kane* or *wahine.* See next words.

MA-KU-A-HO-NO-AI-KA-NE, *s. Makua* and *honoai* (see above), and *kane,* male. A father-in-law. *Lunk.* 1:16.

MA-KU-A-HO-NO-AI-WA-HI-NE, *s. Makua* and *honoai* and *wahine,* female. A mother-in-law.

MA-KU-A-KA-NE, *s. Makua* and *kane,* male. The male parent; a father; the husband of one's mother.

MA-KU-A-KA-NE-KO-LE-A, *s. Makua* and *kane,* male, and *kolea,* to make a friend. A step-father.

MA-KU-A-KE-A-HU, *adj.* The spirit going here and there even to where the clouds and sea meet; o waiho oe auanei a hala loa kou uhane *makuakeahu.*

MA-KU-A-KO-LE-A, *s. Makua* and *kolea.* A parent-in-law, either father or mother.

MA-KU-A-KU-A, *s.* A species of grass growing in bunches; a bunch of grass.

MA-KU-A-LII, *s. Makua* and *lii,* chief. A progenitor; a patriarch. *Ios.* 13:21.

    2. A head of a tribe; a chief. *Kin.* 36:15.

MA-KU-E, *s.* A pale brown or chestnut color; purple; blue; any dark color.

MA-KU-E, *adj.* Dark; brown; blue; green, according to the substance; lole *makue,* purple cloth. 2 *Oihl.* 2:7.

MA-KU-E, *v. Ma* and *kue,* to oppose. To punch, hunch or elbow one; to provoke one to anger; to draw down the eyebrows as if sullen or angry.

MA-KU-E, *s.* Opposition; anger; strife.

MA-KU-E-KU-E, *s.* A kind of grass; the grass with which good adobies are made.

MA-KU-O, *adj.* Brown.

MA-KUU, *s.* A crease around the end of a canoe to hold a rope for dragging it; alaila hoopualiia ke kauwahi mahope o ka waa: ua kapaia kela wahi he *makuu.*

MA-KUU, *adj. Ma* and *kuu,* to let go. Discharging stools involuntarily; lepo *makuu,* involuntary alvine discharges.

MA-KU-KO-AE, *s.* The state of one just dying, formerly worshiped as a god.

MA-KU-LE, *s.* A company of traveling persons; he huakai; a company of horses and riders, &c.

MA-KU-LU, } *v. Ma* and *kulu,* a
MA-KU-LU-KU-LU, } drop of liquid. To drop, as water or a liquid; to shed drops; to drop down, as water from a leaky roof; to drop, as water from the clouds.

MA-KU-WA-HI-NE-KO-LE-A, *s. Makua* and *wahine* and *kolea,* to make a friend. A step-mother.

MA-LA, *v.* To swell; to swell up; to grow large; to puff up, as a swelling.

MA-LA, *s.* A swelling or puffing up, as of the chest; an enlargement; a growing.

    2. The name of a disease.

3. A small patch of ground; a garden; a small plat of ground for cultivation or under cultivation; a field. *Neh.* 5:11. See MALAWAINA.

4. A gentle breeze; the east wind; makani hikina, he aeloa.

MA-LA, *adj.* Swelling; puffed up; enlarging; growing.

2. Exhausted; spent.

MA-LAE, *s. Ma* and *lae,* a calm. A calm; a calmness; a pleasant appearance. See HOOMALAE.

MA-LAE-LAE, *adj.* Clear; serene, as the sky; pleasant, as the weather.

2. Clear; smooth, as a plain; without obstructions.

MA-LAI-O-A, *adj.* Broken fine; scattered, as small particles of a substance.

MA-LAI-LA, *adv. Ma* and *laila,* there. There; at the side of; at that place. *Gram.* § 165, 2: Auialo.

MA-LAI-LE-NA, *s.* Bitterness; ill tasted; what is unpalatable.

MA-LAI-LE-NA, *adj.* Bitter, acrid or sour; unpalatable.

MA-LAI-LU-A, *s.* A goat without horns, derived from the name of a particular goat formerly found at Kona, Hawaii.

MA-LA-O-A, *adj.* Sad; sorrowful, as one sitting and thinking of many sources of grief and imaginary evils as they flit before the mind as real ones; he weli *malaoa* aku no ka lue la.

MA-LAO-LAO, *s.* Twilight; light between day and night.

MA-LAU, *s.* A place in the sea where the water is still and quiet; a calm place in the sea.

2. A place where the bait for the aku or bonita is found.

3. An impious wicked person.

MA-LAU, *v.* See No. 3 above. *Hoo.* To reject good advice or good principles; to treat with contempt one's principles or doctrines.

MA-LAU-E-A, *v.* To hawk about and sell; to peddle.

MA-LAU-E-A, *s.* An indolent person, indisposed to work; *malauea* o ka pililau o lawaia o ke aukaka.

MA-LAU-LAU, *s.* See MALAU. A preparation.

MA-LAU-LAU-A, *v.* To trade; to make market; to peddle. See MALAUEA. See also MAAUAUA, the *l* dropped.

MA-LA-HI, *v.* To be relieved from punishment; to be joyful, as one who has been condemned, but the accuser is reconciled or no longer angry.

2. To be joyful, as one who seeks for a thing and quickly finds it.

MA-LA-HI-A, *adj.* For *malaia.* See MALA 2. Bitter; disagreeable to the taste. See MALAILENA.

MA-LA-LAI-O-A, *s.* Name of an office in the king's train.

MA-LA-LU-A, *v.* To swell, as anything blistered; as fruit exposed to the hot sun; ua *malalua* i ka la o Kawaihoa, Kawaihoa is *blistered* in the sun.

MA-LA-LO, *comp. prep. Ma* and *lalo,* down. Downward; under; below; beneath. *Gram.* § 161.

MA-LA-MA, *v. Ma* and *lama,* light. To keep; to preserve; to watch over. See KIAI.

2. To serve as a servant; to take care of, as one who cares for another. *Kin.* 47:13.

3. To reverence; to obey, as a command. *Kanl.* 5:9.

4. To observe, as a festival; to attend to, as a duty.

5. To be awake to danger.

6. To put and keep things in order.

7. To swell; to be enlarged, as the belly. See MALA.

MA-LA-MA, *s.* Light, as of the sun, moon or stars. See MALAMALAMA.

2. A solar month in distinction from *mahina,* a moon or lunar month.

3. A looking-glass; he aniani nana.

4. One who observes the heavenly bodies; a prophet; a star-gazer; an astrologer.

MA-LA-MA, *adj.* Taking care; giving heed; watching over.

MA-LA-MA, *adv.* A conditional term. Perhaps; it may be, &c.; *malama* e kupu auanei ka hua i luluia, *perhaps* hereafter the seed sown may spring up; *malama* o huli mai, *perhaps* he will turn. *Malama* is often connected with *paha,* which only strengthens the possibility; as, *malama paha* e make ia, *perhaps* he will die; the same as *malia* or *malia paha,* perhaps.

MA-LA-MA-LA, *v.* See MALA, to swell. To swell; to rise up round and full; to be large.

MA-LA-MA-LA, *s.* See MALA. Something swollen; enlarged by swelling; swollen with pride or haughtiness; he poe makau kakou i ka *malamala.*

MA-LA-MA-LA-MA, *v.* See MA and LAMA, a torch; also MALAMA. To shine; to give light, as the sun or a luminous body.

2. *Hoo.* To enlighten; to cause light. *Kin.* 1:14, 15.

MA-LA-MA-LA-MA, *s.* Light; the light of

the sun or of the heavenly bodies; the light of a lamp or of a fire.

2. FIG. Supernatural light; light of the mind; knowledge; knowledge of salvation; opposite to *pouli* o ka naau.

MA-LA-MA-LA-MA, *adj.* Shining, as a light.

MA-LA-NA, *v.* See MANANA. *Ma* and *lana*, to float. To float together, as a body of canoes; to move together, as a drove of cattle or a multitude of men; ke *malana* mai la na kanaka. *Malana* hiki ae i ka ili kai.

MA-LA-NA, *s.* A moving together, as many single things.

2. The name of a fine rain from the northeast at Waimea as it moves along before the trade wind.

MA-LA-NA, *adj.* Tottering; weak; feeble. See LANA.

2. Loose; pulling up easily, as weeds from soft ground.

MA-LA-NAI, *s.* The gentle blowing of the north-east wind.

2. One of the names of the trade wind. See MOAE and AELOA.

MA-LA-NI, *s.* The name of the sixteenth day of the month. See MAHEALANI.

MA-LA-WAI-NA, *s.* *Mala*, a garden, and *waina*, grapes. A patch for grapes; a vineyard. Kin. 9:20.

MA-LE, *v.* To hawk and spit; to raise phlegm; e palahehe; to expectorate.

MA-LE, *s.* Phlegm; mucous raised from the lungs or throat; he huka paa.

MA-LE, *s.* A species of fish; the young of the uhu. See OMALEMALE.

MA-LE, *s.* An incorrect orthography for *mare.* See mare.

MA-LE-A-LE-A, *v.* See MAALEA. To be cunning; to be crafty; to have a forethought for one's advantage.

2. To assuage, as one's anger; to pacify.

MA-LE-HA-LE-HA, *s.* The appearance of the sky at evening.

2. The time of evening. Isa. 5:11.

MA-LE-HU-LE-HU, *s.* The appearance of the sky at dawn of day.

MA-LE-LA, *adj.* Idle; lazy; indolent.

MA-LE-LE, *v.* To distribute or give out to others, as food. *Hoo.* To parcel out; to give to one and to another, as food; pau no ka ai, aole *malele* aku ia mea. E *hoomalele* aku i ka ai ia hai, ame ka palapala.

MA-LE-LE, *v.* To call to one for help; *malele* kuala.

MA-LE-NA, *s.* A burning or preparing medicine; he papaa laau lapaau.

MA-LE-NO, *s.* A rough sea.

MA-LI, *v.* To tie on; to fasten, as a fish-hook on to a string; to tie the end of a rope to keep it from unraveling; to tie up, as a broken limb.

2. To beseech; to beg in a soothing manner.

MA-LI, *s.* See the verb above. A string used in tying the bait on a fish-hook, or for tying the end of a rope to prevent it from unraveling.

MA-LI-A, *adv.* See MALAMA, *adv.* Perhaps; but; then; if then; lest; often followed by *paha* or *o* or both; *malia paha* i hehuia makou i poe nana e kuhikuhi i ka iwi; *malia o*, lest. Kanl. 24:15. *Malia paha o*, lest perhaps. Nah. 22:6.

MA-LI-E, *v.* To be calm; to be quiet; to be still as to noise; to cease an agitation; to be calm, as the sea after a storm. *Hoo.* To make quiet; to still; to hush up.

MA-LI-E, *adj.* Quiet; calm; still; gentle.

MA-LI-E, *adv.* Quietly; calmly; gently.

MA-LI-E-LI-E, *v.* Intensive of *malie.* To hush up a pertubation of any kind. *Hoo.* To soothe one's anger; to entreat quietness; to persuade one to be still. Nah. 13:3.

MA-LII, *v.* A contraction for *malili.* See MALILI.

MA-LI-O, *s.* The opening of the morning; the first rays of light; *malio* pawa o ke kakahiaka. See PAWA.

MA-LI-U, *v.* *Ma* and *liu*, perservative. To attend to one; to regard or listen to one's request.

2. To turn a compassionate eye upon one; to be favorably disposed towards one; to look upon one with kindness when needing compassion. Puk. 32:12.

3. To hearken to advice; to turn from a purpose. Kanl. 21:18.

4. To be accepted as an offering. Oihk. 1:4.

5. To be gracious to one; to turn towards one; to have respect to. Kin. 4:4.

6. *Hoo.* To be entreated for a person or thing. 2 Sam. 21:14.

MA-LI-U, *s.* A chief deified and become an aumakua.

2. A deep sound, as of an ancient deep-toned instrument (shell), like the bellowing of a bull.

MA-LI-U-IA, *adj.* Acceptable; favorable. Hal. 69:13.

MA-LI-HI-NI, *v.* To be or to live as a stranger. Puk. 2:29.

MA-LI-HI-NI, *s.* A stranger; a non-resident; a transient person; a person from another place. Oihk. 20:2. FIG. One that has not been seen for some time.

MA-LI-HI-NI, *adj.* As a stranger; stranger like; new faced; maka hou.

MA-LI-LI, *v.* Ma and *lili* for *lii,* small. To be or become small, as something that is too great.

2. To calm down, as a storm or one in fierce anger.

3. To be consoled, as one indulging in immoderate grief.

4. *Hoo.* To wither; to droop; to lessen down; to make less.

5. To be bereaved of children, as parents, or of parents, as children.

MA-LI-LI, *s.* A blast, as upon fruits; a blasting. 1 *Nal.* 8:7.

MA-LI-LI, *adj.* Lessened; stinted; degenerated; withered; applied to fruits. *Isa.* 37:27.

2. Applied to a wind; huaai *malili,* a wind injuring vegetables. *Kanl.* 28:22.

MA-LI-MA-LI, *v.* See MALI, to beseech. To dissemble through flattery.

2. To flatter for the sake of some advantage.

3. To speak pleasantly in order to make one forget former injuries.

4. To make a defense before an assembly.

5. To talk soothingly; to make friends with those whom we have offended.

6. To persuade. 1 *Nal.* 22:20.

7. *Hoo.* To flatter. *Hal.* 78:36.

MA-LI-MA-LI, *s.* Flattery; dissimulation; pleasant speech for gain or advantage; he poe akamai i ka *malimali,* a company skilled in *flattery.*

MA-LI-MA-LI, *adj.* Soothing in language; flattering; dissembling.

MA-LI-NA, *s.* A calm smooth place in the sea; o ka *malina* a Moi kekahi kahuna nui o ia manawa.

MA-LI-NO, *adj.* Ma and *lino.* See LINO-LINO. Calm; quiet, as one whose spirits have been ruffled; calm, as the surface of water without wind; quiet; gentle. See MALIE. Reflecting light, as calm water. See OLINO.

MA-LI-NO-LI-NO, *adj.* See MALINO above.

MA-LO, *s.* A strip of kapa or cloth girded about the loins of men; in former times the *malo* was the only dress worn by men when at work; a covering for the nakedness of men; ka wawae e paa'i ka mai.

2. FIG. Ua loheia mamua ka olelo a kekahi alii, e kaohi a e moku ka ka *malo.*

MA-LO, *adj.* See MALOO.

MA-LO-E-LO-E, *v.* See LOELOE, feeble.

To be faint; to be weary; to relax, as the joints of animals. *Anat.* 1.

2. To breathe hard; to puff from hard exercise, as traveling, or by hard labor.

3. *Hoo.* To weary one's self in doing evil. *Ier.* 9:5.

MA-LO-E-LO-E, *adj.* Weary; stiffened with labor or traveling. SYN. with oopa. See MAALOELOE.

2. Firm; substantial.

MA-LO-I, *v.* To start in the eyes, as tears for love or affection.

MA-LOO, *v.* To dry up, as water.

2. To wither, as a tree.

3. To become dry, as a river. *Ios.* 3:16.

4. *Hoo.* To cause to dry up, as the sea. *Ios.* 2:10. To dry or season in the sun.

MA-LOO, *adj.* Dry; dry, as land, in opposition to water; dry in opposition to moist or wet.

2. Dead, as a vegetable dried up.

MA-LOO-HA-HA, *v.* To be dry; to be without moisture.

2. To yield no fruit, as dry ground.

MA-LOO-HA-HA, *adj.* Dry; barren; unfruitful, as ground.

MA-LO-HI, *v.* Ma and *lohi,* slow. To be slow; to be lazy; a maluhi, *malohi,* maloeloe.

MA-LO-HI-LO-HI, *v.* See MA and LOHI, slow. To be weary; to be fatigued. See MALOELOE and MALUHILUHI.

MA-LO-HI-LO-HI, *adj.* See MALUHILUHI. Weary from traveling. See MALOELOE.

MA-LO-KA, *v.* Ma and *loka,* not found. To be sluggish in mind; to be slow in giving one's attention to a subject.

2. *Hoo.* To be unbelieving; to be disobedient.

3. To treat sacred things with contempt.

MA-LO-KA, *s.* A disregard to the commands of a chief. *Hoo.* Unbelief in a chief's word or promise; disobedience in practice; under the christian system, an unbeliever; a scoffer.

MA-LO-KA, *adj.* Disobedient; unbelieving in the word of a chief. *Hoo.* Unbelieving; discrediting the christian system. 1 *Kor.* 7:12.

MA-LO-KO, *comp. prep.* Ma and *loko,* within. In; within; inside of; internally. *Gram.* § 161.

MA-LO-LO, *v.* To break off work at the arrival of a la kapu; to rest. *Hoo.* To rest; to be still; to desist from work or labor on account of kapu.

2. To ebb and flow, as the ocean, much more than usual; o Nana no ka malama e

malolo ai ka moana.

MA-LO-LO, *s.* A day of preparation before a la kapu. Hoo. Causing a *malolo* or resting day. NOTE.—At the present time it is equivalent to *Saturday*; ka la *Hoomalolo*, the day before the Sabbath.

MA-LO-LO, *s.* The flying-fish that swims near or on the surface of the sea; ma ka ili kai e holo ai ka *malolo*.

MA-LO-LO, *adj.* Ebbing much further than usual, as the sea, and when this occurs, it is followed by a very high tide called ke *kaimalolo*.

MA-LO-LO-HI, *adj.* Ma and *lohi* or *lolohi*, slow. Sluggish; numb; torpid.

MA-LO-LO-LU-A, *adj.* Malolo and *lua*, second. The reflux of a very low ebb tide of the sea; o ke kai *malololua* kona.

MA-LO-WAI, *s.* Malo and *wai*, wet; water. A wet malo; ina i komo ke kanaka ma ko ke alii hale me ka pale ole i kona *malowai* e make no.

MA-LU, *v.* To shade; to overshadow; to cast a shade; *malu* ka la, the sun in *shaded. Laieik.* 163.

2. To be comfortable, as in a shade when all is heat around; to be in a state of quietness and peace with others.

3. To be favored; to have many enjoyments and privileges.

4. To be fruitful; to be blessed.

5. *Hoo.* To bless; to comfort; to make comfortable.

6. To rule over; to govern, as a chief; to keep in order the affairs of state. 1 *Nal.* 3:9.

7. To make peace, i. e., a treaty of peace with *olelo kuikahi. Lunk.* 3:19.

8. To protect; to govern; to put under a kapu; *hoomalu* iho la o Kamehameha, nana wale no e kuai i ka wahie ala, Kamehameha *prohibited* the sandal-wood; he only would sell it.

MA-LU, *s.* A shade; the shadow of a tree or anything that keeps off the sun.

2. Peace; quietness; protection.

3. Watchfulness; care.

MA-LU, *adj.* Overshadowed; protected; governed.

2. Quiet; without care or anxiety.

3. Wet; cold; damp; soaked in water; i waiho ia maloko o ka wai.

4. Shivering with wet and cold.

MA-LU, *adj.* Secret; not openly; contrary to order; without liberty; unlawful; olelo *malu*, secret conversation. *Lunk.* 3:19.

MA-LU, *adv.* Secretly; unlawfully.

MA-LU-A, *v.* Ma and *lua*, a pit or hole. To dig or prepare holes or hills for planting; to plant, as corn or potatoes.

MA-LU-A, *s.* Hills dug up or places made for planting potatoes.

2. A little spot dug up and prepared for planting.

3. Laziness; indifference about work; he maluwa.

MA-LU-A-HE-LE, *s.* Name of a wind on Kauai from the north-west.

MA-LU-A-KE-LE, *s.* Name of a wind blowing mostly on Kauai; hohola ka *maluakele*.

MA-LU-A-LU-A, *v.* To be rough and uneven; to be up and down, as hilly land; as an uneven road.

MA-LU-A-LU-A, *adj.* Rough; uneven; hilly, as land.

MA-LU-A-LU-A, *s.* Name of the north-west wind at Lahaina.

2. Name of a wind at Kauai.

3. Name of a north wind at Oahu.

MA-LU-O-HI-A, *s.* The sacrifice of a person at the cutting of the tree for a god.

2. The name of the kapu setting apart that tree.

MA-LU-HA, *s. Heb.* A mallows bush. *Iob.* 30:4. Purslain perhaps.

MA-LU-HI, *adj.* Ma and *luhi*, weary. Tired; slow; weary; lazy; dull; drowsy.

MA-LU-HI-A, *v.* Passive of *malu* for *maluia*, *h* inserted. To be at rest; to enjoy peace, &c.; aole i *maluhia* ka aina no ke kaua pinepine, the land did not *enjoy rest* on account of frequent wars.

2. To be under a kapu; to be under the injunction of a solemn stillness or silence, as at some parts of the ancient worship.

3. To be under the fear or dread of the punishment of broken kapus.

MA-LU-HI-A, *s.* Peace; quietness; safety.

2. A sense of the presence and power of the gods.

3. Fear; dread of the gods in ancient times.

4. The solemn awe and stillness that reigned during some of the ancient kapus.

5. The sascredness and solemnity of religious rites.

MA-LU-HI-A, *adj.* Peaceful; quiet, &c.

2. Fearful; troubled with fear during the ancient worship.

MA-LU-HI-A, *adv.* Quietly; silently. *Ios.* 10:21.

MA-LU-HI-LU-HI, *v.* Ma and *luhi*, weary. To be weary from traveling. 2 *Sam.* 16:14. To be weary, i. e., to be inclinded to sleep. *Hal.* 121:3. *Hoo.* To weary; to fatigue.

Kekah. 10:15.

Ma-lu-hi-lu-hi, *s.* Weariness; pain from exertion; fatigue from labor.

Ma-lu-hi-lu-hi, *adj.* Fatiguing; painful; weary; lazy; indolent.

Ma-lu-ko-i, *s.* *Malu,* shade, and *koi,* root not found. The shadow of death, death's shade. See MALUMAKE.

2. The act of going and cutting ohia trees for a heiau; ka maluohia, ka waokele, no mauhaalele.

Ma-lu-le, *v.* *Ma* and *lule,* to shake. To be weak; to be yielding; to be flexible.

2. To be soft, as poi.

3. To change; to vary one's form.

4. *Hoo.* To be changed; to pass to another form. 1 *Kor.* 15:52.

Ma-lu-le, *s.* Weakness; flexibility; a changing from one form to another.

Ma-lu-le, *adj.* Limber; weak; flexible; changeable.

Ma-lu-le-lu-le, *adj.* Intensive of *malule.* Weak; flexible; changing; limber.

Ma-lu-lu, *s.* *Ma* and *lulu,* a calm spot of water. A place where water stands not dried up by the sun nor by drought; he wahi wai, aole kaee i ka la ame ke koeleele.

Ma-lu-ma-ke, *s.* *Malu,* shade, and *make,* death. The shade or shadow of death. *Iob.* 24:17. See MALUKOI.

Ma-lu-ma-lu, *adj.* See MALU. Shady; cool; comfortable; peaceful; hale *malumalu,* a shed; a portico.

Ma-lu-ma-lu, *s.* See MALU. To be shady, &c. *Hoo.* To shade; to overshadow. *Heb.* 9:5.

Ma-lu-ma-lu-hi-a, *s.* See MALUHIA. Peace; quietness; rest. *Puk.* 18:23.

Ma-lu-na, *comp. prep.* *Ma* and *luna,* above. Upward; upon; over, either as to place or office; oia no *maluna* o ka poe kaua. *Gram.* § 161.

Ma-lu-wa, *adj.* Lazy; indifferent about work; idle. See MOLOWA.

Ma-ma, *v.* To be light, in opposition to heavy; to be unoppressed with a burden; to be relieved of a burden, of care or of labor; to be light, i. e., quick in making a journey.

2. To be active; to be nimble; to be affected with wine. *Eset.* 1:10. To revive from a fainting fit. *Laieik.* 165. A *mama* ae la ke alii.

3. *Hoo.* To lighten what is heavy, i. e., to mitigate an affection. 1 *Sam.* 6:5.

4. To lighten or diminish, as a task or hard labor. 1 *Nal.* 12:4.

5. To finish; to have done with a thing;

to set it afloat.

Ma-ma, *v.* To chew with a view to spit out of the mouth; to chew or work over in the mouth; hoomakaukau iho la ia e *mama* i ke kukui; to chew or grind in the mouth, as the Hawaiian doctors do some of their medicines. NOTE.—When the substance chewed is to be swallowed, the action of chewing is *nau.* Hoolale koke ae la ke kuhina e *mama* i ka awa. *Laieik.* 34.

Ma-ma, *s.* Lightness; swiftness in movement. 2 *Sam.* 1:23.

Ma-ma, *adj.* Light; active; nimble.

Ma-ma, *adj.* Chewed; masticated; kona mau *mama* awa, persons whose business it was to chew awa to make intoxicating drink. *Laieik.* 88.

Ma-mae, *s.* *Ma* and *mae,* pain. A kind of pain or uneasy feeling, as of the flesh in cupping; similar to *mae.*

2. A slight involuntary contraction of the muscles when hurt or threatened to be hurt.

Ma-ma-o, *adv.* *Ma* and *mao* (see O), compound preposition. LIT. At there, i. e., at a distance, but not far off; out of hearing. *Puk.* 18:24.

Ma-ma-o, *adj.* Further; distant; far off; palena *mamao* loa, the utmost bounds. *Nah.* 22:35. E ku *mamao* aku, keep at a distance. *Tit.* 3:9.

Ma-ma-o, *s.* A distance of time or space; a long distance; afar off. *Mat.* 8:30. A space between one place and another; something existing or done at a great distance off, or a long time ago.

2. A sticky substance, as tar, pitch, pilali, &c.

3. Name of a species of fish.

Ma-ma-o, *v.* To remove to a distance; to go afar off; to be far from locally and morally.

2. To make clear, explicit or plain.

3. *Hoo.* To remain at a distance; to separate widely from a person or place. *Ezek.* 11:15.

Ma-mau, *v.* *Ma* and *mau,* to continue. To be rough, as a road; to make rough or uneven.

2. To be hard or heavy upon; to overpower, as something opposed.

3. To be heavy; to press down.

Ma-mau, *adj.* Rough; difficult; uneven; narrow, as a path; hard to unloose; rough in treatment, as in contention.

Ma-mau-a, *v.* *Ma* and *maua,* often; repeated. To obtain often; to obtain gratuitously. See MAUMAUA.

Ma-mau-e-a, *s.* Wild kalo growing in uncultivated places. See AWEOWEO.

Ma-ma-ka, *v.* To travel in company; to go in bands; e hele huakai.

Ma-ma-ka, *s.* Name of the stick on which Hawaiians carry burdens across the shoulders. See also AUAMO and AUMAKA.

Ma-ma-ka-kau-a, *s.* *Mamaka* and *kaua,* war. A principal man in battle, such as bears the brunt of a fight.

Ma-ma-kau-a-lu, *adv.* Horizontally; flying off horizontally like a bird; lele *mamakaualu* auhono i ke kai.

Ma-ma-ke, } *v.* Freq. of *make,* to die.
Ma-ma-ma-ke, } To die or perish together or in companies.

Ma-ma-ki, *s.* The bush or plant from the bark of which the mamaki kapas are made.
2. The name of the kapa or cloth thus made.

Ma-ma-la, *s.* *Ma* and *mala,* a small piece of ground. A small piece of any substance broken off from a larger; a fragment. *Luk.* 9:17. He hakina.

Ma-ma-la-ho-e, *s.* *Mamala,* piece, and *hoe,* paddle. Name of one of Kamehameha's criminal laws, a law of the most stringent class; the violation of all such laws was, indeed, punishable with death. The name was derived from the fact that he came near losing his life by a paddle being split over his head. O Kamehameha ka mea nana i kau *mamalahoe* kanawai.

Ma-ma-lu, *s.* *Ma* and *malu,* shade. A shade; a screen from the sun.
2. In modern times, an umbrella. See LOULU. A defense from a storm. *Isa.* 32:2. A covering; a protection.

Ma-ma-lu, *v.* *Ma* and *malu,* to protect. To defend one from evil; to parry off; to hinder one from doing a thing.

Ma-ma-lu, *adj.* Covered; shaded; protected.

Ma-ma-mo, *s.* Name of a species of fish.

Ma-ma-na-la, *adj.* Small; little, as little or light work; little, as the voice; he noho wale iho no na 'lii, he oluolu, he *mamanala,* aole hana nui.

Ma-ma-ne, *s.* Name of a species of tree, wood hard, used for the boards of holuas and for oos.

mamane

Ma-mi-na, *v.* *Ma* and *mina,* grief. To regret the loss of anything; to hold on to it; to withold its loss. See MINAMINA.

Ma-mo, *s.* A descendant; posterity below the third generation. *Kin.* 26:24. Children; descendants generally. *Kanl.* 32:52.
2. A species of bird with yellow feathers, and much valued for its feathers.
3. A yellow war cloak covered with the yellow feathers of the mamo.
4. The name of a species of fish.
5. The name of a tree with beautiful blossoms; he pua nani, he laau.

Ma-mo, *adj.* Yellow, from the yellow bird called *mamo;* aahu *mamo,* a yellow garment; ua aahuia i ka lole ula ame ka aahu *mamo,* he was clothed in a red coat and a *yellow* robe.

Ma-mo-na, *s.* *Chald.,* mamon; *Eng.,* mammon. Riches. *Mat.* 6:24.

Ma-mua, *comp. prep.* *Ma* and *mua,* first. Before; first in time or place; formerly; previously; in front of. *Gram.* § 161.

Ma-mu-li, *comp. prep.* *Ma* and *muli,* after. Behind; afterwards; hereafter; soon; by and by; after; according to; after the example of. *Gram.* §161.

Ma-na, *s.* Supernatural power, such as was supposed and believed to be an attribute of the gods; power; strength; might. See *Oihk.* 26:19. Applied under the christian system to divide power. *Lunk.* 6:14.
2. Spirit; energy of character. 2 *Nal.* 2:9. Official power or authority; o kona mau kaikuahine ka mana kiai. *Laieik.* 101.
3. Glory; majesty; intelligence; ka ihiihi, ka nani, ka ike.
4. A branch of limb of a tree; the cross piece of a cross; a limb of the human body.
5. A line projecting from another line. *Puk.* 37:19. See MANAMANA.
6. Food while being chewed in the mouth, children were fed by taking the food from the mother's mouth and putting it into the child's; a mouthful of food.
7. The name of the place of worship in a heiau; a house in the luakini; hence,
8. The name of a particular class of heiaus.
9. The name of a species of kalo.
10. Name of a species of fish-hook.

Ma-na, *adj.* Powerful; strong. 1 *Sam.* 2:4.

Ma-na, *v.* To branch out; to be divided; to be many.

2. To chew food for infants; e *mana* aku i ka ai na ke keiki.

3. *Hoo.* To reverence or worship, as a superior being, i. e., of superhuman power; a *hoomana* aku la i ua alii la e like me ka *hoomana* akua, they *worshiped* that chief as if they *worshiped* a god.

4. To worship; to render homage to. *Puk.* 20:5.

MA-NA, *s.* *Hoo.* Worship; reverence; adoration.

MA-NAI, *s.* An instrument used anciently as a needle in stringing flowers for wreaths; e ake no lakou e hookuikui i ka *manai*, a uo i ke kaula i lawa; a sharp instrument to make leis with.

MA-NAI-E-A, *s.* A species of sea moss. See MAN-AUEA.

MA-NA-O, *s.* Ma and nao, root not found. To think; to think of; to call to mind; meditate; *manao* io,

manaiea

manao oiaio, to believe as true; to credit; to have full confidence in; to wish; to will. *Rom.* 9:18.

2. *Hoo.* To remember; to consider; call to mind; to please to do a thing; will.

MA-NA-O, *s.* A thought; an idea; a plan; a device; a purpose; a counsel; a stratagem; *manao* kiekie, a high thought; pride; *manao* io, faith; belief; confidence; *manao* oiaio, the same; *manao* kuko, lust *manao* lana, hope; expectation; *manao* akamai, spirit of wisdom. *Puk.* 28:3.

MA-NAO-IA, *s.* or *part. pass.* What is believed, thought or supposed.

MA-NAO-I-O, *v.* *Manao* and *io*, real; substantial. To believe; to credit what one says. *Kin.* 15:6. To have confidence in. *Puk.* 14:31. The same as *manao oiaio*, to think to be truth or true.

MA-NAO-I-O, *s.* Faith; verity; full confidence.

MA-NAO-KU-PAA, *s.* *Manao* and *ku*, to stand, and *paa*, fast. A decree; a fixed plan; a purpose.

MA-NAO-LA-NA, *v.* *Manao* and *lana*, to float. To be buoyed up, as the mind; not to sink, in opposition to *manao poho*, to

sink; to despond; hence,

2. To hope; to trust in; to expect. *Hal.* 71:5.

MA-NAO-LA-NA, *s.* Hope; expectation; a buoyancy of mind.

MA-NAO-LI-A, *s.* See MANAOIA, *l* inserted. What is thought of, or destined, or purposed. *Gram.* § 48.

MA-NAO-NAO, *v.* Freq. of *manao*, to think. To think over; to turn over and over in one's mind; to meditate. *Hal.* 63:6.

2. To lament; to grieve; to pity one; to mourn for one; kumakena.

MA-NAO-NAO, *s.* A meditating; a turning over in the mind; grief; sadness on parting with friends. *Laieik.* 194. Mourning; sadness for the death of one.

MA-NAO-PAA, *s.* *Manao* and *paa*, fast. A plan; a resolution; a design. *Laieik.* 25.

MA-NAO-PAA, *adj.* Just; inflexible; not turned aside by selfish motives; he kaikamahine *manaopaa* no, aole e hoopilimeaai. *Laieik.* 194.

MA-NA-HA-LO, ⎱ *s.* *Mana* and *halo.* See
MA-NA-HO-LO, ⎰ HALO, *s.* The motion of the arms and legs in swimming.

MA-NA-KA, *v.* To be discouraged; to be disheartened in doing a thing.

2. To become indifferent as to the result; to be lazy; to work slackly and carelessly.

MA-NA-KA, *s.* Discouragement; faintheartedness; indifference in one's business; laziness. *Hoo.* Hoomanaka is opposed to *hooikaika.* E hana no me ka hooikaika, aole me ka *hoomanaka*.

MA-NA-KA, *adj.* Faint-hearted; lazy; aole e loaa keia mea, o ka naauao, i ka mea *manaka*, this thing, learning, will not be obtained by the *lazy*.

MA-NA-LO, *adj.* Sweet, as fresh water, in distinction from brackish or salt water; slightly brackish; insipid.

2. Sweet, that is, free from taint; insipid; free from taste.

3. Firm; hard, as good kalo, in distinction from *loliloli.*

MA-NA-LO, *s.* Sweetness; destitute of bad taste.

MA-NA-LO-NA-LO, *v.* To be unseasoned, as food; to be insipid to the taste; to be without tatste, as pure water. See MANA-NALO.

MA-NA-MA-NA, *v.* See MANA, a branch. To branch out; to grow into branches; to form several divisions; to part asunder, as several things from each other.

MA-NA-MA-NA, *v.* A branch; a limb of

a tree or of a person.

Ma-na-ma-na, *adj.* Branching; projecting in parallel or radiated lines; divided; split, as limbs of trees, twigs of branches, &c.

Ma-na-ma-na-li-ma, *s.* I. e., the branching of the arm; the finger. *Puk.* 29:12.

Ma-na-ma-na-nu-i, *s.* The thumb or the great toe as it is connected with the *lima* or the *wawae.*

Ma-na-ma-na-wa-wae, *s.* The toes.

Ma-na-na, *s.* Name of a kind of potato.

2. That which is tottering, weak or feeble. See MALANA.

3. That which is buoyed up; hikike, hapai.

Ma-na-nai, *s.* See MALANAI. A gentle breeze; a pleasant wind to sail with and no motion of the canoe or vessel.

Ma-na-nao, *s.* See MANAO. Thought; opinion; view of a matter; eia ka *manao* o ka poe pono ia lakou. Ina hoi i ole ka pepa, heaha ka pono e loaa mai no ka noonoo ana i *mananao?*

Ma-na-na-lo, *v.* To be pure; to be simple, as a liquid; without mixture of ingredients. *Hoik.* 14:10.

Ma-na-na-lo, *adj.* See MANALO. Insipid; tasteless, as pure cool water; slightly brackish; hence.

2. Sweet, as water. *Sol.* 9:17. Okakai, koekoe.

Ma-na-na-lo, *s.* Name of the planet Venus.

2. Name of a species of fish.

Ma-na-na, *v.* To be angry or displeased with; hoopili aku, a *manana* koke iho la no. *Manana* ke kanaka i ka wahine, i ke keiki, ame na mea e ae.

Ma-na-ne, *s.* A kind of tree.

Ma-na-wa, *s.* Feelings; affections; sympathy. *Kin.* 43:30.

2. A spirit; an apparition.

3. The anterior and posterior fontanel in the heads of young children; the soft place in the heads of infants. *Anat.* 9.

4. A time; a season; a space between two events; a space of place between two material objects, between two localities, &c.; he *manawa* ole, instantly; immediately. *Laieik.* 102. See WA.

Ma-na-wa-e-a, *s.* Childhood before the open place in the head is grown up.

2. Hard breathing; an impediment in breathing.

Ma-na-wai, *adj.* Bent in; crooked; defective internally.

Ma-na-wai-nu-i-kai-oo, *s.* Name of a fabled whirlpool.

Ma-na-wa-i-no, *adj.* See MANAWA and INO, bad. Evil minded; having a bad disposition; unlovely; unfriendly.

Ma-na-wa-nu-i, *s.* *Manawa,* time, and *nui,* much. To be a long time. *Hoo.* To be patient; to be long-suffering; to continue steadfast; to bear up against difficulties; to be persevering; to be awake and active; to be ready.

Ma-na-wa-nu-i, *s.* Steadfast in difficulties; patience; watching. *Hoo.* The resistance of evil appetites or passions; temperance.

Ma-na-wa-hu-a, *adj.* *Manawa,* disposition, and *hua,* jealous. Bad dispositioned; unlovely; evil minded.

Ma-na-wa-hu-a, *s.* Loss of appetite.

2. An unpleasant state of the bowels; the disease called *hailepo.*

3. An evacuation of the bowels. See also KAEA.

Ma-na-wa-hu-a, *s.* *Manawa* and *hua,* envy. Irascibility; anger; evil mindedness.

Ma-na-wa-hu-a-kai-koo, *s.* *Manawa,* time, *hua,* to swell, and *kaikoo,* a high surf. A great perturbation of the sea, wind and current contrary.

2. A great perturbation of the mind, thoughts distracted. See HAKUKAI.

Ma-na-wa-le-a, *s.* Alms; that which is given to the poor; a gift; a present; help in time of need; a present made to assuage one's anger. 1 *Sam.* 25:27.

Ma-na-wa-le-a, *v.* *Manawa* and *lea,* to please. To send or give relief in distress; to give alms; to give willingly, cheerfully and liberally; to bestow something upon another with affection.

Ma-na-wa-le-a, *adj.* Bestowing freely to the needy; generous; liberal; bestowing upon the undeserving; gracious. *Puk.* 34:6. Mea naau *manawalea,* a person of a willing heart, i. e., willing to give. *Puk.* 35:5.

Ma-ne, *s.* *Heb.* Manna, the food of the Israelites in the wilderness of Arabia. *Puk.* 16:31.

Ma-ne-a, *s.* The hoof of a beast, as ox or horse. *Lunk.* 5:22. The nail of a person's finger or toe; the claws of a beast or fowl; the ball of a man's foot. See MAIAO and MAIUU.

2. *Manea* o ka moku, the toes, i. e., the divisions of the island.

Ma-nei, *comp. prep.* Ma and *nei,* here. This; here; in this place. *Gram.* § 161. See MAANEI and MENEI.

Ma-ne-o, *v.* To itch; to feel the sensation of itching.

2. To be bitter or pungent to the taste, as after eating raw kalo or red pepper.

3. To be sharp and pricking.

Ma-ne-o, s. An itching pain; the sensation after eating red peppers or raw kalo.

Ma-ne-o, adj. Itching; pepeiao *maneo*, itching ears, i. e., desirous of hearing new or strange things. 2 *Tim.* 4:3.

Ma-ne-o-ne-o, s. A species of sea-grass.

Ma-ne-le, s.
A sedan chair; a species of palanquin; a bier. 2 *Sam.* 3:31.

2. The name of the pole with which

maneoneo

two men carried a corpse; he laau amo kupapau.

3. Name of a tree found on the mountains.

Ma-ne-le, v. To carry on the shoulders of four men, as a palanquin or a sedan chair. NOTE.—This mode of conveyance is said to have been, formerly, very common among the chiefs; but a certain chief of Kauai, very corpulent and very crabbed to his people, used to make them carry him up and down the palis, until weary with his petulancy, they allowed him to fall, or threw him down a deep pali or precipice; since which time it has not been so fasionable for chiefs to ride in them.

Ma-ne-lo, s. The name of certain large fissures or caves in the bottom of the ocean.

Ma-ne-lo, adj. Free, as land from stones, lava or gravel.

Ma-ne-na, s. Name of a medicinal herb.

Ma-ne-ne, adj. Soft and tender footed; smooth footed.

2. Affected in walking, as with dizziness.

3. Fearful; trembling with fear.

Ma-ne-ne, s. The nervous sensation of one when in a dangerous situation his hands or feet slip.

Ma-ne-ne, v. To tremble for, as for one in danger; manene aku i ka mea aneane haule; manene i ka mea e pepehi ia ana; manene i ka ma kokoke make.

2. To be dizzy or like one intoxicated. See Mania and Ona.

3. To slip, as a man's foot or fingers in climbing a pali or precipice.

Ma-ne-wa, s. A vegetable; a species of grass near the sea beach.

2. The breathing of a fish; the muscular motion of such breathing.

Ma-ni, s. Heb. A Hebrew weight for money; a pound. *Neh.* 7:71.

Ma-ni, v. To diminish, as heat; to fly off, as heat; to cool; e waiho ana ka momoku pi e *mani* ai ka umu.

Ma-ni, adj. Dull; heavy; smooth. See Mania.

Ma-ni-a, v. To be dull; to be blunt, as a dull instrument; to be heavy; to be smooth.

2. To be sharp; to be smooth cutting; to smooth down what is rough.

3. *Hoo.* To set on edge, as the teeth by eating acids, or by any tingling noise, as the filing of a saw.

4. To be affected, as the nerves at any sudden or unpleasant noise.

5. To smooth down a rough road. *Luk.* 3:5.

Ma-ni-a, s. Dizziness; drowsiness; inclination to sleep.

2. The sensation felt when one files a saw.

3. A broad smooth place, as a reef uncovered with water.

Ma-ni-a, adj. See Laupapa. Smooth; dull, as the blunt smooth edge of a knife.

2. Sleepy; inactive; lazy; weary.

3. Straight; even; smooth, as a surface. See Laumania.

4. *Hoo.* Set on edge, as the teeth by eating an acid.

5. Having the sensation occasioned by a grating noise, as the filing of a saw, &c.

Ma-ni-a-ni-a, v. Intensive of *mania* in all its senses.

Ma-ni-a-ni-a, adj. Even; smooth. *Hal.* 26:12.

2. Dull; sleepy; lazy, &c. See Mania.

Ma-ni-a-ni-a, s. Name of a species of grass, soft and smooth. See Manienie.

Ma-ni-a-ni-a-u-la, s. *Maniania*, grass, and *ula*, red. A species of low grass with bearded seeds; it is found on Lanai, and is the same as *pilipiliula* on Hawaii.

Ma-ni-e, adj. Clear; smooth; plain. See Mania, Laumania and Laumanie.

Ma-ni-e-ni-e, s. See Maniania. Name of a species of grass, soft and smooth; it is very tenacious of life.

Ma-ni-ha, adj. Wild; rude; rough; harsh. See Niha and Kamaniha.

Ma-ni-he-u, v. To bruise, as flesh; to injure the surface of a thing.

2. To break; to break off or break in two.

Ma-ni-la, *s.* The name given to Manila hats from the city of Manila.

Ma-ni-ne, *adj.* Scratching with the finger where one itches.

Ma-ni-ni, *v.* *Ma* and *nini,* to spill over. To spill or spatter out, as water in carrying.
2. To overflow; to run over, as water.
3. *Hoo.* To pour out water by little and little.
4. To be dashed, as water against the sides of a container by carrying it unsteadily.

Ma-ni-ni, *s.* Name of a species of fish caught by diving down after it.
2. Name of a species of kalo.

Ma-ni-ni, *adj.* Spilling; overflowing, as water.

Ma-ni-ni-ni, *v.* Freq. of *manini.* To overflow; to spill over; to run over, as water; aleale ka wai, *maninini* mawaho. *Hoo.* The same as *hoomanini.*

Ma-ni-ni-ni, *adj.* Overflowing, &c. See MANINI.

Ma-ni-ni-ni, *s.* The name of a species of fish.

Ma-ni-no, *s.* See MALINO, change of *l* for *n.* A calm or quiet place after a storm; the abating or lulling of strong winds.

Ma-ni-no-ni-no, *s.* Intensive of *manino* above. A calm; a lull of strong wind.
2. A small quiet place sheltered from the wind.

Ma-no, *s.* The number 4,000; hookahi lau ai, hookahi *mano* ia, one 400 bunches of food, one 4,000 of fish. *Gram.* § 116:5. He umi lau ua like ia me ka *mano,* 4,000.

Ma-no, } *s.* A shark; he inoa no ka ia
Ma-noo, } ai kanaka. NOTE.—There are many species of shark, besides some other kinds of fish which Hawaiians call by the general name of *mano,* as the *niuhi* and the *ahi*; they were all kapu to women to eat under penalty of death.
2. The fountain head of a stream of water. See POOWAI.
3. A channel of a brook or stream. See MANOWAI.

Ma-no, *v.* To throw; to cast, as a stone; to throw at a thing; e pehi; to pelt.

Ma-no, *adj.* Thick; multitudinous; many; numerous. See MANOMANO and MANUU.

Ma-no-a, *adj.* Thick, as a board or plank; thick; deep, as a substance having breadth and depth, that is thickness.

Ma-no-a, *s.* Thickness; depth.

Ma-no-a-no-a, *v.* See MANOA. To be thick; to be impenetrable. FIG. Applied to the mind, to be careless; to be dull of apprehension; to be inattentive; to be indifferent. *Oih.* 28:27.

Ma-no-a-no-a, *s.* Thickness. 1 *Nal.* 12:10. Aia no a like pu ka *manoanoa* alii o na kupuna.

Ma-no-a-no-a, *adj.* Thick, as a board.

Ma-no-i, *s.* Cocoanut oil scented.
2. Perfume. *Isa.* 57:9. Oil. *Isa.* 61:3. A Tahitian word perhaps.

Ma-no-he-u, *v.* To bite with the teeth and peel off, as the bark of a tree; hence, to deface; to make a mark in.

Ma-no-ma-no, *v.* See MANO. To be multitudinous; to be or become many.

Ma-no-ma-no, *adj.* Manifold; many. *Hal.* 86:5. Great in number; excessive; magnificent; powerful; numerous.

Ma-no-ma-no, *s.* Greatness; might. *Isa.* 63:1.

Ma-no-no, *s.* Name of a tree, timber used for some parts of canoes.

Ma-no-no, *s.* The sea as the surf dashes against the rocks; o kekaikuihala kui *manono.*

Ma-no-wai, *s.* A channel of a brook or river. *Isa.* 8:7.
2. The material heart; that place whence the blood comes together, as in a fountain, and flows out again. See KUMANO and PUWAI.

Ma-nu, *s.* The general name for fowls or the feathered tribe. *Kin.* 1:20. All winged feathered animals; na mea eheu e lele ana.
2. The name of two gods at the gate of Lono's yard.

Ma-nu, *adj.* Salted; applied to meat and fish.
2. Humming; lightly rumbling; making an indistinct noise.
3. Full of holes, like some worthless thing.

Ma-nu-a, } *s.* The Hawaiian pronun-
Ma-nu-wa, } ciation for the English phrase man-of-war, i. e., ship-of-war.

Ma-nu-ai-hu-e, *s.* *Manu,* bird, and *aihue,* to steal. The thievish partridge. *Ier.* 17:11.

Ma-nu-e-a, *v.* See HANAMANUEA. To make a blunder; to act carelessly; to be dilatory in movement.

Ma-nu-e-a, *adj.* Blundering; careless; indifferent in action.

Ma-nu-io-io, *s.* *Manu,* bird, and *ioio,* to peep. Name of a small bird; a swallow perhaps. *Ier.* 8:7.

MA-NU-I-HU, *s.* The name of a beak, i. e., the end of the bow and stern of a canoe; ina i palahalaha maluna o ka *manuihu.*

MA-NU-U, *s.* Name of a bird; perhaps a crane. *Ier.* 8:7.

MA-NUU, } *adj.* Great; immeasurable; vast; multitudinous; mainfold.
MA-NUU-NUU, }

MA-NUU, *adj.* Sick; painful; weak.

MA-NU-HE-U, *s.* *Manu* and *heu,* wing. A breaking up; a flying away; a setting at variance, as a people; civil commotion or contention.

MA-NU-HU-HU, *s.* *Manu* and *huhu,* angry. A wild ravenous bird. *Isa.* 18:6 and 46:11.

MA-NU-KA, *v.* To mistake; to blunder; to be slow; to be careless; to lag behind.

MA-NU-KO-RA-KA, *s.* *Mana* and *koraka,* Gr. A raven. 1 *Nal.* 17:4.

MA-NU-KU, *adj.* A dove, so called from its noise. *Hal.* 55:6.

MA-NU-MA-NU, *adj.* Rough; irregular, like the surface of a board unplaned.

2. Defective; full of cracks or holes; not solid.

3. Rough; unpolished; want of beauty.

MA-NU-MA-NU, *s.* Civil commotion; a breaking up; a crash in civil affairs; a setting against each other.

MA-NU-NU, *v.* To crack or creak against each other, as broken bones. See HALOKE and UUINA.

MA-NU-NU, *adv.* In pieces; finely, as if broken fine; haki *manunu* ka iwi o ka moku.

MA-NU-NU-NU, *s.* A rumbling; a rustling indistinct noise; a slight tremor.

MA-NU-NU-NU, *adj.* Rumbling; rustling; tremulous, as an indistinct sound.

MA-NU-NU-NU, *v.* To creak; to grate or crepitate, as the finger joints when pulled, or the back when lomied, or as broken bones when they come in contact.

MA-PE-LE, *s.* Name of a tree used in building a heiau in the worship of Lono; alaila, he *mapele* ka heiau e kukulu ai; he heiau pili ka *mapele* i ka hoouluulu ai.

MA-PU, *v.* To rise up, as incense; to rise up and float off.

2. To spatter, as when rowing a canoe.

3. *Hoo.* To set off together, as two persons riding in on the surf on a bet.

MA-PU, *adj.* Moving, as a gentle wind; floating, as odoriferous matter in the breeze; spattering, as water from a paddle.

MA-PU, *s.* The name of a wind.

2. A ring-tailed monkey.

MA-PU-MA-PU, *v.* See MAPU. To fly upwards; to float off in the air.

MA-PU-MA-PU, *s.* A rising upward; a moving off; o ka *mapumapu* aloha o Waialoha e.

MA-PU-NA, *v.* *Mapu* and *ana.* See MAPU. To boil up, as water in the sea near the shore or in other places.

2. To excite or stir up the mind.

3. To turn the affections upon a beloved object.

4. To love ardently.

MA-PU-NA, *adj.* Boiling up and flowing off, as water in a spring; wai *mapuna,* spring water. Fig. Oili mai la ka makemake i ka naauao o ka poe naauao me he wai *mapuna* la e kahe mai ana.

MA-WAE, *s.* A cleft; an open place or opening among rocks; a secret or hiding place; a pit.

MA-WAE, *adj.* Hidden; secreted; stolen.

MA-WAE, *v.* See the substantive. *Hoo.* To crack; to break; to cleave asunder.

MA-WAE-HU-NA, *s.* In the phrase *mawae huna aina,* literally, breaking the land in small pieces. All practices of the people, such as gambling, betting, racing, &c., that induce laziness and its vices.

MA-WAE-NA, *comp. prep.* *Ma* and *waena,* between. Between; among; in the midst of; in the middle; a *mawaena* iho, in the interior; in the space between; between two points. *Ioan.* 4:31.

MA-WAE-NA-KO-NU, *adv.* *Mawaena* and *konu,* center. In the center; in the middle. *Isa.* 24:13.

MA-WAE-WAE, *s.* The fish prepared or food first given to a new born infant; he hanau wale iho na wahine ilihune i ka lakou mau keiki me ka *mawaewae* ole.

MA-WAI, *s.* Any cathartic medicine given to children to carry off the meconium.

MA-WA-HO, *comp. prep.* *Ma* and *waho,* outside. What is outward; outside; opposite to *maloko.*

MA-WA-LE, *v.* *Ma,* to wilt, and *wale,* only. To fade quickly or easily; to pass away, as the beauty of a thing; to come to an end, as earthly glory. *Hoo.* To be destroyed or perish soon. NOTE.—The word in its origin has reference to the fading of a flower or the colors of a kapa; indeed it is applied to everything subject to decay; hence, to perish quickly.

MA-WE-HE, *v.* *Ma* and *wehe,* to loosen. To loosen; to separate; to be loosened; to be separated.

MA-GO-I, *s.* Gr. A magician; a practicer of magic arts. *Puk.* 7:11.

2. A wise man: philosopher. *Mat.* 2:1.

MA-RA-KI, *s.* *Eng.* The name of the third month of the year, March.

MA-RE, *s.* Marriage. *Isa.* 62:5.

MA-RE, *v.* *Eng.* To marry; to take a wife or a husband; to wed. *Puk.* 21:3.

MA-RE, *adj.* Married or to be married; as, kane *mare*, a bridegroom. *Mat.* 25:1. Wahine *mare*, a bride.

MA-RE-KA, *s.* *Eng.* Name of the planet Mars. See the first Hawaiian Alemanaka for 1835. The Hawaiian name of the planet Mars is *Holoholopinaau.*

MA-TE-TE, *s.* *Eng.* Mustard; a plant; hua *matete*, mustard seed. See MAKEKE.

ME, *simp. prep.* With; accompanying; as; like; like as; besides; so. *Gram.* § 68 and 72.

ME, *conj.* With or without other words; with; in company; *a me*, and. It is often followed by *pela*, corresponding with it; as, *me* ia i hana'i, *pela* oe e hana ai. It is frequently connected with *like*; as, e like me oe, *like* you; it then merely strengthens *like*; me nei, *like* this.

ME, *s.* A contraction of *mea*, a thing. See MEA. *Puk.* 17:14.

ME-A, *s.* A thing; an external object; a visible or invisible substance.

2. A circumstance or condition.

3. A person; a thing in its most extensive application, including persons; ame kolaila poe *mea* a pau, and all the *things* belonging to them. *Kin.* 2:1.

4. Having the quality of obtaining or possessing something; as, he wahine *mea* kane, a woman *having* a husband. *Kin.* 20:3.

ME-A, *v.* To do; to say; to act.

2. To have to do; to meddle with. *Kanl.* 22:26.

3. To touch; to injure; to meddle with. *Kin.* 22:12.

4. To trouble with unprofitable business; to hinder. *Sol.* 14:10.

5. To cause to come to. *Ier.* 18:2.

6. To speak; to utter; to ask questions.

7. *Hoo.* To hinder; to stand in the way; mai *hoomea* hoi oukou i ke pai; aka, e hooiaio aku hoi i hiki wawe mai hoi na wahi palapala a kakou.

ME-A-E, *s.* *Mea* and *e*, another. Another in addition; another besides.

2. A stranger; one unknown; a new thing; a wonder; a prodigy.

ME-A-E, *adj.* Wonderful; strange; unaccountable; something new.

ME-A-E, *v.* For *mea ae*. See MEA 6. To speak to one; to address one; to ask one.

ME-AU, *s.* The itch. See MAIAU and MEEAU.

ME-A-HA-LE, *s.* *Mea* and *hale*, house. The owner of a house; a chief.

ME-A-KI-AI, *s.* *Mea* and *kiai*, to guard. A guard; a protection; a preserver; epithet of Jehovah. *Iob.* 7:20.

ME-A-ME-A, *adj.* Yellowish; whitish; ke poae ula, ke koae nui hulu *meamea.*

ME-E, *v.* Contraction of *meae*. See MEAE. To wonder at; to be astonished.

ME-E, *s.* A thing greatly desired; something much wished for; he mea i makemake nui ia.

ME-E, *adj.* Singular; strange; unheard of.

ME-E-AU, *s.* The itch. See MEAU above.

2. Name of a class of insects on trees.

ME-EU, *v.* To jump; to run; to fly; to run away.

MEE-MEE, *s.* Strong desire; the object of desire; the thing desired; o ka *meemee* ui nui o Hanalei.

MEE-MEE, *adj.* Desirous for; longing after; sweet to one's thoughts.

MEE-MEE, *s.* Name of a species of fish.

ME-O, *v.* To shoot or sprout out, as a vegetable; to grow, as a plant.

ME-O, *s.* The voice of crying, as of a child.

2. A sickly crying child.

3. One who is often calling to obtain favors.

ME-O, *adj.* Sickly; weak; crying, as a child; meddlesome; taking hold of everything in one's way.

ME-O-ME-O, *adj.* Reddish, as the bud of a plant; as a feverish swelling on one's finger; ulaula, omeomeo.

ME-U, *v.* To meet; to bring two things together; to stitch together; to meet together, as two persons in kissing.

ME-U-A, *v.* To strike each other, as two persons quarreling; peua, meu.

ME-U-KE-U, *s.* The knuckles of the fist when the hand is doubled up.

ME-U-LA, *s.* *Eng.* A mule; the offspring of a horse and an ass; vulgarly pronounced *piula.* See MIULA.

ME-U-ME-U, *v.* To be blunt; to be round on the edge; to be dull, as a cutting instrument.

ME-U-ME-U, *adj.* Very blunt or dull, as an instrument whose edge or end is beat off till quite round.

ME-HA, *v.* To be solitary; to dwell

alone; to be desolate. *Hoo.* To dwell alone without society; to sit solitarily in a house or at home, as in keeping the ancient kapus.

ME-HA, *s.* Loneliness; the state of being solitary.

ME-HA, *adj.* Solitary; desolate; dwelling alone.

ME-HAI, *s.* Some hair or kapa or other article carried to the sorcerer by which he (sorcerer) might procure the death of the one desired; o ke ola lau *mehai,* o *mehai* kolo.

ME-HA-ME-HA, *v.* See MEHA. To be waste or desolate, as a country. *Ier.* 46:19.

ME-HA-ME-HA, *adj.* See MEHA. Lonely; alone; without society; desolate. *Hal.* 25:16. Alone by one's self; retired; secret; forsaken.

ME-HA-ME-HA, *adv.* Solitarily; without company. *2 Sam.* 13:20.

ME-HA-NA, *v.* See MAHANA. To be or become warm. *Kekah.* 4:11.

ME-HA-NA, *s.* See MAHANA. Heat; warmth. *Isa.* 18:4.

ME-HE, *adv.* Me, conjunction, as, and he, indefinite article. Like a; as a, &c. NOTE.—This is generally written in separate words as *me he.*

ME-HE-U, *s.* A track of the foot; an impression of a foot on the sand or dirt; a scratch on paper; a track of a horse. See KAPUAI.

2. The effects or results of some action or something done.

ME-HE-U, *v.* To make tracks.

2. To walk over ground; aole loa i *meheu* aku na wahi a makou i hana pu ai me na haku, the places are no longer *trodden* by us where we worked with our masters.

3. To walk over a particular spot frequently so as to make a path. See MAA.

ME-HE-U, *adj.* Trodden, as a path through high grass. NOTE.—If it becomes much trodden or a large path it is *maa.*

ME-HE-U-HE-U, *v.* Freq. of *meheu.* To make tracks frequently, &c.

ME-HE-U-HE-U, *s.* Many or frequent tracks.

2. Custom; what is often done.

ME-KI, *s.* The ancient name for iron; the modern term is *hao.*

2. A nail; an iron spike, used for fastening or pinning.

3. A secret pit or pitfall in the mountains into which, if one fell, he never came out.

ME-KI, *adj.* Used with *lua,* pit, as an intensive. Hence, *lua meki,* an unseen (secret) bottomless pit; he lua *meki* ia aina meki, full of deep pits is that land of *pits. Hal.* 88:12. NOTE.—Hawaiians couple the idea of *lua meki* with that of *lua ahi* as they read *lua ahi* in the Bible.

ME-KU, *v.* To reply in scolding terms; to talk back offensively.

ME-LE, *v.* To chant; to cantillate; to sing singly.

2. To sing in chorus or concert. *Puk.* 15:1. To sing with joy; to sing and dance. See HULA.

ME-LE, *s.* A singing; a subject of song.

2. A song; the words of a song. *Kanl.* 31:19. A chorus; a song of praise. *Puk.* 15:2. In modern times, a hymn; a rejoicing expressive of gladness. NOTE.—*Mele* sometimes takes *ke* instead of *ka* for its article.

ME-LE, *adj.* Of or pertaining to song or rejoicing. *Puk.* 32:18. Walaau *mele,* hilarity.

ME-LE, *adj.* Yellow; generally written *melemele.*

ME-LE, *s.* For *meli.* Honey. See MELI. *Isa.* 7:15.

ME-LE-KU-LA, *s.* Eng. for *marigula.* Marigold, a yellow flower.

ME-LE-ME-LE, *adj.* See MELE, *adj.* Yellow. *Oih.* 13:30. Oho *melemele,* yellow hair.

2. Beautiful; handsome; pretty.

ME-LI, *s. Lat.,* mel. Honey. *Kin.* 43:11.

ME-LO-ME-LO, *adj.* Applied to a piece of wood smoothed and oiled over and let down into the water to attract fish; it was called laau *melomelo;* me ka laau *melomelo* a kahekahe paha.

2. Lazy; unemployed; lying in the house; not working.

ME-LU, *v.* To pull out the beard.

2. To swell; to be soft.

ME-LU, *s.* The act of pulling out the beard as Hawaiians did formerly.

2. Softness; a swelling.

ME-LU,   } *adj.* Soft, as fish long
ME-ME-LU, } caught.

2. Bad smelling, as spoiled fish; swelling up.

ME-LU-ME-LU, *adj.* See MELU. Very soft; swelling up large.

ME-ME-KI, *s.* Anger.

ME-ME-KI, *adj.* Angry.

ME-ME-LE, *v.* See MELE. To sing; to sing often, or to sing many together.

ME-ME-LE, *s.* A singer; poe *memele,* concert singers. *1 Oihl.* 15:27.

ME-NA, *s. Heb.* Manna. See MANE.

ME-NE, *adj.* Dull; blunt, as the rounded edge of a knife or axe.

ME-NE, *v.* To shrink or settle down; to pucker up; to contract; aole e *mene* ke poo o ke kohe.

ME-NE, *s. Art.* ke. Any dull utensil, as an oo or axe or koi; o kou no ke *mene.*

ME-NEI, *adv.* Me, as, like, and *nei,* this. LIT. Like this. Thus; so; as follows. See PENEI.

ME-NE-O, *v.* See MANEO. To itch; to tingle; to stagger; to reel as drunk.

ME-NE-O, *s.* An itching; a reeling; a staggering.

ME-NE-U, *v.* To double up, as the arms at the elbows, as the legs at the knees, &c.; ua pelupeluia, ua *meneu* wale.

ME-NE-ME-NE, *v.* To have compassion upon; to pity. *Rom.* 9:15.

2. To regard with kindness one who is in a suffering condition. *Lunk.* 10:16.

3. To curl up; to contract, as a wound. See MENE, *v.*

4. To fear; to shrink with fear; to be afraid; to be sad from fear.

ME-NE-ME-NE, *s.* Fear for one lest evil should befall him; no ka *menemene* o make i ka ai noa, for *fear* lest he should die by eating contrary to kapu.

ME-NE-ME-NE, *adj.* Fearful for one; sad on account of his hazardous situation or his suffering condition.

ME-NU-I, *adj.* Contracted; shortened; curled in; blunted off.

ME-RE-KU-RI-A, *s. Eng.* Name of the planet Mercury; Hawaiian name, *Ukali.*

ME-SA, *s. Lat.,* missa; *Fr.,* messe. The mass, i. e., the consecration and oblation of the host; a service in the Roman Catholic churches.

ME-SI-A, *s. Heb.,* anointed; in *Gr.,* Christos, the same. The anointed or consecrated one, to be a Savior of men, Jesus Christ; ke mea nana e lawe aku i ka hala o ke ao nei.

ME-TO-PI-O, *s.* Name of a spice, galbanum. *Puk.* 30:34.

MI, *v.* To void urine. See MIMI and MIANA.

MI-A, *v.* To make water; to void urine. See MI, MII and MIMI.

MI-A-NA, } *s.* Mi and *ana.* The place
MII,   }   for voiding urine.

2. The member by which it is voided.

MI-A-LA, *v.* To be bold; to be impertinent; to exhibit familiarity; to be forward in asking favors. See KOANA.

MII, *s.* See MIANA above.

MII, *adj.* Good; precious; desirable; ano e.

MI-O, *v.* To be pinched up; to be confined on all sides.

2. To wallow; to roll; to tumble about in the water; to sink out of sight.

3. To leer; to lay back the ears, as a horse or mule when about to kick.

4. To move easily; to move softly; to make no noise.

5. E kio, e mohai ke ananio, e hai ke anau.

6. To flow strongly and swiftly, as water confined in a narrow channel.

7. To be prepared or ready for any event. See LOLII. E lolii e oukou ia oukou iho a *mio.*

MI-O, *s.* A place where a stream of water is confined within very narrow bounds, and hence runs very swiftly, like water in a millrace.

2. The flowing or running of water in the above condition.

3. The moving of the arm in water, as in swimming.

MI-O, *adj.* Ready; prepared; prosperous; doing well.

MI-O,   } *adj.* Confined in a narrow
MI-O-MI-O, }   space; pinched up, as the toes in a tight shoe.

MI-O-I, *adj.* Bold; forward. See MAOI.

MI-O-I-OI, *v.* To stick; to adhere; to meet together; to almost close up the eyes; to wrinkle up.

MI-O-MI-O, *v.* See MIO. To dive in the water; to swim; to move the hands in swimming; to puff; to breathe hard, as in swimming.

MI-O-MI-O, *adj.* Sloping; tapering to a point.

2. Beautiful, like a nicely shaped canoe.

MI-U, *v.* To admire the appearance of a chief, the fine dress of one, or anything remarkable about one.

MI-U-LA, *s. Eng.* A mule; the offspring of an ass and a mare. *Kin.* 36:24. See MEULA.

MI-HA, *v.* To flow along, as a wave; to pass, as a slight breeze over still water, stirring up ripples.

2. To wave along, as a succession of waves; to flow or pass along, as a current.

3. To float off in the air, as miasma.

4. To look dark, as water rippled beside calm glassy water. See AUMIHA.

Miha lana au i kaukahiki ka newa'na.

MI-HA-LA-NA-AU, *v.* *Miha* and *lana*, to float, and *au*, current. E aio, e holo, e ale.

MI-HI, *v.* To be sad in countenance; to express the feeling of sadness or grief in the countenance.

2. To feel or have regret for past conduct.

3. To repent of a past act or acts.

4. To change or break off from a sinful course of life.

MI-HI, *s.* Repentance; sorrow or sadness of countenance; a breaking off from an evil course of life.

MI-HI-MI-HI, *v.* See MIHI. To be sour or cross to one; to look upon one with disfavor; to be inimical to; to be bitter towards.

MI-HO, *v.* To place one thing on top of another.

MI-KI, *v.* To eat poi or other food by putting the fingers into it. *Mar.* 14:20.

2. To pinch; to snatch; to eat in a hurry.

3. To urge on; to act promptly and energetically; to be quick in doing a thing; to hasten on a work to completion.

miki

4. To lick; to sup up. 1 *Nal.* 18:38.

MI-KI, *adj.* Energetic; active; ready to act; diligent. *Sol.* 22:29.

MI-KI, *s.* Readiness; promptness in doing a thing.

2. One ready to ask for anything he sees.

MI-KI-A-LA, *v.* *Miki* and *ala*, to rise up. To arise quickly or early in the morning; to be prompt in getting up; hence,

2. To be in season; to be promptly on the ground and ready prepared; e *mikiala* mai i kakahiaka nui, be here bright and early.

MI-KI-A-LA, *adj.* Early on hand; ready for business.

MI-KI-OI, *s.* *Miki* and *oi*, to excel. Neatness; excellency in work; no ka *mikioi* o ka oukou hana.

MI-KI-OI, *adj.* Neat; nice; neat, as work done in a workmanlike manner; palawaiki, aulii.

MI-KI-LI, *v.* See MAKILI. To perceive internally; to perceive, as the mind; i ka lua o ko'u noonoo ana, *mikili* iki mai la ka maka o ka manao maloko o ko'u naau, on my second thought, the eye of my mind within me *perceived*.

2. To have a little light; to shine, as light through small holes; to be feebly lighted.

MI-KI-MI-KI, *v.* See MIKI. To be quick; to be brisk and dextrous in doing a thing.

2. To pinch or seize hold of readily, as in eating with the fingers.

3. To scoop up and eat fish gravy with the fingers.

4. To nibble, as a fish at a hook.

MI-KI-MI-KI, *adj.* See MIKI, *adj.* Energetic; ready to act; prompt; neat; diligent.

MI-KO, *v.* To be salted; to be seasoned, as food.

2. To be entangled; to be mixed up with something else; to tie up into a knot.

3. FIG. To be tasteful; to be edifying and profitable, as instructive conversation. *Kol.* 4:6. To be advantaged by another; to be benefited. *Ezera* 4:14.

4. *Hoo.* To season; to salt. *Oihk.* 2:13.

MI-KO, *adj.* Seasoned with salt; savory; saltish. *Puk.* 29:2. Na mea miko, spicery used in embalming. 2 *Oihl.* 16:14.

2. Entangled; tied up in a knot. See NAPUU.

MI-KO-LE, *v.* *Miko* and *ole*, not. To eat daintily; to eat fastidiously; to eat temperately.

2. To eat in an awkward manner, like an aged person who had lost his teeth.

3. To suck the fingers, as in eating the inamona.

4. To desire strongly; to wish for very much; to look for something a person wants.

MI-KO-LE-LE-HU-A, *adj.* Thoughtful; skillful; having the power of reflecting pertaining or applying to the subject on hand; ua huli au, ua noke au, ua noii au i manao *mikolelehua* no'u, a.

MI-KO-LO-LO-HU-A, *adj.* See the above. Thinking; reflecting; skillful, wise and intelligent in affairs of difficulty. See AULIKOLOMANU.

MI-KO-MI-KO, *v.* See MIKO. To be tasteful, as well seasoned food; to relish well, as food.

2. To be pungent or bitter to the taste; e mulemule.

3. To be pleasant; to be instructive; to be entertaining in conversation.

4. To be pleased or satisfied with the arrangement of an affair. *Laieik.* 40.

Mi-ko-mi-ko, *adj.* Relishable, as food; seasoned.

Mi-la, *s.* Eng. In *arithmetic*, a mill, the tenth part of a cent.

Mi-le, *s.* Eng. In *measure*, a mile; eight furlongs.

Mi-le-ni-o, *s.* Lat. *Mille* and *annus*, a year. A space of time of a thousand years' duration about to come, when Jesus Christ will reign over the kingdoms and nations of the world. *Hoik.* 20:2, 4, 6. The millennium.

Mi-le-ta, *s.* Eng. Millet, a species of grain. *Ezek.* 4:9.

Mi-li, *v.* To feel of; to handle.

2. To take up and carry; to bear in one's arms.

3. To look at; to examine; to look at carefully or critically.

Mi-li, *s.* A handling; a carrying; a taking up; examining.

Mi-li, *adj.* Sullen; sluggish.

Mi-li-o-na, *s.* Eng. In *arithmetic*, a million; ten hundred thousand; the number 1,000,000.

Mi-li-ka-na, ⎫ *s.* The name of the paw-
Mi-li-ka-ni, ⎭ paw tree; also the name of the fruit; he papaia, he hei.

Mi-li-la-ni, *v.* *Mili* and *lani*, heaven, an intensive. LIT. To lift up; to raise up to heaven.

2. To praise; to celebrate the exploits of one; to exalt. *Puk.* 15:2. See HIILANI.

3. To thank; to praise. 1 *Oihl.* 16:7, 8. To give thanks. *Hal.* 79:13.

Mi-li-la-ni, *s.* Thanksgiving; rejoicing; praise. *Hal.* 100:4.

Mi-li-mi-li, *v.* See MILI. To view; to handle; to look at, as a curiosity; to examine; a e *milimili* nei me he keiki aloha la.

Mi-li-mi-li, *s.* A thing to be looked at as curious; a curiosity; nana iho la maua me ka *milimili*, we two looked at as a *curiosity*.

2. A lord; a chief; a foster-child. *Laieik.* 20. He haku, he alii, he hanai.

Mi-li-mi-li, *adj.* Desirable to look at; worthy of examination; na mea *milimili*, curious things. *Isa.* 2:16. Ipu *milimili*.

Mi-lo, *v.* To twist, as a string, thread or cord on the thighs; to spin, as a thread; to twist into a rope; to twist with the fingers. *Puk.* 35:25.

Mi-lo, *s.* The name of a shrub or tree; laau *milo*. *Laieik.* 40.

2. A species of tree; the fruit contains seeds which are used as cathartics.

Mi-lo-mi-lo, *v.* See MILO, to twist. To roll in the fingers or hand, as a pill to make it round.

Mi-lo-ro-pe, *s.* *Milo* and *rope*, thread. Mea *milorope*, a distaff. *Sol.* 31:19.

Mi-lu, *s.* The name of an ancient chief noted for his wickedness while on earth; he is now, according to Hawaiian mythology, lord of the lower regions, to whose dominions departed spirits go. He is the Pluto of Hawaiians. He alii no lalo o ka po, ka haku o ka pouli.

Mi-lu, *adj.* Soft, as a rotten spot in a melon.

2. Beautiful; grand; splendid; nani.

Mi-lu-mi-lu, *adj.* See MILU. Grand; solemn; shaded.

Mi-mi, *v.* See MI. To void or pass urine, as man or beast.

2. To play tricks upon one; to vex; to make one cry; to be mischievous.

Mi-mi, *s.* Urine; water from the bladder. *Isa.* 36:12. Opu *mimi*, the bladder.

Mi-mi, *adj.* Hoo. Extinguished; put out, as fire; not burning.

Mi-mi-hi, *v.* Intensive of *mihi*. To repent; to change one's course; to cease to do wrong; e hoopau i ka hewa.

Mi-mi-ki, *v.* Freq. of *miki*. To cut or roll up, as a dried leaf.

2. To spring together, as a steel trap; to pinch up tightly.

3. To be industrious; to be constantly at work; e hele mau ma ka hana.

4. To be quick or spry, as men at work; *mimiki* mai kanaka.

5. To reitre; to recede, as a wave from the shore; *mimiki* aku ka nalu.

Mi-mi-ki, *s.* A meeting of a returning wave with another.

2. The same as *mimilo* below.

Mi-mi-lo, *v.* See MILO, to spin. To twist; to spin round; to go round and round, as water in a whirlpool.

Mi-mi-lo, *s.* See MILO. A whirlpool; a great pit in the sea where the water makes a great noise, flowing round and round and destroys everything in its reach.

2. The turning of the hair on the top or crown of the head.

Mi-mi-lo, *adj.* Rolling up like a dried leaf; twisted; curly, as the hair of a negro, described as follows: he kanaka eleele, lauoho pokopoko *mimilo*.

Mi-mi-mi-o, *v.* To dive down; to plunge deep in water; e lululuu.

Mi-mi-mi-hi, *v.* See Mihi, to be sad. To grieve; to be sad; to repent sorely, &c.

> Nani wale lakou e *mimimihi* nei,
> Ua mihi aku, ua mihi mai,
> Ua haakulou wale ka noho ana,
> Ua kalele na lima i ka auwae.

Mi-mi-no, *v.* See Mino. To wrinkle; to curl up; to ruffle, as paper or cloth, in opposition to smooth.

2. To languish; to be weak; to be feeble; to be infirm. *Isa.* 24:4.

3. To wither; to dry up, as grass. *Isa.* 40:7.

Mi-mi-no, *adj.* Wrinkled; faded; withered; immature, as fruit untimely fallen or plucked. *Isa.* 34:4. Or as fruit prematurely fallen before fully grown. *Kin.* 41:23.

Mi-mo, *v.* To be right morally; to be good.

2. To be gentle; to be soft; to be easy in one's manners.

3. To be without noise or confusion.

4. To move off unperceived; to step silently aside; ke ike nei au ua *mimo*, ua panakai ole.

Mi-mo, *s.* Straightness; uprightness; what is morally good; gentleness; aole ma ke ino, ma ke kekee; ma ka *mimo* wale no.

Mi-mo, *adj.* Upright; straight; gentle; good; without noise.

Mi-mo-ka, *s.* Name of a tree, a species of the locust.

Mi-mo-mi-mo, *adj.* See Mimo. Good; gentle; soft.

Mi-na, *s.* Grief for the loss of a thing; mostly found in the compounds *mamina* and *minamina.*

Mi-na-mi-na, *v.* See Mina. To grieve for the loss of a thing; to be sorry for the sufferings of any one, i. e., to have sympathy with. *Kanl.* 32:36.

2. To be sorry on account of the consequences of an event; to pity so as to save from punishment. *Kanl.* 19:13. To spare from persecution. *Oih.* 20:29.

3. To be sorry at sad intelligence; to be sad; to be cast down, as the countenance. 1 *Sam.* 1:18. To be weighed down with sorrow.

4. To grudge what is due to another. *Kanl.* 15:10.

5. To be stingy; to be covetous; to keep closely all one has.

6. To be greedy of property; to be intent on accumulating one's personal conveniences regardless of others.

Mi-na-mi-na, *s.* Regret for the loss of a thing.

2. Sorrow; sadness; regret for an error.

3. Sorrow for others' misdoings. *Hos* 11:8.

4. Covetousness; a strong desire for property; hard, unjust treatment of others in order to get it; ka makee, ka alunu, ka puniwaiwai.

Mi-na-mi-na, *adj.* Much desired; precious; considered valuable; scarce; sorry to lose; ka! he mea *minamma* ka waa.

Mi-ne-ta, *s. Eng.* Name of an herb, mint. *Mat.* 23:23.

Mi-no, *v.* To be loose, i. e., weak; to be unstrung, as a feeble person.

2. *Hoo.* To be sad; to be sorrowful, as one desponding. See Omino. Note.—*Mino* and *mimino* is an expression made use of to children, as much as to say, "cover up your nakedness."

Mi-no, *s.* The turning or curling up, as a dried leaf or wrinkled paper; the curl of the hair, i. e., the crown on top of the head; he mimilo maluna o ke poo. See Milo and Mimilo.

Mi-no, *adj.* Deep down, as a deep pit.

Mi-no-i, *v. Mino* and *i.* See Mino, *s.* To contract towards a center, as the lips of a child in sucking.

2. To suck, as a child; to suck the fingers, as in eating gravy with the fingers where the lips contract around the fingers to secure the gravy.

Mi-no-i-no-i, *v.* See Minoi above. To suck, as a child, &c.

2. To fold and tie up in a narrow compass; to collect a great many things in a narrow space.

3. To come together in one place in great numbers, as flies.

Mi-no-mi-no, *v.* See Mino, *s.* To contract; to wrinkle up; to curl together; to be wrinkled, as cloth or the skin of an aged person; *minomino* na lima, eleele ka lehelehe. See Omino.

Mi-no-mi-no, *s.* A wrinkle in folding a cloth. *Epes.* 5:27. See Mimino.

Mi-nu-te, *s. Eng.* A minute, the sixtieth part of an hour.

Mi-ge-bo, *adj. Heb.* Papale *migebo*, goodly bonnets. *Puk.* 3C:28.

Mi-si-o-na-ri, *s. Eng., Lat.* One sent for any business.

2. In *religion*, the same as the Greek, Apostle; one sent to publish the Gospel and teach men the religion of the Bible; a

missionary; Maraki 31, 1820, hiki mai na *misionari* i holo mua mai.

MO, *v.* To break or to be broken, as a rope; ua *mo* ke kaula; the same as *moku.*

2. FIG. To break or open, as light in the dawn of the morning; ua *mo* ka pawa.

3. *Hoo.* To strike against; to dash. See HOOILI, HOOPAE and HOOMO.

MO is a prefix to many words, but the meaning is not very apparent.

MO-A, *v.* To dry; to roast; i mai la kela, aole i *moa* ka baka, that person said, the tobacco leaf is not *dry*; to bake. *Oihk.* 6:17. To be cooked in an oven or pan. *Oihk.* 7:9. *Hoo.* To be thoroughly cooked or baked. *Oihk.* 23:17. To cook food generally, vegetable or animal.

MO-A, *s.* A fowl of the hen species; *moa* kane, a cock; *moa* wahine, a hen.

2. The name of a stick used in play.

3. Name of a plant, the leaves of which made into a tea are cathartic.

4. Name of a piece of wood made to slide down hill on; so called perhaps from its shape; the practice of using it was attended with gambling; ka hooholo *moa*, he mea pili waiwai ia.

5. Name of a moss-like plant growing in the forests.

6. A kind of banana or plantain.

MO-A, *adj.* Done, that is, cooked thoroughly in any way; ai *moa*, cooked vegetable food; ia *moa*, cooked flesh, &c.; *moa* lea, fully cooked; berena *moa* ole, dough.

MO-AE, *s.* Name of the regular trade winds; he kaomi; no ka mea, he makani ikaika ka *moae.*

MO-AE, *v.* To be cracked; to be broken; to be split; to be full of cracks.

MO-AE, *adj.* Cracked; split; bent; crooked.

MO-A-E-KU, *s.* *Moae* and *ku* or *eku*, to resist. A foreign wind, or a wind from a foreign country; he makani no Kahiki mai.

MO-A-E-LE-HU-A, *s.* *Moae* and *lehua*. The name of a wind that shakes the lehua trees; mai hookoke na maka a ka *moaelehua.*

MO-AE-PE-HU, *s.* *Moae* and *pehu*, swollen. The name of a wind.

MO-AI, *v.* To relish food; *moai* kou puu i ka ai a mea, your stomach *relishes* the food of Mr. ——.

MO-AI, *adj.* Long; bending; arching over.

MO-A-OU-A, *s.* *Moa* and *oua*, unspurred, as a cock. A young cock before his spurs are grown. See OUWA.

MO-AU, *adj.* Long; stretching out.

MO-A-U-LA, *s.* Name of a heiau for offering human sacrifices in time of war.

MO-A-HA, *s.* The name of some white substance connected with a fish line in taking fish; ka *moaha* ka lau o maewa.

MO-A-HI-LE-LE, *s.* See MOOAHILELE.

MO-A-HO-A-HO, *adj.* Afar off; at a great distance.

MO-A-KA-KA, *v.* Mo and *akaka*, to be clear or plain. To make clear; to render explicit, as anything not easily understood.

2. To make things clear or distinct, as colors. *Kin.* 30:37. To be plain; to be clear; to be explicit; to explain or interpret, as a dream. *Dan.* 2:9.

3. *Hoo.* To expound a writing. *Neh.* 8:8. See HOAKAKA.

MO-A-KA-KA, *adj.* Clear; plain; intelligible, as the expression of a thought or an idea; transparent, as glass. See MOLAELAE and KONALE.

MO-A-KA-KA, *s.* *Hoo.* A reasoning; an explaining. *Iob.* 32:11.

MO-A-KA-KA-LA, *s.* *Moa* and *kakala*, points; spurs. A cock with sharp spurs; he moa kane, ua wini kakala.

MO-A-KI-NA-NA, *s.* *Moa* and *kinana*, a hen. A hen that has laid eggs; he moa wahine i hanau i na hua.

MO-A-LA, *s.* Name of a species of fish; he papai.

MO-A-LA-A-LA, *adj.* *Moa* and *ala*, to rise up. Going from house to house; going here and there; forward; without backwardness or modesty in seeking or asking for favors.

MO-A-LE-A, *adj.* *Moa* and *lea*, very. Thoroughly cooked, as food.

MO-A-LI, *v.* To be fine; to be small, as a thread; to be small, as a very little bit of a thing. See MAALI.

2. E helei, e makoe, e pokole. See MOOALI.

MO-A-LI, *s.* The thread or strand of a rope; a fraction or small piece of a thing. See MAALI. A slight track where a person has only once gone. See MAKAALA.

MO-A-LI, *adj.* Small; short; fine; fine marked.

MO-A-MA-HA, *adj.* *Moa* and *maha*, to rest; to cease. Imperfectly or half cooked.

MO-A-MA-HI, *s.* A cock that conquers.

2. A conqueror of any kind.

MO-A-MO-A, *v.* To be or to act the cock among fowls. *Hoo.* To go in company with, as a cock goes with hens to give warning in case of danger; to be intimate with; e hoopunahele.

MO-A-MO-A, *s.* The sharp point at the

stern of a canoe; kahi e oioi ana mahope o ka waa.

Mo-a-mo-a-waa, *s.* The paper nautilus.

Mo-a-na, *v.* *Moe* and *ana,* a lying down. To spread out or down, as a mat.

2. To spread out, i. e., to camp down, as a people or an army; to stop at a resting place, as travelers; e hoomaha, e oioi.

3. *Hoo.* To encamp; to make an encampment; to lodge in a place, as an army or a great number of travelers. *Puk.* 13:20.

4. To bow down; to prostrate one's self, i. e., to worship. *Puk.* 34:8.

5. To rise high; to spread over the shore, as the tide; ua *moana* mai ke kai.

Mo-a-na, *s.* *Moe* and *ana,* a lying down. The ocean; the sea generally; *particularly,*

2. The deep places of the sea; na wahi hohonu maloko o ke kai.

3. A place of rest or a resting place for a company of travelers.

4. A place of meeting for consultation among the chiefs; he wahi ahaolelo.

5. Name of a species of red fish.

6. *Hoo.* Ka poe *hoomoana,* the people encamped. *Neh.* 2:17.

Mo-a-na, *adj.* Broad; wide; extended.

Mo-a-na-a-na, *v.* See **Moana.** To be broad; to be extended.

2. To be opened widely.

3. To leave a thing to its own care or protection.

Mo-a-na-a-na, *adj.* Widely extended; opened widely.

Mo-a-na-kai, *s.* *Moana* and *kai,* salt. The salt sea; *literally,* a salt ocean; epithet of the Dead Sea. *Nah.* 34:3. Applied in *geography* to salt lakes; lilo iho la ia wahi i *moanakai* make, that place became a *dead sea.*

Mo-a-na-paa-kai, *s.* *Moana* and *paakai,* salt. The salt ocean or the salt sea. *Nah.* 34:12. The same as *moanakai.*

Mo-a-na-wai, *s.* *Moana* and *wai,* fresh water. A lake; a lake of fresh water. Syn. with loko. *Mat.* 8:26, 27.

Mo-a-ni, *v.* To emit an odor; to send forth a perfume or fragrance. *Mel. Sol.* 1:12.

Mo-a-ni, *s.* *Mo* and *ani,* a breeze. A breeze; the name of a wind.

Mo-a-ni-a-ni, *adj.* *Mo* and *ani* and *aniani.* Blowing along as the moani; he ua *moaniani* lehua no Puna.

Mo-a-ni-le-hu-a, *s.* *Moani* and *lehua,* a tree. The name of a wind; the lehua breeze.

Mo-a-no, *s.* The name of a species of fish; a dark or reddish color.

Mo-a-pa-la-hu,
Mo-a-pe-la-pe-la-hu,
Mo-a-pe-le-hu,
Mo-a-pe-le-pe-le-hu,
} *s.* *Moa,* a fowl, and *palahu,* swollen. Soft and red; epithet of a cock turkey from its comb and gobble; a turkey, especially a cock turkey; he manu lepe ulaula e hoolewalewa ana.

Mo-a-wi, *s.* *Moa,* fowl, and *wi,* poor in flesh. A poor fowl.

Mo-e, *v.* To lie down; to fall prostrate, as in ancient worship. *Ioan.* 11:32.

2. To lean forward on the hands and knees, as the people in coming into the presence of a chief.

3. To lie down, as in sleep. 1 *Sam.* 26:7. To lie down for the purpose of taking sleep; e *moe* no kaua, a momoe iho la; hence,

4. To sleep; to take rest in sleep.

5. To dream; to dream a dream; e *moe* ka uhane; e *moe* i ka moe.

6. To stretch one's self on a bed; e *moe* hoolei. *Amos.* 6:4.

7. *Hoo.* To lay one's self down to sleep; to cause to sleep.

8. To sit upon, as eggs to hatch. *Isa.* 59:5.

9. To bow down in humble solemn adoration. Note.—*Hoomoe* signifies the observance of that silence, awe and respectful behavior proper for the highest degree of adoration.

10. E *hoomoe* kolohe, to go a whoring after one. *Puk.* 34:16.

Mo-e, *s.* A bed; a sleeping place; *moe* hilinai, a couch.

2. A dream. *Dan.* 2:3, 4. Ma ka *moe,* in a dream. *Mat.* 1:20. Hoakaka no hoi ke alii i ka *moe* ia ia, the kind explained the *dream* to him; ua moe ia ma ka *moe,* he lay on a *bed.*

Mo-e, *s.* The name of one of the six houses of a Hawaiian establishment; eono hale o na kanaka, he hale *moe* kekahi. See **Hale.**

Mo-e-ai-ka-ne, *v.* *Moe* and *aikane,* sodomy. To commit sodomy.

Mo-e-ai-ka-ne, *s.* *Moe* and *aikane,* sodomy. Carnal abuse, male with male. 1 *Kor.* 6:9.

Mo-e-i-ka-hai, *s.* A phrase rather than a word. *Moe,* to sleep, *i,* with, and *ka hai,* another's (wife or husband.) Adultery with another's wife or husband. 1 *Kor.* 6:9.

Mo-e-i-no, *s.* Sleeping uncomfortably for want of room, being crowded; he kahua, he moewaa.

2. An unpleasant dream; a dream of an unpleasant nature, or as we say, *a bad dream.*

Mo-e-i-po, *s.* *Moe* and *ipo,* a lover in a low sense. A fornicator; an adulterer; one who indulges with another, as a kept mistress; a mistress.

2. Fornication; adultery.

Mo-e-o-ne, *s.* *Moe* and *one,* sand. The name of a worm that lives in the dirt; a peelua.

Mo-e-u-ha-ne, *s.* *Moe,* to sleep, and *uhane,* soul; spirit. A dream. *Kin.* 20:3. A dreamer. *Ier.* 27:9. A vision; a trance; he akaku; eia keia mea nui, he *moeuhane* na ka wahine o Liliha, here is a thing of importance, a *dream* by a woman of Liliha.

Mo-e-ha-lau, *v.* *Moe* and *halau,* to stretch out. To stretch one's self out at full length; to lie at full length.

Mo-e-he-wa, *v.* *Moe* and *hewa,* wrong. To be disturbed in one's sleep; to talk in sleep; to get up and do things in sleep.

Mo-e-he-wa, *s.* Talk in sleep; restless and disturbed sleep; somniloquism.

Mo-e-ka-ha-u la, *s.* *Moe* and *kahaula.* A lascivious dream; a dream of sexual intercourse; ka moekolohe ana ma ka moe-uhane. See AIKAHAULA.

Mo-e-ka-hu-a, *s.* See MOEWAA and MOEINO.

Mo-e-ko-lo-he, *v.* *Moe,* to sleep, and *kolohe,* mischief. To have unlawful intercourse between the sexes.

2. To commit adultery or fornication.

3. To sleep at an improper place or time

4. *Hoo.* To cause to commit lewdness. 2 *Oihl.* 21:11.

5. FIG. To practice idolatry, as Jehovah claimed to be the husband and protector of his people as well as their Maker and God, the worship of all other gods was considered as adultery, i. e., a breach of covenant with him. *Ezek.* 16:8, 15.

6. To defile; to pollute.

Mo-e-ko-lo-he, *s.* The unlawful intercourse of the sexes, adultery, fornication, &c.; generally connected with many other vices. *Rom.* 1:29.

Mo-e-ko-lo-he, *adj.* Adulterous; lustful; morally impure. *Nah.* 15:39.

Mo-e-ku-hu-a, *adj.* Sore eyed, so that on waking the eyes cannot be opened, being glued together.

Mo-e-lo-a, *v.* To sleep a long time; to sleep till late in the morning; aole Wakea i ala mai, ua *moeloa.*

Mo-e-lu, *v.* To commit adultery; no ko Wakea makemake no e *moelu* laua me Hoohokukalani—maloko o ia mau po i *moelu* ai o Wakea.

Mo-e-lu-a, *s.* A red kapa, either a malo or pa-u. See PENAUEA. He kapa, he pa-u, he *moelua.*

Mo-e-mo-e, *v.* See MOE. To lie down to sleep; to dream.

2. To lurk; to lie in ambush; to lie concealed for some evil purpose. *Hal.* 10:9.

Mo-e-mo-e, *s.* An ambush. 2 *Oihl.* 13:13.

Mo-e-mo-e-a, *v.* See MOEMOE above. To devise evil against another.

2. To dream an evil dream.

3. To tell an evil dream.

Mo-e-na, *s.* Contraction of *moe* and *ana,* a lying down. See MOANA. A mat; a mattress; a couch; a pillow; the common application is to *mats* of different kinds as Hawaiians use them in their houses.

Mo-e-na-a-hu-ao, *s.* A mat braided from very fine strands of the lauhala leaf.

Mo-e-na-pa-we-he, *s.* A species of fine mat, colored, checkered, and mostly made on the Island of Niihau.

Mo-e-waa, *s.* He moe ino, he moekahua.

Mo-i, *s.* A sovereign; one in whom is supreme authority. *Tito.* 3:1.

2. Sovereignty; majesty; supremacy; it is applied to men and to gods, as *haku, alii* and *akua.* In the Old Testament it is applied to Jehovah. *Heb.* 8:1. In the New Testament it is applied to Jesus Christ. *Heb.* 1:3. *Hoailona moi,* a badge of supreme authority; applied to the Son of God. *Heb.* 1:8.

3. The name of one of the gods in the luakini.

Mo-i, *adj.* Supreme; royal; lordly; pertaining to the gods; haku, alii, akua.

Mo-i, *s.* Name of a species of fish of a white color.

2. White specks on a dark skin.

Mo-i-u, **Mo-i-u-i-u,** *adj.* *Mo* and *iu* or *iuiu,* afar off. Afar off; at a great distance; out of sight; hence, more or less venerated. See POIUIU.

Mo-i-lii, *s.* A small white fish found at Kohala; ka huaili hua *moilii* o Kohala.

Moo, *s.* A general name for all kinds of lizards. *Oihk.* 11:30. Hence, a serpent; a snake; the lizard god of Paliuli, whose name was Kihanuilulumoku, ka *moo* nui. *Laieik.* 104.

2. A narrow strip of land; a division of land next less than an *ili.*

3. A planted patch of food, provided it be much longer than it is wide.

4. Two or three rows of bananas or other food planted between two water courses.

5. A path. See KUAMOO. A line of direction.

6. Ka mea nana *moo,* an observer of times by watching serpents. *Kanl.* 18:10.

7. Name of some long sticks that run length ways of a canoe; penei, e kalai ia na *moo* a pau i ka umeumeia.

8. A history. See mooolelo. A connected story.

9. A bed in a garden; a division made for irrigation. See the compounds.

Moo, *v.* To dry; to become dry. See MALOO. E kuku ma ke kua me ka ie a palahalaha, a kaulai a *moo* a lilo i kapa.

Moo-a, *s.* A narrow or faint path; slight traces of a path where only a few foot-steps are seen.

Moo-ae, *s.* Name of the north wind at Honolulu.

Moo-a-hi-le-le, *s.* Moo and *ahi,* fire, and *lele,* to fly. A fiery flying serpent. *Isa.* 14:29. NOTE.—In the last edition of the Bible the *ahi* is left out; the word there is *moolele.*

Moo-a-ku-a, *s.* Moo, a story, and *akua,* a god. A legend; a story concerning the gods.

Moo-a-li, *adj.* Moo and *ali,* a scar. Small; thin; little. See MOALI.

Moo-a-lii, *s.* Moo, a line, and *alii,* chief. The names of a line of chiefs; a genealogy; a history of one's ancestors.

Moo-o-le-lo, *s.* Moo and *olelo,* discourse. A continuous or connected narrative of events; a history. *Luk.* 1:1. A tradition. *Mat.* 15:2. In modern times, the minutes of a deliberative body; a taxation list.

Moo-o-mo-le, *adj.* Moo and *omole,* round and smooth. Anything having the qualities or round and smooth.

Moo-o-mo-le, *s.* A long, smooth, round bottle, like some oil bottles; a smooth, long calabash.

Moo-hu-e-lo-a-wa, *s.* Moo and *huelo,* tail, and *awa,* bitter: stinging. A scorpion. *Kanl.* 8:15. A poisonous serpent. *Hoik.* 9:3.

Moo-ka-a-la, *s.* Name of the species of lizard found on dry lands running about on the rocks.

Moo-ka-ao, *s.* A historical legend; a tale of ancient times. *D. Malo* 1:8.

Moo-ka-u-la, *s.* A species of black lizard found about houses.

Moo-ka-hi-ko, *s.* Moo and *kahiko,* old. The old serpent; a being spoken of in *Hoik.* 12:9. Satan; Diabolo; Deragona.

Moo-ku-hu-na, *s.* A genealogy of the ancient priests, kept by the priests themselves.

Moo-ka-na-ka, *s.* Moo and *kanaka.* A genealogy or a list of the people for the purpose of taxation.

Moo-ku, *s.* The name of the worship of the god Ku, one of the great gods. See MOOLONO.

Moo-ku-au-hau, *s.* Moo and *kuauhau,* a tax. A story or history or genealogy of the ancestors. NOTE.—The *mookuauhau* has several sources; some believed Kumulipo to stand at the head; others, Paliku; others, Ololo; others, Puanue; others, Kapohihi. *D. Malo* 1:8 and 10. A line of descent for the people, but in connection with taxes.

Moo-ku-pu-na, *s.* Moo and *kupuna,* grandfather. A list or line of the stock or tribe of one's family or ancestors.

Moo-le-le, *s.* Moo and *lele,* to fly. The name of a reptile mentioned in *Kin.* 49:17, *Kanl.* 32:33 and *Isa.* 34:15; a dragon; a flying serpent.

Moo-li-o, *v.* To be small or narrow, as a path.

2. To be small, as a patch weeded by many men.

3. To breeze on one side. See KOLOLIO.

Moo-lo-no, *s.* Name of the worship rendered to Lono, one of the four principal gods; ua kapaia ma ka *moolono,* no ka mea o Lono ke akua nui o ia aoao. See MOOKU.

Moo-lu, *adj.* Olu, noolu, mo and *olu.* Free; unrestrained; quiet.

2. Sinking, as in the mire; loose; yielding.

Moo-ma-ke, *s.* Moo and *make,* death. Name of a deadly reptile in *Isa.* 11:8; asp; viper. *Iob.* 20:16.

Moo-moo, *s.* Kapa of second or third rate; kapa that is not considered valuable.

Moo-na-he-sa, *s.* A boa constrictor.

Moo-ni-ho-a-wa, *s.* Moo and *niho,* tooth, and *awa,* poison; bitter. LIT. A lizard with a poison tooth. A serpent; a viper; a poisonous reptile. *Kanl.* 32:33. See MOOLELE.

Moo-nu-i, *s.* Moo and *nui,* great. LIT. A great lizard. A being several times mentioned in the Scriptures and translated *dragon. Hal.* 91:13; *Isa.* 51:9.

Moo-pe-pe-i-ao-ha-o, *s.* Moo and *pepeiao,* ear, and *hao,* iron or horn. Name of an animal mentioned in *Isa.* 11:8; translated in English *cockatrice.*

Moo-pe-te-na, *s.* Moo and *pethen* (*Heb.*), adder. An adder. *Hal.* 58:4.

Moo-pu-na, *s.* Moo, succession, and *puna,* springing up, as water. A grandchild. *Kin.* 29:5. Posterity generally; *moo-*

puna kuakahi, that is of the third generation: makua first, keiki second, keiki a ke keiki third, i. e., *moopuna*, grandchild; *moopuna* kualua, a grandchild of the fourth generation, i. e., a great grandchild. Note. Descendants were counted down as follows: 1st. *makua*, parent; 2d, *keiki*, child; 3d. *moopuna kuakahi*, grandchild; 4th, *moopuna kualua*, great grandchild; 5th, *moopuna kuakolu*, great, great grandchild, &c.

Moo-waa, *s.* Name of some long sticks belonging to a canoe reaching fore and aft.

Moo-wi-ni, *v.* To be misty; to be dim visioned; to see indistinctly; to be blind.

Moo-wi-ni, *s. Moo* and *wini*, fine pointed. Dimness in vision; misty in seeing.

2. Blindness, natural or moral. *Oihk.* 13:11; *Rom.* 11:25.

3. A blind person; nana mai no na maka, aole nae he ike.

Moo-wi-ni, *adj.* Very small, like the filaments of a spider's web; very fine.

Mo-u, *s.* See **Mouo** below. Eia ka hoolana ame ka *mou* poho ole.

Mo-u-o, *s.* A buoy; a float to show something below the water, as an anchor. Fig. O oe no ka *mouo* nui nana i hoolana i ko'u uhane i ke ao. A piece of wood, board or other substance to float on; o ka *mouo* e ou ai ka naau, a *buoy* for the heart to escape on; a place where anything may float securely, like the poe heenalu when they come in through the surf and float at ease.

Mo-uo-uo, *s.* A float or buoy for a fish net; he lowaia *mououo.* See **Pououo.**

Mo-u-ki, } *adj. Mo* and *uki*, dirty.
Mo-u-ki-u-ki, } Dirty; bad smelling; corrupt.

Mo-u-ki-u-ki, *adj.* Warm, as the effluvia from a corrupting body; bad scented, as the air from a tight room. See **Ikiiki.**

Mo-ha, *adj.* Bright; clear; shining; glistering.

Mo-hai, *v.* To break, as a stick; to break in two; to break off.

2. To sacrifice to the gods; to offer a sacrifice; to present a gift at the altar.

Mo-hai, *adj.* Broken; fractured; broken in two.

Mo-hai, *s.* An expiatory sacrifice; a sacrifice generally; a general name of an offering to the gods, of various kinds and for various purposes. Note.—The most of the following kinds of sacrifices are common to the Levitical and to the ancient Hawaiian priesthood.

Mo-hai-ai, *s.* A meat offering. *Puk.* 40:29.

Mo-hai-a-hi, *s.* An offering made by fire. *Puk.* 29:25.

Mo-hai-a-la-o-no, *s.* A sweet-smelling offering. *Oihk.* 3:5.

Mo-hai-a-lo-ha, *s.* A free-will offering. *Kanl.* 12:6.

Mo-hai-ha-la, *s.* A sin offering. *Nah.* 15:25, 27.

Mo-hai-ho-a-li, *s.* A wave offering. *Puk.* 29:24.

Mo-hai-hoo-ma-lu, *s.* A peace offering. *Puk.* 29:28.

Mo-hai-hoo-lu-li, *s.* A wave offering. *Oihk.* 7:30. See **Mohaihoali.**

Mo-hai-hoo-ko, *s.* A sacrifice on performing a vow. *Nah.* 15:3.

Mo-hai-hoo-ma-na, *s.*

Mo-hai-kai-kai, *s.* A heave offering. *Puk.* 29:27.

Mo-hai-kai-kea, *s.* An offering made by fire of the fat. *Oihk.* 10:15.

Mo-hai-ka-la-he-wa, *s.*

Mo-hai-ku-ni, *s.* A burnt sacrifice; a burnt offering. *Kin.* 22:7.

Mo-hai-la-we-ha-la, *s.* A sin offering. *Oihk.* 4:3.

Mo-hai-ma-ka-na, *s.* A free-will offering. *Puk.* 25:2.

Mo-hai-mi-li-la-ni, *s.* A sacrifice of thanksgiving. *Hal.* 116:17.

Mo-hai-mo-li-a-o-la, *s.*

Mo-hai-pa-nai, *s.* An offering of a hog to a god by a mother on weaning an infant; he *mohaipanai* keia na ka makua, i mea e oluolu mai ai ke akua i ke keiki.

Mo-hai-po-ni, *s.* An offering of consecration. *Oihk.* 7:37.

Mo-hai-pu-hi, *s.* An offering by fire. *Oihk.* 2:3.

Mo-ha-ha-la, *v.* See **Maholahola** and **Alalala.**

Mo-ha-la, *v.* To open; to expand, as a flower; to blossom. See **Mohola.**

2. To be erect; to stand straight; to rise up.

3. To be loosened or set free; applied to that which has been bound, coiled or drawn up tight.

4. *Hoo.* To spread out or smooth, as a kapa or cloth that has been ruffled.

5. To disperse or drive away, as fear.

6. Applied to the mind, to calm; to soothe where the mind has been disturbed.

7. To open or enlighten the mind. See **Mohola.**

Mo-ha-la, *adj.* Raised up, as something

that had been depressed.

2. Opened, as the petals of a flower that has been pressed; open, as a flower; pua *mohala*. 1 *Nal.* 6:18.

3. Devoid of fear, as one in danger.

Mo-ha-la-ha-la, *v.* See Mohala. To break loose; to set free, as something that had been bound or restrained.

Mo-ha-la-ha-la, *adj.* Loose; unbound; set free; lilolilo wale.

Mo-ha-lu, *s.* Clearness; fullness, as the full moon.

2. Name of a day of the month when the moon begins to be round.

Mo-ha-lu, *v.* To be comfortable; to be unrestrained; to be at full liberty.

Mo-ha-lu, *adj.* At ease; quiet; at liberty; unrestrained. See Pohalu.

Mo-ha-lu-ha-lu, *v.* See Mohalu. To be easy; to be quiet; to be at liberty.

Mo-hi-o-lu-o-pe-o-pe, *adj.* Disobedient; unyielding; stubborn, as a child.

Mo-hi-hi, *s.* Mo and *hihi*, a vine. Name of a strong vine used for strings.

Mo-hi-hi-o, *s.* Name of a plant.

Mo-ho, *s.* Name of a species of bird; he *moho* ka mea kani iloko o ka weuweu, the *moho* is a bird that crows in the grass; it seldom flies, but walks about.

Mo-ho, *v.* To evolve or show the upper or top leaf of a plant of sugar-cane, kalo, &c.; to bud out; to break or unfold, as the bud into leaves.

Mo-ho-la, *v.* See Mohala. To evolve; to unfold, as the leaves of a growing plant; to bloom out, as a flower; to blossom. *Kin.* 40:10. See Uhola.

Mo-ho-le, *v.* To bruise; to break up; to crush; to rub off the skin. See Pahole, Pohole and Mahole.

Mo-ho-le, *adj.* Rubbed off; bruised; crushed. Fig. Sad; sorrowful; dejected.

Mo-ho-le-ho-le, *v.* To skin off; to rub off; to polish.

2. To act lazily; to be dejected or cast down.

Mo-ka, *v.* See Oko. To tear in small pieces; to break up fine; to reduce to dust; to blow away and scatter, as dust.

Mo-ka, *s.* Anything torn or broken up small; small fragments of anything; he opala.

2. Refuse matter; that which is thrown away.

3. Something connected with the hole of the squid.

Mo-ka, *adj.* Broken fine, as small dust,

chaff, &c. *Dan.* 3:29.

Mo-kae, *s.* A species of grass or shrub something like the *ahuawa*.

Mo-kai-kai, *adj.* New; sweet; insipid, as poi just made and not become sour; *mokaikai* ka ai.

Mo-ka-pa-wa, *s.* Mo, to break, *ka*, article, *pawa*, morning dawn. Also, *ua moku ka pawa o ke ao.* Lit. The dawn is breaking. The opening dawn; daybreak.

Mo-ki, *s.* A pipe lighter; he *moki* baka; a term of reproach; said to be a late coined word.

Mo-ki-o, *v.* To steal.

2. To pucker up or contract the lips for whistling.

3. To whistle audibly.

4. To take the pipe-stem into the mouth to smoke.

Mo-ki-ha-na, *s.* A species of strong scented wood.

2. A species of mushroom.

3. An odor; a fragrance.

Mo-ki-mo-ki, *v.* To drink water, as a fowl; to suck, as a child; to breathe water, as a fish. See Muki and Mukiki.

Mo-ko, *v.* To fight; to pound with the fist; to box; mako, melu, pauhu.

Mo-ko-i, *s.* Something about the bait in fishing; eia ka mea lealea, o ka *mokoi* akua.

2. The art of deceiving fish and capturing them.

Mo-ko-i, *v.* To be hard; to be stingy; to be cruel.

2. To provoke; to make angry.

3. To tempt; to deceive fish; hence, to catch fish.

4. To be hollow; to be without internal substance; ke ohe, oia ka laau ponapona, o kona kino he *mokoi* aku, the bamboo is a jointed vegetable, *hollow* inside.

Mo-ko-i-ko-i, *v.* See Mokoi. To take fish, &c.

Mo-ko-le, *s.* See Makole. Inflamed eyes; sore eyed.

Mo-ko-le, *adj.* Inflamed, as the eyes; swelled out; not able to see distinctly.

Mo-ko-lo-a, *s.* The name of a species of grass.

Mo-ko-mo-ko, *v.* To box; to fence; to fight; to hold boxing matches as pastimes or as games; i ka makahiki, e *mokomoko* no na kanaka ame na 'lii ame ka wahine ame kamalii, on the first day of the year the people, the chiefs, women and children, *held boxing matches*, i. e., attended on them.

Mo-ko-mo-ko, *s.* A boxer; a man skilled in fighting; a puka mai la kolaila *mokomoko*.

Mo-ku, *v.* To divide in two; to cut, as with a sword; hahau mai la i ka pahi, a *moku* kekahi alii, he struck with a sword and *cut* a certain chief; to cut off, as a member of the body.

2. To break asunder, as a cord, rope or chain. *Oihk.* 26:13.

3. To break, as the neck; a *moku* ko Kiwalao a-i a make no ia, he *broke* Kiwalao's neck and he died.

4. To cut off, as with a sword at a single blow.

5. To rend or tear in pieces, as a furious beast. *Mat.* 7:6.

6. To crack; to burst open with a noise.

7. To hold fast, as an anchor holds a ship.

8. To cast or throw into the sea; *mokuia* i ke kai, aole e make.

Mo-ku, *s.* A part of a country divided off from another part.

2. A district; a division of an island, as Kona on Hawaii, and Hana on Maui.

3. An island, i.e., land separated from other land by water. *Moku* or *mokupuni* is synonymous with aina. *D. Malo* 7:1.

4. A ship; so called from the supposition when first seen that they were islands.

5. A dividing line; boundary between the different divisions of an island. See MOKUNA.

6. A part or piece of anything broken off.

Mo-ku, *adj.* Greatly increased; swollen, as water; running; flowing; breaking down barriers, as water.

Mo-ku-ai-na, *s.* *Moku*, broken off, and aina, land. An island; a land separated from another land. *Laieik.* 110. SYN. with moku.

Mo-ku-a-ha-na, *v.* To be divided, as a kingdom, a city or a family into two or more contending parties; to be split, as a community into factions. *Hoo.* To cause divisions. *Hal.* 55:9. To set one against another, as parties.

Mo-ku-a-ha-na, *adj.* Split into parties or factions, as a people; divided; unfriendly; opposed.

Mo-ku-a-hi, *s.* *Moku*, a part, and *ahi*, fire. A fire brand. See MOMOKUAHI.

2. *Moku*, ship, and ahi, fire. LIT. A fire ship. A name given by some to a steam vessel, but improperly, as a steam vessel is *moku mahu*, which see.

Mo-ku-a-hu-a, *adj.* Evil minded; evilly disposed; injurious; sad at the evil of another.

Mo-ku-a-wai, *v.* To be many; to be multitudinous.

2. To travel in large companies; *mokuawai* na kanaka.

3. To flow along, as a stream with rains.

4. To run; to rush, as a multitude. 2 *Oihl.* 23:12.

Mo-ku-hi-a, *adj.* For *mokuia*, passive of *moku*. Broken; divided. See MOKULIA.

Mo-ku-hi-a, *v.* To drown; to extinguish, as by water. *Mel. Sol.* 8:7.

Mo-ku-hi-ku-hi, *adj.* Mo and *kuhikuhi*, sweet. Sweet; sweet, as sugar

Mo-ku-kau-a, *s.* *Moku*, ship, and *kaua*, war. A war ship; a man-of-war.

Mo-ku-ke-le, *s.* The name of the action of sailing from island to island in a canoe in ancient times. *D. Malo* 7:1.

Mo-ku-ke-le-ka-hi-ki, *s.* A canoe sailing to a foreign country. *Laieik.* 175.

Mo-ku-ki-a-lu-a, *s.* *Moku* and *kia*, mast, and *lua*, two. A vessel with two masts; a schooner; a brig.

Mo-ku-ki-a-ko-lu, *s.* *Moku*, ship, *kia*, mast, and *kolu*, three. A vessel with three masts; a ship.

Mo-ku-le-i-a, *s.* Name of a species of fish of the kahala kind; kahala *mokuleia*.

Mo-ku-li-a, *adj.* Passive of *moku*, *l* inserted. Divided; broken up. See MOKUHIA.

Mo-ku-mo-ku, *v.* See MOKU. To tear up; to rend; to break in pieces; to pluck, as the feathers of a bird.

Mo-ku-mo-ku, *s.* See MOKOMOKO. A striker; a boxer; a fighter. *Tit.* 1:7.

Mo-ku-mo-ku, *adj.* Broken or cut to pieces, as a rope.

Mo-ku-mo-ku-a-hu-a, *v.* See MOKUAHUA. To yearn; to be moved with affection towards one; to yearn with pity for one. *Kin.* 43:30. Ua *mokumokuahua* ka manawa o ke alii i ke aloha, the spirit of the chief *yearned* with affection. *Laieik.* 136.

Mo-ku-na, *s.* *Moku* and *ana*, a breaking; a dividing. A dividing line between two lands.

2. A boundary line of a land; a district; a country. *Sol.* 15:25.

3. A part or piece cut off from something larger.

4. A division of a country; a coast or region.

5. A chapter or division of a book.

Mo-ku-pu-ni, *s.* *Moku*, an island, and *puni*, to surround. The full form for island; i. e., island surrounded (by water.) SYN.

with aina. O ka *mokupuni* oia ka mea nui e like me Hawaii, Maui, ame na moku e ae.

Mo-ku-wa-hi, *v.* *Moku* and *wahi*, to break. To be at enmity or variance, as two men. See **Mokuahana.**

Mo-la, *v.* To turn; to be unstable; to spin round; e milo.

Mo-la, *adj.* Turning; twisting; unstable; paa ole i ka milo ana.

Mo-lae-lae, *adj.* Mo and *laelae*, clear. Clear; explicit; easily understood; unobscure in vision.

Mo-la-le, *s.* Clearness; brightness.

     E ka *molale* ilio ilio lau lani.

Mo-la-le-la-le, *adj.* Clear; bright; plain.

Mo-la-mo-la, *adj.* See **Mola.** Spinning or twisting round; not fixed.

Mo-le, *s.* The principal root of a tree that runs straight downwards; also the large roots of a tree generally. (The small ones that branch out from them are called *aa*.)

     2. The bottom of a pit; the bottom of the sea. *Habak.* 3:13.

     3. Fig. A root, i. e., offspring; descendants from a root. *Rom.* 15:12.

     4. One belonging to a family. *Oihk.* 25:47.

     5. A cause; a means. 1 *Tim.* 6:10. A root; a foundation; aole i loaa ia'u ka *mole* o ka naauao, I have not obtained the *principles* of knowledge.

Mo-le, *v.* To linger; to lag behind; to be slow.

Mo-le-a, *adj.* Drawn tightly; strained, as a rope; hard; severe; tight.

Mo-le-a, *s.* A person so angry that his countenance is distorted.

Mo-le-hu-le-hu, *s.* The shade of the morning or evening; twilight. *Ier.* 6:4. Ka malamalama iki e nalowale ai ka ili kanaka.

Mo-le-hu-le-hu, *adj.* Shady, in time of twilight. *Iob.* 3:9.

Mo-le-mo-le, *adj.* See **Mole** and **Omole.** Round and smooth; cylindrical; smooth, as the skin of a bald head; hence,

     2. Baldheaded.

     3. Sleek and smooth with fatness.

Mo-li, *s.* A sharp instrument to print with on the skin; hahau iho la ka *moli*, pahuhu ae la ke koko, the moli is struck on, the blood flows out.

     2. The name of a large bird.

Mo-li-a, *v.* This word, like the Latin *sacro*, signifies to devote, to give up or give over to a good or bad end, that is, to bless or to curse according to the character of the thing devoted and the purpose to which it is devoted.

     1. To bless or to curse, according to the prayer of the priest.

     2. To bless; to pray for the safety of one.

     3. To be sanctified, i. e., set apart or devoted to the service of the gods; e *molia* ka ai i ke akua.

     4. To worship; to sacrifice; to offer to the gods; to save alive; e hoomana, e kaumaha, e amaama, e hoola.

     5. To curse; to give over or devote to destruction; to be sacrificed.

     6. To anathematize. *Isa.* 34:2. To destroy; e hoomake.

     7. In the use of the word, *molia* is *to bless* or *to curse* according to some following word or phrase. Note.—Some of the forms are as follows: *molia* mai e ola, *bless* him, let him live; *molia* mai e make, *curse* him, let him die; *molia* ka poe kipi, *curse* the rebels; *molia* i ke alii e make, *curse* the chief, let him perish; *molia* i ke kukui e pio, *curse* the lamp, let it go out; *molia* i ka ua e oki, *curse* the rain, let it stop; *molia* i ka hekili aole e hekili hou mai, *curse* the thunder, let it thunder no more.

Mo-li-a-o-la, *s.* An ancient form of worship when the priest offered a sacrifice and prayed for the life or safety of the people.

     2. Applied in modern times to the Jewish passover when a lamb was sacrificed for each household, and the angel of death passed over leaving the children of Israel unhurt. *Puk.* 12:11.

     3. In the New Testament it is figuratively applied to the death of Christ as the sacrifice for the sins of men. 1 *Kor.* 5:7.

Mo-li-a-o-la, *adj.* Of or belonging to the Jewish passover; mohai *moliaola*, ahaaina *moliaola*.

Mo-le-ki-a-ha, *s.* *Mole* and *kiaha*, cup. The bottom of a cup or mug.

Mo-li-o, *s.* See **Molia.** To offer to the gods; to lay upon the altar, as a sacrifice; o ke akua i ka *molio* o ke ahiahi.

Mo-li-li, *adj.* Mo and *lili*, small. Little; small; stinted.

Mo-li-mo-li, *v.* See **Moli.** To use the moli in puncturing the skin in making letters or figures.

Mo-lo, *v.* To untwist; to unbraid, as a rope or string. Note.—This word is found in many compounds, especially proper names, as *Molokai*, *Molokini*, &c., also in *molokamaaha*. See below.

Mo-lo-a,   } *v.* This word is written by
Mo-lo-wa, } Hawaiians in both forms. As it is evidently a compound word, the

second form is preferable. *Molo* and *wa*, time; space. To be indisposed to work; to spend time listlessly; to be lazy; to be idle; to be indifferent whether a thing is done or not; *molowa* iho la ua alii la ia Hawaii, that chief *was indifferent* respecting Hawaii; i aku la, ua *molowa* au i ka aina, he said, I *am indifferent* about the lands. *Hoo.* The same.

Mo-lo-ka-ma-a-ha, *s.* Molokama is the name of a land on Kauai; in singing meles the *aha* protracted would be added.

> Uina ka wai o na *molokamaaha.*

Mo-lo-ku, *adv.* On the back; at the back (of a person); on the backside.

Mo-lo-wa, *s.* Slackness; indifference; carelessness; laziness. *Ios.* 18:3.

Mo-lo-wa, *adj.* Indisposed to make an effort; inactive; lazy; unwilling to do; tiresome to one's patience. *Hoo.* Slothful. *Sol.* 12:24. See MANAKA.

Mo-lo-wa, *adv.* Lazily; deceitfully. *Ier.* 48:10.

Mo-lo-hai, *s.* Laziness; heaviness of head and eyes; drowsiness; i keia manao e huna i ka'u ano, i aku au me ka make, *molohai.* NOTE.—This word is used by the proud or foolish for *molowa.*

Mo-lu-hi, *adj.* Mo and *luhi*, tired. Weary; fatigued. See LUHI.

Mo-lu-lo, *v.* To steal; to take another's.

Mo-lu-lo, *s.* A thief; one who steals.

2. A bloated dead body which floats ashore from the sea; he mea pae wale ma kahakai.

3. A person wrecked and cast ashore.

Mo-lu-lo, *adj.* Fat; plump; bloated; large, so that the fat shakes on one's bones; applied to men.

Mo-lu-lo-lu-lo, *adj.* Fat; plump, &c. See the foregoing.

Mo-lu-lo-le-a, *s.* The voice or wail of a ghost.

2. The wail of one shipwrecked and cast ashore.

Mo-lu-lo-le-a, *adj.* Wailing, crying, &c., of a ghost; of one cast ashore from a wreck.

> Ia uina ai lele hauli e ka manawa,
> Lele-pioe loko i ko aloha—
> Aloha mai nei, hele a hiikua,
> Hoi lanaau ka maha i hana ke-ua,
> I ka uaua o ka pihe *molulolea.*

Mo-lu-na, *v.* To take by force; to rob; to plunder. See MOLULO.

Mo-lu-na, *s.* A thief; one who robs another.

Mo-mi, *s.* A pearl. *Mat.* 13:46. The pearl of the oyster; the hard center of the eye; the hard face of a watch; the eye of a fish; maka ia.

Mo-mi, *v.* See MONI. To swallow, as food; to put in the mouth and swallow.

Mo-mi-o, *adj.* Mo and *mio*, confined; close. Tapering; cramped.

Mo-mi-ku, *v.* *Momi*, to swallow, and *ku*, standing. To swallow standing up; a word made use of by Kamehameha to express contempt of his enemies, meaning, *he would swallow them up.*

Mo-mi-mo-mi, *v.* See MOMI. *Hoo.* To cause to swallow; to receive into the mouth and swallow. See MONI.

Mo-mo, *s.* See MOOMOO. Kapa of an inferior quality; he moomoo, he palaholo, he kiwaawaa.

Mo-mo-a, *v.* To give liberally; to take care of a poor person; to act the friend of one; to be continually giving to others; to take care of, as a guardian takes care of the property of his ward. See MALAMA.

Mo-mo-e, *v.* See MOE. To sleep; to dream; to sleep together, as two persons.

Mo-mo-ka, *s.* See MOMOKU. The rushing and running together of people, as in a popular outbreak.

Mo-mo-ku, *v.* See MOKU. To break; to break up; to separate.

Mo-mo-ku, *adj.* Broken; separated; broken up; greatly increased, as water running in a freshet, breaking or rushing forth.

Mo-mo-ku, *s.* What is broken or torn off or snatched out; *momoku* ahi, a fire brand; e waiho ana ka *momoku* pi e mani ai ka umu. See MOMOKUAHI.

Mo-mo-ku-a-hi, *s.* *Momoku* and *ahi*, fire. The remnants of fire; charcoal; wood charred; a fire brand. *Sol.* 26:18.

Mo-mo-le, *v.* See MOLE and KUMOMOLE. To be round and smooth; to be smooth and plumb up and down, as a smooth perpendicular pali.

Mo-mo-le, *adj.* Round and smooth.

Mo-mo-li-o, *adj.* Narrow; contracted, as a place, or as space.

Mo-mo-mi, *v.* See MOMI. To swallow greedily.

Mo-mo-mi, *s.* Name of a kind of fish; he paopao, he nukumonui.

Mo-mo-mo-e, *v.* See MOE and MOMOE. To sleep; to sleep often or soundly; to be very sleepy.

Mo-mo-na, *v.* See MONA. To be fat; to be round; to be plump.

2. To be swelled out full; to be smooth, as the skin of a fat person or animal.

3. To become fat, that is, independent. *Kanl.* 32:15. *Hoo.* To make one fat. 1 *Sam.* 2:29.

Mo-mo-na, *s.* The fat, i. e., that fat part of an animal. *Oihk.* 6:12. The fat of land, i. e., fertility. *Nah.* 13:20. Fat, as a person or community, i. e., rich; wealthy. *Kanl.* 32:15.

Mo-mo-na, *adj.* See **Mona.** Large; fat; fleshy; generally applied to persons or animals.

2. Fig. Applied to the ground, rich; fertile, &c. *Kin.* 41:34. Note.—*Momona* when applied to food or drink, refers to whatever is good or pleasant to the taste, as rich, sweet, fat, &c.

Mo-na, *adj.* See **Momona.** Fat; rich; good, as a good soil; ua hookupu maikai oia (o Hawaii), he *mona* ka lepo.

Mo-na, *v.* To be fat; to be round and plump with fatness.

2. To be rich or fertile, as land.

Mo-ne-a, *v.* For *moniia*, to be swallowed. To be stuffed; to be filled full with food; to be glutted.

Mo-ne-ha, *s.* A long distance.

Mo-ni, *v.* See **Momi.** To swallow; to consume. *Puk.* 7:12. To swallow, i. e., to drink up, as the earth drinks up water; o ka honua, ua *moni* i ka wai, the earth, it *drinks* up the water; to suck up, as a sponge; e omo; e *moni* i ka ai, to *swallow* food.

Mo-ni, *s. Eng.* Money; the price of a thing sold. *Kin.* 44:12. Syn. with talena. *Mat.* 25:18.

Mo-ni-mo-ni, *s.* A fast eater; one who swallows quickly.

2. *Metaphorically,* one who receives instruction greedily.

Mo-pu-a, *adj.* Fine; melodious, as a voice.

Mo-pu-na, *s.* See **Moopuna.** A descendant of the third generation, including the first, as *makua, keiki, mopuna;* a grandchild.

Mo-wa, *adj.* See **Moa,** cooked. Done, as food.

Mo-wae, *s.* Mo and *wae*, to separate. A rent; a broken place; a furrow; a cleft; an opening among rocks. See **Mawae.**

Mo-wae, *s.* See **Moae.** The name of a wind; the regular trade wind.

Mo-wa-mo-wa, *v.* To carry or send food to others gratuitously.

Mo-ra-ki, *s. Eng.* A mortgage; a deed of conveyance on condition.

Mu, *v.* To shut the lips and hold the mouth full of water. See **Mumu.**

2. To be silent; not to answer. See **Mumule.**

Mu, *s.* A little black bug that eats most kinds of wood; it also eats through and through all kinds of clothing; he mea e popopo ai ka lole; a destroyer of many kinds of property. *Mat.* 6:19. The *mu* bores a hole about as large as a gimlet; a moth. *Isa.* 51:8.

2. The name of a man who lived in the country above Lauhaele and ate bananas.

3. Name of a small bird with yellow feathers; he *mu* kekahi manu, he lena kona hulu.

4. A person employed to procure human victims when a heiau was to be dedicated or a new house built.

Mu-a, *v.* To mumble food, as for a child; to eat with the lips.

Mu-a, *adv.* and *comp. prep.* Of *place*, before; in front of; of *time*, first; previous to; before; usually prefixed with some of the simple prepositions. *Gram.* § 161.

Mu-a, *s.* The name of a house for men only in ancient times; the house was kapu to women.

2. The distinguishing name of one of the six houses constituting a family arrangement. See **Hale.** Eono hale o na kanaka—he *mua*, oia kekahi, men had six houses—a *mua* was one; the *mua* was the eating house for the husband; ai no ke kane ma ka *mua*, the husband ate in the *mua*. See *Mooolelo Hawaii* 59. Holo kiki aku la o Papa a komo i *mua* e paio me Wakea, Papa ran hastily and entered the *eating house* or husband's house to quarrel with Wakea.

2. The front part of a house or room. 1 *Nah.* 6:20.

3. A poor looking calabash.

4. A person with pouting or large lips.

5. The first born of a family.

6. The first; the beginning; the commencement. *Mar.* 1:1.

Mu-a-kau, *adj.* First ripe, as fruits; first born; fish first caught.

Mu-a-ku-a, *adj.* Unfriendly; unsocial; niggardly.

Mu-a-mu-a, *adj.* Drinking water out of a calabash and then spitting it out; oumua-mua, omuemue.

Mu-e, } *adj.* Bitter; bad tasted;
Mu-e-mu-e, } offensive to the palate.

2. Cold; chilly; shaking; trembling.

Mu-e-e-ke, *v.* To shrink; to start from fear or pain. See **Eeke.**

Mu-i, *v.* To collect; to assemble.

Mu-i-a, *v.* Passive of *mui* for *muiia.* To be collected together.

Mu-i-ki-ki, *v.* *Mui* and *kiki,* very. To press close together; to draw in; to cut short.

Mu-i-mu-i, *v.* To collect together; to assemble in one place; to be thick together; to assemble to see something; *muimui aku la na kanaka ame na wahine e makaikai,* men and women *assembled together* to examine.

Mu-i-mu-i-a, *v.* Passive of *muimui.* To be collected together; to be in a compact mass.

Mu-o, *v.* To bud; to open, as a bud into a leaf; to put out a leaf. *Hoo.* To cause to bud; to put forth or enlarge, as buds before the leaves appear.

Mu-o, *s.* A bud. *Isa.* 61:11. A branch. *Isa.* 27:10. A new or fresh leaf. *Luk.* 21:30.

Mu-ou-ou, *v.* *Mu* and *ouou,* short; thick set. To be short; to be low; to be little; to be blunt.

Mu-ou-ou, *adj.* Short; little; blunt.

Mu-o-lo-o-lo, *adj.* See OLO and OLO-OLO. Flexible; swinging; hanging down. See PUALUALU.

Mu-o-mu-o, *v.* See MUO. To swell out; to appear, as the bud of a flower.

2. To cover over as the calyx covers the incipient flower. See OMUAMUAPUA.

Mu-o-mu-o, *s.* The flower covered by the calyx; the place below the *muo* or bud.

Mu-o-ko-le,   } *v.* To cut off the
Mu-o-mu-o-ko-le, } branches of trees or the tops of kalo.

Muu, *v.* To collect; to lay up, &c. SYN. with mui, puu, ahu and waiho. To heap together; to fill up; to set thick together. See MUUMUU.

Muu, *adj.* Collected; laid up in store.

Muu-lu-lu, *s.* Name of a south wind at Honolulu.

Muu-muu, *v.* See MUU. To cut short; to cut off; to shorten.

Muu-muu, *s.* A shirt or under garment worn by females.

2. A lame person; *primarily,* one who creeps, halts or limps; one who has lost or never enjoyed the use of his limbs.

Mu-hee, *s.* *Mu* and *hee,* to slip. A fish that moves two ways like the crab.

Mu-hee, *adj.* Fickle; changeable; unsteady minded.

Mu-hee, *v.* To make an indistinct sound; to hum. See MUMUHU.

Mu-ka, *adj.* Tasteless; insipid; ono ole.

Mu-ka, *s.* A seizing; a swallowing up; a devouring. *Laieik.* 105.

Mu-kae, *s.* Anything jutting or hanging over, as the brow of a precipice. See UMALU.

2. The brim of a basin or tub. 2 *Oihl.* 4:2.

3. The circumference of anything; he poai, he anapuni.

4. The edge of a pit.

Mu-ki, *v.* To apply the lips or mouth to; to kiss; e *muki* baka, to kiss or suck the tobacco pipe; to take a whiff of tobacco smoke; e *muki* i ka wai, to squirt water through the teeth.

2. To peep; to speak indistinctly, as an enchanter. *Isa.* 8:19. SYN. with namu.

3. To play on the hokiokio or pipe, a wind instrument.

Mu-kii, *s.* A pipe lighter; one who waits upon a chief with the pipe. See MOKI. NOTE.—The office of the pipe lighter was to attend the person of the chief with a pipe always lighted; in order to keep it always lighted, the pipe lighter must himself, very frequently, give a little suck or puff or kiss, which was called *muki.*

Mu-ki-ki, *v.* See MUKII. To suck into the mouth, as in smoking.

2. To suck in or drink, as water; to swallow up.

3. To drink or sip water, as a bird drinks from a flower.

4. To squirt water through the teeth.

5. To make mouths at one.

> *Mukiki ka ia lelehuna a ka manu,*
> *Ka awa ililena i ka uka o Kaliu,*
> *Ka manu a haihai kanu awa—e—*
> *Aia ka laau ka awa o Puna,*
> *Mapuna wale mai ana no kona aloha la.*

Mu-ki-ki, *s.* A mouth made at one as a matter of reproach; hoomaka ko oukou *mukiki* i mea henehene, a i mea akaaka.

Mu-ki-mu-ki, *v.* To tie; to bind fast.

Mu-ko-i, *adj.* Sharp and projecting; applied to the forehead. See LAEKOI. *Mukoi* pue kaua.

Mu-ko-le,   } *adj.* Mu and *kole,*
Mu-ko-le-ko-le, } raw; red. Red; inflamed, as the eyes; *mukolekole* na maka.

Mu-ku, *v.* To wrangle; to blackguard; to quarrel. See NUKU.

2. To cut short; to shorten; to cut off, &c.; the same as *moku.*

3. To cease; to diminish, as a sickness; ua *muku* ka hi.

Mu-ku, *s.* A measure of length used by Hawaiians; the length from the fingers of one hand to the elbow of the opposite arm when extended; i. e., the cutting off at the elbow; o ka puaa nui, he anana paha, he *muku* paha, a i ka iwilei paha.

2. A piece cut off; that which is cut off; anything cut short.

3. The outside of a canoe.

4. The name of the night when the moon entirely disappears; i ka po i nalowale ai ka mahina, o *Muku* ia: alaila, pau ka malama, on the night in which the moon entirely disappears, that is *Muku*, then the month ends.

5. The short end of the iako or cross stick of a canoe; hawele koke aku la ia i kana aho i ka *muku* o ka iako mua o kona waa.

6. A short garment, as if the bottom were cut off. See MUMUKU.

MU-KU-MU-KU, *v.* To cut up into pieces; to cut off frequently. See KUMUKUMU, the letters transposed.

MU-KU-MU-KU-WA-HA-NU-I, *s.* The name of a red fish.

MU-LA, *s.* See MURA.

MU-LE, } *adj.* Bitter, as water;
MU-LE-MU-LE, }   bitter, as an berb. *Puk.* 12:8. E paipai i ka laau *mulemule* a pau.

MU-LE-A, } *adj.* Bitter; sharp;
MU-LE-MU-LE-A, }   bitter, as herbs; biting; caustic.

MU-LE-A, *v.* To be bitter, as water of Mulea. *Puk.* 15:23.

ME-LE-LE-HU, *v.* Mu and *lelehu*, weak. To be slightly intoxicated.

MU-LE-MU-LE, *v.* See MULE. To be bitter; to taste bitter.

MU-LI, *comp. prep.* After; according to; behind; afterwards; it relates either to time or place; mostly preceded by o, no, i, ma or mai. *Gram.* § 161.

MU-LI, *s.* The remains; the last of a thing.

2. A successor; *muli* mai, a brother or a sister next younger than one.

3. The last; the hindmost; the youngest of several children.

4. The last one of a series. *Mar.* 12:21. I keia mau la *muli* iho nei, in these *last days. Heb.* 1:1. He kaikaina, he pokii.

MU-LI, *adv.* A *muli* aku, afterwards; after awhile; ka mea e muli *mai*, that which shall be hereafter.

MU-LI-HO-PE, *s.* Muli, last, and *hope*, end. The last; the youngest born; o ke keiki *hiapo*, he mua ia; o ke keiki *muli-hope*, oia ka hope loa; also, *keiki muli iho*, youngest child. *Kin.* 9:34. He panina.

MU-LI-WAI, *s. Muli*, the remains, and *wai*, water. The opening of a stream into

the sea.

2. A frith; a bay at the mouth of a river; hence,

3. In *geography*, a river. *Ios.* 1:4. NOTE. The derivation of the word refers to the fact that at the mouths of most of the streams on the islands there is a bar; at low tides there is some water standing which has not run out; these remains of water are called *muliwai.*

MU-LU-WAI, *s.* An awkward or affected pronunciation of *muliwai*. See the above.

MU-MU, *v.* See MU. To hum; to make an indistinct sound.

2. To be silent; to sit mum.

3. To hold water in one's mouth.

4. To be smooth or round; to be blunt.

5. To cry out indistinctly.

6. To take food into one's mouth and afterward take it and convey it to the mouth of another.

MU-MU, *adj.* Indistinct; blunt; dull; round; smooth.

MU-MU, *s.* An indistinct sound; some noise, not known what; the confused noise of a multitude at a distance; opiopio ku ka laula o ka *mumu.*

MU-MU-IA, *v.* Passive of *mui* for *muiia.* To be collected together; to come together in crowds; to be thick together in one place.

MU-MU-HII, *s.* A whispering; a muttering; a voice in a low tone.

MU-MU-HU, *v.* To be large; to be plump; to be numerous; to sound, as many voices; to hum an indistinct sound.

MU-MU-HU, *s.* An indistinct sound, as of many together; hence, a crowd of people in one place.

MU-MU-KA, *adj.* See PUPUKA. Bad; worthless; unworthy of notice.

MU-MU-KU, *s.* See MUKU. The name of several things cut off, or cut short; a canoe cut in two in the middle; a garment cut short or the sleeves cut off; a wind blowing over land between two mountains as if cut off from the main wind; a maimed person having lost a hand, arm or foot. *Mat.* 15:30. The name of a lady's under garment is *mumuku.*

MU-MU-KU, *adj.* Cut off; separated, as a member of the body, i.e., the body when the limb is separated is *mumuku*; cut short; too short for a designed purpose.

MU-MU-LE, *s.* See MUMU. To be dumb; to be speechless.

2. To be silent; to hold one's peace

through grief or affliction. *Hal.* 39:2. Nolaila, noho *mumule* mai la oia ia mau la, therefore he lived in a *taciturn manner* during those days.

3. To be silent, as one confuted; not having anything to say. *Neh.* 5:8.

4. To be out of one's right mind.

5. *Hoo.* To keep silence. *Oih.* 18:9.

Mu-mu-le, *s.* The gathering around a kapu; the assembling of a company together.

Mu-mu-le, *adj.* Silent; quiet; refusing to speak; taciturn; displeased; sullen; out of one's mind; demented; pupule.

Mu-mu-lu, *v.* To come together in a cluster or crowd; to be thick together; to be numerous; to sit conversing together in a cluster; heaha ka lakou e *mumulu* la? Aole, he pupule wale no.

Mu-na, *adj.* Slow of speech; not quick or ready; maloeloe ka waha.

Mu-ra, *s.* Gr. Myrrh. *Mel. Sol.* 4:14.

Mu-tu-e-la, *s. Heb.* A weasel, an animal. *Oihk.* 11:29.

N.

N, the tenth letter of the Hawaiian alphabet. It represents the same liquid in Hawaiian as in most European languages. It is often commuted for *l* (see the letter L); as, *nanai, lanai; nanahu, lanahu,* &c.

Na, *simp. prep.* Of; for; belonging to. Placed before nouns or pronouns, it conveys the idea of possession, property or duty. It has the relation to *no* that *a* has to *o,* or *ka* to *ko. Gram.* § 69, 1, 2, 3.

Na, *art.,* standing before nouns, represents the plural number; as, *ke* alii, the chief; *na* alii, chiefs or *the chiefs. Na* often answers the double purpose of a plural article (that is, a plural for all the other articles which are singular), and the sign of the plural number of the noun. As an article, it is both definite and indefinite. *Gram.* § 67; also, § 83, 86 and 87.

Na. A particle somewhat frequent, adding strength to an expression either positive or negative; aole *na* he wahine e, o ka moopuna *na* a Waka, she is not *certainly* any other woman, she is *certainly* the grandchild of Waka. *Laieik.* 128.

Na, *v.* To be quiet; to be pacified, as a child; ua *na* ke keiki, the child is *quiet;* to be comforted, as one in affliction. *Ier.* 31:15.

2. To enjoy respite from pain; a pau kana heluhelu, ana, noho iho la ia e *na* aku i ka mea manao ole.

3. To gasp or half breathe, as a dying person.

4. *Hoo.* The same; also, in a *legal sense,* to settle difficulties; to decide between different claimants; as, e *hoona* kumu kuleana aina, to *settle* land claims.

Na, *adj.* Quiet; pacified, as an aggrieved child; calmed; quieted, as one's passions.

Na-au, *s.* The small intestines of men or animals, which the Hawaiians suppose to be the seat of thought, of intellect and the affections.

2. The internal parts, i.e., the inwards of animals. *Oihk.* 1:13. The bowels. 2 *Oihl.* 21:15. Alua ano o na *naau,* o ka mea nui ame ka mea liilii, the *intestines* are of two kinds, the large and the small. *Anat.* 51. Hence,

3. The affections; the mind; the moral nature; the heart; the seat of the moral powers. *Mat.* 22:37. Synonymous in many cases with *uhane,* the soul. NOTE.—The *naau* of animals were formerly used by Hawaiians as strings for various purposes; ka *naau* i mea aha moa, the *intestines* for strings to tie fowls. See the compounds of *naau* below.

Na-au-ao, *s. Naau,* the mind, and *ao,* instructed. An enlightened mind.

2. Instruction; knowledge; learning; wisdom. *Kanl.* 4:6. He ike, he noonoo, he noiau.

Na-au-ao, *adj. Naau* and *ao,* to teach. Wise; knowing; learned; enlightened; having the skill or art of thinking and planning well.

Na-au-ao, *v.* See the noun. To be learned; to be wise; to be intelligent, &c. *Hoo.* To enlighten, as the mind; to instruct; to be instructed.

2. To instruct, i. e., to convince; to be advised; to be warned. *Hal.* 2:10.

3. To attend to that which is right; to give heed to truth and duty.

Na-au-au, *s.* A remission of the strictness of a kapu; used in the phrase *kau naauau;* the suspension of a kapu so far that the people might eat certain kinds of food, thatch houses, &c.

Na-au-au-a,   } *v. Naau* and *aua,* self-
Na-au-au-wa,   } ish desire. To kill one's

self; to commit suicide on account of the death of a friend, or from the feeling that nothing remained worth living for.

2. To mourn for the loss of a friend; to grieve.

3. To be weak; to be bent over, as one in sadness.

NA-AU-AU-A, }

NA-AU-AU-WA, } *s.* The desire to commit suicide on account of the death of a friend; self murder through grief or disappointment; nui na hewa o ka wa kahiko, o ka *naauaua*, many were the sins of ancient times, *suicide.*

2. Anguish; sympathy with one; sorrow for the loss of one dear.

3. Strong desire for the good of one.

4. Depression of spirits; grief.

5. Real sorrow of heart.

NA-AU-KA-KE, *s.* A sausage.

NA-AU-KEE-MO-A, *s. Naau* and *kee,* crooked, and *moa,* cooked, i.e., hardened in any shape. An evil disposition; perverseness; a general disposition to wickedness. See OPUKEEMOA.

NA-AU-KO-PE-KO-PE, *s. Naau* and *kopekope,* morose. Perverseness; a bad disposition; surliness. See NAAUKEEMOA.

NA-AU-KU-HI-LI, *s. Naau* and *kuhili,* blundering. Carelessness; indifference; a disposition to carelessness; inattention.

NA-AU-PO, *s. Naau* and *po,* night. Ignorance; darkness of mind; without intelligence or instruction; a cloudy mind; awkwardness.

NA-AU-PO, *adj.* Dark-hearted; ignorant; unenlightened; dark-minded.

NA-AU-PO, *v.* To be dark-hearted; to be ignorant; to be awkward; to be brutish. *Hoo.* To be willingly ignorant; to remain ignorant while possessing the means of knowledge.

NA-AU-PO-NO, *v. Naau* and *pono,* right. To be upright; to be just. *Hoo.* To be staid in mind; to be fixed; to be sober. *Tit.* 2:6.

NAA-NAA, *s.* A sour disposition; unsociability; ignorance.

NAA-NAA, *adj.* Unsocial; crabbed; sour; unlovely in temper and life.

2. Round and hard, as pills, or as goat's dung; poepoe me he lepo kao la.

NAA-NA-AU, *s.* The stomach; the small intestines; the receptacle of food after it is eaten; kahi e waiho ai ka ai maloko o ke kino.

NAE, *adv.* An elegant expletive, but difficult to define. Truly; indeed; but; however, &c. A mild *but* is perhaps the best definition, though it does not express strong opposition like the English *but.* Aohe alii au, he kanaka *nae,* I am not a chief, *but* I am a man.

NAE, *v.* To breathe hard; to pant, as one laboring or exercising severely.

2. To pant for breath, as one with the phthisic.

3. To give liberally; to distribute; to be liberal, as a landlord to his people. See NAI below.

NAE, *s.* A sickness which occasions hard breathing.

2. The blowing of one's breath when fatigued on stopping to rest. FIG. Applied to the strong affections of the heart. *Laieik.* 142.

3. The phthisic. See NAENAE.

4. The upper regions of the air in distinction from the lower; ua lohe o uka a me kai, a me *nae* a me lalo.

5. The place whence the wind comes; a ihea o mea? Aia ma *nae.*

6. The name of a species of fish net with small meshes.

NAE-I-KI, *adj. Nae* and *iki,* little. Breathing a little, i. e., almost exhausted; near dead.

2. Nearly out of patience or courage.

NAE-E-LE, *adj.* Open; loose; full of holes, as open sleazy cloth; perhaps better spelled *naele,* the same as the following.

NA-E-LE, }

NA-E-LE-LE, } *adj.* Full of holes, cracks or chinks.

2. Rotten, as timber.

3. Moist; damp; applied to that kind of soil which retains moisture and is always rich and good.

NA-E-LE, *s.* Mire; deep mud. See NAKELE, boggy, and NAKA.

NA-E-LE, *v.* To scatter, as men who do not abide by their work; to be distributed by littles; to be dissipated or scattered.

2. To get into a slough or into the mud; to sink down.

3. FIG. To get into difficulty; aia ka kakou e malama ai, o *naele* auanei kakou, it is for us to take heed, lest we *get into the mud,* i. e., into difficulty; o *naele* auanei kakou, a pahemo, a haule ilalo.

NAE-O-A-I-KU, }

NAE-O-WAI-KU, } *s. Nae,* hard breathing, *a-i,* the neck, and *ku,* to stand. A disease where hard breathing causes one to stretch out the neck; a disease of the throat; to croup. NOTE.—The first orthography is the correct one.

NAE-NAE, *v.* See NAE. To breathe like one out of breath by hard exercise; to be out of breath; to pant for breath; to sigh. *Hal.* 38:10.

Nae-nae, *s.* Difficult breathing; the phthisic; the asthma.

2. An offering made to the gods to appease their anger; a sacrifice. See Ka-naenae.

3. The name of a species of fish; he mahamea.

Nae-nae, *adj.* Sweet-scented, as some herbs; he aku pua *naenae* o Waialoha.

Nae-nae, *s.* The name of a shrub bearing sweet flowers.

Nae-mai, *s.* Hard breathing; wheezing mixed with cough.

Nai, *v.* To strive hard to excel another; to urge on; to go ahead.

2. To finish; to make an end.

3. To give or parcel out alike; na ia keiki e *nai* na moku e pau ai. *Laieik.* 10.

Na-ia, *s.* A species of black fish; the porpoise. Note.—The *naia* was forbidden to women to eat, under the kapu system, under pain of death.

2. A kind of sandal-wood. See Naio.

Na-i-o, *s.* A species of sandal-wood; the bastard sandal-wood.

2. The name of the worm often found in horse dung and in that of other animals; the pin worm.

3. Small white specks in the fæces.

Na-i-o-ai-kae, *s.* The name of a famine in former times. See Kaiolekaa.

2. (*Naio*, pin worm, *ai*, to eat, and *kae*, the anus. Lit. That which causes itching in the anus.) A slanderer; a backbiter; a detractor.

Nai-u, *s.* Name of a kind of bush or small tree somewhat odoriferous.

Nai-i-ke, *v.* To be angry; to take in dudgeon; to set off in anger to take revenge. See Hoomaau.

Na-i-ke, *s.* Anger; a repelling from one; aole ike hou aku.

Nai-ko-la, *v.* To boast or glory over one. Hoo. The same. See Akola, Aikola and Hoaikola.

Nai-nai, *v.* See Nai. To exercise or cherish bad feelings; to be sour or crabbed towards others; to be evilly disposed; to struggle against opposition; to hop.

Nai-nai, *adj.* Sour; crabbed, as one's disposition; contentious; envious.

2. Short; low; pokole, haahaa.

Nai-nai-na-mi-mi, *s.* Living in a state of dissatisfaction; a persevering in and cherishing of bad feelings.

Nai-nai-na-mi-mi, *adj.* Unfriendly; unsocial; displeased with everybody and everything; changeable.

Na-o, *v.* To thrust in, as the fingers into an opening; e lalau i ka lima iloko o kahi poopoo. See Nanao.

Na-o, *s.* A slight ripple on the water.

2. The ridges of twilled cloth; lole *nao*; the streaks on kapa.

3. The grain or fibres of wood. *Anat.* 2.

4. The mucous from the nose; he palehehe, he pilau, he hehe.

5. He waiulaula, he waiahulu.

Na-o-a, *adj.* Not relishing food, as one sick; *naoa* oloko, aole ono i ka ai; filled; crammed with food; disgusted or sick at the sight of food from one's own surfeit.

Na-o-a, *s.* A thick ripple on water; writing so thick together that the paper appears black; a covering with what is black.

Nao-ma-ka-lu-a, *s.* Some instrument or method of taking fish; he hinai, he koi kekahi, o ka luina kekahi e *naomakalua.*

Na-o-na-o, *s.* A species of ant; the winged or flying ant; he mau mea eheu liilii loa e lele ana.

Na-o-na-o, *s.* Phlegm; spittle; mucous from the nose.

Na-o-na-o, *adj.* Deep down, as a cavern or pit; deep, as a hole in the earth.

2. Slightly lighted; light of twilight.

Na-o-na-o, *v.* See Nao. To thrust in the hand; to take hold of; to seize; to steal.

2. To look earnestly at; to contemplate. See Manao.

Nau, *pers. pron.* An oblique case (the *auipaewa*) of the personal pronoun, second person singular of oe. For thee; to thine; thine; belonging to thee, &c. *Gram.* § 132.

Na'u, *pers. pron.* An oblique case (*auipaewa*) of *au*, first person singular of the pronouns. For me; belonging to me; mine. *Gram.* § 124.

Nau, *v.* To chew; to chank; to gnash with the teeth. *Mar.* 9:18. To gnash with the eye-teeth or tusks; *nau* hou i ka ai, to chew the cud. *Oihk.* 11:3.

2. To measure time by the slow respiration of the breath.

3. To hold in the breath; to restrain one's self from breathing.

Nau, *s.* The name of a bush or tree affording coloring matter in the fruit.

2. Dye or coloring matter of the *nau.*

3. The holding in or restraining the breath; ka hoopaa ana i ka hanu i ka manawa e napoo ai ka la.

4. Pain; distress, but of a less degree than *hui*.

> He *nau* la kamalii
> Ke kohi la i ke kukuna o ka la,
> Pumehana wale ia aina,
> Aloha wale ke kini o Hoolulu—e.

NAU, *adj.* Chewed over; ground fine, as food thoroughly masticated.

NAU-A, *adj.* Cold; distant; unaccommodating; unyielding; angry; aloha ole, konia aole hoolohe mai, aole ou kanaka *naua* like.

NAU-A, *s.* Noon.

NAU-A, *adj.* Celebrating the birth or residence of a chief; alaila, kukuluia i hale *naua* no ke alii; nawai oe e mea *naua*? owai kou makua *naua*?

NAU-E,   }   *v.* (The first orthography is
NA-WE,   }   preferable.) To shake; to
NAU-WE,   }   move to and fro.

2. To tremble; to vibrate, as the earth in an earthquake. 1 *Sam.* 14:15. Synonymous with *haalulu*.

3. To move away a little; to withdraw from others to a private place; *naue* aku la ka makaula ma kahi kaawale, a pule aku la. PASS. To be moved. *Hoo.* To trouble one when quiet. 1 *Sam.* 28:15. To change one's mind. 2 *Tes.* 2:2.

NA-UE-UE, }   *v.* See NAUE. To vibrate;
NA-WE-WE, }   to shake often or violently; to shake, as an earthquake. *Mat.* 27:51.

NA-UE-UE, }   *s.* A moving; a vibration;
NA-WE-WE, }   a trembling, as of the earth; o ka *nawewe* o ka honua, an earthquake.

NA-U-KI, *v.* See UKI. To fret; to complain. *Hal.* 37:8. *Hoo.* To stir up or excite anger; to cherish ill-will or malevolent feelings.

NA-U-KI-U-KI, *v.* See NAUKI, UKI and UKIUKI. To be vexed; to be out of temper. *Hoo.* To provoke. *Kanl.* 31:29. To vex; to displease; to make one angry. *Nah.* 14:11.

NA-U-KI-U-KI, *s. Hoo.* A provocation; a source or cause of anger. 2 *Nal.* 23:26.

NA-U-LE, *s.* Name of a medicinal plant which forms the medicine called *kuakala*.

NAU-LI-A, *s.* The growling action of a dog while devouring his food; *naulia* aokaaoka pupuhi ka iwi.

NA-U-LU, *v.* See ULU and ULUULU. To vex; to provoke. *Hoo.* To provoke; to displease; to make one angry. *Kanl.* 9:22.

NA-U-LU, *s.* Heavy mists; a shower of fine rain apparently without clouds, or a single cloud; he ua kuhao; he ua *naulu*, he ua uuku ia, he ikaika nae.

2. Name of the sea breeze at Waimea, Kauai.

3. A thick dense cloud.

NA-U-LU, *adj.* Dark; thick, as a cloud. *Iob.* 22:14.

NA-U-LU-U-LU, *v.* Intensive of the above. To vex, &c. *Hoo.* To repeat provocations; to persevere in making one angry, like *hoonaukiuki*. See also HOOULUULU.

NAU-NAU, *s.* See NAU, to bite. The name of several acrid plants, as wild horseradish, cresses, pepper-grass, &c.

2. Ka papala ke lele mai.

NAU-NAU, *v.* See NAU, to chew. To chew; to mince in the mouth.

2. To move, as the mouth in the act of eating.

3. To move, as the lips in talking secretly to one's self. *Sol.* 16:30.

NAU PAHA LA. A phrase expressing the return of a salutation; thine perhaps.

NAU-PA-KA, *s. Nau*, to chew, and *paka* (*Eng.*), tobacco. The name of a plant.

NAU-WE,   }   *v.* See NAUE. All these
NAU-WEU,   }   forms are found with the
NAU-WE-WE, }   reduplications according
NAU-WEU-WE, }   to the writer's fancy; but the simple original form is *naue, naueue*. To shake; to vibrate; to tremble. *Hal.* 18:7. To be moved or shaken, as nations. *Hal.* 46:6. To be shaken often. 2 *Sam.* 22:8. Synonymous with *haalulu*. *Hoo.* To cause to shake or tremble.

> *Nauwe* Kalalau, poniu ka lawakua.

NAU-WE, *s.* See other forms above. A trembling; a shaking; a vibrating.

NA-HA, *v.* To split, crack or open, as the ground. *Nah.* 16:31.

2. To break up or break open, as a house.

3. To be split, cracked or broken, as a dish or any kind of crockery, glass, boards, slates, &c. *Puk.* 32:19.

4. To crack or break, as mason work. 1 *Nal.* 13:3.

5. To break or burst open.

6. To operate, as an emetic or cathartic.

7. To break in pieces.

> Nonoi ae la ka lani iluna,
> *Naha* mai la Kulanihakoi,
> Kulukulu ka ua
> Kapakapa e Kane,
> Akahi akua i nana—
> Ke haupu wale nei ka lani
>   Kau o Hiiaka.
> Wahi ka lani, uli ka lani eleele,
> Ka lau ka hoalii,
> Ka pohaku koii ka hooilo,
> *Naha* mai Kulanihakoi,
> Ke haaloloku nei ka ua,
> Ke neinei ke olai.

Na-ha, *adj.* Bent; broken; separated; scattered.

    2. Pierced; opened.

Na-hae, *v.* See Hae, to tear in pieces. To rend; to tear; to burst.

    2. To break, as the heart with sadness. *Ier.* 23:9.

    3. To rend, as a garment. 1 *Sam.* 15:27.

    4. To tear away; to separate, as a people. 2 *Nal.* 17:21.

    5. Fracta pudenda sicut virginis coitio prima.

Na-hae, *s.* A rent; a torn place; mea *nahaeia*, that which is torn. *Oihk.* 22:8. A piece broken off.

Na-hae, *adj.* Rent; torn; broken off.

Na-hae-hae, *adj.* Torn in pieces, as a welu or rag; broken, as the heart. *Isa.* 65:14.

Na-ha-ha, *v.* Frequentative of *naha*. To break, as a hammer breaks a rock. *Ier.* 23:29. To be dashed or broken in pieces. *Kanl.* 9:17.

    2. To divide up; to separate in pieces.

Na-ha-ha, *adj.* Broken; cracked; broken in pieces; separated.

> *Nahaha* i ke ania e ka makani he puulena,
> He makani kahiko ia no Puna,
> No Puna ka hala me ka lehua,
> Ke kui ana e ke ani lehua,
> Ke kaoo la ia ka moani.

Na-ha-na-ha, *v.* Frequentative of *naha*. To break up; to break fine.

Na-ha-na-wa-le, *s.* The name of a small fish.

Na-ha-we-le, *s.* The mussel shell-fish; he wahi ahi ano pioeoe.

Na-he,   } *adj.* Soft; slow; gentle,
Na-he-na-he, }   as the voice of music. See Unahe. He leo *nahe*, a melodious voice; he makani *nahenahe*, a gentle wind; thin; soft, as fine kapa or soft cloth.

Na-he,   } *v.* To blow softly, as a
Na-he-na-he, }   gentle breeze; stronger than *aheahe*, which is stronger than *aniani*. See Kolonahe.

    2. To be soft, as the voice.

    3. To be thin and soft, as fine cloth or kapa.

Na-he-le, *s.* That which grows; the verdure of bushes or trees; the leaves of bushes or thick trees; *nahele* ooi, thorns; brambles. 2 *Sam.* 23:6.

Na-he-le, *adj.* Pertaining to a thicket or grove; lau *nahele*, green leaves; herbs.

Na-he-le-he-le, *s.* The grass, trees, shrubs, &c., of a wilderness; a wilderness.

Na-he-le-he-le, *adj.* Wild; unculti-vated, as land.

Na-he-le-he-le, *v.* To become wild, as land that has once been tilled; to be overgrown with vegetation. *Puk.* 23:29. *Hoo.* To allow or cause land to be overgrown.

> E kokomo aku ai maua
> I ka pea i Kahiki,
> I ka ukauka laau nahele waokanaka,
> He *nahelehele* okoa hoi ke kanaka,
> Ulu nahele ka oa nahele hiki ke koa,
> Ulu wehiwehi i ka niu po i ke kou,
> Oia uka nahele loloa, a ka puni—e—
> O kou puni iho la ia, ua hala kamalii,
> Kau ka naha ia.

Na-he-le-ma-ne-o, *s.* *Nahele*, a plant, and *maneo*, stinging. A nettle. *Isa.* 34:13.

Na-he-na-he, *adj.* See Nahe. Thin; soft; fine.

    2. Empty, as the bowels from fasting or sickness.

Na-he-sa, *s. Heb.* A serpent. *Kin.* 3:1. Syn. with moolele. *Kin.* 49:17. Hoowale-wale i na *nahesa*, a snake charmer. *Kanl.* 18:11. See Mooomole and Mookahiko.

Na-hi. See Nahe and Lahi.

Na-hi-li, *v.* See Hili. To act awk-wardly; to blunder in doing a thing; to be slow; to lag behind; e lalau, e manuka.

Na-hi-li, *s.* A mistake; a blunder the effect of carelessness; slowness; want of energy; ka lalau, ke kiipua, ka hanamanuia.

Na-hi-li, *adj.* Slow; lagging behind; awkward; blundering.

> O *nahili* ka pololoa ia manu,
> O kapu kau kama ia kea a Kiha.

Na-hi-na-hi, *adj.* See Nahe and Lahi-lahi, soft; thin. Very small or fine; kapa *nahinahi* or *lahilahi*, thin cloth; applied to words or manner of speaking, soft; mild; gentle; soothing; he olelo akahai. Note. The orthography of *nahinahi* and *nahenahe* is used; the meaning is the same, and the pronunciation but slightly varied.

Na-ho, *v.* To overflow; to be deep, as water.

Na-ho, *s.* Depth; an overflowing with water; he manini ku, he manini kai.

Na-ho-a, *v.* To be bold; to dare.

    2. To be strong; to feel one's self to be strong.

    3. *Hoo.* To provoke; to be impudent to one. See Nehoa, *hoo.*

Na-ho-a-ho-a, *v.* To strike one on the head; to break one's head.

    2. To strike the head, as the rays of the sun.

    3. To give pain; to wound the feelings.

Na-ho-a-ho-a, *s.* A wound on the head and the pain connected with it.

    2. The effect of a sun-stroke on the head.

3. Applied to the heart when the mind is in great distress. SYN. with walania and ehaeha.

NA-HO-LO, *v.* *Na* and *holo,* to run. To run along on the ground. *Puk.* 9:23.

2. To run at random, here and there; to run away from, through fear. *Luk.* 8:34.

3. To be absent; to be gone away. 2 *Sam.* 23:9.

4. To flee away from, as from an enemy in battle. 2 *Sam.* 23:11.

5. To run along together, as a company of people desirous of doing something; *naholo* mai la lakou ma keia kapa, they ran along on this side (of the stream.)

> Naholo i ka laula o Puna,
> Ka luhi a ke kalukalu,
> Ku moena a ipo,
> Moku mahole i ka hoa mauu.

NA-HO-LO, *s.* A running; a fleeing; a retreat; a flight.

NA-HO-LO-HO-LO, *v.* See NAHOLO. To run along; to move rapidly; to pass along by something else.

NA-HO-LO-HO-LO, *s.* The Hawaiian name of the planet Saturn.

NA-HO-NA-HO, *adj.* See NAHO. Deep or fistulous, as a sore; deep, as a pit; far down in the earth.

NA-HU, *v.* To bite; to gripe with the teeth; e hoopohole i ka ili me ka niho, to tear up the skin with the teeth.

1. To bite, as a dog; to snatch at; to seize.

2. To bite; to gnaw. *Mik.* 3:5. To gnash the teeth, as in pain; e *nahu* i ke elelo, to *gnaw* the tongue. *Hoik.* 16:10.

3. To bite, as a serpent. *Nah.* 21:6.

4. To bear the short sharp internal pains of colic or of child-birth.

5. To bite off, as a shark; *nahu* mai la ka mano i kona waa a mumuku o hope, a shark *bit* his canoe short off behind.

6. To file; to rasp; e apuapu.

NA-HU, *s.* The pain of biting; the colic; sudden internal pains.

NA-HU, *adj.* Biting; writhing in pain.

NA-HU-A, *s.* The name of a wind which often blows at Kaanapali.

2. The fine rain with the north-east trade winds on the northern part of Maui.

NA-HU-KU-A-KO-KO, *adj.* *Nahu,* pain, *kua,* back, and *koko,* blood. Suffering pain, as a travailing woman. *Mik.* 4:9. See KUAKOKO.

NA-HU-NA-HU, *v.* See NAHU. To bite often.

2. To suffer frequent pains; to writhe in pain; to feel the first pains of child-birth; ia ia nei e *nahunahu* ana hele aku la. *Laieik.* 11.

3. To bite, as a serpent or centipede.

4. To be in, or to suffer the pains of child-birth. 1 *Sam.* 4:19.

NA-HU-NA-HU, *s.* The birth pains of females. *Iob.* 29:3.

NA-HU-NA-HU-I-HU, *v.* To quarrel, as two brothers; to fight or dispute, as an older with a younger brother.

NA-KA, *v.* To tremble; to shake; to be loose.

2. To be fearful; to be afraid; to tremble, as the joints with fear. *Dan.* 5:6.

3. To tremble, as ground not solid. *Ier.* 4:24. To shake, as a quagmire.

4. To crack; to split; to break open, as the ground sometimes in a drought.

NA-KA, *adj.* Trembling; shaking; unsteady; shaky, as a quagmire, in distinction from solid ground; full of cracks; not solid.

NA-KA, *s.* Name of a species of fish.

NA-KA-KA, *v.* See NAKA. To break; to shatter; to shake; to be full of cracks.

NA-KA-KA, *adj.* Split; shattered; full of cracks; split open, as parched grain. *Ier.* 14:4. Cracked and scaling off, as the skin of one after drinking awa; inu i ke awa; mahope, mahuna ka ili, *nakaka* puehuehu, inoino loa.

NA-KA-KA-KA, *v.* Frequentative and intensive of *naka.* To be trembling; to be shaking; to be full of broken places or cracks; to be unsound.

NA-KE-KE, *v.* To move back and forth; to make an indistinct sound.

2. To rattle; to rustle, as paper in the wind, or as new kapa.

3. To shake to and fro. *Iob.* 39:23.

NA-KE-KE, *adj.* Humming; rustling; moving.

NA-KE-LE, *v.* See KELE. To be slippery; to be soft; to sink in, as one in a soft boggy place.

NA-KE-LE, *s.* A soft boggy place, where the earth is not solid or hard.

NA-KE-LE, *adj.* Soft; slippery, as ground where one would be apt to slide.

NA-KI, } *v.* To tie; to tie up; to fasten,
NA-KII, } as a horse. 2 *Nal.* 7:10.

2. To bind fast; to tie round.

3. To tie a knot; to bind, as a criminal.

4. To confine one, as if bound.

NA-KI-KI, } *v.* See NAKI. To bind; to
NA-KII-KII, } tie up; to gird; to tie on. *Puk.* 29:9. To bind, as the hands. 2 *Sam.* 3:34.

NA-KI-NA-KI, *v.* See NAKI. To bind often; to bind fast. *Hal.* 105:22.

2. To swell out; to make large; to swell,

as the belly.

NA-KI-NA-KI, *s.* A person sick in the chest and feels as though he was bound; one filled to surfeiting with food.

NA-KI-LI, *v.* To open a little; to let in a little light, as into the eyes, or to open the eyes a little.

2. To see a little.

NA-KO-LO, *v.* See KOLO. To run; to flow, as a liquid; to spread out, as ink upon unsized paper.

2. To make a noise in falling, as rain upon dry leaves.

3. To move; to make a rustling sound.

4. To make the noise of many feet running.

5. To squeak like the soles of new shoes.

NA-KO-LO, *adv.* In a running, rushing manner; ua nei *nakolo* i ke aloha, my heart is moved *deeply* with love. *Laieik.* 142.

NA-KO-LO-KO-LO, *v.* See NAKOLO and KOLO. To run, as many running together; to move along, as in a rush.

2. To creak, as the sound of friction.

NA-KU, *v.* To root, as a hog; to throw up ground in heaps or ridges.

2. To tread upon; to trample down; to destroy.

3. To seek; to hunt after; to search for; to look or inquire for; oi imi, oi *naku*, oi noke, oi huli wale a! aole he loaa.

4. To follow; to pursue; e *naku* aku ia ia a loaa.

5. To shake; to be in a tremor, as one dying; *naku* iho la a make.

NA-KU, *s.* Takes both *ka* and *ke* for articles. A rush. *Isa.* 9:13. The rush of which mats are made, *akaakai.*

2. A rooting; a throwing up dirt in ridges or hills.

3. A destroying; an overturning.

4. A pursuit after a thing; aia no i kau *naku* ia ia a loaa; no ka imi, ame ka *naku*, ame ka huli, ame ka noii ana; a search; a pursuit after.

> Ami Nuuanu i ka wa waahila,
> Lea ole no ia Lalanihuli,
> Huli ka makani,
> *Naku* i ke oho o ke kawelu.

NA-KU-E, *adj.* Diligent in business; active; not slothful or lazy.

NA-KU-I, *adj.* Joyful; cheerful; full of hope; diligent; active mama ka manao. See NAKUE.

NA-KU-LU, *v.* See KULU, to drop, as water. To drop as water drops, that is, to make the noise of falling drops of water.

2. To make a rattling noise; to crackle,

as the sharp sound of thunder; heaha keia e *nakulu* nei?

3. To shake; to run along, as a sound; to run, as a report or story of a scandal. *Laieik.* 199. To be in a tremor; used adverbially, e nei nakulu ana ia nei.

NA-KU-LU-AI, *adj.* Perfect; good; upright; praiseworthy.

NA-KU-LU-KU-LU, *v.* See NAKULU and KULU. To shake; to make a rustling noise.

2. To move along; to make an indistinct sound.

3. To patter, as drops of rain; to drop, as rain; to rain fast. *Lunk.* 5:4.

4. *Hoo.* To cause to drop down, as rain; to pour down. *Isa.* 45:8.

NA-KU-LU-KU-LU, *adj.* Trembling; moving; emitting a sound; pattering, as falling drops of rain.

NA-LE, *adj.* Movable; unbound; not fast.

NA-LE-NA-LE, *adj.* See NALE. Free to move; unbound; separate from.

NA-LE-NA-LE, *s.* A separation from something else; not sustained by anything else; without obstruction.

NA-LI, *v.* To bite; to nibble; to chank; to seize suddenly.

NA-LI, *adj.* Nibbling; biting; biting off piecemeal.

NA-LI-NA-LI, *v.* See NALI. To bite often; to seize upon.

2. *Hoo.* To be or to act the chief; to enjoy the privileges and honors of a chief. See AIALII.

NA-LI-NA-LI, *adj.* Bright; shining; royal, as a chief.

NA-LO, *v.* To be lost; to vanish. *Luk.* 24:31. To be concealed from one; aka, aole ia i *nalo* ia Papa, but he *was* not *concealed* from Papa.

2. To recede; to pass away; *nalo e*, to be missing. 2 *Sam.* 2:30. To disappear; to vanish in a distance; a *nalo* aku la ke kia o kona moku, o ka *nalo* pu ana aku no ia, and when the mast of his ship *disappeared*, he (Liholiho) *vanished* together with it.

2. To lie hidden; to lie concealed; to hide; to evade; to elude the sight of; e hiki no ia Iehona ke ike, aole no e *nalo* kona mau maka; to be done in secret. *Mat.* 6:4.

4. To pass away; to leave, as a disease; aole i *nalo* keia mai ia ia a hiki aku i ka make, this sickness *did* not *leave* him until he died.

5. *Hoo.* To hide one's self. *Ioan.* 12:36. To cause to disappear.

NA-LO, *s.* The common house fly.

2. Any insect with wings; he mau mea eheu e lele ana.

NA-LO, *adj.* Lost; obliterated; hidden; forgotten; vanished; passed away.

NA-LO-HO-PE-E-HA, *s. Nalo,* fly, *hope,* tail, sting, *eha,* to hurt. Epithet of a hornet. *Puk.* 23:28.

NA-LO-ME-LI, *s. Nalo,* fly, *meli* (Gr.), honey. The honey bee. *Kanl.* 1:44.

NA-LO-NA-HU, *s. Nalo,* fly, and *nahu,* to bite or sting. A stinging fly. *Puk.* 8:17.

NA-LO-NA-LO, *v.* Frequentative of *nalo.* To hide; to conceal. *Hoo.* To disguise or conceal one's real person. 1 *Nal.* 20:38.

NA-LO-PA-KA, *s. Nalo,* fly, and *paka,* the sharp thorn in the tail of the fish kala. The sting of a fly, i. e., *the wasp.*

NA-LO-WA-LE, *v. Nalo,* to vanish, and *wale,* entirely. To be lost sight of; to be forgotten. *Kanl.* 4:8.

    2. To forget; to hide; to secrete.

    3. *Hoo.* To put one's self out of sight; to conceal one's self.

NA-LO-WA-LE, *adj.* Lost; out of sight; out of memory. 1 *Sam.* 9:20. Concealed. NOTE.—*Nalowale* has been supposed to be one of the highest of a series of numbers; as, kauna, kanaha, lau, mano, kini, lehu, *nalowale;* but *nalowale* only signifies that the person can go no further—that his mind fails to comprehend any higher or further combination of numbers, and by *nalowale* the person means, *it is lost, vanished, he knows no more.*

NA-LU, *v.* To be in doubt or suspense; to suspend one's judgement.

    2. To wonder at; not to comprehend speech or language.

    3. To speak secretly, or to speak to one's self; to think within one's self. *Eset.* 6:6.

    4. To talk or confer together concerning a thing.

    5. To think; to search after any truth or fact.

NA-LU, *s.* The surf as it rolls in upon the beach; a sea; a wave; a billow.

    2. The slimy liquid on the face of a new born infant; o ka wai ma ka maka o ke keiki i hanauia ana.

NA-LU, *adj.* Roaring; surging; rolling in, as the surf of the sea.

NA-LU-LI, *v.* See LULI. To shake; to move; to vibrate.

NA-LU-LI, *adj.* Shaking; unsteady; not easily accomplished.

NA-LU-LI-LU-LI, *v.* See LULI. To shake often. *Hoo.* To cause a shaking; to move violently back and forth.

NA-LU-LU, *s.* A severe sharp pain in the head; the headache; he poohuai.

NA-LU-LU, } *adj.* Painful; sad; heavy hearted.

NA-LU-NA-LU, *adj.* See NALU, surf. Roaring, as a high surf; appearing rough, as a high surf or high sea.

NA-MAU-A-HI, *adj.* Few.

NA-MU, } *v.* To speak rapidly;
NA-MU-NA-MU, } to speak unintelligibly; hence,

    2. To speak a foreign language imperfectly.

    3. To speak a foreign language in the presence of one who does not understand it.

    4. To mock one by imitating his manner of speaking; to speak in the manner of another.

    5. To nibble, as a fish at the bait.

NA-MU, *s.* A person of a foreign or different language; a foreigner.

    2. Unintelligible talk, or unmeaning talk; he *namu* ka olelo, the speech was *unintelligible.*

    3. A rapid motion of the jaws.

NA-MU, } *adj.* Unmeaning, as
NA-MU-NA-MU, } language; unintelligible from the ignorance of the hearer, or awkwardness of the speaker; me na lehelehe *namu* e olelo ai, to speak with stammering lips; i na mea *namunamu,* ame na mea ninau kupapau, ame na kupua. *Isa.* 19:3. A charmer.

NA-NA, *v.* To look at an object when it is in sight; to see; to view attentively. 1 *Sam.* 1:12. To examine carefully; e *nana* hoi! look see! behold! E *nana* i ka maka, to respect persons in judgment. *Kanl.* 1:17. He mea *nanaia* mai, a gazing-stock. *Heb.* 10:33. *Hoo.* To cause one to look.

NA-NA, *v.* See NA. To quiet; to console; to be quieted or consoled, as a child.

    2. *Hoo.* To comfort or sympathize with one. *Kin.* 37:35.

    3. To comfort, as a mourner.

    4. To bark; to growl; a snarl.

    5. *Nana,* erroneously for *lana,* to float. See LANA.

NA-NA, *s.* A snarling, growling disposition; a finding fault with one.

NA-NA, *s.* Name of a Hawaiian month answering to the month of March.

NA-NA, *particle.* Erroneously written for *nane;* as, i *nane,* let me see it.

NA-NA-AO, *v. Nana,* to look, and *ao,* clouds. To look at the clouds and observe times, &c. *Oihk.* 19:26.

Na-na-au, *v.* *Nana* for *lana*, and *au*, current. See Lanaau. To roll away; to flow over; to miss the way; too irregularly; to swim in the current.

Na-na-au, *adj.* *Nana* for *lana*, and *au*, current. Rolling; floating, as in a current; floating irregularly, as on the surface of an overflowing stream.

Na-nae, *s.* A person whose breast is greatly swelled out and stomach equally depressed.

Na-nai, *v.* To go lightly; to go carefully; to sail lightly and carefully.

2. To love greatly; to love exceedingly; aole okana mai ka nui o ke aloha.

Na-nai, *s.* A disease in the back like the *hanunu*; a stooping; a bending.

2. The person having such a disease. See mele a Niauliu.

> Aloha hoi kau ka *nanai*,
> Aloha wale kuu uhane kinowailua,
> E ka maua e nonoho nei,
> Aole au i ike oia kekahi,
> Ua ka ilaila e kokohe ai.

Na-nai, *adj.* Empty; void; stripped, as a kalo patch when all the food is taken away; he loi *nanai*, a kalo patch all pulled.

Na-nao, *v.* See Nao. To thrust the hand or fingers into some unknown receptacle.

2. To think deeply; to penetrate, as the mind.

3. To seize hold of, as the mind.

4. To be slippery; to be led astray; to turn aside.

Na-nao, *adj.* Deep; capacious; deep down; poopoo.

Na-nau, *v.* To be bitter; to be sour; to be crabbed.

2. To scratch like a cat; to be wild.

Na-nau, *adj.* Unfriendly; unsocial; refusing admittance to one to the house.

Na-nau-ha, *v.* To force; to compel with strength; to belch or throw up from the throat or stomach. See Kakauha.

Na-nau-ki, *v.* See Nauki and Uki. To provoke; to insult.

Na-na-u-li, *s.* *Nana*, to look, and *uli*, the blue sky. One who predicted the weather by looking at the sky. *Laieik.* 36.

Na-na-ha, *v.* See Naha. To strain; to crack; to break.

Na-na-he, *adj.* Empty, as the bowels from fasting or sickness. See Nahenahe.

Na-na-ho, *adj.* Deep; deep down. See Nahonaho and Naho.

Na-na-hu, *v.* See Nahu. To bite, as a dog; to tear; to seize; to grasp tightly.

Na-na-hu, *s.* See Nahu, a biting; a burning. Hence,

1. A coal, especially *nanahu ahi*, a live coal; charcoal. *Sol.* 6:28. Sometimes written *lanahu*, as *l* and *n* are often interchangeable.

2. The colic; any sudden sharp internal pain.

Na-na-hu-ki, *v.* To compel; to urge; to drive; to go crookedly; to move here and there as without object.

Na-na-ka, *v.* See Naka. To be dry; to be parched, as land.

2. To be cracked; to be full of chinks; to be cracked, as the walls of an adobie house; ke *nanaka* nei ka hale, mamuli paha hina, the house is *now cracked*, soon perhaps it will fall.

3. To separate, as the parts of a material substance.

Na-na-ka, *s.* A crack; a crevice; a defect.

Na-na-ka, *adj.* Cracked; split; rent.

Na-na-ke-a, *v.* To be weak in body; to be pale; to be thin, as a sickly person; to be feeble in appearance. See Lanakea.

Na-na-ke-a, *s.* Name of a species of rush.

Na-na-ki, *v.* To tie; to bind. See Naki and Nakii.

Na-na-li, *v.* See Nali. To make a strong muscular effort, as in pulling up a bush, climbing a steep hill, or rowing hard against the wind.

2. To eat or chew something hard.

3. To seize upon with vigor. See Nali-nali.

Na-na-li, *s.* A seizing; a making an effort or struggle to accomplish something difficult, as rowing against the wind, climbing a precipice, &c.

Na-na-mu, *v.* See Namu. To reproach with vile terms; to speak against one, finding fault with him.

2. To cast one off as worthless; to treat with contempt.

Na-na-na, *s.* See Lanalana. The long legged spider; he olelo no ke akamai o ka *nanana* i ka hana upena ana, a description of the skill of the *spider* in making her web.

Na-na-na, *v.* To swell up, as the abdomen; to grow large, as in the dropsy or other diseases.

Na-na-na-ia, *v.* To lie as a sick person turning on his bed.

2. To walk proudly; to strut.

Na-na-na-ke-a, *adj.* See Nanakea and Lanakea. Weakly; pale; thin in flesh.

Na-na-na-na, *v.* See Lanalana, to float. To walk about; to exercise by walking.

Na-na-na-na, *s.* See Lanalana. A species of spider. See Punanana.

2. The rope that fastens the ama and the ako of a canoe together. See Lanalana.

3. A spider's web.

4. A picture; an image.

Na-na-na-na-i-ea, *v.* To have a film (spider's web) over the eyes; to see very indistinctly.

Na-na-na-pa, *s.* See Napa. To crook; to bend; to warp, as timber; to writhe; to get out of shape.

Na-na-pau, *s.* A tree; he kou, he laau.

Na-na-wa, *v.* See Nanau. To not know one formerly an acquaintance; to be estranged from a friend.

Na-ne, *v.* To speak in parables; to allegorize.

2. To give out or put forth a riddle. *Lunk.* 14:13.

3. To lay stones squarely and smoothly; to lay stones, as in a pavement.

Na-ne, *s.* A riddle; a parable; an allegory; a dark speech; a comparison; a similitude. *Mar.* 4:3. See Nanehai.

Na-ne, *adv.* An adverbial expression equivalent to *let us see; show it to us;* i *nane,* i *nane* hoi, let us see it.

Na-ne-a, *v.* To be of good cheer; to be pleasant; to be easy minded.

2. To be easy; to be regardless of the future; to be indifferent as to good or evil.

3. To live indolently; to loiter about; to take things easy; to allow of no care or anxiety.

4. To live satisfied with one's self.

5. *Hoo.* To pretend; to make pretenses with a view to deceive.

Na-ne-a, *s.* Joy; comfort; quietness; carelessness.

Na-ne-a, *adj.* Easy; quiet; comfortable; thoughtless; indifferent.

Na-ne-a, *adv.* Easily; quietly in one's manner of living; e noho nanea, to live at ease. *Iob.* 12:5.

Na-ne-hai, *s.* *Nane,* riddle, and *hai,* to declare. A problem in mathematics; a question to be solved; he ninau, he pono ke wehewehe ia.

Na-ne-na-ne, *v.* See Nane. To put forth riddles or enigmas for others to search out.

Na-ni, *s.* Glory. *Puk.* 16:10. A high degree of external beauty; splendor; external excellence; i mea *nani,* a i mea maikai, for *glory* and for beauty. *Puk.* 28:2.

Hoo. Glory. *Hal.* 96:8.

Na-ni, *v.* To be glorious. *Hoo.* To extol; to praise; to glorify; to be manifested or known as glorious. *Puk.* 14:4. See Lani.

Na-ni, *adj.* Beautiful; glorious; excellent; numerous; pleasant.

Na-ni. (An intensive particle, intensifying in a high degree the idea of the words with which it is connected.) *Nani* ka maikai! O how beautiful! *Nani* ka uuku! O how little! &c. *Nani* is also used with *ino,* another intensive. See Ino. *Nani ino* kuu makemake! O how much I desire! or how very great is my desire! *2 Sam.* 23:15. How much! how great! how noble! *Ioan.* 11:36. *Nani* is used impersonally; it is extraordinary; it is wonderful; it is unaccountable. *Laieik.* 71.

Na-ni-na-ni, *v.* To bite; to catch hold of with the teeth; to chank.

2. *Hoo.* To be ennobled; to be dignified, as a chief; to enjoy the honors and privileges of a chief or one highly honored.

Na-no, *v.* To snore. See None and Nonoo.

Na-no, *v.* For *nalo.* See Nalo, to be lost; to be forgotten.

Na-nu, *s.* See Nalu. The surf of the sea; pehea ka *nanu* (nalu)? ke wewe o wahulu mai.

Na-nu-e, *s.* A species of sea-weed; also a species of fish.

2. A swelling; a protuberance.

3. A shaking; a trembling; a tremor.

Na-nu-e, *v.* See Nalu and E, greatly. To swell up; to rise up, as the surf.

2. To tremble; to shake; to vibrate. *Hoo.* The same.

Na-nuu-mao-mao, *s.* Name of a place or places in a heiau; ma ke alo aku o ka laua *nanuumaomao,* ma kahi e pili koke aku ana i ka Lele.

Na-nu-ha, *adj.* Hard; stingy; close; oolea. See Nuha and Kanuhanuha.

Na-pa, *s.* A delay; a postponement.

Na-pa, *v.* To writhe; to spring, as timber partly hewed or made straight; to crook; to be crooked.

2. To shake; to be tremulous, as the air or atmosphere under a hot sun over a smooth surface.

Na-pa, *adj.* Crooked; bent; not straight; uneven, as a surface.

Na-pai, *v.* To be bent in; to be depressed; to be internally defective.

Na-pai, *adj.* Warped, as a board in the sun; *napai* i ka hapaiia e ke ae.

Na-pa-na, *s.* The joints of one's limbs, as wrists, elbows, knees, &c.

Na-pa-na-pa, *v.* See **Napa.** To bend; to spring; to be elastic.

2. To bend over, as an arch; to be arching.

3. To be bright; to be shining; to be lucid.

Na-pe, *v.* To bend, as a flexible stick; to yield.

Na-pe-le,
Na-pe-le-pe-le, } *v.* To wound; to make sore; to hurt; to cause a swelling; to soften; to cause softness in any substance.

Na-pe-le,
Na-pe-le-pe-le, } *adj.* Hurt; wounded; bruised; swelled; *napelepele* kalalau owili i ka makani.

Na-pe-na-pe, *v.* See **Nape,** to bend. To be shaken; to be agitated, as by the wind; to vibrate rapidly.

Na-pe-na-pe, *adj.* Soft; flexible; bending; yielding.

Na-po, *adj.* Mashed soft; made fine; finely pounded, as poi.

Na-po,
Na-poo, } *v.* To set; to go down, as the sun appears to; to grow dark; *napoo* ka la. *Kin.* 15:12.

2. To sink down; to sink, as in water.

Na-poo, *s.* The going down or setting of the sun.

2. The place where the sun goes down. *Kanl.* 11:30.

3. The rays of the sun reflected by the water.

Na-poo-poo, *v.* See **Napoo.** To plunge down; to enter out of sight, as in the water.

Na-po-lo, *v.* To straighten. *Hoo.* To make straight.

Na-po-na-po, *adj.* See **Napo,** mashed soft. Made soft; made fine; wali, aeae.

Na-puu, *v.* To be tied up in a knot; to tie up, as a bundle. See **Hipuu.**

Na-puu, *s.* A knot made by tying, as in tying two ends with a string; a bundle tied up. See **Hipuu.**

Na-puu-puu, *v.* To tie up in bundles; to tie up; to make fast for carrying.

Na-puu-puu, *s.* A bundle tied up for carrying.

Na-puu-puu, *adj.* Bundled up; tied up in bundles; fastened by tying.

Na-wa, *s.* See **Wa,** private talk, and **Wawa,** babbling. Indistinct or confused talk; conversation of double or doubtful meaning.

Na-wai, *interrog. pron.* An oblique case of *wai,* who? For whom? by whom? See Grammar § 158.

Na-wao, *s.* Name of a species of small fish found in fresh water streams; kiahimanu.

2. A large red kind of kalo unfit for eating.

3. Fig. Used for that which is bad, in the proverbial phrase ke hui nei *kalo* i ka *nawao,* the *good* is joined with the *evil;* another form is, ua hui aku a ua hui mai *kalo* i ka *nawao.*

Na-wa-li, *v. Na* and *wali,* fine; soft. To be weakly; to be sickly; to be feeble; to be flexible; to be yielding. *Hoo.* The same.

Na-wa-li, *adj.* Sickly; weak; feeble.

Na-wa-li-wa-li, *v.* See **Nawali,** *v.* To pine away with sickness; to be weak. *Hoo.* To be weak; to faint; to relapse; to yield. *Kanl.* 20:3. To weaken; to make weak; connected with *naau,* to discourage. *Ios.* 14:8. With *ikaika,* to cause one's strength to fail. *Hal.* 102:23.

Na-wa-li-wa-li, *s.* Weakness; want of muscular or mental strength. 1 *Sam.* 30:10. Infirmity. *Luk.* 5:15.

Na-wa-li-wa-li, *adj.* Weak; want of strength; feeble; sick.

Na-wa-wa, *v.* To shake to and fro. See **Nawewe** and **Naueue.**

Na-we, *v.* See **Naue.** To shake; to be agitated.

2. To pant for breath, as one dying.

3. To lie a long time near the pains of death, just breathing.

Na-we-le, *adj.* Fine; small, like a thread of a spider's web; ka *nawele* o kahi ike, small of vision; seeing but little.

Na-we-le, *v. Hoo.* To be fine; to be small; thin, as a thread. See **Punawele-wele.**

Na-we-we, *v.* See **Nawe** and **Naue.** To rock; to shake; to tremble; to vibrate.

Na-we-we, *v.* A shaking; a rocking; an earthquake. See **Naueue.**

Na-re-do, *s. Eng.* Nard; spikenard.

Na-ta-pa, *s. Heb.* Stacte. *Gr.* A spice. *Puk.* 30:34.

Na-za-ri-te, *s. Heb.* A Nazarite; a person separated and under a vow. *Nah.* 6:2.

Ne, *v.* To tease; to fret; to make one cry; to ask for food, as a child, i. e., to cry for it.

2. To be sour; to be sad; to be peevish, as when one is crossed in his plans.

3. To droop; to be sickly; to wither.

4. To murmur; to talk low; to whisper, as the gods or ghosts do; to make low sounds, as the ripples of the sea where there is little surf.

5. To gnash or grind the teeth.

NE, *v.* Use for *nee.* See NEE.

NE, *adj.* Crying; fretting; sickly, as a child.

NE-A, *v.* To sweep off everything, as property from a place; to destroy all; to make a place desolate. See NEO and NEO-NEO. *Hoo.* The same.

NE-A-NE-A, *s.* Waste land; destitute of food; everything swept off.

NE-A-NE-A, *adj.* Lonely; desolate; waste.

NEE, *v.* To move along horizontally; to move off; to hitch along.

2. To move, as a large body; to move from one place to another. 2 *Sam.* 7:10.

3. To pass along by for inspection, as soldiers. *Ios.* 7:14.

4. To move, as a mass of people; to remove. 1 *Oihl.* 17:9.

5. *Hoo.* To remove; to push out of place; to change the place of a thing. *Kanl.* 9:14. To remove a landmark. *Hos.* 5:10.

6. To change, as the mind or opinion. *Kol.* 1:23.

NEE-HEE, *v.* See NEE and HEE. *Hoo.* To hitch along; to move slowly; to approach by degrees.

NEE-NEE, *v.* See NEE, to move in various ways and in different directions. To draw near or approach, as a marching army. 2 *Sam.* 10:13.

2. To journey on towards any place. *Kin.* 12:9.

3. To draw near; to approach one to ask a question. *Kin.* 18:23.

4. To approach one to show respect and reverence. *Kin.* 33:7.

5. To go near to one to kill him. 2 *Sam.* 1:15.

6. To crawl on the hands and knees. NOTE.—This was the ancient manner to which the common people approached the chiefs.

7. To go beyond; to separate one's self from others.

8. To go afar off.

NEI, *v.* Similar to *nee,* but with more energy. To move along with noise or tumult; to rush; a *nei* aku la i na kumu o ka lani, and he *moved* the foundations of heaven; e *nei* nakulu ana ia nei, to *move upon* in a rush.

2. *Hoo.* To move, as in a tumult; to shove or urge along.

3. To move; to be forced, as the trees by the wind.

4. To make a confused noise, as a multitude moving together.

NEI, *s.* This place, or time; perhaps it should be classed with adverbs, but it has the attendants of a substantive; aohe akua o *nei,* there is no god *of here,* i. e., *of this place; ia nei,* here abouts, at this place; *iho nei,* just now, time past. See Grammar § 161.

NEI, *adj, pron.* For *neia* or *keia,* this. No ka la auhau a ke alii nona *nei* noho ana ma Hawaii huipuia *nei,* for the tax day of the chief who sits now (as king) over these united Hawaiian (Islands.) E like me *nei* hana a ke kula nui, like *this* exercise of the high school.

NEI, *adv.* When following verbs, *nei* marks the present time; following nouns, it relates to the present place; as, ke hele *nei* au, I am *going;* ma Honolulu nei, at Honolulu *here.*

NEI-A, *adj. pron.* This. Synonymous with *keia.* 1 *Oihl.* 17:16.

NEI-NEI, *v.* See NEI. To draw up; to shrink; to contract.

2. To be too short or too small, as clothes.

3. To slip up; to slip away. See ELEHEI.

NEI-NEI, *adv.* Too short; too low; not fitting, as a garment; moving off; kikenenei.

NE-O, ⎫ *v.* To be silent; to be still
NE-O-NE-O, ⎭ where had been life and activity.

2. *Hoo.* To make silent; to cause to be still, as an assembly; to cuase one to say nothing. *Oih.* 21:40.

3. Used *imperatively,* hush; silence; no noise.

4. To cause silence by desolation. *Mat.* 24:15. Hence, to make desolate, as a house, city or country by destroying the people. *Oihk.* 26:31. Oia ka mea e *neoneo* ai ka aina i kanaka ole, that is what *renders* a land *desolate* without people.

5. To cause to be empty or desolate. *Isa.* 24:1.

NE-O, ⎫ *adj.* Desolate; empty, as
NE-O-NE-O, ⎭ a house or city without inhabitants; solitary, as a path through a wilderness. *Kanl.* 32:10.

NE-O, ⎫ *s. Hoo.* Desolation; ruin.
NE-O-NE-O, ⎭ *Ier.* 25:18. An empty space. *Iob.* 26:7.

NE-U, ⎫ *adj.* Fat; fleshy; plump;
NE-U-NE-U, ⎭ fair; spoken in reference to animals; fat, as beef.

NE-HE, *v.* To make a rustling noise, as shuffling the feet or drumming with the fingers; to rumble slightly; to scratch on something capable of making a noise. See NENEHE, NENEKE and KAMUMU.

NE-HE, *s.* A rustling sound, as in walking; a rumor of a thing done. See NENE.

NE-HE, *s.* A plant having flowers resembling May-weed.

NE-HE-NE-HE, *adj.* Rustling; scrambling, as many; starting, as a single person.

NE-HI, *adv.* Yesterday; inahea kou puka ana mai la? I *nehi* aku la, or i *nehi.* NOTE.—*Nehi* is generally followed by *nei,* and is mostly added to it; as, i *nehinei,* this past day, i. e., yesterday. See NEHINEI.

NE-HI, *adj.* Rotten; ruined; spoiled; applied to food.

NE-HI-NEI, *adv.* See NEHI. Yesterday; the day before the present day; nawaliwali au mai *nehinei* mai no, I have been unwell since *yesterday.* It is generally prefixed by *i* and written as one word, thus, *inehinei;* it is also sometimes spelled *inei-hinei.* See INEHINEI.

NE-HI-WA, *s.* From *wahine* transposed. Name of a lascivious talk; eia ka olelo hewa hou, o ke kake, o ka *nehiwa,* o ka ololeke.

NE-HO-A, *adj.* Hard; strong; bold; able.

NE-HO-A, *v.* To be strong; to be able; to be bold; to be hard. *Hoo.* The same. See NAHOA. Also, to be impudent to others.

NE-HU, *s.* The name of a species of fish.

NE-HU-NE-HU, *s.* See LEHULEHU. A multitude; the mass of people.

nehu

NE-KE, *v.* To scratch; to make the noise of scratching, as marking on a board, writing on a slate or rough paper.

NE-KE, *s.* See NAKEKE. An indistinct rustling sound, as scratching on a rough board; an echo among the hills. See NENEKE and KAWEWE.

NE-KI, *s.* A rush growing beside the water; a bulrush; he akaakai.

NE-KI, *adj.* Full, as a room with people; full, as a container; running over; packed in; crowded one against another.

2. Awkward; unskillful; ignorant.

NE-KO, *v.* To have an offensive smell; to be foul; to be filthy; to emit a stench.

NE-KO, **NE-KO-NE-KO,** } *s.* An offensive smell; a stench; an ill savor.

NE-KO, **NE-KO-NE-KO,** } *adj.* Filthy; bad smelling; pilau, ihuneko.

NE-LE, *v.* To lack; to be without; to be destitute of.

2. To be in want; to be poor. *Kanl.* 8:9. To be deprived of; to need or want a thing.

3. To be bereaved; to be deprived of. *Kin.* 43:14.

4. *Hoo.* To separate or deprive one of his privileges or enjoyments; to suffer loss.

5. To be without, i. e., to be destitute of. *Oihk.* 2:13. NOTE.—*Nele* has this peculiarity: it is followed by the name of the thing wanted, and this name is again followed by *ole,* no, not; as, *nele* na kanaka o Honolulu i ke kumu *ole,* the people of Honolulu *are without* a teacher. The *ole* in our idiom would be superfluous, but the Hawaiian requires it.

NE-LE, *s.* Want; destitution; bereavement; need. 1 *Ioan.* 3:17; *Kanl.* 15:8. See HEMAHEMA.

NE-LE, *adj.* Destitute; deprived of; empty. *Kanl.* 32:28.

NE-LE, *adv.* Destitutely; being without.

NE-LU, **NE-LU-NE-LU,** } *adj.* Fat; fleshy; full fed; plump.

NE-MA, **NE-MA-NE-MA,** } *v.* To rail upon one; to speak evil of; to reproach; to treat with contempt one's views or opinions. See LOILOI.

NE-MO, *v.* To smooth over; to polish; to resemble the smooth skin of a bald head; to be shiningly smooth; e hamo.

NE-MO, *s.* The full protuberant belly of a child.

NE-MO-NE-MO, *adj.* Smooth; smoothly polished; full; large.

NE-MU, **NE-MU-NE-MU,** } *adj.* Plump; large; nice; applied to men, women or children, to animals or vegetables.

NE-NA, *s.* Takes the article *ke.* A species of small plant.

NE-NE, *s.* A goose, a species of which is found on the high lands of Hawaii.

2. A visible appearance; a sign of something about to take place.

3. A report; a rumor; a gossip. *Mar.* 13:7.

4. A species of thick grass; mauu, weuweu.
O ka mauu *nene* aala i ke kula o Kanehou
Ua like paha—ao i like.

NE-NE, *v.* To be on the point of breaking out, as a war.

2. To be excited; to be moved, as a company of person at unexpected news. *Laieik.* 116.

NE-NE-A, *v.* See NEA. To sit together and talk, without care or anxiety or thought for the future; e like me ka ai a laua i poho ai, a o ka mea i *nenea* palaka ka haupu.

NE-NEE, *v.* See NEE. To draw to; to

move along. *Isa.* 5:19.

Ne-nei, *adj.* Turning the face downwards and the back upwards.

2. Steep, as a hill; he alanui *neinei* ohope. See also **Neinei.**

Ne-ne-hu, *adj.* See **Nehu.** Bending out, as a board; warped.

Ne-ne-ke, *s.* See **Neke.** Any low confused monotonous noise made by the moving of the feet, drumming with the fingers or scratching on a board.

Ne-ne-ke, *v.* See **Neke.** To rustle; to move; to make a noise.

Ne-ne-le-a, *s.* Nene and *lea,* joy. Joy; gladness. See **Lealea.**

Ne-ne-lu, *s.* A receptacle of filth; a ditch; a miry place. *Iob.* 30:19.

2. Mire; mud. 2 *Sam.* 22:43. Aole *nenelu* o ka lepo, a he lepo paakiki.

Ne-ne-lu, *adj.* Thick, as a board.

2. Slumpy; miry, as a wet, soft place.

Ne-ne-ne, *v.* See **Nene.** To be on the point of doing a thing; to act as a bird about to fly. *Hoo.* No ka mea, he *hoonenene* nei lakou e lele iho.

Ne-ne-ne-pu, *adj.* See **Nepu** and **Nepunepu.** Full in flesh; round; full.

Ne-ne-pu, *adj.* Fat; full in flesh; plump.

Ne-ne-wa, *v.* See **Newa.** To be dizzy; to stagger; to reel.

Ne-ne-wa, *s.* Dizziness of the head; vertigo.

Ne-pu,
Ne-pu-e, } *adj.* Round, full and plump, as a fat animal;
Ne-pu-ne-pu, full in flesh; fat.

Ne-pu-ne-pu-li-ke, *adj.* The same rotund size throughout.

Ne-wa, *v.* To reel; to stagger, as one drunk; to walk as one who has been drinking *hola.*

2. To be dizzy, as one under the influence of vertigo. See **Nenewa.**

Ne-wa, *s.* A staff; a cane; a cudgel; a war stick; laau kaua.

Ne-wa-ne-wa, *s.* A vertigo; a dizziness in the head; ka *newanewa* ma ka pouli i ka ua.

Ne-wa-ne-wa, *adj.* Reeling; staggering; intoxicated; having a vertigo.

Ne-we, *v.* To suffer; to be in pain from fullness of the stomach.

2. To be large, round and full, as a child's abdomen.

3. To be full, as one who has eaten too much.

4. To be fickle-minded.

Ne-we-ne-we, *v.* See **Newe.** To be swelled unnaturally, as the belly of a child

from over eating; *newenewe* ka hua; to be round, smooth and plump; to look sad; to feel sad.

Ne-we-ne-we, *adj.* Plump; full, as an ear of corn in the husk, or as a round, full grown fruit; plump; full, as a pregnant female; aohe *newenewe* o ka hua, he malili, the fruit is not *full grown,* it is stinted; *newenewe* ka opu.

Ne-we-ne-we, *adj.* Plump; round; thick, as a cloud in the horizon; he ao *newenewe,* a thick cloud near the sea.

Ne-we-ne-we-we, *s.* The exclamations of people when they play at *maika,* while the stone is rolling and they cheer it on.

Ne-ge-ro, *s.* *Eng.* A negro; a black man; often written *nika,* but vulgarly.

Ni-a, *adj.* Bald; baldheaded; round and smooth, as a bald head.

Ni-ao, *s.* The sharp edge or corner of a board, or the middle of a cocoanut leaf.

2. An edge; a groove; a projection.

3. A standing with the head and ears erect.

4. The middle fibre of a cocoanut leaf.

5. The brim of a container, as a box, barrel, tub, &c.

6. Any substance with prominent corners.

Ni-au, *s.* See **Niao.** The stem of a cocoanut leaf.

2. The whale-bone or wood of an umbrella; he iwi ha.

3. He aki *niau.*

Ni-au, *v.* To sail easily; to sail genteelly.

Ni-au, *adj.* Easy sailing.

Ni-au-ka-ni, *s.* *Niau,* cocoanut leaf stem, and *kani,* to sound. A kind of rude jewsharp made of the stem of a cocoanut leaf; he ukeke.

Ni-au-pi-o, *s.* *Niau* and *pio,* a chief of the highest grade. A superior or highest chief; a kapu chief; he alii kapu, he alii moi. *Literally,* it applies to the child of two high chiefs, i. e., father and mother both high chiefs. See **Kupa ai au,** a child who enjoys, eats the land; *au,* region.

Ni-a-ni-a, *v.* To accuse falsely; to accuse by trapping. *Luk.* 11:54. To accuse and bring no evidence. *Luk.* 23:14.

2. To seek occasion against one; to condemn one unheard.

Ni-a-ni-a, *s.* See **Nia.** A smooth surface; a calm and smooth sea.

2. A baldheaded person.

3. Reproach; blasphemy; a false accusation.

4. He poe *niania* wale, false accusers. 2 *Tim.* 3:3.

NI-A-NI-A, *adj.* Calm; quiet; smooth, as the unruffled sea; hence,

2. Shining; reflecting light.

3. Smooth; shorn close, as the head. See MANIANIA.

NI-A-NI-AU, *adv.* *Hoo.* Straightly, as one's course in moving; holo, e hooniau, hele *hoonianiau* lau konale waho.

NI-A-NI-AU, *adj.* Straight; pololei.

NI-A-NI-A-PE, *adj.* See NIAPE. Bending; arching; stretching out long.

NI-A-NI-E-LE, *v.* See NIELE. To ask with surprise; to seek for information by asking to ascertain the fact of a case.

NI-A-PE, *adj.* Long.

NI-E-LE, *v.* To ask; to inquire; to put questions to another; to ask questions generally.

NI-E-LE, *s.* A question; a proposition; a problem to be solved.

2. A questioner; an inquirer.

NI-E-NI-E-LE, *v.* See NIELE and NIANIELE. To ask questions repeatedly; to ask about this and that; a *nieniele* mai la na kanaka i ke ano o ia mea, the people *asked frequently* the meaning of this thing (an eclipse.)

NII-HAU, *s.* Name of one of the Hawaiian Islands, south-west of Kauai.

NI-O, *v.* To sit in the door way in an open door.

2. To lean over and sleep; e hiamoe, e lopio, e kawaikamama.

NI-O, *s.* A kind of handsome kapa or cloth.

NI-OI, *s.* The name of a bush or tree.

2. Red pepper, a species with small round pods.

3. The name of a poison tree which is said to have grown on Lanai and Molokai and whose touch was fatal; it was fabled to have been entered by the god Kalaipaihoa o Kahuilaokalani, and thence became a poison tree and was worshiped as a god. See the kaao.

NI-O-LE, *v.* To eat slowly and lazily; to eat without a desire to eat; to act as in great weakness.

NI-O-LE, *adj.* Eating slowly; eating with weakness; ai malie, hopilole, nawaliwali.

NI-O-LO, *s.* Sleep; drowsiness; one fast asleep.

NI-O-LO-PU-A, *s.* Sleep; drowsiness; lying asleep; he hiamoe kapu.

NI-O-NI-O, *adj.* *Hoo.* Folded; plaited; braided, as hair. 1 *Tim.* 2:9.

NI-O-NI-O, *v.* *Hoo.* To embroider. *Puk.* 28:39. See ONIONIO.

NI-O-NI-O-LO, *s.* *Hoo.* Straightness; correctness; that which is correct, upright; me ka *hoonioniolo* o ka manao kekahi, some with *correctness* of opinion.

NI-O-NI-O-LO, *v.* To make correct one's opinions; to correct one's language.

NI-U, *s.* Name of the cocoanut tree and fruit. NOTE.—Under the kapu system, it was forbidden to females to eat cocoanuts; the punishment was death.

NI-U, *v.* To whirl about in any way; to whirl, as a top.

NI-U-A, *v.* See LIUA. To be intent upon, as the eyes fixed on one object. 2 *Pet.* 2:14.

2. To turn the eyes so as not to see distinctly.

NI-U-A, *s.* Indistinctness of vision; vertigo; a distortion of the eyes.

NI-U-HI, *s.* A species of fish. NOTE.— It was prohibited to women under the kapu system, to eat of the *niuhi* under the pain of death.

2. A shark of the large kind; mano nunui.

NI-U-HI-WA, *s.* A species of banana. See also POPOULA.

NI-U-LE-LO, *s.* A species of niu or cocoanut; hookapu ae le ka puaa, ame ka *niulelo*, pork and *niulelo* were strictly forbidden (to women.)

NI-U-NI-U, *v.* To turn; to twist; to whirl about any way.

2. To be sad; to be sorrowful; to be faint; to languish. *Ier.* 31:25.

NI-U-NI-U, *adj.* Sad; sorrowful; destitute.

NI-U-NI-U, *s.* The skull; the head. See NIU. Poha ka *niuniu*, nakaka ka pali.

NI-HA, } *adj.* Rude; rough; harsh;
NI-HA-NI-HA, } unsocial; wild, &c.; tight in a bargain. See the compound KAMANIHA.

NI-HEU, *s.* A person whose hair as in ancient times was fancifully fixed; he kanaka maoli no, o ka lauoho nae o *Niheu.*

NI-HI, *v.* To walk very softly and carefully, as on tip-toe; to creep quietly and softly. *Laieik.* 96.

2. To turn sideways on entering a house.

3. To abstain from doing certain things through fear of offending the gods.

4. To do a thing quietly, silently or secretly, i. e., unseen by others.

> E hoopono ka hele i ka uka o Puna,
> E *nihi* ka hele, mai hoolawehala,
> Mai noho a ako i ka pua o hewa,
> O inaina ke akua, paa ke alanui,
> Aole ou ala e hiki aku ai.

NI-HI, *adv.* Carefully; quietly; o ka hana palanehe ole, o ka lawe *nihi.* See KUNIHI.

NI-HI-NI-HI, *s.* Anything standing on

the edge; the sharp ridge of a mountain; the corner of a square piece of timber; the corner of a table, &c.

Ni-hi-ni-hi, *adj.* Standing up on edge; narrow ridged, as a mountain sharp at the top; difficult; strait; narrow edged.

Ni-ho, *v.* To bite with the teeth; to indent; to set in like teeth; to lay a stone wall in a bank of earth.

Ni-ho, *s.* A tooth. *Puk.* 21:27. The tooth of an animal, especially a whale's tooth; e malama i ka *niho* palaoa, take care of the *niho palaoa* (an ornament made of a whale's tooth.) See PALAOA. *Niho* elepane, elephant's tooth, i. e., *ivory.* 2 *Oihl.* 9:17. O ka *niho* mano ko Hawaii nei mea e ako ai i ka lauoho, a shark's *tooth* was the Hawaiian instrument for cutting the hair.

Ni-hoa, *s.* See NIIHOA one of the islands.

Ni-ho-a-wa, *adj. Niho,* tooth, and *awa,* poisonous. Poison toothed, as some animals inclined to bite; poisonous; corroding.

Ni-ho-hui, *s. Niho* and *hui,* pain. The toothache; a pain in a tooth.

Ni-ho-kai, *s.* A painful affection of a tooth; the toothache. See NIHOHUI.

Ni-ho-ka-hi, *s.* LIT. One tooth. One tooth remaining, a term for old age; he haumakaiole, he palalauhala.

Ni-ho-mau-o-le, *s.* Name of an office in the king's train.

Ni-ho-mo-le, *s. Niho* and *mole,* smooth. A gap in a row or series; a broken place; places open here and there.

Ni-ho-mo-le, *adj.* Not regular; open; toothless.

Ni-ho-ni-ho, *adj.* Set with teeth; as a saw; projecting; stretching out; rough; full of protuberances.

Ni-ho-pa-la-o-a, *s.* See NIHO and PA-LAOA, an ivory ornament. An ornament worn pendulous from the neck, made from the ivory of the walrus or sea elephant; originally it was an ornament worn only by high chiefs.

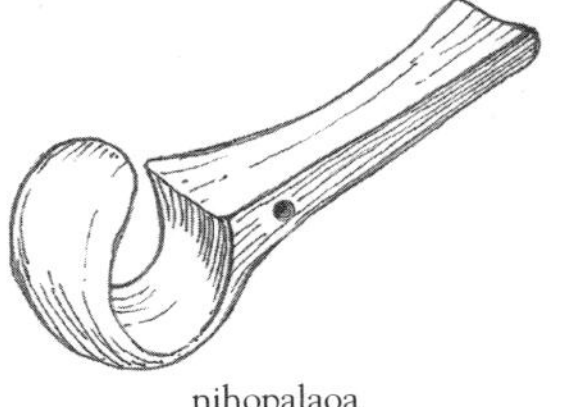

nihopalaoa

Ni-ka, *adj.* Black; deep blue; dark colored.

Ni-ka, *s.* The vulgar orthography for *negero,* as *nigger* is in English for *negro;* a black man.

Ni-ki, *v.* To tie a knot.

Ni-kii, *v.* To tie, as a rope; to fasten; to tie tightly. See NAKII.

Ni-kii-kii, *v.* To tie in knots; to fasten by tying; to bind; to tie fast with ropes or strings. 2 *Sam.* 3:34. See HIKIIKII.

Ni-ki-ni-ki, *v.* Frequentative of *niki.* To tie frequently or tightly; alaila, *nikiniki* iho la ia i ka uha puaa i ke aho, then he *tied* the hams of the hog with a cord. Alaila, *nikiniki* iho la ia i ka makau i ka maunu, then he *tied* the bait on to the hook.

Ni-ki-ni-ki, *s.* The sheath or that which covers and holds fast the bowels; kumu hele.

2. The fat with the inwards. *Oihk.* 3:3.

Ni-ku,   *s.* A bad or offensive
Ni-ku-ni-ku,   smell; a stench. See NE-KONEKO.

Ni-ku-ni-ku, *adj.* Filthy; smelling offensively. See NEKO.

Ni-le-gau, *s.* The name of an animal found in Africa; the nilgau, an animal of the ox kind.

Ni-lu, *s.* See NINILU. Something admired, wondered at, desired.

Ni-na, *adj.* See LINA. Soft to the touch; slippery; adhesive, like poi.

Ni-nau, *v.* To ask a question for information; to inquire concerning a thing; to interrogate. See NIELE. *Ezek.* 20:3.

Ni-nau-u-ha-ne, *adj. Ninau* and *uhane,* ghost. Having familiar spirits; talking with or getting information from ghosts. *Oihk.* 19:31.

Ni-nau-ku-pa-pau, *s. Ninau* and *kupapau,* a corpse. One who consults the dead or the spirits of the dead. *Isa.* 8:19.

Ni-nau-ho-i-ke, *s. Ninau* and *hoike,* to exhibit. A learning by question and answer.

2. The name of a historical catechism formerly in use among the natives.

Ni-na-ni-na, *adj.* See NINA and LINALINA. Very wet; damp; sticky; unctuous; soft; slimy.

Ni-na-ni-nau, *v.* See NINAU. To ask questions repeatedly; to question; to inquire earnestly. *Ioan.* 16:19. To converse by questioning back and forth.

Ni-ni, *s.* That which tends to heal a wound, balm, ointment, oil, &c. *Ier.* 46:11. A medicine for external wounds.

Ni-ni, *v.* To soothe a pain; to heal a wound; to apply *nini* or medicine to a wound.

2. To spill; to spill over; to pour out a liquid.

3. To find fault in a bargain; to complain.

4. To cheat; to ask more for a thing than it is worth.

5. To be hard in a bargain.

6. To lay stones well in a wall; if the stones lie smoothly and tight, the stones are said to *nini.*

NI-NI-AU, *s.* The motion of turning.

NI-NI-AU, *v.* To stretch out; to pull; to overflow; to go wrong.

NI-NI-O, *v.* See NIO, to color. To spot; to print, as kapa. See PANINIO.

NI-NI-O-LE, *s.* Name of a species of fish; he wahi mea ola ano like me ke kualakai.

NI-NI-U, *v.* See NIU. To turn, as a top; to wheel about, as a platoon of soldiers; to whirl about in any direction.

NI-NI-HA, *v.* See NIHA. To be tight in a bargain; to be close; to be hard; to get the better of one in a business transaction.

NI-NI-HA, *adj.* Hard; severe in business with others; tight in a bargain.

NI-NI-HI, *v.* See NIHI. To walk on the edge of a precipice; to set up on edge; to stand up edgeways, as any thin object and sharp at the top.

NI-NI-HI, *s.* A circle.

NI-NI-HU-A, *v.* To play truant, as a child; aole laka mai i ka makua. *Hoo.* To run away from home or from one's parents.

NI-NI-KA, *s.* A bush which spreads out with branches like the *maile.*

NI-NI-LU, *adj.* Soft; mellow.

NI-NI-NI, *v.* See NINI. To pour out, as a liquid; to pour out upon; to give; to imbue; to suffuse.

2. To pour out grain, as from a bag. *Kin.* 42:35.

3. To pour out, as from a bottle. *Puk.* 29:7.

4. FIG. To pour out, as the desires of the heart. 1 *Sam.* 1:15. To pour out, as a complaint, sorrow, weeping. *Iob.* 3:24.

5. In a *religious sense*, to pour out, as the Holy Spirit. *Oih.* 2:17.

6. To exhibit anger, i.e., to pour out fury. 2 *Oihl.* 34:21.

7. To throw away; to squander; e hoolei, e hoopau.

8. To count out, as money. 2 *Nal.* 22:9.

NI-NI-NI, *s.* A casting; a solid from a liquid. 1 *Nal.* 7:37.

NI-NI-NI-A, *v.* See NINI. The passive of NININI. To cast away; to throw out; to pour out; to throw away.

NI-NI-NI-NI, *v.* The reduplication of *nini.* To run off, as a liquid; to move off slily; to go off secretly; to hide.

NI-NI-PO, *v.* See NIPO. To be weak; to be bent over, as one scarce able to walk.

NI-NI-PO-LO, *v.* See NIPOLO. To drum with the fingers and sing.

NI-PO, *adj.* Sleepy; fatigued; languid.

NI-PO-A, *s.* Dullness or numbness of the body; a dizziness; a headache, mostly in the region of the temples.

NI-PO-LO, *adj.* Striking the drum and singing at the same time; o nawenawe *nipolo* lea ka leo.

2. Sick and faint, as one dying.

NI-PO-NI-PO, *adj.* See NIPO. Sick; weak; languid; feeble.

NI-PO-WA, *s.* See NIPOA. Dullness; dizziness; numbness; weakness of body.

NI-SU, *s.* *Heb.* The name of an unclean bird. *Kanl.* 14:15. A hawk perhaps. *Oihk.* 11:16.

NO, *s.* A hole in the ground which draws off water from kalo patches.

NO, *v.* To leak, as water under ground from a kalo patch; e u aku, to ooze out.

NO, *adv.* An affirmative particle; truly; indeed; even so.

2. An intensive, strengthening the idea, connected both with verbs and nouns.

NO, *prep.* Of; for; belonging to; concerning; similar in meaning to o and ko, but used in a different part of the sentence. *Gram.* § 69, 3.

NO-A, *v.* To be released from the restrictions of a kapu; to take off the kapu or prohibition; ko lakou makemake, i *noa* loa na lealea, ame na hana uhauha, their wish was that pleasure and licentiousness *should have no restraint.*

2. To be released from restraint; to be out from under restraint or law; *noa* honua, *noa* loa, all kapus taken off.

3. *Hoo.* To release one from kapu; he wahine *mare,* he wahine *kapu* ia; he wahine *noa,* he wahine kapu ole ia, i. e., a common woman.

4. To cause to become a prostitute, as a man prostitutes his wife or daughter; to be common. *Oihk.* 19:29.

NO-A, *s.* The lower or degraded class of people; a lower servant; a backwoodsman; he kuaaina.

2. The name of a play.

3. The name of the stone used in the game of puhenehene. See KAU.

4. A fire constantly burning like a volcano; ke ahi aa mau, ke ahiaihonua.

NO-A, *adj.* Intermission or cessation from kapu; applied to anything that has been under kapu and the kapu taken off; the removing of the kapu constitutes it *noa.* Sabbath day is a *la kapu,* but Monday is a *la noa.* He makuahine *noa* wale no kou, ma Hamakua, your mother was a mere *common woman* at Hamakua.

2. Constantly burning, as a fire; unquenchable, as a volcano; ahiaihonua.

NO-A-AU-LO-A, *s. Noa,* free from kapu, *au,* time, and loa, long. Applied to Kauikeaouli because he reigned over the people without kapus; o ke alii malama makaainana, he alii ia noaauloa.

NO-A-NO-A, *s.* See NOA. One opposite to a chief by birth; a common man; a countryman; a laborer; one whose ancestors were laboring people.

NO-A-PA-HEE, *s.* See NOA and PAHEE, to slip. The name of a game absorbing one's attention.

NO-E,   ⎫ *v.* To sprinkle a little, as
NO-E-NO-E, ⎬   fine rain; to be damp in the air, as a fog; to rain, yet scarcely discernible to the eye.

2. To blow fresh; applied to the wind *noe.* See the noun, 2. Ke *noenoe* mai la ka makani.

NO-E,   ⎫ *s.* A mist; a spray; small
NO-E-NO-E, ⎬   fine rain; a fog. See AWA and AWAHIA.

2. The name of a wind at Lahaina from over the land; the north-east trade wind.

NO-E-AU, *adj.* See NOIAU. Wise; prudent. *Sol.* 12:23. Skillful; dextrous. SYN. with maiau. O ka poe akamai i ka olelo ame ka hana maoli, he *noeau* ia.

NO-E-U-LA, *adj.* Red eyed; sore eyed from going in the rain or sea; ka maka *noeula* pua i ke kai.

NO-E-KO-LO, *s.* The small, fine rain of the mountains mixed with the thicker of the forest; o ka *noekolo* aualii kapu o Kama.

NO-E-LO, *v.* To ask for; to beg; the same as *noi.*

2. To be bold; to be impertinent; to be mischievous.

3. To collect together what is tangible; e ake no lakou e naauao pu, a e noii pu, a e *nowelo* (noelo) pu.

4. To seek the ground of some accusation; e imi i ke kumu e hewa ai; to search out the merits of a question; to prepare before hand.

NO-E-NO-E, *s.* See NOE, mist. A fog; a fine mist; a rain.

2. A gray head; a gray headed person.

NO-E-NO-E, *v.* See NOE 2. To blow, as the wind; ke *noenoe* mai la ka makani.

2. To sprinkle; to wet, as a fog or a mist; to bedew.

3. To be intoxicated.

NO-I, *v.* To beg; to beseech; to ask for a thing; to ask earnestly; to entreat; to ask, as in prayer; *noi* ikaika lakou, i pu, a i pauda, they *begged strongly,* give us guns, give us powder.

NO-I-AU, *s.* See NOEAU. Wisdom. *Iob.* 12:2. Knowledge. *Sol.* 1:2. Skill in language; he akamai i ka olelo.

NO-I-AU, *v.* To be wise; to be skilled in a thing; e *noiau* ma na mea o ka uhane, *to be skilled* in matters of the soul.

NO-II, *v.* To glean; to collect together little things.

2. To collect one's thoughts; to reflect; to search after a thought or an idea; ua *noii* au i manao mikolelehua no'u, I *gathered up* some wise thoughts for myself.

NO-II, *s.* A collecting; a gathering up; a seeking; me ka huli ana ame ka *noii* ana.

NO-II, *adv.* In a small way; little by little; aole oia i auhau *noii* a pau ka moa, koloa, &c., he did not tax all *little things,* as hens, ducks, &c.

NO-I-O, *s.* Name of a small black bird that lives on fish.

NO-I-LI, *s.* Knowledge; skill; skill in the use of language. See NOIAU and MAIELE.

NO-I-NO-I, *adj.* Small, as a dwarf.

NOO, *v.* To seek; to search after; to reflect; to turn over and over in one's mind; to exercise the thinking powers.

NO-O-A, *v.* For *nooia,* passive of *noo.* To be sought after; to be looked for; to be obtained by searching.

NO-O-LU, *adj.* See OLU. Easy; comfortable; cool; pleasant. See MOOLU.

NOO-NOO, *v.* See NOO. To think; to reflect; to consider in order to give an opinion.

2. To meditate; to think of the past; to think with approbation.

3. *Hoo.* To cause to think; to think and act the man; to act wisely; e hookanaka.

NOO-NOO, *s.* A thought; a device; a subject of meditation; in the *plural,* thoughts; opinions; ua hoopuka ia mai *na noonoo,* the thoughts (opinions) were openly expressed; an invention; seeking something new.

NOO-NOO, *adj.* Thinking; reflecting; skillful; planning; thoughtful.

NOU, *v.* To blow hard, as a gale of wind; *nou* mai ka makani.

2. To puff; to fill with wind. See HAANOU.

3. To send out or abroad, as thunder.

Iob. 37:3.

4. To throw or cast a stone; *nou* aku la i ka pohaku, a pa i ka auwae, he *threw* a stone and it struck the chin; to throw stones. 2 *Sam.* 16:6. Pohaku *nouia*, a stone thrown. *Nah.* 35:17.

5. To strike, as the rays of the sun; to be very hot, as the rays of the sun; e wela nui mai ka la, e ko nui mai; *nou* iho ka la o keia aina o Lahaina, the sun of this land of Lahaina *strikes* down.

6. Haa. To be puffed up; to be self-important. 1 *Kor.* 4:18.

7. To boast. *Ezek.* 35:13.

NOU, *s.* A puff or blast of wind.

NOU, *pers. pron.*, second person. An oblique case of oe, thou. Thy; thine; of thee; for thee, &c. *Gram.* § 132. *Nou* ka nou, or *nau*, yours is the fault; none to blame but yourself.

NOU, *adj.* Epithet of a servant born of a common person and a kauwa aumakua; a hanau mai ke keiki, he *nou* ka inoa o ia keiki.

NO'U, *pers. pron.*, first person. Oblique case of *au* or *wau*, I. My; mine; for me. *Gram.* § 124.

NO'U, *v.* To eat to the full; to glut with food; to gormandize; to eat very often.

NO-U-U, *v.* To be wet with rain; to be suffused with water.

2. To smell the sweet scent of flowers; *nouu* aala ka uha i ka pua.

NO-U-LU, *s.* The fan-leafed palm tree. See LOULU.

2. A covering; a screen from the sun.

3. An umbrella, especially a Chinese umbrella.

4. A thick shade tree.

5. A long heiau.

NOU-NOU, *v.* See NOU, *v.* To throw stones back and forth, as two persons at each other.

2. To appear or show itself red; e puka mai ka ula.

3. E pokoke ka ai.

NOU-NOU, *s.* A species of calabash.

NOU-NOU-NEA, *v.* To rub with the hand or paint one's cheeks to give them beauty; e pakuikui i ka limukala iloko o ke kai ma ka papalina.

NOU-NOU-NEA, *adj.* Reddened, as one's face with some substance to give beauty; i *nounounea* me Hikua.

NO-HA, *v.* See NAHA. To break; to split; to crack; to sever.

NO-HAE, *v.* See NAHAE. To be torn; to be rent; to burst.

NO-HE-A, *adv. No* and *hea.* An oblique case of *hea*, where. Whence? from what place? *Gram.* § 165.

> Ka pio o ke ki kamalena o ke kaunoa
> *Nohea* i ka la kapu o ke aalii?
> Ka onohi uli o ka moo o Kaiona
> O naha ka manu—o—Hili—a.

NO-HE-O, *s.* Some mischievous conduct; i ka uu pekupeku a ka *noheo.*

NO-HI, *v.* To be of a reddish color. See ONOHI, KINOHI and KIIONOHI.

NO-HII-A-LO, *s.* The name of a person who was born with a chief and ever continues to live with him; o ke kanaka i hanau ma ke alo alii, he kanaka *nohiialo* ia.

NO-HII-KU-A, *s.* Name of the people who are born and live on the back part of the island; o ke kanaka i hanau ma ke kua-aina, ua kapaia he *nohiikua.*

NO-HI-LI, *adj.* See HILI. Tedious; slow; of a long time.

NO-HO, *s.* A seat; a bench; a stool; a chair; a place of staying or living.

2. *Noho* lio, a saddle; *noho* kapakahi, a side-saddle.

NO-HO, *v.* To sit; to dwell; to tarry in a place.

2. To be in a certain condition or to exhibit a certain character; e *noho* malie, to live quietly, or to hold one's peace; e *noho* pio, to be in bondage; e *noho* like, to be at peace, as between two people. *Lunk.* 4:17. I. e., to have equal privileges. *Noho* in some positions seems almost to carry the idea of existence; ua *noho* oluolu oia, he *lived* comfortably.

3. *Hoo.* To cause one to sit, i.e., to dwell, or live or stay at any place.

4. To establish or appoint any one in a place or in any business. *Kin.* 47:6.

5. To appoint any one to a particular office. *Puk.* 7:1.

6. To bring one forth, i.e., to produce one before a court for trial.

7. To set forth a declaration of some facts in history. *Oih.* 1:1.

8. E *hoonoho* kepau, to set types; i ke ai *hoonohoia* e ka unu loa.

9. To lay a foundation, as of a building. NOTE.—*Noho* is often used merely to strengthen or intensify the idea; often with *a* or *e* imperative; e *noho* ekemu ole, keep silence, i. e., *be silent*, where it gives force to *ekemu.*

NO-HO is used for various purposes; as, mai *noho* a, a forbidding negative, *do not*; e *noho* nei, *here*, *now*, referring to time present or to present place.

NO-HO, *s. Hoo.* A builder; an architect.

NO-HO-A-LII, *s. Noho,* a seat, and *alii,* chief. A throne. *Puk.* 11:5. A king's seat.

NO-HO-A-LII, *v.* To be or to continue to act as a king. *2 Sam.* 5:4. To reign as a king. *2 Sam.* 8:15. *Nohoalii* iho la o Kamehameha maluna o keia pae aina, Kamehameha *reigned* over these islands.

NO-HO-A-LO-HA, *s. Noho* and *aloha,* compassion. A mercy seat. *Puk.* 25:17.

NO-HO-A-LO-HA, *adj.* Friendly; at peace; on friendly terms; dwelling in unity.

NO-HO-A-NA, *s. Noho* and *ana,* a participial termination. A sitting; a dwelling; a living.

2. Moral character; pehea kona *nohoana?* LIT. How is his sitting? i. e., how is his living? how does he live? what is his character? Me na *nohoana* me na kaliu.

NO-HO-HOO-KO-LO-KO-LO, *s. Noho* and *hookolokolo,* to call to account. A judgment seat; a place for trial.

2. The assembled people at a court of justice; he anaina hookolokolo.

NO-HO-KEE, *v.* To rise up against one without provocation.

NO-HO-NO-HO, *v.* See NOHO. To sit together.

2. *Hoo.* To put together in order; to arrange, as the words or circumstances of a history.

3. To explain things misunderstood.

4. To lay together, as stones in a building. *1 Pet.* 2:5.

5. To lay or place together for the purpose of comparing.

NO-HO-PAA, *v. Noho* and *paa,* firm; tight. To confirm; to establish.

2. *Hoo.* To build firmly; to lay firmly the foundation, as of a building. *Ezera* 6:3.

NO-HO-PIO, *v. Noho* and *pio,* a prisoner. To dwell in captivity; to live a prisoner.

NO-HU,   } *s.* Name of a species of
NO-HU-NO-HU, } fish; the toad fish species.

2. A plant with sharp thorns or burs; a small thorny vine.

3. Name of a species of soft porous stone.

NO-KE, *v.* To seek after; to pursue with success; to search after till found.

2. To be energetic; to be persevering; ua huli au, ua *noke* au, ua noii au i manao mikolelehua no'u.

3. To be filled with anger; to fret; to scold; to exhibit a low kind of anger.

NO-KE, *adj.* Energetic; persevering; searching; seeking.

2. Fretful; cross; stubborn.

NO-KE, *s.* An expression of a mean kind of anger by fretfulness or peevishness.

NO-KE-NO-KE, *v.* To mumble in speaking; to stammer unintelligibly.

2. To make a confused unmeaning noise.

NO-KE-NO-KE, *s.* A murmur; a confused noise; a tremor; a rustling; the grinding of a hard substance in the teeth.

NO-KE-A, *v.* To raise or fill up, as one eating much; to stuff one's self with food; hence, to swell up, as the stomach; to fill full, as a cup; to eat greedily.

NO-KE-A, *s.* The name of a fresh water fish; the *oopu.*

NO-KE-A, *adj.* White; spotted, as the fish *nokea;* he io *nokea* popoolimu.

NO-KE-A-A-HU-LI-U, *s.* The white that appears on stones after they have been heated very hot.

NO-KE-TU-RA, *s. Heb.* Name of an unclean bird; a swan perhaps. *Oihk.* 11:18.

NO-KI,   } *adj.* See NOKE, *adj.* Used
NO-KI-NO-KI, } as an intensive; real; substantial; maoli.

NO-KI. A word often thrown in in poetry without any particular meaning.

NO-KU,   } *v.* To stir up; to trou-
NO-KU-NO-KU, } ble, as water.

2. To give pain; to make one uneasy.

NO-LAI-LA, *adv. No* and *laila,* there. An oblique case of *laila. Gram.* § 165, 2d class. Therefore; wherefore; literally, for there; having reference to something preceding.

NO-LA-LO, *comp. prep.* Oblique case of *lalo. Gram.* § 161. Of or for that which is down or below; from below; belonging to that which is below. *Ioan.* 8:23. The opposite of *noluna.*

NO-LE, *v.* To be surly; to chide; to grumble secretly. *Hoo.* The same.

NO-LU,   } *v.* To deceive; to cheat;
NO-LU-NO-LU, } to outwit, with *puni. Ios.* 9:22. To be disappointed in losing a bet; o kekahi poe, *polunolu* na hai ke eo.

2. To seduce; to bribe; to give property secretly on a wager; to lead astray.

3. To be soft; to be pliable; to be elastic; to be soft like a pillow; to bruise; to make soft by bruising.

4. *Hoo.* To be soft; to be fat, as a fleshy person.

5. To be easily fatigued.

NO-LU, *s.* A bruise; a hurt.

NO-LU, *adj.* Soft; tender; elastic; bruised soft; *nolu* ka ihu o Hopoe i ka makani.

NO-LU-A-KAU-A, *s.* Name of a person

born under one chief, but fights for another chief; o ke kanaka i noho me ke alii e, a kaua mai, he kanaka ia *noluakaua.*

No-lu-na, *comp. prep.* Oblique case of *luna,* above. *Gram.* § 161. Of or from above; respecting that which is above; the opposite of *nolalo. Ioan.* 8:23.

No-lu-no-lu, *adj.* See Nolu, *adj.* Fat, as an animal; hence, soft; elastic.

No-me, *v.* See Nau. To chew; to grind with the teeth.

No-me-no-me, *v.* See Nome and Nau-nau. To chew; to soften in the mouth; e hoowali.

No-na, *pers. pron. No* and *na.* An oblique case of *ia.* His; hers; its; for him; for her; for it. *Gram.* § 139.

No-na-no-na, *s.* A small winged insect; a gnat, a species of ant.

2. Name of a Hawaiian periodical formerly printed at Honolulu. See Anonanona.

No-ne, *v.* To snore in sleep. See Nono and Nonoo.

No-ne, *s.* Laziness; indolence; awkwardness in doing a thing.

> Ka *none* no na ai namunamu,
> Ka huhu paokee laau,
> Ka koi wili kekee olelo manawa.

No-ne-a, *s.* The feeling one has after eating much fat meat, pork perhaps; a fullness; distaste for food, &c.

No-ne-ne-a, *v.* See Nanea. To sit idly; to have no employment, nor desire any.

No-ne-no-ne-a, *v.* See None, *s.* To spend time uselessly; to be lazy; to be indolent.

No-ne-no-ne-a, *s.* Anger; wrath; dissatisfaction; discontent.

No-ni, *s.* A shrub; the bark, and especially the root, is used in coloring; the fruit is large and heavy; he kaua hua *noni* kekahi, some fought with *noni* fruit (for weapons); the root colors red.

noni

No-ni-no-ni, *adj.* Turning the eyes up, down or sideways in attempting to recollect some fact, or in being perplexed, as the mind with something not clear.

2. Attempting to take food when one is too weak or not inclined.

3. Confused, as the mind; doubtful; anxious.

No-ni-nu-i, *s.* Name of a species of soft porous stone.

No-no, *v.* To snore. See None and Nonoo.

2. To gurgle; to make the noise of drinking water out of a calabash; to blow up water, as a hog with its snout under water.

No-no, } *v.* To be fresh or red in the
No-no-no, } face from exercise; to be sunburnt or red from the heat of the sun; e ula na papalina i ka wela o ka la.

No-no, *s.* A dark red or purple color; redness.

No-no-a, *adj.* Indistinct; not correctly heard or understood; not clearly spoken. See Nonononoa.

No-no-e-no-e, *s.* See Noe. The northeast trade winds.

No-no-i, *v.* See Noi. To beg; to ask; to borrow. *Puk.* 22:14.

2. To make a request; to exhort; to urge; to beseech; aole nae ma ka iii loa, a *nonoi* no hoi; aia he uuku nui ae. *Nonoi* uwao, to make intercession. *Ier.* 27:18.

No-no-i, } *adj.* Both forms are used.
No-no-ii, } See also Noii and Noinoi. Small; little; stinted in growth.

No-no-i-ka-wai, *v.* To bend over, as a house or some object leaning.

No-noo, *v.* To snore. See None and Nono.

No-no-he, *adj.* Beautiful; graceful; splendid.

No-no-he, *adj.* Applied to a young woman, beautiful; virtuous; modest; a high state of female excellency; so of an animal.

No-no-hi-u-li, *s.* See the above. Excellency in one's person or character, or both.

No-no-hi-na, *s.* Name of the white blossom of the tree *pua.*

No-no-hu-a, *adj.* Jealous; evil minded; disposed to evil conduct.

2. Flowing from the bowels; o ka wai *nonohua* alii o Kalanuiewakumoku.

No-no-hu-a, *v.* To be evilly minded; to indulge a bad disposition; to be a quick tempered.

2. Fig. To have the disease called *hailepo,* i. e., to evacuate the bowels.

No-no-lau, *s.* Name of the bitter calabash used in medicine. See Oopuhue.

No-no-lo, *v.* See Nono and Nonono. To breathe hard; to snore; e *nonolo* mai ana—a. See nunulu. O ke kapu ia e *nonolo* i ka lani, it is kapu (forbidden) to *snore* in the presence of a chief.

2. To leak fast, as a cask.

3. To be routed in war.

No-no-lo, *s.* The sound of singing birds. See Nunulu.

> E nunulu mai ana—a—
> E *nonolo* mai ana—a.

No-no-lu, *adj.* Soft; shaky; as ground dry on top but muddy below. See Maolu.

No-no-ni, *adj.* See Noni. Burnt red; colored red; wela *nononi* ka io i ke ahi.

No-no-no, *adj.* Full of holes; not strong; pukapuka.

No-no-no-no-ho, *v.* See Noho. To appoint; to fix in a place; to sit firmly; to sit upright.

No-no-no-no-a, *v.* See Nonoa. To speak indistinctly; to be heard indinstinctly; to be almost inaudible, as the voice of one speaking.

No-no-pa-pa, *s.* See Mailoihi.

No-nu, *adj.* Deceitful, as language; not to be trusted. See Nolu.

No-pa,
No-pa-no-pa, } *adj.* Lazy; slow; blundering; mopish.

2. Crooked; very crooked and weak.

No-pa-no-pa, *s.* Slowness; laziness; lolo ke kanaka nui, o ka *nopanopa* ka hewa.

No-pa,
No-pa-no-pa, } *v.* To be crooked; to be perverse.

2. To be lazy; to be blundering; to be slow.

No-po-ho-ka-no, *s. Opohokano.* Name of the kalaimoku under two chiefs.

No-po-lo. See Nipolo and Ninipolo.

No-pu,
No-pu-no-pu, } *v.* To spring or swell up in the mind, as a thought, with a desire to express it; nolaila, *nopu* mai la iloko o'u ka manao e hoakaka wale aku, therefore the thought *swelled up* (sprung up) within me to explain.

2. To swell; to be large round; to be full; e puipui, e momona.

3. To spring up, as a seed planted. Syn. with kupu.

No-pu,
No-pu-no-pu, } *adj.* Thoroughly cooked; soft; spongy.

2. Large; plump; fat; swelled out.

3. Burnt by the sun, as the feet when walking on hot earth or stones.

No-pu-e, *adj.* Plump; round, as a well fed, fat hog.

No-we-lo, *v.* See Noelo. To scrape together.

No-te-ma, *s. Heb.* Juniper roots. *Iob.* 30:4.

Nu, *v.* To groan; to shake; to sound; to roar, as the wind; ke *nu* nei ka makani i na kahawai—makani ala ouaoua e *nu* ana ma na keena nui; to make a long indistinct sound.

2. To groan; to sound like distant thunder.

3. To grunt as a hog; to coo like a dove.

4. Fig. To be agitated, as the mind with unutterable feelings, fears or desires; penei ka *nu* ana mai o keia wahi manao iloko o'u: ina paha he *nu* hekili, ina la paha ua loheia kona haalulu; aka, o ka *nu* iloko o ka naau, aole e loheia kona haalulu, here is the *sound* of the thoughts within me: if it were the *voice* of thunder, the sound, wihtout doubt, would be heard; but the *voice* within the soul is not heard.

5. To think; to reflect upon; to ruminate. Note.—The idea of expressing the deep, intense feelings of the soul by that of sound or a voice is common among the Asiatics. Ke uwe (nu) nei no hoi kakou iloko o kakou iho. *Rom.* 8:23.

> E *nu*, e nei, e haalulu iluna o Waialoha:
> Heaha nei makani o Kapona?
> He lanikua ia no Kalalau—e—
> I Kalalau i Puna nakalau aku,
> Nalowale ka leo o ke kai o Hoohila.

Nu, *s.* The roar or sound of strong wind.

2. An indistinct murmur or groaning sound.

3. The grunting of swine; the cooing of doves, &c.

Nu, *adj.* Sounding; groaning; roaring.

Nu-a, *v.* To tread up, as dirt in a path from much travel; *nua* ke ala a hele ku ke ea.

2. To come together in great numbers as people assemble.

3. To sit down to rest, as a traveling company.

4. To go constantly in the same place.

5. To turn up dirt, as a hog; to root.

6. To be accustomed or practiced in any business.

Nu-a, *adj.* Trodden up, as a road frequently or much trodden.

Nu-a-o, *s.* See Naia. The name of a species of fish forbidden to women to eat, under the kapu system, on pain of death.

Nu-a-nu-a, *adj.* Thick, as a board; fat and soft, as an animal; full; large, as a good looking person. Note.—Hawaiians connected the idea of beauty in persons with their size, fullness of flesh, &c. See Anuanua, rainbow.

Nu-a-nu-a, *s.* See Nua. To tread up dirt; *nuanua* ke ala a ku mai ke ea.

2. Hoo. To act proudly; to boast; to dress up one's self in gorgeous apparel; e aahu nui i na kapa.

Nu-a-wa, *s.* A planting; the act of covering seed in the dirt; ka manu ahai ka *nuawa* e.

NU-I, *v.* To be great; to increase in size; to swell; to be more; to enlarge; to raise, as the voice; heaha kou mea e *nui* nei kou leo? *Laieik.* 22.

   2. *Hoo.* To add to; to increase ; to multiply. *Isa.* 59:12.

   3. To magnify; to extol, as one's kindness. *Kin.* 19:19.

   4. *Haa.* To speak proudly; to vaunt; to brag.

NU-I, *s.* Size; increase; multitude; magnitude; greatness; fullness. NOTE.— *Nui* often takes *ke* for its article instead of *ka*; aole paha o *ke nui* o na kina wale no.

NU-I-NU-I, *v.* See NUI. To be large; to be very great; to increase. *Hoo.* To increase greatly; to raise high, as the voice; e *hoonuinui* aku paha i ka leo maluna.

NU-I-NU-I, *s. Hoo.* An increase; a raising up.

NUU, *v.* To rise or swell up; to be full or high.

   2. *Hoo.* To eat much; to have a swelled stomach; to devour food eagerly. See ANUU.

NUU, *s.* See NUU, *v.* A raised place in the heiau where the god dwelt and where the offerings were placed. See KAPAAU.

   2. Evenness; an evenly raised surface.

NUU-A-NU, *s.* The name of a game at cards; e pepa *nuuanu* kakou.

   2. Name of a valley near Honolulu.

NUU-KO-LE, *s.* Name of a fresh water fish of the oopu kind. See KIAHIMANU.

NU-HA, *v.* To be silent; to be taciturn; to be displeased.

   2. To be or to act as an aged person, deaf, silent, &c.

   3. To be rough; to be uncivil; to be hard or heavy upon one.

NU-HA-NU-HA, *v.* See NUHA. To be disobedient; not to give heed to any one; to render one's self disagreeable; to be hard; to answer a question captiously.

NU-HE, *adj.* See NUHA. Sullen; silent; mixed with anger.

NU-HE, *s.* A species of worm; o Kaelo, oia ka malama e hanau ai na *nuhe.* See ENUHE.

NU-HEI, *adj.* Crooked billed; crooked mouthed.

NU-HI, *v.* To take; to take from; to draw out. See UNUHI.

NU-HOU, *s. Eng. Nu* for new or news, and *hou*, new; recent. A word coined a few years ago and applied as the name of a weekly periodical, and may be translated *Recent News.* He *nuhou* ia i ka mea waa, it was a *new thought* to the owner of the canoe. *Laieik.* 20.

NU-HOU, *v.* To appear, as a new thing; to spring up in the mind, as a new thought or desire.

NU-KA, *adj.* Large; full grown; plump.

NU-KA-NU-KA, *v.* To be fat; to be full; to be plump; to be round and smooth, as a young animal or a young person; to be fleshy.

NU-KA-NU-KA, *adj.* See NUKA. Fat; plump; in good liking, as a young person.

NU-KE, *adj.* For *nuku ee.* Twisted one side; awry; one-sided, as the mouth; he waha *nuke.* See NUKEE.

NU-KE-A, *adj.* White, as the white billed *alae.* NOTE.—The alae is of two varieties, the white bill and the red bill. Muku, keo-keo, alae *nukea.*

NU-KEE, ⎫ *s. Nuku*, mouth, bill, and
NU-KU-KEE, ⎰ *kee*, crooked. A crooked snout; a crooked mouth; mai mai o mea ia'u.

NU-KO-KI, *adj.* Short; low; small.

NU-KU, *v.* To chide; to complain; to provoke; to quarrel. *Puk.* 17:2.

NU-KU, *s.* The bill of a bird; the snout of an animal.

   2. A tunnel; the nose of a pitcher; the nose of a person. *Ezek.* 39:11. The mouth. *Hal.* 108:42.

   3. The mouth of a river. *Ios.* 15:5.

   4. Strife; scolding; contention. 1 *Tim.* 6:4.

   5. Name of a kind of fish-hook.

NU-KU-A-U-LA, *s.* The frame of a fish net.

NU-KU-MO-NE-U, *s.* The name of a fish. See MOMOMI.

NU-KU-NU-KU, *v.* See NUKU. To find fault with one secretly; to complain of one behind his back. *Hoo.* The same.

NU-KU-NU-KU, *adv.* See NUKU, *s.* By the mouth, that is, by the end; endways; kau *nukunuku*, to place endways, as a stick on the shoulder.

NU-KU-WAI, *s. Nuku*, mouth, and *wai*, water. The mouth of a stream of water. See NUKU.

NU-LU, *v.* To rise up, as smoke or steam; to float off in the air, as smoke.

NU-LU-NU-LU, *adj.* Rising up; floating off, as smoke or steam.

NU-NU, *v.* See LUNU, *n* for *l.* To covet, as the property of another, and to use some means of obtaining it. See also ALUNU.

NU-NU, *v.* To provoke.

   2. To swell up; to swell up in places.

3. To roll up, as paper; e owili, e wihi.

Nu-nu, *s.* See **Nu.** A moaning; a groaning; a grunting, as of hogs; a cooing of doves; hence,

2. A dove; a pigeon from the noise they make; *nunu* opiopio, a young pigeon. *Oih.* 1:14.

3. An endearing epithet like my dear *chicken. Mel. Sol.* 2:14.

4. The name of a species of fish; the pipe fish.

Nu-nu, *adj.* Groaning, as of persons in pain; grunting like hogs; cooing like doves.

2. Taciturn; unsocial; sullen; displeased; applied only to persons. See **Nunuha.**

Nu-nu-a, *adj.* See the above **Nunu.**

Nu-nu-i, *adj.* See **Nui.** Very large; kanaka *nunui,* a giant. *Kin.* 6:4. He poe *nunui,* men of large stature. *Kanl.* 2:10, 11.

Nu-nu-i, *v.* See **Nui.** To be large; to be many; to be numerous; to increase; to grow up, as a child.

Nu-nu-ha, *adj.* See **Nuha.** Taciturn; still; unsocial; displeased; quiet; applied to persons. See **Nunu,** *adj.,* 2.

Nu-nu-he, *adj.* See **Nuhe.** Sullen; taciturn; silent; angry.

Nu-nu-ki, *adj.* Rising and falling irregularly, as the sea sometimes.

Nu-nu-lu, *v.* To sound, as the singing of birds; to chirp; to sing, as a bird; to warble.

2. To grunt; to growl. See mele below.

> I ka leo o ka manu—a—
> E *nunulu* mai ana—a—
> E nonolo mai ana—a.

Nu-pa, *v.* To enlarge; to swell; to be full, as one having over eaten.

Nu-pa, *s.* A deep pit; a deep, dark pit; a softening, as of the ground by rain; i ka *nupa* ae lepo a ka ka ua.

Nu-pa-nu-pa, *v.* To be of a deep green like thrifty growing vegetables.

Nu-pa-nu-pa, *adj.* Thriftily growing; full; round; plump. See **Nukanuka.**

P.

P, the eleventh letter of the Hawaiian alphabet. It represents, as in English, a labial sound. Hawaiians are apt to use it for *b* in words derived from English, as *pipi* for *bipi,* or as it should be written, *bifi,* neat cattle, from the word *beef.* It is often used also for *f* in the word *piku* for *fiku,* a fig, &c.

Pa. A distributive particle prefixed to other words, as nouns, adjectives and verbs; mostly however to numeral adjectives; as, *pakahi,* one by one, each one; *palau* or *papalua,* two by two, two-fold, double; *pakolu,* each of the three, three-fold; *pahiku,* by sevens, seven-fold, &c., and so on to any number. These words are sometimes constructed in the sentence as verbs, and thus become verbs; as, ua *pahiku* mai la oia i ka ia ia makou, he *divided* to us the fish *by sevens;* e *paumi* aku ia lakou, *give* them *ten each.*

2. As a *particle, pa,* like *ka, ma, na,* &c., is prefixed to a great many words, but the definite meaning of such particles has not yet been ascertained.

Pa, *s.* The name of any material having a flat surface, as a board (see **Papa**), a plate, a server, a pan; *pa* wili ai, a poi *board; pa* holoi, a *basin* to wash in; *pa* hao, an iron *pan.* NOTE.—With this meaning, *pa* takes *ke* for its article.

2. The extremity; the furthest point of a thing. *Mar.* 13:27.

3. A remnant or piece; the same as *apana.* NOTE.—This meaning also takes *ke* for its article.

4. The wall of a city; an inclosure, including the fence and the space inclosed; *pa* pohaku, a stone *wall; pa* laau, a stick *fence; pa* hipa, a sheep *fold.*

5. A hall; an open court.

6. A pair; as, *pa* bipi, a *pair* or yoke of oxen; *pa* kamaa, a *pair* of shoes, &c. See also **Paa.**

7. A kind of fish-hook for taking the aku or bonito.

8. A species of yam.

9. A kind of shell-fish somewhat large, of the clam or muscle kind.

10. A brazen grate; he *pa* keleawe, manamana, pukapuka.

Pa, *adj.* Barren, as a female; applied to men or animals. 1 *Sam.* 2:5.

2. Dry; parched; cracked, as land; broken.

Pa, *v.* To divide out to individuals, as several things to two or more; e *pa* lima ae oe ia lakou, *divide out five apiece* to them. See **Pa,** particle.

Pa, *v.* See **Pa,** a fence. To hedge in with a fence; to inclose; e *pa* laau, to make a stick fence.

Pa, *v.* See **Pa,** *adj.* To be barren or

childless; applied to females of animals or men.

PA, *v.* To touch; to tap lightly; to strike gently. *Puk.* 19:12.

2. To beat; to strike heavily; to strike suddenly, as a gust of wind. *Iob.* 1:19. Ke *pa* mai nei ka makani, the wind *strikes* us.

3. To strike, i. e., to bite, as a serpent.

4. To strike, i. e., to hit, as a stone thrown. 1 *Sam.* 17:49. A *pa* iho la o Kiwalao i ka pohaku, Kiwalao *was hit* by a stone.

5. To shoot or throw, as an arrow of sugar-cane (a pastime for boys.)

6. To be given up, as property taken in war; nonoi aku la ke kahuna, i aku la, i *pa* ka aina ia kaua, the priest asked a favor, and said, let the land (conquered) be given to us two.

7. *Hoo.* Causative of most of the foregoing definitions. To lay hold of; to cause one thing to approach or touch another.

8. To touch, i.e., to injure or hurt. *Zek.* 2:8.

9. To sound; to ring, as metal struck; to strike upon the ear, as music; to break; to crack.

PAA, *v.* To blow, as the wind. See PA above.

PAA, *v.* To be tight; to be fast; to make tight; hence, to finish a work. *Kin.* 2:1. Ua *paa* ka waha, the mouth *is shut*; he *is silenced. Mat.* 22:34.

2. To confirm; to establish; to continue permanently the same.

3. To lay hold of; to retain; to secure.

4. To retain in the memory; to keep a secret.

5. To affirm; to assert perseveringly; to affirm positively.

6. To be habituated; to be inclined; to be held under the influence of a person or habit.

7. *Hoo.* To finish; to decree; to determine.

8. To establish or confirm, as a covenant. *Kin.* 21:27.

9. To hold fast; to adhere to, as a custom; to affirm strongly. *Oih.* 12:15.

10. To fix; to hold fast; e *hoopaa* i ka waha, to *muzzle* the mouth. *Kanl.* 25:4.

11. To hold back; to be detained from doing a thing; aole i hiki, ua *hoopaa* ia ia Kamehameha, he could not (return), *he was detained* by Kamehameha. See also *Kin.* 20:6.

PAA, *s.* A pair. See PA. A pair; a suit, as of shoes, socks or other clothes. *Lunk.* 14:12. See also *pa lole komo*, a suit of clothes. *Lunk.* 17:10.

2. In *geometry*, a solid. See PAAILI and PAAILILIKE.

PAA, *adj.* Tight; fast; secured; immovable; finished; kahi *paa*, a place of *security*, inward. *Nah.* 15:34.

2. Burnt; scorched; charred.

PAA, *adv.* Steadfastly; perseveringly.

PA-AA, *s.* The rind of the banana; the skin or outside covering of a cluster of bananas; the fibre of a banana stalk; he ili mawaho o ka pumaia. See AA.

PA-AA, *adj.* See AA. Stony, as land; full of stones.

2. Burnt; scorched.

PA-AA-LA-HA, *s.* A memento; a keepsake. See PAUMAUNOONOO.

PAA-I-LI, *s.* *Paa*, a solid, and *ili*, side; surface. A solid with sides according to the number specified. See below.

PAA-I-LI-O-NO, *s.* See PAA and ILI and ONO, six. A solid having six sides. *Ana Hon.* 26.

PAA-I-LI-O-NO-LI-KE, *s.* A solid with six equal sides; a cube.

PAA-I-LI-HA, *s.* *Paaili* and *ha*, four. A solid inclosed by four triangular sides.

PAA-I-LI-HA-LI-KE, *s.* A solid inclosed by four equal and similar triangular sides. *Ana Hon.* 30.

PAA-I-LI-U-MI-KU-MA-MA-LU-A, *s.* *Paaili* and *umikumamalua*, twelve. A twelve-sided solid, the sides being equal, i. e., five-sided polygons.

PAA-I-LI-I-WA-KA-LU-A, *s.* *Paaili* and *iwakalua*, twenty. A twenty-sided solid, the sides being triangles, equal and similar.

PAA-I-LI-KU-PO-NO, *s.* A cube or rectangular parallelopiped. *Ana Hon.* 26.

PAA-I-LI-KAU-LI-KE-HI-O, *s.* An oblique parallelopiped. *Ana Hon.* 27.

PA-AO-AO, *s.* A sickness; a weakness, mostly of children; want of strength; mai *paaoao*, hemo ke kino e.

PA-AO-AO, *adj.* Pa and *aoao*, side. LIT. By sides; sideways; on one side; one-sided.

PAA-OA-OA, *s.* By transposition of letters, the same as *paaoao*, sickness.

PA-AU, *s.* See PAAA. The skin of a banana stalk.

PA-AU-A, *s.* A laborer; a workman; a hired man. *Isa.* 19:10.

PA-AU-A, *adj.* Hired; working as a hired man.

PAA-U-MA, *adj.* Paa and *uma*, to push or draw. Fast to the breast, or pulled towards the breast; pahi *paauma*, a drawing knife; a shave.

PAA-HAO, *v.* Paa and *hao*, iron. To be

iron bound; to be a prisoner. *Ier.* 32:2.

Paa-hao, *s.* *Paa* and *hao*, iron. One bound; a prisoner. *Epes.* 4:1.

2. One bound to work; a servant; one who obeys another.

3. The system of work under the Hawaiian Government in which the common people worked out their taxes; he koele, he hana aupuni.

Paa-hao, *adj.* Made fast; iron bound; bolted. See HALEPAAHAO. Wahi *paahao*, a prison. *Ier.* 37:15. Lua *paahao*, a dungeon.

Paa-ha-na, *v.* *Paa* and *hana*, to work. To be busy; to work constantly.

Paa-ha-na, *s.* One busily engaged; a workman. 2 *Oihl.* 34:10. A mechanic; an artificer. *Kin.* 4:22. A tradesman.

Paa-ha-na, *adj.* Instruments, fixtures, or what belongs or accompanies other things. *Nah.* 7:1.

Paa-he-o, *s.* See HALEPAAHAO. A place of confinement like a prison, dungeon, &c., for criminals; a lele aku kou uhane ma ka *paaheo*, ma kahi make mau loa.

Pa-a-hi, *s.* *Pa*, pan, and *ahi*, fire. A fire pan. *Ier.* 52:19.

Paa-hi-hi, *v.* *Paa* and *hihi*, to spread out. To work here and there; to extend one's operations.

Paa-ho-no, *v.* *Paa* and *hono*, to stitch. To make fast by tying with a string; to splice; to sew together.

Paa-kai, *s.* *Paa* and *kai*, sea water. Salt; that which gives sea water its taste; ke kumu o ke kai. *Oihk.* 2:13.

2. A species of kalo.

Paa-ka-hi-li, *s.* *Paa* and *kahili*, a fly-brush. An officer of a high chief who took care of the kahilis; ma kahi e noho ai na 'lii e noho pu no ka *paakahili*.

Paa-ke-a, *s.* Name of a stone out of which maika stones were made.

Paa-ki-ki, *v.* *Paa*, solid, and *kiki*, intensive, very, exceeding, &c. To be very hard, as a stone or any solid substance.

2. FIG. Applied to the will, to be obstinate; to be self-willed; to be disobedient; to be unyielding to the will of another.

3. Applied to the heart, to be hard-hearted; to be unbelieving through perverseness of disposition; to turn away from the influence of truth.

4. *Hoo.* To harden; applied to substances or to moral qualities.

Paa-ki-ki, *s.* Hardness; compactness; applied to the heart, stubbornness; perverseness. *Kanl.* 9:27.

Paa-ki-ki, *adj.* Hard; compact; difficult to do; perverse; disobedient; unbelieving. 1 *Sam.* 20:30.

Paa-ku-ku, *adj.* *Paa* and *kuku*, to stand. Firmly fixed; immovable; constant.

2. Applied to persons, parsimonious; avaricious.

Paa-lau-ma-ni-a, *s.* *Paa*, solid, and *laumania*, smooth. A regular or smooth, i. e., a plane solid figure. *Ara Hon.* 26.

Paa-la-lo, *v.* To serve as a favorite in any manner in the presence of the chief; *paalalo* malalo ae o ke alii. *Paalalo* malalo ae o ke Akua, or *paalalo* i ke Akua.

Paa-lii, *s.* The name of a medicine.

Paa-lo-ha, *s.* *Paa* and *loha*, love. A keepsake; a memento.

Paa-lu-hi, *v.* *Paa* and *luhi*, fatigue. To work hard; to be overcome with constant hard work.

Paa-mu-a, *s.* A movement of wind in the bowels; a rushing; an opposition to some movement.

2. One who continues daily in prayer.

Pa-a-ni, *v.* To play; to sport. *Puk.* 32:8. To have the enjoyment and pastime of children; to wrestle; to box; to run races, &c.

Pa-a-ni, *s.* A play; a sport; a playing, as among children enjoying a pastime; a general name for play, sport, exercise; the enjoyment of a pastime; he *paani* pono kekahi, he *paani* pono ole kekahi. Note.— The Hawaiians anciently spent much of their time in *paani* or games or *lealea* (sensual gratifications.)

Pa-a-ni, *adj.* Belonging to play or amusement; trifling; hale *paani*, a theater. *Oih.* 19:29.

Paa-paa, *v.* See PAA, burnt. To burn; to scorch; to be consumed by fire; e aiia e ke ahi.

2. To suffer thirst; to be thirsty.

3. To contend in words; to contradict; to dispute contentiously.

4. *Hoo.* To contend in dispute; to chide. *Lunk.* 8:1. To be at strife. 2 *Sam.* 19:9.

Paa-paa, *s.* A dryness; a thirst; a parching or cracking, as the earth in the sun.

2. A disputing; a reasoning. *Iob.* 13:6.

3. *Hoo.* Disputation; altercation; strife. *Kanl.* 1:12.

Paa-paa, *s.* Name of a species of fish.

Paa-paa, *adj.* Burned; baked hard; parched; thirsty.

2. Bound tightly; made fast. See PAA.

Paa-paa-i-na, *v.* See PAINA, to eat. To

eat; to take food.

2. See PAAPAA, to burn. To crackle, as small light fuel in burning. *Kekah.* 7:6.

3. To make any indistinct noise like cracking, parching, &c.

PAA-PAA-I-NA, *s.* The crackling of brush wood or small sticks in burning.

2. The squeaking of shoes; the breaking, snapping, &c., of cords or strings.

3. A separating of one thing from another; lohe aku la au i ka *paapaaina* ana mai o kapuai mahope o maua ma ka lihi o ke kai; alaila, i aku la no hoi au ia ia nei, heaha la hoi neia mea e *paapaaina* mai nei?

PAA-PA-NI, *v.* *Paa* and *pani*, to shut. To stop up; to shut, as a door or a gate; to shut close.

2. To stop one in his speech; to make one shut up and be silent. See APAAPANI.

PAA-PO-E-PO-E, *s.* *Paa*, solid, and *poepoe*, round. A circular solid; a globe. *Ana Hon.* 26.

PAA-PU, *v.* To crowd; to throng; to be thick together, as a company of persons.

2. To be hurried or bustling with business.

3. To be thick; to cover over a surface. *Oihk.* 13:12. To be full of a thing. 2 *Nal.* 6:17.

4. *Hoo.* To fill, as with confusion. *Ezek.* 28:16.

PAA-PU, *adj.* Filled; impervious; solid; not hollow; dark; crowded all together; closely joined; covered up; bound; tied; pouli *paapu*, thick darkness. *Kanl.* 15:19.

PAA-PU, *adv.* Entirely; wholly; thickly; all together; in great quantities. *Puk.* 8:2.

PAA-PU-HE-A, *s.* *Paapu* and *hea*, indistinctness. A mist; fine rain; a fine cloud like fog.

PAA-WA-HA, *s.* *Paa*, tight, and *waha*, mouth. A bridle. *Hal.* 39:1. See KAULA-WAHA.

PAA-WE-LA, *s.* *Paa*, burnt, and *wela*, heat. A burning; a scar from burning. *Isa.* 3:24.

PAA-WE-LA, *adj.* Burnt; scorched, as the skin by the fire; *paawela* kona ili i ke ahi.

PAE, *v.* To flap or shake, as a sail; to turn one side or be loose, as a tooth; as an *adjective*, he niho *pae*, a *loose* tooth.

2. To be carried along by the surf towards the shore; to play on the surf-board; to come to a land, as a boat or canoe; to go ashore from a vessel; to cross a river to the opposite shore. *Ios.* 4:18. To float ashore from the sea; no na laau hao i *pae* mua mai, for the timber with iron that *had* previously *floated ashore.*

3. To lift up; to raise a little.

4. To strip the bark from a tree; to peel off, as the skin of a banana or of a kalo.

5. To strike upon the ear, as a distant sound; to sound, as from a distance.

6. To be published extensively.

7. *Hoo.* To land; to put ashore, as a person or goods from a vessel. 1 *Nal.* 5:9.

PAE, *s.* A cluster; a few; a small company; he pae hao wale, robbers. SYN. with poe and puu.

2. A voice; a sound.

3. A bank of a kalo patch; those parts that are beaten to make them water tight; he mea hana ia ka loi ma na *pae* e pai mua ai—pakui i ka pohaku ma ua mau *pae* la—a paa na *pae* eha.

PAE. A sign of the plural number; as, keia *pae* aina or keia *pae moku*, these islands. *Gram.* § 86 and 92.

PA-E-A, *adj.* Flinty; hard, as a rock. *Isa.* 50:7. Pohaku paea, a carbuncle. *Puk.* 28:17. NOTE.—This word is modern; probably it is the Hawaiian pronunciation for the word *fire* in connection with flint.

PA-E-A, *s.* A flint; a fire stone; he pohaku ahi. See the adjective.

PA-E-A-E-A, *s.* See PAEA. Hardness; severity; cruelty.

2. Conduct contrary to uprightness; ka hana ku like ole me ka pono.

3. The act of catching fish; a iho aku la i ka *paeaea* aweoweo. *Laieik.* 206.

4. The name of a species of fish.

5. Striking for or beckoning to one.

PA-E-A-E-A, *v.* To strike fire, as with steel and flint. *Laieik.* 54.

PA-E-A-E-A, *adj.* Hard; severe; unjust, as a man with his neighbors.

2. Smooth; unruffled, as a smooth sea. See KAIPAEAEA.

PA-E-E, *v.* To peep; to make an unintelligible sound; to gabble; to speak indistinctly; to hear indistinctly; to misunderstand. *Hoo.* To speak so as to conceal the meaning; e hoonalonalo.

PA-E-E, *s.* A bunch of olona; a branch of the olona tree; he apana olona.

PAE-EE, *s.* See PAE. A lying down upon, as one lies down on his surf-board to swim; to lay one's head down on a pillow; he paepae ee, he haiai ulu.

PAE-HI-A, *v.* To thatch; to cover a building by thatching; ke kueneia nei a ke *paehia* nei.

PAE-HU-MU, *adj.* Confining; restraining; e hoopaaia iloko o ka hale *paehumu*, that he should be confined in a *prison house.* *Laieik.* 163.

Pae-kii, *s.* Low clouds; clouds lying on the horizon.

Pa-e-le, *v.* *Pa* and *ele,* black. To be covered with dirt; to besmear; to blacken, as with charcoal; to color the skin black; ua *paeleia* ka hapalua hookahi o ke kanaka a eleele loa; to paint black; e *paele* i ka waa.

Pa-e-le, *s.* A black skin; blackness; a dark color.

Pa-e-le, *adj.* Dirty; besmeared with dirt; black; blackened.

Pae-pae, *v.* To hold or bear up; to support; to sustain. *Puk.* 17:12.

2. To sound; to proclaim; to publish abroad, as a report.

3. To make a great and confused noise; to converse in a loud manner; to gabble; to talk confusedly.

4. To spread; to float off, as a sound.

5. To run along the ground.

Pae-pae, *s.* Any substance upon which another lies to keep it from the ground; a stool; a threshold; a supporter; a prop. 1 *Sam.* 5:4. The plate of a house on which the rafters rest; a pavement of stones.

Pae-pae-ko-mo, *s.* The axle or axle-tree of a wheel; *paepaekomo* i na pokakaa. 1 *Nal.* 7:32, 33.

Pae-pae-pu-ka, *s.* *Paepae* and *puka,* a door-way. A threshold. *Isa.* 6:4. A support or a supporter. 2 *Oihl.* 3:7.

Pae-pae-wae-wae, *s.* A footstool. *Iak.* 2:3.

Pae-pu, *s.* *Pae,* to strike, as a sound, and *pu,* together. The deafening roar of the surf.

2. The setting or placing of things together.

Pae-puu, *s.* The name of several small hills or hillocks standing in a row. See **Lalanipuu.**

Pa-e-wa, *adj.* *Pa* and *ewa,* to crook. Bent; twisted; too short; out of shape.

Pa-e-wa, *s.* Name of one of the cases in Hawaiian grammar. See *Gram.* § 99 and 100. *No* and *na* are its signs.

Pa-e-wa-e-wa, *adj.* Uneven; irregular; crooked.

Pa-e-wa-e-wa, *s.* The fantastic and irregular cutting of the hair formerly practiced on the death of a friend.

Pa-e-wa-e-wa, *v.* To be erroneous or partial in judging or in dealing. *Iak.* 2:4. To be erroneous, unmethodical or one-sided in telling a story or making a report; ma ka *paewaewa* o ka ke alii olelo ana. *Laieik.* 51.

Pai, *v.* To strike or smite with the palm of the hand.

2. E *pai ka lima,* to strike hands, i. e., to take or confirm an agreement. *Puk.* 6:8. E *pai* na lima, a ae na waha, lilo; hence, to make a bargain. *Sol.* 11:15.

3. To strike the hands together expressive of much feeling; a *pai* pu na lima ona, he *smote* his hands one against another.

4. To treat a person harshly or severely; pau ae la lakou i ke *paiia* me ka hewa ole, they were all *hardly treated* without any fault; malama oia i na 'lii, aole *pai* uku i ko lakou aina, he took care of the chiefs, he did not *tax heavily* the land.

5. To strike, i. e., to tax the people or punish them; to lay a tax upon the people for some real or imaginary offense; i ka wa i huhu ai na 'lii i kanaka, o ke *pae* ae la no ia i ka aina, when the chiefs were angry with the people, then they *struck* (taxed) the land.

6. To be bound with one in affection.

7. To appear; to rise up, as out of the water; ike iki lakou ia ia e *pai* wale mai ana no iluna o ka ilikai, he just saw him *rising* above the surface of the sea.

8. To pry up or block up one side of a thing when it is pried up.

9. To stamp; to print; to impress a stamp.

10. To drive or urge one away; e *pai* wale, to exercise in vain; to gain nothing for what one does; a i hopu pu i ka pahu, aole no eo (na kukini). *pai* wale.

11. To stir up sedition; to raise a persecution; *pai* mai la lakou ma ka olelo kaua, they *excited* the people through words of war.

12. To stir up or excite one's desires; *pai* aku la ia i ka makemake nui i na kii.

13. To influence one to evil.

14. To mix together two ingredients, as wine with water. *Isa.* 1:22.

15. To plaster a house; to spread mortar; e *pai* hale.

16. *Hoo.* To strike back; to resist; to revenge; to avenge. *Nah.* 31:2.

17. To punish for some offense; e *hoopai* aku, no ke kaua wale ana o Kahekili ia ia, to *punish* him for Kahekili's making war upon him without cause.

18. To recompense either good or evil; thus, *hoopai* pono, or *hoopai* hewa.

19. To visit or come to one for evil or for good.

20. To administer justice; to requite. *Kanl.* 32:6. To require; to recompense.

21. To end or finish a prayer in the preparation for war.

Pai, *s.* A row; a line.

2. A quantity of food done up in a glob-

ular form in ki leaves; he *pai* ai; a ball; a round loaf of bread; he *pai* palaoa; cakes, &c. *Nah.* 6:15.

3. A cluster or bunch; as, he *pai* maia, a *bunch* of bananas; he pai huawaina, a *bunch* of grapes.

4. A striking; a stamping; an impressing, i. e., a printing, as kapa is printed, or as paper is printed in a press.

5. *Hoo. Hoopai*, a punishment; a judgment. *Puk.* 7:4.

6. A kind of snail shell-fish, said to be poisonous to the touch.

7. A blight; a fading and dying of the leaves of vegetables; the act of decay in vegetables.

8. A shell or cup for scooping up the oopu; he *pai* oopu.

PAI, *s.* A tie or equality of numbers; a drawn game.

PAI, *adj.* Tied up; bound together; connected with; mingled with.

PAI-A, *v.* To wall round; to inclose with a wall, as the body of a house or fort.

2. To be guarded; to be taken care of; to be protected.

PAI-A, *s.* The sides of a house; the surroundings, i. e., the walls of a house. 1 *Sam.* 18:11.

PAI-A, *adj.* Deaf; unable to hear.

PAI-AA, *s. Pai* and *aa*, small roots. The appearance of something not fully developed; *paiaa* koko, the incipient arteries or veins of an embryo branching out from the heart.

2. The small branches of a tree.

3. The branches of the main root of a tree; e oki i ka mole ame ka *paiaa*.

PAI-AI, *s. Pai*, a bundle, and *ai*, food. A bundle of pounded kalo done up in ki leaves in to a round bundle.

PAI-A-U-MA, *v.* To love strongly; to remember with deep and affectionate regret, as one dead; to mourn for; to love and long after the welfare of a friend or a beloved child; to express love strongly, as a wife for a husband; *paiauma* wale aku no i ke aloha i na kane, (the wives of the men who went with Boki) *expressed* unfeigned love for their husbands.

PAI-A-U-MA, *s.* Strong affection; endearing attachment to one dead or long absent; a sorrowing or lamenting the absence of a loved one; a longing after the welfare of one.

PAI-A-U-MA, *adv.* Affectionately; piteously. *Laieik.* 140.

PAI-E-A, *s.* A species of crab with a soft shell; *kuapa*, the hard shell.

PAI-IA, *adj. Pai* and *ia*, passive. Bound up in or mixed together. *Kin.* 44:30.

2. *Pai*, to impress, and *ia*, passive. Impressed; stamped; printed.

PAI-O, *v.* To speak back and forth like persons in a dialogue. See KIKE.

2. To scold back and forth, as two persons.

3. To strive together; to contend; to disagree in opinion. *Kin.* 45:24.

4. To quarrel; to fight with.

5. To turn topsy-turvy; to toss up and down like the sea current.

6. To bend round like a fish-hook.

7. To throw stones back and forth.

PAI-O, *s.* A striving; a quarrel; a strife. 2 *Sam.* 22:14. A combat; a controversy. *Ier.* 25:31.

PAI-O, *adj.* Contentious; disputatious; quarreling.

PAI-U-LA, *s.* Art. ke. A kind of platform used for spreading out *paus*.

PAI-U-LA, *s.* Name of a kind of kapa made by beating up the welus of red kapa with new waoke, which formed a mixture of white and red; kahiko aku la oia i kona mau hookele i na kihei *paiula. Laieik.* 12.

PAI-U-MA-U-MA, *v. Pai*, to strike, and *umauma*, the breast. A play which consisted in striking on the breast; he hula pai ma ka umauma.

PAI-HA-LE, *v.* To thatch houses.

PAI-I-HI, *s.* The tree ohiaha; the bark of the tree used in coloring kapa black; the tree is used for building houses and for fuel.

2. A plant sometimes used for food. See IHI.

PA-I-HI, *adj. Pa* and *ihi*, bark or outside of a vegetable. Clear; unclouded, as the atmosphere.

PA-I-HI-I-HI, *adj.* Neat; tidy.

2. Large; extended; full.

PAI-HO, *v.* To project out beyond, as a broken bone through the flesh.

2. To be crooked outside and not inside.

3. To roll up, as a scroll; to tie up, as a bundle.

PAI-HO, *adj.* Girded, as with a malo; tied up, as a bundle; girded, as one dressed.

PAI-HU-A, *s. Pai*, bundle, and *hua*, fruit. A bundle of fruit.

PAI-HU-A-FI-KU, *s. Paihua* and *fiku*, figs. A bunch of figs. 1 *Sam.* 25:18.

PAI-HU-A-WAI-NA, *s. Pai* and *huawaina*, grapes. A bunch of grapes; *paihuawaina* maloo, a bunch of raisins. 1 *Sam.* 28:18.

Pai-kau, *v.* To exercise with fire-arms.

Pai-kau, *s.* The act of exercising with fire-arms; ao mai la o Vanekouva i ko Kamehameha poe kanaka i ka *paikau,* Vancouver taught Kamehameha's men the *manual exercise.*

Pai-kau-ha-le, *s.* A poor man going from house to house to beg; one wandering from place to place.

Pai-kau-ha-le, *adj.* Wandering about, as a vagabond; having no home.

Pai-kau-lei-a, *s.* *Paikau* and *lei,* a wreath, and *a* for *ia,* passive, wreathed. A woman that puts on a *lei* so as to signify that she is for sale; an abandoned woman going from place to place; a tattler.

Pa-i-ki, *v.* To be cramped; to be confined; to be held close.

Pa-i-ki, *s.* The hollow of the hand; ka poholima.

Pai-ki-ni, *adj.* Bound up; girded; dressed in tight fitting clothes; nani na haumana me na wawae *paikini,* fine looking are the scholars with pants *tight fitting.*

Pai-ko-le, *adj.* See POKOLE. Short; cut off; low.

Pai-ku-mu, *v.* To ask one to go with him to a chief, the one asked to go being familiar with the chief.

Pai-la, *s.* *Eng.* A pile; a heap; he *paila* wahie. NOTE.—A pile of wood in market was formerly a fathom square every way, i. e., a solid fathom; it is now about three-quarters of a cord.

Pai-la-ni, *v.* To praise; to extol; to rejoice in; e hoonani.

Pai-le, *s.* The uncomfortable feeling produced by tattooing the face.

Pa-i-li, *v.* To touch the skin; to slap on the skin with the hand.

2. To stick to the skin, as some animals in the sea when bathing; he aloha ka ia *paili* kanaka o Kawainui.

Pai-lo-lo, *s.* The name of a channel between Maui and Molokai.

Pai-lo-ta, *s.* *Eng. Art.* ke. A pilot; one who directs vessels into ports and out of them.

Pai-lu-a, *v.* To feel sickness at the stomach.

2. To be disgusted at a thing.

3. *Hoo.* To loathe; to abhor. *Puk.* 7:18. To be greatly displeased with; to be an abomination or loathing. *Oihk.* 11:23.

4. To vomit; to retch with nausea.

Pai-lu-a, *s.* Sickness; sea-sickness; nausea. *Hoo.* Sickness of the stomach.

FIG. That which causes disagreeable sensations; that which is disagreeable to one; an abomination. *Puk.* 8:22.

2. The name of a wind from Kamiloloa.

Pai-ma, *s.* To be sea-sick.

Pai-ma-lau, *s.* A living creature having

paimalau

a sting in its tail, and floating on the ocean like the auwaalalua; he wahi mea huelo awa e lana ana ma ka moana me he auwaalalua la.

2. A place in the ocean where the water is calm and clear, sought by those who are fishing for the *aku.*

Pa-i-na, *v.* To eat; to dine. *Kin.* 27:4. To eat; to feed upon. *Scl.* 15:14.

2. To ring; to squeak; to sound, as in tearing or breaking a thing.

Pai-na, *s.* A land; an island.

2. A part separated or broken off.

3. A meal; an eating.

4. The Cape gooseberry.

5. The sound made in tearing a piece of cloth or in breaking a cord.

6. The sound of a flea hopping on a piece of paper.

7. *Eng.* A pine or fir tree. 2 *Oihl.* 2:8. Laau *paina.* 2 *Oihl.* 3:5.

8. Fine white cloth; he lole keokeo makalii; also, broad cloth; paa *paina,* a suit of broad cloth.

Pa-i-na, *adj.* Rotten, as cloth; brittle; easily torn or broken. See POHAEHAE.

Pai-ni-ki, *v.* *Pai* and *niki,* to tie a knot. To dress one up with close fitting garments; to go buttoned up tightly, as a dandy.

Pai-pai, *v.* See PAI, to strike. To rouse; to excite; to put in mind, as one careless or indifferent.

2. To strike with the palm of the hand.

3. To prune; to lop off limbs; to pluck leaves. *Oihk.* 25:3.

4. To chastise; to correct; to smite. *Isa.* 53:4.

5. To bolster up, as a sick man. 1 *Nal.* 22:35.

6. To clap the hands as a sign of rejoicing; a *paipai* lakou i na lima. 2 *Nal.* 11:12.

7. To peel off, as the bark of a tree or

the skin of an animal; to peel off; to separate the flesh from the bones.

8. To act against another thing, as the under jaw against the upper in eating or speaking; to strike against so as to make a noise.

9. *Hoo.* To swell out as if stuffed with food; to strut with sufficiency; to be bold; to dare.

PAI-PAI, *s.* A correction; a chastisement. *Kanl.* 11:2.

2. *Paipai* manao, a remembrancer; a memorial. *Puk.* 30:16.

3. The act of pounding kapa as done by women.

4. Name of a medicine made of the leaves of the ipuawaawa, a kind of gourd; the waiiki diluted with water.

5. A threshold of a door. *Lunk.* 19:27.

6. The name of a kind of hula; he *paipai* kekahi hula.

PAI-PAI, *adj.* He pahi *paipai*, a pruning knife; mea *paipai* waina, any article used in dressing grape vines. See *Isa.* 61:5.

PAI-PAI-KU-KUI, *s.* The name of a species of kapa made on Molokai; its color was pale yellow; he kapa ano like me ka *paipaikukui.*

PAI-PAI-LI-MA, *v.* *Paipai* and *lima*, hand. To clap the hands as a sign of joy. *Isa.* 55:12.

PAI-PA-I-NA, *v.* See **PAINA.** To eat; to take food.

PAI-PAI-NA-HA, *s.* A cloak; a garment; a kapa.

PAI-PA-LA-PA-LA, *s.* *Pai*, to print, and *palapala*, printed or written paper. A printing press.

PA-I-PU, *s.* A set of empty calabashes.

2. A calabash for packing kapas or clothes to keep them dry on a canoe.

3. Basins used as containers. 1 *Nal.* 7:40.

4. A bowl for containing food. *Ier.* 52:18.

Olepe waha *paipu* Kohala na ka ino,
Me he wahine hili haehae la ka makani,
Aole ui hele wale o Kohala,
Ipu hahao ka ipu haa na ka makani.

PA-I-PU, *s.* Name of a hula or dance.

PAI-PU-NA-HE-LE, *s.* Name of a dance.

PAI-WA-LE, *s.* A drawn game, or battle when neither party conquers; ina like pu ka ikaika o na moa, he *paiwale.*

PA-O, *v.* *Pa*, to strike, and *o*, point. To peck with the bill, as a bird; *pao* iho la ka manu, he elepaio i ka huewai o ke kanaka a puka.

2. To dig out with a chisel; to dig, as in a rock. *Isa.* 22:16.

3. To dig down in the ground; to dig deeply, as in digging a deep pit.

PA-O, *s.* An arch of a bridge; the bridge itself; a prop; *art.* ke.

2. An oven or shallow pit; a place dug out.

3. An artificial cavern.

4. A concealed or hidden pit, or a pit to hide things in; he lua huna; a gutter or drain, as that of a cellar stoned in and buried under ground.

5. A species of sweet potato.

6. A species of small and singular looking fish.

PA-O-A, *v.* See **PA** and **OA,** destitute. To be empty; to be destitute; to return without obtaining the object sought; to return destitute, as one who catches nothing at fishing; ua *paoa* ka makou huakai, our company *did not obtain* what they went for,

Paoa wale hoi au—e—
Aole moewaa o ka po—e.

PA-O-A, *s.* Destitution; having obtained nothing after making an effort.

2. Name of a small kind of fish.

PA-O-A, *adj.* Destitute from not having obtained, not from having lost; ua hoikaika, ua imi, a *paoa* no.

PA-O-A, *s.* An unpleasant odor; a bad smell.

PA-O-A, *adj.* Unpleasant to the smell; bad smelling.

PA-OI-OI, *adj.* *Pa* and *oioi*, exceeding. Out of the common order or practice; ungrammatical; incorrect in speaking.

PA-OO, *s.* A species of potato. See **PAO** 5.

PA-OO, *adj.* Of or belonging to the *ama*, a species of sweet potato; ikaika i ka ama *paoo.*

PA-OO,
PA-OO-LE-KAI,
PA-OO-PU-HI, } *s.* The names of several species of fish.
PA-OU-OU,
PA-O-KAU-I-LA,

PA-O-KEE, *v.* To treat one's friend badly; to condemn one's companion; to deal crookedly or perversely with one's friend.

PA-O-KEE, *s.* A slanderer; a detractor; a perverse person.

PA-O-KEE, *adj.* Slanderous; railing; perverse.

PA-O-KO-KE, *s.* The breaking off of one's friendship through fear or rivalship in the estimation of a chief; ka *paokoke* i na io o Hana.

PA-O-LA, *s.* *Pa* and *ola*, recovery from sickness. The opposite of *pamake*; he ola wale no ka mai, aole pamake iki o na kanaka.

PA-O-LI-VE, *s.* *Pa*, fence, and *olive*

(*Eng.*), olive. An olive yard. 1 *Sam.* 8:14.

Pa-o-lo, *s.* See Puolo. A bundle; something folded and carried under the arm or in the hand; i loaa kahi wahi ma ko kakou poholima, a he wahi *paolo* paha.

Pa-o-mo-ni, *v.* To contend, as two parties for victory.

Pa-o-na, *s. Eng.* A pound in money; twenty shillings.

2. A pound in weight. *Oihk.* 19:35.

3. An instrument to weigh with; a balance; scales, &c. This is sometimes written *pauna.*

Pa-o-na, *v.* To weigh; to use the instruments of weighing. *Oihk.* 19:36.

Pa-o-ni, *v. Pa* and *oni,* to move. To envy; to be moved by envy.

Pa-o-ni-o-ni, *v.* Lit. To move; to struggle, as an infant either before or after it is born; hence,

2. To struggle against a person, or against adverse circumstances.

3. To withstand; to contend, as two parties for supremacy.

4. To resist one's influence; to envy.

Pa-o-ni-o-ni, *s.* Envy. *Oih.* 13:45. The act of envying. 1 *Kor.* 3:3. The expression of envy by defaming the envied person.

Pa-o-ni-o-ni, *adv.* Struggling for supremacy; ke haele nei no o manao ole me manao, aole i oi aku, aole i emi mai, noho *paonioni* no laua a hiki mai i keia la.

Pa-o-no, *adv.* See Pa, distributive particle. *Pa* and *ono,* six. By sixes; six-fold; six times; six at once. *Isa.* 6:2.

Pao-pao, *v.* See Pao, to peck; to strike at. To beat or bruise the head.

2. To beat or bruise generally. *Isa.* 53:5. To smite. *Puk.* 3:20.

Pao-pao, *s.* A strife; a beating. *Puk.* 21:25. *Paopaoia,* beaten; bruised. *Oihk.* 22:24.

2. The name of a species of fish.

Pao-pao, *adj.* Bound, as a prisoner; one in bondage. See Pio.

Pao-pao-no-ho-ni-a, *s.* Envy; jealousy; ill-will; living with or indulging in bad feelings towards others.

Pa-o-da, *s. Eng.* Gun-powder. See also Pauda.

Pau, *v.* To all; to be all; to be entire or complete to whatever it refers.

2. To be spent; to be finished or completed.

3. To consume; to pass away. Pass. *Pauia* or *pauhia.*

4. *Hoo.* To destroy; to consume; to put an end to. *Nah.* 14:35.

5. To make an end of; to finish, as an appointed work. *Ios.* 5:8.

6. To end; to terminate; to make up; to fill up, as time; to fullfill, as a specified time. *Kin.* 29:27.

Pau, *s.* A kind of poor kapa, not white nor black, nor any definite color. It takes *ke* for its article.

2. Ink for writing.

3. The black smut of a lampwick; he wahi eleele no ke kukui.

4. A vault; a stone house; lua *pau.*

Pau, *adj.* All; *a pau loa;* all; every one; everything.

Pau, *adv.* Entirely; wholly; completely. Note.—Use has rendered the meaning of this word like the French *tout,* as in *tout le mond,* all the world, everybody, when only a small part is intended.

Pa-u, *s.* The principal garment of a Hawaiian female in former times, consisting of a number of kapas, generally five, wound around the waist and reaching to the knee more or less.

Pa-u, *v.* To put or bind on a *pa-u.*

Pau-a, *s.* Name of a species of oyster; a species of fish; he wahi ano pipi kai; he wahi ia, he papaua.

Pau-a-a-li-na, *v.* To be heavy to carry; to be hard to bear, as a burden; e *pauaalina* me he pookaeo la.

Pau-a-hi, *s. Pau* and *ahi,* fire. Destruction of anything by fire; generally applied to a house, viz.: *a house burning.*

2. Soot from a fire or lamp.

Pau-a-ho, *v. Pau* and *aho,* breath. To be out of breath.

2. To be discouraged; to give up the pursuit of a thing; to forsake it.

3. To be faint-hearted; to be discouraged. 1 *Oihl.* 22:13. To be weary on account of trouble. *Kin.* 27:46.

4. *Hoo.* To labor in vain. *Kin.* 19:11. To despair of success. *Kekah.* 2:20.

Pau-a-ho, *adj.* Breathless. Fig. Faint-hearted; giving up; yielding; wanting perseverance.

Pau-a-ka, *v.* To be weary; to be fatigued with carrying a burden or with hard work.

2. To work without reward; e hana me ka uku ole.

3. *Hoo.* To deride; to reproach one for laboring to no purpose or without reward; e puali, e pauakaaka, e puakaaka.

Pau-a-ka, *adj.* Crooked; deceitful or unjust; lying or deceiving, as giving away what belongs to another.

Pau-a-ka-a-ka, *v.* See **Pauaka** above. To laugh at or ridicule one for laboring without wages.

Pau-a-li, } *v.* To be crooked, per-
Pau-a-li-a-li, } verse or wicked; applied to chiefs and people.

2. E puali me he poo maia la, e pauaa-lina me he pookaeo la.

Pau-a-nei-nei, *v.* See **Pau** and **Neinei,** to shrink up. To shrink; to be too little; to be small.

Pau-a-ni-hi, *s.* Young kalo; the tops of kalo. See **Oninihi.**

Pau-o-hii-a-ka, *s.* Name of a vine like the koali, used as a cathartic medicine.

2. Name of a species of bird.

Pau-o-no, *v. Pau* and *ono,* sweet. To be finished or gone; done complete; applied to food fully cooked; *pauono kahi puaa a kakou, aole malena,* our piece of pork *is finely cooked,* it is not burnt.

Pau-u, *s.* The young of the ulua, a species of fish.

Pau-ha-ka-ki, *adj.* Full; well fed; plump; me kona kino ikaika, puipui *pau-hakaki* no hoi.

Pa-u-ha-na, *adj.* Constantly at work; e hana mau.

Pau-he-o-he-o, *v.* To be small, as a small place between two larger; applied to many things.

2. A person returning from fishing without any is *pauheoheo.*

Pau-hi-a, *v.* Passive of *pau.* To be alike; to be all in the same condition; to be all together. NOTE.—The signification is varied by the words following; as, ua *pauhia* lakou i ka hiamoe, they *were all* asleep. 1 *Sam.* 26:12. Ua *pauhia* mai au e ka makemake nui, I *was overwhelmed* with a strong desire. *Laieik.* 144.

2. To be overtaken by evil; to suffer loss or damage; to be overtaken by any calamity so that there is a general suffering.

3. To sleep soundly; to dream; to have a vision.

Pau-hu, *s.* Name of a shell-fish, a species of the leho.

Pau-hu, *adj.* Small; feeble about the chest and shoulders; panuu, pohuku.

Pa-u-hu-u-hu, *s.* The name of a fish. See **Pauhu,** *s.*

Pau-ke, *v. Pau* and *ke,* to press against. To slander; to belie; to tell lies about one in order to bring him into fault.

Pau-ki-ki, *v.* To be excited; to make a great noise.

2. To slip up; to fall.

3. To all cry out.

Pau-ki-lo, *v.* To know as a *kilo* is supposed to do.

Pau-ki-no, *adj.* Destroyed, as the body of a person by a shark or by fire. NOTE.— *Paukino* is not often used, but is sometimes used for *paumako.*

Pau-ku, *v.* To curve, as the curve of a canoe.

2. To be divided into bits or small parts. *Mel. Sol.* 1:11.

3. To cut up into short pieces.

Pau-ku, *s.* A bit of a thing; a piece cut off; a fraction; a portion.

2. *Specifically,* a verse or stanza of a hymn; a verse or small portion of Scripture; a section of a book. *Laieik.* 111.

3. A small lot of land next less in size than a *moo.*

4. An age; a period of time.

5. The length from the ends of the fingers of one hand to the elbow of the opposite arm when both are extended.

6. In *geometry,* a cylinder. *Ana Hon.* 29.

Pau-la, } *s. Eng.* Gun-powder. See
Pau-da, } **Paoda.**

2. Sand, i. e., *one a,* burning sand: so gunpowder was called at first by Hawaiians.

Pau-la, *s.* A full grown tree when the timber becomes red; he laau oo a ula.

Pau-la-lii-lii, *s.* The watch-word given by Kalanimoku before the battle of Kuamoo.

Pau-le-le, *v.* To trust in; to lean or rely upon; to believe or credit what one has said; to put confidence in; to desire with the whole heart; to believe fully.

Pau-le-le, *s.* Confidence; faith. *Luk.* 7:9.

Pa-u-li, *adj. Pa* and *uli,* blue. Dark colored; blue, as the sea; *pauli* ke kai.

Pa-u-li-u-li, *adj.* Dark blue, as the sky in the evening near the horizon—one of the signs of a kaikoo or high surf.

Pa-u-li-hi-a, *adj.* Accustomed; skillful on account of being accustomed.

Pau-li-hi-ua, *s.* A great thickness of dark, heavy, shining clouds.

He *paulihiua* na ka ua haoa,
He loko papohaku na ke kioao,
Na kuu anae no Lele aanae—
Aia la iluna o Waipuhia
Me au aholehole i Lanihuli.

Pau-li-hi-ua, *adj.* Dark; black with thick darkness.

Kuu pae opua i Awalau,
Kualau ka ua koko,
Paulehiawa (paulihiua) pa ka hoolua,

Pa ke kau malie Kona ua lai lua,
Haki kau hola kahelaka nalu o Kapaelauhala,
Hoaiai ke kaiko o Maliu—e—
Ko maliu ole i ka uolo—e.

Pau-li-na-li-na, *v.* To gird up tightly; to tie fast.

Pau-ma, *s.* *Eng.* A pump; he omowai; he omoliu.

Pau-ma, *v.* To draw; to move along; to push.

2. To turn, as a person turns a canoe to the wind to empty it of water.

Pau-maa-le-a, *adj.* *Pau* and *maalea,* skill; cunning. Given to thought; accustomed to reflection; giving to devising and planning.

Pau-ma-e-le, *v.* *Pau* and *maele,* dirty. To defile; to pollute; to be all over polluted. *Isa.* 59:3. *Hoo.* To defile; to make dirty. *Mel. Sol.* 5:3. To be soft; to be moist; to be unctuous.

Pau-ma-e-le, *adj.* Dirty; defiled; obscured by something black.

2. All over defiled; very filthy.

3. Fig. Sunk in sin or moral defilement; heart unrenewed.

Pau-mau-noo-noo, *s.* A keep-sake; a memento.

Pau-ma-ko, *v.* *Pau* and *mako.* To cry for grief; to be sad for the loss of a friend; to writhe in mental agony; to exhibit deep grief; to be cast down; to be down-hearted; to be disquieted. *Hal.* 42:5, 11.

Pau-ma-ko, *s.* Deep grief; a mourning for the loss of a friend; heaviness of the eyes with sorrow; the being overwhelmed with sorrow. *Hal.* 61:2.

Pau-ma-ko-ko, *s.* Great sorrow; the eyes heavy with sorrow.

Pa-u-me-u-me, *s.* The name of a game.

Pa-u-mi, *dis. part.* Ten apiece; ten each; *paumi* ka apa o kahi, some had *ten* pieces of cloth *each.*

Pau-na-kau-li-ke, *s.* Scales, as from the flesh; baldness. *Isa.* 40:12.

Pau-nei-nei, *v.* To be all moved or excited; to make a great noise; to slip up; to fall; to cry out.

Pau-ni-ni-u, *v.* *Pau* and *niniu.* See Niu, to whirl. To turn about, as a top; *pauniniu* ka lemu o ka laau.

Pau-pau, *v.* See Pau, to cease. To make an end of; to break off. *Hoo.* To cease doing a thing; e *hoopaupau* i kela kamailio keia kamailio e lealea ai, *cease* all conversation that leads to licentiousness.

Pau-pau, *s.* *Hoo.* A breaking off from any practice; a putting an end to it.

Pau-pau, *adj.* Bad; evil; dirty; old or worn out, as mats or kapas; *paupau* kahi kapa; filthy; dirty; unclean.

Pau-pau-a-ho, *v.* *Paupau* and *aho,* breath. To be out of breath; to pant for breath.

2. To be faint-hearted; to give over an undertaking without sufficient effort. *Hoik.* 2:3.

3. To be discouraged through fear. *Ier.* 4:31.

4. To be faint through great exertion. 2 *Sam.* 21:15.

5. *Hoo.* To weary; to trouble; to provoke. *Isa.* 7:13.

Pau-pau-a-ho, *adj.* Breathless; panting for breath, as a dying person.

2. Giving up a pursuit; discouraged; faint-hearted.

Pau-pa-e-le, *adj.* *Pau* and *paele,* defiled. Filthy; defiled; dirty. See Paumaele.

Pau-pu, *adv.* *Pau* and *pu,* together. All together; all in one condition; together in the same circumstances; *paupu* kakou malalo o ka make, we are all alike under sentence of death.

Pau-wa, *s.* Name of a species of fish. See Papaua.

Pau-da, *s.* *Eng.* Gun-powder; variously written *paola, paula* and *paoda.*

Pa-ha, *s.* Pride; haughtiness of bearing. See Pahaha.

Pa-ha, *s.* The name of a plant, the leaf of which is used for food during a scarcity; in some places it is called *kapala.*

2. A surf board; he papa heenalu.

Pa-ha, *v.* To be proud; to boast; to be lofty in one's bearing. See Pahapaha.

Pa-ha, *adv.* Perhaps; it may be so, &c.; expressive of doubt. Note.—It is often used when there is very little or no doubt; a frequent expletive; *ae paha,* yes perhaps, a polite way of assenting to one's opinion while the speaker withholds full belief, or even holds to an opposite opinion.

Pa-haa, } *adj.* Pa and *haa,* low.
Pa-haa-haa, } Very short; low; humble.

Pa-haa-haa, *s.* Shortness; bluntness; rotundity.

Pa-hao, *s.* *Pa,* pan, and *hao,* iron. An iron pan or plate.

Pa-hao, *v.* In a *game,* to lay down your own with another's, and take up at random in order to get a better.

Pa-hao-hao, *v.* Pa and *haohao,* to wonder at. To have another form; to be transfigured. *Luk.* 9:29.

2. To change one's appearance externally; to be changeable.

3. To change one's character.

4. *Hoo.* To transform. *Rom.* 12:2.

Pa-hao-hao, *adj.* Changed in appearance; transfigured; having another external form.

2. That which cannot be laid hold of; not material; not substantial, as a ghost; he mea *pahaohao,* a *bodiless* thing.

3. Wavering; fickle; unsteady, as in feeling or conduct; in doubt or suspense; undecided.

Pa-hau, *v.* To embezzle in a second-hand way; applied to property which is to be distributed, as fish, kapa, &c., among the people of a chief.

Pa-hau-na, *s.* The name of a heiau near Lamaloloa in Hamakua, Hawaii; he heiau kahiko kela mai ka po mai, a hiki i keia manawa. *Laieik.* 27.

Pa-ha-ha, *s.* Name of a species of fish.

Pa-ha-ha, *v.* *Pa* and *haha,* to strut. To strut; to walk about proudly; to play the cock-turkey.

Pa-ha-ha, *s.* A large broad swelling of the neck.

Pa-ha-ha, *adj.* Broad, full and plump, as the neck when one has the mumps.

2. Proud; high-minded; disdainful.

Pa-ha-le, *s.* *Pa* and *hale,* house. An inclosure in front of a house; a court yard; the space around the house inclosed by a fence.

Pa-ha-ne-ri, *distrib. adv.* *Pa,* distributive particle, and *haneri* (*Eng.*), a hundred. By the hundred; a hundred fold; a hundred times.

Pa-ha-pa-ha, *s.* See **Pahaha,** *adj.* Affected stiffness in the gait and address of a person; strutting; me ka *pahapaha* i hele mai ai.

2. A kind of sea-weed; he lipaha, he limu.

Pa-ha-pa-ha, *v.* See **Paha** and **Pahaha,** *adj.* To gird one's self up; to vaunt in fine clothes; to be proud; to boast; *pahapaha* iho la kekahi poe me ka noonoo ole i ka mea e oluolu ai.

Pa-he, *adj.* Soft; easy; flexible.

Pa-he-a-he-a, *s.* *Pa* and *hea,* to call. The voice of whispering like a ghost; a small, thin voice just audible.

Pa-hee, *v.* *Pa* and *hee,* to slip. To slip; to slide, as the feet. *Hal.* 17:5. *Hoo.* To cause to slide; hence; to fall. *Kanl.* 32:35. To let or cause to flow, as blood; mai *hoopahee* koko.

2. To play at the game called *pahee;* ua pono ka *pahee,* no ka mea me ka ikaika nui e *pahee* ai, a ua pono no ke kino ma ia paani.

Pa-hee, *s.* Smooth cloth; silk.

2. The name of a game which consists in sliding a stick either on grass or gravel. See the verb.

3. Slipperiness; smoothness. *Hal.* 55:21.

4. A smooth place.

5. Name of a region on the side of the mountains next below the *ilima.*

Pa-hee, *adj.* Smoothed; polished; slippery; shining, as a polished surface; smooth, as a person without hair. *Kin.* 27:11.

Pa-hee-hee, *adj.* Slippery; liable to fall. *Hal.* 73:18. Muddy, as a road.

Pa-he-le, *v.* To take in a snare; to insnare. *Kekah.* 9:12. Hoo. To be caught in a snare. *Isa.* 28:13. To be insnared. *Isa.* 42:22.

Pa-he-le, *s.* A noose for catching animals; a snare. *Isa.* 8:14.

2. Deceit; treachery; a malama ia oe iho i na *pahele* o ko Hawaii nei.

3. Applied to the deceit of an enemy. *Ios.* 23:13.

Pa-he-le, *adj.* Kahi puka *pahele* ma kahi ana i makemake ai e hei.

Pa-he-lo, *v.* To slip; to slide; to slip and fall.

2. To throw a spear.

Pa-he-lo, *s.* A slipping; a sliding.

Pa-he-ma-he-ma, *adj.* *Pa* and *hemahema,* awkward. Ignorant; awkward in the use of language; ungrammatical.

Pa-he-mo, *v.* *Pa* and *hemo,* to loosen. To loosen; to set or let loose.

2. To slip, as one walking; o naele auanei kakou a *pahemo* auanei a haule ilalo.

3. To slip off, as an axe from the helve. *Hoo.* The same.

Pa-he-pa-he, *adj.* Soft; flexible; rotten; lazy. See **Pa** and **Hepa,** lazy.

Pa-hi, *s.* A knife; any cutting instrument of the knife kind; *pahi* kaua, a sword; *pahi* pelu, a jack-knife, &c. See the compounds.

Pa-hi, *s.* In *Tahitian,* a canoe or ship; no ka mea, aia malaila (ma Tahiti) ka waa nui, he *pahi* ka inoa. *D. Malo* 3:20.

Pa-hi, *v.* Lit. To knife, i. e., to cut a piece of meat thin as a knife; e oki lahilahi i ka io.

2. To stand up on edge.

3. E kulepelepe, e hoolepe.

Pa-hi-a, *int. adv.* *Pa* and *hia,* how many? How many fold? how many to each?

PA-HI-A, *v.* To jump in an oblique manner from a perpendicular height into the water, so that in rising to the surface, the feet come up first.

PA-HI-A, *s.* A mistake; a slipping; a falling.

PA-HI-A-HI-A, *v.* See PAHIA. To slip; to slide; to fall down.

PA-HI-O, *v.* *Pa* and *hio,* to lean. To lean over; to bend over in walking; to move, as a weak person.

PA-HI-O, *adj.* Tall and slender, as a man; leaning over, as a house; stooping, as a person.

PA-HI-OI, *s.* *Pahi* and *oi,* sharp. A sharp knife. *Ios.* 5:3.

PA-HI-OI-LU-A, *s.* *Pahi* and *olo,* to vibrate. A saw, so called from its motion in using. *2 Sam.* 12:13.

PA-HI-U-HI-U, *s.* *Art.* ke. The name of a game like the konane.

PA-HI-U-HI-U, *v.* To move by jumping, as one does in playing konane. See KO-NANE.

PA-HI-U-MI-U-MI, *s.* *Pahi* and *umiumi,* beard. A beard knife, i. e., a razor. See PAHIKAHI.

PA-HI-HA-HAU, *s.* *Pahi* and *hahau,* to strike. A knife to strike with, i. e., a sword.

PA-HI-KAU-A, *s.* *Pahi* and *kaua,* war. A sword; a war knife. FIG. Power; oppressive power. *Kin.* 27:40.

PA-HI-KA-HI, *s.* *Pahi* and *kahi,* to cut. A razor. *Isa.* 7:20. See PAHIUMIUMI.

PA-HI-KA-KI-WI, *s.* *Pahi* and *kakiwi,* bent. A crooked knife; a cutlass; a sickle, &c. *Kanl.* 23:26.

PA-HI-KU, *dist. adv.* *Pa* and *hiku,* seven. Seven-fold; seven times; by sevens. *Kin.* 7:2. He uku *pahiku,* seven-fold punishment.

PA-HI-LAU, *s.* A falsehood; an untruth; o ka like ole o ka olelo me ka oiaio.

PA-HI-LI, *v.* *Pa* and *hili,* to turn; to twist. To blow on different sides, as a flickering wind; *pahili* ka pea i ka makani. Ke *pahili* mai nei ka makani.

PA-HI-LO-KE-A, *s.* *Pahi* and *lokea,* white. A long knife with a white handle. See LOKEA.

PA-HI-LO-LO, *s.* False; untrue; deceitful; aole ka he *pahilolo.*

PA-HI-LO-LO, *adj.* Tall; strutting; proud in one's movements.

PA-HI-MA-KA-LU-A, *s.* *Pahi* and *maka,* edge, and *lua,* two. A double-edged sword or knife.

PA-HI-PA, *s.* *Pa,* yard, and *hipa* (*Eng.*),

sheep. A yard for sheep; a sheep fold. 2 *Sam.* 7:8.

PA-HI-PAI-PAI, *s.* *Pahi* and *paipai,* to prune. A pruning knife. *Isa.* 2:4.

PA-HI-PA-HI-LI-MA, *s.* Name of an ancient play or pastime.

PA-HI-PE-LU, *s.* *Pahi* and *pelu,* to double over. A jack-knife; a pen-knife; any shut knife.

PA-HI-POO-MU-KU, *s.* A knife like a razor; a butcher's knife.

PA-HI-WA-KA-WA-KA, *s.* *Pahi* and *waka-waka,* shining. A polished blade, as a saw, a sword; a flaming sword. *Kin.* 3:24.

PA-HO, *v.* See POHO. To sink; to sink down, as in water or mud; to be out of sight under water; e nalo iloko o ka wai; to settle down in a miry place; e napoo i kahi nenelu.

2. To swim. *Isa.* 25:11. Mea *paho,* a swimmer.

3. To slip off; to slide away, &c. See PAHOLO.

PA-HO, *adj.* Sinking; settling down; pohi, emi, piho.

PA-HO-A, *s.* A sharp stone; a broken piece of a stone with a sharp edge.

2. A short wooden dagger; oo iho la laua ia ia i ka *pahoa,* they two pierced him with a *pahoa* (short wooden sword.) Hookoke ia Lono me ka *pahoa,* he drew near to Captain Cook with a *pahoa.*

PA-HO-E, *s.* A fleet of canoes fishing for the malolo, flying-fish.

PA-HO-E-HO-E, *s.* Smooth shinging lava; flat unbroken lava; he *pahoehoe* a Pele.

PA-HO-E-HO-E-PE-LE, *s.* Name of the hooks used in catching the sea-turtle.

PA-HO-O-LA, *s.* *Pa* and *hoola,* a single kapa. A remnant; a piece; a worthless piece. See PAHOLA. SYN. with pawelu.

PA-HOO-LA-PA-LA-PA, *s.* *Pa,* pan, and *hoolapalapa,* to boil or fry. A frying-pan.

PA-HO-LA, *v.* *Pa* and *hola,* to poison fish. To render useless; to be inactive; to be without effect.

PA-HO-LA, *s.* That which is made useless, ineffectual or of no account; ua hoolilo i ka Olelo a ke Akua i *pahola,* a i pawelu, a i mea ole, i mea lapuwale.

PA-HO-LA-HO-LA, *v.* *Pa* and *holahola.* To poison fish with the auhuhu.

PA-HO-LE, *v.* To peel off, as the skin.

2. To rub; to polish.

PA-HO-LE-HO-LE, *s.* *Pa* and *holehole,* to rub off the skin. A rubbing of the skin; a breaking of the skin; o ka *paholehole* o ka ili; hilahila ino ka poe hana pela.

PA-HO-LO, *v.* See PAHO. To sink in the water or mud.

2. To plunge down out of sight; to drown; to be overwhelmed. 1 *Tim.* 6:9.

3. To fall down.

4. To slip off the handle, as an axe, or off from the finger, as a ring or thimble.

5. *Hoo.* To throw into the sea.

PA-HO-LO-HO-LO, *v.* See PAHOLO. To slip off; to let loose; to be separated from.

PA-HO-NO, *v.* *Pa* and *hono,* to stitch. To sew up, as a rent; to join two pieces of kapa or cloth by sewing; to stitch together.

PA-HO-NO-IA, *adj.* See HONO. Sewed; mended, as old garments. *Ios.* 9:4.

PA-HU, *s.* A barrel, cask, box, chest, &c. NOTE.—A *pahu* was originally a hollow cocoanut or other tree with a shark skin drawn over one end and used for a drum; hence anything hollow and giving a sound when struck is a *pahu.*

2. A coffin. *Kin.* 50:26.

3. A hole dug as a landmark. See the compounds.

4. The name of a species of fish forbidden to women to eat under the kapu system.

PA-HU, *v.* To push or shove on end.

2. To push over; to push down. FIG. To overthrow, as an enemy. 2 *Oihl.* 18:10. To overpower; to tread down, as opposition. *Hal.* 44:5.

3. To burst forth; to run out, as a liquid; to gush or flow out.

4. To burst forth with a noise; to break suddenly; to burst, as a boil.

5. To dig holes for planting.

6. To fall down.

7. To strike or pound. See PAOPAO.

8. To cut, as in bleeding.

9. To blunt; to cut off the end of a thing; to cut into.

10. To throw, as a spear.

11. To stuff food into a person's mouth.

PA-HU, *s.* Small kalo stinted with weeds.

2. The name of a fish.

3. The name of a species of fish net; he upena *pahu.*

PA-HU, *adj.* Round and smooth, as a bald head; applied to a *hula,* hula *pahu.*

PA-HU-A, *v.* To dance; to go through the evolutions of dancing.

2. To beat against the wind, as a ship.

3. To fall off, as a ship sailing against the wind.

4. To refuse to go or to do a thing; to be stubborn; to be angry.

PA-HU-I-HU-I, *v.* See HIU and HIUHIU. To play at a game; to play for pleasure; e hoopiopio, e hoomake i kekahi pohaku me ka hele ana, e kaina.

PA-HU-I-HU-I, *s.* The name of a game or pastime.

PA-HU-U-ME, *s.* *Pahu* and *ume,* to draw out. A bureau; a chest of drawers; a drawer from a larger chest or box.

PA-HU-HO-I-KE, *s.* *Pahu* and *hoike,* to show. The ark of the testimony, so translated from *Puk.* 26:33 and other places.

PA-HU-HO-PU, *s.* The name of a goal where the race-course stopped, opposite to the *pahuku,* where the race commenced; a kukuluia ka laau me ka lepa ma ka *pahuhopu.*

PA-HU-HU, *v.* See PAHU, *v.* To gush out, as blood from a wound; hahau iho la ka moli, *pahuhu* ae la ke koko, the instrument strikes, the blood *flows out.* See MOLI.

PA-HU-HU, *s.* A species of fish; the young of the huhu.

PA-HU-HU-LA, *s.* A kind of drum used at hulas in former times; it was covered with shark skin.

PA-HU-KA-LA, *s.* Name of one of the mock-fights formerly practiced in keeping up the war spirit; he kaua *pahukala* kahi inoa o keia kaua.

PA-HU-KA-NA-WAI, *s.* *Pahu* and *kanawai,* law. The ark of the testimony. *Puk.* 30:6. See PAHUHOIKE above.

PA-HU-KA-NI, *s.* *Pahu* and *kani,* to sound. A drum; a bass viol; a music box. *Kin.* 31:27. Any musical intrument of the pulsatile kind.

PA-HU-KA-PU, *s.* *Pahu* and *kapu,* prohibited. LIT. A sacred box. A sanctuary; a place consecrated to a particular use. *Puk.* 15:17. A place where it was kapu or forbidden to go or to pass. *Laieik.* 101. Some sign or signal was generally put up.

PA-HU-KU, *v.* To turn back an enemy and make the pursuers retreat.

2. To be cut off short; to be round.

PA-HU-KU, *s.* The reserve of an army; a reinforcement that supports the vanguard party and repels the enemy.

2. A soft yielding mass; a round mass.

3. A stick or goal erected at the beginning of a race; hele aku la ua mau kanaka elua a hiki i ka *pahuku.*

PA-HU-KU, *adj.* Short; round. See POHUKU.

PA-HU-LA, *v.* *Pa* and *hula,* to dance. To dance; to hula, i. e., to sing and dance.

PA-HU-LA, *s.* A dance. See HULA.

Pa-hu-lu, *s.* Potatoes of the second growth.

2. A *papu* part of the sea which is much used; he kai kapu, i hoonuaia.

Pa-hu-lu, *s.* Name of an ancient god who lived in the hole of a certain rock on Kauai; he was killed by Kaululaau, a chief from Maui.

2. Name of the goddess who conceived and brought forth Lanai; he akua hapai no Lanai.

Pa-hu-lu-lu, *adj.* Somewhat rainy; a little cloudy and rainy or dripping; not entirely clear.

Pa-hu-ma-na-ma-na, *s.* A market; a market place; haule i ka pahu i ka *pahumanamana*.

Pa-hu-na, *s.* See Pahu, to push, and Ana. A thrusting; a striking, as with a weapon.

Pa-hu-pai, *s.* A drum for beating at a hula; o ka ili mano, he mea ia e hana ia i *pahupai*.

Pa-hu-pa-hu, *s.* Stinted kalo growing among weeds.

2. The name of a game played on a rectangular table, billiards.

Pa-hu-pa-hu, *adj.* Blunt; obtuse; dull; omuku.

Pa-hu-pa-hu, *v.* See Pahu, to strike. To strike or pound; to bruise. See Paopao.

Pa-hu-pa-la-pa-la, *s. Pahu* and *palapala*, writing. *Originally*, a container for the liquor in printing kapas.

2. A writing desk.

Pa-hu-wai, *s.* A cistern; a container of water. *Ier.* 2:13.

Pa-hu-be-ri-ta, *s. Pahu* and *berita* (*Heb.*), a covenant. The ark of the covenant among the Hebrews. *Ios.* 3:3.

Pa-ka, *v.* To make war; to fight; to strike, as large drops of rain upon dry leaves, making a noise.

2. To cut; to pare; to peel off.

3. To fend off or turn aside, as the stern does a canoe to avoid a wave which threatens to fill it.

4. To shoot or slide a canoe or surf-board on a wave.

5. To prepare before hand for any business or any event.

Pa-ka, *s.* Any small round substance, as the head of a pin; a knot at the end of a rope.

2. The sharp projections on the sides of the tail of certain fish, as the kala, the palani and the manini.

3. A flat calabash, so called because large and flat.

4. A stone used by fishermen.

5. *Paka* is sometimes written for *baka*, tobacco.

Pa-ka, *adj.* Lean, as flesh; destitute of fat.

2. Ready; prepared; furnished.

3. Old; aged.

Pa-ka, *adv.* Clearly; plainly; intelligibly; evidently. Syn. with lea, pono and maopopo. Ua oki *paka*, haalele i na mea ino a pau.

Pa-kaa, *v.* To peel off; to skin; to strip off the skin from a vegetable.

Pa-kaa, *s.* Lean flesh.

Pa-kaa-wi-li, *v. Pa* and *kaawili,* to writhe. To encircle; to twine around, as a vine.

2. To turn this way and that.

3. To turn round; to roll in upon itself like a curling flame. *Ezek.* 1:4.

Pa-kai, *s. Art.* ke. An eatable vegetable; he mea ulu, he mea ai; a kind of herb used for food in time of scarcity.

Pa-kai-e-le-lu, *s.* Name of a wind; a strong wind off Waianae.

Pa-kai-e-a, *s.* A species of sea-weed.

Pa-kai-e-le, *s.* Name of a species of fish; he pakaualoa.

Pa-kai-kai, *v.* To pound, as with a pestle.

Pa-kai-kai, *s.* The name of a vegetable. See Pakai.

Pa-kao, *v.* To go about lazily; to live without object; to live solitarily; e hakao, e helewale.

Pa-kau-a, *s. Pa,* fence, and *kaua,* war. A fort; a place of refuge; a stronghold. 1 *Oihl.* 11:5. A garrison. 2 *Sam.* 8:14. A palace; the residence of a king. *Neh.* 1:1.

Pa-kau-a-kee, *s.*

Pa-kau-a-lo-a, *s.* The name of a fish. See Pakaiele.

Pa-kau-ka-ma, *s. Pa,* yard, and *kaukama* (*Eng.*), cucumber. A garden of cucumbers. See Kaukama. *Isa.* 8:1.

Pa-kau-la, *s. Pa,* pair, and *kaula,* rope. A set of ropes for the rigging of a vessel.

Pa-kau-lei, *v.* To be continually changing one's residence; mai noho a *pakaulei*.

2. To move along step by step; to go by little and little.

3. To sit upright.

Pa-kau-lei, *adj.* Unsteady; going from house to house.

2. Destitute of house and untensils. See Kuonoonoole.

3. Living in a loose way or without

method, as one who leaves his wife to follow one, then another.

Pa-ka-ha, *v. Pa* and *kaha.* To be greedy of property; hence, to oppress; to cheat; to be dishonest ln any way.

Pa-ka-ha, *s.* A kind of shell-fish of the sea, rough outside.

2. Greediness after another's property; a seizing what is another's.

Pa-ka-hi, *dist. adv. Pa* and *kahi,* one. One to each. *Ios.* 4:5. One in a place; one by one; *pakahi* i ka makahiki, once a year. *Oihk.* 16:34.

Pa-ka-hi, *v.* To distribute to each one. *Ios.* 4:2. To take turns; to do one at a time; to be numbered one by one. 1 *Oihl.* 23:3.

Pa-ka-ka, *v.* To glide with a canoe on the surf; to ride on the surf.

2. To flow off; to turn off, as a canoe is turned to avoid a sea; to shoot or slide, as a surf-board on a wave; e *pakaka* i ka waa, to *steer* the canoe. See Paka.

Pa-ka-ka, *adj.* Narrow; thin, as the back door of a house; aka, e komo oe ma ka puka *pakaka.*

Pa-ka-ka, *adj.* Swelled; big, as one's person.

Pa-ka-ka-hi, *v. Paka,* to drop, as rain, and *kahi,* one. To drop scatteringly a little rain.

Pa-ka-ke, *v.* See Hoopakake. To talk indistinctly, as a Hawaiian trying to speak English; to use the *kake* language.

Pa-ka-ke-u, *v.* To have the last word in scolding; to chide; to scold often; to act as a scolding woman; to exhibit an evil disposition.

Pa-ka-ki, *v.* To talk irrationally; to act as in a revel; to contend, as a drunkard.

Pa-ka-la-ka-la, *s.* A species of fish; the little kala; he kala liilii.

Pa-ka-na-o-no, *dist. adj. Pa* and *kanaono,* sixty. Sixty-fold. *Mat.* 13:8.

Pa-ka-na-lo-a, *s.* Name of a species of fish. See Olali, same species.

Pa-ka-nu, *s. Pa,* yard, and *kanu,* to plant. A garden; a place where things are planted. *Eset.* 7:7.

Pa-ka-pa-ka, *v.* See Paka. To drop, as large rain drops; to make the noise that such drops make on dry substances; to patter.

Pa-ka-pa-ka, *s.* A heavy shower of rain.

2. The wrinkled skin of the eye.

3. An aged person, from his wrinkles.

4. Weakness; feebleness, as of an aged person.

Pa-ka-pa-ka, *adj.* Coarse or large, as the lauhala leaves with which a mat is braided; he moena *pakapaka.*

2. Numerous, as men.

3. Large and many, as fish, &c., in one's possession; *pakapaka* kanaka o mea; *pakapaka* ka ia ia mea ma.

Pa-ke, *v. Pa* and *ke,* to resist. To push away; to defend off; to resist.

2. To ring; to sound; to sing.

Pa-ke, *s.* Softness; weakness.

2. The name of white kapa.

3. The appellation given to a Chinaman.

Pa-ke, *adj.* Soft; weak; flexible.

Pa-ke-a, *s.* A species of white stone.

Pa-ke-a-ai, *s.* See Pakelaai.

Pa-ke-o, *adj.* Fled; escaped; broken away; agitated.

Pa-ke-o-ke-o, *s.* The people that eat with the chief, as the aialo, in distinction from the *makaainana.*

Pa-ke-u, *v. Pa* and *keu,* to remain over and above. To excel; to be more than was expected; to be over and above; to leave a remainder.

Pa-ke-ke, *s.* See Bakeke, *Eng.* A bucket, &c.

Pa-ke-la, *v. Pa* and *kela,* to shoot out. To exceed; to go beyond; to go before. 2 *Kor.* 11:23.

2. To exceed another in wickedness. 1 *Nal.* 14:9.

3. To be over and above. 1 *Oihl.* 29:3.

4. *Hoo.* To prefer; to esteem more.

5. To excel; to do better than another. *Rom.* 12:10.

6. To abound in wickedness. 1 *Nal.* 14:22.

Pa-ke-la, *s.* Excess; what is over and above; a superfluity. See the compounds. A no ka *pakela* loa i ke akamai i ka hoopuka ana i na olelo pahee, on account of the *very great* skill in uttering smooth words.

Pa-ke-la, *adj.* High; stretching out; excelling.

Pa-ke-la-ai, *v. Pakela,* and *ai,* food. To be a glutton; to be greedy in eating. *Kanl.* 21:20.

Pa-ke-la-ai, *s.* A glutton; gluttony; the practice of eating to excess.

2. In *natural history,* the name of an animal, the glutton.

Pa-ke-la-ai, *adj.* Gluttonous; eating to excess. *Mat.* 11:19. *Pakela* inu waina, a drunkard. 1 *Pet.* 4:3. *Pakela* nani, excess of glory. 2 *Kor.* 3:10.

Pa-ke-le, *v. Pa* and *kele,* to slip. To escape from some evil; to escape punishment. *Heb.* 2:3. To be free from. *Hoo.* To deliver; to cause to escape. *Puk.* 6:6.

PA-KE-LO, *v.* See PAKELE. To slip out of the grasp of a person or thing, as a fish from the hands.

2. To set free; to loosen; to escape.

3. To administer an injection.

PA-KE-LO, *s.* An injection; an enema.

PA-KE-LO, *adj.* Slippery; sliding; slipping up; slipping off.

PA-KE-PA-KE, *adj.* See PAKE. Soft; limber; weak; flexible.

PA-KI, *v.* To smite with the palm of the hand; to spatter, as water.

2. To dash in pieces, as one would break a melon by throwing it on the ground.

3. To ooze through, as water; to leak, as a barrel, or as a kalo patch.

4. To move along; to slip or slide; e hoonee, e hookele.

PA-KI, *s.* The dividing of the water by a ship under sail; plowing the main.

PA-KI-AI, *s.* Epithet of a barren woman; he wahine pa.

PA-KI-AI,
PA-KI-A-KI-AI, } *v.* To forsake wife or husband and live in adultery.

PA-KII, *v.* To mash, as one treading on an egg.

2. To lie with the face down, the belly unsupported, in order to enlarge the abdomen. See PAIPO. E moe papio, e huli ilalo ke alo, i nui ka opu.

PA-KII, *s.* A species of fish.

PA-KII, *adj.* Broad; spread out; fallen flat down; edging along, as one moving on his belly.

PA-KII-KII, *adj.* See PAKII. Broad; extensively spread out; fallen down flatly.

PA-KII-KII, *adj.* Applied to a fish net, a small net; i ka upena *pakiikii.*

PA-KI-O, *v.* To fall continually, as falling rain; to rain continually; to drop constantly; e haule mau, e ua mau, e kulu mau.

PA-KI-O-KI-O, *v.* *Pa* and *kiokio.* See KIO. To break wind often; to void excrements.

PA-KI-HI, *v.* *Pa* and *kihi,* border; edge. To go lightly; to pass softly; to just touch in passing.

> Ke *pakihi* la i ke kai o Huia,
> O ka hui maka wale no ka makou,
> O ka honihoni ana i ke uiuiwi.

PA-KI-KA, *v.* To slip; to slide in walking, as one walking on a slippery place.

PA-KI-KA, *s.* Name of an insect that eats potato leaves and destroys them.

2. A bad pronunciation for *makika,* a musquito; he eleao, he ilo, he mea e make ai ka ulu o ka ai.

PA-KI-KA, *adj.* Smooth; polished; slippery; smoothed, as a thing polished; e kalai a maikai, anai a *pakika;* alaila, hoomaka ke kau.

PA-KI-KE, *v.* *Pa* and *kike,* to speak back and forth. To make a pert saucy reply to something said; to answer back. *Tit.* 2:9.

2. To rail; to cavil; to talk impudently.

3. To answer roughly. 1 *Sam.* 20:10. To be provoking in a controversy.

PA-KI-KE, *s.* A caviling. *Rom.* 10:21. A reviling; he lokoino.

PA-KI-KE-KI-KE, *v.* See PAKIKE. To answer back and forth frequently.

2. To be rough; to be uncivil towards one in conversation.

PA-KI-KI, *v.* See PAAKIKI. *Pa* and *paa,* solid, and *kiki,* intensive. To be very hard; to be solid; applied to substances.

2. Applied to the mind, to be obdurate; to be inflexible. *Hoo.* To harden, as the heart. *Puk.* 4:21.

3. E papaiawa, e hoomana i ke akua.

PA-KI-KO, *v.* *Pa* and *kiko,* a little dot or mark. To eat but little; to be temperate; to be abstemious in diet. 1 *Kor.* 9:25. NOTE.—*Pakiko* is the opposite of *pakela,* spoken in reference to taking (kiko ana) here a little and there a little.

2. To eat quietly or cautiously; to think before hand and not follow the appetite.

PA-KI-KO, *s.* Temperance; regular habits of life. *Oih.* 24:25; 2 *Pet.* 1:6.

2. The name of an instrument anciently used in war.

PA-KI-KO-E-LE, *v.* See KOELEELE. To make a rough sound; to rumble slightly; e kamumu.

PA-KI-PA-KI, *v.* See PAKI, to slip; to slide. To sail along; to divide the water, as the keel of a ship; to move sideways; to spatter the water in rowing a canoe.

PA-KI-PA-KI-KA, *adj.* See PAKIKA. Slippery; muddy; liable to fall in walking.

PA-KO-LE, *adj.* Short. See POKOLE.

PA-KO-LE-KO-LE, *adj.* Short. See POKOLE and PAKOLE.

PA-KO-LE-KO-LE, *s.* A species of fish large and greenish.

PA-KO-LI, *s.* Names of the first three notes in the Hawaiian scale of vocal music; he kumu leo himeni; the whole seven sounds are represented by the syllables *pa, ko, li, ha, no, la, mi.*

PA-KO-LI, *adj.* Singing by notes; he kumu *pakoli,* rudiments of vocal music.

PA-KO-LU,
PA-KO'U, } *adj.* Short. See POKOLE.

PA-KO-LU, *v.* *Pa* and *kolu*, three. Three; three-fold; three by three; to do three times. *Nah.* 22:28.

PA-KO-NI, *s.* *Pa* and *koni*, to beat, as the pulse. An ache, as the toothache; a pain; a strong pain.

PA-KU, *v.* *Pa*, a wall, and *ku*, to stand. To partition off; to guard; to defend; to shield one from harm: manao iho la au e haliu ae i ko kakou Haku me ka i aku, e *paku* mai oe ia'u; to parry off; to defend by some means; a *paku* aku la na kanaka i ka moena no ka pu, and the people *put up* their mats as *a defense* against the guns.

2. To cast away; to drive off; to tread or trample down; e hahi, e hehi, e peku.

PA-KU, *v.* See **PAHU.** To burst out, as grain from a bag, or as matter from a boil. NOTE.—This is perhaps a mistake for *pahu*, but the manuscript was very plain.

PA-KU, *s.* A partition, as of a house.

2. The wall of a small inclosure.

3. A defense; a place of security. *Hal.* 89:18.

4. A shield; a veil concealing something. *Puk.* 26:31. A hanging division; a curtain. *Puk.* 27:15. NOTE.—The partitions or *pakus* in the houses of former times, where the people had any at all, were nothing more than kapas or mats hung up.

5. A division; that which makes a place to be separated from another place.

6. A uniting or joining or sewing of two pieces of kapa.

7. A uniting of two pieces of wauke by beating to make one kapa.

PA-KU-A, *v.* To do over and over again continually; to go to the same place; to travel the same road day after day; e hele mau i kela la i keia la ma kahi i hele mau ia.

PA-KU-A, *adj.* Accustomed; so accustomed as to become second nature; he mea *pakua* wale, a thing become *common*.

PA-KU-EI, *v.* To be present before the time; to commence a job before the time.

PA-KU-I, *v.* *Pa* and *kui*, to join one thing to another. To splice, as timber or a rope.

2. To engraft, as one tree upon another. *Rom.* 11:17.

3. To add one evil deed to another. 1 *Sam.* 12:19.

4. To unite, i. e., to add one story of a building to another; to heap one thing on the top of another; e hou i kekahi mea maluna iho o kekahi mea.

5. To beat against, as an opposing wind. *Mar.* 6:48.

PA-KU-I, *v.* To be unpleasant to the taste; to be sickishly sweet; to send forth an odor; to be odoriferous; e ala, e *pakui*, e kuhinia.

PA-KU-I, *adj.* Added on; joined; hale *pakui*, a house joined to a house above, that is, a tower. *Kin.* 11:4. Engrafted; united. *Iak.* 1:21.

PA-KU-I-KU-I, *v.* See **PAKUI.** To splice or join together timbers that are not long enough for the purpose designed; to fasten together; e hookuikui, e panainai.

PA-KU-I-KU-I, *v.* To beat against; to be contrary to, as a contrary wind; *pakuikui* mai ka makani. *Oih.* 27:4.

2. To beat; to pound fine; to bruise. 2 *Sam.* 22:43.

3. To mix up, as sweet food.

PA-KU-I-KU-I, *s.* Name of a species of yellow fish.

PA-KU-I-KU-I, *adj.* Contradictory; opposing; as, m a k a n i p a k u i k u i, an opposing wind, or a head wind; he olelo *pakuikui*, a contradicting speech.

pakuikui

PA-KU-I-PAI, *adj.* Some quality of a fish net; he upena *pakuipai*.

PA-KU-PA-KU, *adj.* Round; low; short.

PA-LA, *adj.* Mellow; soft; ripe, as fruit; rotten; cooked soft.

PA-LA, *s.* Name of the foreign common disease, the syphilis.

2. The name of a vegetable eaten in time of famine.

3. A hahai mai na kanaka e hele ana me ke akua i ka *pala* a haawe—hai mai ka *pala* mai uka—kii hou ka *pala* ma ia po iho.

PA-LA, *v.* To cook soft; to ripen and be soft, as banana or other fruit.

2. *Hoo.* To anoint; to daub; to besmear.

3. To erase; to blot out.

PA-LAA, *s.* Almost any dark color, such as brown, purple, &c.; lole *palaa*.

PA-LA-AI, *adj.* *Pala* and *ai*. Fat, as animals; *palaai* ka holoholona, *palaai* ka ia, *palaai* ka manu.

PA-LA-AU, *s.* *Pa*, fence, and *laau*, timber. A stick fence; a wooden fence; he *palaau* ka pa kahiko; *palaau* oioi, a thorn hedge. *Mik.* 7:4.

PA-LAI, *v.* For the English *fry*. To cook or fry in a pan. NOTE.—It should be written *parai* or rather *ferai. Oihk.* 7:12.

Pa-lai, *v.* To be ashamed and turn the face away, as one who is conscious of guilt; or conscious of the presence of superiority or dignity, as a poor man when he goes into the house of the rich. *Hoo.* To cause a blush; to feel disconcerted at the presence of superiors; to confuse one; to make ashamed. *Ier.* 7:19.

Pa-lai, *s.* A blush; shamefacedness; he *palai* ka maka, the face *blushes.*

2. Name of a species of fern; he mea ulu, he palapalai; he ieie ame ka *palai. Laieik.* 103.

Pa-lai, *adj.* Adulterous; defaced.

Pa-la-i-e, *adj. Pala,* soft, and *ie,* flexible. Inconstant; not firm; easily tempted to turn from the right; o na kanaka a pau loa ma ka honua nei, he *palaie* no ia na Iehova.

Pa-la-i-e, *s. Art.* ke. A species of play formerly among the people; ua hana na kanaka i ke *palaie* i mea lealea.

Pa-la-i-ki, *s. Pala,* soft, and *iki,* little. The sound of a stone thrown high and falling into the water perpendicularly. See **Palamimo.** Huna *palaiki* ke akamai.

Pa-lai-ma-ka, *v. Palai* and *maka,* face. To put to confusion; to be cast down in countenance; to be confounded. *Isa.* 41:11. Syn. with hilahila. To be turned back. *Isa.* 42:17.

Pa-lai-ma-ka, *s. Hoo.* A blushing; a shame; a sign of shame.

Pa-la-o, *s.* Name of a species of fish.

Pa-la-o-a, *s.* A species of large fish; a whale.

2. An ornament made of a whale's tooth worn pendulous from the neck; e malama i ka niho *palaoa,* take care of the *ornament* (we have no name of it in English); hence,

3. Ivory.

4. The sea-elephant.

Pa-la-o-a, *adj.* Of or belonging to ivory. 1 *Nal.* 10:18.

Pa-la-o-a, *s.* The Hawaiian common orthography and pronunciation for the English word *flour;* hence,

1. Bread; flour, &c.

2. The grain of which flour is made. See **Huapalaoa.** *Palaoa* huluhulu, barley; *palaoa* eleele, rye; *palaoa* hu ole, unleavened bread. *Puk.* 9:31, 32. *Palaoa* wali, fine flour. *Oihk.* 7:12. *Palaoa* kawili, dough. *Neh.* 15:20. Note.—The word should be written *falaoa* or *felaoa.*

Pa-lao-lao, *s. Pa* and *laolao.* A bundle done up short; a bundle of fagots.

2. The name of a species of fish.

Pa-la-o-nu-i, *adj.* Broad, as the eye.

Pa-lau, *v.* To lie; to misrepresent; to deceive; e wahahee, e hoopunipuni.

Pa-lau, *v. Hoo.* To betroth. *Puk.* 21:9. To betroth; to give in marriage; to engage to marry.

Pa-lau, *s.* A lie; a falsehood.

2. An instrument for cutting kalo tops; laau *palau,* me ka laau *palau,* o Kapahielihonua. *Laieik.* 167.

3. A species of yam; the same as the uhi.

4. *Eng.* A plow.

5. A species of fish, purple, striped.

Pa-lau-a-le-lo, *s.* Idleness; indolence; want of disposition to work. 1 *Tim.* 5:13.

Pa-lau-a-le-lo, *adj.* Indolent; unoccupied; lazy; idle; neglecting to cultivate land; low; ill-bred.

Pa-lau-e-ka, *v.* To be obscured, as the sun.

2. To work briskly; to finish a job speedily.

Pa-lau-e-ka, *adj.* Obscure; dim; not white.

2. Expeditious; finishing a work quickly.

Pa-lau-lau, *s.* A species of red fish.

Pa-lau-wi-li, *adj. Pa* and *lauwili,* to change. Changing often: whiffling about, as the wind; *palauwili* ka makani.

Pa-la-ha, *v. Pa* and *laha,* to spread out. To slip; to slide. *Sol.* 3:23. To stumble and fall down by hitting the foot against an object.

2. To fall flat down, as a house or tent. *Lunk.* 7:13.

3. *Hoo.* To fall prostrate in adoration.

4. To stretch out upon; to lie flat upon. 1 *Nal.* 17:21.

5. To be spread or wafted off, as a shower over land; *palaha* aku ka ua ma ka aina.

6. To conceive, as a female; to become large.

Pa-la-ha, *adj.* Smooth and flat, as the back of the shell-fish called *leho;* akahi noa loa ka olu, *palaha,* pauhu, maka ino.

Pa-la-ha-la-ha, *v.* See **Palaha** and **Laha,** to extend. To spread out; to extend generally.

2. To spread abroad, as a report. *Oih.* 4:17. To extend far and wide.

3. To spread or extend, as a sore or disease. *Oihk.* 13:22.

4. *Hoo.* To extend abroad; to increase, as a people. *Kin.* 41:52.

5. To spread out, as the wings of an army. *Lunk.* 20:37.

Pa-la-ha-la-ha, *s.* Breadth; extent, as

of a country. *Isa.* 8:8.

2. A species of the limu. See LIMU.

PA-LA-HA-LA-HA-LAU, *adj.* Having leaves only, as a tree; he *palahalahalau* wale no, aohe hua, making a show of leaves only, but no fruit.

PA-LA-HE, } *adj.* Soft; tender; so
PA-LA-HE-HE, } soft as to flow; flowing, soft and slimy, as the mucous from the nose.

PA-LA-HE-A, *s.* *Pala*, soft, and *hea*, to be dirty. Dirty food.

2. A spot; a stain. 2 *Pet.* 2:13.

PA-LA-HE-A, *adj.* Dirty; filthy; defiled; *palahea* ko lakou naau i ke koko o hai; unclean; besmeared, as a child's hands and face when eating greasy food; blotted, as paper which has ink spilled on it.

PA-LA-HE-A, *v.* To daub; to besmear; to anoint.

2. *Hoo.* To stain; to color, as with blood. *Isa.* 63:3.

PA-LA-HE-A-HE-A, *v.* Intensive of *palahea*. To be unsound; to be weak; to be frail, as a person; to be unsound; to be wanting in strength.

PA-LA-HEE, *v.* *Pala* and *hee*, slippery. See PALAHE above. To shrink away, as a coward from duty or danger.

PA-LA-HEE, *adj.* Dead ripe; rotten.

PA-LA-HI, *v.* *Pala* and *hi*, to flow away. To flow from the bowels; to discharge liquid matter from the bowels.

PA-LA-HI, *s.* The liquid discharge from the bowels in a bowel complaint.

PA-LA-HO, *s.* Corruption. *Iob.* 17:14. Putridity; the action of decaying matter.

PA-LA-HO, } *adj.* Rotten; decayed; sub-
PA-LA-HU, } ject to decay; corruptible.

PA-LA-HO-LO, *s.* *Pala* and *holo* for *hee*, to flow. Paste made from the fern called *amaumau*; the paste was used in pasting kapas.

2. The name of a plant.

PA-LA-HU, *s.* The sickness of fowls.

2. The name of a large fish; the opelu.

3. The epithet of a cock-turkey from the soft elastic red substance on and about his head.

4. A turkey generally. See PELEHU.

PA-LA-HU-KI, *v.* *Pala* and *huki*, to become soft. To become soft and putrid, as a dead body. See PALAKAHUKI. A lilo ae la kona kino i mea *palahuki*, and his body became *putrid*.

PA-LA-KA, *v.* *Pa* and *laka*, to tame. To be inactive; to be inattentive; to be indifferent to what interests others; to be ineffi-

cient.

2. To live without thought or care.

3. To be dull or stupid; to be slow of apprehension; applied to the moral powers. *Mat.* 13:15.

4. *Hoo.* To cause one's self to be indifferent; to harden one's heart; to be unbelieving in great and solemn truths. *Isa.* 6:10.

PA-LA-KA, *s.* A disposition of heart opposed to religious truth; hard-heartedness; stupidity; moral insensibility; indifference.

2. The name applied to a short shirt; he wahi palule pokole.

PA-LA-KA, *adj.* Inactive; stupid; careless; ineffecient; indifferent.

PA-LA-KA-AO, *adj.* *Pala*, ripe, soft, and *kaao*, the fruit of the hala tree. Hence, soft; ripe; having undergone some process of decay; palakahuki, palahu.

PA-LA-KAI, *v.* To wither; to droop, as a vegetable; to produce no fruit; to be stinted in growth; to fade, as a flower; to fail.

PA-LA-KAI, *adj.* Barren; unfruitful; sickly; withered, as a plant; stinted in growing, as a child.

PA-LA-KA-HE-LA, *adj.* *Pala* and *kahela*, bent. Crooked; curved; having crooked legs or neck.

Palakahela ka a-i o Makaukiu,
He kiu ka makani, he alele hooholo na Kokoolau,
Ke kuehu mai la iuka o Pehu,
Ike ke kanaka kahea uolo makani.

PA-LA-KA-HU-KI, *v.* *Pala* and *kahuki*, to decay; to corrupt. To corrupt; to putrefy, as a dead body; to be soft; to rot. See PALAHU and KAHUKI. *Sol.* 10:7.

PA-LA-KA-HU-KI, *adj.* Soft; decayed, as animal bodies; putrid.

PA-LA-KE, *adj.* Mixed up of water and other things; heavy; water-soaked, as kalo or potatoes.

PA-LA-KE-A, *s.* A variety of kalo.

2. A kind of vegetable eaten in time of scarcity.

PA-LA-KE-A, *adj.* *Pala* and *kea*, white. Anything soft and white; white; clear; unclouded; unshaded with any color.

PA-LA-KI, *v.* To brush; to polish, as a shoe; to wash; to cleanse.

2. To smear over; to whitewash a wall.

PA-LA-KI, *s.* *Eng.* A brush generally.

PA-LA-KI-O, *s.* *Pala* and *kio*, excrement from a sore. The name of a disease connected with lasciviousness; he mai pala, he mai haole.

PA-LA-KI-KO, *v.* To steal, especially to steal little things; to pilfer; to take little by little. NOTE.—This appears to be a modern coined word; its derivation is not apparent, except that *kiko* signifies to *pick up* as a fowl eats food.

Pa-la-ki-ko, *s.* Theft; a stealing of small articles; pilfering.

Pa-la-ku, *v.* *Pala* and *ku*, to stand. To be soft; to be rotten, especially rotten internally.

Pa-la-la, *v.* To tax the people for kapa, poi, &c., on the birth of a young chief.

   2. E haki lala ka nalu, e kahi aoao.

Pa-la-la, *s.* A tax paid on the birth of a chief.

   2. A gift; a present on the birth of a child.

   3. A wedding feast. *Kin.* 29:22. Also connected with *ahaaina*. *Luk.* 14:10.

   4. A feast made by a chief for any purpose. *Laieik.* 88.

   5. A tax paid to the chiefs for any purpose; he mea *palala* ia ka hulumanu o na 'lii.

Pa-la-lau-ha-la, *v.* *Pala*, softness, and *lauhala*, a tree. To be weak; to be feeble; to be infirm.

   2. To walk, to see or to move with feebleness.

   3. To be old; to be in the last stages of life.

   4. To swoon; to lie like one dead.

Pa-la-lau-ha-la, *s.* Weakness; infirmity; the feeble state and infirmities of old age; the last stage of life of an old person.

Pa-la-la-ha, *v.* *Pa* and *laha*, to spread out. To be broad; to be widely extended. See PALAHALAHA.

Pa-la-la-ha-lau, *adj.* See PALAHALA-HALAU. Having leaves only, and no fruit; making a show of leaves, as a tree.

Pa-la-la-kai-mo-ku, *s.* A broad plain; land spread out.

   2. An extended land; a country; *figuratively*, a kingdom.

Pa-la-la-lo, *adj.* *Pala*, soft, and *lalo*, below. Soft; rotten, as kalo or bananas; applied to persons, sick; soft; diseased with the *pala*; applied to a kingdom, without strength.

Pa-la-le, *v.* To branch out; to project out.

   2. To put together confusedly.

   3. To speak indistinctly; to make blunders in speaking; to vociferate.

   4. To work in a slovenly manner.

Pa-la-le, *adj.* Scattered; spread out; lying confusedly so as to answer no purpose, as the wheels of a watch when apart.

Pa-la-lei, *s.* The spreading of one's kapa over the head of a chief on entering a house; ka *palalei* o kou kapa.

Pa-la-le-ha, *v.* *Pala* and *leha*, to lift the eyes. To raise slowly the eyes; hence, to be lazy; to be faint-hearted; to be indolent. *Hoo.* To be slothful; to be idle; to be careless. See HOOMOLOWA. *Hoopalaleha* iho la kakou i ka hana maikai.

Pa-la-le-ha, *adj.* *Hoo.* Slothful; idle. *Sol.* 10:4.

Pa-la-li, *v.* *Pa* and *lali*, soft. To sound softly, as a flute or pipe; e kani me he pu hihio la.

Pa-la-lo-li, *adj.* *Pala* and *loli*, to change. Changed from its original state; soft; decayed; corrupted; rotten. See PALALUHIEHU.

Pa-la-lu, *v.* *Pala*, soft, and *lu*, to scatter. To burst out suddenly; to snort like a horse.

   2. E puhuluhulu, e palali.

   3. *Hoo.* To imitate the *palalu* or voice of the *moho*, &c., as men do.

Pa-la-lu, *s.* The noise of the dove as made in the throat; also the voice of the *moho*; applied also to other noises.

Pa-la-lu-e-hu, *adj.* *Pala* and *luehu*, soft. Soft; yielding; flexible; soft, as a ripe boil; rotten; corrupt, as decaying animal or vegetable matter. See PALAKAHUKI.

Pa-la-lu-hi-e-hu, *adj.* Decayed; corrupted; soft. See PALALOLI.

Pa-la-ma, *s.* *Eng.* A palm, name of a tree; the leaf of the tree. *Hoik.* 7:9. See PAMA.

Pa-la-ma, *v.* *Pa* and *lama*, a torch. To watch over; to guard; to keep guard, as soldiers; to be guarded or watched over; e malamaia me na koa e kiaiia.

Pa-la-ma, *s.* A watching; a guarding.

   2. A watch; a guard.

Pa-la-mai-ki, *v.* To gather up into a bunch, as a handkerchief.

Pa-la-me-a, *s.* Plumpness; fatness, as of an animal.

   2. A pure, clear atmosphere.

   3. The splendid appearance of the heavenly bodies with the beautiful blue of the sky; he aaka na mea ma ka lani, a uliuli maikai mai ka lani.

Pa-la-mi-mo, *v.* *Pala* and *mimo*, to move softly. To move off silently; to step aside without noise; to go or to move softly; to move gently; to be small; to enter, as a house, without noise; e uuku, e komo pono.

Pa-la-mi-mo, *adj.* Quickly and easily done; moving easily without noise.

Pa-la-mo-a, *s.* A bluish cloud; seen in the east in the morning it was considered a sign of rain; he papalaoa, he *palamoa* he mau ouli ua ia.

PA-LA-NAI, *adj.* Flat; not deep, as a flat dish; flat, as a vessel or ship which is not deep.

PA-LA-NA-I-KI, *v.* *Palana* and *iki*, little. To be small; to be confined to a small space; to be shrunk or curled up; to fit a place designed.

PA-LA-NE-HE, *v.* *Pala* and *nehe*, to rustle. To be gentle; to be soft and careful in doing a thing; to move softly, without noise.

PA-LA-NE-HE, *s.* Gentleness; uprightness; quietness and gentleness in doing a thing; silence and softness.

PA-LA-NE-HE, *adj.* Gentle; good; without noise; without confusion; o ka hana *palanehe* ole, o ka lawe nihi.

PA-LA-NE-HE-O-LE, *v.* See PALANEHE and OLE, not. To depart secretly; to vanish.

PA-LA-NE-HE-O-LE, *adv.* Silently; quietly; unperceived. NOTE.—It is difficult to see how *palanehe* and *palaneheole* should convey the same idea of a still, quiet movement; the *ole* cannot have its usual meaning of a negative.

> *Palaneheole ia i nalo*
> O lohilohi ku, o ka lohi lani—e.

PA-LA-NI, *v.* To skim; to dip lightly, as an oar; applied to rowing feebly; aole komo ka hoe, dip not deeply the paddle.
   2. To dig slightly, not deeply.

PA-LA-NI, *adv.* Lightly; feebly; kioe *palani*, skim a *little*.

PA-LA-NI, *adj.* Sour, as a melon or other fruit partly eaten, the remainder left and it becomes sour.

PA-LA-NI, *v.* To stink; a word of contempt, applied to dirty, filthy persons, from the fact that the fish *palani* stinks abominably. *Palani* was formerly applied to servants in distinction from chiefs; ua kapaia ka poe kauwa he *palani*, he hohono ke ano.

PA-LA-NI, *s.* The name of a fish emitting a very bad odor.

PA-LA-NI, *s.* *Eng.* The Hawaiian orthography for *barani*, that is, brandy; it should always be written and printed *barani*.

PA-LA-NI, *s.* *Eng.* France, French or a Frenchman; this word should always be written and printed *Farani* or *Ferani*, France; he kanaka *Farani*, a Frenchman.

PA-LA-NI, *s.* A species of sugar-cane.

PA-LA-NI, *v.* To soften. *Hoo.* To paint; to daub.

PA-LA-NI-OA, *s.*

PA-LA-PA-LA, *v.* See PALA, to paint; to spot. To stamp with marks, as in painting or printing kapa. NOTE.—The figures, like calico printing, were cut on pieces of wood or bamboo, dipped in the liquid coloring matter and then impressed with the hand on the kapa.
   2. In modern times, to write; to mark; to draw; to paint. See KAKAU.

PA-LA-PA-LA, *s.* Characters made by impressing marks on kapa or paper like printing or by writing with a pen; hence,
   2. A writing; a book either written or printed; a manuscript.
   3. An incription upon coins; the handwriting of any one; *palapala hemolele*, the Holy Scriptures. NOTE.—The whole system of instruction as first commenced at these Islands was summarily called by the Hawaiians the *palapala*.

PA-LA-PA-LA, *s.* The name of a fish found near banks and shallow places.
   2. The dead dry lauhala leaves; he lauhala maloo wale.

PA-LA-PA-LAI, *s.* The name of a species of fern. See PALAI.

PA-LA-PA-LA-KE-A, *adj.* *Palapala* and *kea*, white. Clear; bright; white; shining. See PALAKEA.

PA-LA-PA-LA-NI, *v.* See PALANI, to paint; to soften. To paint or print kapa and put out to dry.

PA-LA-PO, *adj.* See PALAHO. Rotten; decayed; bad smelling.

PA-LA-PO-HA-KU, *adj.* Small; feebly running, as a small stream of water; he wahi wai *palapohaku*.

PA-LA-PU, *v.* To make a bruise or wound.
   2. To be soft to the touch; to be soft, as a boil ripe for lancing.

PA-LA-PU, *s.* Anything so soft as to run, as matter from a boil.
   2. Softness, as meat or flesh bruised to a jelly.
   3. A wound or bruise. *Puk.* 21:25. A stripe; the wound of a whip or scourge. *Isa.* 53:5.

PA-LA-WAI, *s.* A species of limu or seagrass.
   2. He wahi wai e palapohaku.

PA-LA-WAI-KI, *adj.* Nice; neatly done; polite; done with taste.

PA-LA-WE-KA, *s.* Vain work; much labor and no fruit; applied to fishing all night and catching nothing; o ka hana pua he ahe o ua kula wela nei, hoi *palaweka* ole oukou o kahi hulilau.

PA-LE, *s.* A sheath; an outer garment; an apron; a veil; a curtain. *Puk.* 26:2.

2. Anything that defends or wards off; a partition; the bones are a defense to the brain, the ribs to the vitals, &c. *Anat.* 1.

3. A division; a dividing line; a boundary line. *Puk* 8:19.

4. An interval of time.

5. FIG. A convalescent person, i. e., one whose sickness is warded off.

6. The upper rim sewed to a canoe.

PA-LE, *v.* To refuse; to stand in the way; to hinder.

2. To defend off; to parry, as in the sword exercise; to ward off. *Nah.* 25:8.

3. To strike against; to be opposite to; to oppose; to resist. 2 *Oihl.* 29:11. To fend off a blow, as in boxing. *Laieik.* 41.

4. To make void, as a law; to turn into another meaning from the one designed; to misinterpret.

5. To render useless; to fall upon one; *pale* ka pono, aohe pono i koe, it is useless, we need not try again. *Laieik.* 67.

6. To deliver, as a midwife.

7. *Hoo.* To resist; to reject; to strive against.

8. To cover up; to overlay. 1 *Oihl.* 29:4.

PALE KA PONO. An adverbial phrase. *Laieik.* 140. To refuse obedience to a request; to listen to no advice; to pay no attention to what is right.

PA-LE, *adj.* Hindering; separating; opposing.

PA-LE-O, *v.* Pa and *leo*, voice. To converse together; to converse together, as several persons; to utter or express something with the voice.

PA-LE-O-LE-O-A, } *v.* Pa and *leoleoa*, to
PA-LE-O-LE-O-WA, } wish evil. To listen to vile language; to speak reproachfully of another; to curse another by wishing him dead; to blackguard.

PA-LE-O-PU-A, *v.* To pardon one's offenses, as the priest in former times by offering a sacrifice; e kala, e wailua, e *paleopua.*

PA-LE-U-HI, *s.* Pale and *uhi*, to cover up. A covering; a veil; an article of concealment. *Nah.* 4:5.

PA-LE-U-MAU-MA, *s.* Pale and *umauma*, the breast. A breast plate; an armor of defense. *Isa.* 59:17.

PA-LE-U-MAU-MA-U-NA-HI, *s.* Pale, *umauma* and *unahi*, the scale of a fish. A brigandine; an armor of defense; a coat of mail. *Ier.* 51:3.

PA-LE-HE, *v.* To be slack; to be loose; to hang loosely; to shake; to vibrate; e *palehe*, e alualu, e oloolo, e haaluea, e po-

hemo. See POLEHELEHE.

PA-LE-KAI, *s.* Pale and *kai*, the sea. The railing or bulwark of a vessel; a ku iho la ma ka *palekai*, when he stood upon the *bulwark.*

PA-LE-KAU-A, *s.* Pale and *kaua*, war. A shield; defensive armor. 1 *Sam.* 17:41.

PA-LE-KA-NA, *v.* To rest; to feel secure from danger; to breathe freely, i. e., to feel secure or safe; to be safe, i. e., to have made an escape. *Hal.* 119:117.

PA-LE-KA-NA, *s.* One who has escaped from danger or secure from it.

PA-LE-KA-NA, *adj.* Safe; in a state of safety from danger; escaped from danger; *palekana*, pau ka makau, pau ka luhi, pau ka hele ana i ka hana.

PA-LE-KE-I-KI, *v.* Pale and *keiki*, child. To deliver a child; to act the midwife.

PA-LE-KE-I-KI, *s.* One who acts as a midwife; a midwife. *Kin.* 38:28.

PA-LE-LA, *v.* Pale and *la*, day. To be idle; to be lazy; to refuse to work. *Puk.* 5:17.

PA-LE-LA, *s.* Laziness; indolence.

PA-LE-LA, *adj.* Lazy; going about idly; sauntering here and there; contemptuous.

PA-LE-LE, *v.* Pa and *lele*, separated. To put in another place, as when there is no place vacant; e hele a *palele* wale aku, go and put it somewhere else; the same as *e waiho aku ma kahi e.*

2. To stammer, as when one tries to speak and cannot get the word out.

PA-LE-LE, *adj.* Stammering; he leo *palele*; applied also to dropping water.

PA-LE-LU-A, *s.* The second veil or partition in the temple of Solomon. *Heb.* 9:3.

PA-LE-MA-I, *s.* Pale and *mai.* An undershirt; lolewawae *palemai*, drawers.

PA-LE-MA-KA, *s.* Pale and *maka*, face. A veil; a covering for the face. *Kin.* 38:14.

PA-LE-MO, *v.* To sink down, as into water; to be lost, i. e., to be sunk in the sea or mud. *Hal.* 69:2. To plunge out of sight.

2. To move the head up and down, as fighting cocks before they spring at each other.

3. *Hoo.* To cast down; to hurl; to throw.

PA-LE-MO, *s.* The name of a fish.

PA-LE-NA, *s.* Pale and *ana*, a dividing off. A border or boundary. *Kin.* 49:13. A dividing line between two parts or places.

2. Name of people formerly in Kohala, a particular class of men under Kamehameha, some chiefs, some common people.

PA-LE-NA-AI-NA, *s.* Palena and *aina*, land. The boundary of a land. *Nah.* 33:37.

PA-LE-PA-LE, *s.* See PALE 6. The upper rim sewed to a canoe; the lower or first one is *moe*. See PALIPALI.

PA-LE-PA-LE, *v.* See PALE. To defend off; to separate.

PA-LE-PO, *s.* *Pa*, fence, and *lepo*, earth. An earth fence, i. e., an adobie wall.

PA-LE-WA-WAE, *s.* *Pale* and *wawae*, leg. Greaves; defensive armor for the legs. *Isa.* 9:4.

PA-LI, *s.* A precipice; the side of a steep ravine; a steep hill. *Puk.* 14:22. Whatever stands up like a precipice.

PA-LI, *adj.* Full of deep ravines or precipitate hills; he aina *pali*.

PA-LI-KA-U-LU, *v.* To fall, as heavy rain and wind down a precipice; to shower down, as rain and wind; *palikaulu* ole ka lani. *Laieik.* 175.

PA-LI-KA-U-LU-O-LE-KA-LA-NI. A phrase rather than a word, meaning a clear serene sky; no clouds; all mild above.

PA-LI-KU, *s.* The name of an ancient order of priests on Hawaii, who are said to have come originally from *Paliku*, a foreign country; another order was called *Ka Nalu*.

PA-LI-LI, *v.* To fear; to be in a tremor.
2. To throw up, as on a fence; to throw ashore, as from a boat or canoe.

PA-LI-LI, *s.* Kalo floating up on the sides of the patch; the refuse kalo after the good is taken.

PA-LI-LO-A, *s.* A kind of cloud that lies low near the shore; the same as *kakai*.

PA-LI-MA, *adj.* Hana hou i hale *palima*.

PA-LI-PA-LI, *adj.* Steep down hill, or up and down; a ma kahi *palipali* i holo kiki ai ka waa.

PA-LI-PA-LI, *s.* The upper board on the side of a canoe to keep the water out. See PALEPALE.

PA-LO, *v.* To live idly; e noho wale; loea hana ole ka manawa.
2. To act the hypocrite; to be hypocritical. *Hoo.* The same.

PA-LO-A, *s.* A kind of fish net; called also the upena *pakuipai*.

PA-LOO, *adv.* Thunder without rain; thundering only; i kui *paloo* ka hekili. *Laieik.* 178.

PA-LO-KE,　　　　｝ *v. Eng.* The Hawai-
PA-LO-KE-LO-KE,　 ｝ ian pronunciation of the word *broke*. To break; more generally written *poloke* and *polokeloke*. These words correspond to the Hawaiian words *naha* and *hai*. See POLOKE.

PA-LO-LA-LO-LA, *adj.* See LOLA and LO-LALOLA. Palsied; helpless; stiff; awkward; useless.

PA-LO-LO, *v.* To deceive; to lie; wahahee, alapahi; to circumvent.

PA-LO-LO, *s.* See the verb. A lie; a deceiving; false information.

PA-LO-LO, *s.* Sticky mud; adhesive dirt; hard mud; a whitish clay of the Islands; clay mortar. *Puk.* 1:14.

PA-LO-LO, *adj.* Skilled in language or in speaking; fluent; branching out.

PA-LO-LO-LO, *adj.* Solid or hard, as the dirt; he lepo *palololo*.

PA-LU, *v.* To lick; to lap; to lap water with the tongue, as a dog. *Lunk.* 7:5. FIG. To lick the dust, that is, to be greatly degraded. *Isa.* 49:23. To destroy, as an enemy. *Nah.* 22:4.

PA-LU, *s.* The entrails of fish used in taming fish.
2. The action of an ox's tongue in eating grass.
3. An eating up; a devouring. *Nah.* 22:4.
4. Name of a species of fish.

PA-LU, *adj.* Soft; gentle; kind; flexible. See PALUPALU.

PA-LU-A, *adj.* *Pa*, distributive particle, and *lua*, two. Double; two-fold; two by two.

PA-LU-A, *v.* To double; to give two shares; to dispose of two by two.

PA-LU-HEE, *v.* *Palu* and *hee*, to flow. To soften; to cook so as to be soft; to flow.

PA-LU-HI, *v.* *Pa* and *luhi*, heavy; fatigued. To oppress; to tyrannize over.

PA-LU-HI, *adj.* Oppressed; weary from labor or exertions.

PA-LU-KA-LU-KA, *s.* The name of a fish. See PAUHUUHU.
2. The slimy matter of stools.

PA-LU-KU, *v.* *Pa* and *luku*, to destroy. To strike, as a hammer on an anvil.
2. To pound solid, as the bottom of a kalo patch with stones.
3. FIG. To knock down; to overthrow; aloha oe, e ka naauao, ka mea nana e *paluku* i na kii.
4. To beat; to break in pieces, as stones in the road.
5. To beat another.

PA-LU-KU, *adv.* Heavily; severely, as in striking heavy blows.

PA-LU-KU-LU-KU, *v.* See PALUKU. To bruise the head; the same as *paopao*; to strike; to hit.

PA-LU-LA, *s. Art.* ke. The leaf of the sweet potato.
2. A dish of food made by roasting sweet

potato leaves with hot stones.

Pa-lu-la, *adj.* Still; calm; quiet, as in the lull of the wind.

Pa-lu-le, *s.* Name of the loose under garment for men; a shirt; *palule* onionio. *Puk.* 28:4. A broidered coat; he lole komo kane.

2. Soft cotton or woolen cloth.

Pa-lu-lu, *v.* To resist; to stand against; to oppose. See KOLULU. To refrain from weeping when one is much affected; a *palulu* ae la i kona mau maka imua o ke anaina. *Laieik.* 194.

2. To tremble; to shake; to move; to cause a tremor.

Pa-lu-nu, *s.* Name of a creeping plant like the koali.

Pa-lu-pa-lu, *v.* See PALU. To be tender; to be soft; to be weak; to be flexible.

2. To be tender either physically or morally; to be enfeebled, as the body. *2 Sam.* 4:1. Ua *palupalu* ke keiki, the child is *feeble*; ua *palupalu* kona naau, he is *tender* hearted.

3. *Hoo.* To soften; to fatten; to make weak.

Pa-lu-pa-lu, *s.* Tenderness; softness; flexibility; weakness; want of strength.

2. The name of a pa-u colored yellow.

Pa-lu-pa-lu, *adj.* Weak; feeble; soft. *Kin.* 33:13. Pliable; limber; tender. *Kanl.* 28:54. Large, fat and weak. See POLUPOLU.

Pa-ma, *adj. Eng.* See PALAMA. Of or belonging to the palm tree. *Kanl.* 34:3. Laau *pama.* See also *Puk.* 15:27.

Pa-ma-ke, *s. Pa* and *make,* death. Deaths often repeated, as one dies after another as in a time of general sickness; he ola wale no ka mai, aole *pamake* iki na kanaka. See PAOLA.

Pa-ma-loo, *adv.* See PALOO. Thundering without rain, especially if the weather is good; aia a lohe aku kakou i ka hekili kui *pamaloo. Laieik.* 181.

Pa-na, *v.* To shoot out; to shoot, as an arrow. *Hal.* 11:2. The whole form is *pana pua. Nah.* 21:30. To shoot at; i ole e aihueia (na iwi) a hanaia i mea *pana* iole, that (the bones) might not be stolen and made into instruments for *shooting* mice. NOTE.—Among Hawaiians formerly, the greatest contempt a person could show of his enemy was, to procure some of his bones after he was dead, and make them into fish-hooks for taking fish or arrow heads for shooting mice.

2. To snap, as a person snaps with his finger on any substance.

3. To spread out; to open.

4. To excite; to raise up; to cast; to throw.

5. To give a name or appellation.

Pa-na, *s.* The act of shooting an arrow.

2. The act of the arrow in flying from the bow to the object.

3. A bow to shoot with; a cross bow; kanaka *pana* pua, an archer. *1 Sam.* 31:3. He mau mea *pana,* hunting instruments. *Kin.* 27:3.

4. A portion of land less than an *aina.* See APANA, a piece.

5. The pulse; nawaliwali ka *pana,* the *pulse* is feeble.

Pa-na-pu-a, *s. Pana* and *pua,* arrow. A shooter of arrows; an archer. *Iob.* 16:13.

Pa-nai, *v.* To put one thing in the place of another, i.e., to compensate for something lost.

2. To give a substitute; to redeem. *Puk.* 13:13.

3. To buy one's liberty; to pay a redeeming price; to exchange prisoners. *Isa.* 43:4.

4. To fit one thing to another, as one piece of cloth to another; to cover up a defect, as with a patch.

5. To stitch together; to splice on.

6. To graft; e *panai* aku; the same as *pakui.*

Pa-nai, *s.* A thing substituted for another; a substitute. *Nah.* 3:41.

2. A ransom; a price paid for redeeming. *Isa.* 43:3. SYN. with uku panai.

3. A surety for one. *Kin.* 43:9. He poe *panai,* hostages. *2 Oihl.* 25:24.

Pa-nai, *adj.* Closing up an entrance; filling a place wanting; entering the place of another; substituted; redeemed. *Nah.* 3:49.

Pa-na-i-o-le, *s.* LIT. A shooting of mice; an ancient pastime among Hawaiians.

Pa-na-i-ki, *adv.* Diagonally; from corner to corner; e opiopi *panaiki,* the same as *opiopi lepe,* to fold up catacornered.

Pa-nai-nai, *v.* See PANAI. To lengthen anything out when not long enough; to piece a thing, as kapa when not broad enough; to splice; to lengthen out by splicing. See PAKUIKUI.

Pa-nau, *v.* To be restless; to be uneasy; to act the gad-a-bout; to go about from house to house or from place to place; to act; to exert one's self. *Anat.* 27.

Pa-nau-a, *adj.* Weak; frail; applied to persons or things; nearly synonymous with *maimai;* he auwaa *panaua* la.

Pa-nau-e-a, *v.* To be poor or thin in flesh; to be very lean.

2. To be feeble in walking about.

3. To go slowly or carefully.

Pa-nau-e-a, *adj.* Thin; poor in flesh; weak.

2. Slow; tardy; dilatory.

Pa-na-kai, *adj.* Leaning; crooked; rough in motion; ke ike nei au ua mimo, ua *panakai* ole.

Pa-na-la-au, *s.* A possession of land out of one's own place of residence; holo o Kamehameha e nana i kona aupuni, a e ai i kona *panalaau,* Kamehameha sailed to look at his kingdom and to eat (enjoy) his *colonies,* i. e., receive the fruits or taxes of them.

2. A province; a dependency. *Ezer.* 4:15.

3. A land gained by conquest; he aina i lilo ma ke kaua.

Pa-na-le-a, *adj.* Pleasantly; with pleasure, as in dancing, in practicing the hula; me he hula *panalea* la i haa mai la. *Pana-lea* ka ua i kai o Hilo.

Pa-na-na, *v.* To row a canoe irregularly; to sail crookedly; to go here and there; to go beyond the place intended; to exhibit great awkwardness in steering a canoe or vessel.

Pa-na-na, *s. Pa* and *nana,* to look. A compass, especially a mariner's compass.

2. A pilot; one who directs the sailing of a vessel; he mea kuhikuhi holomoku.

Pa-na-nai, *v.* To touch or strike softly.

Pa-na-pa-na, *v.* See PANA. To snap with the thumb and finger.

2. To shoot, as a marble; lealea kamalii i ka *panapana* hua.

Pa-na-pa-na-ni-au, *s.* The name of a play or pastime anciently in practice.

Pa-na-pa-na-pu-hi, *s.* Name of a shellfish.

Pa-na-poo, *v. Pana,* to strike, and *poo,* head. To strike or scratch one's head, to cause himself to remember something forgotten; oia iho la no ka ko'u wahi a *panapoo* i noonoo iho ai.

Pa-ne, *v.* To open, as the mouth preparatory to speak. *Iob.* 3:1. To utter; to speak.

2. To speak in reply. *Puk.* 19:19. To answer; to answer a question. *Kin.* 44:16. To answer to a call. *Iob.* 5:1.

3. To speak first; to reply back and forth, as in conversation.

4. To strike upon the ear, as a voice; *pane* ole, dumb; silent.

Pa-ne, *s.* The joining of the head with the bones of the neck; he hookuina o ka iwi poo me ka iwi a-i. See PANEPOO.

Pa-nee, *v. Pa* and *nee,* to move along. To move along; to drive back; to push out; to shove along, as a canoe on the sand; *panee* aku la i ka waa i kai, they *pushed off* the canoe into the sea; to move slowly, as in ascending a hill or pali; *panee* i ka pali.

2. To wait a little; to delay.

3. To pass away; to be transient; to be vanishing. 1 *Ioan.* 2:17.

4. *Hoo.* To drive back; to thrust at; to push a thing out of its place.

5. To delay; to procrastinate. *Kin.* 34:19. To put off the time; to procrastinate; hai mai oia (o Liholiho) i kona manao e *hoopanee* aku i ka mihi.

Pa-nee, *adj.* By interest; what is gained for the use of money as interest; money gained by putting off payment. *Isa.* 56:11. Waiwai *panee.* See UKUHOOPANEE.

Pa-ne-e-ha, *v.* To haul long; to drag; to move slowly.

Pa-nee-nee, *v.* To move little by little; to go ahead; to excel.

Pa-ne-poo, *s. Pane* and *poo,* head. The occiput or hinder part of the head. See PANE.

Pa-ne-pa-ne, *v.* See PANE. To answer back; to quarrel; to scold; to be angry; to express anger in words.

Pa-ni, *v.* See PANAI, to put something in a vacancy or in the place of something removed. To close up an opening; to shut, as a window; to shut, as the door of a house; as the gate of a city. *Ios.* 2:5, 7. To shut off, as the light of the sun; ka manu nana e *pani* ka la. *Laieik.* 175.

2. To supply a deficiency; to supply a vacancy; e pani i ka *hakahaka,* to fill the breach; to put one thing in the place of another; a *paniia* iho la ka hilahila ame ka makau ma ka hakahaka o ka huhu, shame and fear *took the place* of anger. *Laieik.* 203.

3. *Hoo.* To close up; to fasten; to muzzle the mouth. 1 *Tim.* 5:18.

Pa-ni, *s. Art.* ke. Something filling a vacancy; that which fills or takes the place of another person or thing. *Nah.* 32:14.

2. That which closes an entrance, as the door of a house, the shutter of a window, the gate of a city, the stopper of a bottle, &c. *Hal.* 24:7. Nui ka poe i make i ke *pani.*

Pa-ni, *s. Eng.* A pan.

Pa-ni-a, *v.* See PANI. *Pania* is for *paniia,* to be shut up. Me he mea la i *pania* mai ka waimaka. *Laieik.* 142.

Pa-ni-o, *v.* To spot; to paint in spots;

to variegate, as colors; to write.

PA-NI-O-NI-O, *v.* See ONIO. To print a kapa in gaudy colors; to variegate in colors; to dye with different colors, but more or less gaudy.

PA-NI-HA-KA, *v.* *Pani* and *haka*, a space. To fill a place or vacancy.

PA-NI-HA-KA, *s.* A supply of a deficiency; that which supplies something wanting; more often doubled, thus,

PA-NI-HA-KA-HA-KA, *v.* To fill a vacancy; to supply or fill a deficiency; *adverbially*, in the place of; to supply a deficiency. *Kin.* 4:25.

PA-NI-HA-KA-HA-KA, *s.* One acting in the place of another. *Kin.* 30:2.

PA-NI-HI, *v.* *Pa* and *nihi*, to turn sideways. To wound slightly; to ruff up the skin; to rub over; e mahinu.

PA-NI-HO-LO-A, *s.* The name of a kind of fish.

PA-NI-KI, *s.* Coloring matter; a dye for coloring kapas; wai hoohinuhinu.

PA-NI-NA, *s.* The youngest born; the youngest of a family of children; the youngest child as *hiapo* is the oldest; ka pokii.

2. A breaking off or cutting short.

3. The *pani ana*; the shutting up, i. e., the *pau ana of the hanau ana.*

PA-NI-NA, *adj.* Having great cheeks, as a man.

PA-NI-NI-O, *v.* To color or dye with gay colors; to paint or print as the *kilohana* was formerly printed. See PANIONIO.

PA-NI-PA-NI, *v.* See PANI. To strike; to strike back, as an echo; to echo. See PINAI.

2. (A lascivious word.) To prostitute; to commit adultery for pay; said to be of Chinese origin by Chasmisso.

PA-NI-PU, *s.* *Pani* and *pu*, a gun. The wad of a gun.

PA-NI-PU-KA, *s.* *Pani* and *puka*, an entrance. That which closes an entrance; a door of a house; the gate of a city or a yard. *Neh.* 1:3.

PA-NI-PU-KA, *s.* A beggar, because beggars often took a seat in the door.

PA-NI-PU-PU, *s.* *Pani* and *pupu*, a bunch. An eye-stone.

PA-NO, *adj.* Black; deep blue; deep dark colored, as heavy clouds; dark, as the appearance of a fathomless abyss.

PA-NO-A, *v.* To make dry; to make solitary, as a dry, barren, desolate place. *Zep.* 2:13.

PA-NO-A, *s.* A wild desert place; a dry desert.

2. A deep place; a cavern. See PANO.

3. A name applied to a woman who cannot obtain a husband; or having a husband, is barren and has no children.

PA-NO-A, *adj.* Dry; applied to a place parched with drought, without water, where no vegetable grows, where no seed will vegetate.

PA-NO-A-NO-U, *v.* To be wet in spots, i. e., damp, as earth, and dry in spots; e huli mau ia, e loli ia, e ku e kuu.

PA-NO-E-A, *adj.* Dilatory; slow.

PA-NOO-NOO, *v.* To be without fish, as the sea beach; *panoonooia* kahakai e ka lawaia moku ke alii.

PA-NO-NO-NO, *s.* That which is full of holes or cracks.

PA-NO-NO-NO, *adj.* Full of holes; full of cracks. See HANONONO and HANONANONA.

PA-NO-PAU, *adj.* See PANA. Black; so black as to have a gloss; glistening black.

PA-NO-PAU, *s.* See PANO. Black streaks in the grains of wood.

PA-NO-PA-NO, *adj.* Intensive of *pano.* Thick; dense, as a cloud; black; glossy black. *Puk.* 19:9. See PAPANO. Dark blue; hence, beautiful; grand; splendidly attired; excellent.

PA-NO-PA-NO, *s.* Blackness; a deep blue color; shining jet blackness.

PA-NUU, *adj.* Growing thriftily, as young plants, while yet young; pauhu, pohuku.

PA-NU-HU-NU-HU, *s.* Name of a species of fish.

PA-PA. A reduplication of the distributive particle *pa.* See PA. It is often used as a verb; as, e *papa* lua, to make twofold, to put two together; e *papa* kolu, e *papa* ha, &c. See PALUA, PAKOLU, &c.

PA-PA, *s.* See PA, *s.* Applied to many substances having a flat, smooth surface, as a flat, smooth stone, a board, a plank, a table, a flat wooden dish, a plate. *Puk.* 39:30. *Papa* pohaku, a slate; *papa* kanawai, tables of the law. *Puk.* 25:16. *Papa* ai, *papa* aina, an eating table; *papa* wili ai, a poi board; *papa* manamana pukapuka, a grate of net work. *Puk.* 38:4. A wafer; a flat cake. *Puk.* 29:2. *Papa* konane, a board for the game of konane. *Laieik.* 115.

PA-PA, *s.* A row; a rank; a company standing or setting in a row; hence, a military band; a division of people; a sect; an order; *papa* inoa, a catalogue of names; a particular office, secular or ecclesiastical; a native born in a place; a story in a building; *papa* lalo, *papa* waena, *papa* luna, lower, middle and upper stories of a building. *Kin.* 6:16.

Pa-pa, *s.* An ancestor some generations back; a race; a family.

Pa-pa, *s.* The wife of Akea or Wakea, the fabled mother of the Islands and of men on them. See Opapa. Na Papa ka haku akea o Lono.

Pa-pa, *s.* A species of fish; a small crab, a species of the paiea.

    2. A term used in relation to a fish net.

    3. A scab; a shell; a slice or piece; *papa* kalo, a piece of kalo; *papa* ipu, a piece of melon.

    4. Name of a species of a soft stone.

Pa-pa, *s.* Name of a certain class of Kamehameha's laws.

Pa-pa, *v.* To prohibit; to forbid. Note. The language or the words of the prohibition generally follow. The rebuke; to reprove. *Kin.* 37:10. To adjure; to request in strong terms. *Nah.* 11:28.

    2. To erect a shade or screen to prevent the light or heat of the sun. See Papai, s.

    3. To shine, as the sun, i. e., to create light and heat.

Pa-pa, *adj.* Perhaps old; ancient; former times.

Pa-paa, *v. Pa* and *paa,* tight. To hold tight; to refuse to give up.

    2. Used for *paapaa,* to be dry; to be parched, as the tongue with thirst. *Isa.* 41:17.

    3. To burn; to burn freely; to be burnt up; to be consumed; e welawela.

Pa-paa, *adj.* Tight; secure, as an inclosure of any kind.

    2. Storing; securing; kulanakauhale *papaa,* a *store* city. 2 *Oihl.* 8:6.

    3. Strong; fenced, as a city. *Puk.* 1:11. Hale *papaa,* a store-house.

Pa-paa, *s.* Anything hard or compact; as, *papaa* lepo, a clod. *Iob.* 7:5.

Pa-pa-ai-na, *s. Papa,* table, and *aina,* eating. A table. *Puk.* 25:23. An eating table.

Pa-pa-a-kai, *v.* To wither, as a vegetable; to bear no fruit; to dry up; to be killed by insects.

    2. To be white on the surface like a salt pond; to become white, as salt granulating.

Pa-pa-a-ka-hi, *s. Papa* and *akahi,* one; first. The first border or rank.

Pa-pa-a-ke-a, *s.* The name of the soft white stone above Lahainaluna.

Pa-pa-a-la, *s.* The hot season; a time of drought; a time of famine; a time of no rain when all is parched with the sun; ka wa ua ame ka *papaala.*

Pa-pa-a-lu-a, *adv.* Doubly; two together; two by two. *Kin.* 7:15. See Palua.

Pa-pa-a-na, *v.* To be quick, as in gaining strength after sickness; *papaana* oe i ka nui, you have grown fleshy quickly; to hasten. *Hal.* 22:19.

    2. To be at ease; to rest; to breathe freely.

    3. To escape from danger.

    4. To overcome; to conquer.

    5. To lay a kapu; to prohibit. See Papa.

    6. To govern; to establish laws.

Pa-pa-a-na, *adj.* Resting; confiding; comfortable; satisfied; overcoming difficulties.

Pa-pa-a-poo, *s.* The name of the company of men sent out first from an army to plunder, to commit murder, steal men, &c.; understood as a commencement of hostilities and a declaration of war.

Pa-paa-pu, *v.* To wound; to hurt; to make a sore.

Pa-paa-be-re-na, *s. Papaa* and *berena* (*Eng.*), bread. A wafer. *Oihk.* 8:26.

Pa-pai, *s.* See Papa, shade. A temporary partition of a house; a house or room for playing a game; papai kilu. *Laieik.* 121. A screen; a roof on all sides; a slight slender house or shed.

    2. A species of crab-fish.

    3. He kikalapai, he pananai, he papa.

Pa-pai, *v. Pa* and *pai,* to strike. To smite with the open hand; to strike.

    2. To strike gently; to touch. *Kin.* 32:25.

    3. To thatch a house or building with grass. Note.—In the act of thatching, Hawaiians in drawing the string tightly around a handful of grass give it a blow with the left hand.

    4. To drive off or expel a tenant from his house and land; to drive off; to banish; a common punishment in former times for real or imaginary offenses.

    5. To make a solemn promise; to take an oath; e hoohiki ma ka ae ana; e *pai* na lima, ae na waha, the hands *strike,* the mouths assent.

Pa-pai-a, *s.* A foreign word. The custard apple; the pawpaw; the carica papaya; ka milikani, ka hei.

Pa-pai-a-a-wa, *s.* A form of worshiping the gods. See Pakiki.

Pa-pai-a-wa, *v.* To clap the hands while singing and praising the gods; i kela wa, *papaiawa* ae la o Aiwohikupua me kona mau kaukaualii. *Laieik.* 109.

Pa-pai-e-u.

Pa-pai-o, *v.* To set up the akua makahiki (the year god) and carry him off; *pa-*

paio ia ke akua a hele aku.

PA-PAI-HO, *v.* To set up above; to fix up on high; e kau iho maluna iho.

PA-PAI-LA-NAI, *s.* The name of a species of small crab.

PA-PA-I-NA, *v.* Pa and *paina*, to eat. To eat; to eat upon a table.

2. To break, as glass or crockery; to be brittle.

3. To crack, as the joints of the fingers.

4. To squeak, as new shoes. See UINA.

PA-PA-I-NA, *s.* The sound of small materials in breaking or cracking.

2. The noise made in eating.

3. The sound of the feet in walking.

4. The ticking of a watch.

PA-PA-I-NA, *adj.* That which may easily be broken; brittle.

PA-PAI-PA, *adj.* Pressed full.

PA-PA-I-PU, *adj.* See PAPAIEU. Barren; nothing in the calabash, especially no fish.

PA-PAI-WA-LE, *s.* *Papai*, to strike, and *wale*. A striking; a smiting; a method of killing in former times.

PA-PA-O, *v.* Pa and *pao*, to dig. To break in; to thrust in; to lay together.

2. To fill up; to cram wood into an oven.

PA-PA-O-HE, *s.* A fish, a species of akule.

PA-PA-O-KO-LE, *s.* See PAPAKOLE.

PA-PA-O-NO, *adj.* Papa and *ono*, six. See PAONO. By sixes; six by six; six-fold. *Hoik.* 4:8.

PA-PAU, *v.* Pa and *pau*, to be all; to be entire. To be deeply engaged in thought; to engage with all the powers of the mind in some research; to have full confidence in.

2. *Hoo.* To be fully engaged; to be all in earnest; to give the whole attention of heart and mind. 1 *Oihl.* 22:19.

3. To be entire; to be altogether or chiefly engaged in some pursuit; e *hoopapau* hoi ma ka hana maikai. *Hoopapau* iho la ke alii ma ka aie, the king's great business was to get into debt. *Hoopapau* loa oia i ka inu i ka rama, he drank rum *with all his might.*

4. To fill up; to raise up a heap; to suck in and fill up the mouth with water like a fish.

5. To be shallow, as water; to flow off, as the sea at low tide, leaving the water on the rocks shallow; to be at low tide; e kai make; a *papau* ae la ka Pele ma Oahu, alaila lele oia i Maui; a *papau* hou iho la ma Haleakala, lele hou oia i Kilauea, when Pele's dominions *became shallow* on Oahu (i. e., when burnt down near to the level of the sea), then she leaped over to Maui;

and when she *became shallow* again at Haleakala, she again jumped over to Kilauea.

PA-PAU, *s.* Shallowness; littleness; no depth, as water.

2. A ford of a river. *Kin.* 32:22. Fewness. *Mat.* 13:15.

3. With *make*, a graveyard. See PAPAU-MAKE.

PA-PAU, *adj.* Shallow, as water; not deep; kahi *papau*, a fording place.

PA-PAU-A, *v.* To compel persons to hard bondage; to weary them day by day with severe labor; to make hard-working slaves of people.

PA-PAU-A, *s.* Name of a species of shellfish; ano o ka pipi noloko o ke kai.

PA-PA-U-KI-U-KI, *s.* The name of a very fierce strong wind; makani ikaika pukiki.

PA-PA-U-KI-U-KI, *v.* To blow fiercely, as a strong wind; ua *papaukiuki* ka makani.

PA-PAU-KU, *v.* See PAPAPAUPU. To be all; to be entire; to be entirely in the circumstances mentioned; a *papauku* wale ka lukuna, the slaughter *was thorough and entire.*

PA-PAU-MA-KE, *s.* A graveyard; a burying ground; ke ku la na kii elua i ka *papaumake.* See KUPAPAU.

PA-PA-U-NU, *v.* To fill up; to cram down; to push in.

PA-PA-HA, *adj.* Papa and *ha*, four. Four by four; four times; by fours. See PAHA. *Ezek.* 1:6.

PA-PA-HE-HI, *s.* Papa, board, and *hehi*, to tread upon. The floor of a house; the boards to be trod on. 1 *Nal.* 6:15.

PA-PA-HI, *adj.* Of or belonging to a kind of lei; as, lei *papahi.*

PA-PA-HO-I-KE, *s.* Papa and *hoike*, to show. A table of witness or testimony to an agreement.

PA-PA-HO-LA, *s.* Papa and *hola*, spread out. The front of a heiau, in other cases called a *kahua*, i. e., mostly an artificial level place on which the heiau was built, but containing a greater surface than the building; hence, a court; a yard in front of a temple. 2 *Nal.* 1:2.

PA-PA-HOO-LE-WA-LE-WA, *s.* Name of a species of fish net.

PA-PA-HU-LU-I, *s.* Name of a species of fish net; he *papahului*, oia no ka upena o na ia ku.

PA-PA-KAI, *s.* A narrow escape of a canoe landing in the surf.

PA-PA-KAU-A, *s.* Name of a division of an army on going into battle.

PA-PA-KAU-KAU, *s.* An eating table.

Pa-pa-ka-na-li-ma, *adv.* By fifties; fifty in a company. 1 *Nal.* 18:4.

Pa-pa-ke-a, *s.* *Papa* and *kea*, white. That part of the sea beach washed by the high tide and not by the low, i. e., if the sand be white.

2. The action of the ocean current against the wind, when the waves stand up; he kupikipikio.

Pa-pa-kee-ha-na, *s.* A floor. 1 *Nal.* 6:30.

Pa-pa-ke-le-a-we, *s.* *Papa* and *keleawe*, copper. Copper plates used in sheathing ships.

Pa-pa-ko-a, *s.* Boards made from the koa tree.

2. *Papa*, row, and *koa*, soldier. A rank or company of an army. *Oih.* 10:1.

Pa-pa-ko-le, *s.* The hip bone; the hip; the joining of the hip bone with the socket bone; ka hookuina o ka iwi uha me ka iwi ka; the os *innominatum*.

Pa-pa-ko-le-a, *v.* To rise; to stand up, as water in a current of the sea; e kupiki-pikio. See Papakea.

Pa-pa-ko-li, *s.* See Papakole. The hip; the loins. *Dan.* 5:6.

Pa-pa-ku, *s.* A disease attended with entire costiveness and always fatal.

Pa-pa-ku-ki-a, *s.* *Papa*, *ku* and *kia*, a mast. The mast of a ship.

2. That which strengthens a mast. *Isa.* 33:23.

Pa-pa-ku-ku-i, *s.* A species of fish.

Pa-pa-la, *v.* Not to be able to sound; to emit sound with difficulty; to make a hoarse sound; to be hoarse.

Pa-pa-la, *adv.* Hoarsely; like a hoarse person; kani *papala* mai la hoi, ua uweka nei.

Pa-pa-la, *s.* The name of a tree.

2. Bird lime, a sticky material by which birds are caught; he kepau kapili manu.

Pa-pa-la, *adj.* Heavy, as a back-load.

2. O ka lahui a ka ipo ahi *papala*.

Pa-pa-la-au, *s.* *Papa*, flat, and *laau*, timber. A board; a plank; o ka *papalaau* ka mea kui poi.

Pa-pa-la-o-a, *s.* A smooth kind of cloud indicating rain or wind, from its resembling the fish *palaoa*.

Pa-pa-la-le, *v.* To do awkwardly or unskillfully; to have things all out of place.

Pa-pa-la-le, *adj.* Awkward; unskill-ful; unthinking; unreflecting; inexpert.

Pa-pa-la-lo, *s.* *Papa*, board, and *lalo*, below. The lower story of a house. *Kin.* 6:16.

2. The floor of a house. *Nah.* 5:17.

Pa-pa-le, *v.* *Pa* and *pale*, to defend off. To be out of place; to put together unskill-fully. See Papalale.

2. To have or to put on a hat or bonnet. *Ezek.* 44:16.

3. *Metaphorically*, to cover up; to hide; ua ulu kou nani a *papale* maluna o kou kaikuaana. *Laieik.* 196.

Pa-pa-le, *s.* *Pa* and *pale*, a defense. A hat; a cat; a bonnet; any covering for the head.

2. A chapiter for the top of a pillar. 2 *Oihl.* 3:15.

3. A shovel. *Puk.* 27:3. *Papale* hainika, a mitre. *Puk.* 28:4. *Papale* kahuna, a mitre. *Oihk.* 8:9. *Papala* laa, a holy crown. *Puk.* 39:30.

Pa-pa-le-a-lii, *s.* *Papale*, hat, and *alii*, chief. A crown; a distinguishing head dress of a king. *Hoik.* 6:2. Same as *leialii*.

Pa-pa-le-ka-pu, *s.* A cap.

Pa-pa-le-laa, *s.* *Papale* and *laa*, conse-crated. A holy or consecrated crown. *Puk.* 39:30.

Pa-pa-le-na, *v.* *Papale* and *ana*. To put out of order; to displace; to do a thing awkwardly. See Papale, *v.*

Pa-pa-li-ma, *adv.* See Palima. By fives; five by five; five in company.

Pa-pa-li-ma, *v.* *Papa*, to strike, and *lima*, hand. To touch or join hands, as in confirming a bargain, or as the sign of an agreement; as in English, *to shake hands* upon it.

Pa-pa-li-na, *s.* *Papa* and *lina*, soft. The side of the face; the cheek. *Kanl.* 18:3. He wahi palahalaha malalo o ka maka ma na aoao o ka ihu.

Pa-pa-li-na-nu-i, *adj.* Large, fleshy and weak.

Pa-pa-lo-le, *adj.* Slovenly done.

Pa-pa-lu, *v.* To bind up; to dress, as a wound.

2. To hide; to put out of sight; to cover up.

3. To go off and hide one's self.

4. To be soft; to be defective; to be rotten; popopo.

Pa-pa-lu, *s.* An occasional dress when employed in dirty work that would injure a common dress.

2. A dress different from the pa-u.

3. An apron. *Kin.* 3:7.

4. The principal covering garment, or covering of a person.

Pa-pa-lu-a, *v.* *Papa* and *lua*, two. To double; to put two things together of the same kind.

2. To be double. *Hal.* 68:17. To be two-fold. *Kin.* 41:32. See PALUA.

PA-PA-LU-A, *s. Papa*, story of a house, and *lua*, two. The second story or floor of a building. *Kin.* 6:16.

PA-PA-LU-A, *dist. adv.* See PALUA. Two by two; two-fold; two at a time; doubly; in pairs, &c. *Kin.* 6:20.

PA-PA-MAU, *adj.* Creaking; grating, as the friction of one thing against another. See EEINA.

PA-PA-MA-NA-MA-NA, *s. Papa* and *manamana*, branching. A grate; a grating. *Puk.* 27:4.

PA-PA-MU, *s.* The name of the board on which the game konane is played.

PA-PA-NA, *v. Papa* and *ana.* To be quick; to be smart; to do things readily.
 2. To be boasting; to be proud of one's own doings.

PA-PA-NA, *s.* Haste; quickness in accomplishing an object.

PA-PA-NE, *v. Pa* and *pane*, to reply. To scold; to chide; to be angry; to answer back provokingly.

PA-PA-NI, *v.* See PANI, to stop up. To shut, as an opening; to close; to shut up. *Isa.* 66:9.
 2. To shut, as a door or other shutter. *Kin.* 7:6.
 3. To hide; to conceal; to veil; to put out of sight.
 4. To close or stop, as the ears. *Oih.* 7:57.
 5. To hide; to close the eyes. *Puk.* 3:6.
 6. To shut up one, as if sick or infected. *Oihk.* 13:4.
 7. To hold fast; to bind; to hinder one from doing a thing.
 8. To turn on the hinges, as a door.

PA-PA-NI, *adj.* Shutting out; parting off, as a partition; closing up.

PA-PA-NO, *adj.* See PANO and PANO-PANO. Thick; black; glossy black.

PA-PA-NO-A-NO-A, *s.* Any substance full of holes or cracked; he hanonanona, he panonono.

PA-PA-NOO, *adj.* See PANO and PAPANO. Dark colored; black, as a black cloud.

PA-PA-NO-NA-NO-NA, *adj.* Thick together; collected; laid up in store; rising up; standing together.

PA-PA-PA, *s.* A kind of food; beans, from the flat pods, also applied to purslain.

PA-PA-PA, *adj.* Low; broken down; flat and smooth, as the smooth surface of lava.

PA-PA-PA-I-NA, *s. Papa* and *paina*, to eat. An eating table; a table. 1 *Kor.* 10:21.

PA-PA-PAU, *v. Papa*, a double reduplication of *pau*, all. To put all together in one; to sum up together.
 2. To consider all alike or all as in one condition; mai *papapau* na kanaka i ka make, nearly all the people died, i. e., they were nearly *alled* by death.
 3. To be all together in one place; mai *papapau* iho kakou ia nei, let us not *all stay* in this place.
 4. To bring to an end, as the end of life; the same as *e pau ke aho*, or *e mamake*, to cause to die or perish together.

PA-PA-PAU, *adj.* All together; consumed; finished; entirely at an end; all dead.

PA-PA-PA-LA-O-A, *s. Papa* and *palaoa* for *falaoa* (Eng.), flour. A cake; a wafer; a flat loaf of bread. *Ier.* 7:18.

PA-PA-PA-LA-PA-LA, *s. Papa* and *pala-pala*, a writing. A writing table. *Luk.* 1:63. A writing desk.

PA-PA-PO-HA-KU, *s. Papa* and *pohaku*, stone. A board on which food or poi is pounded; the pestle is made of stone; he pohaku kui ai; the board or thick plank is slightly hollowed out like a very flat tray. See KUIAI and PAPAWILIAI.
 2. A row or tier of stones. *Ezer.* 6:4.
 3. A slate; a stone for writing on.
 4. A table of stone. *Kanl.* 5:19.

PA-PA-PU, *v. Papa* and *pu*, together. See PAPAPAU. To do all together; to do all alike; a lele mai kekahi poe o kakou, a *papapu* mai mamuli o ke kumu.

PA-PA-PU, *s. Papa* and *pu*, a gun. A row or tier of guns.

PA-PA-WAE-NA, *s. Papa* and *waena*, between. The middle story of a building of three stories. *Kin.* 6:16.

PA-PA-WA-HA-NU-I, *s.* Taking fish with a long net; o ka upena ka mea hana i *papawahanui*.

PA-PA-WI-LI, ⎫ *s. Papa*, board, *wili*,
PA-PA-WI-LI-AI, ⎭ to mix, and *ai*, food. A board for mixing food; a poi board; a very flat tray on which poi is pounded; a kneading trough. *Puk.* 12:34.

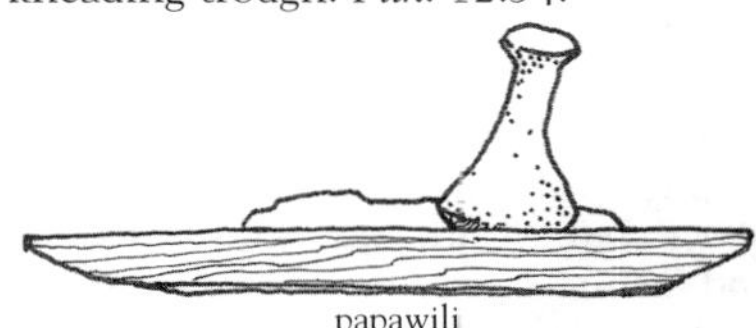

papawili

PA-PA-BE-RE-NA, *s. Papa* and *berena* (Eng.), bread. Flat cakes. *Kin.* 18:6.

PA-PA-GU-LA, *s. Papa* and *gula* (Eng.),

gold. A plate of gold. *Puk.* 28:36.

Pa-pa-rai, *s.* *Pa*, pan, and *parai* (*Eng.*), for *farai*, to fry. A frying-pan. *Oihk.* 2:7.

Pa-pi-o, *adv.* *Pa* and *pio*, an arch. Lying face downward with nothing for the belly to rest on, for the purpose of enlarging the belly; e moe *papio*, e huli ilalo ke alo i nui ka opu.

Pa-pi-o-pi-o, *s.* Name of a fish like the ulua; perhaps the young of the ulua.

Pa-pi-pi, *s.* The prickly pear.

Pa-po-ha-ku, *s.* *Pa*, fence, and *pohaku*, stone. Stones laid into a wall; a stone wall. *Nah.* 35:4.

2. Name of a kind of soft stone.

Pa-pu, *s.* A plain; a level piece of ground of considerable extent. *Nah.* 36:13.

2. *Pa*, wall, and *pu*, gun. A gun fence, i. e., a fort; he pa kaua.

Pa-pu, *v.* To explain; to make clear; to converse freely.

Pa-pu, *adv.* Fully; wholly covered; established; plainly; clearly.

Pa-pu-a, *v.* *Pa*, to throw (see Pa 5), and *pua*, an arrow. To cast or throw an arrow, a pastime or exercise for men, women and children; name of a game played in former times.

Pa-pu-he-a, *s.* A mist; fine rain; a fog.

2. A gray head; a gray headed person.

Pa-pu-he-ne, *s.* A row of men in a certain game. See Puhenehene. O na hewa kahiko, o ka hula, o ka pili, o ka *papuhene* kekahi; he lealea ino o ka *papuhene* i ka po.

Pa-pu-ro, *s.* The Egyptian papyrus. *Iob.* 8:11.

Pa-wa, *s.* A garden; a cultivated patch of ground.

2. The sky; the blue expanse of the heavens.

3. The breaking of the dawn; ka wahi awa o ke alaula; the period early in the morning; kani ana ka bele i ka wanaao, i ka wehe ana o ka *pawa* o ke ao. A ike ke kahuna, ua moku ka *pawa* o ke ao.

4. A watch; a period of time; a particular time of the twenty-four hours. 1 *Sam.* 11:11.

5. Some early part of the morning dawn.

Pa-waa, *s.* Wildness; fearfulness, like that of an untamed animal; rudeness; incivility of uncultivated persons.

Pa-waa, *adj.* Wild; rude; rough in habits and manners; untamed, as an animal.

Pa-wai, *s.* *Pa* and *wai*, water. Lit. A water plate. A watering trough for cattle. *Kin.* 30:38.

Pa-wai-i-nu, *s.* *Pawai* as above, and *inu*, to drink. A drinking trough for cattle. *Kin.* 30:41.

Pa-wai-na, *s.* *Pa*, fence, and *waina*, grapes. A vineyard.

Pa-wao, *v.* To see with indistinctness; to be uncertain; to be in doubt.

Pa-wa-li, *adj.* See Puali. Crooked; deceitful; unjust; perverse.

Pa-wa-pa-wa, *adj.* Fat; plump; muscular; with shaking or rolling muscle.

Pa-wa-pa-wa, *s.* Fatness; muscular fleshed; roundness; i ka *pawapawa* haahaa onikiniki.

Pa-we-o, *v.* See Pawaa. To be wild; to be untamed; to express rudeness; to be uncivilized; to make blunders in everything attempted; to turn askance, as the eyes; to turn away the eyes. *Laieik.* 71. To be displeased with; a ike mai la o Poki ia ia, *paweo* ae la kona maka ia ia.

Pa-we-he, *adj.* A kind of spotted mat made on Niihau; moena *pawehe*.

Pa-we-lu, *s.* *Pa* and *welu*, a rag. Any worthless thing, as *opala*, *pahola* and *pawelu*; anything useless, valueless or of no account; ua hoolilo i ka olelo a ke Akua i pahola, a i *pawelu*, i mea ole, i mea lapuwale.

Pa-wi-wi, *v.* *Pa*, fence, and *wiwi*, slim. To make a very tall, high fence so as to be weak.

Pa-wi-wi, *s.* A tall, slim, weak fence.

Pa-rai, *v.* *Eng.* To fry. *Oihk.* 7:12. The word should be written with *f* instead of *p*, thus: *farai* or *ferai*.

Pa-ra-bo-le, *s.* *Eng.* from Gr. A parable; an enigmatical discourse; he olelo nane.

Pa-ra-dai-so,
Pa-re-dai-so,
Pa-ra-di-so, *s.* *Gr.* Paradise; a happy garden; a happy place. *Luk.* 23:43.

Pa-so-a, *s.* *Eng.* The passover; the name of a feast of the Jews in commemoration of the passing of the Angel of Death over them when he slew all the first born of the Egyptians. *Puk.* 12.

Pa-tau-sa-ni, *adv.* *Pa* and *tausani* (*Eng.*), thousand. By thousands; a thousand fold. *Kanl.* 1:11.

Pe, *adv.* Thus; so; as; in this way; it is often prefixed to *la*, *nei* and *ia*; as, *pela*, thus, so; *penei* or *peneia*, like this, thus; *peia*, this way, like it, &c. It also stands by itself, especially in asking questions, as, *pe keia?* I iho la au, *pe keia?* I said, *how* is this? *Pekeia* are sometimes written together, signifying as this, thus, after this manner, &c.

Pe, *v.* To anoint; to apply odoriferous ointment.

2. *Hoo.* To anoint; to pour on odoriferous ointment.

3. Fig. To scent; i. e., to give tone and character to one's life; applied also to the soul; o ke kupaoa ia e *hoope* ai na uhane. See Kupaoa.

Pe, *v.* To be humble; to crush; to pound fine. See Pepe.

Pe, *adj.* Broken or flatted down; depressed; crushed.

Pe-a, *v.* To make a cross; to set up timbers in the form of a cross; to make four arms or four prominent points; to be opposed to.

2. *Hoo.* To accuse through envy. *Mat.* 27:18. To punish for little or no crime; ame ka *hoopea* wale o ka poe koikoi i ka poe liilii, and the great *accused* (punished) the small.

3. To be in bonds; to suffer, as a prisoner. *Kol.* 4:3. To bind one's hands behind his back or to a post; ua *peaia* kona mau lima i kona kua, no ka aihue.

4. To be bound or restrained from producing an effect. 2 *Tim.* 2:9. Hou aku la i ka hulu i ka inika, kakau iho la, *pea* ae la no, o kohu hele.

Pe-a, *s.* The extremity of a village or settlement; mai kela *pea* a i keia *pea*, from one *end* of the settlement to the other *end*.

2. The name of one of the six houses of the ancient Hawaiians; he hale *pea*, oia kekahi hale. See Hale. E pani i ka puka o ka *pea* kapu, to shut the door of the *pea* kapu, sacred house. *Laieik.* 167.

3. The sail of a canoe or ship.

4. The extreme end of a leaf of a tree.

5. A flying kite; he lupe hoolele.

6. The ground of offense; an entanglement in law, a difficulty.

7. The name of a many-pronged fish in the ocean; he mea ola manamana maloko o ka moana.

8. He hale koko. See Halepea.

9. The excrements of men; the place where they are thrown.

10. A cross or timbers put cross wise thus ✗, formerly placed before the heiaus as a sign of kapu (taboo); e kau pea, to place in the form of a cross. See Kea.

Pe-a, *adj.* Filthy; unclean; kapa *pea*. *Isa.* 64:6. Welu *pea*, a menstruous cloth. *Isa.* 30:22. Defiled; haumia; belonging to menstruation. See Halepea and Kapapea.

Pe-ao, *v.* To roll up, as a piece of paper.

Pe-a-hi, *s.* The bones of the hand distinct from the arm; e malama i kona mau iwi ame na *peahi* lima.

2. The open hand; an open hand as a symbol of power. *Hal.* 44:3.

3. A fan. *Mat.* 3:12. The sign or picture of a fan marked on anything; he *peahi* ko kona poe kanaka, oia o lakou hoailona; ua kakauia ma ko lakou papalina.

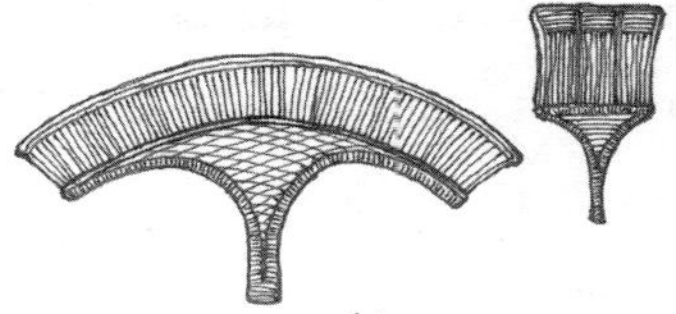

peahi

4. A gentle fanning breeze; a soft wind, as though made with a fan; he koaniani.

Pe-a-hi, *v.* To fan; to sweep; to brush; to make wind with a fan.

2. To motion or beckon to one with the hand or otherwise.

3. To make signs with the hand. See Kunou.

Pe-a-hi-li-ma, *s.* The palm of the hand. See Peahi. A hand's breadth. *Ezek.* 40:5.

Pe-a-pe-a, *v.* See Pea, *v.* To get into a difficulty; to quarrel; to be opposed to; to be entangled.

2. To be crossed together; to be braided or woven, as mats.

Pe-a-pe-a, *adj.* Difficult; perplexed; entangled; twisted; braided or woven together.

Pe-a-pe-a, *s.* Water made dirty by washing fish or other things.

2. The crossing of slats, as in verandas, at an oblique angle.

> Kohola i ka *peapea*,
> Koele iho lena kahakai—e—
> Lena kohola i ka *peapea* ike,
> Holo ia ole ia ka heka,
> Kaheka Hilo ma ka ua,
> He makaha ua i ka lani.

Pe-a-pe-a-a-hi, *v.* See Peahi. To sweep; to brush a floor, as in former times, by striking a kapa down upon it.

2. To fan; to cool; to cause a wind.

3. To flap the wings, as a bird in flying.

Pe-e, *v.* To hide away from some person; to run and hide; to conceal one's self. *Kin.* 3:8. To flee away. *Puk.* 21:13. Ke hoolohe nei ua kanaka la e *pee* ana i ka olelo. See Haupeepee. Kakali na kanaka i kahi a lakou i *pee* ai, the people staid in the place where they hid.

Pee-o-ne, *s.* Pee, to hide, and *one*, sand. A species of crab that burrows in the sand.

Pee-ku-e, *adj.* Thick, as a plank or

board; manoanoa, makolukolu; no ka piha o kona poo i na kahiko *peekue* o ka manao.

Pee-lu-a, *s.* *Pee* and *lua,* hole. A species of worm destructive to vegetation; the same as the *anuhe* or *enuhe.* 2 *Oihl.* 6:28. A caterpillar perhaps.

Pee-pee, *s.* A kind of sea moss.

Pee-pee-a-ku-a, *s.* The play of hide and seek.

Pee-pee-ku-e, *adj.* See PEEKUE. Thick, &c. See MANOA.

Pee-po-li, *v.* *Pee* and *poli,* bosom. To be or to lie in the bosom, as a child.

Pee-pee-pu-e-o.

Pei, *adv.* Thus; so; as follows, &c.; alaila, manao iho la au *pei,* then I thought *thus;* kauoha ia *pei* ia kakou i na la Sabati a pau, he charged us *thus* on every Sabbath day.

Pe-i, *v.* To lift up; to raise up; e hapai, e kaikai.

Pe-i-a, *adv.* *Pe* and *ia,* it. Thus; like it; after this manner. SYN. with penei, peneia, menei, keia, meia, &c. E like me ka moa e hoouluulu ana i kana mau keiki malalo o kona mau eheu, *peia* no hoi keia kula nui.

Pei-pei, *v.* See PEI. To rouse up; to stir up one to duty; to excite to action; to cast off sluggishness.

Pei-pei, } *adj.* Exciting; stirring up;
Pe-pei, } rousing to action. See the verb. He manao *peipei* no keia ia kakou.

Pe-o, *s.* A house with a rounding roof.

Pe-o, *adj.* Round; rounding; globular.

Pe-o-pe-o, *adj.* Round; roundish; without angles or corners.

Pe-u, } *v.* To throw up; to turn up,
Pe-pe-u, } as a hog turns or throws up his nose in rooting; hence, applied to anything of that motion.

2. To hunch or touch for the purpose of attracting attention.

Pe-u, } *s.* Words often used in las-
Pe-pe-u, } civious meles.

Pe-u-pe-u, *v.* To make frequent and many tracks. See MEHEU.

Pe-u-pe-u, *adj.* Tracked or trodden, as through the grass.

Pe-ua, *v.* To meet together; to unite; to kiss. See MEUA and MEU.

Pe-ua, *adj.* Uniting; joining; adhering.

Pe-u-ta, *s.* *Eng.* Pewter; tin. *Nah.* 31:22. See PIUTA and PIULA.

Pe-he, *adv.* See PE, as, in this manner, and HE, indefinite article. As a; so as; like as. See MEHE.

Pe-he, *s.* A snare; a kind of trap for catching owls. See PEHEAPUEO. *Pehe* ma ke kino.

Pe-he-a, *adv. inter.* *Pe,* as, and *hea,* how? In what manner? how? why? what?

Pe-he-a, *v.* See the adverb above. To ask how or in what manner a thing was done; to inquire how a person is; alaila, *pehea* iho la kela? pane mai la ia, *pehea* hoi, then that person *asked how it was done?* he answered, *how indeed.*

Pe-he-a-pu-e-o, *s.* See PEHE, snare, A, of, for, and PUEO, owl. A snare or trap for catching owls.

Pe-he-u, *adj.* *Pe* and *heu,* soft; flexible. Soft and flabby, as flesh; soft and tough; vibrating to and fro.

2. Webbed, as the foot of a duck or goose; he *peheu* ke kapuai o ke koloa ame ka nene.

Pe-he-u, *s.* The wing of a bird. See EHEU. The fin of a shark; a flipper of a turtle; the brim of a hat. See PELELEU.

Pe-he-u-he-u, *adj.* Soft; spongy; flexible, as the muscle of the calf of the leg or of the thigh.

2. Plump or swollen, as the neck in mumps; a-i *peheuheu.*

3. Whiskered; having large whiskers.

Pe-hi, *v.* To pelt with stones; to throw stones at. *Puk.* 21:18. To shoot, as an arrow. *Hal.* 18:14. SYN. with pana. To throw any missle at one; to threaten to stone, as a criminal. 1 *Sam.* 30:6. See NOU, KIPEHI and PANA. E *pehi* i ka ulu, to *throw* the maika stone.

Pe-hu, *v.* To swell, as any part of the body from injury or disease. *Kanl.* 8:4. *Hoo.* To cause a swelling. *Nah.* 5:2.

2. To swell, i. e., to increase in size generally; to enlarge. See UPEHU and UPEHU-PEHU.

Pe-hu, *s.* A swelling; a blain; a boil. *Oihk.* 13:2. *Pehu* nui, a great swelling.

2. The name of a game; o ka *pehu* ma ka hale.

Pe-hu, *adj.* Swollen; enlarged; mai *pehu,* the dropsy. See UPEHUPEHU.

Pe-hu-a. See PEKUA.

Pe-hu-a-koa, *s.* The name of a kind of kapa, colored with the bark of the koa tree.

Pe-hu-pa-la, *s.* *Pehu,* swollen, and *pala,* soft. A scab; the name of a disease. *Kanl.* 28:27.

Pe-hu-pe-hu, *adj.* See PEHU. Swollen; enlarged. See UPEHUPEHU.

Pe-ka, *adj.* A false interpretation in trading; favoring one's self.

Pe-ka, *v.* See PAKA. To teach one specifically something to say or do.

Pe-kaa, *s.* Name of a fruit like a bean; he pipa.

Pe-ka-pe-ka, *v.* To advise one to do wrong.

2. To calumniate another for self advancement; to detract; to find fault with one.

3. To be hard in dealing with one.

Pe-ka-pe-ka, *s.* Slander; detraction; saying hard things of one.

Pe-ka-pe-ka, *adj.* Slanderous; reviling; calumnious; stingy; close; parsimonious.

Pe-ke, *adj.* Short. See Poko. Low; not tall; poupou.

Pe-ke-keu, *s.* The wing of a fowl. See Ekekeu and Eheu.

2. The fin of a fish. *Oihk.* 11:9.

Pe-ke-pe-ke, *adj.* See Peke. Short; low.

Pe-ki, *v.* To send one off in haste on an errand; to send away.

Pe-ku, *v.* To kick with the foot. See Keehi. Elua *peku* ana me ka wawae, he *kicked* him twice with his foot; to kick, or to act as one about to kick; he keehi uuku me he mea hoowahawaha la; applied to a horse or a man.

Pe-ku-a.

Pe-ku-pe-ku, *v.* Frequentative. To kick frequently.

Pe-la, *v.* To tie up a bundle for a pillow of pulu. See Pelamoe.

2. To be unclean; to be filthy; to emit stench. See Pelapela.

3. To be thus, that is, after the manner specified ; to be done as before mentioned. See the adverb.

Pe-la, *adv.* See Pe, thus, so, and La, particle of place. Thus; in that manner. It always refers to a past transaction or something absent as *penei* does to something present. *Pela io no,* adverbial phrase, *so be it;* amen.

Pe-la, *s.* Bones burnt for manure to enrich the ground; he a ahi i kipuluia, he hoomomona i ka lepo.

2. The putrid flesh and bowels of the dead body of a chief after the bones were separated; the mass was thrown into the sea.

Pe-la-mo-e, *s. Pela,* a pillow, and *moe,* to lie down. A pillow for the comfort of sleeping. See Pela, *v.*

Pe-la-ne, *adj. Heb.* Of or belonging to chestnut; na laau *pelane,* chestnut rods. *Kin.* 30:37.

Pe-la-pe-la, *v.* See Pela 2. To be defiled; to be unclean; to stink; to emit a bad smell. See Eka, Haueka, Kaeka and Paupau.

Pe-la-pe-la, *s.* Uncleanness; filth; refuse dirty matter. *Isa.* 4:4; 1 *Kor.* 4:13.

Pe-la-pe-la, *adj.* Filthy; stinking; dirty; mean.

Pe-la-ta-no, *s. Heb.* Name of a tree mentioned in *Ezek.* 31:8; chestnut perhaps. See Pelane.

Pe-le, *s.* The name of the fabled goddess of volcanoes.

2. A volcano; he ahi ai honua; a fire consuming the earth; i neia wa, ua pio ka nui o na *pele;* i ka wa kahiko, he *pele* no ma Maui, at the present time the greater number of *volcanoes* is extinct; in ancient times there was a *volcano* also on Maui.

3. Sulphur proceeding from a volcano.

4. A stone from a volcano used in the play called puhenehene. See Noa.

Pe-le, *v.* To swell out; to be large; to be fleshy; to be fat; to have a large belly.

Pe-le, *adj.* Swelled out; enlarged; fleshy.

Pe-le-u, *v.* To break a kapu; to violate some article of the chiefs that was kapu or sacred; ua *peleuia* ke kapa o ke alii, the dress of the chief *has been defiled.*

2. To hide one's sins or offenses from a chief.

3. To hide the sins of another.

Pe-le-u, *adj.* Hiding or concealing the sins of one; he kanaka *beleu* oia.

Pe-le-hu, *s.* Name of a species of kapa made on Kauai.

2. Epithet of a turkey, from *pele,* to swell, and *hu,* to swell or puff out. See Palahu.

Pe-le-ku-nu, *adj.* Having a rank smell; strong-scented; sour; musty; *pelekunu* ka ia.

Pe-le-le-u, *s.* A fishing canoe of the largest size, made shorter in proportion than ordinary.

2. Name of a large double-canoe used in war.

3. The brim of a hat. See Peheu.

Pe-le-le-u, *v.* To bear away small quantities of a thing; to carry away frequently; to carry a little at a time.

2. To make many separations or divisions of a thing; e hoohikihiki.

Pe-le-le-u, *adj.* Note.—*Peleleu* is used as a noun. See above. But it is also frequently used as an adjective with *waa,* canoe; as, *waa peleleu,* a short canoe; kalai iho la ia ame na 'lii i na *waa peleleu* he nui loa, he and the chiefs hewed out a great many large *war canoes.*

2. As an *adjective,* short and thick.

Pe-le-ta, *s. Heb.* A species of vegetable

used for food; fitches perhaps. *Ezek.* 4:9.

PE-LI-KA-NA, *s. Eng.* A pelican, an unclean bird. *Kanl.* 14:17.

PE-LU, *v.* To double over; to bend or flex, as a joint; to open and shut, as a penknife; to double or fold over, as a cloth. *Puk.* 26:9. To bend or curve up.

PE-LU, *adj.* Doubled; folded over; shut up, as a knife; pahi *pelu*, a shut knife of any kind; crooked; bent; pani *pelu*, a folding door.

PE-LU-A, *s.* Name of a greenish kind of worm which eats and injures vegetables. See PELUE and KAKALA.

PE-LU-E, *s.* See PELUA above. A worm that eats potatoes and other vegetables, between a black and green color.

PE-LU-PE, *v.* To project; to send out.

PE-LU-PE-LU, *v.* See PELU. To double over and over.

2. FIG. To talk here and there; to recapitulate.

3. *Hoo. Hoopelupelu* iho la i kana olelo, he *doubled and twisted* his speech, i. e., he was very repetitious.

PE-LU-PE-LU, *s.* A binding; a doubling; a folding over. *Puk.* 28:32.

PE-LU-PE-LU, *adj.* Doubled over. FIG. Made hard or unfeeling, as the heart.

2. Doubled over, i. e., shortened; thick, &c. See PELELEU. Holo a kihi i ka waa *pelupelu* o lakou, they ran till they arrived at their *short canoe*, i. e., their boat.

PE-NA, *v. Eng.* To paint; to apply coloring matter to anything. NOTE.—The Hawaiian word is *hooluu.*

PE-NA, *s. Eng.* Paint; any substance mixed with oil or water to give another color; *pena* ulaula, vermilion. *Ezek.* 23:14. The Hawaiian term is *wai hooluu.*

PE-NEI, *adv.* See PE, thus, and NEI, here; this. Like this; after this manner; thus. See PEIA, PELA and PENEIA.

PE-NE-TE-KO-TA, *s. Gr.* The fiftieth; Pentecost, i. e., with la, the fiftieth day after the Israelites came out of Egypt, or the fiftieth day after the Passover, one of the three great annual feasts of the Jews. 1 *Kor.* 16:8.

PE-NE-TE-KO-TA, *adj.* The fiftieth; la *penetekota*, the fiftieth day. *Oih.* 2:1.

PE-NI, *s. Eng.* A pen for writing. 3 *Ioan.* 13. The Hawaiian word is *hulu*, quill.

PE-NI-KA-LA, *s. Eng.* A lead pencil. *Ana Hon.* 4. See PENIPOHAKU.

PE-NI-PO-HA-KU, *s. Peni* (*Eng.*), a pen, and *pohaku*, stone. A slate pencil.

PE-NO, *v.* To wet; to moisten; to be mouldy through moisture; hence, to be strong smelling.

PE-NO-PE-NO, *adj.* Wet and strong smelling, as mats with urine; he hohono.

2. Wet and dirty, as a neglected child; he maka *penopeno*, a *smutty* face; *penopeno* oe i ka ua, you are *wet* with rain.

PE-NU, *v.* To wipe one's eyes with a kapa or handkerchief.

2. To dip one's piece of fish that he is eating into the gravy, to absorb as much as it can; e miki, e *penu* kai. Olelo ia, he ono ka malolo, a *penu* no ia i ke kai. *Penu* no ia i ke kai me ka opukao. See OPUKAO.

PE-PA, *s. Eng.* Paper, especially writing paper. The Hawaiian word is *kalana* or *kanana.*

2. The common name for gambling cards; e paani *pepa*, to play at cards

PE-PE, *v.* To throw down; to throw down flat; to spread out.

2. To flatten or spread out after falling.

3. To crush. *Oihk.* 22:24. To bruise.

4. To make small by compression.

5. *Hoo.* To scatter abroad, as things crushed fine. 2 *Sam.* 22:43.

PE-PE, *s.* Any substance crushed fine or flattened down; that which is spread out by pressure.

PE-PE, *adj.* Broken or flattened down; broken fine; bruised; ground fine.

2. Bent; soft; pliable; rotten.

3. *Morally*, soft; kind; gentle; applied to the voice of a friend; ka olelo a na kanaka maikai; he waliwali ka olelo, he *pepe.* See UPEPE and PEPEPE.

PE-PEE, *v.* To be broken but not separated, as the parts of a broken limb; to adhere, though broken; to be bent or doubled over.

PE-PEE, *s. Pepee* baka, a plug of tobacco.

PE-PEI-AO, *v. Pepe* and *ao*, a fresh bud just unfolding leaves; *pe-pe-i-ao*, to flatten down that which might grow more protuberant; hence the name of the ear of man or beast.

1. To shoot or put forth a bud or young twig; to sprout or grow, as a vegetable.

2. To ear out, as corn; to send forth a shoot.

PE-PEI-AO, *s.* Any protuberance not very prominent.

1. The external ear of man or beast; hence,

2. The hearing or audience. *Puk.* 24:7.

3. The projections inside of a canoe to which the iako is fastened.

4. The first shoots or swelling buds of a vegetable.

5. Protuberances of the material heart in men or animals. *Anat.* 44, 45.

PE-PEI-AO, *adv.* By the ear; with the ear; e haliu *pepeiao*, listen *attentively*. *Iob.* 13:17.

PE-PEI-AO-A-KU-A, } *s.* A species of fun-
PE-PEI-AO-LA-AU, } gus or touch-wood that grows from some of the forest trees on Hawaii, and used by the Chinese as a delicate article of food; it has also become an article of commerce.

PE-PEI-AO-HA-O, *s.* *Pepeiao*, ear, and *hao*, horn. Any hard projection; *pepeiaohao*, the horn of an animal.

2. *Pepeiaohao* o ke kuahu, horn of the altar. *Oihk.* 4:7.

3. FIG. Power; strength. *Hal.* 89:17.

4. A horn, i. e., the name of a wind instrument of music. *Hal.* 98:6. *Pepeiaohao* kao, a goat's horn or a goat's ear.

PE-PEI-AO-LA-AU, *s.* See PEPEIAOAKUA above.

PE-PEI-EE, *s.* Name of a breadfruit ripe and baked; ame ka *pepeiee* ua ai nui ia keia.

PE-PE-U, *v.* See PEU. To raise up the nose, as a hog in rooting; to make that motion.

2. To swell; to rise up.

3. To pout; to project the lips or mouth.

4. To project or send out.

PE-PE-UA, *v.* To be hard; to be thick; to be disobedient.

PE-PE-HI, *v.* See PEHI, to pelt. To beat severely; to strike; to smite.

2. To pound a thing until it is soft; hence,

3. To kill; to commit murder. *Puk.* 20:13.

4. To slaughter, as an animal. *Oih.* 8:15.

PE-PE-HI-KA-NA-KA, *s.* *Pepehi* and *kanaka*, man. Killing; murder; manslaughter, &c. NOTE.—*Pepehi kanaka* is now used in *law* for murder in any degree; formerly it was used, as the words imply, for all kinds of striking and beating as well as killing; it was used as synonymous with *hooeha* and *kuikui.* Nui na hewa kahiko— o ka *pepehi kanaka*, many were the ancient sins—*striking men*; this, of course, included murder.

PE-PE-HU, *v.* See PEHU. To swell; to grow large; to become fleshy. See UPE-HUPEHU.

PE-PE-HU-A, } *adj.* Thick; swollen.
PE-PE-HU-E, }

PE-PE-LA, *v.* *Pe* and *pela*, so; thus. To ask is it so? is it in this manner? It ap-

plies to a scholar asking his teacher.

PE-PE-LA, *v.* See PELA and PELAPELA. To be strong smelling or offensive; to emit offensive effluvia.

PE-PE-LE, *s.* A species of kapa made on Kauai.

PE-PE-LU, *v.* See PELU. To bend or double over; to measure round; to double up, as the knee.

PE-PE-LU, *adj.* Doubled over; bent; arched.

PE-PE-MA-KA-WA-LU, *s.* *Pepe* and *maka*, face, and *walu*, to scratch. A kind of spider.

PE-PE-NA, *v.* See PENA (*Eng.*), to paint. To paint; to lay on colors; to make different colors; to apply colors to any object; to daub; to smear; e hamo, e paele.

PE-PE-NO, *adj.* See PENO and PENO-PENO. Dirty; strong smelling; filthy.

PE-PE-PE, *v.* See PEPE. To flatten down; to fall flat; to depress; to humble; to make low.

PE-PE-PE, *adj.* Low; flat; applied to a house; depressed.

PE-WA, *s.* The tail of a fish.

2. The dawn of day. See PAWA.

PE-WA-PE-WA, *s.* The side fins and tail of a fish; the spreading out of the tail of a fish.

PE-RI-O, *adj.* A foreign word, origin not known. Counterfeit, as money; uncurrent. FIG. He dala *perio* maoli no makou iwaena o na dala maikai, we are really *uncurrent* money among good money. He *perio* io no makou, he mea lawe ole ia ma na wahi kuai, we are real *bad money*, we are not taken in market places.

PE-SA-LA-TE-RI-A, } *s.* A psaltery, a mu-
PE-SA-LE-TE-RI-A, } sical instrument among the Jews in ancient times. 2 *Sam.* 6:5; 1 *Nal.* 10:12.

PI, *v.* To sprinkle, as water. *Oihk.* 6:27.

2. To throw water with the hand. See PIPI, KAPII and KAPIPI.

3. To cause water to flow drop by drop; to flow in very small quantities.

4. *Hoo.* To be stingy; to be close; to be hard upon the poor.

PI, *adj.* Green; soggy; incombustible; smoking, as green wood; e mani ai ka umu; e waiho ana aku ka momoki *pi* e.

2. Parsimonious; stingy; close; hard; unkind; ungenerous. See UAHOA.

PI, *s.* Closeness; stinginess; parsimony, &c.

2. *Eng.* Peas; lentiles. 2 *Sam.* 17:28.

PI-A, *s.* Any white substance, as flour or arrowroot, eaten by Hawaiians only in time of scarcity. See HAUPIA.

2. The flour or starch of the arrowroot; the plant tacca pinnatifida.

3. The name of a bird in *Ier.* 8:7; *Lat.* pius; the stork.

4. A kind of stone hammer.

PI-AI, *s.* The fruit of the kukui tree; a kukui nut; i uka la i ka hua *piai* la.

PI-AO, *v.* To curl up, as a leaf in the sun or as paper; *piao* la'i, a leaf folded up for a cup.

PI-AO, *s.* The hot reflection of the sun on a smooth surface or dry land; in the *abstract*, heat. *Isa.* 25:5.

PI-A-LU, *v.* To be heavy, as the eyes; to be almost blind, as an aged person, or an aged person with weak eyes; ua *pialu* na maka.

PI-A-PA, *s.* The name of the first little primer or spelling book printed in the Hawaiian language, January 7, 1822. The first sheet is said to have been pulled by Liholiho himself to his great satisfaction. Ianuari 7, 1822, ua paiia ka palapala *Pi-a-pa* Hawaii, on the 7th of January, 1822, was printed the *Hawaiian Spelling Book.* NOTE.—The word is formed like the English word *alphabet* from the names of the two first letters of the Greek alphabet; or more like our word A B C, meaning the first rudiments of letters. The missionary said to his pupil, b, a—ba; the Hawaiian would repeat, p, a—pa; hence the word and the name of the book.

PI-A-PI-A, *s.* The thick white liquid matter from sore eyes.

2. Sore eyes generally.

PI-A-PI-A, *adj.* Disordered, as the eye; changed from its natural appearance by disease or anger; e wiki iho oe, o hoi e mai kahi maka *piapia* huhu mai.

2. Dirty; watery, as the eyes.

PI-E, *adj.* Slimy. See PIEPIE.

PI-E-LE, *v.* To trade; to traffic. *Kin.* 31:21. Hele ia i Honuaula i ka *piele* ia, he went to Honuaula to *peddle* fish. See PIIELE.

PI-E-LE, *s.* A disease consisting of little bunches on the head; he mai puupuu ma ke poo.

2. A kind of food made by grating kalo very finely and then cooking it.

PI-E-LE-E-LE, *adj.* Cleaned and hung up to dry; clean; pure; makau ana.

PI-E-NA, *adj.* Wild; untamed; angry; disagreeable.

2. Rough; rude in speaking; uncivil.

PI-E-NA-E-NA, *adj.* *Pi* and *enaena,* raging heat. Very offensive to the smell; stink-

ing beyond endurance.

PI-E-PI-E, *v.* To be slippery, as a thing besmeared with slime.

PII, *v.* To ascend; to go up in various ways.

2. To ascend, as a mountain or hill. *Mat.* 5:1.

3. To go up, as from a low place to a higher. *Ios.* 4:16, 17.

4. To mount, as into a vehicle, carriage, cart, &c.

5. *Metaphorically,* to come from darkness to light.

6. To go up, i. e., to strike upon, as the shadow of a substance upon something else; ina e pii ke aka o ke kanaka maluna o ke alii, make ke kanaka, if the shadow of a common man *should fall* upon a chief, the man must die.

7. To throw up from the mouth; to vomit.

8. *Hoo.* To accuse; to charge one with a misdemeanor or crime; to give information against one; *hoopii* kekahi i ke kumu no na haumana.

9. To have a lawsuit; e *hoopii* i ke kanawai.

10. To appeal from the decision of one court to another.

PII, *s.* A small substance on the side of a thing; he wahi apana iki ma ka aoao.

2. Any medicine acting as an emetic; he laau *pii.*

PII, *adj.* Accusing; complaining.

2. Causing to vomit; laau *pii,* medicine causing to vomit.

PII-E-LE, *v.* To sell; to peddle. See PIELE.

PII-E-LE, *s.* A trafficker, including the idea of a peddler; a market man; a merchant, &c. NOTE.—This word is said to have been used mostly on Maui, *maauauwa* on Oahu, and *kalepa* on Hawaii for the idea of traffic.

PII-KO-I, *v.* To go after, as the desire after this and that.

2. To practice onanism.

PII-KO-I-KO-I, *v.* See PIIKOI, also HAA-KOI and PIKOIKOI.

PII-KU, *s.* A drink made from the leaves, branches and fruit of the kukui tree and used as a medicine.

PII-LAE, *adj.* Vain; haughty.

PII-NA, *s.* *Pii* and *ana,* going up. Name of a path ascending a hill. LIT. The going up (a hill.) See also HOOPIINA.

PII-PII, *v.* See PII, to go up. To ascend; to leap up.

2. To flow upwards, as water in a spring. *Kanl.* 8:7. To vomit.

3. To rise up, as waves in a storm. *Hal.* 107:25.

4. To turn or bend up, as the runner of a sleigh.

5. *Hoo.* To turn this way and that; to beat, as a vessel against the wind; hoholo makou me ka *hoopiipii* mau ana ame ka hakalia.

6. To seek for some ground of anger; e imi i kumu e huhu ai.

Pii-pii, *s.* Curls of hair.

Pii-pii, *adj.* Curling, as the hair of a negro.

2. Furious; rushing together, as an angry mob; rushing, as a strong wind.

Pi-o, *v.* To bend; to bend around, as the arch of a rainbow; to curve, as an arch; to bend, as an elastic substance. *Hoo.* The same.

2. To be extinguished; to go out. *Oihk.* 6:13. To be put out, as fire or a lamp. *Ier.* 4:4.

3. To be vanquished or overcome, as an enemy. *Hoo.* To vanquish; to conquer; to reduce to servitude. *Kin.* 34:29.

4. To administer food or medicine to a person far gone in a disease. See PIOO.

5. To alight for want of wind, as a kite; pio ka lupe no ka makani ole; to cease spinning, as a top; ua *pio* ka hu.

6. To cohabit, as a brother with a sister.

Pi-o, *s.* A prisoner; a captive. *Nah.* 14:3. *Pio ana,* bondage; captivity. *Kanl.* 30:3. A state of captivity. *Ier.* 26:6. One enslaved; anything taken by force, as a prisoner; a prey.

2. That which may be quenched or put out.

3. An arc of a circle. *Ana Hon.* 23.

4. In the marrying or cohabitation of two high chiefs related to each other, as brother and sister or father and daughter, the offspring, if any, was called he *alii pio;* hence,

5. The highest grade of chiefs. See NI-AUPIO.

6. The measure of a fathom and a half, i. e., three yards.

Pi-o, *adj.* Extinguished; put out; quenched, as fire or a lamp.

2. Bent; crooked; curved; arched.

3. Superior; highest; chief.

Pi-o, *adv.* Relating to captivity; captively. *Epes.* 4:8.

Pi-o-e-o-e, *s.* Name of a species of mussel or small shell-fish. See NAHAWELE.

Pi-o-o, *v.* To disrelish food, as a sick person.

2. To apply, i. e., to force into the mouth of a sick person a medicine made of potatoes and other things with something fragrant, to be applied when nearly dead; e hanai i ka mai me ka hiki pono ole o ka ai ana.

3. To pour water, as into a calabash; e *pioo* i ka wai.

4. To cast the eyes about, as in confusion.

5. To be in trouble; to be perplexed; i kuu wa i ku ai iluna, *pioo* kuu manao i o a i o i keia hana a oukou.

6. To be out of one's senses, though able to look about; to be wandering, as the mind; e alaalawa na maka a pono ole ka manao.

Pi-o-o, *s.* A wandering state of mind; a state of doubt, anxiety and perplexity; a slight derangement.

Pi-o-lo, *v.* See OLO, to make a motion back and forth, or up and down, as a saw. To rub; to polish; to strike the hand back and forth, as in playing a jewsharp.

Pi-o-le-po, *v. Pio,* bending, and *lepo,* dirt. To fly crookedly, as dirt in the wind; me he anuenue la, hele a pio ka lepo. See PIPIOLEPO.

Pi-o-lo-o-lo, *v.* See PIOO 2. To feed the fruit of the noni to a sick person. See HOOPIOLOOLO.

Pi-o-lo-ke, *v.* To gabble; to make a great noise by confused talking.

2. To be teased or harassed by unnecessary talk.

3. To be in confusion or trouble of mind, as a weak person. *Hal.* 6:3.

4. To be ashamed, as a person confused in mind.

5. To make a mistake; to commit a blunder in confusion.

6. *Hoo.* To vex; to disturb. *Ezek.* 32:9.

Pi-o-lo-ke, *s. Art.* ke. A talk; a confused sound of voices; a gabble; a nui loa ae ke *pioloke* ana; an inquiry about something.

2. A great excitement among people through fear or any cause.

3. Haste without thought or carefulness.

Pi-o-lo-ke, *adj.* Confusedly; without order; e hee *pioloke,* to flee in disorder. *Lunk.* 20:41.

Pi-o-pi-o, *v.* To make a noise, as any young feeble animal; e kani me he mea liilii la. See IOIO.

2. To peep, as a chicken.

3. To pray, as with the pule anaana.

4. *Hoo.* To use curious arts; to practice

jugglery. *Oih.* 19:19. To practice witch-craft. *Gal.* 5:20. See the substantive.

PI-O-PI-O, *s. Hoo.* A practicer of sorcery or witchcraft. *Hoik.* 22:15. I make no i ka *hoopiopio,* he died indeed by *sorcery.*

2. A whoremonger. *Heb.* 13:4.

3. A reveling. 1 *Pet.* 4:3. Wild immod-est behavior; he hiu. NOTE.—*Hoopiopio* is often used for *hooipoipo* in a lascivious sense. In 1 *Pet.* 4:3, some editions of the Testament have *hooipoipo* and others *hoo-piopio.*

4. He hale pio.

5. An old form of prayer; he pule anaana.

PI-O-PI-O, *adv. Hoo.* Examining care-fully, as a prisoner; e ninau *hoopiopio. Oih.* 22:24.

PI-U, *s.* The distance or length of three yards, i. e., the length of the arms extended called *anana,* and then the length from the end of the longest finger to the middle of the chest; generally written *pio.* See PIO, *s.*

PI-U-LA, *s.* A vicious orthography and pronunciation for *miula (Eng.),* a mule, a mongrel breed of the horse and the ass. See MIULA.

2. The name of a game at cards.

PI-U-LA, } *s. Eng.* Pewter; tin, &c.;
PI-U-TA, } any metal the color of pewter. *Nah.* 31:22. NOTE.—*Piula* is an errorneous orthography for *piuta.*

PI-HA, *v.* To be full, as a vessel or con-tainer. FIG. To be full of anger. *Eset.* 3:5.

2. To have conceived, as a female; to be pregnant; ua *piha* anei kela bipi wahine? ae, ua *piha,* is that cow *with calf?* she is.

3. *Hoo.* To fill; to cause to be full, as with water or other things.

4. To overflow its banks, as a river.

5. FIG. To fill, as the heart with joy or sorrow.

6. To be moved or energized by the Holy Spirit. *Oih.* 2:4.

7. To fill to overflowing.

PI-HA, *s.* Fullness; strength, as a high tide. *Puk.* 14:27.

2. Fullness of angry feelings.

PI-HA, *adj.* Full, as a container of any kind.

PI-HA, *s.* Name of a species of small fish.

PI-HAA, *s.* Drift-wood. *Hal.* 102:3. That which floats swiftly by; he wahie na ka waikahe.

PI-HA-LI-MA, *s. Piha* and *lima,* hand. A handful. *Ezek.* 13:19.

PI-HA-NO, *adj.* Sitting still in time of a kapu with no noise; still, as an assembly for worship under the kapu system; na wahine i ke anaina *pihano* kanu awa.

PI-HA-PI-HA, *v.* See PIHA. To swell out; to be full; to swell, as a bud before it opens. See POLAPOLA.

PI-HA-PI-HA, *s.* See PIHA. The lungs or lights of a fish.

2. A ruffle; a fringe of a garment. *Nah.* 15:38. A ruffle, as of a shirt.

PI-HA-PI-HA, *adj.* Full; large; flowing, as a garment. See POLAPOLA.

PI-HA-WEU-WEU, *s.* The name of a flat fish.

PI-HE, *s.* The sound or voice of wail-ing; he *pihe* keia e olo nei. See *Ier.* 7:27. Generally used with olo. See OLO. A lamentation; a confused noise; also with *uwe;* a pau ka lakou *pihe uwe. Laieik.* 142.

PI-HE, *adj.* Lamenting; mouring; wailing with a voice of sorrow. *Ier.* 3:15. SYN. with uwe.

PI-HE, *adv.* Na wahine olo *pihe* ana, the mourning women.

PI-HE, *s.* Takes the article *ke.* A but-ton; a fastening for a garment.

PI-HE-A, *s.* Flood-wood, such as floats down the swollen streams in storms of rain; *pihea* na kahawai, ku ka *pihea* i kai.

PI-HE-A, *v.* To float down a swollen stream, as flood-wood; *pihea* na kahawai.

PI-HE-KA, *adj.* Inflamed, as the eyes.

PI-HE-LE-HE-LE, *adj. Pi* and *helehele,* to divide into small parts. Ground to pow-der; grated off, as a potato, that the sick may swallow it.

PI-HI, *s.* See PIHE above. A button. NOTE.—It is written both ways.

PI-HI, *s.* A species of the venereal dis-ease; a foreign disease.

PI-HI, *adj.* Blunt; dull.

PI-HI-PI-HI, *v.* To be blunt or dull; to have a round or blunt edge; to be without edge, as a cutting instrument.

PI-HO, *v.* To be almost filled with water and swamped, as a canoe; aole make, *piho* wale no. *Hoo.* To plunge under a sea, or a sea to go over a vessel or boat.

PI-HO, *adj.* Sinking or being sunk; moku *piho,* a sinking vessel.

PI-HO-A, *s.* Dizziness of the head affect-ing the eyes.

PI-HOI, *v.* To be surprised at; to be startled at suddenly seeing a stranger; to be agitated.

PI-HOI-HOI, *v.* To admire; to wonder; to be surprised at; to be astonished.

2. To tremble with fear; to be afraid.

Kanl. 20:3.

3. To be troubled. *2 Sam.* 4:1. To speak or act as in great perturbation of mind. *Iob.* 21:5. To be troubled in one's spirit or mind. *Dan.* 2:3.

4. To rejoice; to express gladness; e hauoli.

5. To be excited; to get up an excitement; to talk confusedly; e pioloke. *Mat.* 21:10.

Pi-HOI-HOI, *s.* Astonishment, wonder and fear; a mixed emotion of pleasure and fear; like that occasioned by the presence of a superior.

2. Joy; rejoicing; excitement of a pleasurable kind.

3. Fear; a trembling. *Ier.* 30:5. A state of great anxiety on account of some evil expected. *Kanl.* 28:28.

Pi-HO-LO, *v.* To plunge into the water; to be overwhelmed with water; to sink down.

Pi-HO-LO-HO-LO, *s.* A thin kind of poi made of kalo or potatoes for the sick.

Pi-HO-PI-HO, *v.* See PIHO. To pitch frequently in the sea, as a canoe that takes in water.

2. To sink in the ocean and go out of sight.

Pi-HO-PI-HO, *adj.* Heavy and sinking in the water instead of floating well; applied to a canoe which is heavily loaded; *piho-piho ka waa.*

Pi-KA, *s.* Half of a thing. NOTE.—This word is probably of foreign origin, from *picul.* As two *piculs* of sandal-wood were usually weighed at once, a *pika* (picul) was of course *half*; hence the word as now used means *half.*

Pi-KA-LE, *adj.* Little; a small quantity; a little at a time; *pikale ka ai i ke keiki uuku, little* the food for a little child.

Pi-KA-KA, ⎰ *s. Eng.* A peacock, a for-
Pi-KO-KA, ⎱ eign bird having a long tail.
2 Oihl. 9:21. A peacock. *1 Nal.* 10:22.

Pi-KA-KA, *adj.* Smooth; smoothly polished; nemonemo.

Pi-KA-KA, *s.* The entrance of a chief's house; he puka hale alii.

Pi-KA-NE-LE, *adj.* Probably from *pii-i-ka-nele,* to go up into nothing. Small; diminutive; makalii loa. NOTE.—The word *pickaniny* of very common use among foreigners, and said to be a Chinese word, is from the West Indies, and is in common use among the slaves, meaning *an infant, a little child.*

Pi-KA-WAI, *s. Pika (Eng.),* a pitcher, and *wai,* water. The name given by Ha-

waiians to a water pitcher.

Pi-KE-LE, *s.* A pitcher.

Pi-KI, *v.* To cut short; to shorten; to cut off.

Pi-KI-PI-KI, *v.* See PIKI. To shorten a transaction or an act; to do instantly.

2. To milk, as the sudden squeezing of the teat forces out the milk, which is quickly done.

Pi-KI-PI-KI, *adj.* Rough, like a chopped sea.

Pi-KI-PI-KI-O, *v.* To stand up in heaps, as water in a current of the sea, especially when the wind and current are contrary.

2. *Hoo.* To cause the sea to roll or be rough; to be tempestuous. See KUPIKIPIKIO.

Pi-KO, *s.* The end; the extremity of a thing in cases as follows: *piko o ke kuahiwi,* the top or summit of a mountain. *Isa.* 30:17. *Piko o ka pepeiao,* the tip of the ear. *Puk.* 29:20. *Piko o ke poo,* the crown of the head. *Kanl.* 28:35. The navel; the end of a rope; the extreme corner or boundary of a land; e wehe hoi i ka *piko* la e ka hoahanau. Lawe ae la ke kahuna i ka *piko* o kana hanai a lei iho la ma kona a-i. *Laieik.* 137.

Pi-KO-I, ⎰ *s.* The core of the breadfruit.
Pi-KO-NI, ⎱ 2. Any substance that will cause a fish net to float; small buoys; floats. See PIKONI.

3. A club or a long kind of ball fastened to a rope, and used for robbing and plundering.

Pi-KO-I, *v.* To be proud or high-minded; hookano; he kanaka *pikoi,* a proud man.

2. To follow one's inclination; to go after one's desire. See PIIKOI.

3. To crave or covet what is another's, as food or kapa.

4. To call as to birds by way of enticement; also *pikoikoi.*

Pi-KOI-KOI, *v.* See PIKOI above. To call or entice birds so as to catch them.

2. To collect together; to assemble, as persons for pleasure or business.

3. To suck; to stick together, as by attraction; applied to the organs of speech; hence,

4. To speak inarticulately; to stammer; e omoomo, e eueu.

5. To work and effect but little; to make a great effort and bring little to pass.

6. To practice onanism.

Pi-KOI-KOI, *s.* Hard labor with little produce.

2. The practice of onanism; self abuse.

Pi-KO-KA, *s.* See PIKAKA.

Pi-KO-NI, *s.* The cords connected with

the buoys and sinkers of a fish net; a float connected with a net; a buoy. See PIKOI.

PI-KO-PI-KO, *v*. See PIKO. To be spotted; to be variegated with different colors; mostly appiled to the smooth unruffled spots on the surface of the ocean in a calm. See MAOKIOKI.

PI-KO-PI-KO, *s*. The juice of the squid under the tails. NOTE.—The liquor of the squid when emitted in the water in different degrees causes the water to assume different colors. He waiu no ka hee malalo o ke aweawe.

PI-KU, *s*. *Eng*. A fig; also written *fiku*.

PI-LA, *s*. *Eng*. The Hawaiian pronunciation of the word *fiddle*. A fiddle; a violin.
2. Any musical instrument.

PI-LAU, *v*. To emit a loathsome smell; to emit stench, as a dead body or putrid matter. *Ioan*. 11:39. Morally as *Kin*. 34:30. To stink. *Puk*. 7:21.
2. To be hateful to one; to be disliked. *2 Sam*. 10:6. To fill the air with putrid exhalations; e ino ke ea.

PI-LAU, *s*. A stench; a stink; an unsavory smell.
2. FIG. Evil influence; vileness; ua ku ko'u *pilau* mai Hawaii a Kauai, my *vileness* extends from Hawaii to Kauai.

PI-LAU, *adj*. Dirty; filthy; *especially*, of a bad smell.

PI-LA-HI-LA, *adj*. Broad; wide, as a flat surface.

PI-LA-LA-HI, *adj*. *Pi* and *lalahi*. See LAHI. Broard; wide; extended; flat, as a broad, flat surface.

PI-LA-LI, *s*. The gum of the kukui tree.
2. The gum or sticky substance of any tree; *pilali* palolo, slime; wax. *Hal*. 68:2.
3. Cartilage; kumumumu.

PI-LA-LI-O-HE, *adj*. See PILALI. Having water gathered on the outside, as fish or meat that has been dried; it is applied also to *poi* which has water floating on the top; slimy; juicy, as any substance that absorbs water on the surface.

PI-LA-LI-LA-LI, *s*. See PILALI. The viscid watery fluid that collects on the outside of substances, absorbed from a damp atmosphere or from internal moisture; e kowali a pau ka *pilalilali*, work up (the poi) till the *outside moisture* is gone.

PI-LA-PI-LAU, *s*. A turnip. See LAULELE and ANANU.

PI-LE-KA-LE-KA, *s*. Moisture or water gathered on dry fish or dry meat, &c., on being exposed to moisture; also on *poi* when water settles on top; e kowali a pau ka *pilekaleka*. See PILALILALI.

PI-LE-KA-LE-KA, *adj*. Moist outside, as fish, meat, &c., which has been dried but exposed to moisture; it also applies to *poi* when water settles on the surface. See PILALILALI, *adj*.

PI-LI, *v*. To coincide; to agree with, as boards jointed.
2. To cleave or adhere to, as persons good or bad as friends; to lay a wager; to bet; a *pili* nui mai i ko lakou waiwai a pau; *pili* kekahi wahine i kona kino iho, a lilo i ka pu.
3. To become one's to account for or to take care of.
4. To agree together, as witnesses.
5. To belong to; to accompany; to follow.
6. *Hoo*. To join company with; to adhere to one; applied to persons.
7. To seal up, as a document. *Dan*. 12:4.
8. To approach to one of the opposite sex for defilement.
9. To be united to; to adhere to each other, as husband and wife.
10. To add something else to a thing. *Kanl*. 4:2.
11. To treat badly; to reproach; to cast up to one.

PI-LI, *s*. The name of the long coarse grass used in thatching houses; so called from the easy manner in which the seeds are detached from the stalk and adhere to a person's clothes.
2. The adhering or uniting of one thing with another.
3. The name of shingles from their taking the place of the grass *pili* in covering houses.
4. The name given to nine o'clock in the evening, from the game puhenehene; ka *pili* o ka po. See PILIPUKA.
5. The name of what belongs to one, as his property, children or friends; kona mea *pili*, what belongs to one. FIG. Ka *pili* ame ka mauu, all that belongs to one.
6. Ka *pili* o ke ao ae, nearness; united with; in the morning. *Mar*. 1:35.

PI-LI, *adj*. Of or belonging to a person or thing; ka *pili* ana o ke ahiahi, first of evening; after dark.
2. United; joining.
3. Things adhering or coming in contact that ought not; hence,
4. Topsy-turvy; helter-skelter; huikau.
5. Poor; destitute.

Pi-li-a-a-i-ku, } *s. Pili* and *a-i*, neck,
Pi-li-a-i-ku, } and *ku*, to stand. LIT. That which belongs to a stiff neck. Numbness; stiffness of joints with a lack of warmth. See OPILI and MAILOIHI.

Pi-li-a-lo, *s. Pili*, to adhere, and *alo*, the front. One's bosom friend; one's beloved wife.

Pi-li-a-no, *s. Pili* and *ano*, meaning. A modern form, used in *grammar* for adjective or participle.

Pi-li-hi-hi-a, *v.* In *gambling*, the frequent transfer of property from one to another; alaila, pili nui lakou, *pilihihia*, pili kaakua.

Pi-li-hu-a, *v. Pili* and *hua*, word; pain. To be sad; to be distressed in mind.
2. To be sorrowful; to be cast down; to be dismayed. *Ezek.* 3:9.
3. To be amazed; to be astonished; to wonder greatly. *Oih.* 2:7.
4. To be in despair; to be utterly cast down. *2 Kor.* 4:8.
5. To stick fast, as words in a person's mouth when afraid or astonished; to be unable to speak through fear.
6. *Hoo.* To trouble; to vex with sorceries. *Oih.* 8:9, 11.

Pi-li-hu-a, *s.* Sadness; sorrow; dejection of heart. *Kanl.* 28:65.
2. Astonishment connected with fear and wonder.
3. Perplexity; difficulty; want of something essential.
4. An inability to speak or utter anything through fear or astonishment.

Pi-li-hu-a, *adj.* Speechless; perplexed; sorrowful; astonished. *Ier.* 14:9.

Pi-li-hu-a, *adv.* Sadly; silently from sorrow. *Ezera* 9:3.

Pi-li-hu-ki, *v.* To clash; to have separate interests; to separate.

Pi-li-ka-na, *v.* To be related to one; to have an interest in one.

Pi-li-ka-na, *s.* An interest in one; a relation to one; a friend; a motive; heaha kou kuleana e wena aku ai ia ia? he hoahanau.

Pi-li-kai, *s.* A kind of medicine consisting of some kind of seeds, one handful, beaten up and siften and taken as a purgative.
2. The name of a shrub, the seeds of which are used for medicinal purposes, especially to children as a cathartic.
3. A kind of berry growing near the sea shore.

Pi-li-ki-a, *v. Pili* and *kia*, a mast or post. To be crowded; to be in want of room. *2 Nal.* 6:1.
2. To be in straits; to be in difficulty; to be entangled in any way. *Puk.* 14:3.
3. To be cramped for want of means or instruments for doing a thing.
4. To be stinted in a provision for one's living.
5. *Hoo.* To bring or cause one to be in difficulty. *Kin.* 34:30. To trouble. *Puk.* 14:24.

Pi-li-ki-a, *s.* A difficulty; a hindrance; a perilous situation; extreme danger, as in distress.

Pi-li-ki-a, *adj.* Crowded close together; strait; narrow; difficult.

Pi-li-ku-a, *v. Pili* and *kua*, back. To run upon another's back, as when many flee together; to cleave to the back.

Pi-li-ku-a, *s.* A land or country existing only in the imaginations of men; he aina e manao wale ia e na kanaka.

Pi-li-lo-ko, *v. Pili* and *loko*, internal. To belong to that which is internal; to go close to.

Pi-li-lo-ko, *s.* A friend; a relation; one interested in; one who sympathizes with another. See PILIKANA.

Pi-li-me-a-ai, *v. Pili* and *mea*, purpose, thing, and *ai*, food, living. To live with or follow one for the sake of food or a living as the chiefs in former times had many followers because they fed them. *Hoo.* To live in idleness, pretending to belong to a chief merely to get a living, while indifferent as to his honor or authority or interests.

Pi-li-me-a-ai, *s.* One who followed a chief or other person for the sake of food or a living. NOTE.—Such persons were always spoken of with contempt.

Pi-li-mo-e, *s.* Name of one of the five puu kapus in playing at the game of noa.

Pi-li-mu-a, *s. Pili* and *mua*, before. In *grammar*, an article from its position with the noun; a late coined word.

Pi-li-pa, *s. Pili* and *pa*, fence. A hedge. *Luk.* 14:23. A hedge fence.
2. A joining together; adhering closely.

Pi-li-paa, *v. Pili* and *paa*, fast; tight. To live together in close union or in constant friendship; to be seldom separate from each other.

Pi-li-paa, *s.* Constant friendship; living together in great harmony with unity of sentiment; ka *pilipaa* o ka houpo, the cementing of affection.

Pi-li-pi-li, *adj.* See PILI. Adhering;

sticking to; connected with. *Hoo*. Constantly adhering; never failing; i ka pono pau ole, i ka pono *hoopilipili*, he pono mau loa keia.

Pi-li-pi-li-u-la, *s.* *Pilipili* (see Pili,) and *ula*, red. A species of small, low bearded grass, the beards of which adhere tightly to the dress of one walking through it. See Manianiaula.

Pi-li-pu, *v.* *Pili* and *pu*, together. To unite; to join and adhere together; to come in near contact, as the skin and bone in a poor animal. *Hal.* 102:5.

2. To come together, as the lips, i. e., to shut the mouth; to be silent; to cease answering.

3. To put to silence either by argument or authority. *Mar.* 3:4.

4. To be confounded; to know not what to say through astonishment; to cease replying; to be satisfied with one's answer.

Pi-li-pu-ka, *s.* *Pili* and *puka*, a door or gate-way. The name given to the hour or time of three o'clock in the morning; aia i ka pili o ke kakahiaka, i ka *pilipuka*. See Kau, *s.*

2. Name of one of the puu kapus in playing the game of noa.

Pi-li-wai-wai, *s.* The general name of betting and gambling and obtaining property without work and with more or less deceit. Note.—The ancient forms of *piliwaiwai* were almost innumerable; cards called by Hawaiians *pepa* have taken the place of many of them, but many still remain. See Pepa.

Pi-li-wa-le, *v.* *Pili* and *wale*, gratuitously. To join one's company or party for the sake of living.

2. To live carelessly regardless of the future; to live idly.

3. To be exposed to the weather; to die with hunger.

Pi-li-wa-le, *s.* Poorness or thinness in flesh; wiwi o ke kino.

2. Scarcity of food; suffering on account of famine.

3. An adhering to, or living on another.

Pi-li-wa-le, *adj.* Silenced; awed; unable to answer.

Pi-lo, *v.* To be corrupt; to be impure; to be much injured; ohikihiki i ka niho a *pilo*.

Pi-lo-u-ku, *s.* *Pilo* and *uku*, pay. Aohe *pilouku*, nothing wrong in the pay, any reward is acceptable; I will take anything for pay which you will give.

Pi-lo-li, *v.* See Loli. To make small;

to weaken; to make diminutive.

Pi-lo-pi-lo, *adj.* Corrupt; impure; applied to impure water. *Sol.* 25:26. Fouled; dirty, as water.

Pi-lo-pi-lo, *s.* An offensive smell from any cause. See Pilau.

Pi-lu, *v.* To shake; to vibrate.

Pi-lu-pi-lu, *adj.* Rich, as a woman richly dressed, with her rich turban, or a child adorned with rich presents.

2. Rich; used in ridicule by the poor; also in ridicule of the poor on account of their poverty.

Pi-lu-pi-lu, *v.* See Pilu. To shake; to vibrate strongly.

Pi-na, *s.* A pin or instrument for fastening up the hair on the sides of the head; he mea mahamaha lauoho. Note.—This might seem to be from the English *pin*, but it is a genuine Hawaiian word.

2. The dragon-fly. See Pinau.

3. A pin. *Ana Hon.* 2.

Pi-nai, *v.* To patch a garment; to mend; to fill up a vacancy.

2. To work constantly; e hana mau.

3. To adhere to a chief or rich person for the sake of food or a support.

4. To stand thick together; to crowd each other.

Pi-nau, *s.* The dragon-fly. See Pina above. Kaula *pinau*, the string that holds a dragon-fly.

Pi-nau-e-a, *s.* A species of kapa; a pa-u.

Pi-na-na, *v.* *Pi* for *pii*, and *nana*, to look. To climb up, as a cat climbs up the side of a house.

2. To be mischievous, as a child that climbs where he ought not; to climb up mischievously.

3. To crook; to bend; to bend over; to bend out of shape.

4. To be higher, as one part of an object than another.

5. *Hoo*. To roll away; to flow fast, as a current; to miss the way; to go crookedly. See Hoonanaau.

Pi-na-na, *adj.* Mischievous; acting mischievously; going here and there.

Pi-na-na-e-a, *v.* To have the eyes bedimmed, as with cobwebs; e punawelewele na maka.

Pi-na-nai, *v.* To rise up, as the bow of a ship or canoe in passing over a swell; lanaiea; *pinanai* e ke kaikaina e ka ua.

Pi-na-nai-e-a, *v.* See Pinanai and Lanaiea. To turn aside, as the bow of a ship when struck by a strong sea or wave.

2. To turn one's head aside to look.

PI-NE, *s.* A falsehood; a falsifier; he kanaka wahahee.

PI-NE-PI-NE, *v.* To do frequently; to do often; to repeat.

PI-NE-PI-NE, *adv.* Often; frequently.

PI-NI, *s. Eng.* A pin.

PI-NO-PI-NO, *adj.* See PILOPILO. Bad smelling; corrupt.

PI-PA, *v.* To turn sideways; to edge up to a thing; to dodge; to parry off.

PI-PA, *s.* A pali or precipice.

2. The fruit of the kae, a fruit like a bean. See KAKEE.

3. The name of a medicine given to madmen. See KIPA.

PI-PA-PI-PA, *v.* See PIPA. To sit straddle of a fence; e nihi ma ka pa; to dodge this way and that.

PI-PE, *s. Eng.* A pipe; a large cask; he pahu nui.

PI-PE-WA, *s.* See PEWA. The tail of a fish.

PI-PI, *v.* See PI, to throw water. To sprinkle. *Oihk.* 1:5. To wet by sprinkling water or blood. FIG. For purifying. *Isa.* 52:15.

2. *Hoo.* To smoulder; to continue to burn without a flame, as the wick of a lamp. *Isa.* 42:3. To burn, as green or wet wood.

3. To talk back; to reply in offensive terms to something said; to chide; to quarrel.

4. To be multitudinous or many; to stand thickly together; to be a multitude. See KUPIPI.

PI-PI, *s.* An oyster; he ano paiea, he ano ia; a kind of fish.

2. The center of a sea-shell, that is, the place where the meat adheres to the shell, hence,

3. The center of the eye; the sight.

4. The hen or female of the bird *oo*.

5. O kahi malalo e polipoli ana, he *pipi* ka inoa o ia wahi.

PI-PI, *s. Eng.* More properly written *bifi.* A foreign animal, first introduced by Captain Vancouver in 1793 or 1794 from Mexico; neat cattle generally. See BIPI.

PI-PI, *adj.* Incombustible; smouldering, as fire under green wood.

2. Almost extinguished; not burning easily. *Hoo.* Smoking, like something that will not blaze. *Mat.* 12:20.

3. Thick together; ku *pipi*; set thickly together, as kalo in rows.

4. Thick together without order; huikau.

5. Multitudinous; crowded many together.

PI-PI. NOTE.—With this orthography may be found some words which should have been written *piipii*. See PIIPII, *adj.*

PI-PII, *v.* See PIIPII. To spring up or flow upwards, as water in a spring or fountain.

2. To overflow; to effervesce, as in opening a bottle of beer; e piha me he bia la.

PI-PI-O, *v.* See PIO. To bend over, as a tall, stoop-shouldered man; to bend, as in bowing; to bend forward.

2. To bend, as the rainbow.

PI-PI-O, *s.* A tall, stoop-shouldered man.

2. An arch; a bending line.

3. The name of a species of fish.

PI-PI-O, *adj.* Crooked; bending; arched.

PI-PI-O-LE-PO, *v.* See PIOLEPO. To fly, as dirt or opala in the wind, i. e., crookedly, in whirls, or any way except in straight lines; me he anuenue la, hele a pio ka lepo.

PI-PI-KA, *v.* To flow over; to overflow, as a stream over a bank; e hu ma kapa.

2. To turn aside from the natural course.

3. To rush against the sides of any confining object.

4. To thrust or push against, as a wall. *Nah.* 22:25.

5. *Hoo.* To wander; to go here and there, as without object; to fetch up against something.

PI-PI-KA, *adj.* Turning aside; moving out of the direct line.

PI-PI-LI, *v.* See PILI. To stick fast to, as with pitch; to cleave to. *Kanl.* 13:18.

2. To adhere to one, as a friend; to fasten; to adhere to, as the tongue to the roof of the mouth, i. e., to be speechless. *Hal.* 137:5.

3. To be joined or united with; to belong to.

PI-PI-LI-LI, *s.* A begging repeatedly; if one obtains to go again, like a fly when brushed away it returns again; ike nei poe kanaka i ka *pipilili* o nei kanaka i ko lakou nei kumu.

PI-PI-LO, *adj.* See PILO. Bad smelling; disgusting to the smell. See PILOPILO.

PI-PI-NA, ⎰ *s.* A foreign word applied to
PI-PI-NE, ⎰ girls desired by foreigners; a common girl; ina paha i i mai kekahi, o hele e ke kama e upaa me ka *pipine*, i aku ke kama he kapipine i huiia me ke kamaioa.

PI-PI-NO-KE, *v.* See PIPI and NOKE, to fret. To scold; to quarrel with one; to dispute; to contradict; to go on scolding, as one party when the other party stops. See OLEOLE.

Pɪ-ᴘɪ-ᴘɪ, *v.* See Pɪᴘɪ. To be thick together; to stand thickly together, as people or things; to crowd one against another; kupinai.

Pɪ-ᴘɪ-ᴘɪ, *s.* A species of shell. See Pɪᴘɪ, oyster.

Pɪ-ᴘɪ-ᴘɪ, *adj.* Thickly; near together; crowded.

Pɪ-ᴘɪ-ᴘɪɪ, *v.* See Pɪɪ. To spring or rise up continually, as water in a spring or fountain.

2. To ascend a hill together, as a company of people; to go up.

Pɪ-ᴘɪ-ᴡᴀɪ, *s.* *Pipi* and *wai*, water. A place where water springs up or oozes out of the ground or rocks.

4. The oozing or dropping of water.

Pɪ-ᴡᴀɪ, *s.* A distinctive name of a species of wild duck; manu koloa *piwai*.

2. The name of a species of hard rock out of which kois were made.

Pɪ-ᴡᴇ-ᴋᴀ-ᴡᴇ-ᴋᴀ, *adj.* *Pi*, stingy, and *weka*, hard. Close; stingy; hard in a bargain.

Pɪ-ꜱᴇ-ᴛᴀ-ᴋɪ-ᴀ, *s.* *Eng.* The nut of the pistacia, the kernel eatable. *Kin.* 43:11.

Po, *s.* Night; the time after the going down of the sun; the time of the twenty-four hours opposite to *ao*, day.

2. Darkness; the time when the sun gives no light.

3. Chaos; the time before there was light; mai ka *po* mai, from chaos (darkness) hitherto, that is, from the beginning, from eternity.

4. The place of departed spirits; the place of torment. Nᴏᴛᴇ.—Hawaiians reckon time by *nights* rather than by days; as, *Po akahi*, first night, i. e., Monday; *Po alua*, second night, Tuesday. *Po* was counted as a god among the poe akuanoho.

Po, *v.* To be dark; to darken; to become night; to be out of sight; to vanish; hence, to be slain; to be lost; e *po* i ke kaua, to *be lost* in war.

2. Fɪɢ. To be ignorant; to be wild; to be rude; to be uncultivated.

3. To overshadow, as the foliage of trees.

4. To assemble thickly together, as people; to come together in multitudes.

5. To emit an odoriferous smell. See Pᴜɪᴀ.

Po, *adj.* Dark; dark colored; obscure.

2. Fɪɢ. Ignorant; rude; wild; savage.

3. Unsocial; sour; unfriendly; crabbed.

Po is prefixed to a good many words, and seems to denote an intensive, thus: maikai, *po*maikai; ino, *po*ino; eleele, *po*eleele; pilikia, *po*pilikia, &c.

Pᴏ-ᴀ, *v.* To castrate; to emasculate; to make one a eunuch; i *poaia*, castrated. *Oihk.* 22:44. E hoopau i ke ano kane. 2 *Oihl.* 18:8.

2. To throw water over one's self; to dive, paddle or play in the water.

3. To cast up or spatter water.

4. To wallow and roll in the water like a hog.

Pᴏ-ᴀ, *s.* One castrated; a eunuch.

Pᴏ-ᴀ, *adj.* Castrated; despoiled of virility; he luna i *poaia*. 2 *Nal.* 8:6.

Pᴏ-ᴀ-ᴀ-ʜᴀ, *s.* The bark of the cloht mulberry.

Pᴏ-ᴀ-ᴀ-ʟᴀ, *v.* To thrum with the fingers on a drum head; kilipoipoi e, e *poa-ala* la. See Kɪʟɪᴘᴏɪᴘᴏɪ.

Pᴏ-ᴀᴇ, *s.* A company; a vegetable; he poe, he mea ulu.

Pᴏ-ᴀᴇ-ᴀᴇ, *s.* The hollow place under the arm; the armpit. See Pᴏᴇᴇ.

Pᴏ-ᴀᴇ-ᴀᴇ, *adv.* Obscurely; indistinctly seen; darkly. 1 *Kor.* 13:12. Ike *poaeae*, to have indistinct ideas of a thing. See Pᴏᴡᴇʜɪᴡᴇʜɪ.

Pᴏ-ᴀ-ɪᴀ. Particle passive of *poa*. One castrated; a eunuch. *Dan.* 1:3.

Pᴏ-ᴀɪ, *v.* To encircle; to go round; to encompass, as a city besieged. *Ios.* 6:3.

2. To go round an object in order to see it on all sides; e makaikai.

3. To pass or sail round an island, as a ship.

4. To surround for evil; *poaiia* oia a puni, e make ai oia, he was surrounded entirely that he might be killed.

Pᴏ-ᴀɪ, *s.* A circle real or imaginary; a hoop; a girdle. In *geography*, *poai* waena, the equinoctial line; *poai* anu akau, the arctic circle, &c.

Pᴏ-ᴀɪ, *adv.* A *poai*, round about; ku *poai*, to stand around.

Pᴏ-ᴀɪ-ᴀɪ, *v.* See Pᴏᴘᴏᴀɪ and Pᴏᴀɪ. To go round and round; to surround.

Pᴏ-ᴀɪ-ʜᴀ-ᴘᴀ-ʟᴜ-ᴀ, *s.* *Poai* and *hapalua*, half. A semicircle. *Ana Hon.* 23.

Pᴏ-ᴀɪ-ʜᴇᴇ, *v.* To flee, as a party in battle.

Pᴏ-ᴀɪ-ʜᴇ-ʟᴇ, *v.* *Poai* and *hele*, to go. To travel about from place to place. *Mat.* 23:15. To encompass; to go round, as an island.

Pᴏ-ᴀɪ-ʟᴏ-ɪ-ʜɪ, *s.* *Poai* and *loihi*, long. An oval figure; an elipse. *Ana Hon.* 24.

Pᴏ-ᴀɪ-ᴘᴜ-ɴɪ, *v.* *Poai* and *puni*, around. See Pᴏᴀɪʜᴇʟᴇ. To travel round here and there; to go round a country for any purpose; to circumambulate.

Pᴏ-ᴀ-ᴏ-ɴᴏ, *s.* *Po*, night, and *aono*, six.

LIT. The sixth night, i. e., Saturday. See next word.

PO-A-HA, s. *Po* and *aha*, four. The fourth day (night. See PO, note), i. e., Thursday.

PO-A-HA, v. To encircle; to go round; to go about here and there.

PO-A-HA, s. A circle.

2. A ball wound with a hollow on one side as something to set a calabash in.

3. A smaller ball of the same kind to apply to any swelling.

4. The name of a tree.

PO-A-HA-NU-I, s. The name given by Hawaiians to the hollyhock.

PO-A-HI-A-HI, adj. Dim; obscure.

PO-A-KA, s. A circular paper; he palapala poepoe.

PO-A-KA-HI, s. *Po* and *kahi*, one; first. The name of the first day (night. See PO, s.) of the week, Monday.

PO-A-KO-LU, s. *Po* and *kolu*, three. LIT. The third night, i. e., Wednesday.

PO-A-LA, v. To roll up, as a ball; to wind up string into a ball; e owili i ke kaula, e hana popo.

2. E kani i ka puu i ka ono ana i kekahi mea, e uinaka puu.

PO-A-LA, s. The name of a tree; he puu *poala* i ka moni e.

PO-A-LA-A-LA, adj. Rolling; tumbling over and over.

PO-A-LA-A-LA, adv. Going towards land and out to sea again, as in sailing along a coast in a canoe; mai holo *poalaala* ka waa i uka i kai.

PO-A-LE, v. *Po* and *ale*, to swallow, as a wave. To be open; to be absorbent; to drink in; e hamama, e aleale.

PO-A-LE-A-LE, adj. Open; absorbent; lying useless.

PO-A-LI, adj. *Po* and *ali*, a scar. Dark; confused; obscure.

PO-A-LI-MA, s. *Po* and *lima*, five; the fifth. The name of the fifth day (night) of the week, Friday. Hawaiians counted by *nights* rather than by days. See PO. I ka 21 o Augate oia ka *Poalima*, the 21st of August, that was *Friday*.

2. The name of a religious meeting on Friday of each week, formerly very generally attended by the people throughout the Islands.

PO-A-LO, v. To pluck or dig out the eyes. Mat. 5:29. Ua *poaloia* kona mau maka, a make no ia ma kahiki, his eyes *were dug out*, and he died in a foreign country.

2. To twist round and draw out, as a tooth.

3. To take or force out, as beans from a pod; to shell out beans.

4. To surround; to circumambulate.

PO-A-LU-A, s. *Po* and *alua*, two; the second. The second day (see PO, note) of the week, Tuesday.

PO-A-NA, s. The name of the sea outside of where the surf breaks; also *pueone*.

PO-A-NA-A-NA, adj. Weary; lame; sore, as with walking or lying in one position; fatigued, as with carrying a burden.

PO-A-PO-A-AI, s. Name of a small coiling shell-fish, a species of the pupu.

PO-A-PO-A-AI, v. See POAI. To coil in a circular form, as in winding a ball; to wind round and round; e owiliwili; to surround.

PO-A-PO-A-LA, v. See POALA. To wind frequently; to wind round and round.

2. To go round; to surround; to travel round a city or country.

PO-A-PO-A-PO-LA, v. To go about from house to house.

2. To eat greedily; to swallow down food rapidly.

PO-E, s. A company; a number of persons or animals, from three to any indefinitely large number. It is not so often applied to *things* as to persons and animals; but the idea is that of a certain company or assemblage as distinct from some others. A cluster; a bunch. It is often synonymous with *pae* and *puu*.

2. The name of a vegetable resembling the akulikuli or purslain; a water or sea plant.

PO-E. A sign of the plural number of nouns; synonymous with *pae* and *puu*, but much more frequently used. When applied as a sign of the plural, it still retains the idea of a separate class. *Gram.* § 85, 86, 91 and 92. NOTE.—*Poe* is sometimes used where *na* would be proper.

PO-E, v. To break up; to mash; to pound, as in pounding poi.

PO-E, adj. Round; circular. See POEPOE and POAI.

PO-E-E, s. The armpit. *Ier.* 38:12. See POAEAE.

PO-E-KO, adj. Skillful; clever; intelligent; able to think.

PO-E-LA-MU-KU, s. An officer who attended the person of a chief and executed his orders. See ILAMUKU and LAWEKAHILI.

PO-E-LE, v. *Po*, night, and *ele*, black. To be very dark, as a dark night; to be black colored.

2. FIG. To be sinking in death; to experience the darkness that often precedes

death.

3. To feel the pangs of death.

Po-e-le, *adj.* Dark blue; black as night; dark colored.

Po-e-le-e-le, *v.* See Poele. To be or become dark, as night; to become black. *Hoo.* To cause darkness. *Puk.* 10:21.

Po-e-le-e-le, *adj.* Black; dark as night; benighted.

2. Applied to the mind, ignorant; bewildered.

3. Round; smooth; polished; pokaka, nemonemo.

Po-e-po-e, *v.* To be short; to be low, in opposition to tall, high.

2. *Hoo.* To round; to make round. *Oihk.* 19:27.

3. To throw away from one, as a child is thrown away from the arms.

Po-e-po-e, *adj.* Round; round and smooth; globular; cicular; he mea *poepoe* ka honua, the earth is a *round* thing.

Po-e-po-e-ha-wae, *s.* A flattened sphere. *Ana Hon.* 29.

Po-e-po-e-pi-koi, *s.* A lengthened sphere. *Ana Hon.* 29.

Po-i, *v.* To make clear or explicit.

2. To excite; to stir up; to hurry.

3. To cover; to shut, as a door or book; to cover over; to protect.

4. To cover, as a pot or calabash.

5. To curve and break over at the top, as a high surf. See Popoi. To cover or overwhelm, as the sea. *Hal.* 78:53. *Poi* mai ka nalu; *poi* mai ka ale.

6. To catch flies with the hand; to catch as an owl does mice or small birds; e *poi* no laua (ka pueo ame ke kaio) i ka iole.

7. *Hoo.* To examine by torture or by threatening.

Poi, *s.* The paste or pudding which was formerly the chief food of Hawaiians, and is so to a great extent yet. It is made of kalo, sweet potatoes or breadfruit, but mostly of kalo, by baking the above articles in ovens under ground, and afterwards peeling and pounding them with more or less water (but not much); it is then left in a mass to ferment; after fermentation, it is again worked over with more water until it has the consistency of thick paste. It is eaten cold with the fingers.

Po-i, *s.* A cover of any vessel or container; *especially*, the cover or upper gourd of a calabash; hence,

2. Perhaps the name of the food kept under or protected by it.

3. The cover of a pot or other vessel. *Puk.* 25:29.

4. The top of a curling surf where it breaks; he wahi e haki iho ai ka nalu.

5. A head of cabbage, a foreign vegetable.

Po-i-a-wa, *s.* *Poi* and *awa*, sour; bitter. Sour poi, or poi too much fermented.

2. Fig. A person of a sour or crabbed disposition.

Po-i-a-wa-a-wa, } *adj.* Sour, as poi.
Po-i-a-wa-hi-a, }　　See Poiawa.

2. Sour in disposition; taciturn; refusing to answer when spoken to. See Poipupuu.

Po-iu, *v.* *Po,* intensive, and *iu,* sacred; consecrated. To be under the protection or care of some one having power to protect.

2. To be prohibited or forbidden; to be under a kapu.

3. To be consecrated; to be holy. See Iuiu.

Po-iu, *adj.* Afar off; at a great distance.

2. Grand; solemn, as a sacred place; glorious.

3. Precious; desirable.

Po-iu-iu, *v.* See Poiu above. To be very far off or high up; o ka hoa i *poiuiu* o ka ike nei, the friend who is afar off beyond the sight.

2. To be very kapu or sacred. See Iuiu and Koiuiu.

Po-i-ka-lo, *v.* To cover up kalo (upland), i. e., to spread over the hills dried grass, banana leaves or anything to serve as manure and shade the roots.

Po-i-na, *v.* To forget; to be forgotten. *Kin.* 41:30. Note.—In this form, it is used only in a neuter or passive sense.

2. *Hoo.* To cause to forget; to pass from the mind or memory.

3. To forget a person or an event. *Kin.* 40:23. To forget God. *Lunk.* 3:7.

Po-i-no, *v.* *Po,* intensive, and *ino,* bad; evil. To be in distress; to be in miserable circumstances.

2. To suffer from some cause; to suffer an injury; to be injured.

3. To be ill-fated or destined to suffer.

Po-i-no, *s.* Hard fatigue; suffering; affliction; harm; injury; whatever is unfortunate.

Po-i-no, *adj.* Unlucky; unfortunate; ill-fated.

Po-i-pa-lau, *s.* A kind of food; a mixture of potatoes and cocoanut.

Po-i-po, *v.* To ambuscade; to set an ambuscade for an army.

2. To fall upon, as an enemy in the night; to surprise; mai *poipoia* lakou ilaila, they were near *being surprised* there.

3. To overcome; to conquer. *Kin.* 14:15.

Po-i-po, *s.* An ambuscade; that part of an army which is set for an ambuscade.

Po-i-po-i, *v.* See Poi 3. To cover over with weeds or grass.

2. To quench fire by pouring on water.

3. To interrupt a discourse when one is speaking.

4. To hush or quiet, as a child.

5. *Hoo.* To examine one, as by torture. See Poi, *hoo.*, and also Popoi.

Po-i-pu, *v.* To cover over; to bury with a flood. *Puk.* 15:5.

2. To shade deeply; to shade from the light of the sun so as to be almost dark, as a glen thick with trees.

3. To cover over the heavens with thick dark clouds.

Po-i-pu, *s.* The state of being covered up, overwhelmed or darkened by a thick covering, as with clouds, water, thick shade, &c.

Po-i-pu, *adj.* Covered or buried up, as one overwhelmed with waves or the surf. *Laieik.* 133. Iloko o ka halehale *poipu* o ka nalu.

Po-i-pu-puu, *v.* To be full of hard lumps, like poi not well pounded or made from bad kalo.

2. To be unsocial; to be sour; to be unfriendly.

Po-i-pu-puu, *s.* Food full of lumps.

2. Fig. A sour, morose person.

Po-i-pu-puu, *adj.* Hard; lumpy, as bad poi.

2. Sour; unsocial, as a person.

Poo, *v.* To scoop up, as water; to dip down into the water; to stir up or trouble water, as in bathing, or as a hog in rooting under water.

2. To make a noise by putting the fingers in the mouth and snapping the lips.

3. *Hoo.* To add; to join on; e hookui.

4. To do with the head, i. e., as we say in English, *to do head-work*; e hanaia ka mea akamai e na mea poo noonoo.

5. To dig; to dig deep down; e hoopoopoo; to make a deep hole in the ground; e kohi, e eli.

6. To cause to be light; to swim; to press upon the ama of a canoe; e komi ma ke ama.

Poo, *s.* Takes the article *ke.* The head; the summit, &c.; ke *poo* o ka mauna, the *top* of the mountain.

2. The head of a person; the seat of thought; the seat of the intellectual powers; he wahi e noho ai ka noonoo, ka noho ana o ka uhane.

3. The head or chief point of a discourse; the text of a sermon; ke kumu olelo e hai aku. See Pooolelo.

4. The name of a place under the sand; pehea kau puaa? eia i ka *poo.*

5. A kind of sea-shell. See Poopalaoa.

6. A chief of a number of people; a head, guide or leader. *Kanl.* 1:15. Opposed to *huelo*, a lower class. *Kanl.* 28:13. The head of a people either in civil or military matters; often synonymous with *luna*; o ke alii, nana no e haipule na heiau, *poo* kanaka, oia hoi na luakini.

Poo-e-e, *s.* See Poo above, No. 4.

Poo-o-le-lo, *s.* Poo and *olelo*, speech. The head of a discourse: the text of a sermon; aia kana *pooolelo* ma ka Oihana.

Po-ou, *s.* A species of fish of a reddish color, similar in character to the huli, aawa and ea.

Poo-he-pa-li, *s.* One who has the best of a bargain.

Poo-hi-na, *v.* Poo and *hina*, to fall off, as the hair. To be gray headed; to be old. *Isa.* 46:4.

Poo-hi-na, *s.* The gray hairs of an aged person. *Oihk.* 19:32.

2. A gray haired person. 1 *Nal.* 2:6.

Poo-hi-na, *adj.* Gray haired or gray headed; gray with age. *Kanl.* 32:25.

Poo-hi-wi, *s.* Poo, top, and *hiwi*, to diminish; a diminishing point.

1. The sharp top of anything.

2. Applied to the shoulder. *Kin.* 9:23. The shoulder; hoolei i ke kapa ulaula ma kona *poohiwi*, they cast the red (royal) kapa upon his *shoulders.*

3. The point of union of the upper arm bone with the shoulder blade; he hookuina lewa o ka iwi uluna me ka iwi hoehoe ma kela aoao ma keia aoao.

Poo-hi-wi, *adj.* Of or pertaining to the shoulder. *Puk.* 28:7.

Poo-hoo-le-wa, *s.* Poo and *hoolewa*, to bear or carry. Epithet of a very high chief who was always carried by the people.

Poo-hou, *s.* Poo, head, and *hou*, new. Name of the character § used in writing or printing to designate a new subject or paragraph.

Poo-hu, *v.* To sing; to sound, as a bell or other sounding matter.

2. To crack; to squeak, as shoes.

Poo-hu, *s.* A wound, particularly if swollen; a bruise.

Poo-hu-ai, *s.* A pain; a disease; the headache.

Poo-hu-ku, s. The top point of a hillock, ridge or mound.

2. The sharp tops of the ridges of a file or rasp.

Poo-hu-na, adj. Appellation of one of the lying gods; he wahahee maoli kekahi akua, ua kapaia he *poohuna* i ke aouli, he wahahee ke ano oia inoa.

Poo-ka-eo. E pauaalina me he *pookaeo* la.

Poo-ke-o-ke-o, adj. Poo and *keo*, white. White headed; bald headed; epithet of an aged person.

2. Wry or crooked necked.

3. Prosperous; successful.

Poo-ke-o-ke-o, s. Prosperity; success. *Hal.* 73:3.

Poo-ke-o-ke-o, v. To be prosperous in business; to be successful in an enterprise. *Hal.* 37:7. To make a good bargain.

Poo-ke-la, v. Poo and *kela*, to excel. To excel; to be or act as chief; to be put foremost.

Poo-ke-la, s. A chief; a prince or chief among men. *Nah.* 16:2.

2. A superior either by birth or by great exploits; the greatest, chief, highest among a number of persons. *Kol.* 1:18.

3. Official dignity or insignia. *Ier.* 13:18.

Poo-ke-la, adj. More excellent; exceeding; better; a lilo ai kakou i *pookela* maluna o na holoholona, that we may become *more excellent* than (above) the brutes.

Poo-ke-pa, s. Poo and *kepa*, sideways; edgeways. The hair cut so as to be made to stand differently from what it naturally would.

2. A part of the hair cut and a part left standing.

3. A one-sided head. NOTE.—It was customary among Hawaiians in mourning for the loss of friends, to cut the hair in very fantastical shapes as a sign of sorrow.

Poo-ke-pa-li, s. Probably *poo*, head, and *o ke pali*, of the precipice. The man who makes the best bargain in trade, i. e., he caps the pali.

Poo-ko-i, s. Poo, head, and *koi*, sharp as an axe. A person having a sharp or projecting forehead. NOTE.—Such were supposed to have something supernatural about them and had the power of using the *pule anaana*, that is, of praying people to death.

2. A person lacking good sense; he mea i manaoia he lapuwale.

Poo-ko-ii, v. To be envied on account of one's riches.

Poo-ko-ii, s. One who is envied on account of of his riches.

Poo-ku-a-ke-a, adj. Poo, head, *kua*, back, and *kea*, white. White or bald headed. See POOKEOKEO.

Po-o-la, s. Name of a species of fish.

2. The name of a tree.

Poo-la-pa-la-pa, s. Poo and *lapalapa*, cornered. A square head; a head with many angular points.

Poo-le-lo, s. Poo and *olelo*, the chief speech. The man who makes the best bargain in trading. See POOKEPALI.

Po-o-lo-pu, s. See OOLAPU and OOLOPU. A blister; a rising of the skin.

2. The swelling up of cloth when thrown into the water.

Poo-lu-a, s. Poo, head, and *lua*, two. A child who has two fathers; he keiki na na makuakane elua; a nominal and a real one.

2. A child born out of wedlock; a bastard. *Kanl.* 23:3.

Poo-lu-a, adj. Of a double meaning or sense.

2. Double headed; sinful; adulterous. *Mar.* 8:38.

Poo-lu-lu-hi, adj. Poo and *luhi*, fatiguing labor. Cloudy; dark.

2. Depressed with labor or sorrow.

Poo-mau-nu, s. Poo and *maunu*, bait of a hook. The bait of a fisherman's hook; he maunu lawaia.

2. The end; the remainder.

Poo-mu-ku, v. Poo and *muku*, cut off; the head cut off. To cut off; to sever, as with a knife or sword.

Poo-ni-u-ni-u, } s. Dizziness of the head;
Poo-nu-nu, } the vertigo.

Poo-noo, v. Poo and *noonoo*, to think. To think; to reflect; to turn over and over in the mind.

Poo-noo-noo, s. Thought; reflection; the act of reflecting.

2. A person skilled in thinking; one taught to think; he poonoeau.

Poo-noo-noo, adj. Thinking; reflecting; using the mental powers.

Poo-pa-la-oa, s. Name of a sea shell. See POO.

Poo-poo, } s. A ball of an oval shape.
Po-po, } NOTE.—The orthography of *popo* is the more correct. See POPO.

Poo-poo, v. To be deep; to be lower down; to be sunk in. *Oihk.* 24:37.

2. To be deep down, as a pit dug deeply. *Hal.* 7:15. E hoea aku ai i ka lua nui, i *poopoo* nahonaho.

Poo-poo, *adj.* Deep, as a hole dug deep in the ground; a deep pit; *poopoo* hoi na maka iloko lilo, their eyes were set *deep* within; sunken, as the eyes of a person from disease.

Poo-po-no-po-no, *v.* Poo and *pono,* to put in order. To seat persons in regular order; to arrange sitting places for a great number; to set up near to each other.

Poo-pu-aa, *s.* One of the wooden gods in a heiau whose head resembled a hog's; a like me ke *poopuaa* ke kii, ua kapaia kela kii he puaa kukui ka inoa.

Poo-pu-a-li, *s.* Poo, head, and *puali,* binding. The depression or slight hollow on the crown of the head. See POPUALI.

Poo-puu, *s.* Poo and *puu,* a rise of ground; a hillock. The top of a hillock or mound; the top of a ridge. See POOHUKU.

Poo-wai, *s.* Poo and *wai,* water. A fountain head of water; o ke kahiko *poowai* o Kuaikua.

Pou, *s.* The name of the side posts of a Hawaiian house.

2. A post or pillar of a building. *Puk.* 27:10. E hanaia i paa a kukulu ia ka *pou* ma ka waa akau; e hanaia ka *pou* i ke kaula mai luna a lalo.

3. A disease said to be a hard, long substance lying perpendicularly above the *umbilicus.*

Po-uo-uo, *s.* The substance that fishermen use to bear up their nets, light buoys, floaters, lighters, &c. See MOUO and MO-UOUO.

2. The name of the net thus prepared; upena *pououo.*

Pou-o-ma-nu, *s.* Pou, post, o, of, and *manu,* an ancient god. The post of a chief's house, into the hole of which a man was first put as a sacrifice, and then the post set in. (This was a work of former times.)

Pou-ha-na, *s.* See POU. The long end post of a house to which the ridge pole is fastened.

Pou-ha-nuu, *adj.* Pou and *hanuu,* short protuberances. Short; round; broken in short pieces.

Pou-hi-a, *adj.* See PAUHIA. Overcome with sleep; drowsy; dreaming; in a trance.

Pou-hi-o, *s.* Pou and *hio,* slanting. The corner post of a house.

Po-u-hu, *adj.* Po, head, and *uhu,* groaning. Homely; ugly looking; bad looking, as the countenance; ano inoino ma ka helehelena.

Po-u-hu, *s.* A species of fish; the shell fish *leho* perhaps.

Pou-ki-hi, *s. Pou* and *kihi,* corner. The corner post of a Hawaiian house. See POU-HIO.

Po-u-ki-u-ki, *v.* Po, intensive, and *uki-uki,* wet; mouldy. To be wet; to be damp and cold; to be mildewed; hence, to smell musty; to be bad smelling.

Po-u-le, *s.* Po and *ule,* penis. The ule or stamen of the male flower of the breadfruit; *poule* ulu; he ule no ka ulu i ka hoomaka ana e hua mai.

Po-u-le-u-lu, *s. Poule,* see above, and ulu, breadfruit. The stamen of a breadfruit flower.

2. Something that grows on the extreme branches of the ulu or breadfruit tree; it is used for making kapa.

Po-u-li, *v.* Po, night, and *uli,* black; dark. To be or become dark, as night. *Puk.* 10:22. To be affected with silence or sadness; spoken of the effects of love; aole loaa ia ia ka ono o ka ai, no ka mea, ua *pouli* i ke aloha, she perceived no sweetness in food, because she was in *a dark state* through love. *Laieik.* 205. *Hoo.* To cause darkness; to be darkened.

2. To darken; to blind morally. *Rom.* 1:21. E hoopoeleele mai i ka naau.

Po-u-li, *s.* Darkness; want of light; night; moral darkness; ignorance; generally expressed by the word naaupo.

Po-u-li, *adj.* Dark; obscure.

Po-u-li-u-li, *adj.* The intensive of *po-uli.* Very dark.

Po-u-li-u-li-u, *v.* See LIU and LIULIU, a long time; a great distance off. A great ways off; a far distance; o ka lanipaa oia no kahi e *pouliuliu* ana ke nana aku.

Po-u-lu, *s.* Name of a shrub or small tree from the bark of which a species of kapa was made.

Po-u-na, *s. Eng.* A pound in weight. *Kanl.* 25:13.

2. A pound of money; twenty shillings. *Luk.* 19:13.

Pou-na-kau, } *s. Pouna,* see above,
Pou-na-kau-li-ke, } and *kau,* to put upon or place. A balance for weighing; scales. *Isa.* 40:12. See KAUPAONA.

Pou-na-na-hu-a, *s.* Name of a certain post in a heiau near the door.

Pou-pou, *adj.* Short of stature; low; short generally; pokopoko; ua like ka *poupou* me ka haahaa. NOTE.—This word should not be confounded with *poopoo,* which means *deep down.*

Pou-pou-a-na, *s.* Name of a prayer at the luakini; *o Poupouana ka inoa oia aha.*

Pou-pou-no-ho-ni-o, *s.* Faslehood; evil reports to the injury of one.

Pou-da, *s. Eng.* Powder; gun-powder. The Hawaiian name for powder is *one a*, burning sand. See WAIPAHU. The word is also written *pauda*, and awkwardly *paula.*

Po-ha, *v.* To burst; to burst forth, as a sound; to thunder; *poha ka nanu (nalu), ke wewe o wahulu mai.* See WEWE.

2. To rush upon; to make an irruption, as an enemy. 1 *Oihl.* 14:11.

3. To come upon suddenly, as in anger; to punish. *Puk.* 19:22.

4. To burst or break forth, as a boil or sore. *Puk.* 9:9.

5. To unstop, as the ear of a deaf person.

6. To burst forth suddenly, as light in a dark place.

7. To appear; to come in sight, as the moon; to appear; to flow out, as the menstrual flux; *ua poha ua wahine la.*

8. To appear in sight, as the leprosy under the skin. 2 *Oihl.* 26:19.

9. To burst forth; to overflow, as tears. *Ier.* 9:18.

10. *Hoo.* To burst suddenly, as the sound of thunder. 2 *Sam.* 22:14.

11. To burst or break through opposition, as a torrent. *Iob.* 28:10.

Po-ha, *s.* The crack of a whip.

2. The noise of thunder; the noise of any explosive substance.

3. The bursting or breaking of a boil.

4. The bursting or flashing of light.

5. The name of the Cape gooseberry; article *ke.*

Po-ha, *adj.* Bursting; cracking; sparkling.

Po-hae, *v. Po* and *hae*, to tear. To be torn, as a hole in a bundle.

2. *Hoo.* To tear, as a hole in a package or bundle; to tear a hole in the thatching of a house; *mai hoopohae oe i ka hale e nana.*

3. To make the sound of tearing cloth or kapa.

Po-hae-hae, *adj. Po* and *hae*, torn. Rotten; brittle, &c., as cloth easily torn. See PAKEPAKE and HAEHAE.

Po-hai, *v.* To be surrounded and gathered into an inclosure.

2. To be gathered together in a circular form, as fish inclosed in a net; *ua pohai ka ia; ua pohai na waa; ua pohai na kanaka.*

Po-ha-ha, *adj.* Round; circular, as a sore, as a pit, &c.; round, as the crater of a volcano; deep down, as a pit. See PONAHA.

Po-ha-ka, *s.* A printed or painted kapa.

2. A cincture; a girdle; a belt.

Po-ha-kaa, *s.* The name of a god supposed to live in ravines or precipitous places where stones were often rolled down.

Po-ha-kau, *s.* An anchor by which a ship is fastened by means of the cable; *he heleuma, he mea e paa ai ka moku i ka hekau.*

Po-ha-kau-lei, *v.* To draw in; to contact.

2. To raise or lift up; to raise to a higher place.

Po-ha-kii-kii, *v.* To place and to carry a child on the back part of the neck (not on the shoulder.)

2. To carry anything on the back part of the neck, like a *kihei.*

Po-ha-ki-o-lo-a, *s.* A stone used by fishermen, probably as anchor to the canoe.

Po-ha-koi, *v. Po*, intensive, and *hakoi.* To be very heavy; to bear down. See KOI and KOIKOI.

Po-ha-ku, *s.* The general name of stones, rockes, pebbles, &c.; *pohaku ula*, a brick; a tile. *Ezek.* 4:1. *Pohaku* lepo, an adobie; a sun-dried brick. *Puk.* 1:14. *O na mea paa he pohaku ia.* Large stones were called *pali pohaku*; lesser ones *pohaku uuku*; melted stones or lava was called *aa*; small stones rubbed or worn smooth in the water were called *iliili*; the least of all hard substances was called *one*, sand.

Po-ha-ku, *adj.* Of the nature or quality of stone, hard.

Po-ha-ku-he-le, *s. Pohaku* and *hele*, to go. LIT. A walking stone. A species of crab which has a shell like a stone.

Po-ha-ku-kaa, *s. Pohaku* and *kaa*, to turn. A millstone. *Kanl.* 24:6. *Pohakukaa palaoa. Lunk.* 9:53.

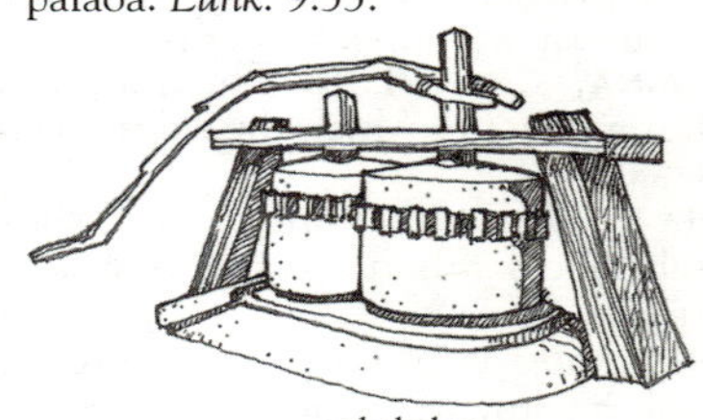

pohakukaa

Po-ha-ku-le-po, *s. Pohaku* and *lepo*, dirt. A brick made of dirt or soil mixed with grass or straw, and dried in the sun. See ADOBIE.

Po-ha-ku-paa, *s. Pohaku* and *paa*, firm; solid. A rock. *Iob.* 28:9. NOTE.—*Pohaku* *paa* is the general name of a hard or solid stones out of which kois were made, and *pohaku paa* stands in opposition to *pohaku luehee*, soft or porous stones.

Po-ha-ku-pa-e-a, *s.* *Pohaku* and *paea*, the Hawaiian pronunciation for the English word *fire*. A fire stone; a flint stone. *Ezek.* 3:9. A flint.

Po-ha-ku-wai-ki, *s.* *Pohaku* and *wai*, water, and *ki*, to shoot, as a gun. A name given to a ball or bullet formed anciently from a stone and adapted to a squirt-gun. See WAIKI.

Po-ha-la, *v.* To be healed; to recover from sickness. *Iak.* 5:16.
2. To recover from a swoon or fainting; alaila, *pohala* ae la kona manao. *Kin.* 45:27. Used also with *naau*.
3. To breathe freely and easily after being relieved from severe pain.
4. To be freed from constraint; to break loose from confinement.
5. To unfold; to burst forth, as the petals of a flower.
6. *Hoo.* To question in a captious manner; to speak against a person or a measure.
7. To object to; to interfere; to reply to; to find fault with. *Luk.* 14:6. To forbid.
8. To use influence with one to prevent a thing; mai hoole, a *hoopohala*, a hana hewa.

Po-ha-la, *s.* Rest; ease after pain or suffering; relief from constraint.
2. *Hoo.* A pretense; a specious course of conduct.

Po-ha-la, *adj.* Quiet; breathing freely; opening, as a flower; relieved from confinement.

Po-ha-le, *v.* See POALE, *h* inserted. To be very full of waves; to be open on top, as a rough sea.

Po-ha-le, *adj.* Absorbent; swallowing up.

Po-ha-le-ha-le, *adj.* See POALE and PO-ALEALE. Open; unprotected; lying useless.

Po-ha-lu, *v.* *Po*, intensive, and *halu*, to sink in or to sink down. To sink down, as something weak or overcome.
2. To lie or be folded up.
3. To rest securely or quietly in a place.

Po-ha-lu, *adj.* Broken; wounded; coiled up; lying quietly.

Po-ha-no, *adj.* *Po*, intensive, and *hano*, hoarse. Hoarse; unnatural, as the voice from a cold or other cause; hard breathing, as one with the phthisic.

Po-ha-po-ha, *v.* See POHA. To burst forth suddenly, as any sound; to parch, as corn; to crack, as a whip; to squeak, as shoes.
2. To burst or break forth, as a boil.
3. *Hoo.* To cause to bubble, as water in boiling; to break up with a noise, as the surface of water.
4. To trouble the water, as the flukes of a whale or other fish. *Iob.* 41:31.

Po-he, *v.* To cut short; to round off, as the corners; to cut into short pieces.

Po-he, *s.* The marshmallows.
2. A small plant like low mallows, the bark of which is used like olona or hemp.

Po-he, *adj.* Cut short, as a rope with a knife or with the teeth; cut smoothly off instead of being broken. *Lam. Haw.* 10:4. He weluwelu ka ka ia, he *pohe* keia.
2. Round; smoothed by cutting off the corners.
3. Cut into short pieces.

Po-hee-ua, *v.* See POHEEPALI. To slip or fall down a steep precipice on account of a great rain.

Po-hee-pa-li, *v.* To die mysteriously, no one knowing the cause; e make me ka poino, aole maopopo ka mai ame ka popilikia.
2. To fall down a slippery pali when alone and be killed.
3. To get the advantage of one.

Po-he-o, *s.* A stone; some hard thing; he mea paakiki.

Po-he-o-he-o, *s.* Any small, round, hard substance.
2. *Specifically*, the head of a nail or pin; the head at the top of a rafter.

Po-he-o-he-o, *adj.* Round; smooth; hard. See POHE.

Po-he-he-o, *v.* To swell up round and smooth; to be round and plump, as a woman with many folds of pa-u on.

Po-he-mo, *v.* To slip out of the hand, as one carries a bundle and it falls; e pu-hemo, e alualu, e ooloic, e haaluea.

Po-hi, *v.* To sink down; to settle away; to grow less. See PAHO, to go out of sight.

Po-hi-hi, *v.* *Po*, intensive, and *hihi*, to be thick and tangled, as vines. To be very much tangled, as a thick growth of vines.
2. To be shady, as with thick leaves and branches of trees.

Po-hi-hi, *adj.* Dark; obscure; intricate. *Sol.* 1:6. Confused, as long tangled hair.

Po-hi-hi-u, *adj.* *Po* and *hihi* and *hiu*, wild. Entangled; puzzling; not plain.

Po-hi-hi-hi, *adj.* See POHIHIU. Obscure, as language; puzzling, as a question; not plain; entangled; mea *pohihihi*, a mystery;

a dark saying; hard questions. 1 *Nal.* 10:1. Forgotten; not known.

Po-hi-hi-hi, *s.* A mist; an obscurity of vision; anything dark or entangled; that which is obscure or mysterious; a mystery. 2 *Tes.* 2:7.

2. Forgetfulness; ignorance; awkwardness.

Po-hi-na, *s.* See POHI and ANA. A mist or fine rain; a fog; a thin cloud.

2. A person with gray hairs; one having white hairs. See POOHINA.

3. Any white substance, as pia, flour, &c.

Po-hi-na, *adj.* White; whitish; having a white appearance.

> Pohina luna i ke ao makani kaluu,
> Naue ka lehua ka pua o ka laau,
> Hakawai ka ohua o Okuauli,
> Uli ke a i na hua e ke akua.

Po-hi-na-hi-na, *s.* A breaking down, as a tree or shrub; he wahia na laau.

2. The name of a plant of a silvery gray color; he hinahina.

Po-hi-we-hi-we, *adj.* By change of letters for *powehiwehi*. Dark; obscure; having but little light; seeing faintly.

Po-hi-wi, *s.* The shoulder, &c. See POOHIWI.

Po-ho, *v.* To sink, as in water. *Puk.* 15:4. To plunge in the water out of sight.

2. To sink, i. e., to lose money or property in business.

3. *Poho* ka manao, to sink, as the mind; to despond; to despair.

4. To blow gently, as the wind; to fill the sails.

5. To clasp hands, as men two and two in carrying a canoe.

6. *Hoo.* To go beyond in a bargain; to overreach. 1 *Tes.* 4:6.

Po-ho, *s.* A slight hollow or cavity; *poho* lima, the *hollow* of the hand. *Oihk.* 14:15. *Poho* wawae, the *hollow* of the foot. See POLI. 2 *Nal.* 19:24. Opposite to *piko* o ke poo, *top* of the head. *Isa.* 1:6.

2. The name of a chalky white earth; hence, chalk as imported; he hauone, he ano keokeo me he puna la.

3. A deep place; a deep pit.

4. A deep basket or container made of the *ie* to put fish in when caught.

5. Loss; damage by loss. *Eset.* 7:4.

6. A goal or base; any such place marked in a game; ke *poho* o ka moku.

Po-ho, *adj.* Lost; dead; sunken. *Sol.* 21:16.

Po-ho-la, *v.* To open; to spread out, as the petals of a flower when blossoming; to open; to expand; to grow larger.

Po-ho-la-lo, *v. Poho* and *lalo*, downward. To give or furnish a thing to be trampled upon; e haawi mai malalo o na wawae.

Po-ho-la-lo, *s.* Mischief done by disturbing one when sitting down; na hana kolohe malalo o ka okole.

Po-ho-la-wa, *v.* To be water-soaked, as kalo; to be worm-eaten, as potatoes; to be internally defective, as vegetables.

Po-ho-la-wa, *adj.* Partially rotten or decayed, as vegetables.

Po-ho-le, *v.* To break forth; to open, as a flower.

2. To wound; to bruise; e hai kona lima, ame ka ihu, *pohole* kona umauma.

3. To peel off, as the skin. *Ezek.* 29:18.

Po-ho-le, *s.* A wound; a bruise; an opening or breaking of the skin; a mark made on the skin by a blow.

Po-ho-li-ma, *s. Poho* and *lima*, hand. The hollow of the hand. *Puk.* 9:8. The palm of the hand. *Isa.* 49:16. Kahi palahalaha o ka lima.

Po-ho-lo, *v.* To slip, sink or glide down into the water, as a piece of lead or other heavy substance.

2. To slip off, as an axe from its helve. 2 *Nal.* 6:5.

3. To cast, as a female her young; to miscarry by premature birth.

Po-ho-lo-ho-lo, *v.* See POHOLO. To adhere only slightly, as a work of many pieces; to be brittle; to be easily broken or separated.

Po-ho-lo-ho-lo, *adj.* Slightly adhering; easily separating; sinking.

Po-ho-lu-a, *v.* To set the sails of a vessel to the wind so as neither to go forward or backward; to lie to.

Po-ho-lu-a, *s. Poho* and *lua*, pit. The deep cavity of the anus.

Po-ho-ni, *s.* A sinking in or sinking down, as with pain; a contraction of the muscles in disease; a sinking of the lips and cheeks from the loss of teeth.

Po-ho-po-ho, *adj.* See POHO. Sinking; marshy; miry. *Ezek.* 47:11.

Po-hu, *v.* See KUPOHU. To be calm; to lull, as the wind; *pohu* loa ka makani, the wind *lulled* greatly; to be or become calm after a storm at sea. *Mar.* 4:39.

Po-hu, *s.* A calm after a storm. *Hal.* 107:29.

2. A calm still place in the sea; aia kekahi wahi *pohu* ma Lanai, ua kapaia o Kaholo mahope o ka hanee ana o ka pali;

calm still water out of the wind; makemake nui ko Hilo poe alii ia Kona, no ka *pohu*, the Hilo chiefs greatly desired Kona for the *calm water* (of the sea.)

Po-hu, *adj.* Calm; still; quiet, as the wind or sea after a storm.

Po-hu-e, *s.* A broken piece of calabash.

2. A water calabash.

3. A piece of the bitter calabash; a potsherd. *Sol.* 26:33. Hookomo i ka apana *pohue* maloko o ka malo; unuhi ae la ia i ke *pohue* mai kona aoao ae: i ae la.

Po-hu-e, *adj.* Of or pertaining to a gourd or calabash; elua ipu, he ipu laau, he ipu *pohue.* Hana hou no i hale *pohue.*

Po-hu-e-hu-e, *s.* The name of a running plant like the koali.

2. The name of the root of a species of the convolvulus growing on sand banks, and used with the koali as a cathartic.

3. The name of a species of stone used in polishing canoes.

Po-hu-hu. See HOOUWAHI.

Po-hu-ku, *adj.* Round and smooth, i. e., without prominent corners; smooth, as the shell of the pauhu; smooth and round, as a baldhead.

Po-hu-ku-hu-ku, *s.* Any white globular substance, as a white baldhead.

2. Anything growing or increasing in size.

3. One having the head larger at the top than at the bottom.

4. The rising up of a large white substance, as a white cloud, a pillar of smoke. See PONUHU.

Po-hu-ku-hu-ku, *adj.* Much in quantity; copious; overflowing, as phlegm in a severe cold when working off; *pohukuhuku* ka male, i ka nui loa.

Po-hu-ku-hu-ku, *v.* To get the advantage in a bargain. See POOHEPALI.

Po-hu-ku-hu-ku, *adv.* Unitedly; acting together.

Po-hu-li, *v.* To plant that which has been dug up for transplanting, as a tree, banana, &c.

2. To transplant. See HULI, to set, as a slip in the ground. *Isa.* 17:10.

Po-hu-li, *s.* The sucker, branch or sprout of any vegetable to be transplanted for producing its kind.

2. Anything which is transplanted, as a banana or other vegetable.

Po-hu-lu-hi, *v. Pohu* and *luhi,* fatigue. To be heavy from fatigue; to be weighed down, as by sleep; to be very sleepy; to be overcome by fatigue.

Po-ka, *s.* A small globular substance; a ball; a bullet.

Po-ka, *adj.* Round; rolling; rolling round.

Po-ka-a, *v. Po* and *kaa,* to roll. To turn; to go round; to surround; to turn, i. e., to make go round, as a rope or band round a wheel.

Po-ka-a, *s.* That which is wound up; a ball, as of rope or twine.

Po-ka-o, *v.* To be poor; to be naked; to be destitute of the comforts of life.

Po-ka-o, *adj.* Very poor, as one destitute of decent clothing; naked.

Po-kao-kao, *adj.* Poor, as land; unyielding, as dry barren soil; destitute of verdure.

Po-ka-ka,   } *s.* A wheel, as of a pulley;
Po-ka-kaa,   }   the wheel of a cart or carriage. *Lunk.* 5:28.

Po-ka-kaa, *adj.* Turning; rolling; turning over and over.

Po-ka-kao, *adj.* See POKAOKAO. Dry and barren, as land; producing nothing.

Po-ka-na, *adj. Poka* and *ana.* The quality of being round; rounded; liable to roll; rolling easily.

2. Rolling in upon; coming to one gratuitously or without care; e loaa wale mai a nui.

Po-ke, *s.* A piece; a part; a portion; he pauku, he apahu, he apana.

Po-ke-o, *s.* The time or period of childhood; the time when one is little.

Po-ke-i-na, *s. Poke* and *ina,* sea egg. A calabash of *ina,* a species of the sea egg; he ia poepoe kalakala.

Po-keo-keo, *s.* The name of property given gratuitously; a present.

2. Roundness; plumpness; smoothness. See POOKEOKEO.

Po-ki, *s.* The name of a worm which destroys vegetables.

2. A standing or setting close together, as a crowd of people.

Po-ki, *v.* The stand or sit thick together, as people crowded.

2. To be united so as not to be separated.

Po-ki-a, *s. Po* and *kia,* a post. A post set up for birds to light on when they are caught; he kia manu, he laau lawaia manu.

Po-kii, *s.* The youngest member of a family; ka hanau muli loa; the youngest born of several children. 1 *Sam.* 16:11. The younger of two children of the same sex; an endearing appellation.

Po-kii-kai-na, *s.* A double epithet for a younger brother or sister. A real dear little brother or sister.

Po-ki-na-hu-a, *s.* Name of an *aha* or assembly for honoring the chief.

Po-ki-ni-ki-ni, *s.* A word used in prayer by the priests.

2. It is also called *pomanomano*, a place where the wicked forever dwell. See PO-LIOIA.

Po-ki-po-ki, *s.* A species of the oniscus, an animal which lives in the mouth of the flying-fish, or attaches itself to the side of the fish; he wahi ano ia ma ka moana, a ma ka ae kai, a ma ka aina.

Po-ki-po-ki, *v.* See POKI. To stand thickly together, as people in a crowd; to sit close together; to be multitudinous.

Po-ko, *s.* See POKO, short. The epithet often applied to the smaller division of a district of country; as, Koolau loa, long Koolau; Koolau *poko*, short Koolau; Hamakua loa, long Hamakua; Hamakua *poko*, *short* or *small* Hamakua, &c.

2. The name of a species of worm, the same perhaps as the *peelua* and *anuhe*; a caterpillar. *Hal.* 78:46.

Po-ko, *adj.* Short; not long; hence, incompetent; insufficient.

Po-ko, *adv.* Shortly; briefly; summarily. *Rom.* 13:9.

Po-ko-a, *adj.* See PAKO'U and PAKOLU. Short; poko; the opposite of long.

Po-ko-hu-ko-hu, *s.* *Po*, intensive, and *kohu.* A red dye made of the noni.

Po-ko-le, } *adj.* See POKO, short.
Po-ko-po-ko, } Short in comparison with something long; not long; hana *pokole*, a *short* work.

2. Insufficient for a purpose; incompetent for a place; low; humble; not tall. See PAKOLE and POUPOU. Ua like ka *pokole* me ka pako'u.

Po-ko-le, *v.* To be short. *Hoo.* To make short. FIG. To be unable to do a thing. *Nah.* 11:23.

Po-ko-ke, *v.* See KOKOKE, to be soon. To be near at hand, as time or place; e *pokoke* ka ai.

Po-ko-ke, *s.* Name of a disease; a chill; he kulu.

Po-ko-po-ko, *adj.* Short. See POKOLE above.

Po-ku, *v.* To cry out, as one of the terms of a public crier; to cry out in the night, as a person making mischief.

Po-la, *s.* The edge or end of a kapa, as a pa-u for instance which is tucked in from above, and hands down after being tucked in.

2. An end of a kapa which hangs over the back.

3. The hanging down of the blossom of the maia or banana.

4. The lower end of a bunch of bananas; o na eka malalo.

5. The high seat between the canoes of a double-canoe. *Laieik.* 112.

6. The Hawaiian pronunciation of the English word *bowl*; a cup. See BOLA.

Po-la-la-wa-hi, *s.* The name given to a certain great darkness over the Islands in ancient times.

Po-la-le, *adj.* Clear; bright; splendid. See MOLALE and MOLALELALE.

Po-la-po-la, *v.* To sprout; to shoot out; to grow, as a bud or leaf.

2. To put on or clothe one in large flowing garments; e aahu *polapola*, e poaka.

3. To recover; to get well from sickness.

Po-la-po-la, *s.* A sense of fullness in the stomach; pihapiha.

Po-la-po-la, *adj.* Well; healthy; *polapola* na maka; bright, as the face of one recovered from sickness; full; flowing, as a garment.

Po-le, *v.* To defend off; to separate; to divide between.

Po-le-a, *v.* To be smooth; to be without edge or points; to be smooth, as the gums without teeth; to sink in, as cheeks without teeth.

Po-le-a, *adj.* Without projections; without sharp edge or border; sunken in, as the face of one without teeth.

Po-le-he-le-he, *adj.* Not bound tightly, as a bundle; paa ole. See ULEHELEHE.

Po-le-hu-le-hu, *v.* To be between darkness and light; to be in a state of twilight; to be a little dark. See MOLEHULEHU.

Po-le-hu-le-hu, *s.* Sunsetting; twilight of morning or evening; partial light.

Po-le-ke, *v.* To be unfortunate; to be stripped of one's property; to lose one's property by authority of a chief.

Po-le-ko, *v.* To be easy and fluent in conversation; e akamai i ke kamailio.

Po-le-mo, *v.* To sink down in the water; to plunge. See PALEMO.

Po-le-na, *v.* To be mixed, as dirt or coloring matter with water; to be discolored, as water; ina e hookomoia ka lepo iloko o ka wai, alaila, ua *polena* ka wai.

Aole lua o ke ki lena i ka ua,
Lena makalena ka maka o ka lehua,
Lena, *polena* a ki lena
I ka hoowiwo e ka makani,
Laaua wiwo ka pua, ka pua makahala,
Hala aku no oe, owau aku no.

PO-LE-NA, *s.* A species of the bird *oo*, yellow feathers made into the *aahu alii*, royal robe.

> O ka *polena* hulu manu hulu la.

PO-LE-NA, *s.* Sails drawn tightly; all the sails of a vessel made fast, tight and secure; hao na pea a pau.

> Hao na *polena* o Haupu,
> Na heke luna o ke olewa.

PO-LE-PO-LE, *v.* See POLE. To ward off; to defend; to separate.

> Polepole i na lihilihi o ka ohai,
> Onoonou kela i ke kula o Makahuna,
> Ahi lapalapa kela i ke pili o Piihonua.

PO-LE-PO-LE, *s.* A kind of child's play which consisted in putting up one hand above another and saying as follows:

> Polepole ka mamalihini, kaa mai, kaa mai
> I kou, i kou kauhale, kauhale ouou,
> Ke akia nei kuu piko e kauleleo la e ko lae.

PO-LE-WA, *v.* To sway to and fro; to flow; to run, as a liquid; to be unsteadfast.

PO-LE-WA, *s.* Anything swinging or loose; that which is not tight.

PO-LE-WA, *adj.* Loose; swinging; not fast.

PO-LI, *s.* The lower part of the belly; the lap when one is sitting; the bosom. *Rut.* 4:16. Wahine o kou *poli. Kanl.* 13:7.

2. A slight concavity, as the hollow of the foot; *poli* wawae; the space between the breasts of females. *Mel. Sol.* 1:13.

3. FIG. Friendly presence; love. See POHO.

PO-LI, *adj.* Having a slight hollow or cavity, as the bosom or lap; ilio moe *poli*, puaa moe *poli*, a dog or pig often carried in the bosom, i. e., greatly beloved; petted.

PO-LI-AI, *v.* To send or call for an absent person on business or conversation; to give in charge to one.

PO-LI-A-HU, *s.* A soft touch; a gentle adherance of one thing to another.

PO-LI-E, *s.* A shining substance; a bright gleam or flash of light.

PO-LI-E-LE, *adj.* Deep blue; black; shining black; panopano.

PO-LI-O, *adj.* Dark, as a place of misery. See POKINIKINI.

PO-LI-O, *s.* A place of torment for wicked men; a place dark and far off from good men. See POMANOMANO.

PO-LI-O-IA, *s.* A distant place of suffering; a place of torment for the wicked; ka po make mau loa, ka lilo i ka make. See POKINIKINI.

PO-LI-U-KU-A, *s.* An imaginary place away in the back part of the heavens, where the stars are fixed; it is supposed to be a very dark place; ma kahi o na hoku i kau ai ma ka paia kua o ka lani, ma kahi poeleele.

2. Thick or gross darkness.

PO-LI-U-LI-U, *s.* Whatever is at a great distance of time or place; something very far off; that which is widely separated from something else.

PO-LI-U-LI-U, *adj.* Far off; widely separated; at a great distance.

PO-LI-HI-U-A, *s.* Resplendency; some shining, glittering substance; a flash of lightning.

2. Shining black; a deep blue.

PO-LI-HI-WA, *s.* A bright shining cloud.

PO-LI-HI-WA, *adj.* Bright; shining; applied to clouds.

PO-LI-KI-A, *s.* Whatever is tied tightly or bound fast; severe suffering; olioli no hoi lakou i ka hiki ana mai o ka *polikia* maluna o lakou. See PILIKIA.

PO-LI-LI-MA, *s. Poli* and *lima*, hand. The hollow of the hand.

PO-LI-NA-HE, *v.* To blow softly, as a light breeze.

2. To exhibit the qualities of softness, fineness, thinness, &c.

PO-LI-NA-HE, *adj.* Soft and gentle, as the voice of affection; soft, as the sound of low music; gentle, as a zephyr.

PO-LI-PO-LI, *s.* Name of a species of soft porous stone.

PO-LI-PO-LI, *v.* To soften, as a stone in the art of making stone adzes; o kahi malalo e *polipoli* ana, he pipi ka inoa.

PO-LI-WA-WAE, *s. Poli* and *wawae*, foot. The hollow of the foot.

PO-LO-AI, *v.* To send orders for one to come.

PO-LO-U-HI-WA, *adj.* Dark brown; deep blue; makue.

PO-LO-HA-NA-O-LE, *s.* Epithet of a woman who will not work but lives upon her husband's earnings.

PO-LO-HI-WA, *adj.* Dark; black, as a black cloud; shining black. *Puk.* 19:16.

PO-LO-HI-WA, *s.* A shining black cloud.

PO-LO-HU-A, *s.* The fruit of the popolo which was eaten in time of scarcity.

PO-LO-HU-KU. See PONOHUKU.

PO-LO-KA, *s.* A bunch of the hala fruit, especially the lower end of the bunch.

> Ka pololu *poloka* oiki halale,
> Na hue maka moku kapa e ka ua,
> Na hakakae nawali i ka ua e he.

PO-LO-KA-NI-KU-A-MAU-NA, *s.* A species of locust. See POLOLEIKANIKUAMAUNA.

PO-LO-KA-WAE, *s.* A long sickness.

2. A long spear.

Po-lo-ke, *s.* New fresh food, as poi just pounded up from kalo. See also POLOLEI, another name. See AIAKAKAI.

Po-lo-ke, *v.* To be fresh, as new pounded poi; ua *poloke* i ke kai ole ka loaa.

Po-lo-lei, *v.* To be straight; to be correct, naturally or morally.

   2. To make straight; to direct.

   3. *Hoo.* To become straight; to make that straight which has become crooked naturally or morally.

   4. To direct; to put in order.

Po-lo-lei, *s.* Uprightness; rectitude of conduct; he *pololei* kona aoao.

   2. A name given to new fresh food (poi.) See POLOKE.

Po-lo-lei, *adj.* Straight; correct; accurate, in opposition to crooked, irregular or perverse.

Po-lo-lei, *adv.* Straightly; uprightly; certainly.

Po-lo-lei-ka-ni-ku-a-mau-na, *s.* A species of locust. See POLOKANIKUAMAUNA.

Po-lo-li, *v.* To sink down with weakness.

   2. To be attenuated or thin for want of food; hence,

   3. To be hungry in opposition to being full.

   4. *Hoo.* To cause to be hungry; to fast for any purpose. *Neh.* 1:4.

Po-lo-li, *s.* That which sinks down in opposition to that which swells up; opposed to *maona*, filled with eating; hence,

   2. Hunger; want of food. *Puk.* 16:3.

Po-lo-li, *adj.* Having lately eaten nothing; hungry; maona ole.

Po-lo-lo-a, *v.* To blunder; to act awkwardly; to miss the mark; to go astray.

Po-lo-lo-hu-a-me-a, *adj.* Green and far off, as the sea at a great distance; ke kai *pololohuamea* a Kane.

Po-lo-lu, *s.* A spear. *Lunk.* 5:8. A long spear; he laau kaua, he ihe loihi. Hina iho la ia no ka hihia i ka *pololu*, he fell, being entangled by the *long spear.*

Po-lo-na, *s.* Sickness at the stomach; nausea; vomiting.

   2. Sense of fatigue; heaviness; sluggishness.

Po-lo-pe-a, *s.* The stem of a bunch of hala fruit.

Po-lo-po-lo-u-a, *s.* A bunch of hala fruit still unripe but growing; he polopea no Haalelea.

Po-lo-po-lo-na, *s.* See POLONA. The offensive smell of a crowded, confined room; the vitiated air of a confined room; a house uninhabited; punahelu.

Po-lo-po-lo-na, *adj.* Mouldy; rancid; worm-eaten; hauna.

Po-lu, *s.* Thick woolen cloth; lion skin.

Po-lu-a, *s.* *Po*, head, and *lua*, two. Dizziness; sickness.

   2. A wind blowing from two directions. See POLOHUA.

   3. Elua ai e oa lilo paha.

Po-lu-e-a, *s.* The sickness felt after intoxication; loss of appetite, &c.

   2. Fullness after eating; a pau iho la kakou i ka luai no ka nui loa o ka *poluea*, a poniuniu mai la na maka.

Po-lu-e-a, *v.* To be heavy; to be dull and stupid, as one coming out of a debauch.

Po-lu-ku, *v.* *Po* and *luku*, to slay in great numbers. To slay and destroy in great numbers, as in a battle; to make a slaughter of men or animals.

   2. To turn over and over; to turn upside down.

Po-lu-ku, *s.* A slaughter; a destruction of many persons, as in battle.

   2. He paia.

Po-lu-ku-lu-ku, *v.* To pound fine; to bruise small; to mash down flat.

Po-lu-lu-hi, *adj.* *Po* and *luluhi*, black and heavy, as clouds. Thick and heavy, as watery clouds hanging in the atmosphere; covering over; shady; foggy; dark; misty; po okoa Hilo e *poluluhi* i ka ua.

   2. Dull; stupid; inactive.

Po-lu-mi-lu-mi, *s.* *Po* and *lumi*, to gather together. A cloth or handkerchief gathered up in the hands.

Po-lu-mu, *s.* A vine.

Po-lu-nu, *adj.* Short; round; globular.

   2. Mahumahu, polunulunu.

Po-lu-nu-lu-nu, *adj.* See POLUNU above.

Po-lu-po-lu, *adj.* See POLU. Thick; fat; gross; heavy, as a very fleshy person; large, fat and weak, as a man; feeble, as one who has been sea-sick. See PALUPALU.

Po-ma, *s.* *Lat.* An apple.

Po-mai-kai, *v.* *Po*, intensive, and *maikai*, handsome; good. To be fortunate; to be lucky.

   2. To be successful in a pursuit.

   3. To be happy; to be blessed; to enjoy peace; to be highly favored.

   4. *Hoo.* To bless; to make prosperous; to be prospered. *Kin.* 39:2. To cause to prosper.

Po-mai-kai, *s.* Good fortune; peace; quietness; enjoying what one desires; comfort; a blessing.

Po-mai-kai, *adj.* Fortunate; successful; prosperous; happy; blessed; ka laka, ke kuonoono.

Po-ma-no, *s. Po* and *mano,* thick; many. A stone wall; that which is set or laid in good order, as stones in a wall. See KUMANO.

Po-ma-no-ma-no, *s. Po,* night or intensive, and *manomano,* multitudinous; eternal. Excessive darkness; the name of the place where the wicked dwell forever in separation; eternal night. See POKINIKINI.

2. A place where pointed clouds arise out of the ocean. See POPUAKII.

Po-me-ge-ra-ne, } *s. Eng.* A pomegran-
Po-me-rai-te, } ate. *Kanl.* 8:8; *Mel. Sol.* 4:3.

Po-na, *s.* The joints, as of the spine and the fingers; the spaces between the bulbs or joints of bones.

2. That part of the stalk of sugar cane which is between the joints.

3. The joints themselves of sugar-cane or bamboo.

Po-na, *v.* To divide off into joints or pieces.

2. To cut into parts; e pauku aku.

3. To show spots differently variegated, as places in the sea in a calm.

Po-na, *adj.* Cut up in pieces; variegated with spots; spotted.

Po-na-ha, *v.* To be in a circular form, as an arc of a circle, or the arm bent a kimbo; as the legs when the knees are separated and the feet together; e o, e poepoe kanoa, e kae kanoa.

Po-na-ha, *adj.* Round; circular as a sore, a pit or a volcano.

2. Deep, as a pit. See ONAHA and PO-HAHA.

Po-na-hai-au-a, *s.* The half of a circle; a semicircle; ponahaiaua ke kihi o ka moku.

Po-na-ha-na-ha, *adj.* Round; circular, as the full moon. See PONAHA above.

Po-na-ha-na-ha, *v.* To surround; to be surrounded by something else; ponahanaha ka moku me ka aina. See ONAHANAHA.

Po-na-lo, *s.* The dying or drying up of potato tops, kalo, &c.; he hoopulu e make ai ka ai.

Po-na-lo-na-lo, *v.* To be dim, as the eye.

Po-na-na, *s.* Dry land.

Po-na-na, *adj.* Lame; sore from traveling; applied only to the calf of the leg.

Po-na-no-na-no, *adj.* Obscure; not plainly seen; blurred; blotted out. See PONALONALO.

Po-na-po-na, *adj.* See PONA. Having many joints; divided up in small parts; variegated with spots.

Po-ni, *v.* To besmear; to daub over.

2. To anoint. *Ioan.* 12:3. To consecrate by anointing, as a priest. *Puk.* 23:41. To anoint, as a king. *Lunk.* 9:8. Mea *poni,* an anointed one.

3. To rub over some odoriferous matter; to cause a pleasant odor.

4. To be cold, as in bathing early in the morning when the water is cold (and the skin turns purple.)

Po-ni, *s.* A variety of the kalo with purple stalks. NOTE.—In using, the outside of the stem is stripped off, squeezed in water, and then lemon juice and poi are added for stiffening, which makes a beautiful red.

2. Color; coloring matter. *Ier.* 10:9.

3. A mixture of colors; purple. *Puk.* 25:4. The light indistinct shades of colors in cloth.

4. The early dawn of the morning.

5. The anointing of a chief or god; ka hamo ana i ka mea ala i alii, i akua; ointment. *Ioan.* 12:3.

Po-ni, *adj.* Of or pertaining to color, as colored cloth or garments; aahu *poni* uliuli. *Eset.* 8:15. Having the changeable colors of silk; hence, lole *poni,* purple. *Oih.* 16:14. Lole *poni* mahana, the warm, sweet-scented (variegated) garments. *Lunk.* 8:26.

2. Sweet smelling; agreeable; odoriferous, as perfumed colored kapa; mea *poni,* ointment.

3. Skillful at diving so as not to spatter water; *poni* ia wahi kanaka.

Po-ni, *adv.* Suddenly; in an instant; without waiting; kaili *poni* ka make o ka puhi baka; kaili *poni* ka hanu.

Po-ni-u, *v. Po* and *niu,* cocoanut, out of which Hawaiians formerly made tops for playthings; hence,

1. To spin round like a top.

2. To have a vertigo or dizziness.

Po-ni-u, *s.* Dizziness of the head; vertigo.

2. Name of a low creeping plant like the koali; he mea ulu kolo ma ke ano koali.

Po-ni-u-ni-u, *v.* See PONIU. To turn like a top; to be dizzy; to be sick from hunger or weakness.

Po-ni-u-ni-u, *s.* A vertigo; a dizziness; a sickness.

2. *Particularly,* the sickness that follows intoxication or a debauch.

3. Forgetfulness of events recently passed

through some disease of the brain.

4. The anguish of trouble and disappointment. 2 *Sam.* 1:9.

Po-ni-ho, *v.* *Po* and *niho*, a tooth. To turn up; to turn off, i. e., to uncover; to lay open what has been covered up; to skin or separate the lips from the teeth.

> *Poniho ino ka lae o Pipa,*
> *Ahu wale ka ina uli ka ina eleele,*
> *Ka wana ku ka wana uhalula,*
> *Ka hakahae akau kihi malama*
> *O na kakaka i hauli poia e ke kai.*

Po-ni-ni-u, *v.* See Poniu. To turn round frequently; to walk by turning round.

Po-ni-ni-u, *s.* A turning; a circular motion, as of a wheel.

2. That which causes dizziness or a vertigo.

Po-ni-po-ni, *s.* See Poni. The different but somewhat blended colors of changeable silk.

2. Kapa painted with different colors.

3. The early dawn of the morning from the mixed colors; hence, purple.

Po-ni-po-ni, *adj.* Mixing; mingling, as of different colors; mixing of different ingredients to make an odoriferous perfume; sweet smelling, as a perfume.

Po-no, *v.* To be good; to be right; to be just; to be morally upright.

2. To be good; to bless; to be for the comfort or convenience of one.

3. To be well, i. e., in bodily health.

4. *Hoo.* To justify one suspected of wrong; to clear or acquit, as an accused person. See Apono.

5. To avenge an injured person.

6. To ordain; to appoint.

7. To use, as money; to trade. Note.— *Pono* is frequently used impersonally and also as a helping verb before an infinitive, and signifies, it is right; it is proper; it ought; it may; it is worthy, &c. The form *e pono ai* or *i pono ai* is used very frequently; the word expressing the thing causing the favor or good or benefit, going before. O ka *naauao ka mea e pono ai* ke aupuni, knowledge is a thing *to bless* a kingdom.

Po-no, *s.* Goodness; uprightness; moral good; rectitude of conduct.

2. That which is right or excellent; *abstract*, righteousness; excellency.

3. Duty; obligation; authority. *Mark* 11:28, 29, 33. Note.—The Hawaiians now speak of the *pono* kahiko and the *pono* hou by way of *comparison* and also of *contrast*.

Po-no, *adj.* Good; right; lawful; acceptable; beautiful; nani.

2. Possible; able; proper; fit; wa pono, a proper time.

Po-no, *adv.* Is used in various senses.

1. As qualifying verbs, and signifies, well; rightly; truly; properly, &c.

2. It is used as an intensive of the preceding verb; as, *haka pono*, to look at earnestly; *ku pono*, to stand opposite to.

Po-no-i, *adj.* That which belongs peculiarly to one's self, either of persons or things, and may be rendered by the terms, *own*, *self*, *only*, &c. Nau *ponoi*, for *yourself exclusively*; kau keiki *ponoi*, thine *own child*, in distinction from an *adopted* one; o ka makuakane ame kana keiki *ponoi*, the father and his *own child*; he poe kanaka *ponoi* nona, a company of people for *himself*, i. e., *at his disposal. Kanl.* 7:6. No wai ia hale? no'u *ponoi* no, for whom is that house? it is for *myself*, i. e., it is for my particular use, or it is my *own* in distinction from the claim of any one else.

Po-no-i, *adv.* Exactly so; truly; exclusively.

Po-no-hu-ku, *adj.* Polohuku, pokeokeo.

Po-no-ki, *s.* A piece of *ki* root cut off, in distributing it out.

Po-no-po-no, *v.* See Pono, *v.* and *s. Hoo.* To put in order; to make right; to prepare; to reform, as a wicked person; to amend; to correct, as something erroneous.

2. To judge; to settle a controversy. *Kin.* 49:16.

Po-no-po-no, *s. Hoo.* Judgment; a declaration of what is right.

2. The practice of what is right.

3. That which is right in itself. *Ier.* 22:3.

Po-no-po-no, *adj.* Just; upright; correct.

Po-nu-hu, *v.* See Punohu. To rise up like a pillar or column of smoke; to have the appearance of a ship when her sails are suddenly set; to ascend, as a mass of smoke from the bottom of the volcano.

Po-nu-hu, *s.* See Punohu. The rising up of a pillar of smoke; the appearance of a ship near by with all her sails set; the rising up of smoke, as from a pit of fire. *Kin.* 19:28.

Po-nu-hu, *adj.* Grand; wide spreading, as a ship under sail, or a column of smoke ascending.

Po-nu-lu, *v.* *Po* and *nulu*. To rise and float off, as smoke; to send out or cause smoke or steam.

Po-nu-lu-lu, *adj.* Thick and short, as a bundle.

Po-nu-lu-nu-lu, *adj.* Large and loosely done up, as a bundle of materials more

than the wrapper will contain; mahu, pahupahu.

Po-nu-nu-nu, *v.* To be short and thick;
to be clumsy; e mahumahu, e poupou, e
polohuku.

Po-nu-nu-nu, *s.* A large bunch or bundle of anything, as poi loosely bound up;
he mahumahu.

Po-pa-hi, *s.* A small man or woman.

Po-pe, *s.* *Lat.* papa. The Father or
highest priest of the Romish Church; ke
Kahuna nui o ka Ekalesia Roma.

Po-pe-la, *adj.* *Eng.* Of or belonging
to poplar. *Kin.* 30:37.

Po-pi-li-ki-a, *s.* *Po,* intensive, and *pilikia,* thick together. Want of room.

2. The want of something necessary for
a particular pursuit.

3. Difficulty; distress; tribulation. *Kanl.*
4:30.

4. Oppression; designed vexation.

Po-pi-li-ki-a, *v.* To cause distress to
one; to oppress; to bear hard upon one;
to cause one to work like a slave. *Hoo.*
To vex; to harass. *Nah.* 33:55.

Po-pi-li-ki-a, *adj.* Distressing; afflict-
ive; difficult.

Po-po, *s.* A mass of matter of a round
or oval shape; he mea poepoe me he poka
la; *popo* berena, a loaf of bread. *Puk.* 29:2.

2. The rot in timber or vegetables; worm
dust; the rust of metals. *Iak.* 5:3. See
POPOPO.

3. A ball for playing ball or for cricket.
See KINIPOPO.

Po-po, *v.* To rot; to be without strength,
as worm-eaten timber; to be rotten, as
ropes or cords. *Lunk.* 15:14.

2. *Hoo.* To make a thing round; to turn
to roundness, as in a lathe.

Po-po, *adj.* See POPOPO. Rotten; decayed; what is eaten by the *mu.*

Po-po, *adv.* For *apopo,* to-morrow. *Popo
hoao. Laieik.* 128.

Po-po-ai, *s.* See POAIAI. A bunch or
bundle of pounded kalo.

Po-po-ai, *v.* To surround; to make a circle.

Po-po-e, *v.* To blossom, i. e., to swell
and shoot out, as a blossom; as plants.

Po-po-i, *v.* See POI, *v.* To cover; to
cover up, as a vessel or container; to stop,
as with a bung.

2. To overwhelm, as water. *Puk.* 14:28.
To come upon suddenly, as a cold breeze;
ia manawa, *popoi* mai la ke anu i ka aha
lealea. *Laieik.* 121.

3. To rise up against, as a robber against

a traveler. *Kanl.* 19:11. To fall upon, as
banditti. *Iob.* 1:16.

4. *Hoo.* To cover up; to overwhelm, as
the sea or as the surf. *Kanl.* 11:4. To
break, as the surf over the reef. See POIPOI.

Po-po-i, *s.* A bung; a stopper for any
orifice.

2. The place where the surf, on approaching the shore, rises high and breaks with
roaring noise; the combing of the surf.

    Popoi haki kauhola,
    Kahela ka malu o ka pae lauhala.

Po-po-i-wi, *s.* A corner of a wall; a
turning place. 2 *Oihl.* 26:9. Ka hookuina
o na aoao; the corner of a room or of a
kalo patch.

Po-po-o-li-mu, *s.* The moss that grows
on stones, especially on the mountains
where there is much rain; he io no ke po.

Po-po-u-lu, *s.* The plantain bearing the
short round fruit. See POPOHE and NIU-
HIWA.

Po-pou-no-ho-ni-a, *v.* To cut frequently.

2. To backbite. See NAIOAIKAE, to slander.

3. To eat the refuse of food.

Po-po-he, *adj.* See POHE. Cut short
and smooth, as a rope cut with a knife.

Po-po-ki, *s.* A species of crab fish.

2. A small animal; perhaps a crab found
on the sea beach.

3. A cat. NOTE.—*Popoki* applies to that
which is *short* and *thick;* and a cat is so
called from its plump, short, thick head.

Po-po-ki, *adj.* Short and thick in opposition to long and slender.

Po-po-li, *adj.* See POLI. Arched or curving over, as a leaning precipice, or one that
curves over beyond a perpendicular; *popoli* mai ka pali; it applies also to a board
warped inward; ka aoao *popoli* o ka papa.

Po-po-lo, *s.* The name of a plant sometimes eaten
in times of
scarcity; it is
also used as
a medicine;
eia kona
laau, o ka
popolo a ke
k o w a h a ,
kapiliia iho
la maluna o kona poo.

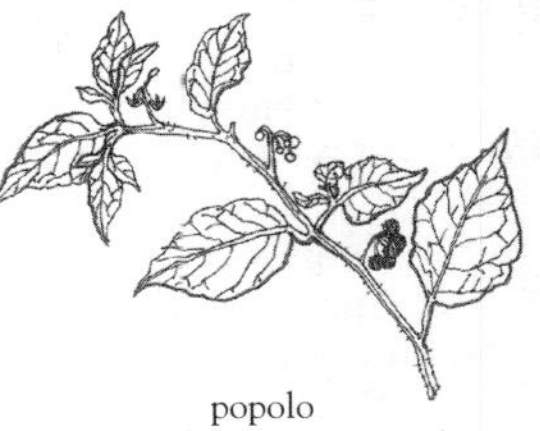

popolo

Po-po-lo-hu-a, *adj.* Blue, as the sky
above in a clear day; puka mai kona hemolele mai loko mai o na ao *popolohua.*

Po-po-lo-na, *adj.* Mouldy; worm-eaten;

rancid. See POLOPOLONA.

Po-po-lu, *s.* See POPOULU. Name of a species of banana; eia na maia a Papa e ai ai, o ka *popolu,* o ka iholena ame ka niuhiwa, these are the bananas of which Papa may eat, the *popolu,* &c.

Po-po-ni, *adj.* Full of fear or dread; weak with fear; hooweliweli ae oia no ka maule *poponi.* See PONI 4.

Po-po-ni, *v.* See PONI 4. To be cold and shivering, the hair erect, &c., through fear.

Po-po-pa-la-o-a, *s.* *Popo,* ball, and *palaoa* (*Eng.*), flour. A cake or loaf of bread. *Oihk.* 7:12. See POPOBERENA.

Po-po-po, *s.* See POPO. The rot in timber and vegetables.

    2. Corruption; decay. *Oihk.* 22:25.

    3. The offal of worms.

Po-po-po, *adj.* Rotten; decayed.

Po-po-po-no, *v.* See PONO, the first syllable twice reduplicated.. To put right; to correct; to justify.

Po-po-po-no, *adj.* Very good; very right; well done; blessed; profited.

Po-po-be-re-na, *s.* *Popo* and *berena* (*Eng.*), bread. A loaf of bread. 1 *Oihl.* 16:3. See POPOPALAOA.

Po-pu-akii, *s.* The place where pointed clusters of clouds arise out of the ocean; kahi e puka mai ai na ao opua mai ka moana.

Po-pu-a-li, } *v.* See PUALI. To girdle
Poo-pu-a-li, }   round; to tie up tightly; to reduce to small dimensions.

Po-pu-a-li, *s.* See PUALI. A hollow on the crown of the head; a depression from tight binding.

Po-wa, *v.* To rob; to kill; to kill and rob.

    2. To castrate; to separate the testicles of a male.

Po-wa, *s.* A robber; a highwayman; a murderer.

Po-we-hi, *v.* *Po* and *wehi,* darkly. To see indistinctly. FIG. To have a feeble or indistinct knowledge of a thing.

Po-we-hi-we-hi, *v.* Intensive of *powehi.* To grow dim; applied to the eyes. *Kin.* 27:1. To be weak sighted.

    2. Applied to the mind, to have obscure and indistinct ideas of a thing. 2 *Pet.* 1:9.

    3. To be obscure; to be uncertain; o ka mooolelo kahiko loa, ua *powehiwehi* ia.

Po-we-hi-we-hi, *s.* Obscure vision; twilight. *Ezek.* 12:6.

    2. FIG. Indinstinct ideas of a truth or fact.

Po-we-hi-we-hi, *adj.* Dark; obscure to the sight; seeing indistinctly; knowing but little; not distinctly manifest; he *powehiwehi* ko ke kanaka aloha.

Po-we-ko, *v.* To be skillful or eloquent in conversation; e *poweko,* e akamai i ke kamailio. See POLEKO.

Po-te-ra, *s.* *Eng.* A potter. *Mat.* 27:7. He mea hana ipulepo.

Po-ti-ko, *s.* *Eng.* A portico; a short veranda.

Pu, *v.* To come forth from; to come out of, as words out of the mouth; to draw out or move off, as a canoe from the place where it was dug out; alaila hele mai ke kahuna e *pu* ia ka waa.

    2. To hold water in the mouth and try to talk; to mumble; to suck wind into the mouth.

    3. To call; to call out; to proclaim; to call upon inanimate matter, as to call upon the mountains.

    4. To cast lots; to choose by lot. See PUU. This was done usually by doubling the hand and one telling whether anything was in it or not.

    5. *Hoo.* To sit with the knees bent up and the hands over them; to sit idly; to do nothing.

Pu, *s.* A shell; a horn; a trumpet; anything that would make a loud noise by blowing into it; na *pu* kiwi hipa ehiku, seven *trumpets* of rams' horns. *Ios.* 6:4.

    2. Anything that would make an explosive noise; a gun, pistol or firelock; na kanaka ame na *pu* kau poohiwi he nui loa, people and *guns* carried on the shoulders, a great many.

    3. A musical instrument made by twisting a leaf: *pu* la'i. *Laieik.* 78.

    4. A lot as in casting lots.

    5. Name of the olona string used in playing at the game called *pukaula;* he wahi kaula olona i hili oioi, a he anana paha ka loa.

    6. A gourd; a pumpkin; a squash; pu lima, the hand *doubled up.* See the verb, 4.

Pu, *adv.* With; together with; along with; in company; ku *pu,* to stand *together;* like *pu, just* alike.

Pu-a, *v.* To blossom, as a plant; to put forth blossoms or flowers. *Isa.* 35:1. To bud, as fruit or flowers. *Mel. Sol.* 6:11.

    2. To appear at a distance; to rise up, as columns of smoke in small quantities.

    3. To raise in the throat in order to feed out of the mouth, as pigeons feed their young; o ka puaa hoi, ua *pua* io ka ai mai ka waha aku o ke kanaka nona ka puaa, e like me ka hanai ana i ka ilio. NOTE.—In

this way Hawaiians fed their pets or favorite animals.

4. To put food into another's mouth from one's own, as into a child's; to spit or spew food into a child's mouth.

5. To tie up in bundles; to bind in bundles, as sheaves of grain. *Kin.* 37:7. To tie in bundles, as the bones of the dead; a paa kona mau iwi i ka *puaia*, when his bones *were tied up.*

6. To lay siege to; to besiege, as a city. 2 *Sam.* 11:1.

7. To bear; to carry.

8. *Hoo.* To make fast; to confine; to establish.

9. To cut or hew off obliquely, as in hewing off the sharp ends of a canoe; penei e kalai ai, e *pua* ia o mua o ka waa ame hope i uuku ai ka ihu.

10. To bunch, as cards when there is a mistake made in dealing them out; e *pua* i ka pepa, no ka mea ua hewa ka haawi ana.

Pu-a, *s.* A blossom; a flower; a carving in imitation of a flower. *Puk.* 25:31.

2. The upper part of the sugar-cane when it blossoms, as *pua ko,* and which was used for arrows, and in modern times by children in play, as *hoolei pua;* hence,

3. The name of a play or game.

4. An arrow for shooting in connection with the *kakaka* or bow.

5. A bundle of sticks; a sheaf of grain or grass. *Kin.* 37:7.

6. Posterity; descendants. *Laieik.* 181. Children; a household. *Puk.* 19:3.

7. A flock; a herd, as of cattle or goats; he *pua* kao; he *pua* hipa; he *pua* bipi; a school of fish; he *pua* anae.

8. A species of small fish; he *pua* amaama.

9. The name of a tree found at Kapua on Hawaii and other islands; the wood is very hard.

10. The name applied to a deranged person.

11. A kind of deity supposed to reside in some person who was called *Kahupua* and who had power to send Pua to do injury to others. He *akuapua* was applied to some kinds of sickness inducing delirium, a sickness supposed to be sent by some individual in anger.

12. The name of a goddess, the sister of Kalaipahoa. She came with him and Kapo from a foreign country, and they entered certain trees.

13. The name of the kind of hook used in taking turtles or the *ea.*

Pu-a, *s.* A pae pu mai a hiki laua (mau mea heenalu) mauka, e lana ana kekahi mouo, ua kapaia kela mea he *pua.*

Pu-aa, *v.* To flee, as a child from its parent to avoid punishment; hoopunipuni—holo, puaa.

2. As if *puaia.* To be gathered into a bundle, as sticks for kindling a fire. See Pua 5.

3. To gird tightly, as in tying up the bones of a deceased person for preservation.

4. To be girded tightly around the throat; e pilikia ma ka puu. See PUAPUAA.

5. To tie up tightly so as to make the substance small; hence,

6. To be small, thin or fine, as a spider's web; me kahi malo, ua *puaa* hilo. See PUAHILO.

Pu-aa, *s.* A hog; a swine; the flesh of a hog. *Oihk.* 11:7. NOTE.—The hog was found indigenous, when the Islands were visited by Captain Cook.

2. A bundle of small wood for fuel; a fagot. See PUA.

3. The name of an unclean bird, *puaa ilioi,* rendered in English bittern. *Zep.* 2:14.

4. Anything very small and easily blown away. See PUEPUEHU.

Pu-aa, *adj.* Small; fine; thin; easily dispersed.

Pu-aa-o-hi, *s.* Name of children whose father had gambled them away. See KUAKI.

Pu-aa-ha-ha, *v.* To call out; to call to some one; to make a vociferous noise.

Pu-aa-he-a, *s.* See HEA, *s.* Name of the last or second hog sacrificed on a certain occasion; kalua kekahi puaa, he *puaahea* ka inoa.

Pu-a-a-ho-le-ho-le, *s.* Name of a small fish.

Pu-aa-ku-mu-lau, *s.* Name of a woman whose husband had gambled her away with all his property.

Pu-a-a-nae, *s.* Name of a species of fish.

Pu-aa-pi-pi, *s.* A name applied to the first cattle brought to the Islands by Captain Vancouver; ua mahaloia kela poe pipi e ko Hawaii, a ua kapaia aku ka inoa he *puaapipi,* those cattle were admired by the Hawaiians and they called them *cattle-hog.*

Pu-a-a-wa, *s.* Name of a species of fish.

Pu-ai, *v.* To flow, as blood from a vein; as water from a fountain.

2. To proceed from one; to fall from one, as an expression, an idea, or as something said. *Mar.* 7:15. To flow from the mouth, as the words of an orator; a *puai* mai la

ka leo ku e.

3. To gag; to heave; to throw up from the stomach; to vomit.

4. To blow water out of the mouth.

5. To cast up; to boil up, as water from a spring. *Ier.* 6:7. Fig. To throw out, as sin from the heart.

Pu-ai, *s.* The gullet.

2. A vomiting; a spitting; a heaving from sickness of the stomach.

Pu-ai-a, *v.* To blow gently, as wind; used at Hawaii the same as *onini* at Maui; ua puaia a *puaia* kae ka pona waa, a mahope pa mai ka makani as it increases in strength.

Pu-ai-li-ma, *s.* Name of a Hawaiian cathartic medicine.

Pu-ai-na-we-le, *adj.* Very small; very fine; thin like spider's webs.

Pu-ai-na-we-le, *v.* To reduce to fineness; to make small or fine.

Pu-ao, *s.* The dashing of two or more waves that meet together; the place where a retreating wave meets one coming in in shallow water; also called *koaka.*

2. The *os tincae* or orifice of the womb.

Pu-a-uu, *v.* To practice onanism on one's self. See Haakoi.

Pu-a-uu, *s.* The name of the same kind of wickedness.

Pu-a-hau, *s. Pua,* blossom, and *hau,* name of a tree. A hau blossom; the blossom of the hau tree.

Pu-a-ha-nu-i, *s.* The name of a tree; also called *akiahala.*

Pu-a-hi, *v.* To do quickly; to be spry. See Hoopuahi.

Pu-a-hi-a-hi, *s.* The name of a foreign flower, four-o'clock; i kuu ike ana i ka *puahiahi* mohala mai la.

Pu-a-hi-o, *v.* To come and go suddenly; to arrive, as a person, and start off again quickly.

Pu-a-hi-o-hi-o, *s.* A whirlwind. 2 *Nal.* 2:1. He mau makani ku elua e ume ana i ka opala iluna.

Pu-a-hi-lo, *v.* To be small; to be fine; to be slender, as a thread of spider's web; e nawali e like me he punawelewele la.

2. To exhibit a fine slender appearance, as the new moon.

Pu-a-hi-lo, *s.* A fine slender appearance; no ka *puahilo* ana o ka mahina, on account of the *slender appearance* of the (new) moon.

Pu-a-hi-lo-hi-lo, *v.* See Puahilo. To break up fine; to crack; to chap or break,

as the human skin.

Pu-a-hi-lo-hi-lo, *s.* The scaly appearance of the scarf-skin; the breaking or cracking of the skin from some disease; the cuticle which peels off from the skin of new born children.

Pu-a-hu-ku, *s.* A word used in blackguard language; ke pii la oe i *puahuku.*

Pu-a-hu-lu, *v.* To hasten; to get ready quickly; to prepare suddenly; to be in a fluster.

Pu-a-hu-lu, *s.* A sudden start; an affright; the doing a thing quickly and without much thought or reflection.

Pu-a-ka-a-ka, *v.* To tie up small; to tie up in a small compass. See Pauakaaka.

2. To compel one to work hard or without reward.

Pu-a-kai, *s.* A journey; a going in company. See Huakai.

2. A dye for coloring red; he wai hooluu ulaula.

3. Hair of the head that has been colored white; he lauoho i hookeokeo ia.

Pu-a-kai-oe, *s. Pua* and *kaioe,* a plant. A blossom of the kaioe.

Pu-a-kai-a-u-lu, *s.* The name of a wind; a light gentle breeze; a dying breeze of the trade wind.

Pu-a-ka-la, *s. Pua* and *kala,* rough. Name of a shrub of the thorn kind, Argemone Mexicana; he laau oioi; a thistle. *Kin.* 3:18.

puakala

Pu-a-ke-a, *v.* To spread out, as the sails of a vessel; to enlarge.

Pu-a-ke-a, *adj.* Pale; wanting color. *Hoik.* 6:8.

Pu-a-ki, *v.* To be stingy; to be close; to treat without compassion.

2. E hiaa, e puka, e hone, i puaki hiaka niho.

3. To sit quietly without speaking; to shut the mouth; e pani i ka waha.

Pu-a-ki, *adj.* Light; swift in running; active.

2. Thin; spare; famished; poor in flesh, as a person; he kanaka wiwi.

Pu-a-kii, *s.* An image for idol worship.

2. He *pouakii,* he ao opuakiikii.

Pu-a-kii, *v.* To take without right; to go wrong; to do wrong.

Pu-a-ko, *s.* The top and blossom part, including the leaves of sugar-cane; oia no ka malama e owili ai ka *puako.*

Pu-a-ko-lii, *s.* Name of a common tree.

Pu-a-la, *v.* To collect together in a heap.

2. To be not sufficiently cooked, as food; to be badly cooked.

Pu-a-lau, *v.* To carry on the hips supported by the arms.

2. E limalau, e puualu, e paapu.

Pu-a-la-wa-hi, *v.* To divide into parts or spaces.

Pu-a-le, *s.* A ravine on the side of a mountain.

Pu-a-lei, *s.* The top leaf or branch of the tree when the lower ones are cut off.

Pu-a-le-na, *v.* To wander; to go about here and there; to be idle; to do nothing because no chief commands to work; to be lazy. See PUANA.

2. To be muddy, as water; to want clearness; *pualena* ka moana, the ocean is *dirty.* Laieik. 163.

Pu-a-le-na, *s.* The glimmering or first dawn of light in the morning. *Puk.* 14:27. A wehe ke alaula, a *pualena,* a ao loa.

Pu-a-le-na, *adj.* Idle; loitering about without any fixed purpose, without business.

2. Obscure, as water when one cannot see the bottom.

Pu-a-le-wa, *v.* To be unfixed; to be unsettled, as an unsteady person; to go from place to place; to be unfurnished with comforts.

Pu-a-le-wa, *adj.* Unsettled; unfurnished; not established; often changing one's residence or employment. Hele a *pualewa* applies to travelers who find no place to lodge, no food, nothing comfortable.

Pu-a-li, *v.* *Pu* and *ali,* a scar; a contraction of the skin. To gird round tightly; to draw in by binding tightly.

2. To be large and small in places, as a rope of uneven size; e pawali, e puaniki, e kualiali.

Pu-a-li, *s.* A place compressed, that is, a small or diminished place between two larger ones.

2. An inclosing about; hence, a neck of land almost surrounded by water; in *geography,* an isthmus.

3. The small part of a wasp.

4. Fig. A woman, from her being girded with a pa-u (much more with corsets.)

5. Anything girded tight and made small.

6. A malo from its use.

Pu-a-li, *s.* A life guard. *Laieik.* 42. A company of soldiers; koi mai la na *puali* ia Kiwalao, the *soldiers* pressed upon Kiwalao.

2. An army; a host. *Lunk.* 7:1.

3. A company prepared for war and pursuing. *Puk.* 14:4.

4. Fig. A great number; a host; as, *puali* o ka lani, the *host* of heaven, that is, the stars.

Pu-a-li-a-li, *v.* See PUALI. To be of irregular size, large and small.

Pu-a-lii, *s.* Name of a person who lived idly with the chief; ua kapaia ka inoa o na kanaka noho wahi alii he *pualii,* he *aialo* kahi inoa. See AIALO.

Pu-a-lo-a-lo, *s.* The name of a tree.

Pu-a-lu, *v.* *Pu,* together, and alu, to combine. To work together; to combine in aid of one or of each other; to act in concert; to work like a multitude at one kind of business.

pualoalo

Pu-a-lu, } *s.* Acting in concert, as
Pu-a-lu-a-lu, } a great number of people working together; a combination in favor or against.

2. The name of a species of fish.

3. A cord for binding.

Pu-a-lu, *adv.* Unitedly in action; unanimously in opinion; no ka hiki ole paha i na kanaka a pau ke malama *pualu* aku i ke aupuni.

Pu-a-ma-na, *s.* A caret (∧) or sign of omission in writing.

Pu-a-na, *v.* To crowd together in great numbers; to rush together, as soldiers in pursuit of one. 2 *Oihl.* 18:31.

2. To surround, as an enemy; to encompass.

3. To try; to begin the recitation of a mele; to act the part of a precentor or leader in singing; to commence a tune that others may follow.

4. To cry out or proclaim in behalf of others.

5. To pronounce distinctly, as in uttering a word or sentence very plainly.

6. *Hoo.* The same.

Pu-a-na, *v.* To be idle; to be lazy; to go from place to place without object.

Pu-a-na, *adj.* Idle; lounging; unsteady;

small; insignificant.

Pu-a-na, *s.* The signal or first words in beginning to recite or cantillate a mele. Note.—The Hawaiians in chanting their meles or songs in ancient times, had some one as leader or chorister who commenced the recitation in so clear and distinct a manner, that, after the enunciation of two or three words, the whole company were able to join in chorus.

2. That which makes the pronunciation plain. Note.—According to the foregoing note, the *puana* must consist in a distinct enunciation, so that others may at once recognize the subject; hence,

3. The pronunciation of a word; pehea ka *puana?* how is the *pronunciation?*

Pu-a-na-a-na, *v.* To swell and diminish frequently, as poorly made ropes; e pauakaaka, e paulinalina.

Pu-a-nae-nae, *s.* The name of a flower growing on Kauai; he ako *puanaenae* no Waialoha. See Naenae.

Pu-a-ne-a-ne, *s.* A stage of extreme old age, when universal decay is coming on, and yet the person is free from pain or suffering. See also Kolopupu.

2. A world of light and life; he ao malama, he wahi e ola mau loa.

3. Eternity.

Pu-a-ne-a-ne, *v.* To live forever; to live eternity; e ola mau loa a hiki i ka *puaneane.*

Pu-a-ni-hi, *s.* See Pauanihi. Young kalo tops; the young of kalo. See Oninihi.

Pu-a-ni-ki, *v.* *Pua,* to bind, and *niki,* tight. To bind up in a small space; to bind tightly.

Pu-a-ni-u, *s.* Kapa colored with the niu or cocoanut.

Pu-a-nu-a-nu, *v.* See Anu, cold. To be cold; to be damp and shivering; to be chilly.

Pu-a-nu-a-nu, *adj.* Cold; chilly, as in foggy or damp weather.

Pu-a-poo, *s.* *Pua,* blossom, and *poo,* the head. A head blossom, i. e., the comb of a cock or other bird; a tuft of feathers on the head of a bird; i ka *puapoo* o ka manu puukoa.

Pu-a-pu.

Pu-a-pu-a, *v.* To force; to urge on; to compel. See Puepue. To overwhelm; to overcome.

2. To hang down like the tail of an animal.

3. To project like the tail feathers of a cock.

4. To be glorious; to be beautiful.

Pu-a-pu-a, *s.* See Pua, bundle. A bundle of brush-wood, sticks or grass. *Oih.* 28:3.

2. The name of a fly that bites.

Pu-a-pu-a, *adj.* Unpalatable; disagreeable; vicious.

Pu-a-pu-aa, *v.* See Puaa. To be gathered up into a bundle, as fagots or sticks for kindling a fire.

Pu-a-pu-aa, *adj.* Collected; gathered together; me he ao *puapuaa* la ke aloha e kau nei, as a *thick* cloud love settles upon me. *Laieik.* 205.

Pu-a-pu-ai, *v.* See Puai. To bubble or spring up, as water from a spring or fountain. *Iak.* 3:11. See Huahuai.

Pu-a-pu-ai, *s.* The ebullition of water; a spring or fountain of water.

Pu-a-pu-a-la, *v.* See Puala. To collect together in small heaps.

Pu-a-pu-a-mo-a, *s.* See Pupumoa, i. e., *puapua* and *moa,* a fowl. A long skirted coat. See Puapua, *v.,* 3.

Pu-a-pu-a-wa, *s.* Name of a long, thin shell out of which they used to drink awa.

Pu-a-wa,   } *s.* The root of the awa
Pu-a-wa-a-wa, } plant; a small awa plant; he wahi puaa, he moa lawa, me ka *puawa. Laieik.* 49.

2. *Abstract,* bitterness; a bitter medicine.

3. The hala, the leaves of which were made into mats; so called when the leaves are young and most fit for mats.

Pu-a-wa, *s.* The Hawaiian pronunciation of *guava,* which see.

Pu-a-wai, *s.* The slaver or spittle of one with a sore moth, as if salivated; the epithet of a slavering, dirty mouthed child.

Pu-a-wai,   } *s.* Name of a hill near
Pu-a-wai-na, } Honolulu.

Pu-a-we, *adj.* Thin; soft; fine, like the threads of a spider's web.

Pu-a-we-a-we, *s.* Thinness; fineness; smallness.

Pu-e, *v.* To thrust, as with a spear; to make an attack, as in battle; to make an onset.

2. To crowd on; to gain what is another's; to force; to compel; a lohe na kanaka, ua make kekahi alii, *pue* lakou e kaua, when the people heard that one of their chiefs was dead, they *were urgent* to fight; to urge; e *pue* ana lakou ia Kamehameha, they *were urging* Kamehameha.

3. To solicit strongly.

4. To manage so as to make it necessary for one to do a thing; a *pue* iho la o Poki

ia Kaahumanu e kaua, Poki urged Kaahumanu to war, i. e., he planned to make a war unavoidable.

5. To force; to compel, i. e., to commit lewdness. *Eset.* 7:8.

6. To solicit to lewdness; to seduce, as a virgin; to commit a rape. *Puk.* 22:16. E hoala i ka mea e moekolohe ai. See PUE-WALE. E *pue* i ka wahine, to ravish; to commit a rape.

7. To make a round elevated hill, as in weeding out and hilling up potatoes.

8. To attack or besiege a city. *Ier.* 32:2.

PU-E, *s.* A round heap of dirt or mud for planting kalo or potatoes; a potato hill.

2. A raised surf of fresh water; he nalu o ka wai.

3. The name of a bush or tree.

PU-E-A, *v.* Passive of *pue* for *pueia.* To be forced, compelled or urged to do a thing.

PU-E-A, *s.* The name of a god worshiped in the night; he akua kii *Puea;* ma ia po ana iho, hoaia ke ahi o *Puea;* maikai ka po o *Puea.*

PU-E-E-KE, *v.* See EEKE. To shorten; to cut off or cut short; to wrinkle up; to contract.

PU-E-O, *s.* An owl. *Isa.* 34:11. He manu lele hihiu. NOTE.— The *pueo* was formerly worshiped as a god: one of the poe akua mana.

2. A shroud of a ship.

3. The strings used to tie around the posts of a house in building.

PU-E-O-NE, *s.* Name of the place in the sea outside of where the surf breaks; also called *poana kai.*

PU-E-HU, *v.* To blow away; to scatter; to disperse. PASS. To be scattered, as dust or light substances by the wind. *Hal.* 1:4.

2. To be routed and scattered, as an army. *Oihk.* 26:36.

3. To be scattered or separated from each other, as a fleet of canoes in a storm.

4. *Hoo.* To scatter or drive out, as a people. *Nah.* 33:5.

5. To remain; to be over and above. *Puk.* 26:12.

PU-E-HU, *s.* A dispersion; a scattering; a flurry of wind when it strikes suddenly anything and puts in motion whatever cannot resist it, as small dust or bits of paper before the shake of a fan.

2. The remainder ; the remnant of a thing; what is over and above. *Puk.* 26:12.

PU-E-HU-E-HU, *adj.* See PUEHU. Scattered; dispersed.

2. Rough; ragged, as the skin after drinking awa; mahuna ka ili, nakaka *puehuehu* inoino loa ke nana aku.

3. Small; fine, as dust.

4. Raw; uncooked; as, ai *puehuehu,* kalo but partially cooked, so that in pounding it, its parts are easily separated or scattered.

PU-E-KO-LE-A, *adj.* Round and plump, as a duck. See MANUKOLEA.

PU-E-LE-HU, *v.* Pue, to force, and *lehu,* ashes. To push into the embers.

PU-E-LE-WA, *v.* Pue and *lewa,* swinging. To be wandering about; to be unfixed; not settled.

PU-E-LE-WA, *adj.* Going here and there; unsteady; unsettled.

PU-E-PU-E, *adj.* Large; thick; plump; ua loihi kona kino a ua *puepue.*

2. Rotten, as timber; worm-eaten; full of holes. See PUIPUI.

PU-E-PU-E, *v.* To be large; to be plump; to be full, as a fat animal. See PUIPUI.

2. To make up into hills, as potatoes or kalo.

PU-E-PU-E, *s.* A round bunch; a hill of potatoes or kalo.

2. The name of a duck from its plumpness. See PUEKOLEA.

PU-E-PU-E-HU, *v.* See PUEHU. To scatter greatly; to disperse frequently. *Hoo.* To cause a great or thorough dispersion.

PU-E-PU-E-LU, *adj.* Hard; tough; applied to potatoes that are paakiki, and perhaps to other food.

PU-E-WA, *v.* To float about; to be carried hither and thither by the wind or current and scattered; e laweia iloko o ka wai me ka puehu.

PU-E-WAI, *s.* Pue and *wai,* water. The waves at the mouth of a stream as the stream rushes into the sea.

PU-E-WA-LE, *v.* Pue and *wale,* without cause. To ravish; to force, as a female. *Zek.* 14:2. To commit lewdness. *2 Sam.* 13:12. To commit a rape.

PU-E-WA-LE, *s.* A rape; ravishment; forcible lewdness.

PU-I, *adj.* Large; swelled out, as a fat person. See PUIPUI.

PU-I-A, *v.* To spread; to diffuse abroad, as an odor; to fill with odor or perfume; e ala, e kuhinia.

PU-I-A, *adj.* Beautiful; grand; full of sweet-scented flowers adding to the beauty.

PU-I-HO, *v.* To start suddenly; to be frightened. See PUIWA.

2. To cry out suddenly; to shout.

3. To hum; to make a humming noise; e hoomumu iho. See PUOHO.

PU-I-KAI-KA, *v.* To be close or crooked in dealing; to be unyielding to another's judgment or opinion; mai noho oe a *puikaika* mai ia'u, don't *be hard upon me*.

PU-I-KAI-KA, *adj.* Close or crooked in dealing; unyielding to the wish or opinion of another.

PU-I-LI, *v.* To gird round; to embrace; to clasp; e *puili* a paa. See PULIKI. E *puili* me ka lima, to *hold fast* with the hand.

PU-I-LI, *s.* One bent on a thing, as pleasure ; one seeking satisfaction in any way.
2. That which gives temporary delight or pleasure; he *puili* pau wale no ia no ka poe hana lealea.
3. A kind of play or game with sugarcane flowers.
4. Name of a smallish kind of rope.

PU-I-LI, *adj.* Seizing; holding fast with the hand.

> Puili ka ohelo ai a ka manu,
> A ka hala i wiliia e ka makani,
> A ka lehua nee i ka papa.

PU-I-LI-PAA, *adj.* Taking strong hold; holding tightly.

PU-I-PU-I, *v.* To be fat; to be full; to be large; to be corpulent; to be thick set, as the body of a person. See PUEPUE.

PU-I-PU-I, *s.* A fat plump person or animal. *Isa.* 10:16. Plumpness; fullness of person; liki i kona mau *puipui* iho.

PU-I-PU-I, *adj.* Fat; plump; flourishing; stout. *Lunk.* 3:29. Aole i pau ke kino *puipui* o ke akamai ia'u i olahonua; large; corpulent.
2. Bitter; pungent to the taste; sour; awaawa.
3. Hard; severe; oolea.

PU-I-WA, *v.* To be taken by surprise; to start suddenly, as a horse when frightened; to be affrighted, as from sleep; to meet with sudden surprise from any cause.
2. To jump or start suddenly.
3. *Hoo.* To cry out or sound an alarm. 2 *Oihl.* 13:12. See PUOHO and PUIHO.

PU-I-WA, *s.* Amazement; a surprise; a stupefaction on account of wonder; a starting from fright; sudden excitement.

PU-O, *v.* To mix up; to put in confusion; huikau.
2. To strike or clasp the hands together; e pai na lima.
3. To lash, as the sea does the shore; *puo* ae la ke kai i ke one.
4. To bend, as a cocoanut leaf in the wind; to yield to the wind, as the spread sails of a ship.

> I *puo* lani i ke kai o Peapea a ka manu,
> O kaioe o Maui ka hookalakua,
> He kupua ka lani no ka moku—e.

PU-O-A, *s.* See PUUOA. A house built with the poles uniting at the top in the shape of a pyramid; hence,
2. In *geometry*, a pyramid. *Ana Hon.* 29.
3. A temporary residence; a small house hastily put up; ua nui na *puoa* ke nana aku, there were many *temporary residences* to appearance.
4. A small inclosure of poles.
5. A plant choked with weeds.
6. A house for depositing a corpse; he halekupapau.
7. He uloa.

PU-O-HO, *v.* See PUIWA. To start and cry out; to start in a fright; to jump suddenly, as from a sleep. *Laieik.* 26. To cry out or sound together.

PU-O-HO, *s.* A sudden start; a fright, i. e., e oho pu.

PU-O-HAI, *s.* The root and body of the ohai shrub; kumuohai.
2. A bunch of the ohai flowers; opuohai.

> He kumuohai, he opuohai,
> Akua pee *puohai* o ke kaha,
> I walea wale la i ke a
> I ka ulu kanu a Kahai,
> Haina oe e ka oo e ka manu o Kanehili.

PU-O-KO, *v.* To rage; to be hot.

PU-O-KO-O-KO, *s.* See PU and OKOOKO, a red heat. A great hot fire; i ka onohi pono o ka la, i ka *puokooko* hoi o ka wela loa. *Laieik.* 176.

PU-O-LA-NI, *v.* To lay upon a consecrated place, as an altar; to lay by as sacred; to bind or tie up, as a sacrifice.

PU-O-LA-NI, *adj.* Set up on high; raised up; set apart.

PU-O-LO, *v.* To tie up, as a bundle tied on top; to bundle up; alaila, *puolo* ae la a paa, awe mai la, then he *tied up a bundle* tightly and brought it.

PU-O-LO, *s.* A bundle of kapa folded and bound up so as to appear round like a pai-ai.
2. A bundle tied at the top for carrying on a stick.
3. A scrip; a bag; a container. *Ios.* 9:4.

PU-O-LO-O-LO-HEE, *s.* A species of grass having a furzed top.

PU-O-NE, *adj.* See PUUONE.

PU-O-NI, *v.* To lay up for a long life or for a future age; e kau i ka puaneane ola; to lay up the means of living forever.

PU-O-PE-LU, *s.* A bunch of stones lying naturally or brought together where travelers or persons heavily loaded stopped to rest; o hoi o'u hoapili i ka la o *puopelu.* See OIOINA.

PU-O-PU-O, *v.* To clap together the hollow hands with a sound. See HOOPUOPUO.

PUU, *v.* To collect together; to lay by, particularly in heaps.

2. To boll; to form a round seed, as flax; to swell and break, as a boil. *Hoik.* 16:2.

3. To cast or draws lots (a Hawaiian custom formerly in practice) by using a knotted string.

4. To gather or dip up water in the hands.

5. E *puu* paha auanei ka lae i ka ua o ka Kawaupuu.

6. *Hoo.* To heap or pile up, as stones.

7. To cast lots; to divide a country by lot. *Ios.* 7:26.

PUU, *s.* Any round protuberance belonging to a larger substance.

2. A small round hill; a peak; a pimple; a wart; the knuckles; the ankle joints; the Adam's apple of the throat; hence, the throat; a knop; an ornament of a candlestick. *Puk.* 25:3.

3. The material heart. *2 Sam.* 18:14.

4. A heap; he *puu* opala, a heap of rubbish; na *puu* huapalaoa, *shocks* of grain. *Lunk.* 15:5.

5. A tower; a citadel; a substance; a portion; a lot in casting lots. *Nah.* 34:18.

6. A quantity; part; property; destiny; appointment; fortune. *Rut.* 2:5.

7. Habit; custom; eia ko kakou wahi *puu* iki, o ka hoohaunaele i ka manawa kula.

8. Any act or thing causing ridicule, contempt, or perhaps anger, as an offense against good manners or morals; he ino, he mea e loiloi ai, a e hoowahawaha ai paha; he kina, no ka hilahila kona holo ana (o Poki), no ka mea, aole he *puu* nui ma ka puka o kona hale, out of shame, he (Poki) sailed away, because there was no —at the door of his house.

9. A hand, i. e., the cards held at a game.

PUU, *adj.* Dying with one for attachment's sake; as when a chief dies some of his people, for love's sake, wish to die also; ke olelo aku nei au ia oukou, o ka moe *puu* oia nei; a i moe ka moe *puu* ilaila; a hiki ae ilaila ka moe *puu.*

PUU. A sign of the plural number. *Gram.* § 86 and 92. It mostly has reference to a collection. Synonymous in some cases with *poe* and *pae.* He *puu* puaa; he *puu* kanaka; this last form is not often found.

PU-U-A, *v.* See PUUWA. To be full; to be choked or suffocated, as in swallowing food; to stick in the throat; to strangle; e keu i ka puu.

2. To be in difficult labor, as in childbirth. *Kin.* 35:16. Mai puhi malu, o *puua* a loaa.

PU-U-A, *s.* Hardness, as in food; difficulty in swallowing; he wai ka mea e inu ai i ka paina ana no ka *puua* ame ka wela o ka ai.

PUU-A-LU, *v.* To carry on the hips. See PUALAU.

PUU-O-A, *s.* A small inclosure of sticks or poles leaning together at the top in the form of a pyramid. See PUOA.

PUU-OI-OI, } *s.* *Puu,* heap, and *oioi*
PUU-OI-OI-NA, } or *oioina,* a resting place for travelers. An elevated spot by the roadside; a heap of stones; a shady tree, or possibly, a pool of water, used as a resting place.

PUU-O-NE, *s.* *Puu* and *one,* sand. A mound of sand; a heap of earth.

2. The name of a heiau; o ka mea kuhikuhi heiau, he kuhikuhi *puuone* ia.

PUU-O-PA-LA, *s.* *Puu,* heap, and *opala,* dirt; dust. Dust, litter, dirt, &c., piled up into a heap.

PUU-HAU, *s.* A hard lump growing on the flesh, particularly on the joints. See OHAKULAI.

PUU-HOO-MA-HA, *s.* *Puu* and *hoomaha,* to rest. See PUUOIOI above.

PUU-HO-LE, *s.* The slight protuberance below the abdomen, or the lower part of the abdomen; ke aaki la i ka *puuhole.*

PUU-HO-NU-A, *s.* *Puu* and *honua,* flat land. A place of refuge for one pursued. *Nah.* 35:6. A place of safety in time of war; a refuge. *Isa.* 25:4.

PUU-KAU-A, *s.* *Puu* and *kaua,* war. A fortification; a hold. *1 Sam.* 22:45. A stronghold; a fort. *Lunk.* 6:2. He mau puu e kaua ai e like me Kauiki.

2. The commander-in-chief; he alii ia ia ka omaka kaua.

PUU-KAU-LA, *v.* In *gambling,* to stake, as a man his wife, or a wife her husband, to be won or lost; e *puukaula* mai oe ia lakou, e Iehova.

PUU-KA-NI, *adj.* Pleasant; sweet, as the sound of a pleasant voice in singing.

2. Sweet, as the tones of a flute or other instrument.

3. FIG. A handsome person.

PUU-KA-NI-LU-A, *adj.* Drawn straight and tight, as a rope.

2. Obstinate, as one who contradicts.

Puu-ka-pe-le, *s.* The name of a tree on Kauai, the *kauwila.*

Puu-ka-pu, *s.* Kukuluia na *puukapu* elima mawaena o na pae kanaka elua.

2. A hand of cards dealt out and left untouched until the other hands are all played out.

Puu-ki-e, *v.* To insnare; to entrap; to get one into difficulty. *Hoo.* The same.

Pu-u-ki-u-ki, *s.* The name of the spots of water dammed by the uki; he wai no ke uki na ka mahu i hookiokio i ka lau o ka uki, he opu uki.

Puu-ko-a, *adj.* Small; diminutive, as fine grass; i ka puapoo o ka mauu *puukoa.*

Puu-ko-a, *s.* Name of a species of grass.

Puu-ko-ko, *s.* *Puu* and *koko,* blood. The heart of an animal which by its muscular action throws the blood through the system.

Puu-ko-le, *s.* The mons veneris. See Hena.

Puu-ku, *s.* One entrusted with the care of goods. *Kin.* 15:20. A steward. 1 *Nal.* 16:9. The office of a steward; a provider; stewardship.

Puu-ku-ku-i, *s.* A kind of kapa made of wauke and pouleulu.

Pu-u-ku-u-ku, *v.* To be many; to be numerous; to be multitudinous. See Puu-luulu.

Pu-u-la-u-la, *s.* *Puu* and *ulaula,* red. A bank or mass of red earth; redness; the color of red earth.

Puu-le-le, *s.* *Puu,* a swelling, and *lele,* to fly. A rupture; a hernia; so called because it disappears suddenly.

Puu-le-na, *adj.* Name of a cold wind on the mountains or at the volcano; ka ahe *puulena* o ka lua. *Laieik.* 34.

Puu-le-po, *s.* A mound of earth; earth used in coloring.

2. A place designated in the game of papua.

Pu-u-li-u-li, *adj.* Dark; black; dark colored. See Pouliuli.

Puu-li-ma, *s.* *Puu* and *lima,* hand. The wrist joints; the knuckles and wrist bones; the palm of the hand; ka peahi lima.

Pu-u-lu, *s.* A great number of men or things; a multitude; an army of soldiers.

Pu-u-lu-u-lu, *v.* To be thick together; to be multitudinous; to be numerous or many.

Pu-u-lu-kau-a, *s.* Name of a division of an army prepared for battle.

Puu-na-ue, } *v.* To divide into par-
Puu-nau-we, } cels or parts; to divide; to give out; to separate. *Kin.* 10:5. To divide, as spoil. *Puk.* 15:9. E *puunauwe* ma ka hailona, to divide (the land) by lot. *Ios.* 13:6. To divide, as property. *Ios.* 22:8.

Puu-no-hu, *s.* The foot of a cloud hanging on a mountain; a thick cloud.

2. The motion of waves succeeding each other. See Punohu.

Puu-pa, *v.* To receive freely or gratuitously; to give freely or gratuitously; *puupa* hiolo wale no ia leo.

Puu-pa, *s.* Name of a stone from which maika stones were made.

Puu-paa, *s.* *Puu* and *paa,* fast. The reins; the kidneys. *Anat.* 53; *Hal.* 7:9. Fig. The affections; the principles of action.

2. An epithet of female purity; virginity; a virgin. *Kanl.* 22:14. *Puupaa ana,* the state of virginity. *Lunk.* 11:38.

Puu-paa, *adv.* In a virgin state; freedom from impurity. *Laieik.* 115.

Puu-pau, *s.* *Puu,* throat, and *pau,* to destroy. The name of a corroding or eating disease in the throat; when the disease is seated in the mouth it has another name.

Puu-po-o-la, *v.* See Aipoola. To eat in a hurry so as to choke; to strangle.

Puu-puu, *v.* To break out into boils and blisters. See Puu.

2. *Hoo.* To heap up; to pile up in heaps.

3. To be or become lumpy; not smoothly soft as good poi.

Puu-puu, *s.* A protuberance; a swelling; a joint. *Anat.* 18. See Puu, *s.*

2. The pimples of the itch; the knuckles; the ankle bones. *Laieik.* 45, 47.

3. A knot of a tree; a hillock; a fist doubled up for fighting. *Laieik.* 47.

4. A bunch; a handful; a knop of a lamp or candlestick. *Puk.* 25:31.

5. A scurvy or scabby person. *Oihk.* 21:20.

6. Poi not well pounded; *puupuu* kaua, a warlike defense on a wall. *Isa.* 54:12. *Puupuu* koko, emerods. 1 *Sam.* 5:9. Ka *puupuu* a kona maka, the eye-ball (perhaps); ua hele ka *puupuu* a kona maka, aole ona eu ae.

Puu-puu, *adj.* Full of blotches or pimples; rough with uneven places.

Puu-puu, *adv.* Roughly; unevenly; holo *puupuu,* to run over rough places.

Puu-puu-o-ne, *adj.* Fortune telling; living in a strange house called *hale puuone;* kukulu oia i hale *puupuuone.*

Puu-puu-wa-wae, *s.* *Puu* and *wawae,* feet. The ankle bones. *Oih.* 3:7. The ankles. *Ezek.* 47:3.

Pu-u-wa, *v.* To have something in the throat; to be choked; to have difficulty in swallowing. See PUUA.

Puu-wai, *s.* *Puu* and *wai*, liquid. The material heart; the active muscle which receives and distributes the blood through the animal system; the heart. 2 *Nal.* 9:24. NOTE.—The ancient Hawaiians supposed that there was nothing but water in the muscle called the heart, hence the name *puuwai*.

2. Food of different kinds of vegetables tied up in bunches and put into the oven; he luau i hana laulau ia a hookomoia i ka pohaku. See LUAU.

Puu-wai-u, *s.* *Puu* and *waiu*, milk. Epithet of the female breast; a milk breast or breast of milk. *Ezek.* 16:7.

Pu-ha, *v.* See POHA. To burst or break open, as a sore or boil; to pass through or out; tourst forth.

2. To hawk as a means of raising phlegm from the lungs.

3. To be loathsome, as a running sore. *Iob.* 7:5.

4. To breathe like a sea-turtle; e hanu me he honu la.

Pu-ha, *s.* Rottenness inside of timber; wood internally defective; the disease gonorrhea. See PUHIKAOKAO. *Puha* laau, a hollow tree. *Laieik.* 77.

Pu-ha, *adj.* Broken or burst open, as a sore or boil; mai *puha*, an issue; a running sore. 2 *Sam.* 3:29.

Pu-ha-a-a, *v.* To be clear; to be light colored; to be white; to appear distinct, as a thing by itself.

Pu-ha-a-a, *adj.* Having large light spots; applied to kalo or potatoes when partially roasted, i. e., the uncooked part having a white appearance distinct from the cooked.

2. Applied to the light spots of the leho.

3. White, as the uncommon whiteness of the eye of men or women; he maka *puhaaa* kona; he leho *puhaaa*, aole e aina ka hee. Aole leho, he *puhaaa* wale no.

Pu-haa-ka-kai,   } *s.* A species of bird
Pu-haa-ka-kai-e-a, } like the noio; a small black bird. See NOIO.

Pu-hai-na-na, *v.* To look only instead of answering a request.

Pu-hau-hau, *adj.* Loose; not bound tightly.

2. Large; fat, as men; *puhauhau* o mea.

Pu-ha-ha, *v.* To wish evil to one; to speak to one; to speak loudly. See LEO-LEOA and LEOLEOWA.

Pu-ha-ha-lu, *adj.* Tough; appied to kalo; kalo *puhahalu*.

Pu-ha-ka,   } *v.* *Pu* and *haka*, a
Pu-ha-ka-ha-ka, } space between two things. To be vacant, as a space between two things.

2. To be destitute; to be wanting; applied variously; he lohe ma Kuapehu nei, a ma Kailua, a *puhaka* mai o a o mawaena, we hear (preaching) here at Kuapehu and at Kailua, but all between is *destitute*.

Pu-ha-la, *s.* The body of the hala tree.

Pu-ha-la-au, *s.* A hollow tree. See PUHA. *Laieik.* 129.

Pu-ha-la-ua, *s.* A covetous person.

Pu-ha-la-uo,   } *adj.* Stingy; parsimo-
Pu-ha-la-wo, } nious; he awa, he pi.

Pu-ha-la-lu, *v.* To burst or break forth suddenly, as the voice. See PALALU. To imitate the voice of a bird.

Pu-ha-la-lu, *adj.* Large; plump; fat and weak, as men or beasts.

Pu-ha-li, *s.* Stinginess; covetousness. See PUHALAUO.

2. Name of a small delicate sea-shell.

Pu-ha-lu-ha-lu, *adj.* Gazing; staring at. See UHALUHALU.

Pu-ha-ni-ha-ni-ha, *v.* To rue what one has done in a bargain; to regret an agreement; to pay an obligation with reluctance; e aua. See PUNIHANIHA.

Pu-ha-nu, *v.* To breathe easier; to rest a little. See HANU.

Pu-hee, *v.* To disperse; to scatter. See HEE.

Pu-hee, *s.* For *poohee*. The head of the hee or squid.

Pu-he-o-he-o, *s.* A sport of children like jumping the rope. See KOHEOHEO. NOTE.—If grown people attended the play it was called *kilu*.

Pu-hee-ua-nuu, *adj.* *Pu* for *puu*, and *hee*, squid. LIT. The large bunch on the head of the squid.

2. Swelling; strutting, as a dandy.

> Ka *puheeuanuu* o Kahai
> Na ke kamakama luahaku,
> Ina i o ka poni alii.

Pu-hee-mi-ki, *v.* A present made to one of two persons, when the one having not received anything seizes the other's and deprives him of it.

Pu-he-mo, *v.* To be slack; to be remiss; to fall behind. *Hoo.* The same.

Pu-he-ne, *v.* To use lascivious words and actions slily; to tempt to different kinds of wickedness, especially to adultery; e loku, e loha.

2. To tie or bundle up food (pai-ai) in the shape of a nest.

PU-HE-NE, *s.* Lascivious gestures and words slily used to excite to adultery; he loku, he loha, he hana, he alea.

2. A bundle made in the form of a nest, for food; a nest-like bundle of food.

PU-HE-NE-HE-NE, *s.* The name of a play performed by hiding a stone called noa (see NOA) under a kapa; and the game consists in guessing where to find it. See KAU, *s.*, 6.

PU-HE-NU, *s.* A breath; a breathing. See PUHANU and HANU.

PU-HI, *v.* To blow or puff wind; to breathe hard.

2. To blow, as to blow the fire; e *puhi* i ke ahi; to burn in the fire; to set on fire; to burn up.

3. E *puhi* i ke kukui, to *blow out* the lamp.

4. To blow the (conch) shell or trumpet. *Nah.* 10:34.

5. To blow, as the wind; as a strong wind. *Kekah.* 1:6. To blow up.

6. To puff tobacco smoke.

7. To puff at one in a way of contempt; to treat insolently.

8. To distill rum or any liquor; e *puhi* rama; to burn incense; e *puhi* i ka mea ala. *Puk.* 30:1. E *puhi* ka awa mai ka awa a hiki i ke koa.

PU-HI, *s.* A puffing; a blowing; *puhi baka,* tobacco smoking.

2. An eel; he ia loihi, mau maka kalalea.

3. Name of a place in the sea where the water is black from depth or from deep holes in the rocks.

PU-HI, *adj.* He mai pulou, he *puhi.*

PU-HI-A-HI, *s.* A man who tends the fires of a steam-engine, &c.

PU-HI-O-I-LO, *s.* *Puhi,* eel, and *oilo,* a small fish. A small white eel.

PU-HI-O-HI-O, *v.* To break wind; to discharge wind audibly; e hookani okole, e pumakani, e puhiu.

PU-HI-O-MO-LE, *s.* A belching up of wind.

2. A white eel; he puhi keokeo.

PU-HI-O-NI-O, *v.* To paint or color in a spotted manner; to stamp with different colors, as kapa in former times.

PU-HI-O-PU-LE, *s.* A small spotted eel.

PU-HI-U, *v.* Contraction for *puhi hihiu.* To go wrong; to get out of the right path; to go far off.

2. To break wind.

PU-HI-U-HI-U, *s.* See PUHIOHIO. He pumakani, e hookani i ka okole.

PU-HI-HI-O, *v.* To sound, as a pipe or wind instrument.

PU-HI-KAO-KAO, *v.* To burst open or break the skin, as the kaokao or some kinds of the venereal disease.

PU-HI-KA-PA, *s.* See KAPA, an eel. An epithet of Kamehameha.

PU-HI-KO-LE, *v.* To act the spendthrift; to lounge about idly; to waste one's property; to become poor.

PU-HI-KII, *s.* A species of small flying-fish, called *kaawilipuhikii;* they swim on the surface of the sea.

PU-HI-LI, *s.* A scar on the face; a scar by burning.

2. A running vegetable; green things; herbs.

PU-HI-PAU, *v.* To be bearer of an accusation against one's self.

2. To revile; to reproach.

PU-HI-PA-KA, *s.* A species of eel.

2. The Hawaiian orthography for *puhibaka,* tobacco smoking.

PU-HI-PA-KA, *v.* For *puhibaka.* To smoke tobacco.

PU-HI-PA-LA-HO-A-NA, *s.* A species of fish of the eel kind.

PU-HI-PA-LA-LU, *v.* To flatter and amuse one that has property in order to obtain; e *puhipalalu* ia kekahi poe waiwai.

PU-HI-PA-LI-LA, *s.* A tall, slim man with little flesh; he like me he kolu la ka linalina.

PU-HI-PU-HI, *v.* To anoint over with anything medicinal.

2. To blow any substance which has been chewed in the mouth into the sea in order to decoy or intoxicate fish.

3. To bind up tightly.

PU-HI-PU-HI-A-HI, *s.* A cross, overbearing person.

PU-HO, *v.* To be broken out in ulcers, as scrofulous legs; he mai *puho.* See PUHA.

PU-HOO-KA-NI, *s.* Name of a shell-fish.

PU-HO-LO, *v.* To roast blood; *puholo* koko. See HAKUI.

PU-HO-LO-HO-LO, *s.* A perspiration produced by the steam of leaves covering over a fire and the patient sits covered with a kapa over it; a o ka *puholoholo* kekahi mea e pono ai, a o ka laau naha kekahi. *Anat.* 54.

PU-HO-LU, *v.* To cook fish with hot stones in a calabash.

PU-HU-E-HU-E, *s.* A species of the convolvulus.

Pu-hu-la-lu, *adj.* Fat and weak, as a man.

Pu-hu-li, *v.* To be full grown, as food or vegetables; to be ripe; hookahe mau no ka wai, a laupai a *puhuli.*

Pu-hu-lu-hu-lu, *adj.* Full grown; full sized, as an animal; as fruit.

Pu-ka, *v.* To enter or pass through a hole, crevice, a gate or door-way.

2. To enter in or to pass out, according as it is followed by *mai* or *aku.* With *aku* it signifies to go out; to go from one place to another; to go forth. 1 *Nah.* 19:11.

3. To rise, as a subject, to obtain the government; to usurp the authority of a ruler.

4. To cheat; to defraud one of what is due.

5. *Hoo.* To appear in sight when at a distance, as the sun rising or a ship appearing at a distance.

6. To bring along, as the wind brings clouds.

7. To utter; to publish; to proclaim a thing. *Kekah.* 5:2.

8. To pass from one state or condition to that of another, as from ignorance to knowledge; o kakou hoi ka poe i *hoopukaia* noloko mai o ka pouli.

9. To end; to finish; e hoopau aku.

10. To separate from; to go away; e hookaawale aku.

Pu-ka, *s.* A door-way; a gate-way; an entrance; a hole; *puka* o ke kui, *puka* o ke kuikele, the *eye* of a needle; *puka* lou, a loop *hole. Puk.* 25:5. Any place of entrance or egress; *puka* pepeiao, the ear; i hoakakaia'ku ma ka *puka* o ko oukou mau pepeiao. NOTE.—*Puka* as a noun takes various forms, as *puka, aipuka, ipuka, upuka* and *kanipuka,* all which see.

2. The art of making spears, ropes, &c., that appear well but really are good for nothing and *vice versa.*

3. A curious art; a trick; the practice of legerdemain; hoopiopio.

Pu-ka-a-ki, *s.* A pile of fish to be divided out.

Pu-ka-a-ki, *v.* To divide out fish according to the shares of several; to share according to a rule agreed on.

Pu-kai, *v.* To paint or color the hair with lime or whitewash, a practice of former times.

Pu-kai, *s.* The name of the wash used in painting the hair.

2. Name of a species of fish.

Pu-kai, *adj.* Stained or colored with the

pukai; a ike oia i ka wahine *pukai* maikai, when he saw a woman beautifully *painted.*

Pu-ka-i-hu, *s. Puka* and *ihu,* the nose. The nostril. *Puk.* 15:8. Ka puka o ka ihu, he mau puka hanu.

Pu-kai-kai-ka, *v.* To rise up, as smoke; to swell; to raise up on high. See KAIKAI.

Pu-kau-a, *s.* An officer in an army; a general; he luna kaua; a champion of a company. *Laieik.* 45.

Pu-kau-la, *s.* A playing of cards; gambling; the name of a game.

2. A bag or bundle tied up for carrying.

Pu-kau-po-hi-wi, *s. Pu,* gun, *kau,* to place, and *pohiwi,* shoulder. A gun carried on the shoulder; a firelock.

Pu-ka-ha-le, *s. Puka* and *hale,* house. A window of a house. *Isa.* 60:8.

2. A gate or door-way of a house; a place for going out and coming in to a house.

Pu-ka-ka, *v.* To ascend in a zigzag direction.

2. To cluck, as a hen; to cackle in sympathy, as a cock with a hen when she has laid. See PUKOKO. E *koko* (pukaka) e like me ka moa kane i ka manawa e hoohemo ai ka moa wahine i ka hua.

Pu-ka-ka, *v.* To go here and there; to go about without object.

> Pukaka na lehua o Mana,
> Auwana wale iho no i ka auwai,
> He ole ka launa me Makalii,
> Ike i na muliwai holo a ka ia
> E holo ana ka oopu, he ia iki—e.

Pu-ka-ka-la, *v. Pu* and *kala,* rough. To be rough; to be jagged; to have sharp points.

Pu-ka-ku, *v.* To go out of a straight line; to run here and there.

2. To overflow, as water over a bank.

3. To lean over out of a perpendicular line; to wander out of the way.

4. *Hoo.* To be smart; to act independently of others; to separate one's self from others in work.

5. To injure one; to make an example of.

Pu-ka-ma-ka-ni, *s. Puka* and *makani,* wind. A window; a place for ventilation. 1 *Sam.* 19:12.

Pu-ka-nae-nae, *s.* Name of an open spot near the summit of Mauna Waialeale on Kauai.

Pu-ka-ni, *s. Pu* and *kani,* to sound. A sounding instrument; a trumpet. 1 *Oihl.* 13:8.

Pu-ka-ni, *adj.* Stingy; hard; severe; unfeeling for others.

Pu-ka-ni-lu-a, *v. Pukani* and *lua* for

loa, very. To be strong; to be energetic.

2. To be hard; to be severe in exactions.

3. To be large; to be plump; to be full fed. NOTE.—These two last ideas were often united in the same person, especially in the second, third and fourth grade of chiefs.

4. To oppose, as the authority of a chief or head man.

5. To contend, as from anger.

PU-KA-NI-LU-A, *s.* The contention of two parties for the prevalence of their respective opinions.

PU-KA-NU-I, *adj.* Applied to a basket used in catching fish; hinai *pukanui*.

PU-KA-PA, *s.* The gate of a yard; the gate of a city. *Ier.* 17:24.

PU-KA-PAA, *s.* *Puka* and *paa*, fast; concealed. The *ossa vagina*; he ulapaa, he puupaa.

PU-KA-PA-HA-LE, *s.* The gate of a city or village. *Hal.* 9:14.

PU-KA-PA-KA-HA, *s.* A window barred with sticks.

PU-KA-PA-KI, *v.* *Puka* and *paki*, to drop, as tears. To shed tears; to drop, as water from holes; aole e *pukapaki* mai ko lakou waimaka.

PU-KA-PU-KA, *v.* Frequentative of *puka*. To get through frequently.

2. FIG. To seek to obtain the ascendency; to get the advantage of.

3. To speculate in trading; to get the best bargain.

4. *Hoo.* I ka *hoopukapuka* dala ame na mea kupono.

PU-KA-PU-KA, *s.* A window having sticks across for a defense.

2. Whatever is full of holes, not joined well together.

PU-KA-PU-KA, *adj.* Full of holes, chinks, cracks, &c.; net-work. *Puk.* 27:4. Mea ulana *pukapuka*, net-work. *Ier.* 52:22. Eke *pukapuka*, a bag full of holes. *Hag.* 1:6.

PU-KA-WA, *s.* A door or window projecting outward; he puka e oili loa iwaho.

PU-KE, *v.* *Pu* and *ke*, to force. To hit; to strike, as one calabash against another; to strike together, as the knees of one in trepidation. *Dan.* 5:6.

PU-KE-A-WE, *s.* A kind of tree.

PU-KI, *v.* To run suddenly; to dash off, as a horse in a race; e holo, e ka i ka holo me he lio la.

PU-KII, *s.* Name of a species of fish.

PU-KI-KI, *v.* To blow strongly or furiously, as the wind; to be stormy or very rough, as the weather.

PU-KI-KI, *s.* A strong boisterous wind; a heavy storm.

2. A name given to tight waisted dresses for females.

PU-KI-KI, *adj.* Strong; furious; stormy, as the wind.

2. Sewed tightly; akamai i ka humuhumu papale pua, me ka papale *pukiki*.

PU-KO, *v.* To be rough like the sea.

2. To be separated; to be scattered; to be driven away.

3. To be daring, able to conquer; *puko* momona. *Laieik.* 41.

PU-KO-A, *v.* To ascend; to rise up, as smoke. *Hal.* 18:8. *Pukoa* ae la ka uahi o ka laupele.

2. To mix and mingle, as smoke; to collect together.

PU-KO-A, *s.* Rocks hidden or sunken under water, but such as ships may strike upon.

2. The coral rocks of the ocean; ka *pukoa* nui e nee ae nai—e! Oh, the great *rocks of the reef* all coming this way!

3. Smoke united in a column and ascending, as from a volcano.

4. The name of a hog with long tushes; ina loloa na niho o ka puaa, he *pukoa* ia puaa.

PU-KO-A-WA-WA-HI-WAA, *s.* The name of a tree like vegetable coral growing in the sea, to the great annoyance of fishermen with their nets and canoes.

PU-KO-HU-KO-HU, *adj.* A red malo or other kapa; e hawele ana me kona aahu *pukohukohu*. *Laieik.* 40.

PU-KO-HU-KO-HU, *s.* The name of a malo colored with the noni or red; a thick red malo.

PU-KO-KO, *v.* To cackle like a cock; ka uwe ana a ka moa kane me ka *pukoko*.

PU-KO-LU, *s.* The name of a triple canoe, i. e., three canoes rigged up abreast; maluna laua o na *pukolu*. *Laieik.* 100. Ua hanaia o Kaenakane i ekolu waa, ua kapaia he *pukolu*.

PU-KU, *v.* To finish; to end; to put out, as fire; e hoopulu ahi.

PU-KU, *s.* Property given by a chief in charge of his servants.

PU-KU-A-WA, *v.* To be troubled in mind through fear of the gods; he hooahi no na akua.

PU-KU-A-WA, *s.* The fear of the anger of the gods.

PU-KU-I, *v.* To sit doubled up; to be

bent up; to fold together, as the arms.

Pu-ku-i, *s.* An assembly or collection of the gods at the luakini; o Waka, o ka wahine i ka *pukui.*

Pu-ku-i-ku-i, *v.* To gather thickly together; to assemble; to become a multitude.

Pu-ku-ka-li-na, *adj.* Wild; whirling; sweeping, as a small whirling wind that removes light things; makani *pukukalina* o Mahikihiki.

Pu-ku-ni-a-hi, *s. Pu, kuni* and *ahi*, fire. A cannon from the manner of firing.

Pu-ku-pu-ku, *v.* To wrinkle the forehead; to draw down the eyebrows; to frown, as in anger; e hoomainoino i ka lae.

Pu-ku-pu-ku, *s.* A crimping; a folding in fine plaits; a wrinkling.

Pu-ku-pu-ku, *adj.* Wrinkled, as the skin by age or otherwise.

Pu-ku-pu-ku-ku-e-ma-ka, *s.* The wrinkles on the forehead between the eyebrows.

Pu-la, *s.* A small particle of anything, as dust; a mote in the eye; aole e ike ka maka i kona *pula* iho; the mucus in the corner of the eye.

2. The leaves of the hala tree when used with a net in catching fish.

3. The name of the stick used in driving fish into a net; laau ululu.

Pu-la-le, *v.* To hurry; to hasten; to excite to do a thing quickly. See Hoolale.

Pu-la-le, *s.* Quickness; dispatch; hurry in doing a thing.

2. An instrument used to scare fish into a net.

Pu-la-ma, *s. Pu* and *lama*, a torch. A light, generally made from kukui nuts; a flambeau. See Lamaku.

Pu-la-pu-la, *s.* A devotee; one who follows another about.

2. Anger; revenge; opposition.

3. The tops of sugar-cane cut for planting.

Pu-la-wa, *v.* To surround, as with a cloud or fog; to be foggy; to cover the heavens with thick fog or clouds; to render the land and mountains invisible.

Pu-la-wa-la-wa, *adj.* See Lawa. Furnished; having a supply of what is necessary; prepared; ready for an emergency.

2. Bound tightly or firmly, as a thatched house with cords from post to post; braced frimly, as a building.

3. Strong and active for work, as a man; *pulawalawa* ka hale; *pulawalawa* ke kanaka.

Pu-le, *v.* To pray; to supplicate; to worship; to call, with adoration, upon some invisible being; e kahea aku, me ka mahalo aku i ka mea ike maka ole ia.

Pu-le, *s.* The act of worshiping some god; conversation with an invisible being; religious service; begging some favor from heaven.

Pu-lei-pu-lu, *v.* To have an offensive smell; to emit a disagreeable effluvia; to stink.

Pu-le-he, *v.* To be loose, as a bundle loosely bound; to hang loosely; to vibrate.

Pe-le-he, *adj.* Loose; not fast; not bound tightly; vibrating.

Pu-le-hi, *v.* To be accustomed to do anything; to know how to do a thing, as a mechanic by practice.

Pu-le-ho, *s.* See Leho. A small shellfish; the shell is used for beads.

Pu-le-ho-le-ho, *s.* See Leho. A string of lehos or shells for beads.

2. A knot or callous place on the shoulder from carrying burdens.

Pu-le-hu, *v.* To roast on coals or embers; to bake on the fire; to roast in the blaze and smoke; hence,

2. To burn; to consume by fire.

Pu-le-hu, *s.* A roasting on coals or embers; cooking food in a hurry by wrapping it in leaves and laying it on the fire, whether it be coals, hot ashes, flame or smoke.

2. A waterspout.

Pu-le-hu-le-hu, *v.* To bring together several different things to one place.

Pu-le-le, *s.* Some disease or complaint about the neck.

Pu-le-le-hu-a, *v.* To be scattered, as water into spray by falling from a great height, or from being blown by the wind.

Pu-le-le-hu-a, *s.* A butterfly; he peelua i hoomaluleia a lilo i kino lele me he manu la.

Pu-le-lo, *v.* To float in the air, as a flag; to wave to and fro in the wind; to hang loosely; i kapa i *pulelo* mai ka lua.

2. To change, as one's opinion; e ake e *pulelo* iki ae na manao o kakou.

Pu-le-lo, *adj.* Floating; changeable; unstable.

Pu-le-na, *s.* Name of the south-east wind at Hilo, Waimea, &c.

Pu-le-na, *adj.* Softly blowing, as a gentle wind. See Puulena.

Pu-le-pe, *v.* To rain heavily. See Kawa.

2. To perspire freely and copiously.

Pu-le-pu-le, *adj.* Spotted; speckled; of different colors.

Pu-le-wa, *v.* See Lewa, swinging. To be changeable; to turn this way and that; to float here and there, as one of unstable opinion; to be varying; to be tremulous, as a quagmire; he *pulewa* ka aina, he naka Hawaii.

Pu-le-wa-le-wa, *v.* To be open; to be porous; to be full of holes. See Pulewa and Lewa.

2. To be empty; to be hungry; e haupolewalewa.

Pu-le-wa-le-wa, *adj.* Weak; feeble; inconstant; *pulewalewa* wale no ka noho ana, aole ikaika.

Pu-li-u-li-u, *s.* A small gourd in which the laau waiiki (a medicine) was made.

Pu-li-hi, *s.* A whirlwind.

Pu-li-hi-li-hi, *s.* The name of an herb.

Pu-li-ki, *v.* *Pu* and *liki*, to bind up. To gird up tightly; to wrap around, as a vest or armor. *Epes.* 6:14.

2. To embrace or fold in one's arms, as an infant. 2 *Nal.* 4:16.

3. To gird or tie round. 1 *Sam.* 22:18.

4. To embrace with affection. *Kin.* 48:12.

5. To hold fast; to make tight.

Pu-li-ki, *s.* A vest; any garment girded around the body.

Pu-li-ki-kau-a, ⎫ *s.* A habergeon; a war
Pu-li-ki-ko-a, ⎬ dress. 2 *Oihl.* 26:14.

Pu-li-ma, *s.* *Pu* for *puu*, and *lima*, hand. The wrist bones; the wrist; *pulima* palule, wristbands of a shirt.

2. The name of a fire kindled for the benefit of a sick person in the practice of the ancient physicians; a ma ke ao ana o ua po la, alaila hoaia ke ahi, he *pulima* ka inoa oia ahi.

Pu-li-ma, *adj.* Pertaining to the wrist; iwi *pulima*, the wrist bones. *Anat.* 19.

Pu-lo, *v.* To pass by; to pass on; to go about.

Pu-lo-a, *s.* A species of fish; he hee; a squid.

Pu-lo-u, *v.* To cover the head; to veil the eyes.

2. To hide or conceal from view; *pulou* iho la ia i ke kapa. *Laieik.* 174.

3. *Hoo.* To blindfold; to veil; to cover with a veil. 2 *Sam.* 19:4.

Pu-lo-u, *s.* A veil; a covering for the head. *Eset.* 5:12.

2. A black kapa; a kapa of any dark color.

3. The act of putting a black kapa over one for the purpose of concealment.

4. Name of a disease; mai *pulou.*

Pu-lo-u, *adj.* Bound up; covered out

of sight; he mai pulou.

Pu-lou-lou, *s.* Bunches or bundles of black kapa. *Laieik.* 112.

Pu-lou-lou, *s.* See Pulou, a veil. A veil; a covering, as of a canoe; me ka *puloulou* alii iluna o na waa.

2. A kapa on a stick (called *pahu*) erected as a sign of kapu.

Pu-lo-hi-wa, *s.* Shining black kapa.

Pu-lo-hi-wa, *adj.* Exceedingly black; shining black.

Pu-lo-ku, *adj.* Tender; soft; delicate; fine looking, as a woman; comely. *Isa.* 47:1; *Ier.* 6:2.

Pu-lo-li-a, *v.* Passive of *pulo.* To be unstable; going here and there.

Pu-lu, *v.* To be wet; to bathe; to wash. *Iob.* 24:8.

2. To be soft as that which is soaked in water.

3. *Hoo.* To wet; to moisten; to soften.

4. To water, as a plant. *Isa.* 16:9.

5. To make soft the material for kapa, that is, wauke, mamaki, &c., by soaking it in water until it becomes wali, paste-like.

Pu-lu, *s.* Any substance partially liquid and soft.

2. That which is soft, as cotton.

3. The soft matter of which kapa is made; so called when made soft by soaking; me he *pulu* kapa i ka hale.

4. *Specifically,* name of the material that grows on and is collected from a species of large fern; it has lately become an article of export.

Pu-lu, *adj.* Wet, as clothes.

2. Soft; cooked to softness.

3. *Hoo.* Deceitful; he kiu *hoopulu*, a *treacherous* spy.

Pu-lu-a, *s.* *Pu* and *lua*, two. A couple of men in a canoe; he *pulua* na kanaka ma ka waa.

2. Two men mutual assistants to each other; he mau kokoolua elua.

Pu-lu-lu, *adj.* Fat, plump and weak, as a man.

Pu-lu-lu-hi, *adj.* Hazy; foggy; cloudy; dull, as the weather.

2. Dull, as a person just waking from sleep.

Pu-lu-na, *s.* The relationship that exists between the parents of a man and the parents of his wife; or the relation of the parents of married parties to each other.

Pu-lu-na-lu-na, *s.* Clothes thrown carelessly together.

Pu-lu-pu-lu, *v.* To warm; to cherish;

to brood over, as a hen her chickens; e hoopunana me he makuahine moa la i kana mau keiki.

PU-LU-PU-LU, *s.* Cotton; he mala *pulupulu*, a cotton field. See HULUHULU.

2. Tinder. *Isa.* 43:17.

3. Fine linen. 2 *Oihl.* 2:14.

PU-LU-PU-LU, *adj.* Wet, &c. See PULU, *adj.*

PU-MAI-A, *s.* A bunch of bananas. See OPUU and OPUU MAIA under *opuu.*

PU-MA-HA-NA, } *v.* *Pu* and *mahana* or
PU-ME-HA-NA, } *mehana*, warm. The first orthography is the most correct. To be warmed, as with clothing. *Iob.* 31:20. To be warm in friendship; to have fellow feeling with a person; aole e *pumahana* ke aloha i waena o ke kane ame ka wahine; to be warm, as in contact with another. *Kekah.* 4:11. *Hoo.* To warm one's self by a fire. *Ioan.* 18:18. To heat a thing in a small degree.

PU-MA-HA-NA, *s.* Warmth physically.

2. Warmth of feeling, of love or attachment. 1 *Pet.* 4:8.

PU-MA-HA-NA, *adj.* Warm; lukewarm.

PU-MA-KA-NI, *v.* *Pu* and *makani*, wind. To blow or rage, as a whirlwind; e puhiohio, e puhiu.

PU-NA, *v.* *Hoo.* To collect or unite with one's self, as two or more wives, friends, favorites, &c. *Haa.* or *hoo.* O kakou no ka lakou poe i *haapuna* ai i ka la o ka makalii, ame ka ua ka hooilo.

PU-NA, *s.* The stone coral; lime unburnt; mortar. *Oihk.* 14:42. He pohaku keokeo no ka moana.

2. Name of a district on Hawaii.

3. A well; a spring; a cavern; a pit; *punawai*, a spring.

4. A joint of sugar-cane or bamboo; also written *pona.*

5. *Eng.* A spoon.

6. The name of a foreign surf-board; he kioe kahiki.

PU-NA, *adj.* Of or belonging to a spring. See WAIPUNA and MAPUNA.

PU-NA-HE-LE, *v.* To be or become an intimate friend of one. *Hoo.* To make one an intimate, a friend or a favorite; to become one's friend; to honor one with presents and dignity; e hoohanohano, e hoowaiwai.

PU-NA-HE-LE, *s.* A friend; a favorite; a beloved one. 2 *Nal.* 25:19. He mea i hoowaiwaiia e ke alii, he mea i hoohanohanoia me ka manao nui ia ia.

PU-NA-HE-LE, *adj.* Beloved, as a child;

honored, as a favorite; he hoalauna *punahele.*

PU-NA-HE-LU, *v.* To have a strong and somewhat rancid smell like that of a variety of articles in a tight, damp room.

2. To be obscure; to be intricate.

3. To be mouldy and full of cobwebs, as a closed, empty room.

PU-NA-HE-LU, *s.* Mould; mildew. *Kanl.* 28:22.

PU-NA-HE-LU, *adj.* Mouldy.

PU-NA-KE-A, *s.* The white sand that a high surf throws up on the beach; ku ka *punakea iuka. Laieik.* 167.

PU-NA-LU-A, *s.* The several husbands of one wife, or the several wives of one husband; he mau kane na ka wahine, he mau wahine na ke kane hookahi; one of two wives, or favorites of same chiefs. *Laieik.* 118.

2. A friend on equal terms with one. *Rut.* 1:15.

PU-NA-LU-A, *v.* To make an equal of one; to come on terms of reciprocity with one; ua *punalua* ole ka pono na ka hewa.

2. To have in common several wives or husbands.

3. To be or to have one for illicit purposes; o ke kii ka hai wahine, ua kapaia i keia manawa he moekolohe; aka, i ka wa kahiko o ka *punalua.*

PU-NA-NA, *v.* To sit on a nest, as a bird; to hatch eggs.

2. *Hoo.* To brood over; to cherish. *Isa.* 34:15.

3. To nestle; to cherish one's self in a comfortable place; ke hoi nei makou e *hoopunana* i ka poli o ko makou mau makua.

4. To live; to dwell; applied to birds.

PU-NA-NA, *s.* A nest; a bird's nest; *punana* manu. *Kanl.* 22:6.

2. FIG. The enjoyment of comforts. *Iob.* 29:18. A place of residence. *Hab.* 2:9.

3. A kind of white kapa.

PU-NA-NA-NA, *s.* A species of spider. See NANANA.

2. A spider's web.

PU-NA-PU-NA, *v.* To scatter; to blow away, as small particles of some substance.

2. To make fine or small as dust.

3. To sit on eggs; to brood, as a hen.

PU-NA-PU-NA, *adj.* Made fine; scattered; blown away.

2. Hard, as food; tough to eat.

3. Dry and mealy or hard, as a potato that is cooked.

4. Weary, lame or sore, as with walking

or lying.

Pu-na-wai, *s.* *Puna* and *wai*, water. A spring of water; a well; a fountain. *Kin.* 7:11.

Pu-na-we, *v.* To divide. See Puunawe.

Pu-na-we-le, *v.* *Pu* and *nawele*, to be fine or small. To be small in size; to be fine as threads of spider's webs.

Pu-na-we-le-we-le, *s.* A species of spider.

2. A spider's web. *Isa.* 59:5. The web of the species of spider called *lanalana*.

Pu-nee, *v.* *Pu* and *nee*, to move along. To come to one; to approach one for the purpose of asking a favor. Note.—This was done in ancient times, in the case of a common person approaching a chief, on the hands and knees, in a slow, hitching manner.

Pu-nee, *s.* A drawing towards one; a riding; a moving; he hukihee, he holopapa; a table. *Mar.* 7:4.

Pu-nee-nee, *v.* To move along, as a shower of rain.

> Puneenee ka ua o Hilo,
> E nee mai ana i ka hapapa,
> E kui mai ana i ka lehua—e.

Pu-ni, *v.* To surround as water does an island.

2. To inclose; to be hemmed in, as one person by multitudes.

3. To surround, i.e., to get round one by deceit; to prevail over; to get the better of.

4. To be surrounded; to be deceived; to be insnared; to be taken.

5. To go around; to encircle; hence,

6. To finish; to complete; to terminate.

7. To close, as an appointed period of time; as the end of the year. 1 *Nal.* 20:22. To finish the period of gestation. 1 *Sam.* 4:19.

8. To gain possession of; hee o Kalanikupule ia Kamehameha, a *puni* Oahu a me Molokai, a me Lanai a me Maui a me Kahoolawe, Kalanikupule fled before Kamehameha, and *he came in possession of* Oahu and Molokai and Lanai and Maui and Kahoolawe.

9. To covet; to desire greatly. See Note below.

10. To be addicted to; to be influenced by, as pleasure or gain; ua *puni* na 'lii ame na kanaka i na hana ino loa, the chiefs and people *were addicted* to very evil practices.

11. *Hoo.* To give false testimony; to deceive.

12. To surround for protection. *Iob.* 1:10. Note.—*Puni* is connected with many other words and signifies, *influenced*, *led by*, or *addicted to*, as well as *deceived*; puni lea-

lea, *addicted* to pleasure; *puni* waiwai, *greedy* of property; *puni* hula, *given to* the practice of the hula, &c.

Pu-ni, *s.* Name of fish nets with small meshes.

2. The termination of a fixed period, as the end of the year; ka *puni* o ka makahiki; the termination of the period of gestation, &c.

3. A desire; a strong inclination for the possession of a thing, or a particular course of conduct; he kii ka *puni* o ua wahine la, an image was the *great desire* of that woman.

Pu-ni, *adv.* Around; on every side; a *puni*; around about.

2. An intensive. Greatly; exceedingly; hotly, as in anger; mai ulu puni mai kou huhu, be not *exceedingly* angry. *Puk.* 32:22. See Ulu.

Pu-ni-a, *s.* A pain in the head above the eye.

Pu-ni-u, *s.* *Pu* and *niu*, a cocoanut. The shell of a cocoanut; ka iwi o ka niu; hence, a small calabash for food; wehe ae la i ua *puniu* la.

2. The skull of man from some resemblance to a cocoanut. 2 *Nal.* 9:35.

3. A knave; a cheat; one who refuses to give up what he has lost in a game; a dishonest gambler.

Pu-ni-u, *v.* To spin round; to turn, as a top; to be dizzy; to have a vertigo.

2. To be hot; to have a fever. See Puniu.

Pu-ni-u-hu-i, *s.* *Puniu*, the skull bone, and *hui*, to unite. The place on the top of the head where the bones unite.

Pu-ni-hai, *adj.* *Puni* and *hai*, to run. Addicted to running; cowardly; full of fear.

Pu-ni-ha-ni-ha, *v.* To refuse; to be stingy; to be close and little in a bargain; to be hard to trade with. See Puhanihaniha.

Pu-ni-ha-ni-ha, *s.* Stinginess; closeness in a bargain.

Pu-ni-ha-ni-ha, *adj.* Stingy; close; difficult to trade with.

Pu-ni-hei, *v.* *Puni* and *hei*, to insnare. To surround with a net; to insnare; to entrap.

2. To lay a plot for one. 1 *Sam.* 28:9. To deceive; to act treacherously; to be deceived; *punihei* aku la ka poe i koho i ka ino, they *are insnared* who choose evil.

Pu-ni-he-le, *adj.* *Puni* and *hele*, to go. Fond of traveling; given to going about.

Pu-ni-hi, *adj.* Lofty; majestic.

Pu-ni-ho, *v.* To force away; to pluck up by the roots; to dislodge a disease.

> Puniho ino ka lae o ka pipa,
> Oohu wale ka ina uli, ka ina eleele.

Pu-ni-ka-la, *v*. *Puni* and *kala* (*Eng*. dala), money. To have a strong desire for money; to have a covetous disposition. NOTE.—This is a modern word come into use with civilization.

Pu-ni-ka-la, *s*. One greedy for money; a strong desire for property; covetousness. *Heb*. 13:5.

Pu-ni-ki-hi, *s*. Name of a game; he hiu, he pahiuhiu, he amo paha, a he lalani, a he *punikihi* paha, aia no i ko laua mau lunamanao.

Pu-ni-ko-ko, *s*. *Puni* and *koko*, blood. A blood-thirsty person; one reckless of murder. *Sol*. 29:16.

Pu-ni-ko-ko, *adj*. Greedy for blood; reckless of murder.

Pu-ni-kuu-a-la, *v*. *Puni* and *kuala*. See KUALA. To long for the time set for payment (of money or a debt) to come; to expect gain for something lent or given; he manawa i oleloia e kuuala ai ka mea i oleloia.

Pu-ni-kuu-a-la, *adj*. Longing for the payment of a debt; expecting gain for something lent or given.

Pu-ni-le-a-le-a, *s*. See PUNI, given to, engaged in, and LEALEA, pleasure. The practice of pleasure; being given or devoted to sensual gratifications.

Pu-ni-ni, *v*. To go here and there out of a straight course; to tack, as a ship; to sail crookedly; to float here and there. *Hoo*. Ke *hoopunini* nei no ke alii i ka moana maluna o ka waapa, the king *floats here and there* over the ocean on a boat.

Pu-ni-pe-ki, *s*. Name of a game like "fox and geese;" the fox they called *Bonepate*—*Punipeki*; a o ka *punipeki*, ua kokoke like me ka hana ana o ke *pahiuhiu*.

Pu-ni-pu-ni, *v*. See PUNI. To deceive; to tell a lie; to speak falsely.
2. To act treacherously in any way so as to deceive one.
3. *Hoo*. To cause one to be deceived. *Oihk*. 6:2. Connected in the next verse with *hoohiki wahahee*. To act deceitfully; to deceive one; e punihei aku ai ma ka aoao ino.

Pu-ni-pu-ni, *s*. A falsehood; a lie; a deceit; he wahahee.

Pu-ni-pu-ni, *adj*. False; deceitful; hypocritical; vain.

Pu-ni-wai-wai, *v*. *Puni* and *waiwai*, property. To desire the acquisition of property; hence, to be covetous; to give one's self to accumulate. NOTE.—*Puniwaiwai* was anciently what *punikala* is now.

Pu-ni-wai-wai, *s*. Covetousness; the strong desire of wealth; he manao nui ma ka waiwai; he hoolilo i ka waiwai i akua nona.

Pu-ni-wai-wai, *adj*. Covetous; greedy after property.

Pu-ni-wa-le, *v*. *Puni* and *wale*, easily. To be overtaken by treachery; to be the subject of deceit; to be insnared by anything; e lilo i ka punihei.

Pu-ni-wa-le, *adj*. Deceived; insnared.
2. Boisterous with anger; overawed.

Pu-no-hu, *v*. To arise or ascend, as smoke. To arise, as a high flame or column of smoke. *Lunk*. 20:40. See PUUNOHU and PONUHU.
2. To make a white appearance, as the sails of a ship quickly set; me he moku la i pau na pea i ka huki iluna.

Pu-no-hu, *s*. The volumes or curls of ascending smoke; he hina me he uahi la no ka lua o Pele; the gray-like smoke (steam) of the volcano; smoke arising from a fire. *Kin*. 19:28. *Punohu* uwahi. *Mel. Sol*. 3:6. See PONUHU.

Pu-no-ni, *s*. Name of a dye, probably of the noni, for coloring kapas.
2. The kapa so colored.

Pu-no-ni, *s*. Name of a dye, probably of the noni, for coloring kapas.
2. The kapa so colored.

Pu-no-no, *v*. See NONO. To be dressed gorgeously. *Hoo*. To be red, as kapa.

Pu-no-no-u-la, *v*. To be spotted, as the skin in some diseases; to be colored white and red.

Pu-no-no-hu, *v*. To swell out; to be large like the sails of a ship. See PUNOHU and HOOPUNOHUNOHU.

Pu-no-no-hu-u-la, *adj*. Blowing the dust; raising the dust, as a strong wind; ka wilikoi ula *punonohuula* i ka lani.

Pu-no-nu, *adj*. Spoiled; rotten; addled, as eggs; he kewakewai.

Pu-no-nu-no-nu, *v*. To be spoiled; to be unfit for use; to be addled, as eggs. See KEWAI. Ua *punonunonu*, ua kewakewai.

Pu-nu-a, *v*. To be without hair or feathers, as some young birds.

Pu-nu-hu, *s*. A cloud apparently standing erect having some of the colors of the rainbow.

Pu-nu-ku, *s*. A halter; a noose passed over the nose of a beast.

Pu-paa-kai, *v*. To eat when there is only vegetable food; a *pupaakai* au.

Pu-pa-na-pa-na, *s*. *Pu*, gun, and *pana*,

to discharge. A pistol; he pu liilii.

Pu-pu, *v.* To be rough; to be uneven, as a road.

2. To be heavy, as a thing drawn or carried.

3. To walk as one carrying a heavy burden; heaha ka oukou mea kaumaha i *pupu* ai oukou makai la?

4. To drag a log or canoe through brush and among rocks, &c.

5. To be slow; to lag behind.

6. To gather and bind up into a bundle; e *pupu* a paa.

7. *Hoo.* The same.

8. To sit still in one place; to sit still, not to go.

Pu-pu, *s.* An old man or woman who walks feebly and carefully for want of strength.

2. A species of snail, the meat of which is eaten by Hawaiians. *Hal.* 58:8. NOTE.— *Pupu* is the general name for shells, both sea and land, though not often applied to large ones.

3. A bunch, as of grass, leaves or flowers; *pupu* husopa, a *bunch* of hyssop. *Puk.* 12:22. See PUU.

4. A bundle or something bound up, as of grass.

5. A glass bead.

Pu-pu, *adv.* Roughly; heavily; disagreeably. *Puk.* 14:25. Hele *pupu*, hele mamau, hele luuluu.

Pu-pu-a, *s.* The rump or tail feathers of a fowl.

Pu-pu-a, *v.* See PUA, a blossom. To open; to unfold, as a blossom; to spread out; ua *pupua*, mohola wale i ke awakea.

Pu-pu-a-hu-lu, *v.* To be in a fluster; to be in a flutter or bustle, as those going but not ready for want of preparation; e pihoihoi.

Pu-pu-a-hu-lu, *adj.* Bustling; in a hurry; not prepared for a duty.

Pu-pu-a-mo-a, *s.* *Pupu* and *moa*, a fowl. A long skirted coat; so called from its resemblance to the tail of a fowl.

Pu-pu-a-wa, *s.* Name of a species of shell-fish.

Pu-pu-e, *v.* To lie in wait; to watch for one to injure or murder him; to be ready for any sudden attack upon one; o *pupue* i ka hao e alii la. *Hoo.* To seize upon suddenly.

Pu-pu-e, *s.* The action of a cat in preparing to seize a mouse; a lying in wait for one.

Pu-pu-i, *adj.* Swelled; enlarged; *pupui* ka maka, a swelled or enlarged eye. See

PUI and PUIPUI.

Pu-puu, *v.* To crouch; to curl up; to be doubled up, as the fingers.

Pu-puu-a-nu, *v.* *Puu*, pimple, and *anu*, cold. To come out in cold pimples; to try to get warm in vain.

2. To be dizzy and feeling cold.

3. To persevere in doing a thing; hoa inea, makaponiuniu *pupuuanu* hoomanawanui.

Pu-pu-hi, *v.* *Pu* and *puhi*, to blow. To blow violently, as a strong wind. *Puk.* 15:10. Ua *pupuhi* wale ia na waa i holo ma ka moana; to blow, as wind from the mouth.

2. To spout water, as a whale.

3. To burn with fire, as incense. 2 *Oihl.* 16:14. To consume in the fire. *Ios.* 7:25. *Pupuhi* aku la lakou i kona io i ke ahi, they *burnt* (consumed) his flesh in the fire.

4. To blow, as a trumpet. *Ezek.* 7:14.

Pu-pu-hi, *s.* A blowing; persons who blow, i. e., the trumpeters; na *pupuhi*. 2 *Nal.* 11:14.

Pu-pu-ho-a-ka, *s.* *Pupu*, shell, and *hoaka*, a crescent. An ornament for the wrist made of small shells.

Pu-pu-hu, *adj.* Large; plump; round; full.

Pu-pu-ka, *s.* An epithet of reproach, signifying *good for nothing*.

Pu-pu-ka, *adj.* See PUKA and PUKA-PUKA, full of holes. LIT. Vain; without substance. *Mat.* 5:22. Anything full of holes; hence, worthless; having an unsightly appearance; of no value.

Pu-pu-ka-hu-li, *s.* Name of a class of small shells. See PUPU.

Pu-pu-ka-ni-oe, *s.* Name of a class of mountain snails having shells, the achatinella. The Hawaiians declare that the animal sings. See PUPU.

Pu-pu-ke-a-we, *s.* The name of a small plant found on the tops of the mountains; o na nahelehele maluna o na kuahiwi, ua kapaia'ku ia he *pupukeawe*. It is also called *maieli*.

Pu-pu-ku, *v.* To curl, as the hair; to shrink; to start from fear; to shrink from pain, as a muscle; to contract.

Pu-pu-ku, *adj.* Wrinkled; shortened; contracted; curled, as hair. See PUKUPUKU.

Pu-pu-le, *v.* To be mad; to be crazy; to act insanely; to be infatuated. *Ier.* 50:38. To make one mad. *Kekah.* 7:7.

Pu-pu-le, *s.* Insanity; madness; infatuated conduct. 2 *Pet.* 2:16.

Pu-pu-le, *adj.* Crazy; insane; bereft of reason.

Pu-pu-lo-lo-a, *s.* Name of a species of shell-fish.

Pu-pu-lu, *v.* To be many; to be multitudinous, as a people; to congregate in masses; to be full; to be crowded, as a place with people.

2. To sit conversing together in a cluster. See MUMULU.

Pu-pu-lu, *s.* A great company; a multitude, as of flies on spoiled meat; a great collection of individual things.

Pu-pu-lu, *adj.* Assembled; thick together.

2. Adhesive; soft.

Pu-pu-ni, *adj.* See PUNI. Greedy; desirous of something and laboring to obtain it, as property, pleasure, grandeur, power, &c.; ka aki lauoho *pupuni* waiwai.

Pu-pu-pu, *v.* To extend; to project; to be prominent.

Pu-pu-pu, *s.* A small out-house; a shelter from the sun. See KAMALA. A small house such as is used for beating kapa; a temporary shed.

2. A kind of white kapa used of pa-us.

3. A heap of refuse, worthless kapa.

Pu-pu-pu, *adj.* Temporary; frail; hale *pupupu. Isa.* 1:8.

Pu-pu-wa, *v.* See PUPUA and PUA, a blossom. To unfold; to open, as a blossom.

Pu-wa, *v.* See PUA. To ascend and remain suspended, as smoke or a cloud. *Puk.* 24:16.

2. To shine; to glitter, as the surface of a thing. *Puk.* 34:30.

3. To reflect brightness, as a red garment, as clouds, or as a bright fire by night.

Pu-wa, *s.* A shining appearance; reflected brightness. *Puk.* 34:29.

2. A small bush; a flower. See PUA.

3. Little fish; he *puwa* ia, he liilii.

Pu-wai, *s.* See PUUWAI, the heart. An alarm; a sound of an alarm. *Ioel.* 2:1.

2. The fountain head of a stream of water; hence,

3. The material heart; the fountain of blood; he mea e hoi ka haalulu o kona *puwai,* strange was the beating of his *heart. Laieik.* 165.

Pu-wai-kau-a, *s. Puwai,* alarm, and *kaua,* war. An alarm of war. *Ioel.* 2:1.

Pu-wa-lu, *v.* See PUALU, to act in concert. To work together, as in lifting; to make a united effort.

2. To cry out all together.

3. To rehearse or speak or recite in concert, as a class in school. NOTE.—This was the general practice in the first schools of the Islands, and helped much to keep up the enthusiasm of the thing.

Pu-wa-lu, *s.* The ancient flag of the Hawaiians placed on the triangular sails of canoes.

Pu-wa-lu, *s.* Name of a body of men who worked together; a gang; a company of fellow-workmen. See LAULIMA.

Pu-ra, *s. Heb.* or *Chal.* A lot in casting lots. *Eset.* 3:7.

W.

W, the twelfth letter of the Hawaiian alphabet. The real sound represented by it is one between the English *w* and *v.* In Tahitian the *v* sound is most universal; in Hawaiian the *w* sound predominates. In many cases the letter *w* is superfluous, the vowel *u* before *a, e, i, o,* producing the same sound as is made by the use of *w;* as, *uwala, uala; uwao, uao; uwa, uä; uwe, uë; uweke, uëke; uwi, uï; uwila, uila; uwo, uö; kawowo, kauouo,* &c. In other places the *w* is an important letter, and sometimes, if the orthography of the language were fully settled, its use would serve to make a distinction in the meaning of words, as *kaua,* war, and *kauwa,* a servant, &c.

Wa, *s.* A space between two objects, as between two rafters or two posts of a house; hence,

2. A space between two points of time.

3. A definite period of time, as the lifetime of a person; i ka *wa* i hiki mai ai o Vanekouva, at the *time* Vancouver arrived; *wa* kamalii, *time* of childhood; ka *wa* ana ao (see WANAAO), the early dawn of the morning. NOTE.—The Hawaiian year was formerly divided into two *was.* Elua no *wa* o ka makahiki hookahi, o ke *kau* a o ka *hooilo,* there are two *was* (periods) in one year, the *kau* (summer) and the *hooilo* (winter.)

4. In *grammar,* a tense.

5. A situation without friends or connexions, as in the phrase *ku i ka wa,* independent. He alii e noho wale ana i ka *wa,* a chief without subjects.

Wa, *s.* Private talk or gossip concerning the characters of others.

WA, *v.* To reflect; to think; to reason. *Mat.* 16:7, 8.

2. To seek to know; to wish. PASS. To be the subject of conversation. *Laieik.* 87.

3. To say to one's self; to ponder; to revolve in one's mind; to consider.

4. To hit as a stone hits a mark; to compass, as a man his designs.

5. *Hoo.* To sicken; to make sick; to cause to vomit.

WAA, *v.* For *waha*, a ditch. *Hoo.* To dig a ditch or pit; to make a furrow.

WAA, *s.* A canoe; a small boat; *waa kome. Puk.* 2:3. NOTE.—The ancient canoes of the Hawaiians were dug out of single logs or trees, generally of the koa; many were large. The specific names were *kaukahi*, a single canoe; *kaulua*, a double canoe; *peleleu*, a short blunt canoe, &c.

WAA-KAU-A, *s.* A division of any army as about to enter into battle; a mahope mai o lakou (huna paa) na *waakaua.*

WAA-KAU-KA-HI, *s. Waa* and *kaukahi*, one place. A single canoe, or a canoe moved with one paddle; he waa hoe hookahi.

WAA-KAU-LU-A, *s. Waa* and *kaulua*, two-fold. Two canoes united; a double canoe; more generally written simply *kaulua*; he mau waa elua i hoapipiia.

WAA-KI-O-LO-A, *s.* A very small handsome canoe.

WAA-KO-I-HI, *s.* A waterspout; a great rush of water from above; he wai nui i iho mai, mai luna mai.

WA-A-NA-AO, *s. Wa*, time, *a* of, *na*, article, and *ao*, light. LIT. The time of the lights, i. e., the first rays of the sun; early morning; the early dawn. NOTE.—In common use, the word is contracted into *wanaao.* See WANAAO.

WAA-PA, *s. Waa*, canoe, and *pa*, a board. A canoe made of boards; a skiff; a boat. 2 *Sam.* 19:18. A *waapa* is shorter and wider than a canoe. He waa pelupelu. A ship boat; he keiki na ka moku , a child of the ship.

WAA-WAA, *v.* To act ignorantly or without forethought, as if a person, without thought, should in a freak of generosity, give away all his property, and afterwards should remember his own act when it was too late.

WAA-WAA, *s.* The upper end of a lobster's leg; also the front side of a lobster's head.

2. The upper part of the thorax; the lower part of the throat.

3. Mischief from ignorance, from badness generally; applied to all classes of persons; ku i ka *waawaa* o ke kapu la.

WAA-WAA, *adj.* Plump, as the shoulders of a young man; hard; full.

2. Dark-hearted; ignorant; unskillful; awkward; naaupo. (See the verb.) *Waawaa* iki naauao kahi keiki; *waawaa* iki naaupo kahi keiki.

3. Full of hillocks or knolls; he *waawaa* ka lae, an expression of blackguardism.

WAE, *v.* To select; to pick out; to choose. *Puk.* 12:21.

2. To sort out the good from the bad; to separate; to set aside; to draw out some from among others; *wae* ae la ke kuhina i na waa kupono ke holo. *Laieik.* 100.

3. To break and separate, as the parts of a thing.

4. To dwell upon, as the mind in thinking of an event.

5. To think; to reflect; to consider a case. See WA.

WAE, *s.* A choice; a thing that suits one's desires; something according to one's wish.

2. The knee; the side timbers in a boat or ship; he *wae* waa, he *wae* moku.

3. Name of a species of kalo.

WA-E-LE, *v.* To clear away weeds, grass, bushes, &c., preparatory to planting.

2. To clear away grass, weeds, &c., preparatory to building a house.

3. To weed; to hoe; to cultivate food. *Ier.* 4:3.

WAE-NA, *s.* The middle; the central point of a substance or of a period of time; i ka *waena* o ka po, midnight. 1 *Nal.* 3:20. With the article, *ka waena*, the middle. 1 *Nal.* 6:6.

2. A space inclosed by bounding lines. *Ana Hon.* 10.

3. A field; a farm; a garden; a cultivated spot. *Kin.* 3:18.

4. A dead body. SYN. with kupapau.

WAE-NA, *comp. prep.* Between; in the middle; in the midst; prefixed by *i, ma, mai, no. Gram.* § 161.

WAE-NA-KO-LU, } *s. Waena* and *konu,*
WAE-NA-KO-NU, } center. LIT. The middle center. The central point; the very or real center. *Puk.* 14:29. The center of a circle. *Ana Hon.* 20. The midst, as of an assembly of people. *Laieik.* 120. NOTE. The first orthography is seldom used.

WAE-NA-KO-NU, *adv.* Through the midst; in the middle; in the center.

WAI, *s.* A general name for what is

liquid; fresh water in distinction from *kai*, salt water; *wai maka*, tears; *wai kahe*, running water, *wai u*, milk; *wai eleele*, ink; *wai hooluu*, dye; *wai puna*, spring water, &c. See the compounds.

Wai, *inter. pron.* Who? It refers only to persons or to the names of persons or things. See the forms in the paradigm, *Gram.* § 156-158.

Wai-a, *adj.* Strong and bad smelling; stinking; foul; filthy; polluted.

Wai-au, *s.* *Wai* and *au*, current. A place where water runs continually; water where one can always bathe.

Wai-au-au, *s.* *Wai* and *auau*, to bathe. A pool; a bathing place. *Ioan.* 5:2.

Wai-a-hu-lu, *s.* *Wai* and *ahulu*, reddish; dirty. Water of a muddy color; dirtyish red water.

Wai-a-le-a-le, *s.* *Wai*, water, and *ale-ale* (see ALE), to ripple; to disturb, as the surface of water. The name of a spring or fountain on or near the top of the highest mountain on Kauai.

2. The name of the mountain above mentioned. See the mele.

> Aloha *Waialeale*
> Ke kuahiwi a Kauai.

Wai-a-li,   *s.* The place assigned to the
Wai-e-li,   king when he speaks on public affairs.

Wai-a-li-a-li-a, *s.* *Wai* and *alialia*, a hard, smooth surface. Water reflecting light.

Wai-a-nuu-ko-le, *s.* Name of a species of soft porous stone.

Wai-a-po, *s.* Water of a dirty reddish color; he *waiapo*, he wainao, he wai me he kukae hao la; water of the color of iron rust.

Wai-e-a, *s.* Name of a class of heiaus.

Wai-e-hu, *s.* A file or rough stone; any substance that will grind or polish iron.

Wai-e-li, *s.* See WAIALI.

Wai-e-le, *v.* To poison or intoxicate fish; to catch fish by making them numb.

Wai-e-le, *s.* *Wai* and *ele*, dark colored. A dye for cloth or kapa.

Wai-e-le-e-le, *s.* *Wai* and *eleele*, black. LIT. Black water, i. e., ink. See INIKA.

Wai-i-ki, *s.* A medicine used in the sickness called haikala.

2. A medicine made of ipu awaawa for injections. See WAIKI.

Wai-o-hi-a, *s.* *Wai* and *ohia*, the Hawaiian apple. The juice or cider from the ohia.

Wai-o-ki-la, *s.* Name of a place in Kahukuloa full of precipices and ravines; hence the verb in the meles.

Wai-o-ki-la, *v.* See KOLOAU. To go up and down, as going across palis.

Wai-o-hu-hu-ki-ni, *s.* Name of a class of Kamehameha's laws.

Wai-o-pu-a, *s.* Name of an internal disease among Hawaiians.

Wai-u, *s.* *Wai* and *u*, the breast. LIT. Breast water. The breast of females. *Mel. Sol.* 4:5.

2. Milk; the ooze of the breast.

3. FIG. Blessings; favors. *Nah.* 14:8.

Wai-u-a, *s.* *Wai* and *ua*, rain. Rain water; water from the clouds; also *wai maoli* in distinction from well or spring water, which is *wai kai*.

Wai-u-paa, *s.* *Waiu* and *paa*, hard. Hard milk; cheese. 1 *Sam.* 17:18.

Wai-ha, *v.* To desire or request of the gods, as in prayer; pela ka'u *waiha* aku ame ka'u waipa aku ia ce e ke akua.

Wai-hau, *s.* A round heap; a bundle done up in small compass; a bundle done up again smaller than before.

Wai-hau, *v.* To do over again; to tie up anew, as a bundle; to compass into smaller compass.

Wai-hau-na, *s.* *Wai* and *hauna*, bad smelling. Water that has been used for different purposes, as washing fish and other matter offensive to the smell.

Wai-hi, *s.* *Wai* and *hi*, to flow down. A cataract; a cascade; a waterfall. See WAILELE.

Wai-ho, *v.* To lay or set down a thing; to lay on, as one in striking. *Laieik.* 44, 45.

2. To place or set aside; to let remain.

3. To leave off doing a thing; to quit; to stop; to let alone; to leave unhurt.

4. To set aside or lay up for future use; *e waiho wale*, to set aside as void or useless.

5. To give up or offer up, as one's life; to trust or commit to another.

6. To carry away to a certain place.

7. To leave; to pass by. *Puk.* 12:13.

8. To give, afford or suggest an idea or expression to another; to put a word into another's mouth. *Nah.* 23:5. *E waiho imua*, to set before one. *Kanl.* 11:26.

Wai-ho-a, *v.* See WAIHO. To lay down; to put down a thing; to give up.

Wai-hoo-luu, *s.* *Wai* and *hooluu*, to dye. Water for coloring; a dye.

Wai-ho-lo-mo-ku, *s.* *Wai* and *holomoku*, ship swimming. A great or deep flood so that a vessel might swim. *Hal.* 124:5.

Wai-ho-na, *s.* *Waiho* and *ana*, participial termination, a laying together. A place for laying up things for safe keeping; the things are designated by the qualifying term.

Wai-ho-na-i-pu, *s.* *Waihona* and *ipu*, cup. A base of a pillar. 1 *Nal.* 7:35.

Wai-ho-na-ka-la, *s.* *Waihona* and *kala*, money; silver. A treasury; a place where money is laid up. *Luke* 21:1. See Waiho-nadala.

Wai-ho-na-ku-ku-i, *s.* *Waihona* and *kukui*, light. A candlestick; a lamp stand. 1 *Oihl.* 28:15.

Wai-ho-na-me-a-laa, *s.* *Waihona* and *mea laa*, consecrated things. A place for sacred things; a treasury of things consecrated to sacred purposes. *Neh.* 7:70, 71. So also in the ancient temples of Hawaii.

Wai-ho-na-me-li, *s.* *Waihona* and *meli* (*Lat.* mel), honey. A honey-comb; a depository of honey. 1 *Sam.* 14:27.

Wai-ho-na-mo-ni, *s.* *Waihona* and *moni* (Eng.), money. A place for keeping money; a treasury. See Waihonadala.

Wai-ho-na-wai-wai, *s.* *Waihona* and *waiwai*, property. A treasury or depository of goods or property. 2 *Oihl.* 5:1.

2. The treasurer, the person who oversees the property of a nation or community.

Wai-ho-na-da-la, *s.* *Waihona* and *dala* (Eng.), coin, dollars, &c. A treasury; a depository of money. See Waihonakala.

Wai-kai, *s.* *Wai* and *kai*, sea. Brackish water; any saltish fluid.

Wai-kau-a, *adj.* Epithet of a robe used in war; no ke alii ai moku ia aahu ula, oia no kona kapa *waikaua*; also of a heiau; he heiau *waikaua* ia na ke alii nui.

Wai-ka-he, *s.* *Wai* and *kahe*, to flow. Running water; a stream. *Hal.* 124:4. A flood. *Isa.* 59:19.

Wai-ka-he, *v.* To flow; to overflow with water; *waikahe* ka aina. *Laieik.* 163.

Wai-ka-kaa, *s.* Name of a waterfall on Kauai one hundred and fifty feet in height.

Wai-ke-a, *s.* Eight fresh kukui nuts burned in water.

Wai-keo-keo, *s.* *Wai* and *keokeo*, white. The *fluor albus*, a disease of females.

Wai-ki, *s.* *Wai*, water, and *ki*, to shoot, as a gun. A medicine made of ipu awaawa for injections.

2. The gonorrhea. See Ulehilo.

3. The sharp end or point of a thing; applied to the *welau ule*.

4. The ball anciently made of stone and projected from a squirt-gun; hai mai, ua make o Kapupuu i ka *waiki*, he said that Kapupuu was killed by the *waiki*, i. e., the wad or ball of the gun. No ka puka o ka *waiki* a kakou i lohe ai, he mea kani, the whizzing of the ball was heard. Ua lohe mua ia he mea kani ka *waiki*, we had heard before that the *waiki* (ball of the gun) made a noise. Note.—Hawaiians supposed at first the sound of a gun (kani pu) had some effect in the execution.

Wai-ki, *s.* The epithet of a person whose father was chief and his mother not. See Kulu.

Wai-lau, *s.* A bundle of food (poi) done up for carrying; a pai-ai.

Wai-la-na, *v.* *Wai* and *lana*, to float. To cast out, as an evil person from society; to banish; to reject as unworthy of confidence.

Wai-la-na, *s.* *Wai* and *lana*, to float. Still, calm water; a quiet place in the ocean.

2. A state of banishment from society.

3. One cast out for bad conduct.

Wai-le-le, *s.* *Wai* and *lele*, to jump; to fly. A cataract; a waterfall. See Waihi.

Wai-le-na-le-na, *s.* *Wai*, water, and *lenalena*, yellow—yellow water. Name of a small valley near the top of Mount Waialeale on Kauai remarkable for the plant apeape found there.

Wai-lii-lii, *s.* Thick striped kapa; the stripes are yellow.

2. Deceitful language; puzzling expressions leading to error.

Wai-lu-a, *s.* A ghost or spirit of one seen before or after death, separate from the body. See Kinowailua and Kinoaka-lau.

Wai-li-u-la, *s.* For *waiiliula*, red surface water. Lit. Water with a red surface. The water in a salt-pond; water with the oxyd of iron on the surface.

2. The reflection of light to the eyes from any body which causes them to close, or wink, or turn away.

3. A flash of light; the hot penetrating rays of the sun.

4. The evening twilight; a mixture of light and darkness.

Wai-ma-ka, *s.* *Wai* and *maka*, eyes. Water flowing from the eyes; tears. *Kekah.* 4:1. E hookahe i na *waimaka*, to shed tears; e haule ka *waimaka*, to drop tears.

Wai-ma-ka-le-hu-a, *s.* *Waimaka* and *lehua*, the lehua tree. Water drops from the lehua trees; o ka *waimakalehua* nonohi e uli.

WAI-MA-NO, *s.* Name of a soft porous stone.

WAI-ME-A, *s.* A species of tree; the same as *olomea.*

WAI-MI-MI, *s.* *Wai* and *mimi,* urine. Urine. 2 *Nal.* 18:27.

WAI-NA, *s. Eng.* A grape vine; grapes; hence,

2. Wine; drunkenness. *Kin.* 9:24.

WAI-NAO, *s.* *Wai* and *nao,* dirty. Dirty water; water with filthy ingredients. See WAIAPO.

WAI-NI-HA, *s.* Name of a stream near the top of Waialeale on Kauai.

WAI-NO-HI-A, *s.* A state of safety.

WAI-NUI, *s.* An injection.

WAI-PA, *v.* See WAIHA. To desire; to request from the gods in prayer; pela ka'u waiha aku ame ka'u *waipa* aku ia oe e ke akua.

WAI-PAA, *s.* *Wai* and *paa,* fast; hard. Name of ice; hard water. *Iob.* 6:16.

WAI-PAU, *s.* The land breeze at Waimea, Kauai.

WAI-PA-HU, *s.* *Wai* and *pahu,* to burst. Gun-powder. LIT. Dust for shooting. See ONEA.

WAI-PE-HA, *s.* A state of safety. See WAINOHIA.

WAI-PII, *s.* *Wai* and *pii,* to ascend. A flood; an overflowing of water. *Ier.* 46:7.

WAI-PU, *s.* Gun-powder; one-a.

WAI-PU-I-LA-NI, *s.* *Wai* and *pui,* forcing, and *lani,* heaven. A watersprout; water drawn up into the clouds or poured down from the clouds. *Hal.* 42:7.

WAI-PU-HI-A, *s.* *Wai* and *puhiia,* blown by the wind. The spray of water blown by the winds when rushing down a pali; water falling in very small drops.

WAI-PU-NA, *s.* *Wai* and *puna,* a spring. A deep spring of water; a place where the water boils up. *Kanl.* 8:7.

WAI-WAI, *s.* Goods; property; that which is possessed or owned; property in distinction from money or cash; *waiwai* auhau, tax; tribute.

WAI-WAI, *adj.* Costly; rich; dear; valuable.

WAI-WAI, *v.* To enrich; to give one property. *Hoo.* To make rich; to supply one's desires.

WAI-WAI-PIO, *s.* *Waiwai* and *pio,* captured. Property taken in war or in robbery; plunder; spoil. *Ios.* 11:14.

WA-O, *v.* See WAU. To scratch; to scrape; to grate; *wao* aku la ke kahuna i ka ipu awa, a me ke kukui, a me ka uala, a me ke ko, a me ka wai maoli.

WA-O, *s.* A space on the sides of mountains next below the *kuahea;* it is also called *waonahele* and *waoeiwa;* a place of spirits; the dwelling place of the gods; a wild place as appears from the compounds. NOTE.—*Wao* and *wau* are similar in some of their meanings.

WAO, *adj.* High; long; a high shady place unfrequented; thick with vines.

WAO-A-KU-A, *s.* *Wao,* place, and *akua,* god. A region on the side of a mountain below the *waomaukele;* it has but a small growth of trees; or perhaps *wa,* space, *o,* of, and *akua,* god, that is, a region of the gods; a desert; a desolate place, generally back from the sea and uninhabited; a place where gods, ghosts and hobgoblins are supposed to reside. See AUAKUA.

WAO-E-I-WA, *s.* Name of a region on the sides of mountains covered with vegetation and small forest trees. SYN. with wao and waonahele.

WAO-KA-NA-KA, *s.* A region on the side of a mountain next below the *waoakua;* it is a region where people may live and where vegetables may be cultivated; *ma'u* is another name.

WAO-KE, *s.* The name of a shrub or bush from the bark of which kapa is made; a species of mulberry; also written *wauke* and *kawauke.*

WAO-KE-LE, *s.* The shadow of death; death's shade. See MALUKOI and MAUHAALELE.

waoke

2. A long tall ohia tree.

WAO-LA-AU, *s.* An upland and uncultivated region, where tall trees grow and thick shades are found.

WAO-MAU-KE-LE, *s.* Name of a region on the sides of mountains next below the *waoeiwa* and above the *waoakua;* the trees are larger than in the *waoeiwa.*

WAO-NA-HE-LE, *s.* *Wao* and *nahele,* covered with vegetation. A place on the sides of mountains overgrown with grass, weeds, bushes, &c.; a wilderness; a *waoakua,* but with vegetation.

WAU, *pers. pron.*, first person. I. *Gram.* § 122, 124. NOTE.—The *w* in this word seems unnecessary; it is formed by the coalescence of the emphatic *o* and *au*, the pronoun proper; thus the simple form *au*, emphatic *o au*, pronounced quickly becomes *wau*. The several forms are *au*, *o au*, *wau* and *owau*.

WAU, *v*. To say I; to answer I to a question; *wau* aku la no hoi *au*, *owau*, I *answered* to him, I.

WA-U, *v*. See **W**AO. To scrape; to scratch; to rub; to polish.
 2. To clean out, as the inside of a calabash which would require scraping. See **W**AUWAU.

WAU-AU, *v*. To go out of the path in traveling; to travel crookedly where there is no road.

WAU-AU, *adv*. Crookedly; perversely; unfeelingly.

WAU-A-HA, *adj*. In prayer; entire deliverance, freedom from, &c.; pali *wauaha* kua makani holo uka.

WAU-A-KU-A, *s*. See **W**AOAKUA.

WAU-KE, *s*. See **W**AOKE. The kapa shrub.

WAU-KE-LE-NU-I-AI-KU, *s*. The name of the chief who killed the fabled bird *halulu*.
 2. The young of the bird that waited on Kiwaa; he keiki na ka manu i lawe na Kiwaa. See the mele.

WAU-WAU, *v*. See **W**AO. To scratch as a cat; to scratch when one itches; to rub; to polish; to scrape. *Iob.* 2:8.

WA-HA, *s*. A mouth; an opening generally.
 2. The mouth of a person; e olelo he *waha* no he *waha*, to speak *mouth* to *mouth*.
 3. The mouth of a cave or pit; ka *waha* o ke ana. *Ios.* 10:18.
 4. The throating in the lower end of a rafter.
 5. The mouth of a bag. See **A**UWAHA, a furrow.
 6. A bundle to be carried on the back. See **W**AHA, *v*.

WA-HA, *v*. To carry on the back, as a child, or a person, or a bundle.
 2. To dig a furrow or a ditch, especially a long one. See **W**AHA, *s*.

WA-HA-A, *v*. To talk or speak with the mouth; to mumble; to dispute.

WA-HA-A-MA, *v*. *Waha* and *ama*, tattling. To tell tales; to reveal secrets.

WA-HA-O-HE, *v*. To talk scandal; to scandalize. See **W**AHAOHI.

WA-HA-O-HE, *s*. A great tattler; a scandalizer.

WA-HA-O-HI, *v*. To talk like a crazy person; to talk confusedly about that and that; to utter many words without meaning.
 2. To scold; to tattle.

WA-HA-O-HI, *s*. Foolish; crazy; loud talk.
 2. The person so talking; applied to females.
 3. A scold; a slanderer; a tale bearer.

WA-HA-U-HAU-HA, *s*. *Waha* and *uhauha*, dirty. A long or hoggish mouth.
 2. A gormandizer; one who eats as long as he can.

WA-HA-U-HAU-HA, *adj*. Hoggish in one's manners; filthy; cramming one's self with food.

WA-HA-U-KAE, *s*. A filthy mouth. See **W**AHAHAUMIA.

WA-HA-HAU-MI-A, *s*. *Waha* and *haumia*, dirty; foul. A foul mouth; a blackguard.

WA-HEE, *s*. A contraction of *wahahee*, which see.

WA-HA-HEE, *v*. *Waha* and *hee*, slippery. To lie; to speak falsely; to deceive in speaking.

WA-HA-HEE, *s*. A lie; a false speech; a deceit in speaking.

WA-HA-HEE, *adj*. Lying; deceitful; deceiving.

WA-HA-HEE, *adv*. Falsely; not truly. *Kanl.* 5:17.

WA-HA-HE-WA, *s*. *Waha*, mouth, and *hewa*, wrong; wicked. The wickedness of the mouth; any false conversation. In a prayer to the gods for the sick, e kala mai i kona hewa, a me kona aiku, a me kona aia, a me kona *wahahewa*, foul mouth.

WA-HA-KO-KO, *v*. *Waha* and *koko*, blood. To contend; to quarrel.

WA-HA-KO-KO, *adj*. Tale bearing; slandering.

WA-HA-KO-LE, *s*. *Waha* and *kole*, red. A long protuberant mouth; waha nuku.
 2. A mouth that belches out filthy matter; a boisterous, raving person.

WA-HA-LE, *s*. The same tree as the loulu or palm tree.

WA-HA-LE-HE, *s*. *Waha* and *lehe*, lips. The outside of a hole or orifice.

WA-HA-LE-HE, *adj*. Wide or broad, as a hole in a board; open wide, as the mouth of a hole.

WA-HA-MA-NA, *s*. *Waha* and *mana*, divided. A screen; a shutter.
 2. A digression in one's speech; a turning off the subject in conversation.

WA-HA-PAA, *s*. *Waha* and *paa*, hard. A

person full of noise in his talk; a raving person; a scold; one who talks angrily and furiously; he *wahapaa* ia; mai hele oe i ka *wahapaa*; o ka *wahapaa*, oia ka hoopaapaa.

WA-HA-PAA, *adj.* Noisy; clamorous; raving.

WA-HA-PIO, *v. Waha* and *pio,* a prisoner. To speak as one that is under constraint and knows not what to say; e like me ka pio.

WA-HA-PUU, *s. Waha* and *puu,* swelled. A person who speaks unintelligibly in conversation; a boisterous person; a loud talker.

WA-HA-PUU, *adj.* Rude; obstreperous in conversation; unintelligible.

WA-HA-WA-HA, *v.* See WAHA, mouth. To make mouths at; to open the mouth at by way of contempt.
2. To be dishonored; to live unhonored.
3. To hate; to dislike; to be ashamed of.
4. *Hoo.* To mock; to scorn; to rail at; to despise. *Nah.* 14:31. To treat contemptuously; to deride.
5. To abominate. *Oihk.* 19:7. To hate. 1 *Nal.* 22:8.
6. To be unbelieving; to be disobedient; ua like ka *hoowahawaha* me ka hoomaloha.

WA-HA-WA-HA, *s.* Dislike; hatred; contempt. *Iob.* 31:34.

WA-HA-WA-HA, *adj.* Disliked; displeased with; objected to; ahu iho ka pua *wahawaha* i Wailua.

WA-HE-A-WA, *s.* The giving up of a plan, device, or intention, as a desire to go to a chief, but on thinking, gives it up; ka *waheawa* o ke alaula.

WA-HI, *art. Gram.* § 63. Some; some little; a few. It unites or takes with it the indefinite article *he*; as, he *wahi* wai, *some* water. It also takes *kau* before it, and both the definite article *ke*; as, lawe ae la ia i *ke kau wahi* leho no ka honua, in which case it means, some; some little; some indefinite quantity. It has no corresponding word in English; as, owau nei o ko oukou *wahi* kaikaina uuku hope loa.

WA-HI, *s.* A place; a space; a situation; *wahi* kaawale, a vacant *place;* synonymous with *kahi,* but used differently in a sentence. See KAHI. *Wahi* hilahila, private parts. *Kanl.* 25:11. Na *wahi* a pau loa, all *places. Ios.* 1:3. Na *wahi* paa, strong *holds* or *places.* 1 *Sam.* 23:14. It is used with *ka* for *kau;* a ka *wahi* (kau wahi) e noho ai, the dwelling *place. Hal.* 26:8.

WA-HI, *s.* Accent on the last syllable. That which surrounds or envelopes anything; a covering; a sheath; a wrapper, as kapa, paper, ki leaf, cloth, &c.; *wahi* pahi kaua, a sword *scabbard.* 1 *Sam.* 17:51.

WA-HI, *s.* A word; a saying; a remark. NOTE.—This word is somewhat anomalous; it has no article and has some of the properties of a verb; *wahi* a wai? *word* of whom? whose *word?* whose *saying,* or who *said it? Ans. Wahi* a ke alii, the king *said so.*

WA-HI, *s.* One that is above law, or is so much a favorite, or is so holy that the law cannot affect him.
2. A favorite or high servant of the king; pepehiia o Kainapau *wahi* alii e Kainapau kuaaina, Kainapau the king's *favorite* was slain by Kainapau the backwoodsman.

WA-HI, *v.* To break by casting out of one's hand. *Puk.* 34:1. SYN. with naha.
2. To break through, as an army; to break or rush through, as through a troop. *Hal.* 18:29.
3. To break, as one's head. *Lunk.* 9:53.
4. To separate; to open; to rend; to break through. *Isa.* 64:1.
5. To open; to cause to flow. *Isa.* 41:18.
6. To break; to cleave; to break, as a rock. *Hal.* 105:41. See WAWAHI.

WA-HI, *v.* To cover over; to bind up, as a wound. *Ier.* 30:26.
2. To wrap up, as a body for burial; to tie up in a wrapper, as a bundle.
3. To roll or fold up in kapa or cloth; to swathe; to wrap up.
4. To surround, as a wrapper; to overlay; to cover up. *Puk.* 36:34.
5. To cover, as the body of a person with clothing. SYN. with uhi. O ka lole ka mea e *wahi* ai i ke kino.

WA-HI-A, *v.* See WAHI, to break. *Wahia* is for *wahiia,* to be broken.

WA-HI-E, *s.* Wood for burning; fuel. *Oihk.* 1:7. *Wahie* is used for *fuel* in distinction from *laau,* timber.

WA-HI-E-A-LA, *s. Wahie* and *ala,* odoriferous. An epithet of sandal-wood; sandal-wood. Its appropriate name is *iliahi.*

WA-HI-NE, *s.* A female in distinction from *kane,* male.
2. A woman; a wife. The term is applied to men and animals, and when applied to animals it merely marks the feminine gender. In *grammar,* ano *wahine, feminine* gender. *Wahine,* he mea ia e nani ai ke kane, he lei alii maikai no ke kane, *woman,* she gives honor to the man, she is a crown of beauty for the husband.

WA-HI-NE-HE-LI-A-KA-EA, *s.* The names of two goddesses.

WA-HI-NE-KA-NE-MA-KE, *s.* *Wahine* and *kane* and *make*, dead. A woman whose husband is dead; a widow. *Kanl.* 16:11.

WA-HI-NE-MA-NU-A-HI, *s.* *Wahine* and *manuahi.* A kept mistress.

WA-HI-NE-PUU-PAA, *s.* *Wahine* and *puupaa*, epithet of virginity. A virgin; *virgo intacta.* *Puk.* 22:17. Hence, purity; a state of undefilement.

WA-HO, *comp. prep.* Out; out of; outside; outward; prefixed by *o, no, ko, i, ia* and *ma.* *Gram.* § 161. *Ia waho*, the outside. *Mat.* 23:25. Opposed to *ia loko.* *Luk.* 11:40.

WA-HO, *adv.* Outwardly. *Esek.* 44:1.

WA-HO-KA-HU-A, *s.* *Waho*, outside, and *kahua*, foundation of a house. What is outside of a house.

WA-HU, *v.* To take by force. *Hoo.* To rob; to take by force.

WA-HU-A, *v.* To set a snare or trap. *Hoo.* To insnare; to entrap.

WA-HU-A, *s.* A snare; a trap for catching small animals.

WA-HU-LU, *v.* To bake food in the oven for a long time till it is burnt or turned yellow or black; poha ka nanu (nalu) ke wewe, o *wahulu* mai ka piko.

WA-HU-WA-HU, *v.* To lean upon a person with the arms across the shoulders. See WAHU.

WA-KA, *s.* Appearance; the personal appearance of one.

WA-KAI-KAI, *v.* To examine; to look at; to look round. See MAKAIKAI.

WA-KA-WA-KA, *adj.* See WAKA. Shining; glistening; flaming. *Kin.* 3:24. *Wakawaka* o Mano e moku ai ka hako.

WA-KE-WA-KE, *s.* See WEKAWEKA. The black liquid of the squid.

WA-KI, *s.* *Eng.* See WATI.

WA-LA, *v.* See HOALA. To excite; to stir up; to throw stones; to pelt; to be or feel hurt.

WA-LAA, *v.* For *walaia.* To be thrown; to be thrown, as a stone; to be pelted; walakike ka ihe, *walaa* ka pohaku, the spears were hurled back and forth, the stones *were thrown.*

WA-LA-AU, *v.* To speak in a boisterous manner, as a crazy person.

2. To cry out, as in fear; to shout, as in battle.

3. To make a noise of lamentation for a deceased person.

4. *Hoo.* To cause or make a noise. *Isa.* 42:2. To make a confused unmeaning noise.

WA-LA-AU, *s.* A noise; a confused noise as of a riotous multitude. *Puk.* 32:17. See UWAUWA.

2. A noise, as a wailing for the dead.

3. Any loud boisterous talk or noise with more or less indistinctness or want of meaning.

WA-LA-AU, *adj.* Noisy; obstreperous; confused; disorderly.

WA-LA-HEE, *s.* Name of a shrub, the leaves used in coloring black.

WA-LA-KI-KE, *v.* See WALAA above. To toss or throw back and forth, as spears in battle; *walakike* ka ihe, walaa ka pohaku.

WA-LA-NI-A, ⎫ *v.* For *walaia, n* inserted,
WA-LE-NI-A, ⎭   to be hurt. To smart, as a wound; to feel pained from an external hurt.

2. To feel pain mentally; to feel the pain of dislike or of hatred by another.

3. To feel revengeful; to feel cut to the heart by something said. *Oih.* 2:37.

4. *Hoo.* To cause pain to another by one's words; to use sharp words. *2 Kor.* 13:10.

WA-LA-NI-A, *s.* A stinging pain, as a burn.

2. Deep anguish of heart at something said.

WA-LA-WA-LA, *v.* See WALA. To be excited; to make a great noise; to shout; to cry out.

2. To fall, as a man from a high place, turning over and over.

3. To refuse; to deny; no'u no ka hewa, aole au e *walawala* ae; ae aku no.

WA-LA-WA-LA-AU, *v.* See WALAAU. To make a noise so as to disturb one's hearing; to make a great noise in talking; e paepae, e lohelohe.

> *Walawalaau* i ka pali o Kolokini,
> Me he hanehane la ka leo i Waialoha.

WA-LE, *adv.* A state of being or existing without qualification; used mostly in an adverbial sense; only; alone; gratuitous, &c.; as, e noho *wale*, to sit *only*, i. e., to sit *idly*; e hana *wale*, to work *only*, i. e., to work *without reward, gratuitously*; e olelo *wale*, to speak *without effect*; e hele *wale*, to go *as one is*, i. e., to go *naked.* As *wale* has no corresponding term in English, it is difficult to define, the idea must be gained by the connection.

WA-LE, *s.* The phlegm or matter coughed up from the lungs.

2. Saliva like that running from the mouth of an infant; kahe ka *wale*, to drool; ka *wale* o kona waha, spittle; saliva.

WA-LE-A, *v.* To indulge in ease; to

please one's self; to dwell in quiet free from care.

2. To be satisfied with one's circumstances. *Puk.* 2:21.

3. To be accustomed or habituated to a thing; to do often.

WA-LE-A, *adj.* Accustomed; frequently doing; constant.

WA-LE-A, *s.* Name of a fish.

WA-LE-HAU, *s.* The name of a medicine.

2. The mucous from the nose.

WA-LE-KE-A, *s.* *Wale*, slime, and *kea*, white. A disease of the eye; a liquid from a sore eye; white mucous.

WA-LE-NI-A, *adj.* Hard; painful; severe. See WALANIA.

WA-LE-WAI-KA-PO, *s.* *Wale*, spittle, and *wai*, i. e., the water is spittle. Used in a prayer; *walewaikapo*; the saliva of the mouth; a prayer for a blessing.

WA-LE-WA-LE, *v.* See WALE. To be deceived; to be led astray by one. *Isa.* 36:14. To deceive; to entrap; to get the advantage.

2. *Hoo.* To tempt; to entice; to insnare; to deceive by flatteries; *hoowalewale* nui mai na haole ia ia (ia Liholiho) i ka inu rama, the foreigners greatly *enticed* him (Liholiho) to drink rum.

3. To suborn; to influence to wrong. *Oih.* 6:11.

WA-LE-WA-LE, *s.* A temptation to evil.

2. A tempter to evil.

3. Forgetfulness of a thing.

4. Indifference; slowness; destitution.

WA-LE-WA-LE, *s.* One set apart as defiled, as a woman having given birth to a child; in her condition she was called *walewale*. A hala na la ehiku, a ma ka wa e pau ai ka *walewale*, alaila hoi mai ma ka hale o kana kane iho; a ma ka la awalu, hoi mai kana kane, noho pu, no ka mea ua pau ka *walewale* keiki.

WA-LE-WA-LE, *adj.* Insnaring; enticing to evil; tempting.

2. Stringy; slimy, as the secretion of the nose; as matter coughed up from the lungs.

3. Slimy, as certain states of the fæces; nearly synonymous with *aweawe*; *walewale* ka lepo.

WA-LE-WA-LE, *adj.* At a venture. 1 *Nal.* 22:34. Without object; hele *walewale* lakou a lilo loa i ka hewa.

WA-LE-WA-LE-NA, *v.* To pinch; to gnash expressive of great anger.

WA-LE-WA-LE-NA-HE-SA, *v.* *Walewale* and *nahesa* (*Heb.*), serpent. To act the part of a sorcerer; to enchant.

WA-LE-RU-SA, *s.* The walrus.

WA-LI, *v.* To grind to powder; to mince fine; to mix. *Puk.* 30:36.

2. To grind. FIG. To oppress; to overbear, as a chief his people. *Isa.* 3:15.

3. *Hoo.* To make soft or pliable; to reduce to powder. *Puk.* 32:20.

4. To break up ground finely.

WA-LI, *adj.* Fine; soft; minced finely; fine, like soft paste; fine, as flour. *Kin.* 18:6.

WA-LI-NA, *adv.* Used in answer to a salutation; as, *walina* wale laua. See WELINA.

WA-LI-WA-LI, *adj.* See WALI. Fine; soft; paste like.

2. Weak; limber; weak from sickness. See NAWALIWALI.

3. Soft; gentle; kind, as language; ka olelo a na kanaka maikai, he *waliwali* ka olelo, he pepe.

WA-LI-WA-LI, *v.* See WALI. To soften, as stone or wood to make it work easily; alaila, hahao (i ka pohaku) maloko o kahi wai i mea e *waliwali* ai.

WA-LO, *v.* See UALO, to cry out; to complain.

WA-LO-I-NA, *v.* To call to a chief with a voice of praise and admiration; *waloina* aku ke alii o Kaakahi.

WA-LO-WA-LO, *v.* To strike, as a sound upon the ear; to hear a sound; to hear indistinctly; to strike back, as an echo. See WALAWALAAU.

> Walowalo e hea ka leo o Kalakua,
> Walawalaau i ka pali o Kolokini,
> Me he hanehane la ka leo i Waialoha,
> Me I ka uwe hoouwe a ka lawakea.

WA-LU, *v.* To scratch, as a cat; to scratch, as a person with his fingers.

2. To rub; to rasp; to polish; to pinch.

WA-LU, *adj. num.* Eight; *ka walu*, the eighth. *Oihk.* 9:1. As a cardinal it is generally prefixed by *a* or *e*; as, *awalu, ewalu,* eight. *Gram.* § 115:4.

WA-LU, *s.* Name of a fish having very hard scales.

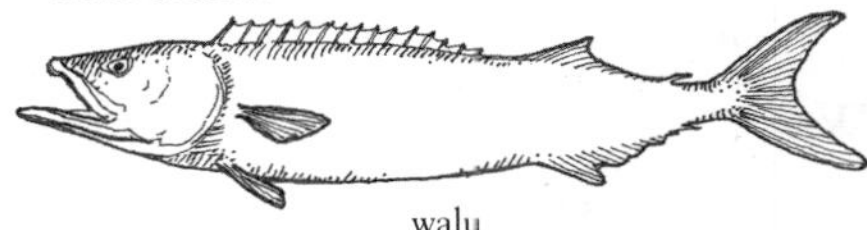

walu

WA-LU-A, *s.* The middle; the interior. *Mel. Sol.* 3:10.

WA-LU-NA, *s.* A prophecy.

WA-LU-WA-LU, *v.* See WALU. To scratch much or frequently; to pinch up with all the fingers. See UMIKI.

WA-NA, *v.* To come; to approach; to appear, as the early dawn. See WANAAO.

WA-NA, *s.* A species of the sea-egg of the size and shape of a turnip; he ia poepoe me he ina la, he oioi mawaho.

Wa-na, *adj.* Pronged; sharp pointed; externally jagged.

Wa-na-ao, *v.* *Wana,* to appear, and *ao,* light. To dawn, as the first light in the morning; to appear, as the dawn. See Waanaao.

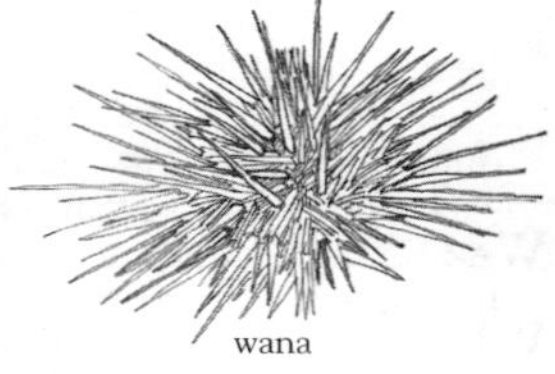

wana

Wa-na-ao, *s.* The near approach of morning. *Kin.* 19:15.

2. The early dawn of the morning; the first light of day. *Ios.* 6:15. Twilight; molehulehu.

Wa-na-oa, *v.* To project; to extend any way beyond the body of a thing.

Wa-na-oa, *s.* A projection or an extension, as the fingers of the sea-egg.

Wa-na-hi-na, *adj.* Becoming gray, as a person; gray headed.

Wa-na-na, *v.* To prophecy; to foretell future events; to preach; to declare the will of the gods. *Nah.* 11:25.

Wa-na-na, *s.* A prophecy; the declaration of the kilo or the kaula; a declaration made before hand of what is to be, which was known by its fulfillment.

Wa-na-wa-na, *v.* See Wana and Wa-naoa. To extend; to stretch out; to project.

Wa-na-wa-na, *adj.* Having sharp points; thorny.

Wa-wa, *v.* To shout in a noisy tumultuous way; to bawl in a vociferous confused manner.

Wa-wa, *s.* A tumult, as the action of a tumultuous assembly.

2. Babbling, vain, foolish talking. 1 *Tim.* 6:20.

3. A confused noise, as of a battle at a distance. 2 *Sam.* 18:29. The confused noise of a multitude.

Wa-wa, *adj.* Noisy on account of great multitudes; tumultuous. *Isa.* 22:2.

Wa-wae, *s.* The leg of a person or animal; the foot. Note.—Hawaiians have no separate words for leg and foot, *wawae* includes both; so *lima* includes both hand and arm. See Lima.

2. A pair of pantaloons; so called from the legs; breeches. *Puk.* 28:42.

3. A post of duty belonging to gods and priests.

Wa-wai, *s.* *Wa,* space, and *wai,* water. A land of water; a well watered land; he auwai, he pipiwai, he uwahiwai e kulu ana, he kowakowau.

Wa-wau, *v.* See Wau and Wauwau. To scratch; to pinch with the fingers; hence, to be quarrelsome; to be unfriendly; *wawau* i ka ili o ke kane ame ka wahine.

Wa-wau, *adj.* Scratching; pinching; cross; unfriendly.

Wa-wa-ha, *v.* Lit. To mouth. See Waha. To rail; to storm at one; to curse with a loud obstreperous voice.

Wa-wa-hi, *v.* See Wahi, to break. To break to pieces; to break down; to demolish, as a house or building. 2 *Nal.* 21:3.

2. To break, as bread; to break open, as a box or chest.

3. To split; to break up, as rocks. 1 *Nal.* 19:11.

4. To break up, as a boat; *wawahiia* hoi ka waapa i kui houhou, the boat also *was broken up* for the nails to make awls.

5. To break down, as idols. *Puk.* 23:24.

6. To break up, i. e., to take down, as a tent. *Nah.* 10:17.

7. To break down, as a tower. *Lunk.* 8:9.

Wa-wa-hi-ia, *s.* Participle passive. A breaking up; a destruction, as of a city. *Ier.* 19:8, 11.

Wa-wa-li, *v.* See Wali and Waliwali. To soften; to make fine; to reduce to pulp.

Wa-wa-li, *adj.* See Wali. Soft; fine; flexible; good humored.

Wa-wa-lo, *v.* See Ualo, Walo and Uwalo. To cry out; to call; to make a noise of calling.

Ua lai hea *wawalo* i ka ohu no na mauna,
Uina ka wai o na molokamaaha.

Wa-wa-lu, *v.* See Walu. To scratch, as a cat or a person; to pinch; to quarrel, as a man and his wife.

Wa-wa-na, *adj.* Rough; thorny, as a road; difficult of traveling. See Wana, *adj.*

Wa-we, *adv.* Quickly; suddenly; hastily; soon; hiki *wawe, quickly* done.

Wa-ti, *s.* Eng. A watch; a clock; a period of time. *Puk.* 14:24.

We, *v.* See Ue and Uwe. To weep; to cry; to salute.

2. To move anything forward or sideways. See Ue, to hitch along.

We-a, *v.* To question for the purpose of eliciting some secret, as theft, or to try to buy stolen articles; to act skillfully in questioning one so that he shall not suspect the design of the questioner.

2. To print or color red.

We-a, *s.* A red dye; red coloring matter; he koho ulaula.

WE-A-WE-A, *s.* A procurer; a pimp; one who acts or bargains for another in licentious matters.

WE-A-WE-A, *adj.* Red; reddish; spotted with red.

WE-O, *s.* See WEA. Redness; freshness; a red color; ua like ka ulaula me ka *weo;* he *weo* ke kanaka, he pano ke alii.

WE-O-WE-O, *adj.* See WEO. Fresh; red, like fresh meat just killed.

WE-U, *v.* To be covered with beard or down, as a young unshaven boy.

WE-U-WE-U, *s.* A general name for herbage; grass; green grass. *Kanl.* 11:15.

2. Name of a fish to be caught only in the night; hence,

3. FIG. Success in night iniquity.

WE-HE, *v.* To open, as a door; to open, as the dawn or advance of light in the morning; a *wehe* ae la ke alaula o ke ao, pau ka pouli.

2. To uncover what is covered up; to uncover, as the head. *Oihk.* 10:6. To uncover for illicit purposes. *Oihk.* 18:6, 7.

3. To strip off the clothes from one.

4. To open, as the eyes. FIG. To open, as the heart.

5. To open, as a well or cave. *Ios.* 10:22.

6. To open, as a book; to unfold, as a scroll. *Neh.* 8:5.

7. To loosen; to untie, as a string or rope.

8. To disregard or disbelieve one's word.

9. To reject a favor. NOTE.—The passive is sometimes written *wehea* instead of *weheia.*

WE-HE, *s.* An opening; an untying; a solving, as a problem; an explanation of a difficulty.

WE-HE, *adj.* Opened; separated; loosened.

WE-HE-A, *v.* Passive of *wehe.* See WEHE, note.

WE-HE-WE-HE, *v.* See WEHE. To open frequently; to open, i. e., to expound, as language; to explain what is mysterious; to explain, as a writing or a passage in a book. *Luk.* 24:27.

WE-HE-WE-HE, *s.* An explanation of anything obscure or intricate; a solving of a problem; explaining the intricacies of language.

WE-HE-WE-HE, *adj.* Loosening; explaining; unfolding.

WE-HI, *s.* Blackness; a black spot; a deep dark color.

2. A wreath for the neck.

WE-HI-WA, *s.* The name of a species of kalo.

WE-HI-WE-HI, *v.* To be deep blue; to be black; to have black stripes.

2. To be thick, as leaves; to be deep shaded.

3. *Hoo.* To braid; to twist, as a wreath for the neck; he launahele i *hoowehiwehiia,* e kaei ana ma ka a i.

WE-HI-WE-HI, *adj.* Thick together, as the leaves of a shady tree.

2. Splendid; beautiful of face; i ka *wehiwehi,* i ka onaona.

WE-KA, *s.* The meconium in children; kukae *weka;* any slimy, mucous substance; the matter in the cyst of the squid.

WE-KA-WE-KA, *v.* See WEKA. To have a foul stomach.

2. To fail in the fulfillment of a bargain.

3. To be hard; to be stingy; to be close; to be slippery.

WE-KA-WE-KA, *s.* Foulness of the stomach; the black substance or liquid in the cyst of the squid.

2. Fat unctuous matter.

WE-KA-WE-KA, *adj.* Stingy; close; hard; refusing to fulfill a contract.

WE-KE, *v.* See WEHE. To crack or open, as the joints of a floor; to separate, as two things united; to open, as a door. See UWEKE. *Hoo.* To cause to be opened.

WE-KE, *s.* A crack; an opening.

2. Name of a species of fish.

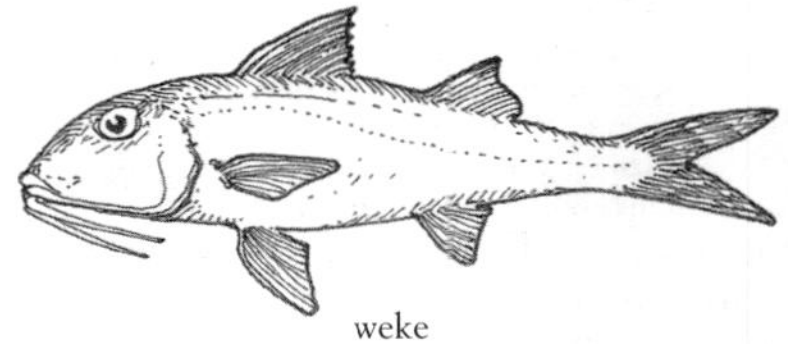

weke

WE-KE-A, *s.* The topmost part of a tree.

WE-KE-WE-KE, *v.* *Hoo.* To cause to blaze up, as a fire; to kindle a flame; to mount upwards, as a pointed flame.

WE-KI-U, *s.* The small branches of a tree that hang down from larger ones; ka lala liilii ma ka lewa o ka laau; the union of the small branches with the larger ones.

2. The top of a tree, house, mountain or other object.

WE-LA, *v.* To burn. *Kanl.* 4:11. To be on fire.

2. To burn or rage, as anger. *Puk.* 4:14. To be hot in mind; mai *wela* ko oukou manao i keia olelo, be not excited at the speech.

3. To be warm. FIG. To be warm, as the heart with affection for one.

4. *Hoo.* To cause to burn; to set on fire; to scorch. *Hoik.* 16:8.

WE-LA, *s.* The heat of fire or of the sun. FIG. The heat of anger. A burning, as of a sore. *Oihk.* 13:25. Warmth. FIG. Strong feelings.

WE-LA, *adj.* Warm; hot; burnt; cooked; burnt very much.

WE-LAU,
WE-LAU-LAU,
WE-LE-LAU, } *s.* The end or extremity of a thing; the top, as of a tree; na *welau* o na laau. *Oihl.* 14:15. The tip end; the ridge; the end of a finger; the ridge or summit of a precipice; the extreme boundary of a country. *Ios.* 15:4. FIG. *Welau* o ka make, *point* of death; *welau* akau, the north *pole*; *welau* hema, south *pole*.

WE-LA-WE-LA, *adj.* See WELA. Hot; very hot; kuu hoa hoi o ka la *welawela* o ke kula o Auwaiowao; i ka la *welawela* o ke awakea.

2. Parched; dried up; scorched.

WE-LA-WE-LA, *s.* A burning; a scorching; a heating.

WE-LA-WE-LA, *v.* See WELA. *Hoo.* To heat intensely; to be very warm; to dry up.

WE-LA-WE-LA, *v.* To give a thing and afterwards to take it back; to regret having given; e aua.

WE-LE, *v.* See WAELE. To clear off land; to cultivate the ground; to pulverize the earth; e mahi, e waele, e *wele* aku i ka weuweu o kona aina.

> Wele iluna ka mala lani a ka ua
> Ke pule ino ka hio a ka makani,
> Ka mahakea ulu lani o pua ke ao
> I paia a kiwaawaa a ulu pehu ke kino,
> Ulu kupu hakakai a malama.

WE-LE-A, *s.* The name of a species of fish which burrows in the sand. See KAWELEA and HALALOA.

WE-LE-HU, *s.* A species of fish.

2. Name of one of the Hawaiian months.

3. Name of one of the days of the month.

WE-LE-LAU, *s.* See WELAU. The end or extremity of a thing; the most distant part of a country. *Ier.* 50:12.

WE-LE-WE-LE, *v.* To refuse to fulfill an agreement.

WE-LE-WE-LE-I-WI, *s.* The extreme end of a thing; the point furtherest off; *weleweleiwi* ka hana a Iehova.

WE-LI, *v.* To branch out, as the roots of a tree; to take root, as a tree; to have many roots.

WE-LI, *s.* A form of salutation. See WELINA and WALINA.

2. The phosphorescent light in the sea; the light of sparks of fire.

3. A long black worm found in the sea;

he mea ola maloko o ke kai ma Ewa, me he puhi la ke ano.

4. A cion or shoot from the roots of a dead plant or tree; the spreading roots of a tree.

5. A fear; a trembling. See WELIWELI. Kau mai ka *weli, fear* fell upon him. *Laieik.* 167.

WE-LI-NA, *s.* See WELI. A reply to a salutation, as *aloha* or *anoai*; it applies to the person of the house when addressed by a stranger.

WE-LI-WE-LI, *v.* See WELI, *s.*, 5. To tremble with fear; to fear; to dread.

2. To be astonished; to be amazed. *Puk.* 15:15.

3. To fear; to reverence as a child should a parent. *Oihk.* 19:3.

4. To fear and obey, as God. *Oihk.* 25:17.

5. To be in anguish through fear. *Kanl.* 2:25.

6. To be afraid of an enemy. *Kanl.* 20:3.

7. *Hoo.* To cause one to tremble; to put one in fear.

8. To give one a charge; to threaten severely in case of disobedience. See OLELO HOOWELIWELI, to threaten. *Oih.* 4:17, 21.

WE-LI-WE-LI, *s.* Fear; dread; a trembling; a tremor through fear; a cause of fear. *Laieik.* 101.

WE-LI-WE-LI, *adj.* Fearful; causing fear; dreadful; terrible. *Dan.* 7:7. Oia no hoi ka pahu kapu *weliweli* loa. *Laieik.* 101.

WE-LI-WE-LI, *adv.* *Hoo.* Fearfully; tremblingly.

WE-LO, *v.* See KOWELO and KOELO. To float or stream in the wind, as an ensign, colors or flag; to flutter or shake in the wind.

> Kowelowelo kihei a *welo* ka ua—e.—*Mele.*

WE-LO, *s.* Name of one of the months of the year corresponding to April; hiki ia *Welo* hoi koi ia nei keiki papa.

2. The setting of the sun (in the ocean); the appearance of the sun floating upon the ocean.

3. The females of men or animals which bring forth young of a large size. See KUMULAU. A good breeder on account of the number and size of the offspring.

4. A breed; a cast or kind, as of hogs, dogs, &c.; he *welo* puaa, he *welo* maikai.

5. Name of a native medicine; the same as waiki or the ipu awahia or pipa.

WE-LO-WE-LO, *v.* See WELO, *v.* To float or flap in the wind; to float, as the tail of a kite; to float, as colors or an ensign.

WE-LO-WE-LO, *s.* Colors or cloth streaming in the wind.

2. A tail, as of a kite.

3. Light streaming from a brand of fire thrown into the air in the dark. *Isa.* 7:4.

WE-LO-WE-LO, *adj.* Floating; streaming, &c.; hoku *welowelo*, a blazing star; a meteor; a comet from its tail.

WE-LU, *s.* A rag; a piece of torn kapa or cloth.

WE-LU-U-LA, *s.* *Welu* and *ula*, red. The name of a kind of kapa made of pieces of red kapa beaten up with waoke; more generally called *paiula*.

WE-LU-WE-LU, *v.* See WELU. To tear; to rend in pieces, as kapa or cloth.

2. To kill a person, as a mob would.

3. To be torn in pieces, as a person by a wild beast. *Kin.* 44:28.

4. To be torn or broken to pieces, as vegetation or trees by a whirlwind. *Puk.* 9:25.

5. To become ragged, as a garment. *Kanl.* 8:4.

WE-LU-WE-LU, *adj.* Torn; broken up; ragged. *Ios.* 9:13.

WE-NA, *v.* To cleave to; to adhere to, as one to another; the same as *pili*, heaha kou kuleana e *wena* aku ai ia ia? He hoahanau keena loa ae nui *wena*.

WE-NA-WE-NA, *adj.* Red; of a reddish color.

WE-PA, *s.* *Eng.* A wafer; it should be written *wefa*.

WE-WE, *v.* Secundines feminarum parturientium; the after-birth; poha ka nanu ke *wewe* o wahulu mai.

WE-WE-O, *v.* See WEO. To be red; to be fresh.

WE-WE-LA, *v.* See WELA. To burn; to be hot, as a feverish sore. *Oihk.* 13:24.

WE-WE-LA, *s.* A burning or feverish boil or sore. *Oihk.* 13:23.

2. A very great heat of anger. *Ier.* 2:6.

3. A burning zeal, i. e., a horror; great fear. *Ps.* 119:53.

4. Great excitement of mind; walania.

WE-WE-LO, *v.* To stream out, as the streamer of a ship; to draw out; to be loose; e *wewelo* ana ka naau o ke kanaka.

WE-WE-NA, *v.* To be of a reddish color; ahiahia; some faded or indistinct color.

WE-FA, *s.* *Eng.* See WEPA. A wafer; a seal. *Puk.* 16:31. *Wepa* palaoa, thin cakes. *Nah.* 6:15.

WI, *v.* To be impoverished, as a country; to be suffering a grievous famine. *Rut.* 1:1. *Hoo.* To reduce one's flesh; to make one poor in flesh; e hoopau i ka momona.

WI, *s.* A famine; a destitution of food. *Kanl.* 8:9. A time of famine.

2. A name given by Hawaiians to the tamarind tree and its fruit.

WI, *adj.* Poor in flesh; lean; famishing; poor; barren, as land. *Nah.* 13:20.

WI-U, *v.* To be dirty, as one engaged in filthy work; to be unclean; to be dirty all over.

2. To be or become entangled, as a kite; ua *wiu* ka lupe.

WI-U, *adj.* Dirty all over; filthy; unclean.

WI-U-IA, *adj.* Grand; solemn.

WI-HI, *v.* To turn one's eyes askance; to wink; to express some idea by a wink, ogle or oblique look.

2. To roll up, as a bundle.

WI-KA-NI, *adj.* Close; hardy; compact; robust.

WI-KI, *v.* To hasten; to be quick in doing a thing. 1 *Sam.* 20:38.

WI-KI, *adj.* Quick.

WI-KI-WI-KI, *v.* See WIKI. To hasten; to hurry; to do quickly. *Ios.* 4:10. *Hoo.* To stir one up to speed.

WI-KI-WI-KI, *adj.* Quick; expeditious; not slow.

WI-KI-WI-KI, *adv.* Quickly; very quick; in haste.

WI-LA, *s.* Lightning. See UILA.

2. A ribbon. See WILI.

WI-LI, *v.* To twist; to wind; to turn, as a crank; to grind at a hand-mill. *Lunk.* 16:21. To bore, as with an auger or gimlet. 2 *Nal.* 12:10.

2. To writhe in pain.

3. To mix, as liquids of different qualities, i. e., to stir them round and round.

4. *Hoo.* To torture; to give pain; to tear; to be in anguish.

WI-LI, *s.* A ribbon. See WILA.

2. A roll; a twist. See OWILI. *Wili* lauoho, a *lock* of hair; o na *wili* o ke poo. *Mel. Sol.* 5:2.

3. Sadness; a writhing in pain.

4. The sickness of hogs; a cough; a strangling.

5. The name of a fish.

WI-LI, *adj.* Winding; tortuous; ala *wili*, a *winding* path; na mea *wili*, *mills* for grinding. *Nah.* 11:8. Mai *wili*, the venereal disease or gonorrhea.

WI-LI-A, *v.* For *wiliia*, passive of *wili*. To be twisted; to be contorted by the wind; ka hala i *wilia* e ka makani.

WI-LI-AU, *s.* *Wili*, to twist, and *au*, to swim. The circular motion of an eddy in a river or in the ocean.

2. The circular motion of the hand in mixing poi.

WI-LI-IA, *adj.* Passive of *wili*. Anything made by braiding or twisting; he hana i *wiliia*, *wreathen* work. *Nah.* 8:4.

WI-LI-O-KAI, *v.* To go or move in great numbers, as a huakaihele; as a small army or the retainers of a high chief.

WI-LI-KA-HEI, *s. Wili* and *kahei*, to tie round. A bit for boring rocks; a bit of any kind of boring.

WI-LI-KO, *v. Wili* and *ko*, sugar-cane. To grind sugar-cane.

2. To manufacture sugar in general.

WI-LI-KO-I, *s.* The substances that are taken up in the center of a whirlwind; me he kanaka la no ka *wilikoi.*

WI-LI-PU-AA, *s.* A cork-screw.

WI-LI-WI-LI, *v.* To stir round; to mix, as different ingredients by stirring.

2. To shake, as a flexible rod. *Isa.* 10:15.

3. To rub the hands hard, as in washing the hands when very dirty.

4. *Hoo.* To be writhing in pain, especially the pains of child-birth; *hoowiliwili* hookokohi e hanau, e hanau mai ana oia nei i na keiki.

5. To be uneasy, as in constant pain; *hoowiliwili* ae oia no ka maule poponi.

6. To loosen; to separate, as in parturition.

7. To brandish, as a sword. *Ezek.* 32:10.

WI-LI-WI-LI, *s.* Name of a tree, the timber of which is, for its buoyancy, made into outriggers for canoes; erythrina corallodendron.

WI-LOU, *s. Eng.* The name of a foreign tree; a willow. *Isa.* 44:4. NOTE.— One species of the willow has lately been introduced into the Islands.

WI-LU, *s.* A disagreeable smell; a stench.

WI-LU, *adj.* Disagreeable of smell; offensive; smelling badly.

WI-NI, *v.* To reduce to a sharp point; to be sharp pointed. *Hoo.* To point; to make sharp.

WI-NI,
WI-NI-WI-NI, } *s.* Sharpness, the result of grinding to a point.

2. The sharp point of any sharp instrument, as the point of a needle, pin, nail, pen, &c.

WI-NI,
WI-NI-WI-NI, } *adj.* Pointed; sharp; reduced to a point, as a needle, pin, or any sharp instrument; e kalai a winiwini.

WI-WI, *v.* See WI. To be poor; to be shriveled up.

2. *Hoo.* To lessen; to diminish; a i ke kalai ana, e hoonui ae o mua, a e *hoowiwi* ae o hope, e kalai a maikai.

3. To grow poor in flesh, as a person or animal. *Zek.* 14:12.

WI-WI, *s.* Leanness of flesh. *Iob.* 16:8.

2. The name of a beer made from sugarcane.

3. A small kind of fish.

WI-WI, *adj.* Poor in flesh; slender; feeble. *Kin.* 41:6. Opposite to *ohaha.*

WI-WI, *adj.* Full; plenty; no want; applied to a chief's plate where there is always plenty; as, pa *wiwi*, a full plate; a sufficiency of food.

WI-WI-KI, *v.* To shine, as a faint light through a small aperature into a dark room; to glimmer faintly.

WI-WO, *v.* To fear; to dread.

2. To be ashamed; to blush. *Ezer.* 9:6.

3. *Hoo.* To become fearful; to be humble. *Isa.* 5:15.

WI-WO, *s.* Fear; shame; disgrace; dread.

WI-WO, *adj.* Afraid; bashful; modest; astonished.

WI-WO-O-LE, *s. Wiwo* and *ole*, not. Boldness; fearlessness. *Oih.* 4:13.

WO-HI, *s.* One who accompanied, i. e., went before or followed after the king, to convey and execute his orders; in his person and office he added to the king's dignity. He was generally some relation of the king.

WO-LU, *s.* Name of a species of fish, sometimes a fathom in length.

B.

NOTE.—The following words have been introduced from foreign languages. Owing to the peculiar structure of the Hawaiian (every syllable ending in a vowel sound), the forms of these words are somewhat modified, by dropping a letter or syllable of the original, but more frequently perhaps by inserting or adding a vowel in order to Hawaiianize them. A sufficiency of foreign letters is retained to show their derivation and distinguish them from native words by their orthography.

B AI-BA-LA, *s. Eng.* Bible; the united inspired books of the Old and New Testaments.

BAI-LA, *v. Eng.* To boil; to seethe. NOTE.—The cooresponding Hawaiian word is hoolapalapa. 2 *Oihl.* 35:13; *Ezek.* 24:5.

BAI-LA, *adj.* Boiled; seethed. *Ezek.* 24:6.

BA-KA, *s. Eng.* Tobacco; e puhi *baka*, to smoke *tobacco.*

BA-KE-KE,
BA-KE-TE, } *s. Eng.* A bucket; a pail; a small cask.

BA-LE, *s. Eng.* Barley, a species of

grain. *Oihk.* 27:16.

BA-LE-SA-MA, *s. Eng.* Balsam, a medicinal vegetable. *Ezek.* 27:17.

BA-MA, *s.* Balm, an odoriferous plant. *Kin.* 43:11.

BA-PE-TI-SO, } *v. Gr.* To baptize; to ad-
BA-PE-TI-ZO, } minister the ordinance of baptism. *Ioan.* 1:25.

BA-PE-TI-SO, } *s. Gr.* Baptism; the rite
BA-PE-TI-ZO, } of baptism. *Mat.* 20:22.

BA-RA-NI, *s. Eng.* Brandy; an intoxicating drink distilled from wine.

BA-RE-KA, *s. Heb.* A carbuncle, a precious stone.

BA-TA, } *s. Eng.* Butter. *Kin.* 18:8;
BA-TE-RA, } *Hal.* 55:21.

BA-TO, *s. Heb.* A bath, a Hebrew measure. 1 *Nal.* 7:26.

BE-A, *s. Eng.* A bear, a wild ferocious animal. 2 *Nal.* 2:24; *Lam. Haw.* 18:1 and 19:1.

BE-A-VA, } *s. Eng.* A beaver; an aquatic
BE-A-WA, } animal.

BE-KA, *s. Heb.* A half shekel, a measure of weight. *Puk.* 38:26.

BE-LA-KI, *s.* Puka kona kaula ma ka *belaki* ma ka ono o ka maha. *Anat.* 28.

BE-LE, *s. Eng.* A bell; *bele* gula. *Puk.* 28:33.

BE-LU, *adj. Eng.* Blue; the color blue. *Ezek.* 23:6.

BE-RE-NA, *s. Eng.* Bread; food generally. *Mat.* 4:4. *Berena* maka, dough.

BE-RE-NA-HO-I-KE, *s. Eng.* with *hoike.* Show bread. *Puk.* 25:30.

BE-RE-NA-HU, *s. Eng.* with *hu.* Leavened bread. *Puk.* 23:18.

BE-RE-NA-HU-O-LE, *s. Eng.* with *hu ole.* Unleavened bread. *Puk.* 23:15.

BE-RE-NA-KU-LA-LA-NI, *s. Eng.* with *ku lalani.* The twelve loaves of bread set by the Jewish priest every Sabbath on the golden altar. *Oihk.* 24:5, 6.

BE-RI-LA, *s. Gr.* A beryl, name of a precious stone. *Hoik.* 21:20.

BE-RI-LA, *adj.* Of or like a beryl. *Ezek.* 10:9.

BE-RI-TA, *s. Heb.* A covenant; the covenant between God and man. *Kin.* 9:9.

BE-RI-TA, *v. Heb.* To covenant; to agree to do something. *Hal.* 65:1. To enter into covenant. *Hal.* 50:5.

BE-RU-LO, *s. Gr.* A beryl. See BERILA. *Puk.* 28:20.

BE-RU-MI, *v. Eng.* To broom; to sweep with a broom. NOTE.—The Hawaiian equivalent is *kahili.*

BE-RU-MI, *s. Eng.* A broom, an instrument for sweeping.

BI-PI, *s. Eng.* The Hawaiian pronunciation for *beef,* and should properly be written *bifi.* An ox or cow; the general name for neat cattle; *bipi* kane, an ox or bull; *bipi* wahine, a cow; *bipi* kaulua, a yoke of oxen; *bipi* kauo, a draft ox; *bipi* wahine hou, a heifer. *Nah.* 19:2.

BI-PI-KAU-O, *s.* See BIPI.

BI-PI-KAU-LU-A, *s.* See BIPI.

BI-PI-KA-NE, *s.* See BIPI.

BI-PI-KU-A-PUU, *s. Eng. Bipi* with *kuapuu,* humpback. The bison (in the United States of America, the buffalo.) *Lam. Haw.* 8:1.

BI-TU-ME-NA, *s. Eng.* Bitumen, a mineral slime. *Kin.* 11:3.

BO-LA, *s. Eng.* A bowl; a dish. *Lunk.* 6:38. The Hawaiian word is *ipu.*

BU-BO, *s. Heb.* A species of owl. *Kanl.* 14:16.

BU-KE, *s. Eng.* A book; a volume. *Puk.* 24:7.

BU-FA-LO, *s. Eng.* A buffalo, a species of ox. *Lam. Haw.* 9:1. See BIPIKUAPUU.

BU-NI-BE-TI, *s.* The name of a game.

BU-SE-LA, *s. Eng.* A bushel, a dry measure of thirty-two quarts. *Ana Hon.* 60.

D.

DAI-A-KO-NA, } *s. Gr.* One who serves;
DAI-A-KO-NO, } a deacon; a deaconess. *Rom.* 16:1.

DAI-MA-NA, } *s. Eng.* A diamond, a pre-
DAI-MO-NA, } cious stone. *Puk.* 28:13.

DAI-MO-NI-O, *s. Gr.* A demon; an evil spirit. *Oihk.* 17:7.

2. A person possessed or ruled by an evil spirit. *Mat.* 8:31.

DA-LA, *s. Eng.* A dollar in money.

2. Silver generally; the Hawaiian orthography is kala.

DA-MA, *s. Lat.* A species of deer; the fallow deer; the pygarg. *Kanl.* 14:5.

DE-A, *s. Eng.* A deer; a stag. *Kanl.* 12:15. See DIA.

DE-LE-U-MA, } *s. Gr.* Bdellium; the
DE-LI-U-MA, } name stands in connection with metals in *Kin.* 2:12. In modern times bdellium is a gum.

DE-MA, *s. Lat.* See DAMA above.

DE-NA-RI, *s. Lat.* The name of a small

Roman coin; a penny. *Ioan.* 6:7.

De-ra-go-na, *s. Gr.* A dragon. *Hoik.* 12:3. He is called a *serpent* and *satan* in verse 9.

De-ra-ma, *s. Gr.* A drachm, a small weight. *Neh.* 7:71.

De-ro-ra, *s. Heb.* Name of a little bird; a swallow. *Hal.* 84:3.

Di-a, *s. Eng.* A deer; a stag. See Dea.

Di-a-ko-na, } *s. Gr.* See Daiakona. A
Di-a-ko-ni-o, } deacon, an officer in a
Di-a-ko-no, } church. Note.—The orthography of this word is not settled: all the five forms are used by different translators of the Bible.

Di-a-bo-lo, *s. Gr.* The devil; the tempter. *Mat.* 4:1, 3, 5.

Di-a-wa-hi-ne, *s. Eng.* with *wahine.* A female deer; a hind. *Kin.* 49:21.

Di-de-ra-ma, *s. Gr.* Tribute; tribute money. *Mat.* 17:24. Note.—The word *hapaha* is used in the late editions of the New Testament.

Di-la, *s. Eng.* A small Hebrew measure; a deal. *Oihk.* 23:13 and 24:5.

Du-ki-ma, *s. Chald.* A dulcimer, an ancient instrument of music. *Dan.* 3:5.

Du-dai-ma, } *s. Heb.* Hua *dudima,* a
Du-di-ma, } mandrake. *Kin.* 30:14.

Du-te, *s. Eng.* In *law,* custom; toll paid for the privilege of receiving foreign merchandise. *Rom.* 13:10. Note.—*Waiwai auhau* is used for *dute* in the last editions of the New Testament.

F.

F. Though Hawaiians easily and naturally run the sound of the letter *f* into that of *p,* yet it is not difficult for them to pronounce *f.* It has been introduced only in a few cases, especially in commencing words.

Fa-la-o-a, *s. Eng.* Flour; ground grain. 2. Bread; baked flour; hua *falaoa,* wheat; grain generally. It is often written *palaoa.*

Fa-le-ko-na, *s. Eng.* The name of an unclean bird; a falcon. *Oihk.* 11:14.

Fa-rai, } *v. Eng.* To fry; to cook in
Fe-rai, } fat. It has been written *parai,* but the *f* should be used instead of *p.*

Fi-ku, *s. Eng.* A fig; laau *fiku,* a fig tree. *Mat.* 21:19. Manawa *fiku,* a time of figs. *Mar.* 11:13.

Fi-ra, *s. Eng.* A fir tree. *Mel. Sol.* 1:17.

G.

G. is used in Hawaiian only or mostly in its hard sound; the word *gini,* gin, is perhaps the only exception; it is easily run into the *k* sound.

Ga-la-ni, *s. Eng.* A gallon, a measure of four quarts; mostly used as a liquid measure; a firkin. *Ioan.* 2:6.

Ga-li-ka, *s. Eng.* A garlic, a plant. *Nah.* 11:5.

Ga-ze-la, *s. Eng.* The gazelle, the name of an animal. *Kanl.* 12:15.

Ge-he-na, *s. Heb.* The name of the valley south of Jerusalem; also called the valley of the Son of Hinnom; it was used as a place of punishment for criminals. *Mat.* 5:22.

Ge-ra, *s. Heb.* A gerah, a small piece of money, or the one-twentieth of a shekel. *Puk.* 3:13. A Jewish coin.

Gi-ni, *s. Eng.* Gin, a distilled intoxicating liquor.

Gi-ra, *s. Heb.* A Hebrew coin. See Gera above. *Nah.* 18:16.

Go-la, } *s. Eng.* Gold. *Adj.* Golden;
Gou-la, } *gula paa,* beaten gold. *Puk.*
Gu-la, } 25:36.

Gu-la-a-i, *s. Eng. Gula* and *a-i,* neck. A golden ornament for the neck. *Puk.* 35:22.

Gu-la-paa, *s.* Beaten gold. See Gola above.

Gu-la-pe-pei-ao, *s. Gula (Eng.),* and *pepeiao,* ear. Gold for the ear, i. e., an earring. *Puk.* 35:22.

J.

JU-re, *s. Eng.* In *law,* a jury; the popular element in a court of justice.

R.

R. The letter *r* as a rolling liquid is easily assimilated with the letter *l;* hence the meaning of many foreign words is mistaken by the orthography.

Rai-si, *s. Eng.* Rice, a plant lately introduced; is now planted and growing at the Islands; Hawaiian pronunciation

RAI-KI,
LAI-KI, } *s.* Rice, &c.

RA-KO-O-NA, *s. Eng.* A raccoon, an animal of the cat genus.

RA-BI, *s. Syr.* A master; Hawaiian, *kumu. Mat.* 23:7.

RA-BI-TA, *s. Eng.* A rabbit; the name of a small animal, a cony. *Sol.* 30:26.

RA-MA, *s. Eng.* Rum; intoxicating liquor.

RA-NA, *s. Lat.* A frog. *Puk.* 7:27; *Hal.* 78:45. Hawaiian, *moolele.*

REI-NA-DI-A, *s. Eng.* A reindeer. *Lam. Haw.* 17:1.

RI-BI-NA, *s. Eng.* A ribbon. See LIBINA.

RI-BI-NA, *adj.* Kaula *ribina* uliuli, a string of blue *ribbon. Nah.* 15:38.

RO-PE,
RO-PI, } *s. Eng.* rope. Thread; sewing thread. *Puk.* 26:36. A line. 1 *Nal.* 7:15. See also LOPI.

RO-SE, *s. Eng., Gr.* A rose. *Mel. Sol.* 2:1.

RO-LE-MA, *adj. Heb.* A Hebrew word translated *juniper. Hal.* 120:4.

RU-E, *s. Eng.* Rue, the name of a bitter herb. *Luk.* 11:42.

S.

S. Hawaiians have no sibilants in their language; hence they naturally run the sound signified by *s* into that of *k*, as *kabaki* or *kapaki* for *sabati*

SA-BA-TI, *s. Heb.* The Sabbath; a resting day; the name of the seventh day of the week among the Jews. *Kin.* 2:2; *Puk.* 20:10. By the Christian Church it is termed the Lord's day. *Hoik.* 1:10. La o ka Haku.

SA-PEI-RO,
SA-PI-RA,
SA-PI-RE,
SA-PE-RA, } *s. Gr.* The name of a precious stone; a sapphire. *Iob.* 28:6; *Puk.* 24:10; *Mel. Sol.* 5:14.

SA-RE-DI-O, *s. Gr.* A sardius, the name of a precious stone. *Hoik.* 21:20.

SA-RE-DO-NU-KO, *s. Gr.* A sardonyx, the name of a precious stone. *Hoik.* 21:20.

SA-TA-NA, *s. Gr.* from *Heb.* An adversary; the prince or leader of the fallen angels; Satan. *Iob.* 1:6, 7, 8.

SA-TA-NA, *v.* To act the part of an adversary or enemy. *Hal.* 109:4.

SA-TO, *s. Gr.* A dry measure among the Jews. *Mat.* 13:33.

SA-TU-DE, *s. Eng.* Saturday, the name of the last day of the week; called more frequently by Hawaiians *Poaono,* the sixth night, or *la hoomalolo,* the day before a kapu day.

SA-TU-RE-NA, *s. Eng., Lat.* Saturn, the name of one of the planets. See Almanac for 1835. The Hawaiian name is *Naholoholo.*

SE-KE-LA,
SE-KE-LI, } *s. Heb.* A shekel, the name of a small Hebrew coin.
  2. Name of a weight. *Kin.* 23:16.

SE-KO-NA, *s. Eng.* A second of time; an instant; a moment. 1 *Kor.* 15:52.

SE-LU, *s. Heb.* A quail, a bird. *Puk.*

16:13. Another orthography is *silo.* See SILO.

SE-ME-NA, *s. Heb.* Name of a tree, some species of pine.

SE-ME-NA, *adj.* Of or belonging to a pine tree. *Neh.* 8:15.

SE-RA-PI-MA, *s. Heb.* Plural of *seraph.* Seraphim, the highest order among the angelic hosts. *Isa.* 6:2, 6.

SE-RU-TI-O, *s.* The name of an unclean bird; a night hawk. *Kanl.* 14:15.

SE-TA-DI-A, *s. Gr.* A furlong, name of a long measure. *Ioan.* 6:19.

SE-TO-RE-KA, *s. Eng.* A stork, a large bird similar to the heron. *Zek.* 5:9.

SI-LI-KA, *s. Eng.* Silk; Hawaiian pronunciation, *kilika.* See KILIKA.

SI-LI-KA, *adj.* Silken; made of silk; laau *silika,* mulberry trees. 2 *Sam.* 5:23.

SI-LO, *s. Heb.* Shiloh, a prophetical name of the Messiah. *Kin.* 49:10.

SI-LO, *s. Heb.* A word translated *quail,* the name of a bird. *Hal.* 105:40. In *Puk.* 16:13 it is written *selu.*

SI-NA-PI, *s. Gr.* Mustard, stalk and plant. *Luk.* 13:19. Hua *sinapi,* mustard seed.

SI-TI-MA, *s. Heb.* Shittim wood, a kind of furniture wood. *Puk.* 25:10; *Kanl.* 10:3.

SO-PA, *s. Eng.* Soap. *Ier.* 2:22. See KOPA, the Hawaiian pronunciation.

SU-KA-MI-NO,
SU-KA-MO-RE-A, } *s. Gr.* These are different orthographies for the same thing. Sycamore, the name of a tree and fruit. See Robinson's Lexicon, *art.,* SUKOMOREA. As an *adjective,* of or belonging to a sycamore tree.

SU-NE-DE, *s. Eng.* Sunday; originally applied among the Saxons as a day for worshiping the sun; the Christians in the dark ages applied it to the Lord's day or Christian Sabbath. With Hawaiians the *po ehiku* is the *la hoomaha* or resting day. NOTE.—Hawaiians do not often use this word, they prefer the word *Sabati* or *la pule*. See SABATI.

SU-PA, *s. Eng.* Soup; gravy, &c.; the Hawaiian term is *kai.* *Isa.* 65:4. Broth or some liquid offering.

T.

T. This letter was introduced in order to distinguish words which were introduced from other languages containing it. It is distinguished from *k* by being pronounced from the end of the tongue; but the ears of Hawaiians do not readily perceive the difference.

TAU-SA-NI, *s. Eng.* A thousand; the number ten hundred. *Kin.* 20:16.

TAU-SA-NI, *num. adj. Gram.* § 115, 4th; *Puk.* 18:21. *Kanaka* understood.

TA-HA-SA, ⎫
TA-HE-SA, ⎬ *s.* Name of an animal in Scripture called a badger.
TE-HA-SA, ⎭ *Puk.* 25:5. It is mostly used with *ili* as an adjective; as, *ili tehasa*, a badger's skin. *Ezek.* 16:10.

TA-LE-NA, *s. Eng.* from *Gr.* A talent, a measure of weight, equal to about fifty-seven pounds. *Puk.* 25:39.

2. A denomination of money, about fifteen hundred dollars.

TA-RE-DE, *s. Eng.* Thursday; originally Thor's day, i. e., a day set apart for the worship of Thor, the god of thunder; among Hawaiians, the fourth day of the week, *poaha.* NOTE.—In English reckoning it is the fifth day of the week.

TE-A-SO-RA, ⎫ *s. Heb.* The name of a
TE-A-SU-RA, ⎭ tree in *Isa.* 41:19 translated the *box tree*; also in *Isa.* 60:13.

TI-LA, *s. Eng.* See KILA.

TI-ME-BE-RA-LA, ⎫ *s. Eng.* A timbrel, a
TI-ME-RA-LA, ⎭ small drum, a very ancient musical instrument, similar to the *kuolokani* of Hawaiians. *Hal.* 68:25. For various other instruments, see 2 *Sam.* 6:5.

TI-DA-RA, *s. Heb.* The name of a tree mentioned by *Isa.* 41:19 and translated *pine.* See also *Isa.* 60:13.

TI-GA, *s. Eng.* A tiger, an animal of the cat kind. *Lam. Haw.* 15:1.

TI-RE-SA, *s. Heb.* A cypress tree. *Isa.* 44:14.

TO-PA-ZA, ⎫ *s. Eng.* from *Gr.* A topaz,
TO-PA-ZO, ⎭ the name of a precious stone. *Mel. Sol.* 5:14; *Hoik.* 21:20.

TU-MI-MI, *s. Heb.* The thummim, something worn on the breast-plate of the Jewish high-priest. *Puk.* 28:30. See URIMA.

TU-SE-DE, *s. Eng.* Tuesday, name of the third day of the week; with Hawaiians the second day, *Poalua.*

V.

V. The sound of the letter *v* is as seldom distinctly heard in Hawaiian as it is in the Tahitian dialect. The real sound represented by *w* from a Hawaiian's mouth is between that of *v* and *w*; but the double-you sound predominates; the letter *v* is therefore used only in words derived from foreign languages.

VE-NU-SA, *s. Lat.* The name of the planet Venus. See Alemanaka for 1835. The Hawaiian name is *Hookelewaa.*

VI-O-LA, *s. Eng.* A viol, a musical instrument. *Isa.* 38:20.

VI-O-LA-U-MI, *s. Viola* and *umi*, ten. A musical instrument of ten strings. *Hal.* 33:2; *Hal.* 144:9.

VI-NE-GA, *s. Eng.* Vinegar. *Mat.* 27:34. He wai awaawa. Hawaiian pronunciation, *pineka.*

VU-LE-TU-RA, *s. Eng.* The vulture, the name of an unclean bird. *Kanl.* 14:13.

Z.

Z. There are but few words commencing with this letter, and those mostly from the Greek.

ZE-PO-RA, *s. Heb.* The name of a small bird; a sparrow perhaps. *Sol.* 26:2.

ZE-BE-RA, *s. Eng.* A Zebra, a species of the horse. *Lam. Haw.* 13:1.

ZE-BU, *s. Eng.* An animal of the ox kind; a zebu. *Lam. Haw.* 10:1.

ZE-LU, *s.* The name of an animal.

ZI-O-NA, *s. Heb.* The name of a hill in Jerusalem, Zion. FIG. The whole city and to the Christian Church. *Hal.* 137:1.

ZI-ZA-NI-A, *s. Gr.* Tares; cockles; plants injurious to the growth of grain. *Mat.* 13:25, 26, 30.

AN
ENGLISH-HAWAIIAN VOCABULARY.

NOTE.—It was not the design of the Author of the foregoing Dictionary to add anything like an English-Hawaiian part, inasmuch as, in his opinion, such a work must be so concise as to be of little avail to Hawaiians or others who might wish to use it in studying English. But on account of the strongly expressed opinions of some whose judgment he respected—that such an addition would be valued—he waived his own opinion and wrote out the following Vocabulary.

The English words are taken from "a Samoan Dictionary, English and Samoan," by Rev. George Pratt, and printed at Samoa, 1862. The Hawaiian definitions are the Translator's, except as the "Hoakaka olelo no na Huaolelo Beritania" printed at Lahainaluna, 1845, was open before him, and to which he had recourse when the proper definition did not readily occur. It is hoped that those who may use this Vocabulary will know how to account for it if they fail in finding the words they need.

L. A.

To avoid confusing English homonyms, note that *e* indicates a verb, *he* (or another article) indicates a noun, and *–ia* indicates a passive or participle. Adjectives are usually unmarked.

A.J.S.

A

A, *art.* he, kahi, kekahi.
A-ban-don, e haalele loa.
A-bash, e hoopalaimaka.
Ab-do-men, ka opu.
Ab-hor, e hoowahawaha.
A-ble, he mea hiki.
Ab-or-tion, o ka hemo e ana o ke keiki.
A-bound, e nui ae, e lako.
A-bout, a puni; aneane.
A-bove, iluna, maluna.
A-bridge, e hoopokole.
Ab-scess, he mai palahee.
Ab-scond, e mahuka.
Ab-scent, nalowale.
A-bun-dance, he lako, he nui wale.
A-buse, e hana ino aku.
Ac-cept, e lawe i ka mea i haawiia.
Ac-cess, ke ala e hiki ai, kahi e hiki ai.
Ac-ci-dent, kahi poino hiki wale mai.
Ac-com-pa-ny, e hele pu, e ukali.
Ac-com-plish, e hooko i ka hana.
Ac-cord-ing, e like me, ka like ana.
Ac-count, he mooolelo, he mooaie.
Ac-cu-mu-late, e hui ae, e mahuahua.

AFFABLE

Ac-cu-rate, e oiaio, e pololei.
Ac-curse, e hooino.
Ac-cus-tom, e maa, e hana pinepine.
Ache, he hui, eha.
A-cid, awaawa e like me vinega.
Ac-qui-esce, e ae aku.
Ac-quire, e loaa.
Ac-rid, wewela i ka waha ke hoao.   [aoao ae.
A-cross, e kau kea, mai kekahi aoao a i kekahi
Act, he mea i hanaia.
A-dapt, e hoopili aku.
Add, e hui, e hoopili hou.
Ad-here, e pipili, e launa.
Ad-journ, e hoopanee a i ka la hou.
Ad-mi-ra-ble, e mahaloia, nani.
Ad-mon-ish, e ao aku.
A-dopt, e hookama.
A-dorn, e hoonani, e kahiko.
Ad-ver-si-ty, he pilikia, ka poino.
A-dult, ka mea i hele i ka nui, he oo.
A-dul-ter-y, he moekolohe.
Ad-vo-cate, he mea uwao, he loio.
A-far, e loihi aku, he mamao.
Af-fa-ble, e kamailio oluolu ana.

Af-fec-ta-tion, he hoike wale ano ole.
Af-fec-tion, aloha, makemake.
Af-firm, e hoooia, e hoopaa.
Af-flict, e hana ino, e hoopilikia.
Af-fright, e hooweliweli.
Af-front, e hoonauki.
A-fraid, makau.
Af-ter, mahope, mamuli.
Af-ter-birth, ka iewe.
Af-ter-noon, mahope o ke awakea.
A-gain, ka wa hou.
A-gainst, e ku e aku.
Age, ka loihi o kahi manawa.
A-ged, *men,* elemakule; *women,* luwahine.
Ag-gres-sor, ka mea hoouka ia hai.
Ag-i-tate, e lulu, e luliluli.
A-go, wa i hala, mamua aku nei.
Ag-o-ny, ka eha nui.
A-gree, e manao like, e launa.
A-ground, ili ka moku, ma ka honua.
A-ha! uwe! aikola!
Aid, e kokua.
Aim, he makemake, ka mea i imi ia.
Air, ke ea, ka makani.
A-las! auwe! aloha ino! poino!
A-like, like, e like me.
A-live, make ole, e ola ana.
All, pau loa, aohe mea koe.
Al-le-vi-ate, e hoomama i ke kaumaha.
Al-low, e ae aku.
Al-lure, e hoowalewale.
Al-most, aneane, kokoke pau loa.
A-lone, oia hookahi.
Al-so, hoi, oia hoi, kekahi.
Al-ter-nate, e hana pakahi na mea elua.
Al-though, ina, ina paha, aka.
Al-ways, oia mau, he mea mau.
A-mass, e ohi a nui, hoouluulu.
A-mazed, pihoihoi, eehia.
Am-bas-sa-dor, he luna, he elele.
Am-big-u-ous, he ano elua, akaka ole.
Am-bi-tion, ikaika ka manao e loaa.
A-mends, he mea e pani ai ka hewa.
A-midst, iwaena, iwaena konu.
A-mongst, iwaena pu.
Am-ple, he lawa, he nui.
An, he, kahi.
An-chor, ka heleuma.
And, a, a me, hoi.
An-ger, huhu, inaina.
An-i-mal, ka mea e ola ana.
An-kle, puupuu wawae.
An-noy, e hoouluhua, e hoonauki.
A-noint, e hamo, e poni.
An-oth-er, e, he mea e, okoa.
An-swer, e pane aku, e hai aku.
Ant, he nonanona.
Anx-ious, he makau o hiki mai ka ino.
An-y, kekahi o na mea he nui.
A-part, kaawale.
A-part-ment, he keena okoa.
A-pol-o-gize, e olelo hooakaka.
Ap-par-el, he lole komo, aahu.
Ap-pa-ri-tion, he lapu, kinowailua.
Ap-pear, e ikeia, e puka mai.

Ap-plaud, e mahalo.
Ap-point, e hoonoho, e wae aku.
Ap-proach, e hookokoke.
Ar-gue, e wehewehe i ka manao.
A-rise, e ku iluna, e ala mai.
Arm, lima.
Arms, he mau mea kaua.
Ar-my, he poe kaua, he puali.
A-round, a puni, a poai.
Ar-rive, e hiki aku i kau wahi.
Ar-ro-gance, he kaena, he hookiekie.
Ar-row, he pua pana.
Ar-row-root, he pia.
Ar-ter-y, he aalele.
Ar-ti-fice, he hana hoopunipuni, maalea.
As, me, pe, penei.
As-cend, e pii iluna, ae.
As-cent, he piina.
A-shamed, i hilahilaia.
Ash-es, he lehu, lehu ahi.
Ask, e ninau, e noi.
A-slant, he hio.
As-sem-ble, e hoouluulu, e halawai.
As-sist, e kokua.
Asth-ma, he nae, he hokii.
As-ton-ish, e puiwa, e ano e ka manao.
A-stray, he auwana, hele hewa.
A-sun-der, kaawale.
A-sy-lum, he wahi e malumalu ai.
At, i, ma.
A-tone, e kala i ka hala.
A-tone-ment, ka uku no ka hewa.
At-tain, e loaa, e hiki aku.
At-tempt, e hoao, e hooikaika aku.
At-tend, e hele pu, e hoolohe.
Aus-tere, he pi, paakiki.
A-vail, e lilo i mea e pono ai.
Av-a-rice, he puni kala, puni waiwai.
A-void, e alo ae, e launa ole.
A-wait, e kali, e noho hoomanawanui.
A-wake, makaala, pau ka hiamoe.
A-way, ma kahi e, kahi kaawale.
Axe, he koi, he koi lipi.

B.

Babe, he keiki uuku, he kama.
Back, kua, mahope ae.
Back-bite, e aki.
Back-bone, ka iwi kuamoo.
Back-side, ma ke kua, muli.
Back-wards, emi hope, mahope.
Bad, ino, he hewa, kolohe.
Bag, he eke, he hipuu.
Bait, he maunu.
Bake, e hooimu, e hoomoa i ka imu.
Bald, ohule.
Bale, he opeope nui he waiwai oloko.
Bale, e ka, e ka i ka liu.
Bam-boo, he ohe.
Band, he kaei, he apo.
Ban-ish, e kipaku i ka aina e.
Ban-ner, ka hae koa.

Barb, kahi e paa ai ma ka makau.
Bark, ka ili o ka laau.
Bark, (me he ilio la) e aoaoa.
Bar-ren, pa, hua ole.
Bar-ter, e hoololi waiwai no kekahi waiwai.
Bas-ket, hinai.
Bat, he opeapea.
Bathe, e auau i ka wai.
Bat-tle, e kaua, he hoouka kaua.
Beach, kahakai, ke one ma kahakai.
Bead, he pupu no ka lei.
Beak, ke nuku manu, nuku moku.
Bear, e lawe, e amo; e hanau.
Bear, he bea.
Beard, ka umiumi.
Beast, ka holoholona.
Beat, e paopao, e pepehi.
Beau-ti-ful, maikai, nani.
Be-calm-ed, e ku malie ana i ka pohu.
Be-cause, no, no ka mea.
Beck-on, e peahi.
Be-come, e lilo.
Be-com-ing, kupono, e lilo ana.
Bed, he moe, wahi e hiamoe ai.
Bed-rid-den, i moe mau ma ka moe.
Be-fore, mamua ae, ma ke alo.
Beg, e noi, e makilo.
Be-get, e ko (me he kane la.)
Be-gin, e hoomaka.
Be-hav-ior, ke ano o ka noho ana.
Be-hind, ma ke kua, mahope iho.
Be-hold! aia hoi! aia la! e nana!
Belch, e luai.
Be-lieve, e paulele, e manaoio.
Bel-ly, ka opu.
Be-lov-ed, i alohaia.
Be-low, malalo, malalo iho.
Belt, he kaei.
Bench, noho loloa, he noho papa.
Bend, e hoopio, e hookeekee.
Be-neath, malalo ae.   [maikai ai.
Ben-e-fi-cial, he mea e pono ai, he mea e po-
Be-nev-o-lence, lokomaikai, hoomanawalea.
Be-night, he hiki e mai ka po.
Be-seech, e noi, e pule aku.
Be-side, he mea a keu, he mea e ae hoi.
Be-siege, e hoopuni i ke kulanakauhale i ka
  puali.
Best, he oi ma ka maikai.
Be-stow, e haawi wale aku.
Be-tray, e kumakaia.
Be-troth, e hoopalau.
Be-tween, iwaena.
Be-wail, e kanikau, e uwe aku.
Be-wil-der, e ike ole i kahi e hele ai, e hoopo-
  uli, ike powehiwehi.
Be-yond, mao aku.
Big, nui.   [hine.
Big-a-my, o ka mare hookahi kane elua wa-
Bil-low, he nalu nui o ke kai.
Bind, e hoopaa i ke kaula, e nakii.
Bird, he manu.
Bite, e nahu, e aki.
Bit-ter, he awaawa, he awahia.
Black, eleele.

Blad-der, opu mimi.
Blas-pheme, e hailiili i ke Akua, e hooino.
Bleed, e hookahe koko.
Bless, e hoomaikai.
Blind, makapo, ike ole.
Blink, e nana powehiwehi, e amo ka maka.
Blis-ter, he pehu ili he wai oloko.
Blood, he koko, he wai ula.
Blood-y, hapalaia me ke koko.
Blos-som, he pua o ka laau.
Blotch, e hapala i kahi luu.
Blow, he hahau ana.
Blow, e pa ka makani.
Blue, uli, uliuli.
Blun-der, he kuhihewa, he lalau.
Blun-der-buss, he pu kau poohiwi pokole.
Blunt, he oi ole, meumeu.
Boar, he puaa kane.
Board, he papa, he laau i olo lahilahi ia.
Boast, e liki, e kaena, e haaheo.
Boat, he waapa.
Bod-y, kino.
Boil, me he wai la e hoolapalapa.
Boil, mai pehu, a hehe paha.
Bold, he koa, makau ole.
Bone, iwi.
Bon-net, he papale wahine.
Bo-ny, paa i na iwi.
Book, he palapala i paiia, he buke.
Bor-der, he palena, mokuna.
Bore, e hou i ka wili.
Bor-row, e noi aole nae lilo loa.
Bo-som, ka umauma.
Both, o laua a elua.
Bot-tle, he omole wai, he hue wai
Bot-tom, kumu, mole, aoao lalo.
Bough, he lala laau.
Bound-a-ry, mokuna, palena.
Bow, e kulou ke poo.
Bow, he kakaka.
Bow-els, he naau.
Bowl, he apu, he bola.
Bow-string, he kaula kakaka.
Box, he pahu.
Box, e mokomoko, e kui me ka lima.
Boy, he keiki kane.
Boy-ish, he ano kamalii.
Brack-ish, mananalo, he wai kai iki.
Brag, e akena, e kaena.
Brain, ka lolo poo.
Branch, he lala, he manamana laau.
Bran-dish, e oniu aku me ka hooweliweli.
Brave, makau ole, he koa.
Bread-fruit, ka hua ulu.
Breadth, he akea, he laula.
Break, *as a law,* hai; *as glass,* &c., naha; *as
  a rope,* moku, &c.
Break-er, he kai koo.
Breast, umauma.
Breathe, e hanu.
Breech-es, he wawae komo, he wawae muku.
Breed, e hanau, e loaa ke keiki.
Breeze, he makani oluolu.
Bridge, he holopapa, he wapo.
Bright, huali, aiai.

Brim-ful, piha, piha a hu.
Bring, e ho mai, e lawe mai.
Brink, he kae, he kapa o ka muliwai.
Brit-tle, mea naha wale, hai wale.
Broad, akea, laula.
Broil, e koala, e pulehu i ke ahi.
Broil, e hakaka ana, e ohumu.
Brood, he ohana, he ohua manu.
Brood, e hoopunana me he moa la.
Broth-er, he hoahanau kane.
Brown, he ano ulaula ahiahia.
Bruise, e hoeha, e palapu.
Brush, e kahili, e kahi.
Brush, he hulu puaa i hana kahili ia.
Bud, e opuu, e opuupuu mai.
Buf-fet, e kui, e kui aku.
Build, e kapili, e kukulu.
Build-er, he kanaka kukulu hale.
Bul-let, he poka pu.
Bunch, he huhui, he ahui, he puu.
Bun-dle, he ope, he puolo.
Bur-den, he ukana kaumaha.
Burn, e aa, e wela.
Bur-nish, e anai, e hoohuali.
Burst, e poha, e hoonaha.
Bur-y, e kanu iho, e uhi i ka lepo.
Bush-y, paapu i na laau liilii.
But, aka.
But, he pahu nui.
But-ter-fly, he pulelehua.
But-tock, he kikala.
But-ton, he pihi.
Buy, e kuai lilo mai.
By, e, ma.
By, kokoke, ma.
By-and-by, mamuli.
By-word, he inoa i kapaia'i kekahi no ka ino.

C.

Ca-ble, he kaula nui e paa ai ka moku.
Cack-le, e alala me he moa la, e pukoko.
Ca-dav-er-ous, me he kupapau la ke nana aku.
Cage, he hale manu, he hale holoholona hihiu.
Cake, he popo berena uuku, he berena liilii.
Ca-lam-i-ty, he poino, he pilikia nui.
Cal-cu-late, e imi ma ka noonoo.
Cal-dron, he ipu hao nui.
Calk, e hoopaa hamama ma ka moku.
Call, e hea aku, e kahea.
Calm, he pohu, he malie, makani ole.
Calm, e pohu, e malu.
Ca-lum-ni-ate, e hoino ia hai, e niania aku.
Camp, he wahi e hoomoana ai na koa.
Can, e hiki, e ikaika.
Can, he ipu tini no ka mea wai.
Cane, ko, ka ohe, he laau kookoo.
Can-non, he pu nui kuniahi.
Can-not, he hiki ole.
Ca-noe, he waa.
Cap, he uhi no ke poo, he papalekapu.
Cape, he lae, he aahu no ka poohiwi.
Cap-tive, he pio, ka mea i lawe pio ia.

Care, ka manao nui e kaumaha ai.
Car-pen-ter, he kamena, he kapili hale.
Car-ry, e lawe, e halihali, e amo.
Carve, e kalai, e mahele pono i ka ia.
Case, he pale, he wahi.
Cast, e hoolei, e hooheehee i ke kepau.
Cas-tle, he hale papu, he pa ikaika.
Cat, he popoki, he owau.
Cat-a-ract, he wailele.
Catch, e hopu.
Cat-e-chise, e ao aku ma ka niele.
Cave, he ana, he lua.
Cav-il, e hoohalahala, e hoopohala.
Cause, he kumu, kumu hookolokolo.
Caus-tic, he aai ana me he mai aai la.
Cau-tion, he makaala, he kuoo.
Cease, e oki, e hoopau.
Cel-e-brate, e hoonani.
Cen-sure, e ahewa, e hoohewa.
Cen-ti-pede, he mea kolo niho awa, kanapi.
Cen-ter, waenakonu, mawaenakonu.
Chain, he kaulahao.
Chair, he noho.
Chal-lenge, e aa aku.
Cham-ber, he keena maluna.
Chance, he mea hiki wale mai.
Change, e ano hou ae, e hoololi.
Chant, e mele heluhelu.
Chap, he nakaka ka ili, he ili naha.
Char-ac-ter, ke ano o ke kanaka.
Char-coal, he nanahu.
Charge, he kauoha, he mea e malamaia.
Char-i-ty, he manawalea, he aloha.
Charm, e hoolealea.
Chase, e hahai.
Chasm, he awawa hohonu.
Chas-tise, e hahau, e haua.
Cheap, he kumukuai uuku, makepono.
Cheat, e epa, e hoopunipuni.
Cheek, ka papalina.
Cheer-ful, oluolu ka manao, hoihoi.
Cher-ish, e malama maikai.
Chest, he pahu papa.
Chew, e nau, e mama.
Chick-en, he ohana moa, moa opiopio.
Chide, e ao, e hoopaapaa.
Chief, he alii, he kiaaina.
Child, he keiki, he kama.
Child-ish, ma ke ano kamalii.
Chill, he anu, he haukeke, he li.
Chin, auwae.
Chip, he apana okiia.
Chirp, e nunulu, e ioio me he manu la.
Chis-el, he kila.
Choice, ka mea i koho ia, ke koho ana.
Choke, e puua, e umi.
Choose, e koho, e wae ae.
Chop, e oki, e kua aku.
Clam-my, he pulupulu a he pili ana.
Clam-or, he walaau, he uwauwa.
Clang, he leo o ke kaua, he leo kani nui.
Clap, *of the hands,* e pai ka lima; *of thunder,* he kui hekili.
Clasp, e apo, e puliki.

Class, he papa, he poe.
Clat-ter, e koele, e kamailio lapuwale.
Claw, *of a bird,* he maiuu.
Clay, he palolo, he lepo pipili.
Clean, maemae.
Cleanse, e huikala, e hoomaemae.
Clear, aiai.
Cleave, e pili aku; *cleave asunder,* e mahele.
Clev-er, akamai, oluolu.
Climb, e pii iluna.
Cling, e puili, e pili aku.
Close, e pi, e paakiki.
Cloth, lole, kapa.
Clothe, e aahu, e komo i ka lole.
Cloud, he ao, he oho paapu.
Cloud-y, paapu i na ao.
Clo-ven, i maheleia.
Club, he newa, he laau e pepehi ai.
Cluck, e koukou aku.
Clum-sy, he hawawa, he mama ole i ka hana.
Clus-ter, he ahui, he huihui.
Clutch, e hopu a paa.
Cob-web, he punawelewele.
Cock, he moa kane.
Cock-crow-ing, ka wa o ka po i kani ai ka moa.
Cock-le, he mea ulu, he zizania.
Co-coa, ka laau niu.
Co-e-qual, he like ke ano me kahi mea e ae.
Cof-fin, he pahu kupapau.
Cog-i-tate, e noonoo.
Coil, e poai, e wili poai me he kaula la.
Cold, he anu, he haukeke, he hui.
Col-ic, he nahu, he eha o ka naau.
Col-lar-bone, ka iwi o ka a-i.
Col-lect, e hui pu, e ohi.
Col-lec-tion, he mau mea i huiia.
Col-lis-ion, he ku, he pili, he anai.
Col-or, ke ano owaho, he eleele paha, he ula-ula, he melemele paha, he mea hooluu.
Comb, he kahi no ka lauoho.
Com-bat, he kaua, he hoouka.
Com-bine, e alu, e hui pu.
Com-bus-ti-ble, he hiki ke hoaaia.
Come, e hele mai.
Com-et, he hoku welowelo.
Com-fort, he oluolu, he maha.
Com-mand, e kauoha, e olelo paa aku.
Com-mand-ment, he kanawai, he kauoha.
Com-mem-o-rate, e hana ma na mea e hooma-nao ai.
Com-mence, e hoomaka.
Com-mend, e hoapono.   [naau.
Com-mit, e haawi aku ia hai, e hoopaa ma ka
Com-mon, he mea i loaa pinepine, he kaulana.
Com-mo-tion, he haunaele, he pioloke.
Com-pan-ion, he hoa, he mea launa.
Com-pa-ny, he poe, he mau kanaka hui.
Com-pare, e hoohalike.
Com-pas-sion, aloha.
Com-pel, e koi aku, e hooikaika.
Com-pen-sate, e pani aku no ka mea i lilo.
Com-plain, e ohumu, e hai i ka pilikia.
Com-plete, e hoopau, e hoopaa i kahi hana.
Com-plex, he mea ano nui, hihia.
Com-ply, e ae aku me ka hana a malama.

Com-pose, e hoooluolu, e kakau manao; *to compose e mele,* e haku.
Com-pre-hend, e ike maopopo.
Com-pute, e helu, e loaa ma ka helu.
Com-rade, he hoa, hoa hele, hoa hana.
Con-ceal, e huna, e uhi.
Con-ceit-ed, he manao nui ia ia iho.   [opu.
Con-ceive, e loaa ma ka noonoo, e ko ma ka
Conch, he pu nui no ka moana mai.
Con-cil-i-ate, e hoolaulea, e hoooluolu.
Con-cise, pokole ma ka olelo ana.
Con-course, he aha kanaka nui.
Con-demn, e hoahewa aku.
Con-de-scend, e hoohaahaa, e ae aku.
Con-duct, ka ano o ka noho ana o kekahi.
Con-fer, e kuka pu, e haawi ia hai.
Con-fess, e hai aku i kahi hana malu.
Con-firm, e hoopaa, e hooia.
Con-flict, he ku e, he kaua.
Con-found-ed, he pili paa, he hoopohihiia.
Con-gre-gate, e hui, e hele nui mai me kanaka.
Con-jec-ture, e koho, e manao wale.
Con-nect, e hui pu, e hoohui.
Con-quer, e lanakila, e hoopio.
Con-science, ka manao oloko e hoomaopopo ana i ka hewa, ka lunaikehala.
Con-sent, ka ae, ka ae ana.
Con-sid-er, e noonoo, e poonoo.
Con-sign, e haawi ia hai e malama ia.
Con-sole, e hoooluolu, e hoona.
Con-spic-u-ous, i ikeia, i maopopo.
Con-spire, e noonoo ku e, e ohumu aku.
Con-stant, mau, paa, kuihe ole.
Con-stant-ly, e mau ana, e paa mau ana.
Con-ster-na-tion, he weliweli, he wiwo.
Con-sti-pa-tion, he paa.
Con-struct, e kapili.
Con-sult, e niele aku ia hai.
Con-sume, e pau i ka ai ia, pau i ke ahi.
Con-sump-tion, he ano mai.
Con-ta-gious, he mai i hoolahaia ma ka pili.
Con-tam-i-nate, e hoohaumia.
Con-temn, e hooino.
Con-tem-plate, e poonoo.
Con-tend, e ku e, e hakaka.
Con-tent, walea, oluolu.
Con-ten-tion, haunaele, hakaka.
Con-tig-u-ous, e pili ana.
Con-tin-u-al, e mau ana, oki ole.
Con-tin-ue, e hoomau, e oia mau.
Con-tract, e hooemi iho.
Con-tri-vance, he mea i loaa i ka noonoo.
Con-tro-ver-sy, he hoopaapaa.
Con-tu-ma-cy, he hoolohe ole.
Con-vene, e hoohalawai.
Con-ver-sa-tion, he kamailio.
Con-vert, e hoohuli, e hoololi i ka manao.
Con-vey, e lawe aku, e hali.
Coo, e uwe me he manu nunu la.
Cook, e kahumu i ka ai, he kuke.
Cool, oluolu, wela ole.
Co-pi-ous, nui wale.
Cop-per, he keleawe melemele.
Cop-u-la-tion, he hui e ai pu ana.
Cor-al, he akoakoa, he puna.

Cord, he kaula liilii.
Cord-age, na kaula moku.
Core, he kaku, pikoi.
Cor-ner, he kihi, huina.
Cor-ner-stone, he pohaku kihi.
Corpse, he kupapau.
Corps, he poe koa.
Cor-pu-lent, he kino puipui, momona.
Cor-rect, he pololei, he oiaio.
Cor-rode, e ai me he popo la.
Cor-rupt, e hoohaumia, e hauna.
Cos-tive, he paa ka lepo.
Cot-ton, he pulupulu.
Cov-e-nant, e ae like ana, he kuikahi.
Cov-er, he ihi, he poi.
Cov-et, e kuko, e iini.
Cough, e kunu.
Coun-cil, he poe e kukakuka pu ana.
Count, e helu.
Coun-te-nance, he helehelena, maka.
Coun-ter-act, e hana ma ka mea e ku e ai.
Coun-ter-feit, e hoohalike kolohe.
Count-less, e hiki ole ke helu ia.
Coun-try, he aina, he aupuni.
Coup-le, elua, papalua.
Cour-age, he makau ole.
Cour-te-ous, lokomaikai.
Cour-te-san, he wahine moekolohe.
Cous-in, he hoahanau.
Cow-ard, he kanaka hee wale.
Cow-er, e kulou iho, e ae wale aku.
Coy, maka hilahila.
Crab, he papai.
Crack, he nakaka, naka.
Crack-le, e paapaaina.
Craft, he maalea, ka oihana.
Cramp, maele.
Crave, e noi me ka ikaika.
Craw-fish, he papai, he wahi ula.
Crawl, e kolo, e hele me he ilo la.
Creak, e uwi, e nakeke.
Cre-ate, e hana, e hoololi hou.
Creep, e kolo me he keiki la.
Crev-ice, he naha, nakaka.
Crew, ka poe luina, ka poe hoholo moku.
Crick-et, he mea ano uhini.
Crime, he hewa e pili ana ke kanawai.
Crim-son, he ulaula loa.
Crip-ple, he mea oopa.
Crisp, e wela a paapaa.
Crock-e-ry, he mau ipu naha.
Crook, e hookekee, e pio.
Crook-back, he kuapuu.
Cross-way, he ala liilii moe kea.
Crouch, e kulou, e moe iho.
Crow, he manu eleele.
Crow, e hookani ka leo me he moa kane la.
Crowd, he poe nui a paapu.
Crown, he papale alii, ka piko o ke poo.
Cru-el, he oolea, he paakiki.
Crumb, he huna liilii, he huna ai.
Crum-ble, e helelei liilii.
Crum-ple, e hoomimino.
Crush, e hoopepe.
Cry, e ue, e uwe.

Cu-bit, he ana ma ka loa 18 iniha.
Cum-ber, e hookaumaha.
Cun-ning, akamai, noiau, maalea.
Cup, he ipu, he apu.
Cure, e hoola i ka mai.
Cur-ly, mimilo, piipii.
Cur-rent, he au, ke kahe wai ana.
Curse, e hooino, e kuamuamu.
Curve, e hookekee, e pelu.
Cus-tom, he maa, he hana mau.
Cut, e oki, e kalai.
Cut-lass, he pahi kaua.

D.

Dai-ly, kela la keia la.
Dal-li-ance, he hoopanee, he alohaloha.
Dam-age, he poino, he kina.
Damp, mau, koekoe.
Dance, e haa, e hula.
Dare, e aa aku.
Dark, poeleele, ke ano o ka po.
Dar-ling, he hiwahiwa, mea i aloha nui.
Dart, he ihi, he pua no ke kakaka.
Dash, he kahamaha.
Daugh-ter, kaikamahine.
Daunt, e hoomakau.
Dawn, he wanaao.
Day, he ao, pau ka pouli.
Daz-zle, e olinolino.
Dead, make, pau ke ea.
Deaf, kuli, aa.
Deal, e mahele aku.
Dear, he nui ke kumu kuai, he aloha nui ia.
Dearth, he wa wi.
Death, he make, he kaili ke aho.
De-bate, e kukakuka, e paio.　　　[lohe me ia.
De-bauch, e hoowalewale ia hai e hoomoeko-
De-bil-i-tate, e hoonawaliwali.
De-cap-i-tate, e hoooki i ke poo.
De-cay, e pala, e maloo, e popopo.
De-cease, e make.
De-ceit, e hoopunipuni.
De-cent, kohu pono.
De-cide, e hoomaopopo, e paa ka manao.
Deck, e hoonani.
Deck, ka inoa o ka papa maluna o ka moku.
De-clare, e hai aku.
Dec-o-rate, e hoonani, e kahiko.
De-coy, e hoowalewale.
De-crease, e emi iho, e hooliilii.
Ded-i-cate, e hoolaa, e hoolilo ia hai.
Deep, hohonu, poopoo.
De-fame, e hoino, e hoowahawaha.
De-feat, e lanakila, e hooauhee.
De-fend, e hoomalu, e pale aku.
De-fer, e hoopanee.
Def-er-ence, he ae aku, he hoolohe.
De-fi-ance, he aa aku.
De-fi-cient, emi iho, he nele.
De-file, e hoohaumia.
De-fine, e hoakaka, e hoike i ke ano.
De-form, e hoomumukuia.

De-form-ed, he hookinaia, he mumuku.
De-fraud, e hoopunipuni ia hai.
De-fy, e aa aku.
De-grade, e hoohaahaa.
De-lay, he hoopanee.
De-lib-er-ate, e kuka, e noonoo.
De-li-cious, ono i ka ai, miko.
De-light, he olioli, he manao lealea.
De-liv-er, e hoopakele.
Del-uge, he wai kahe nui, kaiakahinalii.
De-lu-sion, he manao kuhihewa.
De-mol-ish, e wawahi, e hoohiolo.
De-mon, he daimonio, he uhane ino.
De-ni-al, he hoole, ae ole.
De-part, e hele aku.
De-pend, e kau aku, e pili ana ia hai.
De-pop-u-late, e hooemi iho na kanaka.
De-pose, e hemo i kekahi i kana oihana.
De-prave, e hoolilo aku i hewa.
Depth, he hohonu, he poopoo.
Dep-u-ty, he hope, he pani haka.
De-ride, e hoowahawaha, e akaaka.
De-scend, e iho, e hele ilalo.
De-scend-ant, he mamo.
Des-e-crate, e hooino i ka mea i hoolaaia.
Des-ert, he wao, he wahi kanaka ole.
De-sert, e hele aku, e haalele.
De-sign, e manao e mamua.
De-sire, he makemake, he ake.
De-sist, e hooki, e hoopau i ka hana.
Des-o-late, he mehameha, kanaka ole.
Des-pair, he manao poho, lana ole.
Des-patch, he hana i paa wawe ia.
Des-pi-ca-ble, he mea manao ole ia.
Des-pise, e hoowahawaha, e hooino.
Des-pond, e poho ana i ka manao.
Des-ti-tute, nele, ilihune.
De-stroy, e hoopau aku.
De-tach, e hemo aku, e hookaawale.
De-tail, e hai nui a loihi aku.
De-tain, e kaohi, e hoololohi ia hai.   [i hewa.
De-tect, e loaa ka mea i nalo, e hopu i ka mea
De-ter-mine, e hooholo ka manao.
De-test, e hoowahawaha, e inaina aku.
De-vi-ate, e hele hewa, e huli ae.
De-vice, he manao hana maalea.
De-void, he ole, he neoneo.
De-vote, e hoolaa, e hookapu.
De-vour, e pau i ka ai ia, e ai wikiwiki.
Dew, he hau, he hau o ke kakahiaka.
Di-a-dem, he hoailona alii.
Di-a-lect, ka olelo i hoohuli iki a kekahi poe.
Di-a-logue, he olelo kike a na mea elua.
Di-a-phragm, ka pale mawaena o ka opu.
Di-ar-rhe-a, ka hi.
Dib-ble, he wahi oo.
Die, e make, e kaili ke aho.
Dif-fer, e like ole, e hookoa.
Dif-fi-cult, he oolea, he paakiki.
Dif-fi-dent, maka hilahila.
Dif-fuse, mahuahua, hoonui.
Dig, e eli, e kohi ka lepo.
Dil-a-to-ry, lolohi, hoomolowa.   [ia.
Dim, powehiwehi, maopopo ole ka mea i imi
Di-min-ish, e hele liilii, e hooemi iho.

Dip, e kupenu, e hookomo i ka wai.
Dire, he ino nui, he weliweli.
Di-rect, e kuhikuhi aku, e hoopololei.
Dirt, he lepo, he paumaele.
Dis-a-gree, e like ole, e ku e aku.
Dis-ap-pear, e hoonalowale.
Dis-as-ter, he poino, he lilo, he pilikia.
Dis-cern, e hoomaopopo, e ike.
Dis-charge, e hookuu aku, e hana a paa.
Dis-ci-ple, haumana.
Dis-close, e wehe, e hoohu ae.
Dis-com-pose, e hoopohihi, e hoohuhu.
Dis-cord, kohu like ole, launa ole.
Dis-cov-er, e loaa ma ka imi ana.
Dis-course, he wahi olelo, he haiao.
Dis-cour-te-ous, he oluolu ole.
Dis-crim-in-ate, e ike maopopo lea.
Dis-dain, e hoowahawaha.
Dis-ease, he mai.
Dis-fig-ure, e hooano e i ka helehelena.
Dis-grace, e hoohaahaa iho.
Dis-gust, he hoopailua, ono ole.
Dish, he ipu, he kiaha.
Dis-heart-en, e manaka, poho ana o ka manao.
Dis-hev-el-ed, lauoho i kah ole ia.
Dis-in-ter, e huai i ke kupapau.
Dis-join, e hemo ae, e hookaawale aku.
Dis-like, e makemake ole, e launa ole.
Dis-lo-cate, e hemo i ka ami o ka iwi.
Dis-miss, e hookuu aku.
Dis-mount, e lele ilalo o ka lio.
Dis-o-be-di-ent, hoolohe ole, malama ole.
Dis-own, e hoole, olelo kekahi aole nona.
Dis-perse, e hooauhee, e hele liilii.
Dis-pir-it, he pau ka manao ikaika.
Dis-play, he hoike hanohano.
Dis-please, e pono ole ka manao.
Dis-pos-sess, e hemo wale, e hao.
Dis-pute, e hoopaapaa.
Dis-re-gard, e hoolohe ole, malama ole.
Dis-res-pect, e malama ole.
Dis-sem-ble, e hookamani.
Dis-sev-er, e hooki, e hookaawale.
Dis-sim-i-lar, he like ole.
Dis-si-pate, e hoohelelei.
Dis-solve, e hoohee.
Dis-so-lute, hoomaunauna.
Dis-tant, mao loa, iu.
Dis-tem-per, he mai lele.
Dis-tend, e pehu ae a nui.
Dis-tin-guish, e noonoo i ka like ole.
Dis-tress, he eha, he pilikia.
Dis-trib-ute, e haawi aku.
Dis-trict, he apana moku.
Dis-turb, e mea aku, e haumaele.
Ditch, he auwai i eliia.
Dive, e luu iho i ka wai.
Di-verse, he like ole me ka mea e ae.
Di-vide, e mahele, e puunawe.
Di-vorce, e oki i ka mea i mare ia.
Di-vulge, e hoopuka i ka mea i hunaia.
Diz-zy, he poniuniu.
Do, e hana.
Do-cile, he hikiwawe i ke aoia.
Doc-tor, he kahuna lapaau.

Dog, ilio.
Dol-phin, he ia.
Dolt, he mea lolohi i ke ao ana.
Do-min-ion, ka hoalii ana.
Doom, he hoopai pono ana.
Door, ipuka, he pani puka.
Do-tage, he ano elemakule.
Doub-le, palua, papalua.
Doub-le-mind-ed, he manao paa ole.
Doubt, he kanalua.
Dove, he manu nunu.
Down, lalo, ilalo.
Down-ward, e iho, e imi ilalo.
Drag, e kauo.
Drake, he manu koloa kane.
Draught, ka mea i kauo ia.
Dread, makau, ka eehia.
Dream, he moe uhane.
Dregs, he oka, na mea haule ilalo.
Dress, he kapa komo.
Drill, he mea e hana ai ka puka.
Drink, e inu, e moni iho.
Drip, e kulu uuku.
Drive, e hoeueu, e kipaku aku.
Driv-el, e kahe ka wale.
Dry-dock, he aki hoolana.
Droll-e-ry, he mea hoomake akaaka.
Droop, mae iho.
Drop, e haule iho.
Drop, he kulu wai.
Drop-sy, he mai pehu o ka opu.
Drown, e make iloko o ka wai.
Drow-sy, he ano hiamoe.
Drum, he pahu, he puahu kani.
Drunk, ona.
Dry, maloo.
Duck, he manu koloa.
Dull, oi ole, manoanoa.
Dumb, he aa, he leo ole.
Dung, he lepo kipulu.
Dung-y, me he lepo la.
Du-ra-ble, e mau ana, pau ole.
Du-ring, oiai.
Dusk, he malamalama uuku, molehulehu.
Dust, he lepo makalii.
Dwell, e noho.
Dys-en-ter-y, he hi koko.
Dys-pep-si-a, he wahi mai ma ka opu.

E.

EACH, kela mea keia mea.
Ea-ger, ikaika ka manao.
Ear, pepeiao.
Ear-ly, wawe, e hiki mamua.
Ear-nest, he manao ikaika, papau o ka manao.
Earth, ka honua nei, he lepo.
Earth-quake, olai, haalulu honua.
Earth-worm, he ilo lepo, anuhe.
Ease, maha, oluolu.
East, hikina.
Ea-sy, maha, noho oluolu.
Eat, e ai.

Eat-a-ble, he mea hiki ke ai ia.
Eaves, na umalu o ka hale.
Ebb, e emi ke kai, emi iho.
E-bul-li-tion, e hoolapalapa me he wai la.
E-cho, he kupinai.
E-clipse, ka pouli ana o ka la, mahina paha.
Edge, he kae, he palena.
Ed-i-ble, he mea hiki ke ai ia.
Ed-u-cate, e malama a hoonaauao aku.
Eel, he ia, he puhi.
Ef-fem-i-nate, e hoopalupalu me he wahine la.
Ef-ful-gent, he alohilohi, he nani.
Egg, he hua; *hen's egg,* hua moa.
Eight, awalu.
Eight-een, umikumamawalu.
Eight-y, kanawalu.
Ei-ther, kekahi o na mea elua.
E-late, e hookiekie, e lana.
El-bow, ke kuekue lima.
El-ders, he poe kahiko, mau luna ekalesia.
Eld-est, ka mua loa, maka hiapo.
E-lect, ka mea i kohoia, i waeia.
El-e-gy, he kanikau.
El-e-phan-ti-a-sis, he mai pehu nui.
El-e-vate, e hapai iluna.
E-lev-en, he umikumamakahi.
E-lude, e oni ae, e pakele.
E-ma-ciate, e hoowiwi i ke kino.
E-mas-cu-late, e hoopau i ke ano kane, e poa.
Em-balm, e ialoa.
Em-bas-sy, ka poe i hoounaia i ka aina e.
Em-bel-lish, e hoonani, he mea maikai owaho.
Em-bers, he nanahu ahi ane pio.
Em-brace, e apo aku ia hai a e honi paha.
E-merge, e puka mai.
Em-i-nence, he wahi kiekie.
Em-is-sa-ry, ka mea i hoounaia, he kiu.
Em-met, he naonao, he mea kolo.
Emp-ty, kaawale iloko, he nele.
Em-u-late, e hooikaika e like me ka mea e ae.
En-camp, e hoomoana.
En-close, e kaapuni, e hookomo iloko.
En-com-pass, e poai ae.
En-coun-ter, e hoouka, e kaua aku.
En-cour-age-ment, e hooikaika, e paipai i ka manao.
En-croach, e komo iloko o ko hai wahi.
En-cum-ber, e hookaumaha, e hoopilikia.
End, he hope, he pau ana.
En-deav-or, e hoao aku.
End-less, pau ole, e mau ana.
En-dure, e hoomanawanui.
En-e-my, he mea manao ino mai, he ku e.
En-fee-ble, e hooemi i ka ikaika, e hoopalupalu.
En-force, e hooko, e hoopaa aku.
En-gage, e olelo ae like e hana.
En-grave, e kaha keleawe a mea e ae.
En-join, e kauoha aku.
En-joy, e pomaikai i kekahi mea.
En-kin-dle, e hoaa, e kuni i ke ahi.
En-large, e hoonui, e hoomahuahua.
En-light-en, e hoonaauao, e hoomalamalama.
E-nough, ua lawa, ua nui.
En-rage, e wela ka huhu.

En-sign, he hae, he kanaka lawe hae.
En-slave, e hookauwa, e hoohana uku ole.
En-tan-gle, e hoohihia.
En-ter, e komo iloko.
En-tice, e hoowalewale, e kai i ka hewa.
En-tire, okoa, pau, aohe mea koe.
En-trails, he naau.
En-trance, kahi e komo ai.
En-trap, e upiki, e hopu.
En-treat, e noi ikaika.
En-vel-op, he wahi, he pale.
E-nu-mer-ate, e helu.
En-voy, he elele, he luna.
En-vy, e huahua, e lili wale.
Ep-i-dem-ic, he mai i hoolaha nui ia.
Ep-i-lep-sy, he mai i kau koke mai.
E-qual, e like, e hoohalikeia.
E-quiv-a-lent, he mea waiwai like.
Ere-long, mahope aole nae loihi.
E-rect, ku pololei iluna.
Err, e hele hewa, e lalau.
Er-rand, e hele imi i kahi mea a hoi mai.
E-rup-tion, e poha ana, he puupuu ma ka ili.
Es-cape, he pakele.
Es-cort, he poe koa e hele pu ana me ke alii.
Es-say, e hoao.
Es-tab-lish, e hoopaa.
E-ter-nal, oia mau, aohe mua aohe hope.
E-vade, e pale aku, e alo ae.
E-va-sive, ma ke ano pale ae.
E-ven, laumania, e moe like ana.
Eve-ning, ahiahi.
Ever, i ka manawa a pau.
Ev-e-ry, kela a me keia.
Ev-i-dent, maopopo, akaka.
E-vil, ino, hewa.
E-vil-speak-ing, he ahiahi ia hai.
Eu-lo-gy, he olelo mahalo.
Ex-act, ku pono, pololei loa.
Ex-alt, e hookiekie ae.
Ex-am-ine, e milimili, e huli.
Ex-am-ple, he kumu hoohalike.
Ex-as-pe-rate, e hoonaukiuki.
Ex-ceed, e oi aku, e kela aku.
Ex-cel, e oi aku, e maikai ae.   [heluna.
Ex-cept, he mea kaawale aole e komo i ka
Ex-change, e hoololi, e haawi i kekahi mea no
   kekahi mea e ae.
Ex-cite, e hooala mai, e hooeueu.
Ex-claim, e hooho, e kahea nui.
Ex-cre-ment, he kiona, he kukae.
Ex-cuse, e ae aku, e kala aku.
Ex-e-crate, e hoowahawaha, e hoino.
Ex-e-cute, e hooko.
Ex-em-pli-fy, e hoike maopopo.
Ex-empt, kaawale, pakele.
Ex-ert, e hooikaika.
Ex-hib-it, e hoike aku.
Ex-hort, e paipai.
Ex-ile, e kipaku aku i ka aina e.
Ex-pand, e mohola, e wehe ae.
Ex-pect, e kakali.
Ex-pec-to-rate, e kuha.
Ex-pe-di-ent, e pono ke hana ia.
Ex-pe-dite, e hana koke, e hoohikiwawe.

Ex-pel, e hookuke, e kipaku.
Ex-pert, akamai, hikiwawe.
Ex-pi-ate, e uku aku no ka hewa.
Ex-pire, e make aku, e kaili ke aho.
Ex-plain, e hooakaka, hoomaopopo.
Ex-plode, e naha aku me he pu la.
Ex-pose, e hoike aku.
Ex-pound, e hoakaka i ke ano.
Ex-tend, e kikoo, e hooloihi aku.
Ex-ten-u-ate, e hoemi i ka hewa.
Ex-te-ri-or, o waho, ko waho.
Ex-ter-min-ate, e hoopau.
Ex-tinct, e hoopio ia me he ahi la.
Ex-tir-pate, e uhuki i na aa a pau loa.
Ex-tol, e hoonani, e hoolea.
Ex-tort, ma ka hooweliweli e loaa ai.
Ex-treme, kahi e oi loa ai, ka welau.
Ex-trem-i-ty, ka hope, ka welau.
Ex-tri-cate, e hoopakele, e hoohemo aku.
Ex-u-be-rant, e ulu nui ana, hoohu ana.
Ex-ult, e olioli, e hoaikola.
Eye, maka.
Eye-ball, onohi o ka maka.
Eye-brow, ke kuemaka.
Eye-lid, kuapoi o ka maka.
Eye-sore, ka mea e eha ai ke nana aku.

F.

FACE, ka maka, ka papalina.
Fade, e mae.
Faint, e maule, he nawaliwali.
Fair, maikai, laelae.
Faith, manao io, manaolana.
Faith-ful, hoolohe ana, ku pono.
Fall, e haule, e hina.
Fal-low, mahakea.
False, oiaio ole, hoopunipuni.
False-hood, he wahahee, oiaio ole.
Fal-ter, e hooemi iho, e nawaliwali.
Famed, e kaulanaia.
Fam-i-ly, ka ohua, ka ohana.
Fam-ine, he wi, he nele i ka ai ole.
Fam-ish, e hoowiwi, e make i ka wi.
Fan, he peahi.
Fan, e peahi aku.
Far, mamao aku, loihi aku.
Fare-well, he uwe aloha.
Far-thest, loihi loa aku.
Fash-ion, ke ano e hoomahuiia.
Fast, e hooke ai, e hoopololi.
Fast, he mama, he kiki.
Fas-ten, e hoopaa, e hana a paa.
Fast-ness, he kauwahi e pilikia ai.
Fat, momona, puipui.
Fa-ther, makuakane.
Fath-om, he anana.
Fa-tigue, he luhi, he maloeloe.
Fault, he hala, ha hewa.
Fa-vor, he lokomaikai, he aloha.
Fa-vor-ite, he makamaka, hoa aloha.
Fear, makau, hopohopo.
Feast, ahaaina.

Feath-er, he hulu o ka manu.
Fee-ble, nawaliwali.
Feed, e hanai.
Feel, e haha aku.
Feign, e hoopunipuni.
Fe-li-ci-ty, he oluolu no ka pomaikai.
Fell, ua hina, ua haule.
Fel-low, he hoa.
Fe-male, wahine.
Fence, he pa, pa pohaku, pa laau.
Fer-ment, ka hu ana, ka pii ana.
Fern, he mea ulu ano amaumau.
Fe-ro-cious, hihiu, hihiu hae.
Fer-tile, momona me he lepo la.
Fer-vent, e wela, mahana nui.
Fes-ter, e akoako ka wai maloko o ka eha.
Fetch, e kii aku, e lawe mai.
Fet-id, pilau, hauna.
Feud, he ku e, he hakaka.
Fe-ver, he wela, he kuni.
Few, kakaikahi, he uuku.
Fi-bre, he olona, he kaula liilii.
Fick-le, he manao lolelua, paa ole.
Fierce, he hae me he ilio la.
Fif-teen, he umikumamalima.
Fifth, ka lima.
Fif-tieth, ke kanalima.
Fif-ty, kanalima.
Fig, he fiku, he hua ai.
Fight, e hakaka, e paio.
Fig-ure, he hoailona helu, he helehelena.
File, he apuapu.
Fill, e hoopiha.
Filth, he opala pilau, he lepo ino.
Fi-nal, ka hope loa, ka pau ana.
Find, e loaa ma ka imi.
Fine, he makalii, uuku.
Fin-ger, manamana lima.
Fin-ish, e hoopau.
Fire, he ahi.
Fire (a gun), e ki pu.
Fire-shov-el, he kope ahi.
Fire-wood, wahie.
Firm, paa, naue ole.
First, ka mua.
First-born, ka hanau mua, he makahiapo.
Fish, he ia.
Fish (to), e hopu i ka ia, e kalawaia.
Fish-hook, makau.
Fish-er-man, he kalawaia.
Fis-sure, he wahi naha, he maawe.
Fit, he mai e popilikia ai ke kino.
Five, elima.
Fix, e hoopaa, e paa mau.
Flab-by, alualu, palupalu.
Flag, he hae, he hoailona o ke aupuni.
Flame, he lapalapa ahi.
Flank, ka aoao.
Flan-nel, he lole hulu hipa.
Flap, e kapalili, e kilepalepa.
Flat, lahilahi, honua, iliwai.
Flat-ter, e hoomalimali.
Fla-vor, ke ano o ka honi o ka ai paha.
Flaw, he naha, he kina.
Flay, e lole i ka ili.

Flea, he ukulele.
Flee, e holo aku, e mahuka.
Fleet, he ulu moku.
Fleet, mama.
Flesh, he io.
Flex-i-ble, e hiki ke peluia.
Flinch, e hoohalahala, e hooemi iho.
Fling, e nou aku.
Flint, he pohaku paakiki.
Flirt, e hoomahie.
Float, e lana aku.
Flock, he auna manu, he poe.
Flog, e hahau, e haua.
Flood, he waikahe nui, kaiakahinalii.
Floun-der, e kupaka.
Flour-ish, e ulu nui.
Flow, e kahe me he wai la.
Flower, he pua mohola.
Flu-ent, makaukau i ka olelo.
Flu-id, hehee, kahe me he wai la.
Flute, he ohi kani mele.
Fly, he nalo.
Fly, e lele me he manu la.
Foam, he huwahuwa.
Foe, he mea ku e, he enemi.
Fog, ohu.
Fold, e opiopi, e opi me he kapa la.
Fold, he pa hipa.
Fol-low, e ukali, hahai.
Fol-low-er, he mea hahai ana, haumana.
Fol-ly, he lapuwale.
Fond, e launa ana, a aloha ana.
Food, he ai, he mea e ai ai.
Fool, he mea naaupo, he aia.
Foot, he wawae, he kapuai.
Foot-path, ke ala e hele wawae ai.
For, i, no, na.
For-age, he ai no na holoholona.
For-bear, e oki ae i kahi hana, e alia.
For-bid, e papa aku, e hoole.
Force, he ikaika.
Ford, he wai papau.
Fore-fin-ger, ke manamana lima mua.
Fore-go, e waiho wale, e haalele.
Fore-head, ka lae.
For-eign, he mea kahiki mai.
Fore-land, he aina e oi ana i ka kai.
Fore-most, ka mea e oi e mamua.
Fore-noon, mamua ae o ke awakea.
For-est, he ulu laau.
Fore-tell, e hai e mamua, e wanana.
For-get, e hoopoina.
For-give, e kala i ka hewa.
Fork, he o manamana.
Fork-ed, he mahele manamana ia.
For-lorn, he poino, he nele.
Form, ano owaho, he ano kino.
For-mer-ly, mamua, i ka wa mahope.
For-ni-ca-tion, he moekolohe.
For-sake, e haalele.
Fort, he papu.
For-ti-tude, he manao ku paa, makau ole.
For-tu-nate, pomaikai.
For-ty, kanaha.
Fos-ter, e malama, e hanai.

Foul, eka, paumaele.
Foun-da-tion, ke kumu, ka mole.
Found-er, ka mea e hookumu aku.
Foun-tain, he punawai, kahi e piipii ai ka wai.
Four, aha, kauna.
Four-fold, paha.
Four-foot-ed, wawae eha.
Four-teen, he umikumamaha.
Fowl, he moa, he mea lele.
Fowl-ing-piece, he pu ki manu.
Fra-gile, hikiwawe ke hoonaha ia.
Fra-grant, he mea ala maikai ke honi.
Frail, he palupalu, ikaika ole.
Frame, e kapili laau.
Fran-tic, he huhu loa, piha i ka huhu.
Fraud, he hoopunipuni, he hana epa.
Free, he kaawale, kuikawa, he ku okoa.
Freight, ka ukana o ka moku.
Fre-quent, pinepine, he mea mau.
Fresh, maka, mea hou.
Fret-ful, he walea ole, he uwe wale.
Friend, he makamaka, he hoa launa.
Fright-en, e hoomakau, hooweliweli.
Fright, he hikilele, he weliweli.
Fringe, ka aoao kapa i weluwelu ia.
Frisk, e lele me he ilio la.
Friv-o-lous, he ano paani lapuwale.
From, mai, aku.
Front, alo, ma ke alo, ka aoao mua.
Fron-tier, ka aoao o ke aupuni.
Froth, he huwa.
Frown, he hookuekue o ka maka.
Fru-gal, he malama waiwai ana.
Fruit, hua, he mea ulu i mea ai.
Fruit-less-ly, he hana inea, hua ole.
Frus-trate, e hoolilo i mea ole, e keakea.
Fry, e hoomoa ma ke pa hao, e parai.
Fu-el, he wahie.
Fugh! ka! kahoho!
Ful-fill, e hooko, e hoopaa i ka olelo.
Ful-gent, he alohilohi.
Full, piha, maona.
Fum-ble, e haha, e hana hawawa.
Fun, he paani lealea.
Fur-bish, e hoohuali.
Fu-ri-ous, ukiuki, wela ka huhu.
Fur-ni-ture, he lako no ka hale.
Fur-ther, mamao aku, loihi aku.
Fu-tile, makehewa, lapuwale.
Fu-ture, ka wa mahope.
Fu-tu-ri-ty, ka manawa mahope aku.

G.

Gad, e hele i o ia nei.
Gain, ka mea oi ma ka loaa.
Gal-ax-y, ka leleiona, ke ala waiu o na hoku.
Gall, he mea awaawa iloko o ka opu.
Gall, e hooeha, e anai i ka ili.
Gam-bol, e paani lealea.
Gaol, jail, he hale paahao.
Gape, e hoohamama i ka waha.
Gar-gle, he wai laau e holoi ai i ka waha.

Gar-ment, he lole no ke kino.
Gar-nish, e hoomaikai, e hoonani.
Gar-ru-lous, he kamailio pau ole, alapi.
Gash, he oki ma ke kino.
Gasp, he mauliawa, he hanu paa.
Gate-way, he ala mawaena o ka puka.
Gate, he pani puka no ka pa.
Gath-er, e ohi, e hui pu.
Gaze, e haka pono.
Geld, e poa aku.
Gen-er-al, he alihi kaua.
Gen-er-al, pili i na mea a pau.
Gen-e-ra-tion, he hanauna.
Gen-tle, laka, oluolu.
Gen-tle-man, he kanaka noho a hana pono.
Gen-u-ine, maoli, kaawale i ka mea e.
Ger-min-ate, e ulu, e hookupu.
Get, e loaa.
Ghost, he lapu, he uhane.
Gid-dy, poniuniu, lanalana.
Gift, he makana.
Gill, ka mahamaha o ka ia.
Gim-let, he wili uuku.
Gin-ger, he awapuhi.
Gird, e kaei, e nakiikii a paa.
Girl, he kaikamahine.
Give, e haawi aku.
Glad, olioli.
Glare, e olinolino.
Glass, he aniani.
Glis-ten, e alohilohi mai.
Glob-u-lar, he ano poepoe.
Gloom, he poeleele, he naau kaumaha.
Glo-ri-fy, e hoonani.
Glow, e ula mai me he ahi la.
Glut-ton, he pakela ai.
Gnash, e uwi i na niho i ka huhu nui.
Gnaw, e nau.
Go, e hele, e nee.
God, ke Akua, Iehova.
God-li-ness, he manao i ke Akua, e haipule.
Gog-gles, he aniani uhi maka.
Good, pono, maikai, oiaio, hemolele.
Gore, he koko kahe.
Gore, e o aku i ka pepeiao hao.
Gorge, e ai nui, e moni okoa.
Gos-sip, he holoholo olelo.
Gov-ern, e hoomalu, e hooponopono.
Gov-ern-ment, ka hoomalu ana i ke aupuni.
Grace, he lokomaikai wale, he aloha wale.
Gran-u-late, e oneone.
Grap-ple, e puliki, e apo ikaika.
Grasp, e apo, e hopu.
Grass, he mauu, he weuweu.
Grate, e anai aku, e olo.
Grave, he lua kupapau.   [pau.
Grave-stone, he pohaku i kauia i ka lua kupa-
Grav-el, ka iliili.
Gra-vy, ke kai no ka io moa.
Greas-y, paumaele i ka aila.
Great, nui, nunui.
Greed-y, pakela ai.
Green, omaomao, maka.
Greet, e uwe aku, e aloha aku.
Grey-hair, lauoho ahina.

Grieve, e uwe, e kaumaha ka naau.
Grind, e anai, e wili.
Grind-stone, he hoana, hoana kaa.
Gripe, e lalau a puliki ikaika.
Gris-tle, he kumumu.
Grist-ly, he ano kumumu.
Groan, e kaniuhu, e uwe eha.
Grope, e hele haha me he makapo la.
Ground, he lepo, honua.
Ground-less, kumu ole.
Grow, e ulu, e mahuahua.
Growl, e hookeke, e ohumu.
Grub, he enuhe a me na mea like.
Grudge, e aua, e lili.
Gruff, leo haahaa.
Grum-ble, e ohumu, pono ole ka manao.
Grunt, e uhu me he puaa la.
Guard, e kiai.
Guess, e koho.
Guest, ka mea i hookipaia.
Guide, e alakai.
Guil-ty, hewa io.
Gull, e hoopunipuni.
Gul-let, ka puu, kahi e moni ai.
Gulp, e ai wikiwiki a moni okoa.
Gum, he pilali.
Gun, he pukuniahi.
Gun-pow-der, he one-a, he pouda.
Gut, naau liilii.

H.

Hab-it, he mea mau ma ka hana.
Hab-it-a-tion, kahi e noho ai.
Ha-bit-u-al, he maa ka hana.
Ha-bit-u-ate, e hana a maa.
Hack, e oki hawawa me ka lipi.
Haft, ke au, ke kumu o ka pahi.
Hair, ka lauoho.
Hale, ikaika, puipui.
Half, he hapalua.
Half-full, he hapalua ka piha ana.
Half-way, like alike ke ala.
Hall, he keena halawai.
Hal-low, e hoolaa aku.   [ana i ka la.
Ha-lo, ka ulaula powehiwehi e poai kaawale
Halt, e ku ka hele ana.
Halve, e mahele hapalua.
Ham-per, e hoopilikia.
Hand, lima.
Hand-ful, piha ka poho lima.
Hand-ker-chief, he hainika.
Han-dle, e lawelawe.
Han-dle, he au.
Hand-saw, he pahiolo.
Hand-some, maikai, nani ke nana aku.
Hang, e kau iluna, e li.
Hank, e owili ropi.
Hank-er, e makemake nui.
Hap-py, pomaikai, oluolu ka manao.
Har-angue, e hai aku i ka manao.
Har-bor, he awa, kahi e luuluu ai ka moku.
Hard, paakiki, oolea.

Hard-ly, he aneane hiki ole.
Hark, e lohe, e huli ka pepeiao.
Har-lot, he wahine hookamakama.
Harm, he poino, he hewa.
Har-poon, he o ka mea e hou ai ka ia.
Harsh, he lokoino, he kalakala.
Haste, he hiki wawe, he wikiwiki.
Has-ty, mama, wikiwiki.
Hat, papale.
Hatch, e kiko ka hua.
Hatch-et, he koilipi uuku.
Hate, e inaina aku.
Have, ua loaa.
Haugh-ty, he kiekie ka manao.
Haul, e kauo, e huki.
Haunch, he apana o ka io.
Hav-oc, ka luku ana.
Haze, he omalumalu.
He, oia (pili i ke kane.)
Head, ke poo, ka luna o ke kanaka.
Head-land, he lae.
Head-long, e haule ana ilalo ke poo.
Head-strong, uhu, hookuli.
Heal, e lapaau, e hoola.
Heap, he puu, he ahu.
Hear, e lohe, e haliu ka pepeiao.
Heart, ka puuwai, ke kumu o ke aloha.
Hearth, he kapuahi.
Heat, wela, wewela.
Hea-then, he naaupo, he ike ole ia Iehova.
Heave, e naenae, e pani.
Heav-en, lani, ouli.
Heav-y, kaumaha.
Heel, ke kuekue wawae.
Height, he kiekie.
Helm, hoeuli o ka moku.
Help, he kokua.
Helve, he au o ke koilipi.
Hem, ka pelu ma ka aoao o ka lole.
Hen, he moa wahine.
Her, ia oia (pili i ka wahine.)
Herd, he ohana bipi, puaa, hipa.
Here, maanei, ia nei.
Here-af-ter, ma keia hope aku.
He-ro, he kanaka koa loa.
Her-ring, he ia.
Hew, e kalai.
Hic-cough, he mauliawa.
Hide, e pee, e huna.
Hide, he ili bipi.
High, kiekie.
High-mind-ed, he naau kiekie, hookano.
High-wa-ter, he kai nui, kaikoo.
High-way, alanui.
Hill, he puu, he mauna uuku.
Hil-lock, he puu uuku.
Hilt, ke au, ka mea e paa ai.
Him, ia ia (pili i ke kane.)
Hin-der-most, ka mea hope loa.
Hinge, he ami.
Hint, e kuhikuhi maopopo ole.
Hit, e ku, e pili aku.
Hith-er and thith-er, i o ia nei.
Hoard, e hoahu.
Hoarse, leo ha, hanapilo.

Hob-ble, e hele oopa, e hele puupuu.
Hog, he puaa.
Hoist, e hapai iluna.
Hold, e hoopaa, e malama.
Hold! ua oki! hamau!
Hole, puka, he lua.
Hol-low, kaawale oloko, hakahaka.
Home, kahi e noho ai kekahi.
Hon-or, ka manao nui no ka maikai.
Hoof, he maiuu, ka wawae o ka holoholona.
Hook, he makau.
Hook-ed, ka mea i peluia me he makau la.
Hoop, he apo, me he apo pahu la.
Hope, manao lana.
Hor-i-zon, ka huina aouli.
Horn, he pepeiao hao.
Hor-ri-ble, he mea eehia, weliweli.
Hor-ri-fied, he mea i hoomakauia.
Horse, he lio.
Hos-pi-ta-ble, he hookipa malihini.
Hot, wela.
Hot-head-ed, ikaika ma kona manao iho.
Hov-er, e lele nui mai na manu maluna o kau-
   wahi.
House, he hale.
House-hold, ka poe ohua no ka hale.
House-hold-er, ka mea nona ka hale.
How? pehea? ma ke ano hea?
How-ev-er, aole manao i ke ano.
Howl, aoaoa, e uwe me he ilio la.
Hug, e puliki i na lima, e apo.
Huge, nui, nunui.
Hum, e hamumu.
Hu-mane, lokomaikai, oluolu.
Hum-ble, haahaa.
Hu-mid, pulu uuku, mau.
Hu-mor-ous, pili i ka lealea.
Hump-back, he kuapuu.
Hun-dred, he haneri.
Hun-ger, he pololi.
Hunt, e imi i ka mea i huna ia, e hahai.
Hurl, e nou, e hoolei aku.
Hur-ri-cane, he makani ikaika.
Hur-ry, e hana wikiwiki.
Hurt, he eha, he kina.
Hus-band, he kane mea wahine.
Hush! e kuli! e malie!
Hush-up, e hoomalie, e kulikuli.
Husk, e hemo i ka aa o ke kurina.
Hut, he hale uuku, hale ino, he kamala.
Huz-za, ka leo olioli, he aikola.
Hymn, he himene, he mele i ke Akua.
Hy-poc-ri-sy, ka hookamani.

I.

I, au, wau, owau.
I-di-ot, he hupo, he lola.
I-dle, noho wale, aole hana.
If, i, ina.
Ig-nite, e hooa, e kuni ahi.
Ig-no-rant, naaupo, ike ole.

Ill, mai, nawaliwali.
Im-age, he kii, he aka,
Im-ag-ine, e noonoo.
Im-bol-den, e koa, e makau ole.
Im-i-tate, e hana like, e hoohalike.
Im-ma-ture, pala ole, oo ole.
Im-me-di-ate-ly, ano, hoopanee ole.
Im-merse, e kupenu, e hookomo i ka wai.
Im-mor-tal, make ole.
Im-mov-a-ble, nauwe ole, paa loa.
Im-mu-ni-ty, he noa ke kapu.
Im-mu-ta-ble, hiki ole ke hoololiia.   [elua.
Im-par-tial, e hana like i na mea o na aoao
Im-pa-tient, paupauaho, pauaho.
Im-pede, e hoohihia, e keakea.
Im-pel, e hoonee aku.
Im-per-fect, paa ole, hemolele ole.
Im-pe-ri-ous, e hookiekie ana.
Im-per-ti-nent, maoi, mahaoi.
Im-pet-u-ous, e holo ikaika ana.
Im-plant, e kanu, e hookomo.
Im-plore, e pule, e noi aku.
Im-por-tune, e noi ikaika aku.
Im-pose, e kau maluna o kekahi mea.
Im-po-si-tion, e kau ana maluna o ka mea e,
   e hoopunipuni.
Im-pos-si-ble, he hiki ole ke hanaia.
Im-po-tent, he hiki ole, nawaliwali.
Im-pre-cate, e hoohiki paa.
Im-prop-er, pono ole, pololei ole.
Im-prove, e hoomaikai ae.
Im-pru-dent, malama ole, waiho wale.
Im-pu-dent, maka hilahila ole.
Im-pu-ni-ty, he hana hewa me ka hoopai ole.
Im-pure, paumaele, aole i holoi ia.
In, i, iloko, maloko.
In-a-bil-i-ty, he ikaika ole.
In-ac-ces-si-ble, hiki ole ke hookokoke aku.
In-ac-tive, hana ole, molowa.
In-ar-tic-u-late, he hai leo maopopo ole.
In-ca-pa-ble, hiki ole.
In-car-nate, maloko o ke kino.
In-ces-sant, mau, maha ole.   [ke mare.
In-cest, moekolohe o na hoahanau pono ole
In-cis-ion, he kaha iloko.
In-ci-sor, ka niho i puka mua mai.
In-cite, e hoala, e hoeueu.
In-clin-ed, e hio ana, aole ku pololei.
In-clude, e hookomo pu.
In-com-par-able, aohe mea like.
In-com-pat-i-ble, ku like ole, launa ole.
In-com-pe-tent, hiki ole, makaukau ole
In-com-plete, paa ole, aole hemolele.
In-com-pre-hen-si-ble, hiki ole ke ike lea ia.
In-con-gru-ous, e kohu ole ana.
In-con-sid-er-a-ble, aole nui loa.
In-con-sist-ent, kohu ole.
In-con-sol-a-ble, aole e hooluoluia.
In-con-stant, lauwili, paa ole.
In-cor-rect, hewa, pololei ole.
In-cor-ri-gi-ble, hiki ole ke hoopololei iho.
In-crease, e mahuahua.
In-cum-ber, e hookaumaha.
In-de-cent, maemae ole, pono ole.
In-deed, no, oia, hoi.

In-de-fat-i-ga-ble, hana mau, luhi ole.
In-def-i-nite, maopopo ole.
In-del-i-ble, hiki ole ke holoiia.
In-del-i-cate, kohu ole me ka maemae.
In-dem-ni-fy, e pani i ka mea i lilo.
In-de-ter-min-ed, he mea i kanaluaia.
In-di-cate, e kuhikuhi, e hoike.　　　　[elua.
In-dif-fer-ent, he lewa mawaena o na aoao
In-di-gent, ilihune.
In-dig-nant, huhu.
In-dig-ni-ty, he pakike, hoowahawaha.
In-di-rect, kapakahi, pololei ole.
In-dis-creet, aole hana me ke akamai.
In-dis-crim-in-ate, he hiki ole ke manao ma-
　waena o ka pono a me ka hewa.
In-dis-pos-ed, he manao ku e.
In-dis-tinct, maopopo ole, pohihihi.
In-do-lent, molowa.
In-dus-tri-ous, hana mau.
In-e-bri-ate, ona, he ona pinepine.
In-ef-fi-ca-cious, he mea hiki ole ke hooko.
In-el-o-quent, he hiki ole ke hai pololei.
In-ev-it-a-ble, ka hooko ka mea e pono ai.
In-ex-haust-i-ble, hiki ole ke hoopau ia.
In-ex-pe-di-ent, aole pono ke hanaia.
In-ex-pe-ri-enced, he maa ole, mea hou.
In-ex-pert, maa ole, naaupo.
In-fal-li-ble, kuhihewa ole ana.
In-fa-mous, he mea hoowahawahaia.
In-fant, he keiki, he keiki uuku.
In-fect, e hoolaha i ka mai lele.
In-fe-ri-or, malalo iho.
In-fi-nite, he hope ole, palena ole.
In-firm, ikaika ole, nawaliwali.
In-form, e hoonaauao aku, e hoike.
In-fringe, e haalele i ka ae like.
In-grat-i-tude, he aloha ole no ka lokomaikai.
In-hab-it, e noho ma kauwahi.　　　　[e hanu.
In-hale, e hookomo i ke ea i ke ake mama,
In-her-it-ance, he hooilina.
In-hu-man, he ku e i ka ke kanaka hana.
In-i-qui-ty, he hana kekee, he pono ole.
In-junc-tion, he papa ana, he olelo ao.
In-jure, e hana ino aku.
In-jus-tice, he paewaewa, he pololei ole.
Ink, wai eleele, he inika.
In-land, mauka, iuka.
In-land-er, he kuaaina.
In-most, maloko loa.
In-nu-mer-a-ble, hiki ole ke helu ia.
In-quire, e ninau, e emi aku.
In-sane, he pupule.
In-sa-ti-a-ble, aole maona, walea ole.
In-se-cure, paa ole, hiki ke ohemo ai.
In-sep-a-ra-ble, aole e kaawale, e pili pu.
In-side, maloko loa.
In-sig-nif-i-cant, ano ole, he manao ole ia.
In-sin-cere, aole oiaio, hookamani.　　　[hai.
In-sin-u-ate, e hookomo maalea i ka manao ia
In-sip-id, mananalo, ono ole.
In-sist, e koi aku, e kupaa ka manao.
In-snare, e hoopuni, e hoopahele.
In-so-lent, he pakike.
In-spect, e nana, e huli i ike.
In-spire, e hanu i ka makani.

In-sta-bil-i-ty, he paa ole o ka manao.
In-stant-ly, hiki wawe, emo ole, ano no.
In-stead, kahi o ka mea e ae.
In-sti-gate, e paipai, e hoala i ka manao.
In-sti-tute, e hoomaka.
In-struct, e ao aku.
In-stru-ment, he mea e hana ai.
In-suf-fer-a-ble, hiki ole ke hoomanawanui.
In-suf-fi-cient, lako ole, aole lawa.
In-sult, e hoonaukiuki, e hooino aku.
In-sup-port-a-ble, hiki ole ke hoomanawanui.
In-sur-rec-tion, he kipi ku e i ke aupuni.
In-ten-tion, he manao e hookoia.
In-ter, e kanu me he kupapau la.
In-ter-cede, e uwao ae.
In-ter-cept, e hopu.
In-ter-change, e lilo aku lilo mai.
In-ter-dict, e papa, e hookapu.
In-te-ri-or, iloko, maloko.
In-ter-me-di-ate, he wahi mawaena.
In-ter-min-a-ble, hope ole, pau ole.
In-ter-nal, ko loko.
In-ter-pose, e komo mawaena, e uwao.
In-ter-pret, e mahele olelo.
In-ter-ro-gate, e ui aku, e ninau.
In-ter-rupt, e hoopilikia.
In-ter-val, he wa mawaena.
In-ter-view, he kamailio.
In-tes-tine, ko loko.
In-thrall, e hoopilikia.
In-ti-mate, he hoa aloha.
In-ti-mate, e kuhi aku akaka ole nae.
In-tim-i-date, e hoomakau.
In-to, iloko.
In-tol-er-a-ble, hiki ole ke hoomanawanui.
In-tox-i-ca-tion, ke ona ana.
In-tract-a-ble, hiki ole ke aoia.
In-trep-id, he ano koa, wiwo ole.
In-tri-cate, i hoohihiaia.
In-trude, e hele ma kahi i noi ole ia.
In-trust, e waiho aku me kekahi.
In-un-da-tion, ka halana ana o ka wai.
In-vade, e komo ano kaua i ke aupuni e.
In-va-lid, he oopa, he nawaliwali.
In-vert, hoololi, e huli ka mua i hope.
In-ves-ti-gate, e huli a ike lea.
In-vid-i-ous, he manao lili iki aku.
In-vig-o-rate, e ikaika ae ana.
In-vin-ci-ble, hiki ole ke hoopioia.
In-vis-i-ble, i nana ole ia.
In-vite, e kono aku.
In-voke, e noi aku me he pule la.
In-ward, ko loko.
Ire, he huhu, he inaina.
Irk, e luhi.
Iron, he hao.
I-ron-ic-al, he ano lua.
Ir-re-cov-er-a-ble, hiki ole ke loaa hou.
Ir-ref-u-ta-ble, hiki ole ke hooleia.
Ir-re-me-di-a-ble, hiki ole ke lapaauia.
Ir-rep-re-hen-si-ble, hiki ole ke hoohewa aku.
Ir-re-proach-a-ble, he hoowahawaha ole.
Ir-res-o-lute, kanalua, paa ole ka manao.
Ir-rev-er-ent, manao ole i ke Akua.
Ir-ri-tate, e hoonaukiuki aku.

Isl-and, he mokupuni, he aina puni i ke kai.
Is-sue, he keiki, ka hope.
Itch, ka meau, puupuu, kakio.   [aku.
I-tin-er-ant, ka mea hele ia wahi aku ia wahi

J.

Jagg, he puu, kauwahi oi.
Jan-gle, e hakaka, e ku e.
Jar-gon, he olelo pohihi, he namunamu.
Jaw, he iwi a.
Jeal-ous, lili.
Jeer, e hoino, e nuku.
Jest, he olelo ano lua.
Jin-gle, e kani.
Jo-cose, he olelo e akaaka ai.
Jog, e hele malie, e pahu aku.
Join, e hookui, e pakui.
Joint, he hai, he ami.
Joke, he olelo e lealea ai.
Jos-tle, e hoohaalulu.
Jour-ney, he hele me he poe huakaihele.
Joy, he olioli.
Judge, lunakanawai.
Jug, he ipu lepo, he omole apu lepo.
Juice, ka wai mai ka mea ulu mai.
Jum-ble, e huikau.
Jump, e lele ma na wawae.
Just, kupono, pololei.
Jus-tice, ka pololei iwaena o kanaka.
Jus-ti-fy, e apono, e hoapono.
Jus-tle, e luliluli iki.

K.

Keel, ke kikala o ka moku, ka iwi kaele.
Keen, he maka oi loa o ka mea oki.
Keep, e malama, e kaohi.
Keep-er, ka mea malama.
Ker-nel, ka hua o ke kurina a he mea e paha.
Kick, e keehi, e peku.
Kid, he keiki kao.
Kid-ney, he puupaa.
Kill, e pepehi a make.
Kin, he hoahanau.
Kind, lokomaikai.
Kin-dle, e hoaa, e kuni.
King, he alii moi.
Kins-man, he hoahanau.
Kiss, e honi.
Kit-ten, he popoki opio.
Knee, ke kuli.
Kneel, e kukuli iho.
Knife, he pahi.
Knock, e kikeke.
Knot, he lala, he pona.
Know, e ike, e hoomaopopo.
Knuckle, ka puupuu lima.

L.

La-bor, e hana aku.

La-bor, he hana.
Lan-guish, e nawaliwali iho.
Lan-guor, he nawaliwali.
Lap, ka uha.
Lap, e palu, e palu aku.
Lar-board, ka aoao hema o ka moku.
Lard, he aila puaa.
Large, nui, momona, nunui.
Lar-ynx, kahi o ka a-i.
Las-civ-i-ous, he kuko ana.
Lash, he ili i hiliia i mea hahau.
Lass, he kaikamahine.
Last, ka hope loa.
Last, e hoomau a loihi loa.
Last-ing, e mau ana.
Laud, e hooapono, e hoonani.
Laugh, e akaaka.
Law, he kanawai.
Law-less, e malama ole i ke kanawai.
Lay, e waiho aku, e hanau hua me he moa la.
La-zy, molowa, palaualelo, hana ole.
Lead, he kepau kaumaha loa.
Lead, e kai aku, e alakai.
Leaf, he lau.
League, e hana kuikahi.
Leak, e kulu, e komo ka liu.
Lean, kaha ole, momona ole.
Lean, e hio.
Leap, e lele, e lelele me he lio la e lele i ka pa.
Learn, e ao, e hoonaauao iho.
Least, ka mea uuku iho.
Leath-er, ka ili holoholona i hooluuia.
Leave, e haalele aku.
Leave, he ae aku.
Leave-off, e oki! e hoopau!
Leav-en, he hu.
Leav-ings, na koena, na mea i haaleleia.
Lech-er-ous, kuko ana.
Leer, e hoomoe i ka pepeiao me he lio la.
Lees, na oka o ka waina a me na mea like.
Left, hema; *left hand,* lima hema.
Leg, he wawae.
Le-gis-la-tor, he mea hana kanawai.
Leis-ure, he kaawale, pilikia ole i ka hana.
Leis-ure-ly, me he hana wikiwiki ole la.
Lend, e haawi ia hai a mahope hoihoi hou mai.
Length, loa, ka loloa.
Length-en, e hoololoa, e hooloihi aku.
Len-i-ty, he lokomaikai.
Less, he uuku iho.
Les-sen, e hooliilii iho.
Lest, o, ina i ole.
Let, e ae aku.
Let-ter, he palapala hoouna.
Lev-el, he iliwai.
Lev-i-ty, ke ano akaaka lapuwale.
Lewd, e lilo ana i ke kuko.
Li-ar, he mea wahahee.
Lib-er-al, lokomaikai.
Lib-er-ty, he ku ole ke kanawai i kau wale ia.
Li-bid-in-ous, he manao nui i ke kuko.
Li-cense, e ae aku i kekahi hana.
Lick, e palu iho me ke alelo.
Lid, he poi no ka ipu.
Lie, he wahahee.

Lie, e moe ilalo.
Life, ke ola ana.
Lift, e hapai iluna.
Light, malamalama, he ao.
Light, mama, kaumaha ole.
Light-en, e hoomama iho.
Light-head-ed, e pooniuniu.
Light-ning, uila, ka uwila.
Like, like, e like me, pe, peia.
Like, e mahalo, e manao nui aku.
Like-ness, ma ke ano, he like ana.
Lim-bo, he pilikia nui.
Lime, he puna, he hua awahia.
Lime-tree, he laau lemi.
Lim-it, mokuna, ka aoao owaho.
Limp, he hele me he oopa la.
Limp-id, he aiai, he lepo ole me he wai la.
Line, he kaula, (fishing) he aho lawaia.
Lin-e-age, he ano mamo, he ohana.
Lin-ger, e lolohi, e lohi, e emi ihope.
Lin-i-ment, he laau mea hamo.
Lip, he lehelehe.
Li-que-fy, e hoohee.
Li-quid, he wai, e hee me he wai la.
Lisp, e hai pahemahema i ka olelo.
Lis-ten, e hoolohe.
Lit-tle, uuku, lii, liilii.
Live, e ola, e noho.
Liv-er, ke akepaa.
Liz-ard, he moo.
Lo! eia hoi! e nana!
Load, he ukana, he haawe.
Loaf, he popo berena.
Loathe, e hoopailua.
Lock, kahi lauoho o ke poo; he laka.
Lodge, he hale noho paa ole.
Lof-ty, kiekie.
Log, he kino laau nui.
Loins, puhaka.
Loi-ter, e lolohi, e emi ihope.
Lone-ly, meha, mehameha.
Long, loa, loloa, loihi.
Look, e nana.
Look-ing-glass, he aniani nana.
Loose, e kala, e wehe, e hemo.
Loos-en, e kala aku.
Loose-ness, he paa ole, he hii.
Lop, e oki me ka pokole ae.
Lo-qua-cious, he kamailio nui ana.
Lord, haku, alii.
Lose, e nele me ka lilo aku.
Loud, he leo nui ana, he ikaika ma ka leo.
Love, e aloha aku.
Love, he aloha.
Lounge, e noho wale.
Louse, (head) uku poo, (kapa) uku kapa.
Low, haahaa, malalo iho.
Low-er, haahaa iho.
Low-er, e hookuu iho.
Low-ly, haahaa.
Lu-cid, aiai, akaka.
Luck-y, pomaikai.
Luff, e huli i ka moku i ka makani.
Lug, e halihali i ka mea kaumaha.
Luke-warm, he mahana, aole wela.
Lull, e malie ka makani, e hoohiamoe.

Lu-na-tic, pupule.
Lungs, kahi e hanu ai, he akimama.
Lure, e hoowalewale ia hai.
Lurk, e hoomakaakiu.
Lux-u-ri-ant, ulu nui ana.

M.

MAD, hehena, pupule.
Mag-ni-fy, e hoonui, e hoomahuahua.
Mag-ni-tude, ka nui.
Maid, he wahine puupaa.
Maid-serv-ant, kauwa wahine.
Maim-ed, ua oopa, ua mumuku.
Main, nui, oi ana.
Main, ka ikaika; ka moana.
Main-tain, e malama, e hookipa.
Ma-jor-i-ty, ka nui, ka nui ma ka heluna.
Maize, he kurina.
Make, e hana.
Mal-a-dy, he mai.
Male, he kane.
Mal-e-dic-tion, ka hoino.
Mal-e-fac-tor, he mea hana ku e i ke kanawai.
Mal-ice, he lokoino ka manao.
Man, he kanaka, ka mea uhane.
Man-age, e hooponopono.
Man-gle, e oki weluwelu.
Man-i-fest, e hoike aku.
Man-i-fest, maopopo lea.
Man-i-fold, manomano, nui wale.
Man-kind, na kanaka.
Man-ner, ka aoao, ke ano.
Man-sion, he hale e noho ai.
Man-u-fac-ture, e hana akamai me na lima.
Man-u-mis-sion, e hookuu ana i ke kauwa i hooluhiia.
Ma-ny, nui loa, nui wale.
Mar, e hooino i ko waho.
Mare, he lio wahine.
Mar-gin, kaha, palena, aoao o ka lua wai.
Mark, he kaha, e hoailona aku.
Mar-riage, ka mare ana, ka hoao ana.
Marsh, he aina wai, aina pulu i ka wai.
Mar-vel, e kahaha.
Mash, e hoopepe iho.
Mas-sa cre, e luku, e hailuku.
Mast, he kia moku.
Mas-ter, he luna, he kumu ao.
Mas-ti-cate, e nau, e ai a moni iho.
Mat, he moena.
Match, he like, he hui like ana.
Match-less, he lua ole, aohe mea like.
Mate, he hoa, ka lua o na 'lii moku.
Ma-te-ri-als, ke kumu o na mea hana.
Mat-ri-mo-ny, ka mare ana.
Mat-ron, he makuahine.
Mat-ter, he mea kino, he male.
Ma-ture, he oo, he pala, he makua.
May-be, ae paha, e hiki paha.
Mea-gre, uuku, he wiwi.
Mea-ly, he okaoka liilii loa me he falaoa la.
Mean, he ano ino, he lapuwale.
Meas-ure, he ana e ana ai.

Meas-ure, e ana aku.
Me-di-ate, e uwao aku, e komo iwaena.
Me-di-a-tor, he mea uwao.
Med-i-cine, he laau lapaau.
Med-i-tate, e noonoo, e halalo iho.
Meek, akahai, he naau nohomalie.
Meet, e halawai pu.
Meet-ing, e halawai ana.
Me-li-o-rate, e hooluolu, e hoomama iho.
Mel-low, pala, palupalu.
Melt, e hoohehee.
Mem-o-ry, ka manao hoopaa i ka mea i ikeia.
Men-ace, he hooweliweli.
Mend, e kapili hou i ka mea i haiia.
Men-tion, ka hai ana, ka olelo ana.
Mer-ce-na-ry, he mea i hoolimalima ia.
Mer-chant, he mea kalepa waiwai.
Mer-ci-ful, lokomaikai.
Mer-ci-less, aloha ole, paakiki.
Mere-ly, maoli, wale no.
Me-ri-di-an, awakea.
Mer-ry, olioli, lealea.
Mesh, ka maka o ka upena.
Mess, he huina o na mea ono e ai ai.
Mes-sage, he olelo, he manao i hoounaia.
Met-al, he mea no ka honua mai hiki ke hoo-
  heheeia e like me hao.
Met-a-phor, he olelo nane.
Me-thought, manao iho la au.
Me-trop-o-lis, he kulanakauhale nui.
Mid-day, he awakea.
Mid-way, mawaena, like a like iwaena.
Mid-dle, mawaenakonu.
Mid-dle-a-ged, aole opio aole elemakule.
Mid-dling, aole oi aku aole emi iho.
Mid-night, aumoe, like a like ka po.
Midst, kahi mawaena.
Mid-wife, he pale keiki.
Might, ikaika, mana.
Mild, akahai, oluolu, malie.
Mil-dew, he ponalo.
Milk, he waiu.   [lani.
Milk-y-way, ka leleiona, he ala keokeo ma ka
Mim-ic, e hana like, e hoohalike.
Mince, e oki liilii.
Mind, e malama, e hoolohe.
Mine, ko'u, ka'u.
Min-gle, e hui, e hui pu.
Min-is-ter, he kahunapule, he elele.
Mi-nor-i-ty, ka poe uuku o na poe ku e elua.
Mint, he wahi mea ulu, kahi hana dala.
Min-ute, he hapa kanaono o ka hora.
Mi-nute, he uuku loa.
Mire, he lepo poho, lepo kelekele.
Mir-ror, he aniani nana, he kilo.
Mirth, he akaaka, he lealea.
Mis-be-come, ka hana kupono ole.
Mis-be-have, e kolohe, e hawawa.
Mis-car-ry, e owili wale.
Mis-chiev-ous, kolohe, apiki.
Mis-count, e helu hewa.
Mis-de-mean-or, e hana hewa aku ia hai
Mis-er-a-ble, he pilikia no ka hewa.
Mis-for-tune, he poino, pilikia.
Mis-give, he kanalua, he poho kahi manao.

Mis-guide, e alakai hewa.
Mis-hap, he wahi poino i hiki mai.
Mis-in-form, e hai hewa aku.
Mis-in-ter-pret, e mahele hewa i ka olelo.
Mis-lead, e alakai hewa.
Mis-spend, e uhauha waiwa
Mis-rep-re-sent, e olelo hewa aku.
Miss, e hala, ku ole ka pua ke pana ia.
Mis-sion-a-ry, he misionari, he elele.
Mist, he ohu, ua makalii.
Mis-take, he kuhihewa, he lalau.
Mis-trust, he paulele ole.
Mis-un-der-stand-ing, he kuhihewa.
Mis-use, e hana ino aku.
Mit-i-gate, e hooemi iho.
Mix, e kaawili, e hui pu.
Moan, e uhuuhu, e uwe aku.
Mock, e hoomaewaewa.
Mod-er-ate, e hoomalie, e hoomalili.
Mod-est, akahai, haahaa.
Moist, mau, pulu iki.
Mo-lest, e mea aku, e hoopilikia.
Mol-li-fy, e hoopalupalu.
Mon-ey, he mea dala, he hoailona waiwai.
Month, malama, he mahina.
Mon-u-ment, he kia pohaku.
Mood-y, he ano kaumaha ka manao.
Moon, mahina.
Moor, ka aina paapu i pohopoho.
Mor-al, pono, pololei ma ka noho ana.
More, nui ae, mahuahua ae.
Morn-ing, kakahiaka.
Morn-ing-star, ka hokuloa, hokuao.
Mor-row, apopo, ka la hou.
Mor-sel, wahi mea iki, he kuna ai.
Moss, he limu.
Most, he nui loa ke helu ia
Moth, he mu.
Moth-er, makuahine.
Moth-er-ly, ma ke ano makuahine.
Mo-tion, he nee, he hele, he kapalili.
Mould, he punahelu.
Mould-er, e popo aku.
Moult, ka haule ana o na hulu o na manu.
Mount, he puu, he wahi kiekie.
Mount-ain, he mauna, he kuahiwi.
Mourn, e kaniuhu, e ue.
Mouth, he waha, he nuku.
Mouth-ful, ka piha o ka waha, ka oolopu.
Much, nui loa, nui wale.
Mu-cous, he walewale, he hupe.
Mud, he lepo kaawili me ka wai.
Mud-dy, mea lepo, he ino.
Mul-ber-ry, he laau kilika.
Mul-ti-ply, e hoonui, e hoomahuahua.
Mul-ti-tude, na mea nui wale.
Mum-ble, e uu, maopopo ole ka olelo.
Mu-nif-i-cent, manawalea, lokomaikai.
Mur-der, he pepehi kanaka, ka lawe ole.
Mur-der-ous, ma ke ano pepehi kanaka.
Mur-mur, e ohumu, e hoohalahala.
Mus-cle, he io, he io huki.
Mus-cle, he wahi ia.
Muse, ke akua no ka mele ma Helene.
Muse, e noonoo nui me ka leo ole.

Musk-et, he wahi pu kau pohiwi.
Must-y, punahelu.
Mu-ta-ble, lauwili, lolelua.
Mute, paa, leo ole, kuli, aa.
Mu-ti-late, e oki aku, e hoomumuku.
Mu-ti-ny, he hana ano kipi.
Mut-ter, e namu liilii. [o na mea elua.
Mu-tu-al, hana mai hana aku, hana like iwaena
Muz-zle, e hoopaa i ka nuku.
My, ko'u, ka'u.
Myr-i-ad, lehulehu loa, manomano.
My-self, au iho, wau iho no.

N.

NAIL, maiuu, maiao, he kui hao.
Na-ked, olohelohe, kapa ole.
Name, inoa, he ano kaulana.
Nape, ka ami o ka a-i.
Nar-rate, e hai aku, e olelo aku. [olelo.
Nar-ra-tive, ka olelo e hai ana i kekahi moo-
Nar-row, haiki, ololi.
Nas-ty, haumia, lepo.
Na-tion, lahui kanaka, he aupuni.
Na-vel, ka piko o ka opu.
Naugh-ty, kolohe, ino, hewa.
Nau-se-ate, e liliha, e hoopailua.
Nau-ti-lus, he auwaalalua.
Na-vy, he ulumoku.
Nay, aole, aohe.
Neap-tide, kai make, kai mau.
Near, koke, kokoke.
Near-ly, kokoke, aneane.
Neat, maemae, mikioe.
Ne-ces-sa-ry, he ano nui ke loaa.
Neck, ka a-i.
Neck-cloth, he lole no ka a-i.
Nec-ker-chief, he lole no ka a-i, hainaka.
Neck-lace, he lei no ka a-i.
Need, he nele, he pilikia no ka ole.
Nee-dle, he kuikele, ke kuhikuhi o ke panana.
Nee-dle-work, he mea i hanaia i ke kuikele.
Neg-lect, e waiho wale, e malama ole.
Neigh-bor, he hoanoho.
Neigh-bor-ly, he launa ana.
Nest, he punana.
Net, he upena, he koko.
Neth-er, malalo.
Net-tle, he mea ulu oioi ka heu.
Net-tle, e hoohuhu, e o aku.
Nev-er-the-less, aka hoi.
Neu-ter, aole ia aole keia.
New, hou, kahiko ole.
Next, kokoke loa mai.
Nig-gard, he kanaka aua a pi.
Nigh, kokoke, aneane.
Night, po, wa poeleele.
Night-ly, kela po keia po.
Nim-ble, mama.
Nine, aiwa, eiwa.
Nine-fold, paiwa.
Nine-teen, umikumamaiwa.
Nine-ty, kanaiwa.

Nip, e umiki.
Nip-ple, he maka waiu.
No, aole, aohe.
No-ble, manao kiekie, ano hanohano.
No-bod-y, he mea ole, he kanaka lapuwale.
Nod, e kimo i ke poo, e kunou.
Noise, he leo, he haalulu.
Noi-some, he ino, he mea e poino ai.
Nom-in-ate, e hoike i ka inoa.
None, aole, aole kekahi.
Non-plus, he hiki ole, pohihihi.
Noon, awakea.
Noose, he pahele.
Nor, aole hoi.
North, he kukulu akau, he akau.
Nose, ka ihu.
Nos-tril, ka puka ihu.
Not, ole, aole, aohe.
Notch, nihomole.
Note, he hoailona, he palapala pokole.
No-ted, kaulana.
Noth-ing, he ole, he mea ole.
No-tice, e hooakaka, e hoike aku.
No-ti-fy, e hoike aku.
No-tion, he manao, he mea i noonooia.
No-to-ri-ous, kaulana, he ike lea ia.
Not-with-stand-ing, aka hoi, aole nae.
Nov-el, he mea hou, mea ano e.
Nought, he ole, he mea ole.
Nov-ice, he mea, he kanaka hawawa.
Nour-ish, e hanai, e kokua.
Nour-ish-ment, he ai e ikaika ai ke kino.
Now, ano, i keia manawa.
Now-a-days, i keia mau la.
Nox-ious, he mea e ino ai, he ino.
Nu-di-ty, he olohelohe, he hune.
Nui-sance, he mea e haumia ai, he pilau.
Nul-li-fy, e hoolilo i mea ole.
Numb, maele, lolo.
Num-ber, he helu, he heluna.
Num-ber, e helu; akahi, alua, akolu, aha.
Num-ber-less, hiki ole ke heluia.
Nu-mer-ous, he manomano, he nui wale.
Nurse, e hanai, e malama i ka mai.
Nut, he hua paa iloko o ka iwi.
Nut-meg, he hua ala, he hua laau.
Nut-shell, ka iwi o ka hua.
Nu-tri-ment, he ai, he mea e ikaika ai ke kino.

O.

OAR, he hoe waapa.
Oath, he hoohiki ma ke Akua.
Ob-du-rate, paakiki loa.
O-bey, e hoolohe, e malama.
Ob-ject, e hoole, e hoohalahala, e ku e.
Ob-lig-ing, lokomaikai.
Ob-scene, hilahila ke nana aku.
Ob-scure, powehiwehi, pohihi.
Ob-serve, e nana, e makaikai.
Ob-sta-cle, he mea e hihia ai, he alalai.
Ob-sti-nate, paakiki, lohe ole.
Ob-strep-er-ous, he walaau wale.

Ob-struct, e keakea, e alalai.
Ob-tain, e loaa mai.
Ob-tru-sive, kipa pono ole.
Ob-vi-ous, akaka, maopopo.
Oc-ca-sion, he kumu, he mea e pono ai.
Oc-cult, ike ole, huna ia.
Oc-cu-pa-tion, ka oihana a ke kanaka.
Oc-cu-py, e lawe hana, e noho hale.
O-cean, moana.
Odd, aohe mea like, lua ole.
O-di-ous, hoowahawaha ia, pono ole.
O-dor, he ala oluolu, he mea pilau hoi.
Of, o, a.
Off, aku, mamao, hele pela.
Of-fend, e hana ino aku, e hoohihia.
Of-fense, he hala, he hewa ku e i kekahi.
Of-fer, e haawi.
Of-fer-ing, he haawina, he mohai.
Off-spring, he ohana keiki, he hua.
Of-ten, pinepine.
O-gle, e awihi ke poo, e nana makaleha.
Oh! auwe!
Oil, aila, momona.
Old, kahiko, elemakule.
O-men, he ouli, he haina.
On, iluna, maluna.
Once, akahi, hookahi.
One, akahi.
O-ne-rous, kaumaha.
On-ly, hookahi wale no.
On-ward, mamua ae, imua ka hele.
Ooze, e kulu, e kahe malie.
O-paque, moakaka ole, he paa.
O-pen, e wehe, e hoohamama.
O-pen-hand-ed, lima hoomanawalea.
O-pen-ing, he puka hamama.
O-pen-ly, ma ke akea.
Oph-thal-my, he maka mai, makole.
O-pin-ion, manao.
Op-po-nent, he kanaka ku e mai.
Op-por-tune, kupono i ka manawa.
Op-pose, e ku e aku, e keakea.
Op-po-site, ka mea ku pono aku.
Op-press, e hookaumaha.
Op-tion, he koho ana.
Op-u-lence, he noho waiwa nui ana.
Or, he mea, a i ole ia.
Or-ange, he alani, he hua kahiki.
O-ra-tion, he olelo i haiia i mua o kanaka.
Or-a-tor, he kanaka hai pono i ka olelo.
Or-dain, e hoopaa i ka manao, e hoolilo no kekahi oihana.
Or-der, he hoonoho pololei ana, e kauoha.
Or-der, kauoha aku.
Or-dure, he pilau no ka lepo.
Or-i-fice, he puka liilii, he waha.
Or-i-gin, makamua, kumu.
Or-na-ment, he mea e nani ai, e kahiko ai.
Or-phan, he keiki makua ole, he huahaule.
Os-ten-ta-tious, he ano hoohanohano wale.
Oth-er, he mea e ae, kekahi mea e.
O-ven, he imu, he umu.
O-ver, maluna.
O-ver-aw-ed, i hoomakauia, ua hooweliweliia.
O-ver-cast, e uhi paapu ke ao.

O-ver-come, e lanakila maluna.
O-ver-flow, e kahe ae, e halana ae.
O-ver-hang, e lewalewa ae maluna.
O-ver-head, maluna ae o ke poo.
O-ver-look, e makaikai, e waiho wale.
O-ver-much, nui loa, nui a keu aku.
O-ver-plus, ke koena, ka mea keu.
O-ver-pow-er, e lanakila maluna.
O-ver-run, e lanakila, e hoopio.
O-ver-set, e hookahuli ae.
O-ver-shade, e hoomalu iho.
O-ver-sleep, e hiamoe loa.
O-ver-spread, e hohola maluna ae.
O-ver-take, e hele mahope a loaa no.
O-ver-throw, e hoohiolo.
O-ver-turn, e hookahuli.
Ought, e pono no.
Our, (dual) ko maua, ka maua; ko kaua, ka kaua; (plural) ko makou, ka makou; ko kakou, ka kakou.
Our-selves, ko maua iho, &c., *e nana iluna.*
Oust, e hemo, e kipaku.
Out, mawaho ae, iwaho.
Out-of, mawaho aku.
Out-cast, he mea kipakuia i ka aina e.
Out-cry, he wawa, he walaau.
Out-do, e hana a pakela ae.
Out-er, mawaho loa.
Out-let, he puka e hoopuka aku ai.
Out-rage, he hana kolohe loa.
Out-right, hikiwawe.
Out-root, e uhuki ae.
Out-run, } e oi aku ma ka holo ana.
Out-sail, }
Out-side, mawaho ae, kahi mawaho.
Out-ward, ma ka aoao mawaho.
Owe, e aie, e noho aie ana.
Owl, pueo.
Own, e lilo loa kekahi mea na kekahi.
Own-er, ka mea nona kekahi waiwai.

P.

Pa-ci-fy, e hoona, e hoolaulea.
Pad-dle, e hoe waa.
Pad-dle, he hoe no ka waa.
Pa-gan, he mea hoomana kii.
Page, he aoao o ka buke, keiki lawelawe.
Pain, he eha, he hui.
Paint, e hapala, e hooluu.
Pair, na mea elua i kaulikeia.
Pale, he mae ka hooluu ana, ke keokeo o ka mea mai, nanakea.
Pal-li-ate, e hooemi i ka hewa a uuku.
Palm, he loulu.
Palm, (of the hand) poho lima.
Pal-pa-ble, hiki no ke haha ia.
Pal-pi-tate, e kapalili, e pana.
Pal-sy, he lolo, he mai lolo.
Pal-try, inoino, pupuka.
Pan-der, he weawea, he kanaka ino.
Pang, he hui, he eha nui.
Pant, e naenae.

Pap, ka u o ka wahine, ka ai palupalu.
Pa-paw, he hei, he laau milikana.
Par-a-ble, he nane, he olelo nane.
Par-ade, e paikau me he poe koa la.
Par-a-lyt-ic, he loohia e ka lolo.
Par-a-mount, he oioi ae, he pookela.
Par-cel, he puolo uuku.
Parch, e papaa ke wela ma ke ahi.
Par-don, e kala ana i ka hala.
Pare, e kolikoli, e oki a hemo i ka ili.
Pa-rent, makua ponoi.
Par-ley, he olelo kike.
Par-ox-ysm, ka hoi hou mai ana o ka mai.
Par-o-quet, he manu omaomao.
Par-si-mo-ni-ous, he pi, aua.
Part, hapa, he apana.
Par-take, e lawe pu e like me ka mea e ae.
Par-tial, lawe kapakahi, he paewaewa.
Par-tial-ly, he hapa wale no.
Par-ti-ci-pate, e lawe like me kekahi poe.
Par-ti-tion, he paku e kaawale ai.
Part-ner, he hoa hana.
Par-ty, kekahi aoao o na kanaka, poe okoa.
Pass, e hele ae, e maalo ae.
Pas-sage, he wahi ala hele.
Pas-sen-ger, he mea hele, he ohua.
Pas-sing, he hele ae ana.
Pas-sion, ka eha o ka manao a o ke kino paha.
Past, ua hala, ua pau.
Pas-time, he paani, he hana lealea.
Pat, ku, makaukau.
Pat, he pai malie me ka lima.
Patch, he apana; he mala aina.
Pate, ke poo.
Path, he alanui, he wahi e hele ai, he kuamoo.
Pa-tience, he ahonui, he hoomanawanui.
Pat-ri-ot-ism, ka imi ana i ka pono o ke au-
    puni.
Pat-tern, he kumu e hana like ai.
Pau-ci-ty, uuku, he kakaikahi.
Pave, e kipaepae pohaku.
Paunch, ka opu a me na mea oloko.
Paw, e helu me ka wawae.
Paw, ka wawae mua o kekahi holoholona.
Pay, e hookaa i ka aie.
Peace, he wa kaua ole, he kuikahi.
Peak, kahi oi o ka puu, he wekiu.
Peal, he haalulu nui.
Pearl, he momi.
Peck, e kiko me he manu la.
Pe-cul-iar, e pili ana ia ia wale no.
Ped-i-gree, he kuauhau.
Peel, he ili i ihiia.
Peel, e hooihi i ka ili me he maia la.
Peep, e nana malu.
Peep, ka leo o ke keiki moa.
Peer-less, lua ole, pakela oi.
Peev-ish, huhu wale, na ole.
Pelt, e pehi, e nou aku i na mea liilii.
Pen-al-ty, ka uku hoopai.
Pen-dant, e lewalewa ana.
Pend-ing, e lewa ana.
Pen-e-trate, e komo iloko lilo, e hou.
Pen-i-tence, he manao mihi.
Pen-sive, he noonoo ana, lealea ole.

Pent-house, he hale hoopaa.
Peo-ple, na kanaka, he poe kanaka.
Peo-pled, he aina kanaka, paapu i kanaka.
Per-ad-ven-ture, ina paha.
Per-ceive, e ike, e hoomaopopo.
Perch, e kau ma ka lala laau me he manu la.
Per-chance, paha, ina paha.
Per-di-tion, kahi e poino mau ana.
Per-fect, paa, hemolele, aohe mea koe.
Per-fid-i-ous, malama ole i kana olelo iho.
Per-fo-rate, e hou i wahi puka me ka wili.
Per-force, e koi aku.
Per-form, e hana i kekahi mea.
Per-fume, he mea ala.
Per-haps, paha, ina paha.
Per-ish, e make, e lilo i mea ole.
Per-ju-ry, he hoohiki wahahee.
Per-ma-nent, he mea mau, aole pau koke.
Per-mit, e ae aku i hanaia.
Per-pet-u-al, he oia mau, pau ole.
Per-plex, e huikau, e hoohihia.
Per-plex-ed-ness, he hoopilikia ana ka manao.
Per-se-cute, e hoomaau, e hoohihia wale.
Per-se-vere, e hoomanawanui.
Per-sist, e hookupaa i ka manao.   [paha.
Per-son, ke kino o ke kanaka, wahine, keiki
Per-spic-u-ous, akaka, pohihihi ole.
Per-spire, e kahe ka hou.
Per-suade, e hoohuli ma ke ao aku.
Per-tur-ba-tion, ka aleale ana o ka moana.
Per-verse, paakiki hewa, kekee.
Pe-ruse, e heluhelu.
Pest, he mea kolohe, he mea ino.
Pest-i-lence, he mai lele, he ahulau.
Pet, he mea hiwahiwa, he punahele loa.
Pe-ti-tion, he noi, he pule.
Pet-ty, uuku, liilii.
Phan-tom, he mea manao wale ia, he lapu.
Phy-si-cian, he kahuna lapaau.
Phys-ic, he laau lapaau.
Pick, e wae, e ohi.
Piece, he apana, he hakina.
Pierce, e o aku, e hou.
Pig, he puaa keiki.
Pi-geon, he manu nunu.
Pile, he puu i hoopuuia.
Piles, he mai.
Pil-fer, e aihue i na mea uuku.
Pill, he huaale.
Pill (see peel.)
Pil-lage, e hao, e lawe wale.
Pil-low, he uluna.
Pim-ple, he puupuu ma ka ili.
Pinch, e iniki, e umiki.
Pine, he laau kaa.
Pine, e hokii, e iini nui.
Pine-ap-ple, he hala ai.
Pipe, he ohe, he ipu baka.
Pique, he hoohuakeeo.
Pish! kahaha! he leo hoowahawaha.
Pis-mire, he nonanona.
Pit, he lua.
Pitch, he kepau, he ta (tar.)
Pith, he iho.
Pit-i-ful, aloha, menemene.

Pit-saw, he pahi ololua.
Pit-y, he aloha menemene.
Pla-ca-ble, hiki ke hoolauleaia.
Place, wahi, kahi.
Place, e kau aku, e waiho, e hoonoho.
Pla-cid, oluolu, akahai, malie.
Plague, he mai ahulau.
Plague, e hana ino aku, e hoonauki.
Plain, maniania, maopopo.
Plaint, he leo u, he kanikau.
Plait, e opeope pono, e ulana.
Plan, e manao hoopono i kekahi hana.
Plane, he koikahi.
Plane, e kahe me ke koikahi.
Plank, he papa laau manoanoa.
Plant, he mea kanu.
Plan-tain, he maia popolu.
Plan-ta-tion, he aina nui i mahiia, he kihapai.
Plas-ter, he puna i pai pu ia me ke one.
Plas-ter, e hamo i ka puna.
Plat, he wahi papu iki.
Plaud-it, he hoomaikai ana, he hoolea.
Play, e nonoi, e koi aku.
Pleas-ant, oluolu.
Please, e hoooluolu, e hoolaulea.
Ple-be-ian, he kanaka makaainana.
Plen-ty, he walea, he mahuahua, he nui.
Pli-ant, e ae koke aku, e wili ka manao.
Plot, he manao e hoopuni, he ohumu.
Pluck, e unuhi, e uhuki.
Plug, he umoki, he pani no ka pahu.
Plu-mage, na hulu o ka manu.
Plump, nemonemo, piha, momona, puipui.
Plun-der, he waiwai i hao wale ia.
Plunge, e luu i ka wai.
Plunge, e hou iho.
Ply, e kulou iho i ka hana ikaika.
Pod, ka aa e wahi ana mawaho o na anoano.
Po-et, he haku mele.
Point, kahi oi, he welau, he kiko.
Point, e kuhikuhi.   [akuahanai.
Poi-son, he mea make ke ai ia a inu paha,
Pol-ish, e anai, e hoomaniania.
Po-lite, he ano pili ana i ka hooluolu.
Pol-lute, e hoopelapela, e hoohaumia.
Po-lyg-a-my, ka mare lehulehu ana.
Pomp, he hanohano.
Pond, he loko, he kiowai.
Pon-der, e noonoo, e hoomanao.
Pon-der-ous, he kaumaha, koikoi.
Poor, he ilihune, wiwi.
Pop, e poha aku.
Pop-u-lace, na kanaka, ka lehulehu.
Pop-u-lar, ku like me ka manao o kanaka.
Pop-u-lous, paapu i kanaka.
Pork, ka io puaa.
Por-poise, ka naia.
Port, he awa ku moku.
Por-tent, hoailona o ka poino e hiki mai ana.
Por-tion, he puu waiwai, he puu okoa.
Pos-sess, e paa lima ana, e lilo ponoi.
Pos-si-ble, hiki no.
Post, he pou hale, he laau ku, he elele.
Pos-te-ri-ors, kahi hope o kanaka, kikala.
Pos-ter-i-ty, na hanauna mahope, na mamo.

Post-pone, e waiho aku, e hoopanee.
Po-tent, he ikaika nui, he mea mana.
Pov-er-ty, he ilihune, he noho waiwai ole.
Pound, e paopao, e kuikui iho.
Pour, e ninini.
Pow-der, he one-a, he okaoka, he pauda.
Pow-er, mana, ka pono no ka hana i kekahi
mea.
Pow-er-ful, he ano mana, he ikaika nui.
Prac-tice, he hana mau.
Praise, e hoomaikai, e hoolanilani.
Prate, e olelo wale, e olelo ano ole.
Pray, e pule, e noi aku.
Pray-er, he pule, he noi.
Preach, e hai aku i ka olelo maikai.
Pre-ca-ri-ous, akaka ole ke ko ana.
Pre-cede, he hele ana mamua.
Pre-cept, he kanawai i kakauia.
Pre-cious, nui ka waiwai, makamae.
Prec-i-pice, he pali ku pololei iluna.
Pre-cip-it-ate, e hoolei ilalo i ka pali.
Pre-dict, e hai e mamua, e wanana aku.
Pre-em-i-nent, kiekie maluna.
Pre-fer, e koho e mamua o na mea e ae.
Preg-nant, ko i ke keiki, piha i ka hua, hapai.
Pre-pare, e hoomakaukau.
Pre-pos-ter-ous, lapuwale.
Pre-sage, e hoike mamua, wanana.
Pre-scribe, e kuhikuhi.
Pres-ence, ma ke alo pono.
Pres-ent, e noho hei, e ku nei.
Pres-ent, he haawina, he makana.
Pres-ent-ly, kokoke, aole liuliu aku.
Pre-serve, e malama, e malama o make.
Pre-side, e noho maluna.
Press, e kaomi iho, e hookeke.
Pre-sume, e manao, e kuhi.   [hookamani.
Pre-tend, e hooike wahahee me he oiaio la, e
Pret-ty, maikai ma ka helehelena.
Pre-vail, e lanakila, e laha a kiekie maluna.
Pre-var-i-cate, e hauhili i ka olelo, e lauwili
i ka olelo.
Pre-vent, e hookee, e keakea.
Pre-vi-ous, mamua ae.
Price, ke kumukuai.
Prick, e o aku, e hou.
Prick-ly, ooi, kuku.
Pride, haaheo, he manao kiekie.
Priest, he kahunapule.
Prime, he mua, he oi.
Prince, he alii opio.
Prin-ci-pal, he mea pookela, he mua.
Print, e pai, e pai palapala, e pai kapa.
Pri-or, mamua, hele mua ana.
Pris-on, halepaahao.
Pri-vate, ka noho ana o ke kanaka oia iho
wale no, ka waiwai ponoi o ke kanaka.
Priv-i-lege, he mea i ae ia, he oihana.
Priv-y, malie, e ike malu ana.
Prob-a-ble, oiaio paha.
Pro-ba-tion, he hoao ana i ka oiaio.
Prob-i-ty, he pololei, he oiaio.
Pro-ceed, e hele aku.
Pro-claim, e hai aku, e kukala aku.

Pro-cras-ti-nate, e hoopanee.
Pro-cure, e loaa.
Prod-i-gal, hoomaunauna, hooleilei wale.
Pro-di-gious, nui loa, kupanaha.
Pro-duce, e hoohua, e loaa ma ka hana.
Pro-duc-tive, e pono ke hoohua.
Pro-fane, e hoolilo i ka mea laa i mea laa ole, e hoohaumia.
Pro-fane, e hoohiki ino.
Prof-fer, e haawi aku.
Pro-fi-cient, he makaukau i kahi hana.
Prof-it, ka waiwai i loaa.
Pro-found, hohonu, naauao loa.
Pro-ge-ny, he poe mamo, he poe hanau hope.
Prog-nos-ti-cate, e hoike e mamua i ka mea e hiki mai ana.
Pro-hib-it, e hookapu, e papa.
Pro-ject, he manao ma ke kumu o ka hana.
Pro-ject, e hooi aku iwaho.
Pro-lif-ic, e hua nui ana.
Pro-lix, loloa, hooluhi no ka loloa ana.
Pro-long, e hooloihi ae.
Prom-i-nent, maopopo, oi.
Pro-mis-cu-ous, huikau, huiia.
Prom-ise, he olelo ae hooko.   [he lae.
Prom-on-to-ry, he aina pali e oi ana i ke kai,
Pro-mote, e kokua mamuli o kekahi hana.
Prompt, makaukau.
Pro-mul-gate, e hoolaha, e hoike akea.
Prone, kulou ana imua.
Pro-nounce, e puana, e hai akaka aku.
Proof, he hooiaio ana, he mea e maopopo ai.
Prop, he kia, he koo, he paepae.
Prop-a-gate, e hoolaha aku.
Pro-pel, e pahu aku, e hooholo imua.
Prop-er, kupono, ku like, ponoi.
Prop-er-ty, waiwai ponoi, ano ponoi.
Proph-e-cy, he wanana, he hai e mamua.
Pro-pin-qui-ty, he kokoke ana.
Pro-pi-tiate, e hoolaulea, e hookalahala.
Pro-pi-tious, lokomaikai, laulea.
Pro-por-tion, he like ana, he kuleana like.
Pro-pri-e-tor, ka mea nona kekahi mea.
Pros-e-cute, e hahai aku i mea e loaa ai.
Pros-per-ous, e noho pomaikai ana.
Pros-ti-tute, e hoohuli hewa, e hoohaumia.
Pros-trate, e moe ana ilalo.
Pro-tect, e malama, e hoomalu.
Pro-test, e hoohiki ku e, e hoole aku.
Pro-tract, e hoopanee i ka manawa.
Pro-trude, e hooi aku, e hoopuka aku.
Pro-tu-ber-ance, he puu, he mea oi.
Proud, he manao kiekie ana.
Prove, e hoao a ike, e hoomaopopo.
Prov-erb, he olelo pokopoko a nui nae ke ano.
Pro-vide, e hana a makaukau e.
Pro-vis-ion, he ai i hoahuia.
Pro-voke, e honaukiuki, e hoala huhu.
Prox-im-i-ty, he kokoke ana.
Prox-y, he pani no ka mea nalowale.
Pru-dent, hoopono, he noonoo.
Pshaw! he olelo hoowahawaha, ka!
Pub-lic, i mua o na kanaka a pau.
Pub-lish, e hoike ma ke akea.
Puck-er, he pukapuka, he alu.

Pu-er-ile, ma ke ano kamalii.
Puff, he puhi ana.
Puff, e hoomaikai wale, e haanou.
Pug-na-cious, makemake e hakaka.
Puke, e luai, e hoowa.
Pull, e huki, e kauo.
Pulp, ka io o ka hua.
Pul-pit, he awai kahi e hai ai i ka olelo.
Pulse, ka pana.
Pul-ver-ize, e hoowali a okaoka liilii.
Pun-gent, oi, awahia.
Pun-ish, e hoopai.
Pun-ish-ment, ka hoopai ana.
Pu-ny, liilii, nawaliwali.
Pup, he keiki ilio.
Pu-pil, he haumana.
Pup-py, he keiki ilio.
Pur-chase, e kuai lilo mai.
Pure, maemae.
Purge, e holoi, e hoomaemae.
Pur-loin, e lawelawe, e aihue.   [kue poni.
Pur-ple, he ulaula i paipuia me ka eleele, ma-
Pur-port, ka ano.
Pur-pose, ka manao e hana.
Pur-sue, e hahai mahope.
Pur-u-lent, e pala hehee ana.
Push, e pahu aku, e koo aku.
Push-ing, e pahu ana, e hooneenee ana.
Pu-sil-lan-i-mous, he makau wale.
Pus-tule, he puupuu ma ka ili.
Pus-tu-lous, ma ke ano puupuu ili.
Put, e kau, e waiho.
Pu-tri-fy, e palaho, e popo.
Puz-zle, he pilikia i ka manao.

Q.

QUAD-RU-PED, he holoholona wawae eha.
Quake, e haalulu, e nawe.
Qual-i-fy, e hoomakaukau.   [e ae.
Qual-i-ty, kekahi ano, he like ole me ka mea
Quan-ti-ty, ka nui, ke kaumaha.
Quar-rel, he ku e, he hakaka, he paio.
Quar-ter, he hapaha o kekahi mea.
Quar-ter, e mahele i eha hapa like.
Quash, e hoopau.
Queen, he alii wahine.
Quell, e hoopau, e hooloulu.
Quench, e kinai, e hoopio (i ke ahi.)
Quer-u-lous, he ohumu mau ana.
Que-ry, he ninau.
Quest, ka imi ana, ka huli ana.
Ques-tion, he ninau, he niele.
Quick, e wiki, e hikiwawe.
Quick-lime, he puna moa i hoohu ole ia.
Qui-et, maha, malie, na.
Qui-et, e hoona, e hoomalie.
Quill, he hulu.
Quit, e hooki, e haalele, uoki.
Quite, loa, paa.
Quit-tance, e haalele ana, e hooki ana.
Quiv-er, he aa no na pua, he eke pua.
Quiv-er, he haalulu, he eehia.

Quo-ta-tion, ka olelo a hai i lawe pono ia.

R.

RAB-BI, he kumuao Iudaio.
Rab-id, huhu, haehae, hehena.
Race, he hahai ana, he holokiki ana.
Ra-di-ant, he hoopuka malamalama, olinolino.
Raft, he huina papa e lana ana i ka wai.
Raf-ter, he oa hale.
Rag, he welu kapa, welu lole.
Rage, e enaena, e wela ka huhu.
Rag-ged, he weluwelu ke kapa.
Rail, he laau kaola o ka pa laau.
Rail, e kuamuamu aku ia hai.
Rail-le-ry, he olelo henehene.
Rain, he ua.
Rain-bow, he anuenue.
Raise, e hapai iluna, e hoala ae.
Ral-ly, e hoouluulu i na koa i puehu i ke kaua.
Ram-ble, e hele i o ia nei.
Ran-cor, he inaina, he manao hoino.
Ran-dom, he hana wale, he hana kumu ole.
Range, he wahi i hoopuniia.
Rank, he ku papa ana, he hanohano alii.
Ran-kle, he palahehee me he mai la.
Ran-sack, e huli ikaika ma kauwahi.
Ran-som, he uku hoola i na pio.
Rap, e kikeke, e pai.
Rap-id, holokiki, kahe ikaika.
Rare, kakaikahi loa, moa hapa.
Ras-cal, he kanaka hana hoopunipuni.
Rase, e hokai.
Rash, he hana wikiwiki me ka noonoo ole.
Rasp, he apuapu kalakala.
Rat, he iole nui.
Ra-tan, he ohe mea kookoo.
Rath-er, e aho.
Rat-i-fy, e hooko i ke kuikahi.
Rat-tle, he mea kanikani.
Rav-age, e hao wale, e lawe waiwai pio.
Rave, e walaau ae me ka huhu.
Rav-el, e wehewehe i ka mea i ulanaia.
Rav-ish, e moekolohe me ka limaikaika.
Raw, maka, moa ole.
Raze, e hoohiolo, e wawahi.
Ra-zor, he pahi umiumi.
Reach, e kiko aku, e o aku, e lalau.
Read, e heluhelu.
Read-y, makaukau.
Real, maoli, he oiaio.
Rear, ka hope.   [la.
Rear, e ku iluna ma na wawae hope me he lio
Rea-son, he kumu o ka manao.
Re-as-sem-ble, e akoakoa hou.
Reb-el, he kanaka kipi i ke aupuni.
Re-buke, e ao ikaika ana.
Re-cant, e mihi a e hoopau i ka manao.
Re-ceive, e lawe i ka mea i haawiia.
Re-cent, he mea hou.
Re-cip-ro-cal, kekahi i kekahi.
Re-cite, e hai waha i ka mea i paanaau ia.
Reck-less, noonoo ole, manao ole.

Reck-on, e hoouluulu ma na hua helu.
Re-cline, e hilinai, e moe iki.
Rec-og-nize, e ike me ka poina ole.
Rec-ol-lect, e hoomanao, e hoala manao.
Rec-om-mend, e hoike aku he maikai.
Rec-om-pense, he uku.
Rec-on-cile, e hoolaulea.
Re-cov-er, e loaa hou i kekahi mea i lilo.
Re-count, e hoike liilii a pau.   [mua.
Re-cre-ate, e hana hou i ka mea i hanaia ma-
Re-crim-in-ate, e hoohewa aku i ka mea i hoo-
    hewa mai.
Rec-ti-fy, e hooponopono.
Red, he ulaula.
Re-deem, e uku hoola, e hoopanai.
Re-dress, e hoopuka i ka pilikia.
Re-duce, e hooemi iho, e mahele i uuku iho.
Re-dund-ant, he keu wale ana.
Reed, he ohe.
Reek, e punohu i ka mahu.
Reel, he hikaka.
Re-fer, e kuhikuhi aku.   [me he aniani la.
Re-flect, e noonoo, e hoihoi hou mai i ke aka
Re-flux, ka mimiki ana aku o ke kai hohonu.
Re-form, e hana hou a pono.
Re-frac-to-ry, ku e, hele kekee, hookuli.
Re-frain, e hookaawale, e pakiko.
Ref-uge, he puuhonua, he wahi e pakele ai.
Ref-use, he opala, he koena opala.
Re-fuse, e hoole, e ae ole.
Re-gard, he malama ana, he makemake.
Re-gion, he moku aina.
Re-gret, e minamina, e mihi.
Reg-u-lar, ku i ka pololei.
Reg-u-late, e hooponopono, e hoopololei.
Re-hearse, e hai pakahi i ka mea i paanaau ia.
Re-ject, e hookuke, e haalele.
Reign, e noho alii, e noho aupuni.
Rein, he kaulawaha, he kaula paa lima o ke
    kaulawaha.
Re-joice, e hauoli, e olioli.
Re-join-der, he pane hou ana.
Re-late, e hai aku.
Rel-a-tive, he pili ana, he hoahanau.
Re-lax, e hooluolu, e hooalualu.
Re-lease, e hookuu aku, e wehe ae.
Re-lent, e hooluolu i ka paakiki.
Re-li-ance, e pili i kekahi mea.
Re-lieve, e hookuu, e hoomana.
Re-lieved, ua maha.   [hoomana.
Re-li-gion, he manao i ke Akua, he oihana
Re-lin-quish, e hookuu, e haalele.
Rel-ish, e ono, e honi ala.
Re-ly, e hilinai, e paulele.
Re-main, e koe, e noho hele pu ole.
Re-main-der, he koena.
Rem-e-dy, he laau lapaau.
Re-mem-ber, e hoomanao, e paa ma ka manao.
Re-mind, e paipai manao.
Re-miss, kapulu, nawaliwali.
Re-mis-sion, he kala ana.
Rem-nant, he apana koe.   [iho.
Re-morse, ka ehaeha o ka naau no kona hewa
Re-mote, mamao, loihi aku.
Re-mu-ner-ate, e uku i ke mea poho.

Ren-coun-ter, he hakaka.
Rend, e hoonahae, e hooweluwelu.
Ren-dez-vous, he wahi e akoakoa ai na koa.
Re-nounce, e hoole loa, e haalele loa.
Re-nowned, kaulana no ka maikai.
Re-pair, e hana hou a maikai.
Re-past, he ai ana.
Re-peal, e hoopau i kekahi kanawai.
Re-peat-ed-ly, pinepine.
Re-pel, e pale aku, e kipaku.
Re-pent, e mihi me ka haalele i ka hewa.
Re-pine, e minamina hooino.
Re-plete, piha, paapu.
Re-ply, e pane hou aku, e kike.
Re-port, e olelo hoikeike.
Re-pose, e moe malie, e hiamoe.
Re-pose, he hoomaha ana, he hiamoe.
Rep-re-hend, e ao me ka hoohewa.
Rep-re-sent, e hai hoike.
Re-press, e kinai, e hoopio.
Rep-ri-mand, e ao ikaika aku no ka hewa.
Re-proach, e olelo hoohewa aku.
Re-proof, he hoohewa ana.
Rep-tile, he mea kolo me he enuhe la.
Re-pu-di-ate, e hoole aku, e hoohemo.
Re-pug-nance, he manao ku e, ae ole.
Re-pulse, e kipaku aku e hoi.
Re-pu-ta-ble, manao maikai ia.
Re-pu-ted, he olelo wale ia no kekahi.
Re-quest, he noi, he hoike makemake.
Re-quire, e noi no ka hemahema.
Re-quis-ite, ka mea e pono ai no ka hemahema.
Re-quite, e hoihoi i ka mea like.
Res-cue, e hoopakele i ka pilikia.
Re-search, he imi ikaika ana.   [lena.
Re-sem-ble, e hoohalike, e ku like ka helehe-
Re-sent, e huhu, e ukiuki.
Re-sent-ment, he manao huhu.
Re-serve, e aua, e hoomaka mae.
Re-side, e noho paa ma kekahi wahi.
Res-i-dence, kahi e noho ai.
Res-i-due, ke koena, ka mea i koe.
Re-sign, e waiho i ka oihana o kekahi.
Re-sig-na-tion, ka hookuu ana i kahi oihana.
Res-in, he kepau ta.
Re-sist, e ku e, e pale aku.
Re-solve, e paa ka manao, e hookaawale liilii.
Re-sort, he aha kanaka, he wahi e akoakoa ai.
Re-sound, e kani hou mai, e kupinai.
Re-source, he kumu e loaa mai ai.
Res-pect, e manao pono aku, e mahalo aku.
Res-pire, e ha, e hanu.
Res-pite, ka hoopanee i ka hoopai.
Re-splend-ent, nani loa, hinuhinu.
Res-pond, e pane mai, e olelo kike mai.
Rest, he maha, he hiamoe.
Rest, ke koena.
Re-store, e hoihoi i kahi mua, e hoola.
Re-strain, e kaohi, e keakea, e hoopaa.
Re-sult, ka hua i loaa.
Res-ur-rec-tion, ke ala hou ana.
Re-tain, e kaohi, e hoopaa me ka malama.
Re-tal-i-ate, e hoopai aku e like me ka hana
    ia mai.
Re-tard, e hoohakalia, e hoolohi.

Retch, e hoolualuai.
Re-tire, e hele i kahi e.
Re-treat, e hookaawale i kahi e.
Re-treat, he wahi mehameha e noho ai.
Re-trieve, e loaa hou.
Re-tro-grade, hoi hope ana.
Re-turn, e hoi hou.
Re-turn, e hoihoi hou aku.
Re-veal, e hoike i na mea i ike ole ia.
Re-venge, e hoopai ino i ka hana ino mai.
Re-vere, e hoomaikai weliweli ana.
Re-verse, e hoololi.
Re-view, e nana hou, e huli e ike.
Re-vile, e hoomaino, e nuku, e hooino.
Re-vive, e hoi hou i ke ola.
Re-volt, e kipi, e malama ole i ke alii.
Re-volve, e huli me he kaa la, e noonoo.
Re-ward, e uku aku.
Rheu-ma-tism, ka eha o ka ami iwi.
Rheu-mat-ic, mai eha o ka ami.
Rib, ka iwi aoao.
Rich, he waiwai nui.
Rid, e kaawale ae.
Ride, e holo ma ka lio, ma ke kaa, a mea e ae.
Rid-i-cule, e hoowahawaha, e akaaka.
Ri-fle, e lawe pio i kekahi waiwai.
Right, e hoopololei i ka mea kekee.
Rig-id, ikaika, paa, naue ole.
Rig-or, he ikaika, paa.
Rim, ka lihilihi o keahi ipu.
Rind, ka ili mawaho.
Ring, e hookani, e o me he bele la.
Ring, he apo poepoe.
Ring-worm, he haukeuke, he kane.
Rinse, e hou iloko o ka wai.
Rip, e haehae, e nahae.
Ripe, ua oo, pono ke aiia.
Ri-pen, e oo, e hoopala.
Rise, e ala ae, e eueu, e pii.
Ri-val, he hoa ku e mai me he mau punalua la.
Rive, e honaha, e mahele i ka laau.
Riv-er, he muliwai, he kahawai nui lana malie.
Road, he alanui, he ala akea.
Roam, e kaahele wale, e hele i o ia nei.
Roar, he haalulu nui, e uwo.
Roast, e koala i ke ahi.
Rob, e hao, e kaili wale.
Ro-bust, ikaika, puipui.
Rock, he pohaku nui.
Rock, e hoolulululi.
Roe, he dia wahine.
Roll, e kaa, e olokaa.
Roll, he owili pepa, lole, &c.
Roof, ka uhi maluna o ka hale.
Room, he keena, he wahi akea.
Roost, he wahi e kau ai na manu.
Root, ka mole, ke aa o ka laau.
Root, e eku me he puaa la.
Rope, he kaula nui.
Rose, he pua laau, he rose.
Rot, e pala, e palaho, e hoi hou i ka lepo.
Rough, e kalakala, apuupuu.
Round, poepoe.
Round, a puni.
Rouse, e hoala, e hooeueu.

Rout-ed, i hooheeia me he poe koa la.
Rove, e aea, e kuewa wale.
Row, e ku lalani, he ku papa ana.
Row, e haunaele.
Row, e hooholo ma na hoe.
Rub, e anai.
Rub-bish, he opala.
Rud-der, ka hoeuli.
Rude, hawawa, naaupo.
Rue, he laau kanu awaawa.
Ruf-fian, he powa, he pepehi kanaka.
Ruf-fle, e hooaleale i ka ili o ka wai.
Ruf-fle, he pihapiha lole.
Rug-ged, kalakala, apuupuu.
Ru-in, he hookahuli ana, he hoohiolo ana.
Rule, e hoomalu aupuni, e hoopololei.
Rule, he laau mea hoopololei kaha.
Rum-ble, he kumumu, haalulu.
Ru-mor, he lohe wale, he lono.
Rump, ke kikala, ka hope.
Rum-ple, e hoominomino.
Run, e holo, e kukini.
Runt, ka mea liilii o ka ohana puaa.
Rush, e holokiki aku.
Rush, he kaluha, he mea ulu.
Rust, he popo, he kukae hao.
Rus-tle, e kawewe, e nakeke.
Ruth-less, aloha ole, menemene ole.

S.

Sa-ble, eleele, uli.
Sa-bre, he pahi kaua loloa.
Sack, he eke nui.   [enemi.
Sack, e hao wale i ke kulanakauhale o ka
Sac-ra-ment, sakarema, oihana hoailona eka-
   lesia.
Sa-cred, laa, kapu, hoano.
Sad, kaumaha ma ka naau.
Sad-dle, he noho lio.
Safe, palekana, maluhia.
Sage, he naauao, he noonoo pono.
Sage, he laau kanu.
Sail, he pea o ka moku.
Sail, e holo ae me he moku la.
Sake, he mea e pono ai.   [keia wa.
Sal-a-ry, he kumu e hoouku like i kela wa i
Sale, ka lilo ana i ke kuaiia.
Sa-line, mikomiko me he paakai la.
Sal-i-va, he kuha, he wale o ka waha.
Sal-i-va-ted, hookaheia ka wale o ka waha.
Sal-low, maimai, lenalena ma ka maka.
Sal-ly, he hoopuka nui ana mai kekahi wahi
   aku.
Salt, he paakai.
Salt, e kopi i ka paakai a miko.
Sal-va-tion, he hoola ana mai ka make ae.
Sa-lute, e uwe aloha aku, e honi aloha.
Same, oia hookahi no.
Sanc-ti-fy, e hoano, e hoolaa.
Sand, he one.
Sand-stone, he pohaku oneone, he papaakea.
Sap, he wai iloko o ka mea ulu.
Sa-pi-ent, naauao, akamai.

Sar-casm, he olelo hoohilahila.
Satch-el, he eke lawe buke a na haumana.
Sa-tiate, e maona, e hoopiha a maona.
Sat-is-fy, e hooluolu i ka manao.
Sat-ur-day, ka la hoomalolo.
Sav-age, hupo, lokoino.
Sauce, he inai ai, he olelo pakike.
Save, e hoola, e hoopakele.   [pakele.
Sav-ior, he mea hoola, o Kristo, ka mea hoo-
Saun-ter, e aea wale, e hele a hana ole.
Sa-vor, he hoalaala ana, he ala oluolu.
Saw, he pahi olo, he pahi ololua.
Saw-dust, he okaoka o ka laau i oloia.
Say, e olelo, e hai, e i.
Scab, he papaa maluna o ka eha.
Scaf-fold, he papa kiekie kahi e ku ai na paa-
   hana hale.
Scald, e hoowela i ka wai wela.
Scale, he mea kaupouna.
Scale, e pii i ka pa nui me he papu la.
Scale, he unahi ia.
Scalp, ka ili ma ka piko o ke poo.
Scam-per, e holo ikaika.
Scan-dal, he olelo hoohihia, he aki.
Scant, hapa, lawa ole.
Scar, he linalina o ka ili i moku i ka pahi.
Scarce, kakaikahi, hapa.
Scarce-ly, aneane hiki ole.
Scar-ci-ty, he manawa wi, ai ole.
Scare, e hoomakau, e hoopuiwa.
Scar-let, ulaula.
Scat-ter, e hoohelelei, e lu aku.
Scent, he hohono, he mea honi.
Scent, e honi, e hooala.
Scheme, he manao kumu hana.
Schol-ar, he haumana ao palapala.
School, he kula ao palapala.
School-mas-ter, he kumu kula kane.
Scis-sors, he upa oki uuku.
Scoff, e olelo hoowahawaha aku.
Scold, e nuku, e olelo huhu.
Scope, he kaawale, he akea.
Scorch, e papaa ka ili ma ka wela.
Scorn, e hoowahahwaha loa.
Scour, e anaanai, e holoi ikaika.
Scourge, e hahau i ke kua a eha loa.
Scout, he mea hele a hoomakaakiu i ka enemi.
Scowl, e hoomakainoino.
Scram-ble, e hopuhopu wikiwiki.
Scrap, he apana liilii, he hakina.
Scrape, e koekoe, e wau.
Scratch, e wauwau, e kaha ma ka ili.
Scream, e hooho me ka leo uwa.
Screen, e pale, e hoomalu.
Screen, he paku, he pale.
Screw, he mea nao wili.
Scrib-ble, e kakau wikiwiki me kau lalau.
Scrip-tures, ka palapala hemolele a ke Akua.
Scrof-u-la, he mai alaala ma ka a-i.
Scrub, e holoi ikaika.
Scru-ple, he kuihe, he haohao.
Scru-ti-nize, e emi ikaika i ke ano.
Scuf-fle, he aumeume ikaika.
Sculk, e huna ia ia iho.   [mahope.
Scull, e uneune, e koo i ka waa me ka hoe

Sculp-ture, ka oihana kalai kii.
Sea, ke kai, he moana, he ale nui.
Sea-coast, kahakai.
Sea-sick, ka liliha ma ka holo moku ana.
Sea-side, kahakai.
Sea-wa-ter, kai, wai kai.
Seal, he ilio o ke kai.
Seal, e hoopaa i ka wefa.
Seam, ke kuina o ka lole humuhumu.
Search, e imi, e huli.
Sea-son, he wa pono, he manawa okoa.
Sea-son, e hana a mikomiko.
Sea-son-ing, he mea inai, he hoomikomiko.
Seat, noho, he punee.
Seat, e noho iho, e hoonoho.
Sea-ward, makai.
Se-cede, e hookaokao aku.
Sec-ond, he mea kokua, he sekona.
Sec-ond, e kokua mahope.
Se-cret, huna ia, pohihihi, he hai ole ia.
Sect, he poe e kuikahi ana ka manao.
Sec-u-lar, ma ko ke ao nei aole ma ka lani.
Se-cure, maluhia, paa.
Se-cure, e hoopaa, e hoomalu.
Se-date, nohomalie, oluolu, kuoo.
Sed-i-ment, he oka, he maku.
Se-duce, e alakai iloko o ke hewa.
Sed-u-lous, kaamau ikaika ana, hoomau ana.
See, e nana maka, e hoomaopopo.
See! e nana! aia hoi!
Seed, he hua mea kanu, he anoano.
Seek, e emi, e huli iho.
Seem, e akaka ma ka manao.
Seem-ly, ku i ka pono.
Seine, he upena nui.
Seize, e hopu, e lalau koke aku.
Sel-dom, hiki kakaikahi.
Se-lect, e koho, e wae.
Self, iho, ponoi.
Sell, e kuai hoolilo aku.
Sem-blance, ka like ana, ke ano like.
Sen-ate, he aha kau kanawai.
Sen-a-tor, kekahi o ka poe kau kanawai.
Send, e hoouna, e hoolele.
Sen-ior, hanau mua, he hanau mua.
Sen-si-tive, hiki wawe ka manao.
Sen-su-al, ma ko ke kino.
Sen-ti-ment, he manao, he olelo pili.
Sen-ti-nel, he koa e ku kiai ana.
Sep-a-rate, kaawale, koukoa.
Sep-ul-chre, he hale kupapau.
Se-quel, e pili ana mahope, ka hope.
Se-rene, aiai, malie, oluolu.
Ser-mon, he olelo no ka ke Akua.
Ser-pent, he mooomole, he nahesa.
Ser-vant, he kauwa lawelawe.
Ser-vice-a-ble, ku i ka pono, e pomaikai ai.
Set, e kau, e hoonoho iho, e napoo iho.
Set, he mau mea e ku like ana.
Set-tle, e noho iho ma ka aina hou.
Set-tle, e emi iho malalo.
Sev-en, ahiku, ehiku.
Sev-en-teen, umikumamahiku.   [hiku.
Sev-en-ty, kanaha me kanakolu keu, kana-
Sev-er, e hookaawale i ka mea e kui ana.

Sev-er-al, he mau mea, mahuahua.
Se-vere, oolea, kaumaha, ikaika loa.
Sew, e humuhumu me ke kui a me ka ropi.
Shade, he malumalu, he aka.
Shade, e hoomalu, e uhi ka malumalu.
Shad-ow, he aka, he hoailona.
Shag-gy, paapu i ka huluhulu.
Shake, e lulu, e haalulu.
Shake, he lulu ana, he haukeke ana.
Shal-low, papau, ahua.
Sham, he hana hoopunipuni, he oiaio ole.
Shame, he hilahila.
Shame-ful, ku i ka hilahila.
Shape, e hana aku i ke ano.
Shape, ka helehelena o ke kino.
Share, he hapa o ka mea okoa.
Share, e puunawe i na apana.
Shar-er, ka mea lawe i kekahi hapa.
Shark, he mano, he ia nui, he kanaka epa.
Sharp, oi, ooi.
Sharp-en, e hana a oi.
Shat-ter, e wawahi liilii.
Shave, e kahi ae.
She, ia (pili i ka mea wahine.)
Sheath, he wahi no ka pahi a me na mea oi.
Shed, he hale malumalu maluna a hamama
     malalo.
Sheep, he hipa.
Sheet, he kihei moe.
Shelf, he papa e kauia'i na mea maluna.
Shell, he iwi mawaho o ka io.
Shell-fish, he ia mea iwi mawaho.
Shel-ter, he mea hoomalu, he mea uhi maluna.
Shel-ter, e hoomalu, e pale aku i ka ino.
Shelv-ing, e moe kapakahi ana, e moe hio.
Sherd, hakina ipu.
Shield, he paku e pale ai i ke kaua.
Shield, e paku pale aku, e pale ae.
Shift, e hoololi, e hoolilo.
Shift, ka hoololi ana; ka palule wahine.
Shin, ka lapa wawae.
Shine, e hoomalamalama.
Ship, he moku kiakolu.
Ship-wreck, he ili ana o ka moku a nahaha.
Shirt, palule no ke kane.
Shiv-er, e haalulu, e nahaha liilii.
Shoal, he ia paapu; he wai papau.
Shoe, he kamaa.
Shoot, e ki i ka pu, e pana i ka pua.
Shore, he kahakai.
Short, pokole, poko.
Short-ly, kokoke, emo ole.
Short-wind-ed, naenae.
Shot, he lu, he poka pu liilii.
Shove, e pahu aku, e koo mahope.
Shov-el, he oo palahalaha mea kiola lepo.
Shov-el, e kope a e hoolei aku.
Shoul-der, ka poohiwi.
Shoul-der-blade, ka iwi o ka uha mua.
Shout, he hooho olioli.
Show, e hoike imua o na maka.
Show-er, he ua naulu.
Shred, he apana liilii.
Shriek, e hooho me ka leo uwo.
Shrill, oi loa, kani loa.

Shrink, e emi iho a uuku.
Shriv-el, e emi iho a mimino.
Shud-der, e haalulu, e haukeke.
Shuf-fle, e hoololi wale, e lauwili.
Shun, e maalo ma kekahi aoao.
Shut, e pani a paa.
Shut-ter, he pani mawaho.
Sick, mai, maimai.
Side, aoao.
Siege, he hoopuni ana me na koa kaua.
Sigh, he hanu loloa, e uhu iho.
Sight, ka ike maka ana.
Sight-ly, maikai i ka nana ia.
Sign, he hoailona, he ouli.
Sig-nal, he hoailona hoike, kupanaha.
Sig-ni-fy, e hoike i ke ano.
Si-lence, he nohomalie, walaau ole.
Si-lence! e hoopaa i ka waha, e hoomalie.
Sil-ly, lapuwale, ano ole.
Sim-i-lar, like, he likepu.
Sim-i-le, he hoolike ana, he nane.
Sim-ple, akamai ole, makaukau ole.
Sin, he hewa, he ku e i ke kanawai, he lawe-
  hala ana i ka ke Akua.
Sin, e hana i ka mea ku e i ka ke Akua.
Since, mahope mai.
Sin-cere, oiaio, hookamani ole.
Sin-ew, ke olona ma ke kino.
Sing, e mele, e hoolea me ka leo mele.
Singe, e kuni a wela na hulu ma ke ahi.
Sing-er, he mea akamai i ka leo mele.
Sin-gle, hookahi, pakahi.
Sing-ly, ma ke ano pakahi ana.
Sin-gu-lar, akahi ana, kakaikahi.
Sink, e poho, e poholo, e emi iho.
Sin-ner, he mea lawehala, he kanaka hewa.
Sip, e hoao i ka mea inu, e inu liilii.   [paha.
Sir, he olelo pili i ke kane i ka mea nui a like
Sis-ter, he hoahanau wahine a na makua hoo-
  kahi.
Sit, e noho iho.
Site, he kahua, he wahi pono ke noho.
Six, eono.
Six-teen, umikumamaono.
Sixth, ke ono.
Six-ty, kanaono.
Size, ka nui ana o kekahi mea.
Skate, he hele pahee.
Skill-ful, akamai, makaukau.
Skin, he ili, he alualu.
Skin, e lole, e hemo i ka ili.
Skin-flint, he kanaka alunu paakiki.
Skin-ny, alualu, wiwi, ili wale no.
Skip, e hele me ka lelele, e lele iki ana.
Skip-per, ke kahu o ka moku liilii.
Skir-mish, he aumeume ana, he kaua iki.
Skirt, ka lihi o kekahi mea.
Skit-tish, puiwa wale, makau wale.
Skulk, e holo malie, e pee.
Skull, he puniu, iwi poo.
Sky, ka lani, ke aouli, ka lewa.
Sky-col-or, he uliuli e like me ke aouli.
Slab-ber, e hooluolu ai i ka mea inu.
Slack, alualu, nawaliwali, kapulu.
Slack-en, e hoalualu, e hoolohi.

Slan-der, e aki wahahee.
Slant, e hio, e moe kapakahi.
Slap, e pai ma ka poho lima.
Slate, he papa pohaku, he papa kahakaha.
Slave, he kanaka noho kauwa kuapaa.
Slaugh-ter, he luku, he pepehi nui wale.
Slay, e pepehi a make.
Sleep, hiamoe.
Slen-der, lahilahi loa.
Slide, e pahee, e pakika.
Slight, ololi wiwi.
Slight, e haalele, e hoowahawaha.
Slim, ololi, loloa.
Slime, he wale, he mea palupalu pipili.
Sling, he maa nou pohaku.
Sling, e maa aku, e nou pohaku i ka ka maa.
Slink, e pee aku me ka hilahila.
Slip, e pahee, e pakika, e hina.
Slip-per-y, paheehee.
Slit, he nahae.
Slob-ber, e kahe ka wale.
Slope, e waiho hio ana.
Slope, he wahi pii iki.
Slop-py, kelekele, pohopoho.
Sloth, he lohi, he molowa, he ano hiamoe.
Slov-en, he kanaka lole pelapela, a weluwelu.
Slough, he wahi poho, he nenelu.
Slow, lohi, hakalia.
Slow-ness, he lolohi, he akahele loa.
Slug-gard, he kanaka hiamoe wale.
Slum-ber, e hiamoe, e hiamoe iki.
Slut, he wahine hoopelapela.
Small, uuku, palanaiki.
Smart, wikiwiki, hana koke.
Smear, e hapala i ka lepo.
Smell, e honi; he ala.
Smile, e aka iki.
Smite, e hahau, e papai, e kui.
Smit-ten, hahauia, papaiia.
Smoke, he uahi.
Smoke, e puhi i ka uahi.
Smooth, pahee, laumania.
Smooth, e hana a pahee.
Smoth-er, e hoopaa i ka hanu.
Smut-ty, paumaele, paeleia.
Snail, he pupu o ka honua.
Snake, he mooomole, he nahesa.
Snap, e pana, e haki me ke kani.
Snare, he pahele e hoohei manu.
Snarl, e nana huhu me he ilio la.
Snatch, e hopu, e kaili aku.
Sneer, e aka henehene.
Sneeze, e kihe iho.
Snore, e nono, e hoho.
Snot, he upe, he hupe.
Snout, he nuku.
Snuff, he baka honihoni.
Snuff, e honihoni a komo i ka ihu.
So, pe, pela, peia.
Soak, e hoomau i ka wai.
Soap, he kopa.
Soar, e lele maluna.
Sob, e hauhau, e nae, e uwe.

So-ber, manao pono, aole ona.
So-ci-a-ble, launa, kamailio, oluolu.
Soft, palupalu, pepe, akahai.
Soil, he lepo maikai.
So-journ, e noho malihini.
So-lace, he mea hooluolu.
Sole, akahi, oia hookahi.
So-li-cit, e noi, e koi aku.
So-li-ci-tude, he manao nui ana.
Sol-i-ta-ry, mehameha, noho hookahi.
Solve, e hoakaka, e wehewehe.
Some, he mau mea, kekahi hapa.
Some-bod-y, kekahi kanaka.
Some-thing, kekahi mea, he wahi mea.
Some-times, kekahi manawa.
Son, he keikikane.
Son-in-law, hunonakane.
Song, he mele.
So-no-rous, kani moakaka ana.
Soon, wawe, koke, kokoke ka wa.
Sooth, e hoona, e hoolaulea.
Sooth-say, e hoopiopio, e hai wanana.
Soot-y, pili ka lepo uahi.
Sore, he eha ma ka io.
Sor-row, he eha ma ka naau, kaumaha.
Sov-er-eign, he moi, he kiekie loa.
Soul, he uhane o ke kanaka, he ea.
Sound, he haalulu, he kani, he leo.
Sound, e kani, e kui ae, e poha.
Sour, awahia, awaawa.
Source, ke kumu, he punawai.
South, he kukulu hema.
Sow, he puaa wahine.
Sow, e lulu hua.
Spa-cious, akea, laula.
Spade, he oo palahalaha.
Span, he ana o ka lima, he kiko.
Spare, wiwi, lahilahi.
Spare, e waiho, e hookuu.
Spark, he huna ahi.
Spat-ter, e kopipi i ka wai.
Spawn, na hua o ka ia.
Speak, e hai, e i, e olelo, e ekemu.
Spear, he ihe, he pololu.
Spe-ci-fy, e hooike i kekahi mea pakahi.
Speck-le, e kikiko.
Spec-ta-cle, he mea e makaikaiia ana.
Spec-ta-tor, he mea e makaikai ana.
Spec-tre, he uhane lapu.
Speech, he olelo i oleloia.
Speed, he holo hiki wawe.
Spell, e hookuikui i na hua.
Spend, e hookaa aku i ka waiwai.
Spew, e luai aku.
Spi-der, he lanalana.
Spill, e hanini iwaho.
Spine, ka iwi kuamoo.
Spi-nous, ma ke ano iwi kuamoo.
Spir-it, ka uhane, ka hanu, ke ea.
Spir-it-u-al, ko ka uhane.
Spit, e kuha.
Spite, e huhu, e huhu koke ana.
Spit-tle, he wale o ka waha, he kuha.

Splash, e nou aku i ka wai.
Splen-did, nani, hanohano.
Splin-ter, he hakina laau liilii.
Split, e mahele ma ka loa, e wahi.
Spoil, e hao wale, e hoonele i ka waiwai.
Spoil, he waiwai i lawe wale ia, a i hao ia.
Sponge, he huahuakai.
Spon-ta-ne-ous, ka makemake iho.
Sport, e paani, e lealea.
Spot, he wahi kina, he paumaele.
Sprain, he okupe, he hai.
Spray, he ehu wai, he ehu kai.
Spread, e hohola ae, e hoopalahalaha aku.
Spring, e lele, e lele iluna.
Spring, he wai mapuna.
Spring-tide, kai nui, kai piha.
Sprin-kle, e kapipi, e kopi.
Sprout, e kupu.
Spurn, e kipaku me ka inaina.
Spy, he kiu, he makai.
Spy-glass, he ohe nana.
Squab-ble, he aumeume, he hakaka.
Squal-id, he pelapela, weluwelu ke kapa.
Squall, e uwe aku me ka leo nui.
Squeak, he leo e like me ka iole.
Squeeze, e kaomi iho, e uwi iho.
Squint, e nana kapakahi ka maka.
Squirt, e kiki aku mai ka ohe ae.
Stab, e hou aku, e oo aku.
Sta-ble, paa, naue ole,
Sta-ble, he hale no na holoholona.
Staff, he kookoo, he mea kokua.
Stag-ger, e hikaka, e hele hikaka.
Stag-nant, lana malie, e kahe ole.
Stain, e kohu lepo, e hoohaumia.
Stair, he alapii anuu.
Stale, mananalo, liliha.
Stal-lion, he lio kane hoolaha.
Stam-mer, e olelo me ka namu, e nu.
Stanch, e pani i ke koko kahe.
Stanch-ed, he koko i paniia ke kahe ana.
Stan-chion, kekahi ano koo e paa ai.
Stand, e ku, e ku malie.
Stand-ard, he hae, he kanawai hoopono.
Star, hoku.
Star-board, ka aoao akau o ka moku.
Stare, e haka pono ka maka.
Start, e hikilele, e puiwa.
Starve, e make i ka pololi.
Stave, he laau no ka pahu.
Stay, e noho, e kali ma kahi wahi.
Stay, he kali ana, he alia ana.
Stead-fast, hoomau, paa mau.
Stead-y, paa, luli ole.
Steal, e aihue, e lawe wale.
Steam, he mahu.
Steep, palipali, nihinihi.
Steep, e hoomau i ka wai.
Steer, e hookele, e hoeuli.
Steers-man, ke kanaka ma ka hoeuli.
Stench, he pilau.
Step, he meheu, he kapuai, he hele kuku.
Ster-ile, pa, aole hua mai.

Stern, ka hope o ka moku.
Stern, he huhu ma na maka.
Stick, he pauku laau.
Stick, e pipili, e hou.
Stick-le, e hoopaapaa, e paio.
Stick-y, pipili, linalina.
Stiff, oolea, maloeloe.
Sti-fle, e puua, e uumi i ka hanu.
Still, malie, e kemu ole, nawe ole.
Still, e hoomalielie, e hoona.
Still-born, make i ka wa hanau.
Stim-u-late, e hooeueu i ka ikaika.
Sting, e o, e pahu i ka mea oi.
Sting, he mea ooi mahope o kekahi nalo.
Stin-gy, he pi, he aua.
Stink, e pilau, e hohono.
Stip-u-la-tion, he olelo ae like.
Stir, e oni, e neenee, e naue.
Stom-ach, ka opu naau.
Stone, he pohaku.
Stone, e pehi i ka pohaku.
Sto-ny, paaa, paapu i ka pohaku.
Stool, he noho kua ole.
Stoop, e kulou, e hele pupu.
Stop, e hooki, e oki i ka hele, e ku malie.
Stop, ke ku ana, he kiko hoomaha.
Storm, he ino, he makani ikaika.
Sto-ry, he kaao, he mooolelo.
Stout, nui, ikaika, paa.
Strad-dle, e kihelei ae.
Straight, pololei, pono.
Straight, ololi, pilikia.
Strand, he kahakai.
Strand, e pae wale iuka a kau i ke one.
Strange, kupaianaha, kamahao.
Stran-ger, he malihini.
Stran-gle, e paa ka hanu, e umi i ka hanu.
Strat-a-gem, he hana maalea e hoopuni ai.
Stray, e auwana, e aea.
Streak, he kaha onionio.
Stream, he waikahe.
Strength, he ikaika.
Stretch, e hooloihi aku ma ka huki ana.
Strew, e haalii, e hoolelei.
Strife, he hakaka, he aumeume.
Strike, e hahau, e papai.
String, he kaula liilii.
Strip, he mea weluwelu loloa.
Strip-ling, he kamalii aneane makua.
Strive, e aumeume, e hooikaika nui.
Stroke, he hahau ana, he kaha.
Strong, ikaika.
Strug-gle, e oni ae, e aumeume.
Strum-pet, he wahine hookamakama.
Strut, e hele hoohanohano, e haaheo.
Stub-born, he oolea, he paakiki ka naau.
Stub-by, poupou a puipui.
Stud-y, he ao ana i na mea e naauao ai.
Stum-ble, e okupe, e ku a hina.
Stump, ke kumu o ka laau i okiia.
Stunt-ed, he mea uuku ke kino.
Stu-pid, hawawa, manao ole.
Stur-dy, ikaika nui.

Stut-ter, e uu, e uuu.
Sub-due, e hoopio, e hoolaka.
Sub-ject, e hoolilo malalo iho.
Sub-merge, e hoopoho iloko o ka wai.
Sub-mis-sion, he ae ana i ka na luna.
Sub-se-quent, e pili ana mahope.
Sub-serve, e kokua mai ana mahope.
Sub-side, e hooemi iho, e mimiki aku.
Sub-sti-tute, he pani no ka hakahaka.
Sub-ter-fuge, he mea hoopuka kapakahi.
Sub-tle, maalea, lahilahi.
Sub-tract, e unuhi ae, e lawe i kekahi.
Sub-vert, e hookahuli, e hooauhee.
Suc-ceed, e ko, e kali, e hahai.
Suc-cess, he ko ana, he pomaikai.   [kahi.
Suc-ces-sive, e hahai ana kekahi mamuli o ke-
Suc-cor, e kokua i ka pilikia.
Suc-cumb, e ae aku, e hina malalo iho.
Such, e like ana, like me.
Suck, e omo ma ka waha.
Suck-er, he oha, he ia.
Suck-le, e hanai i ka waiu.
Sud-den, koke, emoole, hikiwawe.
Sue, e hoopii i ke kanawai.
Su-et, ke konahua.
Suf-fer, e hoomanawanui i ka eha.
Suf-fice, e hooluolu, e hana a nui.
Suf-fo-ca-ted, ua hoopaaia ka hanu.
Su-gar-cane, he ko.
Sug-gest, e hai iki i wahi manao.
Su-i-cide, he pepehi make ana ia ia iho.
Suit, he mau mea ku like.
Suit, e ku like.
Sul-ky, mumule, huhu maloko.
Sul-try, wela, mehana.
Sum-mit, kahi oi o ke kuahiwi.
Sum-mon, e kii aku ma ka lunakanawai.
Sun, la.
Sun, e kaulai i ka la.
Sun-day, ka la o ka Haku, he Sabati.
Sun-der, e hookaawale ae, e hookaokoa.
Sun-dires, he wahi mau mea i huiia.
Sun-ny, alo ana i ka la.
Su-per-a-bound, e nui loa ana, e lawa a keu.
Su-per-flu-i-ty, he mea e oi ana i ka mea e
    pono ai.
Su-pe-ri-or, kiekie ae, maluna.
Su-pine, palaleha, molowa.
Sup-per, he aina ahiahi.
Sup-ple, ae wale ana mamuli o kekahi.
Sup-pli-cate, e noi haahaa.
Sup-ply, e hoolako, e kii i na mea e pono ai.
Sup-port, e paepae; he kokua ana.
Sup-pose, e manao, e kuhi wale.
Sup-press, e kinai, e hoopau.
Sup-pu-rate, e kahe ka palahehe.
Su-preme, kiekie loa maluna.
Sure, oiaio, luliluli ole, paa.
Sur-mise, he manao hewa ia hai.
Sur-pass, e hele mao aku, e hooi aku.
Sur-plus, ke keu ana, ka mea e oi ana.
Sur-prise, he kahaha i loaa koke.
Sur-prise, e kau koke aku, e hoohikilele.

Sur-ren-der, e hoolilo malalo, e lilo i pio.
Sur-round, e hoopuni.
Sus-pect, e manao hewa ia hai.
Sus-pense, he manao kanalua, he kuihe.
Swal-low, e moni iho, e ale iho.
Swamp, he aina lepo nenelu.   [e kukai.
Swap, hoololi i kahi waiwai no kekahi waiwa,
Sway, e hoalii, e hoomalu aupuni.
Swear, e hoohiki imua o ke Akua.
Sweat, he hou, he kahe ana ka hou.
Sweep, e kahili lepo ana, e hoe loloa.
Sweet, ono, oluolu.
Swell, e pehu ae.
Swerve, e lalau, e kapae ae.
Swift, hikiwawe, holo mama.
Swim, e au iloko o ka wai.
Swine, he puaa.
Swing, e lewa ae i o ia nei, e lele kowali.
Swing, he lele kowali.
Swoon, e maule, he maule ana.
Swop (e nana *swap*.)
Sword, he pahi kaua, he pahi hahau.
Symp-tom, he hoailona hoike i ke ano o ka mai.

T.

Ta-ble, he papa, papapaina, &c.
Ta-ci-tur-ni-ty, he manao ekemu ole.
Tack, he kui hao uuku.
Tail, ka hiu, ka huelo, ka hope.
Take, e lawe, e lalau lima.
Tale, he kaao.
Talk, he kamailio, he olelo kike.
Talk-a-tive, lilo i ke kamailio ana.
Tall, kiekie ma ke kino.
Tame, laka, makau ole i ke kanaka.
Tan-gle, e kahihi, e hoohihia pu.
Tap, e paipai iki me ka lima.
Tar-dy, lohi, puka mai mahope.
Ta-ro, kalo.
Tar-ry, e kali, e noho liuliu iki.
Tart, awahia, oi, ehaehae.
Taste, e hoao ma ka waha.
Taunt, e olelo ino, e nuku.
Teach, e ao aku, e kuhikuhi.
Tear, he waimaka.
Tear, e nahae, e haehae.
Tease, e hoonaukiuki.
Teat, he u, ka maka o ka u.
Te-di-ous, hoolohi a luhi.
Teem, e hoohua a nui.
Tel-es-cope, he ohe nana.
Tell, e hai aku, e olelo hoike.
Te-mer-i-ty, he aa ana, he wiwo ole.
Tem-per-ance, ka pakiko ana i ka mea ai a
    me na mea inu.
Tem-pest, he makani ikaika, he ino.
Tem-ple, he heiau, he luakini.
Tem-po-ral, pili ana i ko keia ao.
Tempt, e hoao, e hoowalewale.
Ten, he umi; *ten days,* he anahulu.
Te-na-cious, paa i kahi manao, paakiki.
Tend, e malama, e lawelawe.

Ten-der, palupalu, ehaeha.
Ten-don, he olona ma ka lala.
Tenth, ka umi.
Ter-min-a-tion, he oki ana, he paa ana.
Ter-ri-ble, he eehia, he hooweliweli.
Ter-ri-fy, e hooweliweli, e hoomakau.
Ter-ror, he weliweli, he makau nui.
Tes-ti-fy, e hai aku i ka mea i ikeia.
Text, he kumuolelo, he pooolelo.   [mai.
Thanks, he aloha aku i ka lokomaikai wale
That, kela, ua mea la.
Thatch, e ako hale i ka pili.
The, ka, ke.   [laua.
Their, ko lakou, ka lakou; (dual) ka laua, ko
Them, lakou; (dual) laua.
Than, alaila.
There, malaila, ilaila.
There-fore, no ka mea, no ia mea.
These, o lakou nei, o keia mau mea.
They, o lakou, o laua.
Thick, manoanoa, paapu.
Thief, he aihue.
Thigh, he uha.
Thim-ble, he komo lima humuhumu.
Thin, lahilahi, wiwi.
Thing, mea.
Think, e noonoo, e manao ae.
Thirst, e make wai.
Thir-teen, he umikumamakolu.
Thir-ty, he kanakolu.
This, keia, eia.
Thorn, he laau ooi.
Thor-ough, paa pono, pololei.
Those, kela mau mea.
Thou, o oe.
Though, ina, ina paha.
Thought, he manao, he kuhi ana.
Thou-sand, he tausani.
Thral-dom, e noho hooluhi ana.
Thrash, e hahau iho me ka ikaika.
Thread, he kaula makalii, he ropi.
Threat, he olelo hooweliweli.
Three, akolu, ekolu.
Three-fold, pakolu.
Thres-hold, ka paepae puka.
Thrive, e noho me ka pomaikai.
Throat, ke kani a-i, ka puu a-i.
Throb, e panapana, e pana.
Throng, he lehulehu o kanaka.
Throt-tle, e lalau a paa ma ka a-i.
Through-out, mawaena a pau.
Throw, e kiola, e hoolei.
Thrush, ka ea, ka eaea.
Thrust, e kipaku ikaika.
Thumb, ka lima nui.
Thump, e kui aku.
Thun-der, ka hekili.
Thun-der-strike, ka poha ana o ka hekili.
Thus, pe, penei.
Thwart, e keakea, e ku e.
Tick-le, e iniiniki, e opaopa.
Ti-dings, he mea hou, he olelo hoike.
Ti-dy, maemae me ka maikai.
Tie, e nakii a paa.
Tight, paa, oolea.

Till, until, a hiki i ka manawa.
Tim-id, makau wale, palaimaka.
Tin, he kepau keokeo, he tini.
Tin-gle, e kani hookulikuli.
Tin-kle, e kani ooi me he bele uuku la.
Ti-ny, makalii, palanaiki.
Tip, welau, kahi oi.
Tip-sy, ona i ka inu i mea ona.
Tire, e hooluhi, e hoomaloeloe.
Tire-some, kaumaha, hooluhi ana.
Ti-tle, he inoa luna, inoa buke.
Tit-ter, e aka henehene.
To, i, ia, io; before the infinitive e.
Toe, manamana wawae.
To-geth-er, pu; *sit together,* noho pu.
Toil, e hana ikaika, e kamau hana.
To-ken, he hoailona.
Tol-er-ate, e ae e hanaia.
Tongs, he upa ahi.
Tongue, ka elelo, alelo.
Tools, he mau mea paahana.
Tooth, niho.
Top, ka welau, kahi kiekie.
Torch, he lama, he lamaku.
Tor-ment, e hooeha loa, e hoowalania.
Tor-rent, he waikahe ikaika.
Tor-rid, wela loa, maloo i ka wela.
Tor-toise, he honu, he ea.
Tor-ture, e hooeha, e hoowalania.
Toss, e hoolei lima iluna.
To-tal, okoa, pau loa.
Tot-ter, e haalulu.
Touch, e hoopa, e pa aku.
Touch-y, huhu wawe.
Tough, uaua, paakiki.
Tow, e kauo maloko o ka wai.
To-ward, ma, i.
Town, he kauhale kinikini.
Toy, he mea milimili no na kamalii.
Toy, e hoolealea wale.
Trace, e kahakaha aku, e hahai me ka imi.
Tract-a-ble, hiki ke hooponopono koke ia.
Trade, ka oihana paahana.
Trade-wind, ka makani mau.
Tra-di-tion, he mooolelo no na kupuna mai.
Trail, e kauo mahope iho.
Train, e ao i ka paikau, e alakai.
Trait-or, he kanaka kipi, he kumakaia.
Tram-ple, e hehi ilalo.
Tran-quil, malie, maluhia.
Trans-act, e hana.
Trans-cend, e pii iluna, e hoohala aku.
Trans-fer, e hoolilo aku, e lawe mai kahi wahi a i kahi wahi e ae.
Trans-fix, e hou iho a puka.
Trans-form, e hoomalule, e hooloi i ke ano [hou.
Trans-gress, e lawehala, e hele mao aku.
Tran-sient, hele ana, aohe noho loa.
Trans-late, e unuhi i ka olelo e.
Trans-mit, e lawe aku ma kahi e.
Trans-pa-rent, moakaka lea.
Trans-plant, e kanu ma kahi e.
Trap, he mea upiki e paa ai na mea hihiu.
Trash, he opala, he mea waiwai ole.
Trav-el, he hele ana, he holo ana.

Trav-el-er, he mea hele i na aina e aku.
Treach-er-ous, hoopunipuni, wahahee.
Tread, e hehi maluna iho.
Trea-son, he kipi i ke alii.
Treas-ure, he waiwai i ahuia.
Treat-y, he olelo kuikahi.
Tree, he laau.
Trem-ble, e haalulu, e haukeke.
Tre-men-dous, weliweli, kupanaha.
Trem-u-lous, haalulu ana.
Trench, he auwaha.
Trep-i-da-tion, he haalulu ana.
Tres-pass, e komo wale i ko hai wahi.
Tri-al, he hoao ana, he hockolokolo ana.
Trib-u-la-tion, he popilikia nui.
Trick, he hana apiki, he hcopunipuni.
Trick-le, e kahe uuku iho, e kulu.
Tri-fle, he mea liilii, waiwai uuku.
Trig-ger, ke ki e pana ai ka pu.
Trim, e paipai, e hooponopono.
Trip, e hele mama, e okupe.
Trip-le, pakolu.
Tri-umph, e lanakila.
Troop, he poe koa.
Troub-le, he pilikia.
Troub-le-some, hoopilikia ana.
Trough, he papa auwai lolca.
Trow-sers, he lolewawae no na kane.
True, oiaio, pololei.
Trum-pet, he pu kani memele.
Trun-dle, e kaa maluna o na huila.
Trust, e hilinai aku, e paulele.
Try, e hoao.
Tuft, he eka lauoho.
Tug, e huki ikaika, e kauo.
Tum-ble, e kaa ilalo, e hookaa ilalo.
Tu-mid, pehu.
Tu-mult, he haunaele.
Tune, he leo mele.
Tur-bid, paapu i ka lepo.
Tur-key, he manu palahu.
Tur-mer-ic, he olena.
Tur-moil, he wawa, he pioloke.
Turn, e huli ae, e haliu, e wili.
Tur-tle, he honu, he ea.
Tush! ka! kahaha!
Tusk, he niho loloa.
Twelve, he umikumamalua.
Twen-ty, he iwakalua.
Twice, papalua.
Twig, he lala uuku o ka laau.
Twi-light, he wanaao, he wanapoo.
Twins, he mahoe.
Twine, he kaula ropi.
Twin-kle, e imoimo me he hoku la.
Twirl, e kaa, e wili.
Twist, e hilo, e wili.
Twitch, e kaili.
Two, alua, elua.
Two-fold, palua, papalua.
Tyr-an-ny, he hana hookaumaha.

U.

Ug-ly, ino, kekee.

Ul-cer, he mai puha.
Um-brel-la, he mamalu, he loulu.
Un-a-ble, he hiki ole.
Un-at-tend-ed, aohe mea hele pu.
Un-a-wares, me ka ike ole.
Un-be-com-ing, ku ole i ka pono.
Un-bend, e hoalualu.
Un-bind, e wehe i ka mea i nakinakiia.
Un-bound-ed, aole i puniia.
Un-cer-tain, maopopo ole, akaka ole.
Un-civ-il, launa ole, lokoino.
Un-cle, he hoahanau kane o ka makua ponoi.
Un-clean, maemae ole, pelapela.
Un-clothe, e wehe ae i ke kapa.
Un-com-mon, kakaikahi, aole pinepine.
Un-con-stant, aole paa mau, he ano luli.
Un-cov-er, e wehe i ka uhi.
Un-cour-te-ous, aole oluolu ka hana.
Unc-tion, he poni ana i ka aila.
Unc-tu-ous, momona, piha i ka aila.
Un-cul-pa-ble, he hana me ka hewa ole.
Un-cum-ber-ed, aole i hookaumahaia.
Un-curse, e hoino ole aku.
Un-dam-aged, hana ino ole ia.
Un-de-ci-ded, kanalua, paa ole ka manao.
Un-der, malalo, ilalo.
Un-der-go, e hoomanawanui i ka eha.
Un-der-most, malalo loa.
Un-der-stand, e ike maopopo.
Un-der-take, e lawehana.
Un-do, e wawahi iho i ka mea i hanaia.
Un-dress, e wehe i na kapa aahu.
Un-em-ploy-ed, aohe hana e hana ai.
Un-e-ven, like ole, apuupuu.
Un-ex-pect-ed, hiki mai me ka ike e ole ia.
Un-ex-pert, hawawa, hemahema.
Un-fas-ten, e kala, e hemo.
Un-fath-om-ed, he hohonu ana ole ia.
Un-fledg-ed, he manu puka ole ia ka hulu.
Un-fold, e wehewehe i ka opiopi.
Un-for-tu-nate, poino, popilikia.
Un-fre-quent, aole hiki pinepine.
Un-fre-quent-ed, kipa kakaikahiia, mehameha.
Un-gov-ern-ed, hoomaluhia ole ia.
Un-hand-some, maikai ole ka helehelena.
Un-han-dy, hewawa ka hana ana.
Un-hap-py, kaumaha ka naau.
Un-hon-or-ed, aole i hoomaikaiia.
Un-hos-pi-ta-ble, lokomaikai ole i na malihini.
Un-hurt, he eha ole ia.
U-ni-form, e ano hookahi ana.
Un-in-jur-ed, aole i hana ino ia.
Un-in-ten-tion-al, me ka manao ole.
Un-in-ter-rupt-ed, aole i alalaiia.
Un-ion, he hookui ana, e kuikahi ana.
U-nite, e hui pu, e hookui.
U-ni-ver-sal, a pau loa, ma na wahi a pau.
Un-just, ku ole ma ka pono.
Un-kind, lokomaikai ole.
Un-known, i ike ole ia.
Un-law-ful, ku ole i ke kanawai.
Un-less, ina ole, ke ole.
Un-like, like ole, ku like ole.
Un-like-ly, aole paha oiaio.
Un-lock, e wehe me ke ki.

Un-loose, e wehewehe.
Un-luck-y, poino.
Un-man-ner-ed, ku ole i ka naauao.
Un-mar-ri-ed, aole i mareia.
Un-meas-ured, aole i anaia.
Un-mer-ci-ful, aloha ole, menemene ole.
Un-mov-a-ble, paa loa, aole e hiki ke nee.
Un-neigh-bor-ly, launa ole.
Un-ob-serv-ed, aole i ike ia.
Un-paid, uku ole ia.
Un-par-don-ed, aole i kala ia.
Un-prof-it-a-ble, e waiwai ole ana.
Un-rav-el, e wehewehe i ka mea hihia.
Un-ripe, oo ole, opiopio.
Un-roll, e wehe i ka owili.
Un-ru-ly, kolohe, hookuli.
Un-sat-is-fied, aole i oluolu, walea ole.
Un-sight-ly, he ino ke nana aku.
Un-skill-ful, akamai ole.
Un-suc-cess-ful, aole pomaikai.
Un-suit-a-ble, ku ole, pili ole.
Un-thank-ful, aloha ole i ka lokomaikaiia.
Un-tie, e wehe i ka nakinaki o ke kaula.
Un-til, a, a hiki i ka manawa.
Un-true, he oiaio ole.
Un-u-su-al, maa ole, walea ole.
Un-whole-some, pono ole no ke ola.
Un-wil-ling, makemake ole.
Un-wont-ed, laka ole, hihiu.
Up! e ala ae! iluna.
Up-braid, e nuku, e ao ikaika.
Up-hold, e kokua.
Up-on, maluna iho.
Up-per-most, maluna loa aku.
Up-right, kupono, pololei.
Up-roar, he haunaele, he walaau.
Up-root, e uhuki ae, pau pu me ke aa.
Up-side-down, ilalo ka aoao luna.
Up-ward, ma kahi maluna ae.
Urge, e koi ikaika.
U-rine, he mimi.
Us, ia makou, ia kakou, ia maua, ia kaua.
Use, he hana, he oihana.
Use, e hoolilo i kahi mea i mea hana.
Use-ful, pono ke hanaia.
U-su-al, e mau ana, e pinepine ana.
U-surp, e lalau wale i ko hai wahi.
U-te-rus, ka opu.

V.

Va-cant, hakahaka, aole i nohoia.
Vag-a-bond, he mea aea, he kuewa wale.
Vain, makehewa, lapuwale.
Vain-glo-ri-ous, haanou, kaena.
Vale, he aina mawaena o na mauna, he awawa.
Val-e-dic-tion, he aloha o ka mea hele.
Val-iant, makau ole, koa.   [mauna.
Va-ley, he awawa, he wa mawaena o na
Val-u-a-ble, pono e waiwai ai.
Van, he poe kaua hele mua.
Van-ish, e nalowale iho.
Van-quish, e lanakila maluna.

Va-por, he mahu.	**Wag,** e neenee me ka luliluli ae.
Va-ri-a-ble, lauwili, huli i o ia nei.	**Wa-ges,** he uku no kekahi hana.
Va-ri-ance, he ku e ana.	**Wail,** e uwe kanikau, e kumakena.
Va-ri-e-ty, nui ke ano o kela mea keia mea.	**Waist,** ka puhaka.
Vast, nui, nunui.	**Waist-coat,** he puliki.
Vaunt, e kaena wale, e haanou.	**Wait,** e kali, e ukali.
Veer, e haliu ae.	**Wake,** ala, e ala mai ka hiamoe ae.
Veg-et-a-ble, he mea kanu, mea kupu.	**Wake,** ka maawekai mahope o ka moku.
Veil, e uhi.	**Walk,** e hele wawae.
Vein, he aa koko.	**Walk-ing-staff,** he kookoo.
Ve-lo-ci-ty, ka mama ana o ka hele.	**Wall,** he pa pohaku, he paia hale. [paka.
Vend, e kuai aku, e kalepa.	**Wal-low,** e kaa i ka lepo me he puaa la, e ku-
Ven-e-rate, e mahalo nui, e hoomaikai.	**Wan-der,** e aea, e kuewa wale.
Ve-ne-sec-tion, e hookahe i ke koko.	**Wane,** e emi iho.
Ven-geance, he hoopai huhu ana.	**Want,** he nele, he ilihune ana.
Ven-om, he mea awaawa make.	**Wan-ton,** uhauha, makaleho.
Ven-om-ous, he ano o ka mea e make ai.	**War,** he kaua.
Verb-al, ma ka waha, hai waha ia.	**War,** e kaua aku.
Ver-i-fy, e hooiaio.	**Warm,** mahana, pumahana.
Verse, he pauku olelo.	**Warm,** e hoomahana.
Vers-ed, he makaukau, he akamai.	**Warn,** e ao aku i makaala ai.
Ver-tex, kahi i oi maluna.	**Warp,** he ropi e moe ana ma ka loa o ka lole.
Ver-ti-go, he poniuniu.	**War-ri-or,** he koa kaua.
Ver-y, io, oiaio, maoli.	**Wart,** he ilikona.
Ves-i-cate, e hoopohapoha i ka ili.	**Wash,** e holoi, e hoomaemae i ka wai.
Ves-i-cle, he wahi puu ma ka ili.	**Wasp,** he nalo hope eha.
Ves-sel, he ipu, he pahu, he waa, he moku.	**Waste,** e hoomaunauna waiwai.
Vest-ige, he kapuai, he kaha.	**Watch,** e kiai, e makaala.
Vex, e hoonaukiuki, e hoopilikia.	**Watch,** he wati; he poe kiai.
Vex-a-tious, e hoonaukiuki ana.	**Wa-ter,** wai, kai.
Vi-al, he omole aniani uuku.	**Wa-ter-fall,** he wailele.
Vi-brate, e lewa i o ia nei.	**Wa-ter-y,** pulu ma-u.
Vice, he kina, he hewa.	**Wat-tle,** he lala laau uuku.
Vic-tor, he koa lanakila.	**Wave,** he ale o ke kai.
Vic-to-ry, he lanakila ana.	**Wave,** e luli, e ka i o ia nei.
Vict-uals, he mea ai na kanaka.	**Wax,** he kepau ta, he mea pipili.
Vie, e hoolike, e hana like.	**Way,** ke ala, alanui, ka aoao hana.
View, he ike maka, e makaikai ana.	**Way-lay,** e hoohalua.
Vig-i-lant, makaala.	**We,** kakou, makou, kaua, maua.
Vig-or-ous, ikaika.	**Weak,** nawaliwali, palupalu.
Vile, ino, kolohe, haukae.	**Weal,** he pomaikai ana.
Vil-i-fy, e olelo ino, e aki.	**Wealth,** he waiwai.
Vil-lage, he kauhale.	**Wean,** e ukuhi i ka waiu.
Vin-di-cate, e kokua ae, hoopuka ae.	**Weap-on,** he mea kaua, he mea pale i ka enemi.
Vin-dic-tive, manao hoopai wale.	**Wear,** e aahu lole, e hoopau liilii.
Vi-o-late, e uhai, e wawahi, e limaikaika.	**Wea-ry,** luhi, pauaho.
Vi-o-lent, ikaika, huhu.	**Weave,** e ulana.
Vi-per, he moomole, he mea niho awa.	**Web,** ka mea i ulanaia, he punawelewele.
Vir-gin, he wahine puupaa.	**Wed,** e mare, e lawe i wahine, i kane paha.
Vis-it, e hele e ike.	**Wed-nes-day,** wenede, ka poakolu.
Vix-en, he wahine nuku wale.	**Wee,** uuku, lahilahi.
Vo-ca-tion, he oihana.	**Weed,** he mea ulu wale.
Voice, he leo.	**Weed,** e waele i ka nahelehele.
Void, hakahaka, nele. [honua.	**Weep,** e uwe me ka waimaka.
Vol-ca-no, he pele, luapele, he ahi iloko o ka	**Weigh,** e kaupouna.
Vol-ume, he owili palapala, he buke.	**Weight-y,** he kaumaha, koikoi.
Vol-un-ta-ry, no ka makemake iho.	**Wel-come,** e hookipa me ke aloha.
Vom-it, e luai aku.	**Well,** he luawai, he punawai hohonu.
Vo-ra-cious, ai nui loa, aihamu.	**Well,** pono, mai ole.
Voy-age, he holo ana ma ka moana.	**Well-nigh,** kokoke, aneane.
	Well-spring, he puna, he waipuna.
	Wel-ter, e kaa maloko o ke koko.
	Wen, he puu maloko o ka io.
W.	**Wench,** he kaikamahine, wahine mare ole ia.
	West, komohana.
Wade, e auhele.	

Wet, koekoe, pulu i ka wai.
Whale, he kohola.
What? heaha?
Whee-dle, e hoopunipuni.
Whelp, he keiki ilio.
When? (with the past) inahea? (future) ahea?
Whence? nohea mai? ihea mai?
Where? aihea? mahea? aila mahea?
Where-fore? no keaha la?
Whet, e hookala i oi.
Wheth-er, ina paha.
Whet-stone, he pohaku hoana.
Which? he mea hea?
While, } oiai, ia manawa, ma ia manawa.
Whilst, }
Whip, e haua, e hahau a eha.
Whirl, e wili ikaika.
Whirl-pool, he mimilo, he wili iloko o ke kai.
Whirl-wind, he puahiohio.
Whisk-er, he umiumi loloa ma ka papalina.
Whis-per, e hawanawana.
Whis-tle, e hookio, e pio.
White, keokeo, kea.
White-wash, he mea hamo keokeo.
Whith-er? ihea? i kahi hea?
Who? wai? owai?
Whole, okoa.
Whoop, he hooho kaua, he hooho.
Whore, he wahine hookamakama.
Why? no keaha la? i mea aha?
Wick, he uwiki o ke kukui.
Wick-ed, aia, hewa, lawehala.
Wide, akea, laual, palahalaha.
Wid-ow, wahine kane make.
Wife, he wahine mea kane.
Wild, hihiu, laka ole.
Wild-ness, he hihiu.
Wile, apiki, hana maalea.
Will, he palapala kauoha i ka waiwai.
Wil-ling, e ae ana, oluolu.
Win, e loaa, e ko.
Wind, he makani.
Wind, e wili.
Wind-bound, paa i ka makani.
Win-dow, he puka makani.
Wing, eheu, pekekeu.
Wink, e imo, e imoimo.
Wipe, e holoi me ka kawele.
Wise, naauao, akamai, ike.
Wish, manao.
With, i, ma, me.
With-draw, e hoi iwaho.
With-er, e mae a make.
With-hold, e aua, e huna.
With-in, maloko, iloko.
With-out, mawaho, iwaho.
With-out, ke ole, me ole.
With-stand, e ku e, e hooke, e papa.
Wit-ness, e hoike.
Wo, woe, auwe! poino! e poino ana.
Wo-man, he wahine makua.
Womb, ka puao.
Won-der, e mahalo, e kahaha ka manao.
Won-der-ful, kupaianaha.
Wont, maa, walea.

Wood, laau, he wahie, he ululaau.
Woof, na kaula i ulanaia.
Wool, he hulu hipa.
Word, he huaolelo.
Work, hana, he oihana.
Work, he mea i hanaia.
World, ke ao nei, kela ao.
World-ly, lilo i na lealea o ke ao nei.
Worm, enuhe, he mea liilii e kolo ana.
Worm-eat-en, aiia i ka mu.
Worse, he oi i ka hewa.
Wor-ship, e hoomana.
Worst, hewa loa, ino loa.
Worth, ke kumu kuai, ka pono.
Wound, e hooeha.
Wran-gle, e hakaka, e hoopaapaa.
Wrap, e wahi ae, e opeope.
Wrap-per, he wahi no kekahi mea.
Wrath, huhu, inaina.
Wreath, he lei i ulanaia.
Wreck-ed, nahahaia me he moku la.
Wrench, } e huki ikaika, e kaili hewa.
Wrest, }
Wres-tle, e hakoko.
Wretch, he kanaka inoino loa.
Wretch-ed, ehaeha loa, popilikia.
Wring, e uwi, e wili ikaika.
Wrin-kle, he minomino.
Wrist, ka pulima.
Write, e kakaulima.
Writhe, e wili, e oni ae.
Wrong, kekee, pono ole, he hewa.
Wrong, e hana hewa.
Wrong-ing, e hana ino ana i kekahi mea.
Wry, i wiliia, kapakahiia.

Y.

Yam, uhi.
Yawn, e hamama.
Ye, oukou, olua.
Year, he makahiki.
Year-ly, ma ka makahiki.
Yearn, e iini, e makemake nui.
Yell, he hooho me ka leo nui.
Yel-low, melemele, he lenalena.
Yes, e, ae, oia.
Yes-ter-day, inehinei.
Yet, aka, i keia manawa.
Yield, e hoohua; e kuu ae.
Yon-der, mao, mamao.
You, *singular,* oe; *dual,* olua; *plural.* oukou.
Young, opio, opiopio.   [oukou.
Your, *singular,* kou; *dual,* ko olua; *plural,* ko
Youth, he wa keiki, ka wa kamalii.

Z.

Zeal-ous, piha i ka manao ikaika.
Zeph-yr, he makani nawaliwali.
Zig-zag, he kekee i o ia nei.
Zinc, he kepau keokeo.
Zone, he kaei o ka honua.

A CHRONOLOGICAL TABLE

OF

REMARKABLE EVENTS

CONNECTED WITH

THE HISTORY OF THE HAWAIIAN ISLANDS.

PREFACE.

THE following Chronological Table is a translation of a Table compiled by the Rev. A. Forbes, of Molokai, and was designed for a Hawaiian Almanac for the present year, 1865. The Compiler says: "This Table has been made up from the Hawaiian History (Mooolelo Hawaii) and some fifty or more articles added. It is not, however, supposed that all deficiencies are supplied, but only some of the defects of previous tables. There will be fact and dates to be added hereafter."

The first Chronological Table of notable events at these Islands was published in the Hawaiian Almanac for 1835, before the Hawaiian History was written. To that Table additions have been made from time to time, until the present.

L.A.

1716. Keaulumoku was born at Naohaku in Kohala.

1752. Kalaniopuu King of Western Hawaii.

1769. Transit of Venus, observed by Cook and Green.

1774. Keaulumoku was living with Kahahana, King of Oahu.

1775. Kaahumanu became the wife of Kamehameha I.

1776 to 1778. Kahekili, King of Maui, was at war with Kalaniopuu, King of Hawaii.

1778. January 18, Capt. Cook first anchored at Waimea, Kauai, having first seen Oahu.

1778. November, Capt. Cook touched at East Maui.

1778. Kamehameha, a soldier under Kalaniopuu, was on Maui fighting against Kahekili.

1779. January 17, Capt. Cook anchored in the Bay of Kealakeakua, Hawaii.

1779. February 14, Capt. Cook was slain at Kaawaloa, Hawaii.

1782. April, Kalaniopuu died, leaving his Kingdom (Western Hawaii) to Kiwalao, who was his own son.

1782. July, the battle named *Mokuahae*, i. e., the fight of Kamehameha with Kiwalao and his party at Keomo, Hawaii; Kamehameha triumphed, Kiwalao was slain, and Keoua became King of Kau and Puna.

1782. Keawemauhili reigns as King at Hilo, Hawaii.

1782. Keaulumoku composed the mele *Haui*

ka Lani, or a Prophecy of the overthrow of Hawaii by Kamehameha.

1782. Kamehameha reigns King over Kona, Kohala and Hamakua.

1782. December, Kanekoa was slain in battle by Keoua.

1783. March, at Laupahoehoe mua, Kamehameha fought with Keawemauhili and Keoua, Kings of Kau and Hilo.

1784. They fought at Hapuu.

1784. Keaulumoku the Poet died, aged 68 years.

1785. At Laupahoehoe alua, Kamehameha fought with Keawemauhili and Keoua, Kings of Kau and Hilo.

1786. The ship *Lo* anchored.

1787. August, Kaiana sailed to a Foreign Country (China.)

1790. The battle called *Kapaniwai* was fought between Kamehameha and Kalanikupule at Wailuku, Maui.

1790. First American ship (*Eleanor*, Captain Metcalf) visited the Islands.

1790. Keawemauhili was slain in battle by Keoua.

1790. Kamehameha lives at Kaunakahakai, Molokai.

1790. Keoua was taken prisoner by Kamehameha at Koapapaa, Hamakua, Hawaii, and Kamehameha thus became sole King of the whole Island.

1790. John Young and Isaac Davis became attached to Kamehameha.

1791. Kaeo, King of Kauai, and Kahekili, King of Maui, met Kamehameha at Kohala, Hawaii; the battle was called *Kepuwahaulaula.*

1791. Kahekili, King of Maui died.

1791. In this year the battle of Nuuanu was fought, in which Kalanikupule, son of Kahekili, King of Maui and Oahu, was slain; and thus Maui, Molokai, Lanai and Oahu fell into the hands of Kamehameha.

1792. Keoua was slain at Kawaihae.

1792. March 3, Capt. Vancouver first visited the Islands, and left cattle, sheep, &c.

1792. The *Dædalus*, store ship, visits Waimea, Oahu; a Massacre.

1793. Kamehameha attempted a voyage to Kauai, but could not succeed, the wind being against him. That voyage was called *Ieiewaho.*

1793. March 12, Vancouver anchored at Lahaina.

1794. December, first discovery of Honolulu harbor. Entered by *Jackall* and *Prince Leboo*, American.

1795. January 12, last visit of Vancouver.

1795. *Dædalus* visits Niihau. Massacre. January 1, Murder of Captains.

1797. Liholiho (Kamehameha II.) was born.

1797. Namakeha dies at Hilo, in the battle of Kaipalaoa.

1798. The work of digging out a fleet of canoes was commenced; the canoes were of the class called *Peleleu.*

1801. The fleet of canoes called Peleleu arrived at Kawaihae.

1802. The Peleleu arrived at Lahaina.

1802. Kameeiamoku dies at Lahaina.

1803. The Peleleu arrived at Oahu.

1804. The great pestilence called *ahulau okuu.*

1804. Keeaumoku dies.

1808. Ualakaa?

1809. Kanihonui was slain for making an attempt on Kaahumanu.

1810. Kamehameha and Kaumualii, King of Kauai, meet, and Kaumualii gives Kauai to Kamehemeha. Hence all the Islands of Hawaii became one Kingdom under Kamehameha I.

1812. Kamehameha returned to Hawaii. That voyage was called *Niaukani.*

1812. The stone wall of Kiholo was built.

1814. March, Kauikeaouli (Kamehameha III.) was born.

1815. Nahienaena (the Princess) was born.

1816. Some Russian ships arrive.

1816. The building of the Fort at Honolulu commenced by Kalanimoku.

1817. The Fort at Honolulu finished.

1819. May 8, Kamehameha I. died.

1819. May, Liholiho (Kamehameha II.) reigns King.

1819. October, Liholiho breaks kapu on the night of Kukahi.

1819. Kapu broken on Oahu in November.

1820. January, a battle on account of breaking kapu at Kuamoo on Hawaii.

1820. March 30, first Missionaries arrived at Kailua.

1820. April 18, Missionaries first arrive at Honolulu.

1820. July, Messrs. Whitney and Ruggles sailed for Kauai.

1820. December, Liholiho sails for Maui.

1820. First whaler (*Mary*, Capt. Allen) enters Honolulu harbor.

1821. February 4, Liholiho sails for Oahu.

1821. July 22, Liholiho arrives at Kauai.

1821. First house of Christian worship built

in Honolulu.

1822. January 7, Printing first commenced at the Islands. It is said that King Liholiho was allowed to pull the first sheet.

1823. January, Kaahumanu returned from Hawaii.

1823. April 4, Mr. Ellis arrived from Tahiti.

1823. April 27, the second company of Missionaries arrived.

1823. September 16, Keopuolani died.

1823. November 27, Liholiho, his Queen and attendants sailed for England, leaving the Kingdom in the care of Kaahumanu.

1824. May 26, Kaumualii, King of Kauai, died.

1824. July 8, Kamamalu, wife of Liholiho, died in London.

1824. July 13, Liholiho died in London.

1824. August, Humehume (George Tamoree) raised a Rebellion on Kauai.

1824. August 18, Kiaimakani was slain in battle.

1824. August, Kapiolani descended into the Volcano of Kilauea.

1825. May 4, Boki and his companions return from England with the Remains of the King and Queen in the English frigate *Blonde*.

1826. February, the ship *London* was wrecked on Lanai.

1826. February 26, the crew of the war brig *Dolphin* created a great disturbance in Honolulu,—attacked and broke into the house of Kalanimoku.

1826. August, Kaahumanu made her first circuit of Oahu.

1826. September 27, the first Meeting House at Kailua was dedicated.

1826. Kahalaia died.

1827. February 8. Kalanimoku died.

1827. October 23, Capt. Clark fired into the Village of Lahaina.

1827. October, Kinau and Kekuanaoa were married.

1828. March 30, the third company of Missionaries arrived.

1828. The stone Meeting House at Wainee, Lahaina, commenced.

1829. Kaahumanu took the bones of the Chiefs from the "House of Keawe" and deposited them at Kaawaloa.

1829. July 3, first Meeting House at Honolulu dedicated.

1829. Namahana died.

1829. December 2, Boki and his company sailed away from the Islands and were lost.

1829. Piia died.

1830. Kaahumanu and her train made the circuit of Maui and Hawaii.

1830. March, Kaahumanu, the second time, made the circuit of Oahu.

1830. December 11, His Majesty Kamehameha V. was born.

1831. June 7, the fourth company of Missionaries arrived.

1831. September, Kaahumanu made the circuit of Oahu for the third time.

1831. September, the High School at Lahainaluna was commenced.

1831. The erection of the Fort at Lahaina commenced.

1831. December 29, Naihe died.

1832. The second visit of Kaahumanu to Maui and Hawaii.

1832. May 17, the fifth company of Missionaries arrived.

1832. March, the stone Meeting House at Wainee, Lahaina, dedicated.

1832. June 5, Kaahumanu died.

1832. June, Kinau was appointed Premier (Kuhina Nui.)

1832. September, Kaomi begins to make disturbance.

1832. Messrs. Alexander, Whitney and Tinker sail to examine the Marquesas Islands as a field for Missions.

1832. The Fort at Lahaina was finished.

1832. The Oahu Charity School was commenced.

1833. Kuakini returns to Hawaii and Kinau dwells in the Fort as Governess.

1833. March, Kamehameha III. assumes the reins of Government, and Kinau becomes His Minister (Kuhina Nui.)

1833. May 1, the sixth company of Missionaries arrive.

1833. July 2, Messrs. Alexander, Armstrong and Parker sail for the Marquesas Islands.

1833. The Bethel Church built at Honolulu.

1833. Kaomi died.

1834. February 9, Kamehameha IV. (Alexander Liholiho) was born.

1834. Kamanele died.

1834. Keola died.

1834. February 14, first Newspaper printed at the Hawaiian Islands, called the *Lama Hawaii*, at Lahainaluna.

1834. The Newspaper *Kumu Hawaii* commenced at Honolulu.

1835. Leleiohoku and Nahienaena were married.

1835. June 6, the seventh company of Missionaries arrived.

1835. First Hawaiian Almanac printed.

1836. January 2, the Queen Dowager Emma was born.

1836. The Female Seminary at Wailuku, Maui, commenced.

1836. The first Weekly Newspaper in English commenced.

1836. The High School of Mr. Lyman commenced at Hilo.

1836. December, Nahienaena died.

1837. February 4, Kamehameha III. and Kalama were married.

1837. April 9, the eighth company of Missionaries arrived.

1837. Aikanaka died.

1837. The flag was burnt at Kalamakini.

1837. The business of laying out public streets in Honolulu was commenced.

1837. November 7, remarkable rise and overflow of tide throughout the Islands.

1838. August, the Chiefs commence the study of Political Economy with Mr. Richards.

1838. November 1, Victoria Kamamalu was born.

1838. Great attention to religion among the people.

1839. April 4, Kinau died.

1839. April 5, Kekauluohi became Premier (Kuhina Nui.)

1839. May 10, the printing of the First Edition of the Hawaiian Bible finished.

1839. July 9, the French man-of-war *l'Artemise* (Capt. Laplace) arrived.

1839. Kaikioewa died.

1840. The School for the Young Chiefs commenced at Honolulu—Mr. and Mrs. Cooke Teachers.

1840. January, Hoapili, Governor of Maui, died.

1840. The stone Meeting House at Kawaiahao, Honolulu, commenced.

1840. August 3, Mr. Bingham and Family returned to the United States.

1840. October 8, Kamehameha III. gives the first written Constitution to the people of the Hawaiian Islands.

1840. October 20, Kamanawa and others were publicly executed for crime.

1840. September, the United States Exploring Expedition arrived.

1841. May, Kapiolani died.

1841. May 21, the ninth company of Missionaires arrived.

1841. The School for Missionaries' Children at Punahou (now Oahu College) commenced.

1842. January, Hoapili Wahine (Kalakaua) died.

1842. July 8, Haalilio sailed as Commissioner to the Courts of France, England and the United States.

1842. July 21, the Meeting House at Kawaiahao finished.

1842. September 21, the tenth company of Missionaries arrived.

1843. The United States consent to the Independence of the Hawaiian Islands.

1843. February 25, Lord George Paulet seized the Hawaiian Islands and raised the English Flag.

1843. July 31, the sovereignty of the Islands was restored by Admiral Thomas of the English Navy.

1843. September, Bartimeus Puaaiki died.

1844. The Government of Belgium consents to the Independence of the Hawaiian Islands.

1844. November 28, the Governments of England and France recognize the Independence of the Hawaiian Islands.

1844. July 15, the eleventh company of Missionaries arrived.

1844. Silk exported from the Islands—197 pounds.

1844. Haalilio died on his return voyage to the Islands.

1845. April 2, Representatives first chosen from the common people under the Constitution of October, 1840.

1845. Mr. Richards, the Interpreter of Haalilio, returned with his Remains.

1845. Kekauluohi died.

1845. First export of Coffee—248 pounds.

1845. John Young (Keoni Ana) is appointed Premier (Kuhina Nui.)

1846. February 11, Commisioners appointed to settle land claims.

1846. March 20, Mr. Whitney died at Lahainaluna.

1846. November, G. L. Kapeau returned to Hawaii as Governor.

1847. November, Mr. Richards died.

1848. Leleiohoku (William Pitt) died.

1848. Mose Kaikoewa died.

1848. Kaiminaauao died.

1848. The twelfth company of Missionaries arrived.

1848. The Measles (mai puupuu ula) prevailed, and very fatal.
1849. The Fort seized at Honolulu by Admiral Tromelin of the French Navy.
1849. Beef first exported from the Islands—158 barrels.
1851. The Hawaiian Missionary Society was formed.
1851. June, the Court House at Honolulu built.
1851. First Whale Oil and Bone transhipped.
1852. April 2, Kaliokalani died.
1852. First export of Fungus.
1852. The Small-Pox (mai puupuu liilii) swept over the Islands.
1854. The Fort at Lahaina demolished by order of Government.
1854. December 15, Kamehameha III. (Kauikeaouli) died, and Kamehameha IV. became King.
1855. Paki died.
1855. Mr. Hitchcock, of Molokai, died.
1855. Flour exported—463 barrels.
1856. June 2, Kamehameha IV. was united in marriage with Emma Rooke.
1856. J. Aikake was married to Ruta Keelikolani.
1857. The Fort at Honolulu was demolished by order of Government.
1857. Konia (Widow of Paki) died.
1857. John Young (Keoni Ana) the Premier died.
1857. Victoria Kamamalu appointed Kuhina.
1857. William L. Lee, Chief Justice of the Supreme Court, died.
1857. Mr. Armstrong sailed for the United States.
1857. Governor Adams (Kuakini) died.
1857. David Malo died.
1858. May 20, the PRINCE OF HAWAII (Haku o Hawaii) was born.
1859. An eruption of the Volcano on Hawaii, as before in 1840, 1852, 1855.
1859. April 26, Jonas Piikoi died.
1859. July, the Civil Code first published.

1859. September, Gas-light (ea aa) first introduced into Honolulu.
1860. Feb., Custom House built at Lahaina.
1860. March, New Custom House built at Honolulu.
1860. May 27, J.W.E. Maikai died.
1860. Queen's Hospital built; so named from Queen Emma.
1860. The steamer *Kilauea* arrived at Honolulu.
1860. Prince Lot (Kamehameha V.) sailed for California.
1860. September 23, Dr. Armstrong, Minister of Public Instruction, died.
1860. October, G. L. Kapeau, Governor of Hawaii, died.
1860. December, B. Namakeha died.
1862. The PRINCE OF HAWAII died.
1862. October 11, Reformed Catholic Missionaries arrived.
1862. July 18, the building of the Seminary at Lahainaluna burnt.
1862. New building erected.
1863. November 30, His Majesty Kamehameha IV. died, and Prince Lot took the Throne as Kamehameha V.
1864. May 5, Convention of Delegates was called by the King.
1864. June 13, Members of the Convention chosen by the people.
1864. July 7, Convention assembled.
1864. August 13, the Constitution given by Kamehameha III. abrogated by His Majesty and the Convention dismissed.
1864. August 20, the King gives a New Constitution.
1864. September 29, Representatives for a Legislature chosen under the New Constitution.
1864. Oct. 15, the new Legislature assembled.
1864. L. Haalelea died.
1864. October, Act passed the Legislature authorizing the erection of two Distilleries in Honolulu.